AMERICA'S
GARDEN
BOOK

AMERICA'S

NEW · REVISED · EDITION

GARDEN BOOK

JAMES BUSH-BROWN

Member of The American Society of Landscape Architects

LOUISE BUSH-BROWN

Director Emeritus of The Pennsylvania School of Horticulture

CHARLES SCRIBNER'S SONS

NEW YORK AND LONDON

FOREWORD

THIS new edition of *America's Garden Book* has been completely revised and amply enlarged. Several new chapters have been added which extend the scope of the book, but the original purpose remains the same—to provide a ready and authoritative source of reference on all the important phases of gardening.

The authors have endeavored to meet the needs of the gardener for accurate information and sound counsel on the processes of garden making. No attempt has been made to write an inclusive encyclopedia. The aim has been to present the latest and the most satisfactory methods and practices of the craft of gardening, and also to emphasize the importance of artistic design and composition. Throughout the book there runs a strand of recurring selection, dictated by considerations of taste. Lists of plants represent choices of varieties which have merit as material for planting compositions.

With the exception of a few cases, the International Rules of Botanical Nomenclature have been followed, so that the names used agree with those in Bailey's *Standard Cyclopedia of Horticulture* and in Rehder's *Manual of Cultivated Trees and Shrubs*. Where exceptions have been made in recognizing habitual usage in this country the names conform to those in *Standardized Plant Names* prepared by the American Joint Committee on Horticultural Nomenclature.

In designating the relative hardiness of trees shrubs and vines, the map published by the United States Department of Agriculture in the *Atlas of American Agriculture* has been used. The several zones of hardiness represent areas in which similar temperature conditions prevail. The data are based on average annual minimum winter temperatures, and the zone of hardiness of each plant has been derived largely from Rehder's *Manual of Cultivated Trees and Shrubs*.

The material for *America's Garden Book* has been gathered from many sources over a period of years. It would be impossible to list here the names of all those whose kindness and whose willingness to share with us something of their own experience have added so much to the pleasure of our task. Their enthusiasm and wisdom have been an inspiration to us.

Within recent years the interest in gardening has become ever more widespread, and among the home owners of America there is a growing appreciation of the artistic aspects of the garden. And many have discovered that it is the doing of the practical tasks in an artistic way which gives lasting satisfaction and raises the craft of gardening to the status of an art.

JAMES BUSH-BROWN
LOUISE BUSH-BROWN

Ambler, Pennsylvania
September, 1957

CONTENTS

I. THE HERITAGE OF GARDENING 1

II. DESIGN 6
    Style in Landscape Design 6
    Contemporary Design 7
    Creating a Design 10
    The Design of the Home Property 10
    Foundation Planting 13
    Built-in Planting Beds 14
    Trees and Shrubs in the Landscape Composition 15
    Architectural Features in the Garden 18
    Planting Design 19
    Garden Lighting 28

III. PATIOS AND TERRACES 31
    The Terrace 31
    The Patio 33
    Pavements for Patios and Terraces 35
    Plants in Pots 37
    Plants in Tubs and Very Large Pots 44
    Hanging Pots and Baskets 46
    Plants in Portable Boxes 49

IV. CITY GARDENS 51
    Design 52
    Paths 53
    Utility Backyards 55
    Plant Materials 59

V. PENTHOUSE AND ROOF GARDENS 61
    Plant Materials 64
    Maintenance 68

VI. ROCK AND WALL GARDENS 69
    The Rock Garden—Design 70
    Construction 72
    Planting 73
    Winter Mulches 74
    The Wall Garden 76
    Plant Material 78

VII. THE WOODLAND GARDEN 83
    Design 83
    Soil Requirements 85
    Plant Material 85

VIII. WATER AND BOG GARDENS 96
    Plants for Water Gardens 96
    Cultural Requirements 97
    Bog Gardens 99

IX. THE HERB GARDEN 100
    Uses of Culinary Herbs 102
    Herbs for Flavoring and Fragrance 103
    Herb Chart 104

X. GRADING 106
    Top-soil 108
    Lawns for Tennis or Croquet 108
    Water Supply Systems 110

XI. WALLS, STEPS AND BANKS 111
    Garden Walls 111
    Banks 117
    Garden Steps 118

XII. GARDEN PATHS   121

Brick   122

Brick and Cement   123

Flagstone   124

Gravel   127

Stepping Stones   127

Tanbark   128

Turf   129

XIII. GARDEN POOLS AND FOUNTAINS   130

Concrete Pools   131

Lead Pools   132

Copper, Stone and Clay-lined Pools   133

Fountains   135

XIV. THE HOME SWIMMING POOL;

THE GRILL   138

Water Supply and Filter Systems   138

Construction   139

The Grill for Outdoor Meals   143

XV. FENCES   144

Wood Fences   144

Fences of Other Types   151

Maintenance   153

XVI. SOILS AND SOIL IMPROVEMENT   154

Types of Soil   155

Humus   155

The Compost Pile   156

Cover Crops   158

Manures and Fertilizers   159

Soil Testing   168

Lime   170

XVII. LAWNS   173

Establishment of New Lawns   173

Important Lawn Grasses for Cool

Climates   174

Important Lawn Grasses for Mild and

Dry Climates   179

Lawn-grass Substitutes   180

Preparation of the Soil   181

Maintenance of Existing Lawns   187

Control of Lawn Pests   194

Control of Lawn Weeds   197

XVIII. GROUND COVERS   201

Tabular List of Ground Cover Plants   202

XIX. TREES   206

Trees for the Small Place   208

Preparation of the Soil   209

Methods of Transplanting   210

Transplanting Very Large Trees   215

Care of Trees After Transplanting   218

Fertilizing Trees   219

Spraying, Pruning   220

Trees of Merit   220

Trees for Various Uses   226

Tabular List of Trees   229

XX. SHRUBS   237

Planting and Transplanting   238

Pruning   241

Winter Protection   243

Shrubs of Merit   244

Shrubs for Various Uses   264

Tabular List of Shrubs   267

XXI. VINES   279

Support for Vines   279

Maintenance   281

Vines of Merit   282

Vines for Various Uses   292

XXII. HEDGES   293
    Planting   294
    Maintenance   295
    Hedge Plants of Merit   297
    Tabular List of Hedge Material   298

XXIII. INVITING THE BIRDS   302
    Winter Feeding   302
    Nesting Sites   303
    List of Plant Material Attractive to Birds   303

XXIV. ANNUALS   305
    Soil Requirements, Propagation   306
    Thinning, Transplanting, Pinching Back   307
    Annuals of Merit   308
    Annuals for Various Uses   315
    Tabular List of Annuals   322

XXV. BIENNIALS   328
    Transplanting   328
    Biennials of Merit   328

XXVI. HERBACEOUS PERENNIALS   334
    Planning the Perennial Border   335
    Propagation, Preparation of the Soil   340
    General Maintenance   341
    Summer and Winter Mulches   344
    Perennials of Merit   344
    Perennials for Various Uses   374
    Tabular List of Perennials   377

XXVII. BULBS, CORMS, AND TUBERS   384
    Narcissi   384
    Tulips   387
    Hyacinths   391
    Small Spring-flowering Bulbs   391
    Summer-flowering Bulbs   394
    Autumn-flowering Bulbs   409

XXVIII. LILIES   412
    Propagation   414
    Species of Merit   416
    Hybrid Strains   421

XXIX. ROSES   423
    Design of the Rose Garden   423
    Soil Requirements   426
    Planting   428
    Pruning   430
    Winter Production   431
    Roses for Garden Beds and Borders   433
    Roses for Walls, Pergolas, and Trellises   436
    Shrub Roses   439

XXX. PLANTS IN THE HOME   442
    General Care   444
    Control of Pests and Diseases   447
    Flowering Plants of Merit   448
    Foliage Plants of Merit   455
    Flowering Vines   459
    Foliage Vines   460
    House Plants for Various Conditions   461

XXXI. GROWING HOUSE PLANTS UNDER ARTIFICIAL LIGHT   462

XXXII. FLOWER BOXES   466
    Suitable Plants   469

XXXIII. PROPAGATION   471
    Reproduction by Seed   471
    Propagation by Cuttings   481
    Propagation by Division   489
    Propagation by Specialized Shoots   491
    Grafting   493

x   CONTENTS

XXXIV. MULCHES   497

XXXV. TOOLS, TOOL HOUSES, AND
        GARDEN EQUIPMENT   502

XXXVI. COLDFRAMES AND HOTBEDS   508

XXXVII. THE SMALL GREENHOUSE AND
        THE LATH HOUSE   514
        Heating   516
        Watering   518
        Plant Materials   522
        Plants for Special Conditions   538

XXXVIII. THE HOME FRUIT GARDEN   543
        The Orchard   545
        Tree Fruits   548
        Small Bush Fruits   555
        Vine Fruits   561
        Spraying   565
        Control of Diseases and Pests   568

XXXIX. THE HOME VEGETABLE
        GARDEN   570
        Fertilizers   571
        Storing   573
        Cultural Directions   574
        Control of Diseases   595

XL. THE CONTROL OF WEEDS AND
        UNDESIRABLE PLANTS   599
        Trees and Vines   600
        Shrubs   602
        Perennials and Weeds   603
        Weed Control   605

XLI. PLANT DISEASES AND INSECT
        PESTS   610
        Insecticides   614
        Fungicides   616
        Dusts and Sprays   617
        Fumigants   618
        Trees and Shrubs   619
        Flowering Plants   630
        Miscellaneous Insect Pests, Rodents,
            and Animals   673

XLII. GARDEN PRACTICES   677
        Digging, Cultivation   677
        Watering   678
        Feeding, Pruning   679
        Winter Protection   681
        Transplanting   682

GARDENER'S MISCELLANY   687
Notable Gardens Open to the Public   687
Arboretums and Botanical Gardens   692
Available Services   694
State Colleges and Universities   695
Plant Societies   696

GARDEN CALENDAR   698

GLOSSARY   703

MAPS OF GROWING CONDI-
TIONS, FROST DATES, ZONES
OF HARDINESS   705-710

INDEX   711

LIST OF ILLUSTRATIONS

PHOTOGRAPHS

VIEW OF LAKE COMO FROM VILLA BALBIANELLO	3
FORMAL GARDEN WITH CENTRAL POOL	8
FORMAL GARDEN WITH AZALEAS AND DOGWOOD	11
COLONIAL GARDEN OF A PENNSYLVANIA FARMHOUSE	16
TERRACE IN A VERMONT GARDEN	17
NATURALISTIC SETTING FOR A HOUSE	20
FOUNDATION PLANTING	21
SUMMER HOUSE IN THE GEORGIAN STYLE	22
CAPE COD DOORYARD GARDEN	23
A PICTURESQUE GARDEN HOUSE	23
A FLOWER GARDEN IN A CITY YARD	24
A PLEASANT PATIO	25
FOUNDATION PLANTING FOR A SMALL HOME	26
A PATIO AT NIGHT	27
AN ENTRANCE COURT	27
A SMALL PATIO AND POOL IN CALIFORNIA	28
A DRAMATIC EFFECT OF LIGHT	29
A FLORIDA PATIO IN THE SPANISH TRADITION	34
A PAVED CORNER OF THE GARDEN	35
A PATIO IN THE CALIFORNIA MOUNTAINS	36
A SIMPLE TERRACE WITH PLANTING OF ROSES	40
A PATIO IN A SANTA BARBARA GARDEN	43
HANGING POTS OF FUCHSIA	47
STRELITZIA IN PORTABLE PLANT BOX	49
MODULAR PLANT BOXES	49
SPRING BLOOM IN A CITY GARDEN	52
A GARDEN ON BEACON HILL IN BOSTON	53
ARBOR IN A CHICAGO GARDEN	54
BOSTON GARDEN FEATURING A WROUGHT-IRON GRILLE	55
FORMAL CITY GARDEN	56
CITY GARDEN IN SAN FRANCISCO	57
A POOL IN A CITY GARDEN	58
A ROOF-TOP GARDEN	62
A GARDEN AMONG THE TOWERS OF NEW YORK	63
A GARDEN DECK IN CALIFORNIA	64
ROOF GARDEN AT THE CLEVELAND GARDEN CENTER	65
ROOF GARDEN OVERLOOKING SAN FRANCISCO HARBOR	67
NATURALISTIC PLANTING AT THE NEW YORK BOTANICAL GARDEN	71
A ROCK WALL IN SPRING	75
A BANK OF BED ROCK AND FLOWERS	77
A WOODLAND POOL IN CONNECTICUT	85
EARLY SPRING BULBS IN THE WOODLAND	86
A FERN-BORDERED WOODLAND PATH	87
EARLY SPRING IN THE WOODLAND	87
THE CHARM OF A WATER GARDEN	98
RETAINING WALL WITH RAISED FLOWER BED	114
TERRACE WALL AND STEPS	114
A WALL IN A CITY GARDEN	115
A GARDEN WALL AND DOOR	115
TAPESTRY WALL IN A SOUTH CAROLINA GARDEN	116
GARDEN PATH PAVED WITH BRICK	124
GARDEN PATH EDGED WITH BOXWOOD	126
RANDOM FLAGSTONE PAVING ON A TERRACE	126
A GARDEN TERRACE OF FLAGSTONE	127
PATIO PAVEMENT WITH MODULAR BOXES OF REDWOOD	128
A POOL AS THE CENTRAL FEATURE OF A GARDEN	134
WALL FOUNTAIN IN A PENNSYLVANIA GARDEN	136
GARDEN FOUNTAIN IN A CALIFORNIA GARDEN	137
SWIMMING POOL WITH BROAD PAVING	140
SWIMMING POOL ENCLOSED BY A SPLIT REDWOOD FENCE	141
SWIMMING POOL ENCLOSED BY A RUSTIC PICKET FENCE	142
SPINDLE FENCE IN A NEW ENGLAND GARDEN	148
SMALL SCALE POST AND RAIL FENCE	149
DOORYARD GARDEN ENCLOSED BY A PICKET FENCE	150
PLASTIC AND REDWOOD FRAME FENCE	151
REDWOOD BOARD FENCE	152
THE TREE-SHADED LAWN OF A PENNSYLVANIA FARMHOUSE	177
GROUND COVER OF JUNIPERS, HEATHER AND COTONEASTERS	203
OAK TREES IN EARLY SPRING	216
OAKS AND DOGWOODS	217
BLACK LOCUST AND MAPLES	222
LIVEOAK IN A CALIFORNIA PATIO	223
BOXWOOD AS A BACKGROUND	239
BOUNDARY PLANTING OF AZALEAS AND VIBURNUMS	240
AZALEAS AND RHODODENDRON CAROLINIANUM	246
CAMELLIA	249
REDWOOD FENCE WITH SHADOW STRIPS AND TRELLIS	280
HYBRID CLEMATIS	281
CLIMBING ROSES ON A NEW HAMPSHIRE GARAGE	281

TRUMPET VINE IN A CALIFORNIA PATIO	282
CANTERBURY BELLS	329
FOXGLOVES	331
ICELAND POPPIES	332
A PERENNIAL BORDER	335
ABUNDANT BLOOM IN A PERENNIAL GARDEN	
IN VERMONT	342
JAPANESE ANEMONES	346
AQUILEGIA	347
DELPHINIUMS	353
HEMEROCALLIS	356
JAPANESE IRIS	363
NARCISSUS IN A WOODLAND SETTING	386
SPRING BULBS ALONG A GARDEN PATH	387
TULIPS IN A FORMAL GARDEN	388
SPECIES CROCUS	392
ACHIMENES	395
TUBEROUS BEGONIAS	397
FANCY-LEAVED CALADIUMS	401
LILIES IN A PERENNIAL BORDER	414
LILIES IN A FORMAL SETTING	415
LILIUM AURATUM	416
IMPERIAL STRAIN LILIES	419
JAMBOREE STRAIN LILIES	419
IMPERIAL SILVER LILIES	420
ESTATE LILY	420
SHUKSAN LILY	420
LILIUM SPECIOSUM	421
SUNKEN ROSE GARDEN	425
ROSES IN A LATTICED BAY	437
CLIMBING ROSES	438
A WINDOW GARDEN IN A MODERN HOUSE	445
A BROAD WINDOW SILL FOR POTTED PLANTS	451
A DRAMATIC ARRANGEMENT OF HOUSE PLANTS	452
A WINDOW GARDEN	453
A RECESSED SHELF FOR PLANTS	459
A WELL PLANTED WINDOW BOX	468
AN OLD SPRING HOUSE USED AS A TOOL HOUSE	504
AN ATTRACTIVE TOOL HOUSE	504
A WORK YARD WITH POTTING BENCH	505
A TOOL HOUSE IN CALIFORNIA	506
A SMALL GREENHOUSE	517
A WELL PLACED HOME GREENHOUSE	520
A LATH HOUSE IN CALIFORNIA	541

DRAWINGS

PLANTING PLAN FOR A SUBURBAN HOME	12
PLANTING PLAN OF A FORECOURT	14
GARDEN PLAN	18
GARDEN PLAN	19
PLAN OF A PATIO	25
PLAN OF PATIO SHOWN ON P. 28	30
PLAN OF A TERRACE	32
PLAN OF TERRACE SHOWN ON P. 36	37
PLAN OF SAN FRANCISCO ROOF GARDEN	67
SECTION OF LOW DRY WALL	73
SECTIONS OF DRY WALL AND ROCK BANK	76
HERB GARDEN IN THE TUDOR STYLE	101
GRADING PLAN OF A SUBURBAN PROPERTY	107
TWO SECTIONS AND FRONT VIEW OF MASONRY	
RETAINING WALL	112, 113
RAMP AND STEPS	118
STEPS IN A RETAINING WALL	119
CONSTRUCTION OF BRICK PATHS	123
STONE PAVEMENT PLANS	124, 125
TYPES OF FENCES	146, 147
AN OUTDOOR GRILL	153
EFFECT OF ROOT PRUNING	211
TRANSPLANTING A TREE WITH A BALL	213
SHRUBS HEELED IN	241
PRUNING AN ESTABLISHED SHRUB	242
TWIG PRUNING	243
GOOD FORMS OF HEDGES	295
HEDGE FORMS WHICH ARE NOT SATISFACTORY	296
ANNUAL BORDERS	305
PINCHING BACK TO INDUCE BRANCHING	307
PERENNIAL BORDER	337
PERENNIAL BORDER	339
AN IRIS DIVISION READY TO TRANSPLANT	361
DAHLIA CLUMP AND TUBER	403
BULB PLANTING CHART	410
LILIUM REGALE AND LILIUM AURATUM WITH	
BULBETS FORMING	416
PLAN OF A ROSE GARDEN	424
PLANTING, PRUNING AND PROTECTING ROSES	429
SEED SOWING	478
PROPAGATING POT	481
SOFTWOOD STEM CUTTINGS	485
HARDWOOD STEM CUTTINGS	486

xii

BEGONIA LEAF CUTTINGS	487
ST. PAULIA LEAF CUTTINGS	488
LAYERING	492
GRAFTING	495, 496
COLD FRAME	510
CROSS SECTION OF HOTBED	510
HEATING SYSTEMS FOR HOTBEDS	513
ESPALER AND CORDON	544
METHOD OF STAKING ROWS OF TREES	546
PLANTING BOARD	546
GROWTH OF AN APPLE FRUITING SPUR	548
PRUNING PEACH TREES	552
PEACH BUDS	553
A BLACK RASPBERRY BEFORE AND AFTER PRUNING	559
PRUNING A GRAPE VINE	561, 562, 563
ROOT PRUNING	680
PROPER AND IMPROPER METHOD OF CUTTING BRANCHES	681

A GARDEN

The Gardener said: "Speak to us of gardens
and their meaning."
And the Poet answered:
A garden is a place of peace and contentment
wherein one finds refreshment for the spirit.
It is the poetry of the seasons made manifest,
the living music of Nature which sings its melody
to the heart.
It is the soul's striving for beauty, and Nature's answer
to a yearning which lies deep in the heart
of both king and peasant.
The garden knows not the limitations of wealth
or race or time. Where'er man dwells,
in cottage or in castle, it graces his abode.
The garden holds joy for all who come to behold its
loveliness, but for him who labors to create
this beauty, it holds a joy which is two-fold.
The garden is sensitive to the spirit of the artist
who dreams of its beauty, and it is sensitive also
to the hand of the gardener who makes possible
the fulfillment of the dream.
The gardener works not merely with his hands
but with his faith, for faith is the substance of
things hoped for, and he knows that from the seeds
which lie dormant in the furrow there will bloom again
the beauty which is our heritage from the past.
From poppies which flowered centuries ago on the high
Persian plains, from harebells which bloomed beside
some ancient castle wall, from mignonette which shed
its fragrance in some far-distant land, come the seeds
which the gardener holds in his hand, ready for the
sowing. And they bear not only the promise of the
beauty which is to come, but the memory of all the
beauty of the distant past as well.
The gardener counts not the hours of his labor
or the fatigue of his task.
He seeks no reward save the beauty of the garden.
And so, with the coming of the springtide,
let him who would drink deeply of life's
contentment turn his thoughts to the garden,
For there will he find himself near to
the very heart of God.

I

THE

HERITAGE OF GARDENING

"He who plants a garden, plants happiness"
CHINESE PROVERB

GARDENING is an art, a science and a craft. In order to obtain the most rewarding satisfactions from this many-jewelled occupation the gardener should possess something of the creative, buoyant spirit of the artist, the eager, inquiring mind of the scientist, and the skillful hands and diligent zeal of the craftsman.

Gardening is an art near to the hearts of the people. But unlike most other works of art, a garden requires of its owner something more than mere appreciation. He must care for it, renew it, and put his thought and handiwork into its very life.

A garden is ever-changing, for it is a thing alive. And herein lies its fascination, its similarity to all life, and its responsiveness to the efforts of the gardener. The life of a garden flows on in rhythmic sequences. The small trees which a man plants in his youth become the great trees of his old age and a legacy to his grandchildren. The conditions which produce a wealth of bloom in one season must be maintained so that there will be the same radiance of bloom in the next season.

Once begun a garden becomes a loving taskmaster, demanding of the gardener the careful planning of seasonal work, and daily diligence. But it is a rewarding master giving often in fuller measure than was anticipated, for it gives in subtle ways, not foreseen. Through the years it creates in the heart of the gardener an awareness of beauty which becomes a deeply enriching experience in his life; it imparts to him a reverence for Nature and her immutable laws; it teaches patience and humility.

Always in gardening there is a sense of eager anticipation which gives a heightened zest to life. There is not only the fullness of the enjoyment of the present, but always the expectancy of the beauty which is to come. The creative pause of winter is but a prelude to the beauty of the spring, the bounty of the summer gives way to the glory of the autumn.

The well-designed and well-established garden is the fulfillment of the gardener's hopes, his expression of an ideal, his preoccupation and his joy. Seldom is perfection attained but it is ever important to work towards perfection. In this the gardener is one with Nature. And if he can bring to his tasks understanding and humility, industry and patience, he will reap the harvest of beauty and bountiful goodness which only Nature, in her wisdom, can bestow.

Gardens have a universal appeal to the heart of man. The love of gardening knows no boundaries of wealth or station, of race or nationality, or time. It is a tradition deeply rooted in our heritage. The well-informed gardener of to-day will have a knowledge of the history of his craft, an understanding of the flow of tradition through the centuries, an appreciation of what has been accomplished in the past, and a feeling of fellowship with the many who, through the ages, have loved and labored in their gardens, and have passed on to us this rich and precious heritage.

Gardening is one of the oldest of the arts. The ancient Egyptians, the Assyrians and the Persians developed gardens of majestic grandeur and opulence. The Chinese, with their deep

1

sensitiveness to beauty, laid the foundations for a form of garden art which was later to have great influence upon other lands.

The Greeks gave to the world a new concept of gardening. Their homes were adorned with flowers, but it was in their civic design that they most skillfully applied their garden art. Their temples were surrounded by groves of trees, and trees lined the important streets and market places in their principal cities.

Much of the knowledge and skill in garden craft which the Romans possessed was acquired from the Greeks. In the second century A.D. the Romans began to build gardens of tremendous scale, inspired by the precedent of the vast palace gardens of Mesopotamia which they had conquered. They studied hydraulics and brought water from great distances by conduit to supply the ornamental fountains which adorned their villa gardens. These great villas were later to inspire the Italian garden architects to follow the Roman precedent.

Through the Dark Ages, those centuries of almost complete barbarism and ignorance, the art and practices of gardening were kept alive by the monks in the monasteries, those scholarly men of faith who made their work the interpretation of goodness and their study the means of gaining a deeper knowledge of life.

The gradual emergence of Europe into an era of revived culture and intellectual enlightenment; the spread of the study of the classics, brought about by the founding of the universities; the rise of an independent class of citizen craftsmen, unattached to the feudal system; the growing importance of the great free cities of Europe, all combined to usher in an age of greater prosperity and greater accomplishment in the arts. It was a remarkable era, destined to become known as "the Renaissance", the time of rebirth of Western civilization.

It is only natural that while this great surge of rebuilding and rediscovery of learning was taking possession of the ambitions and imaginations of free men, experiments should be undertaken in many fields, each with the hope of capturing something of the unknown and

mastering it. Painting, sculpture, architecture, garden design, music and literature, all supported by the skilled crafts, were the outgrowths of this upsurgent spirit of the times. And all the while the gains in the arts were upheld by the firmer economy, based on a lively production of goods and an ever-expanding commerce.

It was during this period that some of our most notable examples of garden art were produced; the great villas of Italy, the palace gardens of Spain, the vast plaisances of the French châteaux, the careful parterres of the Dutch, and the beautiful manor house gardens of England.

In the 16th century the Italians began to build palatial country villas after the manner of the Romans, and they designed and planted these gardens with all the artistic and poetic refinement of their sensitive natures. The results were marvelous essays of merged architecture, verdure, trees, sculpture, flowers and water-courses, all woven into designs of subtle harmony and perfect proportions. So beautiful were these pictorial compositions that they arrested the attention and won the admiration of the many visitors from all parts of Europe who flocked to Italy; and the Italian style, with some variations, soon spread to other realms and other climates. Italian artists and architects were invited to France and Spain to practice their professions and to teach. Thus the Italian Renaissance garden became the European Renaissance garden.

For two hundred years this formal, architectural style of garden art was practiced throughout Europe. The artist-architects of each nation designed in this grand manner and modified the work of their predecessors to suit their times. In all these gardens formal shapes, symmetrically placed, predominated. The details expressed the basic character of the design, with emphasis on straight pathways, clipped hedges, balustrades, fountains and pools, and sculpture.

The Spaniards copied the geometric patterns of the Moors and, later, the over-ornamented details of the baroque Italian gardens. The French enlarged the scale of garden building to include many acres in their far-spreading

VIEW OF LAKE COMO AND THE ITALIAN ALPS FROM VILLA BALBIANELLO

bosques and tapis-verts. The Dutch reduced the scale in order to fit their gardens compactly into the inevitably small areas available. And the English drew from Italian, French and Dutch styles in developing their formal gardens, adding notable touches of their own, such as the Mount and the long perennial border.

When the early colonists came to America in order to gain greater freedom from the lingering tyranny that still held power in Europe, or in the hope of broader opportunities in the New World, the influence of the Renaissance was still being felt throughout Europe. Each generation was contributing its full force to the wave of intellectual growth, and the break with the old which these settlers made seemed only briefly to interrupt the flow of this energy and the search for a new and a better way of life.

The colonists naturally drew their inspiration from the familiar scenes of their homes in England. The villages of New England resembled the villages of old England, except that most of the houses were built of wood instead of stone or brick or half-timber and plaster. The plantations of Virginia, Maryland and the Carolinas were set out in much the same arrangement as the manors of England. Their conception of garden art was that of seventeenth- and eighteenth-century England.

Thus, precedent for garden design in the colonies was drawn from the English interpretation of the Renaissance spirit, just as the architecture which we know as Colonial was copied by painstaking carpenter-designers in the colonies from the Georgian of England, itself a translation from Italian Renaissance into English methods and materials. The gardens were formal in major lines. Prim, patterned flower beds, straight paths edged with boxwood or with flowers, fruit trees in rows, turf squares bordered with flowers, these were typical features of the colonial garden. As architectural features and purely decorative ornaments were rarely included, the design was expressed almost entirely in plant materials, a medium which greatly softens the regularity of the formal. The gardens at Williamsburg and the garden at Mount Ver-

non which have been so faithfully restored are fine examples of gardens of this period.

In the latter years of the eighteenth century the Spanish tradition of the secluded patio was brought into Southern California by the Spanish missionaries and early settlers, and, with modifications, has remained a feature of most gardens in this area.

The Renaissance tradition in America lost its vitality in the early years of the Republic. In order to infuse new life into the thread of design, Greek forms were resorted to in architecture, as if design could go no further and must return to the ultimate source of classic precedent. The Greek revival had its brief day. But so utterly unadapted was it to domestic needs of the times that it was soon abandoned, and from that time on, for the next seventy years, no serious attempt was made to derive inspiration from the classic monuments of architecture.

This trend of architecture was also the trend of garden design of that period, and was only a phase of what was happening in the mind of the growing nation. The attention and efforts of the people were absorbed in the great tasks of winning the West, extending the railroads, and developing industries, while art was all but lost in the headlong rush, the unceasing competition of the moment. To build up a civilization in the wilderness was, in itself, a work demanding the energies of several generations, and it is small wonder that, until Americans had earned the leisure to travel in Europe and to see for themselves the art heritages of the race, no great demand for art was made, no great appreciation of art was manifest. Briefly, then, we may consider that between the colonist, who came full of knowledge of artistic precedent, and the later traveler who rediscovered it, there was a gap in which little contact was maintained with the older culture of Europe, and little thought given to developing culture here. Lest this seem unappreciative of a century which produced Irving, Emerson and Cooper, let us say that it was a century the very conditions of which focused the minds of the people upon politics, letters, industry and invention, rather than upon art.

Through much of this period the concept of a garden was that of a collection of plants, purely horticultural in purpose. There was great interest in botany, in the introduction of new plants, and in the growing of fine horticultural specimens, and these interests completely occupied the minds of the gardeners of the period. Save for the efforts of Andrew Jackson Downing to introduce into this country the romantic, naturalistic expression of landscape design, as expressed in England by the works of Sir Humphrey Repton, no attempt was made to produce examples of garden art of any significance.

During the last decades of the 19th century and the early decades of the 20th century many educated Americans traveled widely in Europe, and renewed a close contact with that rich culture after a lapse of several generations. During the same period the country home in America was assuming a more important aspect, and gardening was again becoming a field of artistic expression. The garden styles of Italy, France and England were diligently studied and copied. English, Scotch and Dutch gardeners came to this country in great numbers to carry on their craft in a land of widening opportunities. Nurseries expanded to meet the steadily increasing demands for choice plant materials. In this era of prosperity the art and craft of gardening flourished as never before.

But the estate, with its expansive lawns, its woodland, and its well-designed and superbly maintained garden, was the part-time residence of the man of wealth. These were gardens for the few, cared for by professional gardeners.

After the First World War the building of large and magnificent estates continued, but a change gradually became perceptible. In the many small homes being built in the rapidly spreading suburbs more and more people began to take an interest in the development of their grounds, and the owners of small homes took gardening seriously into their hearts. Gardening was no longer for the few, but for the many. Each decade since then has witnessed an ever-increasing number of enthusiastic home gardeners.

These new gardens are of necessity different from the old. They are more free from the tradition of formality and style. They have much charm, but demand less in the way of maintenance, they are more lived in, and perhaps more intimately loved. Thus has evolved the modern garden as a harmonious setting for the modern home.

A garden, more readily than any other artistic expression, reflects the taste of the present and changes with changing ideals. We must not expect garden design to imitate styles of other times or other lands. The very life of art is its power to rise phoenix-like from its own past self. Tradition we have, precedent we have. Knowledge of what has been accomplished in art in past centuries is helpful and often inspiring. But it is not the goal. The purpose of garden design is to create beauty for its own sake and to provide an environment for happy living, seeking at the same time to fulfill the practical requirements of good gardening.

II
DESIGN

THE visual appearance of the natural landscape is the result of many gradual changes through the ages, brought about by changes in its geologic formation, the climate and its vegetation. The use of land for man's occupancy has brought about further changes, each one tending to override the natural causes, or to direct them to different ends. The farm has replaced the forest and the prairie; the town has spread out over the farm.

The design of the landscape for man's use begins with a careful study of the natural conditions of the site. It is the means of guiding the modifications in the use and appearance of the land so that the resulting forms will be harmonious, pleasing and convenient. The preservation of natural beauty and the development of the landscape as a work of art are the important purposes of landscape architecture.

There are certain fundamental qualities inherent in all good design, and a landscape composition should have the same qualities which are found in other works of art. A good design is ageless. It transcends style and outlasts time.

A well-designed landscape should have unity, harmony and fitness to use. A dominant focal point, or center of interest, a consistency of style, and the rhythmic repetition of minor details will contribute to the unity of the composition. There must be a harmonious relationship with the surroundings. The design of the landscape should be in harmony with the architectural design of the house, and with the natural conditions of the site. There should be harmony of line and form, giving balance to the composition, and harmony of scale in the parts and details. Scale is one of the most difficult qualities to maintain. It is so easy for some detail to become too large and over-dominant, or too small, and thus lose its significance.

Each of these relationships has its bearing on the resulting composition. Each must be studied before a satisfying design is possible.

Beauty is a quality to be found in all true works of art. It is elusive, difficult to capture, and in landscape design it may take years of growth for it to become fully evident. If, with the introduction of new concepts and new ideals we are too ready to sacrifice beauty for efficiency, too eager to seek other goals, such as utility and convenience, or newness for novelty's sake, we will lose something more precious than anything which we may attain.

Landscape design is a subtle art. It requires an understanding and an appreciation of natural conditions, imagination in foreseeing the possibilities of the site, skill in creating artistic compositions, taste in selecting materials, and ingenuity in adjusting diverse requirements.

Unless it is well designed, a landscape which is being modified for more special uses is likely to become an inconvenient arrangement of parts, lacking in beauty, dignity and charm. In terms of good living a well-studied design will bring deeply rewarding satisfactions.

Style in Landscape Design

In architecture and in landscape architecture style is intimately connected with social customs, and with the economic and political structure of the times in which it is produced. Indeed, the various stylistic expressions of design, and the evolution of design itself, have come about more as a result of economic trends and the social history of people than by a narrow development within the arts.

6

Every race or generation which has developed a recognizable style has done so out of its environment, and partly out of its own distinctive culture, as well as out of its sense of beauty and order. Habit and tradition tend to fix existing styles, while changing social customs tend to bring about new styles.

The influence of one country upon another has been tremendous at times, but seldom has a style been transplanted without some modification in expression, due to local standards of worth, or to the use of local materials. When the Gothic style of architecture which flourished in western Europe penetrated Italy it did not reach a full expression there. At first it was applied as a sort of veneer to Italian buildings not at all Gothic in form, and it resulted in such compromises as are expressed by the Doges' Palace in Venice. Later, when the classic styles of Renaissance Italy were adopted by other countries of Europe, they became not so purely classic as they had been in the country of their revival. In Northern Europe roofs were steeper, and often contained dormer windows, a holdover from the Gothic tradition. In the stoneless regions of Holland and eastern England it was, from earliest times, necessary to use brick for permanent structures instead of stone. This warmer material gave the designer much freedom and an opportunity for variety in texture not heretofore associated with the austerity of the ancient precedent. The resulting Georgian style of England and the Dutch Renaissance style were, therefore, quite different in character from the precedent which inspired them.

Landscape design, because of the very nature of its material, is even more limited by local conditions than is architecture. Plant materials can be used only in climatic zones which are somewhat similar to those of their place of origin. While an Italian villa can be built in New England and its design may be archaeologically correct, it cannot be embellished by the cypresses, the stone pines and the olive trees traditional in the Italian landscape.

Style is as recognizable in garden art as it is in architecture. Our American heritage includes the simple dignity of the New England colonial village, the restricted, prim yards of the formal town houses in Philadelphia, the spacious formality of the southern plantation home and the secluded patios of the early Spanish Missions in California.

The precedent for these early gardens in America were the abundant gardens of England, both great and small, the stately, architectural gardens of Italy, the measured formality of France, and the serried patios of Spain. All of these older styles were faithfully based on the formal plan: trees in balanced symmetry, straight paths, paved and precisely edged, a flat terrace with a clipped hedge at the outer rim to provide a satisfactory transition between the formality of the garden and the naturalness of the outer landscape. The axis of symmetry was used to emphasize the architectural character of the garden, and often to bring into an artistic unity a wide area under cultivation.

But also strongly rooted in our American tradition is a later art form, the naturalistic style of England. In this graceful, flowing style the axis is discarded in favor of sweeping curves and balanced asymmetry of masses. This style is adapted to wide areas with simple compositions of open lawns and meadows, flanked by groves of trees.

Contemporary Design

As at present widely practiced, landscape design is a method of making compositions which achieve harmony and balance without symmetry. In this type of design there is no evident similarity to established styles, and even not much expectation of evolving a new style. There is such variety in most contemporary work that the essentials of a style—the agreement on an ideal —are lacking. There is emphasis on freedom of expression, on individuality. Startling effects are achieved by combining dissimilar forms and by dramatic accents. Some designers avoid compliance with proven methods of construction, so intent are they on originality.

Throughout the field of design today there is great dependence and emphasis on materials,

THIS IS A GARDEN OF FORMAL
PLAN WITH SYMMETRICAL PARTS,
WELL FRAMED, AND WITH
EMPHASIS ON THE CENTRAL POOL.
IT IS RICH IN COLOR
COMPOSITIONS, AND BECAUSE THE
CENTRAL SECTION IS AT A LOWER
LEVEL THE FLOWERS SHOW TO
BETTER ADVANTAGE.

especially newly developed structural materials. As a consequence plants are sometimes given minor roles in the total design, and such plants as are used are often artificially modified by pruning and shearing. However, plants are often generously used, and with great skill, to produce dramatic and beautiful compositions. In such designs they dominate, just as they so often do in Nature and in traditional designs.

Modern design has various expressions. It cannot be limited within an accurate definition. It is buoyant, surprising, joyous, original, and ever evolving new forms by experiment. At its best it recognizes the demands, limitations and oppor-

8

tunities of the site. It captures something of the mood of the environs. It contributes something fresh to the art of living, and it makes appreciative use of the beauty of created and natural forms.

A work of landscape design should never be judged on the basis of whether it is contem-porary or traditional. Its merit is dependent on something more enduring, on the subtle qualities of harmony and fitness, balance, line and form. In spite of changes brought about by the intro-duction of new materials and new concepts, the basic principles of landscape design remain the same. Utilitarian things must be convenient and economical. Aesthetic things must appeal to the senses as being right because they are harmonious and beautiful.

Creating a Design

Creating a design is an orderly process of thought, a sequence of decisions, resulting in an arrangement of forms and objects in a harmonious composition. It is a method of making decisions between many possible arrangements.

Without a design there is no opportunity, until it is too late, to decide between various alternatives. The creation of a design is a means of evolving and sifting out all possible solutions to a problem in order to reach a satisfactory decision regarding function, form, materials and aesthetic quality. The process of designing crystallizes and makes clearer the image of the composition. It is a systematic method of foreseeing results. A design is evolved out of the practical requirements of the problem, out of the restrictions and opportunities of the site, out of the imagination of the designer.

The design is usually expressed in a series of preliminary sketches, followed by maps, plans, elevations, perspective drawings, and finally working drawings showing details of construction and planting.

In some cases it may be possible to execute the work without plans, but unless one has had long experience one is not likely to solve the problems with good results. Plans are a means to several ends. They are most helpful to the designer in making studies and reaching decisions. They are more definite than a written description can be, although working drawings should always be supplemented by written specifications. They are exact enough to make it possible to compute quantities of materials accurately and to estimate costs. From the finished plans the lines of the work may be staked out on the ground. Above all, the very process of making plans is the best means of foreseeing the problems and of making certain that all of them have been solved.

The first sketches should show the general arrangements but not the details. Several sketches should be made showing alternate schemes. The designer should judge the sketches critically, and coming back to them with a fresh mind, should make whatever revisions will improve the arrangement or the composition. Some of these early sketches may be discarded as better arrangements supersede less adequate ones, or the best elements of several schemes may be combined to make a more satisfactory composition. Ultimately the design as it evolves will incorporate the most desirable ideas of both the owner and the designer. The first step in creating a design is, therefore, to clarify ideas, to make them definite, and to improve upon them by a process of experimentation in pictorial form.

The preliminary sketches should be followed by more exact drawings, done to scale; and at every stage the critical judgment should be applied. These drawings should include a general plan which will provide for all the foreseen conditions of the site and will best meet the desires and needs of the owners. Perspective sketches can be used to further express the design.

The general plan, after it has been carefully considered and approved, should be supplemented by working drawings for grading and planting and by detailed plans of construction, usually drawn at larger scale. The complete set of plans fully expresses the design.

THE DESIGN OF THE HOME PROPERTY

Every problem in the design of a home property is an individual problem the terms of which are dictated by the desires of the owner, the nature of the site and the funds available for development and maintenance.

No two owners are apt to have the same combination of personal desires for their homes, and sites vary in their capacity for development, but in general the successful design is one which provides adequately for all the practical requirements; which has a distinction and individuality, arising either from the nature of the site or from the artistry of the design, or from both; and which reflects the taste of the owners and satisfies their desires most completely.

HERE IS A FORMAL GARDEN WITH
BOXWOOD-EDGED BORDERS IN
WHICH AZALEAS AND DOGWOOD
TREES ARE THE DOMINANT PLANTS.
THE ENFRAMEMENT OF A HEMLOCK
HEDGE GIVES PROTECTION FROM
THE WIND, AND THE PINE IN THE
BACKGROUND AND THE ARBOR
WITH CLIMBING HYDRANGEA AT
THE ENTRANCE FURTHER ENCLOSE
THIS COMPOSITION OF RICH COLORS.

Every site has pictorial assets and liabilities. Some are apparent, some are latent. The creative designer must be able to see through the actual conditions to a number of possible compositions and to a number of solutions of the practical problems. One of the first steps in creating a design is the evaluation of these possibilities and the summing up of the practical facilities which must be provided. One must endeavor to plan for these necessary facilities in such a way as to preserve, as far as possible, the picturesque qualities of the site. Major decisions come first, details later.

In developing a new piece of property one of the first decisions is that of the position of the house. Its orientation in respect to sunshine, prevailing winds and views; its relation to the land forms and its relation to the other units of the design are all important matters for consideration. Many suburban houses are placed on the

11

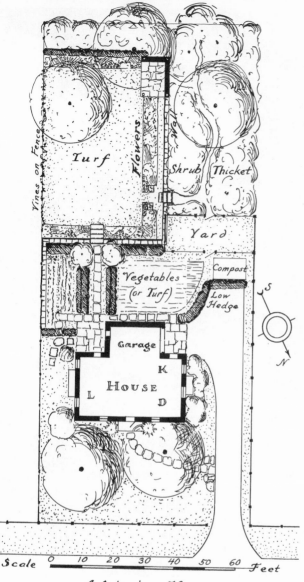

Turf

Flowers

Shrub Thicket

Vines on Fence

Wall

Yard

Vegetables
(or Turf)

Compost

Low
Hedge

S

N

Garage

K

HOUSE

L

D

Scale   0   10   20   30   40   50   60   Feet

A Suburban Home

well. The most functional arrangement and the one most economical of space is that in which the service door, the kitchen, and the purely utilitarian part of the grounds and of the house are grouped together towards the street. The other rooms thus occupy the more remote part of the house and look out upon a secluded area which can be attractively designed and developed for satisfactory outdoor living.

The grounds should be developed in a style in harmony with the character of the house. A Cape Cod cottage requires the compactness and the simple charm of a cottage garden. A house with horizontal lines and low roof suggests a more ample development of the grounds. A home on a wooded hillside offers opportunities for the development of a naturalistic garden, with a mass of azaleas and rhododendrons. A house in the Colonial tradition should be graced with a garden developed with the preciseness and dignity of the period. In contemporary design precise formality usually plays little part and there is more freedom of expression. The creative imagination and skill of the designer has free play and great originality is often displayed in adjusting the design to the site and in meeting the requirements of the owners. Great emphasis is placed on the use of flowers on patio and terrace.

The three major functional units of the home property are the approach, the service area, and the area devoted to living and recreational pursuits. In general, the approach should be reasonably direct, the service area convenient and accessible, and the living area ample, secluded and attractive. Each of these units should be contiguous with the corresponding portion of the house, each should be as complete and as segregated from the others as is practical. Local topographic conditions may dictate compromises in this scheme but wherever it is possible to adhere to this program the plan should result in a convenient, economical and functional arrangement.

After assigning different areas of the ground to certain uses, one of the next steps is to separate these areas from one another and con-

lot which they occupy with utter disregard for the general design of the property. All too frequently the house has been placed very nearly in the center of the lot and the garage at the rear in the hope that it would be less conspicuous. But such a position for the garage often appropriates for the driveway 20 percent of all the land not occupied by the house and, if repeated by the neighbors, results in a panorama of garages as

nect them logically. This is best done by masses of foliage, trees, shrubs, hedges, fences, or walls. The designer should indicate on the plan the position of open lawn and of trees; the position of screen plantings to hide unsatisfactory views; the positions of viewpoints, and the directions of distant views. There is an element of the practical and an element of the æsthetic in each of these decisions.

On a small property space must be very carefully planned and economically used. No amount of embellishment can overcome the inconvenience of an ill-adapted plan or make up for the loss of available space caused by an illogical arrangement of parts. The needs and desires of the family must be carefully considered and one alternative weighed against another—whether a certain space would be of more value if used as a play area than if used as a vegetable garden. And here let it be said that even in progressive and enlightened communities where public playgrounds exist, nothing quite takes the place of a sand pile or a favorite tree to climb in a child's own home yard.

On a very small lot, bounded as it is by straight property lines and the straight lines of the house, a rectilinear design is sometimes the most logical and most effective. This does not imply that the design must be symmetrical. The placing of a few well-chosen trees and the developing of one or two axes will be enough to make the plan harmonize with its semi-artificial site. The planting of the shrubs and flowers may be incidental. Unity of design may be obtained by emphasizing the boundaries, by separating the property from its adjoining neighbors, and by concentrating interest within the area. The boundary may take the form of a hedge, or a fence, or a wall, which sets off and enhances the composition within.

One sees so many examples of efforts wasted because of the lack of a definite plan. Trees, shrubs and flowers are so often planted in haphazard fashion without regard for the beauty of the composition as a whole, or the eventual size of the plants. The same amount of diligent effort and money applied to carrying out a well-conceived plan would result in a much more satisfying and beautiful picture. It is not the amount expended, but rather the exercise of forethought and good taste, which is necessary to create beautiful home surroundings, and the small property deserves as much consideration as any, and perhaps even more.

Foundation Planting

There are probably more poor examples of foundation planting in America than of any other type of planting.

Foundation planting has been practiced with the often expressed purpose of fitting the house to the surrounding area, harmonizing its vertical surface with the horizontal lines of the ground about it, compromising the artificiality of the architecture with the naturalness of the landscape. These purposes are worthy, but how much harmony is there in the monotony of stiffly spotted little evergreens? Does a building fit into its site better if it is surrounded by a smothering mantle of greenery? And will evergreen trees in a variety of form and color and texture, trimmed to resemble croquettes, really serve to harmonize a dignified piece of architecture with its surroundings? A finely designed house that has charm arising from its own design has more in common with a simple, dignified landscape of trees and graceful lawn than it has with what we have come to mean by "foundation planting."

It is time that we stopped thinking about foundation planting altogether, and allowed ourselves to think about the whole setting of the house, its background and foreground, the ground forms, and the play of lights and shadows upon its walls. Then we would let the planting at the base of the walls be as unobtrusive as possible, and so moderate would we be in the use of both quantity and variety of plants that the attention would remain on the structure, where it should rightly be. The planting in the foreground of the house should contain only such plants as harmonize with each other. A few varieties in greater number are more easily harmonized than are many varieties. Yet variety is a quality which enriches, and makes possible a succession of interest as the season advances. With care in the selection, it is possible to use variety and yet keep to a fixed general character. This may be accomplished to a considerable extent by avoiding the use of plants which are conspicuous because they are unique in form or color. A beautiful house needs a beautifully designed setting, one which embraces the whole house as a dominant element in the composition, and subordinates the details to their proper places. A planting which is simple and dignified will always remain satisfying.

Built-in Planting Beds

A modification of the usual foundation planting area is the built-in, raised, planting bed found in an increasing number of homes of contemporary design. This consists of a low retaining wall built about three feet out from the base of the house, and usually of the same material as the house. Such beds are suitable only for houses built of stone, brick or some other form of masonry.

Planting beds vary in height according to the design of the house. They should be deep enough to provide a good bed of soil for the plants to be grown in them. The bed should have no bottom, the soil in the bed being contiguous with the soil below. Thus the capillary movement of water in the soil will prevent an excessive evaporation of moisture from the bed, and will also aid in the drainage of surplus water.

An exposure of partial sun and partial shade is ideal for most plants grown in raised planting beds. Beds exposed to full sun throughout the day tend to dry out very rapidly and many plants are unable to withstand the combination of full sun and the reflected heat from the wall of the building, which can be very intense during the midsummer months. In such an exposure the choice of plant materials is definitely restricted.

The selection of plants for built-in beds must be given careful consideration, thought being given to such points as hardiness, ultimate size, and good year-round appearance. Some of the dwarf evergreens and shrubs meet these exacting requirements well, and certain perennials and

bulbs may be used to bring animation and color into the planting composition during the spring and summer months.

For partial shade in cool climates the following plants are recommended: Azaleas of the smaller types, such as Kaempferi and Kurume; Ilex crenata convexa; Lonicera nitida; and the spreading Junipers. Among the shrubby perennials Iberis sempervirens and Daphne cneorum are particularly good, and tuberous begonias and achimenes may be used along the front of the bed to give a brilliant note of color during the summer months. Patches here and there of early spring bulbs, such as the species crocus, the scillas, the narcissus and the lovely species tulips such as Tulip Kaufmanniana, will give added interest in the spring, as will the colchicums and autumn-flowering crocus in the fall.

For more dense shade Leucothoë catesbaei, Pieris japonica, Ilex glabra and Sarcococca

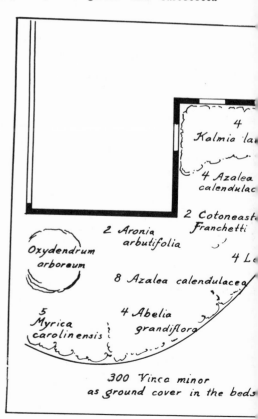

4
Kalmia la

4 Azalea
calendulac

2 Cotoneast
Franchetti

2 Aronia
arbutifolia

Oxydendrum
arboreum

4 L

8 Azalea calendulacea

5
Myrica
carolinensis

4 Abelia
grandiflora

300 Vinca minor
as ground cover in the beds

hookeriana may be used, with Vinca minor and Ajuga reptans as a ground cover in the foreground, enlivened with occasional clumps of violas and primroses in the spring.

In mild climates where frosts are not known there is a wide choice of material: Fatsia japonica, with its striking, large leaves, may be used to achieve very dramatic effects, as may Fatshedia lizei and the lovely fern pine, Podocarpus elongata; Acuba japonica variegata; Phormium tenax, the New Zealand flax; Agapanthus africanus, the Blue lily of the Nile; and Plumbago capensis may also be used very effectively.

Trees and Shrubs in the Landscape Composition

Plantings of trees and shrubs form the masses in the landscape plan. Not only are they important objects in themselves, interesting in outline, texture, and color, but they are one of the best means of marking the boundaries of the place, and separating the various functional areas from each other. A mass of flowering shrubs, a hedge, or a vine-covered fence, each makes an excellent screen about the service yard. Where a view is to be kept open, the most effective means of relating it to the foreground is to frame it within the branches of trees in the middle distance. This separates it from every other scene, fixes the attention upon the distance, and contrasts the shadowy foreground with the light-filled countryside. At the same time, the trees afford shade which makes the house and its adjoining lawn or terrace more livable in summer. Trees and shrubs determine, by their position, the shapes of open areas in the design, contrast the solid masses with the open spaces, the shade with the sunlight. The designers of the Italian villas were masters of the use of this kind of dramatic contrast.

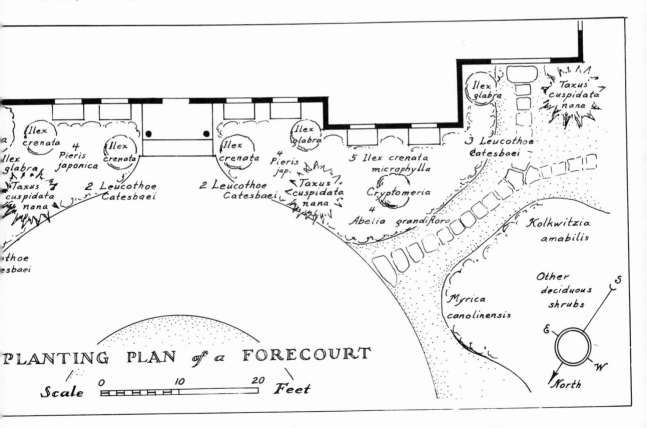

PLANTING PLAN of a FORECOURT

Scale 0 10 20 Feet

THE PLANTS USED HERE ARE LARGELY EVERGREEN SHRUBS WHICH ARE HARDY ON THE NORTHERN EXPOSURE.

THIS SIMPLE COLONIAL GARDEN CONSISTS OF BOXWOOD HEDGES, FLOWER BORDERS AND LAWN. THERE IS NO SYMMETRY HERE, YET A CAREFUL BALANCE OF PARTS IS MOST PLEASING. THE HOUSE IS A PENNSYLVANIA STONE COLONIAL FARMHOUSE WHICH HAS BEEN BEAUTIFULLY RESTORED AND ENLARGED. THE TWO PARTS, THE HOUSE AND THE GARDEN, COMPLEMENT EACH OTHER.

The owner should see that care be taken to protect the existing trees upon a piece of property which is to be developed. It is well to remember what the building of a house is apt to do to trees standing close about. Foundations cut through the root system, the excavations lower the water level of the sub-soil, thus reducing the tree's available water supply, and paved areas of drive, or terrace, deprive the soil of its normal supply of water and air. In many instances, trees become so encumbered with adverse conditions, as a result of building operations, that they die after several years of struggle. Prompt and adequate feeding of the trees may save them. It is an obvious absurdity to compromise a house plan to save a worthy tree and then have it die from lack of consideration of its needs. A new structure should be kept at such a distance from any tree which is to be saved, that

only a very small fraction of the roots is disturbed.

Each new tree should be selected for a variety of purposes—shade, flowers, fruit, or picturesque outline. To fulfill most completely the exacting requirements of the home property, trees should have the following characteristics. They should be in scale with their surroundings; they should have good habits, that is, they should never drop sections of bark (Sycamore) or unpleasant fruit (Ginkgo) on the terrace; or be the habitual home of insects (Wild Cherry), or require much spraying and attention to protect them from insects. They should not produce flowers with a disagreeable odor, like the Hawthorns and Privets; they should not be brittle and lose great branches in the storms; and they should not disperse a quantity of seedlings. If, besides these negative qualities, they possess

16

A GRACIOUS TERRACE IN A VERMONT GARDEN

well-shaped, symmetrical heads or picturesque outlines, if they produce beautiful flowers or fruits, or if they turn to gorgeous hues in autumn, then they are especially desirable.

For the small suburban property the choice is necessarily limited, as the matter of scale must be given consideration. In most designs, a sense of proper scale is one of the most difficult quali-

ties to preserve. A small house may be made to seem still smaller by giving it a big chimney. We say then that the chimney is "out of scale." The same thing applies to the design of a residential property. A small yard may seem even smaller because of the presence of very large trees. This changing of the apparent scale may be just what we wish to accomplish. Certainly there is no

17

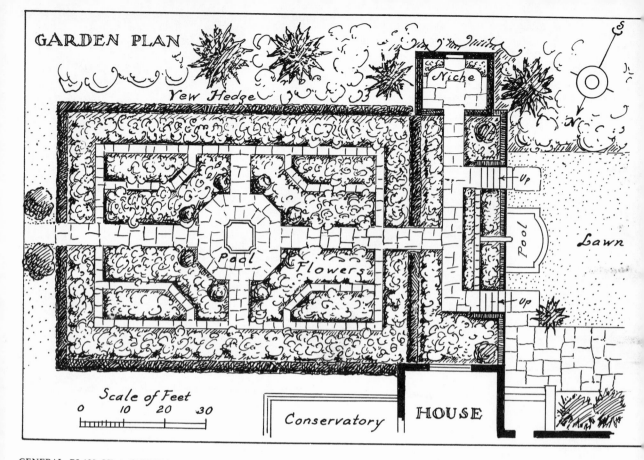

GENERAL PLAN OF A GARDEN. PATTERN OF PAVEMENT AND FLOWER BEDS.

more home-like picture than a little New England farmhouse standing in the shelter of a great elm tree. But some houses do not belong to this type of setting. In the suburbs there is not the open countryside to make the elm tree seem at home and appropriate. Everywhere is evident that saving of space, forced by the high price of land. The lots are narrow, usually too narrow for the houses upon them; the street may be narrow in proportion to the amount of traffic it is to carry. The elm tree in such a situation may very well be too large—much as we love the elm. Smaller trees are better adapted to the small suburban home.

And adequate expenditure on trees and shrubs is an excellent investment. The plants continue to increase in value as the years pass, and to contribute, as nothing else can, to the value of the property.

See page 208 for "Trees for the Small Place."

Architectural Features in the Garden

A garden composed entirely of plant material is apt to lack precision and definiteness of design. An architectural feature placed at the end of an axis, or used as a central motif, will serve to emphasize the major lines of the design, and to impart to it that note of regularity, so important in the more highly wrought surroundings of the house.

Pavements of flagstone and brick have an architectural function, as their regular pattern and outline give form to the plan. Walls and fences, and even hedges, are architectural, and

18

they can be very decorative with their rhythmic repetition of parts. But the principal architectural embellishments of the garden are those structures which are functional as well as beautiful. The picturesque tool-house or dovecote at the corner of the garden wall, the summer house, the potting shed, even the rear of the garage, all offer infinite possibilities for pleasant architectural treatment. Lattices, arbors, trellises and pergolas not only provide practical support for vines but also contribute to the architectural embellishment of the garden. Fountains, sundials, statues, seats and benches may be treated as incidental ornaments or as dominant features, but in either case they are architectural in character and give permanence to scenes made up largely of changing plant forms.

The architectural features in a garden should be in complete harmony with the architecture of the house and its surroundings. If the house is informal in character, the summer house in the garden may be of a somewhat rustic design. If, on the other hand, the architecture of the house is distinctly formal, the architectural features in the garden must carry out the formality of the general scheme. If the house is colonial in character, the dominant features in the garden should be of the same period and in like character.

PLANTING DESIGN

By arranging plants in harmonious compositions it is possible to change an ordinary scene which has no distinction and no natural advan-

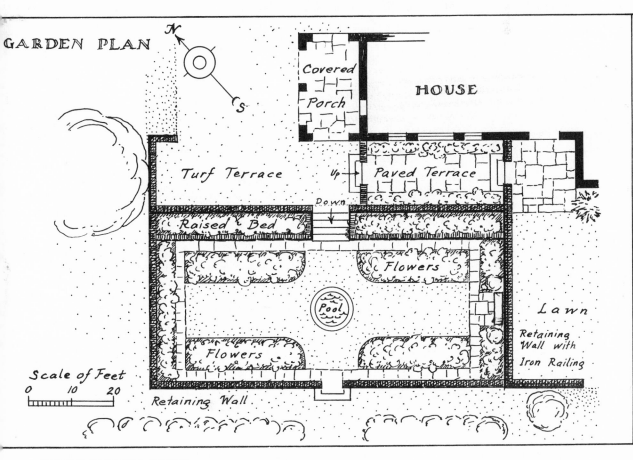

GENERAL PLAN OF A GARDEN

tages to one of rare beauty and charm. The wide variety of form, color, and texture found in plant materials offers infinite possibilities both for harmony and for contrast.

Harmony is one of the principal elements of good design and it is interesting to note that the forces of nature are constantly at work to harmonize the landscape scene, and that they are capable of slowly restoring it to orderliness after man's intrusion. In windy places the plants remain close to the ground, and develop tough stems and tenacious leaves. Even trees which normally grow tall and straight in the forest will adapt themselves to the wind by growing broad and low. On steep banks where the rain at first washes the soil away, vines will begin to spread out over the bare ground, dead leaves will collect under the tangle, and presently all manner of plants spring up from seeds and reclothe the earth with verdure. These are examples of nature's methods of harmonizing life forces with the elements. The result is usually a harmonious composition because the very plant forms have had to adapt themselves to the conditions of the site. Anyone working with plants must understand the forces of nature to which the plants are exposed, and the ability of the plants to thrive under varying conditions.

One of the most important considerations in the arrangement of plants in the landscape composition is the point of view from which the plants will be seen. So important is it that unless the viewpoint is well chosen the beauty of the plants may be greatly diminished, or lost entirely. For example—many small, delicate rock plants are best seen at close range and should preferably be planted on a bank above the path, whereas the best effect produced by other rock plants is that of a broad carpet of color which should be viewed from a distance of many feet. The blossoms of the red maple in early spring are far more beautiful when viewed from a distance with the gray winter forest behind them than they are when seen at close range. Sugar maples in their autumn brilliance are finer when seen in masses at a distance than they are in the foreground. Rhododendrons are more magnificent when viewed at a distance of forty feet than they are at three feet. And so one could recall example after example of the effect of viewpoint upon the appearance and beauty of plants. The interrelation of viewpoint, foreground, objects of principal interest and background is nowhere more important than in the art of landscape architecture. Each affects the other and together set the conditions for making the picture.

EXCELLENT FOUNDATION PLANTING

The simplest aspect of a plant is its silhouette. In some situations the shadowy stems of trees contrasted with a sunny meadow or against an open sea beyond produce a picturesque composition in lines, as, for instance, the twisted trunks of sassafras along a shore line. In other instances

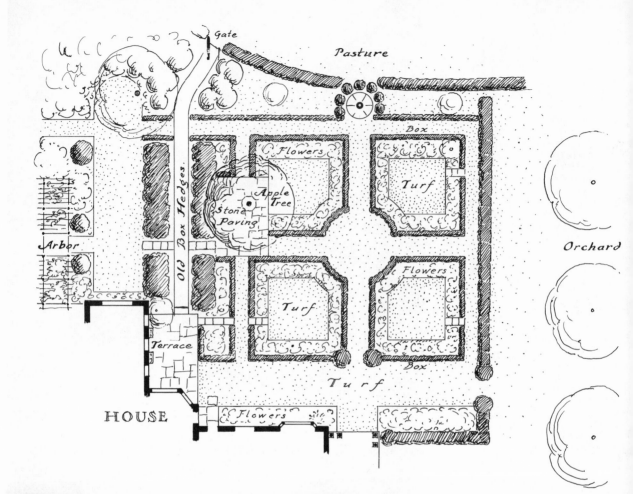

Gate

Pasture

Flowers

Box

Turf

Apple Tree

Stone Paving

Old Box Hedges

Arbor

Turf

Flowers

Orchard

Terrace

Turf

Box

HOUSE

Flowers

SUMMER HOUSE IN THE
GEORGIAN STYLE

THIS LITTLE DOORYARD
GARDEN ON CAPE COD IS A
FINE EXPRESSION OF LOCAL
TRADITION. SIMPLE, SMALL
IN SCALE, AND PRECISE,
IT IS IN PERFECT HARMONY
WITH THE HOUSE. THE
ABUNDANT ROSES, THE
LILACS AND THE BOXWOOD
ARE TIME-HONORED
FAVORITES. THE FLOWERING
ENCLOSURE EXPRESSES THE
WELCOME AND THE
HOSPITALITY OF COUNTRY
LIVING.

A PICTURESQUE GARDEN HOUSE

A FLOWER GARDEN IN A CITY
YARD

trees make a silhouette by spreading dark masses of foliage against the sky, the pines being distinguished for their bold outlines. Another dramatic silhouette is made by white birch seen against a background of hemlocks. Any tree of distinctive outline, such as the American elm, the white oak, or the Lombardy poplar, is excellent in silhouette. Often a mist or a winter's snowstorm will bring into silhouette trees which at other times merge with those about them. Different species of native trees have typically characteristic outlines which make them recognizable by their silhouette alone. Hickory, sugar maple, black walnut, tulip-trees, the white ash

and the Kentucky coffeetree are among the native trees most easily distinguished from a distance.

The three outstanding aspects of plants are form, texture, and color. The outline of a tree seen as a silhouette is a print of its form, but the more subtle modelling is better appreciated by the play of light on the surface of the foliage masses. The importance of form in design can hardly be overemphasized, as it gives balance and substance to the composition. And form is much more than outline. Whereas the outline of Juniperus chinensis Pfitzeriana and the outline of Taxus cuspidata are very similar, their forms

24

A PLEASANT PATIO

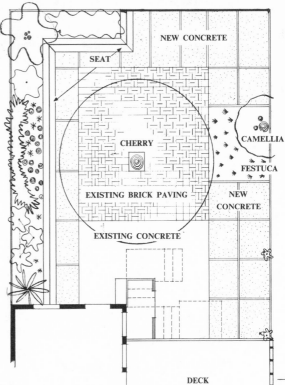

PLAN FOR A PATIO, COMBINING BRICK WORK AND CONCRETE

PLEASANT FOUNDATION PLANTING FOR A SMALL HOME

are quite different, because the branches of the yew are in somewhat flat planes, while the many, fine branches of the juniper are grouped in thick masses.

Texture is a matter of leaf size and distribution. The contribution which some trees and shrubs make to a landscape composition is largely in the texture of their foliage. Notable for this rather subtle beauty are the Katsura-tree (Cercidiphyllum japonicum), the birches, the locusts, the English maple and the English oak. Many of the azaleas have leaves grouped at the end of the branches which make beautiful patterns. The same effect at a larger scale is produced by the compound leaves of the horse chestnut. Trees and shrubs with compound leaves are apt to have finer textures than those with simple leaves. This is not true in all cases,

however, because the ash and cherry are about the same in texture. The leaves of some plants are so large that it is difficult to adjust them to the textures of other plants. In this group we find such plants as the castor oil bean, elephant ears, and Magnolia macrophylla.

Plants are the pigments in a color scheme, and every plant contributes its facet of color to the whole mosaic of colors. Some of the colors, in fact many of them, change with the seasons, the gray of winter merging into the green of spring, with a short period of brilliance at blossom time or at the time of fruiting. Outline, form, mass, and texture are all important elements in the design, but in many compositions, particularly in the flower garden, it is color which has the strongest appeal. The arrangement of plants to produce harmonious color compositions is one

A PATIO GARDEN AT NIGHT

AN ENTRANCE COURT

A SMALL PATIO AND POOL IN CALIFORNIA

of the most fascinating accomplishments of the designer, and it is one of the most joyous expressions of garden art.

GARDEN LIGHTING

In the 18th century the magnificent gardens at Versailles were illuminated with thousands of torches for the delight of Louis XVI and his

28

courtiers as they strolled through the great plaisances.

Today the illumination of gardens is no longer the luxury of kings, as even the most modest garden may achieve that special enchantment which skilled lighting effects can give.

Lighting makes possible more hours of outdoor living, and for many the evening hours are

A DRAMATIC EFFECT OF LIGHT

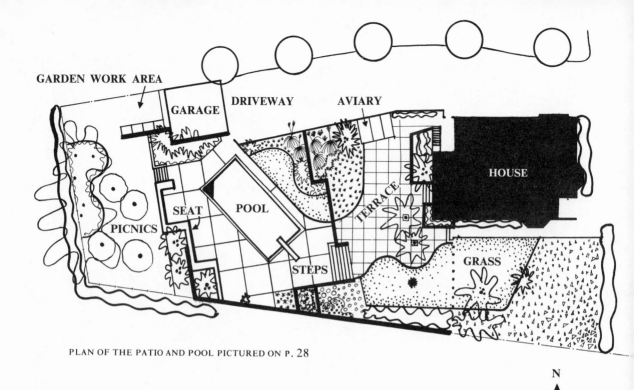

GARDEN WORK AREA

GARAGE   DRIVEWAY   AVIARY

HOUSE

SEAT   POOL

PICNICS

TERRACE

STEPS

GRASS

PLAN OF THE PATIO AND POOL PICTURED ON P. 28

N

the only time for leisure and relaxation. Well-planned lighting extends the usefulness of the terrace and patio, and the recreation areas; it dramatizes the beauty of the garden as viewed from the house or terrace; it highlights special points of interest; and it makes safe and pleasurable the use of garden paths and steps.

Light emphasizes the texture and pattern of foliage silhouetted against the darkness, and it brings out interesting details. A greater feeling of depth and form will be obtained if trees and flowers are lighted from the side rather than from the front, and when dramatic effect is desired it is usually best to concentrate on one or two points of interest, rather than on too broad an area.

With the development of waterproof extension cords, moisture-proof outlets and connections, and attractively designed lamps, garden lighting has become a simple and comparatively inexpensive undertaking. There are fixtures of many types:—there are lamps suitable for the lighting of outdoor dining areas and reading chairs; there

are low, mushroom-type fixtures which direct the light downward, being specially designed for lighting paths or steps; and there are spotlights of various types designed for general overall illumination or for highlighting some special group of plants or some garden feature.

For lighting paths and steps ordinary bulbs are usually satisfactory. A 60-watt bulb in a mushroom-type fixture will light an area about 20 feet in diameter. For larger areas, or for creating dramatic effects at a distance, 150-watt bulbs, or PAR spot or flood lamps may be used. A 150-watt PAR bulb with a bullet-type reflector will illuminate a group of trees or a garden feature at a distance of 40 feet. Some fixtures are portable, others are stationary. Most spotlights are arranged so that they can be turned at any angle. All outdoor lighting fixtures should be of rugged construction and weatherproof.

It is important that the wiring and the laying of the cables meet the specifications of the local electrical code, and it is advisable to have a well-qualified electrician do the work.

30

III

PATIOS AND TERRACES

THE terrace is an important feature of the modern home. It is a transition between house and garden and is often the foreground of an open view. In the great Italian villas the terraces commanded views over the countryside. They often extended across the whole garden scheme, and by the architectural treatment of their outlines with balustrades they pleasantly combined architecture with plant forms. Often they were embellished with sculpture, fountains, potted plants and patterned pavements, and usually they were shaded by large trees. Wherever garden art has felt the Italian influence, terraces have formed an important element in the landscape design.

Architectural Functions of the Terrace

Because of its architectural form, almost every house requires some degree of formality in its immediate surroundings, and the terrace, with its precise outline of clipped hedge, parapet, or balustrade, may well mark the limit of the formal area. The terrace makes a platform for the house and thereby adjusts it to its site in a graceful and easy transition. Furthermore, the terrace is another room to the house, useful whenever it is pleasant enough to sit out-of-doors. In this respect the terrace should be arranged for various weathers, part of it being open to the breezes of summer and part hemmed in by the house so that it is exposed to the warm sunlight of early spring mornings.

Scale and Proportion

The size and proportions of a terrace are a matter of scale. The bulk of the house, the size of the property and the extent of the lawn are factors, and function is also to be considered. It is safe to say that one is more apt to make a terrace too narrow than too broad. The broad terrace has an air of spaciousness and makes a good foreground to a distant view. A narrow terrace is only appropriate on a restricted site where other elements, such as the lawn, are also compact, or where a broader terrace would cut off a pleasant view down into a valley. Unless conditions of the site dictate otherwise, the terrace should be at least as broad as the height of the house façade flanking it.

The Raised Terrace

The house terrace may be raised above surrounding land by a wall or bank; it may be level with the lawn, the separation being made merely by the edge of the pavement; or it may be sunk below the adjacent ground. The grading will be suggested by the conditions of the site. The terrace floor should slope slightly away from the house and the surface water should be collected in drain inlets at the outer rim. The terrace floor may be treated in a number of ways; pavement to accommodate the furniture, smooth turf, small pebble surface, or, what is usually better, a combination of these materials. A broad expanse of stone paving just outside the house can be uncomfortably hot. If only a small part of the terrace is paved and if it is shaded by large trees, summer heat will be greatly mitigated.

The Sunken Terrace

Built upon the side of a hill, the terrace floor is maintained by a masonry wall or by a smoothly graded bank. If the hill ascends above the terrace it, too, must be retained, and the treatment of this wall may be made an interesting feature of the design. A long, unbroken

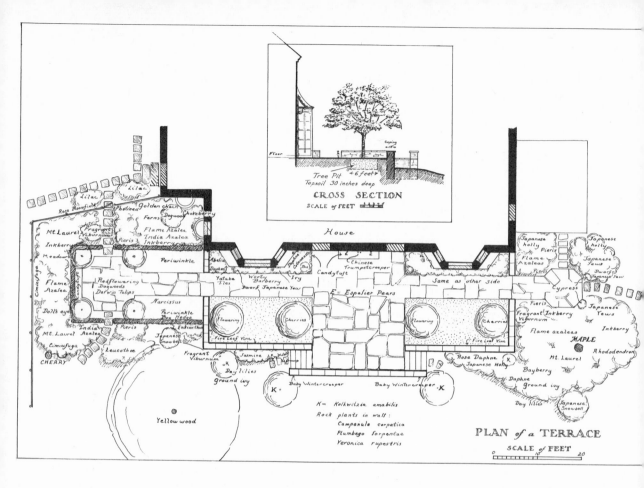

CROSS SECTION

SCALE of FEET

Tree Pit ← 6 feet →
Topsoil 30 inches deep

House

E = Espalier Pears

Same as other side

K = Kolkwitzia amabilis
Rock plants in wall:
Campanula carpatica
Plumbago larpentae
Veronica rupestris

PLAN of a TERRACE

SCALE of FEET
0   10   20

masonry wall may be monotonous; but divided into bays by buttresses or pilasters, or surmounted by a balustrade, it becomes architectural, something in harmony with the artificiality of the place. Vines clinging to the wall or hanging down over it from above, or fruit trees pleached against it, impart a softness of texture in pleasing contrast to the rugged masonry.

Draining the Terrace

Because of the importance of ridding the terrace of rainwater promptly, drain inlets should be placed at frequent intervals. On a terrace eighty or a hundred feet long, four drain inlets at the outer margin are sufficient to carry off the surplus water of a storm. The ground surface should slope toward the drain inlets. The inlet gratings may be small and inconspicuous, 8

inches × 12 inches being ample. For the construction of drains and inlets see Drainage of Surface Water on page 109.

Plants in the Stone Paving

A very pleasant effect of stone paving is produced by planting between the flagstones little flowering plants or herbs. Such a paving is not laid on a concrete base but on a cushion of sand and pockets of soil for the plants are prepared beneath the crevices.

PLANTS APPROPRIATE FOR PLANTING IN SOIL BETWEEN PAVING STONES

Ajuga reptans
Arabis alpina
Arenaria montana
Arenaria verna

Campanula glomerata
    acaulis
Gypsophila repens
Herniaria glabra

32

Mazus rugosus
Sedum acre
Sedum sexangulare
Sempervivum arachnoideum
Sempervivum atlanticum
Silene acaulis
Statice armeria
Statice alpina

Thymus citriodorus
Thymus serpyllum
    vulgaris
Thymus serpyllum
    lanuginosus
Veronica repens
Veronica rupestris
Veronica serpyllifolia

THE PATIO

The patio is derived from an architectural form traditional in Spain, which was introduced by the Moors at the time of their conquest in the 7th century. It was reminiscent of the ancient Moorish courts which were enclosed within walls but were open to the sky and were enlivened with fountains and adorned with plants.

In the elegant homes built by members of the Spanish nobility and the wealthy aristocracy in Seville and Granada and other cities of southern Spain in the 16th century the serried patios were the center of family life, as they are today. The central feature was usually a fountain about which potted plants were grouped, and some special planting was usually featured in each patio which gave to it its name—the patio of the orange trees, or the patio of the box, or of the laurel, or the myrtle. The white stucco walls which divided one patio from another were adorned with gracefully arched openings with delicate, wrought-iron grills or "rejas", through which pleasant vistas were glimpsed. The walks were made of glazed tiles or river pebbles, or of colored earth, such as bright ochre clay, firmly tamped. Vines or trees were pleached against the walls and there were low, clipped beds of ivy and myrtle, and pomegranate and pepper trees for accents. And in the spring the patios were fragrant with the scent of orange blossoms. The rooms of the house opened upon the various patios and picturesque balconies looked down upon the patterned walks and beds, with here and there a descending staircase, its graceful, wrought-iron railing entwined with vines.

The early Spanish explorers and missionaries brought with them the memories of these lovely, secluded patios and when they built their homes and their missions in the New World the enclosed patio was its central feature. This tradition has persisted for many years in some sections of Florida and in Southern California, and in these sunny lands it has come to seem indigenous.

In contemporary garden design, which allows great freedom and originality of expression, the patio has assumed a variety of forms. It may be a paved area open to the sky and either partly or wholly enclosed by the walls of the house. It may be partly covered by a roof or by vines on a latticed support. It is usually adjacent to the house, being the transition between the house and the out-of-doors, although it may be a paved area separated from the house with a supporting wall of its own and perhaps a roof.

A patio may be designed to fulfill a variety of functions. It may be an entrance patio, separated from the street by a wall or fence. Small as such a patio must often be, it can possess great charm and provide a most attractive entrance to a home. A patterned pavement, a choice vine espaliered against the wall, a few well-chosen plants in pots and tubs can bring distinction to such an area.

An area may be designed as an intimate patio, entirely enclosed, and to be entered from but one room—a guest room, or the master bedroom. Here, again, the treatment should be restrained and the planting composition handled with great sensitiveness and skill, for such a secluded patio is for repose and quiet meditation. For a small child's patio opening off of a nursery the treatment would be imaginative and playful.

The most usual type of patio is that designed for the enjoyment of the family and for entertaining. Such a patio is usually of ample proportions and is made gay with plants in pots and tubs and hanging baskets. It has the pleasing aspect of partial enclosure and if it is partly protected by a roof it affords a pleasant place for the enjoyment of social pleasures in sunshine or in shadow. It is usually adjacent to the recreational area—the pool, the outdoor grill, the sand pile—and is the center of family life.

A FLORIDA PATIO IN THE SPANISH TRADITION

A PAVED CORNER OF THE GARDEN

Because of the enclosure and the regulation of sunshine and shade, conditions for plant growth may be made almost ideal on the patio. Shelter from the wind and the concentration of sunshine tend to prolong the season and make this a warm spot in winter where one may grow tender plants without protection. On the other hand, protection from too much sun in summer by vines on a lattice or by a louver roof, and the play of water in a fountain, make possible cooler conditions than would be attained on an open, sunny terrace. The patio has become, in the hands of a skillful designer, a versatile and charming adjunct to the modern home, one which contributes greatly to the comfort and enjoyment of outdoor living.

Pavements for Patios and Terraces

For pavements which are to be in constant use for several months each year, the qualities most desired are firmness, smoothness and water-tightness. In cold climates it is also important

35

A PATIO IN THE CALIFORNIA MOUNTAINS

that the pavement have foundations which will be undisturbed by frost heaving.

The paving materials generally used are brick, flagstone, wood-block and concrete. The construction of brick and flagstone pavings is described in the chapter on Garden Paths (see pages 122 and 124).

Wood-block paving is laid in the same manner as brick, on a foundation of sand. The blocks, which are about the size of bricks, are set close together with the end grain on the surface. Such a pavement will dry rapidly after a summer rain, the moisture draining down between the blocks to the sand beneath.

As it is usually used for pavements, concrete makes a wonderful, firm, smooth, quick-drying surface, durable and therefore practical. Furthermore it is economical and rapid to cast and it is enduring. But it is not in the least interesting, it lacks texture and color, and it imparts a mechanical artificiality to a scene which is quite foreign to the hand-wrought refinement of a garden or patio.

Concrete used with imagination and skill may be quite different. Indeed it can give variety, interesting texture and color to a pavement. One of the most satisfactory methods of using concrete is to substitute small natural pebbles for the crushed stone in the mixture, and then to brush off with a wire brush the upper surface of the cement, before it has finished setting, and thus expose the pebble aggregate. The surface will be made up of the many irregular, rounded forms of the pebbles which will impart their color and roughness to the floor.

Broad expanses of this pavement may be divided into squares of three or four feet by two-inch strips of redwood set on edge in the cement, so that the wood and pebble surfaces are flush. Further variety may be made by using two or three sizes or colors of pebbles, each in a separate square. The result will be a pattern of several hues and an interesting sequence of textures, each catching the light in a different way.

PLANTS FOR PATIOS AND TERRACES

Few outdoor areas offer such dramatic opportunities for the use of plant materials as do the patio and terrace.

Because the area is small and intimate each plant assumes an importance which it would not have in a more expansive setting, and the plants should therefore be chosen with special care.

There can be great variety and distinction in the planting. Plants may be grown in pots and tubs, in portable planting boxes, and in hanging baskets, and there is a wealth of material available from which selections can be made.

Plants in Pots

In the gardens of southern France and in Spain and Italy potted plants are used in gay profusion. Many a low wall or parapet and many a balcony is thus pleasantly adorned and they bring vivid animation to otherwise placid scenes. But nowhere can potted plants be used to better advantage than on the patio or terrace.

With careful planning a succession of bloom may be enjoyed from very early spring, when the first diminutive blooms of iris reticulata unfold, to be followed by the starry flowers of the water-lily tulip, to late autumn when the last of the chrysanthemums are over.

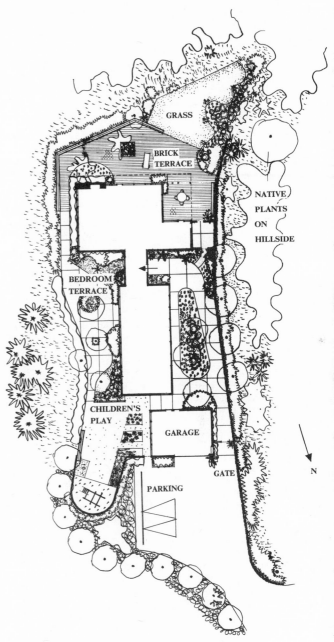

PLAN FOR THE TERRACE SHOWN ON P. 36

In order to be of value for pot culture a plant must measure up to certain requirements. It should thrive under the particular conditions which pot culture necessitates, it should be reasonably easy to grow, and it should flower over a long period. A surprising number of plants adapt themselves quite happily to pot culture. Among them we find not only the usual pot plants such as the geraniums, fuchsias, and begonias, but also many gay-flowered annuals, a number of very decorative biennials such as foxgloves and canterbury bells, and a few of the herbaceous perennials, among them the lovely, old-fashioned bleeding heart, sea lavender and chrysanthemums.

A large number of bulbs and tubers, including the colorful tuberous begonias, the exotic lily-of-the-Nile and many of the early spring bulbs may also be grown as potted plants.

Practical Considerations

In growing potted plants successfully there are a number of points which should be taken into consideration: the selection of the right type and size of pot, the soil mixture, watering, feeding and general care.

Selection of Pots: For centuries plants have been grown, and grown very successfully, in unglazed clay pots. Recently, however, glazed pots, available in a variety of colors, have come into vogue. Each type has certain advantages and disadvantages. The unglazed pot normally provides very good drainage but has the disadvantage of drying out very rapidly in hot weather. However, this is a disadvantage which can be overcome to a considerable extent. Unglazed pots require less frequent watering, but even when a drainage hole is provided there is danger, especially during periods of heavy rains, of having the soil become completely water-logged. Under such conditions some plants suffer seriously.

In many situations the color of the clay pots is more unobtrusive than the brighter colors of the glazed pots, and if one's garden budget is ample enough, beautiful handmade clay pots with fluted or rolled rims may be used. Pots of this type, skillfully molded by hand, lend such distinction and charm to the serried patios of southern Spain and the terraced gardens of Italy. They were the only type of flowerpot available in Colonial days and have been reproduced in this country for use in the garden at Mt. Vernon and in the gardens at Williamsburg which have been so faithfully restored.

Sizes of Pots: Pots are obtainable in various styles and sizes. The standard type of pot, which is the kind most generally used, is always as wide across the top as it is high. A pot 4 inches across the top is also 4 inches high. Standard pots come in sizes beginning at 1 inch and increasing in size up to 14 inches. The increase in the smaller sizes occurs at intervals of half inches, in the medium sizes at intervals of an inch and in the larger sizes at intervals of two inches.

Pots which are commonly referred to as "pans" are one half as high as they are wide, the smallest size of this type being five inches in diameter. Pots known as "azalea" or "three-quarter" pots are three-quarters as high as they are wide. These pots are very popular for shallow-rooted plants such as tuberous begonias, as they are broad at the base and cannot be easily tipped over.

Care of Pots: New clay pots should always be soaked overnight before they are used. Unless this is done the pot will draw water from the soil which is needed by the plant. Old pots should be washed thoroughly before they are re-used. Hot soapy water and a small, stiff scrubbing brush will do a good job. If, because of the possible presence of disease, it seems desirable to disinfect pots, they may be put in a large kettle and boiled for thirty minutes.

Providing drainage: In preparing the pots for planting it is necessary to see that adequate provision is made for drainage. An inverted piece of broken crock placed over the hole in the bottom of the pot will usually be sufficient. In the case of tuberous begonias, achimenes and other plants which demand exceptionally good drainage, an inch of broken crocks or gravel should be placed in the bottom of the pot and a thin layer of damp sphagnum moss should be spread over it.

Potting Mixtures: It is well to have a good basic potting mixture which can be altered, when necessary, to meet the specific needs of certain plants. In general such a mixture should be well supplied with humus and should be light, porous and well drained, being made up of good garden loam, well-decayed compost, a moderate amount of sand, and a small quantity of damp peat moss. For plants which prefer a somewhat heavy soil less sand and more garden loam would be used. For plants requiring a soil exceptionally high in organic matter an additional amount of compost or well-decomposed leafmold would be added. For plants requiring soil of very high fertility well-rotted manure or, if such manure is not available, a small amount of dried cow manure mixed with damp peat moss could be included. If the only garden soil available for use in the mixture is a very heavy clay loam a soil conditioner should be applied before it is used (see page 170 for full details).

Potting: At the time of potting the soil mixture should be damp but not in the least soggy. The usual test may be applied. Take a handful and squeeze it. Then let it drop to the ground. If it crumbles when dropped it is in good condition to handle. If it retains its shape in the ball it is too wet and sticky to use. The soil in the flats, trays or pots, in which the plants to be potted are growing, should also be moderately moist but not saturated with water. If the soil is too wet at the time the potting is done it is apt to form a solid mass through which the delicate feeding roots cannot penetrate, and the supply of oxygen will also be diminished. Consequently the plants will fail to become well established and will not make good growth.

When young seedlings with little soil on their roots are being transplanted from seed bed or flats into pots it is advisable to spray them with a protective plastic spray *before* they are removed (see page 682). This will prevent them from wilting and suffering a set-back.

After plants have been potted they should be watered and kept in semi-shade for a few days until they have become re-established.

Repotting: Young, actively growing plants should be repotted as soon as their roots have filled the pot. This stage may be determined by knocking the plant out of the pot, which is a simple process. Turn the pot upside down, placing the left hand over the top of the pot, with the stem or crown of the plant held between the index and middle fingers. Tap the rim of the plant against a hard, wooden surface. After one or two taps the plant will be dislodged from the pot. If no roots, or only a very few roots, are visible the plant is not ready for repotting.

When plants are being shifted to larger pots the pot next in size should be selected, a plant which has been in a three-inch pot being shifted into a four-inch pot. It is a great mistake to shift a plant into a pot which is too large, as it will not be able to make use of the moisture or nutrients. Consequently the soil in the pot is apt to become soggy and sour and the plant will fail to thrive. If the pots are dry it is wise to soak them before they are used.

When old plants which have become badly potbound are being repotted it is wise to rub off some of the soil on the surface so that the young feeding roots can come into contact with the fresh soil.

As plants reach maturity they can be maintained for long periods without repotting, provided a good program of feeding is put into effect.

Watering: In general, plants in pots dry out more quickly than plants in garden beds. The rapidity with which they dry out depends upon whether the plants are in active growth, whether the pots are in an exposed position in full sun or are protected by other plants, or whether they are in a shady location. It is important to know the requirements of the various plant groups and to endeavor to meet their specific needs. Some plants, such as impatiens and the tuberous begonias, require large amounts of water and suffer seriously if neglected, while other plants thrive well on a moderate amount of moisture, and some, such as lantana, prefer to be kept on the dry side.

If it is necessary to keep potted plants in a sunny location during very hot weather it is possible to reduce the loss of moisture appreciably by using the "pot-within-a-pot" method. The pot containing the plant may be set into a larger pot, the space between the two pots being filled with wet sphagnum moss or with damp peat moss. Potted plants thrive extraordinarily well when this practice is followed and practically never suffer from lack of sufficient moisture. A planting box or tub may be used to serve the same purpose.

Syringing the foliage occasionally with a fog nozzle will help to keep the foliage clean and in good condition and will also help to increase the humidity. This should be done when the sun is not on the plants.

Feeding: As plants in pots have a very restricted soil area from which to draw their nutrients, adequate fertilization plays an important part in a good maintenance program. Here again, it is necessary to understand the needs of the various plant groups, and no general rule can be applied to all types of plants. Geraniums and impatiens will give their best bloom on a rather meager diet, and many a tuberous begonia has suffered and died from the effects of overfeeding. On the other hand, there are plants which require liberal feeding if good growth is to be obtained. The majority of potted plants will benefit from biweekly feedings of a well-balanced, high-analysis, soluble fertilizer. (See page 165.)

General Maintenance: Potted plants require faithful attention and respond well to the thought and care bestowed upon them. Dead blooms and dead leaves should be removed promptly; pinching back to induce bushy growth, and judicious pruning to maintain a shapely form should be practiced, and an ever-vigilant eye should be on the alert to detect the first signs of insect infestation or disease. Shabby, neglected plants are no credit to the gardener.

ANNUALS FOR POT CULTURE

Alonsoa	Marigold
Balsam	Nicotiana
Browallia	Petunia
Calendula	Phlox drummondii
Celosia plumosa	Salpiglossis
Clarkia elegans	Schizanthus
Heliophila	Sweet alyssum
Impatiens holsti	Torenia
Lobelia	Vinca rosea alba

A SIMPLE TERRACE WITH PLANTING OF ROSES

Annuals. Many of our most colorful annuals are admirably adapted to pot culture, and some, with proper care, will continue to bloom over a long period. For fragrance there is nothing which will equal a few pots of nicotiana; the multi-colored beauty of a superbly grown pot of schizanthus is something long to be remembered; and the clear blue of heliophila reflects the blue of summer skies. The soft, velvety tones of salpiglossis are a striking contrast to the more brilliant colors; and the tall, graceful stems of clarkia, studded with their crisp little whorls of bloom, are enchantingly lovely. The golden, feathery spikes of celosia plumosa are very decorative; and the petunias and phlox drummondii, and some of the other low-growing annuals, will provide gay splashes of color for many weeks during midsummer.

All of the annuals may be grown very easily from seed, being started early indoors, in a cold frame or in an outdoor seed bed. The young seedlings may be transplanted into flats and later into small pots, being shifted on into larger pots. Most of the smaller types will flower well in 4 and 6 inch standard pots. Some of the larger ones, such as nicotiana, impatiens and

schizanthus require 8-inch pots for their best development, and are well adapted to the azalea-type of pot. The annuals may be kept in the growing area until they are coming into flower, and may then be brought onto the terrace or patio. During this growing period the pots may be sunk in the soil or in trays of damp peat moss, which will provide excellent conditions for vigorous growth.

A good, general potting mixture will be entirely satisfactory for most annuals and they will respond well to biweekly feedings. Impatiens should not be fertilized too heavily, as it tends to produce such a growth of leaves that the flowers become almost hidden in the foliage. For magnificent specimens schizanthus should be started early indoors and should be fed regularly and generously.

If one does not have facilities for starting plants at home it is usually possible to purchase some of the more commonly grown annuals in pots. If some of the more unusual types are desired it is often possible to arrange with some local nurseryman or florist to grow them on special order.

40

BIENNIALS FOR POT CULTURE

Canterbury bells	Pansies
Foxgloves	Violas
Myosotis	Wallflowers

There are also a number of biennials which thrive well when grown in pots. Some are dramatically beautiful when in flower, such as the foxgloves and Canterbury bells, while others, the pansies and violas, are more modest in the contribution which they make, but are none the less beloved.

These biennials may be grown in the accustomed way, being wintered in the cold frame or, in mild climates, in the open ground. Early in the spring they should be potted up, fed, and grown on with special care until they are ready to come into flower and make their debut on the terrace.

Canterbury bells and foxgloves should be put into large 8 or 10 inch pots, either standard pots or azalea pots being satisfactory. If the plants are of good size one plant per pot should be used. If the plants are small and show little sign of being well branched, three plants per pot is desirable. The general basic soil mixture should be used, and they should be heavily fed, weekly feedings of a high-analysis, soluble fertilizer being given. With proper care and feeding magnificent specimens can be produced, with flower spikes from three to five feet in height. Canterbury bells may be kept in flower for many weeks if the individual bells are picked off as they fade. The small axillary buds will then have an opportunity to develop and will form new blossoms. As both of these plants transplant very easily if sprayed with a plastic spray (see page 682), they may be shifted into pots at any stage of growth, even when coming into bloom, but early potting and special care is the best procedure.

The smaller biennials, such as myosotis, pansies and violas, are most effective when five or six plants are used in a large ten-inch azalea-type pot. If the pansies and violas are not allowed to set seed and are well fed they will continue to bloom over a long period.

These small biennials are colorful and charming, and as they come into flower early in the season when few other flowers are in bloom they are particularly welcome. They may be used in mixture as gay masses of color, or by growing named varieties in separate colors, delightful color composition may be achieved. Lavender violas combined with reddish-purple pansies make a striking combination, and the possibilities are almost limitless.

PERENNIALS FOR POT CULTURE

Included in the group of perennials which are well adapted to pot culture are the commonly grown pot plants such as the geraniums and the begonias, as well as some of the herbaceous perennials usually thought of as garden flowers but which have great decorative value when grown in pots.

All perennials need a period of rest, or in some cases a period of complete dormancy, at some time during the year. Those which are to flower during the summer must be given their rest period during the winter months, while those which are to flower during the winter must be given a rest period during the summer. Many plants determine their own rest period by their habit of growth. Others, however, like the geraniums, may be induced to flower either during the summer months or in the winter, in accordance with the manner in which they are handled.

Garden Perennials

Chrysanthemums: All types of chrysanthemums are exceedingly well adapted to pot culture, and are now available in the autumn in wide variety at most local nurseries or, if desired, plants may be grown at home. Cuttings may be taken in the spring from established plants (see page 484) or may be purchased as rooted cuttings. If early, midseason and late varieties are selected the period of bloom may be extended over several months. The plants may be grown in pots, being shifted from one size into another throughout the growing season, or they may be grown in nursery beds, being lifted with a good ball of earth and potted up when they are just coming into flower. They may be transplanted with the greatest ease, even at this stage. The plants should be kept pinched back during the early part of the season to induce bushy growth, they should never be allowed to suffer from lack of water, and they should be fed at two-week intervals for maximum development.

Dicentra spectabilis: The lovely, old-fashioned Bleeding-heart is an exciting addition to any planting composition on terrace or patio. It will often reach three feet or more in height and the graceful sprays of pendent, heart-shaped flowers will remain in bloom for six or eight weeks. The roots should be potted up in the autumn in a pot of generous size, 10 to 12 inches, and the pots should either be carried through the winter in a cold frame or buried in the ground. A soil mixture rich in leafmold is ideal. Shoots will appear early in the spring and growth is very rapid. Abundant moisture is necessary and an occasional feeding. After the blooming period is over the leaves will die down and the plant will become dormant. The plants may be held over for another year, being repotted in fresh soil in the autumn.

Hosta (Funkia): The Plantain Lily is valued for its ability to grow and flower in fairly dense shade and makes an excellent potted plant for such difficult areas. When not in flower the leaves are interesting and have some decorative value. It is extremely hardy and not exacting in its demands.

Limonium perezii (Statice perezii): This lovely, tall-growing Sea Lavender is one of the most satisfactory perennials for pot culture. The great clusters of diminutive florets, of a soft purple-lavender hue, are borne on stems nearly three feet in height, and the plants continue to flower from midsummer to autumn. It must be given a pot of large size or a small tub, prefers full sun, but will tolerate light shade, and requires a light, well-drained soil. *L. latifolium* is a more dwarf form, reaching a height of 12 to 18 inches and bearing daintier flowers.

Tender Perennials

Among the tender perennials are some of our most decorative and most widely grown potted plants, such as the begonias, the geraniums and coleus.

Begonias: The semi-tuberous and fibrous-rooted begonias are of great value for shady and semi-shady areas and are particularly effective when a number of varieties with contrasting foliage are grouped together. They require abundant water, high humidity and a light, well-drained soil, rich in humus. (For full cultural details see page 456.)

Coleus: Some of the beautiful new varieties and strains of coleus have great decorative value and they may be used effectively to high-light plants with quiet green foliage. They are of extremely easy culture and unexacting in their requirements. Coleus may be grown very easily from seed and from cuttings, and excellent plants may be purchased at most nurseries.

Pelargoniums (Geraniums): All types of geraniums are especially well adapted to pot culture. The two species most widely grown are *P. hortorum*, the common or garden geranium, and *P. domesticum*, the Martha Washington geranium. There are many other interesting types, some with scented foliage, others with attractively variegated foliage.

Geraniums prefer full sun, with slight protection from intense sunlight in very hot climates, and will produce the best bloom if allowed to become somewhat pot-bound. A soil of moderate fertility is best and the pots should be allowed to become slightly dry between waterings. Firm potting is necessary for best growth and a monthly feeding may be given. Too frequent feedings are not advisable. Plants for replacements should be started from cuttings taken in late autumn (see chapter on Propagation, page 484), and young plants should be pinched back frequently to make them bushy and stocky. Cutting back old plants severely, occasionally, will enable them to renew their growth. Mature plants may be given a rest during the winter and brought into growth again in the spring.

Shrubby Plants

Fuchsia: Among the most decorative of plants for patio and terrace are the fuchsias. They may be allowed to assume their naturally graceful habit of growth, or they may be easily trained as standards. They are well suited to pot culture and may be maintained in large 8 to 10 inch pots or, if larger specimens are desired, they may be shifted on into tubs.

Fuchsias have very definite cultural requirements. They are at their best when grown in a rich, mellow soil, well supplied with humus and slightly on the acid side. A soil mixture consisting of equal parts good garden loam, leafmold and well-rotted cow manure is ideal. They require abundant moisture, combined with good drainage of surplus water, thrive particularly well in areas where the humidity is high, and should have filtered sunlight and protection from wind. A mulch of peat moss will help to conserve moisture and keep the soil cool, and in areas where the atmosphere is dry daily sprinkling with a fog nozzle will be extremely beneficial. Mild applications of a high-analysis, soluble fertilizer made at two to four-week intervals throughout the growing season are advisable.

When fuchsias are grown in pots in cold climates they require winter storage in a frost-free place (see page 46). The plants should be cut back before the first frost. The pots should then be allowed to dry out before being placed in storage. Best results will be obtained if the pots are sunk to the rim in boxes containing damp peat moss or sawdust. The mulch should be kept damp throughout the winter.

Fuchsias flower on new wood and when they are pruned all weak branches should be cut back as far as the main stem, and the remaining branches should be cut back to one or two pairs of dormant buds, leaving a good, well-balanced framework. Repotting in fresh soil is advisable in the spring and at this time some root-pruning should also be done.

Lantana: For plants of exceptional vigor, able to withstand intense heat and sunshine, and producing an abundance of brilliant flowers month after month, few plants can equal the lantanas. They require full sun and thrive best in a rather dry soil of moderate fertility. They are well adapted to pot culture but should be pinched back when it is necessary to restrain their too rampant growth.

Lantanas are not hardy in areas where the temperature drops much below 30 degrees F. In Northern areas they may be treated as annuals or the plants may be carried over in winter storage. (See page 46.)

Bulbs

Many of the spring bulbs, and also some of the summer-flowering bulbs and tubers, may be grown very satisfactorily in pots.

A PATIO IN A SANTA BARBARA GARDEN

SPRING-FLOWERING BULBS FOR POTS

Crocus	Iris (Bulbous Type)	Muscari (Grape Hyacinths)	Scillas (many species)
Hyacinths	Leucojum	Narcissus	Tulips

AUTUMN-FLOWERING BULBS FOR POTS

Autumn Crocus Sternbergia Colchicums

For full description of the bulbs refer to Chapter XXVII

Spring and Autumn-flowering Bulbs: The spring bulbs are a particularly happy choice for the patio or terrace as they can be brought into flower when few other things are in bloom, and they are always gay and charming. With careful planning a succession of bloom may be had throughout the spring months, beginning with a few pots of the lovely species crocuses, aureus and tomasinianus, followed in swift succession by iris reticulata, one of the most dainty and charming members of the iris group. Then come the species tulips, T. kauf-

43

manniana being one of the loveliest. These early bulbs hold a very special joy for the gardener and are, in turn, followed by the narcissus and the tulips which, if used with abandon, can create an enchanting spring garden within the confines of a patio.

Practically all of the spring bulbs may be planted in pots in the autumn, and stored over the winter in a cold frame or pit dug in the ground. In late winter or early spring the pots may be brought into the house to be gently forced for early bloom, or after freezing weather is over they may be placed directly on the patio or terrace.

Summer Bulbs and Tubers: Among the bulbs and tubers which add a full measure of beauty to the patio and terrace during the summer months are the superb and colorful tuberous begonias, the caladiums, and the dainty achimenes for semi-shaded areas. For the more open, sunny spaces there are the lilies and the tuberoses, so beloved for their fragrance. In mild climates pots of amaryllis, with their great, showy blooms, can be used effectively in patios during the late winter and early spring months.

SUMMER-FLOWERING BULBS AND TUBERS FOR POT CULTURE

| Achimenes | Caladiums | Tuberoses |
| Amaryllis | Lilies | Tuberous begonias |

Achimenes — See page 394 for description and culture
Amaryllis — See page 449 for description and culture
Caladiums — See page 400 for description and culture
Tuberous
  Begonias — See page 396 for description and culture

Lilies: The lilies add great distinction to any planting composition and there are a number which are well adapted to pot culture. In this group are some of our most beautiful and stately lilies, such as Auratum, Croft, Speciosum, Henryi and Regale.

Lily bulbs should be potted in the autumn as soon as they are received and they may be wintered over in a cold frame or a pit, being placed on a bed of cinders. For bulbs of small to medium size 6 to 8 inch standard pots may be used. For large bulbs 8 to 10 inch pots are desirable. Ample drainage should be provided in the bottom of the pot, and a light potting mixture, containing generous quantities of humus, should be used. When spring growth starts the pots may remain in the frame after the sash has been removed, or they may be placed in a nursery bed, until they are ready to be moved to the patio or terrace when in bud. The base of the plants should be kept heavily mulched or shaded throughout the growing and blooming season. Sinking the pots in peat moss will help to retain moisture and keep the roots cool while in the frame or nursery and the pot-within-a-pot method may be used after they are brought to the patio.

Tuberoses: Although not as showy as many other flowers, the tuberoses are greatly prized for their fragrance, and a few pots will shed a delicate perfume on the air.

The tubers may be potted up at any time during the spring months after the weather is warm, one in a 6 inch pot or two or three in a 10 inch pot. A good potting mixture with the addition of leafmold will give good results. The pots may be held in the nursery until ready to come into flower.

Plants in Tubs and Very Large Pots

There are many shrubs and a few small trees which will make very satisfactory growth in wooden tubs or in very large pots. Such material lends height and substance to the planting on a patio or terrace, and if careful, well-studied selections are made, and the plants are skillfully placed, they will add dramatic distinction to the landscape composition.

Some shrubs and trees are particularly well adapted to growing in tubs while others do not thrive well under such conditions. Some plants may be grown in tubs almost indefinitely, while others may be grown in this way for a considerable number of years and then begin to deteriorate. In Italy, where tubs are used with lavish abandon, one occasionally sees orange trees or laurel trees which have been growing in tubs or huge pots for more than a hundred years.

It is wise to choose plants which are known to thrive well under the restricting conditions of pot and tub culture, and fortunately a wealth of material is available from which selections may be made. Some shrubs are evergreen, others are deciduous, some are valued for their flowers, others for their foliage or for their interesting form.

Unless shrubs are purchased as large specimen plants they usually begin their sojourn on the patio or terrace in medium-sized pots, being shifted on into larger pots and eventually, as they become more mature, into tubs. Some trees and shrubs which normally grow to a considerable size will never attain their full development when grown in a tub, and, with judicious pruning and wise handling, may be kept at almost any desired size.

Practical Considerations

When growing plants in tubs there are many practical points which must be taken into consideration, such as the size and type of tub best suited to the needs of the plant, soil mixtures, methods of shifting from one tub to another, general maintenance requirements, and the wintering of plants in tubs.

Type and Size of Tub: Plant tubs may be purchased in a variety of types and sizes, or they may be constructed at home. Whether purchased or home-made, tubs should be made of durable wood which is resistant to decay. Such a tub will give years of service, whereas a tub constructed of cheap lumber which does not possess the ability to resist decay will deteriorate rapidly and will be worthless after a few years. The best and most durable woods are redwood, cypress, and cedar.

Tubs may be round, square, or hexagonal in shape. The bottom of a tub should always be supplied with holes, approximately five $\frac{1}{2}$ inch holes per square foot, for drainage, and it should be raised slightly above the base of the tub to permit good air circulation which will prevent it from rotting and will facilitate drainage. If the bottom is flush with the tub, the tub may be placed on small blocks of wood, or cleats may be used.

Commercially available tubs range in size from small tubs 8 to 12 inches in diameter, suitable for fuchsias and other small shrubs, to tremendously large tubs 20 to 30 inches in diameter, suitable for growing shrubs of large size or small trees. The depth of a tub will vary according to the needs of the plant for which it is to be used. Plants that are shallow-rooted or that never attain great size, such as the azaleas, bouvardia, fuchsias and lantanas, require tubs from 12 to 15 inches in depth, while such plants as camellias, laurel, crape-myrtle, pittosporum and other plants which grow to considerable size, require tubs with a depth of 18 to 24 inches.

A very satisfactory type of tub which can be made by a good home carpenter is one square in shape, which is fastened together with removable bolts. This makes it possible to remove only one side, if desired, or all four sides, and greatly facilitates the shifting of a plant from one tub to another of larger size. It also makes easier such routine practices as root pruning and the addition of fresh soil or compost.

If ball-bearing casters are placed on the bottom of plant tubs it will greatly facilitate moving them from one location to another.

Determining Size Needed: When a plant is to be shifted from a pot into a tub it is important to select a tub only slightly larger in size than the pot in which the plant has been growing. The same premise holds true in shifting a plant from a small tub into a larger tub. The increase in diameter should not exceed one to two inches. A plant in a 10 inch pot may be shifted into a 12 inch pot or tub; a plant in a 12 inch tub may be shifted on into a 13 or 14 inch tub when its roots have begun to fill the smaller tub.

The size to which a plant develops can be controlled by regulating the size of the tub. If a plant normally reaches considerable size and one wishes to maintain it at a size considerably below the maximum this may be achieved by keeping it in a small container. The procedure, therefore, is to continue shifting the plant from one tub to a slightly larger tub until it attains its normal size *or* until it attains the smaller than normal size which one desires to have it maintain. There are instances in Italy where plants have been kept in the same sized tubs or huge pots for seventy years or more and have still retained their vigor and flowered regularly, although no increase in growth has occurred.

Soil: The soil mixture should be one which will best meet the needs of the specific shrub. The great majority of shrubs will thrive well in a good basic soil mixture such as 2 parts good garden loam, 1 part compost or leafmold and 1 part sharp sand. Some shrubs, such as the rhododendrons and many of the azaleas, require a definitely acid soil (see page 168). Some require exceptionally light, well-drained soils and others prefer slightly heavy soils.

Maintenance: General maintenance requirements include watering, feeding, mulching, and pruning.

Plants in wooden tubs do not dry out as rapidly as plants in pots, and in hot weather the soil remains at a cooler temperature, as wood is a better non-conductor of heat. Most shrubs require a moderate amount of water, while some require a more abundant supply, and some prefer to be kept on the dry side. Frequent, light waterings should be avoided, as this tends to induce shallow rooting. It is best to give a thorough watering once or twice a week, depending upon the weather and whether the tub is in full sun or in shade, and then to wait until the soil appears dry on the surface. A mulch of damp peat moss will help to conserve moisture in hot, dry weather.

If a good soil mixture is used frequent feedings are usually not necessary or desirable. Three feedings of a high-analysis soluble plant food are usually sufficient. The first should be given early in the spring to encourage good growth. If the condition of the plant indicates by the color of its leaves or its general appearance that it would benefit by further feedings additional applications may be given. If plants are to be given a winter rest period no feedings should be given from mid-summer on.

Judicious pruning should be done occasionally to maintain an attractive shape and to remove dead wood or growth which is too twiggy.

Wintering Plants in Tubs: In mild climates it is possible for the plants to remain on the patio or terrace throughout the year, but where winters are severe it is necessary to move the tubs into some suitable area where they will be adequately protected from cold. Success with many shrubs depends upon being able to winter them well. A cool sun porch or a conservatory which may be maintained at a very low temperature provide ideal conditions, but when such a place is not available a *cool* cellar will prove to be a good substitute. The matter of temperature is the chief consideration. It is more important than the question of light, as little light is required during this period of semi-dormancy.

The temperature should range between 45° and 55° F. Warm temperatures in cellars are apt to prove disastrous, as the combination of high temperature and lack of light will cause serious damage to the plants.

Certain plants, such as the fuchsia, require special pruning or other care at the time of winter storage and careful attention must be given to such details (see page 42).

Some plants do not adapt themselves well to a period of winter storage and in selecting plants to be grown in tubs in Northern areas this fact must be kept in mind. Those starred on the following list are recommended as adaptable.

PLANTS ADAPTED TO GROWING IN TUBS

	HEIGHT
*Abelia grandiflora	2' to 5'
*Agapanthus africanus (Lily-of-the-Nile)	3'
*Aucuba japonica	4' to 5'
Azalea (in great variety)	2' to 5'
*Bougainvillea glabra (trained as shrub)	4' to 5'
Bouvardia	3' to 6'
*Buddleia davidii	4' to 5'
*Buxus japonica and sempervirens	3' to 5'
Camellia japonica and sasanqua	5' to 10'
*Ceanothus delilianus	3' to 5'
Citrus aurantium (Seville orange)	4' to 10'
*Datura arborea and D. suaveolens	4' to 6'
Fatsia japonica	4' to 8'
*Ficus carica	4' to 6'
*Fuchsia	4' to 5'
Gardenia florida	3' to 5'
*Hibiscus rosa-sinensis	5' to 8'
Ilex aquifolium (English Holly)	10' – up
*Laburnum watereri	5' to 8'
*Lagerstroemia indica	5' to 8'
*Lantana camara	3' to 5'
*Laurus nobilis	4' to 8'

	HEIGHT
*Ligustrum japonicum	3' to 6'
*Mahonia lomarifolia	3' to 6'
*Myrtus communis	3' to 5'
*Nandina domestica	3' to 6'
*Nerium oleander (Oleander)	4' to 6'
Osmanthus fragrans (Sweet Olive)	6' to 8'
Pittosporum tobira	6' to 8'
*Plumbago capensis	3' to 5'
Podocarpus elongata	8' & up
Podocarpus macrophylla	6' to 10' & up
*Prunus laurocerasus	3' to 6'
*Punica granatum nanum	3' to 8'
Pyracantha (Firethorn)	5' to 6'
*Raphiolepis umbellata (Yeddo-hawthorn)	3' to 5'
*Roses (in great variety)	4' to 6'
Rhododendron (in variety)	5' to 6'
*Strelitzia reginæ (Bird-of-paradise)	3'
*Streptosolen jamesonii	3' to 5'
*Viburnum tinus, laurestinus	4' to 6'
*Vitex agnus-castus (Chaste-tree)	4' to 6'
*Wisteria floribunda macrobotrys (standard)	5' to 6'

Hanging Pots and Baskets

Hanging pots and baskets filled with cascades of bloom have a unique charm quite their own, and may be used most delightfully to adorn a terrace or patio.

Flower baskets are used with great distinction on the West Coast and should be more widely used in other sections of the country, for they add greatly to the charm of outdoor living areas.

In California baskets of tuberous begonias and fuchsias hang from the latticed roofs of patios, and from the picturesque branches of live oak trees arching over white-washed walls. They are used on balconies and porches, are sus-

pended from wall brackets beside entrance doorways and hang from the beams of pergolas and arbors. In New England many a window is adorned with a hanging pot of the lovely Italian Bellflower (Campanula isophylla) with its myriad, star-like flowers. And on the porches of many a plantation home in the South hang pots or baskets of the enchantingly lovely achimenes, with their dainty, richly-colored blooms.

There are flowers to suit every location. For shady areas there are the hanging types of tuberous begonias and fuchsias, both of which may be seen to the best advantage when growing in hanging pots or baskets. A superbly grown basket of begonias with its cascades of exquisite flowers is a thing of exciting, breath-taking beauty, long to be remembered.

For hot, sunny situations on balconies there are the trailing lantanas, so lavish with their lavender blooms, and the gaily-colored portulacas, and anagalis, with its dainty sky-blue flowers. On porches where there are but a few hours of morning sun, and then shade for the balance of the day, the achimenes and the Italian Bellflower will be happily at home.

Practical Considerations

Types of Containers: There are various types of containers which may be used. Pots, wooden baskets, small wooden tubs, and wire baskets are all very satisfactory. Pots especially designed to be used for hanging are available in a number of styles and sizes. In some types small holes just below the rim permit the easy insertion of wire, and some come already equipped with wire hangers. Also available are especially constructed wire hangers which can be attached to the rim of any ordinary clay pot. These are provided with a hook at the top, some having hooks of a swivel type which greatly facilitates the turning of the pot.

Baskets made of small redwood or cedar slats are very popular on the West Coast. They are available in a number of sizes, and are attractive and durable. Small redwood tubs or boxes are widely used in California and are the best type in which to grow tuberous begonias and fuchsias, as they retain moisture better than any other type of hanging receptacle. Some are square in shape, being tapered at the base, others are octagonal and some are round, and they may be obtained in various sizes.

Open-mesh wire baskets are also obtainable in a great variety of shapes and sizes. They are considerably less expensive than the other types and are very satisfactory for many plants if careful attention is given to the method of planting and to watering. Copper wire is superior to galvanized wire as it will not rust and will give more years of service. Baskets of similar type may be fashioned at home, if desired.

Pots, redwood containers and wire baskets are also available with one flat side for use on walls, fences and posts.

Planting: Slatted baskets and wire baskets should be lined either with sheets of wood moss, or with wet sphagnum moss. Osmunda fiber may also be used but is less satisfactory, as it is difficult to pack the soil in firmly and there is more danger of rapid drying out. All of these materials are usually available from florist supply houses. The lining will serve two purposes. It

HANGING POTS OF FUCHSIA

will retain the soil within the basket and it will provide for good drainage of surplus water. Slatted and wire baskets tend to dry out very rapidly and if they are to be used in a sunny location it is advisable to place a flower pot saucer in the bottom of the basket, covering it lightly with a layer of sphagnum moss. This will act as a reservoir for surplus water.

After the baskets have been lined the soil may be added. If one desires to have plants growing out of the sides of wire baskets, as well as drooping down from the top, the planting should be done when the basket is about half filled with soil. The plants should be placed on their sides, the ball of earth about the roots being kept intact. The moss lining should be temporarily pulled aside, and the leaves and stems should be worked carefully through the wires. The remaining soil should then be added.

In planting pots and solid wooden boxes adequate drainage material must be put into the bottom of the

47

container. The soil may then be added, and the flowers planted. The number of plants used will be determined by the size of the container and the ultimate size which the plants will attain.

Watering: Hanging pots and baskets, particularly when in full sun, dry out very rapidly and they require faithful care. Daily watering is usually essential and on days when there are hot, drying winds it may be necessary to water twice a day. Pots and wire baskets dry out much more rapidly than solid wooden boxes. Glazed pots dry out less rapidly than clay pots. If, however, a coat of shellac is applied to clay pots it will reduce evaporation.

One of the most effective ways to overcome the loss of moisture is to follow the "pot-within-a-pot" method or a variation of it—a "pot-within-a-basket" method. A plant such as a fuchsia, a tuberous begonia or a campanula isophylla in a pot of adequate size, may be placed in a larger pot or in a wire basket, the space between being filled with either damp peat moss or damp sphagnum moss. Excellent growth is usually obtained where this method is followed, other conditions being favorable.

If there are quite a number of baskets to be watered a hose attachment may be purchased which will greatly facilitate the task. This consists of a long, metal tube with a spray at the end which is put on at a convenient angle for overhead watering.

PLANTS FOR HANGING POTS AND BASKETS

Abronia umbellata (Sand-verbena) Rosy-lavender flowers: Full sun
Achimenes (for complete cultural details see page 394)
Anagalis (Pimpernel) Annual: Blue flowers: Full sun
Begonia, pendula type (for complete cultural details see page 396)
Beloperone guttata (Shrimp Plant) Showy, pinkish bracts: Partial shade
Browallia speciosa: Tubular, clear blue flowers: Light shade
Campanula
   C. fragilis: Pale blue, star-shaped flowers, gray foliage: Partial shade
   C. isophylla: (for complete cultural details see page 452)
Coleus: trailing types: brilliant foliage: Sun or light shade
Convolvulus mauritanicus: Lavender-blue flowers: Sun or light shade
Dianthus
   D. latifolius Beatrix: double pink flowers: Full sun
   D. plumarius: Spicy fragrance, many colors: Full sun
Dimorphotheca aurantica (Cape-marigold) (for cultural details see page 310)
Fuchsia: hanging varieties (for complete cultural details see page 42)
Hedera helix (English ivy): Many types and varieties: Partial shade
Hoya carnosa (Wax plant): Partial shade
Lantana montevidensis (trailing type) Lavender-purple flowers: Full sun
Lobelia (many varieties) Blue flowers: Sun or light shade
Lotus berthelotii: Gray foliage, scarlet flowers: Sun or light shade
Mimulus tigrinus (Monkey flower) Yellow, trumpet flowers: Shade
Pelargonium
   P. peltatum (Ivy-leaved geranium) Pink and lavender flowers: Sun or light shade
   P. tomentosum (Peppermint geranium) Scented foliage: Light shade
Petunia (Balcony type) (for cultural details see page 312)
Portulaca (Rose-moss) Flowers in many colours: Full sun
Saxifraga sarmentosa (Strawberry geranium) White flowers: Sun or shade
Schizanthus (Poor Man's Orchid) (for cultural details see page 536)
Sedum sieboldii: Blue-green foliage, pink flowers: Partial shade
Sweet Alyssum (for cultural details see page 308)
Thunbergia alata (Clock Vine) Flowers orange, buff, apricot: Sun or light shade
Torenia fournieri (for cultural details see page 315)
Tropæolum majus (Nasturtium) Flowers yellow, orange, gold: Full sun
Zebrina pendula quadricolor (Wandering Jew) Blue flower: Sun or shade

Plants in Portable Boxes

Portable planting boxes are a recent innovation and have increased the opportunities for an ever-changing succession of bloom on the patio and terrace. Indeed, if they are skillfully planted and maintained, one may experience within a small paved area all the pleasures of a veritable garden.

Planting boxes of the portable type have great versatility. They may be moved very easily from one location to another on the patio, and interesting effects may often be obtained by combining boxes of different sizes and shapes. They offer almost unlimited opportunities for dramatic and beautiful combinations of color, texture and form, as plants may be removed as soon as they have completed their period of bloom and be replaced with other plants just coming into flower. Thus in the North a succession of bloom may be maintained from early spring when the first bulbs come into flower until late autumn, and in mild climates a full year's cycle of bloom may be enjoyed. And special gems, such as some of the dainty and exquisite cyclamens, and the lovely Christmas rose, which require special culture, may be grown in small

ABOVE: STRELITZIA IN PORTABLE PLANT BOX

BELOW: MODULAR PLANT BOXES

boxes and used where their beauty will be most fully appreciated and enjoyed.

To the gardener planting boxes offer solutions to many practical problems, as they make it possible, in many instances, to provide conditions which approximate the ideal. Soil mixtures may be prepared which best meet the needs of special plants. One box may contain a rich, woodsy soil in which tuberous begonias will feel most happily at home, while another box may contain a lean, sandy mixture to restrain the often too rampant growth of lantana and thus produce more abundant flowering. And in areas where nematodes are troublesome, sterilized, nematode-free soil may be used. Conditions involving exposure, humidity, watering and feeding may also be controlled more readily than is possible when plants are grown in the open ground.

Practical Considerations

Types of Boxes: The two most satisfactory materials for portable plant boxes are wood and fiberglass.

Wooden Boxes: Boxes made of wood have special advantages. In many areas they may be purchased ready-made, or they may be easily constructed at home by anyone who is handy with tools, as the making involves very simple carpentry. If durable lumber is used, and if the boxes are carefully made, they should last for ten years or more. Wooden boxes may be made, and in some cases may be purchased, in a wide variety of shapes and sizes, and if well designed they may be attractive in appearance. Boxes made of wood also provide good growing conditions for plants.

Some nurseries and garden supply centers offer planting boxes in modular sizes. These are often made up in units of 8 inches, available in the following sizes: 8 × 8 inches; 8 × 16 inches; 8 × 32 inches; 16 × 16 inches and 16 × 32 inches.

Wooden plant boxes should always be made with cleats on the bottom to facilitate lifting and moving, and to provide for the circulation of air and good drainage. Ball-bearing casters may be attached to the cleats if desired and will greatly facilitate the ease of shifting boxes from one location to another.

(For full details concerning selection of wood and details of construction see pages 466 and 467.)

Fiberglass: This new material offers certain advantages. Boxes made of fiberglass are light in weight, are easily handled, and are extremely durable. As it is not easy to attach cleats to the bottom of a fiberglass box the cleats should be placed directly on the paving and the box rested upon them.

Drainage: It is essential that good drainage be provided in planting boxes. A narrow space may be left between the bottom boards, or if a solid board is used drainage holes should be provided. In addition it is advisable to place an inch layer of broken crocks, or bricks or gravel on the bottom of the box over which a thin layer of moist sphagnum moss should be spread.

Soil: A soil mixture should be used which will meet the needs of the plants to be grown in the box. Unless plants have specific requirements a general purpose mixture which is light in texture and contains abundant humus will be the most satisfactory, as it will tend to drain well.

Maintenance: The usual good maintenance practices should be followed. The boxes should never be allowed to dry out completely but they should be watered with care and good judgment, as over-watering can be as harmful as under-watering. Most plants will benefit from feedings of a high-analysis, soluble fertilizer at intervals of two to four weeks.

In the case of tuberous begonias and caladiums it may prove most satisfactory to grow the plants in pots and sink the pots in peat moss, rather than to fill the box with soil. The peat moss should be kept thoroughly damp.

PLANTS FOR PORTABLE BOXES

Ageratum	Dimorphotheca	Marigolds	Stocks
Alonsoa	Echium	Nicotiana	Sweet alyssum
Begonias (tuberous type)	English daisies	Pansies	Torenia
Caladiums	Forget-me-nots	Petunias	Verbena
Calendulas	Impatiens	Phlox drummondii	Vinca rosea alba
Candytuft (Iberis umbellata)	Iris	Salvia farinacea	Virginian stock
Chrysanthemums	Lantana	Schizanthus	Violas
Dahlias (dwarf types)	Lobelia	Snapdragon	Wallflowers

BULBS

Colchicums	Cyclamen (hardy types)	Muscari	Scillas
Crocus	Leucojum	Narcissus	Tulips

IV

CITY GARDENS

IN spite of cramped quarters within the old fortification walls, the mediæval town had many a small garden. And in the 16th and 17th centuries, a formal garden was a common adjunct to the larger houses of London, Brussels, and Paris. But cities grew rapidly with the expanding commerce of the 17th century and the discomfort, dirt and disease of city life in London had become so appalling by the time of the great fire (1666), that it was the sincere hope of many of the colonists to do better with their new towns. This natural striving for improved conditions is expressed in some of the important writings of the times, as is evident in the following quotation.

"Let every house be placed, if the Person pleases, in ye middle of its platt as to the breadth way of it, that so there may be ground on each side, for Gardens, or Orchards, or fields, yt it may be a greene Country Towne, which will never be burnt and will allwayes be wholesome." Thus William Penn gave instructions to the three commissioners whom he sent to lay out the city of Philadelphia on the banks of the Delaware in 1682. In these words he expressed an ideal of town planning which was heartily accepted by the colonists and they were able to maintain their city as a "greene Country Towne" for more than a century thereafter.

But, about the middle of the nineteenth century, Philadelphia, like many other cities, experienced a phenomenal growth of industrial expansion, houses became crowded together on narrow lots, and at the century's close little remained of Penn's "greene Country Towne." People who cherished the old traditions did one of two things. They moved farther out of town in each succeeding generation, or they remained in the city and preserved what they could of that little oasis, the yard garden, against increasing odds.

No garden is more artificially situated, or beset with greater disadvantages, than the garden in the city. It is cramped for space, for the tremendous increase in land values has made ground space almost unobtainable. Neighboring buildings often deprive it of adequate sunshine and circulation of air. In most cases the soil is impoverished and overlaid by dust and soot. Every ton of loam, every load of manure and humus must be hauled in by truck, and carried to the yard in wheelbarrows.

If, by ingenious designing, the space has been well utilized, and a pleasing composition results, and if, by technical skill, the cultural requirements for healthy plant growth have been provided, then such a garden may bring real satisfaction to the owner. It can be a measure of compensation for much that city life fails to provide.

The development of steel frame buildings in the last decade of the 19th century brought about certain solutions of the city housing problem. Group apartment houses now provide many more families with homes than the single houses did on the same land. When the apartment groups are well planned, as they so often are, space remains in great open courts for gardens, playgrounds and trees; and pleasant views from sunny windows make the interiors delightful.

This new era in city building, made possible by modern methods of construction and by rational designing, has already brought the garden back to the city and we are likely, in the near future, to experience further development in this direction. The garden in the city may reach again that place of importance which it formerly occupied.

DESIGN

The surroundings of the town garden make an architectural approach to its design the most logical one. The garden site should be enclosed by a wall or fence, thus securing privacy and framing the composition. Axes should be employed as a framework of the design, giving it strength of form and harmonizing it with the adjoining architecture. However, exact symmetry may not necessarily be important in so small a space. Architectural features such as sculpture, a wall fountain, balustrades, wrought-iron grills, colored tiles, and pavement, all express the formal style and add color and interest of detail to a garden in which flowering plants do not play a dominant part. The design should be simple, straightforward, formal, small in scale and economical of space, and not crowded.

BACKGROUND

As with so many gardens, the background is an important part of the composition. Walls 8 or 9 feet high are an effective means of blocking unsatisfactory views, but in some positions they shut out too much sunshine and air circulation, and they should be used with a careful regard for the points of the compass. Brick, hollow tile with stucco surface, hollow tile with colored-tile surface, or combinations of these, are all satisfactory. The coping on the top of the wall—tile, flagstone or brick—can be made a decorative color note. To mitigate the severity of wall surfaces and the heat radiating from them, vines

SPRING BLOOM IN A CITY GARDEN

should be grown on the walls. Such vines as English ivy and Boston ivy cling to brick by rootlets, but clematis, polygonum, and many other vines require lattices upon which to climb. Lattices of white-painted wood can be of simple decorative patterns. Wood frames are good, but wrought iron is preferred for wisteria, which is so strong that it can wreck wooden trellises in a few years.

A combination low brick wall and high brick piers with fencing between the piers is satisfactory when designed in good proportions. It is more permanent than a fence with wooden posts and the combination of materials makes it an interesting architectural feature.

There are numerous types of wooden fences which may be used very satisfactorily. The close-woven type of fence made of cedar pickets is obtainable in various heights and affords excellent protection. The basket-weave type with a lattice top to provide support for vines is attractive, reasonable in price and easily erected.

Modern louver fences are excellent, as they provide for a good circulation of air and at the same time insure privacy and protection. Well-designed board fences are also very satisfactory. (See Chapters XI and XV for the design and construction of walls and fences.)

PATHS

Concrete is permanent and the most practical and economic material for walks, but it is harsh and glaring and its use should be avoided if possible. Its combination with colored pebbles of a fairly uniform size may give pattern to an otherwise monotonous surface. In this type of pavement, the pebbles are pressed into the surface of the concrete while it is still mobile, and protrude above the surface, forming a knobby, rough floor. Such a pavement may be combined with flagstone. In districts where frost action in the soil is not the usual winter condition, "popple" stones may be used. These are small cobblestones set on edge into the ground and firmed by

A GARDEN ON BEACON HILL
IN BOSTON

ARBOR IN A PLEASANT CITY GARDEN IN CHICAGO

A CITY GARDEN IN BOSTON FEATURING A WROUGHT IRON GRILLE

tamping. The art of laying such a pavement is practiced in southern England; and in Spain, where the passion for decoration is so strong, these stones are placed in patterns of varied colors and sizes, especially in the enclosed courts or patios of town houses.

Brick and flagstone are the most satisfactory materials for paths in the city garden. They are in harmony with the architectural surroundings, and are attractive, and permanent. Paths of loose pebbles or crushed gravel are also appropriate with small formal schemes but require a certain degree of maintenance and are less comfortable to walk upon.

(See Chapter XII for the design and construction of garden paths.)

UTILITY BACKYARDS

Many a city-yard garden is also the means of access from delivery truck to kitchen. As a yard it must provide receptacles for wastes, and an area to be used occasionally for drying lines. A cupboard for containing rubbish cans may sometimes be concealed behind a low wall, the top of which is a broad shelf for potted plants. If the path to the alley is at a slightly lower level than the rest of the garden, this concealment is all the more easily accomplished.

The wall, with its potted plants, as seen from the garden side, is a very decorative feature, and may be the background of the garden pool or fountain. The cupboard, on the back side of the

55

A FORMAL CITY GARDEN

A CITY GARDEN IN SAN FRANCISCO

wall, can be made in two sections, one of which is large enough to accommodate the garden tools. Clothes lines, when in use, may be strung to hooks in the fence or wall or to decorative poles. When not in use they may be rolled up and hung on a peg in the cupboard.

Practical Considerations

As drainage of surface water and air circulation are apt to be poor in city gardens it is advisable to plan for raised planting beds when possible in order to help mitigate these handicaps. Such beds may be held in place by narrow walls of brick, by flagstones set on end, by planks or old railway ties.

Soil is always a problem in a city garden. Usually it must be purchased either by the ton or by the cubic yard and brought in by truck from the country. It is wise to obtain a sample of the soil before the purchase is made as there is a great difference in the quality of topsoil. The ideal soil is a good loam well supplied with humus, such as is found on old pastures or on farm fields which have been well handled. When highways are put through, or when areas are sold for development and roads are put in, such

57

soil may become available and one is fortunate indeed to be able to obtain it. When purchasing soil one should stipulate that it is not to be loaded and delivered when it is too wet. This is particularly important in the case of clay soils as they can become lumpy and extremely difficult to handle if they are loaded and dumped when saturated with water. In the case of heavy soils the use of a soil conditioner is recommended. (See page 170.)

The care of the plants in a city garden poses very special problems. All plants suffer from smoke and soot in city areas. This is particularly true in the case of the broad-leaved evergreens. The best way in which to overcome the harmful effects of soot and other similar residues is to syringe the foliage at frequent intervals with a strong force of water from a hose nozzle.

Since plants are in a more or less restricted soil area in a city garden special care must be

A POOL IN A CITY GARDEN

taken to see that their nutrient requirements are met and that a pH is maintained which will meet their specific needs.

Although the city gardener labors under definite handicaps, much may be accomplished if plants are selected with care and a good maintenance program is followed.

PLANT MATERIALS

Vines on walls and arbors, potted plants on the low coping about a pool, shrubs and small trees as background and accents, early spring bulbs heralding the arrival of spring in the city, roses in flower from June until late autumn, the gay and colorful bloom of petunias, seedling dahlias and lantana, defying midsummer heat, the dramatic coloring of fancy-leaved caladiums, hanging baskets of the lovely achimenes with its cascades of richly colored flowers—much of the beauty of the surrounding countryside may be enjoyed in the small city garden if the plant materials are selected with care.

There are many plants which cannot survive city conditions. There are others, however, which will make themselves quite happily at home in a city garden. Surprisingly, we find in this group some plants which are inhabitants of the wild and yet will thrive well under city conditions if given the proper soil.

Since a city garden is usually a small garden, special thought and study should be given to the planting design, as each individual plant assumes an importance which it would not have in a large-scale planting. Instead of long beds filled with tulip or iris there may be room for only one or two groupings and the varieties to be used should be chosen with great care; instead of a wealth of spring bloom from a variety of flowering trees there may be room for but one tree, and the selection of that particular tree, whether it is to be a star magnolia, a Japanese flowering cherry, a dogwood or a Pekin lilac, is a matter of great importance.

Since comparatively little space can be devoted to flower beds and borders in a city garden, plants in pots and tubs can often be used very effectively, and with careful planning a succession of bloom may be achieved from early spring until late autumn. Pots of early spring bulbs may be following by tulips and bleeding-heart, foxgloves and Canterbury bells. And a gay array of tuberous begonias, fancy-leaved caladiums, geraniums and annuals will carry on until the chrysanthemums come into flower in early autumn. (See Chapter III, Plants for Patios and Terraces.)

The plant materials included in the following lists will thrive under average city conditions and are well suited to the small city garden. The list is not all-inclusive. There are many trees which will grow well in the city and are excellent as street trees, but if planted in a garden would soon become too large and would rob the shrubs and flowers of light and food. And there are other plants which would thrive well but which are of inferior character and have not been included.

PLANT MATERIALS WHICH MAY BE GROWN UNDER CITY CONDITIONS

DECIDUOUS TREES

Betula alba	White Birch	Magnolia soulangeana	Saucer Magnolia
Carpinus betulus	European Hornbeam	Magnolia stellata	Star Magnolia
Cornus florida	Flowering Dogwood	Malus—species and varieties	Flowering Crabs
Cratægus cordata	Washington Thorn	Prunus subhirtella	Japanese Flowering Cherry
Cratægus Oxyacantha	English Hawthorn	Sophora japonica	Chinese Scholar Tree
Ginkgo biloba	Maidenhair Tree	Styrax japonica	Snowbell Tree
Ilex opaca	American Holly	Syringa pekinensis	Pekin Lilac
Magnolia glauca	Swamp Magnolia	Ulmus pumila	Dwarf Asiatic Elm

EVERGREEN TREES

Pinus mughus	Mugho Pine	Taxus cuspidata	Japanese Yew
Pinus sylvestris	Scots Pine	Thuya occidentalis	Arborvitæ

DECIDUOUS SHRUBS

Acanthopanax pentaphyllum	Five-leaf Aralia	Nandina domestica	Heavenly Bamboo
Azaleas	Many species	Philadelphus (most species)	Mock-orange
Berberis Thunbergi	Japanese Barberry	Physocarpus opulifolius	Ninebark
Deutzia scabra	Rough Deutzia	Rhodotypus Kerrioides	Jetbead
Exochorda grandiflora	Pearlbush	Rhus cotinus	Smokebush
Forsythia	All species	Spirea Vanhouttei	Vanhoutte's Spirea
Hibiscus syriacus	Rose-of-Sharon	Symphoricarpos vulgaris	Snowberry
Lagerstroemia indica	Crape-Myrtle	Syringa vulgaris	Lilac
Ligustrum ibota	Ibota Privet	Tamarix varius	Tamarisk
Ligustrum ovalifolium	California Privet	Vitex agnus-castus	Chaste-tree
Myrica caroliniensis	Bayberry	Weigela, hybrids	Weigela

EVERGREEN SHRUBS

Buxus microphylla Koreana	Korean Box	Pyracantha coccinea	Firethorn
Ilex crenata and varieties	Japanese Holly	Rhododendron	
Kalmia latifolia	Mountain Laurel	R. carolinianum	
Osmanthus aquifolium	Holly-olive	R. mucronulatum	
Pieris japonica	Andromeda	R. Hybrids	

VINES

Calonyction aculeatum	Moonflower	Parthenocissus quinquefolia	Virginia Creeper
Cobea scandens	Cup and Saucer Vine	Phaseolus coccineus	Scarlet Runner Bean
Hedera Helix	English Ivy	Polygonum auberti	Chinese Fleece Vine
Humulus japonicus	Japanese Hop Vine	Wisteria floribunda	Wisteria
Parthenocissus tricuspidata	Boston Ivy		

GROUND COVERS

Hedera Helix	Pachysandra terminalis	Vinca Minor
English Ivy	Japanese Spurge	Periwinkle or Myrtle

ROSES

Climbing Roses	Floribundas	Grandifloras	Rugosas	Shrub Roses	Species Roses

FLOWERS

PERENNIALS

Bleeding-heart	Delphinium	Iris	Phlox
Columbine	Eupatorium	Peony	Primrose
Day Lily	Hosta		

ANNUALS

Alyssum, var. Snowdrift	Lobelia	Salvia farinacea
Dahlia (Seedling type)	Marigolds	Snapdragon
Larkspur	Petunias	Torenia
		Zinnias

BIENNIALS

Canterbury bells	Foxgloves	Wallflowers
English daisies	Pansies	
Forget-me-nots	Violas	

POTTED PLANTS

Achimenes	Geraniums
Caladiums	Tuberous Begonias
Coleus	Wax Begonias

LILIES

Candidum Lily
Regal Lily

BULBS

Crocus	Chionodoxa	Muscari	Narcissus	Scillas	Tulips

PLANTS FOR SHADY AREAS
(*partial shade*)

Achimenes	Caladiums	Ferns	Lily-of-the-Valley
Bleeding-heart	Coleus	Hosta	Tuberous begonias

V

PENTHOUSE AND ROOF GARDENS

As the private homes of a few generations ago have gradually been superseded by apartment houses, an entirely new type of gardening has come into vogue. The present trend of modern city living has led to the development of the penthouse garden and there are many charming roof-top terraces high above the canyoned streets.

For an apartment dweller to be able to watch eagerly for the first signs of spring in his garden, to plan with enthusiasm for color harmonies of distinction, and to pick and arrange his own roses would have seemed hardly within the realm of possibility a few decades ago. But to-day there are many skillful and erudite penthouse gardeners who have had the opportunity to discover these joys, and their number is steadily increasing.

The problems and hazards of developing a penthouse garden are many, but many also are the compensations—to be able to step from one's living room on to a sunny terrace; to know the joy of discovering, on some early spring morning, the golden flower of the first species crocus; to prune and tend one's roses and rejoice in the bounty of their bloom; to pick a few sprigs of sweet marjoram from the tiny herb bed to add zest to some particular dish which is to be prepared; to dine on warm spring evenings in the garden with its wide view of city and harbor. These are some of the deeply satisfying rewards which come as a result of one's efforts.

Since a penthouse garden must necessarily have distinct limitations in the use of plant materials, its charm is dependent to a considerable extent upon its design and architectural embellishment. Because of the restrictions of the surroundings the design should be formal, simple, yet interesting. If space permits, a pleasant sitting area and an attractive place for outdoor dining should be provided. Instead of a spacious, overall design it is sometimes possible to design a series of outdoor rooms separated by low hedges or walls with wrought-iron grilles, reminiscent of the serried patios in Spanish homes. Such an arrangement will afford a feeling of intimacy and will provide welcome protection from high winds.

Architectural features such as a wall fountain with a pool below, antique oil jars and carved fruit baskets from Italy, a piece of sculpture, well placed, will contribute greatly to the charm of the penthouse garden.

The areas devoted to outdoor living may be paved with tile or brick or flagstone or they may be carpeted with turf. If turf is used there should be at least four inches of good topsoil, and a good maintenance program is essential. (See Chapter XVII on Lawns.)

Even though the area available for a penthouse garden is small the plant materials selected can be used with distinction, and effects of dramatic beauty can be achieved: trees and shrubs espaliered against a wall, a tall, slender tree as a tapered accent against the sky, a bed of roses, a strawberry jar, the pockets filled with the lovely sedum eversii with its soft, glaucous foliage of indescribable beauty, pots of tuberous begonias in a shady corner where the exquisite colors can be seen to the best advantage.

Practical Considerations

In developing a penthouse garden a consideration of first importance is to make sure that the supporting structure possesses sufficient strength to carry the weight which will be added to it. Most of the materials used in constructing a roof garden such as tile, brick, soil, planting tubs and

A ROOF-TOP GARDEN OF GREAT CHARM

boxes are heavy and the sum total of the weight may reach a considerable figure. Expert advice on this matter may be advisable in order to prevent the possibility of future trouble.

Raised planting beds may be constructed or, if desired, all the planting may be done in tubs or planting boxes. Such boxes should be substantially built of good materials. Redwood, cedar and cypress are the most durable of woods, one-inch boards being used for the construction of the boxes. The outside of the boxes should be painted, the inside treated with cuprinol, which is a good wood preservative non-toxic to plants. For trees, shrubs, roses and vines the planting

boxes should be at least 18 inches in depth and any length and width required. For bulbs and annuals, boxes 10 to 12 inches in depth will be satisfactory. Brass screws should be used in the construction of the boxes and angle irons used at the inside corners. Holes should be bored in the bottom of the boxes to facilitate drainage and at least an inch of drainage material such as gravel or rubble from broken bricks or crocks should be used. The boxes should be raised slightly above the floor in order to facilitate drainage.

Excellent redwood tubs are available in a wide variety of sizes, and casks and hogsheads can be

A GARDEN AMONG THE TOWERS OF NEW YORK

cut down to any desired height and used very satisfactorily for growing trees.

Obtaining good soil for the tubs and planting boxes is a matter of importance. Soil transported to the city and then delivered to a penthouse garden is very expensive, largely because of the high costs of transportation and handling. It costs just as much to transport poor soil as it does to transport good soil and the purchaser should make sure that he is getting good, fertile topsoil.

The greatest hazards of roof-gardening are wind and intense summer sunshine, and in some sections soot may be a problem. It is difficult for anyone who has not experienced it to realize what the full force of a strong wind can be on a roof-top high above city streets, and for many plants some protection must be provided. Above the walls, which are usually part of the structure of the building, it may be advisable to construct a barrier which will provide additional protection from wind. A close-woven cedar picket

63

A GARDEN DECK IN CALIFORNIA

fence, obtainable in sections of varied heights, is excellent for this purpose; a latticed Chinese fence with translucent panels is both decorative and practical; and various types of panel wood fences may be used.

Selection of Plant Materials

The plant materials for the roof garden must be selected with great care as there are many plants which are unable to survive the hazards of strong wind and intense summer sun.

The planting compositions should be carefully studied. There should be trees to give height and scale to the planting; shrubs with good evergreen foliage to provide year-round beauty; vines to adorn and soften the walls that provide enclosure for the garden; bulbs for the special joy that they bring to any garden in spring; and flowering plants to add gaiety and charm throughout the season.

Trees: There are a number of trees which have proved well adapted to the trying conditions on a roof-garden and which can be grown very satisfactorily in large tubs, casks and planting boxes. When the root growth is thus restricted the trees will seldom attain their normal size, but in many cases this is an advantage rather than a disadvantage when they are used in a penthouse garden. The ubiquitous ailanthus will thrive anywhere, under any conditions, but there are so many other trees which are superior that it is hardly deserving of a place in a penthouse garden. The lovely albitzia does well in an eastern exposure and with its feathery, interesting foliage has unique charm, its one disadvantage being that in the latitude of New York it may not survive an extremely severe winter. Both the river birch and the white birch will thrive well and are decorative and full of grace. The beautiful Burford holly will do well if given a location in partial shade, and with its deep green, glossy foliage and red berries it will be a thing

THE ROOF GARDEN AT THE CLEVELAND GARDEN CENTER

of joy throughout the year. The Lombardy poplar is best used as an accent where a tree of slender, tapering height is desired, and although not long-lived even under the most favorable conditions, it will usually remain vigorous and attractive for a good many years on a roof-top terrace. Willows are among the easiest trees to grow and they withstand the wind well. Graceful in form, they will often reach a height of twenty feet or more on a roof-top terrace. Also graceful in form, and lovely when in flower, are the Japanese Cherries.

Some of the fruit trees, such as apples and pears, may be grown in planting boxes and trained to the espalier form against the walls. When trained in this way they become a very decorative feature of the penthouse garden and in time may bear a small quantity of delicious fruit.

Shrubs: There are a number of very choice shrubs as well as many of the more common types which may be grown successfully in tubs and planting boxes in the penthouse garden. Many of the azaleas thrive well and with their abundant and colorful bloom they add greatly to the charm of the garden in spring. Some of the hardiest species of the camellia, such as Camellia Sasanqua, will thrive if grown in a protected corner where they can have partial shade during the summer and some light protection during the winter. They will come into flower in October and remain in bloom for a month or more. Forsythia may be allowed to assume its naturally graceful form, or it may be trained as an espalier against a wall where its branches will form a cascade of golden bloom in the spring. Among the evergreen shrubs which are particularly valued because of their beauty at all seasons, are Pieris japonica, the lovely Andromeda, with its tasseled blooms and beautiful coppery leaves at the tips of its branches, and the Pyracantha or firethorn which, with its brilliant orange berries, is one of the glories of autumn. Pyracantha may be easily trained to any desired form against a wall and is a most decorative feature in a planting composition. Both Regal's privet and the more common California privet also thrive well under roof-top conditions, as does Taxus cuspidata, the Japanese Yew.

Vines: Because of the great expanse of wall which usually completely encloses a penthouse garden, vines play an important part in the planting design. English ivy will usually thrive well against a north or east wall, but will be unable to endure the intensity of the sun on a wall with a southern or southwestern exposure. Japanese honeysuckle is beloved for its fragrance and will give intermittent bloom from June to November, and the decorative Chinese fleece vine (Polygonum auberti) will thrive well under almost any conditions. Fortunate is the penthouse gardener that wisteria, one of nature's masterpieces, will also do well on roof-top

terraces, and it makes the weeks when it is in flower a memorable occasion. For rapid growth and quick shade the Porto Rican Yam is very satisfactory, and many of the annual vines such as the moon flower, the morning glories, the scarlet runner bean and the cypress vine are also excellent and may be used very happily while the more permanent vines are becoming established.

Roses: Some roses, such as the lovely floribundas and the more stately grandifloras, thrive extraordinarily well in the environs of a penthouse garden. In the latitude of New York they are often in full leaf by the middle of March and are in almost continuous bloom from June until late autumn. They may be grown in tubs, in planting boxes or in specially prepared raised beds. Among the most dependable varieties for the penthouse garden are Betty Prior, which will reach a height of 4 to 5 feet and is never out of bloom, Carrousel, Floradora, Spartan and Vogue.

Flowers: With careful planning a succession of bloom may be achieved in the penthouse garden from early spring until late autumn. The spring bulbs, pansies, violas and forget-me-nots, all of which may be purchased in pots or baskets, usher in the season of spring and are followed by greenhouse-grown annuals which have been brought into early bloom. Perennials play a minor role in the penthouse garden. Their period of bloom is usually comparatively short and planting space is at such a premium that it cannot be spared. Some of the perennials such as the lovely old-fashioned Bleeding-heart and some of the biennials such as the Canterbury Bells and Sweet William can be purchased in large tar-paper pots when just coming into bloom and will continue to flower for many weeks. Among the sun-loving annuals there is a wide choice, the ever dependable petunias, which are available in enchanting colors and will give abundant bloom throughout the season, ageratum, alyssum, the new tetraploid giant variety, Snowdrift, which will continue to flower until heavy frost; seedling dahlias in lovely colors, lantana, which thrives in intense heat, zinnias in the new pastel shades, and the marigolds which never fail to be prolific with their blooms.

For fragrance there are nicotiana, night-blooming stock, heliotrope and lavender, and for accents here and there the gay geraniums.

For shady areas there are the foliage plants such as coleus in the lovely, soft rainbow shades, so different from the garish hues of former days, and the exciting new, named varieties of fancy-leaved caladiums. For north and west exposures where they will receive good light but little direct sunshine there are the dramatically beautiful begonias with sculptured blooms and glowing colors, and the fuchsias.

In autumn potted chrysanthemums may be used to replace some of the annuals which have begun to look

ABOVE: A ROOF GARDEN OVERLOOKING
THE HARBOR AT SAN FRANCISCO

PLAN FOR THE SAME ROOF GARDEN

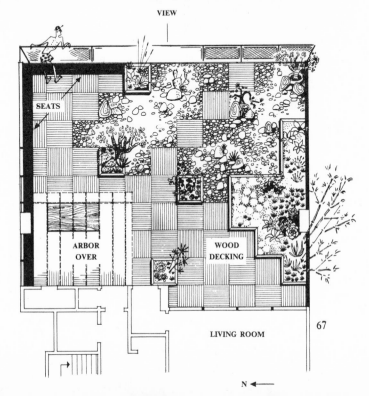

VIEW

SEATS

ARBOR
OVER

WOOD
DECKING

LIVING ROOM

67

N

a bit shabby, and a gay patch here and there of autumn crocus and colchicums, which should be planted in August, will bring a note of added interest into the penthouse garden.

Herbs: Even a few herbs can be grown on a roof-top terrace, and a strawberry jar, the pockets filled with some of the delectable varieties suited only to the home garden, will yield an occasional picking.

Maintenance

It is important that a good maintenance program be followed. The routine care of the plants in a penthouse garden differs somewhat from the care of such plants in the usual type of garden. As the plants on a roof-top terrace tend to dry out very rapidly, due to the effect of wind and brilliant sunshine, more attention must be given to watering. In order to conserve as much moisture as possible in the soil a good system of mulching should be adopted. (See Chapter XXXIV on Mulches.) Because of the shallow depth of soil and the restricted root area in which the plants are grown, special care must be taken to see that the plants are adequately supplied with the nutrients necessary for good growth. A monthly application of a high-analysis, quickly soluble fertilizer is advisable. (See page 165.)

Careful watch should be kept for evidence of disease or insect pests and if trouble occurs prompt measures of control should be undertaken.

VI

ROCK AND WALL GARDENS

THE ROCK GARDEN

SINCE the time when William Robinson, the great English authority on gardening during the late 19th century, introduced the alpine garden into England, rock gardens have had a steadily increasing vogue. The efforts of William Robinson in this vivid, naturalistic expression of garden art began about 1870, and his influence continued and increased through his long career. He was an ardent proponent of the naturalistic school of design, which had been practiced in England along very broad, simple lines for about one hundred and fifty years. Before his time nobody had given to naturalistic design that variety and intricate detail which Robinson, with his knowledge of wild flowers and alpine plants, was able to give. Until brought to their attention, people did not consider wild flowers worthy material for gardens. One outgrowth of Robinson's early efforts is the present very general appreciation of this type of garden art. Robinson was not alone in this work however. Miss Gertrude Jekyll, Lord Henry Bentinck, Miss Ellen Willmott and many others have contributed their skill and enthusiasm to the development of wild and alpine gardens.

One of the first rock gardens in this country was planted on the estate of General Weld in Dedham, Massachusetts. At about the same time Professor Charles S. Sargent built his rock garden at Holmlea in Brookline. Professor Agassiz's daughter first introduced alpine plants from Switzerland to Massachusetts, and descendants of these early introductions are still to be found in many a rock garden in New England. The enthusiasm for alpine gardens was also greatly stimulated by the work and writings of Louise Beebe Wilder, Herbert Durand, George D. Aiken and others, and the demand for rock gar-

den plants became so great that some nurseries made a speciality of them.

A rock garden, at its best, is a collection of alpine plants in a soil environment closely approximating the conditions of their native habitat. The true alpine plants grow in stony soil which is moist, but through which the water passes rapidly, and at high altitudes, which gives them a short but active growing season. In less mountainous regions the soil and drainage conditions may be duplicated by careful construction, but the short season with brilliant sunshine is impossible to reproduce. Some authorities hold the theory that a less rich soil will partly compensate for the long growing season and will prevent the plants from growing too abundantly, and thereby losing their natural form, vigor, and blooming habits. All seem to agree that poor soil is best for alpine plants. However, the emphasis which writers have put on "poor soil" has caused many an amateur to starve his plants to death. Alpines need nourishment, but can get it best from a stony soil containing some humus.

The ideal site for the rock garden should lend itself agreeably to the subject, as for instance an outcrop of rock in the rocky landscape of New England, an abandoned quarry where the rocky cliffs have had time to mellow, or the craggy sides of a natural ravine. If the site does not have any such rock structure as a background, the garden builder must exercise the most subtle skill to create a setting which will assume a natural form and seem appropriate.

The parts of this country which are most favorable to the development of rock gardens are the cooler regions about the Great Lakes, the mountains and hills of the Appalachians, the rugged landscape of New England, the Rocky

Mountain states and sections of the Pacific Coast. In the warmer climate and flat land of the Atlantic Coast plain, the lower Mississippi Valley, the prairies and the great southwest desert, such great climatic difficulties are presented that true rock gardens are unattainable in those regions.

An appropriate and favorable location is the first prerequisite to success with a rock garden. Yet this is the one point on which many failures occur. A bank or a sloping piece of ground is favorable, but not every bank is suitable. If it is under trees it is not going to be a true rock garden, but a shady garden composed of rocks. If it is beside a formal house or otherwise in a sophisticated or artificial surrounding, it will fail from the æsthetic standpoint. It will lack harmony with its site.

A place which is surrounded with artificial things is not appropriate for a rock garden. A concrete sidewalk, the porch of a house, the midst of an open lawn make poor settings. Yet often these places are selected. To be in keeping, the whole environment of the garden should harmonize with the informality and casual character of this specialized garden.

The best location for a rock garden is on sloping ground falling toward the west or northwest, where the enclosure is made by natural trees that separate it from other areas. Thus the plants will not be exposed too directly to the rays of the winter sun. A north or northeast slope is also favorable, because there will be little winter sunshine. Southern exposures may be used in such a case, the plants must be those which tolerate the effect of sunshine and not the more tender specimens from alpine cliffs.

The best treatment of many a bank is not conversion into a rock garden, but simply a carpet of ground cover plants.

General Design

The general form of the garden, its heights, its slopes, and its valleys, should be sketched in advance. The general location of paths and steps should also be planned in order that they may give adequate access among the plants. The paths may be stepping stones in some parts, gravel in others, or a mat of pine needles or tanbark. In the large rock garden which is likely to attract quantities of visitors at the height of the season, there should be a major system of paths, broad enough to accommodate the crowd. For the safety of the plants the visitors should be prevented from picking their way among the rocks and herbs of the lesser paths. Little signs are used in some gardens to steer the throng and protect the plants.

While the general ground-form of the garden should be planned in advance, there is no advantage in detailed planning. Indeed the nature of the material is such that the details are determined by the kind of stones available at the moment, and the way in which they may be placed to produce the general masses and slopes. A few conditions should be avoided: pockets with no outlet, where water will collect in pools; slopes so steep that the soil will wash off; overhanging rocks or caverns under which nothing will grow; and, above all, unstable rocks. Soil pockets may be quite large—a square yard in extent—or very restricted. Variety in arrangement of stones and soil is to be sought. The crevices between rocks may be quite narrow in places, only 2 or 3 inches, but the soil in them must run back and be continuous with the soil beneath and behind the rocks. Indeed the soil, every bit of it, should be rammed into place about the rocks with a pick handle or smaller blunt stick. An air pocket left behind the soil will surely cause the soil to dry out, and the plant growing there will die.

Most rock plants want plenty of moisture in the soil but it must be moisture in motion, constantly draining through, and though the soil looks dry and stony on the surface it must be cool and damp below.

The general arrangement of the plants should also be indicated on the sketch plan, and as the stones and soil are put together, special soil conditions should be prepared for the type of plant to occupy each position. This does not mean an exact planting plan similar to a plan for a perennial border, but a general plan which can be

NATURALISTIC PLANTING AT THE NEW YORK BOTANICAL GARDEN

followed in arranging for groups of plants requiring definite soil conditions. Many rock plants are self-contained, modest creatures which occupy only a small space, while others have the will to spread and occupy adjacent spaces. These aggressive ones should be placed within rock barriers so that their roots cannot overwhelm their neighbors. Some few rock plants require acid soil, and some demand an alkaline soil. Fortunately most are not fussy and are at home in a soil ranging from pH 6 to pH 8. Most rock plants require unmitigated sunshine. Some prefer shade or partial shade, while a few thrive equally well under varying conditions of light and shade. Some plants are happier in a soil more sandy than that generally used for the rock garden. Because of these varying needs of the plants, the spaces which are to be allotted to the more temperamental plants should be designated at the time that the garden is being constructed. Some planning in advance, therefore, is advisable, and some detailed decisions as to the exact position of each plant can be made at the time of planting. The soil preferences of the various groups should be taken into consideration.

Grading

For methods of grading, removal of topsoil, excavating and filling sub-soil, see the section on Grading, page 106.

To provide proper drainage for the rock garden, the sub-soil should be sufficiently porous to allow a constant flow of water down through it. If the sub-soil is heavy it should be broken up by deep plowing and lightened by mixing into it sand or gravel and sand. Tile drains should be laid along the bottom of this sub-soil mixture at a depth of 18 inches to carry off the water. The tile pipe must be laid with open joints and at a grade of not less than 1 percent, and it must empty out upon the surface or into a dry well.

Construction

The best stone for the rock garden is that of local origin. Imported stone, no matter how picturesque in shape, will seem out of place. The stone should not be angular and hard, such as trap rock, or flat and sharp, such as slate and shale, but it should be irregular and somewhat soft. The porousness of the stone is a factor of considerable importance because the stones store moisture and thereby become an equalizer of the ground moisture. In this respect the sandstones and the limestones are the best material for rock gardens. Granite is also good, but hard, and gives an acid reaction to the soil. Quartz is too hard and too conspicuous. Freshly quarried stones are not good, stones from old walls or pastures being more desirable. The stones should be large and should hold their place because of their weight. Small stones will move too easily and permit the air to dry the adjacent roots. For the most satisfactory results, both in appearance and in practical stability, large stones are to be preferred. One of the commonest mistakes in rock gardens is the use of small stones. The best size is what might be termed a "two man" stone, the kind which must be jostled into place with crowbars. Such stones are harder to handle, but should be in the majority if one wants to avoid difficulties later.

To the beginner in rock gardening, the rocks are apt to seem an evident major ingredient of the garden. He usually wants to make the most of the rocks by having most of each rock visible. This is entirely opposed to the real function of the rocks, which is to keep the soil cool and damp, to expose the plant to sunlight increased by the warmth of the exposed surface of the stone, and to prevent the slipping of the soil down steep slopes. Therefore most of the stone should be buried in the ground, only the top surfaces showing. Indeed, to create the proper sub-soil conditions conducive to good drainage, there should be other stones well buried in the ground below the surface stones. The rocks should be partly buried in the sub-soil when they are placed and the final level of the soil kept in mind so that there will be at least 12 inches of prepared soil above the sub-soil.

The rocks should be placed in such a way as to simulate a natural outcropping of ledge, with the strata or grain of the rocks all sloping at about the same pitch. If the rocks are naturally

SECTION of
LOW DRY WALL.

worn boulders, the formation should be that of
a glacial moraine with the stones deeply im-
bedded in the soil.

After the rocks are in place a layer of small
stones or gravel should be spread; then the top-
soil should be spread to a depth of 6 inches.
Above this a 6-inch layer of the specially prepared soil is added, and finally, on the surface, a
thin layer of stone chips or coarse sand.

Soil

The soil requirements of rock plants are quite
different from those of garden flowers or vegetables. No fertilizers or manure should ever be
used, for they supply too strong a diet. The soil
mixture should be one part coarse sand, one
part vegetable fiber, one part garden loam. The
sand should be coarse, rather than fine, and may
contain small gravel. The vegetable fiber should
be well-rotted material, such as old sod that has
been stacked a year or two, leafmold, or the
rakings from beneath the wood pile. Bog peat,
piled and dried for one year, is one of the best
vegetable fibers, because it breaks into small
particles and contains no weed roots or weed
seed. Commercial peat may be substituted for
bog peat. The garden loam should be any
medium loam, low in clay content. As the loam

is the only source of fertility for the plants, the
sand being for drainage and the fiber for water-
holding powers, the loam should be reasonably
good in natural quality. If it is sifted, the weed
roots may be eliminated and thus much trouble
avoided. Weed seeds can only be eliminated
when they germinate and grow during the first
season of the garden.

Planting

Rock gardening is a hobby which demands
very special skill. It combines all the virtues of
a recreational pursuit and becomes, with practice, a field of endeavour with limitless possibilities for exploration, experimentation, and
artistry. There are many stages of attainment in
technique and appreciation. It is a wise program
for the beginner to become acquainted with the
plants which are more easily cultivated, and with
them to practice this craftsmanship. As practice
develops skill and establishes confidence, then
the gardener may prefer to work with the more
difficult plants, and attain those great satisfactions derived from accomplishing a difficult task.
The higher degrees of rock gardening include
establishing conditions in which plants from the
high Alps will thrive, collecting plants from distant mountains, and learning by experiment what
conditions best suit the individual plant. Rock
gardening is a progressive kind of game, and the
experiences of each season, the successes and
failures, add to one's fund of knowledge of the
subject and make possible new delights for the
collector-artist.

Considering plants and planting design in the
rock garden, one is amazed with the wealth of
available material, and intrigued with the infinite
variety of possible arrangements. Selection and
arrangement is largely a matter of personal taste
and judgment.

Good composition with rocks and plants does
not differ in principle from good composition in
other mediums. It should have balance, harmony, and unity. While colors in a rock garden
are apt to be vivid, they must harmonize well
together and be well proportioned. For instance,
a corner of the garden in which blues and

lavenders predominate needs the enlivening of warm colors to compensate for the cool. Pale yellows or pinks may be used in quantity but bright orange and scarlet are better in small spots of color. Deep pinks and oranges are usually an unhappy combination because of the conflict between them, each seeming to spoil the effect of the other.

The lists accompanying this chapter classify the plants according to their soil, cultural requirements, habits, size, color, and season of bloom.

Care and Maintenance

Weeds. If the ground has had the prescribed preparation, the weed roots sifted out of the soil and the bare places covered with stone chips, the weeds should be kept in check without much trouble. Seedling weeds should be removed as soon as they appear, while they are still small. Most rock plants are such little fellows, so slow in growing, that they could be easily lost among weeds. Furthermore, nothing could destroy the good appearance of a rock garden more quickly and completely than a crop of weeds.

Watering. Rock plants require a porous but moist soil. The most satisfactory way to keep the soil in this state is to have the water supply from perforated pipes beneath the surface. Such an installation is not always possible. But in any case frequent watering will be necessary to pull the alpine plants through our long, hot summers.

Winter Mulches

The winter mulch for the rock garden presents a very special problem and unless one exercises wisdom and good judgment, the results may be most disastrous. Many worthy alpines have been literally smothered to death by well-intentioned but unenlightened gardeners. We must bear in mind the fact that most of our rock garden plants come from high mountain regions and in these native haunts they are usually buried under a covering of snow from late autumn until spring. Most of these mountain plants are able to withstand extremely low temperatures but suffer sadly from excessive moisture during the winter months. Therefore, in

providing winter protection for them, it is really dampness against which we must guard, and the ill effects of alternate freezing and thawing, rather than severe cold. In determining which plants to cover and which to leave unprotected, there are a few general rules which may be followed. Plants with heavy mats of foliage which persist through the winter months need no covering. Their own leaves afford sufficient protection and if a mulch is applied, the plants are very apt to rot. In the second group come those plants which are of an entirely deciduous nature, dying back in the autumn and remaining dormant below the surface of the ground. Plants of this type are usually able to withstand very trying winter conditions without protection. On the other hand, plants that form woolly rosettes of leaves seem to be particularly susceptible to winter ailments and will usually come through in more satisfactory condition if afforded some suitable protection.

Various materials may be used for mulches in the rock garden. It is essential, however, that the material be of such character that it will not form a wet, decaying mat about the plants. For this reason manure should never be used and leaves of such trees as maples and elms are very undesirable. Evergreen boughs form one of the best kinds of winter protection as they permit a free circulation of air. Salt hay is excellent if worked in among twigs so that it will not mat down. Oak leaves are also good as they do not rot easily. If oak twigs are broken in the autumn, the leaves will cling to them throughout the winter, and they make an exceedingly good covering. A method of winter protection very commonly employed in English gardens and one which might well be used here with equal success is that of using glass. Large bell jars, or "cloches" as they are called in England, may be used, or ordinary pieces of flat glass such as are used in the glazing of hotbed sash. The glass should be raised at least 6 inches above the plants in order to allow a free circulation of air, being supported on small stones or wooden pegs. This method offers excellent protection for particularly treasured plants, although it would be rather a tedious and expensive undertaking to employ it on a large scale.

In addition to an actual covering of some sort, there are other precautions which may be taken to make one's rock plants safe during the trying winter months. Where plants are particularly subject to injury from extreme dampness a little collar of stone chips may be built up around the crown in order to facilitate good drainage, and a mixture of sand, peat moss and stone chips may be worked into the soil about the plants to serve the same purpose.

When the first freezing weather of autumn has formed a crust of frozen earth a half inch thick, some of the smaller alpines will have been lifted from the undersoil. At such a time a gentle pressing of the soil back into place will prevent

the plants from drying out. The foot is the best means of applying the pressure, but if the space about the plant is small, something smaller must be used. A pick handle or trowel handle will probably be the most useful. After the frost is well into the ground a mulch should be applied to some of the alpines. The crushed fronds of the evergreen fern (Polystichum acrostichoides) make an excellent first covering, because they will not rot or flatten into a dense mat. Above the fronds a layer of autumn leaves may be spread, with a few hemlock branches to keep them in place.

The removal of the mulch in spring should be a gradual process, accompanied by watering. The mulch should not be removed until the frost is out of the bare ground.

A ROCK WALL IN SPRING

THE WALL GARDEN

The underlying principles of construction of a rock garden apply equally to that special adaptation, the retaining wall garden. The soil mixture is identical in each case and the plants to be used are those rock plants which grow in the crevices of cliffs. Since the wall exists to retain the earth behind it, the construction should be solid enough to withstand the pressure of lateral thrust of frost. The crevices where the plants are to grow must be so tightly filled with soil that there is constant contact with the soil behind the wall. Without this contact the soil in the stones will dry out.

As with the rock garden, large rocks are to be preferred. Since no mortar is used, their sheer weight and the friction of stone on stone are the only factors which will hold them in place. A bulging side or a top row of stones thrust out beyond the others not only spoils the appearance of the wall, but destroys its practical value. It is possible to build retaining walls without mortar 12 or 15 feet high, capable of standing a century, provided the stones are large and well placed. Every device for holding the stones together

should be used. The round surface stones should be discarded, and those with reasonably flat surfaces should be placed with the long dimension horizontal. As far as possible stones should be placed in what is called good *bond*, each stone resting on a part of two stones below. Thus, no long vertical crevices are formed and weight is well distributed.

Foundations of the rock-retaining walls need not be below the frost line as in the case of the masonry wall with mortar joints. Here, there is no advantage in avoiding frost heave, because there will be a certain amount of frost action in the wall itself in any case. The footings should be firm and sloping back against the hill, and at the front only 9 or 10 inches beneath the level of the ground at the base of the wall. This depth will be enough to give the wall a hold on the ground and prevent it from sliding on its foundations. The foundations should be constructed of a width equal to the width or thickness of the base of the wall. This is proportioned to the wall's height. A safe rule to follow is to make the width of the base of the wall equal to a third of the height of the wall. Thus a wall 10 feet high will need to be 3 feet, 4 inches thick at the

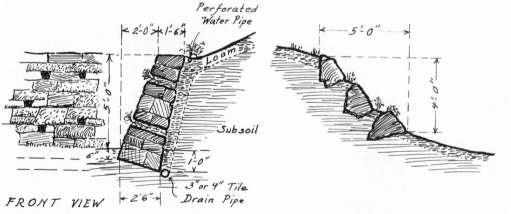

FRONT VIEW of DRY WALL showing position of stones about the earth pockets.

SECTION of DRY WALL showing the slant of stones, and the earth pockets extending through the wall.

SECTION of ROCK BANK showing large stones buried deeply in the earth.

A BANK OF BED ROCK AND FLOWERS

base. Whatever the height may be, the top of the wall needs to be 18 inches across and the wall thickness will thus decrease as the wall goes up. The face of the wall should never be vertical but should slope at an angle, the top face being on a line back of the bottom face. In England the practice is to make the face of the wall slope back as much as 5 inches or 6 inches for every vertical foot. This enables the plants to receive more moisture from rain seeping into the front of the crevices, and tilts the soil pockets back and down so that they will retain the moisture better. Each pocket of earth which is to receive a plant should be so constructed that the stone below is flat, thus holding the soil, and the stones on each side should be placed so that they will bear the weight of the stone above. It is an unnecessary risk to have the soil in the planting pocket actually carry the load of rocks above. With such a construction the action of frost in the wall is much more likely to heave the rocks and plants out of place. Throughout the wall construction, rock should support rock, independent of earth fill, the planting pockets merely representing windows. The soil in the pockets should be continuous back to the earth behind the wall and should be rammed into place so firmly that it cannot possibly separate from the adjacent stones. Air pockets in the wall will serve only to dry the soil and the plants, and these air pockets are difficult to remedy after the wall has been built and planted.

Soil pockets may be very narrow crevices for small plants, but it is easier to get the plant roots properly into place in a pocket 4 inches wide and high.

The shape of the front of the pocket is important. If the pocket is wedge-shaped with the narrow edge down, then the soil as it settles will tend to pack more and more firmly against the sides as well as against the bottom. Also if the pocket and the stone surfaces slope sharply down and back toward the rear of the wall, there will be very little chance for the soil to part from the upper rock.

Plants for the rock wall include all those which form tufts of leaves at the base and send up flower spikes, those of drooping habit, which hang down long leafy branches, and those which cling to the rock surfaces.

SHRUBS SUITABLE FOR THE ROCK GARDEN

Azalea macrantha is of dwarf habit and its foliage is evergreen. It is a rather dense and compact little thing and is considered a gem for the rock garden. The leaves are a deep, glossy green throughout the year and the large single flowers are salmon-red in color. Its growth is comparatively rapid and it is very showy when in flower.

Berberis Wilsonæ (Wilson Barberry) is of very spreading habit, being almost prostrate. The leaves are very small, a dull, pale green in color, becoming a brilliant scarlet in the autumn. The branches are very spiny and the abundant fruits are salmon-red. Because of its low, spreading growth, this Barberry is particularly well suited to the rock garden, and it gives a brilliant note of color at a season when there is little else of interest among the rock plants.

Cotoneaster adpressa (Creeping Cotoneaster) is a low, compact shrub of somewhat creeping habit, with irregular picturesque branches. The small leaves are a deep, shining green, almost waxy in appearance, and it is from its foliage that this shrub derives its great beauty. The small, pink flowers are inconspicuous but are followed by brilliant red berries in the autumn.

Daphne cneorum (Rose Daphne) is a great favorite and is a dainty and exquisite thing. The fine, somewhat needle-like leaves are evergreen and the shell-pink flowers are borne in small clusters at the ends of the branches. They are sweetly fragrant, and they bloom first in April and again in the early autumn. It is of rather trailing habit and seldom reaches a height of more than 12 or 18 inches. There are few things more lovely than the Rose Daphne, and it is a cherished inhabitant of many a rock garden.

Erica carnea (Spring Heath) is a delightful little thing, It is of low, spreading habit, hardly more than 12 inches in height, with fine evergreen foliage. The small rosy-pink flowers are borne through the early spring, from March to May. This small shrub has a certain sprightly charm which is very appealing, and it is universally beloved.

Juniperus chinensis Sargentii (Sargent Juniper) was introduced by the Arnold Arboretum. It is of low, trailing habit with erect branchlets and it seldom attains a height of more than 6 to 12 inches. The foliage is a silvery, gray-green in tone, and it is a shrub which makes a very beautiful ground cover when allowed to develop its natural habit of growth.

Juniperus communis depressa (Prostrate Juniper) is of low, very spreading growth and forms a dense, green mat. It is hardly more than a foot in height and is admirably adapted to the rock garden. The foliage is a soft, cool green, a pleasant foil for the brilliant colors of the rock plants, and during the winter months it takes on a clear, bronzy tone which is very attractive.

Leiophyllum buxifolium (Box Sandmyrtle) is an evergreen shrub with very small, glossy foliage. It prefers an open, sunny position and a sandy soil of high acidity. The clusters of white flowers which open in May and June are borne at the very ends of the branches and possess a dainty quality. The Sandmyrtle is often found growing wild in the pine barrens of southern New Jersey. It is such a charming little thing and so well suited to the rock garden that it should be more widely grown.

Lonicera nitida (Box Honeysuckle) is a graceful little shrub with very small, oval, glossy leaves which are almost evergreen. The foliage is tinted with rich purple in the autumn and is very decorative and lovely. The flowers, which are very small and inconspicuous, are followed by bluish purple fruits which are borne very sparingly and sometimes not at all. Lonicera nitida is hardy in the latitude of Philadelphia and southward.

Lonicera pileata (Privet Honeysuckle) is an evergreen of low, spreading habit with glossy, box-like foliage. The small white flowers which are borne in profusion in April and May are very fragrant and are followed by purple fruits in July. It rarely attains a height of more than 18 inches and is well adapted for planting in the rock garden or for the foreground of a mass planting of broad-leaved evergreens. It will occasionally prove to be only semi-evergreen in habit.

Ononis fruticosa (Rest Harrow) is a rare gem for the rock garden and is not often seen. It is of dwarf growth, seldom more than 18 inches in height. The bark is a soft, silvery-gray in color and the foliage is three-lobed with long, narrow leaflets. The pink flowers which resemble those of the Pea Family are borne in terminal clusters throughout the summer. It is a dainty little shrub and should be more widely grown.

Pachistima Canbyi (Canby Pachistima) forms a dense, evergreen carpet and is particularly well adapted to the rock garden. The small, dark red flowers are rather inconspicuous and its chief beauty is its deep, green foliage. It prefers an acid soil and a partially shaded location.

Potentilla fruticosa (Shrubby Cinquefoil) is a low shrub of dense, somewhat irregular growth attaining a height of from 1½ to 2½ feet. It comes into bloom in June and from then on through the autumn the bush is starred with pale, lemon-yellow flowers which give a pleasant note of color in the rock garden after the riot of spring bloom has passed.

Potentilla tridentata (Wine-leaf Cinquefoil) grows hardly more than 10 inches tall and has dark, glossy foliage

which is almost evergreen. The tiny white flowers are borne in clusters. It makes a very attractive ground cover, as the leaves retain their rich, green coloring throughout many months of the year.

Taxus cuspidata nana (Dwarf Japanese Yew) is a dense, compact shrub of dwarf habit seldom attaining a height of more than 3 feet. It is of irregular and picturesque outline when allowed its free and natural habit of growth, but may be kept symmetrical by occasional shearing. Its great beauty is its evergreen foliage which is a rich, deep color.

ROCK PLANTS FOR ACID SOIL

*(Many of these require special care. Those marked with
* require strongly acid soil.)*

BOTANICAL NAME	COMMON NAME
Achillea moschata	Musk Yarrow
Androsace alpina	Alpine Rock-Jasmine
carnea	Pine Rock-Jasmine
Anemone blanda	Greek Anemone
quinquefolia	Wood Anemone
*Arethusa bulbosa	Arethusa
Astilbe simplicifolia	Star Astilbe
Chimaphila maculata	Striped Pipsissewa
Chimaphila umbellata	Common Pipsissewa
*Chiogenes hispidula	Creeping Snowberry
Coptis trifolia	Goldthread
Dicentra Cucullaria	Dutchman's Breeches
*Epigæa repens	Trailing Arbutus
*Gaultheria procumbens	Wintergreen
Gentiana alpina	Alpine Gentian
Houstonia cærulea	Bluets
Iris verna	Vernal Iris
*Linnæa borealis	Twinflower
Orchis spectabilis	Showy Orchid
Parnassia caroliniana	Carolina Parnassus
palustris	Marsh Parnassus
Potentilla tridentata	Wineleaf Cinquefoil
Primula elatior	Oxlip Primrose
Pyrola elliptica	Shinleaf
Shortia galacifolia	Oconee-bells
Sibboldia procumbens	Creeping Sibboldia
Silene pennsylvanica	Wild Pink
Soldanella alpina	Moonwort
Thalictrum alpinum	Arctic Meadow Rue
dioicum	Early Meadow Rue
minus	Low Meadow Rue
Tiarella cordifolia	Foamflower
Trillium nivale	Dwarf Trillium
grandiflorum	White Trillium
Trollius chinensis	Chinese Globeflower
laxus	American Globeflower

ROCK PLANTS FOR LIME SOIL

BOTANICAL NAME	COMMON NAME
Æthionema (all species)	Stone-Cress
Androsace helvetica	Rock Jasmine
pubescens	

ROCK PLANTS FOR LIME SOIL—(cont).

BOTANICAL NAME	COMMON NAME
Anemone alpina	Alpine Anemone
Anthyllis montana	Alps Anthyllis
Astragalus hypoglottis	Milk Vetch
Aubrietia deltoidea	Wall cress
Dianthus alpinus	Alpine Pink
Draba arabisans incana	Whitlow Grass
Erysimum rupestre	Blister-Cress
Gentiana angustifolia acaulis	Gentian
Clusii	Stemless Gentian
Heuchera sanguinea brizoides	Coral Bells
Hippocrepis comosa	
Hutchinsia alpina	Hutchinsia
Iris pumila	
Lesquerella alpina argentea	
Linaria petræa	Toadflax
Lithospermum linearifolium	Gromwell
Opuntia arenaria humifusa vulgaris	Prickly-Pear
Oxytropis splendens	
Papaver alpinum	Alpine Poppy
Phyllitis Scolopendrium	Harts-Tongue-Fern
Primula (most species)	Primrose
Saxifraga aizoides longifolia	Rockfoil, Saxifrage
Sempervivum (all species)	Houseleek

ROCK PLANTS WHICH THRIVE BEST IF AFFORDED WINTER PROTECTION

BOTANICAL NAME	COMMON NAME
Acantholimon	Prickly-thrift
Adonis amurensis	Amur adonis
Androsace (all varieties)	Rock Jasmine
Anthyllis montana	Alps Anthyllis
Antirrhinum glutinosum	Creeping snapdragon
Arnebia cornuta echioides	Arab primrose Prophet flower
Asperula suberosa	Woodruff
Calandrinia umbellata	Peruvian Rockpurslane
Campanula Allionii alpina pulla	Bellflower
Draba, in variety	Whitlow grass
Eritrichium nanum Wallichii	
Gentiana verna	Vernal gentian
Leontopodium alpinum	Edelweiss
Lithospermum fruticosum prostratum	Gromwell
Lewisia, in variety	Lewisia
Omphalodes Lucilliæ	Navelseed
Onosma, in variety	Borage-wort
Petrocallis pyrenaica	
Phyteuma, in variety	Rampion
Potentilla nitida	Silvery-leaved potentilla

Saxifraga apiculata Burseriana oppositifolia	Saxifrage Burser Saxifrage Twinleaf Saxifrage
Silene acaulis	Moss campion
Soldanella alpina pusilla	Moonwort

ROCK PLANTS WHICH REQUIRE NO WINTER PROTECTION

BOTANICAL NAME	COMMON NAME
Acæna, in variety	New Zealand Burr
Aquilegia, alpina glandulosa	Alpine Columbine Altai Columbine
Alyssum saxatile	Goldentuft
Anemone pulsatilla	European pasqueflower
Arabis, in variety	Rock cress
Arenaria, in variety	Sandwort
Armeria, in variety	Thrift
Aster alpinus	Alpine aster
Aubrietia, in variety	Wall cress
Campanula carpatica rotundifolia	Carpathian bellflower Harebell
Cerastium tomentosum	Snow-in-summer
Dianthus, in variety	Garden pinks
Gypsophila repens	Creeping baby's-breath
Helianthemum	Rockrose
Heuchera, in variety	Alum-root, Coral Bells
Iberis, in variety	Hardy candytuft
Iris, dwarf rock garden varieties	Iris
Linaria	Toadflax
Linum, in variety	Flax
Nepeta Mussini	Nepeta
Papaver alpinum	Alpine Poppy
Phlox amœna divaricata subulata	Amœna phlox Blue phlox Moss phlox
Primula, in variety	Primrose
Saponaria ocymoides	Soapwort
Saxifraga, most varieties	Saxifrage
Sedum, in variety	Stonecrop
Sempervivum, in variety	Houseleek
Silene, most varieties	Catchfly, Campion
Thalictrum alpinum	Alpine Rue
Thymus, in variety	Thyme
Veronica, in variety	Speedwell
Wahlenbergia	Tufted harebell

PLANTS FOR THE ROCK WALL
(Tufted or Ascending)

Æthionema grandiflorum	Cerastium Biebersteinii tomentosum
Alyssum saxatile	
Aquilegia cærulea canadensis	Cheiranthus alpinus Cheiri
Arabis alpina muralis	Dianthus deltoides
Campanula carpatica glomerata rotundifolia	Heuchera americana gracillima sanguinea
Camptosorus rhizophyllus	Iberis sempervirens Pellæa atropurpurea
Centranthus ruber	Saponaria ocymoides

Sedum acre
Ewersii
sexangulare
stoloniferum
ternatum

Veronica repens
rupestris
Woodsia ilvensis
obtusa

(Drooping)

Callirhoë involucrata
Campanula muralis
rotundifolia var. Hostii
Claytonia caroliniana
virginica
Coronilla varia
Dianthus alpinus
arenarius
cæsius
superbus
Euphorbia Myrsinites
Gypsophila repens

Helianthemum Chamæcistus
Heuchera brizoides
Nierembergia rivularis
Platycodon grandiflorum
Mariesii
Polygonum cilinode
vulgare
Scabiosa graminifolia
Sedum Sieboldii
Solidago cæsia
Tunica Saxifraga

DWARF EVERGREENS, SHRUBS AND VINES FOR THE ROCK GARDEN

EVERGREEN
Abelia grandiflora
Arctostaphylos uva-ursi
Berberis Gagnepainii
verruculosa
Calluna vulgaris
Chamæcyparis obtusa nana
obtusa pygmæa
Chamædaphne calyculata

DECIDUOUS
Berberis Thunbergi minor
Wilsonæ
Betula nana
Callicarpa purpurea
Ceanothus Fendleri
Chænomeles Maulei
Comptonia asplenifolia
Cotoneaster adpressa

Cotoneaster horizontalis
microphylla
rotundifolia
Daphne cneorum
Erica carnea
Euonymus radicans
minimus
Hedera helix conglomerata
h. gracilis
Ilex crenata nummularia
c. microphylla
Juniperus chinensis
procumbens
communis depressa
horizontalis
h. Douglasii
Sabina
S. tamariscifolia
squamata
Leiophyllum buxifolium
prostratum (var. Lyoni)
Lonicera nitida
pileata
Pachistima Canbyi
Picea excelsa nana
alba albertiana
Pinus densiflora (var.
umbraculifera)
montana Mugo
Potentilla fruticosa
Taxus cuspidata nana
Thuya occidentalis Reidii
Yucca filamentosa

Cytisus hirsutus
purpureus
supinus
Daphne Mezereum
Epigæa repens
Erica Tetralix
Euonymus nanus
Fothergilla Gardeni
Gaultheria procumbens
Genista pilosa
Hudsonia tomentosa
Ledum grœnlandicum
Menziesia pilosa
Myrica caroliniensis
Philadelphus coronarius
nanus
microphyllus
Rhus canadensis
Rosa rugosa Max Graf
nitida
carolina
spinosissima
Spiræa bullata
Bumalda
Vaccinium pennsylvanicum
Viburnum Opulus nanum

ROCK AND WALL PLANTS COMPARATIVELY EASY TO GROW

(Some will spread too rapidly)

SCIENTIFIC NAME	COMMON NAME	SEASON OF BLOOM	HEIGHT IN INCHES	COLOR	SOIL AND SITUATION (SEE KEY)*
Achillea Clavennæ	Silver Alpine Yarrow	May–June	4	White	E
tomentosa	Woolly Yarrow	June–Sept.	4	Bright yellow	A
Ajuga reptans	Carpet Bugle	May–June	6	Blue	A
Alyssum saxatile	Goldentuft	April–June	12	Bright yellow	A
sax. compactum	Dwarf Goldentuft	May–Sept.	12	Yellow	A–D
argenteum	Silver Alyssum	May–Sept.	15	Yellow	A
Anemone pulsatilla	European Pasqueflower	March–April	10	Purple	A or B
Antennaria dioica	Common Pussytoes	May–June	4	Pink, white, carmine	A
Aquilegia cærulea	Colorado Columbine	May–June	14	Azure	A or D
canadensis	American Columbine (shade)	May	10	Red	A or D
Arabis albida	Wallcress	March–April	8	White	A–D
alpina	Alpine Wallcress	March–April	6	White	A–D
Arenaria grandiflora	Showy Sandwort	June–Sept.	4	White	A
Aster alpinus	Rock Aster	May–July	10	Purple and yellow	A
Mauve Cushion	Japanese Hardy Aster	September	9	Mauve	A
Aubrietia deltoidea	Aubrietia	May–June	8	Bright purple	A–D
Campanula carpatica	Carpathian Harebell	June–Oct.	8	Lilac blue	A–D
rotundifolia	Harebell, Bluebell	June–Oct.	8	Lilac	A–D

* See p. 82.

SCIENTIFIC NAME	COMMON NAME	SEASON OF BLOOM	HEIGHT IN INCHES	COLOR	SOIL AND SITUATION (SEE KEY)
Centaurea montana	Mountain Bluet	May–Sept.	12	Dark blue	A
Cerastium Biebersteinii	Taurus Cerastium (spreads)	May–June	8	White	A–D
tomentosum	Snow-in-Summer (spreads)	June–July	6	White	A–D
Convallaria majalis	Lily-of-the-Valley	May–June	8	White	A–B
Dianthus plumarius	Grass Pink	May–Oct.	8	Rose	A–D
deltoides	Maiden Pink	May–Sept.	4	Bright carmine	A–D
Dicentra eximia	Fringed Bleeding-heart	May	10	Rose	A
Doronicum caucasicum	Caucasian Leopards-bane	May	10	Yellow	A–B
Geranium macrorrhizum	Bigstem Cranesbill	June–Oct.	12	Bright pink	A
maculatum	Wild Geranium	July	8	Pale pink	A
Gypsophila repens	Creeping Baby's-breath	May–Oct.	4	Pink-white	A–D
Helleborus niger	Christmas Rose	Jan.–March	10	Rose, white	A–B
Heuchera sanguinea	Coral Bells, Alum Root	June–Sept.	12	Coral rose	A
Rosmondi		June		Coral pink	A
Hypericum Moserianum	St. John's-Wort	July–Sept.	10	Yellow and Red	ABD
Iberis sempervirens	Evergreen Candytuft	April–June	8	White	A–D
Tenoreana	Tenore Candytuft	April–May	4	White	A–D
Iris cristata	Crested Iris	May–June	4	Lilac-blue	E
pumila	Dwarf Crimean Iris	May–June	4–8	Lilac-blue, yellow	A–D
verna	Vernal Iris	May	4	Blue-lilac	A
Linum alpinum	Alpine Flax	May–Sept.	6	Light blue	A
perenne	Perennial Flax	May–Sept.	20	Azure blue	A
Lewisii	Prairie Flax	July	10	Blue	A
Myosotis palustris semperflorens	Forget-me-not	May	10	Azure blue	A–C
Nepeta Mussini	Nepeta	July	20	Blue	A
Penstemon alpinus	Alpine Penstemon (Beardtongue)	July	10	Blue and white	A
glaber	Blue Penstemon	July–Oct.	10	Blue	A–C
Phlox amœna	Dwarf magenta Phlox	May	10	Magenta pink	A
divaricata	Blue Phlox	April	8	Lilac-blue	A
pilosa	Downy Phlox (Prairie Phlox)	June	12	Bright pink	A
Stellaria	Mauve Phlox	June	8	Pale blue	A–D
stolonifera	Creeping Phlox	May	6	Carmine	A
subulata	Moss Phlox	April	4	Blue or pink	A–D
s. alba		April	4	White	A–D
Plumbago Larpentæ	Leadwort	Aug.–Sept.	10	Bright blue	A
Potentilla alba	Cinquefoil	April	4	White	A–B
pyrenaica	Pyrenees Cinquefoil	May	4	Bright yellow	A
nitida		May	2	Light rose	D–E
Saponaria ocymoides	Rock Soapwort	April–July	10	Bright pink	A–D
Saxifraga cæspitosa	Saxifrage	May–June	3	White and pink	A
cordifolia		April–May	12	Flesh-rose. Part shade	A
Sedum acre	Stone Crop	June–Sept.	3	Yellow	A–D
album		June–Oct.	4	White and pink	A–D
altissimum		June–Sept.	10	Pale yellow	A–D
reflexum		June–Sept.	6	Yellow	A–D
rupestre		June	10	Yellow	A–sand
sarmentosum		June–July	4	Yellow	A–D
Sempervivum (many species)	Hen-and-Chickens or Houseleek	May–June	4	Yellow or red	A–sand
Silene maritima	Sea Campion	June	2	White	D–E
Thalictrum dioicum	Early Meadowrue	May	6	Whitish	A
Tunica saxifraga	Saxifrage Tunicflower	May–Nov.	4	Pink or white	A–D
Veronica rupestris	Cliff Speedwell	June–Aug.	8	Blue	A
Viola cornuta	Tufted Pansy	May–Oct.	10	Dark Lilac	A

EXPLANATION OF SYMBOLS INDICATING SOIL AND SITUATION REQUIREMENTS

A — Plants which do well in garden loam, and need no special soil mixture. They are not particular as to chemical content of soil, and need only ordinary care
B — Shade-loving plants, preferring a soil rich in humus, porous and well drained. Leafmold mixed with loam makes the best soil for this group.
C — Plants which thrive in really wet, marshy soil, with sphagnum moss mixed with loam.
D — Plants that will do well in the crevices of the wall.
E — Rock plants which require the mixture of sand, loam and humus. They need perfect drainage, full sunshine, and require very little care. In dry climates, sphagnum with the soil is advisable.

VII

THE WOODLAND GARDEN

ONE of the most beautiful expressions of landscape art is to be found in the woodland garden. Here the ideals are not those of the flower garden, where perfection of bloom or variety in horticultural forms is the desideratum, but rather a representation of unaltered natural forms. Only wild flowers as they grow in nature should be included, and they should be given a setting closely resembling in appearance and physical condition those of their natural habitat. Since such a woodland is fundamentally a garden, it is not a copy or reproduction of nature, but rather a place for growing wild flowers in their accustomed way. It is, in fact, a garden of flowers either in their native habitat, or so recently brought from the wild that they have changed not at all in appearance or in their cultural requirements.

The Site

The owner of property containing a mature woodland has the ideal situation for a garden of woodland flowers. Indeed, the development of such a tract into a woodland garden is just as logical and natural as the development of the open sunny spaces into gardens of herbaceous flowers. The very conditions of the sunny site favor its development into a sunny garden, and those of the wooded tract favor development of this other type, the woodland garden.

During these many centuries, gardeners have been devoting their effort and skill to developing sun-loving plants, but it is only within the last half century that serious effort has been made with the flora of the forest. We now recognize this as a whole new phase of gardening with its own techniques.

The Design

The limitations of a woodland area should be recognized in the very beginning and every effort should be made to turn into assets those features of the place which might otherwise be regarded as liabilities. A woodland garden must necessarily be developed along naturalistic lines. The informal grouping of the trees themselves determines, to a very large extent, the nature of the design.

There is a very general impression that an informal design is a much more simple and less intricate thing than a formal scheme. On the contrary, quite the opposite is true. There is usually something very straightforward and, in a way, quite obvious about the design of a formal garden, whereas the design of an informal area, if well studied, possesses a subtle quality and charm which it is difficult to define.

Planning the woodland garden does not necessarily require exact plotting of ground areas or the spacing out of plants on a planting plan. But there should be forethought in the planning of major masses of foliage for the sake of good composition and balance, and for the separation of the plants into groups which are congenial and require similar soil conditions. If the site includes areas of varying soil conditions the plants must be assigned to the spaces where they naturally belong. Thus a certain tract might have dry soil on the upper levels, neutral soil in a large area, acid soil where oak trees stand, and wet soil along the stream valley. Whether the plan is actually committed to paper or not, it should be sufficiently definite to keep the plants in the situations where they thrive best and to allot the difficult conditions to those plants which are best able to withstand them.

The person who is a novice in the art of gardening with wild flowers will find that it is possible to develop very attractive groups of plantings by using some of the more easily grown bulbs and perennials which adapt themselves readily to woodland conditions. Masses of pale lavender-blue phlox under a group of white birches in early spring; English primroses and wood hyacinths blooming along a woodland path; foxgloves lifting their stately spires against a background of deep forest green—such delightful pictures may be obtained with a moderate expenditure of time and money.

However, the experienced gardener may not be content to limit his attention to the more easily grown woodland plants. He will want to adventure further and naturalize some of the more fastidious woodland flowers. An adventure of this sort is full of interest and delight.

Woodland Paths

The paths in a woodland area should be as natural in appearance as possible. The surface should be kept free of encroaching growth and sharp stones, small stumps and snags should be removed. A natural surface of fallen leaves is always pleasant but if the paths are frequently used a more permanent surface may be desirable.

The materials best suited for such a purpose are tanbark, pine needles and woodchips. Tanbark is readily procurable in some sections and makes an extremely satisfactory surface. It is pleasing in color, being a reddish, woodsy brown, and provides a soft, springy surface upon which to walk. It also has the advantage of drying out very quickly after a rain and never becomes soggy. Since tanbark will, in time, disintegrate and have to be renewed, it is a wise practice to add a small amount each season. Pine needles are always attractive but soon disintegrate and will give comparatively short service unless a very thick layer is used. And unless one is within easy range of a pine grove they may be difficult to procure. Within recent years wood

chips have become available in many areas and may usually be obtained at small cost. They are easily spread and form a very fine surface. In appearance they are somewhat less attractive than other materials, but this objection to their use may be overcome by applying a light covering of either tanbark or pine needles over the chips. Wood chips disintegrate very slowly and will give good service for a number of years.

Developing Small Areas

One need not necessarily have a piece of natural woodland on one's property in order to have the enjoyment of wild flowers in early spring. Often, even on a small suburban place, there is a semi-shaded spot under a group of trees where some of the denizens of the woodland can be made to feel happily at home. In such an area the dainty little wood Anemone, the Spring Beauty, Hepatica, Dogtooth Violets, Jack-in-the-Pulpit, Solomon's Seal, Mertensia, Bloodroot, Phlox divaricata, Trillium grandiflorum, and many other woodland plants can be naturalized quite easily. And small though such an area may be, one can have the joy of watching for the first flowers of spring—the lovely, glistening white flowers of the Bloodroot which turn always to catch the rays of sunlight, and the exquisite, dainty flowers of the Hepaticas, nestling among the leaves. And later in the spring the delicate lavender-blue of the wild phlox and the gleaming white of the Trilliums will make a lovely harmony.

In a natural woodland area one finds a soil rich in humus which provides ideal conditions for native plants. However, when one undertakes to develop a small wild garden under trees which have but recently been planted one may find that the soil lacks the qualities of a natural woodland soil. The soil may be heavy in texture, and lacking in humus. In such a case it should be carefully prepared before any planting is done. Generous quantities of rotted leafmold and compost should be worked into it, so that it will provide congenial conditions for the woodland plants which are to make it their home.

Soil Requirements

Woodland plants vary greatly in their soil requirements, and in their native habitats they are found growing where the soil, and other conditions, best meet their needs.

Some woodland plants prefer soils which are nearly neutral in reaction, others thrive best in moderately acid soils, a few grow only in soils which are intensely acid, and some are indifferent to soil conditions. The moisture conditions of the soil are also a matter for consideration, as some plants prefer a moist or moderately moist woodsy soil, while others prefer a somewhat dry soil.

It is therefore important to become familiar with the soil requirements of the plants which one wishes to grow and to provide conditions for them which are congenial and which will be favorable for their best development.

All natural woodland soils, especially those of the deciduous hardwood forests, are very rich in humus, due to the decomposition of leaves and branches which is constantly taking place on the forest floor. It is in woodlands of this type, where the shade is not too dense and the soil is well supplied with humus and only mildly acid, that most of our woodland flowers are happily at home. These are the flowers that may be grown so easily in a home woodland area and which, when once well established, will spread very rapidly, as they require only natural woodland conditions.

However, a few of our most beautiful woodland plants such as the pink lady's slipper (cypripedium acaule), the trailing arbutus (epigæa repens) and some of the lovely native azaleas and rhododendrons will thrive only in areas where the soil is very acid. It is useless to attempt to grow plants in this group unless one is willing to make the effort necessary to provide conditions which will meet their specific needs.

This may be done by providing soil which is rich in humus and strongly acid and in maintaining the correct degree of acidity from year to year. This may be accomplished in a number of ways. (See "Increasing the Acidity of the Soil", page 168.)

Increasing the acidity of the soil is important but it is not always the only conditioning process necessary. For rhododendrons, azaleas, mountain laurel, some of the cypripediums and many of the ferns, the soil should be moist, but porous and well drained.

Shrubs and Small Trees for the Woodland

In almost every natural woodland there will be found an undergrowth of native shrubs. Some of these shrubs are of great beauty and should be carefully preserved, while others are of weedy character and should be kept under control or completely eradicated.

85

EARLY SPRING BULBS IN THE WOODLAND

If some of the more desirable shrubs are not found in a piece of woodland they may be purchased from any nursery which makes a speciality of native plant materials, and they will add greatly to the beauty and interest of the planting.

Among the native shrubs most worthy of a place in a woodland planting, because of the beauty of their foliage, fruit or flowers, are the Red Chokeberry (Aronia arbutifolia); the native azaleas such as the Flame Azalea (A. calendulacea), the Pinxter-flower (A. nudiflora), and the beautiful Pinkshell Azalea (A. Vaseyi); the Spice Bush (Benzoin aestivale) with its fragrant yellow flowers in very early spring; Mountain Laurel (Kalmia latifolia), the glory of many a hillside woodland in late spring; the beautiful, dwarf-growing Carolina Rhododendron (R. carolinianum) and the larger R. catawbiense and maximum, if space permits.

86

There are also a number of small trees which should be included, if not already growing in the woodland, such as the Flowering Dogwood (Cornus florida) which is one of our most beautiful small, native trees; the Red-bud or Judas tree (Cercis canadensis) bearing deep, pink flowers in early spring; the lovely Silverbell tree (Halesia tetraptera) with its dainty bell-like flowers; and the Shadbush or Service-berry (Amelanchier canadensis), bride-like when in bloom.

Woodland Flowers

Anemone quinquefolia (Wood Anemone) (Wind-flower). The dainty white blossoms of the Wood Anemone are among the most exquisite of the woodland flowers, blooming from early April to late May. The slender, delicate stems are hardly more than 6 inches in height and the deeply lobed leaves are borne in whorls below the flowers.

Distribution: From Canada south to Georgia and west to the Rocky Mountains.

Preferred Habitat: Open woodlands, hillsides; particularly along the borders of moist, open woods.

Soil Requirements: Moist, moderately acid soil.

Culture: The Wood Anemone is somewhat difficult to establish. Plants should be purchased from a nursery.

Period of Bloom: April to June.

Aquilegia canadensis (American Columbine). Unfortunately Aquilegia canadensis is disappearing from many of its native haunts and perhaps only through its cultivation in wild flower sanctuaries will it be spared to future generations. The small flowers are of a scarlet and yellow hue and are borne on slender stems which vary in height from 1 to 2 feet.

Distribution: From Nova Scotia to the Northwest and southward to the Gulf States.

Preferred Habitat: Rather dry, rocky ledges; partial shade.

Soil Requirements: Thrives best in a soil which is very nearly neutral. It can tolerate neither extreme acidity nor pronounced alkalinity.

Culture: Plants should be purchased from a nursery. Despite its long tap roots Aquilegia canadensis may be transplanted readily and it is not difficult to establish, provided that soil conditions are favorable.

Period of Bloom: April to May.

Arisæma triphyllum (Jack-in-the-Pulpit). This wilding is one of the most beloved denizens of our woods and it is particularly lovely when planted among ferns. It is yellow-green in color, with brown-purple stripes, and is quite pale when growing in the sun. Later the berries turn a bright scarlet.

Distribution: From Nova Scotia westward to Minnesota and southward to the Gulf States.

Preferred Habitat: Moist woodlands among underbrush.

Soil Requirements: Thrives best in neutral soil, being able to tolerate neither extreme acidity nor pronounced alkalinity.

Culture: Plants may be purchased from many nurseries. If soil conditions are congenial, the plants are easy to establish, and they spread rapidly. They may be grown readily from seed.

Period of Bloom: April–July.

Cimicifuga racemosa (Black Snakeroot). So many of our woodland flowers come during the spring months that one rejoices to find something for midsummer bloom, and it is during July and August that the tall stately, white spires of the Snakeroot add their share of beauty to a woodland planting. The plants vary in height from 3 to 8 feet.

Distribution: From Maine to Georgia and westward from Ontario to Missouri.

Preferred Habitat: Deep, moist woods, wooded hillsides, woodland borders.

Soil Requirements: Prefers a rich woodland soil but is indifferent to soil acidity, thriving well in either neutral or acid soil.

Culture: May be transplanted very easily and becomes readily established.

Period of Bloom: July–August.

Claytonia virginica (Spring Beauty). Blooming soon after the Hepaticas, the Spring Beauties are among the earliest of our woodland flowers. The dainty fragile blooms are borne in loose terminal racemes and the slender stems seldom reach a height of more than 8 or 10 inches. The flowers vary from white to pale pink.

Distribution: From Nova Scotia to Georgia and westward.

Preferred Habitat: Moist, open woods, low meadows.

Soil Requirements: Thrives best in soil which is very nearly neutral.

Culture: The plants may be transplanted with care from the wild or they may be purchased from a nursery. They are most effective when planted in drifts or masses. The plants should be spaced from 4 to 6 inches apart.

Period of Bloom: March and April.

Cypripedium acaule (Moccasin Flower) (Pink Lady's Slipper). The clear pink blooms of the Moccasin Flower are startling in their beauty when one comes upon them in some deep forest glade, and one feels a sense of triumph when one achieves this beauty in a woodland planting. The orchid-like flowers are borne on stems hardly more than 10 inches in height.

Distribution: From Canada southward to North Carolina, westward to Minnesota and Kentucky.

Preferred Habitat: Deep, rocky or sandy woods. It is found in both dry and moist situations and it has been known to thrive well in full sun, although it definitely prefers partial shade.

Soil Requirements: Intensely acid woodland soil.

Culture: Plants should be purchased from a nursery. No attempt should be made to transplant them from the wild. During the first season after planting they should be kept constantly moist, the plants being mulched with pine needles. Cypripedium acaule is not difficult to establish provided that the soil conditions are congenial, as the acidity of the soil is the secret of success. In planting cypripediums, the crown should never be entirely buried, the tip being approximately ¼ inch above the surface. Cypripediums may be planted in very early spring while entirely dormant, or in late August and early September, the latter month being preferred.

Period of Bloom: May and June.

Cypripedium pubescens (Yellow Lady's Slipper) (also C. parviflorum). The Yellow Lady's Slipper is of such rare beauty and of such easy culture that it should be included in every woodland planting. The orchid-like flowers are of a soft luminous yellow hue and are borne on slender stems varying in height from 12 to 18 inches.

Distribution: From Nova Scotia to Alabama, westward to Minnesota and Nebraska.

Preferred Habitat: Rich, moist, stony soil in deciduous woods.

Soil Requirements: Rather indifferent to soil acidity thriving equally well in neutral or somewhat acid soil.

Culture: The plants should be purchased from a nursery. They are easy to establish and thrive exceedingly well if the surroundings are congenial. Planting directions as for C. acaule.

Period of Bloom: May and June.

Digitalis (Foxglove). All of the foxgloves do exceedingly well in partial shade and they are well adapted to woodland plantings. They are lovely when planted in great masses along a fringe of woodland or when a few plants are grouped together to give accent to a woodland composition. *Digitalis ambigua* and *Digitalis lutea* are true perennials. They bear dainty yellow flowers which cling closely to the tall, slender stems, reaching a height of about 3 feet. The cultivated types are biennial in habit, and they are obtainable in a wide variety of colors—white, primrose yellow, mauve and apricot—and will often attain a height of 6 to 8 feet.

Distribution: Canada, southward to Georgia, westward to Pacific Coast.

Preferred Habitat: Open woodlands, along a fringe of wood, light shade.

Soil Requirements: A deep, rich, woodsy soil is preferred.

Culture: Foxgloves are of easy culture and when the perennial forms are once well established, they will bloom on year after year. They may be propagated very readily from seed or by the division of old clumps. Being very fibrous-rooted, the foxgloves may be transplanted with the greatest of ease either in the autumn or in very early spring.

Period of Bloom: May and June.

Dodecatheon Meadia (Shooting Star) (American Cowslip). The dainty, cyclamen-like flowers are borne on tall, slender, leafless stems, which often reach a height of 20 inches or more. The blossoms vary in color from flesh-white to pink and are as exquisite as tiny butterflies. The leaves form a rosette-like growth close to the ground.

Distribution: Pennsylvania southward to Georgia and westward from Texas to Manitoba.

Preferred Habitat: Moist hillsides, open woods, tops of cliffs. Thrives in full sun or partial shade.

Soil Requirements: Thrives best in soil which is very nearly neutral. It can tolerate neither extreme acidity nor pronounced alkalinity.

Culture: The plants are listed in many catalogues. They are of easy culture and thrive well if supplied with ample moisture, provided soil conditions are congenial.

Period of Bloom: April and May.

Epigæa repens (Trailing Arbutus) (Mayflower). There are few woodland flowers that are more universally beloved than the Trailing Arbutus, and it is tragic, indeed, that where once it flourished so abundantly it is now all but extinct because of thoughtless vandalism. The fragile beauty of its blossoms and their exquisite fragrance have endeared it to many generations, and now at last, we are able to bring it into cultivation in our woodland gardens.

Distribution: From Newfoundland to Florida, and west to Kentucky and the Northwest Territory.

Preferred Habitat: Wooded hillsides and rocky woods, particularly under or near cone-bearing evergreens.

Soil Requirements: Intensely acid, woodland soil.

Culture: It is advisable to purchase well-established pot-grown plants from some nursery which specializes in the propagation of woodland flowers. It is useless to attempt to grow Trailing Arbutus unless the soil is intensely acid, with a pH of 4.5 or below. During the first season, the plants should be mulched with a light covering of pine needles and the soil about the plants should never be allowed to dry out.

Period of Bloom: April and May.

Erythronium (Troutlily) (Dog-tooth Violet). The narrow, lance-like leaves of the dog-tooth violet are a grayish green, being often mottled or streaked with brown, and they are almost as decorative in the woodland garden as are the flowers themselves. The nodding, slightly fragrant blooms are borne on slender stems, varying in height from 4 to 12 inches. The flowers of E. americanum are a pale russet yellow, occasionally tinted with purple. Some of the California varieties which have been recently introduced into eastern gardens are very beautiful, being obtainable in exquisite shades of pale primrose, mauve and rose.

Distribution: From Nova Scotia to Florida and westward.

Preferred Habitat: Moist, open woods, along brooksides, and stony banks.

Soil Requirements: Prefers a neutral, or very nearly neutral, soil.

Culture: The bulbs may be purchased from a nursery or a few may be carefully dug from an established woodland planting. In their natural habitat the bulbs are usually found at a depth of from 6 to 15 inches. The bulbs are smooth and egg-shaped, and produce small round offsets from the base. The foliage disappears entirely soon after the flowering season is over.

Period of Bloom: April and May.

Hepatica triloba (Liverwort). The Hepaticas are among the first of the spring flowers to appear, sometimes even blooming under the snow. Hardly more than 3 inches in height, the dainty, cup-shaped flowers, in delicate tints of lilac, deep lavender, and white, are borne above the leathery, bronze-tinted leaves. The foliage is evergreen and the new leaves appear after the flowers.

Distribution: From Canada to northern Florida and westward to Missouri, although more common in the East.

Preferred Habitat: Open woodlands and wooded hillsides.

Soil Requirements: Prefers a woodland soil rich in humus and of a neutral or slightly acid reaction.

Culture: Plants should be purchased from a nursery, and they should be planted in clumps, being spaced from 4 to 6 inches apart. They usually succeed well under cultivation in widely varying situations.

Period of Bloom: March and April.

Mertensia virginica (Virginia Cowslip) is one of the most delightful of all our wild flowers, and it may be used in happy combination with woodland ferns and with some of the spring bulbs. The buds are a lavender-pink in color and the open flowers are a clear and lovely blue. The nodding blooms are borne on stems varying in height from 12 to 15 inches. The foliage disappears entirely after the blooming season is over. Mertensia comes into flower at the same time that the Silverbell Tree (Halesia carolina) is in bloom, and it is enchantingly lovely when planted beneath the spreading branches.

Distribution: Southern New York, southward and westward.

Preferred Habitat: Low meadows, banks of streams, moist hillsides, thriving in both full sun and partial shade.

Soil Requirements: Thrives most luxuriantly in soil which is very nearly neutral. Does not tolerate pronounced acidity or alkalinity.

Culture: Plants should be purchased from a nursery and when they are once well established, they increase rapidly from self-sown seed. As soon as the seed has ripened, the foliage begins to wither and soon disappears entirely. Mertensia should be planted in an upright position at a depth of approximately $2\frac{1}{2}$ to $3\frac{1}{2}$ inches.

Period of Bloom: May and June.

Phlox divaricata (Wild Blue Phlox) is one of the most easily grown of our woodland plants and has found its way into many a cultivated garden. The dainty flowers are of a soft lavender-blue and are borne in great profusion. While the plants do well in an open, sunny border, they are most happily at home in a woodland setting and one sometimes sees a wooded hillside carpeted with them. Although the plants are somewhat creeping in habit, the flower stalks reach a height of about 12 inches. Phlox divaricata blooms at about the same time as do many of the spring bulbs, and it combines most delightfully with the large-flowered trilliums and scilla campanulata. There are few woodland flowers more completely accommodating than the wild blue phlox. It asks only a chance to establish itself, and will give generously of its bloom and beauty in the spring.

Distribution: From New York, southward and westward.

Preferred Habitat: Open, rocky woods, wooded hillsides. Thrives equally well in full sun or in partial shade.

Soil Requirements: More or less indifferent to soil conditions, but thrives best in a soil which is very nearly neutral in its reaction.

Culture: Phlox divaricata is of exceedingly easy culture, and when it has become well established in a woodland garden it will increase rapidly and will become more luxuriant and more beautiful each year. The plants may be increased by cuttings and also by the division of old clumps.

Period of Bloom: May and June.

Primula (Primroses). Primroses are always associated with the rare beauty of an English spring. There they grow in gay profusion, and during the month of May the woods are fairly carpeted with them. *Primula vulgaris* is the true English primrose, and it is the one which lends itself particularly well to naturalization. It is a lowly little thing, dainty and piquant; the pale lemon-yellow flowers nestling closely among the leaves. The *Polyantha* type grows considerably taller and bears a cluster of flowers on erect stems from 8 to 10 inches in height. The Munstead strain is an excellent one, the flowers ranging in color from pale yellow to deep orange. Some of the more brilliant types with their red, scarlet, and magenta blooms are very difficult to use in combination with other plants and should be avoided.

Distribution: Canada to Virginia, westward to Pacific Coast.

Preferred Habitat: Open, somewhat moist woods.

Soil Requirements: Rich woodland soil.

Culture: Primroses may be easily grown from seed. One should, however, bear the fact in mind that the seeds germinate very slowly, sometimes requiring six weeks or more. Old clumps may also be lifted and divided shortly after the flowering season. If soil and moisture conditions are favorable, primroses will continue to bloom year after year.

Period of Bloom: May and June.

Sanguinaria canadensis (Bloodroot). Fleeting though the blooms may be, bloodroot contributes its full share of beauty to the spring. The pure white of the petals and the gold of the stamens are lovely in great masses in the filtered sunlight of open woods, though hardly more than a few inches in height.

Distribution: Nova Scotia to Florida, and westward to Nebraska.

Preferred Habitat: Low hillsides, rich, stony ground along the borders of woods and along shady roadsides.

Soil Requirements: Entirely indifferent to soil acidity, thriving equally well in neutral or somewhat acid soil.

Culture: Bloodroot may be transplanted successfully at almost any season, and when it has once become well established, it will spread rapidly. It is most effective when used in large clumps. Plants may be purchased from a nursery or they may be transplanted with care from the wild.

Period of Bloom: April and May.

Trillium grandiflorum (Large Flowering Trillium). There are few woodland flowers more exquisite in form than the large flowering trilliums. The beautiful, pure white blossoms are borne on strong, upright stems which often reach a height of 15 inches or more. As in all the trilliums, the parts are in threes: three sepals, three petals, twice three stamens, and a whorl of three leaves —hence the name, trillium.

Distribution: Massachusetts to North Carolina, westward to Minnesota.

Preferred Habitat: Rich, rocky woodlands, and moist but well-drained woodland glades.

Soil Requirements: Prefers a woodland soil which is very nearly neutral in its reaction. Does not tolerate pronounced acidity or alkalinity.

Culture: Trillium grandiflorum is one of the most easily grown members of this family and when the clumps have become well established, they will bloom happily on, year after year. The tubers should be planted in the autumn, being placed at a depth of about 3 to 4 inches. The bud should point upward.

Period of Bloom: May and June.

SOIL REQUIREMENTS FOR HERBACEOUS WOODLAND PLANTS

GROUP 1

Indifferent to Soil Acidity

SCIENTIFIC NAME	COMMON NAME
Actæa rubra	Red Baneberry
Actæa spicata (alba)	White Baneberry
Anemone canadensis	Canada Anemone
Anemonella thalictroides	Rue Anemone
Cimicifuga racemosa	Black Snakeroot
Convallaria majalis	Lily-of-the-Valley
Cypripedium pubescens	Yellow Lady's Slipper
Habenaria fimbriata	Purple Fringed Orchis
Heuchera americana	Alumroot
Iris cristata	Crested Iris
Lupinus perennis	Blue Lupin
Myosotis laxa	Forget-me-not
Myosotis scorpioides	Forget-me-not
Podophyllum peltatum	May-Apple
Polygonatum biflorum	Solomon's Seal
Polygonatum commutatum	Solomon's Seal
Sanguinaria canadensis	Bloodroot
Tiarella cordifolia	Foam-flower

Trillium erectum	Wake-robin
Viola conspersa	Dog Violet
Viola palmata	Common Blue Violet

GROUP 2

Circumneutral (or very nearly neutral)

Aquilegia canadensis	American Columbine
Arisæma triphyllum	Jack-in-the-Pulpit
Campanula rotundifolia	Bluebell
Claytonia virginica	Spring Beauty
Cypripedium hirsutum	Showy Lady's Slipper
Dicentra Cucullaria	Dutchman's Breeches
Dodecatheon Meadia	American Cowslip, Shooting Star
Epimedium sulphureum	Barronwort
Erythronium americanum	Troutlily, Dog-tooth Violet
Gentiana Andrewsii	Bottle or Closed Gentian
Gentiana crinita	Fringed Gentian
Hepatica acutiloba	Liverwort
Hepatica triloba	Liverwort
Mertensia virginica	Virginia Cowslip
Mitella diphylla	Bishop's Cap
Orchis spectabilis	Showy Orchis
Phlox divaricata	Wild Blue Phlox
Polemonium reptans	Greek Valerian
Smilacina racemosa	False Solomon's Seal
Trillium grandiflorum	Large Flowering Trillium
Trillium stylosum	Southern Pink Trillium
Uvularia grandiflora	Merrybells
Viola blanda	Sweet White Violet
Viola canadensis	Canada Violet

GROUP 3

Moderately Acid

Anemone quinquefolia	Wood Anemone
Aquilegia cærulea	Rocky Mt. Columbine
Cornus canadensis	Bunchberry
Galax aphylla	Galax
Gaultheria procumbens	Wintergreen or Checkerberry
Habenaria ciliaris	Yellow Fringed Orchis
Houstonia cærulea	Bluets or Quaker Ladies
Houstonia purpurea	Bluets or Quaker Ladies
Mitchella repens	Partridge-berry
Viola pedata	Bird's-foot Violet

GROUP 4

Very Acid

Clintonia borealis	Clintonia
Cypripedium acaule	Moccasin Flower
Epigæa repens	Trailing Arbutus
Iris verna	Dwarf Iris

PLANTS FOR THE WOODLAND GARDEN

BOTANICAL NAME	COMMON NAME	HEIGHT	COLOR	SEASON OF BLOOM	SOIL	HABITAT
Actaea rubra	Red Baneberry	1–2'	White	April–June	Well-drained, indifferent to acidity	Open woods
Anemone canadensis	Canada Anemone	1–2'	White	May–Aug.	Indifferent to acidity	Low, moist ground
quinquefolia	Wood Anemone	4–8"	White	April–June	Moderately acid	Moist, open woods
Anemonella thalictroides	Rue Anemone	5–9"	White, tinged with pink	March–May	Indifferent to acidity	Thin, moist woodlands
Aquilegia canadensis	American Columbine	1–2'	Scarlet and yellow	April–May	Circumneutral	Dry, rocky ledges
caerulea	Rocky Mt. Columbine	2–3'	Blue and white	May–June	Moderately acid	Open woods
Arisaema triphyllum	Jack-in-the-Pulpit	12–30"	Yellowish green	April–July	Circumneutral	Moist woodlands
Campanula rotundifolia	Bluebell	6–18"	Light purple	June–Sept.	Circumneutral	Rocky cliffs, sandy fields
Cimicifuga racemosa	Black Snakeroot	3–8"	White	June–July	Indifferent	Sun or shade / Deep, moist woods
Claytonia virginica	Spring Beauty	6–12"	Pale pink	March–May	Circumneutral	Open, moist woods
Clintonia borealis	Clintonia	8–10"	Buff, sometimes greenish tinge		Very acid	Cool, moist woods
Convallaria majalis	Lily-of-the-Valley	6–8"	White	May–June	Indifferent	Sun or shade: rich, moist
Cypripedium acaule	Moccasin Flower	8–12"	Crimson-pink	April–May	Very acid	Wooded hillsides
hirsutum	Showy Lady's Slipper	18–24"	White, stained crimson	June–July	Circumneutral	Swamps, wet woodlands
pubescens (C. parviflorum)	Yellow Lady's Slipper	12–18"	Yellow	May–June	Indifferent	Moist, rich, stony soil
Dicentra canadensis	Squirrel Corn	8–12"	Greenish white	April–May	Indifferent	Fertile, light soil
Cucullaria	Dutchman's Breeches	5–9"	White, yellow tipped		Circumneutral	Thin woods, dry rocky slopes
eximia	Wild Bleeding-heart	12–18"	Pink	May	Indifferent	Rocky ledges in open woods
Digitalis (see Biennials)						
Dodecatheon Meadia	American Cowslip or Shooting Star	8–20"	Flesh-white to pink	April–May	Circumneutral	Moist hillsides, open woods
Epigaea repens	Trailing Arbutus	Trail	Pink	April–May	Very acid	Rocky woods, wooded hillsides under cone-bearing trees
Erythronium americanum	Troutlily, Dog-tooth Violet	4–8"	Yellow	April–May	Circumneutral	Moist woods, along brooks
Galax aphylla	Galax	1–2'	Yellow	April–Oct.	Circumneutral	Open woods and pastures
Gaultheria procumbens	Wintergreen or Checkerberry	2–5"	White	July–Aug.	Moderately acid	Dry, evergreen woods
Gentiana Andrewsii	Bottle or Closed Gentian	1–2'	Violet-blue	Aug.–Oct.	Circumneutral	Borders of woods, banks of streams
crinita	Fringed Gentian	1–3'	Sky blue	Sept.–Oct.	Circumneutral	Low, moist meadows and bogs
Habenaria ciliaris	Yellow Fringed Orchis	18–24"	Orange-yellow	July–Aug.	Moderately acid	Meadows, moist, sandy places
fimbriata	Large Purple Fringed Orchis	To 5'	Lilac or white	June–Aug.	Indifferent to acidity	Wet woods, swampy places
psycodes	Small Purple Fringed Orchis	1–3'	Lilac pink	July–Aug.	Indifferent to acidity	Wet woods, swampy places

Scientific Name	Common Name	Height	Color	Bloom	Acidity	Location
Hepatica acutiloba	Liverwort	3"	Brighter than triloba	March–May	Circumneutral	Open, rich woodlands
triloba	Liverwort	3"	Lilac, white, pale lavender	March–May	Circumneutral	Open, rich woodlands
Heuchera americana	Alumroot	18–24"	Whitish green	May–July	Indifferent to acidity	Moist, open
Houstonia caerulea	Bluets or Quaker Ladies	3–6"	White, tinted w. blue-violet	April–Oct.	Moderately acid	Moist, grassy places and sandy fields
purpurea	Bluets or Quaker Ladies	3–8"	Purple or lilac	April–Oct.	Moderately acid	Moist, grassy places and sandy fields
Iris cristata	Crested Iris	3–6"	Violet with orange crest	April–May	Indifferent to acidity	Hillsides and along streams
verna	Dwarf Iris	4–8"	Violet blue, yellow centers	April–May	Very acid	Needs protected spot in North Wooded hillsides
Lupinus perennis	Blue Lupine	1–2'	Violet-blue	May–June	Indifferent	Barren fields
Mertensia virginica	Virginia Cowslip	1–2'	Sky blue, buds pink	March–May	Circumneutral	Low meadows, banks of streams Sun or shade
Mitchella repens	Partridge-berry	Trail	White and pink	June	Moderately acid	Woods and shaded borders of fields
Mitella diphylla	Bishop's Cap	8–12"	White	April–May	Circumneutral	Damp rocks, deep wooded slopes
Myosotis laxa	Forget-me-not	6–12"	Bright blue, but inconspicuous	May–July	Indifferent	Moist, banks of brooks
scorpioides	Forget-me-not	6–12"	Bright blue, larger	May–July	Indifferent	Moist, banks of brooks
Orchis spectabilis	Showy Orchis	5–10"	Rosy lavender and white	May–June	Circumneutral	Moist stony soil
Phlox divaricata	Wild Blue Phlox	9–18"	Lavender-blue	April–June	Circumneutral	Rocky woods
Podophyllum peltatum	May-Apple	12–18"	White	April–May	Indifferent to acidity	Moist, shaded
Polemonium reptans	Greek Valerian	8–12"	Blue-violet	April–May	Circumneutral	Thin, dryish woods
Polygonatum biflorum	Solomon's Seal	18–30"	Greenish white	April–June	Indifferent to acidity	Thickets, dry wooded slopes
commutatum	Solomon's Seal	8'		April–June	Indifferent to acidity	Thickets, dry wooded slopes
Sanguinaria canadensis	Bloodroot	10"	White	April–May	Indifferent to acidity	Borders of woods Along shaded roadsides
Tiarella cordifolia	Foam-flower	6–10"	White	May–June	Indifferent to acidity	Rich, moist woods
Trillium erectum	Wake-robin	7–12"	Maroon	April–May	Indifferent to acidity	Rich, moist woodlands
grandiflorum	Large Flowering Trillium	10–18"	White, then pink	May–June	Circumneutral	Rich, rocky woods
stylosum	Southern Pink Trillium	12–18"	Rose, pink	May–June	Circumneutral	Rich, rocky woods
Viola blanda	Sweet White Violet	3–5"	White, purple veins	April–May	Circumneutral	Moist or dry situations
canadensis	Canada Violet	5–15"	White, tinged purple	May–June	Circumneutral	Well-drained, upland woods
conspersa	Dog Violet	3–5"	Light blue-purple	April–June	Indifferent to acidity	Moist woods, shady borders of roads and fields
palmata	Common Blue Violet	3–7"	Violet-purple	April–June	Indifferent to acidity	Low moist ground
pedata	Bird's-foot Violet	4–8"	Lilac or blue-violet	April–June	Moderately acid, dry sandy	Open banks, thin woods

FERNS FOR THE WOODLAND GARDEN

BOTANICAL NAME	COMMON NAME	TYPE (DECIDUOUS OR EVERGREEN)	HEIGHT IN FEET OR INCHES	HABITAT
Adiantum pedatum	American Maidenhair Fern	D	2'	Shade
Asplenium platyneuron	Ebony Spleenwort	E	½–1'	Rocky woods
Trichomanes	Maidenhair Spleenwort	E	½'	Clefts in rocks
Athyrium Filix-femina	Lady Fern	D	2–3'	Partial shade or full sun
pycnocarpon	Narrowleaf Spleenwort	D	2–3'	Rich woods
Botrychium virginianum	Rattlesnake Fern	D	1–2'	Open woods
Camptosorus rhizophyllus	Walking Fern	E	4–10"	Limestone cliffs in shade
Cystopteris bulbifera	Berry Bladderfern	D	1–2'	Moist bank or brookside in shade
Dennstaedtia punctilobula	Hayscented Fern	D	2'	Sun or shade
Dryopteris Clintoniana	Clinton Wood Fern	E	2–3'	Moist woods
cristata	Crested Wood Fern	E	1–2'	On hummocks in grassy bogs
dilatata	Mountain Wood Fern	E	2'	Mountain peaks in shade
hexagonoptera	Winged Wood Fern	D	1'	Shade
Linnaeana	Oak Fern	D	½'	Shade
marginalis	Leather Wood Fern	E	2–3'	Rocky woods
Phegopteris	Narrow Beech Fern	D	½–1'	Brookside banks
spinulosa	Toothed Wood Fern	E	2–3'	Shade
Lygodium palmatum	Hartford or Climbing Fern	E	4'	Bogs
Onoclea sensibilis	Sensitive Fern	D	1–2'	Roadsides and damp woods
Osmunda cinnamomea	Cinnamon Fern	D	3–4'	Sun or shade
Claytoniana	Interrupted Fern	D	3–4'	Sun or shade
regalis	Royal Fern	D	3'	Rocky woods
Polypodium vulgare	Common Polypody	E	½'	Rocky woods
Polystichum acrostichoides	Christmas Fern	E	1–2'	Rich woods
Pteretis nodulosa	Ostrich Fern	D	4–6'	Banks of streams, sun or shade

SHRUBS FOR THE WOODLAND GARDEN

BOTANICAL AND COMMON NAMES	EVERGREEN OR DECIDUOUS; HEIGHT	COLOR OF BLOOM AND SEASON	FRUIT AND AUTUMN EFFECT	SOIL AND HABITAT
Aronia arbutifolia Red Chokeberry	D; 9'	Pinkish; May	Red fruit and leaves	Moist
melanocarpa Black Chokeberry	D; 4'	White; May	Black	Well drained
Azalea arborescens Sweet Azalea	D; 9–12'	White; June–July	Leaves Red	Acid
calendulacea Flame Azalea	D; 12'	Yellow-scarlet; June	Inconspicuous	Acid
canadense Rhodora	D; 3'	Rosy-purple; April–May	Inconspicuous	Acid
nudiflora Pinxter-flower	D; 6–8'	Pink; April–May	Inconspicuous	Acid or lime
rosea	D; 9'	Pink; April–May	Inconspicuous	Acid or lime
Vaseyi Pinkshell Azalea	D; 15'	Various; April–May	Inconspicuous	Acid
viscosa Swamp Azalea	D; 4–7'	Pink, white; June–July	Inconspicuous	Moist

Name	Type; Size	Flower; Bloom	Berry/Fruit	Soil/Habitat
Benzoin æstivale / Spice Bush	D; 6-12'	Pale yellow; March–April	Gold leaves, scarlet berries	Fertile; wet woods, swamps
Clethra alnifolia / White Alder or Sweet Pepperbush	D; 4-5'	White; July–August	Inconspicuous	Wet, peaty or acid sandy; edges of woods and fields
Cornus alba / Coral Dogwood	D; 5-10'	Cream; May–June	Bluish white, red twigs	Wet
Amomum / Silky Cornel or Kinnikinnik	D; 5-10'	White; June	Blue	Wet
racemosa / Gray Dogwood	D; 3-15'	Cream; June	White or pale blue	Wet
stolonifera / Golden-twig Dogwood	D; 8'	Dull white; May	White	
Hamamelis virginica / Witch Hazel	D; 8-12'	Yellow; Oct. or Nov.	Black seeds	Indifferent; thickets, edges of woodlands
Ilex glabra / Inkberry	E; 4-8'	White; July	Black berries through winter	Wet
verticillata / Winterberry, or Black Alder	D; 6-15'	Inconspicuous; July	Red	Wet; swamps, wet thickets
Kalmia latifolia / Mountain Laurel	E; 8'	Pink; June	Inconspicuous	Slightly acid and moist; rocky hillsides, woodlands
Leiophyllum buxifolium / Sand Myrtle	E; 1'	White; May–June	Inconspicuous	Acid
Leucothoë Catesbaei / Catesby's Leucothoë	E; 3-5'	White; April	Deep red	Acid; mountains
Pachistima Canbyi	E; 1'	Reddish; April-May		Acid
Pieris floribunda / Mt. Fetter Bush	E; 3-5'	White-pink; April–May	Flower buds about to burst all winter	Acid
Rhamnus cathartica / Buckthorn	D; 12'	White; May–June	Scarlet, good display	Sandy or clay
Rhododendron carolinianum / Carolina Rhododendron	E; 9'	Pink; May–June	Inconspicuous	Moderately acid
catawbiense / Catawba Rhododendron	E; 6-18'	Rosy lilac; May–June	Inconspicuous	Moderately acid
maximum / Rosebay Rhododendron	E; 30'	Pink or white; May	Inconspicuous	Moderately acid
minus	E; 10'	Rosy pink; June–July		Moderately acid
Sambucus pubens / Elder	D; 5-8'	White; June–July	Purple fruit	Swampy
Vaccinium corymbosum / High-bush Blueberry	D; 4-10'	White; May–June	Scarlet leaves, blue berries; Aug. Sept.	Acid; deep swamps, moist woods
pennsylvanicum / Low-bush Blueberry	D; 1½'	White; May–June	Scarlet leaves, blue berries; July–Aug.	Acid; dry, rocky, sandy hills
vacillans / Dwarf Late Blueberry	D; 1-3'	Purple; May	Crimson leaves, berries last later	Acid; open woods (dry), shaded thickets
Viburnum acerifolium / Dockmackie	D; 5'	White; June	Black	Dry
cassinoides / Withe-rod	D; 6'	White; May	Black	Wet
dentatum / Arrow-wood	D; 5-15'	White; June	Blue	
Lentago / Nannyberry	D; 30'	White; May	Black	Moist
prunifolium / Plum-leaved Haw	D; 30'	White; April	Black	

VIII

WATER AND BOG GARDENS

PLANTS FOR WATER GARDENS

THE natural pond or the garden pool may be readily converted into a water garden by the use of water plants. It is often assumed that so exquisite a flower as a water-lily is difficult to grow and that it requires special care. Actually, however, once they are established, the hardy species of *Nymphæa* thrive without much attention. Some of the species are native to this country and are common in the quiet waters of inland ponds. The tender kinds, including *Nelumbium speciosum*, the Egyptian lotus, need more care and are most satisfactorily grown in the greenhouse or removed to the greenhouse for the winter.

It is supposed that water-lilies require abundant space and that one must have a pond of considerable size in which to raise them. While the larger species spread to a circle about 6 feet across, the dwarf species, with small leaves and exquisitely small flowers, are suitable for garden pools hardly more than 3 or 4 feet in diameter.

HARDY WATER-LILIES

Species and Varieties of Merit

Nymphæa odorata, the white, fragrant pond-lily of the Northern States, is hardy and dependable. The leaves are dark green and numerous. The flowers are about 4 inches across, the upcurving white petals encircling yellow stamens.

Many hybrid varieties of *Nymphæa odorata* are on the market.

N. odorata rosea is the pink Cape Cod water-lily.

N. odorata minor is a small plant with tiny flowers. It requires a depth of but 12 inches and spreads to a circle only 3 feet in diameter.

N. odorata caroliniana bears rose-flesh-colored flowers with yellow stamens. The leaves are large, sometimes 12 inches across.

N. odorata Yellow Pigmy has clear yellow flowers. Variety *Helen Fowler* is a good pink. Flowers of *aurora* change color on successive days, yellow the first day, then red-orange and finally red.

N. Marliacea albida and *N. Gladstoniana* are among the best white water-lilies. They are free-growing plants, blooming continuously all season, and they produce large fragrant flowers. Those of *Marliacea albida* have pink sepals. *Gladstoniana* has enormous blooms.

N. Marliacea rosea, similar to *albida* in habit, has deep pink blossoms.

N. alba has large white, floating flowers.

N. alba candidissima has larger flowers than the type and is a vigorous plant with blossoms continuing throughout the season.

Other good pinks are *formosa* and *Pink Opal.*

Attraction, Gloriosa, and *James Brydon* have red flowers. *Comanche* has tones of apricot and red in the petals, and orange stamens. *Sioux* varies from copper yellow to red. *Indian* opens yellow and changes to dark crimson.

N. Marliacea chromatella is still one of the best yellows, bearing blossoms 6 inches across with canary yellow petals and bright yellow stamens in generous numbers. It is a vigorous grower and should be divided every few years to avoid crowding of the leaves in the center of the plant.

All these water-lilies are hardy in Zones V and VI.*

Propagation by Seed

Sow the seeds in pans of sand. Cover the seeds lightly with screened sand and place the pan in water at a temperature of 70 to 80 degrees F. in such a way that the surface of the sand is above the water, but in contact with it. After soaking them all day, submerge the pans to a depth of

*See Zone Map of Hardiness on p. 712.

96

18 inches or more. After the plants have formed the first floating leaf, they may be transplanted to flats with 2 inches of soil containing well-rotted cow manure. Thereafter the young plants should be potted on as they develop and require more space.

Cultural Requirements

The requirements for culture are quiet water with a trickling inlet and outlet, a depth of 18 inches for the smaller sorts and 2 or 3 feet for the larger species, full sunshine, and 2 or 3 cubic feet of prepared soil for each plant.

The soil may be a mixture of two parts good garden soil and one part well-rotted cow manure, or, if natural sources are available, a mixture of equal parts garden soil and pond muck. If neither manure nor muck is obtainable, a half quart of bone meal to each plant may be mixed with the soil.

For convenience in keeping the pool neat, the soil is placed in tubs, half barrels, or boxes. Cypress is the best wood for tubs and boxes but the barrels are usually of oak. The soil bed should be almost 12 inches deep and so placed that its surface is 12 to 18 inches below the surface of the water. In planting, the soil is put into the tub, half filling it, the tuber is placed on the soil so that the growing end is upward and about level with the rim of the tub, being held in this position while more soil is filled in around it. The upper inch or two should consist of sand. In planting water-lilies in a natural pond the tubers may be squeezed down into the muck of the bottom. If the muck does not hold them and they float instead, it may be wrapped about them. The best time for planting is April.

Winter Care

Once established, hardy water-lilies will require no special care. To carry hardy water-lilies through the winter, the only protection necessary is the muck and water above them. If the ice does not freeze to the bottom where the tubers are, no harm will be done to them.

The pool itself may be protected against ice pressure in several ways. If it is small, it may be covered with a floor of boards, with a mound of leaves and litter heaped above it. This will conserve ground heat and delay and mitigate freezing. The larger pool may be protected by a number of floating logs. As the ice freezes, the logs, being somewhat soft, will absorb the pressure and thus relieve the concrete from a strain which might crack it.

Other Water Plants

Other aquatic plants attractive in pools or on pond margins are Floating Heart, which has no roots in the muck; Forget-me-not; Parrot-feather; Primrose Willow; Primrose Creeper; Water-hyacinth; Water Snowflake; Umbrella Palm. Water Snowflake has charming, small white and pale yellow blossoms, which rest on the water like little butterflies.

Oxygenating Plants

Plants which keep the water clear and refreshed by their natural process of charging it with oxygen are known as oxygenating plants. Cabomba and Anacharis are both tiny plants with light green, small leaves—much smaller than those of watercress—floating on the surface, and they grow in shallow water about 4 inches to 12 inches deep. Sagittaria (Arrowhead) is another oxygen plant. It grows from shallow water to a height of 3 feet, and bears arrowhead leaves.

Shore Plants

The shores of a natural pond may be greatly enlivened by groups of Pickerel Rush, Bull Rush, Papyrus, Yellow Flag (Iris pseudacorus), Purple Flag (Iris versicolor), and Arrowhead, most of which grow up from water a few inches deep and stand erect. Such shrubs as Button bush (Cephalanthus occidentalis), Spice bush (Benzoin æstivale), Sweet pepper bush (Clethra alnifolia), are suitable for the larger masses of foliage on the pond side.

Insect Pests

Water plants seem to be troubled by only a few enemies.

THE CHARM OF A WATER GARDEN

Aphids sometimes are found on the leaves. The easiest way to be rid of them is to wash them off into the water with the spray of a hose. The goldfish will then dispose of them.

A *leaf miner* occasionally destroys leaves, making tunnels that are easily seen. The only certain method of coping with it is to cut off all affected leaves as soon as the trouble is detected and burn them. The plant should be able to replace the lost leaves with new ones.

A remarkable insect is the *Leaf-eating Hydrocampa propiralis*, which constructs boats from bits of leaves and cruises about the pond. Picking them off the leaves by hand and catching them in a net while navigating is recommended as the most effective means of control.

Algæ are not damaging but make the pool disagreeable with greenish discoloration. The water can be cleared up by putting copper sulphate in it at the rate of one pound per 500,000 gallons. A pool 3 feet deep and 13 × 30 feet of surface will need only $\frac{1}{8}$ of an ounce of copper sulphate. The crystals of copper sulphate should be crushed, put into a cloth bag like a salt bag, and drawn through the water until dissolved.

BOG GARDENS

A true bog is a flat piece of ground composed largely of peat and covered with living sphagnum moss. It retains the moisture throughout the summer season and yet does not have pools of standing water in it. Permanently wet soil of this nature is difficult to recondition or to drain, and the results of such an attempt may not justify the expenditure. A more logical use of such an area is to grow there the many attractive plants which thrive in saturated soil. And because many of these plants cannot be grown in ordinary garden soil, the possession of a natural bog offers an unusual opportunity for a unique type of gardening.

Lacking a bog, but desirous of growing bog plants, the garden owner may create by artificial means the requisite conditions. The two essentials are a continuous supply of water, and a soil which is capable of retaining it. The first may be provided by water pipes in which tiny holes have been bored at intervals of every 2 or 3 feet, the pipes being buried at a depth of approximately 2 inches. The second requisite may be provided by mixing equal portions of sand and peat moss with generous quantities of humus. The mixture should be deep, 18 inches if possible, and a 1-inch layer of peat moss should be spread over the surface. The only subsequent care of the bog after the plants have become established is the occasional removal of undesirable plants which may have crept in.

PLANTS FOR THE BOG GARDEN

Cardinal Flower (Lobelia cardinalis)
Closed Gentian (Gentiana Andrewsii)
Fringed Gentian (Gentiana crinita)
Iris (Iris fulva)
    (Iris pseudacorus)
    (Iris versicolor)
Jack-in-the-Pulpit (Arisæma triphyllum)
Lilies (L. canadense)
    (L. superbum)
Marsh Marigold (Caltha palustris)

Pickerel weed (Pontederia cordata)
Pitcher Plant (Sarracenia flava)
    (Sarracenia purpurea)
Primulas (P. Bulleyana)
    (P. Cockburniana)
    (P. helodoxa)
    (P. japonica)
Royal Fern (Osmunda regalis)
Troutlily (Erythronium americanum)
Wake Robin (Trillium erectum)
    (Trillium grandiflorum)

IX

THE HERB GARDEN

THE Herb Garden was one of the earliest expressions of garden art during the period of the Renaissance. Throughout Europe physic gardens were found within the cloistered walls of the monasteries and from these gardens were dispensed a variety of medicinal herbs, in an effort, on the part of the monks, to alleviate the suffering and distress of their people. It was an era when the enjoyment of plants for their beauty alone, while not entirely forgotten, was at least secondary in importance to their more practical uses. People were interested primarily in growing plants which were to be used for medicinal purposes, or as flavorings in cookery, or as a source of color for the dyeing of materials, and in some cases for fragrance alone. An intimate knowledge of such plants was general throughout the countryside, as is evidenced by the wealth of plant names in most European languages; and the superstition and folklore regarding these plants were passed on from generation to generation.

The herb garden of the Middle Ages was usually laid out upon simple, formal lines with quaintly patterned beds, narrow paths, and prim edgings, and in many an old monastery garden the "Mint Pool" was a favorite feature. During the Elizabethan era in England the herb garden was an important feature of the grounds and the patterned beds upon the broad terraces surrounding the manor houses became more and more intricate in design.

The early colonists brought with them to this country a knowledge and understanding of the uses of herbs, and it was not long before many of the old, familiar plants were flourishing in the little dooryard gardens of the towns and villages of New England.

During the 19th century the interest in herbs declined steadily and the herb garden, as it had existed in earlier times, became an almost forgotten thing of the past. Within the last few decades, however, there has been a great reawakening of interest in the culture and the uses of herbs and we have again come to appreciate the quaint beauty and charm of the herb garden.

There is a subtle quality about a herb garden which no other type of garden possesses. Perhaps it is because of their long association with man and the many legends which surround them. Or perhaps it is because there are so few bright colors and no large, flamboyant blooms—just the soft gray-green tones of the foliage and the gentle color and form of the flowers which create in the garden a sense of all-pervading serenity and peace.

The Small Herb Garden

Although one occasionally sees a new herb garden with intricate, primly patterned beds, reminiscent of earlier days, most herb gardens to-day are simple affairs. Sometimes the herbs are relegated to the vegetable garden, or are used as a foreground planting in a shrub border where many of them can be made to feel very happily at home. Some gardeners who have no other available space tuck them in here and there among the perennial garden beds and borders.

One of the most ideal locations for a small herb garden is a sunny space near the kitchen door. Such a space may be made very attractive and have a definite charm if a simple design is evolved and if materials are selected with care. Perhaps where space permits a few mellow old bricks could be used to make a small terrace bordered with herbs. Two small bay-trees in tubs and a few pots of rosemary on the terrace, and a simply designed bench would lend added interest; while gay ropes of ornamental gourds, a bunch or two of Indian corn and long strings of red peppers against the wall would be a delightfully colorful and decorative note. If there is no available space for even a small terrace perhaps a walk could be bordered with narrow herb beds, or space found for a little herb patch beside the door, bordered with marigolds and parsley, with tarragon and basil and pineapple sage and lavender with their alluring fragrance planted close against the house wall. Just a few feet of sunny space—that is all that is needed.

It can give a housewife a great deal of pleasure to be able to slip out of her kitchen for a moment and pluck a few fresh sprigs from her herb bed to add flavor or embellishment to her cookery. And few plants will give so generously in return for the time and labor expended upon them as will the herbs.

The selection of the herbs to be grown in a small herb garden will depend to a considerable extent upon personal preference. The variety of different herbs need not be large—a half dozen or so will suffice to give a subtle tang to many a dish. And no matter how small the garden, a few herbs should be included for their fragrance, such as lavender and lemon verbena.

Among the herbs most generally grown for culinary use are the following:

chives	marjoram	summer savory
dill	mint	sweet basil
lemon basil	rosemary	tarragon

Uses of Culinary Herbs

Culinary herbs have a variety of uses in the kitchen of today, and many a cook prides herself on the skill with which she can prepare dishes which might otherwise be commonplace, but which have that special zest and flavor which only herbs can impart.

Borage: leaves floated in a punch bowl or a cold drink, chopped leaves used in salads and in spinach.

Chives: salads, soups, sauces, egg dishes, cottage and cream cheese.

Dill: fish, bouillon, sauces, creamed potatoes, fried summer squash, egg dishes, green salads, cream cheese.

Lemon basil: tomato juice, elderberry jelly, peas, green salads.

Marjoram: roast lamb and pork, egg dishes, sweetbreads, mushrooms, cottage cheese, creamed or fried potatoes and scalloped vegetables.

A bunch of marjoram hung in the kitchen will give a delightful fragrance and will counteract unpleasant cooking odors.

Mint: iced drinks, sauce for lamb, jelly, flavoring for peas and carrots.

Rosemary: fried chicken, fish steaks, roast pork, veal stew, turkey hash, egg dishes, and a few finely minced leaves in baking powder biscuits.

Summer Savory: meat loaf, potato soup, zucchini squash, used sparingly in stuffing for poultry.

Sweet Basil: spaghetti dishes, soups, stews, pot roasts, ragout, chicken livers, stuffed eggs, herb vinegar, a leaf or two in each jar of canned tomatoes.

Tarragon: salads, sauces, herb vinegar.

Thyme: lobster and clam chowder, sauces for veal, pork and tongue.

Classification of Herbs

Herbs are usually divided into several groups, although there is more or less overlapping. The aromatic herbs are those grown for fragrance;

An Herb Garden in Tudor Style
Scale 0 2 4 6 8 10 Feet

the culinary herbs are those grown to be used as flavorings in cookery; the medicinal herbs still play an important part in modern medicine; and those grown for coloring still give us some of our most beautiful dyes.

Cultural Requirements

Most herbs may be grown very easily from seed, or small plants may be purchased. Often there is a friendly exchange of cuttings and divisions among neighbors.

Some of the plants commonly grown in the herb garden will need frequent division and pruning in order to keep them within bounds and to prevent them from crowding out some of the less aggressive plants. The various mints are in this class, and chives will benefit from being lifted and divided each year.

The majority of our herbs prefer a position in full sun and thrive best in a not-too-fertile, sandy loam soil which is well drained. When grown in rich garden beds they make more luxuriant vegetative growth but seem to lose some of their fragrance and flavor.

There are a few herbs which prefer light shade rather than full sun, and a few which prefer a moist location.

Harvesting

If the foliage is to be used either for fragrance or for flavoring, the herbs should be cut just as the flowers are about to open, for with most herbs it is at this stage that the essential oils are the most abundant. The most favorable time for cutting is early in the morning after the dew has dried but before the plants have been touched with hot midday sun. When herbs are to be cut for flowers, as in the case of lavender and chamomile, they should be cut when in full bloom. If the seeds are to be used, the seed heads should be cut when they are no longer green. Those which are harvested for their roots should be dug in the autumn after growth has ceased.

Herbs Grown Indoors for Winter Use

Some herbs can be grown on a sunny window sill during the winter months and offer a wel-come bit of green as well as spicy flavorings. Basil, mint, rosemary and parsley are among those which will thrive well if favorable conditions are provided. They may be grown either in pots or in small window boxes.

For indoor culture the soil should be fairly fertile. A good sandy loam to which some compost has been added will give good results. Herbs will thrive best if they are grown in a south or southeast window in a very cool room, although they will adapt themselves to varied conditions. It is a wise practice to syringe the foliage once a week.

HERBS FOR FLAVORING

Angelica (A. Archangelica)
Anise (Pimpinella Anisum)
Balm (Melissa officinalis)
Basil (Ocimum)
   O. minimum
   O. Basilicum
Borage (Borago officinalis)
Burnet (Sanguisorba officinalis)
   S. minor
Caraway (Carum Carvi)
Catnip (Nepeta Cataria)
Chamomile (Anthemis nobilis)
      (Matricaria Chamomilla)
Chervil (Anthriscus Cerefolium)
Chives (Allium Schœnoprasum)
Coriander (Coriandrum sativum)
Costmary (Chrysanthemum Balsamita)
Cress (Barbarea verna)
Dill (Anethum graveolens)
Fennel (Fœniculum vulgare)
Fennel Flower (Nigella sativa)
Horehound (Marrubium vulgare)
Lovage (Levisticum officinale)
Marjoram (Origanum)
   O. Onites, Pot Marjoram
   O. Majorana, Sweet Marjoram
Mint (Mentha)
   M. rotundifolia variegata, Apple Mint
   M. crispa, Curled Mint
   M. piperita, Peppermint
   M. spicata, Garden Mint or Spearmint
Rue (Ruta graveolens)
Saffron (Crocus sativus)
Sage (Salvia officinalis)
Savory (Satureja)
   S. hortensis, Summer Savory
   S. montana, Winter Savory
Sorrel (Rumex Acetosa)
Sweet Flag (Acorus Calamus)
Tarragon (Artemisia Dracunculus)
Thyme (Thymus)
   T. vulgaris, Common English Thyme
   T. Serpyllum citriodorus, Lemon Thyme
Watercress (Nasturtium aquaticum)

HERBS FOR FRAGRANCE

Ambrosia (Chenopodium Botrys)
Balm (Melissa officinalis)
Basil (Ocimum)
Bergamot (Monarda)
 M. didyma
 M. fistulosa
 M. fistulosa alba
Geranium (Pelargonium)
 P. crispum, Citronella Geranium
 P. denticulatum, Skeleton Geranium
 P. graveolens, Rose Geranium
 P. Limoneum, Lemon Geranium
 P. melissinum, Balm Geranium
 P. odoratissimum, in variety

Lavender (Lavandula)
 L. dentata
 L. spica
 L. vera
Lavender-Cotton (Santolina Chamaecyparissus)
Marjoram (Origanum)
 O. Onites, Pot Marjoram
 O. Majorana, Sweet Marjoram
Mint (Mentha)
 M. citrata, Orange Mint
 M. crispa, Curled Mint
 M. rotundifolia, Apple Mint
 M. piperita, Peppermint
 M. Pulegium, Pennyroyal
 M. Requieni, Creeping Mint
 M. spicata, Garden or Spearmint

Rosemary (Rosmarinus officinalis)
Rue (Ruta graveolens)
Savory (Satureja)
 S. hortensis, Summer Savory
 S. montana, Winter Savory
Southernwood (Artemisia Abrotanum)
Thyme (Thymus), in variety
Verbena, Lemon (Lippia citriodora)
Woodruff, Sweet (Asperula odorata)
Wormwood (Artemisia)
 A. Absinthium, Common Wormwood
 A. pontica, Roman Wormwood
 A. Stelleriana, Beach Wormwood

HERB CHART

COMMON AND BOTANICAL NAMES	ANNUAL, BIENNIAL OR PERENNIAL; HEIGHT	PROPAGATION; USES	EXPOSURE; SOIL REQUIREMENTS
Ambrosia / Chenopodium Botrys	A; 2'	Seed; fragrance	Sunny; any soil
Angelica / Angelica Archangelica	B; 2-3'	Sow seed as soon as ripe; food, perfume	Cool climate; prefers a rather moist soil
Anise / Pimpinella Anisum	A; 2-3'	Seed; food, perfume, medicine	Warm, sunny; moderately rich, well-drained loam
Balm (Lemon Balm) / Melissa officinalis	P; 2½-3'	Seed; medicine, food, perfume	Warm, sheltered position; poor, light soil
Basil / Ocimum minimum	A; 1'	Seed; seasoning, fragrance	Sunny; well drained
Bee Balm / Monarda didyma	P; 2-3'	Seed, division; medicine, perfume, food	Sun or partial shade; dry, well-drained soil
Bergamot / Monarda fistulosa, f. alba	P; 3'	Division; fragrance	Sun or partial shade; any soil
Borage / Borago officinalis	A; 1½-2'	Seed; food	Sunny; dry, well-drained soil
Burnet / Sanguisorba minor	P; 5'	Seed, division; medicine, food	Full sun; any garden soil, prefers lime
Sanguisorba officinalis	B; 2'	Division, seed; flavoring	Sunny; any garden soil
Caraway / Carum Carvi	P; 1'	Seed; medicine, perfume, food	Sunny; dry, well-drained soil
Chamomile / Anthemis nobilis	A; 2'	Seeds, rooting stems; medicine	Sunny; dry, well-drained soil
Sweet or false / Matricaria Chamomilla	A; ½-1'	Seed; flavoring	Full sun; ordinary soil
Chervil / Anthriscus Cerefolium		Seed; food, medicine	Sun or partial shade; any good garden soil
Chives / Allium Schoenoprasum	P; 10"	Bulbs, seeds, division of clumps; flavorings for salads, omelets, sauces	Sunny; any good garden soil

HERB CHART—continued

COMMON AND BOTANICAL NAMES	ANNUAL, BIENNIAL OR PERENNIAL; HEIGHT	PROPAGATION; USES	EXPOSURE; SOIL REQUIREMENTS
Clary / Salvia Sclarea	B; 3'	Seed; perfumes, food	Full sun; rocky, dry soil
Coriander / Coriandrum sativum	A; 1½'	Seed; medicine, perfume, food	Sunny; prefers a warm light soil
Costmary / Chrysanthemum Balsamita	P; 3'	Root cuttings; medicine, food	Sunny; dry, well drained soil
Cress / Barbarea verna	B; 2'	Seed; flavoring for salad	Sun; any meadow soil
Cumin / Cuminum Cyminum	A; 4–8"	Seed; medicine, perfume, food	Sunny; any good garden soil
Dill / Anethum graveolens	A; 2½–3'	Seed (do not transplant); food, for pickling, for vinegars	Sunny; any ordinary garden soil
Fennel Flower / Nigella sativa	A; 1'	Seed; condiment, perfume	Full sun; any garden soil
Florence Fennel / Foeniculum vulgare, var. dulce	A; 6–10"	Seed; food	Full sun; light, well-drained soil
Geranium, scented, in variety / Pelargonium	P*; 1–3'	Cuttings; fragrance	Sunny; any garden soil
Horehound / Marrubium vulgare	P; 3'	Seed; medicine, as a drink	Full sun; poor, light, dry soil
Horseradish / Armoracia rusticana	P; 18–30"	Root cuttings; food, medicine	Sun; any soil
Hyssop / Hyssopus officinalis	P; 18–24"	Seed; medicine, perfume, food	Sunny; ordinary garden soil, not too rich. Prefers lime
Lavender / Lavandula (vera, officinalis, Spica)	P; 2–3'	Cuttings, seed; fragrance, food	Full sun; light, well-drained soil high in lime content
Lavandula dentata	P; 2–3'	Cuttings, seed; fragrance	Full sun; any garden soil
Lavender-Cotton / Santolina Chamaecyparissus	P; 2'	Cuttings; fragrance	Sunny; garden soil, not hardy. Winter over in cold frames
Lemon Verbena / Lippia citriodora	P; 4–5'	Cuttings of half-ripe wood; flavor, perfume	Very sensitive to frost. Best grown in pots; good garden loam
Lovage / Levisticum officinale	P; 6'	Seed; medicine, perfume, food	Sunny; rich, moist soil
Mint, Apple / Mentha rotundifolia	P; 30"	Cuttings, divisions; flavoring, fragrance	Sunny; good garden soil
Mint, Curled / Mentha crispa	P; 3'	Cuttings, divisions; flavoring. fragrance	Sunny; good, deep soil
Parsley / Petroselinum hortense	B; 6–10"	Seed; medicine, food	Full sun; prefers a rather moist soil
Peppermint / Mentha piperita	P; 2–3'	Cuttings, runners; medicine, perfume, food	Sunny; deep, moist soil
Perennial Marjoram / Origanum (Majorana, Onites)	P; 2'	Seed; flavoring, fragrance	Sunny; any garden soil

* Tender; not hardy in North.

Name		Uses	Conditions
Pot Marigold Calendula officinalis	A; 12–15"	Seed; medicine, food	Sunny; any rich garden soil
Pot Marjoram Origanum vulgare	P; 2'	Seed, cuttings; medicine, perfume, food	Sunny; any garden soil
Rosemary Rosmarinus officinalis	P*; 3–6'	Seed, cuttings; medicine, perfume	Sunny, sheltered position; dry well-drained soil
Rue Ruta graveolens	P; 2'	Seed, cuttings; perfume, food	Sunny; prefers a well-drained yet moist soil
Saffron Crocus sativus	P; 4"	Seed, corms; perfume, flavoring, coloring	Sunny; garden soil
Sage Salvia officinalis	P; 2–3'	Seed, cuttings; medicine, perfume, food	Sunny; any well-drained garden soil
Savory Summer Satureja hortensis	A; 1–1½'	Seed; medicine, food	Sunny; any good garden soil
Winter Savory Satureja montana	P; 15"	Seed; seasoning, fragrance	Sunny; any garden soil
Sesame Sesamum orientale	A; 2'	Seed; medicine, food	Full sun; any well-drained garden soil
Sorrel Rumex Acetosa	P; 3'	Seed; salad flavoring	Sunny; any garden soil not too alkaline
Southernwood Artemisia Abrotanum	P; 2–3'	Division; fragrance, medicine	Sunny; any garden soil
Spearmint Mentha spicata	P; 2–3'	Cuttings, runners; perfume, food	Sunny; deep, moist soil
Sweet Basil Ocimum Basilicum	A; 1½–2'	Seed; flavoring, medicine, perfume	Sunny; well-drained soil
Sweet Cicely Myrrhis odorata	P; 2–3'	Seed, division; food	Sun or partial shade; any ordinary garden soil
Sweet Fennel Fœniculum officinale	A; 3'	Seed; food	Full sun; well-drained soil
Sweet Flag Acorus Calamus	P; 5'	Division; perfume	Sunny; moist
Sweet Marjoram Origanum Majorana hortensis	A; 8–12"	Seed; medicine, perfume, food	Sunny; dry, well-drained
Sweet Woodruff Asperula odorata	P; 8"	Division; fragrance, flavoring	Partial shade; thrives well in either moist or dry soil
Tansy Tanacetum vulgare	P; 3'	Seed, division; medicine, perfume	Full sun; any garden soil
Tarragon Artemisia Dracunculus	P; 3'	Root cuttings; perfume, flavoring	Prefers light shade; any good soil
Thyme† Thymus	P; 6–8"	Seed, cuttings; medicine, perfume	Sunny; rocky banks, any well-drained sunny position
Watercress Nasturtium aquaticum	P; 5"	Seed or stem cuttings; salad seasoning	Sunny; pool or stream margins
Wormwood Artemisia Absinthium	P; 2½–4'	Seed, division; medicine, food	Sunny; any garden soil
Roman Wormwood Artemisia pontica	P; B; 4'	Seed, division; fragrance	Sunny; thrives even in poor soil
Beach Wormwood Artemisia Stelleriana	P; 2½'	Seed, division; fragrance	Sunny; any soil

* Tender shrub.

† Sub-shrub. Many varieties.

X

GRADING

THE process of converting land to more intensi-fied use is very apt to make necessary changes in the grades of ground surfaces. Such construc-tions as roadways and the immediate surround-ings of house and play areas need to conform to certain standards of practicality and use. Sloping surfaces, too steep for convenient travel, must be brought down to more gentle grades in order to accommodate new roads. The formality appro-priate for the terraces of a house usually de-mands flat surfaces of ground. The games of tennis, bowls, baseball, etc., require carefully levelled areas. These operations of changing the levels of ground are classed as grading.

Grading for a New House

The subject of grading about a new house usually receives scant attention on the part of the owner. There are so many questions of furnishings and fixtures to be decided that prob-lems of landscape design are sometimes post-poned until these are disposed of. Meanwhile, often the earth from the cellar excavation has been dumped and spread over a considerable area, thus covering up much valuable top-soil, and the floor levels are fixed, regardless of the design of the ground areas round about.

Grading Requirements Influence Design

Adjusting a house to its site is not an easy problem at best. When it has been complicated by postponing its consideration until the house has imposed a new set of conditions, it is ren-dered even more difficult of satisfactory solution. However, when a house and the surrounding areas have been designed together, it is possible to compromise each to accommodate the other. The raising of floor grades by a few inches above the level originally planned may be enough to save several hundred dollars in the grading item alone, or will make possible an easier transition between architecture and landscape. The shifting of the house several feet from the site originally selected may make possible a better grade and an easier curve in the driveway. These results are worth attaining, and can be had by taking pains to make at least a general landscape plan of the property, with a grading plan of the house site, *before* the house is built. All these things may be considered a part of design and, of course, they are. But because there are certain factors such as maximum grade and minimum curve which limit road forms, the problems of grading in many cases determine what the design may be.

Topography

Planning changes in ground form requires careful measurement and the recording of exist-ing grades as a basis for studies. Such a record of the site is called a topographic plan because it represents the ground slopes. By a series of lines called contour lines, each connecting all points on the earth's surface that are at an equal eleva-tion, the plan very readily expresses the con-figuration of the ground. Where the lines are close together, the ground is steep; where they are far apart, the ground is nearly level.

Grading Plan

The finished plan representing the original ground form and the ground levels after they have been adjusted to new requirements, is called a grading plan. It is the working drawing con-trolling the excavating and filling operations. From this plan earthwork quantities are com-puted and the new levels staked out.

106

A GRADING PLAN
OF A SUBURBAN
PROPERTY.
CONTOUR LINES
INDICATE SLOPES.

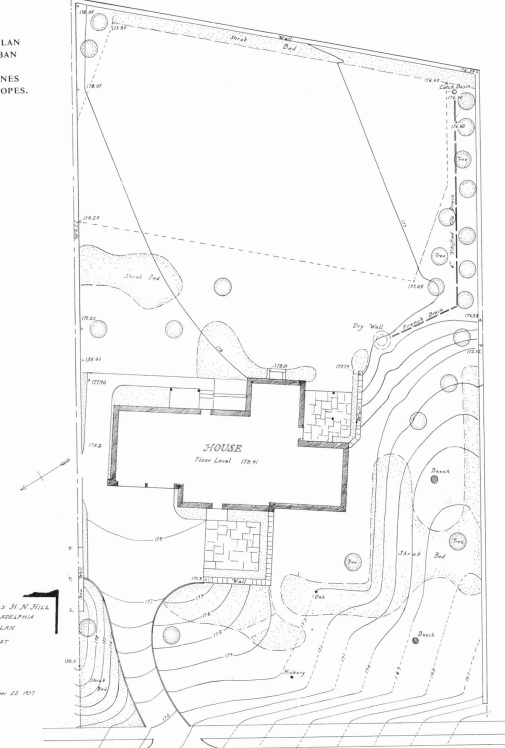

HOUSE
Floor Level 178.41

DENCE OF Mr. AND Mrs H. N. HILL
2 COULTER STREET. PHILADELPHIA
REVISED GRADING PLAN

SCALE 1 INCH = 10 FEET

James Bush-Brown
Landscape Architect
Ambler, Penn,   November 22 1937

Grading Without a Plan

It is perfectly possible to grade land without using a plan. Simply cut where necessary and fill the excavated earth wherever it is most needed, or wherever it will do least damage. The only difficulty with this procedure is that there is no way of knowing in advance how much earth must be handled, whether there will be enough or too much to make the fills required, or even how far the fills will extend. It also results in an uneven layer of top-soil which will show up in uneven growth of whatever planting is done later. If the design is for the environs of a new house, not yet built, the grading plan should be made in order to determine not merely the cuts and fills but the position and floor levels of the house. By adjustment of the floor grade, the quantities of earth excavated and filled may be made to balance, thus reducing to a minimum the cost of grading. If too much earth is cut, the surplus must be hauled away. If not enough earth comes from the cuts, then additional earth must be hauled in to make the fills. In either case more earth is handled than is necessary to do the job.

Top-soil

The importance of top-soil or loam cannot be too strongly emphasized. Every finished surface of the open ground should have a top layer of loam for the support of plant life. The under earth or sub-soil is not productive and will support only the toughest weeds. Even if much of the finished area of the property is to be converted to drives, pavements and house site, the top-soil originally on these areas should be scooped off and saved, and later added to the top-soil in areas to be devoted to garden, terrace and lawn. In this way a natural top-soil only 6 inches in depth may be increased to 12 or 24 inches in special places where extra depth will be an advantage. Garden flowers grow better, bloom better and resist drought better in deep loam than they do in shallow soil. Fertilizer may be used to make up for the lack of proper depth in soil, but its effect is temporary at best, whereas a rich top-soil 15 inches deep is a permanent asset.

When grading begins, all the top-soil should be removed with a scoop from the whole area to be graded and dumped conveniently near, but outside, the field of operations. It is wise to save all available top-soil. If some is left over, the surplus will help make compost, and top-dressing, and renew the soil in the greenhouse and cold frames for several years to come.

Excavation

The next step is to excavate for the foundations and for the areas to be lowered. The earth thus removed should be placed, whenever possible, in its final position, handling the earth only once. The spreading of earth in areas of fill should be done in layers not deeper than 6 inches and each layer should be rolled before the next is spread. This method compacts the earth so firmly that there will be practically no settling of sub-soil during subsequent years.

Settling of Filled Soil

Failure to compact the earth while it is being filled will cause a gradual settling of the earth during three or four years. In some places this settling is no detriment, but in others, adjacent to terrace steps, the settling will cause the steps to appear above their normal position, sometimes as much as several inches, a very awkward condition in a finished landscape.

Sub-grades

The grades of the sub-soil should be brought to levels below the proposed final grade equal to the thickness of top-soil or paving required in these various areas. Thus, if it is intended that a terrace should be furnished with 15 inches of top-soil, the sub-soil should be smoothed off at a level 15 inches below final grades.

Minimum Slope

No area of turf or of pavement should be absolutely level, or be so shaped that a concave surface will collect water. Though they should look level, actually terraces should slope away from the building with a fall of at least one foot (preferably more) to a hundred feet.

Lawns for Tennis or Croquet

Lawns for tennis or croquet should be graded to an even, smooth surface, but they should not be absolutely level. One method is to slope the ground away from the net to the back-stop fence at the minimum degree of slope. This has the effect of making the top of the net actually higher than it should be in relation to players on the base line. Another method is to slope the whole court evenly from end to end. Another is to slope it from the center foul lines toward the sides and from the base lines out to the end fences. Croquet lawns may be graded similarly, from the middle out to the edges.

Drainage of Surface Water

Catch basins and drain inlets are important adjuncts to the drive, court, terrace and flower garden. Properly placed and connected with a drain, they will remove surface water before it has a chance to flood flower beds or wash out banks. The drains should extend in straight lines from one basin to the next and should be at least a foot below the surface. The smallest size practicable for drains is 6 inches in diameter. Drains which take the outflow of three or more basins should be 8 inches or more in diameter. Unless the town has separate storm water sewers, the outlet of drains usually must be taken care of on the property, either by being brought to the surface, distributed through a tile field, or emptied into a dry well, or into a stream.

A Tile Field is a series of tile pipes branching off from the main drain in parallel lines, 10 or 15 feet apart and about 15 inches below the surface. The pipes are laid in trenches and are filled about with crushed stone. The upper few inches of the trench are filled with top-soil. The water flowing through the pipes seeps out into the crushed stone, saturates the soil, and the grass roots absorb the water. It is important to locate the tile field in open ground away from trees. Sunshine keeps the soil in condition to absorb the water. Tree roots are likely to find their way into the drain and clog it. Also important is the grade of the pipe. It should fall at the rate of $\frac{1}{2}$ of 1 percent ($\frac{1}{16}$-inch to the foot). A steep pitch in the pipes will cause the water to run to the end.

A Dry Well is an excavation into the sub-soil, usually 6 or 8 feet deep and 4 or 6 feet in diameter, the sides of which are walled with stone. It is covered by a stone or concrete slab. It fills up in a storm and the water seeps away slowly into the sub-soil.

Filling Trenches

The back-filling of the trenches must be done with the greatest of care. The earth should be filled in layers of 6 inches and each layer sprinkled and tamped into place. This method will avoid future settling. A trench ought to accommodate the pipe and all the soil which came out of it, even if this means a slight mounding up of earth along the trench line. The mound will probably disappear after the first winter.

Top-soil and Finished Grading

After the sub-soil has been brought by excavating and filling to the proper grades, and after the trenches have been refilled, the top-soil may be brought back and spread. If the grading has been in process for several months and the top-soil has been piled up during the house-building operation, many of the old grass roots should be pretty well decomposed, but the pile may be covered with weeds, and the soil will be full of weed seeds. Spreading it out in its final position will give the weeds a chance to germinate. Then if the ground is cultivated before grass seed is sown, many of the weeds may be eliminated. If time permits, it is an advantage to let three or four weeks elapse between finished grading and sowing. Whether such a program can be followed will depend on the time of year the grading is completed. The most favorable time for starting a lawn is August or early September, and the next best is early spring. If top-soil has been spread in the autumn too late for starting a lawn, then the ground should go through the winter with a cover crop of rye which can be sown in October and turned under in the spring. Rye should be sown at the rate of a bushel and a half per acre.

Water Supply Systems and Underground Pipe Lines

After sub-grades are finished, and if possible, before the top-soil has been spread, the utility lines may be laid. House water supply pipes must be in trenches at a depth greater than the maximum frost penetration for the region. House sewers and drains from catch basins and from the roofs need not be as deep, although 15 inches or 18 inches of dirt over the pipes is advisable to keep them out of the way of planting operations.

Water supply pipes leading to garden-hose connections need not be below frost line, if they are constructed in such a way as to permit the emptying of the pipe when the water is shut off for the winter. For this reason the pipes should slope to an outlet at the cut-off valve or at the spigot. An all-season outdoor water supply system must have pipes below the frost line and self-draining hydrants rather than faucets.

Gas pipes may be shallow but they must be so graded that there is a moisture outlet at each low point in the line.

Catch basins are so constructed that the outlet is well above the bottom. The sediment which collects should be removed periodically before it reaches the level of the outlet drain. Neglected catch basins are the principal cause of stoppages in the drainage system.

The size of the drain from the catch basin is dependent on the area of land which it is to drain. The table opposite gives the pipe sizes and grades for draining areas of turf under conditions of rainfall prevailing in eastern North America.

The minimum grade for 6-inch tile drains is 1 percent but 2 percent or more is better because the faster flowing water keeps the pipe clear. Increase in the grade of the pipe increases the flow and capacity.

Under-draining Wet Land

Land which contains too much moisture, or which is so slow to dry out in early spring that spring operations are retarded, may be greatly improved by drainage lines. The tile pipes for draining land should be laid about 18 to 24 inches below the surface, and the ditch should be filled with crushed stone or gravel to within 8 inches of the surface. Strips of roofing paper should be spread over the stone ballast and then covered with top-soil to bring the trench to an even grade. The pipes should be laid at a grade of about 2 percent in parallel lines 15 or 20 feet apart, and the outlet should be carried to a stream. The pipes most often used for this purpose are 3-inch agricultural tile drain pipes, but the main carrying off the outlet from several laterals should be 4- or 6-inch vitrified tile drain pipe.

SIZE OF PIPE	GRADE OF PIPE	AREA TO BE DRAINED	
		IN TURF	IN PAVEMENT
6″ Tile	2%	7,000 sq. ft.	3,500 sq. ft.
8″ Tile	2%	12,000 " "	6,000 " "
10″ Tile	2%	19,000 " "	9,500 " "
6″ Tile	4%	10,000 " "	5,000 " "
8″ Tile	4%	18,000 " "	9,000 " "
10″ Tile	4%	28,000 " "	14,000 " "

XI

WALLS, BANKS AND STEPS

GARDEN WALLS

In olden times, high walls were built around gardens to protect them. Often a moat also surrounded the garden. In some cases the walls were reared as much for shelter against winds as for protection, and they provided supports for fruit trees, trained against them. A southern wall surface stimulated spring growth in the espalier trees and induced earlier flowering and earlier fruiting. Besides these practical functions of garden walls, there is the unescapable charm of the wall as a background for flowers and foliage or as a beautiful evidence of the seclusion which they help to create.

A broad, unbroken surface of masonry is not always interesting, but a wall divided into panels or interrupted by projecting buttresses, or one built with a combination of materials pleasantly blended, has an architectural significance. It is the link which unites the garden and the house as parts of one composition.

Free-standing Walls

It is essential that the top of the wall be protected from the weather. One of the most practical means of preventing the moisture from entering the masonry from above is to cover the wall with a coping of flagstones set in cement mortar joints. This definite edge also gives a finish to the structure. A sharp-pitched roof of slate, brick, shingles or painted boards is sometimes used, the latter being common in Pennsylvania. A brick coping is also frequently used and a wedge-shaped top built of brick courses in diminishing thicknesses is very picturesque. Molded brick set on edge is a favorite wall finish in Virginia.

In the South, walls are sometimes built with some of the bricks omitted, leaving holes in the wall to allow for the passage of air currents. It is important in the South not to exclude all the breezes and the perforated wall is a screen but not an absolute barrier. An unusual wall found in Virginia and supposed to be the invention of Thomas Jefferson is the serpentine wall of brick. Because of its constantly changing direction, it is stronger against wind pressure than a straight wall of the same thickness. Therefore, it may be built only one brick thick and is more economical of material, and far more picturesque than the straight wall. A modern version of the thin wall, one brick thick, is a wall braced at intervals by vertical iron rods built to clasp the brick masonry. It is less expensive than the usual 8-inch brick wall.

A wall typical of South Carolina is a brick wall with arched panels of stucco. The piers are thick and the panels only one brick in thickness.

Retaining Walls

A retaining wall must hold its position against the pressure of the earth behind it. At seasons of alternate freezing and thawing, ground pressure is considerable. We see its effect when paved roads heave in early spring. If the wall is not adequate to hold, the pressure thus exerted may be translated into one of four kinds of movement in the wall. (1) The wall may be forced to bulge out of shape, opening cracks in the masonry. This is apt to happen in dry walls in which there is no mortar to hold the stones together. The pressure and strain is there in all walls. (2) The whole wall may slide away from the hill. This can happen if the footings of the wall are not deep enough to have a firm hold in the soil. (3) The wall can be forced to revolve about its base line and thus made to lean for-

|‹1'-0"›‹1'-6"›‹1'-6"›|

Small Tile Pipe

‹ 4'-0" ›

Width of base equals ⅓ of the height.

ward out of position. (4) The wall may be lifted up vertically by the action of frost beneath the footings. This can happen when the foundations do not extend below the frost line of the region.

Dimension of Retaining Walls

It has been found by long practice that the proportions shown in the sectional sketch are adequate to withstand the pressures in the soil. The footings are below frost line and slope down toward the rear. The thickness of the wall at the base equals one third of the height measured from the lower ground level. The top of the wall is 18 inches thick. Special conditions, such as heavy moving traffic along the top of the wall, will make necessary a greater bulk of masonry than for normal conditions.

Buttresses

By building projections or buttresses into the face of the wall at intervals of 10 or 12 feet, the effective base of the wall is widened, thus making the structure more resistant to the tendency to revolve about its base, and hence more secure. Any revolving of the wall would have to become a lifting of the center of gravity as is shown in the sketch section. The buttresses must be built with the wall as part of the structure. The wider the projection of the base of the buttresses the greater is the resistance to pressure. A buttressed wall may be built thinner and still be as strong as a plain wall of the same height. Buttresses may be made a decorative element, dividing a long wall into bays.

Drainage Holes

Pressure from wet soil is greater than pressure from dry soil. To prevent the soil behind a retaining wall from becoming saturated, or simply to permit the normal flow of water through the sub-soil to continue, uninterrupted by the wall, small holes should be left in the masonry near the base of the wall at intervals of 10 or 12 feet.

Bonding Stones

Stones should be laid into the wall in such a way as to form a strong bond. That is, the long dimension of the stone should be horizontal and each stone should bridge over the joint between the two stones in the course below. In this way no long vertical joint will appear. In any retaining wall some stones should run from the front to the back face across the wall to tie the masonry more firmly together.

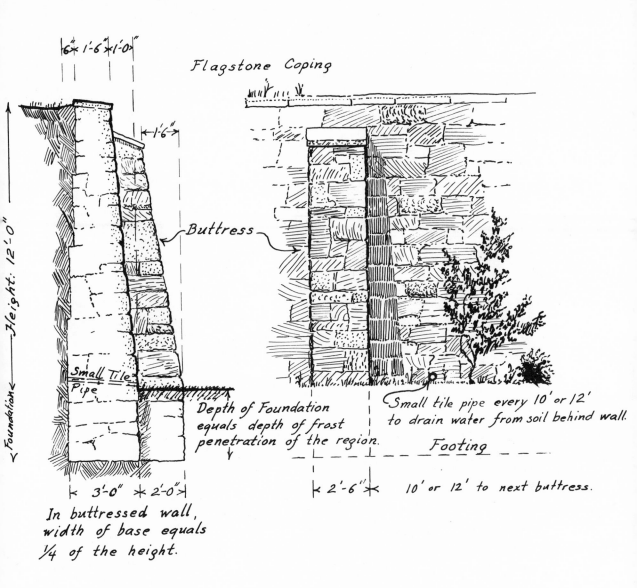

6" | 1'-6" | 1'-0"

Flagstone Coping

← 1'-6" →

Buttress

Height: 12'-0"

Foundation

Small Tile Pipe

Depth of Foundation
equals depth of frost
penetration of the region.

Small tile pipe every 10' or 12'
to drain water from soil behind wall.

Footing

← 3'-0" → ← 2'-0" →

← 2'-6" → 10' or 12' to next buttress.

In buttressed wall,
width of base equals
¼ of the height.

Mixture for Masonry Walls

The mortar should be a mixture of one part
Portland cement and two parts sand.

The masonry wall, well built, is a structure of
great strength, a permanent installation. The retaining walls of the great Italian villas have
remained intact for four or five hundred years.

Dry Retaining Walls

Less expensive to build, but also less secure, is
the dry retaining wall, built without mortar. A
special construction of the dry wall is described
in Chapter VI. Both of these are called "gravity"
walls because they hold their place by reason of
their own weight.

113

RETAINING WALL WITH RAISED FLOWER BED AND FOUNTAIN

A WALL IN A CITY GARDEN

BELOW: A GARDEN WALL AND
DOOR

Reinforced Concrete Wall

Another type, known as the "cantilever" wall, holds partly by the weight of earth upon a broad projecting footing. This is built of reinforced concrete, and is therefore a monolith. It is much lighter and thinner in construction than the gravity wall, and is used in regions where sand is common and stone is scarce. The concrete is poured between temporary forms built of lumber. Steel reinforcing rods form a mesh of 12- or 15-inch squares, which gives the concrete great rigidity, and prevents it from cracking under unequal pressure. The inner surface of a concrete wall should be sealed with an application of a waterproofing compound. Tar is the basis of most waterproof material, and it should be applied when hot. Unless this is done the concrete is likely to become porous and to crack. With this protection from

A TAPESTRY WALL IN A SOUTH CAROLINA GARDEN. SUCH A WALL PERMITS A GOOD CIRCULATION OF AIR.

ground water, a concrete retaining wall may be faced with a coat of stucco or with brick. But unless the wall has been waterproofed, the stucco will peel off and the brick will blossom out with rosettes of lime deposited by moisture coming through the bricks and then evaporating.

BANKS

In many cases an evenly sloping bank, simply treated, will be appropriate and will function as well as a retaining wall. The advantages of the wall are its architectural character, its economy of space, and its permanence. The advantages of the bank are its more natural character and economy of construction costs. The bank sloping down from a terrace or up from a terrace may be planted with interesting ground cover plants to prevent erosion and to reduce maintenance costs. The bank may rise from the top of a low retaining wall. This arrangement of form and material imparts a note of precision which harmonizes with the formality of the terrace.

The Turf Bank

Turf clad banks have been used since olden times and nothing else can present such a finished effect as an accurately graded and well maintained turf terrace bank. Turf banks should not be graded to a steeper slope than one foot of rise to two feet of horizontal dimension. Starting turf on a slope is more difficult than on level land. A heavy rain coming before the turf has formed will erode the soil and will make necessary patching, regrading, and reseeding. Laying turf over the whole bank is the most certain method of starting grass on a bank. If the surface water from the hillside above the bank is diverted by turf gutters, the bank grass may be started with seed sowing. In this case, strips of turf placed in horizontal lines along the banks at intervals of 4 or 6 feet will arrest the washing away of soil. This precaution is worth the additional cost.

The Planted Bank

A bank well furnished with top-soil and covered with densely spreading plants is, perhaps, the most satisfactory and economical treatment of the change in levels. The slope should be 1 foot of rise to 2½ feet of horizontal dimension, or it may be even less steep. By a careful selection of plants the bank may be made very beautiful. Conditions of soil and exposure may affect or even dictate a choice of plants. Such a great variety of plants is suitable for covering a bank that a wide range of choice is possible.

For a bank in sunshine sloping down from the terrace a satisfactory combination is jasmine and Rosa Wichuraiana, with Cotoneaster horizontalis at the margins. For a shady or partially shaded bank periwinkle (Vinca minor), with narcissus coming up among it, is charming in the spring and green throughout the season. A terrace with a planted bank below it should be outlined with a low hedge.

GROUND COVER PLANTS FOR BANKS

WOODY PLANTS

Akebia quinata
Arctostaphylos uva-ursi (Bearberry)
Calluna vulgaris (Heather)
Comptonia asplenifolia (Sweetfern)
Cotoneaster horizontalis (Rock Cotoneaster)
Euonymus radicans (Wintercreeper)
Euonymus radicans coloratus
Euonymus radicans minimus
Hedera helix (English Ivy)
Jasminum nudiflorum (Winter Jasmine)
Juniperus communis depressa (Spreading Juniper)
Juniperus horizontalis (Creeping Juniper)
Juniperus Sabina (Savin)
Lonicera japonica Halliana (Hall's Honeysuckle)
Lycium chinense (Chinese Matrimony Vine)
Pachysandra terminalis (Japanese Spurge)
Rhus canadensis (Fragrant Sumac)
Rosa humilis (Pasture Rose)
Rosa lucida (Virginia Rose)
Rosa multiflora (Japanese Rose)
Rosa Wichuraiana (Wichurian Rose)
Spiræa tomentosa (Hardhack)
Vinca minor (Periwinkle)

HARDY PERENNIAL PLANTS

Ajuga reptans (Bugle)
Arabis alpina (Alpine Rockcress)
Arenaria montana (Mountain Sandwort)

GROUND COVER PLANTS FOR BANKS
—continued

Cerastium tomentosum (Snow-in-Summer)
Convallaria majalis (Lily-of-the-Valley)
Hemerocallis fulva (Tawny Daylily)
Lysimachia nummularia (Moneywort)
Nepeta Mussini
Phlox subulata (Moss Phlox)
Plumbago larpentæ
Sedum acre (Goldmoss)
Thymus Serpyllum (Thyme)

GARDEN STEPS

As a change in levels in a garden necessitates a pleasant and easy transition from one level to another, garden steps may become an important feature. Unless the steps are rustic in character, such as split logs, hewn railroad ties, or long heavy stones, they should rest upon a foundation with footings below the frost line. The steps should be in harmony with the surrounding area, and should be as broad as the path that leads to them.

The angle of ascent of outdoor steps should be less steep than that of interior stairways. In general, the broader the tread, the lower should be the riser. A good formula for proportions in determining the size of individual steps is as follows: one tread plus two risers should equal 27 inches. Thus, steps 6 inches high will require 15-inch treads, while steps 5 inches high should have 17-inch treads. The treads should be constructed so that they pitch slightly toward the front, about $\frac{1}{4}$ of an inch, in order that the water may drain off readily after a rain.

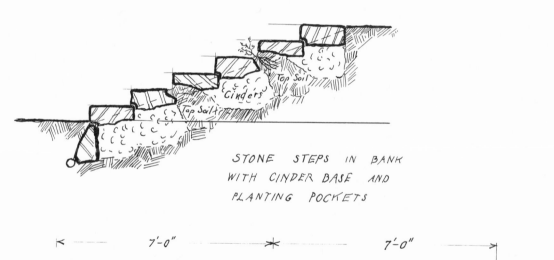

STONE STEPS IN BANK
WITH CINDER BASE AND
PLANTING POCKETS

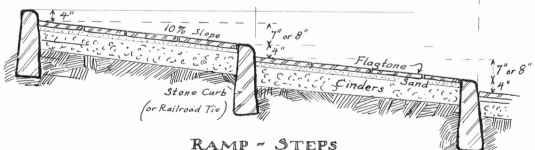

RAMP — STEPS

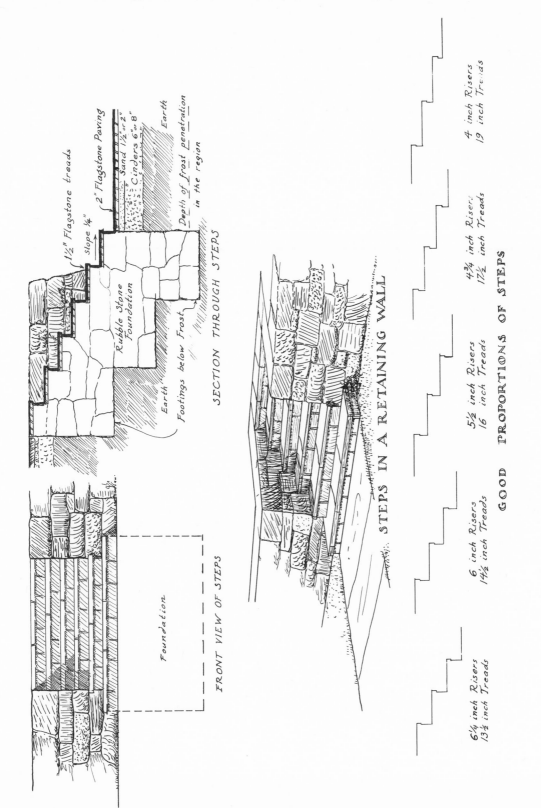

1½" Flagstone treads

Slope ¼"

2" Flagstone Paving

Sand ½" or 2"

Cinders 6" 8"

Earth

Depth of frost penetration in the region

Rubble Stone Foundation

Earth

Footings below Frost

SECTION THROUGH STEPS

Foundation

FRONT VIEW OF STEPS

STEPS IN A RETAINING WALL

6¼ inch Risers
13½ inch Treads

6 inch Risers
14½ inch Treads

5½ inch Risers
16 inch Treads

4¾ inch Risers
17½ inch Treads

4 inch Risers
19 inch Treads

GOOD PROPORTIONS OF STEPS

Foundations

Foundations for stone or brick steps may be built of rubble masonry. Any irregular pieces that are not easily used in finished masonry walls will be good enough for foundations. The stones are thrown in with enough mortar to hold them together. The footings must be below frost line. The foundation for concrete steps, or a concrete foundation for stone or brick steps, need not be so solid. The concrete may be formed like a bridge and reinforced with steel rods. The top and bottom treads rest on footings below frost line, but the others are supported on the concrete slab cast between the supports. The earth between the supporting footings is not even excavated. On such a foundation the stone or brick or tile treads and risers are set upon the concrete base with cement mortar.

The proper mixture for concrete foundation is one part cement, two parts sand and three parts aggregate—crushed stone in sizes from $\frac{3}{4}$ inch to 1 inch. The steel rods should be $\frac{5}{8}$-inch square section placed at intervals of 12 or 15 inches.

Step Arrangements

Long, unbroken flights of steps should be avoided. If the difference in grade between the upper landing and the bottom is greater than 6 feet a landing should be interposed. Steps ascending a terrace held by a retaining wall may project out from the wall or be recessed into the wall, or they may combine both of these arrangements, often with a landing at the wall. If it is a high wall, the most harmonious arrangement is a flight of steps parallel to the wall with landings near the top and bottom. Such a flight should have a hand railing of wrought iron, a balustrade or a parapet.

Ramped Steps

Ramped steps are useful where the sloping hillside of the ascent is too steep for a path (10 percent or more), and not steep enough for a flight of steps. Twenty percent is about minimum for steps. Ramped steps are a series of sloping surfaces alternated with single steps. The risers are formed of narrow stones set on edge and deeply sunk into the ground. The treads or ramps are built of the same material as the pathways, flagstone or brick being the materials most frequently used in this country. The narrow streets of hillside towns in Europe are frequently made into ramped steps, with stone risers and cobblestone ramps. A rustic path in a woodland is frequently stepped by placing logs across the path for the risers. Railroad ties are also good for this purpose.

The proper dimensions for ramped steps may be determined by establishing the distance between the risers at three normal paces, between 6′–3″ and 8′–0″, and the height of the riser as from 3 to 5 inches. The slope of the ramp should be not greater than 12 percent. Obviously the steeper the ramp and the higher the tread, the shorter should be the length of the ramp.

XII

GARDEN PATHS

A GARDEN path—the very words bring to memory old brick walks bordered with box-wood, strips of turf between long flower borders; flagstones set about by tiny herbs and over-arched with spreading branches of magnolias. The path is one of the components of the garden plan which gives expression to the design; in some cases by making a pattern among the flower beds, in some by accenting the lines of symmetry, and in still others by the use of subtle turn and graceful curve.

In considering the construction of paths there are a number of matters which should be given careful thought—the selection of the materials to be used, the suitability, the original cost, and the expense of upkeep.

In many cases, the suitability of one material over another will be the deciding factor. On an area where there is much travel back and forth, turf would not be desirable as it would lack the greatly needed quality of durability. Within the confines of a garden, however, where there is comparatively little passing to and fro, grass paths are entirely satisfactory. On the other hand, if one has a wooded tract, and has conse-quently developed the place along informal or naturalistic lines, a path of tanbark would un-doubtedly be the most suitable. In a setting of this sort paths of brick or gravel would be out of harmony with the surroundings. For a path-way leading from the sidewalk to the door where there is constant passing, some durable material such as gravel, brick, or flagstones should be used.

Costs will vary considerably in different parts of the country. In sections where there are natural outcroppings of rock, and stone is plenti-ful, flagstone paths might be the most econom-ical, while in other sections they might be almost prohibitive in price, due to the expense of ship-ping the materials. In the case of turf and tan-bark paths, much of the work may be done by unskilled labor and the costs may consequently be kept low. On the other hand, a turf path re-quires more upkeep than do most of the other types. It must be kept mowed and it must be kept edged, for nothing detracts more from the trim and pleasing appearance of a garden than straggly grass and frowzy edges. This question of upkeep is one that should be taken into care-ful consideration before the final decision is made.

Lines and Grades

In a formal garden, the lines and dimensions of paths must be laid out with great care. The best way to establish a straight line is to stretch a cord between two stakes. A steel tape or a heavy cloth tape is essential, and a surveyor's transit is a great aid. Lacking a transit, right angles may be marked off on the ground by the 3–4–5 method. This is most easily done by three persons, using a tape and three stakes.

Taking three sections of tape, the lengths of which are proportioned to one another as 3 is to 4 and as 4 is to 5, and placing them end to end in a triangle, the angle between the "3" section and the "4" section will be a square angle or 90 degrees. The reason for this is the old geometric theorem, "The square of the hypot-enuse of a right-angled triangle is equal to the sum of the squares of the other two sides." Thus,

121

$3^2 + 4^2 = 5^2$ or $9 + 16 = 25$. If the lengths of the two lines are to extend some distance it is best to use longer pieces of tape than 3, 4, and 5 feet, because a slight error in holding the tapes together would increase proportionately with the distance to the end of the line. Sections 9 feet, 12 feet, and 15 feet are convenient.

The most direct and satisfactory way of marking a "freehand" curve is to fling a section of garden hose or heavy rope on the ground. The hose may be adjusted until the desired alignment is reached and it may then be marked by frequent stakes.

Grades are important in path building. Surface water must be induced to run off promptly, and this can best be done by making the center of the paths slightly higher than the sides. (On a 6-foot brick path, $\frac{1}{4}$ of an inch; on a 6-foot flagstone, $\frac{1}{2}$ inch; on a 6-foot gravel, 1 inch.) Also, the path must slope slightly lengthwise (at least 1 foot in 100 feet) and there should be catch basins or drain inlets at points where water may be collected and carried off by underground pipes. These subjects have been more fully treated in the chapter on Grading.

Brick

Brick walks are usually very pleasant in character and obtain a mellowness and charm with age which makes strong appeal. The initial cost is comparatively high but if a good quality of brick is used and if the walk is carefully laid it should give service for many years. In some of our old colonial gardens we find paths laid two centuries or more ago which are still in good condition and attest to the worth of the fine craftsmanship of our forefathers.

In sections of the country where there is but light frost action and where there is a natural layer of sandy or gravelly soil, no additional foundation is needed for the path. If frost seldom penetrates more than 2 or 3 inches into the ground it is possible to lay the bricks directly upon a cushion of sand after the sub-grades have been determined. In the North, however, it is necessary to do a much more expensive and

laborious piece of work and a foundation course must be carefully prepared before the bricks are laid. Unless this is done the action of the frost will gradually heave the bricks out of place, causing some to be cracked and broken, and before many years have elapsed one will have an unsightly and entirely unsatisfactory piece of paving. Bricks may be laid either upon a concrete base with a cinder foundation or upon a cushion of sand above a cinder foundation. Where the bricks are to be laid with mortar joints, the concrete base should be used. After the grades have been established and the earth has been excavated to a depth of 12 inches below the finished grade, a 6-inch layer of cinders should be put in place. A 3-inch layer should first be spread, watered thoroughly and then rolled or tamped. The second layer should be handled in the same manner. The base course of concrete should then be prepared and spread over the cinders to a depth of 3 inches. A mixture of one part cement, three parts sand and five parts gravel is recommended for this purpose. After this concrete foundation has set for twenty-four hours, the bricks should be laid according to the desired pattern upon a thin coat of mortar, one part cement to three parts sand. When the mortar has set and the bricks are firmly in place the joints should be filled. This may be done in one of two different ways. If the joints are small, a quarter of an inch or less in width, a dry mixture of cement and sand in the proportion of one of cement to two of sand may be swept into the joints. After the bricks have been swept entirely free of cement, the walk should be watered with a fine, gentle spray until the cement in the joints has become thoroughly wet. Where the joints are large it is advisable to make a very wet mixture of the same proportions and pour it carefully between the bricks until the joints are filled.

When a brick walk is to be laid upon a sand cushion a similar foundation course of cinders is used. Upon the surface of the cinders a 2-inch layer of fine sand should be spread and it should be thoroughly rolled or tamped before the bricks are set in place. After the bricks are laid, the joints should be filled with sand. As the bricks are being laid, the surface of the walk should be kept at an even and uniform level. This may easily be done by placing a wide board crosswise with the path and tamping it until the surface is even. As brick walks which are laid in sand have a tendency to creep, the joints becoming gradually wider and wider, a curb should always be used.

Bricks may be laid in various patterns, the Running Bond, the Herringbone, and Basket patterns being the most usual.

Brick and Cement in Combination

In France one often sees paths constructed of brick and cement. If the workmanship is well done a path of this type is very pleasant and certainly possesses much more character and charm than a plain concrete walk. The construction is comparatively simple and the cost is not unduly high. After the grades have been established the soil should be excavated to a depth of 10 inches. A 6-inch foundation course of cinders should then be laid in the same manner as that prescribed for brick walks. A very thin coat of

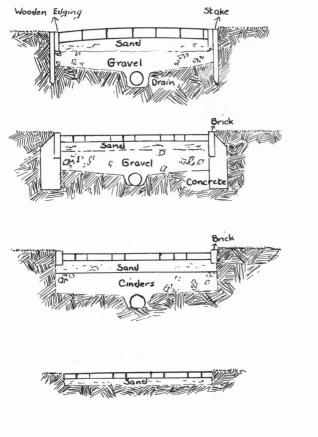

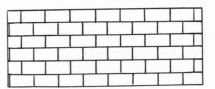

Running bond

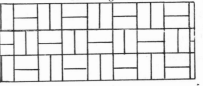

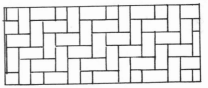

Basket weaves

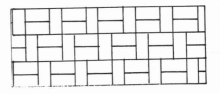

Herring bone

sections

CONSTRUCTION
OF
BRICK PATHS

plans

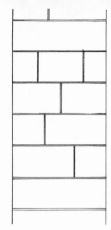

In Porous Soils
Cinders may be om

A GARDEN PATH PAVED WITH BRICK

cement mortar, hardly more than an inch in thickness, should then be spread over the cinders and upon this foundation the bricks should be placed in any desired pattern. The spaces between the bricks should then be filled with cement and the surface should be brought to an absolutely true level. If a small quantity of hematite is mixed with the cement it will give it a slightly reddish tone which will harmonize more pleasantly with the color of the bricks.

The bricks may be placed according to various patterns. In the construction of a narrow path, the area of cement between the patterned bricks should be relatively small, while in a path of more ample proportions the scale could be increased.

Flagstone

Flagstone paths have decided character and charm and are widely used. In sections of the country where there is an abundant supply of local stone they are not expensive and they are very easily laid. There are various types—those made from stones of square or rectangular shape with cut edges which are laid in a perfectly formal or symmetrical manner, and those made from stones of more or less irregular shape laid in a random pattern.

The stones may be laid either upon a sand cushion with dirt joints or upon a cement foundation with mortar joints. Laying them with earth joints makes possible the growing of turf or low-creeping plants between the stones, a

124

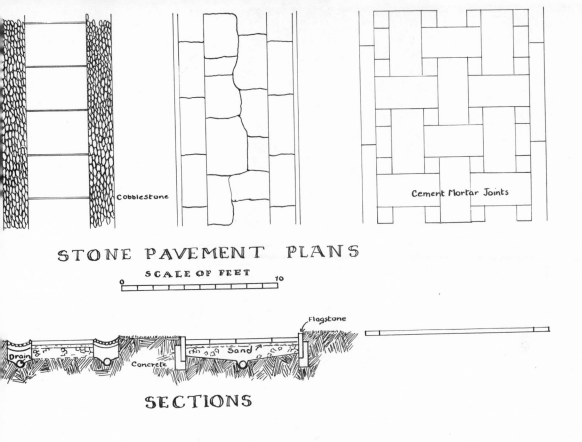

STONE PAVEMENT PLANS

Cobblestone

Cement Mortar Joints

SCALE OF FEET

0   10

Flagstone

Drain   Concrete   Sand

SECTIONS

feature greatly to be desired. The laying of a flagstone path on a sand cushion is a very simple matter and does not require a great amount of skill. The ground should be excavated to a depth which will bring the stones to the desired level and a layer of fine sand about $\frac{1}{2}$ inch in depth should be spread over the surface of the soil. The stones may then be put in place and care should be taken to see that they are very firm, with no tendency to wobble or teeter. If the lower surface of the stone is uneven it will be necessary to remove a portion of the soil directly under the protruding point in order that it may settle firmly into its bed. The surface of the path should be true to the desired grade, and as the stones are set in place a carpenter's level should

be used to check up on the surface. After the stones are in place, good top-soil should be spread over the surface of the path and swept into the joints or, if desired, the joints may be filled with small strips of turf. There are a number of rock plants which are of very low-creeping habit and are particularly suitable for planting between flagstones. Creeping thyme is a dainty little thing and when crushed under foot it emits a sweet, pungent fragrance. Gypsophila repens and Veronica repens are also excellent.

When flagstones are to be laid with mortar joints they must be set in cement. The soil should be excavated to a depth of 10 inches and a 6-inch layer of cinders should be spread in two layers 3 inches thick, each layer being watered,

125

ABOVE: A GARDEN PATH EDGED WITH BOXWOOD

BELOW: RANDOM FLAGSTONE PAVING ON A GARDEN TERRACE

rolled or tamped. A 3-inch layer of cement should be spread upon this foundation course of cinders, being mixed in the proportions of one part cement, three parts sand and five parts gravel. After the cement has set for twenty-four hours a thin coat of cement mortar should be spread over it and the flagstones set in the mortar. After the stones have become firm, mortar should be poured into the joints.

Gravel

Gravel walks were very often used during colonial times and they have maintained their popularity throughout the years. There are numerous methods of construction. If the walk is to have but little travel upon it and if the ground is naturally well drained the gravel may be laid directly upon the soil after the sub-grade has been established. Constructed in this manner, however, a walk will not withstand hard wear and during wet weather it will have a tendency to become very soft and springy. A much better walk will result if an undercourse of slag or crushed stone is used. In the construction of a walk of this type, the soil should be excavated to a depth of 7 inches below the finished grade. A $5\frac{1}{2}$-inch layer of slag or crushed stone of a size which will pass a $2\frac{1}{2}$-inch screen should then be spread and thoroughly tamped or rolled. The gravel should be spread upon this surface and should be well watered and rolled. Gravel known as "pit gravel" is greatly to be preferred to washed gravel for the surfacing of walks and should be obtained whenever it is possible. If it is necessary to use washed gravel, limestone dust to the amount of approximately 15 percent should be mixed with it in order to help bind the surface. Gravel used for the wearing surface of paths should be of a size which will pass a $\frac{1}{2}$-inch mesh.

Stepping Stones

Stepping stones laid in turf make a very pleasant path. Because of their rather informal character they are, perhaps, more suitable for a casual or incidental path than for a walk which is anything in the way of a thoroughfare.

A GARDEN TERRACE OF FLAGSTONE

The stones selected for a path of this type should be of comfortable size, at least 12 to 15 inches square, and the upper surface should be reasonably smooth. It is not necessary that the stones be of absolutely regular shape as very pleasant effects may be obtained with stones of slightly irregular outline. The stones should be placed at even intervals and spaced far enough apart to permit a pleasant, easy step from one stone to the next, 18 inches being the usual distance.

The setting of the stones is a very simple matter. If a new walk is being made they may be set at the same time that the surrounding area of grass is sown or they may be easily set in a piece of established turf. The stones should be placed upon the surface of the ground and their

127

AN INTERESTING PATIO PAVEMENT IN A CALIFORNIA GARDEN WITH MODULAR BOXES OF REDWOOD

final position determined. The outline of each stone should then be marked with the edge of a trowel and after the stone has been lifted to one side the soil within the prescribed area should be removed to the proper depth. A light layer of fine sand should be placed at the bottom of the excavation, as this makes a better bed upon which to rest the stone and settle it into its final position. When placing the stones, care should be taken to see that they are perfectly firm and that they do not teeter from side to side. If the bottom of the stone is uneven it may be necessary to remove it several times and cut one portion of the excavation or build up another until the stone is absolutely firm. The surface of the stone should be level with the area of turf about it. Not only does this make a difference in the general appearance of the path but it greatly facilitates the use of the lawn mower. The soil should be rammed in close around the edges, after the stones have been set in place.

128

Tanbark

Tanbark is particularly suitable for woodland walks and is also frequently used in gardens of formal design. It has much to recommend it as a material for the surfacing of paths. It is comparatively inexpensive; its mellow, reddish-brown color forms a pleasing contrast with the areas of turf and foliage about it; it is easy to handle and under ordinary conditions no elaborate system of underdrainage is necessary; it offers an unusually pleasant and springy surface; and it dries almost immediately after a rain. Even during the heaviest rains tanbark never becomes muddy and it is of such a porous nature that it seldom retains standing pools of water.

A good quality of tanbark should be procured for the construction of paths. A poor grade is not cheap at any price as it is apt to contain large, lumpy pieces and various foreign substances. The best grades usually are obtained from oak and hemlock barks. Unless the path is to be constructed in a very low, swampy area, no underdrainage is necessary. In a case of this sort either a foundation course of cinders or a tile drain may be used. Ordinarily, however, all that is necessary is to see that the ground is levelled to the desired grade before the tanbark is spread. A layer 3 inches in depth makes an excellent and very durable path. Immediately after spreading, the tanbark should be thoroughly soaked and rolled. One ton of tanbark will provide a 3-inch layer for a path 3 feet wide and 60 feet long.

Turf

A turf path has a number of advantages. The initial cost of materials is comparatively low, and the construction requires no great degree of skill. And undoubtedly an area of green, luxuriant turf possesses a beauty and a charm which are difficult to equal in other materials.

Turf paths may be readily established from seeding or, if immediate effect is desired, sod may be laid. In either case the preliminary preparation of the ground is very much the same. If the soil is a medium or light loam no underdrainage will be necessary. If, however, the soil is of heavy clay texture or if the path is to be constructed in a low area which has poor natural drainage some means of artificial drainage should be provided. A 6-inch vitrified tile drain laid 2 feet below the surface of the soil directly under the middle line of the path will usually prove entirely adequate and will add greatly to the enjoyment of a turf walk which might otherwise be soggy and practically unusable after heavy rains or in the early spring when the frost is coming out of the ground. Instead of using tile drains the soil may be excavated to a depth of 12 inches and a 6-inch layer of cinders placed over the sub-soil. A 6-inch layer of good top-soil should be placed above the cinders. This should be levelled off to the proper grade and should then be raked until it is finely pulverized. The first rolling will show up any slight unevenness which may be corrected by subsequent rakings. Where the path is to be seeded approximately one pound of seed

will be required per thirty square yards. Only seed of the very highest quality should be used and it is wise to obtain a mixture which does not contain any clover as it will make a turf of much finer texture. Clover also has the unfortunate tendency to become rather slippery when it is wet which is a decided disadvantage. The various Bent grasses are excellent, and mixtures containing Kentucky Bluegrass, Chewings New Zealand Fescue and Redtop are very desirable. The seed should be sown both lengthwise and crosswise with the path in order to get an even distribution. The ground should be rolled immediately after the seed is sown as a firm seed bed is one of the secrets of success.

If the walk is sodded great care should be taken to obtain sod of the best possible quality. Nothing is more disappointing than to go to the trouble and expense of sodding only to find, later on, that one has a lot of poor, coarse grass that will never make a really good turf. The sod, which usually comes in long rolls, should be laid lengthwise with the path and care should be taken to see that the joints are broken. After it is laid, the sod should be rolled and then thoroughly soaked. It should not be allowed to dry out until it has become well established.

Edgings

The best method of keeping the margins of garden paths permanently neat is to build edgings or small curbs. Many materials may be used for marking the path and separating it from the garden beds. Bricks on edge, or on end, are appropriate for brick or gravel paths. The use of planks dipped in creosote and held at intervals by stakes is an old colonial method, and is appropriate in an old-fashioned garden with gravel paths. It is also good with tanbark. Flagstones set on edge are good with flagstone paving or gravel. Tile is interesting in an architectural garden. Metal strips are also sometimes used and are very satisfactory. After a period of experiment with iron, it has been found that zinc is more durable and unobtrusive. It is excellent for use between driveway and lawn, and also in geometric patterns of garden beds and paths.

XIII

GARDEN POOLS AND FOUNTAINS

WATER is the symbol of life. It is that which makes all life possible. In Persia and in Northern Africa where a garden is a highly developed oasis in an arid land and is considered a paradise, water is indispensable. The sound of a trickling fountain is pleasant indeed to those whose senses are accustomed to the barren dryness of the outer world.

While garden pools had their origin in warm countries and their primary purpose was to cool the atmosphere, the almost universal appeal of sparkling water has made them equally appreciated in Northern climes. The idea of a fountain or pool as a garden feature was first brought to Europe by the Crusaders, after their contacts with the older and more highly developed culture of the East. And even in the comparatively damp climate of England and Scotland the fountain idea has persisted, although with somewhat less elaboration and emphasis than it has received in Italy and Spain.

Besides its original function of providing refreshment in hot weather by cooling the surrounding air, the garden pool fulfills a distinctly decorative purpose. Set in a frame of stone, the gleaming mirror of its surface becomes an object of admiration and attention. It may be used as the central feature of the garden, or it may be used as a terminal motive for a major or minor axis. It often provides a fitting foreground for a piece of sculpture, and, moreover, its usefulness and charm can be heightened by making it the habitation of fish and water-loving plants.

In the design of a garden pool the major decisions are the size, the shape, the material to be used for the coping, the depth of the water, and the color of the bottom.

It is important that the pool should be in harmony with its surroundings, and that it should be in scale as a detail of the garden design. Its setting, in patterned paving or in turf, should be carefully studied. The shape will depend very largely upon the general plan of the garden and, to a limited extent perhaps, upon the personal preference of the owner. In some gardens a round pool would be the most logical and pleasing from a standpoint of design; while in other gardens a square or oblong pool would be more in keeping with the general scheme.

The material to be used in the construction of the coping is largely a matter of personal choice. A simple flagstone coping is always pleasant and is particularly suitable if the garden is small or of somewhat informal character. For gardens of more formal and elaborate design a coping of cut stone might be preferred. Colored tiles are very decorative and lovely, and they may be used both as a coping and as a complete lining for the pool. While concrete may be used as a coping it is decidedly less attractive and less interesting than most other materials.

Special paints are available for painting the interior of cement pools. If the bottom is painted black it gives an appearance of much greater depth. Blue is the most popular color, as it gives a reflection of the sky, but care must be taken not to choose too harsh a tone.

When considering the construction of a pool it must be borne in mind that the first cost is usually the last. A pool is a very permanent feature of the garden, requiring little or no upkeep. When once its construction has been completed, it will be a source of satisfaction for years to come. Fortunately for the home owner,

130

a garden pool need not be an elaborate or an expensive thing. A pool of simple design and small in size may be constructed for a very modest sum and much of the labor can often be done by the owner of the garden.

In constructing a garden pool the major considerations are: absolute watertightness; drainage; and water supply, including the control of inlet, outlet and overflow. The walls of the pool are, essentially, retaining walls, and as such they must be strong enough to withstand the soil pressure against them and to resist the pressure of frost. There must be no heaving, due to the action of frost, as this will crack the walls and throw the coping out of level. A pool which has been poorly constructed, and which consequently is cracked by frost year after year, can become a source of constant annoyance. It is a difficult undertaking to repair a pool that has developed a leak, and it is therefore a matter of sound economy to see that the pool is well constructed in the beginning.

The ground surrounding the pool should be absolutely level. This is a matter of vital importance, which is sometimes overlooked in the construction of a home-made pool. If a pool is constructed on ground that is only slightly uneven the result will be unsatisfactory. If there is no other alternative, and if a pool must be constructed on ground which is slightly sloping, it will be necessary to raise the coping on one side. If this is not done, the surface will have the appearance of a tilted dish.

Construction of Concrete Pools

Concrete is one of the best materials to be used for the construction of garden pools. For a pool of average size, the bottom should be 5 inches thick and the walls 8 inches thick. For very large pools these figures should be slightly increased, while for very small pools they may be somewhat reduced, although it is not wise to reduce them to any appreciable extent. In the construction of the small pool it is not necessary to reinforce the sides. In the construction of a pool which is more than 15 feet in length, however, the sides should be reinforced with steel rods in order to maintain the concrete in a monolith against varying pressures.

The soil should be excavated to a depth of from 12 to 18 inches below the proposed floor level of the pool. The sides of the excavation should be vertical and in line with the outside wall of the pool. A layer of cinders should be spread over the bottom of the excavation and should be tamped firmly into place. If the cinders are sprinkled with water it will help the mass to settle into place. This layer of cinders will act as a drain and will keep the ground-water away from the undersurface of the concrete, thus reducing the danger of heaving, due to the action of the frost. The actual depth of the layer of cinders will depend somewhat upon the character of the soil. In light sandy soils a layer only a few inches in depth will be satisfactory, while in soils of a heavy clay texture a layer 12 inches in depth is advisable.

Forms. After the excavation has been completed the wooden forms should be constructed. They must be built in such a way that no part of the form is in contact with either the sides or the floor of the pit. This is accomplished by suspending the framework from beams extending across the excavation, the beams being held in place at each end by stout stakes driven into the ground well beyond the outside of the pit. The boards used in the construction of the form should be capable of making tight joints, in order to prevent the concrete from leaking through when it is poured. The form should be vertical, and true to the line of the inner edge of the pool. The earth sides of the excavation serve as the form on the outer side, the space between earth and wood being filled with concrete.

Pipes. The piping should be put in place at the time the forms are built as it will be necessary for some of the pipes to extend through the concrete. Wherever a pipe is to pass through the concrete it should be fitted with a flange in order to make a tight joint and to prevent it from working loose. Brass pipes are undoubtedly the most satisfactory for use in the construction of a pool, as they are not subject to rust. Wrought-iron piping is sometimes used and is not as expensive as brass, but it is far less durable and is subject to the corroding effect of cinders when it comes into direct contact with them. The inlet pipe may be brought in below the surface of the water, if desired, or it may be used in the form of a dripping fountain, or as a jet of water rising above the surface of the pool. For a dripping fountain a ¼-inch lead pipe, reduced at the end, is the most satisfactory and most easily handled. For a jet, the pipe should be fitted with a brass nozzle reducer. One pipe may serve both as an outlet and as an overflow if it is fitted with a branch pipe, or gooseneck, which will rise to the height of the water surface and return to the main pipe again. In the portion of the main pipe between the point of branching and the return of the gooseneck there is a valve which, when closed, makes the gooseneck the overflow of the pool. By merely opening the valve the water may be drained entirely out of the pool. A small detail which is of considerable importance, however, is that there should be a small hole in the top of the gooseneck in order to prevent it from becoming a syphon.

Reinforcing. If the walls of the pool are to be reinforced, the steel rods should be put into place before the concrete is poured. The rods should be suspended in such a position that they are two or three inches within the concrete wall. Each rod should extend up into the walls of the pool at either end and the rods should be fastened together with wire at points where they cross, thus forming a network. Five-eighths-inch rods are the usual size.

Concrete. The concrete should be poured in one operation in order to form a monolith. A reliable grade of cement should be used and it should be mixed in the proportions of one part cement, two parts sand and three parts crushed stone or trap rock. Slag, which is very often used for concrete work, should never be used in the construction of a pool because of its porous nature. Soft stones such as limestone and sandstone should also be avoided. The concrete should be mixed in an open box or mixing trough. The required quantity of sand should be measured first and placed in the bottom of the trough. The cement should then be measured and poured on the sand. The dry sand and cement should be thoroughly mixed, being shovelled back and forth, before the crushed stone is added. After all the dry ingredients have been mixed, sufficient water should be added to make a rather mobile mixture, approximately five gallons to every sack of cement. Only enough water should be used to make the mixture flow easily into the forms, but not enough water to make it sloppy or soupy. The quantity of water used has a very direct influence upon the strength and watertightness of the finished concrete. The floor, or bottom, of the pool should be poured first, and before it has finished setting, certainly before twenty-four hours have elapsed, the walls should be poured. The pouring of the walls should be done in one operation in order to alleviate any danger of subsequent cracks. The forms should be left in place for several days while the concrete is hardening. Soon after the forms have been removed, and before the concrete has become thoroughly dry, the surface coating of cement mortar should be applied. A mixture of one part cement to two parts of sand should be used and it should be spread smoothly over the entire surface with a plasterer's trowel and a straightedge template. Since it requires two or three weeks for all the moisture to evaporate out of the concrete, and since the curing process continues during this period, some time should elapse before the pool is filled with water. If the pool is filled before the concrete has been properly cured and while it is still porous, there will be a gradual seepage of water through the concrete and it may never become thoroughly water-tight.

Construction of Lead Pools

For a naturalistic pool with an irregular outline, or for a formal pool with a stone coping, the adaptability of sheet lead is becoming more generally appreciated. Lead is pliable, durable, practically indestructible. The advantages of its use as compared with concrete for the construction of pools are many. In concrete construction, every precaution is taken to prevent the freezing and thawing of the soil from cracking the concrete by exerting irregular pressures. Steel reinforcing rods are necessary in making an immobile structure in all but small pools. With lead the pressure merely bulges the metal but does not open cracks in it. No forms are necessary. The excavation for the lead pool need be no deeper than the required water depth, the metal being only 1/16-inch thick instead of 6 or 8 inches as with concrete. The methods of construction are simple, so that the labor cost is moderate. Lead has no damaging effect on fish or plants, it cannot corrode, and since lead pipes used by the Romans in the age of Augustus are still in good condition, it may be considered permanent.

Excavation and Grades. The work of constructing a lead pool may be done in the following manner. Excavate the soil to the required depth and shape, saving the top-soil for use in making compost or for similar purposes, and disposing of sub-soil by making a fill or trucking it away. The outline of the pool may be determined by levelling. If a surveyor's level is obtainable, this will be the quickest and most accurate help in establishing grades. Otherwise, a line level, which is a spirit level provided with a hook at each end, may be used. A stake is driven into the ground and the water level marked on the stake. A cord attached to the stake at this mark and stretched out tightly may be made horizontal by hanging the line level at its middle and raising or lowering the outer end of the cord until the bubble comes to rest in the middle of the tube. If the level is placed in the middle of the string, the sag will be equalized, the two ends being at the same height.

In portions of the pool margin along which there is to be a bog garden, the excavation should continue out beyond the apparent shore line for whatever width the bog is to have and for a depth of six inches. The same treatment is used on a rocky shore, the shelf being made as wide as the first row of rocks. Where the turf is to come down to the water's edge, the shelf is not necessary.

Material and Its Handling. The sheet lead comes in various thicknesses and widths up to twelve feet wide. The thickness known as "four pound," that is, four pounds to the square foot, or 1/16-inch thick, is pliable enough to bend easily into shape and firm enough to withstand a good deal of pounding. Before it is spread on the floor of the excavation, sharp rocks should be removed so as to eliminate the possibility of puncture. Rocks used along a bank should not have sharp edges which might wear holes through the lead. If the pool is to have a drain, which is a great convenience, the pipe should be laid before the lead lining is spread and it can be soldered to the lead at the lowest point of the floor. The lead is rolled out across the excavation. If the pool is to be broader than the width of the sheet, then two or more sheets may be spliced together. This is done by folding the edges together in a lock joint, the same method used by tinsmiths in joining two pieces of roofing tin. One edge is folded up against a plank so that one inch of metal stands at right angles to the sheet. The edge of the piece adjoining is folded so that two inches of metal are upright, and the two pieces are brought together. Then the longer edge is folded down and around the shorter edge, and the two thus joined are flattened out on the side of the short edge, by blows of a wooden mallet. A strip of solder is then run along the crease to fill the voids in the fold. The solder should be half lead and half tin. A metal worker's tools, torch, solder pot and soldering iron are required for this part of the work, and it would be an advantage to have the services of a tinsmith. The rim of the metal should extend to a level an inch or more above the water and in such a way that it is buried in the bank. The outlet overflow should be arranged over a lip of the lead at the exact level required for the surface of the water. The rim of the formal pool should be arranged with the lead extending under and across the back of the coping stones. The lead may be cut into the sizes required and the edges may be trimmed to the margin line by cutting part way through the sheet lead with a

strong knife blade, and all the way through for the first few inches. Then the sheet may be torn in two.

The pool floor may be painted with a white lead base paint. However, there is no real advantage in painting because the bare lead will soon take on a dark tone quite natural in appearance. In a naturalistic pool a certain amount of sediment collecting on the bottom may be expected.

The pool may remain full of water all winter, and if the depth of water is two and a half feet or more the goldfish may spend the winter under the ice, without danger.

Construction of Copper Pools

Sheet copper is sometimes used as the lining of wall fountains or small garden pools. The metal is put together by lock joints which are then sealed with solder in the same method described for lead pools. Pools which are raised above the ground level by masonry walls or by a cut stone coping may be fitted with a copper lining. The advantage of this method is the avoidance of the necessity of a foundation under the whole area of the pool and the removal of the risk of cracked concrete. Large copper kettles are excellent as garden pools. With a stone coping a kettle makes a very good round raised pool or it may be sunk into the ground so that the rim is flush with the surface.

Water plants are not adversely affected by copper, but goldfish are made sick or are killed by copper impurities in the water.

Construction of Stone Pools

For dripping fountains, no material is more satisfactory than stone. A broad stone, 6 inches thick and slightly concave, makes an excellent shallow pool from the lip of which the water can trickle to a larger basin. The inlet for such a fountain can be a little lead pipe a quarter inch in diameter concealed under a protruding stone at the back of the great stone.

Construction of Clay-lined Pools

A modification of the concrete pool is the pool with a clay bottom. The clay pool is very like a natural pond in its formation because the bottom is a layer of clay. Spread evenly two or three inches thick and worked into the consistency of a mud pie, it will hold water remarkably well. In regions where clay is obtainable it has many advantages as a material for a large pool. No serious injury can come to the clay floor. No forms are required for building, and the actual labor of handling the material in construction is less than for concrete.

Fiberglass Pools

Fiberglass is a light, durable material which is cast to size and shape at the factory and is brought to the job in one piece. The floor and walls form a deep bowl with a smooth, curved surface. It is comparatively inexpensive. The excavation of the pit and the setting of the bowl

A POOL AS THE CENTRAL FEATURE OF THE GARDEN

in sand are the only items of construction. It may be fitted with inlet, outlet and overflow, as with any pool, and the joints may be sealed with liquid fiberglass, which hardens.

Maintenance

With adequate facilities for maintaining a flow of water through the pool, and for emptying it, the care and general upkeep are made easy. An occasional cleaning out of sediment and fallen leaves is practically all that is necessary. In Northern regions the concrete pool should be protected from the action of the frost during the winter months. The water should be drained off before freezing weather, and a few sticks or boards should be placed in the bottom to absorb the thrust of any small amount of ice which may form after snow has melted.

A concrete pool may be arranged for winter with the water level just a little below normal by placing in the water a few large floating logs. The logs will absorb the thrust from the ice, thus relieving the pressure on the concrete walls. Another device is to build the pool with such sharply sloping sides that when the ice forms it merely slides up the sides as it expands, and no pressure is transmitted to the structure.

Ways of Reducing Costs

Those who desire a garden pool and are deterred by the apparently high cost of installation may be interested in methods of reducing the costs. Plumbing is a big item. Its need may be eliminated by using the garden hose to fill and empty the pool. Reinforcing rods comprise a big item. They may be omitted if the pool is small and of simple shape.

Emptying a pool with fifty feet or one hundred feet of garden hose is a simple trick, requiring only a place lower than the pool floor within reach of the hose, whence the water may flow off. To start the working of a syphon, place one end of the hose down the slope at this low point. Hold the other end near the edge of the pool and pour water into it out of a watering can.

When the water begins to flow out of the lower end of the hose and while still pouring water into the upper end, plunge the end of the hose, together with the watering can, into the pool. The flow thus started will continue until the pool is practically empty. The watering can may be removed as soon as the flow from the pool has been established. The flow will continue until the water level reaches the end of the hose.

FOUNTAINS

In centuries past the fountain was the most highly-wrought and most decorative feature of the garden. In dry climates where the presence of water was always highly prized, the garden fountain symbolized the life-giving power of water. At great expense water was piped to the fountains and from the fountains it flowed in little canals throughout the garden to irrigate the soil and make possible the growing of the plants.

During the Italian Renaissance the fountain became an elaborate work of art, combining spouting jets of water with architectural and sculptural forms. The Italian noblemen vied with one another in the display of animated water features in their villas. The water was often piped from streams several miles away to supply a series of fountains which were so arranged that the overflow of one fountain supplied the next fountain on a lower terrace.

The fountain in most American gardens of today is a much less complicated feature, but it is none the less important, and it is often the one note of architectural embellishment. The simplest type is the pool fountain with a single stream rising in a vertical jet from the center. The structure of such a fountain consists merely of a brass nozzle on the supply pipe at the water level. An elaboration of this arrangement is a central pedestal supporting a shallow basin, from the rim of which the water drips into the pool. In such a fountain the central jet is sometimes replaced by a sculptured figure. Greater elaboration occasionally takes the form of minor jets of water near the rim. There is the danger of a

A WALL FOUNTAIN IN A PENNSYLVANIA GARDEN

GARDEN FOUNTAIN IN A
CALIFORNIA GARDEN

fountain design becoming overornamented and fussy, thus loosing both dignity and unity. As with so many other subjects, simplicity and beauty of proportion are the attributes of good design.

The wall fountain as a terminal feature at the end of an axis possesses infinite possibilities for artistic expression. Water coming from a modelled lead spout or through a trough-shaped stone and falling in a narrow stream to the pool below is one of the most satisfactory arrangements for the inlet.

Fountains are definitely architectural in character and they may be used as the dominating motif in the design or as a more incidental feature.

XIV

THE HOME SWIMMING POOL; THE GRILL

A HOME swimming pool beautifully designed, well built and faithfully maintained can be a source of endless pleasure for many people. It can be an investment in healthful recreation for the family and a contribution to happy living.

In early days boys used to walk to the old swimming hole at the edge of the river, take off their clothes and spend the afternoon in the water, diving in from the bank. But the river is not so clear as it used to be; the swimming hole is no longer secluded, and we find that our expanding civilization has deprived many boys of this generation of one of their fundamental pleasures. But a substitute for the river is possible.

The swimming pool first became a feature at the country club and the hotel resort and in some cities public pools were built as part of the recreational system. Thus many people shared the expense and many enjoyed the daily pleasures of the swim. In recent years, however, the improvements in the methods of construction, the standardizing of pre-cast units, the development of new materials, and the perfection of filter systems have all combined to make the swimming pool increasingly attractive, and within the reach of many home owners. Swimming is becoming a thrilling, daily recreation at home, rather than a natural pastime in a country setting. The pool has replaced the river. So it is that thousands of home owners are constructing attractive pools, and their number is ever increasing.

The decision as to whether to build a home swimming pool or not to build one, is one that must be made with full recognition of a number of attendant conditions, the most important considerations being the amount and purity of water

available, the type of filtration system best suited to the water supply, the size and location of the pool desired, the choice of construction materials and methods, construction costs and maintenance expenses, and, finally, the duties and obligations of the owner.

Water Supply and Filter Systems

A swimming pool must have clear, pure water. However, even pure water which remains standing will become clouded with algae in a few summer days. In order to overcome this condition one of two systems must be followed. Either the pool must be drained every week or ten days and filled with fresh water, or the water must be circulated through a filter every few days. In the first case the fresh water will need to be warmed by the sun for a few days before it is warm enough to enjoy. And before long the conditions will be right again for the formation of algae. In the second case the water is pumped out of the bottom of the pool and through a filter and is returned to the pool at the surface. If the water comes from a deep well on the property which has a flow of thirty gallons per minute it will require 19 hours of pumping to fill a standard pool, 20 by 40 feet. If the rate of flow is faster, the time required for filling the pool will be proportionately less. If the water comes from a community water supply which has ample pressure the refilling may be done in three or four hours.

The advantages of the filter system are that the same water can be refreshed and used constantly and will maintain a fairly even temperature. The advantages of the fresh water system are that no filtering will be required and that the water will be naturally fresh. The source of

138

water and its rate of flow will probably be the deciding factor in the choice of the system.

Filters are of two types; the sand filter and the diatomite filter. The first has been in use for many years and requires pumping the water back through the filter in the opposite direction after using it, thus washing out the impurities, and discharging the flow this time into the drain. The second type makes use of a fine-grained or diatomaceous earth, which does not require re-washing but holds the impurities in the filter. The water passes through a series of bags of filter cloth and the collected material is taken out with the filter bags periodically. Because of the capacity of the filter bags through expansion, as the sediment accumulates, long periods of operation are possible between changing or cleaning the filter elements. It is therefore an economical system to operate. But the schedule must be faithfully followed.

Size and Location

In general the size of a pool should be in proportion to the number of people who are expected to use it. But there is a minimum size, fixed by the natural requirements of safety. For diving there should be a depth of $8\frac{1}{2}$ feet and an area not less than 18 × 36 feet. An area a little larger than this is ever so much better, and is well worth the extra cost of construction. A pool 20 or 25 feet wide and 40 or 50 feet long is a far more desirable size. For children and beginners there should be a shallow area at one end of the pool with its floor sloping from a three foot depth to four feet farther out. From this point the floor should slope steeply down to the deep diving area.

The artistic setting of the pool deserves well-studied consideration. Because the swimming pool is likely to be an important and even conspicuous element in the home landscape, we should be concerned with its appearance, its enclosure, its general composition and its relation to other elements. Design, harmony and convenience are as important here as they are in the design of other areas. A simply and generously

designed pool may be a most decorative element in the view from the house. But if it is not well designed it may remain an awkward and inconvenient intrusion. Its horizontality and the need for free circulation about it call for a very simple and level treatment of paving and lawn areas. The composition is usually better for its simplicity; for the pool is to be a frame and a background for joyous activity.

In most situations a geometric shape, rectangle or oval, will be the most harmonious. This simple shape has its advantages, both in construction and in the ease of its use. An oval pool requires less volume of water than a rectangular pool. For swimming races in large pools the rectangular shape is necessary. In an informal or naturalistic setting, when a pool is to be constructed at a distance from the house, an irregular curvilinear outline may be most suitable. Here the shape should be carefully studied in order to avoid restless curves and constricted water areas. It requires study and skill to handle irregular shapes and to keep them rational and harmonious with the surroundings. Concrete and fiberglass are both materials well adapted to the intricate outlines of irregular pools.

The best location for a pool is in open sunshine, sheltered from the winds and unencumbered by neighboring trees. A few falling leaves and twigs can make the task of keeping the water clear all the more difficult. Uninterrupted sunshine is preferred by most swimmers.

Construction

Concrete: Reinforced concrete has been the almost universally used structural material for pools, and today, even though several new materials have been introduced, concrete is often used, sometimes in combination with other materials. It is time tested and has proven satisfactory because of its strength, adaptability and permanence. The construction of a reinforced concrete pool requires the erection of exact forms and the secure placing of the steel reinforcing rods before the concrete is poured. The forms are built of tongue and groove boards held in place by framing which is anchored to stakes in the ground. This frame is hung in such a way that the inner and outer forms produce the required thickness of concrete, usually eight inches at the top and tapering to ten or twelve inches at the bottom. The floor is usually six inches thick.

An improvement on this method of casting concrete consists of using adjustable steel forms instead of wood forms. They can be used over and over again, and thus are an economy for the contractor. For pools longer than forty feet, expansion joints of tar are placed in the walls and floor to separate the concrete into units and to compensate for heat expansion and contraction of the material.

Another improvement in the method of casting concrete was introduced some years ago. By this method the mixed concrete is poured into the mold under pressure from a hose nozzle, and the resulting compactness of the mass increases its strength. This method is called "gunite", and is less expensive than the slower method of filling the forms, but it requires special equipment.

Another method of building concrete pools has also been developed. Pre-cast reinforced concrete slabs are brought to the job and are assembled by cranes. They are fitted together and the joints are sealed with cement mortar. This is a rapid method, but it requires heavy equipment for transporting and handling the units.

New Materials

The several new materials for pool construction include pre-cast fiberglass, plastic lining for pools built of concrete blocks, and steel sections welded together.

Fiberglass has the advantage of lightness and durability. It is pre-cast and brought to the job in very large pieces. Only four pieces are needed to form a thirty foot pool. The joints are sealed with liquid fiberglass which hardens. The unit combines a section of wall with a section of floor in one piece with a curved surface between them. This results in a smooth interior which is easy to clean and it makes a very attractive pool.

A SWIMMING POOL WITH BROAD PAVING

Plastic: Probably the least expensive pool is one built of concrete blocks for walls and a concrete casting for floor. Within this enclosure is placed a flexible plastic lining to hold the water. The material is very durable, and is in use in many other situations where water-tightness, lightness, and flexibility are required. This may prove to be the method and the material best adapted to the homemade pool.

Steel: Like a ship, a pool may be constructed entirely of steel sections, placed on steel frames or on reinforced concrete buttresses. The plates are fabricated at the steel mill true to dimensions and are welded together

at the job. This material requires a waterproof asphalt paint for an outer coating, and an interior surfacing of three coats of base waterproof paint and two coats of finish paint. This method has the advantage of eliminating expensive forms. It is very durable and capable of withstanding the pressures of freezing soil. Its only maintenance requirement is the periodic renewing of the interior paint.

Accessories

For maximum enjoyment, the pool should have a few pieces of equipment, some built into the structure and some movable. There should be on all sides at

CALIFORNIA SWIMMING POOL ENCLOSED BY A SPLIT REDWOOD FENCE

the water level a scum gutter to take off the surface water and drain it into the overflow pipe. The inlet pipe at the surface should flow with fresh water, even if only a small flow. This could, if desired, be made into a small trickling fountain from a raised basin. There should be a ladder or two of brass or other metal for climbing out of the water, and at the shallow end a flight of concrete steps. A springboard reaching out over the water at the deep end is a most important accessory. The rim of the pool should be finished with a coping of cut stone or flagstone fifteen inches wide or wider, and flush with the surrounding ground. This will provide a finish and frame for the panel of water, and will be a convenience for the swimmers. A strip of flagstone paving or other hard paving adjacent to the coping, four feet wide or wider, should also surround the pool. This will be used constantly for running about the pool. A paved area nearby for chairs and tables will be a pleasant convenience for the guests. A post with a coil of rope and a life preserver hanging on it is a wise precaution. It may never be used, but there might come a time when it would be desperately needed.

Enclosure

The owner of a swimming pool finds himself custodian of a serious hazard to the safety of the children in his neighborhood, especially those

A SWIMMING POOL IN A GARDEN SETTING ENCLOSED BY A RUSTIC PICKET FENCE

who are old enough to walk and wander and have not yet learned to swim. It is therefore encumbent upon him to enclose the pool in an impenetrable fence, provided with gates which lock, in order to keep the enclosure safe. The fence is one of a number of supplementary items essential to the pool. It is, in fact, indispensable.

In California, where more people have home pools than anywhere else in the country, there is a state law requiring that either the entire property or the pool be enclosed within a fence, thus insuring complete protection from outside intrusions. Undoubtedly, as swimming pools become more common similar laws will be enacted in other states.

For the pool enclosure, the louver fence, the basket-weave wood fence, the close-woven wood fence, are all satisfactory and attractive. The least expensive of the durable fences is probably the chain link. For pools a fence should be six feet high and a six and a half or seven foot fence is often used to establish privacy. Such fences can be hidden in the foliage of deciduous or evergreen vines. Clematis, silver lace vine, English ivy, Virginia creeper, Akebia quinata, Bougainvillea and Trumpet creeper are among the best.

Obligations

No one should undertake to build and maintain a swimming pool unless he is willing to keep the water renewed or filtered frequently, and unless he will enclose the pool area in a firm fence so that no wandering child can fall into the water. The risk of such a tragedy is always imminent unless this is done. It takes forethought and periodic attention to administer even a small home swimming pool. Its ownership imposes a continuing obligation.

THE GRILL FOR OUTDOOR MEALS

Many a modern home is equipped with a space for enjoying the informality of cooking and serving meals out of doors. The grill and the picnic table have become important features of the home grounds. For some the portable charcoal grill suffices. But the serious cook prefers the permanence of a masonry fireplace with grill top, and perhaps even an oven.

Because of the concentration of use, the area should be paved with flagstone or brick. The edges may be embellished with flower beds or a few well-placed shrubs. In some situations the whole area may be somewhat separated from the rest of the grounds, so that the grill will not be too prominent in the general picture or an intrusion when it is not in use. It is a mistake to crowd it, as the heat from the fire can scorch overhanging branches or a fence which is too near.

The outdoor fireplace should never be used as an incinerator. Its function and dignity should not be compromised for the sake of economy. The incinerator should be in the service yard completely separated visually from the garden, lawn and terrace.

Construction

The foundations should be below the frost line. Side walls and back may be of stone masonry or brick. The firebox should be lined with firebrick, and the grill, 18 inches square or larger, should be of iron rods set about an inch apart. A chimney flue is an advantage because it will take off the smoke, but it is not essential. However, if a chimney is used, let it be high enough to start the smoke up overhead, five feet at least. The draft thus caused will be stronger and more regular than in the flueless fireplace.

The drawing shows the major dimensions.* Larger fireboxes will need larger flues. An oven separated from the firebox by an iron plate, and a box for tinder and fuel are features which will increase the usefulness of the fireplace. But for broiling, frying and boiling the type here shown is all that is needed.

*See p. 153.

XV

FENCES

A FENCE is an element of the landscape capable of great variety of form and with limitless possibilities for distinctive design. Today it has become a background for much of our outdoor living.

Both as barriers and as ornaments, fences are conspicuous. As elements of design and as aids in the use of land they are important and often indispensable. For the home owner, the fence provides a screen against too much publicity and is a barrier against intrusion. Beyond these practical uses a fence should be an expression of pure design, a frame for the grounds and an architectural element in harmony with the house.

Materials and methods have brought about the designs of several distinctive types of fences. In certain regions the abundance of some good material has made a special type of fence structure typical of that locality. Thus the stone wall and the picket fence express New England; the zigzag rail fence, Virginia and Kentucky; the post and rail fence, Virginia; and the post and board fence, Pennsylvania and Maryland.

Today transportation makes available materials other than those from local sources, and has opened markets for the best materials which in earlier times were used only in the regions of their origin. Thus in New England one can have for posts not merely the red cedar of the neighboring pastures, but cypress as well, which will outlast it. Also available are fence materials assembled in manageable units made in Virginia, Michigan, New Jersey, and California, and shipped all over the country.

As with so many other products of modern manufacture and distribution, local tradition in fence design is no longer dominant. The decision as to the type of fence for a certain place should be based on the consideration of strength, durability, appearance and cost.

Requisites of a Good Fence

The practical attributes of a good fence are strength sufficient to hold its place against wind; durability, that is, soundness after many years of exposure to weather; good appearance, the ability to remain neat and trim without much attention to maintenance; economy of construction costs in relation to the life of the fence.

A fence should be so firmly fixed in the ground that it will withstand many years of wind pressure and the effects of summer sun and winter freezing.

Posts should be set into the ground to a depth of $2\frac{1}{2}$ to 3 feet for firm anchorage. In cold climates the base of the post should be below the frost line in order to prevent heaving, due to frost pressures. Fences which are to serve as snow barriers should have an extra anchorage, such as a second post slanting into the ground on the leeward side.

The back-filling of the earth about the posts, after they have been set in the hole, must be accompanied by firm tamping. Any tendency of the post to wiggle will be increased rather than diminished by the force of wind and weather.

All fence corners should be cross-braced to provide additional strength.

TYPES OF FENCES

Wood is the most generally available material for fences and is widely used for the enclosure of home properties. Metal is also used in the form of galvanized iron, wrought iron and woven wire. For posts, wood, concrete, and steel are commonly used.

Wood Fences

There are many types of wood fences, some very simple in design and construction, others more elaborate. Regardless of the type, there are certain points which should be taken into consideration: the durability of the wood selected, the setting of the posts, details of construction, and the upkeep of the fence.

When board fences or picket fences, except those of rustic type, are being constructed, the surfaces of the pickets and rails where they join one another, and the surfaces of the rails and posts where they, in turn, join, should be painted before the fence is put together. It is in these crevices that moisture is most apt to lodge, and the paint will provide protection against decay. At no later time can the painting of these particular spots be done so easily or so effectively. The extra labor required to do this will be more than repaid in the increased life of the fence.

Selection of the Wood: Woods vary greatly in their durability. Some woods will give many years of service while in some climates other wood will last for only a few years under outdoor conditions. The durable woods are usually more expensive but will prove to be the best investment in the end. It is poor economy to select a cheaper, less durable wood which will need to be replaced within a few years.

The decay of wood is caused by certain wood-destroying fungi. In order to function, these fungi must have favorable conditions, the important factors being moisture, air, a warm temperature and food, which is supplied by the wood. If the temperature is too cold, if the supply of air is completely shut off, or if insufficient moisture is present, as in desert areas, the decay of wood is greatly retarded or does not occur. In humid areas with mild climates conditions are particularly favorable and under certain circumstances, such as at the ground line, decay takes place rapidly. It is at this point that posts always decay, and only woods which are extremely resistant to decay or which have been chemically treated should be used for fence posts.

Among the most durable woods are cypress, redwood, red cedar, arborvitæ, white cedar, black locust and sourgum. These woods possess remarkable ability to resist decay and are therefore recommended for posts.

In order to increase the durability of wood it may be treated with a chemical preservative. The chemical, in order to be fully effective, should be applied under pressure so that sufficient penetration may be obtained.

In some cases the entire post is treated, in other cases the treatment extends only to well above the ground line, which is entirely satisfactory. In many areas, treated posts are available. Such treatment will greatly prolong the life of the less durable woods and will sometimes prove to be the best choice if the more durable woods are very high in price or are unobtainable.

For use as rails, pickets, palings, spindles and panels, less durable woods may be used. Although redwood, cedar and cypress will outlast them, such woods as pine, hemlock, spruce and fir will give many years of good service for these purposes, particularly if they are kept painted. For rustic fences redwood, cedar, and imported chestnut are most frequently used.

Split Rail Fence. The "Snake fence" or split rail fence is one of the most picturesque for open farm lands. It originated in Virginia in colonial times, and is often called Virginia rail fence, though more properly the Kentucky rail fence, because of its frequent use in that state. It is made of rails split from poles cut in the woods close at hand. Chestnut and ash were the favorite trees because their wood splits most easily. The rails were put together without nails or wire and were only anchored at the junctions by two slanting rails leaned against the junction of horizontal rails. A great deal of wood is required for the construction of this fence, but no other tool except the axe, and no other materials, are required. It is, therefore, the fence of the pioneer. As forests became depleted, a modification of this fence, which requires less wood, was developed, the Virginia rail fence, strictly speaking. With this the rails are laid end overlapping end in a straight line, their points of junction being kept upright by two posts set in the ground, one on each side, and wired together at the top. A more modern version of this is the post and rail fence with three slots cut in the single post to receive the ends of the rails.

The Post and Rail Fence is a very handsome pasture enclosure, and is suitable for the property lines of country residences. White cedar posts with large slots cut in them are erected at intervals of about 10 feet. The rails, half-round arborvitæ poles 11 feet long, are tapered to flat ends which are thrust through the slots in the posts. There are three sizes of posts, making three-rail, four-rail or five-rail fences. It is an easy type of fence to erect and is most satisfactory for its rugged appearance and durability. The weathering gives it a warm gray color, harmonizing well with the tones of the countryside.

Reinforced concrete posts may be used instead of wooden posts and will outlast them by many years. When concrete posts are used heavy planks may be substituted for split rails and will be more enduring.

ENGLISH HURDLE FENCE

POST AND BOARD FENCE

POST AND RAIL FENCE

SPINDLE FENCE

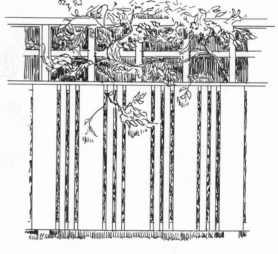

BOARD FENCE WITH LATTICE TOP

The Hurdle Fence was originally developed in England as a pasture fence. It is light, strong and attractive and is excellent for use as a boundary fence on suburban properties of moderate size. It is picturesque, easily erected and easily moved, and it provides an excellent background for climbing roses and other vines. The panels come in 8 foot lengths in both 3 and 4 foot heights. They may be purchased already put together or, at more moderate cost, in a knocked-down state ready for the home-owner to put together. It is one of the quickest and easiest fences to erect. The sharpened posts are driven into the ground with a sledge-hammer and each panel is then pegged to the next.

Post and Board Fence. This type of fence is framed on red cedar or cypress posts erected at 10- or 12-foot intervals. Three or four horizontal rough boards 1 inch × 8 inches, or 1 inch × 6 inches are nailed to the posts

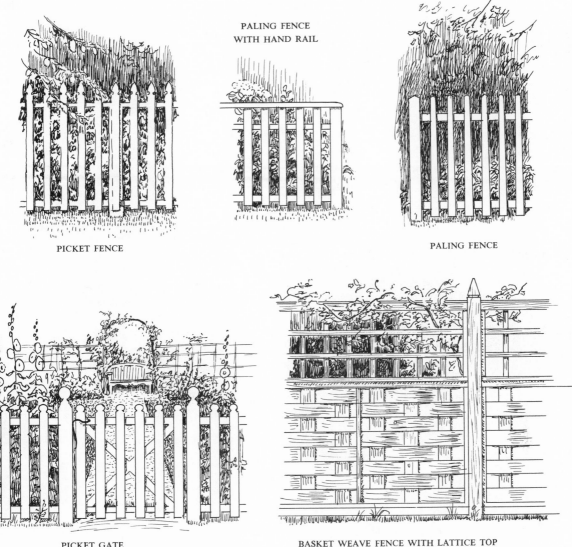

PICKET FENCE

PALING FENCE
WITH HAND RAIL

PALING FENCE

PICKET GATE

BASKET WEAVE FENCE WITH LATTICE TOP

with wide spaces between them. A vertical 6-inch board covers the board ends against each post and a 6-inch square board caps the post like a shed roof. Rough sawed pine boards are usually used. White-washed or better painted white, this makes a very neat type of fence for a suburban property, especially one with a house of colonial architecture.

The Board Fence with lattice top is a very attractive type of fence and is appropriate for town yards, especially where the house is of colonial tradition, and it may also be used as a garden enclosure. Many variations in design and proportion are possible. The posts are usually spaced about 10 feet apart, and several horizontal rails provide a framework to which the up-right boards can be nailed. The lattice top, if strongly built, will provide a support for light, graceful vines, such as clematis and akebia. Wisteria should never be used, as it is too rampant.

SPINDLE FENCE IN A NEW ENGLAND GARDEN

The Louver Fence is a modification of the board fence. The boards are set at an angle to let the breezes through. It is used to achieve privacy and at the same time to provide for a good circulation of air. Fences of this type are very popular in hot climates and they are also an excellent type for city gardens where conditions are often not favorable for good air circulation. Sections of louver fences can be made so that they are adjustable and a slight push will control the breeze. Lightly-con-

structed louver sections are often used as movable wind baffles and can be made quite a decorative feature on a terrace or patio.

The Woven Split Sapling Fence is rustic in character and makes an opaque screen. The construction is simple and strong. Posts are set at 10-foot intervals and are connected with two or three cedar rails. Panels of split saplings about 1½ inches wide, woven together

148

SMALL SCALE POST AND RAIL FENCE. TUBEROUS BEGONIAS AND RHODODENDRONS.

with wire, are nailed on to the rails, so that the finished fence is a continuous wall of rustic vertical lines. With the bark still on, the fence immediately has an old appearance, but with the bark stripped off, a year of mellowing will be required. Fences of this type are usually made of cedar, arborvitæ, or imported French chestnut and are very durable. They may be obtained in various heights and provide an excellent barrier where complete privacy or protection is desired. They are manufactured at the mill and are shipped as panels, with the required number of posts and rails.

The Picket Fence has long been popular and has been used for the enclosure of town yards and gardens since colonial times. In the early New England villages the white, clapboard houses were grouped about the central green and their dignified, spacious yards were always enclosed with picket fences. Within these enclosures flourished pleasant little flower gardens. As were the details of the houses, the fences were often designed with great distinction and gave an architectural expression to the setting of the house.

The picket fence requires careful construction and the proper spacing of parts, as it expresses the qualities of rightness and precision. Great variance in design and proportion may be achieved.

The simplest type of picket fence is one which has natural, round posts. The upper rail, a 2 × 4 inches set flat, rests upon the top of the posts and is nailed to them. The lower rail, a 2 × 4 inches set on edge, is mortised into the face of the post and nailed. The

pickets, $\frac{3}{4}$ × 3 inches or $\frac{3}{4}$ × 4 inches, are nailed to the outer side of the rails and a picket covers each post.

Fences of more carefully studied design may have posts topped by beautiful turned finials. The shafts of such posts are of planed lumber and the bases and caps have appropriate moldings. The pickets, also, may have specially designed tops. A fence of such finished carpentry should be supported on concrete footings under the posts so that the base of the wood is several inches above the ground. This feature will greatly prolong the life of the fence, as there will be no ground rot.

The Rustic Picket Fence has the same structural lines and general character as the picket fence but is less formal. Rustic pickets are made of split wood, usually arborvitæ, cedar or redwood, and the pickets should not be painted.

The Spindle Fence is a refinement of the picket fence and is suitable for the formal dooryard or garden of a colonial mansion. The spindles are round, about $1\frac{1}{4}$ inches in diameter, and pass through holes in the rails at intervals of 5 to 7 inches. Variations from this are made by giving the fence a solid board base, or even a third rail 16 inches above the lower rail and filling the space with a lattice of square bars in diamond pattern, the round spindles extending from the intermediate rail through the upper rail. Such a fence with graceful fenceposts is in keeping with the careful carpentry of modillioned cornices and a carved broken pediment above the door.

149

"*Snow Fences*" consist of pickets woven by horizontal wires and fastened to metal posts driven into the ground. Used as a winter precaution, they are erected at a distance of 50 or 75 feet from the road, toward the prevailing wind; they create enough obstacles to cause snow to form drifts in the lee close to the fence and not in the road. They may be used for any other temporary purpose, to surround play yards or dog runs. The life of the fence is usually about ten years.

Lattice Fences are most closely associated with the French style of garden art for the French developed the lattice to intricate patterns. But very simple lattices were used in colonial gardens as supports for vines, particularly climbing roses. Painted white to harmonize with the frame house or the white trim of brick or stone structure, the lattice is an adjunct of formal design.

The Chinese Lattice Fence, which is used in California with such distinction, has large patterns of irregularly spaced rectangular openings. Only a few of the horizontal bars extend through to both sides of the panel.

The resulting design is balanced but informally unsymmetrical. When used in combination with translucent plastic it makes a pleasing background for flowering plants and also provides protection from the wind.

The Grape Stake Fence is a rustic structure used around many small homes in certain sections of California, and is reminiscent of early pioneer days. The stakes are driven into the ground rather close together, forming a sort of miniature stockade. The tops are cleated together with stakes placed horizontally, or a little on the slant. The tops of the stakes are not cut back to an even saw-line and the effect is most casual. Its great advantages are that the materials are inexpensive, its erection requires a minimum of skill, and it will last for many years. Redwood or cedar are the woods most commonly used. The height may be varied to suit the desires of the owner.

The Basket-weave Fence is becoming increasingly popular and it has much to recommend it. It consists of thin strips of wood woven horizontally between upright supports set about three feet apart. The fencing is made up in panels of several heights, ranging from 4

DOORYARD GARDEN ON CAPE COD ENCLOSED BY PICKET FENCE

A CALIFORNIA PLASTIC AND REDWOOD FRAME FENCE

to 8 feet. It is light in weight, is easily erected, and is comparatively inexpensive. It forms an excellent screen, providing complete privacy and protection, yet permitting some circulation of air. Some types are made with a lattice top which adds greatly to the attractiveness of the fence and which may be used as a support for slender vines such as clematis and akebia. It is not strong enough to support heavy vines.

Fences of Other Types

Plastic Fences: Post fences with top and bottom rails can be finished with sheets of translucent plastic. It is one of the least attractive types of fence, but is inexpensive and requires little skill in its erection.

Canvas Fences are best adapted to dry climates or for use where temporary protection from wind or from the public gaze is desired. The construction requires posts with top and bottom rails between. The sheets of canvas are laced to the posts and rails. The ropes should be loosened in wet weather and tightened on sunny days. Such a fence has a certain novelty and charm when used in appropriate surroundings, as in the environs of an informal summer home.

The Chain Link Fence such as surrounds factory yards is out of place in a finished landscape.

Woven-wire Fences such as are used for pasture are probably the least expensive type of fence as far as initial cost, but their life of usefulness is short when

REDWOOD BOARD FENCE

compared with that of most other types, and they are completely lacking in charm.

If it is necessary to use such a fence its appearance can be greatly enhanced by training English ivy through the wire mesh. If this is faithfully done the fence will eventually become a wall of solid, dark green foliage.

Wrought-Iron Fences and hand railings seem most suitable for the balustrade along the top of a stone retaining wall at the terrace edge. They are strong, light and durable, and combine well with massive stone structures. Capable of great variety of design, wrought iron is a wonderful medium for individual expression. Support-

AN OUTDOOR GRILL—SEE P. 143

ing posts may be placed at long intervals because of the strength of the material in the rails. For the sake of interesting pattern, the spokes may be varied in any number of twistings. A pattern of curved lines may be placed at intervals among the straight uprights. Posts may be $1\frac{1}{4}$ inches square or even only $\frac{7}{8}$ inch square, while the spokes at $\frac{1}{2}$ inch will look and will actually be strong enough. Occasional braces, rods running from near the top to a few inches off the line of fence, will keep it firm. The iron railing is fastened to the stone by drilling holes 4 inches deep in the coping of the wall and fastening the post into the hole by melted lead.

A rust-resisting paint should be applied to the iron work before it is erected, and it should be repainted every three years.

The advantages of such a grill along the terrace or above the garden steps is that views down into the garden or glen are not obstructed as they would be by a parapet wall, and the iron work makes a pleasing patterned silhouette against the distance. A wrought-iron grill fence is expensive in original cost, but is practically indestructible and requires very little care.

The Cast-Iron Fence or grill has much the same qualities as the wrought iron. However, it is not as strong and the pattern is made not so much by a series of narrow pieces making lines, as by a series of flat pieces making masses. The pattern repeats itself in rhythm, like wallpaper, and for this reason it is not as versatile as wrought iron.

MAINTENANCE OF FENCES

Almost all fences, except those of rustic character, require periodic painting.

New wooden fences should have two priming coats of paint and one finishing coat. Repainting should be done *before* the paint has worn off and the wood has become exposed to the weather. The intervals between paintings will depend somewhat upon the climate and also upon the quality of the paint and the quality of the workmanship which goes into the job of painting.

All iron work should receive a coat of special rust-resisting paint before it is erected and should be repainted at intervals of about every three years.

A periodic inspection of fences is a good practice. One broken picket will spoil the appearance of a fence. A few minutes of work with a hammer, saw and paint brush will restore the rhythm and avoid the suggestion of shabbiness.

Posts occasionally become weak and should be tamped firmly into place or, if decay has set in, they should be replaced before the fence is allowed to sag out of place.

XVI

SOILS AND SOIL IMPROVEMENT

THERE is no subject of more fundamental importance to the gardener than that of soil management. In order to handle garden soils intelligently, and to maintain or increase the fertility of the soil, it is necessary to have a thorough knowledge not only of the soil itself, but also of the manner in which plants receive their nutrients from the soil.

There are comparatively few soils which provide ideal conditions for plant growth, but if a wise program of soil management is put into effect, much may be accomplished in improving the structure, the fertility, and the water-holding capacity of soils of widely varying types.

There are certain factors affecting plant growth over which a gardener has very little control, such as climate, rainfall, sunshine and humidity; but over the various factors of soil management he has very definite control. The soil is a heritage which has come to us from the past—a heritage which we in turn will pass on, and it is the privilege of those who work with it to regard it as a trust. Not only for our own immediate benefit should we strive to conserve, and to maintain, and to increase its fertility—it is our obligation to the generations of gardeners who are to follow us.

SOIL FORMATION

The formation of the soil is a process which has continued since earliest geologic times when the surface of the earth was composed entirely of rock. The action of sun and frost, air and water upon these rock surfaces of the earth has resulted in a gradual process of disintegration and the consequent slow formation of soils. Æons ago the first plants grew in the hollows and crevices of the rocks where this newly formed mineral soil had found lodgement. And

as these primitive plants died, they decayed and formed food for other plants, and gradually, as the millenniums passed, this decaying organic matter became mixed with the mineral soil, thus enriching it, and increasing the earth's vegetation. In sections where primeval forest growth abounds we find deep, porous soils, rich in humus, which are classed as peaty soils. Such soils are also found in peat bogs and are composed almost entirely of decayed organic matter. In other sections we find soils which are classed as mineral soils, being composed largely of mineral matter. And in between these two extreme types, the peaty soils and the mineral soils, we find many soils of widely varying character.

Most soils, as we find them in our gardens today, are composed of five intermingled components: the mineral substances obtained from the slow disintegration of rock surfaces; humus or decaying organic matter; minute living organisms such as the bacteria, protozoa and fungi which are present in large quantities in most soils; water, which holds in solution the dissolved mineral salts; and air. In sections where the soil has been under cultivation for many years or where the program of soil management has been poor we find soils which have lost much of their humus content and which, in many cases, have become depleted of their mineral elements. It is these soils which present the greatest problems.

TYPES OF SOIL

Soils are generally grouped into three classes according to structure: sand, silt, or clay. These classes are determined by the size of the soil particles. Sand contains 20 particles or less to a millimeter, silt 20 to 200 particles to a millimeter, and clay 200 or more. A soil of ideal texture is a mixture of sand, silt and clay, being classed as a good garden loam. The structure of the soil has a very direct bearing upon its water-holding capacity, upon its warmth in early spring, upon the ease with which it can be worked or handled, and upon the penetration of plant roots and the consequent nutrition of the plant.

Clay Soils. A clay soil has a water-holding capacity many times higher than that of a sandy soil because each soil particle is capable of holding a film of water upon its surface. Therefore a clay soil possessing 200 particles per millimeter is capable of holding ten times as much water as sand which possesses only 20 particles to the same area. The water-holding capacity of clay soils may be an asset in seasons of extreme drought, but it is, on the whole, almost as much of a liability as it is an asset. A heavy clay soil is very slow in drying out in the spring, and all planting operations and general cultural practices must therefore be delayed. It does not absorb the sun's rays as readily as does a soil of lighter texture and, therefore, does not warm up as quickly in the spring, thus delaying the normally eager spring growth of plants. If left uncultivated too long after a rain, a clay soil will form a hard, baked crust which makes it impossible for either air or moisture to reach the roots of the plants, and in some cases it will form deep cracks. On the other hand, if it is plowed or cultivated or otherwise handled when it is too wet, it will form hard lumps which are exceedingly difficult to break down. A clay soil is one of the most difficult of all soil types to handle wisely, and every effort should be made to improve its structure. Much may be accomplished by the addition of sand, humus, and compost, and even sifted coal ashes will be of some benefit. It is also an advantage to spade or plow clay soils in the autumn, leaving them in a very rough condition throughout the winter. The action of the frost will have a beneficial effect on the close texture of the soil, making it somewhat more mellow and friable.

Sandy Soils possess many of the advantages which are lacking in soils of a decidedly heavy texture. They warm up quickly in the spring, they are easy to work. On the other hand, sandy soils are not retentive of moisture and many of the soluble plant foods may be lost through leaching. It is quite as important, therefore, to improve the structure of sandy soils as it is to improve the structure of heavy clay soils. This may be accomplished most successfully by the addition of liberal quantities of organic matter.

Loam Soils. The ideal soil for most garden operations is a fertile loam, which is a mixture of sand, clay, and humus. It should be porous enough in texture to provide good drainage and adequate aeration; it should be spongy enough to retain an ample supply of moisture; it should contain sufficient humus to provide favorable conditions for the growth of the soil bacteria, which play such an important part in plant nutrition; and it should contain all the mineral elements necessary for the healthy, normal growth of plant life. A soil of this type is the desideratum of every gardener, and with a good program of soil management and an intelligent understanding of the needs of growing plants, much may be accomplished in building a soil which will very nearly approximate the ideal.

HUMUS

An adequate supply of humus in the soil is one of the most important factors in a program of good soil management.

Humus serves many functions in improving the structure and character of the soil. It increases the water-holding capacity of soils; it modifies the soil structure; it readily absorbs the sun's rays and consequently increases and stimulates plant growth in early spring; it prevents the leaching of soluble plant foods; it liberates compounds which, in turn, act upon the chemical elements in the soil, thus making available to the plants mineral nutrients which would otherwise remain in insoluble form; and it promotes the bacterial action in the soil to a very marked degree.

The value of humus in increasing the water-holding capacities of soils can hardly be over-emphasized. It is unlike the particles of mineral soils in that it does not merely hold the water on its surface; it soaks it in like a sponge. In a series of recent experiments to test the water-holding capacities of soils of varying types, it was found that 100 pounds of sand will hold 25 pounds of water; 100 pounds of clay will hold 50 pounds of water, and 100 pounds of humus will hold 190 pounds of water. From 20 to 40 percent of the water-holding capacity of soils is due to their humus content, and in seasons of prolonged drought soils high in humus content will remain moist in both the upper and lower soil horizons far longer than soils which are deficient in humus, and plant growth is correspondingly greater.

Humus is also of great value in improving the texture of soils, as it has the ability to modify the soil structure to a very marked degree. A soil which is of mellow, friable texture, the kind which we class as an ideal garden loam, is made up of crumbs of soil held together in a granule, and it is the humus which furnishes the binding material for these soil particles. A soil of this texture permits the rapid renewal of moisture and food nutrients. It also permits easy root penetration, which is an important factor, as the roots travel to the water and food in the soil, not vice versa. When a clay soil is deficient in humus it becomes tight and compact in structure. The penetration of the roots is therefore restricted and the nutrition of the plant is often seriously limited in consequence. Such a soil has a tendency to become hard and baked when it is dry, and is far less permeable to water than soil of a more open structure. Not only does the water penetrate the soil less readily but it is also more quickly evaporated. Soils of this type may be greatly improved in texture by the application of liberal amounts of humus. When sandy soils are deficient in humus, many valuable plant nutrients are lost through leaching and plant growth also suffers seriously from lack of moisture in times of drought. It is, therefore, quite as important to see that sandy soils are well supplied with humus as it is to maintain an adequate humus supply in clay soils.

Humus and Mineral Fertilizers. Mineral fertilizers supplement, but in no way do they replace, humus. Recent experiments have proved that mineral fertilizers are much more effective if they are applied either with, or immediately following, an application of humus, than if they are applied alone. At the Maryland Experiment Station, crop yields have shown an increase varying from $\frac{1}{5}$ to $\frac{1}{3}$ more when manure and mineral fertilizers were applied together than when double the amount of either was applied alone. This same principle would apply to the building up of soil fertility in the garden.

Sources of Humus

Peat. The various forms of peat provide an excellent source of humus. Technically, peat may be defined as the partially carbonized organic residue of plants, the decomposition of which has taken place under standing water. The peats may be classed into several groups: those of deep water, marsh, swamp, and bog origin. When the process of decay of such substances as tree trunks, mosses, sedges, and grasses takes place under water, the decomposition is greatly retarded because of the exclusion of air, and the resulting product, known as peat, differs considerably from the humus which is found in upland forests.

Peat is rich in organic matter, is highly absorbent and retentive of moisture, and has the added advantage of being comparatively free from weed seeds and harmful fungi. Peat is usually somewhat acid in its reaction and it must, therefore, be used with discrimination. It is of particular value for use in connection with the planting of broad-leaved evergreens, such as rhododendrons, laurel, azaleas, and many of the acid-loving woodland plants, but it should not be used too liberally in connection with plants which are not acid tolerant. The actual fertilizing value of peat is comparatively low. It contains some nitrogen, the amount varying from 1 to 3.5 percent, depending upon the source of the peat, and it is extremely low in phosphorus and potash.

The two kinds of peat most readily obtainable are imported peat and domestic peat. The imported peat comes in tightly packed bales, weighing about 200 pounds. It is largely of bog origin, being a sphagnum type of peat, and it is very low in nitrogen content. When it is to be incorporated in the soil, or used as a mulch, the handling of it will be greatly facilitated if the bale is thoroughly soaked before it is opened. When dry its light, fluffy texture makes it hard to handle.

Domestic peat has a higher moisture content, is darker in color and finer in texture. In general it is considered a better source of humus than the imported peat, as it may be more evenly worked into the soil and its effect is more lasting.

Leaf Mold is an excellent and usually a readily available source of humus. It is highly retentive of moisture, is rich in organic matter, and has the ability to change into a more readily available form various nitrogenous materials in the soil. Leaf mold varies considerably in its reaction upon the soil. Oak leaves and pine needles, when decayed, form a leaf mold which is definitely acid in its reaction. However, the majority of our deciduous trees form a leaf mold which is very mildly acid or entirely neutral in reaction. The best and most abundant source of leaf mold is the natural forest floor. A small but readily available supply may be kept at hand by making a compost of leaves each autumn.

The Compost Pile. A good compost pile is a valuable adjunct to any garden, and no matter how small one's place may be there will always be some organic materials which can be converted into compost. The end product of a compost pile is a soil which is exceedingly high in humus content and rich in plant nutrients. Such soils are of particular value as potting soils for house plants and for use in the preparation of seed flats. Compost is also of value as a top-dressing for lawns and in the preparation of the soil in hot-beds and cold frames, and it is used extensively to enrich and improve the texture of the soil in flower gardens and on vegetable plots. Indeed, there are so many uses for a good compost that the supply never seems to be quite sufficient to meet one's needs.

The building of a compost pile is a simple matter. A partially shaded location is preferable to one in full sun, as it will be possible to maintain a more even degree of moisture. A pile of convenient, workable size is one from 4 to 6 feet in width, 3 to 4 feet in height, and of any desired length. The foundation of the pile should consist of some coarse material, such as inverted sods or weed stalks, and upon this foundation alternating layers of organic refuse and soil should be built up, animal manures being included whenever they are obtainable as they greatly increase the fertility of the compost. Almost any type of organic material may be used with the exception of very woody materials and plants that are diseased. Grass clippings, sod, weeds, refuse from the vegetable garden, and all types of animal manures are excellent materials, and, through the process of composting, may be converted into potential wealth for the gardener.

The decomposition of organic matter is due to the activity of certain organisms, and the rate of decomposition in a compost pile will be greatly accelerated if these micro-organisms are present in sufficient numbers. This may be accomplished through the addition of soil to the pile (a healthy soil is teeming with biologic life); through the use of some well-rotted compost from another pile; or through the use of one of the numerous commercial activators on the market.

Since these organisms which play such an important part in the decomposition of organic materials are not tolerant of acid conditions, it is wise to add an occasional sprinkling of ground limestone to the pile during the process of construction. The moisture content of the pile is also important. The top of the pile should be concave, in order to catch as much rain as possible, and if dry materials such as hay or straw are used the pile should be thoroughly soaked during the process of building. It should have a moist, spongy consistency at all times. An occasional turning is advisable, rebuilding the pile so that the outer portion of the old pile is placed in the center of the new pile.

The time required to convert raw organic materials into a good humus suitable for garden use will depend upon a number of factors, such as climatic conditions, the moisture content of the pile, the type of materials used, and whether or not an activator is used. Bacterial action is more rapid in warm climates than in colder regions; green materials will decompose more rapidly than more woody materials, and some of the new commercial activators will speed the process of decomposition to such an extent that it is possible to obtain an excellent humus in three or four months.

Making Compost Weed-free. When using compost as a top-dressing on lawns, or for a seed-bed in a cold frame, or for flats in which seeds are to be started, it is a great advantage to have material which is weed-free.

There are various methods of producing compost which will be entirely free of viable weed seeds. One of the methods best adapted to the facilities available to the home gardener is a process developed by the University of Rhode Island in which granular calcium cyanamide is used. Not only does this method kill all the weed seeds, but it also increases the nutritive value of the compost, as calcium cyanamide, commonly known as Cyanamid, contains 20 percent nitrogen and the equivalent of 70 percent hydrated lime.

The process is simple. The compost, which should be well decomposed and moderately moist, should be sifted through a $\frac{1}{4}$-inch-mesh wire screen. It should then be mixed thoroughly with the Cyanamid at the rate of 13 pounds of Cyanamid to each cubic yard of compost. The easiest way to measure a cubic yard is to have a bottomless box which holds one cubic yard or an exact fraction thereof. The box may be filled and lifted away and refilled again as many times as necessary. One of the best ways in which to add the Cyanamid in the correct proportion, and to have it well distributed through the compost, is to place the compost in the measuring box layer by layer, adding a proportionate amount of Cyanamid as the layers are built up. If four layers are used, slightly more than three pounds of Cyanamid should be sprinkled over each layer. The Cyanamid should never be applied in excess of 13 pounds per cubic yard, as it might result in the burning of turf or plants when the compost is used.

The mixing may be done by shovelling the material back and forth on a cement floor or some other level surface. After it has been thoroughly mixed it should be screened again and then stored under a shelter in a wooden bin or in some place where the pile will not be disturbed.

It usually requires from four to six weeks to obtain a complete kill of all weed seeds, provided the weather is mild. It requires considerably longer in cold weather. The work should preferably be done during the warm months.

Cover Crops. Cover crops are often spoken of as "green manures." The term is applied to crops which are grown for the sole purpose of being plowed or spaded under, in order to improve the physical texture of the soil, to increase its organic content, and to increase its fertility. Such a procedure is one of the best and also one of the least expensive methods of improving poor, worn-out soils. It is, on the whole, more suitable for large-scale operations than for use on small areas. It may play a very important part, however, in the initial preparation of the soil for a vegetable garden or a fruit orchard, or for a lawn area.

The most valuable cover crops, from the standpoint of increasing the fertility of the soil, are the legumes, such as soybeans, alfalfa, the clovers, and the vetches. The legumes actually increase the nitrogen content of the soil through the aid of the nitrogen-fixing bacteria. These highly specialized bacteria, which have the ability to take nitrogen from the air, are minute, rod-shaped bodies which are found in the soil under certain favorable conditions. When these bacteria come into contact with the roots of certain legume plants, they enter the root hairs, causing a slight irritation which results in the growth of a tiny, round ball called a nodule. These bacteria take nitrogen from the air and supply it to the plant. The plant, in return, furnishes other food matter to the bacteria which enables them to multiply rapidly. This relationship is called symbiosis. There is a slight difference in the forms of bacteria found·on different types of legumes—one form living on one group of legumes, another living only on certain other types. Some legumes, such as alfalfa, are very dependent upon the nitrogen-fixing bacteria and the plants are unable to make vigorous, normal growth, or to survive at all, unless these bacteria are present in the soil. Other legumes, such as soybeans, are considerably less dependent and will make reasonably good growth on soil where no bacteria are present. When grown under such conditions, however, these crops are no more valuable than a non-leguminous crop, as they do not increase the nitrogen content of the soil unless the bacteria are present. In order to insure the presence of these nitrogen-fixing bacteria in the soil all legume crops should be inoculated, previous to planting, with an especially prepared inoculant, carrying the exact type of bacteria needed for the particular legume which is to be grown. Such inoculants are obtainable from any commercial seed house.

The value of legumes as cover crops can hardly be overemphasized. A well-grown leguminous crop which is plowed under at the proper stage of growth will frequently add from 100 to 150 pounds of actual nitrogen to the soil per acre. This would practically equal 10 to 15 tons of good animal manure.

The stage of growth at which cover crops are plowed under has a very direct influence upon the value of the crop. The nitrogen and mineral content are highest shortly before maturity. Therefore, the crop should be plowed under when it is in a slightly immature stage.

If cover crops are to be grown on soils of very low fertility, the eventual value of the crop as a soil improver will be greatly increased if the cover crop receives the benefit of an application of commercial fertilizer, and if conditions are made generally favorable for good growth. There is little to be gained from growing a cover crop on land which is so poor that it can support little in the way of plant growth. Under such conditions, the benefits will hardly justify the cost of seed and labor.

It is a generally accepted fact that the crops which are planted immediately following the plowing under of a cover crop (particularly a non-leguminous crop) will thrive infinitely better if a fairly liberal application of a commercial fertilizer is made at the time that the crop is turned under. The same principle applies to the plowing under of a heavy growth of sod. This is due to the fact that the process of decomposition is carried on by certain of the bacteria in the soil. These bacteria need to use the nitrogen in the soil in order to carry on their activities, and unless a surplus of nitrogen is present the plants suffer in consequence. By applying a highly nitrogenous fertilizer such a surplus may be assured.

DESIRABLE COVER CROPS*

Leguminous Crops

Alfalfa is a perennial crop and consequently requires a longer time to become established than the annual and biennial crops, but there are instances when its use as a cover crop is justified. In a case where a country property is purchased and there are open fields which will eventually be put into lawns, no better use can be made of the land than to put it into alfalfa.

Time and Rate of Seeding: The seed may be sown in early spring or late summer at the rate of 10 to 12 pounds per acre and it should be inoculated. If the field is weedy late summer sowing is preferable.

Soil Requirements: A well-drained soil of reasonably good fertility with a pH of 6·5 or above. (See page 168 for an explanation of pH.)

Time of Plowing Under: Hay may be harvested for a number of years and the crop may be plowed under in the fall or in the spring when the ground is desired for some other purpose, such as a lawn area, garden or orchard. When plowed under, the tops and roots contain approximately 2.65 percent nitrogen and as much as 150 pounds per acre of actual nitrogen may be added to the soil.

Hairy Vetch is a winter annual and is one of the most valuable of all soil builders.

Time and Rate of Seeding: May be sown early in September at the rate of 3 to 4 pecks per acre. The seed should be inoculated.

---

* Dates recommended for plowing under are applicable to the latitude of Pennsylvania and Ohio. In any locality, cover crops should be turned under when slightly immature.

Soil Requirements: It thrives best on a sandy, well-drained soil with a pH of 6.5 or slightly above.

Time of Plowing Under: Should be plowed under about the middle of May. If turned under at this season the top growth and roots will contain approximately 3.75 percent nitrogen.

Mammoth Red Clover. Being a biennial, it is necessary for red clover to occupy the ground for a considerable length of time and it is therefore not as well suited for a cover crop as are some of the other legumes, although it is rated as a splendid soil builder.

Time and Rate of Seeding: It should be sown very early in the spring, preferably with a small grain crop such as oats, or on a wheat crop sown the previous fall. Rate of seeding—8–12 pounds per acre. Inoculate seed.

Soil Requirements: A soil of at least moderate fertility with a pH above 5.5.

Time of Plowing Under: Should be plowed under just before full bloom the year after sowing.

Soybeans are one of the most valuable of all cover crops as they are a summer annual and make rapid growth.

Time and Rate of Seeding: Soybeans should be sown in May or early June at the rate of 2 bushels per acre.

Soil Requirements: If grown on very poor soil a complete fertilizer should be added. Soil should have a pH above 5.

Time of Plowing Under: It is very important that soybeans be plowed under before the vines have become too mature. The most generally accepted practice is to turn them under when the beans in the pods are about half grown. At this stage, the tops and roots will contain approximately 2.65 percent nitrogen.

Sweet Clover is a biennial which possesses tremendous soil building potentialities.

Time and Rate of Seeding: Sweet clover should be sown early in the spring either on, or with, a small grain crop. The usual rate of seeding is 10 to 12 pounds per acre.

Soil Requirements: Sweet clover is one of the few legumes which will grow well on very poor soil. It thrives reasonably well on washed clay land. Its one definite requirement is a soil high in lime content with a pH of 6.5 or above.

Time of Plowing Under: The crop may be plowed under the spring following seeding. In order to secure good results it is essential that it be turned under before it reaches maturity. If plowed under between April 15 and May 1 the maximum percentage of nitrogen will be secured, often running as high as 3.75 percent.

Non-Leguminous Crops

Rye is considered the most valuable of all the non-legumes as a cover crop. Although it does not increase the actual nitrogen content of the soil appreciably, it adds a considerable amount of organic matter.

Time and Rate of Seeding: Rye should be sown during early September, being seeded at the rate of 1½ to 2 bushels per acre.

Soil Requirements: Rye succeeds reasonably well on a soil of average fertility and is almost entirely indifferent to the matter of soil acidity, thriving well on decidedly acid soil.

Time of Plowing Under: Rye should be plowed under in the spring when it has reached a height of approximately 10 inches. At this time the plant contains a greater percentage of nitrogen than at any other stage of its development, sometimes running as high as 1.75 percent.

Rye and Hairy Vetch may be sown in combination, and make a very excellent cover crop.

Time and Rate of Seeding: They should be seeded early in September at the rate of 5 pecks per acre, the mixture containing 60 pounds of rye to 20 pounds of hairy vetch.

Soil Requirements: Soil pH above 6.5 because of the vetch.

Time of Plowing Under: About the middle of May.

ANIMAL MANURES

Long before commercial fertilizers were thought of, the good qualities of animal manures in improving and maintaining soil fertility were known and appreciated. Not only does animal manure increase the fertility of the soil, but it also serves other important functions as well. It increases the organic content of the soil; it improves the physical structure of the soil; it increases the bacterial activity to a very appreciable degree; and it has, in general, a very beneficial effect upon the soil.

Contrary to popular belief, the actual elements of fertility contained in animal manures are very meager when compared with those contained in most inorganic commercial fertilizers. The following table indicates the usual percentages found in various types of manure.

	NITROGEN	PHOSPHORUS	POTASSIUM
Poultry Manure	1.0	0.8	0.4
Sheep Manure	0.95	0.35	1.0
Horse Manure	0.7	0.25	0.55
Cow Manure	0.6	0.15	0.45
Pig Manure	0.5	0.35	0.4

It is even more startling to realize that, low as the above percentages may seem, only one-half of the nitrogen, one-half of the potassium and one-sixth of the phosphorus are readily available for use by the plants. It can, therefore, be seen that the actual fertility added to the soil by an application of animal manure is very slight, and that the benefits derived from such an application are those which are more directly concerned with the physical character of the soil.

The value of animal manure, from a standpoint of fertility, depends to a considerable extent upon the method of handling. If a high percentage of the nutrients which it contains as fresh manure is to be conserved it must be handled with care. The most generally accepted practice is to store manure under cover, to keep it piled in watertight pits and to keep the stack constantly moist, never allowing it to dry out or to become fire-fanged through overheating. If manure is not properly handled it may lose a very large percentage of its nutrients and it may become practically valueless from a standpoint of increasing the actual fertility of the soil.

The rate of application of stable manure varies from what is considered a moderate application of 15 tons per acre to an extremely heavy application of 40 tons per acre; or from 70 pounds per 1,000 square feet to 2,000 pounds per 1,000 square feet.

Fresh manure should never be used where it will come into direct contact with the root formation of the plants as it is liable to cause severe burning. Most gardeners prefer to use manure after it has become partially rotted. In this form the nutrients are more readily available and the danger of any harmful effects is largely mitigated. On large-scale operations manure is usually spread upon the surface of the soil and is then plowed in. On smaller areas it is forked or spaded into the soil.

Dehydrated Manures. There are various forms of dry, shredded and pulverized manures on the market. From the standpoint of economy, such manures are a poor investment. During the process of dehydrating, some of the nitrogen is lost, and comparatively little actual fertility is added to the soil. For the same expenditure, far better results may be obtained from the use of domestic humus and commercial fertilizers.

Liquid Manures. The type of liquid manure formerly used to a considerable extent by gardeners was made by immersing a bushel of manure in a barrel of water. The modern method which consists of dissolving a highly concentrated nitrogenous fertilizer, such as nitrate of soda, urea, or ammonium sulphate, or a well-balanced complete fertilizer, in water and thus applying it to the plant is far superior both from a standpoint of economy, ease of application, and the reliability of the results.

ARTIFICIAL MANURE

In these days when manure is often difficult to obtain, it is a source of satisfaction to the gardener to be able to make an artificial manure which is very similar in every way to the natural product. This may be done by mixing commercial fertilizers and lime with straw, hay, weeds, grass clippings, leaves or any other garden refuse. It is essential that this work be undertaken in the late spring or early summer as the decomposition of the material is dependent upon bacterial action, and correct temperature and abundant moisture are factors of vital importance. To each ton of straw or other litter, the following ingredients should be added—

> 60 pounds sulphate of ammonia
> 30 pounds superphosphate
> 25 pounds potassium chloride
> 50 pounds ground limestone

The method of making artificial manure resembles that for making compost, previously outlined, but for convenience it is repeated here. The pile should be approximately 4 to 6 feet wide, 4 feet high and any desired length. A 4-inch layer of composting material should be placed upon the surface of the ground. This should be liberally sprinkled with the fertilizing ingredients and it should then be thoroughly soaked with water. This process should be repeated until the pile has reached the desired height. The top of the pile should be slightly hollow, or concave, so that it will retain as much water as possible. Unless the rainfall is unusually heavy, the pile should be soaked daily for the period of a week or more in order that the bacterial action may be promoted as rapidly as possible. After the process of decomposition has started, a thorough weekly soaking will usually be sufficient. The sides as well as the top of the pile should be soaked, and the pile should be kept moist at all times. Within three or four months the material should have become sufficiently decomposed, and it will have a composition very similar to a good quality barnyard manure. One ton of straw will produce approximately three tons of organic material.

PLANT NUTRITION

In order to provide for an adequate supply of nutrients in the soil it is essential to understand something of the method by which plants manufacture their food from the elements obtained from the soil and the air.

There are fifteen elements which are known to be essential for the nutrition of plants. Three of these elements, carbon, hydrogen and oxygen, are obtained from water or from the atmosphere. The remaining twelve, nitrogen, phosphorus, potassium, calcium, magnesium, boron, copper, manganese, molybdenum, iron, sulfur and zinc, are normally obtained from the soil. These mineral nutrients in the soil can be utilized by the plant only when they are in solution and can be absorbed through the root hairs. When foliar feeding is practiced there is absorption of the minerals through the leaves.

From these fifteen essential elements a plant is able, in the presence of light, to manufacture sugars, proteins and other complex organic substances which are used for the maintenance of existing tissues and for the production of new tissue. As long as these essential elements are present in sufficient amounts the plant is able to continue this process of food manufacture. However, if one or more of these elements is not available to the plant in sufficient quantity, the

production of food becomes limited and the growth and vigor of the plant is affected.

The twelve mineral elements which are essential for normal growth are divided into two general groups, the major elements, and the minor, or trace, elements. In the first group we find nitrogen, phosphorus, potassium, calcium and magnesium. Since the days of early scientific investigation it has been recognized that these elements are essential for plant growth and each of these elements fulfills an important function.

The three elements which are most likely to be deficient in soils which have been brought under cultivation are nitrogen, phosphorus, and potassium.

Nitrogen

Nitrogen is an essential element for plant growth. Its most important function is to stimulate vegetative development and it is, therefore, particularly necessary in the production of leaves and stems. If an excess of nitrogen is applied, the effects are decidedly harmful, as it will result in an overluxuriant growth of foliage at the expense of flowers and fruit, and maturity will consequently be delayed. The cell walls of the stems will also become weakened and the plant's resistance to disease will be appreciably lowered.

Nitrogen is seldom found in the soil in a free state, it being almost invariably found in combination with other elements. Soils are usually lowest in available nitrogen during the early spring months and it is at this season that quickly available nitrogenous fertilizers are of particular value. It also sometimes happens that in prolonged periods of heavy rains during the summer much of the available nitrogen is leached out of the soil, and when such a condition occurs an immediate application of nitrogen should be made.

Sources of Inorganic Nitrogen

When applying nitrogen in any of the inorganic forms, the material should not come into direct contact with the foliage of the plant as it may cause severe burning. If it is accidentally dropped on to the foliage it should be washed off immediately with a strong spray of water.

Nitrate of Soda. The most quickly available form of nitrogen is nitrate of soda which contains approximately 15 percent nitrogen. Upon application it is almost immediately available to the plant. It is more quickly available in acid soils than in alkaline soils. It should be used only on well-established plants which are making active growth and the soil should be moist when an application is made. Nitrate of soda may be applied in the dry form, the substance being scattered upon the surface of the soil at the rate of 1 pound to 100 square feet, or it may be applied in the form of a solution, being dissolved in water at the rate of 1 ounce to 2 gallons of water. In soils where lime is not present, the long-continued use of nitrate of soda may cause a toxic condition, because of an undue accumulation of sodium carbonate.

Calcium Nitrate contains 15 percent nitrogen. It is readily available, but leaves a decidedly alkaline residue in the soil and it is, therefore, not as generally used as nitrate of soda. The rate of application is approximately the same.

Ammonium Sulphate is a by-product obtained in the manufacture of coal-gas, and it contains approximately 20 percent or more of nitrogen in a readily available form. In warm soils it is often as quickly available as is nitrate of soda, and it has been proven that in alkaline soils its availability is even quicker and greater than nitrate of soda. When it is used over a period of many years it has a tendency to develop an acid reaction in the soil, but any difficulty of this nature may be readily overcome by the use of lime. When ammonium sulphate is applied to acid soils the results will be more satisfactory if it is used in combination with superphosphate, than if it is used alone. The usual rate of application varies from 1 to 2 pounds per 100 square feet, or, in the form of a solution, 1 ounce to 2 gallons of water.

Urea is a synthetic form of nitrogen, being a combination of ammonia and carbon dioxide. It contains 46 percent nitrogen in a form which is quickly soluble, but it is not as quick in its action as nitrate of soda. Being a highly concentrated form of nitrogen, urea must be used with care and discretion. When applied dry it should be mixed with sand, in order that an even distribution may be secured. It is usually applied at the rate of $\frac{1}{2}$ pound per 100 square feet. In the liquid form it is used at the rate of 1 ounce to 7 gallons of water.

Ammonium Phosphate is obtainable in two forms—as mono-ammonium phosphate which contains 10 percent nitrogen and 48 percent phosphoric acid; and as di-ammonium phosphate, which is more highly concentrated and contains 21 percent nitrogen and 53 percent phosphoric acid. A similar material is put out under the trade name of ammophos. The usual rate of application of ammonium phosphate varies from 1 to 2 pounds per 100 square feet.

Cyanamid is another synthetic product of fairly high concentration, being composed of calcium cyanamide and calcium hydroxide. It contains from 20 to 25 percent of nitrogen and it is highly alkaline in its reaction. The usual rate of application is approximately 1 pound per 100 square feet.

Nitrophoska. A series of highly concentrated complete fertilizers have been put out under the trade name of Nitrophoska, and these furnish an excellent source of nitrogen. Several combinations are available, analyzing 15–30–15, 15.5–15.5–19 and 15–11–26. (See page 164 for explanation of this ratio.) The rate of application varies from 1 to 2 pounds per 100 square feet.

Urea-form Fertilizers. A recent advance in the field of chemical fertilizers, and one which will be a great boon to gardeners, is the development of a fertilizer which releases the nitrogen which it contains slowly, over a period of many months, and thereby entirely eliminates the danger of "burning". One of the greatest objections to the commercial chemical fertilizers which have been used so widely in the past has been the danger of burning plant tissues. Many a lawn and many young plants in the vegetable garden and the flower garden have been injured in this way. One of the reasons that organic fertilizers have been preferred by many gardeners is that there is considerably less danger of burning, although in the case of organic fertilizer a delayed nitrogen burn sometimes occurs a month or more after application.

The principal source of nitrogen in the recently introduced urea-form fertilizers is a urea-formaldehyde compound which releases nitrogen slowly and will not cause burning, even under the most adverse conditions.

In extensive experimental tests fertilizers of this type have given most outstanding results when applied to lawns and to ornamental plants, producing vigorous growth and a marked resistance to disease.

One of the great advantages of fertilizers of this type is that the nitrogen needs of a plant for the entire season may be supplied in one application. This is a factor of considerable importance in the management of large areas of turf and in the fertilization of shrub plantings, flower-beds and long-season vegetables. It is of less importance in the case of quickly-maturing flower and vegetable crops.

Sources of Organic Nitrogen

In general the organic forms of nitrogen are less highly concentrated than the inorganic forms and are more slowly available to the plants.

Cottonseed Meal contains approximately 7 percent of nitrogen which becomes slowly available over a long period of time. It is more readily available in warm soils than in cold soils. The usual rate of application varies from 2 to 5 pounds per 100 square feet. There is practically no danger of overstimulation of the plants or of burning when cottonseed meal is used, and in addition to nitrogen it supplies other elements of fertility in small amounts. The usual analysis is 7 percent nitrogen, 2 to 3 percent phosphorus, 2 percent potash.

Castor Pomace is very similar to cottonseed meal in general composition, containing slightly less nitrogen. The nitrogen content usually averages about 5 percent and a somewhat heavier application is therefore made.

Dried Blood is an excellent organic source of nitrogen, containing from 9 to 14 percent. The nitrogen is in a form which is readily soluble and therefore quickly available to the plant. The usual rate of application varies from 2 to 3 pounds per 100 square feet.

Phosphorus

Phosphorus is an essential element in all functions of plant growth and it is particularly associated with the production of fruits and seeds. It also induces good root development, contributes toward the formation of strong cell walls and, in general, hastens maturity. Phosphorus also helps to balance an overabundance of nitrogen in the soil. Phosphorus is fixed in the soil soon after it is applied and it does not leach out. As it does not travel in the soil it must be absorbed by the plant at the point where it falls. There is practically no danger from excessive applications. The acidity of the soil determines to some extent the availability of phosphorus, it being more available in slightly acid soils than in definitely alkaline soils. The presence of ammonium sulphate increases its availability, while the presence of calcium carbonate, sodium nitrate, and iron salts decreases it.

Sources of Phosphorus

Superphosphate is the most commonly used source of phosphorus, and it is obtainable in various grades—

16, 20, or 45 percent. It is the product which results from treating raw phosphate rock with sulphuric acid. The rate of application varies from 3 to 10 pounds per 100 square feet, according to the needs of the soil.

When superphosphate is applied as a top dressing, its penetration is very slow. It is wise, therefore, to work it thoroughly into the soil whenever it is possible to do so, either by lightly forking it in, or by cultivating it in with a hand weeder.

Basic Slag, a by-product in the manufacture of steel, is sometimes used as a source of phosphorus. It usually contains from 10 to 25 percent phosphoric acid and from 40 to 50 percent lime. The phosphorus in basic slag is practically all available, as it becomes water soluble as soon as it is acted upon by carbon dioxide. The rate of application is approximately the same as for superphosphate.

Bone Meal. Raw bone meal is made from finely ground bone and contains from 3 to 4 percent nitrogen and from 20 to 25 percent phosphoric acid. Although the phosphorus content may seem high, it is held in a tricalcium form, and is very, very slowly available. The small percentage of nitrogen is quickly available but the phosphorus becomes available so slowly that, in many instances, the use of bone meal is of doubtful value. It is true that it is one of the safest and most foolproof fertilizers which one can use—but unless it is applied many months before it is needed, the plants will derive practically no benefit from it. Steamed bone meal is of even less value than raw bone meal as during the process of steaming some of the nitrogen is lost. The fineness of bone meal has a very direct effect upon its availability, and weather conditions also have some influence as, regardless of the time of year when it is applied, it seldom becomes available until warm weather. On the whole, when plants are in need of phosphorus, it is wiser to apply it in the form of superphosphate than in the form of bone meal.

Rock Phosphate is the material which is used in the manufacture of superphosphate. While it usually contains from 66 to 80 percent calcium phosphate, its availability is very low and its use is not recommended.

Potassium

Potassium is of particular value in promoting the general vigor of the plant and it increases the resistance of the plant to certain diseases. Potassium also plays an important part in sturdy root formation. In general, it has a balancing influence on other plant nutrients.

Sources of Potassium

Potassium chloride is one of the most commonly used sources of potash. It contains from 48 to 50 percent in a readily available form, as it is immediately soluble. The usual rate of application is 1 pound to 100 square feet.

Muriate of Potash contains approximately 45 percent potash and is applied at the same rate.

Potassium sulphate is another inorganic source of potash, containing approximately 48 percent potash. It is readily soluble, and therefore quickly available to the plant.

Wood Ashes are also a valuable source of potash, although much less highly concentrated than the inorganic forms. Wood ashes vary tremendously in composition. Ash produced from hardwood trees, and which has not been leached by exposure to rain, often runs as high as 10 percent available potash, while wood ashes produced from softwood trees, or wood ashes which have been exposed to rain may contain less than 2 percent potash. Wood ashes also run high in lime content, sometimes containing as much as 40 percent lime. The type of wood ashes most readily available on the market is a high-grade, unleached hardwood ash. Wood ashes are usually applied at the rate of 50 to 75 pounds per 1,000 square feet.

THE TRACE ELEMENTS

The minor or trace elements of essential minerals are boron, copper, iron, manganese, molybdenum, sulphur and zinc. In recent years scientific studies of these elements have brought out the important part which they play in plant nutrition.

The term "trace" refers not to the amount of the element in the soil, but to the amount needed by the plant. Although these elements are needed only in infinitesimal amounts, they are of great importance, and may mean the difference between healthy and sickly, stunted growth. A number of plant diseases are caused by a lack of one or more of the trace elements. In certain crops spectacular increases in yield resulted where the required minerals were supplied to meet the needs of the plants.

Trace elements are usually present in most soils. However, some soils lack one or more of these important minerals, or if present they may be in a form unavailable to the plants. Some soils in Florida and in the Southwest were found to be deficient in some elements. Remarkable improvement in growth of oranges, pecans and other fruits and vegetables occurred when the needed element was supplied.

Many of the complete commercial fertilizers contain the trace elements which are most likely to be deficient in the soil. The manufacturers of high-analysis, quickly soluble fertilizers usually include them in their formulas.

Some organic fertilizers are a poor source of trace elements, while others are a very rich source. Only when the raw materials which are the components of an organic fertilizer contain the trace elements will they be present in the finished product. Thus a good organic fertilizer should contain a variety of organic materials. The best organic sources of trace elements are dried blood and fish emulsion, which contain the major and minor elements in highly soluble form.

The development of the chelating agents have made it possible to make certain trace elements, such as iron and zinc, more readily available to plants than has been possible heretofore.

The best program for the gardener to follow is to use either organic or inorganic fertilizers which contain the trace elements.

COMPLETE FERTILIZERS

For general garden use, for lawns, for the vegetable and fruit garden, for the flower border, and for trees and shrubs, an application of a well balanced complete fertilizer is the most satisfactory method of supplying the needed plant nutrients. Such fertilizers are usually based on a ratio of 1 percent nitrogen, 2 percent phosphorus and 1 percent potash, or 1 percent nitrogen, 3 percent phosphorus and 1 percent potash, or any desired multiple of these ratios—such as 2–6–2, 4–12–4; 5–10–5, 15–30–15. Whenever the analysis of a complete commercial fertilizer is stated in such a way as is outlined above, the first numeral denotes the percentage of *nitrogen,* the second numeral the percentage of *phosphorus,* and the third numeral the percentage of *potash.* In addition to these three essential elements of fertility which are always present in any "complete" fertilizer, there are also usually present some of the minor, or trace, elements which are needed in very small amounts, such as manganese, iron, and sulphur. In the preparation of commercial fertilizers most reliable firms make it a practice to supply the required amount of nitrogen in two, sometimes three, forms; in a quickly available inorganic form, in a somewhat more slowly available form, and in a very slowly available organic form. Such a practice greatly increases the value of any fertilizer from the standpoint of the gardener, as it means that the nitrogen becomes available for the use of the plant over a long period of time.

The time and rate of application of complete commercial fertilizers vary considerably with the individual requirements of the plant and the purpose of the application. The most approved fertilizer practices are discussed in detail in the various chapters on Lawns, Roses, Perennials, Greenhouse Crops, etc.

SOLUBLE FERTILIZERS

The development of high-analysis, quickly soluble, complete fertilizers has solved many problems for the gardener, as they can be applied both to the soil and to the foliage without danger of harming plant tissues, provided they are used in proper concentration.

The quickly soluble fertilizers are water-soluble salts, to be dissolved in water before use. The concentrated solutions are uneconomical, because of the costs of packing and shipping large amounts of liquid. It is wiser to use the salts. Directions given on the package should be followed.

Soluble fertilizers contain the same nutrient elements as do the standard complete fertilizers—nitrogen, phosphate and potash—and often in the same proportions, but usually in higher analysis. Some brands contain most of the trace elements and some also vitamins and hormones. This is an advantage if they are to be used for foliage feeding.

These high-analysis, soluble fertilizers can be used to advantage in many ways. They can be applied directly to the soil to promote the growth and vigor of house plants, flowering plants of all types, vegetables, ornamental trees and shrubs. Being in solution, the nutrients become almost immediately available to the plant. They can be applied as a spray to the foliage of the plant. (See Foliar Feeding, page 167.) They can be used as a pre-planting dip for seeds to quicken germination and promote a more vigorous growth of the young seedlings. They may be used as a dip for leafy, soft-wood cuttings to develop more vigorous plants. They may be used as a solution in which to soak bulbs and tubers, such as tulips and tuberous begonias, in order to increase their vigor and size of bloom. And they may be used very satisfactorily on small lawn areas. They are not practical on extensive areas of lawn unless application can be made by a commercial outfit having the necessary equipment.

It has been found that when young seedlings or rooted cuttings are to be transplanted, or when older plants are to be moved from one location to another, they will suffer less of a setback if given an application of a high-analysis soluble fertilizer. In the case of young plants, best results will be obtained if the fertilizer is applied to the propagating bed, seed bed, or flat in which the plants are growing, about three days previous to the time of transplanting. The benefits will be greater than if the application is made at the actual time of transplanting. In the case of purchased plants it is, of course, not possible to follow this procedure. When the application is made at the time of transplanting one cup of the solution should be allowed for a small plant, two cups for a large plant. The solution should be poured around the plant before the hole has been completely filled.

These starter or booster solutions may be used to great advantage in the vegetable garden when setting out tomatoes, cabbage, cauliflower, broccoli, pepper and celery plants, and they are also very valuable when transplanting annuals, biennials and perennials in the flower garden.

High analysis, soluble fertilizers are more expensive per unit of plant food than the standard complete fertilizers, but they more than justify the additional expense. They are easy to mix and apply; the danger of "burning" plant tissue is eliminated; they are procurable in small quantities and there is no waste.

In handling these soluble fertilizers a number of precautions should be taken. Soluble salts should not be stored in light-weight paper containers, because the container will deteriorate. Glass mason jars with screw tops are excellent for long periods of storage. If a solution is to be kept over from one application to another it should be stored in a glass or earthenware jug, but *not* in a metal container.

UNIVERSITY OF WISCONSIN METHOD OF FEEDING

After years of research the University of Wisconsin has developed a method of feeding plants which is so revolutionary that it has been granted a patent by the U.S. Patent Office.

Highly concentrated fertilizer is packed in a very small plastic bag which resists deterioration in the soil. The plastic is punctured with microscopic holes that allow water to seep in and dissolve some of the fertilizer. The dissolved fertilizer can only be forced out when enough water accumulates inside to create internal pressure.

By controlling the make-up of the fertilizer and the size of the holes in the plastic, a package will continue to supply plant food over a period of from three to five years, as the dissolved fertilizer is released at a rate equal to absorption by the plant. The packet acts as a reservoir slowly releasing the nitrogen, phosphate and potash in correctly controlled proportions. When this method is used there is no danger of injury to tender roots, and it also means a great saving of time and labor.

This method is recommended for the feeding of established trees and for trees at time of planting (page 219), for roses at time of planting and for established beds (page 128), for potted plants (page 444) and for perennials when feasible.

This product is manufactured and sold under license from the Wisconsin Alumni Research Foundation under the name Eeezy-Gro.

The word chelate (pronounced keylate) is derived from the Greek word for claw, as the chelates may be likened to two claws which catch and hold metal ions. When chelates are applied to the soil the metal does not combine with other elements to form insoluble compounds but remains free to be taken up and used by the plants. On the other hand, when simple iron compounds are used they often combine to make insoluble compounds, and thus become unavailable to the plants. This explains why plants sometimes suffer from iron chlorosis or iron starvation when the soil actually contains sufficient iron for normal plant growth, and it also explains why additional applications of simple iron compounds on soils definitely deficient in iron often fail to correct the chlorotic condition. It is their ability to hold the iron in the form in which plants can readily make use of it that gives the chelates their great importance.

The symptoms of iron deficiency in plants are not difficult to detect. In mild cases the veins of the leaf appear to be a darker green than the areas between the veins. If the deficiency is pronounced the areas between the veins gradually become a lighter green, then yellowish in appearance, and, finally, in a severe case of iron chlorosis, the foliage becomes a very pale ivory color. Unless the condition is corrected it will eventually cause the death of the plant.

Iron chelates are used extensively in citrus groves and in the great commercial flower and vegetable growing areas in California and Florida and many other sections. In some instances the effects of an application have been little short of miraculous. In one citrus grove the foliage on the orange trees which were suffering from acute iron chlorosis became green again within six weeks and the vigor of the trees was entirely restored.

Iron chelates are also of great value to the home gardener for the treatment of ornamental plants which are suffering from iron starvation, and for use on orchard trees and vegetable crops.

Among ornamental plants suffering from iron

chlorosis which have responded well to applications of the iron chelates are azaleas, camellias, chrysanthemums, gardenias, gladioli, hydrangeas, magnolias, oaks, rhododendrons, and roses.

Iron chelates may be applied directly to the soil in either powder or liquid form, or may be dissolved in water and applied as a foliar spray. When applied to the soil in the powder form it should be spread evenly over the surface of the soil beneath the plant at the recommended rate, and it should then be watered in thoroughly until the soil is moist to a depth of at least six inches. It will be easier to obtain an even coverage if the powder is mixed with dry sand or fertilizer. The powder may, if desired, be dissolved in water and either sprayed on to the soil or applied with a watering can.

When a foliar spray is applied it is important to make sure that all leaf surfaces are thoroughly covered. When foliar sprays are applied to outdoor plants there will be less danger of injury if the application is made during the middle third of the growing season. It is not advisable to apply foliage sprays to plants when they are in blossom or in fruit.

The iron chelates are available under various trade names such as Perma Green Iron 135, Versene and Versenol. Directions concerning rates of application should be followed with care.

FOLIAR FEEDING

Trees, shrubs, roses, many flowering plants, and vegetables respond well to foliar feeding, and it is becoming a common practice among amateur gardeners as well as among professional gardeners.

Foliar feeding is of particular value in supplying trace elements where a deficiency exists, and often on cold, wet soils nitrogen and phosphorus can be made more readily available to the plant through foliar feeding than through application to the soil.

Scientific research has proved, through the use of radioisotopes, that at least one half of the nitrogen in a good all-soluble, high-analysis fertilizer enters the leaf directly within a few hours after application, and that a reasonable percentage of the phosphorus and potassium is also absorbed in this way. In addition to these major elements (nitrogen, phosphorus and potash) many of the minor or trace elements such as iron, zinc, boron and manganese may also be applied in the form of foliage sprays.

In purchasing soluble fertilizers to be used for foliar feeding it is wise to make sure that they contain these trace elements. In certain soils there may be definite deficiency of some of the trace elements, whereas in other soils they may be present but unavailable to the plant, and one of the most satisfactory ways of supplying them is through foliar feeding.

Experiments have shown that "chelated" (organic) forms of some of these minor elements are very effective in overcoming deficiencies when applied as foliar sprays. Iron in the "chelate" form has proved very effective in controlling chlorosis of lawns, deciduous fruits and vegetables, and zinc in the "chelate" form is effective in controlling a number of conditions attributable to a deficiency of this element.

Some plants can absorb nutrients through their leaves more readily than others. Absorption of nutrients normally takes place more readily through the lower surface to the leaves than through the upper surface. Where the leaves possess a heavily waxed surface it has been found that the absorption of nutrients is usually very restricted or entirely inhibited.

There are many satisfactory types of applicators on the market suitable for applying liquid fertilizers as foliar sprays. It is important not to use too concentrated a solution and the manufacturer's directions should be followed with care.

Excellent results have been obtained from the foliar feeding of many types of plants. Greenhouse and indoor plants seem to respond particularly well. Orchids, Anthuriums, Philodendron, African Violets, Gloxinias, Achimenes, Streptocarpus, Crotons, Ferns, and certain forms of cactus, such as the Christmas Cactus, have shown excellent response. In some cases the increase in the health and vigor of the plants has been spectacular. At the Montreal Botanical Garden where young African Violet plants which were yellowish and sickly in appearance were given a foliar feeding the response was almost immediate. Within a few days the leaves had turned a dark green and the plants had a totally different appearance. The accepted practice in many greenhouses is to give two or three weekly feedings at first, followed by monthly feedings. Sometimes one or two feedings applied at a critical time in the life of a plant are all that is necessary.

Certain insecticides may be applied at the same time that foliar feedings are given, which means a considerable saving of labor.

It must be borne in mind that foliar feedings do not take the place of root feedings; they are definitely a supplementary feeding, not a substitute.

SOIL TESTS

Since it is sometimes difficult to determine deficiencies which are not pronounced, yet which may be of considerable importance, it is well to have an occasional soil analysis made. Soil samples may be sent to any of the State Agriculture Experiment Stations for analysis.

Obtaining Soil Samples

The season when the sample is taken, the method of obtaining the sample, and the preparation of the sample are all factors of importance.

Time of Sampling. The most reliable information concerning the need for fertilization and for the application of lime may be obtained from samples taken either in the early spring or in late fall. During the active growing season the nutrient level of the soil is affected to some extent by the growth of the plants which occupy the area. Heavy rainfalls also very definitely affect the nutrient level and low tests are frequently secured after periods of prolonged leaching. Nitrates and ammonia nitrogen are the most variable, as they are the elements which are the most easily lost by leaching.

Method of Sampling. A trowel or spade may be used to make a V-shaped hole, 6 or 7 inches deep. Remove the loose dirt from the hole and then cut a thin, uniform slice off the straight side of the hole from top to bottom. If the sample is being taken from a lawn area it should represent the zone of the feeding roots, which will vary from 3 to 6 inches. If the area to be tested is of considerable size, or if it varies in texture to any marked degree, it will be necessary to obtain several samples. If there is a decided variance in the general character of the soil, one section being of a sandy texture and another section having a more dense structure, the samples should be kept separate. If the soil is uniform in character, the samples may be mixed together, forming a composite sample.

Preparing the Sample. After the sample has been obtained, the soil should be spread out to dry on a clean sheet of paper. Care should be taken to prevent the soil from becoming contaminated with dust, fumes or chemicals of any kind.

After the soil is thoroughly dry it should be packed for shipment.

SOIL ACIDITY

The relative acidity or alkalinity of the soil is commonly expressed in terms of the symbol pH. The neutral point in the scale is 7. Soil testing below a pH 7 is acid; soil testing above pH 7 is alkaline.

SOIL-TESTING SCALE

pH 9.5	intensely alkaline
pH 9.	strongly alkaline
pH 8.5	definitely alkaline
pH 8.	moderately alkaline
pH 7.7	slightly alkaline
pH 7.	neutral
pH 6.5	very slightly acid
pH 6.	slightly acid
pH 5.5	moderately acid
pH 5.	moderately acid
pH 4.5	definitely acid
pH 4.	strongly acid
pH 3.5	intensely acid

The pH values are based on logarithms, 10 being the base. Therefore, a soil testing pH 5 is 10 times as acid as soil testing pH 6; while a soil testing pH 4 is 100 times as acid as soil testing pH 6. (In going either up or down the pH scale from the neutral point of pH 7, the value of the unit is 10 times greater than the next one approaching 7.)

Most herbaceous plants and the majority of our commonly grown trees and shrubs prefer a soil that is very nearly neutral in its reaction. A few plants seem to be entirely indifferent to soil conditions and will thrive equally well in soil with either a neutral, acid, or alkaline reaction, while some plants definitely prefer a strongly acid soil, and others a soil of pronounced alkalinity. In general garden practice, it is well to maintain a soil reaction as nearly neutral as possible, ranging between a pH 6 and a pH 7.

The reaction of the soil is not a stable factor, as there is a tendency for soils, except in very arid regions, to become, slowly, more and more acid. This is due to the fact that, with the gradual seepage of rainwater through the soil, the elements such as calcium and sodium are dissolved more rapidly than the more strongly acid elements such as carbon and silicon.

Every gardener should know how to make simple, rapid tests to determine the pH of the soil. There are now many very excellent and yet inexpensive soil-testing outfits on the market, and such a kit should be considered an essential part of one's equipment. Complete directions will accompany each outfit and these should be followed with exactitude.

Increasing the Acidity of the Soil

It is a comparatively simple procedure either to increase the degree of acidity in the soil or to bring an acid soil to a more nearly neutral level.

Many woodland plants such as the azaleas, mountain laurel, rhododendrons, trailing arbutus and the pink lady's slipper prefer a definitely acid soil. For such plants a pH ranging between 4.5 and 5.5 is desirable.

When such plants are to be grown the soil should be tested and if it does not fall within this range, measures should be taken to increase the acidity. This may be accomplished in a number of ways.

Method No. 1. The ideal method, and the one strongly recommended if the existing soil is fertile and of good texture, is to incorporate into the soil certain organic materials which will increase its acidity. The following materials may be used for this purpose:

Acid muck from swamps and stream banks
Oak leafmold

Peat moss, of the coarse, *acid* type
Rotting bark and wood from old logs and stumps of hemlock or oak
Sawdust (partly rotted) from hemlock or oak trees
Sphagnum moss, finely ground.

After the organic materials have been worked thoroughly into the soil another soil test should be made to determine whether the acidity has been brought to the desired level.

Method No. 2. Where the existing soil is of poor quality or where raised beds are to be used it is advisable to prepare a special soil mixture which will provide the desired amount of humus and the correct degree of acidity. Such a mixture should contain at least 50 percent decayed organic matter. The following mixture is recommended: 50 percent coarse, acid peat, 25 percent rotted oak leaf mold, 25 percent sandy loam. If, after testing, this does not provide the desired degree of acidity a small quantity of a chemical may be added according to directions given in Method No. 3.

Method No. 3. There are a number of chemicals which may be applied to the soil to increase the acidity. Among the most satisfactory for this purpose are aluminium sulphate and sulphur. They may be used as a surface application, being spread evenly over the area and watered in thoroughly, or they may be mixed with the soil as the bed is being prepared.

The rate of application is given in the accompanying table.

TABLE FOR INCREASING SOIL ACIDITY*

CHANGE FROM pH	SULPHUR, LBS. PER 100 SQ. FT.	ALUMINIUM SULPHATE, LBS. PER 100 SQ. FT.
8.0–7.0	2.0	4.5
8.0–6.5	3.0	7.0
8.0–6.0	4.0	10.0
8.0–5.5	5.5	13.5
8.0–5.0	7.0	17.5
7.5–7.0	1.75	3.5
7.5–6.5	2.0	5.0
7.5–6.0	3.5	7.5
7.5–5.5	5.0	11.5
7.5–5.0	6.5	15.5
7.0–6.5	1.5	2.5
7.0–6.0	2.0	5.5
7.0–5.5	3.5	9.0
7.0–5.0	5.0	13.0
6.5–6.0	1.5	3.0
6.5–5.5	2.5	6.5
6.5–5.0	4.0	10.5
6.0–5.5	1.5	3.5
6.0–5.0	3.0	7.5
5.5–5.0	1.5	4.0

* Laurie, A. and Reis, V. H. *Floriculture*, p. 374, 1942

A number of fertilizers such as ammonium sulphate, ammonium phosphate, cottonseed meal and urea, have an acid reaction and when applied to the soil over a period of years tend to increase its acidity. Therefore fertilizers of this type should be selected for use on plants which are known to thrive best in acid soils. Some fertilizer companies offer special mixtures suitable for such plants. Fertilizers which are known to be definitely alkaline in their reaction, such as nitrate of soda, calcium nitrate, cyanamide, bone meal and wood ashes, should be avoided.

LIME

Lime serves several important functions. It is of particular value in correcting the acidity of the soil, and, in addition to this function, it also changes the structure of the soil, hastens bacterial action in the soil, aids in the liberation of plant foods which would otherwise remain in the soil in unavailable form, hastens the decomposition of organic matter, and supplies a small amount of calcium, which is one of the essential plant foods.

Lime is usually applied either in the form of ground limestone or as hydrated lime. Hydrated lime is quicker in its action but it is not as lasting in its effect.

Lime should never be used in combination with animal manures or with nitrogenous fertilizers, as it causes the rapid release of ammonia.

When lime is applied it should be spread over the surface of the ground and should then be thoroughly mixed with the upper few inches of soil. It should not be plowed or spaded deeply into the soil.

The rate of application depends entirely upon the forms in which the lime is applied, and the texture of the soil. The table opposite will serve as a general guide.

Danger of Excessive Applications

An excessive application of lime has a very injurious effect upon some plants, causing a condition known as lime-induced chlorosis. This is regarded as a physiological disease, and it is due directly to a deficiency of iron in the plant tissues. The symptoms are very marked in most plants, and are most apt to appear on young growth in the early spring, although they may be noticed at almost any time during the growing season. The leaves present a characteristically mottled appearance, being either yellow or whitish in color. The mid-rib of the leaf and the veins remain a very dark green, and the mottling takes place in the areas between the veins.

Iron is absolutely essential for the production of chlorophyll, which is the green coloring matter of the leaf, and when iron is not present in sufficient quantities, the chlorophyll fails to develop. This deficiency of iron in the plant is very closely associated with the lime content of the soil, as the solubility of iron in the soil is dependent, to a large extent, upon the degree of soil acidity. Iron is readily soluble in a definitely acid soil, but as the pH of the soil approaches the neutral point, the iron becomes less and less soluble. In soils which are decidedly alkaline, comparatively little iron, or, in extreme cases, no iron at all is available for the plant. Therefore the long-continued use, or excessive applications, of lime, bone meal, wood ashes, and certain inorganic fertilizers tend to increase the alkalinity of the soil to a point where it is not favorable for certain forms of plant growth, due to this precipitation of iron, which consequently becomes unavailable to the plant.

In general garden practice, it is well to maintain the soil at a pH slightly below the neutral point, and not to increase its alkalinity beyond a pH of 7.5, which seems to be the point of safety for many plants. There are, of course, special plant groups which are definitely more acid or alkaline tolerant, and some which prefer a decidedly acid soil, but for the majority of garden plants a pH slightly below neutral is the safest.

If a condition of lime-induced chlorosis occurs, it may be corrected by the use of the iron chelates (see page 166).

SOIL CONDITIONERS

Soil conditioners are effective in improving the structure and physical condition of certain types

RATE OF APPLICATION OF LIME*

LIGHT SANDY SOIL

SOIL ACIDITY	HYDRATED LIME		GROUND LIMESTONE	
	per 1,000 sq. ft.	per acre	per 1,000 sq. ft.	per acre
pH 4.0	60 lbs.	2610 lbs.	90 lbs.	3915 lbs.
pH 4.5	55 lbs.	2392 lbs.	82 lbs.	3567 lbs.
pH 5.0	45 lbs.	1957 lbs.	67 lbs.	2914 lbs.
pH 5.5	35 lbs.	1522 lbs.	52 lbs.	2262 lbs.
pH 6.0	None	None	None	None

MEDIUM SANDY SOIL

SOIL ACIDITY	HYDRATED LIME		GROUND LIMESTONE	
	per 1,000 sq. ft.	per acre	per 1,000 sq. ft.	per acre
pH 4.0	80 lbs.	3480 lbs.	120 lbs.	5220 lbs.
pH 4.5	75 lbs.	3263 lbs.	112 lbs.	4872 lbs.
pH 5.0	60 lbs.	2610 lbs.	90 lbs.	3915 lbs.
pH 5.5	45 lbs.	1957 lbs.	67 lbs.	2914 lbs.
pH 6.0	None	None	None	None

LOAM AND SILT LOAM

SOIL ACIDITY	HYDRATED LIME		GROUND LIMESTONE	
	per 1,000 sq. ft.	per acre	per 1,000 sq. ft.	per acre
pH 4.0	115 lbs.	5002 lbs.	172 lbs.	7482 lbs.
pH 4.5	105 lbs.	4567 lbs.	157 lbs.	6827 lbs.
pH 5.0	85 lbs.	3697 lbs.	127 lbs.	5524 lbs.
pH 5.5	65 lbs.	2827 lbs.	97 lbs.	4219 lbs.
pH 6.0	None	None	None	None

CLAY LOAM

SOIL ACIDITY	HYDRATED LIME		GROUND LIMESTONE	
	per 1,000 sq. ft.	per acre	per 1,000 sq. ft.	per acre
pH 4.0	145 lbs.	6307 lbs.	217 lbs.	9439 lbs.
pH 4.5	135 lbs.	5872 lbs.	202 lbs.	8787 lbs.
pH 5.0	100 lbs.	4356 lbs.	150 lbs.	6525 lbs.
pH 5.5	80 lbs.	3480 lbs.	120 lbs.	5220 lbs.
pH 6.0	None	None	None	None

NOTE: A light application of lime at the rate of 25 lbs. per 1,000 sq. ft. has proved beneficial on certain soils, even though the soil has a pH value of 6.0.

* As it is not advisable to apply more than 50 lbs. of hydrated lime or 75 lbs. of ground limestone per 1,000 sq. ft. at any one time, it will be necessary to make several successive applications on strongly acid soils and raise the pH gradually. It is often detrimental to plant growth to make an excessively heavy application of lime at one time.

of soil. They should not be used indiscriminately, as it is a waste of time and money to apply them to soils which will receive little or no benefit.

The gardener must bear in mind that soil conditioners are not fertilizers and do not increase the nutrient content of the soil. Soil conditioners have been developed for the purpose of maintaining in porous and loose condition clay soils which are normally heavy and tight in structure. On such soils, which are difficult to handle and which present many problems, soil conditioners have proved of great value. Soils of a light, sandy nature and soils high in organic content show little benefit, and rarely justify their use.

Under tillage conditions heavy clay soils have a tendency to become more and more compact and provide poor conditions for plant growth. They contain little pore space and consequently have low air capacity, they lack the ability to absorb water readily, thus making the application of soluble fertilizers difficult, and they are extremely difficult to handle when the moisture content is high. They are thus problem soils.

If a soil conditioner put out by a reliable firm is used, and if the directions on the package are followed, such soils may be maintained in a crumbly and friable condition throughout the season. Water will percolate freely, there will be sufficient pore space for an adequate supply of oxygen for plant needs, and good response can be obtained from soluble fertilizers. A soil so conditioned can grow thrifty, vigorous plants.

Decaying organic matter is nature's soil conditioner, but such material is not always available to the gardener in sufficient quantity to be effective, and in such cases the chemical soil conditioners fill a long-felt need. One pound of a synthetic soil conditioner is equivalent to several bushels of a natural soil conditioner in improving the structure of fine-particled clay soils. Chemical soil conditioners have several advantages over natural soil conditioners. Results will be obtained more quickly, as within a few days after the application of a synthetic conditioner the soil particles will be crumbly and mellow. Also, this improvement in the soil structure will last over a longer period than will be the case in the necessarily limited use of organic materials.

Soil conditioners can be incorporated into the soil most satisfactorily when the soil is neither too wet nor too dry. The surface of the soil should preferably be slightly dry with moist soil just below the surface. The soil conditioner should be worked into the soil to a depth of six inches, the soil being well pulverized during the process. The more thoroughly the chemical is mixed with the soil the better the results. After the conditioner has been thoroughly incorporated into the soil a moderate watering will speed up the chemical reaction. Best results will be obtained if seed sowing and transplanting are delayed for several days after application.

It is a simple matter to determine whether or not a certain soil will benefit from an application of a soil conditioner. The following test will give a reliable indication: Take a *small* handful of the soil; add four or five drops of water to the soil, using a medicine dropper; mix the soil and water together thoroughly until every tiny granule of soil crumbles; roll the soil between the palms of your hands into the form of a cigarette; if the cigarette holds its shape it is an indication that the structure of the soil will be greatly improved by an application of a soil conditioner. If the soil remains granular and cannot be formed into the shape of a cigarette it is evident that a soil conditioner is not needed and that the soil will derive no benefit from its use. If a weak cigarette is formed which flops over at the end when lifted, this indicates that the application of a soil conditioner will be of enough benefit to warrant its use.

When used on a large scale soil conditioners are very expensive, but in preparing soil for house plants, seed beds, and cold frames, and in special limited areas in the garden and on small areas to be seeded to lawn grasses, great benefit will be derived from their use if the soil is of a heavy clay structure.

In the vegetable and cutting garden treatment may be limited to the actual rows or hills where the plants are to be grown.

XVII

LAWNS

WHEN one plants a tree one does so with the full realization that one may be planting for posterity —that it will increase in dignity as the years pass, and that a century or more hence it may still cast welcome shade for those who linger beneath its branches.

It is difficult to realize, however, that a lawn may be as permanent a planting as the trees that cast their shade upon it. Many of the lawns which surround the beautiful manor houses of England were planted more than five hundred years ago and today the fine quality of this English turf is an inspiration to gardeners throughout the world. There are few achievements which bring more lasting satisfaction to the home owner than a fine, well-maintained lawn. Such a piece of turf, luxuriant in growth, healthy and weed-free, is the result of intelligent study of the requirements of lawn grasses, careful planning, adequate preparation, and the faithful adherence to a program of good management.

ESTABLISHMENT OF NEW LAWNS

In the establishment of a new lawn there are many factors which must be taken into consideration: the selection of the grass or mixture of grasses to be used, the preparation of the soil and the improvement of its fertility, the time and method of seeding, and the program of subsequent feeding, mowing and general management.

SELECTION OF GRASSES

Some grasses thrive best under cool, moist growing conditions, while others will withstand extreme heat and drought. Some grasses require a very high level of soil fertility, other types will grow on relatively poor soils; some will grow well in partial shade, other types prefer full sun;

some are suited to withstand heavy traffic and endure hard wear, while others need careful management.

It is therefore important to select a grass or a mixture of grasses which will be well adapted to the climate and will meet the specific need, whether it be a piece of exceptionally fine turf for a terrace, or a rugged piece of turf upon which strenuous games will be played, or a good general purpose lawn for family use and enjoyment.

Before reaching a final decision it is wise to become familiar with the advantages and disadvantages of the various grasses which are adapted to one's locality.

The quality of the seed is also a matter of importance. In purchasing grass seed it is poor economy to buy cheap or "bargain" seed. A lawn should be viewed as a long-term investment and only the best quality of seed from a reliable source should be considered. Cheap seed will usually be low in germination, and is apt to contain a high percentage of chaff and weed seeds or seeds of inferior grasses. State laws require that all grass seeds be labelled and that the following information be available to the purchaser on the tag: percentage of germination, name of each grass and its percentage by weight.

In purchasing grass seed it is important to note the percentage of germination as stated on the tag. In high quality seed the germination percentage should run not lower than 80 percent and preferably 90 percent or higher.

When grass seed mixtures are purchased it is important to also make certain what type of grasses are included in the mixture and the proportion in which they are used. A mixture which includes a high percentage of grasses such as perennial rye grass, redtop, timothy, Canada bluegrass, sheep fescue, and meadow grass should not be considered, as the first two are not permanent grasses and the others are of inferior quality for use as lawn grasses.

IMPORTANT LAWN GRASSES FOR COOL CLIMATES

Bent Grasses

If one does not have to take into consideration the costs of establishment and maintenance, it is possible to achieve a lawn with turf of such supremely fine quality that it will resemble a putting green. It is sometimes possible to develop such a lawn on a small area such as a house terrace or a grass panel in the flower garden, where it would not be practical to attempt it on a larger scale. For such a turf the bent grasses are the most desirable.

Most of the bent grasses are of low-growing, semi-creeping habit and if given proper care they produce a turf of superior quality and beauty. All of the bents are tolerant of considerable soil acidity and thrive best on soils with a pH between 5.5 and 6.5. They do well on moist soils and they are extremely well adapted to close mowing, it being desirable to keep a bent lawn at a height of $\frac{1}{4}$ to $\frac{1}{2}$ inch. The seeds of the bent grasses are very fine and they should be sown at the rate of not more than 2 lbs. per 1,000 sq. ft.

In general the bent grasses are much more exacting in their demands than are most of the other lawn grasses. In addition to an adequate program of fertilization, watering and mowing, it is necessary to apply frequent top dressings of rich compost in order to provide ideal conditions for vigorous growth. The bent grasses are also more subject to attacks from various fungous diseases than are most other grasses. It is wise, therefore, not to attempt to develop a bent grass lawn unless one is fully prepared to meet the additional requirements of labor and expense which are involved.

The three most desirable types of bent grass are Colonial Bent, Creeping Bent and Velvet Bent.

Colonial Bent produces an excellent quality of turf. It is not tolerant of shade but will grow on soils which vary widely in type, and it is moderately drought resistant. It is frequently used as a component of grass seed mixtures and may also be sown alone. A number of strains of Colonial Bent have been developed in various parts of the country to meet specific conditions, the most widely used being Astoria, Highland, New Zealand, Oregon, Penncross, and Rhode Island. The Highland strain is often used as a companion grass with Bermuda grass in the coastal areas of California where it retains its green color throughout much of the winter. It is also recommended as a companion grass for Merion bluegrass in the north central and eastern states.

Creeping Bent: The various strains of Creeping Bent may also be sown alone or in mixture with other grasses. These are the bent grasses most commonly used for putting greens on golf courses. For satisfactory growth they require a cool climate, abundant moisture and high fertility, and they are exacting in their maintenance demands, requiring extremely close cutting. They will thrive in light shade but prefer full sun. Because of their susceptibility to various fungous diseases they are not as well suited to lawn areas as are some of the other types. The most popular strains are Cocoos, Metropolitan, Washington and Seaside. Polycross Creeping Bent is a hybrid which possesses exceptionally desirable qualities, as it produces a turf of fine quality under a wide range of conditions and is more resistant to disease than some of the other strains.

With the exception of Seaside and Polycross, seed is not available and it is necessary to propagate the other strains by stolons. Stolons are the prostrate shoots, characteristic of the bent grasses. These shoots creep along the surface of the ground, forming roots at frequent intervals. The stolons are usually sold in sections of sod, 1 square foot of nursery sod being sufficient to plant from 5 to 10 square feet of area. The ground must be thoroughly prepared before the stolons are planted (see page 181). The sod is cut into small pieces and scattered over the surface of the ground at the rate of 100 pounds per 1,000 square feet. The stolons should be covered immediately with $\frac{1}{2}$ inch of sifted top-soil and they should never be allowed to dry out, either before or after planting.

Velvet Bent is the true aristocrat among lawn grasses and is considered one of the most desirable of all the bent grasses. When once well established it is persistent, vigorous and hardy, and it produces a remarkably fine-textured turf with a velvet-like quality. It is more tolerant of heat than the Creeping Bents, is also more drought-resistant and thrives fairly well in light shade. In addition it has the decided advantage of being more resistant to fungous diseases. Velvet Bent may be grown either from seed or from stolons. It may be grown alone, or in mixture with other grasses. As the seed germinates quickly it does not require a nurse grass when it is sown alone.

Bluegrasses

Kentucky Bluegrass: The majority of home owners wish to have a lawn of luxuriant green turf which will withstand a reasonable amount of wear and which may be easily maintained. If climate and soil conditions are favorable, Kentucky bluegrass will meet these requirements more completely than any other type of grass. There is no other lawn grass which can equal Kentucky bluegrass in its ability to produce a fine dense turf under average conditions of care and maintenance.

However, Kentucky bluegrass has a few very definite requirements for satisfactory growth. It prefers a cool climate, it requires abundant moisture, it thrives best on a mellow, loam soil of good fertility, and it requires a neutral or very slightly acid soil with a pH between 6.0 and 7.0. Kentucky bluegrass is not satisfactory in shady areas, it does not thrive well on sandy, droughty soils, or on soils of low fertility and it is not tolerant of intense midsummer heat. Under such conditions it soon develops into a thin, unsatisfactory turf and is eventually crowded out by inferior grasses and weeds. Kentucky bluegrass makes luxuriant growth during the cool, moist weather of early spring. It tends to go dormant when temperatures remain above 80° F. for any length of time, and during prolonged periods of summer heat and drought it makes little or no growth, often becoming parched and brown in appearance. However, with the coming of cooler weather it revives and continues growth until late in the autumn.

Kentucky bluegrass germinates more slowly than many other lawn grasses and also requires a longer time to become established. It does not begin to form a dense, springy sod until the second year after sowing.

The results will usually be most satisfactory if Kentucky bluegrass is sown in combination with other good lawn grasses, but it should form 50 percent or more of the seed mixture. It is an extremely long-lived and persistent grass and in time, if conditions are favorable, it will often crowd out the other grasses and become completely dominant.

Merion Kentucky Bluegrass: Merion Kentucky bluegrass is the first improved strain of Kentucky bluegrass. This deep-rooting, somewhat creeping strain of bluegrass was observed at the Merion Golf Club in Ardmore, Pennsylvania, by Mr. Joseph Valentine who noted a small patch of it there in 1936. After watching it closely for a few years Mr. Valentine sent samples of it to the Green Section of the U.S. Golf Association at Beltsville, Maryland, where it was developed and tested under the direction of Dr. Fred Grau. Merion Kentucky bluegrass has a wider climatic range than Kentucky bluegrass. It thrives well in the more southern sections of the bluegrass region where Kentucky bluegrass is sometimes difficult to maintain and it also thrives well on the West Coast. It does not do well on very light, sandy soils.

Merion Kentucky bluegrass is a deeper green in color than Kentucky bluegrass, is more spreading in habit of growth, and slightly coarser in texture. It has a deep root system, requires a good soil and liberal feeding. It is more drought-resistant than Kentucky bluegrass, red fescue or the bent grasses, and will remain green during periods of heat and dry weather when most other grasses are brown and dormant. Merion Kentucky bluegrass does not go dormant in the summer until the temperature reaches the upper 90's. Merion Kentucky bluegrass also retains its green color during the winter better than almost any other grass. It is in active growth every day during the year when the temperature is above freezing. When planted alone Merion Kentucky bluegrass forms a beautiful, dense turf which is reasonably resistant to wear. When grown under favorable conditions it will produce a better turf than any other species of grass commonly used for home lawns. In a well-managed Merion Kentucky bluegrass turf there should be few, if any, weeds.

The seed of Merion Kentucky bluegrass is usually of high quality, but is slow in germination and even under very favorable conditions it sometimes requires from eight to ten weeks to become established. The usual rate of seeding is considerably lower than for most other grasses, which helps to compensate for the higher cost of the seed. A rate of one to two pounds per 1,000 square feet is recommended.

Seeding and Combinations

When a lawn area is to be seeded with Merion Kentucky bluegrass the preparation of the soil must be done with care. A pH of 6.5 to 7 is considered optimum. (For preparation for seeding see page 181.) Merion Kentucky bluegrass should be seeded as soon after the 15th of August as possible. This is earlier than most autumn seedings are made but is advisable as it will give the young grasses a chance to become established before winter. Seeding may also be done in very early spring but results are usually far less satisfactory, and autumn seeding is strongly recommended.

For best results Merion Kentucky bluegrass should be seeded alone or in combination with some other grass which is known to be a good companion. It has very slow starting habits and when it is seeded with an ordinary lawn-grass mixture it sometimes fails to get started at all, or is crowded out before the young seedlings become established. The fact that its cultural requirements differ from those of the more common lawn grasses also make such a seeding inadvisable.

Merion Kentucky bluegrass makes an excellent turf when sown in combination with Pennlawn Fescue, a very superior strain of Creeping Red Fescue. It may also be seeded with one of the upright bent grasses. Sown with 10 percent of Highland Bent it will produce a fine turf. A combination which shows great promise of producing a superior turf of good density and appearance through the year is a mixture of Merion Kentucky bluegrass and Meyer Zoysia. Excellent results have been obtained by starting the Meyer Zoysia in the early summer and seeding Merion Kentucky bluegrass over the area in the very early autumn.

On the West Coast an excellent turf which will remain green throughout all or most of the year can be obtained by seeding Merion Kentucky bluegrass and U 3 Bermuda grass in combination. It is advisable, however, to make regular applications of fertilizer throughout the autumn months in order to encourage the growth of the Merion Kentucky bluegrass which is the dominant grass during the winter months while the U 3 Bermuda is dormant.

When attempts are made to seed Merion Kentucky bluegrass in already established turf the results are apt to be disappointing, although under ideal conditions one may meet with success. The most favorable time for seeding Merion Kentucky bluegrass on established turf is during late winter, from the middle of February to the middle of March, when the soil is undergoing alternate freezing and thawing and is in a honeycomb condition. At this time no coverage is necessary. If an attempt is made to seed Merion Kentucky bluegrass on established turf in the autumn the existing grass should be cut very close. $\frac{1}{2}$ inch or less, and the soil should be thoroughly aerified. Lime and fertilizer should be added before the seed is sown. The seed

should be worked into the soil with the back of an iron rake, or with a rough fiber doormat, which may be used as a drag. The soil should be kept moist until germination has taken place and the young seedlings have become established. During this period the existing grass should be kept cut very short. When Merion Kentucky bluegrass is seeded on established turf it may take two or three years before it begins to take hold and becomes at all evident.

Merion Kentucky bluegrass may also be established by the vegetative method, either sprigs or plugs being planted. (See page 180.)

In the management of a Merion Kentucky bluegrass turf mowing, fertilization and aerification play important parts. As Merion Kentucky bluegrass thrives on close cutting, the mower should be set to cut at a height of $\frac{1}{2}$ to $\frac{3}{4}$ of an inch. When a cut higher than an inch is maintained Merion Kentucky bluegrass fails to form a dense, closely-knit, weed-free turf. Mowing should begin as soon as it has reached a height where there is anything to cut. It should not be mown when wet, however. It must be borne in mind that close mowing is possible only in pure stands of Merion Kentucky bluegrass or when it is in mixture with bent grasses, U 3 Bermuda grass or Meyer Zoysia. If a Merion Kentucky bluegrass turf is well fertilized and is mown closely, a dense turf will be formed which will resist the invasion of weeds and weedy grasses.

Merion Kentucky bluegrass requires heavier applications of fertilizer than many other grasses and is particularly dependent upon an adequate supply of nitrogen. (See page 189.)

It has been found that if too much water is applied to Merion Kentucky bluegrass it tends to become shallow rooted and fails to do well. It requires a well-drained soil and rather infrequent watering, a thorough soaking about every ten days during periods of prolonged dry weather.

It is recommended that Merion Kentucky bluegrass turf be aerified thoroughly in the spring and again in the early autumn. It is not advisable, however, to aerify the turf the first spring following fall planting.

While Merion Kentucky bluegrass is not immune to disease it is highly resistant to leaf spot, a disease which is common to Kentucky bluegrass. Rust occasionally appears on Merion Kentucky bluegrass in the autumn but under a system of good management it is seldom serious. Merion Kentucky bluegrass possesses high sensitivity to phenylmercury compounds and their use should be avoided in a program of disease control. As grubs make no distinction between the roots of Merion Kentucky bluegrass and other grasses the usual precautions should be taken. (See page 195.)

Roughstalk Bluegrass (Poa trivialis)

This grass is of value chiefly because it is one of the few lawn grasses which will grow in moist, shady locations. It is a light-green in color and forms a reasonably good turf under rather unfavorable conditions. It is often included in shady mixtures.

THE TREE-SHADED LAWN OF A PENNSYLVANIA FARMHOUSE

Fescues

The fescues are among the most adaptable of lawn grasses and while they do not form a turf of superior quality they are valuable in specific lawngrass mixtures and for use under certain adverse conditions where better grasses would fail to thrive. The fescues will thrive almost equally well in sun or in shade and when used in a general purpose mixture they will usually become dominant in the shady areas beneath the trees on the lawn. They are tolerant of both moist and dry conditions, and although appreciative of good fertility they will thrive surprisingly well on soils low in nutrients. A pH between 5.5 and 6.5 best meets their needs but they will do reasonably well on more acid soils. The fescues are cool climate grasses and will not endure extreme heat well.

The turf formed by the fescues is deep green in color, dense and fine in texture, but somewhat stiff and wiry. However, these very qualities which make it less desirable as a lawn impart to it a ruggedness which makes it of special value on areas subjected to rough usage, such as playing fields and park areas where there is heavy foot traffic. It is also one of the best grasses for dry slopes. The fescues should not be mown closer than 2 inches.

Creeping Red Fescue: The improved strains of Creeping Red Fescue are best suited for general use and are included in many all-purpose lawn mixtures. The Illahee and Pennlawn strains are considered two of the most superior in the East. Rainier is a strain popular on the West Coast. Other excellent strains include Penn State Chewings, and Trinity.

Redtop is a comparatively short-lived grass and its chief value is as a nurse-grass. It germinates very quickly, within a few days after sowing if conditions are favorable, and gives a newly seeded lawn the appearance of green while the other more slowly germinating grasses are becoming established. It is fine-textured when young but somewhat coarse when mature. When used in a mixture it disappears as soon as the superior grasses have formed a good sod. The proportion of Redtop in a general-purpose lawn mixture should not exceed 10 percent.

Zoysia

The improved strain of Zoysia, known as Meyer Zoysia, is one of the most valuable lawn grasses in the South and is gradually coming into more extensive use in the North, having been grown successfully in Massachusetts, New York, Pennsylvania, Michigan, Iowa, Nebraska and Colorado. However, in the North Zoysia has very definite limitations as it turns brown with the first heavy frost and does not become green again until the warm days of spring. This limitation can be overcome, however, by planting Zoysia as a companion with Merion Kentucky bluegrass. (See page 176.) Zoysia is of particular value in the North where a good turf is desired during the summer months and it makes an excellent lawn grass for summer homes and resort areas. Being exceptionally well adapted to sandy soils it can be used very satisfactorily along the coast. Meyer Zoysia must be grown vegetatively. In the North the plugs may be planted at any time between late spring and mid-August.

For full cultural requirements of Zoysia see page 179.

MIXTURES FOR SPECIFIC PURPOSES FOR COOL CLIMATES

GENERAL PURPOSE MIXTURE

Kentucky Bluegrass	50%
Creeping Red Fescue, Illahee or Pennlawn Strain	25%
Rhode Island Bent	15%
Redtop	10%

MIXTURE FOR MOIST SHADE

Chewings Fescue	50%
Poa Trivialis	30%
Kentucky Bluegrass	10%
Rhode Island Bent	10%

MIXTURE FOR DRY SHADE

Chewings Fescue	70%
Colonial Bent	15%
Redtop	15%

MIXTURES FOR A SUPERIOR TURF

1. Merion Kentucky Bluegrass   90%
   Highland Bent   10%

2. Merion Kentucky Bluegrass   50%
   Pennlawn Fescue   30%
   Highland Bent   15%
   Redtop   5%

IMPORTANT LAWN GRASSES FOR MILD AND FOR DRY CLIMATES

Bermuda Grass: Bermuda Grass is one of the most widely used lawn grasses throughout the southern states and in the Southwest. It possesses many admirable qualities but also has very definite limitations. It is tolerant of intense summer heat and of drought conditions, it is comparatively free from pests and diseases, it is resistant to wear, and, if well managed, it makes an excellent and attractive turf with good summer color. Its chief disadvantages are that it is an extremely invasive grass and can become a serious pest in flower beds and in the vegetable garden unless restrained, it does not thrive in shady areas, and in most areas where it is grown, it turns a dead-looking brown during the winter months.

Bermuda grass may be propagated either by seed sown at the rate of one pound per 1,000 square feet, or by planting sprigs or plugs of sod. (See page 180.) It makes the best turf when it is mowed very closely, being kept at almost a putting green height, not over $\frac{3}{8}$ of an inch. If kept at this height there is less tendency for it to mat badly. If permitted to grow too tall before it is cut the turf loses its green color and remains brown until new growth occurs.

Liberal feeding is required for best results. Two feedings of a good complete fertilizer, at the rate of 20 pounds per 1,000 square feet should be given, one in the early spring and another in the early autumn, and additional nitrogen should be applied during the early summer. The urea-form type will give a slow release of nitrogen over a long period. (See page 188.)

During periods of prolonged dry weather Bermuda grass should be watered thoroughly every week or ten days. Several improved strains of Bermuda grass have been developed. Ormond and Tifton 57 are two strains which are popular in the Gulf states and will make a very satisfactory lawn under average conditions.

U 3 Bermuda grass is a very superior strain which was developed in Savannah, Georgia. It is a fine-textured grass and produces an excellent, tight, velvety turf. The seed germinates quickly and makes rapid growth, forming a fairly good turf six weeks or more after sowing. U 3 Bermuda grass is very hardy and will survive zero temperatures and can therefore be grown further north than any of the other strains. Like common Bermuda grass, it turns brown during the winter months but retains its green color for a longer period.

On the West Coast it produces a year-round green turf when grown in combination with Merion Kentucky bluegrass.

U 3 Bermuda grass requires very close mowing and liberal feeding for best results.

Buffalograss is one of the best grasses for the dry-land regions of the West. There are few grasses which can endure the difficult conditions found in these areas but this native grass of the Great Plains will make a very satisfactory lawn if given good care. It is very adaptable, being able to withstand extremes of heat and cold, and it has the ability to endure long periods of drought, making vigorous growth under very adverse conditions. It is low-growing and produces a dense turf, a soft, gray-green in color.

Buffalograss may be seeded in the spring at the rate of 1 pound per 1,000 square feet, or it may be established vegetatively through the use of sod. The plugs should be set out during late spring 1 to $1\frac{1}{2}$ feet apart. The soil should be well prepared and moist at the time of planting and should be kept well watered until the plugs have become established. When once well started the lawn will require no watering and little or no mowing.

St. Augustine Grass is adapted only to frost-free areas, being used extensively for lawns in Florida and the Gulf states. It thrives well in either sun or shade, requires abundant moisture and moderate fertility. The turf is coarse in texture, and under good management retains its deep green color throughout the year. It requires little mowing. St. Augustine sod does not withstand heavy wear. Since seed is not available it must be planted vegetatively with plugs or sprigs.

Zoysia: The Zoysia grasses, natives of Japan and Korea, are among the most valuable of all lawn grasses throughout the South.

An improved strain of the common Zoysia japonica has been developed through the cooperative efforts of the U.S. Golf Association Green Section and the U.S. Department of Agriculture. This superior, fine-textured strain is known as Meyer (Z-52) Zoysia, and is gaining rapid popularity as a desirable lawn grass. Another excellent strain, introduced under the name Emerald, has been developed by the Georgia Improvement Association.

Meyer Zoysia produces a firm, resilient turf with a pleasing texture and color, closely resembling a Kentucky bluegrass sod. A Zoysia lawn is durable and very resistant to wear when it is in active growth. When grown under favorable conditions Meyer Zoysia forms a very dense turf and has the ability to crowd out summer weeds and undesirable grasses.

Meyer Zoysia will grow on soils of almost any type, thriving equally well on very sandy soils and on rather heavy clay soils. Being exceptionally well adapted to sandy soils it is widely used in coastal areas. It is also more tolerant of low soil fertility than most grasses. However, if a turf of superior quality is desired, regular and liberal applications of a high nitrogen fertilizer must be made.

Meyer Zoysia is deep rooted and is extremely drought-resistant. It is primarily a warm climate grass, being tolerant of extreme heat, and it thrives best during the heat of midsummer. In Florida Meyer Zoysia remains green during the entire year, and throughout the lower South it retains its green color during much of the year.

Meyer Zoysia must be grown vegetatively. Either plugs of sod or sprigs, consisting of roots and stolons with no soil, may be used. Plug-planting is preferred. Meyer Zoysia is sometimes rather slow to establish itself and may take several years to cover an area. If two-inch plugs are used, planted twelve inches apart each way, a good solid turf may usually be obtained within two years' time. Plugs are removed from a pure stand of Meyer Zoysia sod with a simple tool designed for this purpose and with the same tool are plugged into a freshly prepared lawn area or into an existing lawn. Plugs may be purchased from a nursery and, for reasonably small areas, the cost is not excessive. If desired, a home owner may obtain a few packages of plugs and establish his own turf nursery upon which he can later draw. Most nursery plugs measure about two inches in diameter. The plugs should be pressed firmly into the soil and should be kept watered until established, one or two soakings usually being sufficient except in very hot, dry weather. Plugs should be set from six to twelve inches apart, usually being planted on twelve-inch centers. Plug-planting may be done at any time when the ground is not frozen or is not baked hard by drought.

Sprig-planting is a simple process but is suited only to newly prepared lawn areas. If sprigs are planted on established turf the competition of the other grasses will be too great and such a procedure is seldom successful. Plugs can be divided into sprigs having two to three joints each. The sprigs should be spaced from two to three inches apart and should be pressed firmly into the soil. They should be only partially covered, with as much leaf growth left exposed as possible. The soil should be kept moist until the young sprigs have taken root. Sprigs may be planted at any time from spring to midsummer.

Meyer Zoysia makes rather slow growth, and therefore requires mowing at less frequent intervals than most grasses. It forms the best quality of turf when $\frac{1}{2}$ to $\frac{3}{4}$ inch cut is maintained. When it is cut too high it is inclined to develop more slowly and produces an inferior turf which will permit the encroachment of weeds and undesirable grass.

Since Meyer Zoysia makes its most active growth in midsummer it requires its fertility at this time. If luxuriant growth is desired three applications during late spring and early summer are recommended.

Meyer Zoysia seems to be unaffected by turf insects and the various diseases that affect other lawn grasses.

Zoysia Matrella, variety Emerald: This is an excellent type of Zoysia grass which is particularly well adapted to the deep South. It is fast growing, fine in texture, deep green in color and makes an attractive turf. It is also tolerant of shade. Under favorable conditions it becomes established rapidly and it is one of the best varieties for use in the Gulf States. It may also be grown successfully further north.

LAWN-GRASS SUBSTITUTES

There are numerous low-growing plants which are sometimes classed as lawn-grass substitutes but many of these plants actually belong in the category of ground covers. In order to justify its use as a lawn-grass substitute a plant should be of extremely low growth, should have the general appearance of a green lawn, and it should have some of the same attributes which the lawn grasses possess. In order to function as a lawn it should be able to withstand at least a moderate amount of tramping and use, it should maintain a pleasing green color throughout the major portion of the year, it should not be unduly expensive to establish, and its maintenance requirements should be moderate.

If one prefers to grow a ground cover *instead* of having a lawn there is a wide choice of material available. (See Chapter XVIII on Ground Covers.)

The following plants meet the requirements of a lawn-grass substitute reasonably well, although each has its special limitations.

Anthemis Nobilis (Chamomile) is a low-growing herb of dense, compact growth, with finely-cut foliage. It thrives well in full sun, prefers a light, well-drained soil and is particularly well adapted to planting on sunny slopes where it is difficult to maintain a satisfactory stand of grass. It retains its beautiful green color throughout the year. It will withstand moderate use but is not well suited to areas that are subjected to constant wear, as under such conditions it has a tendency to become shabby and die out, leaving bare, brown patches which require renovation. Its appearance will be improved if it is cut and rolled once or twice a year.

Arenaria Verna, *Variety Caespitosa* (Irish Moss). A moss-like plant of dense, compact growth. Its color is a pleasing shade of bright green, and it bears tiny white flowers during the summer. It is very hardy, prefers partial shade but will also grow in full sun, and requires a moist, friable soil well supplied with organic matter. It withstands some trampling and does not usually require any clipping. It has a tendency to become humpy, but this may be controlled by occasional thinning out. Plants may be obtained from nurseries and should be spaced 6 inches apart. It is best suited for small areas in partial shade where a bright green carpet is desired.

Dichondra Carolinensis (D. Repens) (*Lawn Leaf*). This is one of the most widely grown and most satisfactory of the lawn-grass substitutes, its chief limitation being its lack of hardiness. It suffers serious damage at temperatures below 20° F. and is killed by a hard freeze. However, young self-sown seedlings sometimes replace the plants which have been killed. Dichondra is a very low, spreading, mat-like plant with small rounded or heart-shaped leaves. It thrives well in sun or partial shade, is as tolerant of traffic and wear as most lawn grasses, and has a pleasing appearance. It prefers a moist but well-drained fertile soil and is tolerant of both acid and alkaline conditions. It withstands intense summer heat well, provided it has plenty of moisture. Weeds are often a problem until it has become established. It may be readily grown from seed, or plants may be obtained from nurseries. In areas where root-knot nematodes are prevalent seeding is preferable, as there is danger of introducing the nematodes with purchased plants. Mowing is not necessary, but an occasional clipping will improve the appearance of the turf and will prevent bunching up.

Dichondra is well suited to the milder areas in California and to the Gulf Coast and the Middle South.

Lippia Canescens (L. Repens). This low-growing, mat-like plant will withstand extreme heat and thrives well under desert conditions. The foliage is grayish in tone, and tiny, pinkish-lilac flowers are borne during the summer. The plants appear shabby and dead looking for about two months in the winter. It is tolerant of any type of soil, is highly drought-resistant and grows well in either sun or shade. No mowing is necessary unless growth becomes too vigorous. It withstands hard wear well. New areas are established by setting out young plants in the spring 4 to 6 inches apart. There is some danger of the plants spreading to other areas and becoming difficult to eradicate.

PREPARATION OF THE SOIL

It is a far easier task to improve the condition of the soil before planting than it is to improve either the texture or the fertility of the soil after planting. The importance of adequate preparation of the soil before the seed is sown can hardly be overemphasized. The establishment of proper grades, the need for more adequate drainage, the physical texture of the soil, the fertility of the soil, and the degree of soil acidity must all be taken into consideration.

If grading is to be done the top-soil should be carefully removed, and after the grading has been completed it should be replaced. This procedure will increase the cost of the grading but will prove to be a matter of sound economy in the end. (Refer to instructions in regard to grading in Chapter X.)

Unless the area which is to be seeded possesses low spots which are apt to be soggy at some seasons of the year, underdrainage will not be necessary. Frequently such low spots can be improved with proper grading but if this is not possible they may be effectively drained with agricultural tile. Four-inch tile drains should be used, the trenches being from 15 to 24 inches deep and approximately 20 feet apart. There should be a fall of at least three inches in every 50 feet. The tile should be laid end to end and the joints covered with strips of tar paper in order to keep the soil out of the tile.

Organic Matter

The physical texture of the soil plays a very important part in the establishment of a fine turf. It may be improved to a very marked degree by the addition of organic matter. Most soils, with the exception of woodland soils, are deficient in humus. Soils with a marked deficiency of organic matter present very serious problems as they are low in water-holding capacity, are poorly aerated, become too readily compacted, tend to be less fertile, and, in general, provide a very poor medium for the healthy, vigorous growth of lawn grasses. It is a well accepted fact that practically all of our better lawn grasses thrive best on a soil which is well supplied with organic matter.

Organic matter may be supplied in the form of well rotted manure, spent mushroom soil, compost, cover crops, raw native peat, and the peat moss of commerce.* Manure has the disadvantage of introducing weed seeds into the lawn area and in many communities it is not readily available at a reasonable price. The great point in its favor is that it increases the fertility of the soil as well as adding organic matter. If it is applied several months previous to planting, the weed seeds will germinate and can be controlled by cultivation before the grass seed is sown. Spent mushroom soil is a mixture of rotted manure and soil and is of particular value in improving the texture of sandy and shaly soils. In sections of the country where mushrooms are grown commercially it is readily available at a very reasonable price and it is one of the most satisfactory forms in which organic matter can be supplied. Good garden compost is somewhat similar to mushroom soil and is also an excellent source of organic matter. If it is possible to plan the program of work well in advance and to devote several months to the preparation of the soil one or more cover crops may be grown and the organic content of the soil may be increased in this way with comparatively little expense. When a new home is being built it is frequently possible to do this during the process of construction. The following cover crops are recommended:

Fall Sowing—per acre, 1 bushel rye and 1 peck winter vetch; per 1,000 square feet, 1½ quarts rye and ½ pint vetch. Sow in September or early October. Plow or spade the crop under in the spring when it has attained a height of 12 inches.

Early Spring Sowing—per acre, 2 bushels oats and 1 peck Canada field peas; per 1,000 square feet, 1½ quarts oats and ½ pint Canada field peas. Sow as early in the spring as possible and plow or spade under about the middle of June.

Late Spring Sowing—per acre, 1 bushel soybeans, 1 peck of millet; per 1,000 square feet, 1 quart soybeans, 1 cup of millet. Sow between the middle of May and the middle of June. Inoculate the soybeans before planting in order to gain the full benefit of their nitrogen fixing abilities. Plow or spade under at least one month before the time of lawn seeding.

* Obtainable under various Trade names.

Peat moss is a less desirable source of organic matter than some of the other forms of peat, as it supplies practically no plant food, decomposes more rapidly than any other form, and leaves the smallest supply of permanent humus in the soil. Raw native peat decomposes more slowly than peat moss and is consequently of more value. It is advisable to apply both peat moss and the raw native peat sometime previous to planting in order to allow them to become partially decomposed, as the benefits will be decidedly greater. Cultivated peat decomposes more slowly than any of the other forms of peat and the beneficial effects are consequently more lasting. Peat moss should always be thoroughly moistened before it is applied to the soil. If applied dry it may actually do more harm than good, as it will take up the moisture from the soil. On areas where grass is to be sown it should never be allowed to remain as a layer on the surface of the soil. It should always be thoroughly worked into the upper few inches of top-soil.

The rate of application of organic matter will depend upon the character of the soil. Light sandy soils will require liberal applications in order that they may become more retentive of moisture. Soils of a dense, heavy texture will also be greatly improved and the drainage of the surface water will be facilitated if liberal quantities are applied. Manure should be applied at the rate of 1,000 to 1,500 pounds per 1,000 square feet of lawn area, or 20 to 30 tons per acre. Peat moss should be applied at the rate of 4 bales per 1,000 square feet of lawn area, or approximately 170 bales per acre. Native moist peat should be applied at the rate of 2 cubic yards per 1,000 square feet of area, 86 cubic yards per acre.

It is essential that the organic matter, in whatever form it may be applied, be thoroughly incorporated with the upper five or six inches of top-soil. The organic matter, particularly when it is applied in the form of peat moss, should never be allowed to form a definite layer, either upon the surface of the soil or below the surface, as such a layer has a very undesirable effect on plant growth. The organic matter should be thoroughly plowed, forked, or spaded into the upper five or six inches of top-soil. A rototiller is excellent for this purpose and leaves the soil in fine tilth.

Fertilizers

The fertility of the soil is one of the most important factors in the establishment of a new lawn. It is a widely accepted premise that all of our most desirable lawn grasses require a soil of fairly high fertility if they are to produce a fine quality of turf. It is well, therefore, to see that adequate nutrients are supplied before planting. The application of a well balanced complete fertilizer will usually give the most satisfactory results, the amount required depending upon the natural fertility of the soil. On soils of medium fertility an application of 15 to 20 pounds per 1,000 square feet will usually be sufficient, or approximately 650 to 700 pounds per acre. On soils of low fertility the application should be increased to 25 to 30 pounds per 1,000 square feet or 1,000 to 1,200 pounds per acre. (See page 168 for details concerning Soil Tests and the type of fertilizer which should be used.)

Soil Acidity

The majority of our better lawn grasses prefer an almost neutral or very slightly acid soil. A few types, such as the bent grasses and the fescues, while tolerant of rather strong soil acidity, will also make healthy growth on soils which are more nearly neutral. For practically all types of desirable lawn grasses it is therefore advisable to have an acidity which does not fall below a pH value of 5.5* and which preferably ranges between pH 6 and pH 7. Soil tests should be made to determine the existing degree of acidity. If the tests show that the soil is too acid the condition may be readily corrected by an adequate application of lime.

Lime may be applied in the form of hydrated lime or ground limestone. Hydrated lime is more rapid in its action than the other form. One pound of a good quality of hydrated lime is equal in value to $1\frac{1}{2}$ pounds of ground limestone. When the application is made it is important

* See page 168 on Soil Acidity and pH values.

that the lime be distributed very uniformly over the surface of the soil and worked lightly into the upper few inches of top-soil. The lime will move downward in the soil but not laterally and, therefore, any soil areas which are not directly covered by the lime will receive no benefit from the application. There are various outfits on the market for the distribution of lime but on very small areas where the use of machinery is not justified one of the most satisfactory methods of application is to place the hydrated lime in a coarse, loosely woven burlap bag and to drag it back and forth over the area. If one prefers, the bag may be held a few inches above the soil and the lime shaken out on to the surface.

The importance of applying lime at the time that the seed bed is prepared can hardly be over-stressed. If applications are delayed until after the sod has become established it will require several years to entirely correct any marked degree of acidity, whereas this condition may be rapidly and thoroughly overcome if an adequate application is made at the time of planting.

The rate of application will depend entirely upon the degree of soil acidity. On soils of extremely high acidity it is advisable to make several applications as the heavy liming of strongly acid soils is detrimental to normal plant growth. This extreme condition would be met only very occasionally. Soils testing over pH 6 will require no application of lime. Soils testing between pH 5 and pH 6 should receive an application of 50 pounds of hydrated lime or 75 pounds of finely ground limestone per 1,000 square feet, or 1 ton of hydrated lime per acre or $1\frac{1}{2}$ tons of ground limestone. Soils testing between pH 4 and pH 5 or below should receive two or more applications, the total amount varying from 60 pounds to 145 pounds per 1,000 square feet of hydrated lime, or $2\frac{1}{4}$ to 3 tons per acre. Only in very extreme cases would as much as 145 pounds per 1,000 square feet be necessary. In general, sandy soils of a given degree of acidity require lighter applications of lime than do heavy clay soils of the same pH value. Applications should therefore be slightly adjusted to meet the various soil types. Not more than 50 or 60 pounds of hydrated lime or its equivalent in ground limestone should be applied at one time to 1,000 square feet. If heavier applications are necessary the amount should be divided. It must be borne in mind that not only does lime correct conditions of soil acidity, but it serves other functions as well. It helps to improve the physical structure of the soil, and consequently increases its water-absorbing capacity, and it also provides both calcium and magnesium, which are essential elements for normal plant growth.

Preparation of the Seed Bed

After the organic matter, fertilizer and lime have been thoroughly incorporated with the soil, the seed bed may be prepared for planting. On large areas this is done with the use of spike tooth and drag harrows and a smoothing board. On small areas it may be very easily accomplished with an iron hand rake. The surface should be reasonably firm and it should be absolutely even with no hollows or small depressions.

Preparing a Weed-free Seed Bed

It has long been the goal of the home owner and of the turf specialist to be able to produce a weed-free lawn and now, at last, with the introduction of new chemicals and new methods of weed control, it is possible to prepare a weed-free seed bed, which is a big step toward weed-free lawns.

Calcium cyanamide: One of the most effective ways of killing weeds and destroying weed seeds on areas which are to be seeded to lawn grasses is to apply calcium cyanamide (sold as Lawn and Garden Cyanamid). This chemical has the amazing ability to destroy weed seeds and plant growth and later to supply nitrogen and calcium to the soil for the nutrition of the plants which are to follow. An application of calcium cyanamide, therefore, constitutes a double-barreled program.

When calcium cyanamide is applied to the soil and comes into contact with moisture, "free" cyanamide is formed which is toxic to seeds and growing plants. A heavy application of calcium cyanamide will kill all weed seeds near or on the surface of the soil and will also destroy all young weed seedlings and all other plant growth. However, due to the fact that this "free" cyanamide is unstable, it breaks down within a short time into ammonia and nitrate nitrogen, valuable plant nutrients.

In preparing a weed-free seed bed directions must be carefully followed. A month before the lawn seed is to be sown the area should be graded and made ready for seeding, including the addition of organic materials and fertilizers. It is essential that a three-week interval elapse between the application of the calcium cyanamide and the sowing of the grass seed. The calcium cyanamide should be applied at the rate of five pounds per 100 square feet, or 50 pounds per 1,000 square feet of lawn area. It may be applied with a regular lawn fertilizer spreader or, if necessary, by hand. Even distribution is very important if complete weed control is to be obtained. Care must be taken not to spread the calcium cyanamide within two feet of the root spread of trees, shrubs or flowers. The material may be left undisturbed on the surface, or may be raked in *very lightly*. On sloping areas it is advisable to rake it in, in order to prevent it from washing off. After the calcium cyanamide has been spread the soil should be watered thoroughly to the depth of at least an inch, and it should be kept moist throughout the period. This is essential in order to have the proper chemical reaction take place.

After the three-week period has elapsed the surface of the soil should be raked *very lightly* in order to break the crust and the lawn may then be seeded, the area being rolled to provide coverage for the seed. In the process of seeding the soil should be disturbed as little as possible. The toxic effect of the calcium cyanamide does not penetrate into the soil to a depth of more than an inch. The weed seeds are therefore destroyed only in this top inch of soil but not at a greater depth and it is important during seeding not to bring weed seeds to the surface from the lower level.

If directions are carefully followed a weed-free seed bed should be obtained and the young lawn grasses should have no competition from crabgrass, goosegrass, plantains, dandelions or any of the other troublesome lawn weeds.

Lawns for Poor Soils

In establishing a lawn on soil which is definitely low in fertility and which cannot be immediately improved to a point where it will be able to support the better types of lawn grasses, it is wise to use some of the varieties which are less exacting in their demands. The fescues are the most satisfactory grasses for this purpose as they thrive well on poor, sandy soils, are tolerant of acidity, will endure considerable shade, and will withstand long periods of drought. The leaves of the fescues are tough and wire-like, and in habit of growth the plants are low and inclined to be somewhat bunchy. It is advisable, therefore, to sow the fescues in mixture with other grasses in order to obtain a better quality of turf. Of the many varieties Chewings Fescue and True Creeping Red Fescue are the most desirable for lawn purposes. The seeds of the fescues lose their vitality rapidly and as a poor percentage of germination is frequently secured it is necessary to make rather heavy seedings. For a lawn on poor, sandy soil or on extremely acid soil the following mixture is recommended:

	PERCENTAGE
Chewings Red Fescue	35
Redtop (recleaned)	20
Colonial Bent	15
Kentucky Bluegrass	10
Ryegrass	15
White Clover	5

(N. J. Agricultural Experiment Station)

Lawns for Shady Areas

For shady areas it is necessary to choose grasses which are tolerant of such conditions. It must be borne in mind that all grasses require some sunlight for satisfactory growth, and if the shade is too dense it is well to resort to some evergreen ground cover rather than to attempt to produce a lawn. A careful program of pruning will frequently mitigate the density of the shade sufficiently to make it possible to grow lawn grasses under large trees. If the pruning program is carried out over a period of several years it may be done without injuring the form or beauty of the trees. The program consists of gradually removing the lower branches of the trees so that the morning and afternoon sun may reach the grass. The tree will put on additional growth at the top to compensate for what has been cut away and will continue to maintain its natural form. Two or three feet of the lower branches may be cut away entirely each year and at the end of five years the foliage level will have been raised as much as 10 feet.

For suitable grass mixtures for shady areas see page 178.

Temporary Lawns

It occasionally happens that one desires to plant a purely temporary lawn. In moving into a new home late in the spring it would be folly to attempt to plant a permanent lawn at a season of the year when it is most difficult for the better types of lawn grasses to establish themselves, and under such conditions it is wise to resort to temporary measures. Within the space of a few brief weeks it is possible to obtain a rich and almost luxuriant growth of turf if the correct type of seed is used. Either the perennial rye grass or the domestic rye grass should be selected for this purpose. The growth is somewhat coarse and rank, but at least the grass will form a welcome covering of green on ground that might otherwise be bare. Before planting, a complete fertilizer (6-8-4 analysis) should be worked into the soil at the rate of 10 pounds per 1,000 square feet in order to stimulate growth. The seed should be sown at the rate of 6 pounds per 1,000 square feet. The soil should be kept moist until the seed has germinated and the grass should be mown when it has reached a height of 2 inches. This temporary grass may be plowed or spaded under when the time approaches to prepare the seed bed for the permanent lawn, and it will benefit the soil by adding a small amount of organic matter.

SEEDING

Time of Sowing Grass Seed

The one point upon which all authorities seem to agree is that the most desirable time for sowing lawn grasses is in late August or early September. If it is not possible to do the work at this season of the year, seed may be sown in *early* spring. Late spring and summer sowings are not recommended except in the case of purely temporary lawns. Early autumn sowing has several advantages over spring sowing. Practically all of the lawn grasses make their best growth during cool, moist weather and the autumn months usually provide very favorable conditions for good germination of the seed and for the sturdy, vigorous growth of the young grass. There is comparatively little competition from weeds at this season of the year and by the following summer the autumn-sown turf should be so well established that it will not suffer seriously from drought or other adversities.

Method of Sowing

In sowing grass seed the chief aim is to provide for an even distribution of seed over the lawn area. The seed may be sown by hand, or with a hand-operated seeder, or with a mechanical seeder mounted on wheels.

For small areas sowing may be done very satisfactorily by hand if care is taken to get an even distribution. Hand sowing should be done on a calm day when there is little or no wind as it is otherwise impossible to make an even sowing. It is wise to divide the quantity of seed in half and to sow in two directions, walking first north and south and the second time east and west, thus covering the area twice.

Seeding with a hand-operated seeder is much more rapid than sowing by hand and a fairly accurate distribution can usually be obtained. The most approved method, however, is to sow the seed with a mechanical distributor. Such a machine represents a small investment, but as it can also be used for the annual applications of fertilizer its purchase is often justified even for lawns of moderate size. Such a machine can be adjusted to sow the seed at the desired rate.

After it has been sown the seed should be raked into the soil *very* lightly with an iron rake, being covered not more than $\frac{1}{8}$ of an inch. It is very important not to cover it too deeply, as poor germination will result. After raking, the area should be lightly rolled to establish good contact between seed and soil.

From the time of sowing until the grass seed is well up the area should be kept moist. Water should be applied in the form of a fine, mist-like spray. A fog nozzle is ideal for this purpose. A heavy spray will tend to cause a crust to form on the surface of the soil which may seriously interfere with germination.

Rate of Seeding

The quantity of seed required will depend upon the type of grass seed or the mixture used.

TYPE OF GRASS	SEED REQUIRED PER 1,000 SQ. FT.
Bent grasses	2 lbs.
Bermuda grass	1 lb.
Kentucky bluegrass	4 lbs.
Merion Kentucky bluegrass	1–2 lbs.
Fescues	3–6 lbs.
	(the heavier seeding on dry, sandy soil)
Poa trivialis	3 lbs.
General Purpose Mixture (for cool climates)	4 lbs.

Mowing New Grass

Young, newly sown grass (with the exception of the bent grasses, Bermuda grass and Merion Kentucky bluegrass) should not be cut until the blades have reached a height of 2 inches. The mower blades should be carefully set so that the final cut will not be closer than $1\frac{1}{2}$ inches. If young grass is mown too closely it will prevent the formation of a vigorous root system and will seriously injure the quality of the turf.

Sodding New Areas

Undoubtedly, the most rapid method of establishing turf is sodding. It consists of cutting strips of sod from an existing lawn, laying them carefully together on the new area and encouraging the grass roots to re-establish themselves in the soil. Under certain conditions, this method may be preferable to starting grass from seed or stolons, because it has the advantage of being so quickly accomplished that there will be no opportunity for a hard rain to wash away the soil and ruin the surface of newly prepared ground. On banks or steep slopes this is an advantage. It is seldom possible to make as fine a lawn by this method as it is with the slower processes. However, where an immediate effect is desired, sodding is the only sure way.

Turf selected for cutting and transplanting should be well-established grass growing in open ground and free from crabgrass and weeds. The best source is a lawn that has been grown from seed and is composed of a mixture, bluegrass predominating over redtop and fescue, with little or no clover.

Pastures which have been well cared for also provide an excellent source of good sod.

Sodding should be done at a time when there will be four or five or more weeks of good growing weather before the beginning of winter or summer. Unless the roots become established well enough to supply moisture and nourishment growing weather before the beginning of winter frosts will kill the grass altogether.

When sod is to be purchased it is very important to make sure that it is of good quality. At best, sod is expensive, due to the high labor costs involved, and it is very disappointing to go to the expense of buying sod only to find that it is composed of inferior grasses and weeds.

Before cutting sod, the area should be mown closely. The edges of the sod strips are then cut by a rotary blade or by a spade held in a vertical position. The sod is thus divided by these vertical cuts into strips 12 or 15 inches wide and 10 feet or more long. If the job is a small one, cutting sod into squares may be more convenient. A specially built sod spade with its handle at an angle with the blade is forced under the sod, cutting off the lower roots and lifting up a mat of upper roots about 1½ inches thick. The strips are then rolled up and loaded into a truck or wheelbarrow. It is important to keep the edges of the strips straight and parallel and at a uniform distance apart. To facilitate this, a wide plank is laid on the sod with its edge at the last cut, and the new cut is made along the opposite side. This regularity will make more easy the task of laying the sod.

The ground on which the sod is to be laid must be graded to an even surface, cultivated, raked, and rolled, and any irregularities smoothed out. The turf is then laid, the strip being unrolled into place, firmed with blows of the back of the spade. Any irregularities caused by an uneven thickness of the sod should be adjusted at this time by rolling back the strip and filling or cutting the soil below as required. This is the part of the work in which skill and patience are important and which will make the difference between an uneven turf and a smooth one. After rolling with a hand roller, the whole area should be watered until it is thoroughly soaked, and it should not be allowed to dry out until it has become well established.

MAINTENANCE OF EXISTING LAWNS

It is advisable for every home owner to work out a careful program of lawn maintenance and to adhere faithfully to the schedule. The majority of the lawns in this country suffer sadly from neglect. After a lawn is once established the owner is all too apt to assume that the only subsequent care which it requires is that of periodic mowing. Under such conditions of neglect, however, it does not take many years for a good lawn to deteriorate into a poor lawn. The fertility of the soil becomes gradually depleted to the point where it can no longer support the better types of lawn grasses, and the inferior grasses consequently become more and more dominant; the soil becomes increasingly more acid in its reaction and therefore more impervious to water; the lawn becomes less resistant to injury from drought and from insect attacks; and weeds gradually creep in and will, in time, almost entirely crowd out the grasses. It is therefore a matter of sound economy to follow a carefully planned program of lawn maintenance.

The most important considerations in such a program are: rolling, fertilization, liming, mowing, weed control, and disease and insect-pest control.

Rolling

The question of lawn rolling is a much debated one and one upon which authorities fail to agree. It is undoubtedly true that rolling is an operation which has been much overdone in the past, and the present consensus of opinion seems to be in favor of one or two light rollings in the spring. Rolling should not be done until all possibility of alternate thawing and freezing is past. It should be done when the soil is moderately moist—never when it is soggy. Too frequent rolling is apt to cause an undesirable compaction of the soil which tends to interfere with the normal, thrifty growth of the turf. This danger is much greater on heavy soils than on soils of a more sandy character. A water-ballast roller is the most desirable type for lawn use as the weight may be adjusted to meet varying conditions. The roller should be just heavy enough to press the crowns back into the soil without making the soil unduly compact.

Fertilization

The maintenance of soil fertility is one of the major considerations in any program of lawn management. All of our most desirable lawn grasses require a soil of reasonably good fertility for satisfactory development. It is wiser, and better economy, to maintain this fertility from year to year by periodic applications of commercial fertilizers and composts than it is to allow the soil to become depleted.

The three most important elements of fertility needed by lawn grasses for satisfactory growth are nitrogen, phosphorus, and potash. Nitrogen produces a vigorous growth of leaves and stems, phosphorus is needed for good root development, and potash is valuable in promoting general vigor and resistance to disease. A complete commercial fertilizer contains these three essential elements. The true value of a commercial fertilizer, however, depends not only upon the actual content of plant food, but also upon the form in which the nutrients are supplied. This point is of particular importance in the fertilization of lawn grasses.

Nitrogen may be supplied in the form of ammonia compounds, nitrate compounds, urea-formaldehyde compounds, and organic compounds. The ammonia compounds, such as sulphate of ammonia, are quickly available after application. When used year after year, sulphate of ammonia will tend to increase the acidity of the soil appreciably but this may be overcome by sufficient application of lime. Nitrate compounds, such as nitrate of soda, are also quickly available and do not tend to increase the soil acidity. They are, therefore, preferred for use on soils that are strongly acid or for grasses that require a nearly neutral soil. The urea-formaldehyde compounds, known as urea-form fertilizers, release nitrogen very slowly over a period of many months. This is one of the best forms in which to supply nitrogen to lawn grasses as there is no danger of "burning" and the nitrogen needs of the plants for the entire season can be supplied with one application. This is a matter of considerable importance in the management of large areas of turf. The various organic forms of nitrogen, such as cottonseed meal, soybean meal, dried blood, tankage, fish meal, and sludge, decompose slowly and are not active in releasing plant nutrients except under conditions of warmth and moisture. Even although they may be applied in early spring they supply very little nitrogen until the beginning of summer. If organic nitrogen is derived from but one source it may cause what is known as "delayed nitrogen burn" if it is released during a period of hot, dry weather. Therefore organic fertilizers which are to be applied to lawns should supply nitrogen from a number of sources so it will be released over a period of time rather than all at the same time, thus avoiding the danger of delayed nitrogen burn. In general the organic compounds are more valuable for use on sandy soils than on heavy, clay soils as they are not lost through leaching as are some of the more readily available inorganic forms.

Phosphorus is usually supplied in the form of superphosphate and it is an important ingredient of a complete lawn fertilizer.

Potash is commonly supplied in the form of muriate of potash and is included in all complete fertilizer mixtures for turf areas.

Method of Application: Even distribution of the fertilizer is essential, as areas not covered will receive little or no direct benefit from the application.

If fertilizers are used in the dry form they should be applied with a fertilizer distributor which can be adjusted to apply the material at the desired rate and which will make possible an even coverage. This is an essential piece of equipment for the establishment and maintenance of a good lawn and if it is well cared for it should last for many years.

Fertilizer in the dry form should always be applied when the grass is dry in order to avoid the danger of burning the leaves.

Planning a Fertilization Program

Soil Tests: The kind of fertilizer which should be applied and the amount required can be most accurately determined by soil tests. The advisability of having such tests made can hardly be over-emphasized. Unless this is done one is working in the dark. A reliable soil test will indicate whether or not an application of lime is needed, and the amount required to obtain the desired pH can be readily figured. (See page 170.) Whether or not a deficiency of nitrogen, phosphorus, potash or any of the minor elements exists can also be accurately determined, and a fertilizer program can be worked out which will best meet specific needs.

Most State Colleges and State Universities offer a Soil Testing Service. In some states this service is free to residents of the state, while in other states there is a nominal charge. For details concerning the method of taking soil samples see page 168.

Requirements of a Good Lawn Fertilizer: A good lawn fertilizer should contain the essential elements of fertility—nitrogen, phosphorus and potash in the correct proportions. In general, a ratio of 2–1–1 (2 parts nitrogen to 1 part phosphorus and 1 part potash) will best meet the needs of the average lawn. A fertilizer with an analysis of 10–5–5 (10 parts nitrogen, 5 parts phosphorus and 5 parts potash) is an example of a 2–1–1 ratio. If a heavier application of phosphorus than of potash is needed a ratio in which the sum of the phosphorus and potash equals the amount of the nitrogen may be used, such as a 10–6–4 analysis. Adjustments of these ratios may be made very readily if indicated as advisable by soil tests. However, they form a good basis upon which to develop a program.

In addition to the above requirements, a good lawn fertilizer should contain nitrogen in several forms, derived from both quickly available and slowly available sources. The most favorable ratio is 1 to 3, one part from quickly soluble sources and three parts from slowly available sources. This makes it possible to avoid having more nitrogen available than is needed shortly after an application of fertilizer and a deficiency of nitrogen later in the season. And it also makes it possible to reduce the number of applications required per season.

Rate of Application: The rate of application will depend upon the analysis of the fertilizer used, the fertility requirements of the soil as indicated by soil tests, the kind of grasses which compose the turf and, to some extent, upon the structure of the soil.

Without the benefit of soil tests only very general recommendations can be made. The amount of fertilizer to apply can best be figured on the basis of the actual nitrogen required, the level of fertility, and the type of grass being taken into consideration.

The amount of fertilizer which it will be necessary to apply per 1,000 square feet in order to supply one pound of nitrogen may be obtained by dividing 100 by the percentage of nitrogen contained in the fertilizer.

Analysis of fertilizer 5–10–5; $100 \div 5 = 20$

Therefore it would require 20 lbs. of a 5–10–5 fertilizer to supply 1 lb. of nitrogen per 1,000 sq. ft.

Analysis of fertilizer 10–5–5; $100 \div 10 = 10$

Therefore it would require 10 lb. of a 10–5–5 fertilizer to supply 1 lb. of nitrogen per 1,000 sq. ft.

A fertilization program may be worked out for any type of grass, on soils of varying fertility, and with fertilizers of varied analyses, if this procedure is followed and the proper ratio maintained.

RATE OF APPLICATION CHART

General Recommendations

KIND OF GRASS	SOIL FERTILITY	LBS. OF NITROGEN REQUIRED PER 1,000 SQ. FT. PER YEAR	LBS. OF FERTILIZER TO APPLY PER YEAR PER 1,000 SQ. FT. ANALYSIS 10–5–5 OR 10–6–4
Kentucky Bluegrass predominating in the mixture	High	2 to 3 lbs.	20 to 30 lbs.
	Medium	3 to 5 lbs.	30 to 50 lbs.
	Low	5 to 6 lbs.	50 to 60 lbs.
Merion Kentucky Blue-grass sown alone	High	3 to 4 lbs.	30 to 40 lbs.
	Medium	4 to 5 lbs.	40 to 50 lbs.
	Low	6 to 6½ lbs.	60 to 65 lbs.
Fescues predominating in the mixture	High	1 to 1½ lbs.	10 to 15 lbs.
	Medium	1½ to 2 lbs.	15 to 20 lbs.
	Low	2½ to 3 lbs.	25 to 30 lbs.
Bermuda Grass	High	1½ to 2 lbs.	15 to 20 lbs.
	Medium	3 to 4 lbs.	30 to 40 lbs.
	Low	4½ to 5 lbs.	45 to 50 lbs.
Zoysia Grass	High	1½ to 2 lbs.	15 to 20 lbs.
	Medium	2 to 3 lbs.	20 to 30 lbs.
	Low	3 to 4½ lbs.	30 to 45 lbs.

Time of Application: The time of application will depend upon the type of grass, the fertility of the soil and the kind of fertilizer used.

Bluegrass Mixtures: On soils of high fertility one application in the autumn (late August to mid-October) will be sufficient, provided the fertilizer contains ⅔ of its nitrogen in a slowly available form, such as urea-form. On soils of low fertility it is advisable to make two applications of fertilizer of this type—two-thirds of the total amount in the autumn and one-third in late spring. If the fertilizer used does not contain slowly available forms of nitrogen three applications should be made, the first very early in the spring, the second in early May and the third in early autumn.

Bermuda Grass: First application in early spring, second application in early autumn. Additional application of nitrogen in early summer if the need is indicated.

Zoysia Grass: First application in early spring; second in late spring or early summer.

Fescue Mixtures: Same program as for Bluegrass.

Top Dressing

One method of supplying additional fertility to lawn areas and of improving the texture of the soil is through the use of top dressings.

Top dressings in the form of rich top-soil, compost or spent mushroom soil are widely used on many golf courses to keep the putting greens, which are composed largely of bent grasses, in the best possible condition.

In using top-soil and compost for this purpose it is extremely important that it be free of weed seeds. It is a disheartening experience to go to the labor and expense of applying a top dressing only to find that one has introduced new weeds into the lawn area. It is, however, possible to destroy the weed seeds in the soil before it is spread so that there will be no danger of having this occur. The chemicals most satisfactory for this purpose are calcium cyanamide and Vapam.

See page 157 for the method to be followed.

The top dressing, which may be applied at any time during the growing season, should be spread as a thin layer over the surface of the lawn and worked into the turf with the back of an iron rake.

Use of Lime on Lawns

In order to promote a vigorous, healthy growth of the lawn grasses the soil reaction should be kept as nearly neutral as possible. While it is true that the bent grasses and the fescues are decidedly tolerant of acid soil, they will make better growth on more nearly neutral soils.

Normally, grasses produce a new crop of roots each year. The old roots die, adding humus to the soil. On extremely acid soil, however, these old roots fail to decay and the soil tends to become seriously sod bound.

Another point in favor of maintaining a neutral soil reaction is the recently discovered fact that on highly acid soils the grasses are unable to use nitrogen in the form of ammonium compounds. Under such conditions the grass apparently absorbs the nitrogen but cannot assimilate it, and a toxic reaction occurs. It is also a well-known fact that when soils become highly acid something happens to the structure of the soil itself, and it gradually becomes less and less permeable to water. An adequate application of lime therefore not only overcomes the acidity of the soil, but also improves the structure of the soil and increases its water-absorbing capacity, as well as supplying small quantities of plant food in the form of calcium and magnesium.

If soil tests indicate a degree of acidity below a pH of 6, an application of lime should be made, either in the form of hydrated lime or in the form of finely ground limestone. The most favorable seasons for applying lime are autumn, winter and very early spring, when the alternate freezing and thawing of the ground will enable the lime to penetrate more deeply into the soil. It may, however, be applied at any season of the year. Lime is slow in its reaction and no appreciable benefits will be noticed until five or six months after the application has been made. However, the eventual beneficial effects of lime are of long duration and will be apparent for several years. Unless the soil is intensely acid, which occurs infrequently, an application of lime once every two or three years will be sufficient to maintain the correct soil reaction. (For the rate of application refer to the table on page 171.)

Mowing

The height at which a lawn should be maintained depends upon the type of grass or grasses which compose the turf. Some grasses thrive best, and present the most attractive appearance, when they are cut very close, while other grasses must be maintained at a greater height in order to produce a healthy, vigorous turf.

	HEIGHT AFTER MOWING
Bent Grasses	$\frac{1}{4}$ to $\frac{1}{2}$ inch
Bermuda Grass	$\frac{3}{16}$ to $\frac{3}{8}$ inch
Fescues	2 inches
Kentucky Bluegrass	1 to $1\frac{1}{2}$ inches
Merion Kentucky Bluegrass	$\frac{1}{2}$ to $\frac{3}{4}$ inch
Zoysia	$\frac{1}{2}$ to $\frac{3}{4}$ inch

The lawn mower should be checked periodically and adjusted whenever necessary. In order to adjust a mower so that it will cut at a given height, set the roller which is on the back of the mower so that the bedknife, which is the long flat blade against which the blades on the revolving reel cut, is at the desired height.

Frequent and wisely regulated mowing tends to produce a fine-textured turf, as new leaf growth is stimulated. If a lawn is neglected and the grass is allowed to become too tall before it is cut the results are very unfortunate, as the growth becomes coarse and tough and the leaves lose their healthy, deep green color. This is particularly true in the case of Bermuda grass.

Extremely early mowing should be avoided on lawns which are predominantly Kentucky bluegrass, as the root system is entirely renewed each spring and if the grass is closely mown early in the season there will be a decided reduction in root development. The quality of the turf will suffer considerably in consequence, and the grass will be less able to withstand the vicissitudes of summer droughts. In order to insure vigorous root growth, the first spring mowing should not be done until the grass has reached a height of two inches.

Under normal conditions the grass clippings should be allowed to remain on the lawn, thus helping to maintain the humus supply in the soil. If, because of a long period of wet weather or for some other unavoidable cause, the grass has become unusually long and rank in growth the clippings will have a tendency to form a mat on the surface of the newly mown lawn and will have a detrimental effect on the growth of the turf. If the clippings are heavy they should be raked up with a light bamboo rake and removed. If the lawn mower is equipped with a grass catcher the necessity of raking will be eliminated.

In selecting lawn mowers of the motor type it is advisable to avoid those which are equipped with heavy rollers, as they have a tendency to make the soil too compact. The danger of soil compaction is far greater on heavy soils than on light, sandy soils.

Growth Inhibitors

Maleic hydrazide (MH) or (MH40). This chemical, which has come into horticultural use within recent years, possesses the ability to retard the growth of plants without causing any permanent harm. The degree of retardation obtained is in direct proportion to the rate of application.

Maleic hydrazide has proved valuable in slowing down the rate of growth of grasses, thus reducing the number of mowings on turf areas along parkways and in cemeteries.

It is not recommended for general use on home lawns or for turf areas subjected to heavy foot traffic, such as playgrounds and certain park areas. Experiments have shown that when an entire lawn area is treated with MH the various types of grasses found in the average home lawn mixture react differently to it, some varieties being retarded more than others. This results in a ragged, unkempt

appearance. However, occasional areas which are difficult to mow, such as areas along fences, and narrow strips bordering paths or flower beds may be treated satisfactorily with MH and will help to reduce the costs of maintenance.

Aeration

Many soils tend to become very compact and when this occurs on lawn areas conditions become less favorable for the vigorous growth of the turf. Clay and clay-loam soils are more subject to compaction than are soils of other types, but even sandy soils may become somewhat compact and crusted on the surface.

On lawns which are too compact water fails to penetrate down into the soil, and in time of heavy rains there is apt to be considerable surface run-off. Grasses on such soils tend to become shallow rooted, since there is such meager percolation of water through the soil, and the turf suffers seriously in time of drought. When fertilizers are applied on the surface of heavily compacted soils they often fail to penetrate down to the lower root levels where they are most needed, and on such soils the grasses also suffer from a lack of oxygen due to the fact that sufficient air cannot enter the soil.

Adequate aeration of lawn areas therefore serves many functions. It reduces surface run-off of water, and by permitting water to percolate down into the soil it encourages a deeper and more vigorous root system which results in a dense, luxuriant turf. It makes it possible for fertilizers to penetrate to a depth where the roots can readily make use of the nutrients, and it provides for a better circulation of air in the soil which lessens the danger of oxygen starvation.

Aeration is usually done at the time that fertilizer is applied in the spring and again in the early autumn.

There is a variety of tools which are suitable for the aeration of lawn areas. The simplest is an ordinary garden fork, practical only on very small lawns as it is laborious to use. The fork should be inserted into the turf at a 45 degree angle to a depth of four to six inches and a slight downward pressure should be exerted on the handle before it is withdrawn. This procedure should be followed at a distance of every foot. A fork especially designed for this purpose, known as an Aeri-fork, is also available. Another simple method is to drive spikes through a board. The board may be placed on the turf and by walking along it the spikes will be driven into the ground. This procedure is repeated over the area and is an effective method, but practical only on very small lawns. Flat wooden sandals with spikes on the bottom may also be purchased which may be strapped on the feet and in the natural process of walking will perform much the same function as the board. For larger lawn areas there are numerous excellent tools on the market of the spike-disc type which may be pushed like a hand lawn mower. For extensive park and golf areas power-driven machines are available.

Watering

The watering of a lawn must be done with intelligence and discretion. Otherwise more harm than good may result from one's efforts. A thorough watering once a week during dry weather is of far greater value than daily sprinklings. Frequent, light waterings tend to make the plants shallow-rooted and consequently less vigorous, and by keeping the surface constantly moist ideal conditions are provided for the growth and spread of fungous diseases and for the germination of weed seeds and also for the growth of crabgrass.

Water should be applied in the form of a fine, mist-like spray which will fall gently and evenly upon the surface. If an ordinary garden hose is used a fog nozzle should be attached rather than the usual type. Perforated hoses are excellent for supplying water to small areas as they deliver small, mist-like jets of water and they can be easily shifted from one section to another. The oscillating type of sprinkler is also very satisfactory, as it applies water evenly and slowly.

It is important not to apply water faster than the soil can absorb it, or in the form of a coarse, heavy spray, as the surface then becomes so thoroughly saturated that normal percolation is hindered. In order that the grass roots may derive the fullest benefit, the water should penetrate to a depth of at least 4 to 6 inches.

Sub-Irrigation Systems

Before the introduction of plastic pipe an irrigation system for the lawn was seldom within the range of possibility for the small home owner, due to the high cost not only of materials but also of installation. However, there are now on the market a number of excellent outfits which are moderate in price and which may be easily installed by the "do-it-yourself" method.

Polyethylene plastic pipe has many advantages over the various types of metal pipe. It is light in weight, pliable and easy to handle; it will not rust, rot or corrode; it does not need to be buried in a deep trench, as it will not freeze and crack; and it contains no substances which are toxic to plants.

Most of the outfits on the market are equipped with non-corrosive brass fittings, and the sprinkler heads are set flush with the turf so that they will not interfere with the mowing of the lawn. These home outfits are suited to low pressure water systems as well as to high pressure systems, and they are obtainable in various sizes, covering from 1,000 square feet upward. The sprinkler heads deliver a fine spray similar to a gentle rainfall.

Since most lawn grasses are very dependent upon an adequate supply of moisture in order to maintain active, vigorous growth it is a tremendous advantage to be able to supply water *when* it is needed, and although an irrigation system involves an initial outlay it may be considered as a permanent investment and the cost is relatively small when spread over a period of years.

Renovation of Old Lawns

The renovation of old lawns presents special problems. If, through neglect, a lawn has become shabby, and if the better grasses have been crowded out by grasses of inferior quality and by encroaching weeds, it is important to determine how far this process of deterioration has progressed. If it is evident that the existing sod still contains a fair proportion of good grasses much may be accomplished through the initiation of a good program of fertilization, careful mowing, watering and weed control. In all probability the lack of adherence to such a program was the cause of the deterioration of the lawn. For the procedure to be followed see Maintenance of Existing Lawns, page 187.

If, however, the weeds and inferior grasses have become so dominant that they have almost entirely crowded out the good lawn grasses, more drastic measures will have to be taken and the entire area should be prepared for reseeding. This may be done in a number of ways. If the area is small it may be spaded or forked over by hand and a good seed-bed prepared. If it is a comparatively large area a rototiller or some similar implement may be used which will leave the soil in excellent tilth. In most communities such work may be done on the custom basis.

Another method which is recommended and which has the great advantage of eliminating the subsequent germination of weed seeds is the use of Lawn and Garden Cyanamid. When this method is followed it is necessary that the work be started early in August in order that the area may be ready for seeding by September, as the new grass will then have an opportunity to become well established before cold weather.

The procedure is as follows. The existing turf should be mown as closely as possible and all old growth should be raked off. The area should then be watered thoroughly to a penetration of at least 4 inches, and as soon as the surface has dried sufficiently it should be scratched well with an iron rake. The cyanamid should be spread evenly over the surface at the rate of 5 lbs. per 100 sq. ft. It is important to make an even distribution, and this can be best accomplished with a fertilizer distributor.

After it has been spread the cyanamid should be raked *very* lightly into the surface with an iron rake, so that it will come into close contact with the soil. If the soil is at all dry it should be watered lightly and should be kept moist, but not too wet, throughout the entire period. The area should remain undisturbed for three weeks. During this period all existing growth of weeds and grasses will be killed off and all weed seeds in the upper inch of soil will be killed. In addition the cyanamid will have broken down into ammonia and nitrate nitrogen compounds which will provide valuable nutrients for the new grass, and the lime content of the soil will also have been appreciably increased, as each 100 lbs. of cyanamid supplies the equivalent of 70 lbs. of lime.

At the end of the three week period the area should be watered well and the soil raked very lightly preparatory to sowing. The seed should be sown in the usual manner (see page 186), and the area should either be rolled or raked lightly, just enough to bring the seed into good contact with the soil.

Precaution: When cyanamid is applied in the quantity recommended above it is highly toxic to all plant life for a period of several weeks until the "free" cyanamid has broken down. It is therefore not advisable to apply it within two feet of trees, shrubs or flowers which border the lawn area.

CONTROL OF LAWN PESTS

Precaution: As is true of many insecticides, the chemicals recommended for the control of lawn pests are poisonous and must be handled with care. Special care should be taken not to inhale the dusts or the wettable powders and not to let the materials come into contact with the skin as, in some cases, there is danger of absorption through the skin. If these simple precautions are observed there should be no danger in applying the materials which are recommended.

Chinch Bug (Hairy Chinch Bug)

Identification: The adults are about $\frac{1}{8}$ of an inch in length. The body is black with short, white wings. The young nymphs are very small, bright red with a white crossband. As they mature they become brownish, then black. Upon very close examination both the adults and the young nymphs may be seen, in infested areas, at the base of the stems near the crown.

Injury: The young nymphs feed at the base of the grass blades, sucking the juices from the plants. The turf becomes brown, and irregular, somewhat circular, dead patches are formed. The margin is usually a sickly yellow and it is in this area that the young nymphs may be found feeding. The injury from chinch bugs is differentiated from injury caused by beetle grubs in that the infested grass cannot be rolled back like a piece of carpet, as is the case with grub injury.

Life History: The adults usually winter in tall grasses and weeds. In the spring they migrate to the lawn and the females lay their eggs at the grass roots. The eggs hatch during June and the young nymphs begin feeding on the turf. They pass through several molts before becoming adults. A second brood, which is often more damaging than the first, appears in August and the nymphs and adults continue to feed until well into October.

Control: There are several chemicals which will give excellent control. When dusts are applied they should be worked well into the turf with the back of an iron rake.

The first application of the chemical should be made in June. If there is still evidence of infestation a second application should be made in August. Close cutting and a top-dressing of fertilizer following treatment will aid the recovery of the injured turf.

Chlordane is a quick-acting and effective control. It may be applied either as a dust or as a spray.

1. Apply a 5 percent dust at the rate of 5 lbs. per 1,000 sq. ft. It will be easier to obtain an even distribution if the dust is mixed with sand or fertilizer. It may be applied with a fertilizer distributor or by hand.
2. Apply as a spray at the rate of 4 oz. of a 50 percent wettable powder to 10 gal. of water per 1,000 sq. ft.

DDT is slower in its action than chlordane, but has a longer residual effect. It may be applied as a 10 percent dust at the rate of 6 lbs. per 1,000 sq. ft.

Dieldrin has a longer residual effect than most other chemicals. It can be applied in the form of a 5 percent dust at the rate of $2\frac{1}{2}$ lbs. per 1,000 sq. ft. After the dust has been worked into the turf with the back of a rake

it should be sprinkled lightly with a fog nozzle. The area should not be watered heavily for at least 24 hours.

Grubs

There are numerous grubs which cause severe damage to lawns. Among them are the grubs of the Asiatic Beetle, the European Lawn Chafer, the Japanese Beetle, the May Beetle or June Bug, the Oriental Beetle, and the Southern Masked Chafer.

Identification: The grubs are whitish with dark, yellowish brown heads and three pairs of legs. They vary in size from $\frac{1}{4}$ inch to $1\frac{1}{2}$ inches in length.

Injury: The grubs feed upon the roots of the grasses. If they are present in great numbers they seriously injure the growth of the turf and if measures of control are not taken they may kill the grass entirely. Badly infested turf appears brown and dead and can be rolled back like a carpet.

By cutting out a square foot of sod to a depth of 3 to 4 inches and examining it, one may readily determine whether it is seriously infested with grubs. The presence of 5 to 10 grubs would be indicative of light infestation, but enough to warrant treatment. A count of 30 to 50 grubs would indicate very heavy infestation.

Life History: The adult beetles lay their eggs in the green turf or under the grass roots during the summer months. The grubs hatch and begin feeding on the roots immediately. During the winter they move downward in the soil to a depth which will protect them from freezing, moving upward in the spring where they feed again prior to passing into the pupa stage. Some types, such as the May Beetle, require two years to complete their life cycle.

Control: Complete control of grubs may be obtained through the use of chemical insecticides. These may be applied at any time of the year except when the ground is frozen. Application during April and early May is recommended. One application of some chemicals will provide effective control for a period of 3 to 5 years. All grub-proofing insecticides should be watered in with a heavy spray as soon as possible after application in order to become immediately effective and to lessen the danger of harm to birds and pets.

Chlordane will control most species of grubs and is effective when applied in any of the following forms:

1. 5 percent dust at the rate of 5 lbs. per 1,000 sq. ft.
2. 50 percent wettable powder at the rate of 8 oz. to 10 gal. of water per 1,000 sq. ft.
3. 2·5 percent granular form at the rate of 10 lbs. per 1,000 sq. ft.

DDT is effective against Japanese Beetle grubs but is not effective against May or June Beetles or the Chafers. It may be applied as a

1. 5 percent dust at the rate of 12 lbs. per 1,000 sq. ft.
2. 50 percent wettable powder at the rate of 20 oz. to 10 gal. of water per 1,000 sq. ft.

Dieldrin is extremely long-lasting in its residual effect and will provide protection over a period of several years. It may be applied in any of the following forms:

1. 1 percent dust at the rate of 8 lbs. per 1,000 sq. ft.
2. 25 percent wettable powder at the rate of 5 oz. to 20 gal. of water per 1,000 sq. ft.
3. 2 percent granular form applied at the rate of 3·5 lbs. per 1,000 sq. ft.
   This may be applied as purchased, or may be mixed with fertilizer and applied with a distributor.
4. Some lawn fertilizers contain dieldrin for grub control.

Moles

Moles often cause severe damage to lawns. As beetle grubs are one of their chief sources of food the best measure of control is to deprive them of their food supply in the lawn area by eradicating the grubs. See above section on "Grubs".

For measures of control see page 674.

Sod Webworm (Lawn Moth)

The sod webworms are most prevalent on bent grass and bluegrass lawns and are more damaging in warm climates than in the North. There are a number of species which cause damage to lawns.

Identification: Although the adult moths and the caterpillars differ somewhat in appearance, according to the species, they all have certain common characteristics. The small moths are usually seen at dusk, flying low over the grass where the eggs are dropped. The small, thick-bodied caterpillars, from $\frac{1}{4}$ to $\frac{3}{4}$ of an inch in length, make silk-lined tunnels between the grass blades near the ground.

Injury: When young, the caterpillars skeletonize the grass blades while feeding but as they mature they chew off the blades, causing the lawn to become ragged in appearance. If the infestation is heavy and measures of control are not taken, large areas of turf may be killed out.

Control:

Chlordane in any of the following forms:

1. 5 percent dust at the rate of $1\frac{1}{4}$ lbs. per 1,000 sq. ft.
2. 50 percent wettable powder at the rate of $2\frac{1}{2}$ oz. to 10 gal. water per 1,000 sq. ft.

DDT—5 percent dust at the rate of $2\frac{1}{2}$ lbs. per 1,000 sq. ft.

Dieldrin—5 percent dust at the rate of $2\frac{1}{2}$ lbs. per 1,000 sq. ft. Water lightly with a fine, mist-like spray.

LAWN DISEASES

Brownpatch

Brownpatch is a fungous disease caused by Rhizoctonia solani. Many species of lawn grasses are affected, the bent grasses being particularly susceptible to injury. Some soils seem to be comparatively free from the fungus causing brownpatch, while other soils are badly infected. The disease is particularly prevalent during long periods of hot, humid weather. An excessive supply of nitrogen, overwatering, poor drainage conditions, and high soil acidity are contributing factors in the spread of the disease.

When the turf first becomes affected it turns a very dark green in color, and then gradually becomes a light brown, having the appearance of dead, dried grass. The patches are somewhat circular in outline, although very irregular in shape, and they vary in size from a diameter of a few inches to a diameter of several feet.

Control: There are a number of preventive measures which should be followed to lessen the occurrence of brownpatch.

1. Excessive applications of quickly available fertilizers high in nitrogen should be avoided.
2. Watering should be done in the morning in order to avoid having the grass wet during the night.
3. Good air circulation should be provided for the lawn area, even if it means sacrificing some trees and shrubs.
4. Adequate drainage should be provided for low areas.

There are a number of effective measures for the control of brownpatch. Under ordinary conditions it is the practice to treat a lawn only upon the appearance of the disease. However, in sections where it is very prevalent, periodic treatments are advised.

Acti-dione Ferrated (cyclohexamide) is an antibiotic which has proved very effective in the control of brownpatch. It is obtainable in a dual package containing a small bottle of the antibiotic and a larger bottle of ferrous sulfate. These should be mixed together, diluted according to the manufacturer's directions, and applied to the affected area. Applications should be made at intervals of 10 to 15 days.

Corrosive Sublimate plus a *calomel fungicide* is one of the most effective controls. It is put out under various trade names such as Calocure and Calo-clor. When applied during very hot weather a slight yellowing of the turf may occur but the injury is only temporary. The manufacturer's directions should be followed with care.

Phenyl Mercuric Acetate will give good control. It is put out under the trade names PMAS, and Tact-C-Lect. Follow manufacturer's instructions with care.

Thiuram—sold under the trade name Tersan, is also an effective control and will not cause injury to the turf.

Copper Spot

This fungous disease sometimes appears on bent grass lawns after a prolonged rainy spell during the late spring or summer months. Upon close observation salmon-pink spores may be observed on the grass blades.

Control: There are several chemicals which are effective:

Cadmium compounds such as Cadminate.

Captan.

Phenyl mercury compounds such as PMAS and Tact-C-Lect.

Dollarspot

This is a form of brownpatch, causing small, circular patches hardly more than 2 inches in diameter. The patches are of a somewhat lighter color than those which are typical of brownpatch. The measures of control are identical.

Fading-out (Curvularia) (Black Mold)

A fungous disease usually occurring on bent grasses, the fescues and annual bluegrass. Velvet bent is particularly susceptible.

The injury is most severe during the heat of midsummer but the disease may also occur in late spring or early autumn. Lawns affected with the fungus develop a yellowish-green dappled appearance, similar in some respects to iron chlorosis, and the grass eventually dies out. Upon examination under a lens a black mold may be observed on affected blades.

Control:

Phenyl mercury compounds such as PMAS or Tact-C-Lect applied at 10 day intervals will usually give effective control. Injury to the turf may occur if applications are made when the temperature is above 80 degrees F. During periods of hot weather applications should be made in the evening after the sun has gone down.

Leaf Spots

The various leaf spots, which cause the diseases commonly known as Melting-out and Going-out, seriously damage lawns in some sections. Kentucky, Canada and annual bluegrasses are particularly susceptible. Merion Kentucky bluegrass is highly resistant.

Going-out disease, sometimes called Foot rot, occurs in the spring from March through May and occasionally reoccurs in the autumn. The leaves attacked by the fungus shrivel, the crowns turn brown and the rhizomes and roots rot away. Large areas of turf may become affected unless measures of control are undertaken.

Control: Phenyl mercury compounds such as PMAS or Tact-C-Lect will give excellent control if applied at two week intervals from the last of March until early May.

Melting-out disease occurs during the midsummer months. The control is the same as for the Going-out disease.

Slime Molds

During periods of heavy rain in midsummer slimy, yellowish or grayish molds may appear on patches of turf, and in some instances will smother the grasses.

Control: The most satisfactory measure of control is to wash off the mold with a strong force of water, and when the grass is dry to dust it with fine, dusting sulfur.

Snow Mold (Winter Scald)

When the last of a heavy snow has melted, patches of turf may be found which are covered with a grayish-white or pinkish mold. This is caused by a fungus which thrives at low temperatures, and serious damage to the turf may occur. Low areas are particularly susceptible to attack.

Control:

Acti-dione Ferrated, one of the antibiotics, has proved very effective in the control of Snow Mold. It should be applied to the turf late in the autumn before the first snow.

Corrosive Sublimate plus a *calomel fungicide* such as Calocure or Calo-clor will give excellent control if applied before the first heavy snow.

Phenyl mercury compounds such as PMAS and Tact-C-Lect are also effective controls. Application should be made in the autumn before the first heavy snowfall.

CONTROL OF LAWN WEEDS

On areas where a sound program of turf management is faithfully carried out, there will be comparatively little trouble with weeds.

Vigorous, rapidly growing grass is capable of crowding out many of the existing weeds and is also capable of preventing new weeds from gaining a foothold. Many excellent lawns which are entirely free from weeds have been established and are maintained solely through the application of the fundamental practices of good lawn management.

If, however, these practices have been neglected and if a lawn area has become badly infested with weeds, very definite measures of weed eradication should be adopted, along with a general improvement in the management program for the lawn.

On very small areas hand weeding may be practiced with excellent results. It is of vital importance, however, that the weeds be removed before seed has formed. After the hand weeding has been completed, all bare areas should be prepared for reseeding in accordance with the general principles involved in the seeding of new lawns.

While hand weeding may be practical on small areas or where the infestation is very light, it is not a feasible practice for large areas, as it is far too tedious and costly a method. On large areas effective weed control may best be obtained through the use of various chemicals. Within recent years a great deal of research has been carried on by the various experiment stations in regard to the chemical control of weeds, and it has been proved conclusively that practically all of our common lawn weeds may be entirely eradicated through the proper and timely use of various chemicals. The factors contributing to the success of this method are: the selection of the chemical most effective for the control of each particular weed or group of weeds; the method and time of application; the rate of application; and the subsequent method of the re-establishment of the turf.

Most lawn weeds may be divided into three classes according to their general habit of growth. It has been found that for each of these groups some one method of chemical control will give the best results. It is, therefore,

important to select the chemical which is most effective for the particular type of weed to be eradicated.

Weedy Grasses

Crabgrass

Of the weed-like grasses which infest lawn areas, crabgrass is by far the most troublesome. In order to eradicate it or to keep it under control, it is well to know something of its habit of growth. Crabgrass is a tender annual, thriving in full sun and unable to endure shade. The seed germinates late in the spring, the plants make slow growth during early summer, grow rapidly during late July and August, reseed most prolifically, and are killed by the first light frost. In controlling crabgrass, we have three points of attack: to hand-weed the young plants if the area is small; to provide for such a luxuriant growth of the better lawn grasses and to maintain the lawn at a sufficient height ($1\frac{1}{2}$ inches) so that the young crabgrass seedlings cannot gain a foothold; or to use some chemical measure of control, which will either kill the crabgrass or will prevent it from reseeding.

The three chemicals which have proved the most effective in the control of crabgrass are disodium methyl arsonate, phenyl mercuric acetate, and potassium cyanate.

Disodium methyl arsonate (available under various trade names) is one of the most effective controls. If four applications are made during the season it is possible to obtain almost complete eradication. The first application should be made early in July, the second a week or ten days later. The third application should be made about the 10th of August and the last should follow a week or ten days later.

When used under favorable conditions, the soil being moist and temperature moderate, disodium methyl arsonate will not injure the permanent lawn grasses. However, where the soil is dry and temperatures are high serious injury may occur from its use. It is therefore wise to take due precautions. If the soil is dry it should be watered thoroughly the day before the spraying is to be done so that there will be a penetration to a depth of at least four inches. Spraying when the temperature is excessively high, 90° F. or over, should be avoided if at all possible. During periods of hot weather it should be a practice to spray on cloudy days or late in the afternoon in order to avoid direct sun upon the turf.

Disodium methyl arsonate is comparatively non-toxic to warm-blooded animals. It is non-corrosive and may be applied with a sprayer, a watering can or a syphoning device. The manufacturer's directions should be followed with care.

Phenyl mercuric acetate is available under a number of trade names in both the liquid and dust forms. In the liquid form it may also be obtained combined with 2,4–D, which increases its usefulness, as in this form it is effective against some of the broad-leaved lawn weeds as well as against crabgrass. Some grasses are much more sensitive to the effects of phenyl mercuric acetate than are other grasses. Fortunately, crabgrass and goosegrass are in this class, while Kentucky bluegrass, the bent grasses, and most of the other desirable lawn grasses suffer no permanent injury if the material is applied at the recommended rate. Merion Kentucky bluegrass is an exception, as it is sensitive to phenyl mercury compounds and serious injury may occur. In the case of the other grasses there may be a temporary browning of the turf but they will recover quickly.

Phenyl mercuric acetate is an effective control for all species of crabgrass, and in addition it helps to hold certain fungous diseases, such as brownpatch and dollarspot, in check. It also has the advantage of leaving no harmful residue in the soil, and the area where the crabgrass has been killed may be prepared immediately for reseeding.

In the liquid form, phenyl mercuric acetate may be applied with a sprayer or with a watering can. During the early part of the season, when the crabgrass seedlings are just beginning to germinate, a weak solution should be used, and if weekly applications are made at this time the crabgrass plants will die in the seedling stage and the lawn will suffer very little disfigurement. Later in the season, when the plants are making more vigorous growth, a stronger solution should be used. On newly established lawns the weaker solution should always be used. The dry form of phenyl mercuric acetate may be applied most satisfactorily with a small lawn-fertilizer spreader which will insure an even and accurate distribution. If such a piece of equipment is not available, however, a small kitchen collander may be used very successfully. A total of three applications of the dust should be made; the first not later than the middle of July when the young crabgrass plants are in active growth, the other two applications following at intervals of a week or ten days. At the time that the application is made the temperature should not be above 90 degrees, the soil should be reasonably moist but the grass itself should be dry, and there should be no expectation of rain for at least 12 hours. If a heavy rain occurs immediately following an application, an additional treatment should be made

several days later. The grass should be about 1½ inches tall at the time that the application is made, and any recently mown clippings should be raked off. Applications should preferably be made in the late afternoon or early evening. The action of phenyl mercuric acetate is through absorption by the leaves, and the dew will help dissolve the chemicals and make the application more rapidly effective. The lawn should not be mown for several days following the application, and it should not be watered for at least 48 hours.

Potassium cyanate is also recommended as a control for crabgrass and it is effective against chickweed, veronica, knotweed, and goosegrass as well. It possesses the additional advantages of being of very low toxicity to human beings and to animals, and of having some fertilizing value. When potassium cyanate comes into contact with the soil it is rapidly broken down into potash and nitrogen. Two or three applications are recommended, the first early in July, the last by mid-August. On large areas applications may be made with a power sprayer, while on small areas a hand sprayer may be used very satisfactorily. Applications of potassium cyanate should be made only when lawn grasses are making active, vigorous growth. Under such conditions there will be little injury to most lawn grasses other than a slight and very temporary discoloration of the tips. However, if application is made during periods of extreme heat, or when growth is stunted because of drought, severe injury may result. Bent grasses are susceptible to injury and potassium cyanate is not recommended for use on bent grass lawns. Potassium cyanate may be combined with 2,4–D, but when this is done there is greater danger of injury to the turf.

Pre-emergence Weed Killers (available under various trade names) have been used with varying success on lawns. The purpose of applying sprays of this type is to prevent the germination of the crabgrass seed and to kill the small seedling plants before they have had time to make any growth. As crabgrass seeds continue to germinate over a period of six weeks or more, from mid-spring to early summer, two to four applications are necessary. In some instances the pre-emergence sprays have given excellent control, while in other situations they have been less satisfactory. The manufacturer's instructions should be followed with care.

Mat-forming Weeds

In this group we find several weeds which are sometimes very troublesome on lawns and which, if no measures of control are undertaken, may utterly ruin an area of turf. There are, fortunately, several chemicals which will give effective control of the mat-forming weeds.

Chickweed. Both the common chickweed (Stelaria Media) and the Mouse-ear chickweed (Cerastium) may be controlled by spraying with potassium cyanate. Control is most effective when the application is made during moderately warm weather. If spraying is undertaken during the cooler months it should be done on a warm, sunny day and hot water should be used when mixing the spray.

For further details concerning potassium cyanate see page 199.

Knotgrass may be most effectively controlled by spraying with 2,4,5–T plus 2,4–D, obtainable under such trade names as Improved Weedone. Directions given on the container should be followed with care.

See precautions on page 608.

Lawn Pennywort (Hydrocotyle rotundifolia). Sodium Arsenite has proved to be one of the most effective chemicals for the control of this very troublesome lawn weed. As it is a dangerous poison it should be handled with extreme care.

Treatment may be made at any time during the growing season. The lawn area which has been treated will become uniformly brown for a period of 5–6 days, but will fully recover within the following few weeks.

1. Mix 6 ounces of Sodium Arsenite with 12 quarts of dry sand and sift over the infested area. An ordinary kitchen sifter is very satisfactory. Apply at the rate of 6 ounces of Sodium Arsenite to every 1,000 square feet of lawn area, and it is important that an even application be made. At the time that the application is made the soil should be moderately moist and the grass should be in good, growing condition.

2. Dissolve 4 ounces of Sodium Arsenite in 20 gallons of water and apply as a spray. This quantity is sufficient for 1,000 square feet (10 lbs. per acre).

Rosette-forming Weeds

Dandelion. Very effective control may be obtained by spraying with 2,4–D, one of the hormone weed-killers (available under various trade names). Applications are most effective when made in the spring shortly before the plants come into full bloom, or in the autumn from mid-October to early November. Results are not as satisfactory from applications made in late spring or during the summer. If the infestation is light, spot treatment may be done, but if the infestation is heavy it will be advisable to treat the entire lawn area.

2,4–D may be used as a spray or in the dry form, being applied with a fertilizer distributor.

See precautions under Plantain on use of 2,4–D on lawn areas.

Plantain. Both the broad-leaved plantain and the narrow-leaved plantain, or buckhorn, may be effectively controlled by treatment with 2,4–D (available under various trade names). Applications are most effective when made during the spring or early summer. When the infestation is light spot treatment may be done, but if the lawn is heavily infested the entire area should be treated.

2,4–D may be used as a spray or in the dry form, being applied with a fertilizer distributor.

Precautions: Most lawn grasses are extremely resistant to the effects of 2,4–D and will show practically no injury if it is applied at the prescribed rate. It will, however, definitely depress the growth of bent grasses and clover, and in some cases they will be seriously injured or killed.

Young seedling grasses of all species will be seriously injured or killed out entirely by an application of 2,4–D. A new lawn should not be sprayed until it has been mown at least twice and the plants have begun to form a crown. The same precautions should be observed in cases where an established lawn has been seeded with a superior grass such as Merion Kentucky bluegrass.

When applying 2,4–D on lawns precautions must be taken to prevent the material from drifting onto other areas as many flowering plants, vegetables, trees and shrubs are very susceptible to 2,4–D and serious injury may occur. Applications should be made on a day when there is little or no wind.

A sprayer used for 2,4–D should be used for no other purpose except for the application of the hormone sprays.

See page 607 for the general use of 2,4–D.

Garlic

In many sections of the country garlic has become a serious weed pest on lawns. It is particularly unsightly in the early spring and gives a lawn a very unkempt and shabby appearance. Mowing does not offer an effective means of control, as it is only a temporary measure and the garlic will reappear the following spring, more vigorous than before. The most effective means of eradication is to spray with the ester form of 2,4–D. Complete eradication requires a three year spraying program. This is necessary because of the nature of the growth of the garlic plant which consists of the mother bulb, the young bulbs clustered about the mother bulb and the tiny bulblets. If one year in the three year spraying schedule is missed it will start the cycle again. Best results will be obtained when spraying is done during January, February or March. Later sprayings are much less effective, as it becomes more difficult to kill the plants as they reach maturity.

XVIII

GROUND COVERS

THE type of plant which is chosen for the special task of providing low, attractive verdure is known as a ground cover. Actually many plants in their natural state are ground covers, being low-growing and spreading in habit, but some of these are coarse and weedy in character, others are difficult to establish or maintain, and some are so aggressive that they cannot be kept within bounds. However, a few plants possess so many desirable qualities that they have come to play an increasingly important part in the landscape scheme. When ground covers are carefully chosen and are used with distinction and skill they greatly enhance the beauty of a planting composition.

In addition to their landscape value ground covers fulfill other important functions. Wherever planted they help protect the soil, conserving moisture and, during periods of extreme heat, maintaining lower temperatures in the soil, a matter of considerable importance in hot climates. When planted on steep banks they protect the soil from heavy rains and thus reduce the dangers of erosion. And by spreading their green carpet of foliage over areas of bare ground they prevent the encroachment of weeds.

In the development of the home property ground covers can be used in many ways. They can be planted as a pleasant foreground for the shrubbery border, and are of particular value for use among plantings of broad-leaved evergreens. Cultivation of the soil disturbs the roots of rhododendrons and laurels and ground cover plants afford welcome protection, serving much the same purpose as a mulch, as they keep the soil cool and moist. Ground covers may also be used very successfully on narrow or odd-shaped areas which often present a maintenance problem. Some are well suited for use as a green carpet on areas where it is difficult to establish good turf, as under trees which cast dense shade, or on banks where mowing would become a difficult problem. Most ground covers are not a substitute for lawn grasses, as they do not possess the same appearance or qualities, but they may often be used as a substitute for a lawn and will provide pleasant verdure on such areas.

It sometimes requires a year or more for a ground cover to become established, but once established it will usually require little care and attention. Some ground cover plants make fairly rapid growth and look well at the end of the first season, while with others it may require several seasons before a good coverage is obtained. The spacing of the plants has some bearing on this, and in every case the advantages of immediate results should be weighed against those of economy.

Selection of Ground Cover Plants

The selection of an attractive and suitable ground cover will depend, to a considerable extent, upon the area where it is to be used. There are ground covers which will grow well only in partial shade, others which will thrive only in full sun, while some are tolerant of both sun and shade. Some prefer moist soils rich in humus, others are particularly well adapted to dry, sandy soils. Some are low and mat-like, hugging the soil closely, while others are somewhat tall and spreading and of a shrubby character. Some are evergreen and are lovely at every season of the year, whereas others are deciduous and present a pleasing appearance only during the growing season.

It is therefore important that selections be made with care in order that the ground cover best adapted to the location may be chosen. Where a low evergreen ground cover is desired for a lightly shaded area there are a number which meet the requirements and from which a selection could be made, among them ajuga reptans, English ivy, pachysandra and vinca minor. For clothing a sunny bank some of the lovely prostrate Junipers with their ascending but ever-spreading branches and foliage of interesting texture would be a worthy choice, or, in very mild climates, gazania or one of the mesembryanthemums could be used. For a neat planting around a formal pool the lovely little campanula garganica would be a happy choice. For use on the north side of buildings where there is continual shade the choice is more limited, the most dependable ground covers for such a location being English ivy, lily-of-the-valley and ajuga reptans.

Occasionally two ground covers can be grown as companions. One of the pleasantest of such associations is that of periwinkle, (Vinca minor) and leadwort (Ceratostigma plumbaginoides). The soft, lavender-blue flowers of the periwinkle come in late spring and the brilliant blue flowers of the leadwort carry the period of bloom well into the autumn. During the spring months one is hardly aware that the leadwort forms a part of the planting, but in late summer it begins to assume a more important role and by September it has become completely dominant.

Spring-flowering bulbs, such as snowdrops and narcissus, and the autumn-flowering colchicums may be planted among some of the low-growing ground covers such as periwinkle and are very effective.

There are a few plants which are so invasive that they should never be used as ground cover plants. Some of them are occasionally used to clothe steep banks along highways but they should never be used on the home property as they are extremely difficult to restrain and to eradicate.

GROUND COVER PLANTS WHICH ARE INEXPENSIVE BUT TROUBLESOME

(*They become weeds and are difficult to restrain or eradicate*)

Lonicera japonica (Japanese Honeysuckle)
Lonicera japonica Halliana (Hall's Climbing Honeysuckle)
Lycium chinense (Chinese Matrimony Vine)

Lycium halimifolium (Matrimony Vine)
Lysimachia nummularia (Moneywort, Creeping Charlie)
Nepeta Glechoma (Ground Ivy, Gill-over-the-ground)

GROUND COVER PLANTS OF MERIT

NAMES, HEIGHT AND SPACING	REQUIREMENTS	TYPE AND USES	NOTES
Ajuga reptans (Carpet Bugle). 4″ high. 18–20 plants per sq. yd.	Sun, partial or dense shade. Any garden soil, even poor soil.	Perennial. On banks and in shrub border.	A very rapid grower, rich green foliage turning bronze in autumn. Blue flowers in May.
Arctostaphylos uva-ursi (Bearberry). 6–8″ high. 4 plants per sq. yd.	Partial shade or sun. Acid, sandy soil.	Native evergreen trailing shrub. On banks or in wild garden.	A slow grower. Rich, dark green foliage, and red berries in September and October.
Campanula garganica. 4″ high. 9 plants per sq. yd.	Sun or partial shade in good garden loam.	Perennial which hugs the surface of the ground.	Star-shaped, blue-violet flowers through the summer and autumn.

NAMES, HEIGHT AND SPACING	REQUIREMENTS	TYPE AND USES	NOTES
Cerastium tomentosum (Snow-in-summer). 10″ high. 8 or 9 plants per sq. yd.	Sun or light shade, in any soil.	Perennial, useful for covering bank or massing at edges of beds.	A rapid grower which forms solid mounds of foliage and bears an abundance of white flowers in June.
Ceanothus grisens horizontalis (Carmel Creeper). Plant 6–8′ apart.	Sun or partial shade. Suited only to mild climates.	Evergreen trailing shrub, native to California.	Blue flowers in dense clusters in spring.
Ceratostigma plumbaginoides (Plumbago Larpentæ) (Blue leadwort). 9″ high. 9 plants per sq. yd.	Partial or dense shade. Rich soil.	Perennial. Use under trees or as foreground for shrubbery or on shady banks.	Rich green leaves with blue flowers in August and September.

GROUND COVER OF SPREADING JUNIPERS, HEATHER AND COTONEASTERS IN A NATURALISTIC SETTING

NAMES, HEIGHT AND SPACING	REQUIREMENTS	TYPE AND USES	NOTES
Convallaria majalis (Lily-of-the-valley). 8″ high. 9 plants per sq. yd.	Dense or partial shade. Rich humus soil.	Perennial, native to woodlands in the N.E.	This vigorous plant forms solid masses of broad upright leaves and bears white bell-shaped fragrant flowers.
Cotoneaster horizontalis (Rock spray). 2′ high. 3 plants per sq. yd.	Sun or partial shade, in rich loam.	A deciduous shrub for covering banks or open spaces.	The small leaves are persistent and the bright red berries last until freezing weather.
Euonymus radicans (Winter creeper). 2–3′ high. 1 plant per sq. yd.	Light shade. Rich soil.	Evergreen vine good under trees or on banks.	This hardy vine forms permanent cover, but it may ascend trees. Showy orange fruit in clusters.
Euonymus radicans coloratus. 2′ high. 1 plant per sq. yd.	Light shade. Rich soil.	Evergreen vine. Use under trees or on banks.	This variety has rich bronze leaves in autumn.
Euonymus radicans kewensis. 1′ high. 3 plants per sq. yd.	Light shade. Rich soil.	Evergreen vine. Good under trees and on banks.	This variety has very small leaves and forms a dense mat.
Gazania splendens (gazania). 8″ high. 15 or 20 plants per sq. yd.	Full sun in good soil. Suited only to mild climates.	Perennial. Used on banks and in parking strips. Will not stand tramping.	The light green foliage is white beneath. Orange, yellow and cream color flowers through spring and summer.
Hedera helix (English Ivy). 10″ high. 3 plants per sq. yd.	Light or dense shade, good soil.	Evergreen vine. Use as cover under trees. Do not use with shrubs. Can be used as a lawn substitute.	This makes an even solid carpet, will last for years, and will climb up and over anything it can reach.
Hypericum moserianum (St. Johnswort). 1½′ high. 4 plants per sq. yd.	Sun or partial shade. Light, sandy soil.	Deciduous shrub. Evergreen in the south. Use on banks and open areas.	The bright yellow flowers are a welcome sight in summer.
Iberis sempervirens (Candytuft). 6″ high. 4–5 plants per sq. yd.	Sun, rich soil.	Evergreen sub-shrub for banks or foreground.	Masses of white flowers in May, on dense little bushes.
Juniperus horizontalis (Prostrate Juniper). 10″ high. 1–2 plants per sq. yd.	Sun, light soil.	Evergreen shrub for banks on edges of drives or open hillsides.	This is slow growing and will require several years to form a dense mat, but it lasts for many years.
Juniperus horizontalis Douglasi (Waukegan Juniper). 10″ high. 1 or 2 plants per sq. yd.	Sun, light soil.	Evergreen shrub for banks or edges of drives or open hillsides.	Similar to J. horizontalis but with rich purple foliage in the winter.
Lantana callowiana (Trailing Lantana). 3′ high or less. 2 plants per sq. yd.	Full sun. Good soil. Mild climate.	Shrubby vine for sunny banks or rock walls.	A graceful vine with deep green leaves and saffron yellow flowers. Used in California.
Mazus reptans. 4″ high. 9 plants to the sq. yd.	Sun or partial shade. Any soil.	Perennial. Use under trees or shrubs.	Dark green foliage with spikes of lavender-blue flowers in May.

NAMES, HEIGHT AND SPACING	REQUIREMENTS	TYPE AND USES	NOTES
Myosotis palustris semperflorens (Forget-me-nots). 8″ high. 9 plants per sq. yd.	Partial shade in wet or moist soil.	Perennial. Use as cover along stream banks or in moist areas.	Light green foliage; pale blue flowers in June and July.
Mesembryanthemum crystallinum (Ice plant). (Many varieties). 1 plant per sq. yd.	Full sun. Grows well in poor sandy soil. Frost-free climate.	Annual succulents with fleshy stems. Use on banks.	Daisy-like flowers in bright colors. Fast growing.
Nepeta mussini (Persian Nepeta). 15″ high. 4–5 plants per sq. yd.	Sun or partial shade; any soil.	Perennial, forming broad mats. Use on banks and in open areas.	The pale, gray-green foliage is aromatic. The flowers are lavender-blue.
Pachysandra terminalis (Japanese Spurge). 8″ high. 6–12 plants per sq. yd.	Partial or dense shade. Any soil.	Evergreen plant, forms dense carpets under trees	Establishes itself rapidly and is permanent. One of the most reliable ground covers.
Phlox divaricata (Blue phlox) 12″ high. 6–9 plants per sq. yd.	Partial shade in rich soil.	Perennial evergreen, use under trees and in shrubby foreground.	Lovely, soft lavender, exquisite flowers in spring. The plants spread by horizontal stems, but form irregular patches.
Phlox subulata (Moss Pink). 6″ high. 6–9 plants per sq. yd.	Sun, any soil.	Perennial. On banks.	Pink flowers in masses in April. The plants form little mounds of foliage which merge into solid carpets.
Rosa Max Graf. 2′ high. 1 plant per sq. yd.	Sun in any soil.	A trailing rose. Excellent for banks.	Single pink roses in June.
Rosa Wichuraiana (Wichura Rose). 1½″ high. 1 plant per sq. yd.	Sun in any soil.	A trailing rose. Excellent cover for banks.	Small, single white roses in clusters in June. Glossy foliage.
Sedum acre (Stone Crop). 4″ high. 9 plants per sq. yd.	Sun or partial shade. Any soil, prefers sandy loam.	Perennial succulent.	Forms solid masses of gray-green foliage with small yellow flowers in June. (Many other Sedums may be used as ground covers.)
Thymus citriodorus (Lemon Thyme). 4″ high. 18 plants per sq. yd.	Prefers full sun. Any soil.	Perennial. Among rocks, on banks or for open areas.	Low, mat-like growth. Small spikes of purple flowers. The leaves exude a pleasant fragrance when stepped on.
Thymus serpyllum (Mother-of-Thyme). 4″ high. 18 plants per sq. yd.	Prefers full sun. Any soil.	Perennial. Among rocks on banks or for open areas.	Gray-green foliage. Will tolerate some trampling. Low, spreading, mat-like growth.
Vinca minor (Periwinkle or Myrtle). 8″ high. 9 plants per sq. yd.	Dense or partial shade. Good soil.	Evergreen, trailing vine. Use under trees and shrubs or as foreground for shrubs.	One of the most dependable ground covers. Dark green leaves. Lavender-blue flowers in May and June.
Zanthorhiza apiifolia (Yellowroot). 15–18″ high. 9 plants per sq. yd.	Dense or partial shade. Soil rich in humus.	Deciduous shrub. Under trees and as borders of shrubs.	Good foliage and feathery spikes of tiny, brownish-purple flowers in May.

XIX

TREES

EVER since the dawn of civilization the forest and its products have been natural resources affecting the economics of human life, and man has come to understand the importance of trees in relation to his welfare and happiness. Like so many fundamental truths, we are aware of it long before we can ascribe reasons for it. Our love of trees is one of these instinctive affections which has its origin in racial history, and it finds expression in our urge to plant and care for them. The benefits, both physical and æsthetic, derived from trees are so many and so obvious that homes in the country and in the suburbs are invariably sheltered by trees. In the great arid regions of the Southwest where summer suns and desert sands combine to develop terrific heat every ranch homestead and watering place for cattle has a few Cottonwood trees for shade.

Uses and Usefulness

Trees may be grown for many purposes. They may be grown for the sheer beauty of their form, foliage or flowers. They may be grown to provide shelter from the wind or to provide shade; they may be grown for the production of fruits, nuts, timber, sugar, turpentine or other products which may be derived from the forests. And in addition to these many uses trees fulfill other important functions. There are many degrees of usefulness among trees. Some must be considered as weeds or pests, but the good far outnumber the unworthy. We can encourage one group and diminish the other, thus bringing about a gradual change toward a better environment.

Importance of Forests

It is becoming increasingly evident that the presence of forests, or their absence, is an important factor in determining climate. In a country well furnished with forests the climate is more even, and the seasonal changes more gradual than in a comparatively treeless region. It is now well recognized that there is a direct connection between the severity of floods in the Ohio Valley and the condition of the mountainsides of the Alleghenies. The absorbing power of a natural forest floor is so great that there is practically no run-off of surface water, whereas in cornfields and denuded hillsides the run-off during a heavy rain is 80 percent or more. The reduction of forest area by the cutting of timber has permitted the rapid funnelling of rain water and melting snow into the valleys, and the consequent increase in the frequency and severity of floods. This water, moving over the land, carries with it the surface soil, the only soil which has any nourishment for plant growth. Thus the forest is not merely a source of lumber but an equalizer of water-flow, a preventer of floods and a conserver of soil fertility.

As civilization and its demands for forest products spread over southern Europe, one country after another has used up its forests. Every country in which civilization has flourished for many centuries has become deforested in the process, and the exhaustion of the soil has been one of the factors in the cycle of changing fortunes of those nations. China, Mesopotamia, Palestine, Greece, Italy, and Spain, have all experienced this change toward a drier climate, and a less productive soil.

It is believed that Columbus was sent westward not so much to discover new sources of gold, as to find a country abounding in forest land. Probably the reason that the Spaniards began colonizing the new world a hundred years before the English did, was that their country had become at an earlier date unable to support the people, and this was due in part to the loss of the Spanish forests.

Native Trees

In a landscape composition the trees native to a region are usually to be preferred to exotic trees. In New England and the northern states, the Elm, Sugar Maple, White Oak, and White Pine are typical trees dominant in the landscape, and their use in plantings here is appropriate and satisfying. On the other hand, on the coastal plains where Spruce trees are not native, Norway Spruces and Blue Spruces will always look artificial and out of place.

Foreign Trees

This does not mean that no foreign trees should be used. In formal designs there is no such restriction. But if a naturalistic scene is desired, then the trees selected should be either native or kinds the appearance of which has much in common with the native trees. For instance, the Scholar-Tree, Sophora japonica, though it comes from the Orient, blends agreeably with the foliage of native deciduous trees, and will be pleasing as a specimen flowering tree or as a member of a grove. But Sciadopitys verticillata, the Umbrella-Pine, another Oriental, being unlike anything we have in this country, would seem an intrusion if placed in a naturalistic setting.

Trees in a Landscape Design

As an element in landscape composition, trees are very important and they are used for various purposes in design. Groups of them form the masses in the design as contrasted with the open area, as for example, the bosques and tapis-verts of France. Many trees together make a background for the structure and for the more intimate details of the design. Individual trees may be accents in the design or incidental notes of the picturesque. By their shapes trees express line as well as mass in the composition. Thus the famous group of Cypresses at Villa Falconieri gives dominant vertical line to the composition. The wind-swept Monterey Cypresses of California make horizontal lines against the sky and sea.

Many trees produce flowers in profusion, thus giving the garden picture greater scale and variety and more richness of color. Many trees are adorned with ornamental fruit, and with some the foliage turns a glorious color in autumn. Still others have picturesque branching forms which are particularly interesting in winter.

Trees, especially ornamental trees, should be considered as a long-time, though continuous, crop. The mature trees about the house will eventually become aged and subject to decay, and home owners with forethought will plant young trees to take their place, long before the old trees go. In this way the general form of the composition and the essential shade will be maintained, although individual members of the group may change. Seedling trees come up constantly in places not requiring them. If they are not removed while young, they may spoil the appearance of the hedge or shrub border or rob the soil in the flower bed.

Distance Apart

In planting new trees, their eventual proportions should be considered. Nothing is more futile than the planting of many trees on a small place. Within a few years, the inevitable crowding will have an unfavorable effect upon the beauty of the individual trees and upon the general arrangements. It is sometimes hard to cut down trees we enjoy, and the crowding is allowed to continue. It is an advantage to plant woodland trees closely because young trees benefit by mutual protection.

A young forest thus started may be thinned out with an axe later. But there is no justification for crowding specimen lawn trees.

Planting Mature and Young Trees

Sometimes it is a great advantage to transplant mature trees and to place them where they are most needed. Thus is avoided many years of waiting for the trees to develop, but in most cases, especially when economy of investment must be considered, smaller trees are better. On the other hand, it is a great mistake for an owner to postpone planting trees for several years. The money invested in small trees the first year of his possession of a new home will enhance its value more certainly than it could were it put to any other use. The trees themselves will increase in value. A twenty-five-dollar tree may be worth fifty dollars after six years of growing.

Selection of Trees

In selecting trees for a place, there are many points which should be considered. Not merely the size of the tree when mature, but its hardiness in the climate, its resistance to wind, its adaptability to soil conditions, its habits and rapidity of growth, its production of flowers and fruit, its undesirable habits such as shedding bark or poisonous fruit—these points should all be taken into account.

From a list of fairly dependable trees a great variety may be selected which together will produce bloom over a period from April to August, then a succession of ornamental fruit and rich autumn coloration. There are trees which are suitable for unusual conditions, such as wet soil, dry gravelly soil, city atmosphere, wind, heat, and drought, and there are trees which for one reason or another are not dependable or satisfactory.

Trees for the Small Place

Trees for the small home property should become intimate friends of the family. Each tree should be chosen with care, either for the beauty of its bloom in springtime, its picturesque form, its brilliant autumn coloring, or the welcome shade which it will cast.

Few features will enhance the surroundings of a home more than the flowering trees. And, fortunately, many of our most beautiful flowering trees are not large and are therefore well adapted to planting on the small property, as they will not outgrow the restrictions of the site. There is the lovely Star Magnolia which greets the spring with its display of delicate white flowers; the Dogwoods with their wealth of ivory-tinted bloom and their picturesque, horizontal branches extending outward in rhythmic waves; the lovely Silverbell tree, hung with a myriad white bells in May; the flowering crabs and cherries with their deep pink buds and their profusion of bloom; the Snowbell tree from Japan with its dainty, pendent bells which open early in the summer after the flowering period of most of the other trees has passed; and the Sourwood which in autumn brings to the small suburban home a touch of woodland glory, for there are few trees which have more beautiful fall coloring or retain their leaves over so long a period. And there are many other flowering trees from which selections may be made.

There are also a number of small trees which do not bear conspicuous flowers but which, because of their picturesque form or because of other desirable characteristics, deserve to be considered. In this group are the English Maple and the White Birches. The English Maple is a sturdy tree and offers to children welcome opportunities for climbing and for building tree houses among its branches. A clump of White Birches on the edge of the lawn area is always picturesque, and when a planting of primroses and early spring bulbs is grouped beneath their branches it makes a lovely composition.

When space permits it is desirable to have one or two larger trees for shade. Considerable thought should be given to the selection of such trees, however. A tree should be selected which will cast high shade and under which grass will grow well. It should be a tree which is graceful in form and which does not attain too great a size. Trees with wide-spreading branches which sweep the ground are not suited to the small place, as year by year they diminish the area needed for lawn and recreation, and gradually the property becomes too heavily shaded. And it should be a tidy tree which does not shed its bark or drop objectionable fruits upon the lawn. Among the trees which are excellent as shade trees on the small home property are the Moraine Locust, the Augustine Ascending Elm, the Sweetgum and the Ginkgo.

TREES FOR THE SMALL PLACE*

	HEIGHT	SPREAD
Acer campestre	30 to 40 ft.	40 to 50 ft.
English Maple, Hedge Maple		
Betula alba (B. pendula)	50 to 60 ft.	25 to 30 ft.
White Birch		
Cornus florida	15 to 25 ft.	12 to 18 ft.
Flowering Dogwood		
Cornus Kousa	15 to 20 ft.	15 to 18 ft.
Japanese Dogwood		
Cratægus oxyacantha	12 to 15 ft.	12 to 15 ft.
English Hawthorn		
Ginkgo biloba	100 to 125 ft.	40 to 50 ft.
Maidenhair Tree		
Gleditsia triacanthos inermis moraine	100 to 125 ft.	30 to 40 ft.
Moraine Locust		
Gordonia alatamaha	15 to 20 ft.	12 to 15 ft.
Franklinia Tree		
Halesia carolina	20 to 30 ft.	25 to 30 ft.
Silverbell Tree		
Koelreuteria paniculata	20 to 30 ft.	20 to 30 ft.
Goldenrain Tree		
Liquidambar styraciflua	70 to 90 ft.	35 to 40 ft.
Sweetgum		
Magnolia kobus	15 to 25 ft.	15 to 18 ft.
Kobus Magnolia		
Magnolia soulangeana	20 to 30 ft.	15 to 25 ft.
Saucer Magnolia		
Magnolia stellata	12 to 15 ft.	12 to 15 ft.
Star Magnolia		
Malus floribunda	20 to 25 ft.	20 to 25 ft.
Flowering Crabapple		
Oxydendrum arboreum	20 to 30 ft.	12 to 18 ft.
Sourwood, Sorrel Tree		
Pinus nigra	80 to 90 ft.	30 to 35 ft.
Austrian Pine		
Prunus subhirtella	25 to 30 ft.	15 to 20 ft.
Japanese Flowering Cherry		

* For a complete description of Trees for the Small Place see pages 220 to 225.

Sorbus aucuparia	30 to 35 ft.	20 to 25 ft.
Mountain Ash		
Styrax japonica	20 to 25 ft.	15 to 25 ft.
Snowbell Tree		
Syringa japonica	20 to 25 ft.	12 to 20 ft.
Japanese Tree Lilac		
Ulmus americana ascendens, var. Augustine	80 to 90 ft.	20 to 25 ft.
Augustine Ascending Elm		

Preparation of Soil for Planting

Trees growing in the woods have a soil rich in humus, porous but moist, all the conditions most favorable to growth. Trees growing in lawn or field have a soil usually less rich in humus, less porous and more full of grass roots. Preparing the soil before trees are transplanted is one of the essentials to success. Rich soil stimulates the vigor of trees, thereby equipping them with abundant vitality that will make them less subject to disease and less vulnerable to attack by insects. Undernourished trees start with a handicap in the battle for existence. The proper preparation of soil for tree planting will include plowing and harrowing to eliminate turf roots, or deep hand-digging if on a small scale; addition of humus or peat moss to lighten the soil and make it porous but moisture-conserving; adding sand to a soil that is too heavy with clay; and breaking up the clay sub-soil with deep plowing. Well-rotted manure may be added to improve the soil texture and increase the available nourishment.

In preparing soil for the planting of large deciduous trees, the top-soil should be removed, sub-soil excavated to a depth of 18 inches or 2 feet below the final grade, and the hole filled with additional top-soil. The shock of transplanting is more severe with a mature tree than with a young tree and the added depth of rich soil will be a wonderful help in re-establishing the root system. The planting bed should be round and 3 feet wider than the diameter of the ball of earth that will come with the roots. If possible, this preparation should be done six months or a year in advance of planting to allow the soil to settle.

In preparing the soil for tree planting, if rock is encountered at a depth too shallow to permit the proper soil preparation, one of three alternative procedures must be chosen. In some situations, the grade of the ground may be raised by filling in top-soil over a wide area to a depth that will cover the rock by 18 inches of earth. In other cases, the position of the tree may be changed, without seriously affecting the pictorial composition, to a place where the underlying rock is deeper. But if a tree must be planted at a certain position where rock is near the surface, the rock will have to be removed. Blasting a hole in the rock, removing the pieces and filling the place with soil is the best method. But if blasting cannot be performed, the rock may be broken by an old method. On a cold day, build a wood fire on the rock, heating it. Rake away the ashes and pour water on the rock. The rapid change of temperature will crack the rock and the pieces can be pried up with a crowbar and wedge.

Preparation of Trees for Transplanting

Plastic Sprays

The use of plastic sprays has appreciably reduced losses after transplanting. Diluted in water, the plastic may be sprayed over the entire tree so that not only the trunk but the whole tree is covered with a thin film which is flexible, colorless and lasting. While it retards evaporation it does not arrest transpiration. It can be applied to large trees with a power sprayer or to small trees and bushes by a hand spray. This method is so effective that when it is used on deciduous stock in a dormant state pruning is seldom necessary; and it makes better bark protection than wrapping the trunk with paper. One spraying is usually enough. Spraying should be done when the temperature is 50 degrees F. or warmer. In transplanting evergreen trees the spraying of plastic before digging is an enormous help in retarding evaporation.

While the transplanting of deciduous trees in full leaf is not recommended, it may be done with good success if the whole plant is sprayed with plastic to cover both sides of the leaves.

The use of plastic sprays enables one to prolong the planting season into the late spring and to commence it earlier in the autumn, and reduces the need for severe pruning or eliminates it altogether.

Defoliation

Another method of preparing trees for transplanting is called defoliation. This consists of cutting with shears (not pulling off from the twigs) all of the leaves of the tree, or all but one-fourth of the leaves. This method is used particularly on the hollies, both American and English, when they are being transplanted in northern regions. New leaves will grow out in due time and meanwhile the tree will not be losing moisture. Nurserymen report that they have never lost a holly from transplanting if it has been defoliated.

Methods of Transplanting

(A) *Bare Root Transplanting.* Bare root transplanting, the method used in moving most deciduous shrubs and young deciduous trees from the nursery to their permanent location, depends for success on taking up a large proportion of the root system, placing it in the ground again as soon as possible, and removing enough of the top (branches and foliage) to compensate for the temporary reduction of activity in the roots. This operation is best accomplished in early spring when the twigs are bare or in the autumn when the plant is losing its leaves.

In digging up a tree, the plantsman begins by digging into the ground in a circle at the outer ends of the roots, and works in toward the trunk, spading and forking the earth from the roots. Thus, practically all the important main roots and a large portion of the fibrous roots remain intact. What earth clings to the roots is carried with them, and is a great benefit to the plant while it is re-establishing itself in the new place. These little particles of soil held by the fine roots keep the contact and hence capillary action uninterrupted during transportation and they continue to function unless they become very dry while out of the ground.

The time which elapses between digging in the nursery and planting in the new position should be reduced to a minimum. The roots should never be exposed to the sun or wind during this interval. If a group of plants must be kept waiting for several hours, as is usual on a large planting job, they should at least be in the shade of a tree or building and their roots should be covered with burlap. A better precaution against drying of the roots is to heel the trees in at once in a convenient place. Then if planting work is interrupted or delayed, the trees can wait until all is ready. To heel in trees or shrubs, dig a trench large enough to accommodate the roots, throwing the soil to one side. Place the roots of the plants in the trench in such a way that the stems are inclined at an angle of 45 degrees or lower, and cover the roots with the loose soil. If the roots are very dry when the plants are received, they should be soaked in a barrel of water for a half hour before being heeled in. And the soil covering the roots should be kept wet. In such a situation trees and shrubs may be kept safely for several weeks.

When the trees are dug in the nursery, they are bundled, labelled, and gathered for shipment. The risk of injury from chafing of the bark on the side of the truck may be minimized by the placing of a wad of burlap bagging where the trunk rests on the brim. An injury to the bark at this time is apt to cause a lowering of vitality in the plant and consequent failure.

Transplanting trees from the woods or from your own grounds entails more risk than transplanting from the nursery, because in the nursery each tree has been transplanted or root-pruned once or twice to induce the growth of fibrous roots in a concentrated mass. The roots of forest-grown seedlings are rangy and it is difficult to dig them up and make them stay together. If a tree is to be transplanted from the woods it should be prepared for the journey by pruning its roots a year in advance. This is done by digging a trench around the tree at a distance from the trunk equal in feet to the diameter of the trunk in inches. The trench should be deep enough to cut through all the lateral roots, 18 or 24 inches, according to the size of the tree. The soil is then returned to the trench and new roots will develop within the circle and in the trench. When the tree is taken up it should be done according to one of the methods of transplanting described in this chapter.

In placing the tree in the ground, the hole should be large enough to accommodate the

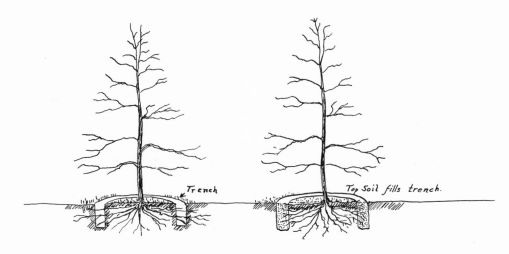

THE EFFECT OF ROOT PRUNING IS TO CONCENTRATE THE ROOTS IN A BALL.

roots without bending them. The roots should be spread out evenly and the top-soil thrown in among the roots and allowed to settle. When the roots are covered with loose dirt, but the hole not yet filled, the earth should be packed in among the roots by treading on it. More earth must be added and firmed by treading, and the hole thus filled. Deciduous trees should be planted in an inch or two deeper than they were in the nursery. This permits the roots to be better protected from drying, pending the establishment of the plant. Evergreens should be planted at the same level, never deeper than their former position. Deep planting of evergreens may result in depriving the roots of adequate air in the soil.

The top of the tree should be cut back quite severely, to equalize the rate of evaporation with the ability of the reduced root system to supply water. This is particularly true of oaks and other slow-growing trees. The top should be pruned the same day that the tree is planted. Postponement of this part of the work permits the plant to lose moisture and vitality. When the tree is pruned later, the pruning will need to be even more severe and the results will not be so satisfactory. The amount of pruning required will depend on the kind of tree, and on the season, *early* spring planting needing less pruning than later planting. (See page 220 for pruning.)

The ground about the newly planted tree should be shaped like a saucer to receive a generous supply of water the first day and on succeeding days. The function of the water is not so much at first to give the plant the extra water which it needs but to firm the soil about its feeding roots and to drive out the air pockets which inevitably remain in newly turned soil. The roots can take up only so much water, no matter how much is put on the soil, but the air in the soil can dry out the little roots before they become established. Water should be frequently given after planting and for the remainder of the growing season. But watering should be intermittent with intervals of several days between for drying and aëration of the soil.

Trees which are 12 feet or more high should be held in place by three or five guy wires fastened to stakes radiating from the trunk. The upper end of the wire should be looped through a piece of old garden hose and passed around a lower crotch. The wires are tightened by twisting two strands about a stick. Loose guy wires are of no use at all, because they will not prevent the tree trunk from shaking and the roots from being loosened in the soil.

Use of Peat Moss. In a series of experiments conducted at the New York State Agricultural Experiment Station, the value of peat moss in planting trees has been proven. Two-year-old apple trees were planted in clay loam. In one row a pail of damp granulated peat moss was mixed with the soil used to fill each tree hole in planting. In the other row the trees were planted as usual with no peat moss. At the end of the growing season, during which there was adequate rainfall, the peat-treated trees had made an average terminal growth of 82 inches as compared with 14 inches for the other trees. This superiority of the trees planted with peat moss continued during the three succeeding seasons as shown by larger top growth, larger trunk diameter, and greater root development. At the end of this time the roots of the peat-treated trees were found to be extended far beyond the limits of the peat in the soil, while the roots of the untreated trees were meager and restricted. The following year a similar test was started using dry peat moss unmixed with soil spread in the hole before planting. During this season a continued drought made growing conditions far from ideal and in this case the peat-treated trees showed little superiority over the untreated trees. Further tests showed the superiority of damp peat moss mixed with soil over the dry peat moss unmixed.

The conclusion reached from these trials is that in a clay loam the peat moss improves aëration in the soil and gives it a more constant water-holding capacity.

In a wet season aëration in the clay loam soil is decidedly diminished, and it is assumed that the presence of peat in the soil is a means of adequate circulation of oxygen to the roots. This may be the principal function of the peat moss in the soil. Certain it is that great benefits to root development and top-growth result from its use, and that these benefits are evident year after year.

(B) *Transplanting with a Ball of Earth.* Most evergreen trees, some deciduous trees and some large shrubs require a more painstaking method of transplanting. The slowness of growth of the evergreens prevents them from becoming established after transplanting with bare roots.

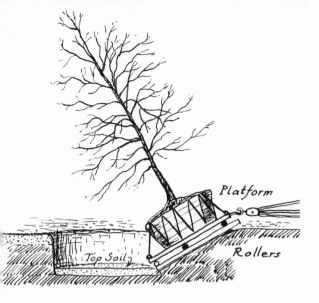

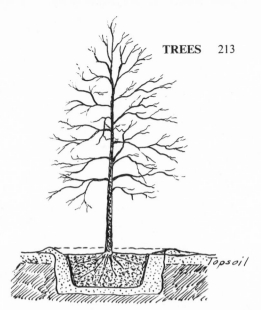

TRANSPLANTING A TREE WITH A BALL

1. The tree is lowered into the hole on skids, by block and tackle.

2. With platform and burlap removed, it is planted in top-soil.

For this class of trees and for a few species of shrubs transplanting is done with a ball of earth, wrapped tightly about with burlap. The roots of such plants as Box and Hemlock form a dense mass in the soil and it is easy to keep the earth together with burlap and hemp cord, but in moving plants with more loosely arranged roots, such as many of the Junipers, it is more difficult to prevent the ball from cracking. A broken ball or crumbling earth is apt to mean a dead tree. The ground must be in good condition before the trees are dug. If it is too dry the earth will crack away from the roots in balling or while moving. This condition may be remedied by a thorough watering several days before transplanting. If it is too wet, the earth will cling and cannot be worked.

The method used by nurserymen in transplanting evergreens which are to be handled in this way is to dig a trench around the specimen at a distance outside the ends of the fibrous roots and as deep as the roots may penetrate. When carefully done the side of the trench is beyond the root ends and the earth is then gradually cut away until the roots are en-

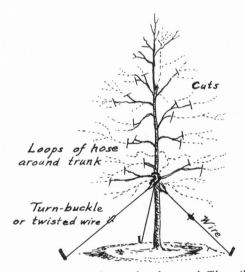

3. The tree planted, guyed and pruned. The soil is graded in the form of a dish, to conserve water.

countered. In digging deciduous trees, the outer roots are cut off and the ball made smaller. The trench is usually wide enough for a man to work in, and this space enables him to get his pick and spade well under the rim of the ball. By digging a gallery under and all around the rim, he carves out the undersurface of the ball, leaving it perched on a pedestal in the center. An incline is dug at one side to the floor of the hole up which the ball is to be dragged. Burlap bagging is wrapped about the sides and bottom of the ball and laced with hemp twine very tightly to the ball. When all is in readiness to take the tree out of the ground, a chain is passed around the ball, the end of the chain is hooked on to one of its links at a point about one-third or one-fourth of the circumference from the direction of pull. In other words the pulling chains start to work tangent to the edge of the ball. The pull twists the ball off its perch and thus frees it from the ground. A steel or wooden platform is then placed under the ball while the ball is tipped up on edge. The ball is firmly fastened to the platform by ropes passing over the ball from rings at each of the four corners of the platform. A block and tackle fastened to the platform and anchored in the direction of pull helps drag the plant out of the hole. The power may be a team of horses, three or four men, or a truck with a power winch.

The tree is loaded on to the truck or on an underslung wagon by skidding or rolling the platform up heavy planks. The planks are used again to unload it, to roll it across lawns, and to ease it into the new hole. Metal rollers on the planks make moving easier. The planks hold the ball while the platform is yanked out from beneath the ball and by sliding out the planks the ball is allowed to settle to the floor of the hole. If the hole has been properly prepared it will have a flat floor covered by a layer 2 inches thick of top-soil (in the case of Box bushes and Hemlocks, top-soil and humus is better) and at such a depth that the top of the ball will be flush with the grade of the ground around it. Deciduous trees may be placed 2 inches lower. The hole will be about 2 feet wider in diameter than the ball of earth, and the soil thrown out of the hole will be in two separate piles, one all top-soil and the other sub-soil. Top-soil, or top-soil and humus, should be used in filling in around the ball. The sub-soil should be carted away.

When the tree is in the hole, if the ball does not come to the proper level, which sometimes happens in spite of careful measuring, the ball should be tipped up on one side and more soil added or removed from beneath it. The specimen can then be revolved by winding so that it faces in the desired direction. Not until then should the twine and burlap be removed. After removing the burlap the space about the ball may be filled with humus and top-soil. The filling should be accompanied by tamping with a tamper (or if the plants are small, with a pick handle), anything to get the soil firmly packed against the roots. Watering and puddling is not satisfactory because it is apt to make a loose soup of soil around the tree in which the tree and its ball may be moved and tipped over by the wind. Water may be applied later after the hole is almost filled with firm soil, but not during the filling. If the outer surface of the ball has become dry and caked during transportation then this condition should be remedied by soaking the ball in water before the earth is filled in. The plantsman must in this case decide between two risks, that of having unstable soil about the ball saturated with water, or of permitting the tree roots to suffer from being encased in a hard crust of dry clay soil.

After placing the ball in the hole the burlap is carefully removed. If the earth has not held well and the ball is about to crack, one is tempted to avoid the broken ball by not removing the bagging, cutting away the burlap at the base and leaving a circle of burlap beneath the ball, to rot during the two or three succeeding years. If this expedient is adopted the lateral roots will not be affected and the down-growing roots will eventually find their way through the bagging. This practice is not favored by plantsmen because of the interference with root growth. Recent experiments show that the rotting bag forms a solvent that is poisonous to the plant.

Placing top-soil about the ball must be done in such a way as to assure firmness of the plant in the ground and the exclusion of air pockets in the soil. A layer of soil should be thrown in and trodden and tamped until it is firm. Then another layer should be added and made compact, the process repeated until the hole is filled. If the soil is all tossed in to fill the hole and then tamped, the lower soil cannot be firmly packed and there will be too much air remaining in the soil.

After planting is finished, the precautions and technique described for planting with bare roots should be employed. Evergreen trees and broad-leaved evergreen shrubs will benefit by a permanent mulch of peat moss or a carpet of rotting leaves to retain moisture and retard evaporation from the soil.

Trees which should be Transplanted with a Ball of Earth

Any tree with a trunk larger than 6 inches in diameter should be transplanted with ball and burlap. Smaller sizes of the following trees also should be transplanted by this method.

Japanese Maples	Birch
Hickories	Magnolia
Persimmon	Sourwood
Beech	Sassafras
Sourgum	Sugar Maple
Walnut	Dogwood
Tulip-tree	Oaks (nearly all)
Sweetgum	Evergreens (nearly all)

Trees which should be moved only when they are very young, three or four years old, are Tulip-tree and Sourgum. The Sourgum especially is difficult to re-establish after transplanting.

Transplanting Very Large Trees

Transplanting large mature trees is a job to be undertaken only by experienced men with adequate equipment. The same precautions must be taken with large trees as with shrubs. The roots must be kept moist during the time when they are out of the ground, and they must be carefully placed and firmly packed about with soil. The amount of leafage (evaporation surface) must be reduced in proportion to the loss of feeding roots. The task is made more difficult by the great weight of soil that must be moved with the roots, and by the longer period of time that the tree is out of the ground, but the principles remain the same. The size of the ball of earth required for proper transplanting is proportionate to the tree. It is out of the question to take all the roots of a large deciduous tree, but for most species the diameter of the ball in feet should at least equal the diameter of the trunk in inches.

Transplanting is a shock to the tree but a shock that may be reduced by preparing the tree for its removal. A year in advance of the transplanting, the circle of the ball is marked out and a trench is dug to a depth of two feet, cutting through the existing roots. The trench is then filled entirely with top-soil. During the year, the tree will form a dense mat of fibrous roots in the top-soil, which will be ready to grow out into a new layer of top-soil in the new location. When the tree is lifted, the new fibrous roots will hold the soil firmly together. The transplanting may be done in early autumn or in spring. It has also been found possible and satisfactory to transplant trees in winter with the ground frozen solid. This is best done in a series of operations beginning the previous year by preparing the ball as described. In the late autumn the trench is dug and the tree ball twisted off its ground base. There it is left with the open trench around it, until the ground is frozen. During the winter the tree can be bound up with burlaps and cord, tilted up and placed on a platform and removed to the new position, put into the hole and left there still unplanted until spring weather thaws the ground. Then the space about the tree is filled with good top-soil.

In handling trees of large size, all the sliding, lifting, rolling on rollers, and skidding of the ball down into the hole should be done without sudden jostling or bumping. A block and tackle anchored to a "dead-man" will transmit the power of the winch and motor or the pull of a gang of men to a slow steady motion. The descent into the hole by an inclined plane is the part which is most apt to bring disaster. Unless the power is strong enough to hold it back, the tree ball may roll with great force down the sloping planks and strike the earth side of the excavation, thus cracking the ball. If the platform is on rollers, it may be gently eased down into the hole by slacking up slowly on the rope of the block and tackle.

Transplanting Seasons

The best times for transplanting trees, shrubs and vines are early spring and early autumn.

THE MAJESTY
OF OAK TREES
IN EARLY SPRiNG

Because of severe winters in Canada, northern New England, Michigan, Wisconsin and west of Omaha, spring planting is preferred. The spring planting season cannot be fixed by calendar. It begins as soon as the ground is dry enough to work, and continues until the buds of deciduous trees have sent forth their young leaves to ½ or 1 inch long. Thus, oaks, which leaf out late, may be transplanted later than horse chestnuts. The evergreen planting season continues longer. The autumn season begins in late August for evergreens, and with the turning color of the leaves for deciduous plants, and continues until freezing weather, except for evergreen trees and broad-leaved evergreens which should not be moved after the middle of October. Many evergreen trees and most deciduous trees may be transplanted with a frozen ball of earth during the winter as described for transplanting large trees.

Some trees can be transplanted safely only at one season; notably magnolias, which should be moved only in very early spring. The magnolia roots are very easily broken, and

OAKS AND DOGWOODS

since loss of root activity is to be expected after transplanting it is wise to move them when root growth is most active, before flowering in spring. Other trees for which early spring planting is preferred to autumn planting are flowering dogwood (Cornus florida), canoe birch (Betula papyrifera), sweetgum (Liquidambar Styraciflua), tupelo (Nyssa sylvatica), black walnut (Juglans nigra), bald cypress (Taxodium distichum), tulip-tree (Liriodendron tulipifera).

Grading Around a Tree

If the grades about a tree are to be altered by filling soil over the original ground level, then special precautions should be taken to prevent the smothering of the roots. A fill of 4 inches of good top-soil over the roots of deciduous trees will do no damage, although it might affect evergreens unfavorably. A fill of a foot or more would be very harmful. The quantity of air and also of water in the soil diminishes in accordance with the depth. Thus, when roots growing at a depth of 18 inches are covered so that they are 36 inches from the surface, they are deprived of their normal oxygen and water rations. To overcome this handicap it is advisable to construct some device for maintaining a contact between the air and the root-containing soil. It is important to do this before the fill is made. First, the original soil is loosened by forking. Then a dry stone wall is built up around the tree, if possible at a distance of several feet from the base of the trunk and to the level of the new grade. Several 4-inch agricultural tile drains are laid in lines radiating from the inner surface of this wall. Over the whole area is spread a course of crushed slag, or coarse crushed stone, or large gravel. This material is put on to a depth of 6 inches or to within 12 or 15 inches of the final grades. Above this is spread a layer of straw or preferably manure to prevent the soil above from sifting down through the stones or slag. Finally a layer of top-soil is spread to a depth of 6 or 8 inches. This construction should cover the whole area of tree

roots. The tile pipes may be used to conduct water to the roots and may be filled by a hose.

If soil has been washed away from the roots of large trees, as sometimes happens on steep slopes, or if the ground is worn down by passing feet, the damage to the trees may eventually be fatal. Restoration of the natural grade by filling a layer of top-soil to cover the roots and establishing a turf or a ground cover crop to retain the soil is the only permanent remedy.

Care of Trees after Transplanting

Transplanting is a shock to a plant. It necessarily interrupts or somewhat retards the life processes. The diminished vitality of the tree renders it more open to attack by insects and diseases, and less able to withstand the effects of unusual weather conditions, which may ensue.

Moisture Requirements. The greatest danger during transplanting and the subsequent weeks is from desiccation, or excessive loss of moisture through natural transpiration of foliage while the disturbed roots are unable to replace water and thus maintain a normal moisture content in the tissues. The function of pruning is to diminish the area of foliage and hence reduce the rate of evaporation.

Watering the tree at intervals is a very important part of after-care. The soil should be thoroughly soaked once a week if rain is insufficient, because the soil should never be allowed to become really dry. On the other hand, in a soil kept constantly saturated, the water will exclude the air from the roots. Proper watering will enable the roots to take up the soil-moisture rapidly and will encourage root growth. Evaporation through the bark is another outlet of plant moisture. A method long in use by plantsmen to retard this evaporation during the first year after transplanting is to wrap the trunk and larger branches with burlap. It is effective, especially against winter drying, but has the disadvantage of harboring insects, and in some positions the objection of unsightliness.

Mulches: To keep the soil about newly planted trees in condition mulching is advisable. For method of application and materials to be used, etc., see Chapter XXXIV on mulches.

Ground Covers as Root Protection. A treatment beneficial to trees, and one which may be used in certain situations where lawn is not essential, is a planting of pachysandra, periwinkle or English ivy. These plants have the ability to thrive in even dense shade, in many places doing better than grass, and what is most important for the tree, they will collect fallen leaves, thus adding annually to the leaf mold in the soil. This subject is more fully discussed in the Chapter on Ground Covers.

Fertilizing Trees

In their natural habitat in the forest, trees are nourished by a soil rich in organic material which is annually replenished by the decaying of fallen leaves. Under conditions where leaves are raked up, this renewing does not take place.

To make up for the lack of soil fertility, it is a benefit to put into the soil solutions of nitrates, phosphates and potash. This should be done every two or three years.

No commercial fertilizer should be placed in the hole in which a tree is to be planted, as the risk of burning the roots is too great.

Time of Application. Applications of fertilizer may be made at any time from early spring until midsummer and from the middle of September until late November. No applications should be made between July 15 and September 15 as there is danger of stimulating a late, succulent growth which will be subject to winter-killing. Tree roots take in nutrients most readily during the period of early spring growth and they continue to absorb nutrients in the autumn long after the leaves have been shed.

Method of Application. The feeding roots of most trees extend from the trunk to a considerable distance beyond the ends of the overhead branches, and the fertilizer should be applied over this entire area. Holes, varying in depth from 12 to 15 inches, should be drilled, being spaced from 15 to 18 inches apart. A mature tree will need about a hundred holes. Into each of these holes is put from one-tenth to one-fourth of a pound of complete fertilizer, and the holes are then filled with water to dissolve the fertilizer.

Kind and Amount of Fertilizer. A 10–6–4 complete fertilizer is recommended for trees, and it should be applied at the rate of 5 pounds per inch of trunk diameter. For a soil markedly deficient in phosphorus and potash, a 4–8–7 mixture is recommended. A soil test is a help in determining what mixture to use.

When feeding trees, according to the method developed by the University of Wisconsin (page 166) the directions are as follows:

Established trees: Use 5 to 8 packets, depending upon the size of the tree. Bore holes 6 to 8 inches deep encircling the tree midway between the trunk and the dripline. Place a 2-oz. packet in each hole and refill hole. Repeat in 3 to 5 years.

Trees at Planting Time: Place one or two 2-oz. packets in contact with the lower root system at time of planting. Repeat at end of 3 to 5 years.

Doctor Carl G. Deuber gives the following table of symptoms and their causes:

SYMPTOMS	CAUSES
1. Poor leaf growth which causes:	
a. Dwarf plants, yellowish color	lack of nitrogen
Dwarf plants, grayish color	lack of phosphorus or potash
b. Tall, spindly plants	lack of light
2. Chlorosis or yellowing of leaf	
a. Uniform all over leaf	lack of iron, excess of lime, magnesium, sodium, potash, carbonates, manganese
b. Patchy, spreading from midrib outward	lack of magnesium
c. Mottled	lack of lime
d. Spotty	lack of potash
e. Leaf yellowing, then drying at tip and from edges inward	lack of potash
f. Leaf yellowing, then drying from midrib outward	lack of nitrogen
3. Patches on leaf	
a. Brown patches like "scorching"	lack of potash
b. Brown patches chiefly in center	lack of magnesium
4. Rich green leaves and large thick stems	large supply of nitrogen
5. Dark colored leaves, tendency to crinkle	lack of potash in relation to nitrogen
6. Patchy appearance of foliage, some dark green, others lighter	acidity of soil

Water

Lack of adequate water in the soil is a very frequent cause of trees' distress. On a warm summer day a mature tree often loses, by evaporation through its foliage, as much as 10 barrels of water. To make up this loss during dry weather, trees should be watered thoroughly at intervals of about 10 days. Frequent light watering accomplishes no good because the water does not sink deeply into the soil.

Spraying to Diminish effect of City Soot and Gas

Sulphur dioxide and other gases often present in the air in cities are detrimental to many of our finest trees. The accumulation of soot on the surface of leaves clogs the pores and retards respiration. These conditions are particularly hard on the evergreen trees, the leaves of which remain active for several years. To minimize the damage to the trees from these atmospheric impurities, the foliage may be washed with hose spray about once a week during the growing season. This treatment will be helpful with such evergreens as Arborvitæ and Chamæcyparis as well as with deciduous trees.

Pruning

Shade trees require comparatively little pruning. The removal of dead or diseased wood and the cutting out of crowded or interfering branches is usually all that is necessary. Pruning of small dead branches will often prevent the rotting of large branches or of the trunk. The cut should be made through live wood and close to the junction with the larger stem. In removing small branches cut from below, part way through, then from above. This lower cut will prevent the weight of the branch, in falling, from ripping off a section of bark below the branch just before the saw cuts through. Larger and heavier branches need even more precaution to prevent this splitting of the bark. (See sketch Chapter XLII.)

First cut part way through from below in the position of the final cut. Then cut through from above at a distance of a few inches out from the crotch. After the limb is cut off leaving this stump, cut the stump to a flat surface and paint it with pruning paint. Small cuts may be protected either by grafting wax or by pruning paint. The purpose of the painting is to avert decay by preventing the entrance of fungi or other damaging organisms.

Trees which have been injured by storm or which have begun to decay will require more attention than mere pruning. The rotted wood should be removed in the cavity down to the live wood. A hammer and chisel may be used to cut away the decayed wood. The surface of the sound wood thus exposed should be painted with pruning paint, or the whole cavity should be filled with prepared cavity cement, a plastic substance which remains flexible and never becomes absolutely hard.

For control of insect pests and diseases, see Chapter XLI.

TREES OF MERIT

DECIDUOUS

Acer campestre (English Maple or Hedge Maple). This pleasant shade tree forms a broad dome with branches near the ground, and dense, dark green foliage. The leaves are small with five rounded lobes. It is a handsome lawn tree and is excellent for children to climb in because of its broad, spreading sturdy branches. Very slow growth. Height 40 feet. Zone IV.

Acer saccharum (Sugar Maple) is one of the noblest of American trees. Its dense habit and its gorgeous autumn foliage make it a tree to remember. This is one of the trees which bring color to the New England mountainsides in October. It is much used as a street tree and it shades many a New England village green. It cannot be surpassed as a shade tree on a broad home lawn or as a forest tree. It is not a rapid grower but it is permanent. Plant this tree for your children, and they will be able to pass it on to their grandchildren. Height 125 feet.   Northern limit.   Zone III.

Albizzia julibrissin (Silk Tree) comes from the semi-tropical regions of Asia. The spreading branches form a flat top and the foliage has the fragile delicacy of tree ferns. It is much used as a street tree. The doubly compound leaves are made up of hundreds of pale green leaflets, about a quarter inch long. The flowers are balls of pink, thread-like stamens in clusters that appear above the foliage early in July, and the pods follow soon after the flowers. The Silk Tree requires full sunlight and much water, will tolerate poor soil, but thrives better in loamy soil.   Height 35 feet.   Zone VII.

A smaller form with brighter pink flowers is hardy in Zone VI, where it reaches a height of only 15 feet.

Betula pendula (B. alba), the European white birch, and **Betula papyrifera,** the canoe birch, are among the most picturesque trees. They have bright, smooth, white stems and in autumn clear yellow foliage. They are much planted as accents and are at home among evergreen trees and with mountain laurel.

Height 60 feet. Zone II.

Other birches, especially the river birch and the yellow birch, are picturesque but not as striking as the white birches.

Cercidiphyllum japonicum (Katsura-tree), a native of Japan, is planted for its beautiful foliage. It usually grows with several stems to form a broad, spreading dome with leaves and branches to the ground, a most graceful structure. The delicate, heart-shaped leaves turn to bright yellow and scarlet in autumn.

Height 60 feet, spread 100 feet. Zone IV.

Cercis canadensis (Judas tree, or Red-bud) is an under-growth tree, common in the woods of Maryland and southward where it blooms with the dogwood. Its deep pink buds cling to the branches for several weeks before opening into rose-pink, pea-like blossoms.

It does best in shade of larger trees, in rich, humus soil. Height 30 feet. Zone IV.

Cladrastis lutea (Yellow-wood) is native to a small region in the mountains of North Carolina and eastern Tennessee. It is a tree with smooth, gray bark very like a beech. The leaves are compound and turn a brilliant yellow in late September. Its glory is its large hanging panicles of cream-white fragrant flowers in June.

Height 50 feet. Zone III.

Cornus Florida (Dogwood) is a native of our eastern forests, and is one of the most beloved and most beautiful of our flowering trees. It is a sturdy, small tree with spreading, drooping branches. Its quantities of white flowers, consisting of four spreading bracts, greet the spring before the leaves appear. In October the leaves turn crimson and the twigs are adorned with tight bunches of scarlet fruits.

Height 25 feet. Zone IV.

Cornus kousa (Kousa Dogwood) is a native of Japan and Korea. Its broad, spreading habit and dense foliage make it an excellent tree for background and screen. Its chief beauty is its white blossoms which cover the top branches in June. Unlike our native dogwood the bracts end in short, sharp points. The pink fruits ripen in August and hang on through the autumn and the foliage turns scarlet in October.

Height 20 feet. Zone V.

Cratægus Cordata (Cratægus Phænopyrum) (Washington Thorn) is one of the best native hawthorns. It is excellent as an untrimmed hedge, as a windbreak and as a specimen. Its horizontal branches and drooping twigs bear quantities of small, bright scarlet apple-like fruits in September which hang on half the winter. The leaves also turn scarlet and orange in the autumn. The thorns are two or three inches long and are sharp. The tree grows well in the valleys.

Height 30 feet. Zone IV.

Fagus Sylvatica (European Beech) has a dignity and refinement deriving from its rugged form and smooth bark. The leaves are finely toothed, the buds long and sharp and tapering, the twigs small and wide spreading. The tree reaches up to a hundred feet, yet the lower branches touch the ground. The autumn color is at first a clear yellow turning to a rich brown, and the lower leaves hang on all winter. Numerous forms have appeared, the most notable of which is the Copper beech. Height 100 feet. Zone IV.

Ginkgo biloba (Maidenhair-Tree) was brought from China two centuries ago and has been distributed widely in Europe and America. The growth is sparse, usually with upward-reaching branches of rather angular outline. The leaves are its chief beauty. They are little fans with conspicuous, radiating veins and an undulate outer rim. In autumn the tree is a glorious, clear yellow. It is used as a street tree especially in Washington D.C., but its value as a lawn tree is well recognized. It is dioecious, and the odor of the fruit is so unpleasant that one should be careful to obtain the male form. Height 125 feet. Zone IV.

Gleditsia triacanthos inermis moraine (Moraine Locust) is valued for its rapid growth, lacy foliage, vase-like form and freedom from disease. It has no thorns and is well adapted for use as a street tree and on the home lawn. It thrives well in many types of soil.

Height 100 feet. Zone IV.

Gordonia alatamaha (Franklinia) is a small tree of very slow growth, native to Georgia, where it was discovered by John Bartram in 1770. It has not been found wild since 1790, and all the trees we have today are descended from the seedlings which Bartram raised. It prefers the sheltered valleys and partial shade of large trees. Its lovely flower is a pure white cup of 5 petals with golden stamens, measuring about 3 inches across. The flowers appear in late summer and open in succession over a period of many weeks. It is a rare and lovely small tree and deserves to be more widely grown. The leaves turn crimson in the autumn.

Height 30 feet. Zone VI.

Halesia carolina (Silverbell Tree) is a lovely small tree, a native of the south. In late spring it bears thousands of small, white, bell-shaped flowers which are followed by interesting four-winged fruits which are greatly relished by squirrels. Rapid in growth, and not subject to diseases, this shrub-like spreading tree is excellent

BLACK LOCUST AND MAPLES

for the small property. The leaves turn clear yellow in October.   Height 30 feet.   Zone IV.

Koelreuteria paniculata (Goldenrain tree or Varnish tree) is a most picturesque Oriental tree. Its rather wide-ranging and twisted branches and its feathery, compound, light green foliage give it a characteristic contrast to our familiar forms. But its great beauty bursts forth in the last week of June when its large panicles of bright yellow blossoms open. Later, when the blooms fall, they cover the ground with a carpet of yellow. The autumn foliage is yellow.   Height 35 feet.   Zone V.

Liquidambar styraciflua (Sweetgum). A native forest tree which forms extensive stands in the lowlands of New Jersey and Maryland. It is a tree with a conspicuous central trunk and a tapering apex. Its star-shaped leaves turn a brilliant crimson in September. The crooked, corky-barked branches are picturesque in winter, as are the hanging fruit balls which persist until spring.   Height 90 feet.   Zone IV.

Liriodendron tulipifera (Tulip-tree) is a majestic tree with a straight trunk often rising thirty feet to the first branch. It is a very fast grower, making fifty feet in 25 years. The large, four-lobed leaves turn clear yellow in

PICTURESQUE LIVEOAK IN A CALIFORNIA PATIO

September. The blossoms which are cream white and tulip-shaped stand erect at the twig ends at the top of the tree where they are not easily seen. An excellent tree for planting on the home grounds as it casts high shade and permits grass to flourish beneath it. It is used to line the avenues of southern plantations and to shade the mansions.

Height 120 feet.   Zone IV.

Magnolia soulangeana (Saucer Magnolia) is one of the most spectacular of flowering trees. The whole tree is covered in May with lavender, cup-shaped blossoms. The bark is light gray and smooth, and the rich foliage is a medium green. The magnolias are remarkably free from disease, and usually live for many years. It thrives extremely well under city conditions.

Height 30 feet.   Zone V.

Magnolia stellata (Star Magnolia) is a much loved tree. It is a true dwarf of very slow growth, but it begins to bloom when it is only three feet high. The white flowers, with many ribbon-like white petals, open in early spring before the forsythias and unless they are frost-touched remain open for many weeks. It is one of the loveliest of the small trees and deserves to be widely planted.

Height 15 feet.   Zone V.

223

Malus floribunda, one of the finest of the many flowering crabs, is a most beautiful sight when in full bloom in mid-spring. Thousands of carmine-pink buds open into pure white flowers which resemble small apple blossoms, and which remain in bloom for several weeks. In September the tree is covered with small, pale yellow apples about a third of an inch in diameter. It will thrive for about fifty years.   Height 30 feet. Zone IV.

Oxydendrum arboreum (Sourwood) is a small, deciduous tree, native to the forests in the Alleghenies from Pennsylvania southward. It is a member of that large family, the Ericaceae, and is thus related to the Rhododendrons. Its blossoms, hanging in branched tassels, resemble the white bells of the Pieris, but its great glory is its autumn coloring. By late August the leaves are beginning to turn and remain a bright crimson until mid-October. It is very slow in growth, occasionally reaching an eventual height of 40 feet, but is usually much smaller.   Zone IV.

Platanus acerifolia (London Plane tree), a hybrid of the American and the European sycamores, is a dependable street tree, thriving in almost any soil and in the restricting conditions of city pavements. Its picturesque cream or white trunk and branches give it a great distinction, but the shedding bark and the fruit heads clutter the ground beneath it. However, it is one of our best shade trees, branching very broadly, casting a deep shade and living for a hundred years.
Height 100 feet. Zone V.

Prunus subhirtella (Higan Cherry), one of the several Japanese flowering cherries, is a tree of graceful habit and great beauty. Its pink buds and pale pink blossoms cover the tree in April. A pathway beneath a double row of these trees is a very impressive sight. A weeping form is also very popular.   Height 30 feet. Zone V.

Quercus alba (White Oak) is almost in a class by itself. Its light gray bark and rugged branches make it easily distinguishable from the other oaks, and its magnificent proportions in maturity give it a dignity beyond that of all other native trees. This is a tree to plant for one's grandchildren. It will live hundreds of years and will grow very slowly. The leaves are deeply indented with rounded lobes. In autumn the colors range through pink-scarlet to deep bronze-brown. It will grow on almost any soil except wet bottomland. A fine tree for the home property of ample size.
Height 125 feet. Zone IV.

Several other oaks are worthy of special mention. Among the best for shade and autumn color are:

Quercus borealis	Red Oak
Quercus coccinea	Scarlet Oak
Quercus laurifolia	Laurel Oak
Quercus palustris	Pin Oak
Quercus virginiana	Live Oak

Except for the Pin Oak, the oaks are rather difficult to transplant. It is therefore prudent to purchase small, young trees, not more than 2 inches in diameter.

Salix babylonica (Weeping willow) has long been a popular tree with romantic association, the subject of Chinese and occidental art. In this country it rarely reaches a height of more than 40 feet. Its long, hanging twigs moving in the wind are most graceful and as winter begins to give way to spring the twigs suddenly turn a light yellow, bringing life to the somber landscape. The leaves are long and narrow and remain green until late autumn.   Height 35 feet. Zone V.

Sophora japonica (Chinese Scholar-tree). Brought from China two centuries ago the Scholar-tree is still not well known. It is a graceful and wide-spreading tree when growing alone. The leaves are compound and resemble those of the locust. In August and September great panicles of white, pea-like blossoms are produced in profusion, and these are followed by picturesque green pods. It is a very handsome shade tree suitable for the home lawn of spacious proportions.
Height 75 feet. Zone IV.

Sorbus aucuparia (European Mountain-ash) is a small tree with compound leaves, white blossoms in flat clusters followed by gorgeous, orange-vermilion fruit in August and September. This is an excellent tree for the small property, graceful and distinctive, but it is slow to mature.   Height 40 feet. Zone II.

Sorbus americana (American Mountain-ash) is seldom used because it is so extremely difficult to transplant.

Styrax japonica (Snowbell tree) is a compact tree with wide-spreading, horizontal branches and deep green leaves. In June and July the branches are hung with little, white, bell-like flowers and in August the oval, green fruits appear which turn brown as they ripen.

This is an excellent tree for the small home grounds, neat and attractive.   Height 30 feet. Zone V.

Syringa japonica (Japanese Tree Lilac). This attractive small tree which is so well-suited to the suburban home property, is compact in habit of growth and in June bears large trusses of white flowers. It is remarkably free from pests and diseases and requires little maintenance.
Height 25 feet. Zone IV.

Taxodium distichum (Bald cypress). Although this deciduous conifer grows in the swamps of the south from Maryland to Louisiana it is, nevertheless, hardy in upland soil as far north as central Pennsylvania. One of the most beautiful sights of the southern spring is the cypress trees with their new feathery leaves of pale green covering them like a mist.

Height 150 feet.   Zone V.

Tilia cordata (European Linden) has been planted as a shade tree since ancient times. It has a broad, spreading base with branches close to the ground and a rounded head. The leaves are small, broad and irregularly heart-shaped.   Height 100 feet.   Zone III.

Ulmus americana (American Elm) is a noble tree beloved and revered by all who know it. The branches spread and divide in a high-arched canopy, the whole a symphony of graceful, curving lines. It is a shade tree of magnificent proportions which often lives for 400 years. Common in the northeast, it was one of the first native trees to be planted for the sheer enjoyment of its beauty. For a few brief days in October the elm foliage takes on a clear yellow, but it is not spectacular. It is planted as a street tree, and it shades many a New England village green. It is of particular value as a lawn tree as it casts high shade and grass grows well beneath it. It is attacked by the Dutch elm disease. (See page 624.)

Height 150 feet.   Spread 100 feet.   Zone II.

Ulmus americana ascendens, var. Augustine (Augustine Ascending Elm). This variety, instead of spreading sideways, maintains the upward thrust of its branches. It is especially well adapted to the narrow street where the space between curb and sidewalk is very restricted, and its columnar form also recommends its use where buildings stand close to the street. It will grow much faster than the type, making fifty feet in ten or fifteen years, and is very resistant to diseases. It is well adapted to the home place.   Zone III.

EVERGREEN

Abies concolor (Colorado Fir) is one of those adaptable trees which seem to make themselves at home in almost any situation. Native to the Rocky Mountains, it is capable of standing dry soil and windy exposures. Its great beauty is its majestic, columnar form and soft, blue-green needles, which are long and waxy smooth. In the West it attains 125 feet.   Zone IV.

Other fir trees, including *Abies balsamea* (Balsam Fir), are grown by the nurseries. They are graceful shafts of rich, green foliage.

Cedrus atlantica (Atlas Cedar) is the hardiest of the three true cedars, and comes from the mountains of Spain. Because the needles are arranged in star-like clusters covering the twigs and branches with a fine pattern, this cedar is a beautiful symphony of line. In maturity the tree is 125 feet tall and very broad at the base, with branches to the ground. Variety *glauca* is much planted for its bluish needles.   Zone VI.

Cedrus libani, the Cedar of Lebanon from Syria, and **Cedrus deodara,** the Deodar Cedar from the bases of the Himalayas, are even more beautiful, with longer needles, but they are less hardy and are suited only to mild climates.   Zone VII.

Chamæcyparis pisifera (Sawara Cypress) was brought from Japan, and with its varieties *plumosa* and *squarrosa*, is used frequently in suburban plantings. It keeps a neat shape and density without shearing, though shearing will thicken the foliage. It should not be planted where it will outgrow a restricted space. It is a good, erect, tapering column of feathery evergreen foliage. *Plumosa* is very fine in texture, and *squarrosa* has bluish scales which stand out as needles in fluffy masses. In Japan it grows to 150 feet but in this country it is rarely higher than 50 feet.   Zone III.

Ilex opaca (American Holly) is a tree beloved by every generation of Americans, but unfortunately it has been exterminated in many regions by the vendors who fill the markets with its branches for Christmas greens. In maturity this magnificent, slow-growing evergreen reaches a height of 60 feet, usually much less in the North, and it will live for two hundred years. The leaves are stiff, a deep dull green with several spines on the rim. The bright, red berries ripen in October and remain all winter.   Zone V.

Ilex aquifolium (English Holly), because of its glossy leaves, is more handsome than our native holly.

Height 75 feet.   Zone VI.

Juniperus virginiana (Red Cedar) is not a cedar at all, but a juniper. It is familiar to all in the Northeast as a shaft of deep green, fine in texture. In the North it normally matures at about 35 feet and widens at the base. In Maryland, Virginia and southward, where it grows more rapidly, it is often 80 or 90 feet tall and very broad at the base. The wood is very hard, and it is one of the best woods for farm fence posts as it resists decay for fifty years or more.

The best variety is *Canærtii* which has a richer green and a denser mass of foliage.   Zone II.

Laurus nobilis (Sweet Bay) is a small evergreen tree of slow growth used for hedges and as specimens on the coasts of the Mediterranean and in the Pacific Northwest. Its picturesque branching and compact form produce a rather tapering outline. It may be pruned into any formal shape. This is the Laurel of history and poetry.   Zone VII.

Magnolia grandiflora (Bull Bay) is the magnolia of the Southern plantations. Its height, and its large, lustrous dark green leaves give it great distinction. But the great, waxy-white, cup-shaped blooms which adorn the upper branches from May to August are its rarest beauty. A native throughout the lower South, it is hardy only as far north as Virginia except in very sheltered locations.   Height 70 feet.   Zone VII.

Pinus nigra (Austrian Pine) is the old reliable among the pines. Hardy in exposure, almost free from insects and diseases, this pine with a rugged character is also a thing of simple beauty. Masses of stiff, long needles cover the twigs and outer branches. Small, broad, dark brown cones cling close to the stems, decorating the top. This tree is used as specimen, as a shade tree and as a windbreak.   Height 100 feet.   Zone IV.

Pinus strobus (White Pine) is one of the glories of New England. Since earliest colonial years it has been sought for its timber and it was famous as the mast tree of the sailing ships of Britain and America. As a home tree it is unsurpassed. One towering white pine by the house can be a joy through winter and summer. It is the gathering place of warblers and finches, the shelter for juncos and the home of nuthatches. In the carpet of its fallen needles in the forests grow the pink lady's slipper, the Indian pipe and Clintonia borealis. Its soft needles clothe the twigs in a rich, green verdure.
Height 100 or even 150 feet.   Zone III.

Several other pines are of landscape value. Among them are *Pinus sylvestris* (Scots Pine), a tree of picturesque outline, and *Pinus thunbergi* (Japanese Black Pine), which will stand terrific wind.

Pseudotsuga taxifolia (Douglas Fir) is one of the valuable timber trees of the Pacific Northwest where it grows to 300 feet. In domestic use it is a graceful spire of rich green, far more beautiful than the spruces and more dependable than the true firs.
It is best as a specimen or as one of several ascending evergreens in a group.   Zone VI.

Quercus virginiana (Live Oak) was often planted along the avenues of the plantation homes, where it has attained great age. The tree has wide, horizontally-spreading limbs but it does not reach great height. It is of rapid growth and will adjust itself to almost any soil; a forest tree, but also a magnificent specimen for the lawn. Native from Virginia to Mexico.
Height 60 to 70 feet.   Zone VII.

Thuya occidentalis (Arborvitae) is a tree for many climates and for a wide range of soil conditions. Normally the arborvitae is a solid shaft of rich dark green with scale-like leaves arranged in broad fans or fronds which hang irregularly on the twigs.
It is best as an ornamental, in groups or as a single accent, but it is often used in hedges or windbreaks.

Hardy, persistent, healthy, it gives satisfaction in heavy soil, damp or dry. Height usually 35 feet but occasionally 60 feet.   Zone II.
Be watchful for bagworm infestations (see page 620).

Tsuga canadensis (Hemlock), in the forests and glens, grows to 100 feet or more with a trunk six feet through. In suburban settings it reaches half these proportions. The sparse nodding top and the drooping branches give it a gracefulness not seen in any other evergreen tree. The lower branches spread widely, and sweep the ground. It is important therefore to give it plenty of room. This tree is excellent as a background, as a clump, or among pines in a grove. It may be clipped into a very dense hedge. It is sometimes wrongly used next to a house where in ten years it will have outgrown the location. Do not compromise its beauty by crowding it. It is not subject to insects and diseases but deserves good care and consideration. Water it during a dry season.   Height 100 feet.   Zone IV.

TREES FOR DRY, SANDY SOIL *

DECIDUOUS

Acer campestre	Hedge Maple
Ginnala	Amur Maple
Negundo	Box Elder
tataricum	Tatarian Maple
Ailanthus glandulosa	Tree of Heaven
Betula alba	European White Birch
Maximowicziana	Monarch Birch
populifolia	Gray Birch
Carya glabra	Pignut
Populus alba	White Poplar
grandidentata	Largetooth Aspen
tremuloides	Quaking Aspen
Prunus cerasus	Sour Cherry
serotina	Black Cherry
Ptelea trifoliata	Wafer Ash, Hop Tree
Quercus coccinea	Scarlet Oak
Robinia Pseudoacacia	Black Locust

EVERGREEN

Juniperus chinensis	Chinese Juniper
virginiana	Red Cedar
Picea alba	Canadian Spruce
excelsa	Norway Spruce
Pinus montana	Swiss Mountain Pine
rigida	Pitch Pine
strobus	White Pine
sylvestris	Scots Pine

* In these lists of trees, scientific names appear in the left-hand column and the corresponding common names in the right-hand column.

TREES OF RAPID GROWTH

DECIDUOUS

Acer dasycarpum	Silver Maple
Negundo	Box Elder
platanoides	Norway Maple
rubrum	Red Maple
Ailanthus glandulosa	Tree of Heaven
Betula Maximowicziana	Monarch Birch
populifolia	Gray Birch
Catalpa speciosa	Western Catalpa
Fraxinus americana	White Ash
Ginkgo biloba	Ginkgo
Gleditsia triacanthos	Honey Locust
Gymnocladus dioica	Kentucky Coffeetree
Larix decidua	European Larch
Liriodendron tulipifera	Tulip-tree
Magnolia acuminata	Cucumber Tree
tripetala	Umbrella Magnolia
Paulownia tomentosa	Empress Tree
Platanus acerifolia	London Plane Tree
Populus alba	White Poplar
nigra italica	Lombardy Poplar
Prunus serotina	Black Cherry
Quercus palustris	Pin Oak
Robinia Pseudoacacia	Black Locust
Salix alba	White Willow
vitellina	Golden Willow
Sorbus aucuparia	European Mountain Ash
Syringa japonica	Japanese Tree Lilac
Tilia americana (T. glabra)	American Linden
Ulmus americana	American Elm
glabra	Scots Elm

EVERGREEN

Picea excelsa	Norway Spruce
Pinus resinosa	Red Pine
rigida	Pitch Pine
strobus	White Pine
sylvestris	Scots Pine

TREES FREE FROM INSECT PESTS AND DISEASES

(Seldom attacked, and not seriously affected)

DECIDUOUS

Ailanthus glandulosa	Tree of Heaven
Cercidiphyllum japonicum	Katsura-Tree
Elæagnus angustifolia	Russian Olive
Ginkgo biloba	Ginkgo
Gleditsia triacanthos	Honey Locust
Gymnocladus dioica	Kentucky Coffeetree
Halesia carolina	Silverbell Tree
Kœlreuteria paniculata	Goldenrain Tree
Liquidambar styraciflua	Sweetgum
Magnolia (all species)	Magnolia
Nyssa sylvatica	Sourgum
Oxydendrum arboreum	Sourwood
Phellodendron (all species)	Cork Tree
Sophora japonica	Chinese Scholar-Tree

EVERGREEN

Pseudotsuga taxifolia	Douglas Fir
Sciadopitys verticillata	Umbrella Pine
Tsuga (all species)	Hemlock

TREES FOR THE SEASHORE

(Will withstand strong wind)

DECIDUOUS

Acer pseudoplatanus	Sycamore Maple
rubrum	Red Maple
Betula papyrifera	Paper Birch
Carpinus betulus	European Hornbeam
caroliniana	American Hornbeam
Cratægus oxyacantha	English Hawthorn
Gleditsia triacanthos	Honey Locust
Platanus occidentalis	American Plane Tree
Populus alba	White Poplar
balsamifera	Carolina Cottonwood
tremuloides	Quaking Aspen
Prunus maritima	Beach Plum
serotina	Black Cherry
Quercus borealis (Q. rubra)	Red Oak
laurifolia	Laurel Oak
virginiana	Live Oak
Salix alba	White Willow
Sassafras variifolium	Sassafras

EVERGREEN

Juniperus horizontalis	Creeping Juniper
virginiana	Red Cedar
Pinus montana	Swiss Mountain Pine
nigra	Austrian Pine
pinaster	Cluster Pine
rigida	Pitch Pine
thunbergi	Japanese Black Pine

SHADE TREES FOR STREETS

(Will withstand restricted city conditions)

Acer Ginnala (for Narrow Street)	Amur Maple
platanoides	Norway Maple
pseudoplatanus	Sycamore Maple
saccharum (North)	Sugar Maple
tataricum	Tatarian Maple
Catalpa speciosa	Western Catalpa
Celtis occidentalis (Mid-west)	Hackberry
Cratægus oxyacantha (Narrow Street)	English Hawthorn
cordata (Narrow Street)	Washington Thorn
Crus-galli (Narrow Street)	Cockspur Thorn
Fraxinus americana	White Ash
Ginkgo biloba	Ginkgo
Kœlreuteria paniculata (Narrow Street)	Goldenrain Tree
Liquidambar styraciflua (South)	Sweetgum

Magnolia grandiflora (South)	Magnolia
Populus alba Bolleana (Narrow Street)	White Poplar
nigra italica (Narrow Street)	Lombardy Poplar
Platanus acerifolia	London Plane Tree
Quercus borealis (Q. rubra)	Red Oak
coccinea	Scarlet Oak
falcata (South)	Spanish Oak
laurifolia (South)	Laurel Oak
macrocarpa	Mossycup Oak
palustris	Pin Oak
Phellos	Willow Oak
velutina	Black Oak
virginiana (South)	Live Oak
Sophora japonica	Chinese Scholar-Tree
Syringa japonica (Narrow Street)	Japanese Tree Lilac
Tilia cordata	Littleleaf European Linden
glabra (T. americana)	American Linden, Basswood
vulgaris	European Linden
Ulmus americana	American Elm
U. americana ascendens, var. Augustine	Augustine Ascending Elm

Quercus bicolor	Swamp White Oak
palustris	Pin Oak
Phellos	Willow Oak
Salix alba	White Willow
babylonica	Weeping Willow
fragilis	Brittle Willow
nigra	Black Willow
pentandra	Laurel Willow
vitellina	Golden Willow
Taxodium distichum	Bald Cypress
Tilia americana (T. glabra)	American Linden

EVERGREEN

Abies balsamea	Balsam Fir
Chamæcyparis thyoides	White Cedar
Picea mariana	Black Spruce
rubra	Red Spruce
Thuya occidentalis	American Arborvitæ
Tsuga canadensis	Hemlock

TREES WHICH WILL FORM GOOD WINDBREAKS

DECIDUOUS

Acer Ginnala	Amur Maple
Negundo	Box Elder
Cratægus mollis	Downy Hawthorn
Maclura pomifera	Osage Orange
Morus alba	White Mulberry
Populus alba	White Poplar
balsamifera	Balsam Poplar
Quercus palustris	Pin Oak

TREES WHICH THRIVE IN VERY WET SOIL

DECIDUOUS

Acer dasycarpum	Silver Maple
Negundo	Box Elder
rubrum	Red Maple
Alnus glutinosa	European Alder
Betula lutea	Yellow Birch
nigra	River Birch
populifolia	Gray Birch
Carpinus caroliniana	American Hornbeam
Carya ovata	Shagbark Hickory
Fraxinus caroliniana	Water Ash
lanceolata	Green Ash
Gleditsia aquatica	Water Locust
Larix americana	American Larch
Liquidambar styraciflua	Sweetgum
Magnolia glauca	Sweet Bay
Nyssa sylvatica	Sourgum, Tupelo
Platanus occidentalis	Buttonwood
Populus balsamifera	Carolina Cottonwood
grandidentata	Largetooth Aspen

EVERGREEN

Juniperus virginiana	Red Cedar
Picea alba	Canadian Spruce
excelsa	Norway Spruce
rubra	Red Spruce
Pinus nigra	Austrian Pine
ponderosa	Western Yellow Pine
resinosa	Red Cedar
rigida	Pitch Pine
Strobus	White Pine
sylvestris	Scots Pine
thunbergi	Japanese Black Pine
Thuya occidentalis	American Arborvitæ
Tsuga canadensis	Hemlock

LIST OF DECIDUOUS TREES

SCIENTIFIC AND COMMON NAMES	ZONE OF HARDINESS; HEIGHT IN FEET; PREFERRED SITUATION AND SOIL	BLOOM; SEASON OF BLOOM; FRUIT	NOTES
Acer campestre / Hedge Maple	IV; 40 (round, low)	Greenish; May; 2-winged samara	Beautiful foliage
dasycarpum (A. saccharinum) / Silver Maple	IV; 125 (narrow)	Greenish; Feb. and March; 2-winged samara	Branches are brittle
Ginnala / Amur Maple	IV; 25	Yellowish white; May; 2-winged samara	Bright red autumn leaves
japonicum / Japanese Maple (7–11 lobed)	VI; 12 (shrubby); rich	Purple; May; 2-winged samara	Crimson autumn leaves
Negundo / Box-elder	II; 60; woods or field	Yellowish green; March; 2-winged samara	Rapid growth; excellent windbreak
palmatum / Japanese Maple (5–9 lobed)	V; 25; rich	Purple; June; 2-winged samara	Many varieties
pennsylvanicum / Moosewood	IV; 35 (narrow); forest in mt.	Yellow; May; 2-winged samara	Clear yellow in autumn
platanoides / Norway Maple	IV; 90 (round headed); rich	Yellow, showy; April and May; 2-winged samara	Very dense shade
pseudoplatanus / Sycamore Maple	V; 90 (round headed)	Yellowish green; May; 2-winged samara	Thrives in exposed place
rubrum / Red Maple	III; 125; low damp soil	Red; March and April; 2-winged samara	Leaves scarlet and yellow
saccharum / Sugar Maple	III; 125; forest or pasture	Red; April; 2-winged samara	Brilliant red or yellow autumn foliage
spicatum / Mountain Maple	II; 30; stream bank	Greenish yellow; June; 2-winged samara	Orange and scarlet autumn foliage
tataricum / Tatarian Maple	IV; 30	Greenish white; May; 2-winged samara	Red fruit in August
Aesculus carnea / Red Horsechestnut	V; 60; rich moist soil	Pink to red; May and June; shell containing glossy brown nut	
glabra / Ohio Buckeye	V; 30; rich moist soil	Greenish yellow; May; shell containing glossy brown nut	
Hippocastanum / Horsechestnut	V; 80; deep rich soil	White, tinged red; May and June; shell containing glossy brown nut	Very dense shade, superb flowers
Ailanthus altissima (A. glandulosa) / Tree-of-Heaven	V; 60; any	Small green; May; samara	Stands smoke and city conditions
Alnus glutinosa / Common Alder	IV; 70; moist	Catkins; March; cones peduncled	Will thrive in wet places
incana / Black Alder	IV; 30; moist	Yellow catkins; March; very dark, conelike	Many forms; picturesque
Amelanchier canadensis / Shadbush; Serviceberry	IV; 30 (narrow); wooded hillsides	White, nodding; May; purple, sweet berry	Excellent forest tree
Aralia spinosa / Hercules Club	V; 40	Small white or cream in large panicles; August; small blue drupe	Very thorny
Betula alba (B. pendula) / European White Birch	II or III; 60; poor, sandy	Powdery yellow; cylindrical	Short lived, 30–40 years. Many varietal forms
lenta / Sweet Birch (Black Birch)	III; 75; stony hillside or forest	Long catkins	
lutea / Yellow birch	III; 90; damp, upland forest	Strobiles wide	

LIST OF DECIDUOUS TREES—continued

SCIENTIFIC AND COMMON NAMES	ZONE OF HARDINESS; HEIGHT IN FEET; PREFERRED SITUATION AND SOIL	BLOOM; SEASON OF BLOOM; FRUIT	NOTES
Maximowicziana Monarch Birch	V; 90; damp	Very long yellowish catkins; April; strobiles large	Catkins 9″ long
nigra River Birch	III; 90; wet, rich soil of valleys	Cylindrical	
papyrifera Canoe Birch (White Birch)	I or II; 90; mt. or northern forest		Not happy at coast. Many natural varieties
populifolia Gray Birch	IV; 30; dry, gravelly soil and old pastures		Weedy tree
Broussonetia papyrifera Paper-mulberry	VI; 50	Staminate catkin 3″–dioecious; Orange and red in Sept.	Naturalized in eastern states, Pa. and southward
Carpinus Betulus European Hornbeam	V; 60	Nut held by bract	For hedges; slow grower
caroliniana American Hornbeam Ironwood	IV; 40; forest and stream valley	Nut held by bract	Forest undergrowth
Carya alba Mockernut	IV; 100; hillside, poor	Edible nut	Hard, tough wood
glabra Pignut	IV; 130; hillside, poor	Edible nut	
laciniosa Shellbark Hickory	V; 130; hillside, poor	Edible nut	Gorgeous yellow autumn color
ovata Shagbark Hickory	IV; 130; hillside, poor	Edible nut	
Catalpa speciosa Western Catalpa	V; 50 (irregular)	White, spotted purple; June; very long pod	Picturesque and rugged
Celtis occidentalis Hackberry	II; 100; any		Hardy in cities
Cercidiphyllum japonicum Katsura-tree	IV; 50 (broad with lower branches to the ground); rich	Inconspicuous; pod 1″ long	For city streets
Cercis canadensis Red-bud	IV; 35 (broad); shade, acid or neutral	Purple bud, deep pink flower; April and May; pod—Sept.	
Cladrastis lutea Yellow-wood	III; 50; forest or lawn, rich	Cream; late June; clusters of pods	Yellow autumn foliage
Cornus florida Flowering Dogwood	IV; 25; partial shade pH 6.0–7.0	White; late April and May; Crimson	Irregular rangy growth
kousa Japanese Flowering Dogwood	V; 20	White; late June; Crimson	Excellent flowering tree
Crataegus phaenopyrum Washington Thorn	IV; 30; rich soil of meadows	White; May; Scarlet, ¼″	Excellent flowering tree
Crus-galli Cockspur Thorn	IV; 40; rich soil of meadows	White; May; Red, ⅓″	Excellent flowering tree
mollis (C. coccinea) Downy Hawthorn	IV; 30; rich soil of meadows	White, large; April and May; Scarlet, ½″	Quantities of fruit. Scarlet autumn leaves
oxyacantha English Hawthorn (May tree)	IV; 15; rich soil of meadows	Rose; May; Scarlet, ½″	Long thorns
punctata Dotted Thorn	IV; 30; dry pasture land	White; May; dull red and dotted	Several varieties with deeper color
Davidia involucrata var. Vilmoriniana Dove tree	V or VI; 65	Cream white; May; Green, pear-shaped, ½″	Flowers of exquisite beauty

Name		Flower; Fruit	Remarks
Diospyros virginiana	Persimmon	V; 60 (irregular)	White; May; Orange. Edible when fully mature	A magnificent tree with glossy foliage
Elaeagnus angustifolia	Russian Olive	V; 20; any well drained	Fragrant; June; Yellow	Free from disease
Euonymus europaeus	European Spindletree	IV; 30 (broad)	Yellow-green; May; Pink or red-orange	Subject to scale
Fagus americana (F. grandifolia)	American Beech	IV; 100–125; forest or lawn	Inconspicuous; edible nut	One of most beautiful native trees
Fagus sylvatica	European Beech	IV; 100 (low spreading branches); lawn as specimen	Inconspicuous; edible nut	Many varieties
Fraxinus americana	White Ash	III; 130; forest or field. Rich soil	Red, dioecious; March; winged samara	Beautiful pink and purple autumn color
Fraxinus caroliniana	Water Ash	VIII; 50; swamps		For wet places
Fraxinus lanceolata	Green Ash	II; 60; field		Will stand wet soil
Ornus	Flowering Ash	V; 65	White, fragrant; May; winged samara	
Ginkgo biloba	Ginkgo tree	IV; 130; rich soil	Staminate flower. Catkins. Dioecious; May; nuts 1″ long	Fruit has disagreeable odor
Gleditsia aquatica	Water Locust	VI; 60; wet	Greenish; May–June; handsome pods	Will grow in very wet soil
Gleditsia triacanthos	Honey Locust	IV; 100 (narrow, irregular); rich	White pea-blossoms in clusters; June; crooked pods, 12″ long	Picturesque, thorny
Gordonia alatamaha	Franklin tree	VI; 30; rich	Cream white; August; globose	Highly prized flowering tree
Gymnocladus dioica	Kentucky Coffeetree	V; 100 (irregular); rich	Green-white; June; Brown pods, 10″	Beautiful foliage
Halesia diptera	Two wing Silverbell	VI; 30; rich forest	White in clusters; May; 2-winged dry fruit	Beautiful flowering tree
Halesia carolina	Silverbell	IV; 30; forest or lawn	White; May; 4-winged dry fruit	Beautiful flowering tree
Hovenia dulcis	Raisin tree	VI; 30; sandy loam	Greenish in clusters; June	Elm-like tree
Juglans cinerea	Butternut tree	II; 100; rich stream banks	Catkins; edible nut	Subject to fungus
Juglans nigra	Black Walnut	IV; 100; forest or field	Catkins; edible nut	Stately tree but subject to caterpillars
Juglans regia	English Walnut	V; 100; rich	Catkins; delicious nut	
Juglans sieboldiana	Japanese Walnut	IV; 65; rich	Catkins; edible nut	
Koelreuteria paniculata	Goldenrain tree	V; 35; rich soil. Sheltered	Yellow panicles; late June; hollow pod	Beautiful flowering tree
Larix americana (L. laricina)	American Larch	II; 80; damp, swampy land	Small cone	Exquisite in early spring with young foliage
Liquidambar styraciflua	Sweetgum	IV; 90; damp, rich soil	Round barbed	Crimson and purple autumn leaves
Liriodendron tulipifera	Tulip-tree, Tulip Poplar	IV; 120; valley, wood or upland	Cream-green, tulip-shaped; June; dry, winged	Stately, tall tree. Gorgeous yellow autumn foliage
Maclura pomifera (Toxylon pomifera)	Osage Orange	VI; 40	Dioecious; April; Fruit, large green; wrinkled in September	Excellent windbreak

LIST OF DECIDUOUS TREES—continued

SCIENTIFIC AND COMMON NAMES	ZONE OF HARDINESS; HEIGHT IN FEET; PREFERRED SITUATION AND SOIL	BLOOM; SEASON OF BLOOM; FRUIT	NOTES
Magnolia acuminata Cucumber tree	V; 100; gravelly	Inconspicuous, yellow-green; May; Red in September	Grows like an oak
denudata (M. conspicua) Yulan	V; 50; rich	White, fragrant; April and May; Brownish	An old favorite
grandiflora Bull Bay	VII; 100; rich	Large, white, fragrant; May and Aug.; rusty brown	Evergreen
Kobus Kobus Magnolia	IV; 30; rich	White; April and May; cylindrical	Quantities of blossoms
macrophylla Bigleaf Magnolia	VI; 50; rich soil of valleys	Cream-white; fragrant; May and June; Rose-red	Enormous leaves
Soulangeana Saucer Magnolia	V; 30 (spreading); rich	Purple to white; May	Several varieties
stellata Star Magnolia	V; 12; rich	White; March and April; small	Earliest to bloom
tripetala Umbrella tree	V; 40 (wide spreading); rich	White; May and June; rose-colored	
virginiana (M. glauca) Sweet Bay (Swamp Magnolia)	V; 60 in S., 20 in N.; damp	White, fragrant; June and July; dark red	Half evergreen (evergreen in South)
Malus Arnoldiana Arnold Crab	V; 30; rich	Pink, large; Yellow, 1"	A hybrid
atrosanguinea Carmine Crab	V; 15; rich	Rose-purple, small; Red	A hybrid
baccata Siberian Crab	II; 45; rich	White; Red or yellow	Very hardy Asiatic species
coronaria Fragrant Crab	II; 30; rich, moist, but well drained	Bluish pink, fragrant; Green, 1"	
floribunda Japanese Flowering Crab	IV; 30	Rose-pink; Red	
Halliana Parkmanii Parkman Crab	V; 15	Bright rose; Purplish	
ioensis plena Bechtel's Crab	III; 30	Double rose, fragrant; Green, 1"	
Neidzwetzkyana Redvein Crab	IV; 50	Red; Red	Var. of M. pumila
Scheideckeri Scheidecker Crab	V; 25	Large, pale pink semi-double; Yellow	
spectabilis Chinese Flowering	IV; 50; any	Deep rose bud, pale pink flowers; Yellow, 1"	
Morus alba White Mulberry	IV; 25; sunny hillside, gravelly soil	Catkins; early spring before leaves; very sweet, variable in color	Forms a good windbreak
Nyssa sylvatica Sourgum (Tupelo)	IV or III; 100 (narrow); damp, rich	Inconspicuous; May and June; Black, small, fleshy	Crimson autumn foliage, turns early
Ostrya virginiana Hop Hornbeam	V; 65; gravelly uplands	Inconspicuous; hanging bunches, yellowish strobiles	
Oxydendrum arboreum Sourwood (Sorrel)	IV (usually 30); well drained uplands in forest, or swamp margins. Acid	White in panicles; July and Aug.; capsule	Early crimson autumn color
Paulownia tomentosa (P. imperialis) Empress tree	VI; 50 (wide spreading); sun and shelter from wind	Violet tubular panicles; May; dark brown capsule	Has run wild in East
Phellodendron amurense Cork tree	IV; 50; any	Inconspicuous; Black, berry-like	Handsome foliage

Platanus acerifolia, London Plane tree	V; 110	Inconspicuous; usually in pairs. Globose	Hardy street tree in cities
occidentalis, Buttonwood, Sycamore	IV; 165; damp, rich soil of valleys	Inconspicuous; Solitary globose	Very massive trunk with shedding outer bark and white inner bark
Populus alba, White Poplar	III; 100	In catkins like spikes emitting cottony fluff; before the leaves; seeds surrounded by silky hairs	White under surface of leaf
alba, var. pyramidalis (P. Bolleana)	III; narrow form of above	In catkins like spikes emitting cottony fluff; before the leaves	
balsamifera (deltoides), Balsam Poplar Cottonwood	II; 90; any	In catkins like spikes emitting cottony fluff; before the leaves; seeds surrounded by silky hairs	Will grow in wet soil
candicans, Balm of Gilead	IV; 130	In catkins like spikes emitting cottony fluff	Long-lived. Massive trunk
grandidentata, Largetooth Aspen	III; 75; variety of conditions	In catkins like spikes emitting cottony fluff; before the leaves; slender, long pedicelled	Will grow in wet soil
nigra italica, Lombardy Poplar	II; 75	In catkins like spikes emitting cottony fluff	Very rapid grower
tremuloides	I; 100; northern forests and uplands	In catkins like spikes emitting cottony fluff	Forms dense thickets
Prunus maritima, Beach Plum	IV; 8; sandy	White; April; Red-purple	Will withstand strong winds
serotina, Black Cherry	V; 100; rich	White; May and June; Black	Massive tree attaining great age
serrulata, Japanese Cherry	V; 80; rich	White; April and May; Black	Short-lived. Thrives 60 years
Sieboldii	V; 25; rich	Pink double, 1"; May	
subhirtella, Early Japanese Cherry	V; 30; rich	Light pink; April	
tomentosa, Nankin Cherry	IV; 10 (compact); rich	White-pinkish; March–April; Light red	
yedoensis, Yoshino Cherry	V; 50; rich	White to pink, fragrant; late March, April	Several varieties
Pterostyrax hispida, Epaulette tree	V; 50; sun or partial shade. Rich	Cream-white in hanging clusters; June; dry drupe	Little known, very beautiful tree
Quercus alba, White Oak	III or IV; 150 (wide spreading); rich soil. Dry or moist uplands or valleys	Catkins; acorn	Very light bark
bicolor, Swamp White Oak	IV; 70; rich, moist	Catkins	Good for wet places
borealis (Q. rubra), Red Oak	IV; 80; rich uplands and valleys	Catkins	
coccinea, Scarlet Oak	IV; 80; sandy or gravelly valleys	Catkins	Brilliant color in autumn
falcata, Spanish Oak	VI; 100; rich woods	Catkins	Common, Del. southward
laurifolia, Laurel Oak	VII; 100; rich, moist	Catkins; acorns ½" long	Will withstand wind; for the South
macrocarpa, Burr Oak	II; 90–170; rich valley lands	Catkins; acorn nearly covered by cup	
nigra, Water Oak	VI; 80; rich valley lands	Catkins	Avenue tree in South
palustris, Pin Oak	V; 80–125; rich valleys	Catkins	
Phellos, Willow Oak	V; 80; sandy uplands or margins of streams	Catkins; small acorns	Dark bark

LIST OF DECIDUOUS TREES—continued

SCIENTIFIC AND COMMON NAMES	ZONE OF HARDINESS; HEIGHT IN FEET; PREFERRED SITUATION AND SOIL	BLOOM; SEASON OF BLOOM; FRUIT	NOTES
Prinus Basket Oak	V; 100; low swamps	Catkins	
Robur English Oak	IV; 80–120; rich	Catkins	Leaf small
velutina Black Oak	V; 100–150; rich hillsides	Catkins	Beautiful foliage
virginiana Live Oak	VIII; 65 (spreading)	Catkins	Rapid growth, evergreen
Robinia Pseudoacacia Black Locust	V; 80; not particular	White, scented; May–June; pods	Rapid growth
Salix alba White Willow	II; 80; moist	Catkins	
babylonica Weeping Willow	V; 30; moist or stream banks	Catkins	Will thrive in wet soil
fragilis Brittle Willow	V; 60; moist	Catkins	
nigra Black Willow	III; 30–40; moist	Catkins	
pentandra Bay Willow	IV; 65; moist	Catkins	Leaf shining dark green
vitellina Yellow Willow	III; 75; moist	Catkins; catkins with the leaves	Rapid growth
Sassafras variifolium Sassafras	IV; 30–60; light	Yellow; May; Dark blue	Fine autumn color
Sophora japonica Chinese Scholar-tree	IV; 80; rich, protected from wind	White in terminal panicles; August; pods	
Sorbus Aucuparia Rowan tree	II; 40; rich	White in flat clusters; May; Red pome, Aug.–Sept.	Compound leaves
Stewartia Pseudo-Camellia Japanese Stewartia	V; 60; rich	2″ broad, white; July; 5-angled capsule, 1″ long	Very beautiful fruit
Styrax japonica Japanese Snowbell	V; 30; rich	White, hanging, bell-shaped; June and July; dry drupe, ¾″ long	Japan
Obassia Fragrant Snowbell	V; 30; rich	White in racemes; May and June; dry drupe	Japan, fragrant flowers
Syringa japonica Japanese Tree Lilac	IV; 25; rich	White; June	Rapid growth
Taxodium distichum Bald Cypress	V; 150; wet saturated	Small rounded cone	Beautiful in early spring
Tilia glabra (T. americana) American Linden	IV; 130; rich, moist	Fragrant yellow; July; pendulous from large bract	Rapid growth
cordata Small-leaved Linden	III; 100; rich	Yellow-white, fragrant; July; pendulous from large bract	Beautiful shade tree
vulgaris European Linden	V; 130; rich	Flowers hanging in clusters; June; pendulous from large bract	
Ulmus americana American Elm	II; 130; rich meadows	April; elliptic disk	Excellent shade tree
glabra Wych Elm	IV; 130		Many forms
pumila Dwarf Elm	IV; 50; rich lowland		Leaves small, smooth, dark

TABULAR LIST OF EVERGREEN TREES

SCIENTIFIC NAME	COMMON NAME	HEIGHT	ZONE OF HARDI-NESS*	NOTES
Abies balsamea	Balsam Fir	70	III	Will thrive in wet places
concolor	White Fir	130	IV	Best fir for specimen
homolepis	Nikko Fir	100	IV	
Nordmanniana	Nordmann's Fir	165	IV	
Veitchii	Veitch's Fir	80	III	Under side of foliage brilliant white
Cedrus atlantica	Atlas Cedar	130	VI	Beautiful foliage in whorls
Deodara	Indian Cedar	160	VII	Beautiful foliage in whorls
libani	Cedar of Lebanon	130	VI	Beautiful foliage in whorls
Chamæcyparis Lawsoniana	Lawson's Cypress	200	VI	Beautiful foliage
obtusa	Hinoki Cypress	130	III	Beautiful foliage
o. compacta		8	III	Dwarf broad conical
o. Crippsii		40	III	Young foliage pale yellow
o. gracilis	Slender Hinoki Cypress	100	III	Compact and slightly pendulous
o. nana	Dwarf Hinoki Cypress	8	III	Very compact and dwarf
pisifera	Sawara Cypress	165	III	Narrow pyramid
pisifera plumosa	Plume Cypress	100	III	Feathery foliage
pisifera squarrosa	Moss Cypress	60	III	Bluish fluffy foliage
thyoides	White Cedar	80	III	Picturesque tree with purple cones
Cryptomeria japonica Lobbii	Temple Cedar	165	VI	Handsome tufted branches
Ilex aquifolium	English Holly	50	VI or VII	Spiny broad leaves and red berries
opaca	American Holly	50	V	Spiny broad leaves and red berries
Juniperus chinensis	Chinese Juniper	65	IV	Leaves sharp needles
chinensis Pfitzeriana	Pfitzer's Juniper	10	IV	Spreading to 20 feet wide
chinensis pyramidalis		30	IV	Very narrow compact shaft
communis	Common Juniper	30	II	Leaves white-marked
communis depressa	Prostrate Juniper	4	II	Spreads to broad patches
communis suecica	Swedish Juniper	25	II	Narrow columnar
excelsa stricta	Greek Juniper	40	VI	Very compact pyramidal form
horizontalis	Creeping Juniper	1½	II	Very low training stems
horizontalis Douglasii	Waukegan Juniper	1½	II	Foliage purple in winter
procumbens		1½	V	Stiff ascending branches
Sabina	Savin	15	IV	Spreading low form
Sabina tamariscifolia		10	IV	Similar, with bluish foliage
squamata var. Meyeri		5	V	Dense bright blue foliage
virginiana	Red Cedar	60–90	II	Upright, narrow form, broadening with age
v. Canærtii		30	II	Compact rich green
v. elegantissimia		30	II	Tips of twigs yellow
v. glauca		40	II	All foliage glaucous
v. Schottii		30	II	Bright green twigs
Libocedrus decurrens	Incense Cedar	150	VI	Slender tree, long leaf scales
Magnolia grandiflora	Bull Bay	100	VII	Leaves shining dark green, flowers waxy white and fragrant
Picea alba (P. glauca)	White Spruce	100	II	Dense pyramid
Engelmanni	Englemann's Spruce	165	II	Dense, light blue-green leaves
excelsa	Norway Spruce	165	II	Rapid growth, dark leaves
mariana (P. nigra)		60	II	Rather sparse habit
orientalis	Oriental Spruce	135	IV	Needles glossy, very short
pungens	Colorado Spruce	100	II	Several blue varieties
rubra	Red Spruce	100	II	For cool damp climate
Pinus Bungeana	Lace-bark Pine	80	V	Broad spreading
Cembra	Stone Pine	80	IV	Dense narrow pyramid
densiflora	Japanese Red Pine	115	IV	Bright green foliage
densiflora umbraculifera	Japanese Table Pine	15	IV	Broad flat-topped
excelsa	Himalayan Pine	160	VI	Broad pyramid
flexilis	Limber Pine	80	V	Needles white-lined
koraiensis	Korean Pine	100	V	Dense slow growth
montana	Mountain Pine	35	III	Broad, irregular form
montana Mugo	Dwarf Mountain Pine	10	III	Dense, compact, broad
nigra	Austrian Pine	100+	IV	Dense, dark foliage
parviflora	Japanese White Pine	100	V	Needles short in tufts

* See Zone Map of Hardiness on page 706.

TABULAR LIST OF EVERGREEN TREES—continued

SCIENTIFIC NAME	COMMON NAME	HEIGHT	ZONE OF HARDI-NESS*	NOTES
Pinaster	Cluster Pine	100	VIII	Will withstand wind in the South and southern California
ponderosa	Western Yellow Pine	160+	V	Narrow pyramid
rigida	Pitch Pine	70	IV	Withstands wind
resinosa	Red Pine	80+	II	Rich green needles
Strobus	White Pine	100+	III	Graceful, vigorous growth
sylvestris	Scots Pine	80	II	Short, bluish needles
Thunbergi	Japanese Black Pine	100	V	Hardy in windy places
Pseudotsuga taxifolia	Douglas Fir	330	VI	Slender, compact, graceful
Sciadopitys verticillata	Umbrella Pine	130	V or VI	Handsome, pyramid, slow
Taxus baccata	English Yew	60	VI	Ascending and spreading
baccata adpressa		12	VI	Dwarf, spreading
baccata fastigiata	Irish Yew	35	VI	Narrow, columnar
baccata repandens		4	VI	Dwarf and drooping
canadensis	Canadian Yew	5	II	Low, spreading shrub
cuspidata	Japanese Yew	15	V	Vigorous, spreading
c. capitata		50	V	Broad pyramid
c. Hicksii		20	V	Broad columnar
c. media		30	V	Cross of C. baccata and C. cuspidata
c. nana	Dwarf Japanese Yew	6	V	Compact, slow growing
Thuya occidentalis	American Arborvitæ	65	II	Rich green, dense column
o. compacta		5	II	Slower and more dense
o. Douglasii pyramidalis		20	II	Narrow pyramid, rich foliage
o. globosa		5	II	Rounded dwarf form
o. Hoveyi		6	II	Rounded dwarf form
o. pyramidalis		30	II	Very narrow dense shaft
o. Vervæneana		13	II	Dense with slender twigs
o. Wareana	Siberian Arborvitæ	15	II	Broad pyramid; slow; dense blue-green
orientalis	Oriental Arborvitæ	30	VI (V)	Foliage in vertical planes
o. compacta (Sieboldii)			VI	Compact oval form
o. elegantissima		30	VI	Compact, bronzed in winter
plicata	Giant Arborvitæ	200	V	Rapid growth
Tsuga canadensis	Hemlock	100	IV	Graceful and fine texture
canadensis microphylla		50	IV	Leaves very short
canadensis pendula	Weeping Hemlock	20	IV	Broad weeping form
caroliniana	Carolina Hemlock	70	V	More compact habit
diversifolia	Japanese Hemlock	100	V	Slow growth; difficult to transplant

* See Zone Map of Hardiness on pages 706.

XX

SHRUBS

IN the planting design for a home property shrubs should be given an important place, not merely because they function so well as a natural screen but for the sake of their own beauty. In wealth and color of bloom, in range of flowering season, in richness and variety of foliage, in vivacity of fruit effect, in individual interest of twig color in winter, there is no other plant group which can surpass the shrubs.

Shrubs form the intermediate plantings on the home property. They may be used with restraint and distinction in the planting about the house; they may be used as low ornamental hedges to form the boundary of the property or as a high hedge to screen unsightly objects; they may be used as specimen plants where the beauty of their bloom or foliage can be enjoyed to advantage; they may be planted in groups or as shrub borders to bring a variety of form and bloom and autumn coloring into the landscape picture, and to provide a nesting place for birds. They may be used as a background for tall perennials and lilies, and some of the smaller species may be used in the rock gardens to give character and form to the planting. Some types may be grown in tubs or planting boxes to be used for decorative effect on terrace or patio, and a few, such as the evergreen Firethorn (Pyracantha coccinea) and the Winter creeper (Euonymus radicans) can be trained as vines against the house wall. Few plant groups are as versatile or as adaptable as are the shrubs.

Most shrubs are long-lived and, like the trees, are considered a permanent or long-time investment. However, unlike the trees, they mature in a very few years and thus begin early to pay dividends. Four or five years after planting, a shrub border or a boundary screen should be high enough and dense enough to obliterate whatever lies behind, and mature enough to bear blossoms and fruit in profusion.

Before winter is really over, some shrubs are already in bloom, followed by others which carry on through the season uninterruptedly until autumn frosts or even later. The great majority of shrubs bloom in spring or early summer. From mid-July on there is only an occasional shrub in flower, but by careful selection a home owner may have some bloom every season. Shrubs with interesting fruit begin to produce it in late June or July and the succession continues without intermission until midwinter or early spring. Some of the fruits are pure colors of red, purple, orange, yellow, or blue. Some are but dry capsules, interesting, however, because of their form. Many shrub fruits are used frequently in flower arrangements for the house. Color, form, texture, line; all the essentials of composition are to be found in twigs and fruit as well as in leaves and blossoms of shrubs. The leaves of some shrubs, though not many, turn to brilliant colors in the autumn, some of the Viburnums and Euonymus being as beautiful as any tree.

Like any other type of plant, shrubs should be adapted to the soil and other conditions of the site. Some shrubs thrive in dry soil, others in wet soil, while the majority prefer a medium between. Some respond to cultivation and enrichment of the soil; others prefer a meager diet. Some are hardy on exposed summits; others require protection from the wind. Some like shade, while most prefer plenty of sunshine. And then there is an easily satisfied group of shrubs which seem not to care what their environment is and seem oblivious to neglect. All of these factors, while they limit in one way the use of shrubs, enlarge the possibilities of their use.

SELECTION OF SHRUBS

Half a century ago the lists of shrubs offered in our nursery catalogs were very limited and the selection of a few reliable kinds presented little difficulty. However, plant explorers have discovered rare and beautiful new species and many new varieties have been introduced.

The subject of selecting shrubs for the site may be approached in either of two ways or a combination of the two. In the first, the existing conditions of the site are (and very often must be) accepted, and only the shrubs which thrive in those conditions are used. In the second, existing conditions are modified to make possible a wider range in the use of shrubs. Sometimes conditions cannot be changed except at great expense. Sometimes it requires time to effect the change. But usually growing conditions may be improved by the application of fertilizer, by cultivation and the removal of grass and weeds, by drainage or by irrigation. If the second method is used shrubs may be selected solely for their quality and for their special contributions to the general composition.

If on a bare, open ground with alkaline or neutral soil we insist upon having rhododendrons and azaleas, then we will have to make changes in the site, underdrain the soil, plant oak trees for shade and for acidity of soil, add humus and leaf mold to the soil, and mulch every year with a carpet of oak leaves. Only then, when these changed conditions are established, may we plant rhododendrons and laurel with any possibility of success.

If we accept existing conditions without making any changes, we must be content with the shrubs which are happy under such conditions. If conditions are favorable, *i.e.,* ordinary garden soil, some sun, not too much shade, and protection from wind, then the range of selection is very wide and our choice may be made entirely on climatic and æsthetic consideration.

To prepare shrubs for transplanting using plastic sprays, see pages 210 and 683.

PLANTING AND TRANSPLANTING SHRUBS

Shrubs which have been grown in the nursery should be transplanted either in early spring, which is the more favorable time, or in autumn. Each planting season has its advantages. Except for the early spring flowering shrubs, the spring transplanting is preferred by many plantsmen because it gives the shrubs increasingly good growing weather in which to re-establish themselves. However, spring is a breathlessly busy time for all gardeners and in apportioning the year's work it often is advisable to plan the transplanting of new shrubs and trees in the autumn when the work may be spread over a longer period of good transplanting weather. In sections of the country from the shores of Chesapeake Bay southward through the coastal plains to Texas, in the central valley of California and on the coast of Oregon, transplanting operations are safely carried on through the winter months, many parts of these regions having six months of continuous good transplanting weather. In northern New York and New England the seasons for transplanting are very short, September and May for evergreens and October and May for deciduous plants.

The best days for transplanting are cloudy, cool days, with a high degree of humidity and no wind. Seldom are we able to pick ideal weather, however, and reasonable precautions against the rapid drying of stems and roots must be taken if satisfactory results are to be expected.

Transplanting is a shock to the plant, even if the man in charge of the job solemnly swears that the "thing will never know it has been moved." Unless the humidity of the air is 90 percent or more, the plant is losing moisture all the time that it is out of the ground, not only through its stems and leaves, but what is more harmful, through its roots. At best, some of the roots are cut and a proportionate part of the top should be cut off to equalize the loss. Dry roots cause more failures after transplanting than any other factor. Whatever precaution we can take to prevent or retard this loss of moisture will reduce the effect of the shock on the vitality of the plant. As with trees, shrubs may be transplanted with a ball of earth or with bare roots. Most deciduous shrubs and some evergreen shrubs are hardy enough and grow rapidly enough to stand bare-root transplanting perfectly well.

The following exceptions should be handled by the method here recommended for each:

Abelia grandiflora	Ball and Burlap
Ceanothus	" " "
Corylus	" " "
Cotoneaster horizontalis	Potted plants
" adpressa	" "
" microphylla	" "
Exochorda	Ball and Burlap
Hibiscus syriacus	" " "
Ilex serrata	" " "
Magnolia glauca	B. & B. special care (see p. 212)
Myrica	Ball and Burlap
Pyracantha	Potted plants
Rhamnus	Ball and Burlap
Tamarix	" " "
Viburnum tomentosum plicatum	" " "
Broad-leaved evergreens *all*	Ball and Burlap, except those noted here for potted plants and except for collected stock

Nursery-grown plants are usually sold at prices in accordance with their height. While the nurserymen's association have made every effort in recent years to standardize quality, there is still a marked difference in the general robustness of the plants. This is caused by the various degrees of upkeep in different nurseries, or even in different parts of the same nursery. Where shrubs have grown too large in the nursery row and have become crowded, height is no indication of value; on the contrary it may even be a detriment, the crowding having caused the loss of good form. Likewise, the encroachment of weeds in the nursery rows affects the growth of the plants and sometimes provides the purchaser of the plants with the introduction of a variety of weed he does not possess. In selecting plants price certainly should not be the governing factor. Well-grown nursery

BOXWOOD AS A BACKGROUND

stock cannot be had at a bargain.

The practice of shipping nursery stock by truck to the site not only saves time and labor costs, but for the plants it reduces the shock of transplanting to a minimum. If other considerations are about equal the best nursery is the nearest one.

Transplanting shrubs with bare roots is done by the same method described for tree transplanting. The same general precautions are taken to get the plants into the ground as soon as possible, to water soon after planting and frequently thereafter, to prune back severely, to shade them from sunshine at first, to mulch the ground about the more tender ones. Shrubs

239

will stand even more pruning than seems
necessary for trees. It is the roots which count
most at first, and healthy roots will send up
enough new shoots to balance the intake and
evaporation of moisture. If the shrubs are not
pruned enough at first, the tops will wilt and
gradually die. Much more severe pruning will
then be required to save the plants, and in the
meantime much vitality has been lost. Shrubs
should be moved before the leaves appear in
spring or certainly while the leaves are yet very
small. Some shrubs are much more subject to
wilting after transplanting than others. The
Honeysuckles are particularly fast wilters and
should never be transplanted while in leaf.
Forsythias, on the other hand, may be moved
while in full flower.

In recent years nurserymen have devised
methods of prolonging the planting season to
permit the late spring planting of stock. All
these methods are dependent on some form of
retarding growth such as storing in root cellars
or heeling in with loose earth in close formation. Plants thus stored may be planted after
leaves are formed, but the plants must be dug
up and planted without loss of time.

Normally, shrubs should not be moved while
in flower, but Forsythia, which blooms before
the leaves come, does not mind it. The Azaleas
also may be handled at this time with ball and
burlap, and as the root growth is rapid at
blooming season, the results are satisfactory.
Shrubs which should be moved only in spring
include: Buddleia, Abelia, Magnolia (very

early). Shrubs which should be moved only in the autumn include: Chænomeles japonica, Cornus mas, Hamamelis vernalis.

Heeling-In

So important is it to keep the roots of shrubs and trees from drying out that when a shipment of plants is received they should be placed in trenches, and the roots should be covered with soil. This should be done even if the final planting of this material is to be undertaken a few hours later. On cloudy damp days this degree of care is not so essential, but if the planting job will require several days, it should always be done.

Preparation of Beds for Planting

Areas to be planted with shrubs should be plowed or dug to a depth of 12 inches, and the soil thoroughly broken up and loosened. Well-rotted manure should be worked into the soil by forking. Heavy soils should be improved by the addition of sandy loam, and sandy soil should have an application of humus or decomposed vegetable matter. The whole planting bed should thus be prepared, not merely little pockets where each shrub is to go. After all, this preparation and improvement of the soil is the last this area is likely to receive for some years and a good soil is essential to the good growth of any plant.

After planting, the top of a shrub should be pruned enough to equalize the loss of roots. With Box bushes, no trimming is necessary because of the dense mat of roots which have remained intact in the ball. The plant should be watered lavishly at first and frequently through the remainder of the season, the foliage being watered as well as the soil, ending with a generous application of water in mid-autumn. Especially is this autumn watering important for Rhododendron, Mountain Laurel, broad-leaved evergreens in general, and Box bushes. These plants all lose moisture through their leaves during the winter. They therefore have to store up a supply of water before winter freezing of the ground about their roots sets in. After freezing the roots cannot replenish the plant's water supply.

The real test of success in transplanting shrubs which have been moved comes the second year after planting. In the first year the new growth comes from the vitality in the plant, stored up from previous years. In the second year its growth is dependent on the nourishment taken in from the new roots made that first year. If the root growth is satisfactory the first year, top growth and general vigor should be good the second year. The importance of good rich soil about the roots of the newly planted shrub cannot be too strongly emphasized.

Pruning

The best time to prune shrubs depends upon their flowering habits. Those shrubs which bear blossoms on *new* growth in late spring or summer should be pruned in early spring or during the last weeks of winter. In this group are:

Abelia	Hydrangea	Rosa
Acanthopanax	Hypericum	Salix
Berberis	Indigofera	Spiræa
Buddleia	Kerria	Staphylea
Callicarpa	Lagerstrœmia	Stephanandra
Caryopteris	Lespedeza	Tamarix, late-
Ceanothus	Ligustrum	flowering kinds
Clethra	Lonicera	Vitex
Colutea	Neillia	
Hibiscus	Rhus	

SHRUBS "HEELED IN"

Trench — *Roots covered*

The shrubs which bear blossoms on last year's wood should be pruned soon after blooming. This prevents the formation of seed pods and thus conserves the vitality of the plant, and in the case of some plants improves their appearance. In this group are:

Amygdalus	Deutzia	Spiræa
Azalea	Exochorda	Syringa
Caragana	Forsythia	Tamarix, early
Cercis	Magnolia	flowering kinds
Chionanthus	Philadelphus	Viburnum Carlesii
Cydonia	Ribes	V. Lantana
Cytisus	Roses (climbers)	

A few shrubs should be pruned lightly after blooming and again lightly in early spring.

Cornus stolonifera	Sambucus	Viburnum
C. paniculata	Spiræa Bumalda	tomentosum
C. alba siberica	Symphoricarpos	V. Opulus
Lonicera		Weigela (Diervilla)

Many jobbing gardeners seem to think that the way to prune shrubbery is to cut off all the branches to an even length. This practice ruins the grace of the shrub and does little to improve its vitality or blooming habits. Branches should be removed by cutting each branch off at its base, and only about 1/5 or 1/4 of the branches should be removed. The purpose of this kind of pruning is to give new stems a better opportunity to develop from the bottom, thus improving the whole plant. The pruning of this sort requires less time than cutting a multitude of stems near the tops, and it maintains the natural shape of the shrub.

The primary purpose of pruning most shrubs is to keep them young, and thus maintain their blooming ability. This is done by removing old wood, although it may be perfectly sound, and with it the parts of the stems which have finished blooming. The preponderance of roots will increase the growth of young stems the following year and thus increase the quantity of stems which will bear blossoms. This is particularly effective with the Spiræas, Loniceras, Hydrangeas, and Philadelphus.

If shrubs have to be pruned to keep them from growing too large for their situation, then something is wrong with the planting scheme. Such shrubs should be transplanted to more ample situations and their place taken by smaller sorts.

Some kinds of shrubs need annual pruning to keep them in good condition. Those shrubs especially which habitually have dead branches or often are winter-killed must have old, mature wood thinned out. Some Deutzias, Hydrangeas, Privets, Mock-orange, Buddleia, Spiræas, Snowberry, Tamarix, Chaste-tree, Kerria, and Stephanandra, Cornus stolonifera and C. sanguinea are all in this class. Those which winter-kill in the north will need a spring clearing of dead stems. They include some of the preceding list plus Abelia, Callicarpa, Corylopsis pauciflora, Genista germanica, Hypericum Moserianum, English Holly, Kolkwitzia, Meratia præcox, Jasminum nudiflorum, Osmanthus Aquifolium, Mahonia Aquifolium, Pieris japonica, Azalea indica, Azalea pontica, and a few less well known shrubs.

Some shrubs are better for the pruning off of the flower heads after blooming and before seeds are set. These include Lilacs, Azaleas, Rhododendrons, Kalmia, Magnolia, Buddleia, and Stephanandra.

1. Shrub with an accumulation of crowded stems.

2. Shrub after pruning, surplus stems removed at the base.

3. Wrong—shrub with flowering parts amputated. This is not pruning.

PRUNING AN ESTABLISHED SHRUB

Proper cut.

TWIG PRUNING

Too slanting.   Too far.   Too close.

bending its branches to the ground and covering the whole plant with a veritable mattress of leaves, a Crape Myrtle has been brought through twenty winters at Philadelphia; but these are exceptions.

One of the most satisfactory methods of providing winter protection for broad-leaved evergreens is through the use of a plastic spray. The spray should be applied between mid-November and early December, a thin film being applied to the leaves and twigs. A spray of this type will give excellent protection from winter sun which often causes a burning of the foliage of broad-leaved evergreens, and it will also reduce transpiration of moisture from the leaves which will enable the plants to come through the winter in better condition. For further details concerning the plastic sprays see pages 210 and 683.

For the protection of half-hardy shrubs or for newly planted shrubs some protection from wind is advisable, and a wind screen should be constructed.

This may be constructed of any material which will remain in place and which will not rot. Mats of straw are often used and are manufactured and sold commercially. They may be rolled up and put away at the end of the season and may be used year after year. Cornstalks, flanked against a rough barrier, offer very effective protection, and are usually readily available at a nominal price in country areas. By weaving stout wire in and out among the stalks, a thick, firm matting of any desired width can be made. This may be fastened to a fence made of stakes driven into the ground with two horizontal wires strung between. Burlap, tacked securely on to lath frames, may also be used very satisfactorily.

The winter screen should not be removed in the spring until all danger of a return to winter has passed. March is one of the most trying months, with much wind and brilliant sunshine, and as the screen is to serve as a protection against these factors, quite as much as against cold, it should remain in place until the weather is springlike and settled.

Some shrubs sucker badly and are improved by the periodic removal of the suckers—Lilacs particularly.

Some shrubs may be cut to within a few inches of the ground and will grow again from the root. Such shrubs as Lilac, Sumac, Lycium, Lonicera, Privet, Forsythia, Myrica, Box, are in this group. On the whole, shrubs have great vitality. Many will stand utter neglect and even much abuse, living for years without attention. Those which are particularly self-reliant are Forsythia, Berberis Thunbergi, the Loniceras, Hypericums, the broad-leaved evergreens in general, Sumacs, Wild Roses, Viburnums, Elæagnus, and Aronia.

Many shrubs are greatly benefited by a good mulch. For materials to be used, method of applying, etc., see Chapter XXXIV on Mulches.

Winter Protection

So many are the hardy shrubs that there seems little justification in trying to maintain shrubs which are not really hardy in the region. Those which may be induced to survive the winters by protecting them and which reward the gardener for this extra care are rare indeed, for an occasional exceptionally cold winter may make the protection of no avail.

Box hedges carefully covered with canvas tents every winter have survived in a garden near Boston for seventy-five years. By carefully

Winter protection is often of great value for newly planted evergreen shrubs, such as Rhododendron, Leucothoë, and Mahonia, and as a general practice it is wise to provide some protection for the two years following transplanting.

Some shrubs suffer seriously from the weight of heavy snow upon their branches. Box is particularly subject to such injury, and suffers also from the action of sunshine on melted snow which has frozen again to ice. In many sections it is therefore wise to cover the bushes with roofs of wood, cornstalks, or heavy canvas in order to prevent the snow from falling on the foliage and branches. If no covering is provided, careful vigilance should be practiced, and snow should be swept from the branches as soon as it has fallen.

SHRUBS OF MERIT

Abelia grandiflora is a dainty and lovely thing, evergreen in the South, leaves persistent in the North. The foliage is glossy and somewhat coppery in tone. The small, pink, tubular flowers are borne in terminal racemes and continue in bloom from midsummer through the autumn. The shrub is dense in habit of growth and at maturity will reach a height of 6 to 8 feet. It is useful in a shrub border, in foundation planting or as a specimen.

Zone of Hardiness: VI.

Soil Requirements: A good garden loam.

Exposure: Sun or partial shade.

Culture: Requires light pruning to maintain the natural, graceful shape of the shrub. Prune in late winter or very early spring.

Arbutus unedo (Strawberry Tree). An evergreen of picturesque habit of growth. Tolerant of a wide range of soil and climate conditions but best suited to mild areas. May be grown under desert conditions and thrives also along the sea-coast. The growth is slow, the branches irregular and the form wide-spreading. The foliage is a dark green and dense. The clusters of white flowers and the small, strawberry-like fruits are borne during the autumn and winter. Height varies from 10 to 20 feet.

Grown widely on the West Coast. May be used as a dense shrub screen or trained as a small tree.

Aronia arbutifolia (Chokeberry) is a shrub of upright growth, varying in height from 6 to 9 feet. The dense flower clusters which are produced in late May are white with pinkish tints and are followed by bright red fruits, ripening in the early autumn. The foliage turns a glorious and brilliant red in the fall and is very decorative. It is conducive to the production of a more naturalistic and less domesticated type of effect than characterizes the usual small home grounds. It may also be used in the wild garden.

Zone of Hardiness: V.

Soil Requirements: Not particular, but thrives best in rich soil on moist side.

Exposure: Sun or shade.

Propagation: Stratify* seeds in the fall, removing the pulp first. Suckers. Layers (not considered the best way). Softwood cuttings under glass.

Culture: Although tall, slender and somewhat irregular growing, this shrub should not be pruned, as it is best used in naturalistic form.

Azaleas (Rhododendron).† The azaleas are among the most beautiful of the flowering shrubs. Native to Eastern Asia, North America and Southern Europe, they have been developed in the skillful hands of the plant hybridizers until today we have many varied and brilliantly flowered forms. There are both evergreen and deciduous types. Most forms possess considerable hardiness, while a few are suited only to mild climates.

Azaleas and other rhododendrons are more exacting in their cultural requirements than are most of the other commonly grown flowering shrubs, but with their profusion and beauty of bloom, their wide range of glorious colors and their dependable flowering year after year, they will more than repay the extra effort expended upon them.

Exposure: Most azaleas prefer a sunny exposure, or a location where they will receive direct sunlight for at least a portion of the day. Some types may be grown successfully under trees which cast high shade and provide filtered sunlight. Some will make satisfactory growth in areas where they are in partial shade, but no azaleas will grow in dense shade. Most azaleas withstand exposure to wind extremely well.

Soil Requirements: Most azaleas require an acid soil. A pH range of 4.5 to 5.5 is considered optimum for most types.

The texture of the soil is also important. Azaleas require a soil which is abundantly supplied with humus, mellow and fibrous in texture, retentive of moisture yet well drained. They will not thrive in heavy, poorly drained, water-logged soil.

---

* See Chapter XXXIII on Propagation for explanation of term.

† Botanically, azaleas are classed as Rhododendrons but they are so distinctive in character and have so long been listed, and continue to be listed, in nursery catalogs as azaleas that we here retain this name.

If the soil in the area where azaleas are to be planted does not meet these requirements measures should be taken to correct its deficiencies. For methods which may be used to increase the acidity of the soil see page 168. If the soil is a good garden loam its texture may be improved by incorporating into it liberal quantities of compost, acid peat and other suitable organic materials. If, however, it is a heavy clay, or a very light sandy soil, it would be wise to remove it and fill the bed or the planting hole with a good mixture—peat, oak leaf mold and humus such as is recommended on page 169. The area should be excavated to a depth of 12 to 15 inches and refilled with the planting mixture. It requires considerable labor to accomplish this but it must be borne in mind that an azalea planting is a very permanent planting and will be a source of satisfaction over a period of many years. The cost of the plants is also comparatively high, and it is a matter of poor economy and unsound judgment to fail to provide congenial soil which will be conducive to their best growth. If this is not done the results will be disappointing. The plants will fail to flower well and will tend to die out after a few years.

Planting: Except in the case of extremely small plants, azaleas should always be planted with a ball of earth. They may be purchased in pots or tubs or with the ball of earth wrapped in burlap. In the North spring planting is advisable. In the South azaleas should preferably be transplanted during the period between the time they have set their flower buds in the autumn and spring. The deciduous azaleas should, if possible, be planted after they have dropped their leaves and while they are completely dormant. It is very important that azaleas be planted at the same depth at which they were growing in the nursery. Too deep planting is the cause of many failures. The ball of earth should not be allowed to dry out between the time of digging and planting and after the bushes are in place the area should be well watered, and a good mulch of acid leaf mold or peat should be applied.

Fertilization: In order to maintain an azalea planting in vigorous, healthy condition and to insure abundant bloom two annual applications of fertilizer are desirable, one early in the spring and the other between the middle of June and the middle of July. Fertilizers which are acid in their reaction upon the soil should be used. See page 169. A commercially prepared complete fertilizer for acid-loving plants may be used if available, or a mixture such as the following may be prepared at home:

10 pounds ammonium sulphate
35 pounds superphosphate
17 pounds sulphate of potash
28 pounds cottonseed meal
10 pounds aluminium sulphate

An application of 2 to 3 pounds per plant is recommended.

Cottonseed meal applied alone is an excellent fertilizer on soils which are not low in potash. The same rate of application is recommended. The fertilizer should be spread evenly over the surface of the ground about the bush, extending out slightly beyond the spread of the branches, and should be watered in.

Culture: The soil about azaleas should never be cultivated, as the feeding roots are very near the surface and might be severely injured. A good mulch of acid peat or oak leafmold should be maintained which will help to keep the soil cool and moist and provide conditions favorable to good growth.

For control of insect pests and diseases see page 620.

SPECIES AND HYBRIDS OF MERIT

Azalea calendulacea (R. calendulaceum). This lovely azalea, known as the Flame Azalea, is one of the most beautiful of our native shrubs. It grows wild in the Appalachian Mountains from northern Georgia to Pennsylvania and in the spring the woods are aglow with its beauty. The flowers vary in color from pale yellow to brilliant orange and a well-grown specimen is a glorious sight when in full bloom. It requires an acid soil, rich in humus and well-drained, and under favorable conditions it will attain a height of 8 to 9 feet. It thrives best in light woodland shade but will withstand considerable exposure to sun and wind. The foliage is deciduous. Zone V, Northern limit.

Azalea—Ghent Hybrids. The Ghent hybrids are noted for their wide range of beautiful colors. The flowers are smaller than those of some of the other types but are borne in great profusion, the colors ranging from white to lilac-pink, deep pink, golden yellow, orange-red and brilliant scarlet. The Ghent hybrids are hardy, dependable and of easy culture, reaching a height at maturity of about 6 feet.

Azalea—Glendale Hybrids. These lovely, large-flowered, evergreen azaleas were developed by Mr. B. Y. Morrison. Most varieties which have been introduced are hardy from Baltimore southward. The plants range in height from 4 to 8 feet, according to variety. Many of the varieties produce flowers which are flecked, striped or blotched with a contrasting color, making them distinctive in appearance. Others are clear self-colors. Most varieties are single, some are of the hose-in-hose type.

Azaleas—Indian Group. This group of azaleas includes many of the beautiful large-flowered, evergreen varieties which are grown so widely in the South and have made famous many of the gardens in that section of the country. More than 50 varieties in this group are available for planting in the South, the colors ranging through white, lavender, rose-pink, salmon and orange-red to the variegated types. Although most of the members of this diverse group are suited only to mild climates a few are very hardy, among them Indica alba (Ledifolia alba), one of our best white azaleas.

Azalea Kaempferi (R. obtusum var. kaempferi). In its native habitat in Japan, A. Kaempferi grows in thickets and along the edge of woodlands, and it is therefore well adapted to growing in light shade. The A. Kaempferi hybrids offer a wide range of color—from soft lilac and pink to lilac-rose, deep mauve, orange-pink, and pale orange, light rose to rose-red and bright, brick-red. The flowers are produced in large clusters. The plants are vigorous, hardy and free-flowering, and attain a height of 8 to 10 feet at maturity. The deciduous foliage turns a brilliant orange-scarlet in the autumn.

Kurume azaleas. The Kurume azaleas were introduced into this country from Japan by the great plant explorer, Dr. E. H. Wilson. Fifty varieties were shipped to the Arnold Arboretum in 1919 and since their introduction they have gained tremendous popularity in many sections. The plants are evergreen, the leaves small, and the characteristic growth is dense and twiggy. The height varies from 4 to 8 feet according to variety.

The flowers, which are smaller than those of many other types, are produced in great profusion. Most are single, others of the type known as hose-in-hose. Among the many varieties there is a wide range of color, from white, pale pink, lavender and salmon to brilliant scarlet. Some of the more brilliant colors are difficult to combine harmoniously with other plants and if used at all should be used with great restraint. Many named varieties are available.

The Kurume azaleas are widely grown from Pennsylvania southward and on the Pacific Coast. In colder sections they require a sheltered location or some winter protection.

Azalea—Mollis Hybrids. The Mollis hybrids are vigorous and hardy, prefer full sun but will grow fairly well in light shade, are less exacting in their soil requirements than are many other types, and may be transplanted when small without a ball of earth. In this group there is a wide range of unusually beautiful colors, some being soft, pastel shades, others of a more brilliant hue—delicate yellow, deep Indian yellow, apricot-yellow, and brilliant, coppery-flame. The Mollis hybrids are excellent for a mass planting in beds or for the foreground of shrubbery borders, and they may

AZALEAS AND RHODODENDRON CAROLINIANUM

also be used in foundation planting and as specimens. The plants vary in height from 3 to 6 feet, depending upon the variety.

Azalea nudiflora (Pinxter-Flower). This lovely azalea is a native of the woodlands in the East from North Carolina to Massachusetts. It is one of the most satisfactory azaleas for under-growth planting in wooded areas. In early spring, before the leaves appear, it brings a touch of color to the gray woods with its masses of small, pink flowers which are delicately fragrant. It is upright in habit of growth, reaching a height of 6 to 10 feet.

Azalea Schlippenbachii. This beautiful azalea from Eastern Asia blooms in early spring before the leaves unfurl. The wide-open flowers are very large, a lovely shade of soft pink, and they are borne in clusters at the tips of the twigs. Its growth is slow and widely branched, but after many years it sometimes attains a height of 15 feet. It is hardy and well adapted to cool climates. It thrives in very light shade and it is tolerant of a greater range of soil acidity than some other types.

Azalea Vaseyi (Pinkshell Azalea). This is one of our most beautiful native azaleas, its natural habitat being the ravines and swampy areas in the mountains of North Carolina. The clear pink flowers are borne in clusters in early spring before the leaves unfold. In habit of growth it is upright, spreading, but somewhat irregularly so, and attains a height of about fifteen feet. It begins to flower when quite small. In autumn the foliage turns a bright crimson. It is hardy, and is best adapted to cool climates and high altitudes. It requires a soil which is abundantly supplied with moisture.

Berberis Julianæ is one of the best of the hardy, evergreen barberries. Its rather dense foliage and its height, six feet or more, make it a dependable background shrub. The yellow flowers are borne in conspicuous clusters in spring and have a most decorative value.

Zone of Hardiness: V, northern limit.

Soil Requirements: A good garden loam.

Exposure: Full sun.

Buddleia Davidi (Orange-eye Butterfly bush) is a welcome addition to any planting as it blooms during the summer months when few other shrubs are in flower. The foliage is a soft gray-green and the tall, slender, wand-like branches are gracefully arched. The beautiful, fragrant flowers are borne in terminal clusters and are violet-purple in color with a small orange eye. The flowering period extends from early July well into the autumn. It often reaches 8 feet in height, and from 6 to 8 feet in diameter. The Butterfly bush is excellent as a source of cut flowers and is considered good for smoky places.

Zone of Hardiness: VI, sometimes V. The wood is not very hardy so that in most northern gardens the plants almost die to the soil each year. See Culture.

Soil Requirements: Rich, well drained.

Exposure: Sunny.

Propagation: Softwood cuttings taken in summer and wintered in coldframes are considered the easiest way. Hardwood cuttings taken in the fall and stored out of danger of frost, also good.

Culture: Given a protection of litter, the rootstock will survive most winters and send up vigorous shoots that flower in late summer. Spring is the best time to cut the plants to the ground. If the plants lack bushy or symmetrical shape, a good practice is to pinch the tips of the branches.

Buxus (Box). Beloved and cherished in the gardens of our ancestors, Box is as highly appreciated now as it ever has been. Indeed its popularity has so increased that collectors search the countryside for fine old specimens, and nurserymen raise it from cuttings by the thousand.

Box is native to southern Europe, parts of Asia and Japan. It has been in cultivation since the times of the Roman Empire. In ancient gardens it was cut into geometric or fantastic shapes and occupied conspicuous positions in the formal gardens. Through the Middle Ages it was cultivated in the Cloister garths, in the castle bowers, and in the town yards, and it has played an important part in English garden art. Because of its very general use in England during the seventeenth and eighteenth centuries, it was brought to America by the colonists who established gardens here similar to those which they had known and loved in the old country.

The climate of Virginia, Maryland and the Carolinas is particularly favorable for the growing of Box, and in southeastern Pennsylvania, Delaware, New Jersey, Long Island, while its growth is slower, it is hardy. In these regions many specimens growing since long before the Revolution have attained great size.

Box is, beyond question, one of the most valuable plants for landscape purposes and it possesses many excellent qualities. Not only is it evergreen, but it retains its deep green color and freshness throughout the year. When well established, it will thrive for many years, and will endure considerable neglect. It withstands severe pruning and clipping better than almost any other cultivated plant, and some varieties can be kept at any desired height. Box hedges 10 inches high and 75 years old are a matter of record. Broken off one inch above the ground, box will send up new shoots and recover with surprising vigor.

It is not a voracious feeder and for this reason it is particularly well suited for edging garden beds, as it will not rob the flowers of food and moisture or send its roots out to encroach upon the roots of neighboring plants. The wood is strong, heavy and very enduring, has close, almost indistinguishable grain of a rich yellow hue. It is highly prized for fine cabinet work and is used for the most delicate sculpture tools, and for architects' scales.

The foliage of Box has a delightful odor. As an individual specimen plant it possesses great dignity and beauty, as well as individual character, the billowy foliage masses in some cases taking irregular forms, always expressive of great vitality. Indeed it is this tremendous vitality, this ability to overcome adversity, this marvellous longevity, linking past to present, which is one source of its enduring charm.

SPECIES AND VARIETIES

Buxus japonica, the Japanese Box, has broader leaves than the European form which are borne rather less thickly and on somewhat pendulous twigs. The main stems are stiff and upright. The growth is fairly rapid but the plant lacks the beauty of the other types. It is more hardy than Buxus sempervirens, and is adaptable to Zone V.

Soil Requirements: Deep rich loam with plenty of humus and a porous sub-soil is ideal for Box. A constant supply of moisture is indispensable to good growth. For the transplanting of large specimens a clay loam is preferable to a sandy soil.

Exposure: Partial shade is better than full sunlight in the North, but in the South either sunshine or shade is satisfactory. While these conditions are ideal, Box will grow and thrive in a great variety of soil and in many kinds of exposure.

Propagation: Box is most easily propagated by cuttings, and layering is also occasionally practiced. Cuttings may be taken at almost any time of the year. Unbranched shoots 4 to 8 inches long are usually selected for cuttings. The leaves of the lower half of the shoot are removed and the cutting is inserted into the soil of the propagating frame, a light, sandy loam or pure sand. A coldframe affords ideal conditions for propagating. The cuttings should be shaded until they have rooted, and the propagating bed should never be allowed to dry out. Cuttings may also be made from branched shoots. These larger shoots do not root as readily as the small ones, but when once rooted they make more rapid growth and soon develop into sturdy bushes.

Culture: Box has a fibrous and extremely compact root system. It may, therefore, be transplanted with ease.

For Zones of Hardiness, see map on page 706.

Except for small plants up to 12 or 15 inches high, it should be transplanted with ball and burlap; large specimens 3 feet high being moved with a platform.

Where a Box hedge is to be trimmed, the pruning should be done in August. Box bushes which have been recently transplanted, especially in regions north of Philadelphia, should be given winter protection. A fence of cornstalks, or straw matting as shelter from the wind, and even a roof to keep off the weight of snow are reasonable precautions during the first few winters. The barriers should not be removed until late March. If Box bushes are not protected, but are acclimatized, snow should be carefully brushed off the foliage as soon as it has fallen. Snow damage by breaking and by freezing into ice is the most serious winter hazard for Box.

Buxus sempervirens var. suffruticosa is the True Dwarf Box, most highly prized, most beautiful in form, but slower in growth. The foliage is a deep glossy green, the leaves are small and oval, and in habit of growth it is extremely compact. When left unclipped it is capable of reaching a height of 12 or 15 feet (after many years of growth) and a spread occasionally of 25 feet. In Virginia its rate of growth is 2 or 3 inches a year. Farther north, one inch per year is normal. It may be clipped annually and kept to a constant height.

In beauty of form, in texture and in rich quality of color, no other variety of box compares with suffruticosa. It is the variety which reached such perfection in the colonial gardens of Virginia. There are several strains varying from one another slightly in leaf form, but the differences are not sufficient to warrant further classification. It is hardy in Zone VI, to Lancaster, York and Bethlehem, Pennsylvania, Long Island, Nantucket, and if given thorough winter protection will survive at Boston, but it is not hardy there.

Buxus sempervirens var. arborescens is the Tree Box. The foliage is very deep green and in habit of growth it is loose, open, irregular, but graceful, the branches being somewhat pendulous. The leaves are larger and longer than those of the type, and taper toward the apex. The growth is rapid, and at maturity it will attain a height of 30 feet. It is at its best when used as a specimen, untrimmed, growing free and natural in picturesque outline. In Virginia, pathways between two rows of tree box are entirely enclosed under its canopy.

Buxus microphylla var. koreana is a compact evergreen shrub with small leaves, reaching a height of 2 feet or more. It is reputed to be the hardiest of all the boxwoods, and has come from the Orient. It is hardy in Zone V.

Calycanthus floridus (Strawberry shrub—Common Sweet shrub) is particularly beloved because of its association with old-time gardens and the delightful and pungent fragrance of its flowers. It is rather coarse and open in its habit of growth and is, therefore, better adapted to mass planting than for specimen purposes. It attains a height of about 8 feet. The flowers which come in June are a dull, reddish brown in color and when crushed give off a very spicy fragrance. The branches also exude a strange, almost camphor-like odor.

Zone of Hardiness: V.

Soil Requirements: Rather rich, moist loam.

Exposure: Shade or open sun.

Propagation: Softwood cuttings taken early root easily; must be protected during the first winter. Root cuttings in early winter. Suckers and division. Layers.

Culture: Mulch in winter.

Camellia. Few flowers have enjoyed such an upsurge of popularity as have the camellias within recent years. And it is a popularity which is well deserved, for the blooms of the camellia have a chaste and sculptured beauty which few other flowers possess.

A generation ago one seldom saw camellias except in the gardens of the great plantations of the South, where they have been grown and cherished for more than a century, and in gardens on the Pacific Coast where they were highly prized as choice ornamental shrubs. In these old gardens one frequently comes upon camellia bushes which are 50 or 60 years old, attesting to the longevity of the plant. And although camellias are of slow growth some of these old bushes have, in the course of time, attained a height of thirty feet or more.

Today camellias are not confined to old Southern gardens or to gardens on large estates. Wherever the climate favors their growth one sees them in small town and suburban gardens as well as on large plantations and estates, and they are grown in many public parks.

With the introduction of hardier varieties the camellia belt is gradually being extended northward. Whereas a few decades ago an occasional Southern or West Coast nursery listed perhaps a dozen varieties, there are now numerous large nurseries devoted entirely to the propagation of camellias and more than 1,800 varieties are listed. Some of these new varieties are of breath-taking beauty and are the sensation of many camellia shows held throughout the country. Camellia japonica is the species which has been most widely grown but within recent years two other species, Camellia reticulata and Camellia sasanqua, have been gaining rapidly in popularity.

CAMELLIA

Camellia japonica

History: Camellia japonica is a native of Eastern Asia its natural habitat being hilly, thinly wooded areas. It was introduced into this country by way of Europe about 1820 and soon became one of the most cherished shrubs on the plantations of the South. In the North it has been grown to a limited extent in greenhouses. With the settlement of the West it was found that the climate of the Pacific Coast was ideally suited to Camellias and with the importation of new and very beautiful varieties from Japan early in the century camellias found a place in numerous large gardens in California, Oregon and Washington.

Description: C. japonica is an evergreen shrub with dark, glossy foliage. There are several distinct types of flowers: single; loose semi-doubles; large peoniforms; and imbricated sorts. Some varieties are stiffly formal, others charming and dainty, and some gracefully un-symmetrical in form. The flowers range in color from white to cream, through shades of pink to brilliant scarlets and deep reds.

Uses: C. japonica is most frequently used as a specimen shrub where the beauty of its flower can be seen to best

advantage. It is also used in shrubbery borders and in foundation plantings. With over 1,300 varieties from which to choose, selections may be made to suit specific needs. Habit of growth, hardiness, period of bloom, color and form of flowers should be taken into consideration. In small gardens varieties may be selected which are compact in habit of growth. If succession of bloom is desired, varieties may be chosen which will extend the period of bloom from late fall well into spring with a slight interruption during periods of severe cold. At the Descanso Gardens in California there are only four months without bloom. Flowering begins in early October, reaches its peak between February and April and continues through May. The blooms of C. japonica usually last extremely well when cut and have great decorative value.

Climatic Requirements: C. japonica thrives best under subtropical conditions with moderate temperatures and high humidity. It is grown in the southeastern portion of the United States from Florida to Texas and northward along the coast to Virginia. It does not bloom well in the southern portion of Florida. Some of the hardier varieties may be grown in the northern part of Georgia and Alabama and in Tennessee, and, if planted in sheltered locations, certain varieties of exceptional hardiness may be grown as far north as Pennsylvania, Long Island and Westchester County, New York. C. japonica is also well adapted to the Pacific Coast area from California to Washington.

Exposure: C. japonica prefers a semi-shaded location and there are only a few varieties which will thrive in full sun. Dense shade is not desirable, as it results in a heavy growth of foliage and but sparse bloom. Camellias should not be planted under trees that are heavy surface feeders, as they will be robbed of nourishment and moisture, two of their chief requirements. They thrive well in the shelter of liveoaks and pines and other needled evergreens. When planted adjacent to a building or a wall, a northern or eastern exposure is considered best. This does not hold true in more northerly areas where plantings on the north and west sides usually show less injury from severe cold than those with southern or eastern exposures. This is due to the fact that they are protected from the morning sun which, if the temperature has fallen below freezing during the night, hastens thawing and seriously injures the foliage, particularly if it is wet. When plants are protected from the sun they will thaw gradually and little damage will result. C. japonica should never be planted where it will be exposed to strong winds.

Soil Requirements: C. japonica requires a light, acid soil which is abundantly supplied with organic matter. Soils with a pH ranging from 4.5 to 6.5 are suitable for C. japonica, a pH of 5.5 being considered the optimum.

Good drainage is absolutely essential, as C. japonica will not thrive in water-logged soil. Camellias will endure many adverse conditions provided this requirement is adequately met. If the only available location is where the water table is high, camellias should be planted in raised beds. The following soil mixtures are recommended:

1. 2 parts acid loam
    1 part leafmold (oak)
    1 part peat moss
    1 part coarse sand

2. 1 part rotted manure
    1 part peat moss
    1 part sandy loam

3. 2 parts peat moss
    2 parts sandy loam
    1 part sharp sand
    1 part leafmold (oak)

Culture: Planting: In the camellia belt of the South camellias are usually planted in the autumn. In more northern latitudes spring is sometimes preferred, although most growers still follow the practice of fall planting.

Fertilization: After the blooming period is over two or three feedings are recommended, to be given about six weeks apart. This will stimulate new growth and a good production of flower buds for the following year. An acid type of fertilizer should be used. The following mixtures are recommended:

1. 5 parts cottonseed meal
    3 parts superphosphate
    2 parts sulphate of potash

2. 35 pounds superphosphate
    28 pounds cottonseed meal
    17 pounds sulphate of potash (high-grade)
    10 pounds ammonium sulphate
    10 pounds aluminum sulphate (used as an acidifier)

No applications of a nitrogen fertilizer should be given after late spring or early summer. This period of less active growth is important, as it allows the new spring shoots to harden and reduces the danger of winter injury. An application of one part sulphate of potash to five parts superphosphate in August will be of benefit in hardening new growth and improving the quality of the flowers.

When applied in the dry form the fertilizer may be spread as a top dressing on top of the mulch and watered in. The application should reach the outer spread of the branches.

Over-fertilization of camellias should be guarded against, as it can be disastrous in its effects.

Watering: The soil should be kept moist at all times but should never be allowed to become soggy. Thorough waterings should be given as needed, rather than frequent, light waterings which encourage surface root growth and lessen the vigor of the plant. An adequate supply of moisture is of particular importance during the period when the plants are making new growth and when they are in flower.

Frequent syringing of the foliage increases the humidity in the atmosphere, keeps the leaves clean and glossy in appearance and improves the general condition of the plant. A fog nozzle on a garden hose is excellent for this purpose. Syringing should be done when the sun is not on the foliage.

Mulching: Camellias should be mulched in order to conserve the moisture in the soil, and to afford protection for the roots which tend to be near the surface. The following materials are recommended; peat moss, partially rotted oak leafmold, pine needles, sawdust, and acid compost.

Disbudding: On one- or two-year old plants all but one or two buds should be removed in order to conserve the vigor of the plant.

On older plants disbudding should be practiced if blooms of maximum size are desired. One bud should be left to every two to four inches of stem.

Pruning: Camellias require little or no pruning, merely the removal of dead wood and the cutting back of an occasional shoot to improve the shapeliness of the bush. Where particularly compact dense growth is desired, it may be encouraged by judicious pruning.

Protection from Cold: It is important to know how to protect camellias from unexpected cold spells. This is particularly important if they are grown along the northern limit of the camellia belt.

A sudden drop in temperature is far more damaging than a gradual decline in temperature, and cold weather during or following a long, dry spell is particularly harmful. Under such conditions the danger of injury can be lessened by watering the soil and spraying the foliage with a mist-like spray of water. Plants that are in active growth have less resistance to cold than those that have been gradually hardened to it. An early freeze after a long spell of warm weather can be particularly disastrous. If a freeze occurs the following precautions should be taken. As soon as the temperature rises above freezing the foliage should be watered with a fine mist-like spray, and should be protected from direct sun. This will greatly reduce the danger of severe injury.

Control of Insect Pests and Diseases (see page 623).

Camellia reticulata

History: Camellia reticulata was discovered in the Yunnan Province of China by French plant explorers during the 17th century. The name "reticulata", given it by these early French botanists, is derived from the netted or reticulate veinings of the leaves.

About 1820 one variety of C. reticulata was brought to England from China and was named Captain Rawes in honor of the captain of the old sailing ship. For more than a century this was thought to be the only variety of C. reticulata. However, in 1947 the discovery was made that some magnificent specimens of C. reticulata

were growing behind the 30-foot walls of an old temple garden in the city of Kunming in Yunnan Province in China. One variety, Lion Head, had attained a height of 50 feet, with a trunk 20 inches in diameter, and when in flower was such a spectacular sight that its blooming was a festive occasion.

Through the efforts of Dr. Walter E. Lammerts and Ralph S. Peer, arrangements were made to import some of these newly discovered C. reticulatas, and 18 varieties were brought into California. These have been propagated by means of cleft grafts and are now listed in some catalogs.

Description: The wild species of C. reticulata bears single flowers of a medium pink color which are three to four inches in diameter. The foliage is a dull green, lacking entirely the glossy sheen of the other species.

The flowers of the modern varieties, the result of hybridization, are of spectacular beauty, being semi-double in form, five to eight inches in diameter, with superb texture, grace and richness of color. C. reticulata is considered by many to be the "Queen" of the camellias.

The reticulatas bring the camellia season to a close, as they are the last to bloom, coming into flower in March and continuing until May. The flowers open quite slowly, some varieties requiring a week or ten days, but they remain in bloom over a long period.

Exposure: C. reticulata tolerates more sun than does C. japonica and will thrive well in a half-sunny exposure.

Fertilization: The reticulatas do not thrive on heavy feeding and will sometimes show signs of leaf burn even under conditions of moderate feeding.

For planting and further cultural requirements see C. japonica.

Camellia sasanqua

History: The native habitat of C. sasanqua is the mountainous region of the Southern Japanese islands. In Japan C. sasanqua has been greatly prized for centuries and over the years more than 150 varieties have been developed by the skilled gardeners of Japan. C. sasanqua was introduced into Europe about the middle of the 19th century but was not grown in this country until half a century later. During the first decade of this century a number of named varieties and a small quantity of seed of C. sasanqua were imported from Japan and laid the foundation for future development in this country. It is only within comparatively recent years, however, that C. sasanqua has begun to attract wide attention. Many new varieties have been introduced and it is becoming increasingly popular.

Description: Like the other camellias, C. sasanqua is an evergreen shrub. The flowers are smaller and more fragile in appearance than are the blooms of C. japonica and C. reticulata, but they are borne in profusion, are obtainable in a wide range of beautiful colors, and are delicately fragrant. The typical form of the flower is single with wide-open petals and prominent stamens. There are also semi-double and a few fully double varieties. The flowers of C. sasanqua do not have the substance or the long-lasting qualities when cut which the blooms of C. japonica possess, but for landscape effects their value is unequalled. In color the flowers of C. sasanqua range from white through various shades of pink to deep red, with some blendings of color. Varieties of C. sasanqua vary considerably in habit of growth, some varieties being much more compact than others. The sasanquas are predominately autumn flowering, coming into bloom in September and continuing into December.

Uses: The C. sasanquas have great decorative value in the landscape scheme. They may be used as specimen plants, in shrubbery borders and in foundation plantings. They make exceedingly handsome hedges and are often used in this way in California. A C. sasanqua hedge, with its dark, glossy foliage, is attractive at any season of the year, but in the autumn when it is in flower, it is a thing of exciting beauty. C. sasanquas can also be trained very readily to an espalier form and can be used as a decorative feature against a wall or garden fence.

Climatic Requirements: C. sasanqua can be grown successfully throughout the same range as C. japonica. It can, however, withstand greater extremes of heat and cold and it may therefore be grown farther south as well as farther north. In southern Florida it is far more satisfactory than C. japonica, and it has played an important part in extending the camellia belt northward. Within recent years the hardier varieties of C. sasanqua have been found more and more frequently in gardens in southeastern Pennsylvania, in New Jersey, and on Long Island, on the highlands of the Hudson and in Westchester County, New York. For northern areas the earlier blooming varieties should be selected.

Exposure: The C. sasanquas require more sun than the japonicas for their best development and they will thrive in full sun as well as in light shade. When grown in the north they should, however, be planted in a location where they will be protected from full winter sun, and from winter winds. C. sasanqua can also be grown successfully along the Gulf Coast and the seacoast, as they possess considerable tolerance to salt spray and can be planted within a few feet of open water, provided other conditions are favorable.

Soil Requirements: C. sasanqua will tolerate a rather poor soil better than any of the other species. It will often thrive reasonably well on soils where C. japonica would not make satisfactory growth. It does, however, respond to good soil preparation and its general soil requirements are similar to those of C. japonica.

Culture: While the C. sasanquas are less exacting in their cultural requirements than are the other species, their general requirements for fertilization, watering, mulching, and protection from cold are very similar to those of C. japonica (see above).

Planting: In the north spring planting is recommended for C. sasanqua.

Pruning: If C. sasanquas are to be used as a hedge and compactness is desired, some pruning back of the shoots may be necessary. When sasanquas are trained to an espalier form it will require only a minimum of pruning to keep them within desired limits. On slow-growing varieties all that is usually necessary is a mere tip pinch during the blooming season.

Carpenteria californica (Californian Mock-orange) is a very beautiful evergreen shrub similar in habit of growth to the Mock-orange (Philadelphus), to which it is related, and it varies in height from 6 to 10 feet. It flowers from early June on through the summer. The blossoms are white with yellow stamens and are produced in loose terminal clusters of from three to seven flowers. They are delightfully fragrant and resemble an anemone in appearance, the individual flowers being almost 3 inches across. This lovely shrub is not very well known and it should be more extensively planted wherever climatic conditions permit.

Zone of Hardiness: VIII. Needs protection in vicinity of Philadelphia.

Soil Requirements: Well drained.

Exposure: Protected from sun and high winds.

Propagation: Seeds sown in spring. Greenwood cuttings in summer under glass. Suckers.

Caryopteris incana (*Mastacanthus*) (Common Bluebeard) is an interesting plant of shrubby nature and gives variety and character to a foundation planting. In the vicinity of Philadelphia it seldom attains a height of more than 3 feet, but in warmer climates it grows considerably taller. The gray-green foliage is a bit coarse in texture and the chief beauty of the plant is its bloom, the violet-blue flowers being produced in abundance in late August and early September when few other shrubs are in bloom. Var. candida has white flowers and recently a pink form has been offered.

Zone of Hardiness: VII. During northern winters, the tops are usually killed back, but the new growth flowers the same summer.

Soil Requirements: Well drained.

Exposure: Open, sunny.

Propagation: Cuttings taken in the spring from stock plants grown indoors during the winter; each of these young plants will bloom the same year. Seed gathered in the fall may be sown in the spring, keeping seedlings in pots. Division.

Culture: Protecting the plants with a light mulch during the winter is advisable. The shrubs should be pruned to the ground each spring and new shoots will bear flowers abundantly.

Chænomeles japonica is a close cousin of the lovely Japanese Quince but is less widely known. It is a low-growing shrub, seldom over 3 feet, and it is of very picturesque outline. The flowers which are borne in great profusion during the month of May are an orange-scarlet in color, a most striking shade. It is a shrub of great beauty and individuality and gives a note of brilliant color when used in a foundation planting.

Zone of Hardiness: IV.

Soil Requirements: Any good soil.

Exposure: Sun.

Propagation: Seed, root cuttings and graftings.

Fruit: The fruit, resembling quinces, is hard and green and not edible raw, but is occasionally used in preserving.

Chænomeles lagenaria (Japanese Quince). Blooming in late April, the myriad, brilliant blossoms of the Japanese Quince are very striking. In color they are of various shades, ranging from white to orange-scarlet and are borne close to the stem before the leaves unfold. The shrub is of irregular and rather picturesque growth, varying in height from 4 to 6 feet. As a specimen plant it is a thing of unique and brilliant beauty. It also lends itself well to mass planting and makes a most attractive flowering hedge. Branches may be cut in late winter and readily brought into bloom indoors.

Zone of Hardiness:
Soil Requirements:
Exposure: } See *C. japonica.*
Propagation:
Fruit:

Chionanthus virginicus (Fringe Tree) is one of the finest of our native shrubs. It resembles a small tree in its habit of growth and is particularly well suited for specimen purposes or for planting along a fringe of woodland. It usually attains a height of from 10 to 12 feet but occasionally grows considerably taller if conditions are very favorable. In late spring it is a glorious mass of bloom, the cream-white flowers being borne in large, drooping panicles. The fruits are small, blue in color, and are produced in clusters. There are few shrubs more beautiful or more showy than the Fringe tree when it is in flower, and in habit of growth it is also decorative and graceful. A literal interpretation of this name "Chionanthus", coming from the Greek word "chion" meaning snow and "anthos" flower, would give this plant the name "snowflower." Endures smoky and bad atmosphere well.

Zone of Hardiness: V. Native from Pennsylvania to Texas. Farther north, they need protected situations.

Soil Requirements: Sandy, fertile loam. Likes sub-acid, 5.0–6.0.

Exposure: Open, sunny location. Does reasonably well in partial shade.

Propagation: Seeds sown in the fall or stratified, take one year to germinate. Grafting on ash (Fraxinus Ornus) is a quicker process.

Culture: This shrub should never suffer from lack of moisture.

Clethra alnifolia (Sweet Pepperbush) is valued for its fragrant white flowers in midsummer when few other shrubs are in bloom. A shrub of slender, erect habit, it reaches a height of 4 to 5 feet. It should be kept well mulched with leaves or peat moss as it suffers under dry conditions.

Variety *Rosea* bears flowers of a charming shade of pink, and is a choice thing.

Zone of Hardiness: Northern limit Zone IV.

Soil Requirements: Thrives best in moist, acid soil.

Exposure: Prefers partial shade, but also thrives in full sun.

Cotoneaster horizontalis (Rock Cotoneaster) is one of the finest of this large and aristocratic family. The branches are horizontal in habit of growth, being almost prostrate, and it seldom reaches a height of much more than 2 feet. The foliage is small, dark green and very glossy. In the North, the leaves turn a brilliant red in the autumn and drop, while in the South they are practically evergreen. The flowers, which are white with a pinkish tinge, are small and are not in the least showy but are followed by myriad bright red fruits which are very decorative.

Zone of Hardiness: V. Evergreen in the South.

Soil Requirements: Likes a well-drained soil.

Exposure: Sunny.

Propagation: By seed, stratified at 40 degrees F. for five to six months before sowing. Softwood cuttings taken in August carried through winter in warmth. Layering in the fall.

C. divaricata: spreading growth to a height of 6 feet; quantities of small, red fruits in the autumn.
C. Francheti: reaches a height of 6 feet; orange fruits.
C. microphylla: evergreen to semi-evergreen, low growing, reaching a height of 3 feet, scarlet fruits.
C. salicifolia: open habit of growth with arching stems; evergreen foliage, height 10 to 15 feet; red fruits.

Deutzia gracilis (Slender Deutzia) is a dainty and lovely thing and as it seldom grows more than 3 feet tall it is particularly desirable for foundation planting. It is of dense, upright growth with gracefully arching branches which, in late May, are festooned with flowers. The pendulous, bell-shaped blossoms are borne in clusters. In the type they are white, but there are numerous varieties with rose, pink, and carmine tints.

Zone of Hardiness: V. Needs protected location farther north.

Soil Requirements: Well drained with plenty of humus.

Exposure: Partial shade as well as in full sun.

Propagation: Division. Softwood cuttings in summer (very easy). Hardwood cuttings just before freezing.

Culture: In general, prune as little as possible in order to maintain the grace of the sweeping branches. The wood of the Deutzia is not long-lived; therefore, it must be renewed. This is done by cutting out the old shoots from the base of the plant and allowing new branches to take their places. Shearing should not be practiced on this shrub as it promotes too bushy and top-heavy an appearance. If the new tender growth has been killed by cold in the spring in northern climes, it should be pruned back early in order to allow new growth to take its place.

Deutzia Lemoinei (Lemoine Deutzia) is one of the beautiful hybrid Deutzias and it is particularly desirable as a specimen shrub because of its graceful habit and its profusion of bloom. It seldom attains a height of more than 3 or 4 feet. It blooms about the middle of May and the masses of white flowers which are borne in thickly clustered panicles are very showy and attractive.

Zone of Hardiness, Soil, etc. See *Deutzia gracilis.*

Elæagnus angustifolia (Russian Olive) is a fast-growing, hardy shrub which will endure extremely difficult conditions. It is often used as a windbreak in the Great Plains section and in the West. The foliage is a soft, gray-green, the flowers which are not showy are a yellowish-orange, the fruits red. It attains a height of about 20 feet.

Zone of Hardiness: II.

Soil Requirements: Tolerant of almost any soil.

Exposure: Will withstand sun, wind and drought.

Elæagnus longipes (Cherry Elæagnus) is noted particularly for the silvery sheen of its leaves and for its brilliant fruit. It is a shrub of upright, spreading growth often reaching a height of from 9 to 10 feet. The small,

greenish white flowers, which are very fragrant, are borne in the axils of the leaves and are not showy. The fruits, which ripen through the summer, are orange-red and somewhat cherry-like in appearance. They are edible but very tart, and are sometimes used for making jelly.   *Zone of Hardiness:* V.

Soil Requirements: Well drained. Sandy or clayey. A good drought-resistant shrub.

Exposure: Sunny.

Propagation: Seed, cuttings of mature or half-ripened wood, and by grafting.

Enkianthus subsessilis (Nikko Enkianthus) is a very striking shrub because of its beautiful glossy foliage which is bronze in color through the early part of the season, turning a brilliant red in the autumn. In habit of growth it is compact and upright, reaching a height of about 9 feet. The dropping clusters of white, bell-shaped flowers are borne at the ends of the branches in May and June.

Zone of Hardiness: V.

Soil Requirements: Acid, moist, sandy soil.

Exposure: Sunny.

Propagation: Seed, cuttings or layers.

Euonymus alatus (Winged Euonymus). For either individual or group planting the Winged Euonymus is a lovely thing. It is of regular, rather horizontal growth, 6 to 8 feet in height. The small, delicate flowers are borne in late spring and are followed by purple fruits. The curious corky bark on the branches gives it a winged effect, hence the common name. The leaves are small and finely toothed and in the autumn they turn a deep rose in color, a most beautiful and unusual shade.

Zone of Hardiness: IV.

Soil Requirements: Not particular.

Exposure: Sunny.

Propagation: Hardwood cuttings.

Euonymus japonicus (Evergreen Burning-bush) is a very handsome evergreen shrub. Unfortunately it is not hardy north of the latitude of Philadelphia except in very protected places and commonly fails to set fruit except in warm latitudes. It is of upright growth, reaching a height of 8 to 10 feet and is well adapted for specimen purposes or for hedges. The broad, oval leaves are thick and glossy and it is a shrub of unique character and great dignity.

Zone of Hardiness: VII or VIII.

Soil Requirements, etc. See *E. alatus.*

Forsythia intermedia spectabilis (Showy Border Forsythia) is one of the best of this large group. It reaches a height of from 8 to 10 feet and in early April, before the leaves unfold, it is a mass of glorious, golden bloom. The flowers are larger in size and more perfect in form than in some of the other types and it also has the advantage of coming into bloom just late enough to escape any danger from severe frosts.

Zone of Hardiness: V.

Soil Requirements: Any soil.

Exposure: Full sun.

Propagation: Hardwood or softwood cuttings. Layering.

Culture: Forsythias require pruning immediately after blooming, cutting several of the oldest stalks a few inches above ground level in order to allow new growth to take its place. This method allows the shrub to bear its blossoms on gracefully arching branches making a compact appearance of bloom, rather than far out on old heavy branches.

Forsythia ovata, a Korean species, has ascending branches which arch gracefully. The flowers are pale primrose-yellow, borne singly, and are produced ten days to two weeks before any other. Its advantages are in the time of bloom and hardiness.

Zone of Hardiness: V. It is said to be much hardier than the others, the buds withstanding a temperature of zero.

Soil Requirements, etc. See *F. intermedia.*

Forsythia suspensa (Drooping or Weeping Forsythia) grows to 10 feet or more with slender branches often bending to the ground and rooting at the tips. In bloom it forms a golden yellow mound. Var. *Sieboldii* has more slender branches and can be used effectively to clothe a wall or arbor. It is also very effective when trailing over a rock or trained on a wall.

Zone of Hardiness: V.

Soil Requirements, etc. See *F. intermedia.*

Gardenia jasminoides: This evergreen shrub with handsome, glossy foliage and beautiful waxy white flowers is a native of China. It may be used as a specimen or in mass plantings and thrives well when grown in a tub or large pot to grace a patio. Under very favorable conditions it will attain a height of 5 to 6 feet. It can be grown out of doors only in sub-tropical climates, requires abundant moisture and liberal feeding from March to September in order to insure good bloom.

Zone of Hardiness: IX and X.

Soil Requirements: Requires an acid, fibrous soil with a pH below 6.0. Gardenias are sensitive to a lack of iron in the soil (see page 166).

Exposure: Gardenias have very high light requirements and thrive best in full sun.

Propagation: Terminal cuttings from healthy plants root readily in sand or in sand and peat. A closed propagating case should be used where high humidity and a temperature of 75° can be maintained.

Culture: Gardenias thrive best in climates where there are hot days and warm nights, the humidity is high and the soil very moist.

Ilex crenata, and its several varieties, are among our most useful shrubs. The leaves are small, dark green in color, and dense; the flowers inconspicuous. It combines well with other evergreens in the shrub border, and may be used in foundation planting and for hedges. Attains a height of 10 to 20 feet.

Zone of Hardiness: VI.

Soil Requirements: Rich loam, acid or nearly neutral.

Exposure: Sun or partial shade.

Culture: Should be watered during periods of drought. Prune only to thicken growth and to remove dead wood.

Varieties:

I. c. convexa: low growing to 4 to 6 feet; broader, convex leaf.
I. c. latifolia: tall growing to 12 to 20 feet, wider, larger leaf.
I. c. microphylla: upright growth to 10 feet, smaller leaf.

Euonymus Corlissi (Emerald Leader) and several other hybrid, evergreen Euonymus, such as Emerald Pride and Emerald Cushion, are appreciated as being superior to the Euonymus radicans group. These excellent introductions have dense, bushy forms and glossy, evergreen foliage. They are very hardy, resistant to disease, withstand dry seasons, thrive in most soils, and in sunshine or partial shade. *Euonymus Corlissi* produces clusters of red fruits in quantities in September.

Zone of Hardiness: V.

Soil Requirements, etc. See *Euonymus alatus.*

Ilex verticillata (Winterberry). One of the best of the native shrubs in the East. It is a deciduous member of the holly family, producing quantities of red berries which remain throughout the winter. A few twigs tucked into a Christmas wreath will brighten it with its sparkle. As a cultivated shrub it is dense and handsome, reaching a height of 12 feet.

Zone of Hardiness: IV.

Soil Requirements: Moist, rich, woodsy, somewhat acid or neutral.

Exposure: Sun or light shade.

Jasminum nudiflorum (Winter Jasmine) is a shrub of trailing, almost vine-like habit. The long, slender stems are green throughout the winter months and in February or very early March, almost before the snows have gone, the small clear yellow flowers begin to open. They are borne very close to the stem and appear well before the leaves. It is a shrub which may be readily trained upon a trellis as a vine and is often very happily used in this way. Its habit of early flowering endears it to the heart of every home-owner, for in its golden cup of bloom it seems to hold the very promise of spring.

Zone of Hardiness: VI. As far north as New York, with protection.

Soil Requirements: Good loam.

Exposure: Sunny position.

Propagation: Cuttings and layers.

Juniperus chinensis Pfitzeriana (Pfitzer Juniper) is one of the larger of the spreading forms, reaching a height of 5 to 10 feet. It is very graceful in its habit of growth, rather open and vase-shaped. The dense foliage is a soft, cool green and retains its fresh coloring throughout the year. It is adaptable to any position where low bulk is required and it is considered one of the best of the spreading Junipers.

Zone of Hardiness: IV. Withstands extremely hard winter conditions.

Soil Requirements: Thrives in poor soil. Preferably sandy and dry.

Exposure: Nearly any exposure. Prefers sun.

Propagation: By seed which germinates second or third year, therefore must be kept moist in sand for over a year.

Culture: Cultivation improves the condition of the plant. If there is evidence of bruise on lower branches which have died, investigate for gnawing mice.

Juniperus horizontalis plumosa (Juniperus depressa plumosa) (Andorra Juniper).

Of all the spreading junipers this is the most satisfactory and the most generally used. Hardy, compact but graceful, long-lived, low, it has a feathery texture and a pleasing appearance. It requires almost no care. Year after year it is dependable. It may be used for covering banks, for foundation planting, and as foreground to larger evergreens. Height 1½ feet.

Zone of Hardiness: II—Northern limit.

Soil Requirements: Light, sandy soil.

Exposure: Full sun.

Juniperus Sabina (Savin Juniper) is a graceful, low evergreen with branchlets which ascend at a high angle and flare out at the top, producing a goblet shape. It grows 3 to 4 feet high and is useful on soil which is too light and sandy for some of our more choice things. Yet it is excellent in itself without a suggestion of the coarseness noticeable in some of the other Junipers. The foliage is a soft, light gray-green in color.

Zone of Hardiness: IV.

Soil Requirements: Prefers sandy and dry soil.

Exposure: Sun.

Propagation: Seed.

Culture: The Savin Juniper sometimes shows evidence of a dead branch which may give the entire plant an appearance of weakness. If the dead branch is due to injury of bruise or mice, it may be cut off and the shrub will regain its healthy condition.

Kalmia latifolia (Mountain laurel) is one of the most beautiful of our native evergreens. It is a very valuable shrub for mass planting and is also well adapted for foundation planting under certain conditions, and for underplanting in woodland areas. It has a decided preference for an acid and rather sandy soil and under favorable conditions the plants often attain a height of 8 feet. The handscme foliage is a dark, glossy green and the lovely flower clusters which open in late May and June vary in color from rose to pure white. There are few shrubs more beautiful than our native Mountain laurel.

Zone of Hardiness: IV, sometimes III.

Soil Requirements: Sandy, acid soil.

Exposure: Dense or semi-shade. Or in sun with a mulch.

Propagation: Seed, cuttings, and layers are all slow.

Culture: Transplanting should preferably be done with ball and burlap. If this is not possible, the plants should be cut down to the ground, allowing them to make more bushy growth.

Kerria japonica (Kerria) is a dainty and very useful shrub. The slender, wand-like branches retain their soft, green color throughout the year and are particularly lovely during the winter months after the leaves have fallen. The flowers are a deep golden yellow and there are both single and double forms. It is particularly good for foundation planting because it is not too dense and heavy in texture and rarely grows more than 4 or 5 feet high.

Zone of Hardiness: V. Tops will be killed back if exposed to much below zero temperatures.

Soil Requirements: Well drained.

Exposure: Sheltered, partial shade, to preserve color from bleaching.

Propagation: Softwood cuttings in summer, protected in coldframes during winter. Hardwood cuttings of good-sized wood.

Culture: Pruning is done for two reasons. One, to prolong the length of bloom by cutting the branches back to various lengths and thus delaying the bloom on some. Two, to cut off any wood that was winter-killed. This last should be done very early in the spring.

Kolkwitzia amabilis (Beauty bush) is of recent introduction and is a very showy and decorative shrub. Of upright habit, with arching branches, it reaches a height of about 6 feet. The flower buds are deep pink in color while the open blooms which are borne in such profusion in May and June are somewhat paler with delicate orange veins in the tubular throat. The flowers are borne in pairs, from twenty-five to fifty in a single cluster.

Zone of Hardiness: V.

Soil Requirements: Soil of poor fertility and good drainage.

Exposure: Full sun and open position for free air circulation. Without free circulation, Beauty bush is apt to winter-kill.

Propagation: Half-ripened wood cuttings in August.

Leucothoë Catesbæi (Drooping Leucothoë) is a low, evergreen shrub with gracefully arching branches. The foliage is a dark, deep green and in winter turns a rich bronze with purple tints. It seldom grows more than 3 feet tall and is often broader than it is high. The flowers, which are borne in late April and May, resemble those of the Lily-of-the-Valley, and are very lovely. The little clusters of drooping, bell-shaped waxy flowers appear at the tips of the branches and are quite fragrant. Leucothoë is a very choice thing and is particularly useful as a filler between large evergreen shrubs or for foundation planting.

Zone of Hardiness: V.

Soil Requirements: Rich loam soil of considerable acidity. Sub-acid, pH 5.0–6.0.

Exposure: Partial shade.

Propagation: Division. Seed sown in sphagnum moss and sand under glass.

Culture: Set plants in spring 2 to 4 feet apart, moving with a ball.

Ligustrum lucidum (Glossy Privet) is a native of the Orient. It is a handsome evergreen with lustrous leaves. Like most of the privets, it grows rapidly and attains a height of over thirty feet. Useful as an untrimmed hedge and windbreak in the South, and it is also often used as a specimen shrub.

Height 30 feet. Zone VII—Northern limit.

Lilac (See Syringa).

Lonicera Morrowi (Morrow Honeysuckle) is one of the loveliest of our bush honeysuckles. It is of wide, spreading growth with crooked, angular branches, and it reaches an ultimate height of about 8 feet. The foliage is a soft gray-green and the myriad cream-white flowers which appear in May are followed by brilliant red berries. As the fruits are greatly relished by the birds, it is a particularly desirable shrub for planting in a bird sanctuary.

Zone of Hardiness: V.

Soil Requirements: Not particular providing soil is good. In poor soil, flowers are deficient in size. Circum-neutral, pH 6.0–8.0.

Exposure: Open, sunny.

Propagation: Hardwood cuttings. Layers. Stratified seed (pulp removed as soon as ripe).

Culture: New plantings should be made preferably in late fall or very early spring. If medium or late spring deliveries are made and leaf growth has started, the transplanting is somewhat of a shock. In this case, hard pruning should be done to avoid a scraggly appearance the first year. After the shrub is established, pruning should consist of only removing dead branches and sometimes the oldest, thick branches in the spring. This will invigorate the bush and start new growth.

Lonicera tatarica (Tatarian Honeysuckle) is of much more graceful form than L. morrowi. It reaches a height of from 8 to 10 feet and is excellent for mass effect. The flowers which are borne in great profusion are rose, pink or white in color and are followed by bright red fruits which are very decorative and last well into the winter months.

Zone of Hardiness:
Soil Requirements:
Exposure: } See *L. Morrowi.*
Propagation:
Culture:

Mahonia Aquifolium (Oregon Hollygrape) is an evergreen shrub, of rather dwarf habit, seldom attaining a height of more than 3 or 4 feet. The handsome foliage is glossy, rather leathery in texture and prickly. It closely resembles the foliage of our Christmas Holly although it is much more shining. The young growth has a very characteristic bronze tint and the leaves turn a reddish bronze during the winter months. The flowers are yellow and are borne in dense clusters at the ends of the branches in late April and May. The small blue-black fruits ripen in September.

Zone of Hardiness: V.

Soil Requirements: Any soil (Circumneutral pH 6.0–8.0), even dry and sandy. Likes moisture. Manure or bone meal will keep plants from becoming straggly.

Exposure: In dense or partial shade. Foliage burns in sun.

Propagation: Seed (pulp removed) sown as soon as ripe, takes two years to germinate. Suckers. Layers. Softwood cuttings under glass.

Culture: Better if moved with ball of earth, but not absolutely necessary.

Myrica Gale (Sweet Gale) is a very useful thing for foundation planting and its merits are, perhaps, not fully appreciated. It is of very upright form and grows only 3 to 4 feet tall. The foliage is a medium green, smooth, glossy and very attractive in appearance, having a delicious and pungent fragrance. The flowers are inconspicuous and the small gray-green fruits are clustered close to the stem.

Zone of Hardiness: I.

Soil Requirements: Prefers a moist, peaty soil. Subacid pH 5.0–6.0.

Exposure: Open, sunny.

Propagation: Suckers freely.

Culture: Rather difficult to establish; therefore, the plants should be balled and burlapped.

Philadelphus grandiflorus (Big Scentless Mock-orange) is very valuable for mass planting because of its substance and its height. It is of large, spreading habit with graceful branches and frequently reaches a height of 12 feet. The large white flowers which are borne in May and June lack almost entirely the fragrance which we associate with most of the other members of the Mock-orange family. P. grandiflorus has a tendency to become leggy with age and is, therefore, much better adapted to mass planting than for use as a specimen shrub. Birds like the fruit.

Zone of Hardiness: IV.

Soil Requirements: Not particular, as long as it is not soggy.

Exposure: Can stand shade better than most flowering shrubs.

Propagation: Softwood cuttings inserted in summer. Hardwood cuttings taken as soon as leaves fall and stored in a cold pit during winter and planted in the spring.

Culture: Prune after flowering.

Philadelphus virginalis (Virginal Mock-orange). This lovely variety of Mock orange was produced by the famous French hybridizer, Victor Lemoine, and it is without doubt one of the most beautiful of the group. The white flowers which are large and semi-double in form are borne in profusion and are very fragrant. It blooms during the month of May and occasional flowers are produced later in the season. The ultimate height varies from 6 to 8 feet. Like many of the other hybrids of this family, it has the advantage of flowering while still quite small.

Zone of Hardiness: V.

Soil Requirements:
Exposure:
Propagation: } See *P. grandiflorus.*
Culture:

Photinia villosa (Christmas Berry) is a very desirable thing wherever it can be grown. It is a large, upright shrub reaching a height of 12 to 15 feet. The oval leaves are sharply toothed and are lustrous and glossy in appearance, turning a scarlet or deep red in the autumn. The white flowers which are borne in May in rounded panicles resemble those of the hawthorn, and are followed by bright red berries which last well into the winter.

Zone of Hardiness: V.

Soil Requirements: Light, sandy, loamy soil; requires perfect drainage and likes plenty of leaf mold.

Exposure: Prefers sun.

Propagation: Seeds; cuttings of half-ripened wood under glass; hardwood cuttings; layers.

Pieris japonica (Japanese Andromeda) is one of the most beautiful, as well as one of the most dependable, of evergreen shrubs. It is almost always adorned with gracefully hanging tassels which in winter are the flower buds, for six weeks in April and May waxy, white, bell-shaped blossoms, and for the rest of the season picturesque seed capsules. The foliage is gracefully spreading in clusters of somewhat glossy leaves.
Height: 10 feet.

Zone of Hardiness: V.

Soil Requirements: Neutral or acid.

Exposure: Sun or partial shade.

Culture: Very easily transplanted and requires no particular attention.

Pittosporum. The Pittosporums are widely used in the South and on the Pacific Coast. They are large, evergreen shrubs and may be used as background plants or as accents.

P. phillyræoides is of slow growth, graceful and willowlike in form, reaching a height of about 20 feet. It will withstand long-continued heat.

P. tobira is of spreading form, reaching a height of about 15 feet. The foliage is thick, leathery and dark green. The creamy-white flowers which are borne in clusters are fragrant.

Zone of Hardiness: VII and VIII.

Soil Requirements: Rich garden loam.

Exposure: Sun or partial shade.

Pyracantha coccinea Lalandi (Scarlet Firethorn) is a shrub of striking beauty and should be included in every collection. It is of tree-like growth, somewhat resembling the Hawthorns in character, and it reaches a height of 8 to 10 feet. The evergreen foliage is dark and glossy and the branches are thorny. The white flowers are borne in clusters and are followed by brilliant orange-scarlet fruits which last well into the winter. For its beautiful evergreen foliage, its flowers, and its highly ornamental fruits, this is a most desirable and highly prized shrub. It may be used as an individual specimen and in group plantings, or it may be trained against a building or over a doorway, where it creates a very unique and handsome effect.

Zone of Hardiness: VI.

Soil Requirements: Well drained. Likes lime. Circumneutral, pH 6.0–8.0.

Exposure: Open sun.

Propagation: Seed; cuttings; grafting on Cotoneaster or Cratægus; layers.

Rhododendrons: There are few shrubs which can compare with the dramatic beauty of the rhododendrons when they are in full flower. More than 800 species of rhododendron have been classified and more than a thousand hybrids have been developed in this country and in England, where rhododendrons have long been highly prized. The hybrids offer a wide range of beautiful colors and have great landscape value as specimen plants and for mass effects. Some sections of the country, such as the Pacific Northwest and the central mountainous region of the East, are particularly well suited to their culture but so highly valued are the rhododendrons that gardeners in the South and Midwest, where conditions are less favorable, make every effort to meet their exacting requirements in order to enjoy their spectacular beauty.

Exposure: Some rhododendrons, such as R. maximum, are tolerant of rather dense shade, but the majority prefer light shade. In their native habitat rhododendrons are denizens of the forest. On the home property the most favorable exposure is a location where they will be protected from hot afternoon sun in the summer and where early morning sun will not strike them in the winter. A northeastern exposure meets these requirements well. Such a location may be in the shelter of buildings, or in an area protected by trees.

Where climatic conditions are not naturally favorable to the growth of rhododendrons, such as in the South and the Midwest, a northern exposure is always desirable in order that the plants may have full protection from intense sunshine and searing winds. They will thrive well in areas where they receive good light, but no direct sun. In the Midwest honey locusts afford an excellent overhead canopy for rhododendron plantings and in the South pines and oaks provide favorable conditions, if the lowest branches are about 12 feet above the ground.

Soil Requirements: In growing rhododendrons a congenial soil is one of the most important factors for success. They require a soil rich in humus and high in acidity. For methods of meeting these requirements see pages 168 and 169.

Planting: Rhododendrons should be planted in very early spring before growth starts or in August and September.

When rhododendrons are to be grown in uncongenial climates it is advisable to purchase own-root plants rather than grafted plants, as they will prove to be definitely superior. Plants which are about 15 to 18 inches in height and well branched, with foliage low to the ground, are the most desirable for planting. If special soil preparation is required, an area of at least twice the depth and width of the ball of earth surrounding the plant should be prepared for each plant used as an individual specimen. If a mass planting is to be done, the entire area may be prepared at one time. In areas where the soil is definitely alkaline, or where it is poorly drained and there is danger of its becoming waterlogged, it is advisable to plant rhododendrons in raised beds. This will not only provide for good drainage but will prevent surface water from seeping into the bed.

This is the method followed so successfully in England when rhododendrons are grown in areas where the soil is highly alkaline.

Rhododendrons must always be planted at the same depth as they were growing in the nursery and after planting they should be thoroughly watered and then mulched with peat moss or acid leaf mold.

Culture: The soil beneath rhododendrons should not be cultivated. It should be kept mulched at all times. During dry periods a thorough soaking every 10 days or 2 weeks is recommended with light, daily sprinkling of the foliage in the intervening interval. Rhododendrons suffer seriously from a lack of oxygen when the soil becomes water-logged.

In severe climates winter protection is advisable. A heavy 8 inch mulch of oak leaves may be applied in the fall or early winter, a portion of the mulch being removed in the spring and the rest left to decay. A snow fence or burlap protection should be provided in areas where winter winds are severe.

If the faded blooms are removed and seed pods not allowed to form it will encourage better bloom the following season. This is, of course, possible only in small plantings.

Fertilization: See page 245.

Control of Insect Pests and Diseases: See page 629.

SPECIES AND HYBRIDS OF MERIT

Rhododendron carolinianum (Carolina Rhododendron). This lovely, low-growing rhododendron seldom attains a height of more than 5 or 6 feet. The flowers, which are borne in great profusion in mid-spring, are a pale, rose-pink in color and possess an unusually dainty and decorative quality. Although native to the mountains of North Carolina this is a hardy species, and because of its habit of growth it is one of the best rhododendrons for the small place. It may be used, provided the exposure is favorable, in foundation plantings and in the foreground of large mass plantings, as underplanting in a grove of trees, or as a specimen shrub. The evergreen foliage is attractive throughout the year. Protection from wind and strong sunshine is advisable.

Zone of Hardiness: V.

Rhododendron catawbiense is one of the finest of the native rhododendrons, its natural habitat being the mountains of Virginia, the Carolinas and Georgia.

Many beautiful hybrids have been developed from this species, and among them there are a number of named varieties of exceptional merit, the colors ranging from white through light lavender to crimson, purple and red. The plants usually reach a height of about 6 feet.

Zone IV is the Northern limit of hardiness without some protection.

HARDY HYBRIDS OF MERIT

R. catawbiense
   alba; a beautiful blush white
   grandiflora; lavender pink
   Boule de Neige; an early white, low growing
   Mrs. C. S. Sargent; a rich crimson
   Lee's Dark Purple; a fine, rich shade
   President Lincoln; a good lavender
   Roseum elegans improved; clear orchid, a beautiful
      English hybrid
   Roseum superbum; clear, soft coral-rose

HYBRIDS FOR MILD CLIMATES

Betty Wormald, pink	Marinus Koster, pink
Countess of Athlone, mauve	Loder's White, white
	Naomi, shades of pink
Earl of Athlone, blood red	Pink Pearl, pink
	Unknown Warrior, bright red

Rhododendron maximum (Rosebay Rhododendron). This is one of the best known of our native rhododendrons and is a shrub of great beauty. It is extremely hardy, is of dense growth and although it is generally seen at a height of about 10 feet, under very favorable conditions it will grow considerably taller. The leaves are larger than in any of the other hardy species and the flowers, which vary in color from white to rose-pink, are produced in large clusters during June and July. R. maximum is particularly well adapted for mass plantings, for underplanting in woodlands and along wooded walks and drives, as it thrives best in shaded areas. It is not suitable for foundation planting, or for the small place, as its growth is too bold and vigorous.

Zone of Hardiness: IV.

Rhododendron mucronulatum (Korean Rhododendron). This beautiful rhododendron from Korea is of particular value because of its early flowering. It is one of the first shrubs to come into bloom in the spring. The soft, rosy-lavender blooms, which are borne in great profusion, open before the leaves unfold and when in full flower it is a dramatically lovely thing. In the autumn the handsome foliage is scarlet-tinted. It attains an ultimate height of about 6 feet. Unlike most other members of the rhododendron family, R. mucronulatum will thrive well in rather dry soils which are not strongly acid. It is one of the few rhododendrons which can be grown in slightly alkaline soils.

Rhus Cotinus (Cotinus coggygria) (Common Smoke Tree) is a very decorative and ornamental shrub. It is somewhat tree-like in its habit of growth and reaches a height of about 15 feet. The foliage is a soft, cool green and in July and early August the shrub is a mass of plumy, mist-like bloom, delicately tinted with purple. A few ripening fruits are usually scattered through the panicles of bloom giving a unique and rather striking effect. Rhus Cotinus is a handsome thing either for mass planting or when used as a specimen.

Zone of Hardiness: V.

Soil Requirements: Well drained, not too rich soil.

Sarcococca hookeriana humilis is a small, evergreen shrub which has proven itself of value in planting compositions. Its dark, glossy leaves and compact form make it an excellent ground cover in semi-shaded areas and it may also be used very effectively as a foreground planting in an evergreen shrub bed or border. The flowers are white, inconspicuous. The leaves are 3 to 4 inches long and taper to a slender point. It is a shrub which makes slow growth, eventually, after many years, attaining a height of 3 to 4 feet.

Zone of Hardiness: VI.

Soil Requirements: A good loam.

Exposure: Prefers partial shade. Does well on the north side of a building.

Culture: Mulch with leaves and do not disturb the roots by cultivation.

Spiræa prunifolia (Bridal wreath) is a comparatively small shrub, seldom growing more than 4 or 5 feet tall. It is of upright, spreading growth with graceful branches which are wreathed with bloom in early spring. The small white flowers are quite double in form and are borne in great abundance. It has a tendency to become a bit leggy near the ground and is most happily used in mass or foundation plantings. In spite of this fault it is desirable because of its daintiness, and when it is in flower it seems to have about it the very breath of spring.

Zone of Hardiness: VI, sometimes V.

Soil Requirements: Any good soil, but thrives best in a rich, moist loam.

Exposure: Sunny position.

Propagation: Best by softwood cuttings taken in late spring or early summer.

Culture: Pruning is necessary to keep the shrub from becoming too leggy below. Cut out all dead wood from the center which does not bear bloom, allowing new growth to come up. Pruning for this early spring-blooming type should take place after flowering, inasmuch as bloom is borne on previous year's growth.

Spiræa Thunbergii (Thunberg Spirea) is well adapted for the foreground of mass plantings as it grows hardly more than 3 feet tall. It is of bushy habit with very slender, twig-like branches. The leaves are small, being narrow and quite pointed, and they are a slightly yellowish green, turning orange and red in the autumn. It blooms very early in the season, in March or early April, the myriad small white flowers coming before the leaves unfold.

Zone of Hardiness: V.

Soil Requirements: $\left.\right\}$ See *S. prunifolia.*
Exposure:

Propagation: Seed.

Culture: Prune immediately after blooming.

Spiræa Vanhouttei (Vanhoutte Spirea) is a veritable fountain of bloom when it is in flower and the chief objection to it seems to be that it has been so extensively planted that we have come to look upon it as something rather ordinary. It is a shrub of very graceful form, 5 to 6 feet in height, and the finely cut, delicate foliage is attractive throughout the season. The large white flower clusters are borne in the most lavish profusion during the month of May. It may be used as a specimen shrub, for both foundation and mass planting and as a flowering hedge.

Zone of Hardiness: IV.

Soil Requirements: $\left.\right\}$ See *S. prunifolia.*
Exposure:

Propagation: Hardwood cuttings taken in August, stored in cold pit and inserted in the spring.

Culture: Pruning for this early spring-blooming type should take place after flowering, inasmuch as bloom is borne on previous year's growth.

Symplocos paniculata is valued for its brilliant blue fruit borne in hanging clusters in the early autumn. The small white flowers which appear in late spring are borne in panicles. The height varies from 15 to 25 feet. The foliage, although small, is dense, and the shrub can be used either as a background or as an accent in a formal setting.

Zone of Hardiness: V—Northern limit.

Soil Requirements: A rich garden loam.

Exposure: Full sun or partial shade.

Syringa microphylla superba (Daphne Lilac) is a small, compact shrub. The mahogany-red buds open to soft, pink flowers in large panicles in May in such quantities that the whole shrub becomes a large bouquet. The leaves are very small. It sometimes blooms again in the autumn. Height 5 feet.

Zone of Hardiness: V—Northern limit.

Syringa vulgaris (Lilac), a native of the mountainous regions of Roumania, Jugo-Slavia, Bulgaria and Greece, was highly prized by the Turks, and from Constantinople was introduced into Europe about 1550. It is a vigorous shrub growing to a height of 15 feet or more, bearing large trusses of blossoms. Its ability to naturalize and thrive caused it to run wild throughout western Europe so that by 1780 it was a common hedgerow shrub in parts of Italy and France. When or how it was brought to America is not known but it is likely that it reached the colonies before 1750. It was greatly appreciated by colonists because of its ability to survive severe winters and long periods of neglect. By 1823 its name appeared in American nursery catalogs. It is hardy in Zone III.

By the early years of the nineteenth century horticulturists were experimenting with lilacs, producing new varieties and discovering sports with distinctive characteristics. Hundreds of varieties have been produced, in France, Belgium, Holland, Germany, Canada, and the United States, and many of these are now offered by American nurseries.

Soil Requirements and Exposure: Lilacs are not exacting about soil, but they thrive best in rich garden loam with a pH value of 6·0 to 8·0 (slightly acid or slightly alkaline). Though lilacs endure shade, they should have plenty of sunshine and moisture to bloom well. When well established they withstand wind, deep snows, hard winters and years of neglect.

Culture: Young lilac bushes should be trained to several main stems. The likelihood of loss by the damage of borers is thereby reduced. If borers are detected in one stem, it may be removed and burned and the borers with it, while the other stems carry on. Many lilacs have a habit of suckering. This should be checked by annual pruning. Likewise the central or interior stems tend to become crowded and should be thinned out occasionally. Overgrown lilacs may be cut down to any desired height after blooming; then feed generously with well-rotted cow manure to promote new growth.

Dead flower clusters should be removed to prevent the formation of seed. With abundantly blooming shrubs, the flowering stems may be cut long to include much foliage and may be used in decorating the house. This is one of the best methods of pruning. Failure to bloom regularly may be due to too severe pruning or to no pruning the preceding season, or to the accumulation of suckers.

Lilacs are subject to borers and scales. The borer is most active in June and July, and its presence is evident by piles of sawdust and by dying branches.

Oyster shell scale and San José scale are both damaging to lilacs. Their presence in clusters on the twigs and branches results in the shrivelling of leaves and general lack of vitality. Measures of control for borers and scales are described on page 626.

VARIETIES OF MERIT

Adelaide Dunbar, double, purple
Congo, single, reddish purple
De Miribel, single, violet
Edith Cavell, double, white
Ellen Willmott, double, white
Katherine Havemeyer, double, pinkish
Lucie Baltet, single, pinkish
Ludwig Spæth, single, purple
Maréchal Lannes, double, violet
Mont Blanc, single, white
Oliver De Serres, double, bluish
Paul Thirion, double, reddish purple
President Lincoln, single, bluish
Vestale, single, white
Victor Lemoine, double, lilac

Syringa Species. Besides the Syringa vulgaris, there are a number of species native to different parts of Asia and Europe, but none native to America.

S. persica, or Persian Lilac, which for centuries was supposed to have originated in Persia, really comes from Kansu, and was early brought over the great caravan route to Persia where it has been cultivated ever since. The plant is smaller than S. vulgaris, rarely over 10 feet tall, and the leaves are smaller and narrower. The principal difference is in the arrangement of flowers which are borne on lateral leafy branches, in small clusters of pinkish bloom. Its existence in Europe is recorded as early as 1660 Zone V.

S. villosa (China) is a very hardy shrub 11 feet high, with broad leaves often 7 inches long and pale rose or flesh-colored flowers in late May. To some the odor of the bloom is disagreeable. This bush was discovered in China about the middle of the eighteenth century, but was not introduced to Europe until a century and a half later and was offered for sale first by Lemoine in 1890.

S. chinensis, or Rouen Lilac, is not a Chinese species at all but a natural hybrid between S. persica and S. vulgaris. It appeared in the nurseries of a grower at Rouen about 1777 and was first supposed to be an imported species when it was named. Its blossoms are larger, more compact than those of S. persica, reddish purple, dark red, or white. The leaves are larger and broader than those of S. persica. Height 15 feet. Zone V.

Two tree-like forms are *S. japonica*, and *S. pekinensis*.

S. japonica is a rapidly growing plant 25 or 30 feet tall with a central stem, low forked branches and cherry-like bark. The cream-white blossoms are borne in enormous, loose panicles in June and July. The odor resembles that of privet, to which it is related. Zone V.

S. pekinensis, though 20 feet tall, has a shrubby form. Its bark is yellowish brown and peels off like birch bark. The flowers are yellowish white in large panicles in June. It was introduced from China about 1880 and is hardy in Zone V.

Tamarix africana (African tamarix) is noted particularly for its light, feathery foliage which forms a pleasant contrast when used in combination with other shrubs of more dense texture. It is slender, graceful, upright in habit, reaching a height of slightly more than 12 feet. The flowers which are a clear warm pink are borne in May in long slender racemes and are very decorative and lovely. It is a shrub of very unusual character and great charm.

Zone of Hardiness: V.

Soil Requirements: Light sandy soil, with lime but not too much.

Exposure: Sun. Good for seashore—tolerates salt spray and wind.

Propagation: Seed, and both softwood and hardwood cuttings.

Culture: For garden use, it is generally best to keep them in bushy form by annually cutting back the long growth. Prune after flowering.

Viburnum Carlesii (Fragrant Viburnum) is a recent introduction from Korea and it is noted particularly for the sweet fragrance of its blossoms. It is a shrub of somewhat rounded form, reaching a height of about 5 feet. The flowers which form a close, compact head are a delicate pink in color when they first open in early April, gradually fading to white, and their fragrance is suggestive of the trailing arbutus.

Zone of Hardiness: V.

Soil Requirements: Not particular, but likes a cool, moist, fertile soil.

Exposure: Full sun.

Propagation: Softwood cuttings, graftings and budding.

Culture: Shrubs of large size do not stand transplanting any too well, so when making a purchase it is wise to choose small specimens.

Viburnum carlcephalum is one of the most choice of recent introductions. It is a hybrid from v. carlesii and v. macrocephalum and possesses many of the best characteristics of both parents. It is hardy and vigorous in growth, reaching a height of 6 to 7 feet. It combines the fragrance and early season of bloom of v. carlesii

with the large, rounded white flower clusters of v. macrocephalum. The blooms are borne in great profusion and in the autumn the foliage turns a brilliant color.

Zone of Hardiness: V.

Soil Requirements: Thrives equally well in acid or neutral soils.

Exposure: Full sun or light shade.

Viburnum dilatatum, like the other viburnums, is a vigorous shrub of dense habit. It is covered with panicles of white flowers in May and June, and in September and October it bears masses of showy scarlet berries, which hang on most of the winter. Excellent in the mixed shrub border. Height 10 feet.

Zone of Hardiness: V—Northern limit.

Viburnum rhytidophyllum (Leatherleaf Viburnum) is one of the few members of this large family which is evergreen. It is a shrub of vigorous growth with strong, stout branches and it reaches a height of about 10 feet. The yellow-white flowers open in May and June and are borne in broad heads well above the foliage. The fruits are characteristically red, changing to black. The handsome foliage is a deep, dark green, very shining and somewhat wrinkled in texture.

Zone of Hardiness: VI and sometimes in V. Hardy in North, but kills back in below-zero weather. Needs protected position for foliage.

Soil Requirements: } See *V. Carlesii.*
Exposure:

Propagation: Softwood cuttings taken in July, wintered over in the frames.

Viburnum setigerum (v. theiferum) is a shrub for special consideration. It is not dense but has beautiful slender leaves and a profusion of white flowers in midsummer. In autumn the clusters of brilliant red berries give it distinction and beauty. It is slow to mature but reaches an eventual height of about 12 feet.

Zone of Hardiness: VI.

Soil Requirements: Thrives equally well in acid or neutral soils.

Exposure: Sun or partial shade.

Viburnum tomentosum (Doublefile Viburnum) (Japanese Snowball) is a strikingly handsome shrub in flower. In the autumn the dark green leaves take on a somber bronzy purple. It is of upright habit, with wide-spreading, horizontal branches. The white flowers which come in May are borne in flat clusters and line the upper side of the branches, producing an unusually interesting effect. The small fruits which are red at first turn gradually to a bluish black. It is a very desirable shrub both for specimen use and for mass planting.

Zone of Hardiness: IV.

Soil Requirements: ⎱
Exposure: ⎰ See *V. Carlesii.*

Propagation: Easily from seed. As soon as ripe, wash pulp from seed and sow.

Culture: More care should be used when transplanting, as it is moved with difficulty.

Weigela amabilis (Rose Weigela) is a tall, somewhat rank growing shrub, reaching a height of from 6 to 9 feet and it is well adapted to mass planting. The foliage is a soft, cool green and the large tubular flowers which are borne in great profusion in late May and early June are deep rose on the outer side of the petals and paler within. Needs considerable room for its wide spread.

Zone of Hardiness: V.

Soil Requirements: Any good garden soil which is moist.

Exposure: Full sun.

Propagation: Softwood and hardwood cuttings.

Culture: Weigelas will bloom intermittently throughout the summer if pruning is done immediately after flowering and if the stronger shoots are cut back at different times.

OLD-FASHIONED SHRUBS

(Appropriate for Colonial Gardens)

ORIGIN AND DATE OF INTRODUCTION

Buxus sempervirens suffruticosa (Box)	Ancient	Philadelphus coronarius (Mock-orange)	S. Europe, cult. 1560
Calycanthus floridus (Sweet Shrub)	Va. to Fla., 1726	Rhus cotinus (Smoke Tree)	S. Europe to C. China, 1656
Chionanthus virginica (White Fringe)	Penn. to Fla. and Texas, 1736	Rosa alba	1597, origin unknown
Hibiscus syriacus (Rose of Sharon)	China-India; intro. Europe before 1600	Rosa centifolia (Cabbage Rose)	Ancient
		Rosa cinnamomea (Cinnamon Rose)	Europe and N. Africa, 1596
Ilex glabra (Inkberry)	Nova Scotia to Fla., 1759	Rosa damascena (Damask Rose)	Asia Minor, 1550
Ilex verticillata (Black Alder) (Winterberry)	Canada to Florida, 1736	Rosa gallica (French Rose)	Cent. and S. Europe, Ancient
Lagerstrœmia indica (Crape Myrtle)	China, 1759; hardy to Wilmington, Del.	Rosa moschata (Musk Rose) Rosa palustris	S. Europe, Medieval E. North America, 1726
Ligustrum vulgare (Privet)	Europe and N. Africa, Ancient	Syringa vulgaris (Lilac) Tamarix gallica (Tamarisk)	S.E. Europe, 1550 Mediterranean, 1596

SHRUBS FOR FINE AUTUMN FOLIAGE

Acanthopanax pentaphyllum	Yellow	Forsythia viridissima	Purple (late)
Amelanchier canadensis	Red or bright yellow (mid-season)	Fothergilla	Yellow
		Hamamelis	Yellow
Aronia arbutifolia	Red	Itea virginica	Deep purple
Azalea Kæmpferi	Crimson	Leucothoë Catesbæi	Bronze (late)
" mucronulata	Crimson	Ligustrum ibota Regelianum	Purple
Berberis Thunbergii	Red	Mahonia Aquifolium	Bronze (late)
" (many others)	Red	Nandina domestica	Crimson or scarlet
Cercis canadensis	Yellow (early)	Photinia villosa	Rose or yellow
Chionanthus virginica	Yellow	Rhus canadensis	Red (mid-season)
Cornus sanguinea	Red	" copallina	Red
" paniculata	Purple	" typhina	Red
Cotoneaster horizontalis	Red	Ribes alpinum	Red
Enkianthus campanulatus	Red or Yellow	Spiræa prunifolia	Yellow
Euonymus alatus	Deep rose (late)	" Thunbergii	Yellow
„ radicans, var. coloratus	Blood-red or bronzy in winter	Vaccinium corymbosum	Crimson

Viburnum acerifolium	Rose-purple		Viburnum Lentago	Deep red
" affine	Purple-red		" Opulus	Red
" americanum (trilobum)	Red		" prunifolium	Purple
" cassinoides	Crimson		" tomentosum	Purple (late)
" dentatum	Yellow		" Wrightii	Red

SHRUBS WITH FINE FRUIT EFFECTS

(*Conspicuous Fruit*)

Aronia arbutifolia	Red	Sept.–winter	Lonicera Maackii	Crimson	Sept.–Nov.
" " brilliantissima	Red	Sept.–winter	" tatarica	Crimson	July
Berberis Thunbergii	Bright red	Winter	Mahonia Aquifolium	Blue	Sept.
" vulgaris, etc.	Red or purple	Winter	Myrica caroliniensis	Gray	Sept.–April
Callicarpa purpurea	Purple	Oct.–Nov.	Nandina domestica	Bright red or	Sept.
" japonica	Purple	Oct.–Nov.		purple-red	
Chionanthus virginica	Blue	Sept.	Photinia serrulata	Red	Oct.
Cornus florida	Red	Sept.–Oct.	" villosa	Bright red	Oct.–Nov.
" mas	Scarlet	August	Pyracantha coccinea	Orange-scarlet	Winter
" paniculata	Blue	Sept.–Oct.	" " Lalandi	Orange-scarlet	Winter
Cotoneaster divaricata	Red	Sept.–Nov.	Rhodotypos kerrioides	Black	Oct.–Nov.
" horizontalis	Bright red	Sept.–winter	Rosa multiflora	Red	Winter
" hupehensis	Bright red	Aug.–Sept.	" rugosa	Red	Winter
" Simonsii (and others)	Scarlet	Oct.	Sambucus canadensis	Black	Sept.
			" racemosus	Red	Sept.–Oct.
Elæagnus longipes	Orange vermilion	July	Symplocos paniculata	Blue	Sept.
			Symphoricarpos vulgaris	Red	Oct.–Dec.
Euonymus alatus (E. multiflorus)	Red and orange	Sept.–Oct.	" racemosus (S. albus)	White	Sept.–Nov.
" americanus	Light scarlet	Aug.–Oct.	Vaccinium corymbosum	Blue	July–Aug.
" atropurpureus	Crimson	Oct.	Viburnum dilatatum	Red	Nov.
" europæus	Pink or red	Sept.–Oct.	" Lantana	Purple	July–Sept.
Ilex lævigata	Orange-red	Sept.	" Opulus	Red	Aug.–early winter
" opaca	Red	Winter			
" serrata (I. Sieboldii)	Red	Oct.–winter	" prunifolium	Blue-black	Sept.–Oct.
" verticillata	Bright red	Oct.–winter	" Sargenti	Red	Sept.–Oct.
Ligustrum ibota	Black	Sept.–Dec.	" theiferum	Red	Nov.
" vulgare	Black	Sept.–Dec.	" Wrightii	Red	Sept.–Oct.

RELIABLE SHRUBS

(*Those which thrive without care, and even in spite of abuse. Rarely attacked by insects.*)

Acanthopanax pentaphyllum	Benzoin æstivale	Hamamelis (all)	
Aronia arbutifolia	Berberis Thunbergii	Hypericum aureum	Lycium chinense
Azalea calendulacea	Clethra alnifolia	Ilex crenata	Myrica (var.)
" canadense	Corylus americana	" glabra	Potentilla fruticosa
" Kæmpferi	Diervilla florida	" verticillata	Rhododendron maximum
" nudiflora	Elæagnus angustifolia	Ligustrum ibota	" carolinianum
" Vaseyi	" argentea	Lonicera fragrantissima	" minus
" viscosa	Forsythia Fortunei	" tatarica (most of the bush Loniceras)	Viburnum (most)
	" intermedia		

SHRUBS FOR DRY PLACES

(*Survive in poor, sandy soil*)

Acanthopanax pentaphyllum	Betula glandulosa	Ceanothus americanus	Cornus Baileyi
Amorpha fruticosa	" nana	" Fendleri	Coronilla Emerus
Arctostaphylos uva-ursi	Caragana arborescens	Colutea arborescens	Cytisus scoparius
Baccharis halimifolia	" Chamlagu	" orientalis	" supinus
Berberis Thunbergii	" frutex	Comptonia asplenifolia	Elæagnus angustifolia

SHRUBS FOR DRY PLACES—continued

Elæagnus longipes
Gaylussacia baccata
Genista tinctoria
"   germanica
Hudsonia ericoides
"   tomentosa
Myrica caroliniensis
Lespedeza bicolor
"   formosa
Hypericum prolificum
Juniperus communis
"   horizontalis

Ligustrum vulgare
Lonicera Morrowi
Lycium chinense
Potentilla fruticosa
Prunus Besseyi
"   maritima
"   pumila
Rhamnus Frangula
Rhodotypos kerrioides
Rhus canadensis
"   copallina
"   glabra

Rhus trilobata
"   typhina
Ribes Cynosbati
Robinia hispida
"   viscosa
Rosa carolina
"   gallica
"   nitida
"   rugosa
"   spinosissima
"   virginiana
Rubus cuneifolius

Rubus procumbens
Salix tristis
Shepherdia canadensis
Symphoricarpos vulgaris
Tamarix parviflora
"   gallica
Viburnum Lantana

SHRUBS FOR WET PLACES

Alnus (various)
Amelanchier canadensis
Aronia arbutifolia
Azalea Vaseyi
"   viscosa
Benzoin æstivale
Calycanthus floridus
Cephalanthus occidentalis

Chamædaphne calyculata
Clethra alnifolia
Cornus stolonifera
Dirca palustris
Hypericum densiflorum
Ilex glabra
"   verticillata
Itea virginica

Kalmia angustifolia
Myrica Gale
Pieris floribunda
Rhododendron maximum
Rosa palustris
Salix (various)
Sambucus canadensis

Spiræa tomentosa
Vaccinium canadense
"   corymbosum
Viburnum cassinoides
"   dentatum
"   Lentago
"   Sieboldii

SHRUBS FOR CUT FLOWERS

Buddleia
Caryopteris Mastacanthus
Chænomeles
Cornus mas
Corylus maxima

Deutzia
Diervilla
Forsythia
Philadelphus

Physocarpus
Prunus
Salix Caprea
"   discolor

Sorbaria
Spiræa
Syringa
Tamarix

SHRUBS OF RAPID GROWTH FOR QUICK SCREEN OR WINDBREAK

	HT.		HT.		HT.		HT.
Acanthopanax		Forsythia intermedia	10'	Ligustrum lucidum	15'	Philadelphus coronarius	15'
pentaphyllum	10'	" suspensa	12'	" ovalifolium	15'	Salix pentandra	30'
Elæagnus angustifolia	25'	" viridissima	10'	" vulgare	15'	Viburnum dentatum	15'
" argentea	12'	Ligustrum amurense	15'	Lonicera fragrantissima	10'	" Lentago	20'
Euonymus				" Maackii	15'	" prunifolium	20'
europæus	25'–30'						

LOW SHRUBS OF NEAT HABIT

(Will never grow too tall for a position under windows)

	HT.		HT.		HT.		HT.
Abelia grandiflora	5'	Juniperus communis		Lonicera nitida	4'	Taxus baccata repandens	3'
Cotoneaster		depressa plumosa	3'	Mahonia (var.)	3'	" canadensis	4'
horizontalis	2½'	Juniperus horizontalis	1½'	Myrica Gale	3'	" cuspidata	
Cotoneaster adpressa	3'	Juniperus Sabina		Pieris floribunda	5'	brevifolia	5'
Deutzia gracilis	3'	tamariscifolia	4'	Sarcococca hookeriana		Viburnum Opulus	
Ilex crenata microphylla	6'	Juniperus squamata		humilis	2'	nanum	2'
" nummularia	4'	Meyeri	5'	Stephanandra flexuosa	4'		
" glabra	6'	Kerria japonica	6'	Symphoricarpos			
Jasminum nudiflorum	4'–5'	Leucothoë Catesbæi	3'	racemosus	3'		

LOW SPREADING SHRUBS FOR COVERING A BANK
(Ground Covers)

Arctostaphylos uva-ursi	Cytisus scoparius	Lonicera japonica	Rosa Max Graf	Stephanandra flexuosa
Callicarpa purpurea	Erica carnea	" pileata	" multiflora	Symphoricarpos vulgaris
Comptonia asplenifolia (Sweet Fern)	Euonymus radicans kewensis	Lycium chinense	" spinosissima	Vinca minor
Cotoneaster horizontalis	" coloratus	Myrica Gale	" Wichuraiana	Zanthorhiza apiifolia
" adpressa	Genista tinctoria	Pachysandra terminalis	Spirea arguta	
Cytisus hirsutus	Jasminum nudiflorum (S. exposure)	Pieris floribunda	" Thunbergii	
		Rhus canadensis	" tomentosa	

SHRUBS FOR SHADY PLACES
(Will grow well in dense shade)

EVERGREEN

Euonymus radicans
Ilex glabra
Kalmia latifolia
Leucothoë Catesbaei
Mahonia Aquifolium
Pieris floribunda
Rhododendron (var.)

DECIDUOUS

Acanthopanax pentaphyllum	Clethra alnifolia (damp)	Myrica (var.)
Amelanchier (var.)	Cornus alba	Rhodotypos kerrioides
Aronia (var.)	" mas	Rhus canadensis
Azalea nudiflora	" paniculata	Ribes alpinum
Benzoin aestivale (damp)	Corylopsis spicata	" odoratum
Ceanothus americanus	Hamamelis virginiana	Stephanandra flexuosa
Cephalanthus occidentalis	Hypericum (var.)	Symphoricarpos racemosus
Chionanthus virginica	Ilex verticillata	" vulgaris

TABULAR LIST OF SHRUBS
KEY FOR TABULAR LIST OF SHRUBS

S	Sun
Sh	Shade
Part. Sh	Partial Shade

I to VIII	See Zone Map of Hardiness, p. 706.
( )	Numeral in ( ) indicates possible hardiness only

SCIENTIFIC AND COMMON NAMES	ZONE OF HARDINESS; HEIGHT	EXPOSURE; SOIL	COLOR AND SEASON OF BLOOM	COLOR OF FRUIT; REMARKS
Abelia grandiflora Abelia	VI; 6-8'	S or Sh, protected; light, peaty	White, flush pink; June–Nov.	Inconspicuous
Acanthopanax pentaphyllum	V; 4-6'	S; rich, heavy	White; June	Inconspicuous
Amelanchier canadensis Shadbush	IV; 30'	S Sh; limestone, loamy or leaf	White; May	Maroon-purple
Aralia spinosa Hercules Club	V; 30'	Sh	White; August	Black
Arbutus unedo Strawberry Tree	VIII; 8-20'	S; porous	White; Sept.	Red, yellow. Evergreen
Aronia arbutifolia Red Chokeberry	V; 9'	S Sh; moist	White, pinkish; May	Red
var. brilliantissima	V; 10'	S Sh; moist	White; April	Red, persistent
Aucuba japonica Greenleaf Aucuba	VIII; 6-10'	Sh; heavy	Maroon; March	Red. Evergreen

TABULAR LIST OF SHRUBS—continued

SCIENTIFIC AND COMMON NAMES	ZONE OF HARDINESS; HEIGHT	EXPOSURE; SOIL	COLOR AND SEASON OF BLOOM	COLOR OF FRUIT; REMARKS
Azalea arborescens — Sweet Azalea	V; 9–12'	Half Sh; acid	White; June–July	Inconspicuous
calendulacea — Flame Azalea	V; 9'	Half Sh; acid	Yellow to scarlet; June	Inconspicuous
canadense	IV; 3'	Half Sh; acid	Rosy purple; April–May	Inconspicuous
indica — Indian Azalea	VII (VI); 6'	Half Sh; acid	Pink to white; May–June	Inconspicuous. Evergreen
Kaempferi — Torch Azalea	V; 12'	Half Sh; acid	Orange-red; May	Inconspicuous
mollis — Chinese Azalea	VI (V); 3–4'	Half Sh; acid	Yellow; May	Inconspicuous
nudiflora — Pinxter Azalea	V; 6–8'	Half Sh; acid or lime	Pink; April–May	Inconspicuous
pontica hybrids — Ghent hybrids	VII; 6'	Half Sh; acid	Yellow, orange or red brown; May–June	Evergreen
rosea — Downy Pinxter A.	IV; 9'	Half Sh; acid or lime	Pink; April–May	Inconspicuous
Schlippenbachii	V; 15'	Half Sh; acid	Pink; May	Inconspicuous
Vaseyi — Pink Shell Azalea	V; 15'	Half Sh; acid	Various; April–May	Inconspicuous
viscosa — Swamp Azalea	IV; 4–7'	Half Sh; moist	Pink, white; June–July	Inconspicuous
Benzoin aestivale — Spicebush	IV; 6–15'	S Sh; wet	Greenish yellow; March	Red
Berberis buxifolia var. pygmaea — Dwarf Magellan Barberry	VI; 3'	S	Orange-yellow	Dark purple. Evergreen, compact
Julianae	(V); 5'	Neutral	Yellow; April	Bluish black. Evergreen
koreana — Korean Barberry	V; 6'	S	Yellow	Red, persistent. Deciduous
mentorensis	V; 6'	S; rich	Yellow; April	Red. Evergreen in Zone VI
Sargentiana	VI; 6'	Neutral	Yellow; April	Bluish black. Evergreen
Thunbergii — Japanese Barberry	V; 3–6'	S Sh; neutral	Yellow; April	Red
var. erecta — Columnberry	V; 6'	Half Sh; neutral	Yellow; April	Red
var. minor — Dwarf Jap. Barberry	V; 1½'	S; neutral	Yellow	Red. Very dense growth
verruculosa — Warty Barberry	VI (V); 2'	S, protected; neutral	Yellow; April	Violet-black. Evergreen
Wilsonae — Wilson's Barberry	VI (V); 1½'	S; neutral	Yellow; April	Salmon-red
Buddleia Davidi — Butterfly Bush	VI (V); 8'	S; well drained	Lilac; July–autumn	Inconspicuous
var. Veitchiana — Veitch's Bush	V	S; rich	Mauve, dense spikes; July	More vigorous than the type
Buxus microphylla var. japonica	V; 6'	Half Sh; rich	Cream; inconspicuous, axillary	Inconspicuous. Evergreen

microphylla var. koreana Korean Box	V; 2'	Half Sh; rich	Cream, inconspicuous, axillary	Inconspicuous. Evergreen
sempervirens var. suffruticosa Dwarf Box	VI; 10'	Half Sh; rich in humus		Evergreen
var. arborescens Tree Box	VI; 30'	Half Sh; rich	Inconspicuous	Inconspicuous. Evergreen, grows rapidly
Callicarpa japonica Jap. Beautyberry	(V); 4'	S; well-drained for hardiness	Pink; August	Violet
purpurea Chinese Beautyberry	(V); 4'	S; well-drained for hardiness	Pinkish; August	Lilac-violet
Calluna vulgaris Heather	VI; 3'	S or Part. Sh; semi-acid	Rosy pink; July–Sept.	Evergreen
Calycanthus floridus Sweet Shrub	V; 8'	S; moist loam	Purplish red-brown; June–July	Inconspicuous
Caragana arborescens Siberian Pea Tree	I or II; 20'	S pref.; sandy	Yellow; June	Green pod profuse but not showy
Carpenteria californica California Mock-orange	VIII; 10'	Protected from sun, high wind; sandy, well drained	White, fragrant; June–July	Evergreen
Caryopteris incana (C. Mastacanthus) Bluebeard	VII; 2–6'	S; well drained	Violet-blue, rarely white; Sept.	Inconspicuous. Winter kills but survives in Zone IV
Chaenomeles japonica (Cydonia Maulei) Lesser Jap. Flowering Quince	IV; 4'+	S	Brick red; March–April	Yellow
lagenaria Jap. Flowering Quince	IV; 6'+	S	Brilliant scarlet; March–April	Yellowish green
Chamaedaphne calyculata Leatherleaf	I; 1–3'	Sh; wet (peaty or acid)	White; April–May	Inconspicuous
Chionanthus virginica Fringetree	V; 10–30'	S; moist, sandy loam	Greenish white; May–June	Blue
Citrus trifoliata Hardy Orange	VI; 10'	S; neutral	White; April	Orange. Green twigs and thorns
Clethra alnifolia Sweet Pepperbush	IV; 3–8'	Sh; wet, peaty or acid, sandy	White, pink tinge; July–Sept.	Inconspicuous. Flowers fragrant
Colutea arborescens Bladder Senna	V; 12'	S Sh; dry	Yellow; June–Sept.	Bronze-red
Comptonia asplenifolia Sweetfern	II; 2–4'	S Sh; peaty, sandy or sterile	Inconspicuous	Inconspicuous
Cornus alba Tatarian Dogwood	II; 5–10'	S Sh; wet	Creamy white; May or June	Bluish white
var. sibirica Coral Dogwood	IV; 10'	S Sh; wet	Creamy white; May–June	Bluish white. Bright coral-red branches
Amomum Silky Dogwood	V; 3–10'	S; wet	White; June	Blue
mas Cornelian Cherry	V; 10'+	S Sh	Golden yellow; March	Scarlet. Often treelike

TABULAR LIST OF SHRUBS—continued

SCIENTIFIC AND COMMON NAMES	ZONE OF HARDINESS; HEIGHT	EXPOSURE; SOIL	COLOR AND SEASON OF BLOOM	COLOR OF FRUIT; REMARKS
Cornus paniculata Gray Dogwood	IV; 3–15′	S	Creamy white; June	White or pale blue
sanguinea Blood-twig D.	V (IV); 10′+	S; wet	White; May–June	Green
stolonifera Red Osier	II; 8′	S; wet	Dull white; May	White. Bright red twigs
Corylopsis spicata Winter Hazel	VI; 6′	Sh; peaty, sandy	Yellow, fragrant	
Corylus americana American Hazelnut	IV; 10′		Drooping catkins	
Avellana fusco-rubra Purple Hazel	(III); 15′	S; moist	Catkins; March	Green. Leaves purple or brown
rostrata Beaked Hazelnut	V (IV); 9′	S; moist	Catkins; March	Beaked green
Cotinus coggygria (Rhus cotinus) Smoke-Tree	V; 15′	S; well drained	Mist-like; June–July	Small drupe
Cotoneaster adpressa Creeping C.	V; Creep	S;	Pink; June	Red
apiculata	V; 3′	S;	Pink; June	Red. Evergreen in the South
Dielsiana Diel's C.	VI (V); 6′	S;	Pinkish; June	Scarlet
divaricata Spreading C.	V; 6′	S;	Pink; June	Red
Francheti Franchet's C.	VII; 6′	S;	Pink; June	Orange
horizontalis Rock Cotoneaster	V; trail	S;	Pink; June	Red
microphylla	VI; 3′	S;	White; May	Scarlet
rotundifolia Round-leaf C.	V; 6″	S;	White; June	Scarlet
salicifolia	VI; 15′	Part. Sh	White; June	Red. Evergreen
Cydonia japonica See Chænomeles japonica				
Cyrilla racemiflora Leatherwood	VII (VI); 30′		White; June–July	Inconspicuous. Beautiful dense foliage
Cytisus hirsutus Broom	V; 2′	S; neutral	Yellow; May–June	Inconspicuous
scoparius Scotch Broom	VI; 10′	S; limy	Yellow; May or June	Inconspicuous
Daphne Cneorum Rose Daphne	V; 1–1½′	S; peaty or sandy alkaline	Rose; April and Sept.	Yellowish brown
Genkwa Lilac Daphne	VI (V); 3′	S; peaty or sandy alkaline	Violet; April	Inconspicuous
Mezereum February Daphne	IV; 3′	S; alkaline	Pink, rose, purple; April	Scarlet

Note (spanning the Cotoneaster group, EXPOSURE; SOIL column): Well-drained soils preferred

Name	Zone; Height	Flower; Bloom	Soil	Remarks
Deutzia gracilis / Slender Deutzia	V; 3–6'	Pink, white; **May**	S; well drained for greater hardiness	
Lemoinei / Lemoine Deutzia	V; 3–6'	White; May	S; well drained for greater hardiness	
Diervilla hybrida (Weigela)*	V; 10'	Pink; May–June	S; well drained for greater hardiness	Capsule
florida (Weigela florida) / Pink Weigela	V; 6–9'	Various (Pinks); May–June	S; well drained for greater hardiness	Inconspicuous
Elæagnus angustifolia / Russian Olive	II; 20'	Yellow; June	S; sandy, clay	Yellowish
argentea / Silverberry	I; 6–12'	Yellow; June	S; sandy, clay	Silvery
longipes (multiflora) / Cherry Elæagnus	V; 9'	Yellow; June	S; sandy, clay	Red
Elæagnus pungens / Silverberry	VII; 8–15'	White; October	S; rich	Red. Evergreen, thorny
Elsholtzia Stauntoni / Mintshrub	V; 3–5'	Red-purple; Sept.	S; well drained	Inconspicuous
Enkianthus campanulatus / Bellflowertree	VI; 6'	Pink; May	S Sh; acid	Inconspicuous
subsessilis / Nikko Enkianthus	V; 9'	White; May–June	S; acid, moist, sandy	Brilliant autumn coloring
Erica carnea / Spring Heath	V; 1'	Rose-red; March	S; sandy, acid	Inconspicuous. Evergreen
Euonymus alatus / Winged E.	IV; 6–8'	Yellowish; May	S; well drained	Purple
var. compactus / Dwarf Winged E.	IV; 6'	Yellow; May	S or Sh; any	Purple
americanus / Strawberry Bush	VI; 5–8'	Greenish purple; June	S Sh; well drained	Light scarlet
atropurpureus / Burning-bush	IV; 25'	Purple	Well drained	Scarlet
japonicus / Evergreen Burning-bush	VIII (VII); 10–12'	Inconspicuous; June	S†	Inconspicuous
patens	VI; 9–10'	White; June–July June	S Sh; well drained	Pink. Spreading
radicans / Wintercreeper	V; climber		S Sh; well drained	Evergreen
var. acutus	V; Shrubby		S Sh; well drained	Orange. Evergreen
var. Carrierei	V; climber	Greenish; June	S; well drained	Evergreen
var. coloratus	V; climber		S Sh; well drained	Evergreen
var. kewensis	V; climber		S Sh	Orange. Evergreen
var. vegetus	V; climber	Greenish; June	S Sh; rich	Evergreen
Exochorda grandiflora / Pearlbush	V; 15'	White; April–May		Five-ribbed capsule
Forsythia intermedia / Border Goldenbells	V; 9'	Yellow; April	S Sh; indifferent	Inconspicuous
var. spectabilis / Showy Border Forsythia	V; 10'	Bright yellow; April	S Sh; indifferent	
ovata	V; 5'	Yellow; April	S Sh; indifferent	Inconspicuous

* Collective name for large group of hybrids.

† Hardier in dry or sandy soil.

TABULAR LIST OF SHRUBS—continued

SCIENTIFIC AND COMMON NAMES	ZONE OF HARDINESS; HEIGHT	EXPOSURE; SOIL	COLOR AND SEASON OF BLOOM	COLOR OF FRUIT; REMARKS
Forsythia suspensa / Drooping Goldenbells	V; 9'	S Sh; indifferent	Yellow; April	Inconspicuous
var. Fortunei	V; 8'	S; indifferent	Yellow; April	Vigorous grower
viridissima / Green-stem Goldenbells	VI (V); 9'	S Sh; indifferent	Yellow; April	Inconspicuous
Fothergilla Gardeni / Fothergilla	V or VI; 4'	Sh; light	White; April	Inconspicuous
monticola / Alabama Fothergilla	V; 6'	S; damp	White; May	Larger flower
Gaylussacia baccata / Black Huckleberry	I; 3'	Sh; dry, sandy		Black, shiny
Hamamelis japonica / Jap. Witchhazel	V; 30'	S; indifferent	Lemon-yellow; Feb. or March	
mollis / Chin. Witchhazel	V; 30'	S; indifferent	Golden yellow; Feb. or March	
vernalis / Spring Witchhazel	V; 6'	S; indifferent	Light yellow; Feb. or March	
virginiana / Common Witchhazel	IV (III); 10–25'	Sh; indifferent	Yellow; Oct. or Nov.	Black seeds
Hibiscus syriacus / Rose of Sharon	V or VI; 20'	S Sh; not too sandy	White, red, purple; August	Brown
Hydrangea arborescens	III; 10'	Neutral	White; June–July	Inconspicuous*
paniculata / Panicle Hydrangea	IV; 25'	S Sh	White, pink, greenish bronze; July	Inconspicuous*
quercifolia / Oak-leaf Hydrangea	VI (V); 10'	S Sh	Pinkish white-purplish; July	Inconspicuous*
Hypericum Moserianum / Goldflower	(VII); 1½'	Sh; sandy	Yellow; Aug.–Sept.	Inconspicuous
prolificum	IV; 5'	Sh; sandy, rocky	July–Sept.	Evergreen
Ilex cornuta / Chinese Holly	VI or VII; 9–15'	S; well drained	June	Red. Evergreen
var. Burfordii	VI; 9'	S; well drained	White; June	Red. Evergreen
crenata / Japanese Holly	VI; 10–15'	Part. Sh; peaty (acid)	White; June	Black. Evergreen
var. microphylla	IV; 4'	Sh; rich, well drained	May–June	Evergreen
var. convexa / Convex Japanese Holly	V; 4'	S; rich	White; July	Black. Evergreen
glabra / Inkberry	V; 8'	Sh; wet (acid)	White; July	Black. Evergreen
verticillata / Winterberry	IV; 8'	S; wet	White; July	Red. Deciduous
Jasminum nudiflorum / Winter Jasmine	(VI); 4–6'	S or Part. Sh; rich	Yellow; Feb.–March	Inconspicuous. Green stems, 3 parted leaves
Juniperus chinensis / Pfitzeriana / Pfitzer's Juniper	IV; 10'	S; dry, sandy		

* Flowers of some horticultural forms may be changed from pink to blue by adding iron filings to the soil.

Name	Height	Soil	Flower; Time	Fruit / Notes
communis / Common Juniper	I; 30'			Dark blue
horizontalis / Creeping Juniper	II; 1½'			Blue
depressa plumosa / Andorra Juniper	III; 3–4'	S; porous		Blue. Evergreen
Douglasii / Waukegan Juniper	IV; 1½'	S; porous		Blue. Evergreen
Sabina var. tamariscifolia	IV; 3'			Evergreen
squamata var. Meyeri	V; 5'			Upright, dense, evergreen
Kalmia latifolia / Mountain Laurel	IV (III); 8'	Sh; sandy, acid	White, pink; June	Inconspicuous
Kerria japonica / Kerria	V; 4–6'	S Sh	Golden yellow; June–Sept.	Inconspicuous
Kolkwitzia amabilis / Beauty Bush	V; 6'	S; good drainage	Pink and orange; June	Inconspicuous
Laburnum vulgare	V; 20'		Yellow; May–June	Pods
Lagerstroemia indica / Crape Myrtle	VII; 15–20'	S	Purple to white; Aug.–Oct.	Inconspicuous
Laurus nobilis / Sweet Bay	VII; 12–30'	S; rich	Greenish white	Black. Evergreen
Leucothoë Catesbaei / Drooping Leucothoë	V; 2–3'	Sh; acid	White; April–May	Inconspicuous
Ligustrum amurense / Amur Privet	V; 15'	S Sh; indifferent	White; June–July	Black
Ibolium / Ibolium Privet	V; 15'	S Sh; indifferent	White; July	Black
Ibota (obtusifolium) / Ibota Privet	V; 15'	S Sh; indifferent	White; July	Black
japonicum / Japanese Privet	VII or VIII; 10–15'	S Sh; indifferent	White; August	Black. Evergreen
lucidum / Glossy Privet	VII; 25'	S Sh; indifferent	White; Aug.–Sept.	Black. Evergreen
obtusifolium var. Regelianum / Regel's Privet	V; 15'	S Sh; indifferent	White; July	Black
ovalifolium / California Privet	(V); 15'	S Sh; indifferent	White; July–August	Black
Lonicera fragrantissima / Fragrant Honeysuckle	(V); 4–5'	S; indifferent	White; March–April	
Korolkowii / Blueleaf Honeysuckle	IV; 12'	S; indifferent	Rose; May	Red
Maacki / Amur Honeysuckle	IV; 12–15'	S; indifferent	White; May	Red
Morrowi / Morrow Honeysuckle	V; 8'	S; indifferent	White; May–June	Blood red
nitida / Shiny Honeysuckle	VII or VIII; 6'	S; indifferent	White; June	Blue, purple. Evergreen
pileata / Privet Honeysuckle	VI; 2'	S; indifferent	Whitish; May–June	Purple. Evergreen

TABULAR LIST OF SHRUBS—continued

SCIENTIFIC AND COMMON NAMES	ZONE OF HARDINESS; HEIGHT	EXPOSURE; SOIL	COLOR AND SEASON OF BLOOM	COLOR OF FRUIT; REMARKS
Lonicera tatarica / Tatarian Honeysuckle	V; 10'	S; indifferent	Rose, white; May	Red.
Mahonia Aquifolium / Oregon Hollygrape	V; 2–3'	Sh; dry, sandy	Yellow; April	Black. Evergreen
Bealei / Leather-leaf Hollygrape	VI (V); 2–3'	Sh; dry, sandy	Yellow; April	Black
Myrica Pennsylvanica / Northern Bayberry	IV; 12'	S; dry	Inconspicuous	Gray
Gale / Sweet Gale	I; 4'	S; moist	Inconspicuous	Gray
Nandina domestica / Nandina	VII or VIII; 3–6'	S Sh; peaty loam	White; June–July	Red. Evergreen
Osmanthus Aquifolium (O. ilicifolius) / Holly-olive	VI; 7–20'	Protected peaty spots	White; June–July	Bluish. Evergreen
Philadelphus coronarius / Mock-orange	IV; 10'	S; lime to neutral	White; June	
grandiflorus / Big Scentless Mock-orange	IV; 12'	S Half Sh; dry, neutral	White; May–June	Mass planting
Lemoinei "Avalanche"	V; 6'	S; lime to neutral	White, fragrant; June	Large flower
virginalis / Virginal Mock-orange	V; 6'	S; lime to neutral	White	Racemes of white semi-double flowers
Photinia serrulata	VII; 30'	S; light, sandy, well drained	White	Red. Evergreen
villosa / Christmas Berry	V; 15'		White; May	Red
Pieris floribunda / Mt. Andromeda	V; 3–5'	Sh; acid	White; April–May	Inconspicuous
japonica / Jap. Andromeda	VI (V); 8'	Sh; acid	White; April–May	Inconspicuous
Pittosporum phillyræoides / Willow Pittosporum	IX; 10–20'	S or Sh	Yellow	Evergreen
Tobira / Japanese Pittosporum	IX; 8–15'	S or Sh	White	Brown. Evergreen
Potentilla fruticosa / Shrubby Cinquefoil	I; 3'	Dry or wet	Yellow and white; June–Oct.	Inconspicuous
Prunus laurocerasus / Cherry Laurel	VI; 18'	S; rich	White	Purple, black. Evergreen
maritima / Beach Plum	IV; 6'	S; sandy	White	Red or yellow. Seashore
tomentosa / Nankin Cherry	IV (III); 5'	S; good, well-drained loam	White; April	Scarlet
Pyracantha coccinea Lalandi / Firethorn	VI or VIII; 6–20'	S; limestone, well drained	White; May–June	Orange-scarlet. Evergreen, and bunches of fruit

Name	Zone; Height	Soil	Flower; Season	Fruit / Remarks
Rhododendron carolinianum Caro. Rhododendron	V; 9'	Sh; subacid	Pink or purple; May	Inconspicuous. Evergreen
catawbiense Catawba Rhododendron	V; 6–18'	Sh; subacid	Red and purple; May	Inconspicuous. Evergreen
maximum Rosebay Rhododendron	IV; 36'	Sh; subacid	Pink or white; May	Inconspicuous. Evergreen
minus	V; 10'	Sh; acid	Pink, spotted with green; June–July	Evergreen
Rhodotypos kerrioides White Kerria	V; 4'	S Sh; indifferent	White; May to Fall	Black
Rhus Cotinus (see Cotinus coggygria) Smoke Bush	V; 15'	S; well drained	Mist-like, tinted with purple; July–Aug.	Small drupe
glabra Smooth Sumac	II; 15–20'	S Sh; dry	Greenish; June–July	Crimson and hairy
typhina Staghorn Sumac	IV; 15'	S Sh; any	Greenish; June–July	Purplish brown
Ribes odatorum Flowering Currant	V; 6'	Sh; moder. fertile	Yellow; April	Inconspicuous
Robinia hispida Rose Acacia	V; 3'	S; limy	Rose-pink; June	Pods
viscosa Clammy Locust	VI; 40'		Pink; May–June	
Rosa alba	V; 6'	Heavy clay	White or pinkish; June	Red
blanda	II; 6'	S; heavy clay	Pink, single; May–June	
carolina Pasture Rose	IV; 3'	S; heavy clay	Pink; June–July	
centifolia Cabbage Rose	V; 6'	Heavy clay	Pink, very double; June	
cinnamomea Cinnamon Rose	IV; 6'	Heavy clay	Red, fragrant; June	
damascena Damask Rose	V; 8'	Heavy clay	Pale pink to red, fragrant; June	Red
Eglanteria (rubiginosa) Eglantine Rose	V (IV); 6'	S; heavy clay	Pink; June	Flower 3" wide
gallica French Rose	V; 4'	S; heavy clay	Pink to crimson, solitary; June	Red
Harisonii Harison's Yellow	V; 9'	S; heavy clay	Orange-yellow; June	Red
Hugonis Father Hugo's Rose	V; 8'	S; heavy clay	Sulphur yellow; May	Red
moschata Musk Rose	VIII	Heavy clay	White; June	
multiflora Japanese Rose	V	S; heavy clay	White; June	Red
nitida	III; 1½'	S; heavy clay	Pink; Spring	Red
palustris Swamp Rose	IV; 6'	Swampy	Pink; June–August	
persica Persian Yellow	(VII); 9'	S; heavy clay	Yellow; June	Red

TABULAR LIST OF SHRUBS—continued

SCIENTIFIC AND COMMON NAMES	ZONE OF HARDINESS; HEIGHT	EXPOSURE; SOIL	COLOR AND SEASON OF BLOOM	COLOR OF FRUIT; REMARKS
Rosa micrantha	V; 6'	S; heavy clay	Pink or white in clusters of 3 or 4; June	
rugosa Rugosa Rose	IV; 6'	S; heavy clay	Pink; white; Spring	Red
setigera Prairie Rose	V; 15'	S; heavy clay	Pink; June–August	Red
spinosissima Scotch Rose	IV; 3'	S; heavy clay	Yellow, white; June	Black
virginiana	III; 6'	S; heavy clay	Pink; June–July	Red
Wichuraiana Memorial Rose	V; prostrate	Heavy clay	White, fragrant; June	Half evergreen
Salix Caprea Goat Willow	V; 25'	S; wet	Catkins; March	Inconspicuous. Hardy to Nova Scotia
discolor Pussy Willow	II; 20'	S; wet	Catkins; March	
Sambucus canadensis American Elder	IV; 5–8'	S Sh; swampy	White; June–July	Black
racemosus European Red-berried Elder	IV; 6–8'	Sh; indifferent	White; April–May	Red
Sarcococca hookeriana humilis	VI; 1½'	Sh; rich	White; Oct.–March	Black. Evergreen
Sorbaria Aitchisonii Kashmir False-spirea	VI (V); 6–8'	S; indifferent	White; June	Inconspicuous
Spiraea arguta Garland Spirea	IV; 6'	S*; neutral	White; April	Inconspicuous
Billiardii Billiard Spirea	V; 6'	S; neutral	Rose; July–August	Inconspicuous
Bumalda Bumalda Spirea	V; 3'	S; neutral	Pink; June	Inconspicuous
var. Froebeli	V; 4'	S; neutral	Deep rose; early June	Inconspicuous
prunifolia Bridalwreath	(V); 4–6'	S; neutral	White; April	Inconspicuous
Thunbergii Thunberg Spirea	V; 3'	S; neutral	White; March–April	Inconspicuous
Vanhouttei Vanhoutte Spirea	IV; 3–6'	S; neutral	White; May	Inconspicuous
Staphylea colchica Bladdernut	VI; 10'	Sh; moist, rich	Yellow-white; May–June	Green
Stephanandra incisa (flexuosa) Cutleaf Stephanandra	V; 3–6'	S Sh; peaty	White; June	Inconspicuous
Stewartia pentagyna	V; 15'		White stamens, orange anthers	
Stranvæsia davidiana	VIII; 6–20'	Sh; poor	White; May	Red. Evergreen

* Prefer sun but most are tolerant of some shade.

Name	Zone; Height	Soil	Flower color; time	Fruit / Remarks
Symphoricarpos albus (S. racemosus)				
Snowberry	IV; 4'	Half Sh; lime and clay	Pink; August	White
vulgaris	V; 4'	Sh	August	Red
Coralberry				
Symplocos paniculata	V; 15–25'		White; May–June	Blue. Very fine fruit cluster
Asiatic Sweetleaf				
Syringa chinensis	V; 10–12'	S; neutral	Reddish lilac; June	Inconspicuous
Rouen Lilac				
japonica	V; 30'	Neutral	Yellowish white; June–July	Tree-like
persica	V; 8'	S; neutral	Lavender, white; June	Inconspicuous
Persian Lilac				
villosa	V; 15'	S; neutral	Lilac; July	Inconspicuous
Himalaya Lilac				
vulgaris	III; 15'+	S; neutral	Various; June	Inconspicuous
Common Lilac				
Tamarix parviflora	V; 15'	Salt air and wind; not too much lime	Pink; April	Inconspicuous
Tamarisk				
pentandra	V; 15'		Pink; Aug.–Sept.	Inconspicuous
Fivestamen Tamarix				
Taxus baccata repandens	VI; 4'			Evergreen
English Yew				
canadensis	III; 6'			
Ground-Hemlock				
Vaccinium canadense	IV; 1–2'		Greenish white to reddish	Blue. Edible fruit; crimson autumn leaves
corymbosum	IV; 12'	Moist; acid	White; April	Blue. Edible fruit; crimson autumn leaves
Highbush Blueberry				
pennsylvanicum	III; 1½'	Dry; acid	White; April	Blue. Edible fruit; crimson autumn leaves
Lowbush Blueberry				
Viburnum acerifolium	III or IV; 5'	Sh; dry	White; June	Black
Dockmackie				
americanum				
(see V. tribolum)				
burkwoodi	V; 6'	Sh; moist	White; April	Black
Burkwood Viburnum				
carlcephalum	V; 7'	S; rich	White; April	Black
Carlesii	V; 4–6'	S	Pink; April	Black
Fragrant Viburnum				
cassinoides	III or IV; 6'	S; wet	White; May	Black; crimson autumn leaves
Withe-rod				
dentatum	IV; 10'	S or Sh	White; June	Black
Arrow-wood				
dilatatum	V; 10'	S	White; June	Red. One of the best red-fruited shrubs
Linden V. or Jap				
Bushcranberry				
Lantana	IV; 15'		White; June–July	Black
Wayfaring Tree				
molle	V; 12'	S	White; May	Black
Kentucky Viburnum				

TABULAR LIST OF SHRUBS—continued

SCIENTIFIC AND COMMON NAMES	ZONE OF HARDINESS; HEIGHT	EXPOSURE; SOIL	COLOR AND SEASON OF BLOOM	COLOR OF FRUIT; REMARKS
Viburnum Opulus Highbush Cranberry	III; 10'	S Sh	White; May–June	Red
var. nanum Dwarf Cranberry Bush	III; 3'	S Sh	No flowers	Good accent plant
prunifolium Blackhaw	V; 30'	S Sh	White; April	Black
rhytidophyllum Leatherleaf	(V); 10'	Shaded in winter; well drained	White; May	Red to black. Evergreen
setigerum (var. theiferum)	VI; 12'	S Sh	Cream white; May–June	Red
Sieboldii Siebold V.	IV; 10'	S; damp	White; May–June	Black. Leaves lustrous
tomentosum Doublefile V.	IV; 10'	S	White; May or June	Blue-black. One of the best white-flowering shrubs
tomentosum plicatum Japanese Snowball	V; 10'	S	White; June	
trilobum (americanum) American V.	II; 12'	S Sh	White; May	Red
Wrightii Wright or Oriental	V; 6–8'	S	White	Red
Vitex Agnus-castus Chaste-tree	VII (VI); 10'	S; slightly acid	Lilac; July–Sept.	Inconspicuous. Stems winter-kill at Phila.
Weigela (see Diervilla)				
Zanthorhiza apiifolia Yellowroot	IV; 1–2'	Sh; wet or dry	Maroon; April	Inconspicuous. Excellent ground cover

XXI

VINES

IN a garden design vines have an important place, as they are both decorative and functional. Probably the earliest use of vines was for fruit and wine production, but the decorative value of the grapevine was so apparent that the garden builders of Italy occasionally used grape arbors as part of the scheme in the formal garden. The arbor in the Villa Medici at Fiesole is a good example.

Each specie and variety of vine possesses distinctive characteristics which make it well adapted to certain locations in the general landscape plan. Some vines are valued for the welcome shade which they cast when trained upon arbors or pergolas. There are others which will lend distinction to a planting when skillfully trained against the wall of a house or patio, or when used to frame a doorway gracefully. Some vines can be used to relieve the monotony of a large expanse of wall, being trained to a definite pattern, or allowed to clothe completely a wall with leafy green. With their bloom and delicate tracery of leaf-form some vines can make an otherwise commonplace fence seem a thing of exciting and sometimes exotic beauty, and there are others that will form a cascade of bloom on rough, steep banks, while holding the soil in place.

Some vines are valued for the rich texture of their foliage, some for their decorative habit of growth, others for the fragrance of their blooms or for the spectacular beauty of their flowers; some for the graceful tracery of their supple stems or for the beauty of their leaf patterns. In the hands of the skillful designer and gardener vines offer a rich source of material with which to create compositions of striking beauty.

Support for Vines

Most vines must have support. And since the various vines differ according to their habits of growth and climbing equipment, the support must be suitable to the type of vine selected. Those which climb by stems, twining around the support, as the Wisteria, and those which have tendrils which reach out and grasp small objects in the manner of the grape vine, need the lattice, arbor or fence type of support. Those which cling to things by means of roots or modified fruit stems need brick or stone masonry walls or great boulders as support. Boston Ivy and Ficus repens are examples.

Some vines will grow without supports, but the amazing fact about many of them is that when grown in this manner they lose their vine characteristics and become shrub-like in form. Euonymus radicans is an outstanding example of this modification. In some cases such vines will send out quantities of long, straight stems along the surface in an effort to find a support. Such are the tactics of Wisteria. Many others, like Virginia Creeper, Rosa Wichuraiana, and English Ivy, are quite content to scramble on the ground and often make good ground covers. However, when they reach a support, up they go, for vines are essentially outlaws. They are opportunists in the plant kingdom. If they did not grow rapidly up and over their neighbors they would not reach the light. The vine's self-preservation comes from its capacity to grow up rapidly without taking time to produce wood strong enough to support itself. It depends on its neighbors for support, and eventually it may even kill the very tree which offers it support by smothering its foliage. Furthermore, vine roots range as widely and

279

freely as their stems. This makes them bad neighbors for many plants. A gardener should understand these tendencies in vines and make provision for them.

The best type of support for vines is the one which gives the required structural strength and stability, and at the same time makes a neat appearance.

In a sophisticated garden, the more architectural arbor has its place, but in many cases the growth of the vines will so completely cover all but the posts that such embellishment seems unwarranted.

Vines which clamber up a trellis on a frame house are a serious obstacle to the periodic painting which the house requires. If rambler roses are trained on the trellis, the painting is both difficult and uncomfortable. To overcome this trouble, the trellis should be built so that, together with the vines, it may be detached from the building. One of the best ways to accomplish this is to hinge the trellis at the bottom and fasten the top to a cleat on the house wall by means of a bolt. When the painting begins, the bolt may be removed, the trellis swung out and held in a slanting position by a strut. There will be sufficient pliancy in the stems of the vine to bend along with the hinge.

For the support of rather small twining vines or shrubs against a stone or brick wall, a special nail is manufactured. From the head projects a strip of soft metal, which is bent around the vine stem to hold it in place. The nails are driven into the cement mortar joint and, because of the rough surface of the metal, hold firmly in the mortar. This is a most satisfactory device for training jasmine, forsythia or firethorn against a masonry wall.

For the support of large, stem-twining vines against a masonry wall metal frame lattices are good. Less expensive is a large mesh network of wire cables fastened to expansion bolts which project out about 8 inches from the face

HIGH REDWOOD SCREEN FENCE WITH SHADOW STRIPS AND TRELLIS FOR STAR JASMINE VINES

of the wall. The wires are made tight by turn buckles. This is suitable for such strong vines as wisteria and actinidia and if the wires are placed 3 feet apart, forming squares, a very pleasing pattern of greenery and masonry is produced. This is a satisfactory means of covering a large bare wall surface flanking a city garden.

Maintenance

Pruning vines to produce better bloom or to keep the plants within bounds is an annual task requiring patience and skill. The removal of the old wood may require several cuts to each stem so that they can be untangled. The same principles of pruning apply to flowering vines as to fruit trees. Prune to guide future growth.

Vines like wisteria produce quantities of large stems which tangle in grotesque knots. As the stems grow and expand, the knots become tighter, and in this way the vine is apt to strangle itself. This may be avoided in part by reducing the number of major stems when the vine is still young, and by training the early growth in such a way as not to form heavy

HYBRID CLEMATIS
VARIETY: NELLIE MOSER

twisted ropes made up of several stems. If the central part of the plant is well branched, the formation of tangles in the outer parts is not so serious. They can be removed without spoiling the vine.

Spraying against insects should be done as part of the general spraying program for the place.

CLIMBING ROSES ENHANCE THE SIMPLE DIGNITY OF THIS GARAGE IN THE HILLS OF NEW HAMPSHIRE

A LUXURIANT TRUMPET VINE CLAMBERS OVER THE CHIMNEY ON THIS CALIFORNIA PATIO.

VINES OF MERIT

Actinidia polygama (Silver Vine) is a vigorous and tall-growing vine with handsome foliage which is remarkably free from insect pests and diseases. It produces small, white flowers in cymes of three blossoms at the axils of the leaf in June, and the fruit, which ripens in September or October, is a greenish-yellow berry about an inch long. As the plants are sometimes dioecious there occasionally occurs a vine which does not bear fruit.

Height: to 30 feet.

Exposure: Sun or shade.

Culture: Occasional thinning out of the mass of stems to improve appearance.

Uses: Makes an attractive pattern on trellis, fence or wall.

Akebia quinata is a charming, slender vine, with beautiful foliage made up of five-parted leaves. The flowers are deep rosy purple, waxy in texture, opening valve-like into three parts. They are not conspicuous or fragrant but as cut flowers they are delightful. The vine is rather low growing and is excellent on a trellis or for covering a low wall. It needs the support of a wall or wires.

Exposure: Sun or shade.

282

Culture: Occasional thinning out of the mass of stems to improve appearance.

Uses: Forms a pleasant, delicate tracery against a wall or fence.

Caution: May become a pest. See page 600.

Allamanda cathartica is an evergreen, shrubby vine adapted only to climates which are frost free. It is sometimes grown in greenhouses in the north. Noted for the beauty of its large, golden flowers, trumpet-shaped, with flaring petals. Blooms in June.

Height: to 10 feet.

Exposure: Full sun; very warm exposure preferable.

Uses: As a decorative vine on trellis or pillar.

Ampelopsis brevipedunculata (blue-berry climber) is a hardy, deciduous vine of rampant growth. The three-lobed leaves are large and handsome, flowers inconspicuous, the fruit a metallic-blue berry.

Height: 20 feet.

Exposure: Full sun or shade.

Culture: Thrives in any good garden soil.

Uses: On trellis or arbor.

Antigonon leptopus (Queen's Wreath) (Coral Vine) (Rosa de Montana): An evergreen vine bearing long, trailing sprays of rose-pink flowers from midsummer to autumn. Foliage heart-shaped, open and airy. Rapid grower. Adapted only to frost-free areas.

Height: 40 feet.

Exposure: Thrives in high summer heat; should be given the hottest exposure possible.

Culture: Any good garden soil; water liberally while in bloom. Keep it on the dry side during the rest of the year.

Uses: On a trellis; as a frame around a doorway or along edge of roof where summer bloom is desired.

Aristolochia durior (A. sipho) (Dutchman's Pipe) is an old-fashioned favorite, not often seen nowadays. It is a foliage vine, with large heart-shaped leaves thickly overlapping one another. If grown on a series of horizontal slats or wires it will form an opaque wall of green. The flowers, although not conspicuous, are very entertaining. They resemble a Dutchman's pipe, and from this comes its common name. It is native to the woodlands of the eastern United States from Pennsylvania and Minnesota southward to Georgia and has long been in cultivation.

Height: 20 feet.

Exposure: Sun or partial shade.

Culture: A good, garden loam with a pH between 6.0 and 7.0. Water well in dry weather.

Uses: On arbor, trellis or wires. Makes a dense shade. Excellent for screen or barrier.

Beaumontia grandiflora (Herald Trumpet) (Easter Lily Vine): An evergreen vine adapted only to frost-free areas. The leaves are large, oval in shape, dark green in color, and glossy. The white flowers, which are borne from May to September, resemble an Easter Lily, and are very fragrant.

Height: 10 feet.

Exposure: Full sun.

Culture: Good, garden soil. Blooms are produced on two- or three-year-old wood.

Uses: As a decorative feature on a wide trellis, as it sometimes attains a spread of ten feet. It may also be trained to an espalier form on a south or west wall.

Bougainvillea: A showy, evergreen vine adapted to frost-free areas. The inconspicuous flowers are surrounded by three bracts which give the vine its brilliant coloring. The height of bloom is reached in midsummer. A variety of colors are available, some of great brilliancy, others of more subtle hue, reddish purple, magenta, scarlet, lavender and salmon-coral.

Height: to 20 feet.

Exposure: Full sun. Thrives best against a south wall.

Culture: Requires a rich soil and heavy feeding for best results. Can be easily shaped or restrained by pruning.

Uses: As an accent against a wall. Can be trained to an espalier form. Care must be taken to avoid clashes of color.

Calonyction aculeatum (Moonflower): A perennial vine usually treated as an annual. Makes rapid growth. The heart-shaped leaves are large and form a dense mass of foliage. The fragrant, flaring, tube-like flowers are often 5 to 6 inches across and are borne in profusion from July until frost. The white variety remains open until noon and then closes until evening. Other varieties usually remain closed throughout the day, opening after sundown.

Height: 20 to 30 feet.

Exposure: Full sun or partial shade.

Culture: Soak seeds for several days until they are twice or three times normal size before planting, or notch seeds on the side with a knife.

Uses: May be trained against a wall on strings or wire; may be used as a decorative feature on a trellis or fence; excellent for penthouse gardens; thrives under city conditions.

Campsis grandiflora (C. Chinensis).

The Chinese Trumpet Creeper has very few aerial rootlets and, therefore, requires the support of a trellis. It may be distinguished from its relatives by the fact that it has fewer leaflets, seven or nine. The flowers are larger, bright scarlet, and open in August and September. By many, it is considered superior to the native trumpet creeper. Less vigorous in habit of growth.

Height: to 20 to 25 feet.

Exposure: Full sun.

Culture: Adaptable to ordinary culture.

Uses: On a trellis against a wall or fence; on arbors.

Campsis radicans: The native Trumpet Creeper, variously named Campsis radicans, Tecoma radicans and Bignonia radicans, is a wonderful vine with orange and scarlet tubular blossoms in terminal clusters in summer, each blossom 3 or 4 inches long. The rich foliage is very dense and consists of compound leaves of nine or eleven leaflets. It is native to forests from Pennsylvania to Texas and has been in cultivation since colonial times. Several varieties exist, some with deeper red blossoms, some blooming earlier.

Height: 20 to 40 feet.

Exposure: Sunshine.

Culture: Requires no attention; good garden soil.

Uses: Against brick, stucco, stone and wood walls to which it clings by means of aerial rootlets. Can be trained along the edge of a roof, over arbors, along sturdy fences. It can also be used as a flowering hedge, as the branches become self-supporting after the first year if they are pruned and guided correctly. In Italy trumpet creepers are often grown in huge, ornamented pots, being trained to a shrub form.

Celastrus (Bittersweet)

C. orbiculatus (or C. articulatus): An Oriental species, which is more vigorous than the native Bittersweet and produces an abundance of brilliant orange and scarlet fruit. The flowers being in axillary clusters are somewhat hidden in the leaves and the fruit is not really conspicuous until the leaves fall. Conditions and requirements are similar to those of C. scandens.

C. scandens (Waxwork or Climbing Bittersweet): Another native of our forests, is an old favorite and still very popular. It is closely related to Euonymus, which it resembles in its fruit formation. This vigorous, high-climbing vine, with rich foliage in a great variety of shapes, has strong, twisty stems. The orange and red fruit which ripens in October lasts all winter even when brought into the house to decorate the mantel or table. The fruit is borne on terminal panicles, which fact makes it conspicuous. It will ascend to the top of any deciduous tree, and is at home in the shadiest forest glade. This vine is dioecious, the pistillate and staminate flowers being on separate plants.

Height: 20 to 40 feet.

Exposure: Shade or sunshine.

Culture: Requires no attention.

Uses: On fences and arbors, and clambering over rocks.

Clematis: The various species of Clematis are among the most decorative and beautiful of vines. Some species are of vigorous growth and will do well under widely varying conditions, while other types are somewhat temperamental and will thrive only when their specific cultural requirements are met.

Some species of Clematis have bell-shaped or urn-shaped flowers, other species bear their blooms in panicles or loose spreading clusters, and some bear large, star-like blooms. The flowering season is long, beginning when Clematis Montana unfolds its lovely

blossoms in May and drawing to a close when the last white blooms of the large-flowered hybrid, the Duchess of Edinburgh, have shed their petals in late autumn.

Of the nearly 300 species of Clematis there are comparatively few that are widely grown, but these add grace and charm to a garden composition wherever they are used.

C. armandii: This lovely, evergreen Clematis is hardy in mild climates and is greatly valued for both its foliage and flowers wherever it can be grown. The leaves are a dark, glossy green and the glistening white, star-like flowers are borne in clusters in early spring.

Height: to 20 feet.

Exposure: Sun or light shade.

Culture: Slow in becoming established, but makes rapid growth later on. Should be trained at frequent intervals to prevent the branches from becoming tangled. It is wise to remove all branches except those desired to form a pleasant pattern.

Uses: To train over doorways, along a cornice, or to outline a gable. May also be used along fence tops if carefully trained.

C. crispa (Marsh or Curly Clematis): This lovely species is a native of the southern swamps, but is hardy in northern New York. The dainty steel-blue flowers are bell- or urn-shaped, and are borne from July to September.

Height: to 8 feet.

Exposure: Full sun or light shade.

Culture: Thrives well in ordinary soil.

Uses: On trellis, fence or stone wall.

C. lanuginosa (Woolly-leaved Clematis): Variety candida. The very large, pure-white flowers are borne in profusion throughout the summer. Of vigorous growth, and flowering over a long season, from June to September, this Clematis bears flowers of rosy-mauve flushed with bluish-purple.

Height: 6 to 15 feet.

Exposure: Full sun.

Culture: Flowers borne on new wood; can be pruned severely.

Uses: Arbor, pergola, trellis.

C. montana: This lovely, vigorous vine is completely covered with anemone-like flowers in June. The flowers are small, about 2 inches across, and are white when first open, turning to a pale pink.

C. m. Variety rubens is sometimes called the Pink-anemone Clematis, the flowers being a deep, rich pink.

Height: 10 to 15 feet.

Exposure: Full sun or light shade.

Culture: The flowers are borne on old wood produced the previous season. Very light pruning recommended.

Uses: On arbor, trellis or fence.

C. paniculata (Sweet Autumn Clematis): One of the most vigorous and fast-growing of all the Clematis. In September and October it bears an abundance of small, white, fragrant flowers which are followed by a profusion of feathery, twisted seed pods.

Height: 10 to 20 feet.

Exposure: Sun or light shade.

Culture: The flowers are produced on new growth; therefore severe pruning may be practiced.

Uses: On arbors or trellis; clambering over old stone walls.

Large-Flowered Hybrid Clematis: The most beautiful and the most widely grown of the Clematis are the large-flowered hybrids which have been developed from the various species. These lovely hybrids are both the joy and despair of many a gardener. They are so decorative that one longs to be able to grow them to perfection, yet they are fastidious in the extreme and perfection is hard to obtain.

General Cultural Requirements of Clematis

Exposure: Full sun should be provided wherever possible. Recent research has shown clematis to be in the group of plants requiring a maximum of sunlight in order to produce the fullest amount of bloom. However, when planted in very lightly shaded locations many of them will make reasonably satisfactory growth and flower well. They will not thrive in full shade or on the north side of the house where they would receive little sunlight. The location selected should be protected from strong winds.

Soil: Clematis prefers a soil which is neutral or slightly alkaline in its reaction. A test for acidity should be made, preferably before planting, and lime should be applied if it is needed (see pages 168, 170). A sandy loam well supplied with organic matter is considered ideal for clematis. Heavy loam or clay soils do not provide favorable growing conditions. Good drainage is essential.

The soil should be carefully prepared before planting. It is well to dig a hole of generous size, from 18 to 24 inches deep. If drainage is likely to be a problem a layer of gravel or rubble should be placed in the bottom. The soil which has been removed may be mixed with well decomposed leaf mold, compost, and dampened peat moss, with a little bone meal or superphosphate added to the mixture. The advisability of using manure is a debatable question. Some growers prefer not to use it, while many others make it a practice to use well-rotted cow manure if it is available, or to substitute driconure. It is generally agreed that if manure is used it should be very well rotted and should not come into direct contact with the roots at time of planting.

Planting: Autumn is considered the most favorable time for planting. It is wise to purchase plants which have been grown on their own roots, as they are considered superior to grafted plants. Most nurseries supply young, vigorous own-root plants in pots. The crown of the plant should be set from two to three inches below the level of the soil, and all plants should be watered thoroughly at the time of planting. Some type of support, such as a bamboo stake or a bit of wire mesh, must be provided immediately. It is very important that this be done at the time of planting as the stems twist and break very easily. The young plant should also be protected at the base from possible injury. A circle of small stakes may be used. A large flower-pot broken in half vertically provides an excellent protective collar.

Mulching: Regardless of its location, whether it be planted in full sun in an exposed situation or in light shade, it is essential that a clematis vine be protected at the base in order that the roots may be kept cool and moist. A mulch 2 inches in depth and extending out at least a foot from the plant is recommended. Dampened peat moss or rotting leaf mold may be used. In some cases a shallow-rooted shrub or other low-growing plants near the base of the vine will give sufficient protection.

Fertilization: In early spring a good complete fertilizer, such as a 5-10-5, may be applied at the rate of 1 tablespoonful per square foot of area and watered in well; or an application of a high-analysis, soluble fertilizer may be made. Repeat every six weeks during the growing season.

Pruning: It is wise to allow young clematis plants to become well established before any pruning is done. The amount of pruning advisable for established plants will depend upon the type. Vines that flower early on old wood produced during the previous year require only the removal of dead, weak or crowding stems. Vines which flower later on the new growth of the current season should be pruned more severely. Pruning should be done in late winter or early spring. Maintaining six to eight vigorous stems will result in an attractive vine. Unless height is desired for some special purpose, the stems should be cut back to 12 to 18 inches in order to encourage vigorous growth and more abundant bloom.

Even when killed to the ground during a particularly severe winter clematis will usually renew itself.

Support: Clematis vines require some type of support in order to prevent them from becoming a tangle of stems. The stems should be encouraged to spread out on the trellis or wire so that all parts will receive maximum sunlight and also so that a pleasant pattern may be maintained. A light trellis, a fence, a post, or wire mesh may be used very satisfactorily for support. Sometimes adjacent shrubs are used as support.

Winter Protection: In cold climates where winter protection is needed, soil, sand, peat moss or coal ashes may be mounded about the base of the plant and covered with a layer of leaves or straw.

Uses: The various clematis are among the most versatile of vines. They are lovely when trained on a trellis against the wall of a house or a patio, or when used to frame an entrance. Intermingled with not-too-rampant varieties of climbing roses on a fence they prolong the season of bloom, and when carefully trained on their own support they lend added interest to a perennial border. Planted in large pots or tubs they add distinction and charm to the planting on a patio or terrace. Such plants should be trained on bamboo stakes and the tips should be pinched out when the shoots are 2 feet high to encourage lateral branching. The soft, exquisite coloring and texture of the flowers, the delicate tracery of the stems and tendrils and the long-lasting quality of the blooms make clematis a favorite among those who delight in arranging flowers.

Common Causes of Failure:
   Too shallow planting.
   Too much shade.
   Soil that is too high in acidity.
   Soil that is too heavy and poorly drained.

VARIETIES OF MERIT

(Large-flowered Hybrids)

Comtesse de Bouchard: satiny rose to pink, gracefully curved petals.
Duchess of Edinburgh: double, white, vigorous. Blooms on old wood.
Henryi: very large, cameo-like white flowers, vigorous.
Jackmani: velvety, violet-purple flowers, very vigorous, profuse bloom.
Lord Neville: plum-purple flowers of rich texture.
Mme. Edouard André: red with purple cast, slow grower, profuse bloom.
Mme. Baron-Veillard: lilac-rose to dark lavender, long season of bloom.
Mrs. Cholmondeley: wisteria-blue, profuse bloom.
Nelly Moser: pale mauve with reddish markings.
Prins Hendrik: rich azure-blue, ruffled petals.
Ramona: lavender-blue, rapid grower, profuse bloom.

Clytostoma callistegioides (Bignonia speciosa) (B. violacea) (Violet Trumpet Vine): A half-hardy, evergreen trumpet creeper. The flowers vary from a lavender-violet to a pale purple in color and are borne in sprays at the ends of the shoots in spring and early summer. It is a strong-growing vine and needs adequate support.

Height: 20 feet.

Exposure: Sun or partial shade.

Culture: Requires no special care.

Uses: On arbors or strong trellis. May be used to frame architectural features. It should be planted where one can look up at the blossoms.

Cobea scandens (Cup-and-Saucer Vine): A perennial vine which is usually treated as an annual. Makes rapid growth and will cling to rough surfaces without support. Violet or rosy-purple, bell-shaped flowers. A white variety is also available.

Height: 20 to 30 feet.

Exposure: Full sun, and a warm exposure.

Culture: As the seeds rot easily in cold, damp soil it is best to start them indoors in pots. Seeds are hard and should be notched with a knife before sowing. Press seed edge-wise into moist soil and cover very lightly. Keep soil moist but not too wet. Do not transplant to garden until weather is warm.

Uses: As a fast-growing annual cover for walls, trellis or arbors.

Distictis lactiflora (D. Cinerea) (Vanilla-scented Trumpet Vine): This lovely, evergreen trumpet vine is, unfortunately, adapted only to mild areas, as it is injured by temperatures below 24° F. It is less rampant in habit of growth than most of the other trumpet vines and may be easily restrained with light pruning. The foliage is attractive throughout the year and the beautiful, trumpet-shaped flowers, in shades of violet, lavender and white, make the vine a thing of exceptional beauty for a period of almost eight months.

Height: 20 to 30 feet.

Exposure: Full sun and partial shade.

Culture: Judicious pruning.

Uses: To frame architectural features such as a doorway or a bay window, to train along the cornice of a house, along the edge of a patio lath roof, or along the top of a high fence.

D. Riversi (Royal Trumpet Vine): A hybrid of D. lactiflora with large leaves and flowers. The blooms are six inches long with flaring petals of royal purple with orange throat.

Dolichos Lablab (Hyacinth Bean): A perennial vine which is often treated as an annual. The flowers, resembling those of the sweet pea, range in color from purple to white and are borne on stiff stems above the broad leaves.

Height: to 10 feet.

Exposure: Sun.

Culture: May be grown readily from seed.

Uses: On small trellis or on a fence. Makes a good, quick screen.

Euonymus Fortunei:

Variety E. F. radicans: An evergreen vine of exceptional merit. Hardy, vigorous and handsome at all seasons of the year. The foliage is a fine, glossy green, and in autumn and winter the bright red berries add a note of welcome cheer to a planting composition.

Height: to 30 feet.

Exposure: Sun or partial shade.

Culture: Extremely hardy and of easy culture. Euonymus is often slow at starting but after the first year or so it makes vigorous growth. It is semi-shrubby in form and if it is desired to train it as a vine it must be given support when first planted and induced to grow upward. Otherwise it has a tendency to remain bushy. Subject to attack by oyster shell scale. (See page 626.)

Uses: Valued for its ability to cling to brick, stone and stucco walls, and it is one of the best evergreen vines for planting against the wall of house, patio or garden.

Variety E. F. vegeta: Similar to E. F. radicans in every respect with the exception that the leaves are slightly larger and the berries an orange-red. Considered by some to be superior to radicans. It also requires support until it starts to climb.

Ficus pumila (F. repens) (Creeping Fig): An excellent vine for mild climates. Clings tenaciously to bricks, stone, cement and wood. The leaves are very small and the young growing shoots make a delicate pattern on a wall.

Height: 20 feet up.

Exposure: Partial shade. Will not thrive well on south or west walls where heat is too intense.

Culture: Sometimes slow in starting to climb but when once established grows well if exposure is favorable. May be kept pruned back to any desired height or may be left to climb to the top of supporting wall.

Uses: Excellent on walls of buildings or on the foundations of a house. In the north often used in conservatories.

Gelsemium sempervirens (Carolina jessamine): A much beloved evergreen vine suited to mild climates. The leaves are a glossy green and the fragrant, tubular, yellow flowers are borne in profusion in early spring. In the south it clambers over tree trunks and is one of the glories of the woodland in springtime.

Height: 20 feet.

Exposure: Sun and partial shade.

Culture: A vine which is native to the south and adapts readily to cultivation.

Uses: On light trellis against the wall of the house; as frame for a doorway; on garden walls and fences.

Hedera:

H. canariensis (Algerian Ivy) (Canary Island Ivy): This ivy from the Canary Islands is adapted only to mild climates. It is more tolerant of hot sun than is English ivy and is therefore more satisfactory in southern areas. The leaves are more widely spaced on the stems than are those of the English ivy, and are three to five lobed, measuring from five to eight inches in width. The variety *variegata* bears leaves edged with greenish white.

H. helix (English Ivy): This sturdy, evergreen vine has many uses and is widely grown. It clings by means of aerial rootlets and the handsome, dark green, somewhat glossy foliage is attractive throughout the year when grown under favorable conditions.

Height: Will eventually reach the top of a building or tree trunk.

Exposure: Does best on a north or east wall where it is protected from too much sun. Susceptible to sunburn in winter if given a southern exposure.

Culture: An annual trimming and pruning back is advisable in order to prevent the vines from becoming too bunchy at the top.

Uses: On brick, cement and stucco walls where it clings tenaciously when once established. May also be used as a ground cover (see Chapter XVIII). English Ivy may also be used very satisfactorily as a fence or screen by weaving the shoots through a woven wire live-stock type fence. In a brief time the wire will be completely covered.

There are many varieties of English Ivy, each having distinctive characteristics of leaf form and habit of growth which make it suitable for specific uses. Among the most valuable of these varieties are:

baltica, which is noted for its hardiness. The leaves are somewhat smaller than those of the type.

conglomerata which has very closely spaced leaves, and is a slow-growing, dwarf variety. It makes a very dense, opaque hedge. When variety conglomerata ivy is trained along a low-set horizontal support it forms an unusual and attractive boundary for garden paths.

hahnii has a very dense, branching habit of growth and is effective when used as a ground cover. The foliage is a lighter green than the type.

minima, a variety with very small leaves which is used chiefly for decorative purposes indoors.

Hibbertia volubilis (Guinea Gold Vine) is an evergreen vine adapted only to frost-free areas. The foliage is a waxy, dark green and the clear yellow flowers, which are borne in profusion in late summer, resemble small single roses.

Height: 8 to 10 feet.

Exposure: Sun or partial shade.

Culture: Grows well under ordinary garden conditions.

Uses: Light trellis or on an arch over a doorway. May also be grown in a large tub or similar container.

Humulus japonicus (Japanese Hop Vine) is an annual vine which makes very rapid growth. The leaves are large and deeply lobed. The variety *variegatus* bears foliage which is streaked and blotched with creamy white.

Height: 20 to 30 feet.

Exposure: Full sun or partial shade.

Culture: Sow the seeds in open ground where they are to grow. Growth will be most luxuriant in a light, fertile soil.

Uses: As a quick screen, or on a wall or fence, being trained on wire or string.

Hydrangea petiolaris (Climbing hydrangea): This climbing form of the hydrangea, which clings by means of aerial rootlets, is a hardy, vigorous vine. The leaves are heart-shaped and the creamy flowers, which are borne in June in wide, flat clusters, are very decorative.

Height: 15 to 20 feet.

Exposure: Full sun or partial shade.

Culture: No special care.

Uses: Handsome when used against the wall of a building. Clings to stone, masonry and wood.

Ipomoea purpurea (Morning Glory): One of the most colorful and easily grown of any of the annual vines. The blooms are borne in profusion from early summer until frost. The named varieties such as Heavenly Blue,

Scarlett O'Hara, and Pearly Gates are far superior to the old-fashioned type.

Height: 10 to 15 feet.

Exposure: Full sun.

Culture: Soak or notch seeds before sowing to hasten germination. Sow where they are to flower after danger of frost is over, or start seeds early indoors in small pots or plant-bands and transplant. Will produce flowers most abundantly on soil which is not too high in nitrogen.

Uses: On arbor and trellis; trained on strings or wires against a wall; on fences of any type; clambering on stone walls.

Jasminum: All the jasminums are adapted to general garden culture.

J. mesnyi (Primrose jasmine): A strong-growing evergreen vine with long, arching branches. The bright, lemon-yellow flowers are borne from February to April.

Height: to 20 feet.

Exposure: Sun or semi-shade.

Uses: Because of the arching habit of growth best used when a cascade of foliage and flowers is desired.

J. nudiflorum (Winter jasmine): A gentle, lovely vine with slender, green willowy branches. Among the first vines to bloom, often flowering in January or February when in a protected position. The flowers are borne before the foliage unfolds.

Height: 10 to 15 feet.

Exposure: Sun or partial shade.

Uses: Carefully trained against a wall or on a trellis where it will be enjoyed for its early bloom, also lovely when allowed to cascade over a wall or bank.

J. officinale (Poet's jasmine): One of the most beloved of the jasmines with small, fragrant white flowers. Blooms throughout the summer. Not hardy where the climate is severe. Semi-evergreen.

Height: to 30 feet.

Exposure: Sun or partial shade.

Uses: On trellis, arbor or pergola.

J. o. grandiflora, known as Spanish jasmine, is an improved variety of officinale with very fragrant, larger flowers.

J. Stephanense: This semi-evergreen hybrid form is a vigorous vine bearing fragrant, pale-pink flowers in terminal clusters. Hardy in mild climates.

Height: to 20 feet.

Exposure: Sun or semi-shade.

Uses: On trellis, arbor or fence.

Lonicera (Honeysuckle)

L. heckrottii, Variety Gold Flame: A deciduous honeysuckle of vigorous growth. The fragrant flowers are borne in profusion from spring until autumn. The blooms are tubular in form, cream-white within and pink to rose on the outside. This is a variety which is widely grown in the Pacific Northwest.

Height: to 15 feet.

Exposure: Sun or partial shade.

Culture: Adaptable.

Uses: On trellis and arbor.

L. hildebrandtiana (Giant Burmese Honeysuckle): An evergreen fast-growing honeysuckle adapted to mild climates. The foliage is a dark, glossy green. The very long, tubular flowers are creamy white, changing to yellow.

Height: 20 to 25 feet.

Exposure: Full sun.

Culture: Adaptable.

Uses: On trellis or arbor.

L. japonica chinensis (L. Chinensis) (Purple Japanese Honeysuckle): A fast-growing, semi-evergreen honeysuckle. The fragrant, tubular flowers are borne in pairs, and are white inside and purplish on the outer side.

Height: to 30 feet.

Exposure: Full sun.

Culture: Adaptable.

Uses: On trellis or arbor.

L. japonica Halliana (Hall's Climbing Honeysuckle): An evergreen to semi-evergreen honeysuckle of rampant growth. Leaves deep green. The axillary flowers are borne in pairs and are white at first, changing to yellow as they mature. The flowers are fragrant and are in almost continuous bloom throughout the summer.

Height: to 30 feet or more.

Exposure: Full sun or partial to dense shade.

Culture: A rampant grower and *must* be kept within bounds.

Uses: On trellis or arbor; as a cover on rough banks.

Caution: When left undisturbed this honeysuckle is capable of making a wild tangle and of smothering or strangling anything with which it comes in contact. See page 601 for measures of control and eradication.

L. sempervirens (Scarlet Trumpet Honeysuckle): This is one of the most showy and most desirable of the honeysuckles. It is semi-evergreen. The scarlet flowers have very long tubes and are borne in long clusters of six. The flowers are not fragrant. The period of bloom lasts from May to August.

Height: 15 feet.

Exposure: Full sun or light shade.

Culture: Subject to attacks of aphids and requires spraying for protection.

Uses: On trellis or arbor.

Mandevilla suaveolens (Chilean Jasmine): A vine of rapid growth adapted to mild climates. The leaves are heart-shaped and the wide-flaring, trumpet-shaped white flowers are borne in clusters. The blooms are very fragrant and are produced in profusion throughout the summer months.

Height: 15 feet.

Exposure: Full sun.

Culture: No specific requirements.

Uses: Should be planted where the gardenia-like fragrances will be enjoyed.

Pandorea jasminoides (Bignonia Jasminoides): A fast-growing vine reaching considerable height and providing an interesting foliage effect. The flowers, which are borne in clusters, are white with red throats and have the appearance of frilled tubes. The flowering period extends from late summer through early autumn. There is a rose-colored form, variety *rosea*.

Height: Up to 30 feet.

Exposure: Sun or partial shade.

Culture: Adapted to ordinary garden conditions.

Uses: On walls and sturdy arbors.

Parthenocissus:

P. quinquefolia (Ampelopsis Quinquefolia) Virginia Creeper: Is a well-known native vine, which clambers over stone walls and fences, clinging by rootlets with disk-like ends. This special equipment for climbing, which is really a modified fruit cluster, enables it to ascend masonry walls as readily as does English Ivy. It has been much used since colonial times. Its compound leaves make a beautiful pattern and turn a brilliant crimson in the autumn. The bluish-black fruit ripens in September. It is a very useful foliage plant, grows well in shade or sun, is hardy as far north as Ottawa and is a common native from Maine to Florida.

Height: to 30 feet.

Exposure: Full sun, partial or deep shade.

Culture: Prune in early spring if it is necessary to keep it within restricted bounds.

Uses: On masonry walls, on arbors and fences, as a ground cover, clambering over old stone walls in a natural setting.

P. q. engelmannii: Leaves much smaller and foliage more dense than P. quinquefolia.

P. Tricuspidata (Ampelopsis Tricuspidata) (Boston Ivy) Japanese Creeper: This is one of the strongest and most rapidly growing of vines, being able to completely cover the entire façade of a large building within a few years. The leaves are large, with long petioles. It clings tenaciously to almost any surface and makes a very dense pattern on a wall. The foliage turns a brilliant color in the autumn.

P. t. Lowii: Foliage is small and deeply lobed.

P. t. Veitchii (small-leaved Boston Ivy): A more desirable form than P. tricuspidata. Makes a more attractive pattern and has the ability to cling to even the smoothest surface.

Height: 30 feet and up.

Exposure: Full sun and partial shade.

Culture: Vigorous, and needs little care.

Uses: Where the complete coverage of a stone, stucco or brick wall is desired few vines can compare with Boston Ivy.

Passiflora (Passion Vine):

P. alato-caerulea (P. Pfordtii): One of the hardiest of the passion vines. The flowers are white, shaded with pink and lavender, the crown being a deep blue or purple. The blooms are fragrant and are borne throughout the summer.

P. incarnata (Maypop Passion Flower): Adapted to mild climates. Flowers small, white with purple crown. Bears yellow fruits which are edible.

P. manicata (Red Passion Flower): Adapted only to frost-free areas. The flowers are most spectacular when in bloom, being a vivid scarlet with a blue crown.

P. mollissima (Softleaf Passion Flower): Suitable only for mild, frost-free areas. The flowers are a beautiful, clear rose-pink.

Height: 12 to 30 feet.

Exposure: Full sun.

Culture: Prune severely after the second year. Provide ample water during growing season.

Phaseolus coccineus (Scarlet Runner Bean): A fast-growing, colorful annual vine bearing brilliant, scarlet blossoms throughout the summer. The young beans are edible in the green stage.

Height: 10 to 12 feet.

Exposure: Full sun.

Culture: Abundant moisture, soil of fair fertility. Sow seed in open ground.

Uses: Trained on strings or wire against a wall or fence; or on a light trellis or arbor.

Plumbago capensis (Cape Plumbago): A shrub, adapted to mild climates, which may be readily trained as a vine. The flowers are a soft, powder blue and are borne throughout the summer in phlox-like clusters.

Height: May be trained to a height of about 12 feet.

Exposure: Full sun or partial shade.

Culture: Requires adequate support. Suckers should be removed in order to encourage the growth of the main stem.

Uses: Trained on a trellis against a wall or on a fence it is a gentle, lovely thing and a pleasant foil for flowers of brighter hue.

Polygonum Auberti (Chinese Fleece Vine) (Silver Lace Vine): A rapidly growing vine which blooms abundantly for a long period. In general disposition it resembles Clematis paniculata. The flowers are cream-white and are borne in long, thread-like panicles which completely cover the top of the vine. It is prolific in the production of seedlings which spring up everywhere, and should be planted only where its vigorous growth will not become a threat to other plants.

Height: Will reach the top of almost any structure.

Culture: Water thoroughly during the blooming season. Its growth may be restrained by severe pruning.

Uses: On trellis against a wall, on fence, and on arbors. It does extremely well under adverse city conditions.

Quamoclit pennata (Cypress Vine): A dainty, annual vine of rapid growth. The foliage is fern-like and the small tubular flowers come in shades of orange, scarlet and white and resemble a star.

Height: 10 to 20 feet.

Exposure: Full sun or partial shade.

Culture: Seeds should be notched or soaked in warm water to hasten germination. They may be sown in the open ground when the soil is warm, or may be started indoors in pots and transplanted later.

Uses: Against a wall or on trellis or arbor, being trained on string or wire.

Stephanotis floribunda (Madagascar Jasmine): A beautiful evergreen vine suited to frost-free areas. The leaves are a deep, glossy green and the fragrant, white, funnel-shaped flowers are borne in loose, open clusters.

Height: 10 to 15 feet.

Exposure: Full sun.

Culture: Ordinary garden conditions.

Uses: Trained against a wall or fence. Should be planted where the fragrance and beauty of the flowers can be enjoyed.

Tecomaria capensis (Tecoma Capensis) (Cape Honeysuckle): An evergreen vine adapted to mild climates. The foliage is a dark, glistening green which forms a pleasant background for the brilliant orange-red, tubular blossoms which are borne in clusters. The flowering period extends throughout the winter months.

Height: 15 to 25 feet.

Exposure: Full sun.

Uses: Trained against a wall or fence. Very effective when espaliered. Will form a casade over a bank or low wall.

Thunbergia grandiflora (Sky Flower): A beautiful vine adapted to frost-free areas and to *very* protected locations in mild climates. The leaves are heart-shaped and the lovely, flaring, tubular flowers, which are borne in clusters, are a delicate blue in color. The period of bloom covers many months and the flowers are borne in great profusion.

Height: When unrestrained reaches a considerable height.

Exposure: Full sun.

Culture: A vine of vigorous habit which requires little care except pruning to keep it within bounds or to train it as desired.

Uses: Against the wall of a building where it can be trained along the cornice or to outline a gable or frame a doorway. Can be used very effectively along the edge of a lath shelter over an outdoor recreation area.

Trachelospermum jasminoides (Rhynchospermum Jasminoides) (Star Jasmine): A lovely, evergreen vine adapted to mild climates. The leaves are a glossy, deep green and make a pleasant background for the clusters of small, white, starry flowers which are very fragrant.

Height: Up to 20 feet.

Exposure: Full sun or partial shade.

Culture: Requires good support and should be trained on heavy string or wire.

Uses: On walls, fences, trellis, posts and arbors. Also frequently used as a ground cover.

Wisteria: The Wisterias are superbly beautiful vines with great, hanging panicles of lavender-purple flowers which are borne in profusion during the spring. The vine is hardy, vigorous and high-climbing and is remarkably long-lived.

W. floribunda (Japanese Wisteria): This species blooms somewhat later than W. sinensis, and thus extends the season of bloom for the Wisterias. There is a white form and a variety *W. floribunda macrobotrys* (W. f. multijuga) which bears exceptionally long flower clusters, sometimes as much as three feet in length.

W. sinensis (W. chinensis) (Chinese Wisteria): This species from China is the one which is most widely planted. The flowers are of exquisite beauty and are slightly fragrant. There is a white variety, W. s. alba.

Height: Wisteria will climb to almost any height, to the top of any support or to the top of the tallest tree.

Exposure: Full sun or partial shade.

Culture: It is essential that Wisteria have a strong support and that it be kept within bounds. When planted on the wall of a building it should preferably have a metal support. Because Wisteria has such great vitality and so easily outgrows its situation it should be pruned back severely every year. This pruning will induce it to bloom more abundantly and will also restrain the venturesome stems before they do any damage to shutters, cornice or roof. It is imperative that the pruning be done every year. If it is omitted, up the vine goes, over the roof, working its way under shingles and gutters and the contest is on. But because of the beauty of its bloom Wisteria is more than deserving of this annual care. Pruning should preferably be done after the blooming season and before the growth of new wood. And one should also be watchful to see that no side runners are sent out by the parent trunk at the base.

Vines which have failed to bloom should be pruned during the summer, reducing new growth to about six buds.

As the tendency to produce abundant bloom seems to be an inherited characteristic, it is wise, when purchasing plants which have been produced from cuttings, to make sure that they have come from freely-blooming vines. Grafted plants, produced from scions taken from heavy-blooming plants, are apt to bloom at an earlier age than plants grown from cuttings.

Uses: On walls of buildings, adequate support being necessary; on stoutly constructed arbors and pergolas.

Caution: Wisteria may become a very serious problem if allowed to get out of bounds. See page 602 for measures of control.

VINES FOR MILD CLIMATES

Allamanda cathartica
Antigonon leptopus (Queen's Wreath, Coral Vine, Rosa de Montana)
Beaumontia grandiflora (Easter Lily Vine, Herald Trumpet)
Bougainvillea
Clytostoma callistegioides (Violet Trumpet Vine)
Distictis lactiflora (Vanilla-scented Trumpet Vine)
Ficus pumila (F. repens) (Creeping Fig)
Hibbertia volubilis
Jasmine
   J. Mesnyi (Primrose jasmine)
   J. nudiflorum (Winter jasmine)
   J. officinale (Poet's jasmine)
   J. o. grandiflorum (Spanish jasmine)
   J. stephanense
Mandevilla suaveolens (Chilean jasmine)
Passiflora manicata (Red Passion Flower)
Passiflora mollissima (Soft-leaf Passion Vine)
Stephanotis floribunda (Madagascar jasmine)
Thunbergia grandiflora (Sky Flower)
Trachelospermum jasminoides (Star jasmine)

ANNUAL VINES

(including perennials usually treated as annuals)

Calonyction aculeatum (Moonflower)
Cobea scandens (Cup and Saucer Vine)
Dolichos Lablab (Hyacinth Bean)

Humulus japonicus (Japanese Hop Vine)
Ipomea purpurea (Morning Glory)
Phaseolus coccineus (Scarlet Runner Bean)

VINES FOR CITY CONDITIONS

Calonyction aculeatum (Moonflower)
Cobea scandens (Cup and Saucer Vine)
Hedera Helix (English Ivy)
Humulus japonicus (Japanese Hop Vine)
Parthenocissus tricuspidata (Boston Ivy)
Phaseolus coccineus (Scarlet Runner Bean)
Polygonum Auberti (Chinese Fleece Vine, Silver Lace Vine)
Quamoclit pennata (Cypress Vine)
Wisteria

VINES SUITABLE FOR ESPALIER EFFECT

Beaumontia grandiflora (Easter Lily Vine, Herald Trumpet)
Bougainvillea
Pyracantha coccinea (Firethorn)
Tecomaria capensis (Cape Honeysuckle)

EVERGREEN VINES

Allamanda cathartica
Antigonon leptopus (Queen's Wreath, Coral Vine)
Beaumontia grandiflora (Easter Lily Vine, Herald Trumpet)
Bougainvillea
Clytostoma callistegioides (Violet Trumpet Vine)
Distictis lactiflora (Vanilla-scented Trumpet Vine)
Euonymus radicans (Winter Creeper)
Hedera canariensis (Algerian Ivy)
Hedera Helix (English Ivy)
Hibbertia volubilis (Guinea Gold Vine)
Jasmine Mesnyi (Primrose jasmine)
Pyracantha coccinea (Firethorn)
Stephanotis floribunda (Madagascar jasmine)
Trachelospermum jasminoides (Star jasmine)

XXII

HEDGES

THE hedgerow has been a familiar feature of the landscape in Europe since mediæval times. But the hedge antedates the mediæval garden. The ancient Romans used hedges of myrtle, laurel, and box in their gardens. Indeed so important a feature was the hedge in gardens of this period that the gardeners who cared for it and kept it faithfully trimmed to the desired form and height were given the dignity of a special title, being known as "topiarius."

The designers of the Italian villas used hedges of ilex and cypress as great walls of green and made them architecturally important components of the design. The French gave the hedge greater scale to conform to their vast plaisances by using large trees such as elm, linden, hornbeam and beech, trimming them to vertical form. In England hedges played an important part in the design of the "knott" gardens, laid out in geometric patterns. Sometimes the spaces within the hedges were flower beds, but more often they were bits of turf. Herb gardens were frequently designed in this style, each plot being planted to a single herb, and the whole forming a pleasing pattern. In the gardens which surround the Elizabethan manor houses of England, there are magnificent yew hedges which were planted more than four hundred years ago and which have been carefully tended throughout the years.

The primary purpose of a hedge is protection. Another purpose is shelter from the wind, and the third is enclosure. In landscape design, the hedge is one of the best means of enclosing a formal area and separating it from the outer world. But not only does a hedge enclose and frame the garden; it may also be used to frame the vistas within the garden and to provide a background for flowering plants. It would be difficult indeed to find a more satisfactory background for masses of bright flowers than the deep green of an evergreen hedge. The colors of the blossoms are contrasted effectively with the dark green of the background. The hedge is interesting enough in texture, but is not conspicuous or obtrusive.

Furthermore, a hedge has the great attribute of permanence. It fixes the major lines of the design. It establishes the background for the garden, against which the succession of color and mass moves in ever-changing sequence. The hedge is not changeless in itself, but it grows in a slower cycle, and thereby imparts an air of stability to the scene—invites confidence. By its continued existence it links the past with the present. There is the hedge. Season after season the flowers come and go. Generation after generation those who care for the garden come and go—but the hedge remains.

Types of Hedges

Hedges vary in size from small edging plants hardly a foot in height to towering trees. They may be extremely formal in outline, being trimmed to even surfaces and regular lines, or they may be natural in growth, with billowing masses of foliage and a profusion of flowers. Every kind has its particular adaptation.

The width of a hedge is something not always easy to predict. Theoretically, most hedges can be kept at any desired dimension of height or width. In actual practice it is not possible to do this, for the plants must be allowed to make some growth each year or they will suffer both in vigor and in appearance. It is essential that adequate space be allowed for the eventual spread of the hedge. One occasionally sees box hedges, planted originally beside the garden paths as edgings of the flower beds, which have grown so wide that they entirely close the path.

Hedge materials may be derived from many sources; from deciduous trees of naturally thick growth, branching close to the ground; from evergreen trees which have a fine texture and closely massed foliage; from deciduous shrubs which have dense foliage and which make vigorous growth; from evergreen shrubs; from herbs; and from vines which may be trained to grow on a frame of any desired shape. In order to be satisfactory as a hedge plant a tree or shrub must meet certain very definite requirements. It must possess thick foliage of fine texture, it must be capable of even growth, it must produce branches and foliage close to the ground, and, in the case of trimmed, formal hedges, it must have the ability to withstand cutting.

Planting

As the roots of hedge plants are bound to be restricted, it is important to have the soil well prepared before planting is done. To soil of average fertility the addition of manure at the rate of 1 ton to 200 linear feet is recommended. Since hedge plants are to form a dense wall of green, the individual plants should grow so closely that they are not distinguishable in the general mass. The plants are, therefore, set much more closely than they would be in the usual shrubbery border. There should be good light and air on each side of the hedge in order to make up for this deficiency in the interior of the hedge. A hedge which is placed too close to a wall not only looks out of place but seldom does well. Hedges under trees are rarely satisfactory. The root system of a hedge is necessarily crowded. When to this handicap is added the competition of tree roots, it is impossible to obtain vigorous growth and development. We have frequent examples of this in the case of privet hedges which thrive well in the open but which become weak and spindly at the point where they pass under trees. A few hedge plants such as Taxus cuspidata and Ilex glabra are exceptions, and thrive reasonably well under the shade of trees.

In order to increase the density of the growth, hedges are sometimes planted in double rows, the plants being either staggered or paired. The advantages to be gained are somewhat doubtful and a single row is usually adequate.

When planting, the trench should be opened to a depth approximately equal to the depth of the balls of earth, or, in the case of plants which are not balled, to the depth of the root system. After the plants have been spaced in the trench each individual plant should be adjusted for depth and the earth should be filled in about the plants, as in any planting operation. A tape stretching along the side of the trench will aid in the correct spacing of the plants. Care should be taken to see that the plants are in an absolutely vertical position and in line with each other. The usual watering and trimming should follow planting.

Protection Against Encroaching Roots

Some of the more vigorous hedge plants have root systems which reach out long distances in search of the nourishment they require to maintain their rapid growth and abundant foliage. Privet is one of the most greedy in this respect, and for this reason it is a bad neighbor for the flower border. The bush honeysuckles, the viburnums and the lilacs are also greedy feeders. If close proximity of such hedges to flower beds is unavoidable, then it is wise to interpose a barrier between them. One device is to dig a trench along the garden side of the hedge 18 inches deep and as wide as the spade. Fill the trench with rocks and a lean mixture of cement, about one part cement, three parts sand, and five parts coarse aggregate (gravel or crushed stone). This will keep the roots from intruding into the garden, but it will be necessary to watch for surface roots hurdling over the wall. A modification of this scheme possible on sloping land is to have the garden on ground higher than that outside and in this case the wall becomes a retaining wall, with its foundation below the frost line. The same results could be obtained from burying sheet zinc in a vertical plane parallel to the hedge.

No precaution need be taken against the roots of box, arborvitæ, or red cedar because these roots are confined closely under the tree in a dense mat. Hemlock roots are a little more rangy but are not very damaging to other plants. A separation of 3 feet of space (path or turf), will be enough protection against hemlock roots.

Care

Untrimmed hedges require no more care than any ordinary planting of the same material. A hedge that is to be trained to a certain form, however, requires periodic care. Formal hedges should have one clipping or more each year, depending upon the type of material which has been used. Yew, arborvitæ and hemlock may be kept in excellent condition with one trimming a year, although two clippings are sometimes given. Privet should have three or four clippings a season, being trimmed whenever it has outgrown its prescribed size. Box and lilacs require but one clipping; beech one clipping—never more. The purpose of trimming is to keep the hedge thick and neat and within bounds. Sometimes an informal hedge may be trimmed lightly to help thicken the mass of foliage. For most evergreen hedges the best season of the year is spring, before new growth starts. But because this is a very busy time for gardeners summer trimming is often resorted to and the results are entirely satisfactory. In this case trimming is done after growth has practically ceased. Lilac hedges should be trimmed in June; box hedges in August. The only tool necessary for the clipping of a small hedge is a pair of shears with long blades and handles. The type with the handles placed at an angle with the blades is the most desirable as it enables the worker to reach the lower parts of the plant without undue bending. There are a number of excellent mechanical hedge trimmers on the market which are of great value if extensive hedges are to be kept trimmed. The blades are set in a series, cutting much as do the blades of a hay

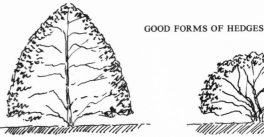

GOOD FORMS OF HEDGES

Hemlock
White Pine
Japanese Yew

Mugo Pine
Japanese Barberry

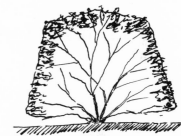

Beech and
Hornbeam

Spreading form
of Japanese Yew

Privet, best form

mower, and the work can be done rapidly and efficiently. Ladders on wheels are a great aid in clipping high hedges and are used extensively on English estates where the trimming of old yew hedges and trees is one of the important seasonal jobs. The wheel type of ladder is so convenient a piece of equipment for a variety

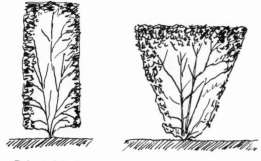

*Privet, fair form, but
it easily becomes the
next type with sparse
lower branches.*

*Privet, poor form,
because the lower
branches, deprived of
light, become sparse.*

HEDGE FORMS WHICH ARE NOT SATISFACTORY.

of garden operations that it seems strange that it is so rarely used in this country.

Hedges of regular and geometric outline require more frequent clipping than the more simple forms. Nothing gives a garden an appearance of neglect more quickly than a formal hedge in the stages of reverting to the wild. The trimming of hedges into definite forms and shapes requires endless patience and no little practice. Topiary work has never been as popular here in this country as it has been in France and England. Perhaps it is that we have not patience enough, or perhaps it is that even our formal estates are not so formal as to require this extreme expression of the dominance of will power over nature.

The general care of hedge plants does not differ appreciably from the usual routine. An occasional cultivation is beneficial and prevents the intrusion of large weeds or encroaching trees. Nothing spoils the beauty of a hedge more surely than seedling trees which have been allowed to grow up beside it, or within it. At first they are unnoticed. Then by the time they are well above the top of the hedge they are difficult to remove, and their removal leaves an unsightly gap in the hedge.

The yearly application of a complete fertilizer is one of the best means of promoting vigor and growth. A mulch of manure applied in the autumn will not only increase the fertility of the soil but will give protection to the roots during the winter. Box hedges respond remarkably well to an application of humus. This should be worked into the soil along the two sides of the hedge just outside the root ends. In order to rejuvenate an old box hedge which has suffered from neglect, the soil should be trenched along each side of the hedge, at the outer edge of the roots. The soil should be removed to a depth of about 15 inches and the trench should be refilled with a mixture of humus and top-soil. The amount of humus will depend upon the quantity available; any proportion up to one part humus to one part top-soil will be satisfactory—the more humus the better.

If a box hedge has been killed to the ground by an unusually severe winter, do not make the mistake of having it dug up. Cut it back to stubs about 3 inches high and wait. Box has wonderful vitality and often has the power to recuperate, if given a chance. This salvaging job should be done early in the spring before the rush of spring work begins. If it is not done then it will probably be postponed until summer and in the meantime the box, in trying to regain life, will send its sap feebly into all the twigs instead of concentrating its efforts on a few adventitious buds at the end of the stubs. The same treatment will often save a privet hedge which has been injured by severe cold.

The Use of Growth Inhibitors

The chemical, Maleic Hydrazide, known as MH, has come into use within recent years as a growth inhibitor, and has proved a great boon to gardeners who are faced with the problem of keeping hedges properly pruned. At best, hedge pruning is a tedious operation, whether it is done with hand shears or with electric hedge shears.

By spraying hedges of certain types with Maleic Hydrazide the number of prunings required during the season can be substantially reduced. Privet and pyracantha hedges have been successfully treated in this way. A hedge of California privet at the New York Botanical Garden which was sprayed early in June, and again three weeks later, with a 0.5 percent solution of Maleic Hydrazide (one ounce of the proprietary compound put out under the trade name of "Slo-Gro" in two quarts of water) required only one clipping during the remainder of the season.

HEDGE PLANTS OF MERIT

Abelia grandiflora makes an excellent, graceful hedge, which is evergreen in mild climates but deciduous in the North. The leaves are glossy and the small, pale pink, tubular flowers are borne almost continuously throughout the summer and fall. It should not be trimmed, but be allowed to maintain its natural grace. Height 6 to 8 feet. Spacing of plants, 4 feet.

Berberis mentorensis, a semi-evergreen, hybrid barberry which has dark green leaves and a dense habit of growth. It is very adaptable, being tolerant of heat and dry conditions, and from Baltimore southward it is evergreen. Height 6 feet. Spacing of plants, 2½ feet.

Berberis thunbergi is one of the old reliable hedge plants. It is hardy, stands exposure well, and because of its thorns it affords good protection against intruding animals. As a hedge it forms a dense foliage mass close to the ground. In autumn the foliage has beautiful tones of orange, red and yellow and the bright red berries hang among the gray twigs well into the winter. It can be maintained at any desired height but naturally reaches a height of about 5 feet. Spacing of plants, 3 feet.

Berberis thunbergi minor is a dwarf form, 2 feet high, but similar to the species in all other respects. Spacing of plants, 2 feet.

Buxus sempervirens suffruticosa is the boxwood of antiquity and of English and colonial gardens, and makes one of the most satisfactory hedges. Dense, but gracefully irregular, and with foliage close to the ground, boxwood makes an excellent hedge for bordering paths and terraces or as a background in the flower garden. Boxwood hedges may be trimmed to exact lines, or left to develop their picturesque, undulating surfaces. The rate of growth is hardly more than one inch a year in the North, but more than twice this in the South where it is so generally used that it has become almost a symbol of the stability and charm of those ancestral homes. Many a box hedge in the South was planted before the Revolution and has been kept to low proportions by careful trimming or by being cut down to short stumps about every 30 years and allowed to grow up again. The "sempervirens" in the name means that it lives always. Its northern limit of hardiness is Zone VI. A few old hedges in Massachusetts have survived 75 winters by being protected each year. Height 6 feet. Spacing of plants, 2 feet. In Zone V Buxus microphylla Koreana, a true dwarf type, is a good substitute.

Cotoneaster divaricata is a wide-spreading, dense shrub which will form a compact hedge when trimmed, and it can be kept at any desired height. The leaves are small, oval and a lustrous dark green, and in the autumn it is bright with small, red berries. Height, 6 feet. Spacing of plants, 2½ feet.

Euonymus alatus compactus is a dwarf form of the winged Euonymus. Its great glory is its brilliant crimson autumn color and its scarlet fruits. It is deciduous but forms a dense hedge and even in winter the thick twigs give it a special solidity. Height 5 feet. Spacing of plants, 3 feet.

Ilex crenata convexa makes a fine, evergreen hedge. It is a low shrub with leaves convex on the upper surface, and it is compact and dense in habit of growth. It will need an annual trimming back of the more vigorous branches, but it will maintain itself without further attention for years. Height 5 feet. Spacing of plants, 2 feet.

Ilex crenata microphylla is one of the best varieties of the Japanese holly for use as a hedge. With careful pruning it forms a dense, evergreen hedge with foliage close to the ground. It is slow growing but it lives for many years and improves with age. It reaches an ultimate height of about 20 feet and can easily be maintained at any desired height. Spacing of plants, 3½ feet.

Laurus nobilis (Grecian Laurel). This tree of classic poetry is an evergreen shrub or small tree. Slow in growth, its leaves make a dense wall, and its tapering form and upright growth provide an ascending screen. It may be sheared into formal outlines. It reaches an eventual height of about 30 feet but may be maintained at any desired height by judicious pruning. It is widely used in the Pacific Northwest. Spacing of plants, 4 feet.

Ligustrum sinense is one of the best of the privets. It remains evergreen in most winters in Zone VII and is definitely evergreen farther south. Less rapid in growth than other privets, it forms a dense hedge, and can be trimmed to formal lines, with leaves right down to the ground. May be maintained at any desired height. Ultimate height 12 feet. Spacing of plants, 3 feet.

Pittosporum tobira (Japanese Pittosporum), is an evergreen shrub which makes an interesting hedge. Although it is not agreeable to shearing it will form untrimmed hedges up to 15 feet, and by selective cutting of branches it can be kept to a lower height. Suited to California and the South. Height 15 feet. Spacing of plants, 4 feet.

Pyracantha coccinea (Firethorn), is a useful and versatile evergreen shrub closely related to the hawthorns. It is notable for its generous clusters of orange-vermilion fruits which hang on all autumn. Because it is not discouraged by severe pruning and because of its evergreen foliage it will form a dense hedge. It is widespreading in habit of growth and requires plenty of space. It should not be used where a narrow hedge is desired, but where it can develop its natural form it makes a magnificent hedge. Height 10 feet. Spacing of plants, 4 feet. It will require a little annual pruning and possibly some spraying against scale.

Sarcococca hookeriana humilis, a very choice, dwarf, evergreen shrub related to the boxwood, which can be trained into an attractive hedge. The dark green, narrow, tapering leaves make solid masses of foliage close to the ground. It is at home in continuous shade and partial shade, but it will be scorched on a sunny bank. Height: Often only 1½ feet high, it can grow to 4 feet. Spacing of plants, 15 inches.

Spiræa Vanhouttei is one of the best shrubs for an informal flowering hedge. It is best not to prune it at all, because any cutting back will spoil the effect of the graceful, arching branches. Covered with small clusters

of white flowers in May, it is a gay background for flowers or may be used as a border for the lawn. Height 9 feet. Spacing of plants, 4 feet.

Taxus canadensis stricta is a variety of the Canadian yew. Its upright branches and rich green needle-like foliage make it appropriate for low hedges. It is very hardy, being at home in Zone II. It may be clipped, but it is more interesting in its natural form. Height: usually 3 feet high, occasionally 5 feet. Spacing of plants, 12 to 15 inches.

Taxus media Hatfieldi is a hybrid yew with upright branches and radially-spreading needles. Its dark green foliage is an excellent background for bright flowers, and its columnar form makes it adaptable for a hedge in a narrow space. Height 6 feet. Spacing of plants, 2½ feet.

Thuya occidentalis (American arborvitae), is the old and trusted hedge plant used ever since the early settlers first domesticated it. Hardy, persistent, slow-growing, it has an air of serenity. Old hedges of 100 years or more and 30 feet in height still persist in New England and elsewhere. Height 60 feet at maturity. Spacing of plants, 4 feet.

Thuya occidentalis pyramidalis is a narrower form, equally lovely in texture. Spacing of plants, 3 or 4 feet.

Tsuga canadensis (American hemlock), makes an excellent dense hedge. It should be sheared only lightly in order to thicken the foliage, but not deeply enough to discourage growth. Old hedges 20 feet high have remained in excellent condition for years. Once established it can be kept at any desired height above 8 to 10 feet, but for low hedges some other plant should be chosen. Height 100 feet. Spacing of plants, 4 feet.

HEDGE MATERIAL

EVERGREEN TREES

SCIENTIFIC NAME	COMMON NAME	SUITABLE FOR CLIPPED OR UNCLIPPED HEDGE	EVENTUAL HEIGHT	MINIMUM HEIGHT BY TRIMMING	SPACING
Chamæcyparis obtusa	Hinoki Cypress	C & U	20′	8′	2–3′
obtusa Crippsii	Cripps Golden Cypress	C & U	20′	8′	2–3′
obtusa gracilis	Slender Hinoki Cypress	C & U	12′	6′	2–2½′
pisifera	Sawara Cypress	C & U	30′	6′	2–3′
pisifera plumosa	Plume Cypress	C & U	30′	5′	2–3′
pisifera squarrosa	Moss Cypress	C & U	20′	5′	2–3′
Lawsoniana	Lawson Cypress	U	30′		2–3′
Ilex Aquifolium	English Holly	U	8′		2–2½′
opaca	American Holly	C & U	8′	4′	2–2½′

SCIENTIFIC NAME	COMMON NAME	SUITABLE FOR CLIPPED OR UNCLIPPED HEDGE	EVENTUAL HEIGHT	MINIMUM HEIGHT BY TRIMMING	SPACING
Juniperus virginiana	Red Cedar	C & U	25'	6'	2½–3'
v. Canærtii	Cannart Red Cedar	C & U	25'	6'	2½–3'
v. glauca	Silver Red Cedar	C & U	20'	6'	2½–3'
excelsa stricta	Greek Juniper	U	12'		2½–3'
chinensis Pfitzeriana	Pfitzer's Juniper	C & U	8'	4'	3–4'
chinensis pyramidalis	Columnar Chinese Juniper	U	20'		2–3'
Laurus nobilis	Grecian Laurel	C	40'	6'	4'
Picea excelsa (P. abies)	Norway Spruce	C & U	30'	6'	3'
alba (P. glauca)	Canadian Spruce	U	30'		3'
Pinus Strobus	White Pine	C & U	40'	10'	3–6'
sylvestris	Scots Pine	U	20'		3–5'
thunbergi	Japanese Black Pine	U	40'		3–6'
Pseudotsuga Douglasii	Douglas Fir	U	30'		3–5'
Taxus baccata	English Yew	C & U	20'	10'	3–5'
cuspidata	Japanese Yew	C & U	12'	4'	2½–4'
cus. fastigiata		C & U	12'	5'	2–3'
cus. capitata		C & U	20'	8'	2–3'
media Hicksii		U	8'		2–2½'
Thuya occidentalis	American Arborvitæ	C & U	30'	8'	2–3'
occ. Wareana	Siberian Arborvitæ	C & U	30'	8'	2–3'
occ. Douglasii		C & U	20'	8'	2–3'
occ. pyramidalis		C & U	20'	8'	2–2½'
orientalis	Chinese Arborvitæ	C & U	25'	8'	2–3'
orientalis elegantissima		C & U	25'	8'	2–3'
Tsuga canadensis	Canada Hemlock	C & U	30'	10'	3–4'
caroliniana	Carolina Hemlock	C & U	30'	10'	3–4'

EVERGREEN SHRUBS AND DWARF EVERGREEN TREES

SCIENTIFIC NAME	COMMON NAME	SUITABLE FOR CLIPPED OR UNCLIPPED HEDGE	EVENTUAL HEIGHT	MINIMUM HEIGHT BY TRIMMING	SPACING
Berberis Julianæ	Barberry	C & U	6'	3'	2'
verruculosa		C & U	3'	2'	1½'
Buxus semp. suffruticosa	Dwarf Box	C & U	6–8'	1½'	6"–1½'
Chamæcyparis obtusa nana	Dwarf Cypress	C & U	10'	2½'	1½–2'
obt. compacta		C & U	6'	3'	1½–2'
Euonymus radicans		C & U	4'		2–2½'
rad. minimus (kewensis)		C & U	3'		1½'
rad. vegetus		C & U	5'		2–2½'
Ilex crenata	Japanese Holly	U	8'		2'
c. convexa		C & U	4'	2'	1–2½'
c. microphylla		C & U	6'	2½'	1–2'
c. latifolia		U	8'		2–2½'
Juniperus depressa plumosa		C & U	4'	2'	2½–3½'
Lonicera nitida	Evergreen Honeysuckle	C & U	5'	1½'	15–21"
Picea excelsa Maxwellii	Dwarf Norway Spruce	U	2½'		1', less
Pinus montana Mugo	Mugo Pine	C & U	10'	4'	2–4'
Pittosporum tobira		C	12'	6'	4'
Pyracantha coccinea	Firethorn	C	12'	4'	3'
Taxus canadensis stricta		C & U	3'	1'	1½'
baccata repandens	Dwarf English Yew	U	3'		2'
cuspidata brevifolia	Dwarf Japanese Yew	C & U	6'	2'	1¼–2'
cuspidata densa		C & U	4'	2'	1¼–2'
Teucrium chamædrys		C & U	1'		1½'
Thuya occidentalis Hoveyi		C & U	6'	4'	2–3'
occidentalis Reidii		C & U	6'	3'	1½–2½'
orientalis Sieboldii (T. orien. compacta)		C & U	5'	3'	2–3'

HEDGE MATERIAL—continued

SCIENTIFIC NAME	COMMON NAME	SUITABLE FOR CLIPPED OR UNCLIPPED HEDGE	EVENTUAL HEIGHT	MINIMUM HEIGHT BY TRIMMING	SPACING
		DECIDUOUS TREES			
Acer campestre	Hedge Maple	U	25'		3–6'
Ginnala	Amur Maple	U	25'		3–4'
Carpinus Betulus	European Hornbeam	C	20'	6'	2–3'
caroliniana	American Hornbeam	C	20'	6'	2–3'
Cratægus cordata	Washington Thorn	U	20'		3'
Crus-galli	Cockspur Thorn	C & U	20'	10'	3'
Oxyacantha	English Hawthorn	C & U	20'	10'	3'
Elæagnus angustifolia	Russian Olive	U	25'		4–6'
Fagus sylvatica	European Beech	C	30'	8'	4–5'
Maclura pomifera	Osage Orange	U	25'	May be cut to 1' and will sprout again	3–4'
Malus floribunda	Japanese Flowering Crab	U	20'		4–6'
ioensis	Prairie Crab	U	20'		4–6'
spectabilis	Chinese Flowering Crab	U	20'		4–6'
Ostrya virginiana	Hop Hornbeam	C & U	25'		4–6'
Populus Bolleana (P. alba pyramidalis)		U	40'		5–10'
nigra italica	Lombardy Poplar	U	50'		5–8'
Quercus imbricaria	Shingle Oak	C	20'	6'	3–5'
Salix pentandra	Shiny Willow	U	25'		3–6'
Tilia cordata	Small-leaved Linden	C	30'	10'	4–6'
Ulmus pumila	Dwarf Elm	C	25'	8'	4'
		DECIDUOUS SHRUBS			
Abelia grandiflora	Glossy Abelia	U	8'		3'
Acanthopanax pentaphyllum	Fiveleaf Aralia	C & U	5–6'	3'	2–3'
Berberis Thunbergi	Japanese Barberry	C & U	4–6'	3'	1½–2'
Thunbergi minor	Dwarf Japanese Barberry	C	1½'	1'	9"–1'
Thun. atropurpurea	Red-leaved Barberry	C & U	4–5'	3'	1½–2'
Caragana arborescens	Pea-tree	U	10'		2½–3'
Cotoneaster adpressa	Rockspray	U	3'		1–2'
divaricata		C & U	5'	3'	2–2½'
microphylla		C & U	3'	2'	1–1½'
Chænomeles japonica	Japanese Quince	C & U	12'	5'	2–4'
Citrus trifoliata	Hardy Orange	C & U	15'	5'	2½–3'
Deutzia gracilis	Slender Deutzia	U	3'		1½–2'
Lemoinei	Lemoine's Deutzia	U	4–5'		2'
Euonymus alatus	Winged Burningbush	U	6'		3–4'
Hydrangea arborescens grandiflora		U	4'		2'
paniculata grandiflora		U	15'		2½–3'
Ligustrum amurense	Amur Privet	C & U	15'	4'	1–2'
ibota Regelianum	Regel's Privet	C & U	6'	3'	1½–2'
ovalifolium	Cal. Privet	C & U	15'	3'	1–1½'
vulgare	European Privet	C & U	15'	3'	1–1½'
Lonicera fragrantissima	Winter Honeysuckle	U	10'		3–6'
tatarica	Tatarian Honeysuckle	U	10'		3–6'
Maackii		U	18'		4–6'
Morrowii		U	6'		3–5'
Myrica pennsylvanica	Bayberry	C & U	12'	4'	2–3'

SCIENTIFIC NAME	COMMON NAME	SUITABLE FOR CLIPPED OR UNCLIPPED HEDGE	EVENTUAL HEIGHT	MINIMUM HEIGHT BY TRIMMING	SPACING
Philadelphus coronarius	Mock-orange	U	10′		3–5′
cor. nanus		C & U	2′	1½′	1′
Lemoinei	Lemoine's Mock-orange	U	6′		2′
Physocarpus opulifolius	Ninebark	U	10′		3′
o. nanus		C & U	3′	2′	1½–2′
Rhamnus Frangula	Buckthorn	U	15′		2½–3′
Rhodotypos kerrioides	Jetbead	U	6′		2–3′
Rosa Harisonii	Harison's Yellow Rose	U	6′		2–3′
Hugonis	Father Hugo's Rose	U	6′		2½–3′
rubiginosa	Sweet-Briar	U	6′		2½–3′
rugosa		U	8′		2–3′
Ribes alpinum		U	7′		1½–2′
Salix purpurea nana	Dwarf Arctic Willow	C	3′	1′	1′
Spiræa Bumalda Froebeli		U	3′		1½–2′
arguta		U	5′		2½–3′
Thunbergii		U	4–5′		2–3′
Vanhouttei	Van Houtte's Spiræa	U	8′		3′
prunifolia	Bridal Wreath	U	10′		3–4′
cantoniensis		U	4–5′		2′
Syringa persica		U	6′		2½′
vulgaris		U	15–20′		3′
Viburnum Lantana	Wayfaring Tree	U	15′		3′
Opulus nanum	Dwarf Highbush Cranberry	C & U	3′	1½′	1–1½′
prunifolium	Black-haw	C & U	18′	8′	3–4′
tomentosum		U	10′		3–4′
Sieboldii		U	25′		3–5′
dilatatum		U	12′		3′

XXIII

INVITING THE BIRDS

WE live in a world blessed with an abundance of life. The seasons come and go. Growth, fruition, and decay follow in unending sequence. The birds remind us with their amazing migrations and their songs that nature's laws are unchanging, and that they, too, are subject to the protection as well as the stern necessities of these laws. For all God's creatures have need of shelter, nourishment, freedom and joy. Life is full of beauty, and the birds, more than most living things, interpret the beauty of living.

Almost all species of songbirds and game birds are our friends and allies in the never-ending process of controlling insects. The warblers, flycatchers, thrushes, creepers, thrashers, mocking-birds, woodpeckers and grackles are busy most of the time, eating the eggs, larvae and mature insects. A pair of yellow-billed cuckoos will consume thousands of tent caterpillars in a season.

If we provide conditions which the small birds seek we will have quantities of resident birds and many of the migrants as well. The most important considerations are water, an open area of lawn or meadow, a thicket of shrubs, some trees and *no* cats. Water is essential even if it is only a small pool with an inlet that can be opened periodically to keep the water fresh. A meadow or lawn and a nearby copse of bushes for cover, for berries and for nesting places will satisfy the ground birds. A few tall trees in a grove will delight the twig-inspecting birds who feed on insects, borers and young buds. Such birds as vireos, warblers, thrushes, woodpeckers and titmice seek tall trees in a grove. The meadowlark, quail, field sparrow, goldfinch and bobolink need pastures and hay fields. Bluebirds, nut-

hatches, downy woodpeckers and flickers prefer old orchards with broken or hollow branches for nesting places. Many of the songbirds are content to live close to our homes, especially if there are mature trees and shrubs and gardens nearby. The house wren, phoebe, robin, catbird, cardinal, song sparrow and chipping sparrow all nest in confidence as our close neighbors.

A constant and varied food supply is as important as good locations for nests. If we will plant the trees and shrubs and garden flowers which provide the birds with the food they like, we will have many birds. In the year round life of birds, all species of trees and shrubs seem attractive in one way or another. But those listed at the end of the chapter have associations which are noteworthy.

Winter Feeding

Winter feeding, if it is kept up regularly, is a great benefit to the winter residents and migratory birds. A feeding tray, or a tray with a hopper from which the seeds pour out as they are needed, well off the ground and protected by a collar of fine mesh wire to keep off the cats and squirrels, will provide a safe and happy spot for the birds to gather. Casting crumbs and seed upon the snow is inadequate, temporary and wasteful.

The junco, nuthatch, chickadee, titmouse, fox sparrow, song sparrow, cardinal, downy woodpecker, hairy woodpecker, flicker, and blue jay are the most frequent feeders at a winter station in Eastern states. But in some winters, bluebirds, white-throated sparrows and robins will stay all winter in the latitude of Philadelphia. If a feeding station is established, the birds must have the assurance that the food will be supplied all winter, for winter is no time to migrate.

Fully as important as the grain and seed supply is the fruit of bushes which will stay fresh in the cold weather. The best of these are Cratægus cordata (Washington thorn), Ilex verticillata (Winterberry), and the cotoneasters. If we would have the birds through the winter we should provide for them. (See lists at end of chapter.)

Nesting Sites

Nesting houses are also a means of attracting birds, especially the species whose habitual home sites have been destroyed or curtailed by modern developments.

The purple martins prefer colony houses on very tall poles.

The barn swallows will settle for a porch roof if there is no barn available.

The phoebe, who loves a running stream and likes to build her nest under a stone bridge, will accept a ledge under an accessible roof.

The house wren prefers a box with a hole just its size. But if it cannot have perfection it will drive out the English sparrows and occupy a box with a larger hole.

The bluebird loves a hollow branch in an apple tree. But it will accept a deep nesting box on a post if it is placed from four to six feet above the ground. The box should be provided with a perch, and the entrance should face south or southeast.

Birds are very suspicious of cats. If you give them every inducement and do not keep the cats away you are not really inviting the birds to make their home with you. Every post which supports a bird box should be provided with a flaring collar of tin or wire mesh several feet above the ground. A well-established climbing rose on the post will do almost as well as the wire.

One final precaution; leave natural places natural. Woodpeckers carve out nesting holes in dead branches of trees. Leave a few dead branches for them. Red-winged blackbirds and marsh wrens love to build in swamps. Do not drain all of the swamps. Chimney swifts like abandoned chimney flues. Do not use your fireplaces until the young birds have left the nest. Great blue herons, little green herons and mallard ducks need secluded ponds. Do not cut down the trees beside the pond. Preserve the woodland for the hermit thrush, the vireo, the wood thrush, the oven-bird, the ruffed grouse and woodcock. Keep all these natural areas as sanctuaries for the birds.

FLOWERS ATTRACTIVE TO BIRDS

Few garden flowers are attractive to birds, but those which are bring the rare and colorful humming bird. This remarkable little creature poises beside a blossom and reaches its bill down to the base of the tube for the nectar. Its favorite flowers are Columbine, Flowering Tobacco, Heuchera, Petunia, Phlox and Vesper Iris.

The goldfinches come to the seed trays of the Sunflowers and to the Goldenrod and Thistle Bloom. Humming-birds and butterflies hover over the blooms of the Butterfly Bush.

TREES ATTRACTIVE TO BIRDS

Apple	Nesting sites for bluebirds. Feeding for nuthatches, flickers and chickadees
Arborvitæ	Nesting sites for catbirds and waxwings
Black cherry	⎱ Fruits for most of the small birds
Cherry (orchard var.)	⎰ Jays, robins, catbirds, cardinals (70 species of birds have been counted)
Chokecherry	
Elm	Nesting sites for orioles. Seed for many song birds, bark insects for woodpeckers and creepers
Flowering crabs	Fruits for song birds
Flowering dogwood	Fruits for many birds

TREES ATTRACTIVE TO BIRDS—continued

Hemlock	Shelter in storms. Nesting sites for hummingbirds
Hackberry	Fruits for many birds
Hawthorns	Fruits in quantity in autumn and early winter
Holly	Fruits for the winter residents and migrants
Larch	Feeding for creepers, chickadees
Mountain ash	Fruits in quantity in August and early autumn
Mulberry	Fruits in quantity in summer
Pines	Cones for crossbills, robins, white-throated sparrows, warblers, kinglets and many other birds
Red cedar	Berries for waxwings, catbirds and sparrows
Shadbush	Fruits for many species
Spruces	Shelter in storms and nesting places
White birch	}Feeding for warblers, finches, chickadees
Yellow birch	

SHRUBS ATTRACTIVE TO BIRDS

Blueberry	Berries	Red chokeberry	Berries
Boxwood	Shelter and nesting	Rosa multiflora	Fruit
Bush dogwoods	Berries	Sumac	Fruit
Butterfly bush	Flowers for hummingbirds	Sweetleaf	Berries
Cotoneasters (all var.)	Berries	Trumpet creeper	Flowers for hummingbirds
Elderberry	Berries	Viburnum (most var.)	Berries
Firethorn	Berries and shelter	Virginia creeper	Berries
Junipers	Berries and shelter	Winterberry	Berries

XXIV
ANNUALS

PLANTS classed as annuals are those which complete their life cycle within the space of one year and in this group we find some of our most useful garden flowers. We also commonly place in this class a few flowers such as the snapdragons (antirrhinum) and the ageratums which are not true annuals but which are best handled as such.

The annuals have many uses. They are indispensable in the cutting garden, giving a wealth of bloom throughout the summer and early autumn months; they are of value in the herbaceous border, coming into flower after the first riot of spring bloom has passed, and carrying gallantly on through the heat of midsummer when many of the perennials are quiescent; and if a garden is to be but a temporary affair, to be enjoyed for the space of but a single season, the annuals may be used as the only material in the planting scheme. For window boxes and porch boxes, for potted plants on the terrace or on the low coping of a wall, for the indoor window garden, and for winter bloom in the small greenhouse the annuals can hardly be equalled.

In form and coloring they offer us an extra-

Cosmos, Orange	Marigold t. Yellow	Nicotiana, White	Marigold t. Orange	Cosmos, Orange
Celosia plumosa, Yellow	Salvia farinacea, Blue	Celosia plumosa, Yellow	Zinnia, t. Orange	Salvia farinacea Blue	Nicotiana White
Marigold m. Yellow	Zinnia m. Pale yellow	Lantana Yellow	Marigold m. Yellow	Arctotis grandis	Marigold m. Yellow
Antirrhinum m. Yellow	Cynoglossum amabile	Antirrhinum m. white	Zinnia m. Pale yellow	Antirrhinum m. Copper
Ageratum t.	Marigold d. Orange	Candytuft Lavender	Aster m. Purple	Dimorphotheca Orange	California Poppy Orange
California Poppy Orange	Torenia Purple	Marigold d. Yellow	Torenia Purple	Marigold d. Yellow

t. tall
m. medium
d. dwarf

ANNUAL BORDER. Yellow, orange and lavender predominating.

Cleome spinosa White	Annual Larkspur Pink	Cosmos Lavender	Lavatera Pink	Annual Larkspur Lavender	Cleome spinosa Pink
Salvia farinacea Blue	Nicotiana White	Zinnia t. Lavender	Salvia farinacea Blue	Zinnia t. Pink	Salvia farinacea Blue
Antirrhinum m. Pink	Zinnia m. Pink	Scabiosa	Salpiglossis	Antirrhinum m. Lavender	Zinnia m. Lavender	Antirrhinum m. Pink
Ageratum t.	Arctotis grandis	Shirley Poppy Pink	Phlox drummondi t. Art shades	Petunia White	Arctotis grandis
Vinca rosea alba	Petunia Pink	Viscaria Blue	Petunia Pink	Verbena Pink
Torenia. Purple	Sweet Alyssum Lav.	Phlox drummondi	Lobelia Cambridge Blue	Torenia White	Ageratum d.

FEET
1 2 3

ANNUAL BORDER. Pink, lavender and blue predominating.

305

ordinarily wide range. As edging plants we have the lobelias, the dainty little Virginia stock, sweet alyssum, phlox drummondii and the low-growing petunias; for border plants of medium height we have a wealth of material from which to choose—the asters, the marigolds, the poppies, salpiglossis, larkspur, zinnias and countless others; and for the background plants we have the tithonia and the exotic castor bean plant.

In recent years tremendous advances have been made in the production of new and superior types among many of the more widely grown annuals. The miracle drug, colchicine, in the hands of skilled plant breeders, has made possible the doubling of chromosomes which has resulted in plants with greater vigor, larger flowers, longer stems, and foliage of a more luxuriant green, such as the Giant Ruffled Tetraploid Snapdragons and the lovely Tetraploid Alyssum, Snowdrift.

Among the petunias, the begonias, the snapdragons and a few other annuals the F_1 hybrids have produced new varieties which show marvellous uniformity and perfection of bloom. These new hybrids are the result of the hand pollination of carefully selected parent plants and are noted for their vigor, their abundant bloom and their wide range of beautiful colors.

Exposure

Annuals are essentially sun-loving plants and there are comparatively few members of this group which will thrive in even partial shade. In selecting a site for the annual garden or flower border, it is, therefore, well to choose an open, sunny location where there is a reasonably good circulation of air.

Soil Requirements

The majority of annuals will thrive well in a soil of reasonably good fertility which is well supplied with organic matter, a good, mellow garden loam with a reaction varying from pH 6.5 to pH 7.5, being considered ideal. A few annuals will grow well on extremely poor soils, some will tolerate a considerable degree of acidity and some seem to be entirely indifferent to soil conditions. For the annual garden, the soil may be prepared in the autumn or in the early spring as soon as the ground is workable. Adequate preparation will bring increased rewards in the way of more vigorous growth and more abundant bloom. If well-rotted manure or good compost is available it may be spread over the surface of the beds and may then be forked or spaded in, or if time and labor do not have to be taken into consideration the beds may be prepared by double digging (see page 677). If the beds are prepared in the autumn the surface of the soil should be left rough during the winter. If, however, it is prepared in the spring, the surface of the bed should be carefully levelled and raked with an iron rake until the soil is of fine tilth.

If it seems advisable to further increase the fertility of the soil a top-dressing of commercial fertilizer may be applied early in July and again in early August. A 4-12-4 or a 5-10-5 complete fertilizer will give excellent results and it should be applied at the rate of 2 pounds to every 100 square feet. When the application is made, care should be taken not to get any of the fertilizer on the foliage of the plants as it might cause severe burning. It should be sprinkled lightly on the surface of the soil and watered in.

The high-analysis, quickly soluble fertilizers are also of great value. They may be applied as a booster application at the time of transplanting (see page 165) and again in midsummer when the plants are flowering heavily.

If the soil tests below a pH of 6.5, lime should be applied. See Chapter XVI, pages 168–170.

Propagation

Practically all annuals are propagated by seed. For full and detailed directions for seed sowing, both in the open ground and under glass, see Chapter XXXIII on Propagation.

The time of sowing will depend to a considerable extent upon the group to which the plants belong.

Thinning

When annuals have been sown in the open ground the young seedling plants will frequently require thinning, as it is essential that each individual plant be allowed ample space for its full development if good bloom is to be obtained. If the seedlings are not thinned out and are allowed to become overcrowded, the plants will make poor and spindly growth and the quantity and quality of the flowers will suffer seriously in consequence. The ultimate space required by the plants should be determined (see tabular list on pages 322–327) and the thinning should be done before the plants have become in the least overcrowded. In some cases, as with zinnias and marigolds, the plants which are thinned out may be transplanted to some other section of the garden. In the case of seedlings which do not transplant readily (poppies, mignonette, etc.) it is best to discard those which are thinned out. It is advisable to do the thinning out of the young seedlings on a cloudy day when the ground is moist, as those which remain will suffer less shock if their root systems are slightly disturbed, and they will also suffer less from sudden exposure to full sunlight if they have been somewhat shaded by the close proximity of other seedlings.

Transplanting

When annuals are transplanted from seed flats or from the coldframe into the garden they should receive as little set-back as possible. Transplanting should preferably be done on a cloudy day or late in the afternoon. A plastic spray (see page 683) will prove of great value in reducing the danger of serious wilting. The plants may be sprayed while still in the flat or seed bed, or if small and not in flower, they may be dipped in the spray.

Pinching Back

Some annuals should be allowed to develop their natural habit of growth and will either produce a spire of bloom or will branch quite freely if they are allowed ample space for their full development. There are a number of annuals, however, that are definitely benefited by judicious "pinching back"—as the operation is called in common garden parlance. If left entirely to their own devices these seedlings will make rather tall, spindly growth and will produce but scanty bloom. It is, therefore, wise to nip out the terminal bud or the tip of the plant when two or three sets of leaves have developed along the main stem, in order that the plant may have an opportunity to become bushy and well branched. In some cases further pinching may be desirable after the side shoots have developed. See list, page 317.

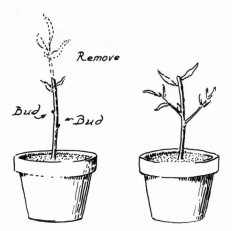

PINCHING BACK TO INDUCE BRANCHING

Culture

The cultivation of the soil plays an important part in the success of the annual garden. Frequent, shallow cultivation should be given, the most satisfactory tool for this purpose being the small type of weeder with three flexible prongs. The soil should be kept in excellent tilth throughout the season and a hard crust should never be allowed to form upon the surface of the bed.

Some annuals, such as the poppies, portulaca and phlox drummondii do not mind a high soil temperature and a minimum supply of moisture in the soil, while many other annuals such as zinnias, marigolds and snapdragons may be greatly benefited by a summer mulch of peat moss or some similar material which will help to conserve the moisture in the soil and will maintain a lower soil temperature. (See page 500).

The period of bloom of most annuals may be greatly prolonged if the fading flowers are removed. This detail of good garden maintenance is of more importance when one is dealing with annuals than it is in the case of any other group of flowers. The chief function of an annual plant is to blossom and produce seed, and having fulfilled this function it has no further reason for existence. In the case of low border plants such as sweet alyssum it is sometimes wise to shear the plants back if they become somewhat shabby, and vigorous new growth will thus be induced.

Diseases and Pests of Annuals

Specific recommendations for the treatment of diseases and pests of annuals are given in Chapter XLI on "Plant Diseases and Insect Pests."

Selection of Varieties

From the long lists of annuals in the seed catalogues, it is difficult to make wise selections unless one has had an opportunity to become familiar with them. They are all listed there; the dependable ones and the fickle ones; the sturdy ones and the temperamental ones; the ones with flowers of exquisite daintiness and the ones with flowers of a garish hue. In the space of one chapter it is impossible to discuss them all, and only those have been selected which are, because of some particular merit, worthy of a place in the general garden scheme.

African Daisy (Arctotis grandis). Arctotis is classed among the worthy annuals because of the simple beauty of its flowers, which resemble a white daisy with long pointed petals, lavender on the under side, with a steel-blue center. The flowers are borne on long, graceful, almost leafless stems and are excellent for cutting, as they last extremely well. The plants reach a height of 15 to 18 inches and they will continue to bloom throughout the summer if the fading blooms are removed. Arctotis grandis is of value as a plant for the front or middle of the flower border.

Culture: The plants are very tolerant of poor soil and of drought, which makes them of particular value for the gardener who must struggle against such handicaps. Arctotis is classed as a half-hardy annual. The seeds may be sown early in the spring indoors, or later in the season either in the frames or directly in the garden where they are to flower. The plants should be spaced from 10 to 12 inches apart. The plants are remarkably free from pests and diseases and since they are so modest in their demands regarding soil and moisture, they may be classed among the most easily grown annuals.

Ageratum, Floss Flower. Ageratum varies in size from the very dwarf, compact type hardly more than 3 inches high, to the tall, branching varieties which often reach a height of from 15 to 18 inches. The pale lavender-blue flowers of the larger types are lovely in the flower border and are also excellent for cutting. White and dark blue varieties are also obtainable but are less satisfactory.

The tetraploid variety, Blue Mink, is an excellent dwarf variety. Vigorous and uniform in growth, the plants are crowned with a myriad of small, lavender-blue flowers.

Culture: Ageratum is classed as a tender annual. For early bloom the seed should be sown indoors in March and the young seedlings transplanted to the garden when all danger of frost is over. Sowings made in the open ground after it has become warm and mellow will give later bloom. The plants reseed so abundantly that they will often establish themselves in a garden, new plants appearing year after year. If the faded blooms are removed and the plants are not allowed to reseed, ageratum will remain in bloom over a period of many months, until the plants are killed by the first frost. The dwarf varieties may be used as edging plants and should be spaced from 4 to 6 inches apart. The taller varieties are excellent for the front of the flower border and should be spaced from 10 to 12 inches apart.

Alyssum, Sweet. Sweet Alyssum is one of the most popular of the annual edging plants. Several of the exceedingly dwarf forms attain a height of hardly more than 3 inches, while some of the larger types are fully 9 inches. The plants begin to flower when still very small, and they are covered with a profusion of bloom throughout the summer months. The varieties most commonly used are white, although there are several strains which bear flowers of a deep lavender hue. The plants are very uniform both in height and in habit of growth.

The dwarf variety Royal Carpet, which received the coveted All-American award in 1953, is a lovely shade of royal purple and makes an excellent edging. The tetraploid giant alyssum, Snowdrift, reaches a height of almost 10 inches and bears a profusion of snowy flowers, continuing in bloom until late autumn.

Culture: Being a hardy annual, sweet alyssum may be sown out of doors as soon as the frost is out of the ground, the plants being thinned to stand 6 inches apart. The young seedlings make rapid growth and will begin to bloom in less than 6 weeks from the date of planting. Seeds may also be sown indoors or in the frames, being later transplanted to the garden, and very early bloom may thus be obtained.

Asters have long been one of the most popular of annual flowers. They are obtainable in a wide variety of form and colorings and will give abundant bloom throughout the season. They are lovely in the flower garden and are quite indispensable in the cutting garden. If early, mid-season and late varieties are selected the period of bloom may be extended from late June until frost.

Culture: Asters thrive best in a fairly fertile soil, and while they prefer full sun they will also do reasonably well in light shade. In the North the seed should be sown indoors or in a cold frame. As asters are shallow-rooted close cultivation should be avoided, and they require ample moisture during periods of drought. Wilt-resistant varieties should be selected.

Browallia. Blue is a color which is found none too frequently among the annuals and for this reason Browallia is especially prized for its abundant bloom throughout the summer. The small, tubular flowers are a clear violet-blue, and they are excellent for their decorative value in the garden, for cutting, and as potted plants. *Browallia elata* is excellent for bedding purposes, attaining a height of about 1½ feet. *B. speciosa* (*major*) produces larger flowers, and it is of especial value as a potted plant, for window boxes and for hanging baskets.

Culture: The seeds may be planted early in the season under glass or later in the open ground. The young seedlings should be pinched back when about 6 inches tall to induce a bushy, well-branched plant. The plants prefer a position in full sun and will thrive well in any good garden soil. They should be spaced from 6 to 8 inches apart, and throughout the season they will give a profusion of bloom.

Butterfly Flower (Schizanthus). Schizanthus is sometimes called the poor man's orchid because of the form and color of its dainty flowers and because it may be so easily grown. The foliage is a soft light green, finely cut, and the myriad, delicate flowers form a pyramid of bloom, in tints of lavender, rose, and brown.

Culture: The seed may be sown either out of doors or under glass, and the plants come into bloom in less than six weeks from sowing. They are so profligate with their flowers, however, that the period of bloom is somewhat short. Schizanthus is exceedingly well adapted to pot culture in the greenhouse, and beautiful plants may be produced which are charming for decorative purposes in the house. The taller types which grow from 2–3 feet should be planted from 1 to 1½ feet apart. The more dwarf varieties reach a height of about 1 foot, and 9 inches is sufficient between the plants.

Calendula or **Pot-marigold.** There is a jauntiness about the great golden and orange blooms of the calendulas which is very appealing. The plants are extremely hardy, and in the South they may be grown out of doors during the winter months. In the North, calendulas are popular both as a greenhouse plant to supply flowers for cutting during the winter, and as a summer flowering annual.

Culture: The plants are of easy culture and are not exacting in their demands. The seeds may be sown indoors for early bloom or directly in the garden as soon as the ground can be worked in the spring. The plants reach a height of from 12 to 18 inches, and they should be spaced about 1 foot apart. They offer excellent material for the front of the border and for the cutting garden.

California Poppy (Eschscholtzia). The California Poppies are among the gayest of our summer-flowering annuals and are beloved by many a gardener. They were named in honor of Doctor Eschscholtz, a Russian ship-surgeon, who found them growing wild on our western coast more than a century ago. While some members of the genus are true perennials in their native habitat, they are not able to survive the extreme cold of Northern winters, and they are therefore usually treated as annuals.

Types and Varieties: The plants vary considerably in height, some of the miniature varieties being hardly more than 6 inches, while the larger, more vigorous types often reach a height of from 12 to 15 inches. The foliage is finely cut, a soft gray-green in color, and the lovely flowers are borne on slender, upright stems. During the night and on dull, cloudy days the petals remain closed, but with the magic touch of the sun, they open wide. The flowers are lovely both in the garden and for cutting as they last exceedingly well when cut and require no special attention. The flowers of the true California Poppy (E. californica) vary in color from a soft cream to a deep golden orange. Many of the varieties which we have today, however, are hybrid forms and offer a much wider range of color, being obtainable in shades of ivory, shell pink, salmon, rose, scarlet, crimson and deep tawny orange. Several seed firms offer Eschscholtzias in named varieties which are very beautiful. *Orange Prince* is very fine, the flowers, which measure nearly three inches across, being borne in great profusion. *Flame* is a gorgeous orange-scarlet; *Gaiety* a brilliant cherry-red on the outer side of the petals and pure white within. *Queen of the Buffs* is a lovely, clear apricot-buff in color; *Rosy Queen* a deep rose on the outer side of the petals and a lighter shade within.

Culture: The Eschscholtzias are of very easy culture. Although they prefer a light, sandy soil they will thrive well in soil of almost any type and they will give an abundance of bloom provided that they are planted in full sun. The seeds may be sown in the autumn, shortly before freezing weather sets in, or they may be sown in the open ground in very early spring. The plants make their most rapid growth during the cool, moist days of early spring. The seeds should always be sown where they are to flower, as the Eschscholtzias do not take kindly to transplanting. If the blooms are cut off as soon as the petals have fallen and no seed pods are allowed to form, the plants may be kept in flower for many months. The plants should be thinned out so that they are spaced from 8 to 10 inches apart.

Cape-marigold (Dimorphotheca). This gay little orange daisy deserves a place both in the cutting garden and in the flower border. It may also be grown very successfully in the greenhouse, and although the flowers are modest in form and size, they are lovely for mixed bouquets. In the garden, the plants seldom reach a height of more than 12 inches. The flowers are daisy-like in form with long, slender, somewhat pointed petals, which seem to shimmer in the sunlight. Several new hybrids have recently been introduced which range in color from pale lemon yellow to deep orange and salmon pink.

Culture: The seed may be sown in the open ground or the young seedlings may be started under glass. The African Daisies prefer an open, sunny location in the garden and will thrive well in very poor soil. They are also more tolerant of drought than some of the other annuals. The plants should be spaced 8 to 10 inches apart.

Clarkia. Clarkia is a native of our own Northwest and was first discovered at the time of the Lewis and Clark expedition, being named in honor of the explorer. There are two types, Clarkia elegans, which bears its flowers in long, loose sprays, and Clarkia pulchella, which bears its flowers in clusters. The stems are of a coppery tone and the dainty flowers are beautiful both in form and in coloring, ranging from white through salmon pink to purple and crimson. The blooms are excellent for cutting and as the plants do extremely well under greenhouse conditions, they are often grown for cut flowers during the winter months.

Culture: The seeds may be sown in the autumn in the open ground, in the greenhouse or in frames for very early bloom, and directly in the garden as soon as the soil is mellow and workable. The plants reach a height of 15 to 18 inches and they should be spaced from 10 to 12 inches apart.

Cornflower, Bachelor's Button (Centaurea cyanus). The Cornflowers may be classed in the group of hardy and absolutely dependable annuals. They are of vigorous habit, will thrive on poor, sandy soil and ask almost nothing in the way of care and cultivation.

Culture: If the seed is sown outdoors late in autumn it will lie dormant during the winter and will germinate with the first warm days of spring. The lusty, vigorous seedlings make rapid growth and will soon come into bloom. Seed may also be sown in the open ground at any time during the spring months. As the period of bloom is rather short, successive sowings should be made. The plants reseed readily and young seedlings will often appear as volunteers year after year. Cornflowers are especially recommended for the cutting garden and for children's gardens. They seem to hold a special delight for children and are so dependable and of such easy culture that they make failure almost impossible. The plants reach a height of about 18 inches, and as they are of a rather branching habit of growth, they should be spaced at least 1 foot apart.

Cosmos. Cosmos is of particular value because of its height, the giant varieties often reaching a height of 5 or 6 feet. If both early and late varieties are planted, bloom may be had from July until frost. In habit of growth, cosmos is somewhat spreading and spindly and lacks the grace and charm of many of our other flowers. It is best adapted to the rear of the border and to the cutting garden. There are single, crested, and double forms, coming in tones of pink, mauve, white and crimson. The recently introduced variety, Orange Flare, is a distinct departure from the usual types, the color being an intense golden orange, and the flowers are very decorative.

Culture: Cosmos is classed as a tender annual and the seeds should not be sown until all danger of frost is over. If early bloom is desired the seedlings may be started under glass. As the plants are of a decidedly branching habit of growth, they should be allowed ample room to develop. The dwarf varieties should be spaced 2 feet apart, the tall varieties from 2½ to 3 feet apart. The tall varieties frequently require staking.

Flowering Tobacco (Nicotiana). The flowering tobacco is one of the most valuable of the tall growing annuals and it is so well adapted to a variety of planting compositions that it should be widely grown. In the evening as the lovely white, tubular flowers recede into the twilight, its delicate fragrance pervades the garden and the night moths hover above it in the dusk.

Some varieties remain closed during the day but many of the newer varieties, such as Sensation Daylight, remain open. A wide range of color is now available among the nicotianas, including such lovely shades as lavender, coral, soft pink, rose-mahogany, and crimson.

Culture: The plants are easily grown, and when once well established in a garden they reseed very readily and the young seedlings will come up year after year. The seed is exceedingly fine and may be sown under glass for early bloom or in the open where the plants are to flower. The plants may be transplanted with ease, and they may be moved into the garden when they are in full flower if they are lifted with ample soil, and if the transplanting is done on a cloudy, moist day. The plants bloom over a long period and may be used very satisfactorily in the herbaceous border after some of the early flowering biennials have been removed. The flowering tobacco is also lovely when used as a house plant during the winter months. Young seedlings may be potted up in the autumn before frost and will give generous bloom throughout the winter.

There are several rather distinct types—*N. affinis* with white, tubular flowers; *N. sylvestris* with drooping, tube-shaped flowers, borne on a stout, central stem; and *N. Sanderæ* with flowers of red and carmine hue.

Incarvillea variabilis. Although the annual form of Incarvillea is not widely known, it possesses many delightful qualities, and it has the ability to withstand the intense heat of Southern summers remarkably well. The plants reach a height of about 18 inches and the tubular flowers are produced in great abundance. The colors range through delicate shades of cream, pink, salmon and rose.

Culture: Incarvillea prefers a position in full sun and thrives in widely varying types of soil. The seed may be sown under glass for early bloom, or it may be sown in coldframes or in the open ground later in the season. The plants should be spaced from 8 to 10 inches apart.

Larkspur. The annual larkspurs are among the loveliest and most decorative of our garden flowers. The stately spires of bloom add their full measure of beauty to any garden composition, and they are highly valued for cutting as well. Several new and greatly improved varieties of annual larkspur have been introduced within recent years. The plants reach a height of from 3 to 4 feet, and the massive spires of bloom are very beautiful, being obtainable in a wide range of colorings—white, shell pink, rose, lavender and purple. The plants should be given ample room to develop. They should be spaced about 18 inches apart.

Culture: The plants are exceedingly hardy, and the seed may be sown in the open ground late in the autumn, germinating with the first warm days of spring; or it may be sown as soon as the ground is workable in March. Autumn sowing and early spring sowing are desirable, as seedlings started later in the season do not thrive as well and the plants do not make as vigorous growth. It is possible to start the seedlings under glass for early transplanting to the open ground.

The annual larkspurs are extremely popular, and deservedly so, for greenhouse culture during the winter months. The lovely spikes of bloom are very decorative as cut flowers and require no special care or attention in the greenhouse benches.

Lobelia. The intensity of the blue found in the lobelia is equalled in almost no other flower. But it has been this very intensity of hue which has made them difficult subjects for the flower border. With the introduction of the lovely *Cambridge Blue* variety, however, and of other varieties such as Blue Gown, the lobelias have gained rapidly in popularity and are now highly valued as edging plants. There are several types, the exceedingly dwarf form suitable only for edgings; the trailing form, which is of particular value for porch and window boxes; and the upright form which reaches a height of almost 15 inches. One of the loveliest of edgings for flower beds during the summer months is a combination of Lobelia, variety Cambridge Blue, with Phlox Drummondii of a clear pink tone.

Culture: The plants are tender and the seeds should be started under glass early in the season, the young seedlings being transplanted into the garden when all danger of frost is over. The plants are of simple culture and will thrive well in any good garden soil. They should be set 4 to 6 inches apart.

Lupine. Although the annual forms are not as large or as decorative as are the perennial types, they possess a certain distinction and charm, and they are well worth growing. The plants do well either in full sun or in partial shade, and if the seed pods are not allowed to form, they will bloom over an exceedingly long period. The tall spikes of bloom are graceful and lovely, coming in tones of clear soft blue, pink, mauve and white. And because of the decorative value of the blooms as cut flowers the annual lupines are frequently grown in greenhouses during the winter months.

Culture: The seeds may be planted in the open ground where they are to flower or they may be started under glass. As they do not bear transplanting as happily as some of the other annuals, an ideal method of growing the plants, if they are to be started indoors for early bloom in the garden, is to sow the seeds in peat moss pots. The plants may then be moved into the garden when they are almost ready to flower. As the roots will be undisturbed, the plants will suffer no set-back. The plants grow from 2 to $2\frac{1}{2}$ feet tall and should be spaced from 12 to 15 inches apart.

Marigold (Tagetes). Although we know them as French and African marigolds, the names are not significant of their origin, as both of these types have come to us from Mexico, where they are found growing in luxuriant abundance.

From midsummer until frost the marigolds may be counted upon for generous bloom. They may either be used as the dominant note in the late summer garden or they may play a minor role by filling in an occasional gap here and there. In the cutting garden they are indispensable. They are so profligate with their bloom that they may be cut with lavish abandon and great bowls of them will carry the rich yellow and orange tones of late summer into the house, until the first frost has touched the garden.

Culture: The marigolds are of the most simple culture. The seeds are large and germinate readily and the young plants may be transplanted with the greatest ease, it being possible to move them into the garden when they are in full flower. They are tolerant of poor soil, and will thrive under almost any conditions, in full sun or in partial shade, and in wet or dry soil. The seeds may be sown in the open where they are to flower or they may be sown early under glass.

The African marigolds may be obtained in tall and intermediate types, ranging from 18 inches to 4 feet in height, and the colors range from palest yellow to deep glowing orange. The African marigolds should be planted $1\frac{1}{2}$ feet apart.

The French marigolds are more dwarf in habit of growth, 6 to 15 inches in height, and are useful for the front of the border, forming bushy, spreading plants. The colors range from pale lemon-yellow, through deep orange to dull, tawny reds. The French marigolds should be planted from 9 to 12 inches apart.

Painted Tongue (Salpiglossis). The trumpet-like flowers of the Painted Tongue come in shades of dusky purple, deep wine-red and ivory, with stencillings of gold, and they are very decorative both in the garden and for cutting, as they last unusually well in water.

Culture: The plants reach an ultimate height of from 2 to $2\frac{1}{2}$ feet and should be given ample space in which to develop, being spaced from 8 to 10 inches apart. Salpiglossis is not of as easy culture as are many of the annuals, and the young seedlings require considerable pampering. The seeds should be sown indoors early in the spring, and the young plants should not be set out until all danger of frost is over. The seedlings should be kept growing on rapidly and should not be allowed to suffer from overcrowding in the seed bed or from lack of moisture. The plants prefer a position in full sun and a deep, rich, loam soil.

Petunias. In the skillful hands of the hybridizers, petunias have been developed into one of our most useful flowers. Always dependable, demanding almost nothing in the way of care and cultivation, thriving under most adverse conditions of soil and climate, they offer us an abundance of bloom and beauty throughout the long summer season. For porch and window boxes, for gay masses of bloom about a summer cottage, as border plants in the flower garden, they are quite indispensable and there is no other flower that can take their place. Single or double, ruffled or fluted, they offer a wider range of color than almost any other flower. Some of the new shades of velvety purple, pale rose, and deep wine-red are exceedingly lovely when used in pleasant color harmonies with other annuals. The lovely F_1 hybrids attest the skill of our modern plant breeders. They are extraordinarily uniform in habit of growth and possess a perfection of bloom which places them quite in a class by themselves.

Culture: For early bloom the seeds should be sown indoors and the young plants may be transplanted into the garden when they are ready to come into flower. Seed may also be sown in the open ground, being covered very lightly with finely sifted soil, since it is so fine. Petunias have a longer season of bloom than most flowers, and if the plants become spindly at any period in their growth they may be cut back and will soon branch out again. The tall and spreading varieties which reach from 1 to 2 feet should be spaced about 1 foot apart. The dwarf varieties reaching a height of 6 to 8 inches should be spaced about 6 inches apart.

Phlox, Annual (Phlox Drummondii). Phlox Drummondii was found growing wild in Texas. Since its introduction into cultivation it has become one of our most useful edging and low border plants. Some of the new "art" shades are very beautiful, both in the garden and for cut flower arrangements.

Culture: In the South it is often grown as a winter annual, and being extremely hardy it can survive many a sudden cold snap and bloom blithely on. In the North the seeds may be planted in the autumn or in very early spring in the open. Sowings under glass are also frequently made. The plants may readily be transplanted and, if they are not allowed to reseed, will remain in bloom for many months. Seed is now obtainable in a wide range of colors, white, soft buff, shell pink, clear deep pink, lavender, scarlet and deep red. Some varieties have a distinctly marked eye or center and are less attractive than the self-colors. There are low-growing, dwarf types reaching a height of about 6 inches, which should be spaced about 6 inches apart. The larger, more spreading types which attain a height of from 10 to 12 inches should be planted about 9 inches apart. Phlox Drummondii thrives best in an open, sunny position and does exceedingly well on poor, sandy soil.

Pincushion-Flower—Mourning Bride (Scabiosa). The flowers of the annual scabiosa are borne in profusion from midsummer until frost. The plants are of rather thin growth with but scant foliage, but the flowers are excellent for cutting and they are attractive in the garden as well. The plants reach a height of about 2½ feet and the flowers are borne on long, wiry stems.

Culture: The scabiosas are hardy, and the seeds may be sown in the open where the plants are to flower, or under glass for early bloom. The flowers come in a wide range of colors—white, lavender-blue, flesh-pink, rose, crimson, purple, and deep maroon. They should be planted about 1 foot apart.

Pinks, Annual (Dianthus chinensis). The annual pinks have long been popular. They will produce generous bloom throughout the summer months. Both single and double varieties are obtainable in a wide range of colorings—white, salmon-pink, crimson and deep red. The plants are branching in habit of growth and reach a height of about 1 foot, being useful in the front of the border.

Culture: The seeds may be sown in a coldframe or in the open ground after the soil has become warm and mellow. The plants prefer a sunny location, and they thrive well in a rich, rather moist garden soil. They should be spaced from 8 to 10 inches apart.

Poppies. Of all the annual poppies the Shirley poppies are the most appealing. Their flowers are of exquisite daintiness and they are lovely both in the garden and for cutting. The Shirley poppies are a distinct strain developed from the little corn poppy which is found growing wild throughout Europe, and they owe their origin to that wonderful student of plant life, the Rev. W. Wilks, who, in the year 1880, found a modest little corn poppy with a fine line of white along the edge of the petals, growing in his garden at the Shirley Vicarage in England. He saved the seed from this little poppy, and the following year from the two hundred seedling plants he obtained four or five others with the same fine white line. For many years he worked patiently with these poppies, gradually developing a new and very beautiful strain known as the Shirley poppies. In habit of growth the plants are somewhat branching, reaching a height of almost two feet, and they bear a profusion of flowers of beautiful form. The single varieties are far more exquisite than the heavy-headed double types, and there is a wide color range—white, salmon-pink, apricot, rose and deeper shades of red and crimson. *Wild-rose Pink* is one of the loveliest varieties.

Culture: The Shirley poppies thrive best in full sun in a light, sandy loam soil, and require a free circulation of air. If planted in a damp, poorly drained situation the young plants have a tendency to rot off. The plants are also apt to suffer badly during a rainy season, as the flower buds frequently rot before they open. The flowers of the Shirley poppy are borne on long, slender, hairy stems, and nature endeavors to protect the buds from too much moisture by allowing them to remain in a drooping position until a few hours before they are ready to open. If, however, because of extreme dampness, the calyx which encloses the bud fails to break away, the bud will rot before opening.

The Opium poppies (Papaver somniferum) differ from the Shirley poppies in that the stems are smooth and glaucous and somewhat thicker. The plants attain a greater height and the flowers are larger. There are single and double types, carnation and peony-flowered forms—and they are all decorative and lovely.

All members of the Poppy family are very hardy. The seeds may be sown either in the autumn or very early in the spring. As it is impossible to transplant the young seedlings with any degree of success, the seeds should be sown in the location where the plants are to flower. As the seed is very fine it should be covered lightly with sifted soil. The young seedling plants should be thinned out to a distance of 6 or 8 inches apart before they become in the least crowded.

Poppies thrive best during the cool, moist, growing weather of spring, and they should, therefore, be sown as early in the season as possible. Particularly is this true in sections of the country where the summer heat is intense.

Snapdragon (Antirrhinum). There are few annuals that are more useful than the antirrhinums. They are indispensable in the flower beds and borders, and are almost equally valuable in the cutting garden. They are lovely in form, and the colors are infinitely varied, ranging from delicate apple-blossom pink through shades of salmon and apricot, to tawny yellow and deep wine-red. The intermediate type, reaching a height of about 18 inches, is the most popular, but for the rear of the flower border the giant types are superbly fine, often reaching a height of 3 feet or more. There are few color compositions in the flower garden more beautiful than the rich tones of apricot antirrhinums massed against the stately spires of the *Giant Primrose* foxgloves. For a border planting of striking color tones, the variety *Bonfire*, a rich tawny red, may be planted in combination with the *Arkwright Ruby* Viola and Delphinium chinense. The F_1 hybrids and the wonderful Giant Ruffled Tetraploid varieties have become tremendously popular. They are striking in their beauty of form and coloring and their vigor of growth.

Culture: For early spring bloom the seeds may be sown in August and the young plants wintered over in the frames, or the seeds may be sown in the greenhouse in January or February or in hotbeds in March. The young seedlings should be pricked out as soon as they have reached sufficient size, and, as they develop, they should be pinched back in order that they may become well branched. The young seedlings may be transplanted to the garden as soon as the soil has become warm and mellow, being spaced about 1 foot apart.

If the faded flowers are removed and if the plants are given good care and cultivation, they will give generous bloom over a period of many months. Antirrhinums prefer a rich, mellow soil rather high in lime content, but they are tolerant of widely varying conditions. In mild climates, antirrhinums will live through the winter, and they may be regarded as perennials.

Since the introduction of the rust-proof varieties, the gardener need suffer no concern over this disease, which formerly took such a heavy toll.

Stocks (Mathiola). Stocks are beloved for their fragrance and for their association with old-fashioned gardens. When grown in the greenhouse during the winter months the flowers are lovely for mixed bouquets

and they are lovely, too, in the garden if the plants are well grown.

Culture: The plants are a bit more temperamental than many of the annuals and sometimes fail to flower well. For most satisfactory results, the seeds should be sown indoors or in frames and the young plants set out in the garden, when danger of frost is over. There are tall-growing types and dwarf-growing types, and both single and double forms, and there is a wide range of color: white, cream, lavender, purple, pink, rose, and a dusky shade of antique copper as well as red and crimson. The tall-growing types, reaching a height of from 2 to $2\frac{1}{2}$ feet, should be planted from 1 to $1\frac{1}{2}$ feet apart, while the dwarf varieties of 1 to $1\frac{1}{2}$ feet in height should be planted from 6 to 9 inches apart.

Sunflower (Helianthus). Although many of the members of this family are of such coarse and ungainly growth that they are ill-suited to the flower border, there are a few varieties which are worthy of consideration. The lovely little sunflower, *Primrose Stella*, introduced by Sutton's, is a delightful thing. The plants reach a height of about 2 feet and the flowers are of a pale, primrose yellow with dark central disks. It is lovely in the garden, and the flowers are very decorative for cutting.

Culture: The seeds may be sown in the greenhouse or in the frames for early bloom, or they may be sown in the open ground after all danger of frost is over. The plants should be spaced from 15 to 18 inches apart. The sunflowers are among the least exacting of plants and require little in the way of cultivation. They prefer full sun, but will tolerate poor soil and drought to an extraordinary degree.

Swan River Daisy (Brachycome). The Swan River Daisy is a winsome little thing, bearing small, daisylike flowers of a soft blue tone with a brilliant yellow center. The plants are useful near the front of the border or as an edging, as they reach a height of hardly more than 12 inches.

Culture: The seed may be sown either indoors for early bloom or directly in the garden. The plants come into flower within six weeks of the time of sowing. They should be spaced from 6 to 8 inches apart. As the period of bloom of the Swan River Daisy is not long, successive sowings should be made every 4 or 6 weeks if bloom is desired throughout the summer.

Sweet Peas (Lathyrus odoratus). Early sowing is one of the secrets of success with sweet peas. If greenhouse space is available the seeds should be sown in January, in small flowerpots. If seed is to be sown in the open ground, it should be planted as early as possible in the season. In the South autumn sowing is preferred. In order to facilitate early spring sowing it is wise to prepare the trench in the autumn. Sweet peas require a deep, rich, soil, and a trench at least 18 inches deep should be prepared with liberal quantities of well-rotted manure and rich compost. A comparatively short trench which has been well prepared will produce vigorous plants and abundant bloom. It is, therefore, wise to prepare a small area thoroughly, rather than to attempt too much. In the spring the trench should be opened to a depth of 6 inches and the seeds placed in the bottom of the furrow, 4 inches apart, being covered with about an inch of soil. If the seeds are either nicked or soaked in water for 24 hours previous to planting, germination will be hastened. As the young plants develop, the trench should be gradually filled until it is almost level, a slight depression being left to conserve moisture. Sweet peas make their best growth during the cool, moist days of early spring and are seriously affected by heat and drought. Wire or brush may be used as a support for the vines.

Torenia (Wishbone flower). The quaint little blossoms of the Torenia are borne in profusion throughout the summer and the plants remain quite undaunted in the face of heat and drought. Attaining hardly more than a foot in height, Torenia is excellent as an edging plant or when planted in drifts along the front of the border. The small flowers are semi-trumpet-like in form and come in shades of lavender and deep violet with a yellow blotch on the lower petal. There is also a white form. The plants are admirably adapted to pot culture.

Culture: Torenia is a tender annual. The seed may be sown in the greenhouse or in the frames early in the spring or in the open ground after all danger of frost is over. The seed is very fine and should be covered but lightly. The young seedling plants may be transplanted readily. If they have been started indoors they may be moved to the garden when danger of frost is over, being spaced from 6 to 8 inches apart. Torenia thrives well either in full sun or in partial shade, and the plants will continue to bloom throughout the season, until killed by autumn frosts.

Verbena. Like the petunias, the verbenas are classed among the ever-dependable annuals. There are dwarf types suited to the front of the flower border and taller types which are remarkably free-flowering. There is a wide range of lovely colors and verbenas are generous with their bloom, continuing until frost.

Culture: They are of easy culture and will give generous bloom throughout the long summer season. The seeds may be started under glass or they may be sown in the open where they are to flower. The young seedlings are sturdy and bear transplanting well. Of low, somewhat spreading growth, the verbenas are of particular value as border plants. The parti-colored types with white eyes are far less lovely than the self-colors which come in shades of pink, rose, lavender and deep purple. The dwarf varieties, reaching a height of about 6 inches, should be planted 9 inches apart, while the taller varieties should be planted 1 foot apart.

Zinnias. In spite of their somewhat ungraceful habit of growth, zinnias are one of the most popular of the annuals, and they have much to recommend them. They offer wide variations in form and coloring; they bloom over a long period; they will endure drought and neglect, and will succeed when all else fails; and the brilliantly colored flowers add greatly to the beauty of many a midsummer and early autumn garden. In size, zinnias range from the tiny Lilliput varieties suitable for edgings and borders, to the giant, branching types which reach a height of over three feet. There are single and double forms, crested, curled and quilled forms—and there are few flowers which offer as wide a range of color; white, shell-pink, salmon, rose, scarlet, deep red, mauve, yellow and tawny orange. There are varieties to suit every color planting and they may be had in soft pastel tints or in shades that are fairly vibrant with color.

Culture: Zinnias are of the easiest possible culture and will thrive under widely varying conditions. They are classed as tender annuals, and the seed may be started under glass for early bloom, or sown in the garden after all danger of frost is over. Zinnias may be transplanted with ease, and it is possible to move the plants when they are in full flower. Although they thrive best in full sun, they will also endure partial shade. The dwarf varieties, reaching a height of 1 to 1½ feet, should be planted about 9 inches apart, while the taller 3-feet varieties should be spaced about 1 foot apart.

ANNUALS WHICH WILL ENDURE LIGHT SHADE

Basketflower (Centaurea americana)
Chinese Forget-me-not (Cynoglossum amabile)
Clarkia (Clarkia elegans)
Drummond's phlox (Phlox Drummondii)
Lupine (Lupinus Hartwegii)

Pansy (Viola tricolor)
Snapdragon (Antirrhinum majus)
Sweet Alyssum (Alyssum maritimum)
Sweet-sultan (Centaurea suaveolens)
Sweet-sultan, Royal (Centaurea imperialis)

ANNUALS WHICH WILL ENDURE CONSIDERABLE SHADE

Balsam (Impatiens)
Calliopsis (Coreopsis tinctoria)
Cockscomb (Celosia plumosa)
Flowering Tobacco (Nicotiana)
Godetia (Godetia amœna)

Lobelia (Lobelia erinus)
Monkeyflower (Mimulus)
Periwinkle (Vinca rosea)
Stock, Virginia (Malcomia)

ANNUALS WHICH WILL GROW ON VERY POOR SOIL

Bartonia (Mentzelia aurea)
California Poppy (Eschscholtzia californica)
Calliopsis (Coreopsis tinctoria)
Corn Poppy (Papaver Rhœas)
Feather Cockscomb (Celosia plumosa)
Four-o'clock (Mirabilis jalapa)
Gaillardia (Gaillardia Lorenziana)
Garden Balsam (Impatiens balsamina)

Godetia, Whitney (Godetia grandiflora)
Love-lies-bleeding (Amaranthus caudatus)
Nasturtium (Tropæolum majus)
Petunia (Petunia hybrida)
Rose Moss (Portulaca grandiflora)
Spiderflower (Cleome spinosa)
Sweet Alyssum (Alyssum maritimum)
Sweet-sultan (Centaurea moschata)

ANNUALS WHICH TOLERATE ACIDITY

Calliopsis (Coreopsis tinctoria)
Flowering Tobacco (Nicotiana)

Marigold (Tagetes)
Verbena (Verbena)

ANNUALS WHICH REQUIRE A NEUTRAL OR ALKALINE SOIL

Balsam (Impatiens)
Candytuft (Iberis)
Corn Poppy (Papaver Rhœas)
Drummond's phlox (Phlox Drummondii)

Mignonette (Reseda odorata)
Nasturtium (Tropæolum majus)
Zinnia (Zinnia elegans)

ANNUALS WHICH WILL ENDURE HEAT AND DROUGHT

Calliopsis (Coreopsis tinctoria)
Cape-marigold, Winter (Dimorphotheca aurantiaca)
Convolvulus, Dwarf (Convolvulus tricolor)
Cornflower (Centaurea cyanus)
Drummond's phlox (Phlox Drummondii)
Four-o'clock (Mirabilis jalapa)
Ice Plant (Mesembryanthemum crystallinum)
Larkspur, Rocket (Delphinium ajacis)
Morning-glory (Ipomœa purpurea)

Perilla, Green (Perilla frutescens)
Pricklepoppy, Showy (Argemone grandiflora)
Rose Moss (Portulaca grandiflora)
Sage, Scarlet (Salvia splendens)
Sanvitalia (Sanvitalia procumbens)
Snow-on-the-mountain (Euphorbia marginata)
Summer-cypress (Kochia trichophylla)
Sunflower (Helianthus annuus)
Zinnia (Zinnia elegans)

ANNUALS WHICH MAY BE SOWN IN THE FALL

California Poppy (Eschscholtzia californica)
Calliopsis (Coreopsis tinctoria)
Candytuft (Iberis)
Clarkia (Clarkia elegans)
Cornflower (Centaurea cyanus)
Cosmos (Cosmos bipinnatus)
Cow Soapwort (Saponaria vaccaria)
Gypsophila (Gypsophila elegans)
Herb Treemallow (Lavatera trimestris)

Larkspur, Rocket (Delphinium ajacis)
Love-in-a-mist (Nigella damascena)
Pansy (Viola tricolor)
Pink, Chinese (Dianthus chinensis)
Poppy (Papaver)
Pot-marigold (Calendula officinalis)
Snapdragon (Antirrhinum majus)
Sweet Alyssum (Alyssum maritimum)
Sweet Pea (Lathyrus odoratus)

ANNUALS WHICH USUALLY SELF-SOW

Browallia (Browallia)
California Poppy (Eschscholtzia californica)
Calliopsis (Coreopsis tinctoria)
Cornflower (Centaurea cyanus)
Cosmos (Cosmos bipinnatus)
Four-o'clock (Mirabilis jalapa)
Gypsophila (Gypsophila elegans)
Larkspur, Rocket (Delphinium ajacis)
Morning-glory (Ipomæa purpurea)

Petunia (Petunia hybrida)
Pot-marigold (Calendula officinalis)
Rose Moss (Portulaca grandiflora)
Sage, Mealycup (Salvia farinacea)
Snow-on-the-mountain (Euphorbia marginata)
Spiderflower (Cleome spinosa)
Summer-cypress (Kochia trichophylla)
Sweet Alyssum (Alyssum maritimum)
Tobacco (Nicotiana sylvestris)

ANNUALS WHICH ARE SLOW GROWING

(Requiring a Long Season to Bloom)

China-aster (Callistephus chinensis)
Everlasting, Winged (Ammobium)
Flax (Linum)
Goldencup (Hunnemannia)
Immortelle, Everlasting (Xeranthemum)
Lobelia (Lobelia)
Petunia (Petunia)

Pincushion-flower (Scabiosa)
Rhodanthe (Helipterum Humboldtianum)
Salpiglossis (Salpiglossis)
Snapdragon (Antirrhinum)
Strawflower (Helichrysum)
Sweet-sultan, Basketflower (Centaurea)
Verbena (Verbena)

ANNUALS WITH A SHORT SEASON OF BLOOM

(Several Sowings should be made for Succession of Bloom)

Calliopsis (Coreopsis tinctoria)
Candytuft, Purple (Iberis umbellata)
Cape-marigold, Winter (Dimorphotheca aurantiaca)
Cornflower (Centaurea cyanus)
Forget-me-not (Myosotis)
Gypsophila (Gypsophila elegans)

Love-in-a-mist (Nigella damascena)
Mignonette (Reseda odorata)
Drummond's phlox (Phlox Drummondii)
Poppy (Papaver)
Sweet Alyssum (Alyssum maritimum)

ANNUALS DIFFICULT TO TRANSPLANT

(Should be Sown where they are to Flower)

California Poppy (Eschscholtzia californica)
Evening-primrose (Œnothera Drummondii)
Godetia, Whitney (Godetia grandiflora)
Gypsophila (Gypsophila elegans)
Herb Treemallow (Lavatera trimestris)
Laceflower, Blue (Trachymene cærulea)
Love-in-a-mist (Nigella damascena)
Lupine (Lupinus)

Nasturtium (Tropæolum)
Poppy (Papaver)
Pricklepoppy, Showy (Argemone grandiflora)
Rose Moss (Portulaca grandiflora)
Scarlet Runner (Phaseolus coccineus)
Sunflower (Helianthus annuus)
Sweet Pea (Lathyrus odoratus)

ANNUALS WHICH BENEFIT FROM PINCHING

Ageratum (Ageratum Houstonianum)
Browallia
Calendula (Calendula officinalis) or Pot-marigold
Chrysanthemum, Annual
Petunia
Phacelia
Phlox

Pinks (Dianthus chinensis)
Salpiglossis (Salpiglossis sinuata)
Schizanthus (Schizanthus pinatus)
Snapdragon (Antirrhinum)
Verbena
Zinnia

ANNUALS WHICH SHOULD NOT BE PINCHED BACK

Balsam (Impatiens)
Cockscomb (Celosia)
Everlasting (Miscellaneous)

Poppies
Stock

WHITE ANNUALS

Ageratum Houstonianum (Mexican Ageratum)
Alyssum maritimum (Sweet Alyssum)
Ammobium alatum (Winged Everlasting)
Antirrhinum majus (Snapdragon)
Arctotis grandis (Bushy Arctotis)
Argemone grandiflora (Pricklepoppy)
Brachycome iberidifolia (Swan River Daisy)
Browallia demissa (elata)
Campanula (Annual Canterbury Bells)
Centaurea (Royal Sweet-sultan, Cornflower, etc.)
Centranthus macrosiphon (Spur-valerian)
Chrysanthemum
Clarkia
Cleome spinosa (Spiderflower)
Clintonia pulchella
Collinsia bicolor (Chinese-houses)
Crepis barbata rubra (Hawkweed)
Datura fastuosa (Yellow Floripondio)
Dimorphotheca aurantiaca (Cape-marigold)
Echium plantagineum hybrids
Gilia tricolor
Godetia amœna and grandiflora
Gypsophila elegans
Helichrysum bracteatum (Strawflower)
Iberis amara (Candytuft)

Impatiens (Balsam)
Lathyrus odoratus (Sweet Pea)
Lavatera trimestris (Treemallow)
Limonium sinuatum (Statice or Sea-lavender)
Lobelia erinus and tenuior
Lupinus mutabilis (Lupine)
Malcomia maritima (Virginian-stock)
Mathiola incana (Stock)
Nemesia strumosa
Nemophila maculata
Nicotiana (Flowering Tobacco)
Œnothera americana (Evening primrose)
Papaver somniferum (Opium Poppy)
Petunia hybrida
Phlox Drummondii
Portulaca grandiflora
Saponaria vaccaria (Soapwort)
Scabiosa atropurpurea
Schizanthus pinnatus (Butterfly Flower)
Senecio elegans (Purple Groundsel)
Verbena erinoides (Moss Vervain)
Vinca rosea (Periwinkle)
Viola tricolor (Pansy)
Xeranthemum annuum (Immortelle)
Zinnia elegans

RED, ROSE, AND PINK ANNUALS

Abronia umbellata (Sand-Verbena)	Rose
Adonis	Red
Alonsoa acutifolia (Maskflower)	Scarlet
A. Warscewiczii	Orange to scarlet
Amaranthus caudatus (Love-lies-bleeding)	Crimson
Antirrhinum majus (Snapdragon)	Shades red to pink
Calandrinia grandiflora	Rose
C. speciosa	Ruby-red
Callistephus chinensis (China Aster)	Shades red to pink
Campanula (Annual Canterbury Bells)	Pink
Celosia (Cockscomb)	Crimson
Centaurea cyanus	Pink
C. imperialis	Pink
C. moschata	Rose
Centranthus macrosiphon	Rose
Clarkia	Rose, pink
Collinsia bicolor (Chinese-houses)	Pink
Collomia coccinea	Scarlet
Cosmos bipinnatus	Crimson to white
Crepis barbata rubra	Rose
Cuphea ignea (Fiery Cuphea)	Scarlet
Diascia barberæ (Twinspur)	Pink
Echium creticum	Red
E. plantagineum hybrids	Pink
Emilia flammea and sagittata	Scarlet
Eschscholtzia californica (California Poppy)	Red, pink
Gilia	Scarlet
Godetia	Rose to white
Gypsophila muralis	Rose

Helichrysum bracteatum	Red, pink
Helipterum Manglesii and roseum	Rose
Iberis umbellata (Candytuft)	Carmine, pink
Impatiens (Balsam)	Rose, pink
Lathyrus odoratus (Sweet Pea)	Rose, pink
Lavatera trimestris and rosea (Treemallow)	Rose
Leptosiphon hybrida	Rose to carmine
Limonium Suworowi (Statice or Sea-lavender)	Rose
Linaria bipartita (Toadflax)	Crimson, pink
Linum grandiflorum (Flowering Flax)	Crimson
Lupinus Hartwegii (Hartweg Lupine)	Pink
Lychnis cœli-rosa (Rose-of-heaven)	Flesh
Malcomia maritima (Virginian-stock)	Pink
Malope trifida grandiflora (Mallow-wort)	Rose-red
Mathiola (Stock)	Rose, pink
Mimulus (Monkeyflower)	Scarlet
Myosotis dissitiflora (Forget-me-not)	Pink
Nemesia strumosa	Rose, pink
Nicotiana Sanderæ and sylvestris	Crimson to white
Papaver Rhœas (Shirley or Field Poppy)	Crimson to pink
P. somniferum (Opium Poppy)	Red to white
Petunia hybrida	Bright rose to pink
Phlox Drummondii	Rose to white
Portulaca grandiflora (Portulaca)	Purplish-crimson to white
Rehmannia angulata	Rose

Salvia splendens	Scarlet	Silene Armeria (Sweet-William	
Saponaria calabrica (Calabrian		Campion)	Rose
Soapwort)	Rose	Tropæolum (Nasturtium)	Scarlet, rose
Scabiosá atropurpurea	Rose to white	Vinca rosea (Madagascar	
Schizanthus pinnatus (Butterfly-		Periwinkle)	Rose to white
flower)	Rose to white	Zinnia elegans	Scarlet to white
Senecio elegans (Purple Groundsel)	Rose to white		

BLUE, LAVENDER, PURPLE, AND MAUVE ANNUALS

The effect of light and shadow, the difference in varieties, the changing color of the flower itself as it blooms and fades, and personal opinion, often make difficult the drawing of an exact line of demarcation between lavender and blue. The following is a list generally considered correct.

Ageratum Houstonianum	Blue	Limonium sinuatum (Statice or	
Anagallis indica (Blue Pimpernel)	Blue	Sea-lavender)	Lilac
Anchusa var. Blue Bird	Blue	Linaria	Purple
Asperula azurea setosa (Blue		Lobelia	Violet and blue
Woodruff)	Blue	Lupinus (Lupine)	Purples and lilacs
Brachycome iberidifolia (Swan		Malcomia maritima (Virginian	
River Daisy)	Blue	Stock)	Purple
Browallia demissa (elata)	Lavender	Martynia fragrans	Mauve
Callistephus (China Aster)	Blue and lavender	Mathiola (Stock)	Lilac and purple
Campanula (Blue Bellflower or		Myosotis (Forget-me-not)	Blue
Annual Canterbury Bell)	Blue	Nemophila insignis (Baby Blue-eyes)	Blue
Centaurea	Blue and lavender	Nigella damascena (Love-in-a-mist)	Blue
Clarkia elegans and pulchella	Lavender	Papaver Rhœas (Shirley or Field	
Collinsia bicolor (Chinese-houses)	Blue	Poppy)	Blue
Cosmos diversifolius	Lilac	Petunia	Purple and lilac
Cynoglossum amabile		Phacelia	Lavender and blue
(Houndstongue)	Blue	Phlox Drummondii	Purple and lilac
Datura fastuosa	Purple	Salpiglossis sinuata	Purple
Delphinium ajacis (Larkspur)	Blue	Salvia (Sage)	Blue
Echium plantagineum	Purple to blue	Scabiosa atropurpurea	Purple and blue
Felicia bergeriana (Kingfisher		Schizanthus pinnatus	Purples and mauve
Daisy)	Blue	Senecio elegans	Purple
Gilia	Purple and blue	Torenia Fournieri	Blue and purple
Godetia grandiflora	Purple	Trachymene cærulea (Laceflower)	Blue
Heliophila	Blue	Viola tricolor (Pansy)	Varied purple and
Iberis (Candytuft)	Lilac shades		blue
Impatiens (Balsam)	Lilac shades	Xeranthemum annuum	Purple
Lathyrus odoratus (Sweet Pea)	Lilac and purple		

YELLOW AND ORANGE ANNUALS

Alonsoa Warscewiczii	Orange to scarlet	Emilia flammea (Tasselflower)	Orange
Antirrhinum majus	Orange, yellow	Eschscholtzia californica (California	
Argemone mexicanum (Mexican		Poppy)	Yellow, orange
Poppy)	Yellow or orange	Gaillardia pulchella (Rose-ring	
Calendula officinalis (Pot Marigold)	Gold, sulphur	Gaillardia)	Yellow
Callistephus chinensis (China Aster)	Yellow, orange	Gamolepsis tagetes	Orange to yellow
Celosia (Cockscomb)	Yellow, orange	Helianthus (Sunflower)	Golden, red to
Chrysanthemum	Yellow, orange,		brown
	bronze	Helichrysum (Strawflower)	Yellow
Coreopsis (Goldenwave and	Yellow, brown to	Hunnemannia fumariæfolia (Tulip	
Calliopsis)	red	Poppy)	Yellow
Cosmos sulphureus (Yellow Cosmos)	Yellow	Lathyrus odoratus (Sweet Pea)	Yellow, orange
Datura chlorantha (Yellow		Layia elegans (Tidytips)	Yellow
Floripondio)	Yellow	Leptosyne Stillmanii (Stillman	
Diascia Barberæ (Twinspur)	Orange	Coreopsis)	Yellow
Dimorphotheca aurantiaca (Cape-		Limonium Bonduellii (Statice or	
marigold)	Orange, lemon	Sea-lavender)	Yellow

YELLOW AND ORANGE ANNUALS—continued

Linaria bipartita (Toadflax)	Yellow
Lupinus luteus (European Yellow Lupine)	Yellow
L. mutabilis	Yellow
Mimulus luteus (Monkeyflower)	Yellow
Nemesia strumosa	Orange
Œnothera Drummondii	Yellow
Papaver Rhœas (Shirley or Field Poppy)	Orange
Portulaca grandiflora	Yellow
Reseda odorata (Mignonette)	Greenish yellow
Rudbeckia bicolor (Pinewoods Coneflower)	Yellow

Salpiglossis sinuata	Variegated yellow
Sanvitalia procumbens	Golden yellow
Sphenogyne speciosa	Yellow
Tagetes (Marigold)	Yellow, tawny
Thunbergia alata (Clockvine)	Yellow
Tithonia rotundifolia (Mexican Sunflower)	Rich Orange
Tropæolum (Nasturtium)	Yellow, orange
Ursinia anethoides	Orange
Venidium fastuosum	Orange
Viola tricolor	Yellow
Zinnia elegans	Yellow

ANNUALS FOR SEASHORE AND MOUNTAIN

(For cooler and more moist regions)

Alonsoa (Maskflower)
Brachycome (Swan River Daisy)
Chrysanthemum (Annual sorts)
Clarkia
Collinsia
Cosmos
Eschscholtzia (California Poppy)
Gilia

Godetia (Satinflower)
Hymenoxis
Layia (Tidytips)
Leptosiphon
Lupinus (Lupine)
Mentzelia (Blazing-star)
Mimulus (Monkeyflower)
Nemesia

Nemophila (Love-grove)
Nigella (Love-in-a-mist)
Papaver
Phacelia
Reseda (Mignonette)
Saponaria (Calabrian Soapwort)
Scabiosa (Sweet Scabious)

EDGING ANNUALS

Ageratum (dwarf varieties)
Alyssum maritimum (Sweet Alyssum)
Anagallis Monelli
A. Phillipsii
Antirrhinum, dwarf (Snapdragon)
Asperula azurea setosa
Brachycome (Swan River Daisy)
Calendula, dwarf (Pot-marigold)
Centaurea candidissima (Dusty Miller)
Celosia, dwarf
Collinsia bicolor
Coreopsis tinctoria (Calliopsis)
Dianthus sinensis
Eschscholtzia californica (California Poppy)
Iberis umbellata (Candytuft)

Kaulfussia amelloides (South African Daisy)
Linum grandiflorum (Scarlet Flax)
Lobelia erinus (dwarf)
Matricaria inodora (a double daisy)
Mesembryanthemum crystallinum (Iceplant)
Nemophila insignis
Phacelia campanularia
Phlox Drummondii
Sanvitalia
Saponaria calabrica
Silene pendula
Tagetes (Marigold)
Torenia (Wishboneflower)
Tropæolum (Nasturtium)
Verbena (Vervain)

ANNUALS FOR WINDOW AND PORCH BOXES

Ageratum
Alyssum
Browallia speciosa
Centaurea (Dusty Miller)

Lobelia erinus
Maurandia
Petunia
Phlox

Portulaca (Rosemoss)
Tagetes signata var. Pumila
Thunbergia (Clockvine)
Tropæolum majus (Nasturtium)

Verbena
Vinca rosea (Periwinkle)
Zinnia

ANNUALS FOR TEMPORARY HEDGES

Helianthus debilis (Cucumber Sunflower)
Helichrysum (Strawflower)
Impatiens (Balsam)

Kochia trichophylla
Mirabilis (Four-o'clock)
Pennisetum (Fountain Grass)

ANNUALS FOR MOIST PLACES

Ionopsidium (Diamondflower)   Nemophila (Love-grove)   Mimulus (Monkeyflower)

ANNUALS FOR POTS IN GREENHOUSE OR CONSERVATORY

Browallia speciosa
Campanula (Canterbury Bells)
Celosia
Cobæa
Diascia

Helipterum (Everlastings)
Impatiens (Balsam)
Ipomœa purpurea (Morning-glory)
Nicotiana (Flowering Tobacco)
Penstemon gloxinioides (Beard-tongue)

Reseda odorata (Mignonette)
Schizanthus (Butterfly Flower)
Torenia
Tropæolum (Nasturtium)

ANNUALS AS EVERLASTINGS

Acroclinium
Catananche (Cupid's-dart)
Gomphrena (Globe-Amaranth)
Grasses, Ornamental

Helichrysum (Strawflower)
Limonium (Statice or Sea-lavender)
Rhodanthe
Xeranthemum (Immortelle)

ANNUALS FOR COOL OR SHADY PLACES

Anchusa
Campanula (Annual Canterbury Bells)

Impatiens (Balsam)
Nemophila (Love-grove)

Nicotiana (Flowering Tobacco)
Œnothera (Evening Primrose)

Omphalodes
Polygonum

ANNUALS FOR CUT FLOWERS

†Acroclinium (Everlasting)
 Amaranthus caudatus (Love-lies-bleeding)
*Antirrhinum (Snapdragon)
 Arctotis grandis (Bushy Arctotis)
 Argemone (Pricklepoppy)
 Browallia demissa
 B. speciosa
*Calendula officinalis (Pot-marigold)
*Callistephus (China Aster)
*Centaurea moschata (Sweet-sultan)
 Chrysanthemum
 Clarkia elegans
 Coreopsis tinctoria (Calliopsis)
*Cosmos
*Delphinium ajacis (Rocket Larkspur)
*Dianthus chinensis (China Pink)
 Dimorphotheca aurantiaca (Cape-marigold)
 Emilia flammea (Tasselflower)
 Eschscholtzia californica (California Poppy)
 Gaillardia
†Gomphrena globosa (Globe-Amaranth)
*Gypsophila
 Helianthus annuus (Sunflower)
†Helichrysum (Strawflower)
 Lathyrus odorata (Sweet Pea)
 Lavatera trimestris (Treemallow)

Leptosyne Stillmanii (Stillman Coreopsis)
†Limonium sinuatum (Notchleaf Statice)
†L. Suworowi (Suworow Statice)
*Lupinus (Lupine)
 Matricaria inodora (a double daisy)
 Mathiola bicornis
 M. incana
 Nicotiana (Flowering Tobacco)
 Nigella (Love-in-a-mist)
 Papaver glaucum (Tulip Poppy)
 P. Rhœas (Corn Poppy)
 P. umbrosum (Field Poppy)
 Phacelia campanularia
 P. tanacetifolia
 Phlox Drummondii
 Polygonum orientale
 Reseda odorata (Mignonette)
 Salpiglossis sinuata
 Scabiosa atropurpurea (Sweet Scabiosa)
 Senecio elegans (Jacobæa)
 Tagetes (Marigold)
 Verbena erinoides (Moss Vervain)
 V. hybrids
 Zinnias elegans
 Z. Haageana

* Salable cut flowers.   † Everlasting flowers.

SCENTED ANNUALS

Ageratum Houstonianum (Mexican Ageratum) delicate
Alyssum maritimum (Sweet Alyssum) delicate
Antirrhinum (Snapdragon) delicate
Calendula (Pot-marigold) pungent
Centaurea moschata (Sweet Sultan) delicate
Heliotropium peruvianum (one of the loveliest)
Iberis coronaria (Candytuft)
I. umbellata (Purple Candytuft)
Lupinus luteus (Yellow Lupine)
*Mathiola bicornis (Night-scented Stock)
 M. incana (Ten-weeks Stock)

Mimulus moschata (Muskplant)
*Nicotiana affinis (Flowering Tobacco)
*Œnothera Lamarchiana (Evening Primrose)
 Petunia—heavy
 Reseda odorata (Mignonette) delightful
 Scabiosa—dainty
 Tagetes (Marigold) pungent
*Verbascum phlomoides (Tall Mullein)
 Verbena erinoides (Moss Vervain)
 V. hybrida

* Night-scented.

TABULAR LIST OF ANNUALS

SCIENTIFIC NAME	COMMON NAME	HEIGHT IN INCHES	DISTANCE APART	COLOR	DATES OF SOWING I. = INDOORS O. = OUTDOORS	REMARKS
Abronia umbellata	Sand-verbena	6	6	Rose	I. March	Really a perennial but usually treated as an annual
Acroclinium (see Helipterum)						
Adonis aestivalis	Summer Adonis	12	6	Crimson	I. March	
aleppica		18	6	Red	O. April	Not easy
Ageratum Houstonianum	Mexican Ageratum	18–24	12	Blue, white	I. March	Reseeds prolifically and when once established it comes up year after year from self-sown seed
intermediate		9–12	9	Blue, white	I. March	
dwarf		4–8	6	Blue, white	I. March	
Alonsoa acutifolia	Maskflower	24	9	Scarlet	I. April	Also good as potted plant. Does not endure a hot, humid climate
Warscewiczii		18	6	Orange-scarlet		
Alyssum maritimum	Sweet Alyssum					
compact varieties		3–4	6	White	I. March, O. April	Fine edger
spreading varieties		6–10	9	White	I. March, O. April	Fine edger
Amaranthus caudatus	Love-lies-bleeding	48–72	18	Crimson	O. May	
Ammobium alatum	Winged Everlasting	24	12	White	I. April	
Anagallis indica	Blue Pimpernel	6	6	Blue	O. April, May	
Anchusa, var. Blue Bird	Blue Bird Anchusa	18	9	Bright blue	O. May	One of the best of the blue annuals
Antirrhinum majus	Snapdragon					
dwarf varieties		6	6	Orange, yellow, white, pink, red, purple shades	I. March, O. April	Select rust-proof varieties
intermediate varieties		18	10		I. March, O. April	
tall varieties		36	12–18		I. March, O. April	
Arctotis grandis	Bushy Arctotis	24	10	White, bluish eye	I. March, O. April	Excellent for cutting
Argemone grandiflora	Pricklepoppy	36	12	White	O. May	Likes warm soil and hottest exposure
mexicana	Mexican Poppy	24–36	12	Yellow or orange	O. May	
Asperula azurea setosa	Blue Woodruff	9		Gray-blue		Does well in poor soil or light shade
Aster (see Callistephus)						
Bartonia		36–48	24	White, yellow	O. May	Opens in the evening, fragrant
Brachycome iberidifolia	Swan River Daisy	12	6	Blue, pink, white	I. April, O. May	Good edger. Short period of bloom. Sow for succession
Browallia demissa (elata)		12–18	9	Purple-blue, white	I. April, O. May	Good pot plant for terrace or conservatory
speciosa major		12–24	9	Purple-blue	I. February	
Cacalia (see Emilia)						
Calandrinia grandiflora		18	10	Rose		
speciosa		9	6	Ruby-red		
Calendula officinalis	Pot-marigold	12–24	12–15	Gold, sulphur	O. April	Very hardy. May be grown in South for winter bloom
Callistephus chinensis	China Aster	18	10	Various (blue, lavender, white, pink, red, yellow)	I. March	

Campanula ramosissima	Bluestar Bellflower	12	6	Blue	I. March	
Annual Canterbury Bells (in variety)		24	12	Blue, pink, white	I. March, O. April	Bloom in late summer and early fall
drabifolia (attica)		6	6	Blue, white	O. April	
Celosia argentea (plumosa)	Feather Cockscomb	36–48	12–18	Yellow to crimson	O. April	The yellow and orange varieties are very effective for autumn bloom in border
all var. of argentea, dwarf argentea,		12	9	Yellow to crimson	O. April	
cristata	Cockscomb	24		Yellow to crimson	O. April	
Centaurea americana	Basketflower	36–48	18	Lavender	O. April	
Cineraria	Dusty-Miller	24	15	Purple-rose	I. March	
Cyanus	Cornflower	36	12	Blue, pink, white	O. Sept. or April	Short period of bloom
imperialis	Royal Sweet-sultan	36	12	Blue, pink, white	I. April, O. May	
moschata	Sweet-sultan	12	10	Blue, pink, white	I. April, O. May	
Centranthus macrosiphon	Spur-valerian	24	9	Rose, white	O. April	
Chrysanthemum carinatum	Annual Chrysanthemum	24	12	White, marked variously	O. April	
coronarium	Crowndaisy	12–30	9	Sulphur yellow	O. April	
Parthenium	Feverfew	24	12		I. April	
segetum	Corn-marigold	12–24	9	Golden	I. April	Excellent for cutting. Prefers cool, growing weather
Clarkia elegans		12–24	9	Rose to white and purple	O. April	
pulchella				Rose to white and purple	I. April	
Cleome spinosa	Spiderflower	48–60	24	Magenta, white	O. April	Excellent in border because of its height
Clintonia pulchella		4–6	9	White, marked with blue	I. April	
Collinsia bicolor	Chinese-houses	18	6	Blue, pink and white	O. April	
Collomia coccinea		12	6	Scarlet	O. April	
Coreopsis Drummondii	Goldenwave	24	12	Yellow	O. April	
tinctoria	Calliopsis	36	15	Yellow; brown-red	O. April–June, Sept.	
tinctoria var. Crimson King		8	6	Yellow; brown-red	O. April–June, Sept.	
Cosmos bipinnatus	Cosmos	48–62	18–24	Crimson to white	O. April	Valuable for cutting
diversifolius	Black Cosmos	36	18	Lilac	O. April	
sulphureus	Yellow Cosmos	48–72	18–24	Yellow	I. March	
Crepis barbata rubra	Hawkweed	12	6	Rose, white (daisy-like)		
Cuphea ignea	Fiery Cuphea	18	12	Scarlet	I. June	
Cynoglossum amabile	Houndstongue	24	9	Blue	I. April, O. May	
Datura chlorantha	Yellow Floripondio	24	18	Yellow	I. April	
fastuosa (D. cornucopia)	Cornucopia Floripondio	18–24	18	White, purple reverse	I. April	
Delphinium Ajacis	Rocket Larkspur	24–36	9	Various blues	O. Sept., March	
Consolida	Field Larkspur	18–24	9	Various blues	O. Sept., March	
Dianthus chinensis	China Pink	12–18	6	Various	O. Sept., April, I. March	
Diascia Barberœ	Twinspur	18	6	Pink, orange	I. March	
Didiscus (see Trachymene)						
Dimorphotheca aurantiaca	Cape-marigold	12–18	9	Orange, lemon to white	I. March	Excellent for hot, dry position

TABULAR LIST OF ANNUALS—continued

SCIENTIFIC NAME	COMMON NAME	HEIGHT IN INCHES	DISTANCE APART	COLOR	DATES OF SOWING I. = INDOORS O. = OUTDOORS	REMARKS
Echium creticum	Viper's Bugloss	12–18	12	Red	I. Jan.	Very effective in border
plantagineum		18–24	15	Purple-blue	I. Jan.	
plantagineum hybrids		18–24	15	Pale blue, pink, mauve, white	I. Jan.	
Emilia flammea sagittata	Tasselflower	18+	9	Scarlet, orange	O. April	
		18	9	Scarlet	I. March, O. May	
Eschscholtzia californica	California Poppy	12	9	Yellow, pink, red	O. March, Sept.	Do not transplant. Good cut flower
Euphorbia heterophylla	Painted Spurge	36	12	Red leaves at tips	O. April	Milky juice is poisonous
marginata (E. variegata)	Snow-on-the-mountain	36–48	12	Leaves margined white	O. March	
Felicia bergeriana	Kingfisher Daisy	6	6	Blue with yellow disks		Daisy-like flower
Gaillardia amblyodon	Maroon Gaillardia	18–24	9	Brown-red or maroon	O. April	
pulchella	Rose-ring Gaillardia	18–24	9	Yellow and rose-purple	O. April	
Gamolepis tagetes		12	10	Orange-yellow	I. March, O. May	
Gilia capitata	Globe Gilia	24	9	Blue	I. March, O. April	
coccinea	Scarlet Gilia	36	12	Scarlet	I. March, O. May	
coronopifolia	Texasplume	36	9	Scarlet	I. March, O. May	
tricolor	Bird's-eye Gilia	24	9	White, purple	O. April	
Godetia amoena	Farewell-to-Spring	24	12	Rose to white	O. April	
grandiflora	Whitney Godetia	18	9	Purple, rose to white	O. April	
Gomphrena globosa	Globe-Amaranth	24	12	Magenta, amaranth, salmon-white	I. March, O. May	
Gypsophila elegans	Baby's-breath	12–18	6	White	O. April	
muralis	Cushion Gypsophila	12	6	Rose	O. April	
Helianthus annuus	Sunflower	96–108	3	Golden	O. April	
debilis	Cucumber Sunflower	48	2	Golden, sulphur	O. April	
dwarf varieties		12–36	12	Yellow or red-brown	O. April	
Helichrysum bracteatum	Strawflower	36	9–12	Red, pink, yellow, white	I. March, O. May	Excellent for winter bouquet
Heliophila		18	10	Blue, white-eyed	I. March, O. May	
Heliotropium	Heliotrope	10	12	Lavender, purple	I. March	Sweet scented
Helipterum Manglesii	Mangles Everlasting	18	6	Rose	I. March, O. May	
roseum	Rose E. (Acroclinium)	12–18	6	Rose	I. March, O. May	
Hunnemannia fumariaefolia	Goldencup or Tulip Poppy	18–24	9–12	Soft yellow	I. April pots	
Iberis affinis	Candytuft	16	16	White, lilac tinge	O. April	
amara		12+	12	White	O. April	
umbellata		16	16	Purple, carmine, pink	O. April	Sometimes fragrant
Impatiens Balsamina	Garden Balsam	12–18	9	Various—pink, rose, purple, violet, white	O. April	
Sultani	Sultan, Patience	15	9	Rose or white	O. April	
Incarvillia variabilis		18	8–10	Yellow, pink, white	I. March, O. May	
Jacobea (*see* Senecio)						

		Height	Spread	Color	Sowing	Remarks
Kochia scoparia	Belvidere or Summer Cypress	18–24	12–18		O. May	
trichophila	Summer Cypress	18–24	12–18	White, pink, rose, purple, yellow, peach, orange	O. May	Makes an excellent low hedge
Lathyrus odoratus	Sweet Pea	48+ (climbing)	6		O. October, April	Prefers cool growing weather
Lathyrus dwarf varieties		8	6	Same	Same	
Lavatera trimestris	Treemallow	24–60	12–18	Rose, white	O. May	
alba splendens		36	18	White	O. May	
rosea splendens		36	18	Rose	O. May	
Layia elegans	Tidytips	12	10	Yellow, tipped white	O. May	
Leptosiphon hybrida		12	10	Rosy carmine	I. April	
Leptosyne Stillmanii	Stillman Coreopsis	18	15	Large yellow, resembling coreopsis	O. April	
maritima		24–36	12	Yellow	O. April	
Limonium Bonduellii	Sea-lavender or Statice	18–24	15	Yellow	I. March	
sinuatum	Notchleaf Sea-lavender	18–24	15	Violet to white	I. March	
Suworowi	Suworow Sea-lavender	18	15	Rose	I. March	
Linaria bipartita	Toadflax	18–24	15	Yellow to crimson, pink and purple	O. April, May	
maroccana		12	4	Bright purple with yellow spot	O. April, May	
Linum grandiflorum	Flowering Flax	8–12	9	Crimson	O. April	Excellent as an edger
Lobelia Erinus, dwarf var.	Edging Lobelia	4–6	6	Violet, blue, white	I. Feb., March	
Erinus, trailing var.		4–6	9	Violet, blue, white	I. Feb., March	
Lobelia tenuior		12–18	6	Bright blue or white	I. March, O. April	
Lunaria annua	Honesty	18	12	Magenta	I. March, O. April	
Lupinus Hartwegii	Hartweg Lupine	36	12–18	Purple, pink	I. pots March, O. May	Very effective in the border and good for cutting
hirsutus	Blue Lupine	24	12	Blue	I. pots March, O. May	
luteus	European Yellow L.	24	12	Yellow	I. pots March, O. May	
mutabilis		24	18	Violet, yellow and white	I. pots March, O. May	
dwarf varieties		12	9	Violet, yellow, pink and white	I. pots March, O. May	
Lychnis Cœli-rosa (Viscaria)	Rose-of-heaven	12	6	Flesh	O. April	
Malcomia maritima	Virginian-stock	4–8	3	Purple, pink, white	O. April	
Malope trifida grandiflora	Mallow-wort	30	12	Rose-red	O. April	
Martynia fragrans		24	12	Mauve	O. April	Woolly foliage, sweetly scented
Mathiola bicornis		12	6	Lilac	I. March, O. April	Night-blooming, grown for fragrance
incana dwarf	Stock	12–18	9	Tones of rose and purple, also white	I. March, O. April	
incana tall	Stock	24–30	12–18		I. March to April	
Mimulus luteus	Monkeyflower	18	9	Scarlet, crimson, yellow mottled	I. March, O. May	
tigrinus		12–18	9	Red and yellow	O. May	
Mirabilis jalapa	Four-o'clock	24	12	Pink, white, yellow	I. March, O. May	Flowers open at four o'clock
Myosotis dissitiflora	Forget-me-not	12	6	Blue, pink	I. April	Lovely as an edger

TABULAR LIST OF ANNUALS—continued

SCIENTIFIC NAME	COMMON NAME	HEIGHT IN INCHES	DISTANCE APART	COLOR	DATES OF SOWING (I. = INDOORS, O. = OUTDOORS)	REMARKS
Nemesia strumosa	Nemesia	18	9	Orange, rose to white	I. March	Prefers cool growing weather
Nemophila insignis	Baby Blue-eyes	9	12	Clear blue	O. April	
maculata	Spotted Nemophila	10	8	White, black spotted	I. April	
Nicotiana alata (N. affinis)	Winged Tobacco	36–48	12	White	I. March, O. April	Delightfully fragrant
Sandere	Flowering Tobacco	24–36	12	Red	I. March, O. April	
sylvestris		36–48	12	White to crimson	I. March, O. April	
Nigella damascena	Love-in-a-mist	18–24	9	Blue	O. April	Short season of bloom
Œnothera Americana	Evening-primrose	12	6	White	O. May	
Drummondii	Drummond E.	12	6	Yellow	O. May	
Papaver Rheas	Shirley Poppy, Field	18–36	12	Tones of scarlet, orange, pink, blue	O. Nov. or March	Hairy stems and buds
somniferum	Opium Poppy	24–36	9	Various (white to red)	O. Sept., March	Source of opium. Smooth stems and buds
Penstemon gloxinioides	Beard-tongue	24–36	10	Many		For use in pots for the greenhouse
Petunia hybrida, dwarf	Petunia	6–8	6	White to bright rose and purple	I. March, O. April	Long season of bloom
tall and trailing		12–24	12	White to bright rose and purple	I. March, O. April	
Phacelia campanularia	Harebell Phacelia	12	9	Blue	I. March, O. April	
ciliata		12	9	Blue	O. April	
viscida		12	9	Blue	O. April	
tanacetifolia		24	12	Light purple	O. April	
Phaseolus	Scarlet Runner		8	Red	O. May	Rapid climber
Phlox Drummondii dwarf varieties	Drummond Phlox	6	6	White, magenta, rose, tawny and purple	I. March, O. May	Plan for successive plantings
tall varieties		6–12, 12–18	9		I. March, O. May	
Portulaca grandiflora	Portulaca	8	6	Purplish-crimson, yellow, white	O. April	Excellent for hot, dry situations
Rehmannia angulata		48	18	Rose	I. March	Lovely perennial treated as annual
Reseda odorata, dwarf	Mignonette	6	12	Greenish-yellow	I. pots April	Lovely fragrance. Does not like transplanting
tall varieties		12–18	12	Greenish-yellow	I. pots April	
Rudbeckia bicolor	Pinewoods Coneflower	24	18	Yellow, black center	O. April	
Salpiglossis sinuata	Salpiglossis	18–24	9	Purples and yellows variegated	I. March, O. May	Rather temperamental
Salvia patens	Gentian Sage	18	12	Deep blue	I. March	A most intense and lovely blue
farinacea	Mealycup Sage	24	9	Blue	I. March, O. May	Half-hardy P. treated as A. Very useful for the border
splendens	Scarlet Sage	36	18	Scarlet	I. Feb., March, O. May	Should be used in moderation
splendens var. Welwyn	Welwyn Sage	36	18	Pink	I. March, O. May	
Sanvitalia procumbens		6, Tr.	9	Golden	I. March, O. May	
procumbens flore pleno		6	9	Golden	I. March, O. May	Double-flowering

Botanical name	Common name			Color	Sowing	Remarks
Saponaria calabrica	Calabrian Soapwort	12+	10	Rose	I. March, O. April	
Vaccaria		18		Pink, white	I. March, O. April	
Scabiosa atropurpurea	Sweet Scabious	36	12	Purple, blue, mahogany, rose, white	I. March, O. April	Attract hummingbirds
Schizanthus pinnatus	Butterfly Flower					
dwarf varieties		12	9	White, rose, purple spotted	I. June, April, O. May	
tall varieties		24–36	12–18	White, rose, purple spotted	I. June, April, O. May	
Senecio elegans	Purple Groundsel	18	6	Purple, rose to white	I. March	
Silene Armeria	Sweet-William Campion	12	6	Rose	O. April	
Solanum integrifolium		36	24	Inconspicuous	I. March	Grown for orange-red fruit for indoor decoration
Sphenogyne speciosa		10	6	Yellow, daisy-like		
Statice (see Limonium)						
Stock (see Mathiola)						
Tagetes erecta	Aztec or African Marigold	48	12–18	Gold, lemon	I. March, O. May	Excellent for cutting
patula	French Marigold	18	9	Gold, spotted maroon	I. March, O. May	Very effective in fall garden
signata pumila	Mexican Marigold	12	6	Gold	I. March, O. May	
Thunbergia alata	Clockvine	9	12	Yellow with dark center	I. March, O. May	Trailer
Tithonia rotundifolia (T. speciosa)	Mexican Sunflower	72–100	36	Rich orange	I. March, O. May	Coarse; spectacular flowers
Torenia Fournieri	Blue-wings	9–12	6	Blue and velvety purple	I. March, O. May	Sun or partial shade. Endures intense heat well
Trachymene cærulea	Laceflower	24		Soft blue	I. March	
Tropæolum majus	Nasturtium	48, Cl.	12–15	Scarlet to yellow	O. April	}Pungent odor
minor	Dwarf Nasturtium	12	6	Scarlet to yellow	O. April	
Ursinia anethoides		12	6	Orange, daisy-like	I. March, O. April	Good for very sunny border
hybrids		12–24	10	Orange, daisy-like	I. March, O. April	Good for very sunny border
Venidium fastuosum		24–36	12	Orange with dark centers	I. March, O. April	Spectacular, spiny-looking foliage
Verbena erinoides	Moss Vervain	8, Tr.	9	Magenta to white	I. March	
hybrida		8, Tr.	9	Magenta to white	I. March	}Long season of bloom
tall varieties		12	12	Magenta to white	I. March	
Vinca rosea	Madagascar Periwinkle	18	9	Rose, white	I. Jan., Feb.	
Viscaria zerantheum (see Lychnis)						
Viola tricolor	Pansy	8–12	9	Varied purple, blue, yellow, or white	I. Feb, O. April, or O. August	Usually B., but may be treated as an A.
Xeranthemum annuum	Immortelle	24–36	9	Purple, white	I. March	Everlasting
Zinnia elegans	Giant Zinnia	36	12	Scarlet, rose, white, orange and yellow	I. March, O. April	
dwarf	Dwarf Zinnia	15	9		I. March, O. April	Long season of bloom
Haageana	Orange Zinnia	18	9	Yellow, blotched maroon	I. March, O. April	

XXV

BIENNIALS

BOTANICALLY, a biennial is a plant which completes its life cycle within the space of two years. During the first year vegetative leaf growth is produced, and during the second year the plant blooms, produces seed, and dies.

In this group we find some of our most beautiful garden flowers, and yet, because they are not permanent residents of the garden, we are inclined to disregard their potentialities. It is true that they are but transients in the flower border—that few, if any of them, may be counted upon for even one full season of bloom, and yet during the space of the few brief weeks when they are in flower they will contribute a full measure of beauty to any planting composition.

Indeed, this transient quality of the biennials may be considered as one of their greatest assets, for it makes it more easily possible to plan for a long succession of bloom. Whereas the perennials, such as the columbines, iris, phlox and peonies, must be left undisturbed in the border throughout the season, even after their period of bloom is over, the biennials may be moved into the garden a few weeks before they are to flower and then, without a qualm, they may be ruthlessly uprooted as soon as their blooming period is over, leaving welcome space for the planting of annuals and summer flowering bulbs and perennials. Foxgloves may be followed by hardy chrysanthemums, gladioli may be planted as soon as the Canterbury bells have been removed, and pansies and English daisies, which make such a colorful spring border, may be followed, later in the season, by some of the gay little annuals such as phlox Drummondii, lobelia, and torenia.

So, while we may continue to consider the perennials as the pièce de résistance of our flower gardens, and while some of the annuals, particularly those which can be counted upon for a long season of bloom, may be considered almost equally invaluable, we must not overlook the possibilities of the biennials, for they have much to offer.

Transplanting

Most biennials may be very easily transplanted. Whenever possible the transplanting should be done on a cloudy day and the plants should be moved with sufficient soil about the roots. An application of a high-analysis, quickly soluble fertilizer at the rate of $\frac{1}{4}$ cupful for small plants, $\frac{1}{2}$ to 1 cupful for medium-sized and large plants, will help to prevent a setback at time of transplanting (see page 165).

When weather conditions are not favorable for transplanting, as during periods of intense sunshine and hot, drying winds, or when transplanting hollyhocks and other plants which are difficult to move, and when large plants already in flower are to be transplanted, the use of a plastic spray is recommended. It will prevent excessive loss of moisture, there will be little danger of wilting, and the plants may be moved with confidence of success (see page 682).

For the control of Insect Pests and Diseases see Chapter XLI.

BIENNIALS OF MERIT

Canterbury Bells (Campanula medium and C. calycanthema). Canterbury Bells are among the most beautiful and most showy of the biennials. In the South they come into bloom in March and April, while in the latitude of Philadelphia and New York they reach their height

328

of bloom during June. Coming as they do, just after the columbines and iris and foxgloves are over, they may be used as the dominant planting in the garden or they may assume a minor roll by filling in an occasional gap here and there.

Culture: Canterbury Bells may very easily be grown from seed. The seeds should be sown in June, either in frames or in a carefully prepared seed bed. The seed has excellent vitality, and a high percentage of germination is usually secured. The seedlings should be transplanted before they have become in the least crowded. Young Canterbury Bells are not entirely happy if exposed to full summer sunshine and after the first transplanting they will make much more rapid growth if they are protected by a lath frame, through which the mitigated sunlight may filter. A coldframe sloping to the north which does not receive sunlight throughout the entire day, offers a very satisfactory location for the growth of the young plants.

Canterbury Bells have a very fibrous root system and they may consequently be transplanted with the greatest ease. If the plants are lifted with ample earth about the roots and if the transplanting is done on a damp, cloudy day, Canterbury Bells may be moved into the garden when they are in full flower. As one cannot always be sure of good transplanting weather, however, it is advisable to move them into the garden after growth has started in the spring and before the plants come into bud. They will then have an opportunity to become well established before flowering. If the fading blooms are pinched off at the base, smaller auxiliary flower buds will develop and the flowering period may be considerably prolonged. In the border, the plants may be set 1 foot apart.

Canterbury Bells may be obtained in both single (Campanula medium) and double (Campanula caly-canthema) forms and in a wide range of color; delicate pink, deep rose, white, pale lavender-blue and a deep bluish-purple.

Soil Requirements: The plants thrive well in almost any soil, provided that it is well drained, but they will

CANTERBURY BELLS

attain a greater size and will give more abundant bloom if given a soil of high fertility.

In mild climates, Canterbury Bells may be wintered in the open ground, if the soil is well drained, but where the winters are severe they require the protection of a coldframe. If only a few plants are being grown and if a frame is not available, large inverted flower pots placed over the plants will afford excellent protection. No covering should be used which will mat down over the crowns, as the plants are rather sensitive to crown rot.

English Daisies (Bellis perennis). In England these winsome spring daisies reseed so prolifically that they are apt to infest the lawns and they are frequently regarded as a pest. Since they do not reseed abundantly enough in this country to become a nuisance and are so gay and charming in the spring border, they have endeared themselves to many gardeners. Coming in shades of pink, deep rose, and white, they may be used in pleasant combination with pansies, violas and forget-me-nots in the planting of a Botticelli border—which is always so colorful and gay.

Culture: English daisies are of very easy culture. The seeds should be sown in July or early August in flats or in frames, and the young seedlings should be transplanted when small, being spaced from 4 to 6 inches apart. In the North they will require some winter protection, in the South they may be wintered in the open ground. In the spring the plants may be transplanted very successfully when in bud or in full flower. They have no decided soil preferences and no pests or diseases, and yet, modest and humble though they may be, they add their share of bloom and beauty to the spring border.

Forget-me-nots (Myosotis). Some species of forget-me-nots, such as Myosotis palustris, are true perennials, while others are commonly classed as biennials. For spring bloom in the garden the seed should be sown in late July or early August, the seedlings being transplanted and wintered over in the frames or in the open. As the young seedling plants are rather susceptible to damping-off every precaution should be taken to see that the soil in the seed bed is free from contamination. For the control of damping off, see Chapter XXXIII. The plants may be transplanted to the flower border in spring, and may be moved with great ease. While forget-me-nots prefer a damp, woodsy soil, they will settle down quite happily in any location in the garden. They may be set from 6 to 8 inches apart.

Varieties: The most desirable variety for spring bloom is the large-flowered Myosotis dissitiflora. The flowers are of a more delicate shade of blue than some of the other types and are borne in graceful sprays, the plants reaching a height of from 8 to 9 inches. The plants bloom over a long period, from April well into June, and they sometimes reseed so abundantly that they seem to be almost perennial in habit, coming up year after year. The pale blue of the forget-me-nots is lovely in combination with other flowers in the spring border. They may also be used very delightfully as an under planting in tulip beds.

Foxgloves (Digitalis). Although there are several species of Digitalis which are true perennials, those which are most commonly grown in the flower garden are of a distinctly biennial habit of growth, and they are, perhaps, the most beautiful members of this group.

In England one sees foxgloves everywhere. The steep banks along the country lanes in Devonshire and Cornwall are gay with them in springtime, great drifts of them may be found in the open woodlands, and in the English gardens they are a glory to behold. There is no other flower which can quite take the place of the foxgloves in the spring border. They are among the first flowers of the season to give height and substance to the garden composition, and the stately spires of bloom against a background of hedge or wall add beauty and distinction to any planting. Coming into flower just as the first exultant ecstasy of spring bloom has passed, they may be used as the dominant note in the garden until the delphiniums and roses are ready to claim the stage.

Types and Varieties: Digitalis purpurea is the wild foxglove of England, and it is from this species that most of our improved strains have been developed. *Gloxiniæflora* is an old-fashioned variety which is still popular. It closely resembles the wild type, being more vigorous in habit and bearing longer spikes of bloom. The flowers are always spotted and may be obtained in a variety of colorings—white, rose, purple and mixed. While it is lovely in itself, it cannot compare in size or in beauty of coloring with some of the more recent introductions. The *Giant Shirley Hybrids* were developed by the Rev. W. Wilks at his home in England and bear witness to his skill as a plant breeder. The plants are of extraordinary size and vigor, often reaching a height of 6 feet, and the large, drooping flowers which are clustered closely along the flower spikes range in color from white to dark rose and purple, many of them being blotched and spotted with crimson and maroon. The *Lutz Hybrids* offer an entirely new and very charming color range, the flowers varying from a delicate cream pink to a light salmon. *Sutton's Apricot* and *Sutton's Giant Primrose* are two varieties of unusual coloring and great beauty, and may be used in pleasant combination with some of the perennials.

Culture: As the seeds of foxgloves are exceedingly fine, the seed bed should be well prepared. If the seeds are sown in June and if the young seedlings are given good care they will develop into large, vigorous plants by autumn and will give generous bloom the following spring. It is unwise to delay the sowing of the seed until August as the plants will be so small that they will not be capable of giving good bloom the following season. The seed should be sown either in flats or in a cold-frame. The seeds are usually of excellent vitality and germinate within a week or ten days after sowing. Care should be taken to see that the young seedlings are transplanted before they become in the least crowded. The young plants need an abundance of water during the growing season, and they should never be allowed to become stunted. If growth is at any time seriously checked, due to overcrowding, insufficient moisture, or lack of nourishment, the young plants have difficulty in making a full recovery. If conditions are favorable, however, the seedlings make rapid growth. They should be pricked out soon after the first true leaves have formed, and about a month or six weeks later they will again require transplanting, as it is essential that they be given ample room to develop. Where the climate is mild, foxgloves may be wintered over in the open ground, but where the winters are severe it is advisable to give them the protection of a frame, which not only protects them from extreme cold but also from excessive moisture. The thick fleshy leaves and the crown buds rot very easily if the soil remains soggy for any length of time. When the plants are wintered in frames they should be spaced well apart, at least 8 to 10 inches, in order that the air may circulate freely between the plants. In spring the plants may be moved from the frames to their permanent location in the garden. If the plants are lifted with an ample quantity of earth and if the transplanting is done on a cloudy day, they will suffer practically no check and will continue perfectly normal growth. If, however, the soil falls away from the roots or if the plants are exposed to wind and brilliant sunshine at the time of transplanting, they will suffer seriously and will never reach full perfection of bloom. They may be set from 10 to 12 inches apart.

Foxgloves will thrive well in almost any type of good garden soil provided that it is well drained, but they prefer a rich friable loam, and will make good use of a hearty diet of well-rotted manure or rich compost.

Hollyhocks (Althæa rosea). Picturesque and lovely, the hollyhocks are reminiscent of old-time gardens, and they seem equally at home beside a humble cottage doorway or in the long herbaceous borders of a formal garden. There are both single and double forms, and the flowers may be obtained in a wide range of colors—white, rose, salmon, pale primrose yellow, scarlet, crimson, purple and maroon. Hollyhocks are among our most useful background plants, attaining a height of from 6 to 8 feet. They are particularly lovely when planted against an old wall or picket fence. The period of bloom extends through the month of July into early August.

Culture: Although hollyhocks thrive best in full sun they will also do reasonably well in partial shade, and they may be grown very successfully in a flower border with a northern exposure.

STATELY FOXGLOVES

Preferring a light, well-drained soil of a neutral or slightly alkaline reaction, hollyhocks will thrive well in almost any garden, provided that the soil does not remain too saturated with moisture throughout the winter months. The plants respond well to good fertility but they will make fair growth on very poor soil.

Hollyhocks may be grown very easily from seed. The seeds may be planted either in a coldframe or in the open ground in late July or early August. The plants will bloom the following season. As hollyhocks produce a strong tap root it is very difficult to move the plants after they have attained any size. It is, therefore, wise to transplant the young seedlings to their permanent position in the garden while they are still quite small. Seedling plants, from seeds sown in July, may be transplanted to the garden in early autumn or early the following spring. Hollyhocks reseed so readily that after they are once established it is seldom necessary to make additional sowings. If a few flower stalks are allowed to produce seeds, these self-sown seedlings may be transplanted to any desired position in the garden. The chief disadvantage of this method is the fact that these self-sown seedlings will produce a variety of colorings and it is not possible to carry out a definite color planting. However, if only soft, pastel shades are used in the original planting, the colors usually blend harmoniously and mixed seedlings are often very lovely.

Because of their robust habit of growth, hollyhocks should be given ample space for their development, and should be planted from 2 to 2½ feet apart. As soon as the blooms have faded, the flower stalks should be cut down unless seed is to be produced.

For the control of insect pests and diseases, refer to Chapter XLI.

Iceland Poppies (Papaver nudicaule). Although the Iceland poppies are true perennials in their native habitat, they have assumed all the characteristics of the biennials when grown in our gardens and they are best treated as such. They bloom luxuriantly the year following sowing, and then they usually die out, an occasional plant surviving through another year.

The soft, gray-green leaves form a rosette-like growth just above the ground, and the delicate, lovely flowers are borne on long, slender, leafless stems. The plants vary in height from 12 to 20 inches, and as many as fifty blooms may be produced upon a single plant. The flowers are very lovely in form, being cup-shaped, with delicately crinkled petals.

Iceland poppies may be obtained in a wide variety of colorings ranging from pure white to salmon pink and from pale yellow to deep orange. Some of the named varieties are very fine: *Gibson's Giant Orange* is one of the best; *Tangerine* bears large flowers of a deep orange hue, and *Miniatum* is a bright orange scarlet. But perhaps the most beautiful of all is the lovely *Coonara Pink* variety which was originated in Australia. The flowers vary in color from a delicate shell pink to a warm apricot-salmon and are exquisite in their daintiness, being particularly lovely when planted in combination with the blue flax (Linum perenne), that enchanting flower which reflects the blue of the soft spring skies.

The Iceland poppies come into flower in spring, about the time that the late narcissus are in bloom, and if the seed pods are not allowed to develop, the plants will give scattered bloom throughout the season.

Culture: The seeds may be sown in August, or under glass in January or February. If the seed is sown during the summer, the young plants may be wintered over either in the frames or in the open. As the Iceland poppies are natives of the Arctic regions, they are extremely hardy and will withstand the most severe winter cold. The plants may be set a foot apart.

Pansies. No spring garden is quite complete without the piquant blossoms of the pansy, upturned to the sun. Many types and strains are now available and although the giant types have lately come into vogue, the smaller, quainter kinds will probably always be preferred by many gardeners. In planning special color schemes, it is a decided advantage to be able to obtain pansies in separate shades: blue, deep purple, wine red, maroon and yellow.

ICELAND POPPIES

Culture: Pansy seeds germinate most satisfactorily when there are wide fluctuations in temperature. Best results will therefore be obtained if sowing is delayed until cool nights follow warm days, as in late August and early September. Sowings may also be made in January in the greenhouse. Such plants will come into bloom later than the fall-sown plants but will continue in flower throughout most of the summer.

Fall-sown seedlings may be wintered over in the cold-frame or, in mild climates, in the open ground. If wintered in the open some protection against rabbits should be provided. They may be transplanted with the utmost ease, being moved when in full flower with no apparent setback to the plant. If the seed pods are not allowed to form, pansies may be kept in flower over a period of several months. When they begin to appear spindly and leggy, the plants may be cut back almost to the ground and a handful of fertilizer may be cultivated into the soil about them, and in reward for one's labor there will be a second blooming.

Pansies may be readily propagated by cuttings as well as by seed, the cuttings being taken in late spring or early summer.

The plants may be set from 6 to 8 inches apart.

Sweet William (Dianthus barbatus). The Sweet Williams are among the most useful of the biennials and now that they may be obtained in lovely pastel shades of pink, salmon and rose as well as in the deeper tones of red and scarlet, they may be given an important part to play in the spring garden. Among the most beautiful varieties are *Newport Pink*, *Fairy*, and *Sutton's Pink Beauty*.

Culture: The seeds should be sown in June in order that the young plants may reach a good development before winter. If the seeds are not sown until August the plants will be too small to give good bloom the following spring. In the South the plants may be wintered in the open. In the North they should be carried over in frames, being moved into the garden in early spring and set 9 inches apart.

Verbascum phœniceum. Verbascum phœniceum is a member of the Mullein family, and while it is not as well known as many of the other biennials it has distinct character and charm. The leaves form a prim rosette of green upon the surface of the soil, and the flowers, which come in soft shades of rose, mauve, and lavender, are borne on erect flower stalks, which vary from 12 to 15 inches in height.

Culture: The plants should be grown from seed sown in July. Because of the long, fleshy tap root the plants are moved with difficulty and must be handled with extreme care at the time of transplanting. The plant must be lifted from the soil in such a manner that the tap root is not broken, and the soil about the roots must be disturbed as little as possible. The verbascums are reasonably hardy and may be wintered in the open except in locations where the climate is of extreme severity. They may be used as individual accents or massed 18 inches apart.

English Wallflower (Cheiranthus cheiri). Throughout England wallflowers grow in cracks and crannies in the walls, and in Ireland one sees their tawny yellow blossoms upon the very rooftops of the peasant cottages. They are, indeed, a poignant part of an English spring, and it is to be regretted that they are not more widely grown in our gardens in America.

Culture: The plants may be easily grown from seed sown in July or very early August, and the young seedlings should be twice transplanted in order that they may develop good, fibrous root systems. The young plants should also be pinched back occasionally in order that they may become stocky and well branched as they have a tendency to make a rather spindly growth if they are left entirely to their own devices. If the plants are wintered over in frames they will be among the first of the spring flowers to come into bloom, and they may be moved into the garden as soon as the ground is workable. They may be set 10 to 12 inches apart.

When mixed seed is sown many of the flowers are apt to be streaked and blotched, and it is more satisfactory to obtain the seeds in self colors such as pale lemon, buttercup-yellow, deep wine red and mahogany. Both single and double forms are obtainable.

Siberian Wallflower (Cheiranthus allioni). The Siberian wallflowers are among the most effective of our spring plants for the low border, and their bright orange blooms may be used in pleasant contrast with flowers of a more subtle hue. They may be used very effectively in combination with the late Narcissus and the lovely, early-blooming tulip, *General De Wet*, with an occasional clump of phlox divaricata and mertensia as a foil for the brilliant tones of the tulips and wallflowers.

Culture: The seeds should be sown in July and the young seedlings should be transplanted when of sufficient size. In mild regions the plants may be wintered in the open very successfully, but in the north the protection of a coldframe is advisable. Being fibrous rooted, the plants may be moved easily in the spring to the desired location in the garden, and as soon as their period of bloom is over the plants may be discarded, making room for other flowers.

Set the plants a foot apart.

XXVI

HERBACEOUS PERENNIALS

THE large group known as herbaceous perennials includes many of our most beloved garden flowers. Although very diverse in form and habit of growth there is one characteristic which members of this group share in common, they die down to the ground in winter and renew their growth again in the spring. Some herbaceous perennials live on almost indefinitely, while others have a tendency to die out after a few years.

Ever since plants were first grown for the beauty of their flowers, perennials have made an important contribution to the garden scene. The long life of most herbaceous perennials and their relative permanence in the garden have been their principal cultural assets, and in this group we find many of our most beautiful and most dependable garden flowers.

All of these common and familiar garden flowers came originally from wild flowers. They were brought into cultivation because of their beauty, and by selection and hybridization many of them have been developed and improved to such an extent that their relationship to their ancestors is difficult to recognize. Indeed with some flowers it is impossible to determine their place of origin or their line of descent, so dissimilar are they to wild species. In the case of most of these domesticated plants, cultivation has stimulated growth, with the result that the plants are more vigorous, the flowers larger and more varied, and in some instances the blossoms have become so specialized that they no longer set seed.

Some perennials have been in cultivation for many centuries, even since ancient times, while others have been introduced more recently, following the era of extensive exploration. Many of them have come from distant lands, and in our gardens we find plants whose original habitats were the bleak shores of Iceland, or the glaciersides of Switzerland; the forests of Mexico, or the mountains of China and Japan; the valleys of India or the veldt of South Africa.

Those plants which have been cultivated in gardens since ancient times were grown first in the countries of their origin and were later introduced into Europe by the returning Crusaders or by travellers or explorers. The flowers thus gathered together in the monastery gardens, and later in the public botanic gardens, gradually became the familiar flowers of the European flower garden.

It is the herbaceous perennials which have made the gardens of England so famous for their abundance of bloom and beauty. Indeed, the long perennial border as developed in the English garden has become one of its most typical features, characteristic of the English style of garden art. Some of these perennial flowers originated in the English countryside and were invited into the gardens, some few were introduced in mediæval times, but the majority were brought into England by botanists and horticultural explorers, beginning in the first Queen Elizabeth's reign and continuing up to the present time.

The early colonists who established homes in the New World brought with them many of the perennial flowers which they had known and loved in their native lands. Their qualities of hardiness and long life, and their thriftiness under adverse and widely varying conditions, made these perennials particularly welcome to the early settlers of this country, and these same sturdy qualities in the perennials recommend them to us today.

Planning the Perennial Border

No planting problem is more diverse and intricate than that of the perennial flower border. No planting plan requires more careful thought, more detailed study, more creative skill. It is the aim of the designer to produce a succession of color harmonies which will merge imperceptibly, one into the other, as the season advances. No other type of plant material offers such infinite possibilities for color compositions as do the perennials, and the gardener finds in this ever-changing medium wide scope for his artistic skill.

It must be borne in mind, however, that perennials alone will not produce as full an effect of bloom and color throughout the season as will perennials when supplemented with

335

spring and summer flowering bulbs, and with annuals and biennials. Therefore, in planning the border for continuous bloom, it is an advantage to include a few plants of these other valuable groups as well.

In planning the perennial garden the entire life cycle of each plant must be taken into consideration when determining its position—its period of growth, blossoming, and retrogression. In the selection and arrangement of plant material the most important factors are the ultimate height of the plants, the color range, and the season of bloom; but there are other factors which must be taken into consideration, such as the texture and color of the foliage, the longevity of the plant, and the cultural requirements. All of these considerations may at first seem confusing but they need not be so if the decisions are made in logical sequence.

The usual procedure in preparing a planting plan for a perennial garden is first to draw to scale a plan showing the outline of the various beds or borders. A scale of $\frac{1}{2}$ inch to the foot will usually provide for a plan of workable size, unless the garden is unusually large, in which case the scale may be reduced to $\frac{1}{4}$ inch to the foot. The next step is to compile a list of the plants and bulbs which one desires to in-

clude in the planting plan. On this list they may be jotted down quite at random, as they come to mind, or they may be listed alphabetically, or in some other logical sequence. Such a list, set down at random, might appear as follows:

> Anemone japonica (Japanese Anemone)
> Aquilegia (Columbine)
> Artemisia lactiflora
> Asters
> Chrysanthemums
> Delphinium
> Dicentra spectabilis (Bleeding-heart)
> Hemerocallis (Daylily)
> Heuchera (Coral Bells)
> Iris
> Linum perenne (Blue Flax)
> Lupinus (Lupine)
> Peony
> Phlox divaricata
>   paniculata
> Salvia farinacea (Mealycup Sage)
> Thalictrum aquilegifolium
> Violas

When this tentative list has been completed, it should be broken up into a number of sub-groupings, according to season of bloom, color, and height.

Biennials, bulbs, annuals and tubers may be added to the list to provide more abundant bloom at certain seasons, or because they are particularly good companions.

ACCORDING TO SEASON OF BLOOM

SPRING	EARLY SUMMER	MIDSUMMER	AUTUMN
PERENNIALS	PERENNIALS	PERENNIALS	PERENNIALS
Aquilegia	Delphinium	Artemisia lactiflora	Anemone japonica
Dicentra spectabilis	Hemerocallis	Hemerocallis	Asters
Iris	Heuchera	Lupine	Chrysanthemums
Peony	Linum perenne	Phlox paniculata	
Phlox divaricata	Peony	Salvia farinacea	
Thalictrum aquilegifolium	Phlox paniculata		
BIENNIALS	BIENNIALS	BULBS	ANNUALS
English daisies	Canterbury bells	Lilies	Ageratum
Pansies	Foxgloves	Gladioli	Antirrhinum
	Sweet William		Cleome
		ANNUALS	Marigolds
BULBS	BULBS	Ageratum Nicotiana	Nicotiana
Narcissus	Lilies	Antirrhinum Torenia	Petunias
Scillas		Cleome Zinnias	Torenia
Tulips		Marigolds	Verbena
			Zinnias
		TUBERS	
		Dahlias	

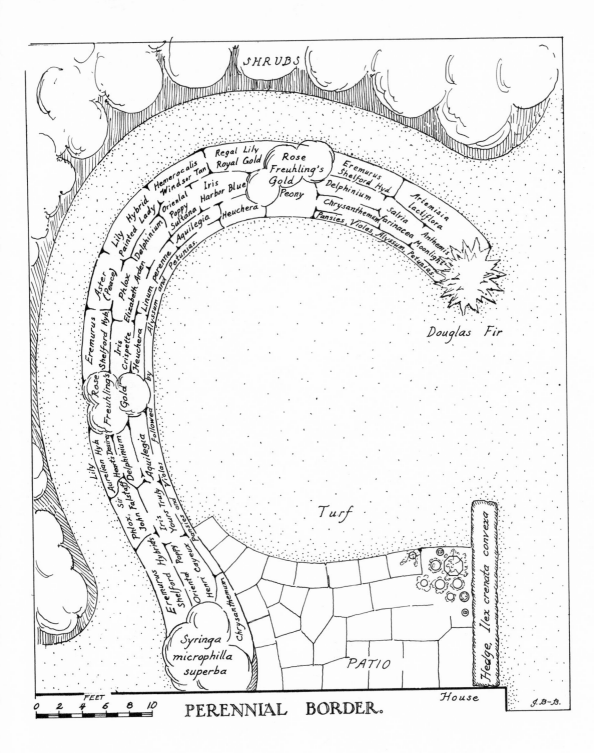

SHRUBS

Regal Lily
Royal Gold

Hemerocalis
Windsor Tan
Iris
Harbor Blue
Oriental
Poppy
Sultana
Aquilegia

Rose
Freuhling's
Gold

Peony

Eremurus
Shelford Hyb
Delphinium

Artemisia
lactiflora
Salvia
Chrysanthemum farinacea
Pansies, Violas, Alyssum, Petunias

Anthemis
Moonlight

Lily Hybrid
Painted Lady
Delphinium
Elizabeth Arden
Phlox
Linum perenne

Heuchera
by Alyssum and Petunias.

Aster
(Peace)

Eremurus
Shelford Hyb

Iris
Crispette

Heuchera

Rose
Freuhling's
Gold

followed

Douglas Fir

Lily Hyb
Aurelian Desiry

Sir John Falstaff
Phlox.

Delphinium

Aquilegia

Iris Truly Yours and Violas

Eremurus Hybrids
Shelford Poppy
Oriental
Henri Cayeux pansies

Chrysanthemum

Turf

Hedge, Ilex crenata convexa

Syringa
microphilla
superba

PATIO

House

g.B-B.

FEET
0 2 4 6 8 10

PERENNIAL BORDER.

337

ACCORDING TO COLOR

WHITE	BLUE, LAVENDER PURPLE, MAUVE	PINK, SALMON ROSE, RED	YELLOW, ORANGE BRONZE
PERENNIALS	**PERENNIALS**	**PERENNIALS**	**PERENNIALS**
Anemone japonica	Anemone japonica	Anemone japonica	Aquilegia
Aquilegia	Aquilegia	Aquilegia	Chrysanthemums
Artemisia	Asters	Asters	Hemerocallis
Asters	Chrysanthemums	Chrysanthemums	Iris
Chrysanthemums	Delphinium	Dicentra spectabilis	
Delphinium	Iris	Heuchera	
Iris	Linum perenne	Iris	
Peony	Phlox divaricata	Lupine	
Phlox paniculata	Phlox paniculata	Peony	
	Salvia farinacea		
	Thalictrum aquilegifolium		

WHITE		BLUE, LAVENDER...		PINK...		YELLOW...
ANNUALS		**ANNUALS**		**ANNUALS**		**ANNUALS**
Antirrhinum	Torenia	Ageratum	Torenia	Antirrhinum	Petunias	Antirrhinum
Cleome	Verbena	Antirrhinum	Verbena	Cleome	Verbena	Marigolds
Nicotiana	Zinnias	Nicotiana	Zinnias	Nicotiana	Zinnias	Zinnias
		Petunias				

WHITE		BLUE...		PINK...		YELLOW...	
BIENNIALS		**BIENNIALS**		**BIENNIALS**		**BIENNIALS**	
Canterbury bells		Canterbury bells	Pansies	Canterbury bells		Foxgloves	Pansies
English daisies		Foxgloves		English daisies			
Foxgloves				Pansies			
Pansies				Sweet William			
Sweet William							

WHITE		BLUE...		PINK...		YELLOW...	
BULBS		**BULBS**		**BULBS**		**BULBS**	
Gladioli	Narcissus	Gladioli	Scillas	Gladioli	Tulips	Gladioli	Narcissus
Lilies	Tulips	Lilies	Tulips	Lilies		Lilies	

WHITE	PINK...	YELLOW...
TUBERS	**TUBERS**	**TUBERS**
Dahlias	Dahlias	Dahlias

ACCORDING TO HEIGHT

LOW	MEDIUM	TALL
PERENNIALS	**PERENNIALS**	**PERENNIALS**
Asters (dwarf var.)	Anemone japonica	Artemisia lactiflora
Linum perenne	Aquilegia	Asters
Phlox divaricata	Chrysanthemums	Delphinium
	Dicentra spectabilis	Hemerocallis
BIENNIALS	Hemerocallis	Thalictrum aquilegifolium
English daisies	Heuchera	
Pansies	Iris	**BIENNIALS**
Violas	Lupine	Foxgloves
	Peony	
BULBS	Phlox paniculata	**BULBS**
Narcissus	Salvia farinacea	Lilies
Scillas		
	BIENNIALS	**ANNUALS**
ANNUALS	Canterbury bells	Marigolds (giant var.)
Ageratum	Sweet William	Zinnias (giant var.)
Marigolds (dwarf var.)		
Petunias	**BULBS**	
Verbena	Gladioli Tulips	
	Lilies	
	ANNUALS	
	Antirrhinum Marigolds	
	Cleome Zinnias	
	Nicotiana	

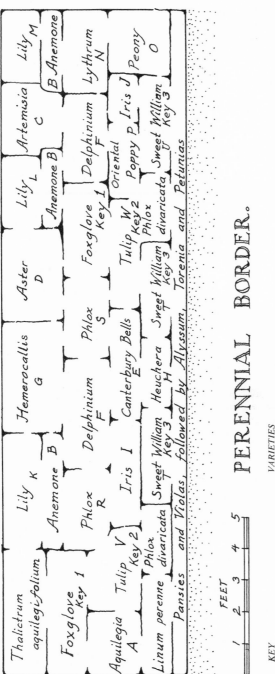

PERENNIAL BORDER.

FEET
1 2 3 4 5

KEY

1. Followed by Salvia farinacea.
2. Followed by gladioli.
3. Followed by chrysanthemums.

VARIETIES

A. Aquilegia, long-spurred hybrids.
B. Anemone japonica, alba.
C. Artemisia lactiflora.
D. Aster, Ryecroft Purple.
E. Canterbury bell, pink.
F. Delphinium, hybrid strains.
G. Hemerocallis, hyperion.
H. Heuchera s. Rosamondie.

I. Iris, Violet Harmony.
J. Iris, Enchantment.
K. Lily, L. auratum.
L. Lily, T. A. Havermeyer.
M. Lily, L. formosanum.
N. Lythrum s. Morden's Pink.
O. Peony, Krinkled White.

P. Oriental Poppy, Salome.
R. Phlox, Columbia.
S. Phlox, White Admiral.
T. Sweet William, Newport Pink.
U. Sweet William, Giant White.
V. Tulip, Carrara.
W. Tulip, Insurpassable.

With these lists at hand one is ready to make the selection of plant material for the plan. A piece of tracing paper may be laid over the outline plan which has been carefully drawn to scale and the notation of the plant names may be made upon this rough sketch sheet. The most orderly and logical sequence is to begin with spring bloom and to place on the plan the names of the plants in the relative positions which they are to occupy. In this early stage of the design the exact outline of the clumps need not be indicated, nor should the quantity of each group be considered. The designer is concerned at present only with the color harmonies, the sequence of bloom and height.

The selection of plants for early summer, late summer, and autumn bloom is then made and the names indicated upon the plan. If it is not possible to indicate the interplanting of annuals because of lack of space on the plan, the name may be written outside the area of the border with an arrow pointing to the spot which they are to occupy.

After the color harmonies and the sequence of bloom have been determined, and the sketch plans and all final decisions have been made, the plant names should be placed on the final plan, the outline of the clump should be indicated, and notation should be made of the number of plants to be used in each group. The groups should be large enough to give an effective display and prevent an appearance of spottiness. Low-growing plants, such as violas and phlox divaricata, may be used in long drifts along the front of the border, the taller plants may be used in groups of five, eight, or ten, depending upon the size of the garden, and an occasional plant, such as bleeding-heart, may be used as an accent, being planted alone, rather than in a group.

Propagation

Herbaceous perennials may be propagated by seed, by cuttings, by the division of old clumps, by layering, by the division of tubers and rhizomes, and in a few very exceptional cases, by grafting. Some perennials may be readily propagated by several methods, some by only one method. For detailed directions concerning seed sowing, division and other methods of propagation, see Chapter XXXIII on Propagation.

Preparation of the soil

Since perennial beds and borders constitute a more or less permanent type of planting, the soil should be adequately prepared. Most herbaceous perennials attain their maximum perfection in a fertile well-drained loam, which is high in organic content, neutral or very nearly neutral in reaction, and which has been deeply and thoroughly prepared previous to planting.

As many perennials are deeply rooted, and as it is well to induce the more shallow rooted types to send their feeding roots downward, the soil should be prepared to a depth of at least 15 inches, preferably to a depth of 24 inches. Trenching and double digging are the most approved methods for the preparation of the soil in perennial beds and borders. For detailed information concerning these practices, consult Chapter XLII, page 677. If the soil is poorly drained, this condition should be remedied at the time that the beds are prepared. Refer to Chapter XXIX, page 426.

Soil Reactions

A few perennials definitely prefer a soil that is slightly alkaline in reaction, others are acid tolerant, and some are entirely indifferent. The vast majority, however, prefer a soil which is neutral or very nearly neutral in reaction, with a pH ranging from 6.5 to 7.5. In preparing the soil for perennial beds, samples should be taken and the soil reaction should be definitely determined. For full and detailed directions, see Chapter XVI, page 168. If the soil tests show that the reaction is below a pH of 6.5, an application of lime should be made. The chart on page 171, Chapter XVI, will indicate the exact amount which should be applied. The application should be made after the beds have been prepared for planting. The lime should be sprinkled over the surface of the bed and should then be cultivated lightly into the soil. In order to meet the needs of those perennials which definitely prefer a slightly alkaline soil, a sufficient quantity of lime should be applied over the area where they are to be planted to bring the reaction to a pH of approximately 7.5.

PERENNIALS WHICH PREFER A SLIGHTLY ALKALINE SOIL

Anemone japonica	Hollyhocks
Gypsophila	Iris

PERENNIALS WHICH ARE ACID TOLERANT

Baptisia	Platycodon
Coreopsis	Silene

Almost all other perennials may be grouped among those which prefer a neutral or nearly neutral soil, or those which are entirely indifferent to soil conditions.

General Maintenance

A perennial garden requires faithful care and maintenance throughout the season. In the spring a general inspection of the garden should be made. Any plants which may have been partially heaved out of the soil during the winter should be pressed gently back into place and notations should be made of any plants which have failed to survive the winter. During this first spring survey, the needs of each individual group of plants should be carefully studied, and the plans for spring work should be outlined. Some plants will need to be divided (see section on Renewing Perennial Plants, page 344), other plants will need to be replaced with younger, more vigorous stock, and plans must be made for the spring feeding (see section on Maintenance of Fertility, page 343). It is also wise to make a few soil tests at this time in order to determine whether an application of lime is advisable. During the days of early

spring any remaining dead leaves and stalks should be removed and the beds and borders should be edged, in order that the garden may have a neat and trim appearance.

The first cultivation should be given as soon as the soil is warm and mellow and has become sufficiently dry. The soil should never be cultivated when it is too wet, as that will seriously injure its physical condition, causing the formation of many hard lumps. An excellent way to test the workability of the soil is to take a small amount and squeeze it tightly in the hand. If it crumbles when it falls to the ground, it is in good condition to be cultivated. If, however, it remains in a firm, compact mold, it contains too much moisture and should not be worked until it has become more thoroughly dry. Subsequent cultivations should be given throughout the season at intervals of every week or ten days unless a summer mulch is applied. A small weeder of the type which has three flexible prongs is one of the most convenient and efficient tools for the cultivation of perennial beds. It is possible to cultivate very close to the plants without damage to the roots or crown; the soil is left in excellent tilth, and the work may be done very rapidly, provided that the soil is in good condition for cultivating, being neither too wet nor too dry.

In order that perennials may be kept in vigorous, healthy condition, it is necessary to be constantly alert to detect the first signs of disease or insect infestation, and as soon as trouble is noticed measures of control should be put into effect immediately. For the control of Insect Pests and Diseases, see Chapter XLI.

Throughout the season all flower stalks should be cut down as soon as the blooms have faded. Not only will this improve the appearance of the garden, but it will also help to conserve the vigor of the plants, as the production of seed is a heavier drain upon the vitality of a plant than any other function which it is required to perform. There are other advantages to be gained as well: in the case of some plants, it is possible to prolong their blooming season to a considerable extent if seed pods are not allowed to form, and, with other plants such as the Delphiniums, it is possible to induce a second period of bloom.

Included also under the term of general maintenance are the tasks of watering, staking, feeding, and the occasional division and replanting of established plants.

Watering. For their best development most perennials require an adequate but not an over-abundant supply of moisture throughout the season. A few perennials thrive well on very dry soils, and there are others which have the ability to thrive under extremely moist conditions, but the vast majority prefer a moderate and fairly constant supply of moisture. In most sections of the country these requirements are met by normal rainfall. If, however, the rainfall is insufficient at any time during the season to meet the needs of the plants, it is advisable to resort to artificial watering. Frequent, light waterings are of little value and usually do far more harm than good as they tend to draw the feeding roots toward the surface. A very thorough watering should be given once in every four or five days and the moisture should penetrate to a depth of at least a foot.

Late afternoon and early evening are the most favorable times for watering as there is less evaporation and the soil retains the moisture more readily. There are a number of excellent sprinkling attachments which may be used on an ordinary garden hose which make it possible to cover a considerable area. If the garden is large it is possible to water a section of it each evening and thus to cover the entire area with comparatively little effort.

Staking. Staking appears to be such a very simple operation; yet it is a task which is seldom done in an entirely satisfactory manner. Staking is necessary for two purposes: either to provide support for weak and floppy stems or to protect tall flower spikes from being bent and broken by winds and heavy storms. Whatever the purpose, the staking should be done in such a way that the natural form and beauty of the plant are preserved.

Some perennials produce a quantity of small stems which have a tendency to be floppy and which consequently need some support. In this group we find Achillea ptarmica, Coreopsis grandiflora, Gypsophila, Platycodon, and the Veronicas. For such plants twiggy shoots may be used very successfully. While the plants are still young, the twigs may be stuck into the ground

ABUNDANT BLOOM IN A PERENNIAL GARDEN IN VERMONT

close beside them and as the foliage develops the twigs will be entirely concealed. Such twigs offer a very satisfactory framework for the support of weak, floppy stems.

Plants such as Delphiniums, Asters, Dahlias, and many others, require fairly tall, strong stakes. Bamboo stakes may be obtained in a variety of sizes and are very satisfactory. Those which are stained a soft green become almost invisible after they are in place. Strong wire stakes are also satisfactory and are obtainable in various styles and sizes. The type with spiral turns is of particular value for supporting individual flower stalks. Wooden stakes are often used, and if they are painted green they are reasonably unobtrusive in appearance. They lack the suppleness of bamboo and wire and unless they are made of suitable wood, such as hickory, ash or lemonwood, they have a tendency to snap off. It is wise to keep a variety of stakes on hand in order to have one to meet every need. Some plants require stout stakes for adequate support, while others will require more slender stakes. When staking large clumps it is usually advisable to use more than one stake. When tall flower stalks are to be staked, they should be tied to the stake at several points. The tape should be wound firmly about the stake and should then be wound about the stalk, being brought back and tied to the stake rather loosely. A flower stalk should never be tied tightly to a stake, as the beauty and grace of the plant are impaired. When a large clump is to be staked, the tape may be attached first to one of the stakes and may then be woven through the clump, being wound about each individual stalk until it reaches the far side of the clump where it is attached to the opposite stake. Clumps of Peonies may be supported by special wire hoops which may be placed about the entire plant, the legs resting upon the soil.

Care must be taken in the selection of the material to be used in tying. Stems which are hollow and brittle must be tied with some very soft material which will not cut or bruise the stalk. Asparagus tape is excellent for this purpose. Green in color, soft in texture, strong and durable, it has much to recommend it. There are a number of similar tapes on the market which possess many of the same good qualities but are somewhat more expensive. Raffia is reasonably satisfactory but is more conspicuous if used in the natural shade.

Maintenance of Fertility

In order to maintain the perennial border at its best from year to year, the fertility of the soil must be kept at a constantly high level. Two applications of a good complete fertilizer should be given during the season, one in spring after the plants have started into active growth and one early in the summer. Late summer and fall applications are not advisable as they tend to stimulate a rather succulent growth which would cause the plants to enter the winter in an immature condition.

The fertilizer may be applied in the form of a standard analysis complete fertilizer such as a 4-12-4 or a 4-8-6, or it may be applied in the form of a high analysis, quickly-soluble fertilizer. The standard complete fertilizer should be applied at the rate of 3 ounces per square yard or 2 pounds per 100 square feet. It should be sprinkled over the surface of the bed, cultivated lightly into the soil, and watered in thoroughly. Fertilizers such as bone meal and cottonseed meal have been used very generally in the past but as they become available very slowly and do not become active until warm weather, they are less efficient than a well-balanced complete fertilizer.

The quickly-soluble fertilizer should be one which contains the trace elements as well as the major elements. For details concerning the use of high-analysis, quickly-soluble fertilizers see page 165.

During periods of prolonged rain it may be necessary to supply additional amounts of nitrogen as all the available supply of nitrogen in the soil is leached out rapidly under such conditions. This may be applied in the form of a top-dressing of nitrate of soda or sulphate of ammonia.

At the end of every five or six years, it is usually advisable to entirely remake the perennial garden. If the garden is large, a small section may be renovated each year. The work may be done either in the autumn or in the early spring, autumn being preferable not only because there is usually more leisure to undertake such work but because new bulbs may be planted and old bulbs may be divided at this season. The plants should be lifted from the beds, the soil should be retrenched or double-dug, liberal quantities of well-rotted manure being incorporated, and, where necessary, the plants should be divided before they are reset. Such permanent things as Peonies and Bleeding-heart which resent being moved may be left undisturbed during this process of rejuvenation without any serious interference to the work.

Renewing Perennial Plants

Although the term "perennial," when applied to plants, denotes permanence, it cannot be assumed that when perennial plants have once become established they will bloom on year after year without further thought or care on the part of the gardener. A few of the exceedingly robust types, such as Golden Glow, might measure up to such an expectation, but the vast majority of our more desirable perennials require a reasonable amount of care if they are to make satisfactory growth and give an abundance of bloom.

Some perennials are comparatively short-lived, and new plants should be grown to take the place of those which have served their period of usefulness in the garden. In this group we have the beautiful hybrid Columbines, which have a tendency to die out after several years of luxuriant bloom; the Lupines; the glorious hybrid Delphiniums, which often fail to carry on over a period of many years unless conditions are extremely favorable for their growth; Linum perenne and the lovely but temperamental Daphne cneorum. As some of our most choice perennials are to be found in this group it is well to recognize the fact that they are more or less transient in the garden and that new plants should be propagated at intervals of every few years.

Other perennials will thrive well for a year or two after they are planted and will then begin to deteriorate rapidly unless the clumps are divided. In this group we have the Chrysanthemums, Physostegia, the hardy Asters, Iris and Phlox. Chrysanthemums should be lifted and divided each year, or new plants should be started from cuttings, as the old clumps usually produce inferior blooms. Physostegia should also be lifted and divided each year, not only for the sake of better bloom but also in order to prevent it from en-croaching upon its neighbors and becoming a pest. Hardy Asters should be lifted and divided every two or three years. Iris should be divided every three or four years, Phlox every five or six years.

There are a few perennials which will thrive for a period of many years without being divided and replanted; in fact in some cases they seriously resent being disturbed. In this group we find Dicentra spectabilis (Bleeding-heart), the Peonies, and the Oriental poppies.

In maintaining a perennial garden, it is well to know the requirements of each individual group and to meet these needs as adequately as possible.

Summer Mulches

A summer mulch may be used very advantageously in the perennial garden and fulfills several functions. It reduces to a minimum the labor required for general care and cultivation, it conserves the moisture in the soil, and it helps to maintain a more even soil temperature.

For details concerning the use of a summer mulch in the flower garden see Chapter XXXIV on Mulches, page 500.

Winter Mulches

In the successful maintenance of the perennial garden, the question of the winter mulch plays an important part. Which plants should be mulched and which plants should be left un-protected; what materials should be used and how heavily they should be applied; when the mulch should be put on and when it should be removed—all these points must be taken into consideration.

For details concerning the use of a winter mulch see Chapter XXXIV on Mulches, page 501.

PERENNIALS OF MERIT

Aconitum (*Monkshood*). The aconites derive their common name of Monkshood from the characteristically hooded or helmet-shaped flowers, and there are a number of varieties which are valued for their rich autumn effect in the garden. The aconites are also well adapted to a semi-naturalistic setting, being suitable for use in the foreground of a shrubbery border or along a fringe of woodland.

A. autumnale reaches a height of from 3 to 4 feet and bears racemes of large, dark blue flowers in late September and October.

A. Fischeri. This species as listed in most catalogs is a dwarf type reaching a height of hardly more than 2 feet. It blooms in early autumn and is one of the hardiest of all the aconites.

A. Napellus blooms in July and August and the dark blue flowers are borne on an upright, single spike about 3½ feet in height.

Spark's Variety blooms at the same season as Napellus but is somewhat taller and bears its abundant, deep-blue flowers on strongly branching spikes.

A. Wilsonii, which blooms in late autumn is distinct both in form and in coloring. The flowers are of a delicate violet-mauve and the tall spikes often reach a height of 6 feet or more.

Exposure: Semi-shade is preferred although the plants will also grow well in full sun.

Soil Requirements: The aconites will thrive in any good garden loam but they prefer a moist soil well supplied with organic matter.

Propagation: The aconites may be propagated by the division of old clumps and by seed. The seed is very slow to germinate, often requiring a month or more, and the viability of the seed is apt to be poor unless fresh seed is secured.

Culture: During dry seasons the aconites should be watered liberally. As the plants are difficult to move they should be left undisturbed for many years after they have once become established. Planting distances vary from 8 to 10 inches.

Anchusa italica (Bugloss). The tall-growing anchusas are useful plants for the perennial border, but being of a robust and somewhat branching habit of growth they require ample space and are not suitable for small garden beds. The small, intensely blue flowers are borne in rather loose clusters on ascending, heavy stems, being produced abundantly in June, and intermittently throughout the summer.

VARIETIES OF MERIT

Dropmore—The flowers are of a deep, gentian-blue. The plants are very vigorous in habit of growth and reach a height of nearly 5 feet.

Opal—The flowers are a clear, pale blue in color and the plants range in height from 3 to 4 feet.

Pride of Dover—One of the most desirable of the recent introductions, the flowers being of a true heavenly-blue shade.

Exposure: Full sun.

Soil Requirements: A fertile garden loam, moist, yet well drained, is considered ideal. Although the plants will make reasonably good growth on soils of moderate fertility they respond remarkably well to liberal feeding.

Propagation: Anchusa italica may be propagated by the division of old clumps, by root cuttings or by seed.

Culture: Transplanting should be done with care as the roots are very brittle. As the plants attain considerable size, they should be spaced from 15 to 18 inches apart. During the growing season, the anchusas require large quantities of water.

Anemone japonica (Japanese Anemone) (Windflower). The Japanese Anemones are among the loveliest of our autumn flowers. The cup-shaped blooms with their brilliant golden stamens are borne on tall, slender stems which rise far above the dense clumps of foliage, often attaining a height of 3 feet or more. The plants are in flower almost continuously from early September until late autumn when they are cut down by heavy frosts. The flowers are exceedingly decorative in the garden and they are also very lovely for cutting.

VARIETIES OF MERIT

Alba—white   *Margarette*—Tyrian-rose
Alice—rose-pink   *September Charm*—silvery-pink

Exposure: Full sun or partial shade. The Japanese anemones do exceedingly well at the edge of a shrubbery border where they are protected from strong winds and have the benefit of light shade for a portion of the day.

Soil Requirements: The Japanese anemones thrive best in a cool, moist, yet well-drained soil, rich in humus and of a slightly alkaline reaction. The soil should be deeply prepared and liberal quantities of well-rotted cow manure, leaf mold or commercial humus should be incorporated previous to planting.

Propagation: Japanese anemones may be propagated by the division of old clumps in the spring, by root cuttings taken at any time during the growing season, or by seed. In purchasing plants from a nursery young, pot-grown plants will usually give the best results.

Culture: The plants should be spaced from 15 to 18 inches apart. They require liberal quantities of moisture throughout the growing season, and will benefit tremendously from a summer mulch of half-rotted leaves. When once well established the plants should be left undisturbed, as they do not transplant readily and resent interference. Where the winters are of considerable severity a mulch of leaves or salt hay should be provided.

Aquilegia (Columbine). The columbines are among the most beautiful of our garden flowers. They possess an exquisite daintiness and charm equalled by few other perennials, and no spring garden is quite complete without them. Within recent years many new and very beautiful strains have been introduced and there is a vast difference between the heavy, short-spurred columbines which our grandmothers grew in their gardens and the graceful types which we have today. It is as if the columbines had undergone an almost complete metamorphosis. From dull, uninteresting blooms with but little grace or charm they have been miraculously transformed into flowers as beautiful as butterflies.

There are many species of Aquilegia and they vary considerably in form, in coloring, and in adaptability. Some are definitely perennial in habit and will bloom on year after year, while others are comparatively short-lived. Some are particularly well suited to the rock garden, others thrive best in a woodland setting and some are happily at home in the herbaceous border. Of the many species there are less than a dozen in common cultivation today.

A. alpina—comes to us from the high mountain steeps of Switzerland, and it is one of the most cherished plants in many a rock garden. It seldom reaches a height of more than 9 inches and the flowers which are borne in May and June vary in color from clear blue to white. The spurs are short and stout and distinctly incurved. The plants prefer a light, well-drained, rather stony soil which is not too rich, and they thrive in either full sun or partial shade. They may be spaced from 6 to 8 inches apart.

A. cærulea—which is known as the Rocky Mountain Columbine is one of the most beautiful of all species. It is a native of our mountain regions from Colorado south to Mexico. The lovely, long-spurred flowers are a clear blue with a white cup and golden anthers and they are borne in great profusion. The plants are considered short-lived in eastern gardens as they frequently die out after two or three years, but recent experiments tend to show that they will persist considerably longer if given a soil of moderate acidity. Many of our beautiful hybrid strains have been developed from this species.

A. canadensis—is a native of this country east of the Rocky Mountains and is usually found growing on dry, stony ledges. It prefers partial shade and a neutral soil, as it will not tolerate either extreme acidity or

JAPANESE ANEMONES

extreme alkalinity. It is a modest little flower, seldom growing more than 10 or 12 inches high. The blooms are of a scarlet and yellow hue. It is most happily at home in a woodland setting or in some partially shaded corner of the rock garden. There is also a very dwarf form known as A. canadensis nana.

A. chrysantha—bears flowers of clear yellow, tinted with claret, and the spurs are long, slender and graceful. It comes into flower a little later than some of the other species but has the pleasant habit of blooming intermittently throughout the season. In fact it is sometimes in flower when cut down by frost in the autumn. The foliage is particularly good, being a deep, glossy green and usually retaining its healthy, vigorous appearance through the summer months. The plants reach a height of from 18 to 24 inches and are well adapted either for the woodland or for use in the garden.

A. glandulosa—is a rare and beautiful species which comes from the mountain regions of Siberia. The large, pendent, wide-spreading flowers are a bright, lilac-blue in color, tipped with white, and the spurs, like those of A. alpina, are short and distinctly incurved. A. glandulosa is one of the first of the columbines to come into flower, blooming from early May until well into June. The foliage is very lovely, having a soft, velvety quality with rich, coppery shadings. The plants vary in height from 12 to 15 inches and are lovely both in the herbaceous border and in the rock garden, thriving either in full sun or in light shade.

A. vulgaris—is the common columbine of Europe and is the one which is so frequently found in old-time gardens. It reaches a height of from 18 to 24 inches and the blooms are heavy, short-spurred and lacking in grace and beauty. There are, however, a number of improved varieties, and some of our lovely hybrid strains have been developed by crossing A. vulgaris with other species.

Hybrid Strains: Many of our most beautiful columbines today are hybrids, and among the most choice of these recent introductions are several distinct strains. The Mrs. Scott Elliott strain bears flowers of large size with long, graceful spurs, the colors varying from deep purple through violet and pink to deep, wine-red. The outer petals are often of one color and the corolla of another color, and many of the flowers offer the most subtle and exquisite harmonies and contrasts.

Sutton's selected long-spurred hybrids are an excellent strain. The plants are hardy and vigorous and the lovely, long-spurred flowers, which vary in color from light to deep colors, are borne in great profusion.

The Rainbow Blend is a strain which was introduced several years ago by one of our Western growers. The flowers are very large with long, slender spurs and for brilliancy of color they are quite unsurpassed. Pink, rose, scarlet, deep reds and purples and many other

AQUILEGIA

unusual and very beautiful shades are found among them.

Dobbie's Imperial Hybrids is a strain which is offered by the famous Scotch firm whose name it bears. It is the result of many years of careful selection and re-selection. The flowers are of beautiful form and the range of color almost defies description.

Propagation: Columbines may be propagated by seed and by the division of old clumps. It is advisable to grow new plants from seed, as the division of old clumps is not very satisfactory and the results are often disappointing. In order to have plants which will give good bloom the following season, it is essential that the seeds be sown early. If greenhouse space is not available they may be sown in frames or in a seed bed in the open later in the season. It is well to have the seed sown before the middle of May in order that the seedlings may have as long a growing season as possible. The seed bed should be carefully prepared. A mixture of equal parts good garden loam, peat moss, and sand provides excellent conditions for germination. The bed should be partially shaded after sowing and the soil should never be allowed to dry out. Growth is rather slow for the first month or so, but after the seedlings have been transplanted they will begin to develop more rapidly. If the young seedlings are protected by a lath shade during the summer months, they will make much more rapid and vigorous growth than they will if exposed to full sunlight. The young plants need a light, mellow soil with excellent drainage. They should be given good cultivation and abundant water throughout the season and they should never be allowed to become stunted, due to overcrowding. If given good care they will develop into thrifty, vigorous plants by autumn, and they may then be moved to their permanent position in the garden or may be wintered over in the nursery beds.

Soil Requirements: Although one or two species among the columbines have decided soil preferences, the long-spurred hybrids, which are those most commonly grown in our gardens, will thrive well in any good garden loam. They appreciate a moderate quantity of well-rotted manure but fresh manure should never be allowed to come into direct contact with the plants. They are, on the whole, most happily at home in a loose, friable soil. In poorly drained locations they are apt to die out during the winter and are also more subject to root rot.

Culture: Most of the hybrid columbines will thrive well either in full sun or in light shade. As the mature clumps attain considerable size they should be allowed ample room for development and the plants should be spaced from 15 to 18 inches apart in the flower border. During the first year when the plants are small, interplantings of Phlox divaricata may be made. Even under the most favorable conditions many of the new hybrid strains of columbines are comparatively short-lived and will die out after a few years of bloom. It is well, therefore, always to have a few young plants coming on to take the place of those that have failed to survive.

Columbines may be transplanted with the greatest ease and large clumps may be moved when in full flower, provided they are watered well and are taken up with a generous quantity of soil. In fact there are very few other perennials that may be moved with such certainty of success.

Season of Bloom: If each individual bloom is nipped off as it fades, new buds will develop along the stems and columbines may be kept in flower for a month or six weeks. By prolonging their blooming season in this way one greatly increases their value in the spring garden. The bloom of some of the perennials is so fleeting that it hardly seems worth while to grow them, but when plants may be kept continuously in flower for nearly a month and a half, they soon come to be looked upon as indispensables. Columbines are particularly lovely when grown in combination with Lupines, Blue Flax, Nepeta Mussini, and Thalictrum, and the most exquisite color harmonies may be obtained.

Not only are columbines lovely in the garden but they are among the most choice of all our flowers for cutting. They last unusually well and their daintiness and their soft and lovely colorings make possible the most beautiful cut flower arrangements. The pink varieties are lovely when arranged with Nepeta Mussini and those with deep purple tints make a lovely contrast when arranged with sprays of Bleeding-heart.

Winter Protection: Columbines are very hardy and need no winter protection except in severe climates. Dry oak leaves which will not mat down over the crowns afford an excellent covering and may be held in place by small evergreen boughs. Salt hay is also good as a winter mulch.

Insect Pests and Diseases: See Chapter XLI.

Artemisia lactiflora. With its creamy-white blossoms which are borne on tall, graceful stems, Artemisia lactiflora is one of the most useful background plants for the perennial border. When grown under favorable conditions the plants reach a height of 5 feet or more. The soft tone of the flowers is a pleasant foil for blossoms of a more brilliant hue, and they may be used very effectively in combination with Gladioli, Salvia farinacea and S. azurea. The foliage is somewhat coarse and heavy and forms a dense background mass.

Exposure: Artemisia lactiflora thrives best in full sun.

Soil Requirements: If the plants are to reach maximum development they should be grown in a fertile, deeply prepared, fairly moist soil. On poor soil, and with an inadequate supply of moisture Artemisia will make spindly growth and will produce but little bloom.

Propagation: Usually by the division of old clumps in early spring or in the autumn. The plants may also be propagated by seed or by cuttings.

Culture: Artemisia lactiflora is one of the few tall border plants which usually do not require staking. The plants must, however, be given ample room and they should be spaced at least 15 inches apart.

Asclepias tuberosa (Butterflyweed). There is hardly a flower of greater decorative value in the garden than the brilliant and beautiful Butterflyweed which blooms during the midsummer months. The myriad orange flowers are borne in broad, flat umbels of irregular outline, and they are lovely both in the garden and for cutting, being particularly striking when planted in combination with some of the tawny Daylilies and the dwarf Tritomas. The plants reach a height of 12 to 18 inches and remain in flower for many weeks.

Exposure: Full sun is essential.

Soil Requirements: A light, sandy, exceedingly well-drained soil of medium fertility. If soil conditions are favorable the plants will continue to thrive year after year, but in a heavy, poorly drained soil they are short-lived.

Propagation: The plants may be grown very easily from seed which may be sown in the coldframe in early spring or in the open ground later in the season. The young seedlings must be transplanted with care as they suffer seriously if the fleshy tap root is broken or unduly disturbed. The seedling plants should be placed in their permanent location when still quite small as the transplanting of old, established plants is very difficult and is seldom successful.

Culture: The plants should be spaced from 10 to 12 inches apart and when they have once become well established, they will give generous bloom year after year provided that conditions of soil and exposure are favorable. They will withstand long periods of drought better than almost any other perennial.

Asters. There are few perennials which will give such a lavish display of autumn bloom as will the hardy asters. In England one sees them used in gay profusion, and it is in England that many of our most beautiful hybrid varieties have been developed. In the herbaceous garden, as a foreground for a shrubbery border, or along the edge of a woodland, the hardy asters are happily at home. In the rock garden, the dwarf varieties which have recently been introduced are a welcome addition because they bloom at the end of the season and thus bring color in autumn to a garden which has too often been considered only for its springtime effect.

VARIETIES OF MERIT

CUSHION TYPE
(8 to 12″ high)

Constance: shell-pink	Niobe: white
Lilac Time: lilac	

DWARF TYPE
(12 to 15″ high)

Pacific Amaranth: purple	Purple Feather: purple
Pacific Horizon: light blue	Twinkle: amaranth-rose
Princess Margaret Rose: rose	Violet Carpet: blue-violet

INTERMEDIATE TYPE
(18 to 30″ high)

Arctic: white	Eventide: blue-violet
Beechwood Beacon: red	Janet McMullen: clear pink

TALL TYPE

Barr's Pink: crimson-rose	Peace: pinkish-lavender
Harrington's Pink: soft pink	Ryecroft Purple: purple
Incomparabilis: fuchsia-red	Survivor: bright pink
Mt. Everest: white	

Exposure: Most of the hardy asters prefer full sun but will thrive reasonably well in very light shade.

Soil Requirements: Asters will thrive under almost any soil conditions, provided that the soil is not too saturated with moisture during the winter months. A medium to heavy loam is considered ideal—there are few perennials which are less exacting than the hardy asters. A soil that is exceedingly high in fertility is less desirable than one of moderate fertility as the plants have a tendency to make too rank a growth and become somewhat leggy.

Propagation: Although hardy asters may be propagated very easily from seed this method is seldom used. The usual method of propagation is by the division of the clumps in early spring, the young vigorous shoots being used. Cuttings may also be made from young shoots in the spring. New plants are usually purchased as rooted cuttings, but sometimes are field-grown divisions.

Culture: About every three years the clumps should be dug up, divided and replanted. Thus frequently renewed, the plants will not deteriorate. The dwarf varieties may be placed one foot apart in the beds, and the larger growing ones two feet. The cushion types sometimes attain a spread of two feet and should be given ample room.

To increase the size of the blooms and to restrain the sometimes over-rampant growth on the intermediate and tall types, many of the young shoots may be pruned away in spring, leaving only five to eight stalks to develop. In the flower garden the taller varieties usually require staking in order to prevent them from encroaching upon other flowers; but in the shrub border or at the edge of the woods the natural growth is preferable. A clever device for keeping tall asters within bounds in a small garden is to stake the shoots while they are still young and pliable in a horizontal position near to the ground, using small wire wickets. The stems will send up short lateral branches and the bloom will thus be spread over a wide area and will remain low.

In England, one frequently sees whole borders devoted entirely to hardy asters and the display of color is magnificent. To attain this effect the cultural procedure is as follows: All of the old clumps are lifted early in the spring as soon as the soil is in suitable condition, and the strong-growing outer shoots are removed. These are planted singly, 1 foot apart, over the entire area, the desired space being allotted to each variety. The ground is well prepared before planting, being enriched with liberal quantities of well-rotted manure. When the plants have reached a height of from 12 to 18 inches a few of the front leading shoots are nipped out. This will greatly improve the form and appearance of the individual plants and will produce a wonderfully fine display of bloom in the border, as each shoot will produce a pyramid of perfect blossoms. One stout stake about two-thirds of the height of the plant will give the plants the needed support. The opportunities for color harmonies which a planting of this nature offers are almost unlimited, and a most glorious display of autumn bloom may be obtained if this method of planting is followed.

Bocconia cordata (Plumepoppy). Bocconia cordata is a magnificent perennial with large, deeply lobed, glaucous leaves, and with tall, handsome flower spikes which often reach a height of 6 to 8 feet. The individual flowers, which are cream-white in color, are small, but are borne in large showy terminal panicles. In late summer these panicles bear quantities of small, almost transparent, pale-green pods which become suffused with reddish-purple, and these fruits are almost as beautiful as the flowers. Bocconia cordata should be used only where it can have ample space. At the rear of a deep, long border its huge spires of bloom and its gray-green foliage are magnificent. In a small garden it would be entirely out of scale, but when planted in bold masses with a background of evergreens or against a high wall it produces a striking effect. Both the flowers and the seed pods are excellent for bold, decorative arrangements in the house.

Exposure: Full sun or partial shade.

Soil Requirements: A rich, moist, deeply prepared soil is considered ideal although the plants will thrive reasonably well in any garden soil of moderate fertility.

Propagation: By seed, by the division of old clumps and by suckers. The plants will attain a height of 3 or 4 feet the first year from seed.

Culture: Bocconia cordata may be planted either in the autumn or in early spring and the plants should be given ample room to develop, being spaced from 2 to 3 feet apart. As the plants produce suckers very freely they are capable of becoming a pest unless they are kept within bounds.

Campanula (Bellflower). The Campanula is a large and varied genus, and its members range in size from the tiny Campanula cæspitosa of the rock garden to Campanula pyramidalis, which grows to a height of 6 feet or more in the border. The flowers of all the species are bell-shaped; in some species they are produced singly, while in others they are borne in clusters. A few campanulas bloom in May, most of them bloom in June and July, with several lasting into August. Blue is the dominant color among the campanulas, with some white forms and pink in a few species. Many are perennial, some are annual or biennial. So varied and adaptable is the genus that few modern gardens are without some form of Campanula.

C. cæspitosa, Tufted Harebell, 4 to 6 inches high, has bright blue flowers in May and June. Plant about 5 inches apart.

C. carpatica. the Carpathian Harebell, which grows 12 inches tall, is delightful as an edging in the flower border, or along the top of a rock wall. It is graceful, yet compact, with quantities of upturned blue bells. Plant from 8 to 10 inches apart.

C. garganica is a trailing plant spreading to broad tufts. The flowers are wide blue bells that are divided into five petal-like points. Plant from 8 to 10 inches apart.

C. glomerata has rather stiff stems bearing closely clustered, blue, funnel-form flowers. Plant from 8 to 10 inches aaprt.

C. persicifolia, the Peach-leaved Harebell, attains a height of 2 to 3 feet and produces violet-blue, wide, bell-like flowers in June and July. An improved variety with large purple-blue flowers known as *Telham Beauty*, is even more beautiful. Variety *Moerheimi* is semi-double, cream-white. The plants should be spaced from 12 to 15 inches apart, and they should be lifted and divided every second year.

C. pyramidalis is a narrow, columnar form which reaches a height of 5 or 6 feet. The flowers, which open in August, are a clear deep blue and continue in bloom for five or six weeks. Plant from 15 to 18 inches apart.

C. rotundifolia, Bluebells of Scotland, is a compact plant, 6 inches or more high, which sends up thin stems bearing hanging blue, bell-shaped flowers from June to September. Plant from 4 to 6 inches apart.

Exposure: Most of the campanulas prefer a sunny location, although several of the dwarf species will thrive well in partial shade.

Soil Requirements: The campanulas prefer a rich garden loam with a neutral or slightly alkaline reaction. The soil should be well prepared previous to planting.

Propagation: Almost all campanulas may be raised from seed, by cuttings made from young growth in spring, or by the division of old clumps. Seedlings raised to partial growth by autumn are carried over the winter in coldframes and transplanted to the garden in the spring.

Chrysanthemum. The brilliant tones of the ash and oaks and maples in the woodlands and the deep bronze and golden russets of the chrysanthemums in the garden bring to a close the season's pageantry of color and bloom. There is no other flower which can take the place of the chrysanthemum in the autumn garden, and from mid-September on they hold the center of the stage. With the introduction of hybrids which are noted both for their earliness and for their winter hardiness, the season of bloom has been greatly extended, and it is now possible to grow chrysanthemums in northern gardens with every assurance of success.

Chrysanthemums may be handled very satisfactorily in several ways. They may be grown throughout the season in beds or borders of mixed perennials, or they may be grown in the nursery plots until they are almost ready to come into bloom, and may then be lifted and moved into the garden. If facilities permit, it is wise to follow the latter procedure, as the plants may be grown under more carefully controlled conditions and will consequently make better growth and will give a greater abundance of bloom, which will usually more than compensate for the additional labor involved.

The essentials for the successful culture of hardy chrysanthemums are: vigorous, healthy plants for spring planting, a sunny location, a well-drained, fertile soil, an adequate supply of moisture throughout the growing season, careful attention to the pinching back of the plants, and protection against insect pests and diseases.

Exposure: Chrysanthemums thrive best in a sunny location. If grown in partial shade the plants have a tendency to become spindly and the lower leaves are apt to shrivel and turn brown.

Soil Requirements: A light rich, well-drained soil is considered ideal for chrysanthemums. The plants are notoriously rank feeders and require abundant quantities of plant food if they are to attain their maximum development. Liberal quantities of manure or compost should be incorporated in the bed previous to planting and the condition of the soil may be further improved by an application of a 5–8–6 complete fertilizer, applied at the rate of 1 pound to every 30 square feet. The application of fertilizer should be made in early spring at least a week or more before planting. Chrysanthemums thrive best in a soil with a pH which is just below the neutral point, and lime should be applied if the soil has a tendency to be acid. During the summer months, from the time of the last pinching back until the time when the buds begin to show color, it is wise to make weekly applications of liquid manure. This practice will greatly stimulate growth and will prove to be of decided benefit to the plants. If liquid manure is not readily available a biweekly application of a high-analysis, quickly-soluble fertilizer may be made (see page 165).

Propagation: Well-rooted cuttings, sold as small pot-grown plants, may be purchased in the spring from any reliable nursery, and after a selection of desirable varieties has been obtained it is possible to maintain or increase the stock by propagating new plants each spring. This may be done either by the division of old clumps or by cuttings taken from the young shoots as they start into growth in the spring. (See Chapter XXXIII on Propagation.)

Culture: Chrysanthemums make their maximum growth during hot weather, and throughout this period they require a liberal supply of moisture. If the plants suffer a serious check at any time during this period of their growth, it will often result in a loss of the lower leaves, which seriously injures the general appearance of the plant.

The pinching back of the plants, which is sometimes spoken of as summer pruning, is a factor of great importance in the culture of garden chrysanthemums. After three or four pairs of leaves have formed, the growing tip of the shoot should be pinched back. From three to five side shoots will then develop and these, in turn, should be pinched back to induce further branching. For the early-flowering varieties no pinching should be done after the middle of July; the late-flowering types should not be pinched back after the early part of August. The importance of this summer pruning can hardly be overemphasized. If it is neglected, the plants will assume a spindly habit of growth, sprawling out over the garden in an ungainly fashion, and they will produce but little bloom. If the pinching

VARIETIES RECOMMENDED FOR THE HOME GARDEN

CUSHION TYPE

Apricot Glow: bronze-apricot
Powder Puff: white
Red Cloud: red
Yellow Cushion: golden yellow

DECORATIVE TYPE

Ashes of Roses: rich old rose
Betty: peach-pink to old rose
Carnival: burnt-orange
Charles Nye: yellow
Chippewa: aster-purple

Christopher Columbus: cream
Glen Star: purple
Lavender Lady: true lavender
Mrs. P. S. duPont: peach-pink
Red Velvet: dark crimson

POMPOM TYPE

Angelo: pink
Burma: bronze
Masquerade: silvery rose
Thyra: purple

SPOON TYPE

Golden Spoon: clear gold
Ivory Spoon: ivory white
Orchid Spoon: orchid
Rose Spoon: shining rose

SINGLE AND DAISY-FLOWERED TYPES

Arctic Queen: golden-salmon
Astrid: white with pink tints
Bittersweet: orange-red
Crimson Splendor: crimson

Kristina: rose-purple
Pollyanna: pink
Silver Moon: white
Viking: orange-red

is done systematically, however, the plants will develop into broad, spreading bushes, bearing many strong, flowering stems.

Hardy varieties may be left in the garden during the winter while the more tender types will need the protection of a coldframe. Many gardeners prefer to dig such clumps as may be needed for propagation as soon as the flowering season is past and to heel them in, in a coldframe. In the spring as soon as the plants start into growth they may be lifted and divided, or cuttings may be taken.

For the control of insect pests and disease on chrysanthemums, see Chapter XLI.

Delphinium. June has always been called the month of roses, but the rose now shares this honor with the delphinium. The low-growing types with their starry, single flowers of clear sky-blue are delightful when used in great drifts along the front of the border, and the towering, majestic blooms of the larger types are a veritable glory during the days of early summer. Delphiniums contribute great distinction to a garden composition by the sheer beauty of their form and the richness of their coloring.

Many fine hybrid strains of delphinium have been developed within recent years, both in this country and in England. The flower spikes of these new hybrids are broad at the base and taper toward the tip, the blooms being clustered closely along the stem. The plants are of extraordinarily vigorous growth and often attain a height of 6 to 8 feet. There is considerable variance in the seedlings, both single and double forms being common, and the flowers range in color from deep purple and maroon through the lighter shades, many very beautiful contrasts being found.

Although the spectacularly beautiful new hybrid types have largely superseded the older types, there are still many gardeners who love the dainty form and the clear, sky-blue coloring of the old-fashioned Delphinium belladonna. It most surely deserves a place in the cutting garden, as it is generous with its bloom, and is lovely when used in combination with roses and other June flowers. It is also less exacting in its cultural requirements and less susceptible to disease than some of the newer types, and it will often thrive well in sections where the giant hybrids have proved difficult of culture. Connecticut Yankees, a 1965 All American selection, is a distinctly new type. Blooms first year, base branching, often 25 spikes on mature plants; lilac, purple, light, medium and dark blue. Excellent for cutting; 2½ to 3 feet.

There are also several intermediate and low border types which are of great merit and deserve to be more widely grown. The very dwarf forms are hardly more than 8 to 10 inches in height, the intermediate forms about 15 inches. The colors range from a deep gentian blue to the lovely, soft, clear blue known as Cambridge Blue. There is also a pure white variety. The plants are branching in habit and the single flowers are borne in great profusion. The plants remain in flower for many weeks and are particularly lovely when grown in combination with some of the annuals along the front of the border. If the seeds of these dwarf and intermediate types are sown early in the spring they will usually bloom well the first season.

Climatic Range: Delphiniums thrive best in a moderately cool climate, and they do exceedingly well in high altitudes. They are unable to withstand intense summer heat and are therefore not well adapted to the South. If grown in southern climates they are usually treated as annuals.

Propagation: Delphiniums may be propagated by seed, by cuttings, or by the division of old clumps. As the plants seldom come true from seed, unless careful hand pollination is practiced, it is necessary to resort to cuttings or to the division of old clumps if one desires to secure new plants of a given variety. It is possible, however, to obtain many exceedingly beautiful plants from carefully selected seed, and it is the most universally employed method of propagation. There are several large firms in this country and in England which have made a speciality of delphiniums. For years they have maintained extensive trial grounds, and by crossing desirable varieties they have produced some very fine hybrid strains. If seed is obtained from any of these reliable sources one will usually find that a large percentage of the plants are of excellent type and possess great beauty. A few may be disappointing, but these can readily be discarded. It is an excellent practice to allow the young seedling plants to produce one or two blooms during the first season while they are in the nursery rows as it is then possible to select those of outstanding merit and to discard those which are less desirable.

By Seed—Delphinium seed looses its vitality very rapidly if kept under average storage conditions, but if stored at a cold temperature it will retain its viability for many months. If delphinium seed, whether home-produced or purchased, is to be kept for any length of time before it is sown it should be stored in the refrigerator in a moisture-proof container.

There are a number of flower seeds which require low temperatures for best germination and delphinium seeds are in this group, the optimum temperature range being 42° to 55° F. Reasonably good germination can usually be obtained by sowing under ordinary conditions, provided the seed is viable, but the nearer one approaches the optimum temperature the better the germination will be. An excellent way for the home gardener to obtain maximum germination is to mix the seed with sterile damp sand and moist peat moss and to place it in the refresher pan in the refrigerator. It must be watched carefully and as soon as the seed sprouts it should be removed, and the sand, peat moss and sprouted seeds may be sown immediately in drills in flats or seed bed, where the medium is sterile, being handled from this point on in the usual way. When delphinium seeds are sown under ordinary conditions every effort should be made to keep the temperature as cool as possible. If sown in late summer in a frame or out-of-doors the seed bed should be shaded. If sown indoors early in the spring the seed pan or flat should be placed in the coolest place possible until after germination has occurred.

As delphinium seedlings are very susceptible to damping-off every precaution should be taken to insure protection. The seeds should be treated before they are sown, in order to control pre-emergent damping-off, and the medium in which the seeds are sown should be sterile. (For complete details of seed sowing see Chapter XXXIII.)

By Cuttings—Within recent years much experimental work has been carried on to determine the most satisfactory methods of propagating delphiniums by means of cuttings, as it is the method most commonly used for the propagation of named varieties and choice hybrids. It has been found that some delphinium plants may be propagated very readily from cuttings, while an attempt to secure rooted cuttings from other plants results only in failure. In the case of occasional individual plants it is possible to secure from 75 to 100 strong, vigorous cuttings in a single season, and from other plants it will be impossible to secure even a single cutting which will strike root. Better results will be secured from plants which are brought into the greenhouse and forced slowly, than from those which are left in the open ground, as more cuttings will be produced, and they will root more readily. Those plants which are to be used for propagation should be lifted in the autumn after the first killing frost and placed in a coldframe where they should be allowed to remain until late in January. When brought into the greenhouse they should be placed in a moderately cool temperature. Cuttings may be taken when the shoots have reached a height of from 2 to 3 inches, each cutting being taken with a very small heel. (See Chapter XXXIII on Propagation.) The cuttings should be soaked in water for an hour before they are placed in the propagating bench. Either pure sand or a mixture of sand and peat moss may be used as the rooting medium, and every precaution should be taken during the first few days to see that the cuttings do not wilt. After the first week watering should preferably be done by sub-irrigation, as it is wise to keep the foliage and stems free from moisture. The shading should be gradually diminished, and as soon as new leaf growth appears, the shade may be entirely removed. When the cuttings have become

well rooted they may be lifted with care and planted in pots.

By Division—Old clumps of delphiniums may be lifted and divided in early spring. (See Chapter XXXIII on Propagation.) The work must be done with care if success is to be assured. The soil should be shaken away from the roots and the plants should be gently pulled apart with the fingers. If the clump is cut or torn roughly apart the crown is apt to be badly bruised and various forms of fungus and bacterial rot will gain easy entrance.

Exposure: Delphiniums thrive best in a sunny location where there is sufficient protection from severe wind. Good air circulation is essential. If delphiniums are planted in a shady position, or where the circulation of air is poor, the growth tends to be weak and spindly and the blooms are inferior.

Soil Requirements: Delphiniums require a mellow, well-drained, deeply prepared soil of a neutral or slightly alkaline reaction. They are not acid-tolerant and if the soil has a pH lower than 6.0 an application of lime should be made to bring the soil reaction up to neutral or slightly above neutral. The application should prefer-

DELPHINIUMS

ably be made several months previous to planting. (See Chapter XVI, page 170.)

The texture of the soil does not seem to be a matter of great importance, as delphiniums thrive almost equally well in a fairly heavy clay or in a light, sandy loam, provided that the soil is well drained and that other conditions are favorable.

The question of soil fertility is one which is open to great controversy and many theories have been advanced. It is generally agreed, however, that the small-flowered, small-spiked types give the most satisfactory results when grown on a soil of moderate fertility. If such plants are grown on an exceedingly rich soil or if they are fed heavily, they have a tendency to become floppy and leggy and the size and quality of the blooms show little or no improvement. The large-flowered types which normally produce tall, massive spikes of bloom present quite a different problem. If maximum development of the plant, and flower spikes of superior quality are desired, the soil must be of high fertility and heavy annual feeding is necessary. For many years it was the common practice to use manure in liberal quantities in the preparation of delphinium beds but the present consensus of opinion is in favor of commercial fertilizers, as it has been found that manure is conducive to the spread of crown rot and other fungous diseases and that its use is not advisable. Some of the most successful growers of delphiniums of exhibition quality follow the practice of mixing a 12-16-12 complete fertilizer with the soil at the time of planting. A top-dressing of the same fertilizer is applied to established clumps early in the spring and after the first blooming period an application is made of a fertilizer with a lower nitrogen content, a 4-16-20 complete fertilizer being recommended.

Culture: Delphiniums are very dependent upon an adequate supply of moisture during their active period of growth and the soil should receive a thorough soaking at least once a week. In many seasons the natural rainfall will supply the needed moisture but if this is not adequate it is wise to resort to artificial watering.

It is possible to transplant delphiniums either in the autumn or in the spring, and since the plants have a fine and fibrous root system they may be moved with comparative ease. As delphiniums are among the first herbaceous plants to start growth in the spring, autumn planting is generally preferred as the plants undoubtedly suffer less shock. If the work is done with extreme care it is possible to move quite large plants when they are just coming into bloom. The plants must be lifted with a generous quantity of earth in order that the root system may remain practically intact, and the work should preferably be done on a cloudy day, otherwise it will be advisable to provide light shade for a few days. The use of a plastic spray will prevent wilting if applied

before the plants are lifted (see page 682). The plants should be kept thoroughly watered until they are well established.

When planting delphiniums it is advisable to use a mixture of sand and charcoal about the crown of each plant as this facilitates drainage and consequently lessens the danger of crown rot.

If blooms of superior exhibition quality are desired, not more than three flower stalks should be allowed to develop on a single plant. The remaining stalks should be cut away before they have had an opportunity to make any growth. When grown for mass effect in the garden, healthy, vigorous plants should be capable of producing from 6 to 8 good spikes of bloom.

The large-flowering types should be given adequate room for development and the plants should be spaced from 18 inches to 2 feet apart. The more dwarf types such as *Porcelain Blue* and *D. chinense* should be spaced from 12 to 15 inches apart.

As soon as the flowering period is over the plants should be given a top-dressing, as recommended under Soil Requirements, and the flower stalks should be partially cut down. A small portion of the stalk and the lower leaves should be left until new growth has appeared at the base of the plant. The old stalks should then be cut down level with the surface of the ground, in order that water may not collect in the hollow tubes projecting above the soil. If new growth has already started at the base of the plant before the flowering period is over, as occasionally happens, the stalks may be cut down to the ground as soon as the blooms have faded. The second bloom will never quite equal the first in size or quality, but through the late summer months the blue of the delphiniums is a very welcome note in the garden and the plants will offer a welcome material for cutting.

It is becoming a common practice among some of our most expert growers to lift and divide delphinium clumps every second year. If this procedure is followed a stock of young and vigorous plants is constantly maintained and the most desirable types and varieties may be retained.

Staking: The proper staking of delphiniums is a matter of great importance. Unless one is fortunate enough to have an unusually sheltered location, staking is absolutely necessary, and even in positions which may seem very protected the wind will occasionally work havoc. The stems of delphiniums are rather hollow and brittle and as the flower spikes of some of the improved varieties are exceedingly heavy when wet, the plants present little resistance to a combination of rain and wind. An excellent method of staking is to place three light bamboo stakes close to each plant and, at a distance of about 18 inches above the soil, to tie a loop of raffia or tape, winding it securely about each stake. During heavy storms, when there is driving wind and rain, it may be necessary to temporarily protect some of the individual flower spikes by tying them as far up as the very tip to a stout stake.

Winter Protection: Delphiniums are far more sensitive to heat than they are to cold and they are capable of withstanding severe winter weather with very little protection. It is the alternate freezing and thawing of the ground and excessive amounts of surface water which are usually responsible for losses during the winter months. It is, therefore, advisable to provide good drainage about the crown of each plant. A little mound of sand or coal ashes placed over the crown late in the autumn will facilitate drainage and will afford excellent protection.

For control of Insect Pests and Diseases see Chapter XLI.

Dicentra spectabilis (Bleeding-heart). Bleeding-heart is an old favorite, associated with gardens of long ago, but its popularity has remained undiminished through the years. It is one of the most beautiful of our spring-flowering perennials and it deserves a place in every garden. Its graceful form, the beauty of its bloom and the quality of its foliage make it one of the most valuable plants for the spring border. Even in a small garden Bleeding-heart does not seem out of place in spite of the wide spread of its arching branches. The foliage is a delicate green in color with a glaucous sheen, and the graceful stems bear hanging, deep pink, heart-shaped flowers which diminish in size towards the tip of the branches. It flowers in spring, with the Tulips and the late Narcissus, and it remains in bloom for almost six weeks. By midsummer the foliage begins to die down and gradually disappears entirely. The plants reach a height of from 2 to 4 feet with an almost equal spread.

Exposure: Full sun or partial shade.

Soil Requirements: A deep, rich loam, well supplied with organic matter is desirable, and an adequate supply of moisture is essential.

Propagation: Bleeding-heart may be propagated by seed, by division, by root cuttings or by stem cuttings. Cuttings may be taken from the young shoots as they start into growth in the spring or soon after flowering. (See Chapter XXXIII.)

Culture: When in flower, the plants need ample room and they should be spaced at least 2 feet apart. They are seldom planted in clumps, being used as accent plants in the general planting scheme. After the leaves have begun to die down, shallow-rooted annuals or chrysanthemums may be planted to fill the vacancy left by the disappearing foliage of the Bleeding-heart. The plants resent frequent moving and when once well established they may be left undisturbed for many years. The roots should be planted in an upright position, being placed at a depth of 2 to 3 inches.

Gypsophila (Baby's-breath). The wiry, twisted stems of the Gypsophilas bear their narrow, gray-green leaves so sparsely that the plants seem almost transparent. The myriad, small flowers are borne in great profusion, and the effect is that of a veil thrown over a portion of the garden, a fairy-like foil for the more colorful flowers of the border.

G. paniculata is the old-fashioned type, forming a symmetrical mass almost 3 feet in height and with an almost equal spread. There are both single- and double-flowered forms, blooming in late summer.

G. p. Bristol Fairy is one of the finest of the recent introductions, flowering almost continuously throughout the summer. The flowers are much larger than those of the type, being fully double and pure white in color.

G. repens is a dwarf, trailing type suitable for the rock garden, bearing myriads of tiny flowers in July and August.

G. repens, var. Rosy Veil is a new dwarf form bearing double flowers of a clear, soft pink. It comes into bloom fully two weeks earlier than the larger types and flowers almost continuously throughout the summer. It reaches a height of about 2 feet and is excellent for use in the front of the border.

Exposure: Full sun is essential as the plants will not thrive in even light shade.

Soil Requirements: A light, well-drained soil of medium fertility and high in lime content. The very name, Gypsophila, meaning gypsum-loving, denotes the preference which these plants possess for limestone soils. Gypsophilas are noted for their ability to grow well on dry, rather poor soils.

Propagation: By seed, by cuttings, and by the division of old plants. The double-flowered varieties are usually grafted on the roots of the single-flowering types.

Culture: The Gypsophilas require very little in the way of care and attention. The dwarf types should be spaced from 15 inches to 2 feet apart, the larger types from 2½ to 4 feet, as they form large masses.

Hemerocallis (Daylily). The modest lemon lily, long a favorite in old-time gardens, is now available in lovely new forms and in enchanting colors. The botanical name, derived from two Greek worlds, *hemera,* meaning "day", and *kallos,* meaning "beautiful", was bestowed upon it because of the fleeting beauty of the flowers, which last only for a day. The daylilies are native to Asia. The lemon lily was introduced into England in 1596 from Siberia and was brought to this country by the early colonists. Other species were later brought in by the captains of the early clipper ships and thus found their way into the gardens of New England.

SPECIES HEMEROCALLIS

Hemerocallis flava, Lemon Daylily, has lemon or canary flowers in May and June which are fragrant; grows about 3 feet high.

Hemerocallis aurantiaca, Orange Daylily, has rich orange flowers shaded to brown in June and July.

Hemerocallis Middendorffii has deep orange flowers in June and July.

Hemerocallis Thunbergii is a late-blooming lemon-yellow sort with fragrant blossoms, blooming in July.

Hemerocallis Dumortierii has flowers of rich yellow inside and bronzy yellow outside, blooming in May.

Hemerocallis fulva, Tawny Daylily, is a deep coppery-orange, darkening to crimson, with flowers in great numbers, in July and August. It is this species which has naturalized itself so much in the eastern states.

Hemerocallis citrina (Citron Daylily) has pale yellow blossoms in June and July, and is very fragrant.

HEMEROCALLIS

During the latter years of the nineteenth century interest in the daylily waned and not until the development of the new hybrids did it again become appreciated. The pioneer work in breeding, which resulted in the introduction of the first hybrid daylilies to be developed in this country, was done by Dr. A. B. Stout at the New York Botanic Garden. Work in hybridization is now being carried on in every section of the country and there is a steadily increasing demand for varieties of proven merit. One Texas grower produces over two and a half million plants per year which is an indication of the current interest in hemerocallis.

Among these beautiful new hybrids there is considerable variance in form and a wide range of colors. There are varieties with wide, overlapping petals, others with slightly recurved petals, some which have frilled, crinkled and ruffled petals. Some of the blooms resemble wide, flaring trumpets, others are graceful, chaliced cups and some are almost bell-like. The colors range from palest lemon-white through tones of ivory-buff to soft yellow, golden yellow, apricot and orange; and from rose-pink, delicate shrimp-pink and violet-pink to wine red, Indian red, claret, deep maroon and dark, ebony-purple. And there are many lovely intermediate pastel shades and polychromes.

There are tall, intermediate, dwarf and midget types. The dwarf varieties have large blooms but low-growing foliage, and attain a height of 18 to 24 inches. The midget varieties have small flowers, slender, grass-like foliage and seldom reach a height of more than 12 to 18 inches.

The blooms of most varieties last but a single day. Toward evening the flowers close and wither. But always the bloom of today is replaced with a fresh bloom on the morrow as long as flower buds continue to form, many varieties continuing to bloom for six weeks or more. The flowers of some of the new hybrids remain open until very late in the evening, while the flowers of a few varieties remain open a full 24 hours. Some of these are evening bloomers which open at dusk and remain open until the following evening. These varieties are very popular in some sections of the South.

By selecting early, mid-season and late varieties it is possible to obtain a succession of bloom throughout the season. The very early varieties will come into bloom with the iris, and some of the late varieties will continue to flower until severe frosts bring the season to a close.

Daylilies can be used with dramatic effect in many planting compositions: in the perennial border, in the foreground of shrubbery plantings, as an accent in a foundation planting or beside a pool. They are particularly effective when planted in sweeping drifts or masses against a wall or fence, or when used to clothe an unsightly bank. A clump planted at the base of a small tree has an informal charm, and they will adapt themselves very happily to odd corners which might otherwise be bare and uninteresting.

The daylily, beautiful when in bloom, can also be enjoyed for its foliage. The foliage is attractive, appealing when the young growth is pushing upward in the spring and valued, too, for its lush, all-season effect. Some varieties have foliage which is evergreen, but with most the foliage dies down in the autumn.

VARIETIES OF MERIT

Angie: ruffled, peach color
Capri: light rose-apricot
Colonial Dame: rose-tan to apricot
Evelyn Claar: bright rose
Frances Fay: melon pink
Gold Strike: golden yellow
Hyperion: citron yellow
Mission Bells: yellow gold
North Star: near white
Pink Prelude: soft-pink
Salmon Sheen: salmon-blend
Step Forward: flesh-pink, ruffled
Sugar Plum Fairy: apricot-pink, frilled

Climate and Exposure: The daylily is one of the few perennials, if not the only perennial, which will flourish and give a good account of itself in every one of our 48 States. It is immune to heat, is completely winter hardy, and possesses an extraordinary capacity to survive floods and drought.

Most daylilies will thrive well in either full sun or partial shade. There are only a few varieties which will do even reasonably well in heavy shade. The flowers of some of the new hybrids have a tendency to fade or wilt in very intense sun and are at their best when grown in a location where they will receive light shade, or shade for at least a portion of the day. In general, most daylilies prefer morning sun and some afternoon shade.

Soil Requirements: A good, sandy loam is considered ideal, but most daylilies will thrive on soils of widely varied types and are not exacting in their demands. Good drainage is, however, an important consideration.

Propagation: Daylilies are very easily propagated by the division of old clumps. The plant should be lifted with a spading fork and the clump should be gently pulled apart. The most favorable time for dividing old clumps and resetting the plants is from late summer to late autumn. Planting may also be done in very early spring but is less advisable.

When planting divisions or newly purchased plants the hole should be made large enough to accommodate the entire root system when it is spread out in a natural position. A little cone of soil should be made in the center of the hole to support the crown, as this will permit the roots to fan outward and downward. The soil should be worked in carefully among the roots. The crown should be set so that it is not more than an inch below the surface of the soil.

Tall varieties should be spaced about 30 inches apart, small varieties from 18 to 24 inches apart.

Culture: Daylilies are among the most adaptable of plants and there are few perennials less exacting in their demands. Indeed they rate at the top among perennials requiring little care. They have practically no pests and diseases, and therefore require no spraying. The stems are strong and supple and require no staking. Daylilies thrive and bloom well on a meager diet and the foliage shades the ground so completely that they require almost no cultivation. When the clumps become crowded they benefit from being lifted, divided and replanted, and this should be done every few years if possible. But if it is not done the plants carry cheerfully on with somewhat less abundant bloom.

The daylilies are among the most self-sufficient plants ever invited into the garden, and they are also among the most versatile and charming.

Heuchera (Coral-Bells) (Alumroot). The Heucheras are charming, graceful plants with geranium-like, evergreen foliage which forms a broad mat close to the ground. The wiry stems, rising above the leaves, bear panicles of tiny, nodding bells. The brilliant hue of the flowers, dispersed as it is into many small particles, makes a delightful sparkle of color and gives life and vivacity to the garden. The Heucheras are excellent border plants, and they are also frequently used in rock gardens with pleasing effect. The flower stems vary in height from 12 to 18 inches.

SPECIES AND VARIETIES OF MERIT

H. lithophila (H. brizoides). The flowers are a pale pink in color and are produced freely in May. The plant is robust in habit of growth, with excellent foliage.

H. sanguinea—The best known of all the Heucheras. The brilliant crimson flowers are lovely for cutting and they are produced in abundance over a period of several months, beginning in June.

H. s. Rosamondie—One of the finest of the hybrids. The brilliant coral-pink flowers are borne in profusion over a period of several months. It is strong and robust in habit of growth.

H. s. Perry's White—Pure white flowers from June to September.

Exposure: Full sun, or partial shade.

Soil Requirements: A rich, well-drained loam is considered ideal as the plants will not thrive in a heavy, clay soil.

Propagation: The most satisfactory method of propagation is the division of established plants. The plants may be lifted and divided either in the spring or in the autumn. If the divisions are made in the autumn, the young plants should be wintered over in a coldframe, and they should be kept well watered until they have become established. Heucheras may also be propagated by seed but the seeds are usually of poor vitality and do not germinate well. Leaf cuttings may also be made. The leaf should be cut at the base of the leaf stalk with a sliver of the main stem attached.

Culture: The Heucheras may be planted in the autumn or in early spring and the plants should be spaced from 6 to 8 inches apart. Spring planting is preferred in sections where the winters are severe.

As Heucheras have a tendency to be heaved out of the soil during the winter, due to the alternate freezing and thawing of the ground, it is well to give them extra attention in the early spring. If the plants have suffered from heaving they should be pressed gently back into the soil and a light mulch of compost should be placed about the crowns.

If plantings of Heuchera are to be maintained in good condition the plants should be lifted and divided every third year, the soil being well enriched before the plants are reset.

Hosta (Funkia) (Plantain Lily). The Plantain Lily is valued both for its foliage and for its flowers. The flower spikes rise above the dense masses of broad, green leaves, reaching a height of $1\frac{1}{2}$ to 2 feet, and bear small tubular flowers in shades of lavender and white. Funkias will flourish at the foot of a wall or on the north side of a building where little else will grow, and they are, therefore, of particular value for positions in semi-shade.

Exposure: Partial shade.

Soil Requirements: Funkia does well in any ordinary garden soil but prefers a soil with a high moisture content, and makes its most luxuriant growth on a rich, moist loam.

Propagation: The plants may be lifted and divided in early spring.

Culture: The plantain lily requires ample space for its best development and the plants should be spaced from 2 to 3 feet apart. The plants are of exceedingly simple culture, demanding little in the way of care and cultivation.

Irises contribute to the garden a quality distinctively their own. They have long been important garden flowers, and with their grace and delicacy of form and their luminous colors they impart a radiance to the garden which is not equalled by any other flower.

In mediæval times the iris was so beloved by the people of France that it was given a special distinction and became the symbol of the royal house of France, and hence the symbol of the realm. It appears in many an illuminated manuscript, and in the heraldry, architecture and jewelry of the early Renaissance in France, where it was affectionately called *"Fleur-de-Lis"*.

Not only are irises valued, today, for the rare quality which they contribute to a planting composition, but they are also greatly prized for their decorative qualities as cut flowers.

During the past quarter of a century remarkable progress has been made in breeding new and superbly beautiful varieties of iris. The color range has been extended to include dramatically lovely shades of pink and also many subtle and muted tones of rose, tawny sunset reds and violets, as well as exquisite blends.

Each year new varieties of iris are introduced. Medals and certificates of merit are awarded by the American Iris Society to varieties considered worthy of these coveted honors. Thus, over the years, a great number of varieties of exceptional merit, vigorous in growth and indescribably beautiful in form and color, have gradually replaced the older types and have brought charm and distinction to many a garden. When new varieties are first introduced they are often very high in price, but within a few years, when stock has become more plentiful, they become available at more modest figures, which are well within the budget of the average gardener.

There are many species, groups and subgroups of iris, each endowed with a special charm. Some are stately and majestic, others are diminutive in size; some prefer dry situations, others are at their best when grown by the waterside; some grace the spring garden with their bloom, others bring dramatic beauty to the garden in midsummer, and the new fall-blooming irises are often in flower until late in the autumn.

With careful planning many months of iris bloom may be obtained in the garden. A succession of bloom can be achieved, however, only through the planting of many species, groups and varieties. The diminutive and enchantingly lovely I. reticulata, blooming in very early spring, is the herald among the irises and is followed in due succession by the Dutch iris, the dwarf bearded, intermediate bearded and tall bearded groups. During the summer months the Siberian, Spuria, Louisiana and Japanese groups carry on the gay pageantry of bloom and the fall-blooming irises often continue to flower until cut down by heavy frosts.

Irises are classified into several groups according to their root characteristics and their flower forms. Most of the more commonly cultivated types have fleshy roots known as rhizomes, while some types are bulbous, and a few have fibrous root systems.

Many of our garden irises, which originally came from Central Europe, have a bearded tongue on the lower petal of the flowers. These are known as the Pogoniris Group, "pogon" being the Greek word for beard. The beardless iris group, which includes many species from the Orient, is known as the Apogoniris Group, meaning "without a beard." Iris belonging to the Crested Group have a ridged growth on the lower petals in place of the beard.

Pogoniris Group

Dwarf Bearded: This group includes several species, such as I. pumila, as well as many hybrid forms. Some types are miniature in size, hardly more than 3 or 4 inches high, while others reach a height of 10 inches. There is also considerable variance in the form of the flowers, and a wide color range. The blooms of some varieties are of exquisite daintiness, while others are more voluptuous, resembling in form the blooms of the tall, bearded group.

The dwarf irises are happily at home in well-drained pockets in the rock garden and are very effective when planted in drifts along a path or when used as an edging in a flower border, being particularly happy companions for primroses and narcissus and the early tulips. They are lovely, also, when planted in masses on a sunny slope, either alone or in combination with arabis alpina, phlox subulata, arenaria and some of the other rock plants. Most dwarf irises bloom early in the spring, several weeks before the tall, bearded type, and there are also several autumn-blooming varieties.

The popularity of the dwarf irises has increased so rapidly during recent years that a Dwarf Iris Society has been formed to guide the destiny of this much-loved group, and through hybridization many lovely new varieties have been introduced.

The culture of the dwarf, bearded irises is similar to that of the tall, bearded group. Good drainage and a position in full sun are essential to their happiness. If conditions are favorable they increase very rapidly and a single plant will develop into a large clump within a few years. In order to prevent crowding they should be divided and replanted about every three years.

(*See* page 360 *for detailed culture of Bearded Iris*.)

VARIETIES OF MERIT

April: early, light blue
Atroviolacea: reddish purple
Blue Flash: wedgwood-blue

Fairy: azure blue
Lavender Dream: clear lavender
Path of Gold: golden yellow

Rose Mist: deep mauve-pink
Schneecuppe: pure white

Intermediate Group: Many of the varieties in this group have been developed by hybridizing some of the dwarf types with the tall, bearded types. The flowers are lovely in form, possessing many of the characteristics of the tall, bearded group, but are smaller and more delicate. Some varieties have ruffled or frilled petals, giving them especial distinction and charm. In height and season of bloom they are intermediate between the two groups, ranging in height from 12 to 18 inches and blooming with the mid-spring tulips. There are also several autumn-blooming varieties within the intermediate group.

(See below for detailed culture of Bearded Iris.)

VARIETIES OF MERIT

Abelard: chestnut and purple
Black Hawk: blackish purple
Crysoro: ruffled yellow
Day Star: cream-white, orange beard
Kansas Ingleside: coppery-red
Red Orchid: red-purple
Snow Maiden: pure white
Zua: frilled ice-white

Tall Bearded Group: The decorative landscape value of the tall bearded irises remains unchallenged through the years.

It is in this group that we find many of our most magnificent garden irises, superb in form and indescribably beautiful in color. No garden is complete without them, and in spring they bring dramatic beauty to many a planting composition.

VARIETIES OF MERIT

Amethyst Flounce: bright violet, ruffled
Breathless: large, flamingo-pink flowers
Carved Alabaster: cream yellow with yellow beard
China Maid: a blending of pink, buff and lilac
Crinkled Gem: a soft lavender
Crystal Blue: a bright, frosty blue
Elmohr: reddish violet to mulberry purple
Fairy Rose: rich, orchid-pink
Frost and Flame: pure white flower with
          tangerine beard
Great Lakes: pure blue
Happy Birthday: flamingo pink
Harbor Blue: sapphire blue
Laced Charm: blend of cream, apricot and pink
Prairie Sunset: apricot, rose, copper-gold blend
Royal Tapestry: wine red to royal purple
Whole Cloth: pure white standards, blue falls

Autumn-Flowering Group: After years of patient effort on the part of plant hybridizers, a new race of iris has been introduced which extends the flowering period through the autumn months. These new irises have two or more distinct flowering periods, blooming in the spring and again in autumn, beginning in September and continuing until growth is checked by heavy frosts. Some varieties also flower intermittently throughout the summer months. Although hardy in Northern gardens, these autumn-flowering irises are specially recommended for the South where the fall-blooming season may extend over many months. The plants vary in height from 15 to 30 inches.

VARIETIES OF MERIT

Autumn Queen: pure white
Eleanor Roosevelt: purple
Jean Siret: chrome-yellow
Lieut. Chavagnac: violet
Olive White: cream color
Sangreal: pale yellow
September Morn: mauve pink

Culture of Bearded Iris

Climatic Range: The bearded irises have an extraordinarily wide climatic range as they are able to endure the intense heat of Southern summers as well as the extreme cold of winters in the Far North.

Exposure: The bearded irises should be planted in a sunny location if they are to be grown at their best. If planted on the north side of a building or in an otherwise shady location they seldom thrive well, the plants being weak and spindly in growth and the flowers decidedly inferior in size and in quantity of bloom.

Soil Requirements: The bearded irises may be grown successfully on soils of widely varying types, and it has been found that they do almost as well on heavy clay soils as on sandy loam, provided that the soil is well drained. Good drainage is absolutely essential, as the bearded irises cannot thrive on soils which are saturated with moisture. Unless the soil is naturally well drained some provision must be made for artificial drainage. (See Chapter XXIX, page 426.) While it is true that many irises will do reasonably well on rather poor soils, the fact must not be overlooked that the most thrifty plants capable of producing an abundance of bloom are to be found on soils of good fertility. If special beds or borders are to be devoted to irises, the soil should preferably be prepared several months in advance of planting. Well-rotted manure, compost, or some commercial form of humus should be thoroughly incorporated into the soil and the soil should be deeply prepared. Although the bearded irises are generally classed among the more shallow-rooted plants, many of the feeding roots penetrate to a considerable depth. At the time of planting an application of commercial fertilizer should be made at the rate of ½ pound per square yard. The bearded irises prefer a soil which is very nearly neutral in reaction, although they will tolerate a very mildly acid soil as well as one with a considerable degree of alkalinity. As a general rule, they are classed among lime-loving plants.

Propagation: The bearded irises are propagated by the division of the rhizomes. The clump should be lifted from the soil with a spading fork and the rhizomes either cut or broken apart. Each fan of leaves should have a short, sound piece of rhizome with a number of strong, vigorous feeding roots attached. Any dead or shrivelled leaves should be removed and in the case of the tall bearded group, the foliage should be cut back to within 6 to 8 inches of the rhizome. The dwarf and intermediate types should be cut back proportionately. The ideal time for the division of bearded irises is the period immediately after flowering. As new root growth is made at this time, new plants will, therefore, have an opportunity to become well established before winter and will usually produce a few blooms the following year. Late autumn planting is not advisable as the plants have had no opportunity to become anchored and are likely to be heaved out of the soil during the winter. Clumps may be divided in the early spring, but the bloom is then sacrificed for that season as the plants will not flower until the following year.

Planting: The dwarf types of bearded iris may be planted from 5 to 6 inches apart if the effect of a large clump is desired. The intermediate and tall-growing types should be planted from 15 to 18 inches apart. If immediate mass effect is desired, the rhizomes may be placed as closely as 8–10 inches apart, but this practice is not recommended except as an occasional expedient, as the clumps soon become crowded and growth and vigor are sacrificed. When planting irises, the rhizome should not be covered deeply. The feeding roots should be spread out in a natural position, a hole of sufficient size having been opened, and the upper portion of the rhizome should be barely covered with soil. Deep planting, particularly in heavy soils, makes the rhizomes more susceptible to rot. The newly planted rhizomes should always be well firmed into the soil.

Culture: The cultural requirements of the bearded iris are not exacting. The plants require an abundance of moisture during the blooming season but are able to endure long periods of drought at other periods. The best bloom is usually produced the second, third and fourth years after planting. As soon as the rhizomes show evidence of becoming crowded, the clumps should be lifted and divided. Most iris plantings will continue to bloom well and will remain in good condition for a period of about five years. After this period

the rhizomes in the center of the clump usually become so crowded that the plants begin to deteriorate.

Each spring, the soil about the clumps should be lightly cultivated and if it seems advisable to improve the fertility of the soil an application of commercial fertilizer may be applied at the rate of ½ pound per square yard. This should be sprinkled on the surface of the soil about the plants and cultivated lightly in, and the soil should then be thoroughly watered.

In the autumn the foliage should be cut back to within 4 or 5 inches of the rhizome and all dead or shrivelled leaves should be removed. Winter protection is not necessary except in sections where the winters are of extreme severity.

Throughout the season one should be constantly alert to detect the first signs of insect infestation or disease. See Chapter XLI.

Apogoniris Group (The Beardless Iris)

Japanese Iris (I. Kæmpferi). The Japanese Irises have become increasingly popular within recent years and the plants possess great beauty and dignity. The flowers are characteristically flat and broad, the standards and falls being horizontal rather than ascending and descending. The flowers possess colors dominantly in the red-purple, purple, lavender, blue and white sector of the color scale. Some are a mahogany red and a few have a gray background tone with deep purple, violet or wine-red markings. The leaves are narrow and reed-like and the blooms, with their broad, crepe-like petals, are borne on tall, erect stems which attain a height of 2½ to 5 feet. With the exception of the fall-blooming bearded varieties they are among the last of the irises to flower, blooming in late June and throughout July.

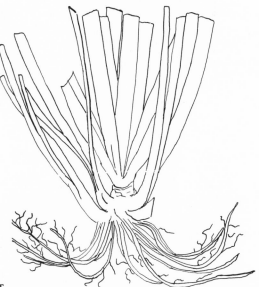

AN IRIS DIVISION
READY TO TRANSPLANT

VARIETIES OF MERIT

Eleanor Parry: hyacinth-violet
Great White Heron: tall, white
Iso-no-Kamone: medium, white

Mountain Grotto: orchid-blue
Nishike Yama: pansy-violet
Repsime: azure-blue

Suehiro: deep lavender
Summer Storm: deep purple

Exposure: Full sun for at least the major portion of the day.

Soil Requirements: The Japanese Irises require an abundance of moisture until after their flowering season is over. They are then able to withstand considerable drought, but should never be allowed to dry out completely. During the winter months they prefer a soil which is free from excessive moisture. It is the almost universal custom in Japan to flood the iris plantings during the period when the plants are in bud and in bloom, but during the balance of the year the soil is kept comparatively dry. Japanese Irises should never be planted in a location where the water table rises to the surface of the ground during the winter months as such a condition will usually prove fatal.

Japanese Irises thrive best in a rich, highly fertile soil well supplied with organic matter and definitely acid in reaction. In preparing the soil liberal quantities of leaf mold (preferably oak leaf mold), peat moss and rotted cow manure (if obtainable) should be used.

Propagation: Japanese Irises may be readily propagated by the division of old clumps, the ideal time being late August or early September. If the divisions are made at this season the young plants will re-establish themselves quickly and may give some bloom the following summer. Clumps may also be divided early in the spring, but the results are not as satisfactory. Many of the divisions may fail to grow and only a small percentage will flower the following year. An entire clump may be lifted and divided, being pried apart with two strong spading forks until it is sufficiently loosened to fall into many natural divisions, or large pieces may be removed from established clumps without lifting them. It requires a stout spading fork with considerable pressure behind it to accomplish this feat. The rhizomes should not be allowed to dry out before planting. If immediate effect is desired in the garden, the divisions should consist of three fans of leaves. If, however, rapid increase of stock is desired, single fans may be planted. The foliage should be cut back to within 5 to 6 inches.

Japanese Irises may also be propagated by seeds. If the seeds are sown out of doors in the autumn as soon as they are ripe they will germinate in the spring and will bloom in 2 to 3 years. They do not, however, come true from seed.

Planting: The rhizome of the Japanese Iris is very slender with many fibrous roots. At the time divisions are planted, these roots should be shortened to 5 or 6 inches. The new roots develop from the backs of the leaf fans and the crowns should be planted 2 inches below the surface of the soil in order to make it easy for these new roots to gain anchorage. For mass plantings which will remain undisturbed for many years, the plants should be spaced from 18 inches to 2 feet apart. If clumps of Japanese Irises are to be used in herbaceous borders or in other similar locations more immediate effect may be obtained if three, four or five divisions are planted about 10 inches apart.

Winter Protection: With the exception of newly planted divisions, Japanese Irises require no winter protection. Young plants which have not had an opportunity to become established are liable to suffer severely from the effects of heaving and it is, therefore, wise to protect them during the first winter. Oak leaves are excellent as a mulch if they are held in place by evergreen boughs. Stable manure may also be used. The Japanese Iris is one of the very few members of the Iris family for which a mulch of manure can be used with impunity.

Siberian Iris (I. siberica). The Siberian Irises are of great decorative value in the garden and are enchantingly lovely as cut flowers. They are lavish with their bloom, a well established clump sometimes producing more than 50 flowers. The blooms are borne well above the narrow, sword-like leaves, each slender stalk bearing from five to ten graceful flowers on branching pedicels. Varieties vary from 2 to 4 feet in height and there is a wide range of colors, from pure white through delicate blue, lavender and violet to rich, velvety purple, with a few deep reds and reddish purples.

VARIETIES OF MERIT

Cæsar's Brother: pansy-purple
Congo Drums: deep purple
Eric The Red: deep red
Gatineau: clear, light violet

Mountain Lake: clear blue
Periwinkle: porcelain blue
Seven Seas: violet-blue
Snow Crest: pure white

Snow Egret: ruffled petals, white
Tycoon: rich, velvety purple
Summer Sky: wisteria blue
White Dove: tall, pure white

JAPANESE IRIS

Exposure: The Siberian Irises are at their best when grown in full sun but will thrive fairly well and give some bloom in partial shade, such as locations where they receive several hours of sunlight during the day. In dense shade the plants will usually continue to exist but will not flower.

Soil Requirements: For best development, the plants prefer a fairly moist, highly fertile soil. Good drainage is, however, essential, and Siberian Irises should never be planted in a location where the crowns might be covered with water during the winter as they cannot survive the effects of a saturated soil during freezing weather. Previous to planting, the soil should be well enriched with rotted cow manure, rich compost, or leaf mold. The plants are acid-tolerant but prefer a soil within the near neutral range.

Although Siberian Irises are appreciative of soils which are high in fertility they will make a remarkably good showing on rather poor soils. This is particularly true of some of the old varieties such as Snow Queen, which will thrive well under the most adverse conditions.

Propagation: The clumps may be lifted and divided very readily, late August and early September being

considered the ideal time. Divisions may be made in spring or immediately after flowering but the percentage of plants which survive is far less than when divisions are made in late summer. The methods of making the divisions and of planting are the same as those for the Japanese Iris, described in detail on page 362. The rhizomes should be planted 2 inches deep and the plants should be spaced from 15 to 18 inches apart.

In order to achieve a clump effect as quickly as possible in the garden a small section containing from five to seven slender rhizomes should be selected for planting. If, however, rapid increase in stock is desired, smaller sections should be used. The Siberian Irises have long, fibrous roots and when planting the divisions it is important to see that the hole is of ample size so that the roots will not be cramped. Long-established clumps are sometimes very difficult to divide, as their roots have often formed a very dense mass.

The Siberian Iris may be propagated by seed but wide variation is found among the seedlings and it is a method seldom employed except by hybridizers.

Culture: Siberian Irises are of extremely easy culture and are almost certain to do well under average conditions. They require abundant moisture before and

363

during the flowering period if maximum bloom is to be obtained, but beyond this they need little care. They are rarely attacked by pests or diseases and the clumps may be left undisturbed for many years. No winter protection is necessary except in very cold climates, or in the case of young plants which have not become established. Under such conditions a light mulch of salt hay or some similar material will prove helpful.

Spuria Iris Group (I. spuria). The lovely Spuria irises, often called the Butterfly iris, are prized not only for their landscape value but also for their distinction as cut flowers. They have a unique and sprightly charm and are considered by many to be the best of all the irises for use in flower arrangements.

In height the spurias range from 2½ to 5 feet. Each flower stalk usually produces four pairs of buds, the flowers being similar in form and size to the larger types of Dutch iris. The colors range from white through shades of yellow and bronze to deep brown, and from pale blue and lavender to deep blue. Some of the new hybrids are very beautiful in coloring.

The spurias bloom in midsummer, following the Siberian irises and overlapping the Japaneses irises. In the South the period of bloom often lasts two months or more.

The Spuria irises may be grown in all sections of the country and have proved to be of particular value in the lower Rio Grande Valley.

VARIETIES OF MERIT

Azure Dawn: light blue
Cherokee Chief: velvety brown
Dutch Defiance: blue
Fifth Symphony: buff-yellow
Golden Gate: rich yellow
Gold Nugget: golden yellow
Lark Song: yellow and white
Pastoral: orange-yellow and lavender
Two Opals: tones of blue and tan
Wadi Zem Zem: greenish buff

Exposure: The Spuria irises prefer a position in full sun but will thrive well in semi-shade. They are tolerant of large amounts of water but also have the ability to withstand long periods of drought.

Soil Requirements: Spurias reach their best development in a fertile soil which is retentive of moisture, but they are much less exacting regarding soil conditions than are many other iris. They are tolerant of some acidity as well as mild alkalinity.

Propagation: The Spuria irises may be easily increased by division, the clumps being lifted and divided in late summer or early autumn.

Culture: These hardy irises are of easy culture. To be brought to perfection they require abundant moisture throughout the growing season. They will form large clumps and may be left undisturbed for years.

Louisiana Iris. The beautiful Louisiana irises, although native to the swamps and bayous of the lower Mississippi, have proved extraordinarily hardy and adaptable and are now widely grown in many sections of the country. Unique in color and form, many of these species and their hybrids are startling in their beauty. They range in height from 2 to 4 feet. Many of the flowers are flat in form, while others have flaring or hanging segments. In color the blooms range through velvety tones of deep garnet, rosy apricot, rose-petal pink, deep pansy-violet, pale lavender and ivory white.

VARIETIES OF MERIT

Bayou Sunset: reddish coral
Cajun Joyeuse: rose-red and copper
Delta Treasure: buff yellow
Gay One: rose-violet and gold
Jeune Fille: white
Mary S. Debaillon: orchid-pink
Reflected Light: chamois-buff
Royal Highness: blue-violet
Ruth Marsalis: soft blue
The Khan: black-violet

Exposure: The Louisiana irises will do well in sun or semi-shade.

Soil Requirements: Members of this group prefer an acid soil with a very high moisture content.

Culture: Before planting the soil should be well and deeply prepared and liberal quantities of peat moss of the coarsest grade, coarse leaf mold, unscreened compost and rotted cow manure, if available, should be thoroughly worked into it to a depth of 12 to 18 inches. Although Louisiana irises can hardly be supplied with too much water during the growing season, care must be taken when they are being planted in a Northern garden not to select a location where water would freeze about their roots during the winter, as this would prove fatal.

Vesper Iris (I. dichotoma). The lovely Vesper iris is unique among the irises, both in its habit of bloom and in the character of its root system. The flowers open in mid-afternoon and remain open until late in the evening. During the night the petals droop and curl into a small spiral, the faded flowers falling to the ground, to be followed the next afternoon by crisp, fresh blooms. There are sometimes as many as 50 to 100 blooms on a single plant. The flowers, which are borne on candelabrum-like branches are dainty and graceful in form, hardly more than two inches across, and the flaring petals, in shades of blue, lavender or wine-red, are marked with touches of orange and tyrian tones. In height the plants range from two to three feet, some being slightly taller. The vesper iris comes into flower in late July or early August and continues to produce its bountiful bloom until frost. The flowers are very attractive to hummingbirds, as well as to honeybees.

Exposure: The Vesper iris will thrive well either in full sun or in partial shade. It is extremely hardy and after it is well established it will withstand temperatures as low as 15° F. below zero.

Soil Requirements: A rich, heavy loam will provide soil conditions most favorable to good growth, but the Vesper iris will thrive reasonably well in almost any type of soil.

Propagation: Unlike most members of the iris family, the Vesper iris has a fibrous root system and does not produce a definite rhizome. It may be propagated both by seed and by the division of old clumps. Each division should have two or three strong eyes. The clumps should always be divided and the division replanted in the spring. If done in the autumn the young plants will not have time to become established before winter and their chances of survival are slight.

Growth is slow at first, after the divisions have been planted, but when they are well started growth is more rapid and there is often some bloom the first year.

Culture: The Vesper iris is of very easy culture. It is subject to few pests and diseases and will do well under ordinary garden conditions. It prefers abundant moisture but will tolerate long periods of dry weather. If, during the blooming period, it suffers from lack of sufficient moisture it will cease flowering, but will bloom again when it receives the moisture which it requires.

Iris pseudacorus. The rich yellow blooms of I. pseudacorus are of striking beauty, being borne on tall, erect stems from 3 to 4 feet in height. There is no finer iris for the water garden or for naturalization along the banks of a stream.

Exposure: Full sun.

Soil Requirements: I. pseudacorus will thrive in almost any location but prefers a very damp soil.

Propagation: Readily propagated by division of the rhizomes.

Culture: As I. pseudacorus is very hardy it demands little in the way of care and cultivation after it has once become established.

VARIETIES OF MERIT

P. alba: a beautiful pure white form
P. gigantea: a giant-flowered form
P. immaculata: pure yellow without throat markings
P. sulphurea: sulphur-yellow form

American Beardless Species

Iris versicolor. I. versicolor is the beardless marsh iris of our Northern states. It is of particular value for the water garden or for naturalization along the banks of streams. The flowers are of a lavender-purple hue.

Exposure: Sun or semi-shade.

Soil Requirements: Rich, very moist soil.

Propagation: The division of the rhizomes.

Culture: As I. versicolor is, perhaps, the most rugged of all the members of the large family of Iris, it requires no special culture. It thrives well in almost any location and is most amazing in its adaptability.

Crested Iris

Iris cristata. This lovely native of the southern highlands is found growing on thinly wooded hillsides and along stream banks from Virginia southward to Georgia. It is an exquisite thing, hardly more than four inches in height. The diminutive flowers, their lavender petals touched with crested gold, spread their bloom above the carpet of soft green leaves in late spring, and sun-splashed patches of it along a woodland path hold joy for all who pass.

Exposure: Partial shade is preferred and I. cristata thrives best in open woodlands. It also does reasonably well in full sun, although it definitely prefers afternoon shade.

Soil Requirements: A gravelly, well-drained soil, rich in humus is ideal, although I. cristata will succeed well in almost any good garden soil.

Propagation: I. cristata is readily propagated by division of the small rhizomes. This may be accomplished with a fair degree of success at almost any time during the growing season, but very early spring is preferred. The roots should be spread out in a natural position and the rhizomes should be barely covered with soil.

Culture: The rhizomes should be planted from 5 to 6 inches apart. When the clumps become too crowded the plants should be lifted and divided. Careful weeding must be done throughout the season in order to prevent more vigorous plants from crowding out the small, delicate rhizomes of I. cristata.

In its native habitat I. cristata is accustomed to an annual leaf cover and if grown in cultivated ground where leaves do not provide such a covering it has a tendency to grow itself out of the ground. In such locations it should be given an annual top-dressing of screened compost or leaf mold.

As slugs have a special fondness for members of the iris family and are capable of destroying large clumps of I. cristata in an incredibly short time, one should be on the alert to detect the first signs of infestation. Fortunately, with simple precautions, damage from slugs can be easily prevented (see page 671 for Measures of Control).

Iris gracilipes (Japanese Crested Iris). In Japan, this dainty little crested iris is found growing in the woodlands and although it is a bit temperamental when transplanted from its native habitat, it may, with a little coaxing, be made to feel quite happily at home with us either in the woodland or in a partially shaded spot in the rock garden. The foliage is slender and grass-like and the miniature flowers, of a pinkish lavender hue, are borne on branching stems hardly more than 8 inches in height.

Exposure: Light shade is essential, as it will not thrive in a hot, dry position. Good air circulation is also necessary.

Soil Requirements: A fairly moist but well-drained soil, loose in texture and well supplied with humus, is considered ideal. I. gracilipes is not tolerant of any degree of alkalinity and thrives best in a slightly acid soil.

Propagation: The division of the rhizomes should preferably be done in July when new root growth is active. If attempted at other seasons of the year, it is less apt to be successful.

Culture: As the plants are somewhat frail, careful weeding is necessary throughout the season in order to prevent more vigorous plants from encroaching upon the clumps of I. gracilipes. In early spring and again in late June, the plants should be given a top-dressing of domestic humus or well-decayed leaf mold.

Iris tectorum. I. tectorum is the roof iris of China and Japan, so famed in song and story. The flowers are a clear blue in color. The foliage is broad and heavily ribbed, and the flower stalks reach a height of 12 to 15 inches.

The white form, I. tectorum alba, is considered one of the most exquisite of flowers. Anyone who has once seen it will never forget the chaste perfection of its bloom, which resembles a magnified snowflake. The

flowers are fragile and suffer from wind and rain but during periods of unfavorable weather they may be cut in bud and allowed to open in the house. The white form is less hardy than the type.

Exposure: Full sun or light shade.

Soil Requirements: Iris tectorum will grow well in soils of widely varying types. It grows extremely well in the strong limestone clay soil of the Shenandoah Valley, and it thrives equally well in the well-drained, sandy-loam soils of Connecticut hillsides. It prefers rich garden loam, well supplied with humus.

Propagation: I. tectorum should be divided shortly after the flowering period is over. It may also be readily propagated by seed.

Culture: I. tectorum is considered rather temperamental, sometimes thriving in one location and not in another. It is one of the most shallow rooting of all the members of the iris group and it requires frequent division and enrichment of the soil. It may be planted in clumps or in drifts, the rhizomes being spaced from 6 to 8 inches apart. It should preferably be lifted and divided every second year. Where the winters are severe it should be given the protection of leaves and brush.

For Bulbous Iris, see Chapter XXVII on Bulbs.

Linum perenne (Blue Flax). This lovely flower which reflects the blue of soft spring skies is of particular value in the perennial border because of its airy grace and its long season of bloom. The fine, delicate foliage is a pale bluish green and the lovely, single-petalled flowers of soft azure blue are borne in great profusion on slender, graceful stems. On days of brilliant sunshine the petals fall before evening, but in cloudy weather they remain open throughout the day. The plants vary in height from 12 to 18 inches. Linum perenne is particularly charming when grown in combination with the dainty little Iceland Poppy, Coonara Pink, and with the Columbines.

Exposure: Full sun.

Soil Requirements: A light, sandy, well-drained garden loam of moderate fertility is considered ideal. Linum perenne will not thrive in a heavy soil which becomes saturated with moisture.

Propagation: Linum perenne is readily propagated by seed. The seeds are of excellent vitality, germinate well, and the young seedlings make rapid growth. The seeds may be sown in the coldframes early in the spring or in the open ground later in the season and will produce vigorous flowering plants the following year.

Culture: The plants should be spaced from 8 to 10 inches apart. Being fibrous rooted, Linum perenne may be transplanted with the greatest ease and large, established plants may be moved with a fair degree of success if they are lifted with a sufficient quantity of earth and if the root system remains intact. If half of the flower stalks are cut back early in the season, being allowed to grow up later to take the place of those which are ready to go to seed, the flowering period will be greatly prolonged and the energy of the plant will not be exhausted. Under such treatment the plants will sometimes flower almost continually from May until September.

Winter Protection: No winter protection is required if the plants are grown in light, well-drained soil. Serious losses sometimes occur where the soil is heavy and badly drained.

Lythrum superbum (Purple Loosestrife). Because of their long season of bloom and their showy flower spikes, the lythrums are an asset in the perennial garden during the summer months. A dozen or more flower spikes will often be produced on a single plant and they make a brilliant note of color in the midsummer garden, blooming from late June to well into September. There are several varieties which reach a height of three to four feet, while some are more dwarf in form, not exceeding a foot and a half.

Exposure: Lythrum superbum will thrive well in full sun or in partial shade. It is, however, usually at its best in a moist, sunny location.

Soil Requirements: Any ordinary garden soil will give good results. Although reasonably tolerant of drought, lythrums reach their height of perfection in a moist soil well supplied with organic matter.

Propagation: Lythrums are usually propagated by the division of old clumps. The clump may be lifted and divided either in early spring or in the autumn as soon as the flowering period is over.

Culture: As the lythrums soon form large clumps they should be given plenty of room to develop without encroaching upon their neighbors. The tall varieties should be spaced from 2 to 3 feet apart, small varieties somewhat closer. The best bloom will be obtained if the clumps are lifted and divided every third year.

The lythrums are hardy and vigorous and will repay with generous bloom the care which is bestowed upon them.

VARIETIES OF MERIT

Dropmore Purple: fuchsia-purple
Morden's Pink: deep pink   Robert: fuchsia-pink

Lupinus (Lupine). In English gardens, Lupines may be grown to perfection and any one who has seen and admired the beauty of their stately blooms and their glorious colors comes away with a longing to produce lupines in America which are as superbly fine. But, unfortunately, we do not have a combination of English soil and English climate, and in many sections of our country these lovely hybrid lupines will not thrive. In gardens along the New England sea-coast, in some sections along the Great Lakes, and on the Pacific coast, where the atmosphere is moist, they do exceedingly well, but where the summers are hot and dry and where soil conditions are not to their liking, it is almost useless to attempt to grow them, for in spite of all one's efforts to provide favorable conditions, they will only sicken and die. With the introduction of the magnificent Russell Lupines, there is an increased desire on the part of many gardeners to attain success with these rather temperamental perennials.

Exposure: Full sun and a somewhat sheltered location are considered ideal.

Soil Requirements: A light, moist, yet well-drained soil of good fertility and with a slightly acid reaction is considered ideal. As the lupines belong to the great family of legumes, the Leguminosæ, they will benefit from the activity of the nitrogen-fixing bacteria in the soil if they are inoculated.

Propagation: Lupines may be propagated very readily from seed. At the time of sowing, the seeds should be inoculated with a specially prepared culture of nitrogen-fixing bacteria. Such a culture may be obtained from most large seed firms and will be accompanied by full directions.

Culture: As lupines are of a somewhat spreading habit of growth the plants should be allowed ample room for development and should be spaced from 12 to 15 inches apart. They require an abundance of moisture throughout the growing season, and they respond well to an annual top-dressing of well-rotted cow manure.

Pæonia (Peony). The Peony has long been a favorite among gardeners, and it is one of the hardiest and most easily grown of any of the perennials. When once established, peonies will continue to flower year after year. Indeed, some of the old-fashioned types are still blooming in gardens where they were planted more than a century ago.

In a small garden peonies are often out of scale. The blooms are so large and the plants themselves require so much room that they should be used but sparingly, if at all. However, in a large garden where quantity of bloom and mass effect are desired peonies may play an important part in the planting composition. They are lovely, also, when planted in groups along the front of a shrubbery border, or when used as specimen or accent plants, and they may be used very effectively as a low, herbaceous hedge.

With the selection of early, mid-season and late-blooming varieties, six weeks of bloom may be enjoyed.

Exposure: While peonies prefer a position in full sun, they will thrive reasonably well in light shade.

Soil Requirements: Peonies thrive fairly well in almost any soil, but prefer a rather heavy clay loam which is well drained. The soil reaction should be as nearly neutral as possible, as peonies do not grow well in a definitely acid soil. The soil should be deeply prepared and well enriched at the time of planting. At no future time will it be possible to supply fertility so effectively, and the plant will derive benefit from it for years to come. A hole of generous proportions should be dug. Well-rotted manure or rich compost should be mixed with the top-soil and placed in the bottom of the hole and firmed well to prevent too much later settling. Over this a few inches of good top-soil should be spread to prevent the roots of the plants from coming into direct contact with the manure before they have become established.

Planting: Peonies should be planted in the autumn, September and October being the most favorable months. Spring planting is sometimes done but is much more of a shock to the plant and is not recommended as a desirable practice. Depth of planting is a matter of great importance with peonies, as more failures are probably due to too deep planting than to any other cause. The division should be placed in the hole so that the tip of the buds will be from one to two inches below the surface of the soil. Good top-soil should be filled in about the roots and firmed well and the plant should be watered thoroughly immediately after planting. It is wise to allow the plants ample room for full development, and they should be spaced approximately three feet apart.

Fertilization: Although peonies make reasonably good growth in rather poor soil, they respond remarkably well to good care and to high soil fertility. If blooms of the finest quality are to be produced it is necessary to see that conditions most favorable to the full development of the plant are provided.

Two applications of a complete fertilizer, such as a 5-10-5, are recommended. The first application should be made in the spring when the new shoots are about 12 inches high. The second application should be made after the period of bloom is over.

The fertilizer should be applied at the rate of approximately $\frac{1}{4}$ cupful per plant. It should be sprinkled on the surface of the soil about the plant, and worked into the soil lightly with a small hand weeder. The ground should then be watered thoroughly so that the fertilizer will go into solution and be made immediately available to the plant. In making the application care must be taken to see that the fertilizer does not come into contact with the stems or leaves as it might result in severe burning, particularly if the foliage is wet.

Culture: Peonies resent being moved and when once well established they may be left undisturbed for many years.

Some varieties do not produce stems strong enough to hold the full-blown flowers erect and for such plants some form of support should be provided. Stakes may be put in at intervals about the plant and a loop of tape used to encircle the plant, or a ready-made support may be used.

For general garden effect peonies are not usually disbudded. However, if exhibition blooms are desired, all of the side buds on the flower stems should be removed, leaving only the large central bud.

When cutting blooms it is wise to leave two or three leaves on each stem in order that the foliage of the plant may not become too depleted, as the leaves are needed for the manufacture of food.

Old blooms should be removed as soon as they have faded in order to conserve the vigor of the plant.

After the foliage has died down in the autumn the stems should be cut off *just* below ground level, raked up and burned, as a precautionary measure against the spread of blight.

If ants are troublesome on the buds of peonies an application of 5 percent chordane dust on the soil about the plant will provide excellent control.

For control of Insect Pests and Diseases, see Chapter XLI.

Classification

There is considerable variability in the flower forms of peonies. The following classification has been drawn up by the American Peony Society.

Single: These consist of a ring of a few broad petals, the center being filled with pollen-bearing stamens and seed-bearing carpels.

Japanese: These show the beginnings of doubling. The outer ring or guard petals are like those in the singles but some of the filaments of the stamens have become petaloid. As long as anthers are present, class as Japanese.

Anemone: The next step in doubling: the anthers have disappeared from the petal-like filaments. The central petaloids still are narrow and short.

Semi-double: Similar to the anemone, except that instead of the petaloids being uniformly wide, they occur in all stages of transformation, the formation being loose.

Crown: The carpels are partly or fully transformed into petaloids which differ from the guard petals and from the petaloids derived from stamens.

Bomb: The next step in doubling finds the petaloids much wider but still differentiated in form from the guard or outer petals, and no anthers are found scattered through the center of the bloom. No collar or crown is in evidence.

Semi-rose: The carpels are fully transformed. The only thing that differentiates this class from the rose is the fact that an occasional pollen-bearing stamen is found.

Rose: This is the fully doubled type, in which the stamens and carpels are completely transformed to more or less evenly arranged petaloids, which are not distinguishable from the guard petals. If the guard petals are distinct, the flower is classed as a bomb, the line of division being arbitrary.

VARIETIES OF MERIT

Among the most desirable varieties are those listed by the American Peony Society with their official ratings. The score is based on a scale of 10 points. Those listed below have received a score of over 9 points.

WHITE		PINK	
Le Cygne	9.24	Myrtle Gentry	9.06
Kelway's Glorious	9.56	Nick Shaylor	9.35
Festiva Maxima	9.13	Mrs. F. D. Roosevelt	9.38
Mrs. J. V. Edlund	9.51	Walter Faxon	9.3
Isani Gidui	9.3	Therese	9.8
Krinkled White	9.4	Tourangelle	9.4
Elsa Sass	9.46	Ama-No-Sode	9.3

DARK RED			
Philippe Rivoire	9.46	Nippon Beauty	9.27
Matilda Lewis	9.19		

SINGLE WHITE	DOUBLE WHITE
Krinkled White	Festiva Maxima
LeJour	Kelway's Glorious
Mildred May	Le Cygne

SINGLE PINK	DOUBLE PINK
Harriet Olney	Alice Harding
Helen	Moonstone
Wild Rose	Mrs. Franklin D. Roosevelt

SINGLE RED	DOUBLE RED
Gopher Beauty	Burma
Kickapoo	Longfellow
President Lincoln	Mary Brand

JAPANESE PEONIES

WHITE	LIGHT PINK
Lotus Queen	Akashigata
Shaylor's Sunburst	Apple Blossom
Toro-no-maki	Kathalo

RED	DARK PINK
Mikado	Filagree
Nippon Beauty	Nippon Gold
Red Star	Tamate Boku

HYBRID PEONIES

Alexander Woollcott: semi-double, crimson
Campagna: single, white with greenish shadows
Chalice: single, large, pure white
Eros: single, salmon or coral pink
Great Lady: single to semi-double, China-rose
Laura Magnuson: semi-double, pink suffused with salmon

Tree Peonies

History: Tree peonies are native in the Orient where they have been cherished and greatly honored since the sixth century. They have figured in the art and literature of these Oriental countries since ancient times, and in the garden they were always accorded a special place of honor. In the imperial gardens, where they were regarded as great treasures, they were usually grown on stepped terraces, and in other gardens they were often planted in high, raised beds, enclosed with stone or marble. Today tree peonies grace many a temple and monastery garden in the Orient, where they are still regarded as sacred plants, and in these gardens specimens are sometimes found which are three hundred years old.

The tree peony was not imported into this country until the early 1800's, and for more than a century it remained a plant cherished by connoisseurs and collectors, and was seldom seen except in Botanic Gardens and in a few gardens on large private estates. Within recent years, however, tree peonies have become increasingly popular and are now more widely grown.

Description: Tree peonies have an ornamental value throughout the year, and lend distinction to any garden. The deciduous foliage is deeply-cut, soft in tone and texture and very decorative; the shrub-like, woody stems have a picturesque quality in the winter landscape picture, and the flowers are of superb beauty. The blooms possess both delicacy and elegance. The texture and sheen of the petals has been described as "like Oriental silk, ruffled taffetas or crimped and glistening satins." The flowers vary in size from 6 to 10 inches across and also vary considerably in form. There are the beautiful single-saucered types, the semi-double, and the fully double types. And there is a wide color range from white through pink to rose, scarlet and red, deep mahogany and maroon; lilac and purple, and occasional yellows in the hybrid species. Plants vary in height from 3 to 6 feet, with a spread often equal to the height. Some varieties are compact in form, others spreading, while some have an upright habit of growth. Well established plants sometimes bear as many as 40 or 50 blooms.

Climatic Requirements: Tree peonies have a wide range of adaptation. Their native home in the Orient is in mountainside forests, in sections where the climate is rigorous and subject to extremes of heat and cold. They have, however, readily adapted themselves to the wind-swept hills of northern New York, to the more mellow, humid climate of Philadelphia and to the burning summer heat of St. Louis and the Midwest. Tree peonies are not hardy in the sub-zero areas of northern Minnesota and Canada.

Exposure: Tree peonies thrive well in light shade but are not suited to heavily shaded areas. They also do well in full sun. In general, plants grown in full sun are larger, more vigorous and tend to hold their leaves longer in the autumn than those grown in partial shade.

Uses: One of our early horticultural writers, Charles Mason Hovey, referred to the tree peonies as "those truly magnificent under-shrubs". And in the general landscape scheme this is one of their greatest values. They are particularly well adapted for planting toward the front of shrub borders and they may also be used in foundation plantings when choice plant materials are desired. Tree peonies are also often grown as specimen plants or as accent plants in the garden. For a dramatic display of bloom in late spring they may be planted in a specially prepared bed.

Soil Requirements: Tree peonies prefer a deep, sandy loam soil which contains an abundance of organic matter. Good drainage is essential. A pH between 6.5 and 7.0 is considered the most satisfactory, although plants will do reasonably well within a somewhat wider range. Since tree peonies are noted for their longevity it is wise to see that the soil is well prepared prior to planting. If ideal conditions are to be provided the soil for each plant should be deeply prepared to a depth of 2 feet. A bushel of leaf mold and 5 pounds of bone meal, worked well into the soil, will provide excellent conditions for good growth.

Planting: Tree peonies may be planted either in the autumn or in the spring, provided the plants are dormant. Plants of small size are usually available as pot-grown plants. Field-grown plants are usually shipped with bare roots, and large, specimen plants are best transplanted with a ball of soil wrapped in burlap. Occasionally fine specimen plants may be obtained in tubs or large pots. Small, potted plants may be transplanted with little difficulty, the only precaution recommended being the removal of flower buds in order to encourage good root and leaf growth while the plant is becoming established. If flower buds are removed during the first season after planting it will

increase the vigor of the plant and will insure more abundant bloom the following season. The depth of planting is a matter of great importance. For years shallow planting (2 to 3 inches) has been advocated, but recent research has proved conclusively that deep planting is to be preferred. It is recommended that the crown of the plant should be set at least 6 inches below the surface of the ground. Deep planting results in a much more vigorous root system than shallow planting and it is one of the keys to success in growing tree peonies.

Fertilization: Well-rotted cow manure and bone meal are regarded as the best fertilizer for tree peonies.

Pruning: Mature tree peonies require little pruning. Dead wood should be cut out, and an occasional shoot should be removed to improve the shape of the plant. A good specimen plant should have from three to seven vigorous stems. When large, bare-root plants are transplanted in the spring some growers prune them severely, cutting the stems back almost to the ground. Some authorities also recommend that where fine specimen plants are desired it is sometimes advisable to cut the plant back to the ground three or four years after it was set out. This should be done in the early autumn and will result in a new growth of vigorous, healthy stems the following spring.

Mulches: In areas where there is excessive summer heat frequently accompanied by drought, as in the Midwest, the mulching of tree peonies is definitely advisable. Under a heavy mulch it is possible to maintain the soil in a reasonably cool and moist condition. Sawdust has proved one of the most satisfactory materials for mulching, although other materials such as straw, leaves, buckwheat hulls, peat moss and corncobs may be used. In more humid sections of the country mulching is not necessary and may tend to encourage fungous diseases.

Staking: When the production of blooms is unusually heavy it is a wise measure to stake some of the lateral branches in order to relieve them of excessive weight.

Pests and Diseases: See page 658.

Oriental Poppies (Papaver Orientale). The Oriental Poppy is a native of Persia and has long been a popular garden flower. In June, the large, flamboyant blooms are borne in profusion above the rough, hairy leaves and there are few perennials which can equal the Oriental poppy in intensity of hue. The old-fashioned varieties vary from pure scarlet to deep red in color but many of the newer hybrids offer flowers of more delicate and more pleasing tones. Mrs. Perry is a soft salmon-pink and is particularly striking when grown in combination with Anchusa italica. Princess Ena is of similar coloring and is a very robust and vigorous grower. Fairy and Princess Victoria Louise are a delicate pink in color and Silver Queen is a pure white. Among the new varieties of more brilliant coloring we have Oriental King, which bears scarlet flowers of marvellous size and substance, Beauty of Livermere, a deep rich red, and Goliath, a vivid orange-scarlet in tone.

Soil Requirements: Oriental poppies will thrive well in any well-drained garden loam. If they possess any definite preference it is for a sandy, gritty loam rather than for a soil of a heavier type.

Exposure: Full sun.

Culture: There are no special cultural requirements for Oriental poppies, for they do well under average garden conditions. As they have a large, fleshy tap root they are very difficult to transplant except when they are dormant. This period of dormancy follows the blooming season and if transplanting is necessary it should preferably be done at this time. If spring transplanting is necessary it may be accomplished successfully if great care is taken not to bruise the roots. The plants should not be kept out of the ground for any length of time and they should be shaded for at least a week after being transplanted. It is also essential that they be kept thoroughly watered until they have become well established.

As Oriental poppies require ample room for development during the period when they are in bloom, they should be spaced from 15 to 18 inches apart. Annuals and summer-flowering bulbs may be planted between the poppies in order to carry on a succession of bloom after the poppies have become dormant.

As the Oriental poppies reseed readily, it is important to see that the flower stalks are cut down before the seed pods form. If this is not done the chances are that the following year colonies of sturdy young plants will develop which will bear flowers of every hue, most of them reverting to the brilliant flame of the old-fashioned type.

Propagation: As the Oriental poppies seldom come true from seed, they should be propagated either by the division of old clumps or by root cuttings. After the blooming period is over, the plants die down entirely and remain practically dormant for a month or more. About the middle of August new growth begins and a little tuft of green leaves appears. The plants should be lifted and divided while they are dormant or just after the new growth begins. Root cuttings may also be made at this time and are very easily handled. The roots should be cut into small pieces 1 to 2 inches long, each piece containing at least one joint. These should be placed on a bed of soil, either in a flat or in a cold-frame, being laid in a horizontal position. A light covering of sand or sandy loam should be spread over them to a depth of about $\frac{1}{2}$ inch and the bed should be kept well watered and partially shaded until active growth has started. If conditions are favorable roots will develop from each joint and in a short time the leaves will begin to appear. This is undoubtedly the most satisfactory method of propagation. A single plant will yield a large number of cuttings.

VARIETIES OF MERIT

Barr's White: pure white
Cerise Beauty: cerise pink
Cowigan: oxblood red
Helen Elizabeth: LaFrance pink

Henri Cayeux: ashes of roses
Indian Chief: mahogany
Salmon Glow: salmon-orange
Salome: French-rose

Souvenir: vivid poppy-red
Sultana: watermelon-pink

Phlox. The tall, hardy types of phlox are the pièce de résistance of most midsummer gardens and with the careful selection of varieties the period of bloom may be extended from June until early September. They are among our most useful plants for the perennial garden and give lavish bloom when color and mass effect are most needed.

The two types of hardy phlox most valuable for summer bloom are *Phlox suffruticosa* and *Phlox paniculata*. The plants in the suffruticosa group bloom early, have glossy, deep green foliage and are very resistant to disease. The members of the paniculata group prolong the season of bloom through the summer.

Phlox paniculata (sometimes listed by nurseries as p. decussata)

Augusta: brilliant cherry-red
Caroline Vanderberg: lavender-blue

Charles Curtis: sunset red
Columbia: light pink
Elizabeth Arden: rhodamine pink
Mary Louise: white
Pinkette: delicate pink
Purple Heart: deep, blue-purple
Sir John Falstaff: salmon-pink
White Admiral: white

Phlox suffruticosa

Miss Lingard: white
Reine du Jour: white with crimson eye

Climatic Requirements: The garden type of phlox is best adapted to areas where the summers are warm and the winters are cold. It does not thrive in hot, dry climates or where the winters are extremely mild.

Exposure: Phlox plants will thrive well either in full sun or in light shade. In sections where the summer sun is intense, partial shade, or shade for a portion of the day, is preferable, as the colors of some varieties tend to bleach in brilliant sunlight.

Soil Requirements: Phlox has long been recognized as a voracious feeder. For maximum growth and for a fine quality of bloom phlox requires a rich, well-drained garden loam, high in organic content and very slightly acid. It is important that the fertility be readily available to the plant in the upper 8 inches of top-soil, as phlox plants are very shallow-rooted. Phlox responds well to heavy applications of potash, therefore a fertilizer should be used which has a high potash content. An application of wood ashes worked into the soil about the plants is very beneficial. A summer mulch of rotted manure or rich compost will supply additional nutrients and keep the roots cool and moist.

During the growing season, phlox plants require an abundance of moisture and suffer seriously from the effects of drought. However, an extremely wet soil and poor air circulation are very injurious and are conducive to poor growth and the spread of various diseases.

Propagation: Phlox may be propagated by the division of old clumps, by root cuttings, and by cuttings made from young, growing shoots. Old clumps may be lifted and divided either in the spring or in the early autumn. New root growth is made in the autumn, shortly after the flowering season is over. September is considered the most favorable time for dividing old clumps and replanting, as it is then possible to take full advantage of this new root formation. The earth should be shaken away from the roots and the clumps should be pulled gently apart into small divisions containing from one to three stems. Only the young shoots on the outside of the clump should be used for replanting, the hard, woody center of the old clump being discarded. In replanting the divisions, a hole of sufficient size should be dug and the roots should be carefully spread out, the crown of the plant being covered with not more than 1 inch of soil. The soil should be firmed well about the roots and the plants should be watered thoroughly until they have had an opportunity to become well established. If planting is done in the autumn, a light mulch of strawy manure may be placed over the crowns, being worked into the soil about the plant in the spring. The plants should be spaced from 15 to 18 inches apart. The largest flower trusses are usually obtained from newly made divisions. Clumps of phlox are at their best from the second to fourth years after planting. After this period the plants usually begin to lose their vigor. The clumps should therefore be lifted, divided, and reset every fourth or fifth year.

Culture: If blooms of exhibition quality are desired, not more than three stalks should be allowed to develop from one crown. Under ordinary garden conditions, however, where a mass of bloom is desired, the stems are allowed to develop naturally. As soon as the plants have completed their flowering period, the fading blooms should be cut off in order to prevent the plants from reseeding. Phlox plants reseed prolifically and these young, self-sown seedlings are a great liability in a planting composition, as they seldom come true to color, usually reverting to an ugly magenta shade. If the fading flower stalks are removed promptly a second period of bloom will sometimes be induced. Another method of extending the blooming season is to pinch back from one fourth to one half of the stems before the flower buds have begun to form. The remaining stems will produce bloom at the normal time while those which have been cut back will bloom several weeks later.

For insect pests and diseases, see Chapter XLI.

Salvia azurea. This hardy perennial is well worth growing. The flowers, which are borne on long spikes, are a clear, azure blue and are very decorative and lovely both in the garden and for cutting. Salvia azurea is particularly charming when grown in combination with pink gladioli, artemisia lactiflora, white phlox, and pale pink snapdragons, and it may be used in generous quantities for late summer and early autumn bloom.

Exposure: Salvia azurea is very hardy and will withstand long periods of drought with no ill effects. A position in full sun is preferred.

Soil Requirements: Salvia azurea has the happy faculty of doing extremely well on poor soil. Indeed, it seems to reach its best development on soils of medium or low fertility. When it is given an excessively rich diet it attains too great a height and has a tendency to become floppy and untidy.

Propagation: The plants may be propagated either by seed or by cuttings. The seeds are usually of excellent vitality and germinate readily. They may be sown in the greenhouse in February or March or they may be sown later in the season either in a coldframe or in the open ground. If sown before the middle of April, the young plants will give some bloom the first year. The seedlings should be transplanted before they become crowded, and when they reach a height of 6 or 8 inches they should be pinched back in order that they may become bushy and will be well branched.

Culture: After the plants are once well established, they will thrive for many years. Each year they should be cut back severely when they have reached a height of about 8 inches and staking is occasionally necessary in order that the plants may be pleasing and symmetrical in form. The plants vary in height from 2 to 4 feet, and they should be spaced from 12 to 15 inches apart.

Salvia farinacea (Mealycup Sage). There are few flowers that bloom over as long a period as does Salvia farinacea, and it is one of the loveliest members of this group. The flowers are a soft, lavender-blue in color and are borne on slender, graceful spikes. The plants are upright in habit of growth, branching freely, and attaining a height of 3–4 feet. The flower stems are held erect and have no tendency to become floppy. The foliage is a cool, rather light green. From midsummer until frost the plants will give generous bloom and they are lovely both as part of the garden composition and for cutting.

Although a true perennial, Salvia farinacea is often treated as an annual in the North, as it is not hardy where the winters are of extreme severity.

Exposure: The plants thrive best in full sun but will make reasonably good growth in partial shade.

Soil Requirements: Salvia farinacea will grow well on almost any type of soil.

Propagation: The plants may be raised very easily from seed. For early bloom the seeds may be sown in the greenhouse or hotbed in March. For later bloom they may be sown either in the coldframe or in the open ground. The seeds germinate readily and the young plants make rapid growth. They should be transplanted or thinned out before they become in the least crowded and when they have reached a height of about 6 inches they should be pinched back, unless very early bloom is desired.

Culture: Salvia farinacea may be transplanted with ease, and the plants should be spaced from 8 to 10 inches apart.

For insect pests and diseases, see Chapter XLI.

Thalictrum (Meadow Rue). Light and graceful in form, the Thalictrums contribute to the garden a quality quite their own. Of the many species and varieties there are four which are of particular value in the garden of herbaceous perennials.

T. adiantifolium: The foliage resembles that of the Maidenhair fern and the myriad small, cream-white flowers are produced in abundance in June and early July. The plants attain a height of from 3 to 4 feet, and as they develop into large clumps, they should be spaced from 15 to 18 inches apart.

T. aquilegifolium: The flowers are borne on tall, graceful stems which rise above the foliage to a height of 3 feet or more. They may be obtained in shades of pink, lavender and creamy white, and they are in bloom throughout the month of June. The foliage bears a striking resemblance to that of the Columbines. The plants should be spaced from 12 to 18 inches apart.

T. dipterocarpum is by far the most beautiful of all the Thalictrums and yet it is so temperamental that in many gardens it will not thrive. In English gardens it is so utterly enchanting in its delicacy and beauty that one longs to see it more successfully grown in America. It thrives well along the sea-coast in northern New England, and may be grown to perfection in the fog belt in California. The tiny flowers are a soft shade of lilac-mauve with brilliant yellow stamens and anthers, and they are produced in abundance during July and August. When grown under favorable conditions the plants reach a height of about 4 feet, and they should be spaced about 18 inches apart.

T. glaucum: The glaucous leaves are a soft blue-gray in color and the fragrant yellow flowers are borne on tall, erect stems, varying from 3 to 4 feet in height. The plants are more compact and erect in habit of growth than most of the other Thalictrums and they should be spaced from 12 to 15 inches apart.

Exposure: Full sun or partial shade.

Soil Requirements: A well-drained, moderately fertile garden loam.

Propagation: By seed or by the division of established clumps.

Culture: The Thalictrums may be planted either in the autumn or in the early spring. With the exception of T. dipterocarpum no winter protection is required. In the latitude of Philadephia and northward it is well to winter this more tender variety in the coldframe.

Violas. The Violas are invaluable as edging plants and are particularly lovely when used in great drifts along the front of the herbaceous border. Most of the varieties of small violas which are grown today are a cross between the quaint little Horned Viola (Viola cornuta) and the Pansy, and they may be obtained in a wide range of colorings—white, lavender, deep purple, yellow, apricot and deep wine-red.

VARIETIES OF MERIT

Among the many lovely varieties are: *V. Jersey Gem*, of a pure rich violet hue; *White Perfection*, producing an abundance of pure white flowers; *Sutton's Apricot*, one of the most beautiful of all, with flowers of a rich apricot shade; *Blue Perfection*, which is very similar in color to the lovely *Maggie Mott* used so extensively in English gardens, a light lavender-blue shade; and *Arkwright Ruby*, a glorious deep wine-red which is very striking when used in combination with Delphinium chinense and Antirrhinum variety Bonfire.

Exposure: Full sun is preferred, although most violas will thrive reasonably well in light shade.

Soil Requirements: Violas will do well in almost any good garden soil but for luxuriant bloom and maximum growth a highly fertile soil is desirable. A cool, fairly moist soil, rich in organic matter, is ideal.

Propagation: The plants may be readily propagated either from seed or from cuttings taken soon after the period of spring bloom is over. Some of the named varieties do not come entirely true from seed but the variations in color are usually so slight that it is not a serious matter unless plants of an absolutely uniform shade are desired. Seeds sown in July or August and wintered over in the coldframes will give abundant bloom the following spring.

Culture: Violas may be planted either in the autumn or in the spring, the plants being spaced from 6 to 8 inches apart. If the plants are not allowed to form seed they may be kept in bloom over a long period. Some gardeners follow the practice of cutting the plants back severely after the spring bloom is over, fertilizing the soil about the plants, and giving them an abundant supply of moisture, thus inducing a second period of bloom. Excessive moisture about the plants during the winter is very harmful and is frequently the cause of winter-killing.

PERENNIALS ENDURING SEMI-SHADE

Aconitum Fischeri (Azure Monkshood)
Ajuga (Bugle)
Anemone japonica (Japanese Anemone)
Anemonella thalictroides (Rue Anemone)
Asperula (Woodruff)
Convallaria majalis (Lily-of-the-Valley)
Cornus canadensis (Bunchberry)
Dicentra eximia (Fringed Bleeding-heart)
Dicentra spectabilis (Bleeding-heart)
Dictamnus (Dittany or Gas Plant)
Epimedium alpinus (Barrenwort)
Eupatorium (Thoroughwort)
Geranium sanguineum (Blood Red Cranesbill)
Helleborus niger (Christmas-rose)
Hemerocallis flava (Daylily)
Heuchera sanguinea (Coral-bells)
Hibiscus Moscheutos (Swamp Rose-Mallow)
Hosta, in variety (Plantain Lily)
Hypericum (St. John's-Wort)
Iberis sempervirens (Candytuft)
Liatris pycnostachya (Cattail Gayfeather)
Lobelia cardinalis (Cardinal flower)
Lychnis chalcedonica (Maltese Cross)
Mertensia virginica (Virginia Bluebells)
Myosotis palustris semperflorens (Dwarf Perpetual
    Forget-me-not)
Œnothera missouriensis (Missouri Primrose)
Phlox divaricata
Platycodon (Balloon Flower)
Polygonatum biflorum (Smaller Solomon's-seal)
Primula, in variety (Primrose)
Thalictrum, in variety (Meadow Rue)

Trillium (Trillium)
Trollius europæus (Globeflower)
Veronica rupestris (Creeping Speedwell)

PERENNIALS ENDURING LIGHT SHADE

Althæa rosea (Hollyhock)
Anchusa italica (Bugloss)
Aquilegia hybrids (Columbine)
Campanula rotundifolia (Harebell)
Chelone Lyoni (Pink Turtlehead)
Cimicifuga racemosa (Cohosh Bugbane)
Doronicum plantagineum (Leopard's-bane)
Linaria (Toadflax)
Monarda didyma (Bee-balm)
Pæonia (Peony)
Physostegia (False Dragonhead)
Polemonium (Valerian)
Pulmonaria saccharata (Bethlehem Lungwort)
Pyrethrum (Chrys. coccineum) (Pink Daisy)
Saxifraga (Saxifrage)
Silene pennsylvanica (Peatpink)

PERENNIALS WHICH WILL GROW IN POOR SOIL

Achillea serrata (Millfoil or Yarrow)
Ajuga genevensis (Geneva Bugle)
Alyssum saxatile (Goldentuft)
Arabis albida (Wallcress)
Cerastium tomentosum (Snow-in-Summer)
Dianthus deltoides (Maiden Pink)
Dianthus plumarius (Grass Pink)
Eryngium campestre (Hundred Thistle)
Euphorbia Myrsinites (Myrsinites-like Spurge)
Geranium sanguineum (Blood Red Cranesbill)
Geranium maculatum (Spotted Cranesbill)
Gypsophila paniculata (Baby's-breath)
Helianthemum vulgare (Rock or Sun Rose)
Iberis sempervirens (Evergreen Candytuft)
Linaria vulgaris (Toadflax)
Phlox subulata (Moss Phlox)
Potentilla tridentata (Wineleaf Cinquefoil)
Salvia azurea (Azure Sage)
Saxifraga pennsylvanica (Penn. or Swamp Saxifrage)
Sedum acre (Goldmoss)
Sedum stoloniferum (Running Sedum)
Sempervivum (Roof Houseleek)
Sempervivum arvernense (Auvergne Houseleek)
Verbascum Thapsus
Veronica rupestris (Creeping Speedwell)
Viola cucullata (Blue Marsh Violet)

PERENNIALS FOR DRY, SANDY SOILS

Achillea Ptarmica (Sneezewort)
Ajuga reptans (Carpet Bugle)
Anthemis tinctoria (Yellow Camomile)
Asclepias tuberosa (Butterflyweed)
Aster novæ-angliæ (New England Aster)

Callirhoë involucrata (Poppymallow)
Cassia marilandica (Wild Senna)
Coreopsis grandiflora (Tickseed)
Dianthus plumarius (Grass Pink)
Echinops Ritro (Steel Globe Thistle)
Euphorbia corollata (Flowering Spurge)
Helianthus, in variety (Sunflower)
Limonium latifolium (Statice)
Lychnis chalcedonica (Maltese Cross)
Papaver nudicaule (Iceland Poppy)
Rudbeckia laciniata (Goldenglow)
Yucca filamentosa (Common Yucca)

PERENNIALS REQUIRING WELL-DRAINED SITUATIONS

Arabis alpina (Alpine Rockcress)
Asclepias tuberosa (Butterflyweed)
Aubrietia deltoides (Purple Rockcress)
Coreopsis grandiflora (Tickseed)
Delphinium hybrids (Delphinium)
Dianthus barbatus (Sweet William)
Digitalis purpurea (Common Foxglove)
Echinops Ritro (Steel Globe Thistle)
Eryngium maritimum (Sea-holly)
Gaillardia aristata (Blanket-flower)
Globularia trichosantha (Globe Daisy)
Helianthus Maximiliani (Maximilian Sunflower)
Iris germanica (Bearded Iris)
Liatris pycnostachya (Cattail Gayfeather)
Papaver nudicaule (Iceland Poppy)

PERENNIALS FOR WET SITUATIONS

*Arundo Donax (Giant Reed)
 Asclepias incarnata (Swamp Milkweed)
 Boltonia asteroides (White Boltonia)
*Caltha palustris (Marsh Marigold)
 Eupatorium purpureum (Joe-pye-weed)
 Helenium autumnale (Sneezeweed)
 Hibiscus Moscheutos (Swamp Rose-Mallow)
*Iris pseudacorus (Yellowflag)
 Iris versicolor (Blueflag)
 Lobelia cardinalis (Cardinal Flower)
 Lysimachia clethroides (Clethra Loosestrife)
 Lythrum Salicaria (Spiked Loosestrife)
 Miscanthus sinensis (Eulalia)
 Monarda didyma (Bee-balm)
 Myosotis palustris (True Forget-me-not)
 Onoclea sensibilis (Sensitive Fern)
 Osmunda cinnamomea (Cinnamon Fern)
*Osmunda regalis (Royal Fern)
 Sarracenia purpurea (Pitcherplant)
 Saxifraga pennsylvanica (Penn. or Swamp Saxifrage)

* May be grown in water.

PERENNIALS FOR BORDERS OF PONDS AND STREAMS

(*Well-drained soil*)

SUNNY LOCATIONS

Brunnera macrophylla [Anchusa myosotidiflora] (Siberian Bugloss)
Chrysanthemum uliginosum (Giant Daisy)
Cimicifuga racemosa (Cohosh Bugbane)
Grasses (Ornamental Grasses)
Hemerocallis, in variety (Daylily)
Iris, in variety
Lythrum Salicaria (Spiked Loosestrife)
Myosotis palustris semperflorens (Dwarf Perpetual Forget-me-not)
Tradescantia virginiana (Spiderwort)
Trollius europæus (Globeflower)

SEMI-SHADY LOCATIONS

Anemone japonica (Jap. Anemone)
Cimicifuga racemosa (Cohosh Bugbane)
Epimedium macranthum (Longspur Epimedium)
Eupatorium purpureum (Joe-pye-weed)
Iris cristata (Crested Iris)
Lythrum Salicaria (Spiked Loosestrife)
Tradescantia virginiana (Spiderwort)

PERENNIALS FOR EDGING

Achillea tomentosa (Woolly Yarrow)
Ægopodium Podagraria (Goutweed)
Ajuga reptans (Carpet Bugle)
Alyssum saxatile compactum (Dwarf Goldentuft)
Arabis alpina (Alpine Rockcress)
Arabis albida (Wallcress)
Bellis perennis (English Daisy)
Aubrietia deltoides (Purple Rockcress)
Campanula carpatica (Carpathian Bellflower)
Cerastium tomentosum (Snow-in-summer)
Dianthus deltoides (Maiden Pink)
Dianthus plumarius (Grass Pink)
Festuca glauca (Blue Fescue)
Heuchera sanguinea (Coral-bells)
Iberis sempervirens (Evergreen Candytuft)
Papaver nudicaule (Iceland Poppy)
Phlox subulata (Moss Phlox)
Phlox procumbens (Hairy Phlox)
Primula veris (Cowslip Primrose)
Sedum reflexum (Jenny Stonecrop)
Sedum stoloniferum (Running Stonecrop)
Statice Armeria (Thrift)
Stellaria Holostea (Greater Stichwort or Starwort)
Tunica Saxifraga (Tunicflower)
Veronica incana (Woolly Speedwell)
Veronica Teucrium (Rock Speedwell)
Viola, in variety (Violas)

PERENNIALS FOR BACKGROUND PLANTING

Althæa rosea (Hollyhock)
Aster novæ-angliæ (New England Aster)
Aster tataricus (Tatarian Aster)
Bocconia cordata (Plumepoppy)
Boltonia asteroides (White Boltonia)
Campanula pyramidalis (Chimney Bellflower)
Cimicifuga racemosa (Cohosh Bugbane)
Delphinium hybrids (Delphinium)
Helenium autumnale (Sneezeweed)
Helianthus Maximiliani (Maximilian Sunflower)
Hibiscus grandiflorus (Great Rosemallow)
Rudbeckia laciniata (Goldenglow)
Valeriana officinalis (Common Valerian)

FRAGRANT PERENNIALS

Arabis, in variety (Arabis)
Artemisia Abrotanum (Southernwood)
Asperula odorata (Sweet Woodruff)
Centranthus ruber (Jupiter's-beard)
Convallaria majalis (Lily-of-the-Valley)
Dianthus plumarius (Grass Pink)
Dictamnus albus (Dittany or Gas Plant)
Hemerocallis flava (Daylily)
Hesperis matronalis (Sweet Rocket)
Hosta plantaginea grandiflora (Funkia or Big Plantain Lily)
Iris, Pallida section
Lathyrus grandiflorus (Everlasting Pea)
Lychnis Viscaria (German Catchfly)
Monarda didyma (Bee-balm)
Œnothera, in variety (Evening Primrose)
Pæonia, in variety (Peony)
Phlox paniculata (Phlox)
Rosa species (Roses—Cabbage and Sweet Briers)
Valeriana officinalis (Common Valerian)
Viola cornuta (Tufted Pansy)
Viola odorata (Sweet Violet)
Herbs
    Anethum graveolens (Dill)
    Thymus, in variety (Thyme)
    Lavandula vera (True Lavender)
    Origanum Majorana (Sweet Marjoram)
    Rosmarinus officinalis (Rosemary)

HARDY PLANTS FOR BOLD OR SUB-TROPICAL EFFECTS

Acanthus latifolius (Acanthus)
Bocconia cordata (Plume Poppy)
Cimicifuga racemosa (Bugbane)
Dipsacus fullonum (Teasel)
Echinops Ritro and exaltatus (Globe Thistles)
Elymus arenarius (Wild-rye)
Eulalia japonica (Eulalia)
Helianthus orgyalis (Sunflower)

Heracleum giganteum (Cow-parsnip)
Kniphofia Uvaria (Torchlily)
Onopordum Acanthium (Scotch Thistle)
Polygonum sachalinense (Sacaline)
Silphium perfoliatum (Rosinweed)
Spiræa Aruncus (Spirea)
Telekia cordifolia (Telekia)
Verbascum olympicum (Mullein)
Yucca filamentosa (Yucca)

PERENNIALS FOR OLD-FASHIONED GARDENS

Aconitum, in variety (Monkshood)
Althæa rosea (Hollyhock)
Arisæma triphyllum (Jack-in-the-Pulpit)
Asters, old varieties
Campanula, in variety (Bellflower)
Convallaria majalis (Lily-of-the-Valley)
Delphinium belladonna (Delphinium)
Delphinium formosum (Formosa Delphinium)
Dianthus arenarius (Sand Pink)
Dianthus barbatus (Sweet William)
Dianthus plumarius (Grass or Garden Pinks)
Dianthus superbus (Lilac Pink)
Dicentra spectabilis (Bleeding-heart)
Dictamnus (Dittany or Gas Plant)
Digitalis, in variety (Foxgloves)
Hemerocallis (Lemon Lily)
Hepatica triloba (Hepatica, or Liverwort)
Hesperis matronalis (Sweet Rocket)
Lilium candidum (Madonna Lily)
Lilium tigrinum (Tiger Lily)
Lunaria (Honesty) (Biennial)
Lupinus, not new varieties (Lupines)
Lychnis chalcedonica (Maltese Cross or Scarlet Lychnis)
Mertensia (Mertensia or Blue Bells)
Myosotis, in variety (Forget-me-nots)
Pæonia officinalis types (Peony)
Primula veris (Primrose)
Trillium, in variety (Trillium or Wake Robin)
Viola odorata (Sweet Violet)
Viola, in variety (Pansies)

PERENNIALS HAVING ESPECIALLY LONG BLOOMING SEASONS

Anchusa italica (Bugloss)
Aquilegia chrysantha (Golden Columbine)
Campanula carpatica (Carpathian Harebell)
Delphinium, if cut back
Heuchera sanguinea (Coral-bells)
Iris, fall blooming varieties
Lathyrus latifolius (Perennial Pea)
Lychnis Coronaria (Dusty Miller)
Phlox, if cut back
Scabiosa graminifolia (Pincushion or Mourning Bride)
Scabiosa sylvatica
Verbascums, if cut back (Mullein)
Viola cornuta (Tufted Pansy)
Viola tricolor (Heart's-ease)

TABULAR LIST OF GARDEN PERENNIALS

SCIENTIFIC NAME	COMMON NAME	HEIGHT IN INCHES	DISTANCE APART	SEASON	COLOR	REMARKS
Acanthus mollis	Bear's-breech	36		July–Aug.	Lilac, rose	Deeply toothed leaves. Sun. Drainage
Achillea filipendulina	Fernleaf Yarrow	36	12	June–Aug.	Yellow	Ferny foliage. Any soil
Millefolium	Yarrow	18	spreading	June, July	White, rose	Will thrive in poor soil
Ptarmica	Sneezewort	24	spreading	July, Aug.	White	Any soil. Cut flower. Profuse
Aconitum Fischeri	Azure Monkshood	36		Sept., Oct.	Pale blue	Shady places
autumnale	Autumn Monkshood	36	9	July	Pale yellow	(See A. Fischeri)
lycoctonum	Wolfbane	24	9	June	Blue, white	
Napellus	Aconite	48	6	September	Blue	
Wilsonii	Violet Monkshood		12			
Adonis amurensis	Amur Adonis	12		April	Yellow	
vernalis	Spring Adonis	8–12		April	Yellow	
Æthionema coridifolium	Lebanon Stonecress	9	6	April	Pink	
grandiflorum	Persian Stonecress	12	6	May	Pink	
Alyssum argenteum	Silver Alyssum	15	12	June–Aug.	Yellow	Silvery leaves
montanum		15	12	May	Yellow	
saxatile	Goldentuft	18	12	May	Yellow	Sheets of yellow
sax. citrinum	"Lemon Queen" Alyssum	12	12	May	Citron	Rarer color
sax. compactum	Dwarf Goldentuft	8–10		May	Yellow	Most popular
Anaphalis margaritacea	Pearl Everlasting	12	9	June	White	Gray leaves. Dry spots
Anchusa Barrelieri	Early Bugloss	24	12	May	Dark blue	
italica	Dropmore Bugloss	36–60	36	June, July	Deep blue	Shade tolerant
myosotidiflora [Brunnera]	Siberian Bugloss	12–18	12	May–June	Blue	
Anemone huphensis	Anemone	12	12	Aug.–Sept.	Rosy	Resembles A. japonica. Partial shade
japonica	Japanese Windflower	36	15	Sept.–Oct.	Various	Popular Fall flower. Partial shade
Anthemis tinctoria	Yellow Camomile	18	12	June	Yellow	Poor soil
Aquilegia cærulea	Colorado Columbine	18	12	April	Blue and white	Graceful. Good color. Long spur
canadensis	Amer. Columbine	18	9	April	Red and yellow	Self sows
chrysantha	Golden Columbine	24	12	May–Aug.	Yellow	Long spur. Blooms longest of any
glandulosa		12	9	May–June	Blue and white	
sibirica		12	9	May–June	Blue	
Skinneri	Mexican Columbine	12	9	April	Yellow and red	Short spurs
vulgaris	European Columbine	18	12	April	Violet	
vul. nivea	Munstead Columbine	18	12	April	White	
Arabis albida	Wallcress	12	9	April	White	Carpet of bloom
alpina	Alpine Rockcress	12	spreading	April	White	
aubrietioides		12	spreading	April	Pink	More tender
Artemisia Abrotanum	Southernwood	24		August	Yellow	Common in old gardens
Absinthium	Common Wormwood	24		August	White, yellow	An everlasting. Grown for gray foliage
albula	Silver King	24–36	18	Summer	White	
lactiflora	Piedmont Wormwood	48–72	24	Aug.–Sept.	White	Fragrant cut flower
montana	Cudweed Wormwood	36		September	White	
Purshiana	Beach Wormwood	18		August	Whitish	
Stelleriana		18		June–July	White	

TABULAR LIST OF GARDEN PERENNIALS—continued

SCIENTIFIC NAME	COMMON NAME	HEIGHT IN INCHES	DISTANCE APART	SEASON	COLOR	REMARKS
Aruncus sylvester	Goat's-beard	60	24	June–July	White	Tallest herbaceous Spirea
Asclepias incarnata	Swamp Milkweed	36	12	July	Pink	Moist places
tuberosa	Butterflyweed	24		July–Aug.	Orange	Dry, sunny places
Asperula odorata	Woodruff	12	9	July	White	Partial shade. Small, fragrant, spreading plant
Aster Amellus		18	12	July–August	Purple	
cordifolius		48	30	Sept.–Oct.	Lavender	
novæ-angliæ		48–72	24 (spreading)	Sept.–Oct.	Purple	
novi-belgii		12–96	12–36 (spreading)	Sept.–Oct.	Various	
subceruleus		15	9 (spreading)	June–July	Blue	
Astilbe Davidii	David's Astilbe	60	18	June–July	Rosy	
japonica		24	12	June–July	Pink or white	} Like moist soil
grandis	Great Astilbe	60		June–July	White	
Aubrietia, in variety						(*See* list of "Rock and Wall Plants Comparatively Easy to Grow")
Baptisia australis	Wild-indigo	24–48	24–36	June	Indigo	Lupine-like flowers; handsome foliage
tinctoria	Yellow Wild-indigo	24–48	24–36	June–July	Yellow	
Bocconia cordata	Plumepoppy	72–96	48 (spreading)	July	Cream-white	Among or back of shrubs
Boltonia asteroides	White Boltonia	60–72	36 (spreading)	September	Creamy	Useful in back of large border. Like Wild Aster, grayish leaves
latisquama	Violet Boltonia	48–72	24 (spreading)	September	White	
nana	Dwarf Pinkray Boltonia	24	12 (spreading)	September	Pink	Best of all
Brunnera macrophylla [Anchusa myosotidiflora]	Siberian Bugloss	12–18	12	May–June	Blue	Sun or shade
Campanula carpatica	Carpathian Bellflower	8	12	June–Oct.	Blue, white	Edging
glomerata	Danes-blood	18	9	July–Aug.	Violet	
lactiflora	Milky Bellflower	36–74	12–36	June–Sept.	Blue, white	
persicifolia	Peachleaf Bellflower	24–36	9	June–July	Blue, white	Good cut flower
punctata	Spotted Bellflower	18		June	White	
Caryopteris incana	Bluebeard	36		September	Lavender	Often called Blue Spirea
Cassia marilandica	Wild Senna	60		July	Yellow	Good background
Catananche caerulea	Cupid's-dart	18		September	Blue	Dry places. Everlasting
Centaurea babylonica	Syrian Centaurea	36		June–August	Yellow	
gymnocarpa	Velvet Centaurea	18		June	Pale purple	Silver leaves
macrocephala	Globe Centaurea	18	18	July	Yellow	White leaves. Edging
montana	Mountain-bluet	48	12	June–July	Violet	Good cut flower
Centranthus ruber	Jupiter's-beard	18	24	June–Aug.	Crimson, white	Needs lime in soil
Cephalaria alpina	Yellow Cephalaria	72	48	June–Aug.	Sulphur	Flowers like Scabiosa
Cerastium Biebersteinii	Taurus Cerastium	8		June	White	Edging
tomentosum	Snow-in-summer	6		June	White	Edging, ground cover
Chelidonium majus	Celandine-poppy	24		May	Yellow	Poppy-like

Botanical Name	Common Name	Height	Spread	Blooming Time	Color	Remarks
Chrysanthemum arcticum	Arctic Daisy	6		September	White	Good, dark foliage
coccineum	Painted Lady (Pyrethrum)	24	12	June	Various	Cut flowers. Pyrethrum in catalogs
Leucanthemum	Oxeye Daisy	24	12	June	White	Wild Daisy
maximum	Shasta Daisy	24	12	June–Sept.	White	Cut flower
morifolium (hortorum)	Garden Chrysanthemum	12–48	12–18	September	White	
nipponicum	Nippon Oxeye Daisy	24	24	September	White	Background
uliginosum	Giant Daisy	60	spreading	September	White	
Cimicifuga cordifolia	Bugbane	60	24	September	White	Graceful, good cut flower
foetida simplex	Kamchatka Bugbane	36–60	24–36	September	White	
racemosa	Cohosh Bugbane	48–60	24–36	July	White	
Clematis heracleaefolia	Tube Clematis	36–48	36–48	August	Lavender	Border
integrifolia		18–24	12	June–Oct.	Blue	Border, needs support
recta	Ground Clematis	48	24	June–July	White	Border, needs support
Coreopsis grandiflora	Tickseed	36	18	May	Yellow	Cut flower { Valuable for long blooming habit and for cut flowers }
rosea	Rose Coreopsis	12		Aug.–Sept.	Pink	Fine foliage { for cut flowers }
verticillata	Threadleaf Coreopsis	18		July–Aug.	Yellow	Good cut flower
Delphinium Belladonna	Larkspur	24	12	June–Sept.	Light blue	Rather tender
Bellamosum		24	12	June–Sept.	Dark blue	
cardinale	Cardinal Larkspur	36	12	August	Scarlet	
grandiflorum	Siberian Larkspur	18	18	July–Sept.	Blue, white	Fine foliage
hybrids		60	9	June–Sept.	Various	Named varieties
nudicaule	Orange Larkspur	18	9	July	Orange	Rather tender. Not easy in all gardens
Zalil	Yellow Larkspur	12–24	9	June–July	Yellow	Tuberous
Dianthus Allwoodii	Allwoods Pink	12–18	9	June–July	Various	Trifle tender in North
barbatus	Sweet William	18	9	June	Various	Always popular
caesius	Cheddar Pink	8–12	9	June–July	Rose	
cruentus	Blood Pink	4–5	6 spreading	July	Scarlet	
deltoides	Maiden Pink	6–9	9 spreading	June	Rose	
latifolius	Double Cluster Pink	12–18	9 spreading	July–Oct.	Crimson	Edging
plumarius	Grass Pink	12–18	12 spreading	June	Various	Edging
Dicentra eximia	Fringed Bleeding-heart	18	12	May–Sept.	Rose	Edging. Sun or partial shade
spectabilis	Bleeding-heart	24–36	36	May	Pink	Likes partial shade
Dictamnus albus	Gas Plant	36	24	June–July	Rose, white	Does not like transplanting
Digitalis ambigua	Yellow foxglove	36	24	May	Yellow	Perennial
amb. Isabellina		36	12	June–July	Tawny	Perennial
Doronicum austriacum	Leopard's-bane	24	12	May–June	Yellow	Earliest yellow daisies
caucasicum		24	9	May–June	Yellow	
plantagineum		24	12	June	Yellow	
Dracocephalum Ruyschiana	Dragonhead	24	9	June–July	Purple	Mintlike
Echinacea purpurea	Purple Coneflower	36	24	September	Rosy purple	Popular
Echinops humilis	Low Globe Thistle	12	9	July	Blue	Globular heads. Spiny plants. Drainage
Ritro	Steel Globe Thistle	36	24	July	Blue	
sphaerocephalus	Common Globe Thistle	60	24	July–August	White	
Erigeron multiradiatus	Fleabane	6	12	July	Pink	
speciosus		18	12	July–August	Violet	Purple daisies
Eryngium alpinum	Bluetop Eryngo	24	12	July–August	Amethyst	Prickly foliage, teasel-like heads
amethystinum	Amethyst Eryngium	24	12	July–August	Amethyst	
maritimum	Seaholly	12	12	July–Sept.	Pale blue	
Oliverianum		36	18	July–August	Blue	
planum		24	12	July–August	Steel blue	

TABULAR LIST OF GARDEN PERENNIALS—continued

SCIENTIFIC NAME	COMMON NAME	HEIGHT IN INCHES	DISTANCE APART	SEASON	COLOR	REMARKS
Eupatorium cœlestinum	Mistflower	24	12	Sept.–Oct.	Blue	Popular in fall
purpureum	Joe-pye-weed	72	24	August	Purple	Wet places
urticæfolium	Thoroughwort	36	18	August	White	Common wild. Likes shade. Stands dryness
Euphorbia corollata	Flowering Spurge	36	12	July	White	Cut flowers. Stands dryness
Cyparissias	Cypress Spurge	12	9	June	Yellow	Fine foliage
epithymoides	Cushion Spurge	24	12	May	Yellow	Border foliage
Filipendula hexapetala	Dropwort	12–24	12	June–July	White	Edging
palmata	Meadowsweet	24–36	18	July	Pink, white	Plumy heads
Gaillardia aristata	Blanketflower	12–15	12	May–Oct.	Red, orange	Ever popular. Does not mind poor soil
Galega officinalis	Goatsrue	36	18	June–July	Purplish blue	
Galium boreale	Bedstraw	12	12	June	White	
verum		12	12 spreading	June–August	Yellow	Tiny flowers in sprays good for cutting
Geranium armenum	Armenian Cranesbill	24	12	May–July	Purple	
Fremontii	Rocky Mountain C.	12	12	June	Rose-purple	
grandiflorum	Lilac Geranium	12	9	June	Violet	Quite evergreen
ibericum	Iberian Geranium	12	9	June	Blue, white	
pratense	Meadow Cranesbill	24	18	June	Purple, white	
Geum chiloense florepleno	Avens	24	12	July–Sept.	Scarlet	⎫ These varieties do not like poor, dry soil
Lady Stratheden	Lady Stratheden	24	12	July–Sept.	Yellow	
Mrs. Bradshaw	Mrs. Bradshaw	24	12	July–Sept.	Scarlet	
montanum Heldreichii		12	9	May–June	Orange	⎭
Gypsophila paniculata	Baby's-breath	30	36	June–July	White	Background
Helenium autumnale	Sneezeweed	48–60	18	Aug.–Sept.	Yellow	Cut flower
aut. pumilum		30	12	Aug.–Sept.	Yellow	Cut flower
Hoopesii		30	12	June	Orange	Graceful foliage
Helianthus atrorubens	Sunflower	36–72	36 spreading	September	Yellow, reddish	Semi-double usually
angustifolius	Swamp Sunflower	36	24	September	Yellow	⎫ Good for back of a large border but must be watched lest weaker plants are smothered.
decapetalus	Thinleaf Sunflower	72	36	August	Sulphur	
Maximiliani	Maximilian Sunflower	84	36	October	Gold	
orgyalis		84	36	October	Yellow	⎭
scaberrimus	Prairie Sunflower	48	24	Sept.–Oct.	Gold	
Heliopsis Pitcheriana	Pitcher Heliopsis	36	36	July–August	Orange	
scabra excelsa		36	36	July–August	Orange	
Helleborus niger	Christmas Rose	12	12	Winter	White	
Hemerocallis aurantiaca	Orange Daylily	36	24	June	Orange	⎫ Good for border or waterside. Like semi-shade. Narrow, grass-like leaves
Dumortierii		18		June	Bright orange	
flava	Lemon Daylily	24		June	Canary	
fulva	Tawny Daylily	36		July	Bronze	
Middendorffii	Amur Daylily	24		June	Gold	
Thunbergii	Japanese Daylily	48		July	Canary	⎭
Hesperis matronalis	Rocket	36	12	June–July	Purple	
Heuchera sanguinea	Coral-bells	12–24	9	July	Crimson	

Botanical name	Common name	Height	Distance	Season	Color	Remarks
Hibiscus Moscheutos	Rose Mallow	48–60	36	Aug.–Sept.	Pink, crimson, white	Wet or normal soil
Iberis sempervirens	Evergreen Candytuft	9–12		March–April	White	Good for shade
Hosta caerulea	Funkia, Plantain Lily	24–36	24	July–August	Blue	Good for shade
japonica		12–24	12	July–August	Pale lavender	
plantaginea		24	24	July–August	White	
Sieboldiana		30	24	June–July	Mauve	(See descriptive list)
Iris	Iris					
Kniphofia foliosa	Early Torchlily	24–36	18	June–July	Orange and yellow	Probably the hardiest
rufa	Torchlily	18	12	June	Yellow	Showy, popular, needs winter protection
Uvaria		36–48	18	Aug.–Sept.	Orange	
U. var. Pfitzeriana	Bonfire Torchlily	36	18	September	Orange-scarlet	Trifle tender
Lavandula Spica	Spike Lavender	24	24	August	Lavender	Bloom from top of spike downwards.
vera	True Lavender	12–24	12	July	Blue	Trying color.
Liatris graminifolia	Grassleaf Gayfeather	24	24	August	Rose-purple	Narrow spikes.
pycnostachya	Cattail Gayfeather	48		Aug.–Sept.	Rose-purple	Needs moisture at root
scariosa		24	12	August	Purple	
spicata	Spike Gayfeather	24–60	9–12	August	Purple	
Limonium Gmelini	Statice	20		August	Lavender	Everlastings. Dainty flower sprays
latifolium	Bigleaf Statice			August	Lavender	
tataricum	Tatarian Statice			August	Lavender	
Linaria macedonica	Macedonian Linaria	36		June	Yellow	Gray leaves
Linum flavum	Golden Flax	12	9	June–August	Gold	
narbonense	Narbonne Flax	24	12	May	Blue	Evergreen
perenne	Perennial Flax	18	12	June–August	White	Evergreen
perenne album	White Perennial Flax	18	12	June–August	White	
Lobelia cardinalis	Cardinalflower	24–36	9	Aug.–Oct.	Scarlet	Grows naturally in wet soil but stands ordinary soil
Lupinus polyphyllus	Washington Lupine	36–48	12–24	June	Various	Very desirable
Lychnis chalcedonica	Maltese Cross	24–36	12	July–August	Scarlet	Popular. Prolific
Flos Jovis	Flower-of-jove	18	12	June	Rose	
viscaria	Clammy Campion	12	9	June	Magenta	
Lysimachia clethroides	Clethra Loosestrife	24	1	July–August	White	Excellent
Lythrum superbum	Purple Loosestrife	30–40	24–30	Summer	Purple to pink	Hardy, vigorous
Meconopsis cambrica	Welsh-poppy	12	9	June	Yellow	Rare. Desirable
Mertensia virginica	Virginia Bluebells	18	9	May	Blue	Best in shade. Dies to ground
Monarda didyma	Bee-balm	36	12 spreading	July	Scarlet	Popular. Stands considerable shade
Myosotis alpestris	Alpine Forget-me-not	6		June	Blue	Always admired
dissitiflora	Swiss Forget-me-not	9		May	Blue	
scorpioides (palustris)	True Forget-me-not	9		June	Deep blue	
Nepeta Mussini	Mussin Catmint	12		May–Sept.	Lavender blue	Edging
Œnothera cespitosa	Tufted Sundrops	4		May	White	Leaves like dandelion
fruticosa	Sundrops	18		June–July	Yellow	Very large flowers and seed pods.
missouriensis	Ozark Sundrops	12		June–Aug.	Yellow	Prostrate with flower 4″ in diameter
Pæonia	Peony	18–48		May–June	White, pink, red	(See descriptive list)

TABULAR LIST OF GARDEN PERENNIALS—continued

SCIENTIFIC NAME	COMMON NAME	HEIGHT IN INCHES	DISTANCE APART	SEASON	COLOR	REMARKS
Papaver alpinum	Alpine Poppy	8–10		June	Yellow	
nudicaule	Iceland Poppy	12		June–Oct.	Yellow, orange, white	Small, but profuse
orientale	Oriental Poppy	36		June	Various	
pilosum	Olympic Poppy	24		June–Oct.	Orange	
Penstemon barbatus	Pink Beauty	36	12 spreading	June–July	Scarlet	Long tubular flowers. Popular
grandiflorus	Shell-leaf Penstemon	24		July	Purple	
laevigatus	Smooth Penstemon	24		June	Rosy lilac	(All good for cut flowers)
digitalis	Foxglove Penstemon	36		June–July	Purple	
Torre,i	Torrey Penstemon	36		June–July	Scarlet	Trifle tender
Phlox Arendsii	Arends Phlox	24	9	May–June	Various	
divaricata	Blue Phlox	12	9	May	Lavender	Wild, but splendid in cultivation
paniculata	Garden Phlox	24	12	July–August	Various	
suffruticosa (glaberrima)	Smooth Phlox	24	12	June–Sept.	Various	Smooth leaves, earlier than standard types of garden Phlox. Disease resistant
Physostegia virginiana var. Vivid	False-dragonhead	36–60	18	July–Sept.	Pink	Good cut flower
		18	12	July–Oct.	Brighter pink	
Platycodon grandiflorum	Balloonflower	24	12	May–Oct.	Violet, white	
Mariesii		12	9	May–Oct.	Violet, white	Superior
Polemonium ceruleum	Greek-valerian	18	9	June	Blue, white	
reptans		9	spreading	May	Blue	Flat flowers in spikes
Potentilla nepalensis	Nepal Cinquefoil	18	9	June–August	Rose	
Warrensii		24	12	June–August	Yellow	
Primula acaulis	English Primrose	6		April–May	Various	
auricula		12		June	Various	
denticulata	Himalayan Primrose	10		May	Violet	
japonica	Japanese Primrose	24	12	June	White to crimson	Moist soil. Cool places
polyantha		6–10	9	April–May	Various in combination	
pulverulenta	Silverdust Primrose	30	12	June	Rosy purple	
Sieboldii		10–12	6	May	White, rose, purple	
veris	Cowslip Primrose	9		April–May	Yellow	
vulgaris						(See P. acaulis)
Pulmonaria officinalis (maculata)		6–12	9	April	Purple	
saccharata	Bethlehem Sage	6–18	9	April–May	Reddish Violet	
Pyrethrum roseum						(See Chrysanthemum coccineum)
Romneya Coulteri	Canyon Poppy	48		June	White	Large poppy
Rudbeckia laciniata	Golden Glow	60		July–Sept.	Orange	Cut flower. Double
maxima	Great Coneflower	60		June–Sept.	Yellow	
nitida	Autumn Sun	60		August–Oct.	Primrose	
purpurea						(See Echinacea)
speciosa	Showy Coneflower	36	12	July–Oct.	Golden	
subtomentosa	Sweet Coneflower	48	18	July–Aug.	Golden	

Botanical name	Common name	Height	Distance	Bloom	Color	Remarks
Salvia azurea grandiflora	Azure Sage	48	24	Aug.–Sept.	Light blue	Trifle leggy
argentea	Silver Sage	24–48	12	June	Rosy white	Half-hardy
farinacea	Mealycup Sage	36	24	Aug.–Sept.	Light blue	
Pitcheri	Pitcher Sage	48	12	Aug.–Sept.	Deep blue	Similar to S. azurea
pratensis	Meadow Sage	24	18	June–Aug.	Blue	Good cut flower
uliginosa	Bog Salvia	36		Aug.–Sept.	Pale blue	Silver leaves
Scabiosa caucasica	Japanese Scabiosa	24	12	June–Sept.	White, lavender	
graminifolia		18	9	June–July	Violet	
japonica		24	12	June–Sept.	Lavender	
Scutellaria alpina lupulina	Skullcap	9	6	August	Yellow	
baicalensis	Baikal Skullcap	12	6	July	Blue	
Sidalcea candida	Prairiemallow	36		July	White	
malvaeflora	Checkerbloom			June–July	Rose-pink	
mal. Listeri	Satin Checkerbloom	12–60		June–July	Rose-pink	Fringed petals
Solidago alpestris	Alpine Goldenrod	4–18		August	Yellow	Popular wild flowers worthy of cultivation. Stand drought
altissima	Tall Goldenrod	48–72		August	Yellow	
cesia	Wreath Goldenrod	24		September	Yellow	
canadensis	Canada Goldenrod	36		August	Yellow	
rigida	Stiff Goldenrod	60		September	Yellow	
Virgaurea	Goldwings			September	Bright yellow	
Stachys Betonica grandiflora	Betony	12–36	6	June	Purple	(See S. grandiflora)
lanata	Woolly Betony	12		July	Purple	White, silky leaves
Statice Armeria	Thrift	6	9	June–July	Pink	Good for edgings. Useful for seashore planting. See also Liminium
Laucheana	Rosalie Thrift	9	9	June–July	Rose	
montana (Alpina)		8		June	Pale pink	
plantaginea (dianthoides)		18		June	Pink	
Stokesia laevis	Stokes-aster	12–24	12	July–August	Lavender, white	Good cut flower
Teucrium Chamaedrys	Germander	12		July	Rosy purple	
Thalictrum aquilegifolium	Columbine Meadowrue	12–36	18	May–June	White, purple	Dainty foliage; plumy flowers. Excellent border plants
dipterocarpum	Yunnan Meadowrue	48	18	Aug.–Sept.	Lilac	
glaucum	Dusty Meadowrue	24	12	June–July	Yellow	
minus	Low Meadowrue	18		June–July	Yellow	
polygamum	Tall Meadowrue	36	24	May	White	
Trollius europaeus	Globeflower	24	12	April–June	Yellow	Very popular. Excellent cut flowers. Need moist soil
asiaticus		24	12	May–June	Orange	
sinensis		24	12	July	Orange-yellow	
Ledebouri		36	18	June	Golden	Flat flower
Tunica Saxifraga	Tunicflower	6	6	July–Oct.	White, blush	Edging
Valeriana officinalis	Valerian	36–60	12 spreading	June–July	Blush white	Fragrant, subject to plant lice
Verbena canadensis		9–12	12 spreading	June–Sept.	Red-purple	
Veronica incana	Woolly Speedwell	12	6 spreading	July–Aug.	Rosy purple	Effective mat of gray foliage
maritima	Clump Speedwell	24	9	August	Violet	
spicata	Spike Speedwell	12	9	June–July	Purple	
spuria	Bastard Speedwell	18	9	June–July	Violet	
virginica	Culvers-physic	48–60		July	White	
Viola cornuta	Tufted Pansy	6–10	6	April–Oct.	Various	Unexcelled garden sorts
Yucca filamentosa	Adam's-Needle	72	36	June–July	White	Coarse; use as accents in shrubbery

XXVII

BULBS, CORMS, AND TUBERS

In the pageantry of the seasons bulbs play an important part. From the first flowers of the diminutive snowdrops in late winter to the last lingering blooms of the autumn crocus there is an ever-changing succession. The fleeting beauty of the crocus, the scillas and the grape hyacinths gives way to the far-flung loveliness of the narcissus, and as the season advances the tulips, with their sculptured beauty, hold the center of the stage.

There are few flowers which give so generously of their bloom and beauty as do the bulbs. Many of the spring-flowering bulbs, when once established, will increase rapidly and will form large colonies. This is particularly true of the early bulbs, such as the snowdrops and scillas, the grape hyacinths and the narcissus. Widespreading clumps of snowdrops along a woodland path in very early spring, the intense blue of a carpet of squills beneath the spreading branches of a great beech tree, a meadow with a myriad grape hyacinths in bloom, a bank where hundreds of narcissus sway in the spring breeze—these are among the joyous ecstasies of spring.

SPRING-FLOWERING BULBS

Narcissus

The narcissi, with their wealth of gay and lovely flowers, are among the most adaptable of bulbs, and deserve a place in every garden. They are hardy and dependable, demand little in the way of care and will bloom blithely on, year after year. They are the prelude to all the beauty that is to come; long drifts of them in the garden, masses of them along the edge of the woodland, grassy slopes clothed with them, gay pots of them in the windows, pushcarts laden with them on the street corners—one

384

sees them everywhere and one loves them none the less for the fact that they are to be found in such gay profusion.

Classification of Narcissus

DIVISION I—*Trumpet Narcissi*

Distinguishing characters: One flower to a stem; trumpet or cup as long as or longer than the perianth segments.

- (*a*) Perianth colored; trumpet colored, not paler than the perianth.
- (*b*) Perianth white; trumpet colored.
- (*c*) Perianth white; trumpet white, not paler than the perianth.
- (*d*) Any color combination not falling into the other groups.

DIVISION II—*Large-cupped Narcissi*

Distinguishing characters: One flower to a stem; cup more than one-third but less than equal to the length of the perianth segment.

- (*a*) Perianth colored; cup colored, not paler than the perianth.
- (*b*) Perianth white; cup colored.
- (*c*) Perianth white; cup white, not paler than the perianth.
- (*d*) Any color combination not falling into the other groups.

DIVISION III—*Small-cupped Narcissi*

Distinguishing characters: One flower to a stem; cup not more than one-third the length of the perianth segments.

- (*a*) Perianth colored; cup colored, not paler than the perianth.
- (*b*) Perianth white; cup colored.
- (*c*) Perianth white; cup white, not paler than the perianth.
- (*d*) Any color combination not falling into the other groups.

DIVISION IV—*Double Narcissi*

Distinguishing character: Double flowers.

DIVISION V—*Triandrus Narcissi*

Distinguishing characters: Characteristics of Narcissus triandrus clearly evident.

(*a*) Cup not less than two-thirds the length of the perianth segments.

(*b*) Cup less than two-thirds the length of the perianth segments.

DIVISION VI—*Cyclamineus Narcissi*

Distinguishing characters: Characteristics of Narcissus cyclamineus must be clearly evident.

(*a*) Cup not less than two-thirds the length of the perianth segments.

(*b*) Cup less than two-thirds the length of the perianth segments.

DIVISION VII—*Jonquilla Narcissi*

Distinguishing characters: Characteristics of any of the Narcissus Jonquilla group clearly evident.

(*a*) Cup not less than two-thirds the length of the perianth segments.

(*b*) Cup less than two-thirds the length of the perianth segments.

DIVISION VIII—*Tazetta Narcissi*

Distinguishing characters: Characteristics of any of the Narcissus Tazetta group clearly evident.

DIVISION IX—*Poeticus Narcissi*

Distinguishing characters: Characteristics of any of the Narcissus Poeticus group without a mixture of any other.

DIVISION X—*Species and Wild Forms and Hybrids*

All species and wild, or reputedly wild, forms and hybrids.

DIVISION XI—*Miscellaneous Narcissi*

All Narcissi not falling into any of the foregoing divisions.

Time of Planting: When grown under natural conditions narcissi produce their new root growth in the late summer and early autumn, and by the time the ground becomes frozen a strong root system has been developed. The ideal time for planting is during the dormant or rest period which occurs after the foliage has died down and before active root growth commences. If old clumps of narcissi are to be lifted and divided, it should preferably be done at this season. Bulbs which have been purchased from commercial growers are usually shipped early in the autumn and should be planted as soon as possible after their arrival, in order that full advantage may be taken of the good growing weather. If, for some unavoidable reason, planting must be delayed until late in the season, the ground should be kept mulched with straw or fresh manure to prevent it from freezing and the mulch should be replaced again after the bulbs have been planted, in order to give them an opportunity to make as much root growth as possible. Late planting is never very successful. Both the quantity and quality of the spring bloom are dependent to a considerable extent upon the root development which the bulb has made the previous autumn. Good root development means good flowers, other conditions being favorable.

Method of Planting: The depth of planting will vary according to the size of the bulb. A generally accepted rule is to cover each bulb with twice its own depth of soil. The small bulbs of the Jonquil type should, therefore, be planted from 1 to 3 inches deep, while the very large bulbs of some of the Trumpet varieties should be planted at a depth of 6 inches or more. The smaller varieties should be spaced from 3 to 4 inches apart, the larger varieties from 6 to 8 inches apart. If the bulbs are to be planted in well-prepared soil in a garden bed, a trowel or a bulb planter may be used to open the holes. Care should be taken to see that the base of the bulb is resting upon firm soil in order to avoid an air pocket beneath it. If bulbs are to be planted in an area of sod, or in a woodland, the digging of the holes is often very tedious and difficult. The work can be done more rapidly and efficiently with a mattock than with any other tool. A sharp stroke with the mattock should be used to pry up a piece of sod; it should not be torn entirely loose. The bulb should then be placed in the hole and the sod pressed back into position.

Soil Requirements: Narcissi may be grown successfully in almost any type of soil. A well-drained, sandy loam is considered ideal. An application of well-rotted manure is beneficial in increasing the fertility of the soil and in improving its structure, but fresh manure should never be used as it is apt to cause serious injury. Some varieties of narcissus are more sensitive than others, but it is wise never to use manure in any form until it has become thoroughly rotted. Bone meal is the most satisfactory fertilizer for narcissus and may be applied at the rate of $\frac{1}{2}$ pound to every 25 square feet, being worked into the upper 2 or 3 inches of soil in the autumn.

After the period of bloom is over the flower stalks should be cut off in order to prevent the formation of seed pods. No leaves should be removed until the foliage has turned a yellowish-brown and has died down. The vigor of the bulbs will be seriously affected if the foliage is removed while still green. If the bulbs have been planted in an area of sod, the grass should not be cut until the foliage of the bulbs has matured. If the yellowing foliage becomes unsightly in the garden, the leaves may be braided or rolled into a small mass and tucked under the foliage of neighboring plants.

Narcissus bulbs increase very rapidly, and when the bulbs have become too crowded, they should be lifted, divided and replanted as soon as the foliage has ripened. In naturalistic plantings, where the size and perfection of the flowers are not matters of great importance, the bulbs may be left undisturbed for a period of many years. In the garden, it is advisable to lift them every 6 or 8 years, as the blooms have a tendency to become smaller, and the bulbs are less thrifty when they have become overcrowded.

VARIETIES OF MERIT

DIVISION I—*Trumpet Narcissi*

(*a*) Aerolite, Lord Wellington, Unsurpassable
(*b*) Bonython, Patrici, Spring Glory
(*c*) Beersheba, Mount Hood, Mrs. E. H. Krelage

DIVISION II—*Large-cupped Narcissi*

(*a*) Aranjuez, Copper Bowl, Fortune, Royal Crown
(*b*) Dick Wellband, Flower Record, John Evelyn, Polindra
(*c*) Gyrfalcon, Tenedos, White Nile

NARCISSUS IN A WOODLAND SETTING

DIVISION III—*Small-cupped Narcissi*

(*a*) Edward Buxton, Mangosteen
(*b*) Firetail, Kansas, LaRiante, Mystic

DIVISION V—*Triandrus Narcissi*

Niveth, Shot Silk, Thalia, Tresamble

DIVISION VI—*Cyclamineus Narcissi*

Beryl, February Gold, Garden Princess, March Sunshine

DIVISION VII—*Jonquilla Narcissi*

Campernelli Orange Queen, Jonquilla Single, Trevithian

DIVISION VIII—*Tazetta Narcissi*

Admiration, Geranium, Scarlet Gem, St. Agnes

DIVISION IX—*Poeticus Narcissi*

Actæa, Recurus, Sarchedon

Miniatures and Species

Bulbocodium conspicuus, Hawera, Triandrus alba, W. P. Milner

Tulips

There are few flowers which offer to the gardener so great an opportunity for color harmonies as do the tulips. In the skillful hands of the artist they may be used to create the most subtle and beautiful compositions in the spring garden. If some of the lovely species tulips are grown, a succession of bloom may be had extending from very early spring, when Tulip Kaufmanniana, the exquisite Waterlily tulip, opens its graceful flowers, to late May when the last of the stately Breeder tulips bring the season to a close.

Exposure: Tulips prefer a sunny location where they will be protected against strong winds. Partial or heavy shade is not desirable, as the stems have a tendency to

SPRING BULBS ALONG A GARDEN PATH

bend towards the light and to become weak and floppy. Tulips will, however, do well where they receive shade for a few hours each day, and in some cases the colors seem to fade less when the flowers are thus protected from full sun.

Soil: The ideal soil for tulips is a light, fertile, well-drained loam. Fresh manures should never be used in the preparation of tulip beds. Very well-rotted manure or compost may be used in fairly liberal quantities. Bone meal is one of the best fertilizers and may be applied to tulip beds at the rate of $\frac{1}{2}$ pound per 25 square feet.

Planting: Where soil conditions permit, deep planting is recommended, the bulb being placed so that the tip is from 10 to 12 inches below the surface. Deep planting has a number of advantages over shallow planting. The bulbs will continue to flower well for a greater number of years; there is less danger of injury from botrytis blight; it is possible to plant annuals and gladioli in the same space after the tulips are over without running the risk of injuring the bulbs; and there is less danger of losses from mice. However, in planting tulips at this depth it is essential that the soil be well drained, and there must be no danger of having standing water near the surface at any season of the year. There must also be a sufficiently deep layer of top-soil to provide a fertile soil of good texture beneath the bulb. In soils which are not well-drained, or where there is only a shallow layer of topsoil, it is wiser to plant tulips at a depth of 4–6 inches.

The early-flowering varieties may be spaced 4 inches apart, the later varieties, such as the Darwins and the Breeders, 6 inches apart. If tulips are to be planted in drifts in the herbaceous border a trowel or a bulb planter may be used to open the holes, care being taken to see that the base of the bulb is resting on firm soil in order to avoid an air pocket beneath it. When a large bed or border is to be planted entirely with tulips, it is sometimes a wise plan to remove the upper 4–6 inches of top-soil. The floor of the bed may then be slightly loosened and raked until the surface is level. The bulbs may be placed in position, being pressed firmly into the soil, and the top-soil may then be carefully replaced. This method will assure absolute uniformity of planting, which is necessary if precise regularity is desired.

Tulips should preferably be planted between the middle of October and the middle of November. If the bulbs are planted too early in the autumn, they are apt to start into active growth, and will suffer a severe setback during the winter. Tulips should, therefore, not be planted as early as narcissus. It is important, however, that the bulbs be planted far enough in advance of freezing weather to enable them to make sufficient root growth. A strong, vigorous root system produced during the autumn has a very direct effect

TULIPS IN A FORMAL GARDEN

upon the quality of the bloom the following spring. If planting must be delayed until very late in the season, the same procedure may be followed as that recommended for narcissus.

Mice are extremely fond of tulips, and if they are prevalent they can completely destroy an entire planting in a single season. In gardens where mice are known to be troublesome it is wise to use every possible measure to eradicate them (see page 673). And where it is not possible, because of soil conditions, to plant the bulbs at a depth of 10–12 inches, it is recommended that the bulbs be planted in wire baskets which will afford excellent protection. Such baskets can be purchased from garden supply stores.

Care after blooming: Tulips will produce their best bloom the spring following planting. Some varieties will bloom well over a period of years, while other varieties deteriorate rapidly and show a decided decline after the first season. Some varieties possess much greater longevity than others. Some of the older varieties such as Clara Butt, William Copeland and Rev. Ewbank will continue to flower for twenty years, while some of the newer varieties are comparatively short-lived. If tulips are planted in a bed with herbaceous perennials or as a foreground to a shrubbery border the foliage may be allowed to die down naturally. If young plants of quick-growing annuals such as snapdragons, petunias and verbenas are planted among the tulips the yellowing of the foliage will hardly be noticed. If tulips are planted in solid beds or borders, and if the space which they occupy is desired for other plantings, the bulbs may be lifted very carefully after blooming, the roots and leaves remaining intact, and they may then be heeled in in a partially shaded spot. They should be left thus, to ripen. When the leaves have turned brown and the bulbs are thoroughly mature they may be placed in storage until planting time in the autumn. The bulbs should be stored in a cool, dark, dry place.

VARIETIES OF MERIT

SINGLE EARLY GROUP: Brilliant Star, DeWet, Hobbema, Rose Luisante, White Hawk, Yellow Prince

DOUBLE EARLY GROUP: Maréchal Niel, Murillo, Peach Blossom, Mr. Van der Hoef

MENDEL GROUP: Athleet, Emmy Peeck, Her Grace, Orange Wonder

TRIUMPH GROUP: Bruno Walter, Elizabeth Evers, Johanna, Nivea, Spring Song

COTTAGE GROUP: Advance, Barbara Pratt, Beverly, Carrara, Dido, Good Gracious, Ivory Glory, John Ruskin, Marjorie Bowen, Rosey Wings

DARWIN GROUP: Afterglow, Anton Mauve, Charles Needham, Cum Laude, Duke of Wellington, Glacier, Insurpassable, Niphetos, Princess Elizabeth, Queen Bartigous, Smiling Queen

LILY-FLOWERING GROUP: China Pink, Ellen Willmott, Marcellina, Marietta, White Triumphator

DOUBLE LATE GROUP: Eros, Golden Lion, Moonglow, Mount Tacoma, Symphonia

BREEDER GROUP: Bacchus, Bronze Queen, Chappaqua, Dillenburg, Louis XIV, Pontiac, Southern Cross, Velvet King

Tulips for Southern Gardens

It has long been a matter of regret to Southern gardeners that tulips were among the flowers which would not thrive in Southern climates, and for generations those who have gardened in the South have had to be content with miserably weak and floppy specimens, or have had to forgo their beauty entirely.

It is only within comparatively recent years that the discovery has been made that tulips may be grown quite as successfully in the South as in the North, provided that the bulbs are placed in cold storage for a period of several months before they are planted. If they are held in storage at a temperature of 45 degrees for a period of 6 months previous to planting, excellent results may be obtained. The bulbs may be planted during December, January and early February, and in the case of late plantings, active growth will begin almost immediately. If this method is followed an abundance of tall, strong-stemmed blooms may be had.

As soon as the foliage has died down and the bulbs have ripened they should be lifted and placed in storage. Some bulbs will flower well for several seasons if accorded this treatment, while others deteriorate rapidly and must be replaced by new stock, which has been specially prepared for Southern planting.

Species Tulips and Hybrids

The species tulips and their hybrids possess a sprightliness and charm which is quite distinctive. Most of them flower early and when once well established they will usually bloom on year after year. As a group they prefer dry, sunny locations and are most happily at home when planted in some sheltered nook where they add a welcome touch of bright color in early spring.

Among the most appealing and beloved in this group are T. biflora; T. clusiana; T. dasystemon; T. fosteriana and its hybrids, which includes T. f. Red Emperor; T. kaufmanniana and its many lovely hybrids; and T. sylvestris.

Hyacinth

Hyacinths lack the grace and charm of the tulips and narcissi and it is sometimes difficult to find a place in the garden where they may be used with artistic effect. If planted as a foreground for a shrubbery border they will present a striking display of color, and they are more effective in such a location than in the garden.

The bulbs should be planted in the autumn between the middle of September and the middle of October. The depth of planting will vary according to the size of the bulb. The tip of the bulb should be approximately 3 inches below the surface if the soil is of a heavy texture; 5 inches in a light, sandy soil. They may be set from 6 to 8 inches apart.

Hyacinths will produce good bloom in any type of moderately fertile soil provided that it is well drained.

After the bulbs have flowered the foliage should be allowed to ripen. If desired, the same treatment may be accorded the bulbs as that recommended for tulips.

SMALL SPRING-FLOWERING BULBS

These early harbingers of spring hold a very special place in our affections, and they may be planted in drifts along the edge of the flower borders, or they may be naturalized in great masses. Gay and jaunty, winsome and charming, they usher in the spring.

All of these small bulbs should be planted during the early autumn. They may be spaced from 3 to 4 inches apart and the depth of planting will vary from 2 to 3 inches, depending upon the size of the bulb. After they have once become established they will increase rapidly, and they may be left undisturbed for many years. They thrive well in any type of well-drained soil and require no care or attention after they have been planted.

Anemone blanda

Dainty and charming, this little anemone comes into flower in very early spring, soon after the snowdrops and winter aconites are over. It is a winsome thing, hardly more than 3 inches in height, and the star-shaped flowers are nestled in a spreading growth of fern-like leaves. It prefers light shade and is lovely in the rock garden, and when naturalized under trees or in the foreground of shrub plantings. A little patch near the house will become a joy for a few brief weeks each succeeding spring. A. blanda atro-coerulea is a rich violet-blue in color. There is also a pink shade.

The little bulbs should be planted 3 inches deep, being spaced about 2 inches apart. It is most effective when the bulbs are planted in clumps of six or more.

Crocus

Among the most beloved and most widely grown of the small, spring-flowering bulbs are the crocuses. The "Dutch" crocus is the garden type most commonly grown and, when planted in masses, gives a lavish display of color. The jaunty, erect, cup-like flowers come in a variety of colors—white, deep violet, porcelain-blue, dark lilac and golden yellow.

Lovely as are the Dutch crocuses, any gardener who has never grown some of the smaller, more dainty Species Crocuses has missed one of the greatest joys of very early spring. They come into flower soon after the snowdrops are over, and they possess a sprightliness and a piquant charm which is very endearing. A little patch of species crocuses near the house, in some sheltered corner where they will catch the first warm rays of spring sunshine, will be a source of joy year after year. They may be tucked into all sorts of places, along a path, on a bank, in front of shrub plantings, anywhere, provided they can be left undisturbed after they have flowered, and each spring one will find oneself eagerly watching for the first blooms. Colors vary according to the species. Aurius is a deep golden-yellow; Korolkowi, the very earliest to bloom, is a brilliant yellow, shading to orange, the reverse of the petals touched with bronze; Chrysanthus is pale yellow with brilliant orange stamens; the flowers of Sieberi are a delicate blue with a golden throat; and Tomasinianus, one of the most charming of all the species, is more than generous with its bloom, the flowers being a soft, pale lavender.

Culture: All types of crocus are of easy culture. They prefer a light, somewhat sandy soil, not too rich a diet, and an exposure in full sun or very light shade. The corms of the Dutch crocuses should be planted about 4 inches deep, the Species from 2 to 3 inches, and they should be spaced from 2 to 4 inches apart.

Where crocuses are planted in a lawn the grass should not be cut until after the foliage has matured and begins to die down.

Crocuses increase very rapidly, both by the production of new corms and by reseeding. Most of the species crocuses reseed readily and sometimes appear in the most surprising places. From a modest initial planting large colonies will often develop.

Eranthis hyemalis (Winter Aconite)

Blooming with the snowdrops, this endearing little flower seems to hold within its golden cup the very promise of spring. Hardly more than 2 to 3 inches tall, each little flower is surrounded by an Elizabethan ruff of green leaves, and has a sprightly, winsome charm. They reseed readily and large colonies soon develop from a small planting. Patches of them are lovely in an open woodland, on a bank, or in the foreground of a shrub planting. They will thrive in full sun or partial shade but prefer light shade during the summer. The little tubers should be planted immediately upon arrival at a depth of about 2 inches and should be spaced about 3 inches apart. If they appear shrivelled and dry it is advisable to bury them in moist sand or in wet peat moss for a few days before planting them.

Galanthus (Snowdrop)

Because the Snowdrop is the true harbinger of spring, often coming into flower while there is still snow on the ground, it is especially cherished and beloved. Diminutive in size, hardly more than 3 or 4 inches in height, it possesses the ability to survive a heavy snowfall quite unharmed and will bloom blithely on after the snows have melted. Preferring partial shade and a rather cool, moist, heavy soil, they will increase slowly over the years until large clumps are formed from an original planting of a few bulbs. The small, drooping, white blooms are of great daintiness, and clumps of snowdrops are lovely when naturalized in open woodland areas, or at the base of trees on the lawn, or in the foreground of a planting of evergreen shrubs. A patch by the door or below a window will bring to those within a message that spring is soon to come.

Iris reticulata (see page 409)

Leucojum (Snowflakes)

The leucojums resemble the snowdrops, having pendent, bell-shaped flowers, tipped with green. They bloom later than the snow-

THE LOVELY SPECIES CROCUS

drops and are much taller and more robust. They may be naturalized in a woodland planting, or used in the foreground of a shrub planting, and they are also quite happily at home in the perennial border, being pleasant companions for tulips, phlox divaricata and bleeding-heart. They are very long-lived and when once established will continue to bloom on year after year, requiring an occasional dividing. The bulbs should be planted in the autumn about 3 inches deep, being spaced 4 to 5 inches apart. There are several types and varieties, some blooming earlier than others.

Lily-of-the-Valley (Convallaria)

This lovely little member of the lily family is an old-time favorite. The nodding cream-white bells are very fragrant and a few stalks tucked into a flower arrangement will bring a pervading perfume into a room. The pips should be planted in the autumn, and when once established they spread very rapidly if conditions are favorable. They prefer a fertile soil well supplied with humus, abundant moisture, and a position in partial shade. They are one of the few flowering plants which will thrive well in really dense shade, although they do not flower as abundantly as when grown in partial shade. In time the clumps tend to become crowded and bloom becomes sparse. In order to prevent this the clumps should be lifted, divided and replanted occasionally.

Muscari (Grape Hyacinths)

Always dependable and bountiful with their bloom are the lovely little grape hyacinths. Some species flower in very early spring, others come later with the narcissi and tulips. Amazingly adaptable, they will do well in full sun or partial shade and will increase rapidly, soon forming large colonies. And they will bloom on year after year with no care or attention. For many years there was a meadow in the countryside near Philadelphia, Pennsylvania, where grape hyacinths had naturalized themselves and in spring there were thousands of them in flower, spreading their expanse of blue over an acre or more.

M. armeniacum is one of the largest species bearing flowers of a deep, cobalt-blue on sturdy stems 5 to 6 inches in height. It is one of the best for mass plantings and comes into flower with the daffodils.

M. azureum is the earliest to flower, blooming with the early species crocuses. It is a dainty, lovely little thing with flowers of a bright, azure blue.

M. botryoides caeruleum bears flowers of bright blue, coming into bloom with the late crocuses. It is more compact in growth than most of the other species and is especially well adapted to the rock garden. There is a white variety.

M. plumosum (Feather-hyacinth or Plume-hyacinth) is quite different in character from the other species. The little feathery plumes are a clear violet color and are borne on stems about 7 inches in height. It flowers in May with the tulips and remains in bloom over a long period.

Scillas

The various species of scilla are among the loveliest of the small, spring-flowering bulbs. When once established the scillas will increase rapidly and will bloom on almost indefinitely. They are particularly fine for naturalizing in a woodland area or on shady banks. They prefer partial shade but will also do well in full sun.

S. hispanica (S. campanulata in many catalogs) is commonly known as the Wood-hyacinth or Scotch Bluebell. It comes into bloom with the Darwin and Cottage tulips and is lovely in flower beds and borders or for naturalizing. Patches of them here and there in a woodland or along a wooded path are lovely in springtime. The dainty flowers are borne on stalks about 10 to 12 inches tall and are excellent for cutting. They come in several colors, deep blue, pale blue, porcelain-blue, white, pale pink and deep pink.

S. nonscripta (S. nutans) is the true English Bluebell. Taller and more robust than S. hispanica, it comes into flower a week or ten days later, with the last of the late tulips. It is particularly valuable for naturalizing and will, in time, completely cover a bank or a wooded area. The banks along Hobby Drive in the lovely little Devonshire village of Clovelly in England are carpeted with bluebells and are an enchanting sight during the month of May.

S. siberica (Squills) is the smallest of the Scilla species and the first to come into flower. The color is a very intense, bright blue and the bell-like, drooping flowers are borne on slender stems hardly more than 3 or 4 inches in height. There is also a white form, S. siberica alba. Squills are most effective when planted in masses. A sheet of blue squills beneath the newly unfolding leaves of a copper beech is a thing of breath-taking beauty. They are also effective when used to border prim garden paths in a colonial garden, or in the foreground of a planting of evergreens.

SUMMER-FLOWERING BULBS AND TUBERS

Achimenes (pronounced a-kim'e-nez)

This lovely member of the *Gesneraceae* family, to which the Saintpaulias and Gloxinias belong, is gaining very rapidly in popularity. It has long been highly prized in Europe and has been grown in a few of the old gardens of the deep South for many years, but it is only recently that it has come to be widely grown in this country. It is a dainty, charming thing, prodigal with its bloom, and adapted to many uses. It offers delightful material of distinction and charm for porch boxes and window boxes, and for hanging pots and baskets. It is colorful and gay when used in flat containers against the wall of a patio, or in small strawberry jars or decorative pots on the terrace. It is lovely on low walls along the edge of terraced beds, or at the edge of raised planting beds by the house. It may be grown under deeply rooting trees which cast high shade, and will thrive well in the foreground of shrub plantings, provided the exposure is favorable. And it may be used to grace many a window sill during the summer months.

There are numerous types and varieties of achimenes, and there is considerable variation in the size and shape of the blooms, as well as in their coloring, and also in the general habit of growth. Some types are dwarf and compact, others taller and more robust, reaching a height of 10 to 12 inches; most types are definitely trailing in habit. Some, however, may be easily trained on small stakes to upright form if desired for use on window sills. The flowers are most attractive in form. A few varieties are slipper-shaped, resembling the flower of the gloxinia, but most varieties have a curved tube, the petals opening into dainty pansy-faced or petunia-like flowers. The colors range from white through delicate mauve, violet, and pale lavender-blue to deep purple, with a few pink and scarlet types.

After the plants come into bloom they will continue to flower without cessation until the end of the season, often flowering over a period of four or five months.

Exposure: Achimenes are native to tropical America, from Mexico southward to Brazil, and they are unable to withstand cold. The very name indicates this, being derived from the Greek word *achaimenis* meaning "suffers from cold". In very mild climates they may be grown out-of-doors, remaining in the ground throughout the year. In cooler regions they should not be planted outside until all danger of sudden drops in temperature are over, as the plants are injured by a temperature below 45° F. They thrive well within a temperature range of 55° to 80° F. Locations where the plants would be exposed to high winds or to heavy rains should be avoided.

One of the most important requirements of achimenes is that of shade. It is essential that semi-shade be provided. They require plenty of light, and will not thrive in dense shade, but must be protected from midday sun. Sun in the early morning and in late afternoon, but no direct sun between 9 o'clock and 5, is a safe rule to follow. Plants will usually thrive well in the foreground of shrub plantings on the north and east sides of the house.

Soil Requirements: A coarse, loose soil mixture is ideal, and good drainage is essential. The pH is not a matter of importance, as achimenes thrive equally well in neutral or strongly acid soils. The following soil mixtures are recommended:

(1) 1 part sandy loam, 1 part sifted peat moss, 1 part leaf mold

(2) 1 part coarse sand, or fine gravel or vermiculite
1 part fibrous loam, rich in humus
1 part milled sphagnum moss, or sifted peat moss or coarse leaf mold

(3) A loose, fibrous, sandy loam, rich in humus

Propagation: Achimenes may be propagated by the division of the tuber-like rhizomes, by stem cuttings and by little axillary cones. The tubercles which form on the roots in late summer and fall vary, according to variety, from $\frac{1}{2}$ to 1 inch or more in length. Some are oval, some roundish, others long and slender. Stem cuttings should be taken just below a node and will root very readily in moist vermiculite or some similar rooting medium. During the latter part of the growing season little axillary cones, which are dark in color and covered with a waxy substance, develop in the axils of the upper leaves. These should be gathered just before they are ready to drop off the plants, and stored in vermiculite during the winter, until time for planting in the spring. They are slow to sprout but will develop into good plants.

Planting: The tubercles and the axillary cones may be planted at any time from February to late May. In mild climates they may be planted out of doors or in suitable containers in lath houses. In the north they must be started indoors.

In outdoor beds the tubercles should be spaced 3 to 4 inches apart. In pots or hanging baskets they should be spaced as follows: 1 in a 2″ pot; 2 to 5 in a 4″ pot; 3 to 7 in a 5″ pot; 5 to 6 in a 6″ hanging basket; 10 to 12 in a 12″ basket; 20 to 25 in a 16″ basket. When planting the more vigorous types or varieties use the smaller number; for the more dwarf and more delicate types use the larger number per pot or basket.

Several planting methods may be followed.

Method 1. Plant directly in the pot or basket in which they are to be grown. If a pot is used, provide at least 1 inch of good drainage material, such as broken crocks or gravel in the bottom. Add the soil to within 1½ to 2 inches of the rim. Place the tubercles in a horizontal position on the surface of the soil. Cover with ¾ to 1 inch of soil. Water *sparingly* until growth starts and maintain a temperature of 70° to 75° F. if possible. After shoots appear shift to a slightly cooler temperature and keep pots always moist but never soggy.

Method 2. If the tubercles have not started to sprout when received, growth may be hastened by placing them on milled sphagnum moss or vermiculite or screened peat moss which has been thoroughly moistened. The container should be kept in a warm place with a temperature between 75° and 90° F. until the shoots appear. They should then be planted in pots or baskets according to the procedure followed in Method No. 1.

If the plants are to be used in beds out-of-doors the tubercles may be started in flats and later transplanted.

Culture: The young plants need warmth and care in watering. The pots should be turned regularly in order that growth may be symmetrical, and when a few inches high the plants may be pinched back to make them more bushy. High humidity is desirable throughout the growing season, and abundant moisture is essential. If the plants are allowed to become completely dry when in active growth they may become prematurely dormant. Cold water will cause a spotting of the leaves. Tepid water should therefore be used and it is advisable to avoid wetting the leaves. A very fine, mist-like spray is not harmful.

THE CHARMING ACHIMENES

The size and quantity of the bloom will depend to a considerable extent upon the nutrients available to the plant. An application of a high-analysis, quickly soluble fertilizer (1 heaping teaspoonful to 1 gallon of water) every few weeks will encourage good bloom.

In the autumn when the lower leaves begin to shrivel it is a sign that the period of dormancy is approaching and water should be withheld. As soon as the stems are completely dry they should be cut off and the pots or baskets should be stored in a cool, dry place. A temperature of 60° F. is ideal. The temperature should never drop below 50° F. In the spring (from February to May) the containers may be placed in a warm temperature, given good light and watered sparingly until the shoots appear. Plants may usually be grown for two seasons in the same pot, or for three years in the same hanging basket, before being divided and re-planted.

Hanging Baskets: Achimenes are well adapted to pot culture but are at their best when grown in hanging baskets. Home-made baskets of various shapes and sizes may easily be made out of hardware cloth (¼-inch mesh wire), or wire baskets may be purchased. The baskets should be lined with a good layer of coarse sphagnum moss and then filled with the soil mixture.

A row of tubercles, with tips pointing outward, should be placed close to the edge of the basket, being spaced about 3 inches apart, and a few should be planted in the center. The tubercles should be covered with $\frac{3}{4}$ to 1 inch of soil. If very large wire baskets are used a row of tubercles may be planted near the edge when the basket is half filled with soil and others planted at the top in the manner outlined above. This method will give a charming effect.

TYPES AND VARIETIES OF MERIT

Adelaide: pale blue
Galatea: medium size, showy, blue flowers. Early
Jaureguia maxima: white
Margaritæ (Purity): white
Mauve Queen: large flowers of delicate mauve
Pink Beauty: clear pink flowers
Pulchella: small, scarlet flowers, fern-like foliage
Purple King (Royal Purple): sturdy, free blooming, of easy
   culture
Violetta: a lovely, trailing variety from Holland
Vivid: Purple with bright orange tube

Anemones (Anemone coronaria)

The anemones are delightful for cutting and may be had in a wide variety of colorings—white, deep purple, lavender, and brilliant scarlet. The cup-shaped flowers are borne on slender, graceful stems which attain a height of from 12 to 15 inches. The St. Brigid strain is considered one of the finest.

Exposure: An eastern exposure is ideal, where they may be protected from afternoon sun.

Soil Requirements: A soil mixture of 1 part loam, 1 part leaf mold and 1 part sand is considered ideal.

Propagation: Tubers. Care must be taken to see that the tubers are not planted upside down. The top of the tuber may be recognized by its fuzzy appearance. The bottom of the tuber is usually pointed.

Culture: In warm climates the tubers may be planted in the open ground from August to November. In sections where the climate is severe, anemones may be planted in coldframes or they may be grown in the greenhouse.

Tuberous Begonias

The tuberous begonias are among the most beautiful and most decorative of flowering plants. The blooms, which vary widely in form, have a sculptured quality, and the glowing colors will highlight a planting composition with great distinction.

Tuberous begonias may be grown in garden beds, in pots, and in hanging baskets. When planted in beds it is wise not to attempt to combine them with other flowers because of their specific cultural requirements. When grown in pots tuberous begonias offer exciting material for the decoration of terrace or patio, and in such a location the rare beauty of the blooms can be enjoyed to the fullest extent. On the West Coast the pendula type is used extensively in hanging pots and baskets, being hung on balconies and porches, suspended from the beams of patio roofs and arbors, or hung from the picturesque branches of live oak trees arching over patio walls. A large pot or basket with its cascade of drooping branches and its myriad blooms is a thing of breathtaking beauty, and when used in great numbers, as on a long balcony or beneath the beams of a pergola, the effect is dramatic.

Types: The tuberous begonia is often spoken of as the "mockingbird flower" because in its widely varied forms the flowers of the camellia, the rose, the carnation, the hollyhock and even the daffodil have found their counterparts.

From the various wild species discovered in the western hemisphere many beautiful forms of the tuberous begonia have been developed through hybridization and careful selection. In most types there is a wide color range—unusually beautiful shades of pink, salmon, apricot and orange; brilliant scarlets, crimsons and deep reds; pure, glistening white, and pale yellow.

The types most popular with commercial growers and with home gardeners include: the double camellia and the ruffled camellia types, the rose form, the picotee, and the carnation or fimbriata types, the pendula or hanging type, and the small, multiflowered type.

Culture: The essential cultural requirements of tuberous begonias are: partial shade, good air circulation, abundant moisture at all times, a congenial soil, and protection from heat.

Exposure: Except in the coolest of summer climates tuberous begonias require *partial* shade. The ideal type of shade is that provided by the high, arching branches of trees through which the plants receive filtered sunlight. This type of sunlight and shade is provided when begonias are grown in lath houses. In dense shade tuberous begonias do not make satisfactory growth or flower well. A northern or north-eastern exposure which receives early morning and late afternoon sun usually provides satisfactory conditions for good growth. When grown in pots or in porch or window boxes tuberous begonias will do well when they receive strong light but little or no direct sunlight.

Tuberous begonias make their best growth in moderately cool climates where there is an abundance of moisture in the atmosphere. It is because of these factors that they reach their maximum perfection in the fog-belt on the Pacific Coast, and the northern New England coast, and sometimes in high altitudes. They do not do well under conditions of intense or prolonged summer heat.

Soil Requirements: Tuberous begonias require a mellow, fibrous soil, rich in organic matter and slightly on the acid side, a pH of 6.5 being satisfactory. Good drainage

is essential. When preparing garden beds liberal quantities of coarse leaf mold should be worked into the soil and rich compost or very well rotted cow manure may be added, if available.

For soil mixtures for plants grown in pots and baskets see page 398.

Propagation: Tuberous begonias may be grown from seed, from stem cuttings and from the division of tubers. However, such methods are commonly used only by commercial growers and hybridizers. The amateur gardener usually purchases tubers or potted plants grown from tubers.

Selection of Tubers: The starting point of success in raising tuberous begonias is to obtain fine, young, healthy tubers from a reliable source. Tubers offered at bargain prices are apt to be small and from very ordinary stock, and they will seldom prove satisfactory.

The price of tubers usually depends upon the size, commercial grades varying from small tubers three-

TUBEROUS BEGONIAS

quarters of an inch in diameter to very large tubers three inches or over. The size of the tuber has a very direct influence upon the size of the plant and the size and number of the flowers. Where tuberous begonias are to be used in considerable quantity for bedding purposes tubers one inch in diameter will usually be satisfactory. For potted plants to be used as a decorative feature on the porch, terrace or patio, tubers one and a half to two inches should preferably be selected, and for blooms of top exhibition quality tubers two and a half to three inches will give the best results.

Most reliable dealers offer tubers which have been produced from seed in one year. Such tubers are young and vigorous, provided they have been well grown, whereas older tubers, although they may be large in size, have, in many cases, begun to lose some of their vitality. The exception to this rule is in the production of tubers of the pendulous or hanging type of tuberous begonia, as it requires two years to produce tubers which will give satisfactory results.

A few named varieties of tuberous begonias are offered, but are usually very expensive, and most gardeners make their selections according to the type desired, and the color preferred.

Starting the Tubers: If a long season of bloom is desired it will be necessary to start the tubers indoors, except in very mild climates. Tubers may be started at any time during the late winter and early spring months.

Old tubers which have been carried over in storage from the previous year will usually begin to sprout in February, whereas purchased tubers which have been raised from seed during the previous year will often not sprout until somewhat later. Old tubers will therefore usually produce earlier blooms.

If one does not have a greenhouse and it is necessary to start the tubers in the house it is not wise to start them too early unless one has ample window-sill space to keep them indoors after they have been shifted into pots, as it will not be safe to put them outside until all danger of frost is over.

Any type of shallow container, such as a greenhouse flat, may be used for starting the tubers. The new composition plastic flats are very satisfactory for this purpose, as they are clean, can be easily disinfected, come in a variety of shapes and sizes, are light and easy to handle and can be nested together when not in use.

Various mediums may be used in which to start the tubers. On the West Coast most commercial growers use a mixture consisting of one part fine loam, one part coarse sand and two parts oak leaf mold. Many growers have found bulb fiber and peat moss to be very satisfactory materials. The chief requirements are that the medium be fibrous and friable so that it will drain readily and not become soggy, and will cling to the roots at the time of transplanting. Sand and vermiculite would not meet this latter requirement.

The container should be filled within an inch of the top with the medium, and should be thoroughly moistened. The tubers should be spaced evenly on the surface with the concave side up. Large tubers should be spaced about five inches apart, small tubers somewhat closer. Some growers recommend having the top of the tuber level with the growing medium, but not covered by it. Other growers, and among them some of the most successful commercial growers, recommend covering the tubers lightly with the rooting medium, claiming that more buds on the tubers will produce shoots if this practice is followed.

The rooting medium should be moist, but not in the least soggy at the time of planting. It should be watered sparingly until growth starts but should always be moist.

The ideal temperature for starting tubers is within a range of 60° to 65° F., but considerable variation seems to do no harm. The flats should be placed where they will receive good light, but a minimum of direct sunlight. A window sill with either an eastern or western exposure will prove satisfactory. They should be turned frequently to prevent the young plants from leaning towards the light.

The plants may be transplanted either into pots or, if the weather permits, into garden beds when top growth has reached a height of about 4 inches. At this stage the roots are usually well developed and form a network several inches in extent.

If the begonias are to be grown as potted plants it is possible to start the tubers in the pot, but it is not considered as desirable a practice as starting them in flats, since they are not likely to make as vigorous growth.

Growing in Pots: When removed from the starting flats the plants may be transplanted into small pots, later being shifted into pots of larger size, or they may be transplanted directly into the pots in which they will continue their growth to maturity. If space is limited indoors, or in the greenhouse, the former practice may be necessary but requires more handling and labor. The pot should always be of sufficient size to permit good growth.

As tuberous begonias are shallow rooted many growers prefer the azalea-type pot which has less depth than the standard pot. For tubers from $1\frac{1}{2}$ to 2 inches in diameter an 8-inch pot is usually sufficiently large. For larger tubers 10- to 12-inch pots are best.

The potting mixture is of great importance in growing fine quality tuberous begonias. It should be rich in humus, friable and slightly on the acid side with a pH about 6.5.

POTTING MIXTURES

(1) 2 parts well rotted leaf mold	(2) 2 parts leaf mold
1 part coarse sand	1 part loam
1 part well rotted cow manure	1 part compost
1 part good loam	

Ample drainage should be placed in the bottom of the pot.

Growing the Pendula type: This is the type which is suitable for hanging pots and baskets. The flowers are considerably smaller than those of the large-flowered types but they are beautifully formed and are borne in great profusion, some plants producing more than a hundred blooms.

It requires a longer time to produce a flowering-size tuber of the pendula type than it does to produce a tuber of the large-flowered types and most commercial growers offer two-year-old tubers. Some offer three-year-old tubers.

The tubers may be started in flats or may be planted directly in the container in which they are to be grown. If started in flats they should be transplanted into the permanent pot or basket when 3 to 4 inches high.

Adequate drainage should be provided and the same potting mixture may be used as that recommended for the large-flowered types. If wire or slatted redwood baskets are used they should be lined with coarse sphagnum moss or with fresh green sphagnum, if available. About two inches of coarse sand should be placed in the bottom of the pot or basket before the soil is added. (See page 46 for complete description.)

There are several types of containers which may be used. Hanging pots and baskets are not attractive unless they are well filled with graceful, drooping branches and abundant blooms. It is therefore necessary for a tuber to produce several shoots. Very large tubers are preferable to small ones, as they will produce a greater number of shoots, the stems will be longer and the branching better. The best practice is to plant one large tuber in each container. However, several small tubers may be used if large tubers are not available. If only one or two shoots develop they should be pinched back to induce branching.

The shoots will be upright at first and will then gradually droop down over the sides of the container. They should not be staked or trained in any way, being allowed to arrange themselves naturally.

Fertilization: As the nourishment for the plant during its early stages of growth is contained within the tuber, it is wise not to apply fertilizers until growth is well started. Over-fertilization when the plants are young will often result in spindly, leggy plants with weak stems. When the plants are being grown in a good soil mixture many growers prefer to delay supplementary feedings until the flower buds begin to form. In the case of potted plants many growers begin feeding when the pot is well filled with roots.

The appearance of the plant will give some indication whether fertilization is desirable. If the leaves are dark green in color and tend to crimp downward, and if the stems are strong and vigorous it will be an indication that satisfactory growth is being made, whereas if the leaves are light green or yellowish, and tend to cup upward it is evident that the plant is suffering from lack of food and an application of fertilizer should be made. One of the safest fertilizers to use is a solution of liquid cow manure, made by soaking one pound of dried cow or sheep manure in five gallons of water. The solution should be diluted until it is the color of weak tea before it is applied. Application may be made every three weeks. Fish meal is an excellent fertilizer, and commercial fertilizers are also used.

Certain precautions should be observed in fertilizing tuberous begonias. The soil should always be thoroughly moist before an application of fertilizer is made, and care should be taken to see that the fertilizer does not come into contact with the foliage.

Over-fertilization should be avoided, as it may cause the flower buds to fall, and if fertilizers are used in great excess it will cause the death of the plant.

Watering: Tuberous begonias require an ample supply of water and the plants suffer seriously if they are allowed to become too dry. Good drainage is essential, whether the plants are grown in beds or in pots, for although abundant water is needed the soil should never become soggy. Over-watering may cause the flower buds to drop.

Disbudding: When begonias are grown in garden beds disbudding is seldom practiced. However, when they are grown in pots, and when exhibition blooms are desired, disbudding will result in larger, better developed plants and more spectacular flowers. The first flower buds should be nipped off when they are small and very immature. If early flowering is desired this practice should not be followed.

Tuberous begonias normally bear three blossoms on each flower stem. The large flower is the male blossom which produces the pollen and the two small flowers on either side, which are often single, are the female flowers which produce the seed. If blooms of maximum size are desired the female flowers should be removed in the early bud stage. When the effect of a mass of flowers is desired this is not done. In some of the newer types the female flowers are double and almost as large as the male flowers.

Wintering dormant Tubers: If given proper care tubers may be carried over from one year to another. Although tubers tend to become less vigorous with age and to loose their vitality after a number of years there are instances where tubers have flowered satisfactorily over a period of 10 to 15 years. However, in the hands of the amateur, their longevity is usually considerably less.

In the autumn when the foliage begins to turn yellow it is evident that the plants are preparing for their period of dormancy. At this time water should be gradually withheld but should not be omitted entirely. If plants have been grown in a greenhouse or indoors they should, at this time, be moved to an open shed or on to a porch. The foliage will gradually die down and drop off and it is wise to remove it from the plants before it begins to decay. At this stage water should be withheld entirely. The main stem will eventually drop off or may be carefully severed by hand. It should never be cut off at the point of junction with the tuber or forcibly broken off. If a portion remains it is wise to leave it on until it will disjoint easily during the curing process.

If the tubers have been growing in garden beds they should be dug with care and prepared for storage. If the tubers have been grown in pots some growers merely turn the pots on their sides and store them in this manner in a dry, cool place. However, the majority of growers prefer to remove the tubers from the pots after the plants have lost their foliage and become completely dormant. After the tubers have been dug from outdoor beds, or turned out of pots, the soil should be removed with care. Some growers recommend that the tubers be washed so that all soil is removed before it dries, as there is then less danger of injuring the skin of the tuber and the larger attached roots.

It is essential that the tubers be completely dry before storage. The best method is to spread them out in flats and place them in the sun. If this is not possible they may be cured in any dry, well-ventilated place. The purpose of the drying process is to permit all excess moisture to evaporate from the tubers and to obtain a completely dry, clean crown before storage. After about two weeks of drying the tubers are usually ready for storage.

During the winter months the tubers should be stored one row deep in shallow trays or flats in a cool, dry place where the temperature can be maintained between 45° to 50° F. There should be as little fluctuation in temperature as possible. The tubers may be left uncovered or may be very lightly covered with dry peat moss, vermiculite or dry sand, just enough being used to sift down between the tubers and to give the barest covering.

In late winter or very early spring the tubers should be uncovered and moved to a warm, light place so that the buds will begin to sprout and show color, preparatory to planting.

Diseases and pests: See page 671.

Caladiums

The fancy-leaved caladiums have been grown to a limited extent in some sections of the country for many years, but it is only recently that they have attained wide popularity among florists and home gardeners. The fancy-leaved caladiums are among the most decorative of foliage plants and some of the new varieties with their distinctive colorings, ranging from silvery whites, through translucent rose to brilliantly variegated reds and greens, are of exotic and exciting beauty.

In mild climates the fancy-leaved caladiums may be grown out-of-doors, and in Florida and Texas and along the Gulf Coast extensive plantings are often made in gardens and parks, and private drives are sometimes bordered with them. The foliage remains beautiful from spring until frost, and in semi-tropical climates they often retain their beauty until late December or early January.

In less favorable climates caladiums may be started indoors and grown on in pots until the weather is warm enough to transfer them to the garden. They may then be shifted from the pots to the garden bed or the pots may be sunk directly in the ground. Pots of fancy-leaved caladiums are very decorative when grouped in a shady corner of a terrace or when placed on a low, shady ledge by a fountain. They may also be used effectively as a foreground planting in shrubbery borders, provided they are not exposed to too much sun.

As house plants caladiums may be used effectively in many ways and add a touch of dramatic beauty to the decor. They thrive best in low light intensity and may therefore be grown in windows where they receive little or no sun. They are also of great decorative value in room dividers and niches when they can be grown under artificial light (see page 465).

Exposure: The natural habitat of the caladium is the tropical forest region of South America. They therefore thrive under conditions of great heat and prefer a temperature which ranges well into the nineties. In areas where the summer temperature ranges around 70° F. or lower caladiums do not make satisfactory growth.

The caladiums require a semi-shaded location. If the shade is too dense it will prevent a full coloration of the leaves, and in full sun the leaves of some of the more delicate and most beautiful varieties tend to burn.

Planting: When grown out-of-doors the dormant tubers should be planted when all danger of frost is over. The tubers should be planted about 2 inches deep and they should be spaced from 8 to 10 inches apart. Good drainage is essential, as the tubers will rot in water-logged soil or in soil that is cold and soggy.

In regions where the climate is not mild enough to plant caladiums in the garden they may be started indoors in pots or in flats, being shifted to pots after the leaves begin to develop. One tuber can be started in a 4-inch pot or several tubers in a larger pot. A deep greenhouse flat with an inch or so of sand on the bottom, covered with a deep layer of milled sphagnum moss, makes an excellent medium for starting the tubers. The tubers should be started in a temperature ranging between 80° and 85° F. In the house such conditions can best be obtained by placing the pots or flats on a piece of tin or on a board directly over a hot-water radiator. The tubers should be watered sparingly but should never be allowed to dry out. When good root growth has been made and the first leaves reach a height of 4 to 8 inches the tubers, if being grown in flats, should be carefully shifted into 6- or 8-inch pots.

Soil: The soil for fancy-leaved caladiums should be rich in humus and well drained, slightly on the acid side, the optimum pH being from 6.2 to 6.5. High fertility is essential, as caladiums do not do well in poor soil. When the tubers are to be planted in garden beds the soil should be well prepared. If obtainable, well rotted cow manure should be forked into the bed. As a substitute compost or leaf mold may be used.

When the tubers are grown in pots the following mixtures are recommended:

(1)	25% rotted cow manure	(2)	1 part leaf mold
	20% peat moss		1 part rotted cow manure
	20% sand		1 part good garden loam
	35% good garden loam		

The pots should be kept in the greenhouse or indoors on a window sill until all danger of frost is over and the weather is warm and settled. They should never be allowed to dry out and liberal feeding with a good soluble fertilizer is desirable.

In the autumn when the foliage begins to droop, water sparingly until the leaves are dry and slough off. During the winter the pots should be stored in a dry, warm place where the temperature ranges around 70° F.

If the tubers are removed from the pots, or are lifted from garden beds after the foliage has ripened, they should be spread out on shallow trays or flats and kept in a dry warm place.

Cannas

In Victorian days cannas were so over-used for mass plantings and the colors were so garish that they gradually lost favor and for years were relegated to formal beds around railway stations or to dreary city parks. Within the past few decades, however, new strains and hybrids have been developed which may be obtained in glowing shades of apricot, coral, watermelon-

FANCY-LEAVED CALADIUMS

pink and other dramatic colors. There are both dwarf forms and tall-growing varieties, such as the Grand Opera Series. The giant forms make excellent accents for the rear of wide perennial borders, and the dwarf forms may be used effectively in the foreground of shrubbery borders and in large tubs as part of the decor on terrace or patio.

Climatic Range: As cannas are native to the tropic and sub-tropic regions they should not be planted in the North until all danger of frost is over.

Soil Requirements: A fertile, moist, well-prepared soil will provide ideal conditions for good growth.

Culture: Old roots should be divided in the spring with a sharp knife, allowing a bud to each piece. Set 12 to 24 inches apart and from 3 to 5 inches deep. Lift in the fall when the tops have been killed by frost and store like dahlias. For pests and diseases, see page 637.

VARIETIES OF MERIT

DWARF	GIANT
Pfitzer's Chinese Coral	Salmon Beauty
Pfitzer's Shell Pink	La Boheme
	Mme Butterfly

Dahlias

There are few flowers which offer us such variety in form and coloring as do the dahlias. All the glorious, translucent tones of a sunset sky, all the warm rosy hues of a summer's dawn are to be found among them, and they bring a richness and a glory to the late summer garden that nothing else can equal. The tall-growing varieties may be used very delightfully at the rear of the herbaceous border, the dwarf sorts are more suitable for bedding purposes, and all types and varieties are invaluable for the cutting garden.

Classification

Dahlias are grouped into several distinct classes according to the form and size of the flower. The classification adopted by the American Dahlia Society is as follows:

Class 1, *Incurved Cactus.* Fully double flower with the margins of the majority of the floral rays revolute (rolled or quilled) for one-half or more of their length; the floral rays tending to curve toward the center of the flower.

Class 2, *Recurved and Straight Cactus.* Fully double flowers with the margins of the majority of the floral rays revolute for one-half of their length or more; the floral rays being recurved or straight.

Class 3, *Peony.* Open-centered flowers with not more than three rows of ray florets regardless of form or number of florets, with the addition of smaller curled or twisted floral rays around the disk.

Class 4, *Semi-Cactus.* Fully double flowers with the margins of the majority of the floral rays revolute for less than one-half their length.

Class 5, *Formal Decorative.* Fully double flowers, rays generally broad, either pointed or rounded at tips, with outer floral rays tending to recurve and central floral rays tending to be cupped, all floral rays in somewhat regular arrangement.

Class 6, *Informal Decorative.* Fully double flowers, floral rays generally long, twisted or pointed and usually irregular in arrangement.

Class 7, *Ball.* Fully double flowers, ball-shaped or slightly flattened, floral rays in spiral arrangement, blunt or rounded at tips and quilled or with markedly involute margins; 2 inches or more in diameter.

Class 8, *Anemone.* Open-centered flowers with only one row of ray florets regardless of form or number of florets, with the tubular disk florets elongated, forming a pin-cushion effect.

VARIETIES OF MERIT

FORMAL DECORATIVE

Bride's Bouquet	Darcy Sainbury	Supreme Command
Clariam Luray	Golden Treasure	Victory
Class	Jersey's Beauty	Virginia B. Taggert

INFORMAL DECORATIVE

Cherokee Brave		Ogden Reid
Dr. John F. Morse		White Winner

CACTUS

Clariam Royalty	Jaune LaBelle	Lady Alice
Connie Casey	Jersey's Dainty	Mme. Elizabeth Sawyer

SEMI-CACTUS

Capitol City	Flaming Sunset	Nay Aug
Clariam Forever	Lynn Fontanne	Prairie Fire

INCURVED CACTUS

Allways	Bertha Shone	Oakleigh Champion

POMPON

Betty Ann	Rothout	Sherry
Bronze Beauty	Morning Mist	Yellow Gem

MINIATURE

Andrea's Orange	Dusky	Lilly Bell
Bishop of Llandaff	Fuchsia Gem	Princess Royal

Class 9, *Single*. Open-centered flowers, with only one row of ray florets regardless of form or number of florets.

Class 10, *Duplex*. Open-centered flowers, with only two rows of ray florets regardless of form or number of florets.

Class 11, *Pompon*. Fully double flowers, ball-shaped or slightly flattened, floral rays in spiral arrangement, blunt or rounded and quilled or with markedly involute margins; less than 2 inches in diameter.

Class 12, *Collarette*. Open-centered flowers with only one row of ray florets, with the addition of one or more rows of petal lids, usually of a different color, forming a collar around the disk.

Class 13, *Miniature Decorative*. All dahlias which normally produce flowers that do not exceed 3 inches in diameter, pompons excluded, to be classified according to the foregoing definitions.

Climatic Range and Exposure: Although dahlias are natives of the mountainous sections of Mexico and thrive luxuriantly in the hot, high, dry climate of that region, they are remarkably adaptable and may be grown in almost every section of America. They prefer an exposure in full sun. If grown in a shady location the plants have a tendency to become spindly and the blooms are poor in quality.

Propagation: By division of the tubers, by cuttings, by seed.

(1) *By Tubers.* Dahlia tubers are produced in clumps which are attached very firmly to the parent stems. If the entire clump is planted the results are unsatisfactory, as a mass of thin, weak stems will be produced and the flowers will be poor in quality. The tubers should, therefore, be divided, previous to planting. Dahlias seldom produce buds on the tuber itself, the buds being found only at the neck of the tuber. When dividing the tubers it is essential to include the neck, which will usually produce from one to three buds. Many gardeners find it an advantage to cover the clumps with damp earth, moist peat moss, or sand, and to place them in a warm temperature for a week or ten days previous to planting. Under these favorable conditions the buds or eyes will start into growth and when the tubers are divided those may be selected for planting which have strong, well-developed buds. The clumps should not be kept under these conditions for too long a period as the actual sprouts will begin to develop, which will necessitate very careful handling at planting time.

(2) *By Cuttings.* If a rapid increase of stock is desired cuttings may be taken from the sprouted shoots produced by the tubers. Where this method is to be followed, the tubers should be started into growth during February or March. They may be planted in flats in the greenhouse, being given ample light, heat, and moisture in order to induce quick growth. When the shoots have formed two sets of leaves, cuttings may be taken. A clean, sharp cut should be made just below the first set of leaves. These lower leaves should then be carefully cut from the stem and the cutting should be inserted in the propagating case. If conditions are favorable, dahlia cuttings root very readily, and as soon as roots have developed, the cuttings may be potted up in small 2½- or 3-inch pots, a mixture of 2 parts loam, 1 part sand, and 1 part leaf mold being used. If the cuttings make rapid growth and transplanting seems advisable, they may be shifted on to larger pots before they are planted in the open. When planted in the garden, they should be set from 1 to 2 inches deeper than they were when growing in the pot.

(3) *By Seed.* Dahlias do not come true from seed. New varieties are always produced by seed, and some of the small bedding types are frequently grown from seed. A few seed firms offer these bedding types in separate colors, but most of such seed comes in mixed packets and the flowers vary greatly. The seed may be sown under glass early in the season or it may be sown in the coldframe later in the spring. The young seedlings may be transplanted into small pots when the second pair of leaves has developed, and they may be set in the open ground after all danger of frost is over.

Soil Requirements: Dahlias have very definite soil preferences. They thrive best on a sandy loam with a gravelly sub-soil and they require a soil which is abundantly supplied with organic matter. It is unwise to attempt to grow dahlias on a heavy, clay soil which is poorly drained, as they will make but little growth and will produce blooms of an inferior quality. The texture of a heavy soil may be greatly improved by the addition of liberal quantities of well-rotted manure, rich compost, and sand, or through the use of a good soil conditioner (see page 170). If the natural drainage is exceedingly poor the entire area upon which the dahlias are to be grown may be underdrained by a tile drain, or the soil where each individual tuber is to be planted may be excavated to a depth of 15 inches and 3 inches of coarse cinders, gravel or some form of rubble may be placed in the bottom.

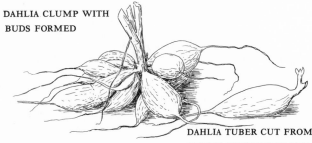

DAHLIA CLUMP WITH
BUDS FORMED

DAHLIA TUBER CUT FROM
CLUMP TO INCLUDE BUD

Dahlias are notoriously heavy feeders and if blooms of superior quality are desired, the plants must have an abundant and well-balanced supply of nutrients throughout the season. An excess of nitrogen should be avoided as it encourages too rank a growth of leaves which are produced at the expense of flower buds. Phosphorus and potash may be supplied in more liberal quantities as they are the nutrients most needed. Unless the soil is naturally fertile and is well supplied with humus and with the necessary nutrients, it is well to prepare it thoroughly, previous to the planting of the tubers. The exact location where each tuber is to be planted may be marked off by a stake and the soil may be excavated to a depth of 8 inches. The soil below this depth should be loosened with a spading fork and a shovelful of humus, rich compost or well-rotted manure may be worked into it. The top-soil which was removed should be enriched with a similar amount of humus, and the hole should be refilled until the soil is within 6 inches of the surface.

Planting Tubers: As dahlias are very sensitive to frost, the tubers should not be planted until the ground is warm and mellow and there is no danger of a sudden drop in temperature. In the vicinity of New York, dahlias are usually planted between the middle of May and the middle of June. Little is to be gained from very early planting as the tubers make but slow, unhealthy growth if the soil remains cold and wet. The stakes which are to provide future support for the plants should be driven into the ground at the time the tubers are planted. If this operation is delayed until the plants have made growth enough to actually require staking the tubers may be seriously injured. Dahlias of the large type require ample space for their best development, and they should be planted at least 3 feet apart in the rows, the rows being spaced from $3\frac{1}{2}$ to 4 feet apart. The dwarf types require less space, but as they are inclined to be somewhat bushy in habit of growth, they should be allowed a minimum of 15 to 18 inches each way. After the ground has been prepared in accordance with the directions given under the section on *Soil Requirements*, and the stakes have been driven into the ground, the tubers may be planted. The excavation should be approximately 6 inches in depth. The tuber should be placed on the prepared bed, the buds or shoots pointing upward, and it should be covered with 2 inches of earth. It is well to have the neck of the tuber from which the shoots arise near the point where the stake was driven. As the shoots develop, the soil may be filled in about the plant, until the surface of the ground is level. The tuber should be approximately 6 inches below the surface.

Culture: If the finest quality of bloom is desired, only one stalk should be allowed to develop from each tuber. If several shoots have developed the strongest should be selected and the remaining shoots should be dis-

carded. When the main stalk has reached a height of about 1 foot and has formed two or three pairs of leaves, the tiny growing tip may be nipped out. Care must be taken not to cut the stalk back too severely, as the hollow stem will have difficulty in healing—just the growing tip should be removed. From four to six strong, vigorous stalks will then develop.

If exhibition blooms are to be produced, disbudding is advisable. The lateral or side buds on each terminal branch should be pinched out in order that the middle bud may have every chance to produce a flower of perfect size and substance. The two series of buds below the terminal buds should also be pinched out in order to increase the length of the stem. If the flowers are desired for cutting, severe disbudding is not usually practiced.

Frequent, shallow cultivations are advisable until the middle of July. At this time cultivations should cease, an application of fertilizer should be made and a good mulch should be applied. A fertilizer mixture consisting of 1 part bone meal, 1 part pulverized manure and 1 part commercial fertilizer (a 2-10-6 or a 4-8-6) may be applied at the rate of 3 handfuls per plant, being broadcast over the surface of the soil about 6 inches away from the base of the plant. The fertilizer should be watered in thoroughly and a good mulch 2 to 3 inches in depth should be applied. (See Chapter XXXIV on Mulches.)

At no time during the growing season should dahlias be allowed to suffer from lack of moisture. A thorough soaking once a week should be sufficient. A soil soaker is excellent for this purpose.

One of the most important factors in the culture of dahlias is to keep the plants in vigorous, continuous growth. If growth is seriously checked at any time due to lack of sufficient moisture or lack of nutrients the stems tend to become hard and woody, the plants remain stunted, and produce poor bloom.

As the plants grow, the stems should be securely fastened to the stakes. Dahlia stems are hollow and pithy and they are easily broken by heavy winds.

Autumn Care: Being extremely sensitive to cold, the plants will be killed with the first heavy frost. The stalks should then be cut off to within 6 inches of the surface of the ground and the tubers should be left in the ground for a week or ten days to become thoroughly ripened. They should then be dug and prepared for storage. A spading fork should be thrust into the ground beside the tubers, and they should be pried loose from the soil with the greatest of care in order that no injury to the tubers may occur. The clump of tubers should be turned upside down in order that any sap or moisture may drain from the stalk and should be exposed to full sunlight for several hours until thoroughly dry.

During the winter dahlia tubers should be stored in a dry, frost-proof place where the temperature ranges between 45° and 55° F. One of the best methods of storing dahlias is to dip the tubers in Wilt-Pruf, using 1 of Wilt-Pruf to 4 parts of water. Allow the tubers to dry and then store them in dry peat moss. This method prevents the loss of moisture and the tubers come through the storage period in excellent condition.

Insect pests and diseases: See Chapter XLI.

Eremurus (Foxtail Lily) (Desert Candle)

Coming to us from the deserts of Persia, the Himalayas and Turkestan, the giant blooms of the Eremurus are dramatic when planted against a background of deep green, where they can be viewed from a distance. They are, however, ill suited to planting in a small garden as they are entirely out of scale. The flower spikes often attain a height of 8 feet or more, the individual, bell-shaped flowers being closely set upon the stalk. The plants flower during June and July and vary in color from cream white through yellow, rose and pink.

SPECIES AND HYBRID VARIETIES

SPECIES	HYBRIDS
Altaicus—yellow, very hardy	Isabellinus—apricot-rose
Bungei—citron yellow	Shelford—pastel shades
Himalaicus—pure white	Rosalind—pink
Robustus—rosy pink	Isobel—coppery orange

Exposure: A sunny and somewhat sheltered position is desirable. The roots are not particularly hardy and in the latitude of New York and northward, the crowns should be protected with a heavy mulch of straw. An inverted box filled with straw affords an excellent means of protection.

Soil Requirements: The Eremurus prefers a rich, moist, but well-drained soil.

Planting: The fleshy roots of the Eremurus should be planted in the autumn. A hole of ample size should be dug in order that the roots may be spread out in a natural position and the plants should be entirely surrounded with sand. The crown of the plant should be only just beneath the surface of the soil. As the roots are very brittle they must be handled with great care. The plants should be spaced from 18 inches to 2 feet apart.

Culture: As growth begins very early in the spring, the winter mulch should be removed as soon as weather conditions permit. The young growth is very subject to injury from frost and during any cold spells which occur after the mulch has been removed, the plants should be protected by a burlap covering or an inverted receptacle of some kind. During the growing season the plants require an abundance of moisture. After flowering the leaves disappear entirely and during this period of dormancy practically no water is required. After the plants are once established, they will thrive for many years, if conditions are favorable. Large plants do not transplant easily and they should be left undisturbed. When the Eremurus is grown in the flower border, great care must be taken not to injure the roots when cultivating after the leaf growth has died down.

Propagation: Eremurus may be propagated either by the division of the root clumps or by seed, the latter process being exceedingly slow and seldom practiced.

Galtonia candicans (Summer Hyacinth)

The creamy white, bell-shaped flowers of the Galtonia, which is a native of Africa, are decorative and lovely either in the perennial border or against a background of deep green shrubbery. The flowers come into bloom in late August and frequently continue until cut down by frost. The flower stalks usually attain a height of 18 inches, sometimes growing as tall as 3 feet, and the flowers hang suspended from the tall, leafless stems.

Exposure: Full sun.

Soil Requirements: A deep, rich garden loam.

Culture: The bulbs may be planted in the spring at a depth of approximately 6 inches, and they should be spaced from 8 to 12 inches apart. The bulbs are not hardy in the latitude of New York and should be lifted in the autumn and stored in a frost-proof place. As the old bulbs frequently fail to bloom a second season, it is wise to replenish one's stock.

Propagation: Galtonias may be grown very easily from seed as well as from bulbs. It requires two years to produce flowering bulbs from seed and during the winter the small bulblets must be lifted and stored.

Gladiolus

Gladioli are amazing in their adaptability, and because they demand so little in the way of care and cultivation and give so generously of their bloom and beauty they are looked upon as one of our most useful flowers. They are invaluable for cutting and may be had in bloom during every month of the year; and they are equally prized for their decorative value in the garden. They may be planted in great drifts through the garden beds and borders, becoming the dominant note in the planting composition from midsummer on; or they may be used in an incidental way to fill in an occasional gap here and there.

VARIETIES OF MERIT

LARGE-FLOWERED TYPE

Apple blossom	Picardy
Dirk Bouts	Purple Burma
Elizabeth the Queen	Red Wings
Elsie Poulsen	Royal Stewart
Golden Arrow	Vagabond Prince
Lorelei	White Goddess

MINIATURES

Atom	Golden Trills
Bopeep	Loveliness
Burnt Orange	Lullaby
Dolores	Peter Pan
Fairy	Starlet
Fifth Avenue	Wedgwood
Flicker	Zona

Climatic Range: There are few flowers that have a wider climatic range than do the gladioli, for they may be grown in every section of America. During the winter months one sees them blooming in gay profusion in Southern Florida and in California, and during the summer one finds them in the little dooryard gardens of some remote Canadian village.

Soil Requirements: Gladioli will thrive well on almost any soil of medium fertility. On soils of a slightly heavy texture the flowers are of a superior quality but only a comparatively small number of cormlets are formed. On a light, sandy-loam soil, the flowers are not quite as fine but a large number of cormlets are produced.

Gladioli are moderately acid tolerant and prefer a soil with a pH of approximately 6.0. If the soil is extremely acid the condition should be remedied with an application of lime the autumn previous to planting. Gladioli will not thrive well in a soil with a reaction of more than pH 7.0, and if the alkalinity runs as high as pH 7.5, the growth will be decidedly inferior. See Chapter XVI, page 170.

Superphosphate has proved to be the most effective fertilizer for gladioli as it will increase production and will produce earlier and better bloom. It should be applied in the furrow at the rate of 5 pounds to every 100 feet of row. The fertilizer, which is best applied in the form of 16 percent superphosphate, should be covered lightly with soil before the corms are planted in the furrow. A complete fertilizer such as a 4-12-4 may be used instead of the superphosphate, but nitrogenous and potassic fertilizers should never be used unless they are liberally supplemented by phosphorus, as the results are definitely detrimental and growth will be seriously checked.

Planting: Gladioli may be planted at any time after danger of frost is over and the soil has become warm and mellow. In order to provide for a succession of bloom, they may be planted at intervals of every 2 weeks until midsummer. The corms come into flower from 8 to 10 weeks after planting. Gladioli corms are graded according to size. The blooming sizes are Nos. 1, 2, and 3. No. 4 will sometimes bloom. The smaller sizes are considerably less expensive than the No. 1 grade, and will give equally good results. If grown in rows in the cutting garden, the corms may be planted 4 inches apart in rows 18 inches apart. In garden beds and borders the corms should be spaced about 6 inches apart. The depth of planting will vary somewhat according to the texture of the soil. In light, sandy soil, the corms may be planted 6 inches deep; in heavy, clay soil a depth of 4 inches is preferable. If the corms are planted as deeply as possible, the stalks will be held more firmly in position and less staking will be required.

Culture: Gladioli require no special care. They thrive best in a sunny location, require a moderate amount of moisture, respond to a reasonable amount of cultivation. They will reward one generously for the small amount of time which must be spent upon them.

When gladioli are to be used for decorative purposes in the house, they should be cut as soon as one or two of the blossoms have opened, as the remaining buds will open after the spikes have been placed in water. When cutting gladioli, it is very important to leave two or three of the broadest leaves at the base of the stalk. If all of the foliage is cut away the development of the new corm and the cormlets will be seriously injured. All flower stalks should be cut as soon as the flowers have faded, as the development of the seed pods also affects the vitality of the corm.

Winter Care: As soon as the foliage has turned yellow, which usually occurs about 6 weeks after the period of bloom is over, the corms are ready to be dug. The leaf stalks should be cut off within about 2 inches of the ground. The corms should then be lifted carefully with a spading fork or spade, care being taken to scatter as few of the small cormlets as possible. The corms should be placed in flats and stored in an airy, frost-proof shed for several weeks in order that they become thoroughly mature. If, as sometimes happens in the case of late-planted corms, the foliage has failed to ripen before mid-autumn, the leaf stalks may be allowed to remain on the plant when the corms are dug.

After the period of ripening is over, the leaf stalks should be cut off and the corms should be prepared for winter storage. The old mother corm which was planted in the spring and the roots should be removed from the new corm and the little cormlets should be separated. The corms may be placed on shallow trays and should be stored in a cool, well-ventilated cellar. The temperature should range between 40° and 45° F. and the air should have a humidity of approximately 80 percent. If the trays are piled one upon another, a free circulation of air must be provided.

Propagation: Gladioli are propagated by means of the small cormlets which are produced at the base of the corm. These may be separated from the corm at the time of harvest, and they may be stored in paper bags during the winter. In the spring they may be planted in shallow furrows, being lifted in the autumn and stored during the winter. The cormlets will produce flowering-size corms the second or third year.

Insect Pests and Diseases: See Chapter XLI.

Ismene (Hymenocallis calathina)

The funnel-shaped white flowers of the Ismene, with their fringed crown and long, thread-like stamens, are unique in form, and they add a note of interest to a planting composition. The flowers are borne at the top of a stout, leafless stem which often attains a height of 15 inches or more.

Exposure: Full sun.

Soil Requirements: Any ordinary garden soil.

Propagation: By offsets.

Culture: The bulbs should be planted in spring at a depth of approximately 3 inches, being spaced from 8 to 10 inches apart. In the early autumn the bulbs should be lifted, and they should be stored during the winter in a cool, dry, frost-proof place.

Kniphofia (Tritoma) (Red-hot Poker Plant)

The decorative value of the Kniphofia is appreciated by the florist and the gardener alike. The brilliant flowers of red and yellow hue are borne on stout, fleshy stems above the sword-shaped leaves and are unique in form and striking in appearance. The dwarf types reaching a height of 18 to 24 inches are of more value as cut flowers in the home than are the larger types, and they combine well

with Asclepias tuberosa and the tawny Daylily, Hemerocallis fulva.

Exposure: A sheltered, sunny location.

Soil: A loose, well-drained soil of moderate fertility is considered ideal. A soil which is too rich causes an over-rampant growth.

Propagation: By seed, by the division of the rhizomes, and by offsets. If the seed is sown under glass in January or February, flowering plants may be produced the same season.

Culture: The rhizomes may be planted in the spring after all danger of frost is over, being set from 9 to 12 inches apart. In the North the rhizomes should be dug up in the autumn and stored in dry earth in a cool but frost-proof place.

Tigridia (Tiger Flower) (Mexican Shellflower)

The brilliant blooms of the Tigridia, a native of Mexico, Central and South America, are unique in form and coloring and although the individual flowers last only for a day, the blooms are produced in succession over a period of nearly two months.

VARIETIES OF MERIT

SPOTTED VARIETIES

Alba grandiflora: white with brilliant carmine spots
Canariense: yellow with purplish spots
Lilacea: deep crimson-rose with red spots
Melissa Joan: brilliant scarlet with crimson spots
Mary Gray: apricot-orange with crimson spots

SPOTLESS VARIETIES

Giant rosea: clear, deep rose   Lutea: pure yellow
Giant scarlet: rosy scarlet

Exposure: Full sun.

Soil Requirements: A light, rich garden loam.

Culture: Tigridias require a warm temperature and abundant moisture during the growing season. The bulbs should be planted in early spring about 2 inches deep, being spaced from 6 to 8 inches apart. In warm regions where there are no heavy frosts the bulbs may be left undisturbed for many years, and they will give generous bloom each season. Where the climate is severe the bulbs should be dug before the ground freezes. It is essential that the bulbs be stored in a cool, airy, dry, frost-proof place. One of the most satisfactory methods of handling them is to tie the dried leaves and stems into small bundles and to hang them up in a cool, dry room. Care must be taken to see that mice cannot reach them. If the top growth is cut off the bulbs may be stored in wire trays. The bulbs are very sensitive to dampness and if they are not kept properly dry, they will decay.

Propagation: Tigridias may be grown very readily from seed, as well as from bulbs. If the seed is sown early in the season about 20 percent of the plants will bloom the first year.

Tritonia (Montbretia)

The brilliant, colorful flowers of the Montbretias, natives of South Africa, are among the most beautiful and most decorative of all the summer-flowering bulbs. The flowers are borne on tall, graceful spikes varying in height from 2 to 4 feet, and they are lovely for cutting, as they last extremely well, often remaining fresh for two weeks or more. Some of the recently introduced varieties of the Earlham Strain are of striking beauty with their wide, flaring flowers in lovely tones of orange and apricot.

VARIETIES OF MERIT

His Majesty: deep scarlet, shading to gold
Lady Gwenn: brilliant orange-scarlet
Lady Oxford: apricot overlaid with salmon-rose
Lemon Queen: buds deep orange, flowers cream-yellow
Marjorie: orange-yellow with crimson center
Peter: rich apricot
Pocahontas: coppery scarlet with golden luster
Una: rich apricot with carmine blotch

Exposure: Full sun.

Soil Requirements: Montbretias prefer a rather sandy soil well supplied with rotted manure or some other form of humus.

Planting: In sections of the country where the climate is mild, Montbretias may be planted in the autumn. In sections where the temperature is apt to drop much below 20 degrees above zero it is wise to plant the corms in the spring. The depth of planting is approximately 4 inches and the corms may be spaced from 5 to 6 inches apart.

Culture: Montbretias require an abundance of moisture during the growing and flowering season. After the flowering season is over the foliage will ripen more quickly if moisture is reduced to a minimum. After the first frost, the corms may be lifted and stored for the winter in the same manner as are gladiolus corms.

Bulbous Irises

Exquisite in form, varied and lovely in coloring, the bulbous irises are unexcelled as cut flowers and their decorative value in the garden is coming to be more and more appreciated. The erroneous and widespread impression that these lovely bulbous irises are not hardy has meant that they have been used to only a very limited extent for outdoor planting, and it is indeed unfortunate that many of them are known to us only as cut flowers which have been grown in the greenhouse during the winter months.

After a series of extensive trials at the Massachusetts Agricultural Experiment Station, it has been conclusively proven that the bulbous irises are quite as hardy as tulips, that they are able to withstand sub-zero temperatures with no ill effects, and that they are practically never injured by the most extreme cold.

There are several species and types of bulbous iris belonging to the same botanical sub-genus, Xiphium. Those which are considered the most desirable for garden plantings and for cut flowers are the Spanish Iris, the English Iris, the Dutch Iris, and Iris tingitana.

Spanish Iris (Iris Xiphium). The leaves are narrow and grass-like, about 1 foot in height. The flowers are predominantly blue but vary somewhat in color, and they may be readily distinguished by the characteristic yellow blotch on the falls. Period of flowering, late May and early June.

VARIETIES OF MERIT

Blanche Fleur	Canary Yellow
Bronze Queen	Prince Henry
Cajanus	Queen Emma

English Iris (Iris xiphioides). The foliage is more abundant than that of the Spanish Iris, and the leaves are somewhat larger. The flowers are produced in various colors, blue predominating, and they are large and showy. The flowering period is slightly later than that of the Spanish Iris.

VARIETIES OF MERIT

Bleu Amable	Grand Vainqueur
Bleu Celeste	Mont Blanc
Duke of Clarence	Prince of Wales
Emperor	Royal Blue
Grand Lilas	Sunset

Dutch Iris. Most of the varieties listed in the catalogs as Dutch Iris are hybrids which have been originated by crossing I. tingitana with I. Xiphium, I. Boissieri and other species. In general character, they resemble the Spanish Iris, the foliage being somewhat broader and more abundant and the plants more vigorous in their habit of growth, flowering a few days earlier.

VARIETIES OF MERIT

A. Bloemaard	Early Snow
Abraham Storck	Hart Nibbrig
Anton Mauve	Hobbema
Dirk Daleus	Indian Chief

Iris tingitana. In this group we find the exquisite variety known as Wedgwood which is so familiar as a cut flower during the winter months. It is unexcelled for forcing and is equally lovely in the garden, being fully as hardy as the other bulbous irises. Another meritorious variety is The First.

Exposure: A position in full sun is essential in order that the foliage may become fully ripe after the flowering season is over.

Soil Requirements: A moderately fertile, well-drained soil is desirable, a light, sandy loam being considered ideal. The bulbs are decidedly indifferent to the reaction of the soil and will thrive equally well in slightly acid, neutral, or mildly alkaline soils.

Planting: Shipment of bulbs is usually made in late September or early October. The bulbs should be planted immediately, being spaced from 6 to 8 inches apart and at a depth of 4–5 inches. As the bulbous irises are apparently considered a great delicacy by field mice, some protection should be given if they are planted in an area where rodents are troublesome. (See Chapter XLI, page 673).

Culture: Active growth begins soon after the bulbs are planted and most varieties will send up several green, spear-like shoots during the autumn. After the flowering period is over in late June the foliage should be allowed to ripen and it is essential that it be exposed to full sun during this period. After the leaves have become brown, the bulbs may be lifted. They should be placed on shallow trays, covered with dry sand, and stored in the hottest attic available, where conditions will approximate as nearly as possible the conditions found in their native habitat. If the bulbs are not lifted, being left undisturbed after the foliage has died down, some few varieties will persist for several years while others will fail to reappear after the first season of bloom. If the flowers are used for cutting it is necessary to reduce the foliage to such an extent that the vigor and vitality of the bulb are seriously impaired, and new bulbs should be planted the following year.

Winter Protection: Little winter protection is required. Salt hay may be used, or small evergreen boughs, placed over the areas where the bulbs have been planted, will be sufficient.

Iris reticulata. This lovely species iris is often in bloom with the Snowdrops and the Crocus, and it may be used very delightfully in the rock garden or in some sheltered spot in the flower garden. The blooms resemble those of the Spanish and Dutch Iris in miniature, the plants being of a decidedly dwarf habit, seldom reaching a height of more than a few inches. The flowers are a rich pansy-violet in color and have the delightful fragrance of violets.

Exposure: A somewhat protected position with a sunny exposure is desirable.

Soil Requirements: A moderately fertile, and very well drained, neutral or slightly alkaline soil is considered ideal.

Planting: The bulbs should be planted in the autumn, in late September or October, being spaced from 4 to 6 inches apart. When once established, the bulbs will continue to bloom year after year and under favorable conditions will increase rapidly. In exposed situations light winter protection should be given.

AUTUMN-FLOWERING BULBS

Colchicum (Meadow Saffron)

The crocus-like blooms of the colchicums are dainty and appealing, and bring a shy, bright touch to the autumn landscape. They come into flower in September and October and as they bloom on naked stems with no foliage at this season they are at their best when planted among vinca (periwinkle or myrtle) or some other low ground cover. They are charming in the foreground of a shrubbery border or along the outer fringe of a woodland or in the rock garden. A small patch near the terrace or the entrance will lend added interest to the planting.

Culture: The corms are usually shipped in August and should be planted immediately upon arrival. If they are held even for a few days the flowers may begin to appear. They should be planted at a depth of three to four inches. Colchicums bloom a few weeks after planting but the foliage does not appear until the following spring. It is very important that the foliage be allowed to mature and die down naturally.

VARIETIES OF MERIT

C. autumnale: lilac-rose
C. autumnale album: white
Giganteum: soft violet
Speciosum
    Autumn Queen: rose-purple
    The Giant: lilac

Crocus

Autumn-flowering Species. There are a number of delightful species crocus which flower during the autumn months, the early ones blooming in September and others carrying the period of bloom through October and November. The flowers are piquant and dainty, and when once established they will bloom year after year. They are lovely when planted along the edge of a shrub border or in little patches at the base of trees or near the terrace.

Culture: The corms should be planted as soon as they have been received, being planted at a depth of 2 to 4 inches. Loving full sun, they will also adapt themselves quite happily to light shade, and they prefer a rather light, sandy soil.

SPECIES OF MERIT

C. lævigatus: white, late   C. speciosus albus: white
C. medius: deep lilac   C. Zonatus: pale lilac
C. speciosus: bright blue

Lycoris squamigera (Amaryllis Halli)

This interesting flower is often called the Hardy Amaryllis or Magic-lily. The lily-like pink flowers, with a tint of lavender, are borne

BULB PLANTING CHART

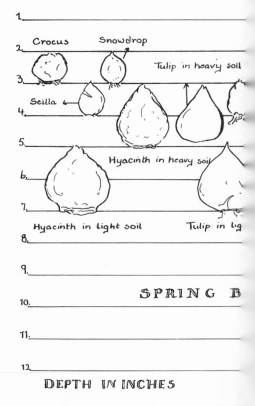

DEPTH IN INCHES

on three-foot stalks in clusters of six to nine, and are delicately fragrant. They flower during August and September and are lovely when planted among ferns or in the foreground of a shrubbery border.

Culture: Lycoris prefers a position in partial shade and a fertile soil, well supplied with humus. The bulbs should be planted in August as soon as they arrive, at a depth of 5 inches. The following spring large, strap-like leaves will appear. They make remarkably rapid growth and after reaching their full height of about $2\frac{1}{2}$ feet they begin to mature, turn brown, and disappear entirely. In August the naked flower stalks emerge and within a week or two will reach full height and come into bloom. The bulbs will live on almost indefinitely and should not be disturbed.

Sternbergia lutea

This brings a touch of lovely autumn color to the garden. The crocus-like flowers, surrounded by glossy foliage, are a clear, golden yellow. They come into bloom in October and remain in flower for several weeks. They are lovely when planted in patches under trees or along the edge of a walk and they will bloom bountifully year after year.

Culture: The bulbs should be planted just as soon as they arrive at a depth of about 4 inches. They prefer a light, well-drained soil and a warm, sunny exposure, although they will also thrive well in light shade.

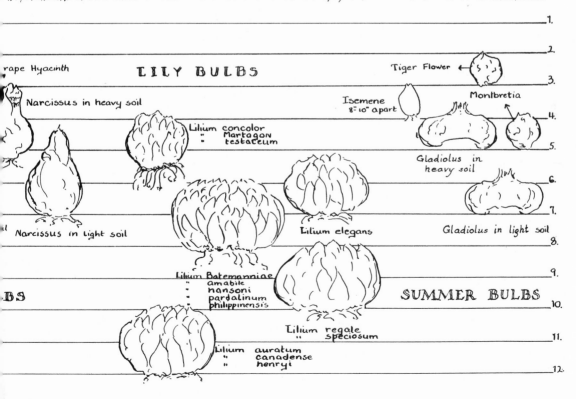

XXVIII
LILIES

FEW flowers have more decorative value in the garden than the lilies. Their stateliness, their beauty of form and their subtle color harmonies make them one of the most highly prized flowers in a landscape composition. In the hands of a skillful designer lilies may be used to achieve dramatic and superbly beautiful effects.

When planning for their use in a planting design there are a few points which should be borne in mind. Lilies are far lovelier when planted in groups of three or more than when they are used as individual specimens. Tall lilies are seen to best advantage against a pleasing background, such as a garden wall, a shrub border or a planting of low-branching evergreens. Tall lilies are also more effective when viewed from a distance rather than at close range, as the full form and beauty of the stately stalks with their myriad blooms can then be enjoyed.

Lilies which are to be used in the perennial border should be selected with care. The colors should be in harmony with the surrounding plants, and the height and the character of the flowers should also be considered. Lilies which would tower above the other plants in the border would be out of scale and would be apt to mar the beauty of the composition rather than contribute to it. The size and general character of the blooms is important for the same reason. In a small garden where most of the flowers are light and airy in form a group of lilies bearing great numbers of large, voluptuous trumpet blooms would be overpowering, whereas varieties with smaller, reflexed flowers on graceful stalks would lend charm and distinction to the planting.

There are lilies to suit every location and every purse. The novice in the art of gardening will be wise to select some of the more easily grown varieties, many of which are very beautiful, while the more experienced gardener will find keen interest and joy in growing some of the more temperamental types.

Within recent years there has been a great upsurge of interest in the culture of lilies. This is due in large measure to the fact that remarkable progress has been made in the hybridization of lilies during the past few decades, resulting in the production of many hybrid strains which offer to the gardener new types possessing vigor, hardiness and resistance to disease, as well as perfection of form and exquisite colors.

Prior to World War II most of the lily bulbs in this country were imported. Many of the bulbs were diseased, many suffered seriously during the long shipment and often arrived too late to permit fall planting, making it necessary to carry the bulbs over until spring. Consequently losses were high and many gardeners gave up the struggle in despair.

However, the great majority of lily bulbs now on the market are American grown, and hence are in excellent condition for planting when they reach the gardener. Many varieties are grown from seed which makes it possible to offer them at reasonable prices and also gives the gardener the confidence of having disease-free bulbs. And the new hybrids are so robust and dependable, as well as so beautiful, that success is almost assured, even under average conditions.

Culture: The essential requirements of success with lilies are: a well-drained soil, abundantly supplied with organic matter; good air circulation; shelter from high winds; disease-free bulbs; the correct time, method and depth of planting; an adequate mulch during the winter and a protective covering for the surface of the bed during the growing season; full sun or partial shade, to meet the requirements of the individual groups; and protection against rodents and disease.

Soil Requirements: Good drainage is an absolutely essential factor, as there is nothing more fatal to the life of a lily bulb than standing water or a soggy, saturated soil. Even those native lilies which are known to prefer a moist situation are unable to endure standing water; they must have their moisture in motion, rapidly trickling through the soil. Therefore, unless the soil is naturally well drained, artificial drainage must be provided. The bed may be drained by the use of 4-inch agricultural tile laid 2 feet below the surface of the soil, or the soil in the bed may be excavated to a depth of $2\frac{1}{2}$ feet and a 6-inch foundation of crushed stone or coarse hard-coal cinders may be placed in the bottom. If the bed is raised slightly above the surrounding area drainage will also be facilitated.

Lilies thrive best in a good loam soil supplied with an abundance of organic matter. If a new bed is being made, the humus should be incorporated into the soil well in advance of planting, and may be supplied in the form of leaf mold, good compost, cultivated peat, or well-rotted cow manure. If the soil is naturally heavy its physical texture will be greatly improved by the addition of liberal quantities of humus, and it will thus be made a more suitable medium for the growing of lilies. Most lilies thrive best in a soil which is nearly neutral, with a pH ranging between 6·5 and 7·5. There are a few exceptions, as philadelphicum prefers a soil of high acidity, canadense will thrive equally well in either an acid or a neutral soil, and Lilium candidum prefers a slightly alkaline soil. For the majority of lilies, however, a neutral soil will provide conditions which are most favorable.

Exposure: Good air circulation is closely related to the problem of disease control, and it will be found that most lilies, except those which are definitely shade-loving, will thrive best in a sunny, airy situation. Disease is much more apt to be prevalent in a low, badly drained spot where there is poor air circulation than on gently sloping, well-drained ground.

Healthy Bulbs: The importance of obtaining clean, healthy, disease-free bulbs can hardly be over-stressed. The vast majority of failures in the growing of lilies are due to the inroads of disease, and it is a problem which faces every grower. It has been found that lilies grown from seed are more free from disease than those propagated directly from the bulbs. Therefore, many gardeners and nurserymen now make a practice of growing from seed as many varieties as possible.

Planting: The time of planting as well as the method and depth of planting will depend to a considerable extent upon the type of lily being grown, although there are a few general rules which apply to practically all members of the lily group. Lily bulbs mature, or ripen, after the flowering period is over, and should be dug as soon as possible after the bulbs have ripened.

Most lily bulbs resent being out of the ground, and some varieties deteriorate rapidly during the process of shipment. It is essential, therefore, that the bulbs be planted without delay as soon as the shipment has been received. The ground should be prepared well in advance, and everything should be ready for immediate planting as soon as the bulbs arrive. The more promptly the shipment can be made after the bulbs have ripened, and the more promptly the bulbs are planted, the greater are the chances of success. Because of long shipments it is sometimes impossible to plant the bulbs at the most favorable time. Another problem with which the gardener is faced is that of shipments which arrive late in the autumn when the ground is no longer in suitable condition for planting, being either frozen or soggy. This situation may be met in either one of two ways.

The bed may be prepared well in advance, and the area where these late arrivals are to be planted may be mulched with fresh manure, leaves, or straw, to prevent the ground from freezing and to maintain it in a favorable condition for planting. Even when this is done, however, the bulbs frequently arrive too late to make sufficient autumn growth to carry them through the winter and they suffer seriously in consequence. In handling bulbs which arrive after the middle of November (in the latitude of Philadelphia) a more favorable procedure seems to be to pot the bulbs in fairly dry soil and to store them during the winter in a root cellar where the temperature will range between 38 and 50 degrees. The pots may be buried in dry sand, being kept without moisture during the winter. In early spring the pots should be set out of doors, being covered with straw or half-rotted leaves until growth has started. Later in the season, when the ground is in good condition the bulbs may be gently removed from the pots and placed in their permanent position in the garden, care being taken not to disturb the roots. This method of winter storage has given excellent results at the Boyce Thompson Institute and is preferable to the use of cold frames for the wintering of bulbs which arrive too late to be planted in the open.

Some growers supply lilies for spring planting which have been dug in the autumn, placed in a plastic bag filled with slightly damp peat moss, and then stored in an air-conditioned warehouse at a temperature of 34° F. Such bulbs give excellent results when planted in the garden in the spring or when used as potted plants. They offer an alternative to late autumn planting under unfavorable conditions. They also make it possible for anyone establishing a new garden to have lilies in flower the first season. And they are of special value as potted plants on terrace or patio.

The method and depth of planting are discussed in detail under cultural requirements of each species.

Winter Mulches: In the North, most lilies, with the

exception of a few exceedingly hardy varieties, require the protection of a winter mulch. Well-rotted leaf mold makes an excellent mulch for lilies as it can be left on the ground throughout the year and will aid in increasing the organic content of the soil. Salt hay is also excellent. (See Chapter XXXIV on Mulches.)

Summer Mulch: Lilies prefer a cool, moist root-run, and there are but few which will thrive in a soil which becomes hard and parched during the growing season. A soil well supplied with organic matter will naturally be more retentive of moisture than a soil deficient in humus and will, therefore, provide more favorable growing conditions. The surface of the soil, however, should have some form of protective covering. When lilies are grown in the herbaceous border this covering is provided by the natural growth of other plants which, in many cases, will afford sufficient ground cover for the bulbs. If lilies are grown in beds or borders by themselves, the surface of the soil should be kept mulched throughout the growing season. Peat moss, well-rotted leaf mold, lawn clippings and buckwheat hulls may be used successfully for this purpose. (See Chapter XXXIV on Mulches.)

Protection Against Rodents: Mice are, unfortunately, passionately fond of most varieties of lily bulbs and in gardens where mice are apt to be troublesome it is useless to attempt to grow lilies unless some adequate protection is provided. The most effective protection is afforded by the use of $\frac{1}{4}$-inch mesh galvanized wire. If the lilies are to be grown in a bed or border by themselves it is the part of wisdom to line the bottom, sides and ends of the entire bed with wire. When the wire is purchased by the roll it is not prohibitively expensive, and it will afford absolute protection from rodents over a period of many years. It may be put in place at the same time that the bed is prepared for planting, and will, therefore, not require much extra labor. If the lilies are to be planted in groups in the border, wire baskets of any desired size may be made or purchased and the bulbs may be planted within the basket. Although many other means of protection have been tried, such as planting the bulbs in camphor or in medicated peat moss, no method of affording protection has been found which is as entirely dependable as the use of wire. For the control of field mice by the use of poison baits, see Chapter XLI, page 673.

Propagation

Lilies may be propagated by seed, by scales, by bulbils and by bulblets. Some lilies may be propagated more readily by one method than by another.

Propagation by Seed: Many lilies may be grown very readily from seed, and if one does not mind the years of waiting which intervene between the sowing of the seed and the flowering of the plant, the success of this method of propagation will usually far outweigh its disadvantages. Lily seeds may be sown in the autumn as soon as they are ripe, or they may be held over for spring sowing. The seed of most varieties, with the

LILIES
IN A
PERENNIAL
BORDER

exception of auratum, speciosum, and Henryi, will ripen in time for autumn sowing. A well-drained cold-frame with deeply prepared, mellow soil offers ideal conditions for the germination of lily seeds. A soil mixture consisting of one part loam, one part leaf mold and one part peat moss will give excellent results, and the seeds may be sown either broadcast or in rows, being covered with about 1 inch of soil. If the seeds are sown in the autumn the seed bed should be mulched with straw or salt hay during the winter. A lath frame will afford excellent protection for spring-sown seedlings until they have become well established. Some growers prefer to keep their lily seedlings partially shaded throughout the first and second season of growth as it prevents the soil from drying out and promotes more vigorous development. About twelve months after sowing, the young seedlings should be transplanted to

another deeply prepared frame in order to have more space in which to develop, and the second summer after sowing, the strongest, most vigorous seedlings should be transplanted to their permanent position in the garden or in the nursery. The majority of lilies will flower the third summer after sowing, some will flower considerably sooner, while a few will require a longer period of growth. Formosanum, which is one of the lilies most easily grown from seed, will flower the following summer if it is sown in the autumn and is carried over the winter in a greenhouse. Regale lilies will frequently produce one flower the second season, several flowers the third season; and they are at the height of their glory during the fifth and sixth years. Among the lilies most easily grown from seed are canadense, candidum, concolor, Henryi, Formosanum, regale, and speciosum. Of these, canadense and specio-

LILIES
IN A FORMAL
SETTING

sum will make no growth above ground until the second spring after planting.

Propagation by Scales: Many lilies may be increased very readily by scales. The bulbs should be lifted in early autumn and the scales should be carefully removed from the outside of the bulbs. A shallow trench should be opened in a well-drained, partially shaded spot, and a thin layer of sand should be placed in the bottom of the drill. The scales should be placed in the trench, being spaced several inches apart, and they should be covered with an inch or two of sand. Peat moss may be substituted for the sand if desired. The young bulbs form about the edges of the scales, and when they have become crowded, they should be transplanted into nursery rows or into coldframes.

Propagation by Bulbils: In some species of lilies small bulbils are produced in the axils of the leaves. When the bulbils are ready to be gathered, they will drop from the stem almost at the touch of the fingers. They should be sown in shallow drills in light, well-prepared soil, and they may be handled in very much the same manner as are lily seedlings.

Propagation by Bulblets: Most of the stem-rooting lilies produced bulblets on the underground stem. When these bulblets are left undisturbed, they produce a cluster of small leaves about the base of the main stem and they soon become overcrowded. It is well, therefore, to remove them, even though one does not wish to use them for the purpose of propagation. In the autumn, the earth should be carefully dug away from the main stem with a trowel and the small bulblets removed. In some cases the stem may be ripe enough so that it may be gently pulled out without harming the bulbs, in which case the bulblets may be picked off. These bulblets may be planted in shallow drills, being handled in the same manner as are the bulbils.

Diseases and Insect Pests—see page 654.

DEFINITION OF TERMS

Genus: A group of plants with closely related characteristics. All lilies have certain characteristics in common and belong to the Genus Liliaceae.

Species: A group belonging to the same genus which has certain characteristics distinguishing it from other members of the same genus: Examples L. auratum, L. candidum.

Hybrids: A hybrid is obtained by the cross pollination of two species of lilies, or by back-crossing a hybrid with the parent stock of another species. Hybrids usually possess what is termed "hybrid vigor", which includes robust growth, greater resistance to disease, larger blooms, such as is found in the Aurelian Hybrids, Fiesta Hybrids and Olympic Hybrids.

Clone: The term "clone" is applied to a lily which has been propagated by vegetative means from a selected plant, usually one having superior characteristics. Such a clone may result in a superior strain of lilies or in a named variety. All plants produced vegetatively from clones bear the identical characteristics of the original parent. Thus all bulbs of the variety "Black Dragon" trace their ancestry to one superior clone selected from hundreds of seedlings resulting from a series of cross pollinations made by the great Oregon lily breeder, Jan de Graaff.

Strains: Many fine strains are produced by cross pollinating superior clones with other superior clones with similar characteristics. In some cases many of the seedlings will closely resemble the parent clones and will continue to pass on these characteristics with some slight variations. Many excellent strains of lilies have been produced such as the Angel Wings Strain, Jamboree Strain, White Champion Strain, Golden Clarion Strain.

Varieties: Named varieties of lilies are produced from clones and although they may be many generations removed from the parent plant they possess the same characteristics. When first put on the market new, named varieties are always very expensive but become less so each year as the supply of bulbs increases.

LILIUM REGALE WITH
BULBLETS FORMING
ALONG UNDERGROUND
STEM

LILIUM AURATUM WITH
BULBLETS FORMING ON
STEM AND SCALES

LILIES OF SPECIAL MERIT

Species

L. amabile is one of the finest of the low-growing lilies, seldom reaching a height of more than 2 to 3 feet. It flowers in June and July and the brilliant, waxy, orange-scarlet flowers are very decorative, the reflexed petals being spotted with black. Amabile prefers a sunny position and thrives well when grown among low shrubs. It is stem-rooting and should be planted at a depth of about 6 inches in a well-drained, sandy-loam soil.

L. a. Luteum: This lovely sport from L. amabile is a golden-yellow in color. In form and in its requirements it is similar to L. amabile.

L. auratum: This lovely lily has proved short-lived in many gardens due to the fact it is more subject to disease than most other lilies, being particularly susceptible to mosaic, a much dreaded virus disease (see page 654).

Many of the hybrid strains and varieties which have been developed from L. auratum have proved much more resistant to disease and have retained the beauty and quality of the species. It is therefore far wiser to make selection from among these.

All lilies of the auratum type thrive best in regions where there is a long, cool growing season. They require ample moisture, particularly during the flowering period, and for satisfactory results they should be grown in a deep, rich, well-drained soil. Being stem-rooting the bulbs should be planted at a depth of about 6 inches. Prefer partial shade except in cool climates.

L. auratum—var. Platyphyllum is a fine, vigorous form, broad-leaved, hardy and much more resistant to disease than the type. The magnificent, bowl-shaped, fragrant, waxy-white blooms, with a golden band on each spotted petal, are borne on stout stems after reaching a height of 6 to 8 feet. Mid to late summer flowering.

L. auratum—var. Virginale: This is a beautiful pure white form with no spotting on the petals. Dark, glossy leaves. Possesses great vigor. Is well suited for pot culture in a cool greenhouse.

L. auratum Strains, Hybrids and Varieties.
Angel Wings Strain: Exquisite white flowers with golden band. Hardy and vigorous, disease resistant, height 4 to 5 feet.

Flying Cloud Strain: A very superior strain among Auratum-speciosum hybrids. The pure white flowers possess great substance and beauty. Medium height 4 to 5 feet. Great vigor.

Jamboree Strain: Award of Merit, Holland, 1961. Superb, fragrant flowers, crimson and silver, crinkled petals. A magnificent addition to any garden. Hardy, disease resistant, tolerates adverse conditions, height 5 to 6 feet.

LILIUM AURATUM

Pink Glory Strain: An excellent pink strain, the result of crossing Auratum x Speciosum x Japonica. Flowers are a beautiful salmon pink and are produced in abundance in July and August. Height 4 to 6 feet.

Empress of China: Magnificent flowers often 9 inches across. The reverse of the petals is pure chalk-white, the interior being heavily spotted with maroon-purple spots.

Empress of India: A sweepstake winner at international shows. Developed from a hybrid clone this is one of the most spectacular of all lilies, both in form and in coloring. The flowers are open, bowl-shaped, as much as 10 inches across. The color is a deep water-melon crimson, the re-

417

verse of the petals being a warm pink. Height 4 to 5 feet. Vigorous, disease resistant, long-lived.

Empress of Japan: A flower of great distinction. White with a gold stripe, the petals being spotted with deep maroon. Blooms in late August. Height 4 to 5 feet.

L. candidum, known as the Madonna Lily, is one of the most beautiful and one of the most beloved of all lilies. A native of south-eastern Europe, it was first introduced into this country many years ago and it is widely grown. It blooms during June and early July, the white glistening flowers being borne on tall, straight stalks from 4 to 6 feet in height. It should be planted in August whenever it is possible to do so. Bulbs produced in this country are available for planting at this season, but imported bulbs coming from France usually do not arrive until late in September. The bulbs are base-rooting and should be planted not more than 2 inches deep. Shallow planting is one of the essentials of success. Candidum lilies prefer a sunny location, and a slightly alkaline, well-drained soil. During the autumn months a growth of basal leaves is produced which remain green throughout the winter. Candidum lily bulbs are among the few bulbs which are not troubled by mice.

L. concolor comes to us from central China and is a semi-dwarf species, varying in height from 12 to 18 inches. The dainty star-like blossoms, borne upright upon the stalk, are a crimson-scarlet in color. L. concolor comes into flower in June and July, following tenuifolium in season of bloom. A sunny position is preferred and the bulbs should be planted at a depth of 3 inches. It is a hardy, adaptable little lily and is frequently grown in rock gardens.

L. Formosanum comes to us from the Philippine Islands and is gaining rapidly in popularity. There are two distinct forms, the early flowering variety which blooms in August and the late flowering type which does not bloom until October. The late-flowering type is sometimes severely injured by frost in the North and is, therefore, particularly recommended for Southern gardens. The flowers are long and trumpet-shaped, pure white, with a tinge of pinkish-purple along the ribs. The early flowering type seldom reaches a height of more than 18 or 20 inches and the stems are slender and wiry. The late-flowering type grows normally to a height of about 3 feet, sometimes attaining a height of almost 6 feet. It is heavily stem-rooting and the bulbs should be planted from 6 to 8 inches deep. It thrives in either full sun or partial shade. L. Formosanum is one of the easiest of all lilies to grow from seed. From seed sown in the greenhouse in March blooms will be produced the following summer.

L. Henryi comes to us from central China where it is found growing wild on limestone cliffs. It is often called the "yellow speciosum" as it is somewhat similar in form. The flowers are a soft golden-orange in color with a tinge of green through the center, and the petals are decidedly reflexed. The flowers are borne on stems ranging from 5 to 9 feet in height and are excellent for cutting, opening in water even to the tiniest bud. They bloom late in the season, in August, and the flowers remain in bloom over a period of many weeks. L. Henryi thrives best in partial shade, and as the bulbs are stem-rooting they should be planted at a depth of at least 10 inches. The bulbs are extremely hardy, are seldom troubled by disease, and are usually untouched by field mice.

L. Martagon: flowers are a dull purple.

L. M. album is far lovelier than the type. The recurving, faintly scented flowers are a glistening, waxy white and are borne on stalks 4 to 6 feet in height from mid-June to early July. Prefers partial shade and a well drained soil. Bulbs are base rooting and should be planted 4 inches deep.

L. Martagon hybrids

Achievement: This lovely lily is a very pale yellow, almost ivory white. Possesses hybrid vigor, increases rapidly, soon forming large clumps. Height 3 feet. Flowers in mid-June.

Gay Lights: This beautiful pinkish, golden-bronze lily bears as many as 30 flowers on a single stalk. Height 3 to 4 feet. Flowers in June.

L. regale. The Regal lily is one of the most popular and most widely grown of all lilies, and it has much to recommend it. It is absolutely dependable under widely varying conditions; it is hardy and vigorous; and it is practically disease-proof. It is undoubtedly one of the most satisfactory of all lilies for the amateur. The large, trumpet-shaped flowers are creamy white, lilac outside, with a golden throat and brilliant golden anthers, and are very fragrant. The flowers are borne in profusion upon tall, straight stems which often reach a height from 6 to 8 feet. The Regal lily thrives best in full sun and is one of the few lilies that can be grown successfully in a dry, harsh, unmulched soil. It blooms during late June and well into July. As the Regal lilies are stem-rooting the bulbs should be planted not less than 8 inches deep. At the rear of an herbaceous border, or against a background of shrubbery, the majestic, stately beauty of the Regal lily is superb. They are well adapted for use in parks and other public places, as well as in the garden. They may be grown easily from seed and will often flower the second summer after sowing. Regal lilies start growth rather early in the spring and it sometimes happens that during a sudden and unexpected cold snap the young shoots are injured by frost. A light protection of straw or an inverted flower-pot placed over the shoots will obviate this danger.

L. r. Royal Gold. This beautiful golden Regal Lily was developed by Mr. de Graaff. It is a soft, Empire yellow, the petals having a rich substance and a glistening sheen. The plants possess the vigor and adaptability of the white Regal Lily.

L. speciosum is a native of the Orient and is one of the most beautiful and appealing of all our cultivated lilies. Although it is far less voluptuous and showy than some of its cousins, there is about it a grace and charm which make it of distinct value as a cut flower and for the garden. The typical form is white, touched with deep pink and spotted with carmine. There are many varieties, varying in color from pure white to deep carmine. The lovely flowers, with gracefully recurving petals, are borne on stems about 4 feet in height and bloom late in August and on into September. The bulbs are stem-rooting and should be planted from 5 to 6 inches deep. The speciosum lilies thrive equally well either in full sun or in partial shade, but have a tendency to be short-lived in most gardens. All of the speciosums are well adapted to forcing and may be grown very successfully in the small greenhouse.

L. s. album novum: Beautiful large, pure white flowers with golden anthers. Height 2½ to 4 feet. Flowers about 2 weeks later than most Speciosums.

L. s. Lucy Wilson: The recurving flower is a soft pink with white margins, spotted deep rose. Very vigorous, heavy bloomer. Height 5 to 6 feet. August flowering. Cut blooms remain fresh for 10 days.

L. s. Magnificum: This is an improved form of s. rubrum. Flowers a rich, ruby-carmine with white margins. Very vigorous. August-September flowering.

L. s. Superstar Strain: Large, crimson flowers bordered with silver, vigorous, free flowering, holds foliage well.

L. s. White Champion: Vigorous grower, multiplies rapidly, flowers white: Excellent for pot culture and in the garden.

L. s. White Pearl: The orchid-like white flowers are excellent for cutting and for corsages. Requires light shade in warm climates.

Hybrid Strains

Aurelian Hybrids

Golden Clarion Strain: Lovely trumpet lilies, ranging in color from pale, lemon-yellow to deepest gold. Dependable and hardy, they are of easy culture and well suited for the amateur gardener. (*Award of Merit Royal Horticultural Society and Massachusetts Horticultural Society.*)

LEFT: IMPERIAL CRIMSON, IMPERIAL GOLD AND IMPERIAL SILVER

RIGHT: AN EXAMPLE OF THE JAMBOREE STRAIN

ABOVE, LEFT: THE BEAUTIFUL ESTATE LILY

ABOVE, RIGHT: ENCHANTMENT

RIGHT: IMPERIAL SILVER LILIES

African Queen Strain: Award of Merit, London. Beautiful, apricot and orange-tinted, trumpet-type flowers, vigorous growth, height 5 to 6 feet, mid-summer bloom.

Golden Clarion Strain: Lovely trumpet lilies, ranging in color from pale, lemon-yellow to deepest gold. Dependable and hardy, they are of easy culture and well suited for the amateur gardener. (*Award of Merit Royal Horticultural Society and Massachusetts Horticultural Society.*)

Heart's Desire Strain: The flowers are widely flared, shallow, bowl-shaped, being intermediate between the trumpet and reflexed types. Colors range from near-white through cream and yellow to apricot.

Sunburst Strain: The blooms resemble L. Henryi in shape but are larger and the petals are more reflexed. Twenty or more blossoms are often borne on a single stem. Colors range from creamy white through yellow to apricot.

Bellingham Hybrids were developed from native Western species. The reflexed flowers are borne on tall, slender stems, with sometimes as many as 20 blooms on a single stalk. The colors range from light, clear yellow, through orange to bright red. Most flowers are spotted with deep brown or maroon. Bulbs soon develop into vigorous clumps. Ideally suited to the dappled shade of a woodland, although they also thrive well in full sun in soil well supplied with humus and protected by a mulch or ground cover. Height varies from 4 to 5 feet. Period of bloom, mid-June to early July. (These hybrids are not as well adapted to the East as are many other types.) Excellent as cut flowers.

> *Peter Pugat:* yellow, shading to red at the tips. 3 to 4 feet.

> *Shuksan:* a lovely lily with flowers of cadmium yellow, faintly flushed with red. Irregularly reflexed bloom. 4 to 6 feet.

Fiesta Hybrids: The lovely, pendent, bell-shaped flowers are borne on strong, wiry stems, 4 to 6 feet in height. Colors range from golden yellow through brilliant orange to dark, rich red and deep maroon. Gay and charming, the Fiesta lilies bloom during July and prefer a position in full sun. They are excellent for cutting. (*Award of Merit, Massachusetts Horticultural Society.*)

Golden Chalice Hybrids: Blooming early in June the Golden Chalice Hybrids bear cup-shaped flowers varying in color from lemon to gold through apricot and buff to a muted orange. These hybrids prefer a warm location in full sun and are excellent for the middle or foreground of the border. They are of easy culture and resistant to disease. Height 2 feet.

LILIUM SPECIOSUM

Golden Harvest Hybrids: Flowering from mid-August well into September these lovely hybrids are a joy both in the garden and for cutting. The colors range from creamy-white through buff to soft and deep tones of yellow. Very vigorous and adaptable, they are of easy culture, preferring light shade. Height 5 to 7 feet.

Green Mountain Hybrids: The trumpet-shaped flowers, white with green-tinted throats, are borne on stems 4 to 6 feet high and are lovely against a background of evergreens. Hardy, adaptable and free-blooming.

Olympic Hybrids: Extremely vigorous and hardy, the Olympic Hybrids are adapted to every section of the country. In form the flowers vary from the usual trumpet to the more widely flared bowl shape. Colors range from a pure, icy white to creamy yellow and soft fuchsia-pink tones. Will grow in full sun or partial shade.

Pink Perfection Strain: one of the loveliest of the Olympic hybrids, flowers are a deep fuchsia pink. Height 4 to 6 feet.

421

Painted Lady Hybrids: Their beautiful and unusual coloring and their free-flowering habit make these lovely hybrids an asset to the garden. Sometimes more than 60 blooms are produced on a single stalk. The colors range from pearl-white to yellow with a few soft orange and reddish tones. Vigorous and long-lived.

Shellrose Hybrids are a selection of trumpet hybrids in shades of shell and cameo-pink and pale rose. Vigorous in growth, and preferring partial shade, they are adaptable and of easy culture. Excellent for cutting.

Temple Hybrids: Vigorous and free-blooming these hybrids are excellent in the garden and for cutting. The flowers are large and trumpet-shaped.

Amethyst Temple: Amethyst-pink to deep red
Jade Temple: Pale, moonlight greens and lime whites
Marble Temple: White, ivory and pearl
Sun Temple: Soft, light yellow to warm gold tones

HYBRID VARIETIES OF MERIT

Afterglow: rich crimson with gold centers, robust, multiplies rapidly, height 6 feet.

Black Dragon: A magnificent trumpet lily; inside white, reverse a purple brown, vigorous, height 5 to 8 feet.

Enchantment: This is one of the fine hybrids developed by Mr. de Graaff. The upright flowers are a glowing nasturtium-red. A vigorous grower, blooming in early summer. (*Awards of Merit from the Royal Horticultural Society and the N. American Lily Society.*) Height 3 to 5 feet.

Green Dragon is considered one of the finest trumpet lilies ever produced. The great, bowl-shaped flowers which are borne on stems 5 to 6 feet in height, are an unusual chartreuse color. Developed by Mr. de Graaff, Green Dragon is a triumph of the hybridizer's skill.

Jillian Wallace: Few lilies have ever received the acclaim awarded this lovely hybrid from Australia. Developed by Mr. Roy Wallace, it is a cross between L. speciosum and L. auratum, variety "Crimson Queen". The large, beautifully formed flowers are a rich carmine-red with white, wavy petal margins. The blooms, which are very fragrant, are borne on stems 5 feet in height during August. (*Awards of Merit from the Royal Horticultural Society, the Mass. Horticultural Society and the N. American Lily Society.*)

Joan Evans is another fine de Graaff hybrid with upward-tilted, golden blooms. Blooming in July, it reaches a height of 3 to 4 feet.

Palomino: The lovely pendent flowers, in a most unusual tone of soft yellow, are partially recurved. It blooms in early July on 5 foot stems. Developed by Mr. de Graaff.

Sunset Glow: Dainty and choice, this lovely hybrid bears flowers which combine sunset pink with a glowing yellow center. Hardy and vigorous, blooming in late June. Developed by Dr. Skinner.

T. A. Havemeyer is considered one of the most beautiful of all lilies. The flowers are large, sometimes as much as 7 inches across, and are an exquisite ivory-yellow, suffused with apricot. It is vigorous and free-flowering, thrives in full sun or partial shade, and flowers from mid-August into September. It is unusually fine as a cut flower. Height 7 to 8 feet. It is particularly beautiful against a background of evergreens.

Winter Sunset: A fine rose-toned trumpet type, a hybrid of L. regale developed by Mr. Abbey. (*Award of Merit, Royal Horticultural Society.*)

XXIX

ROSES

SINCE ancient times the rose has held a place in the hearts of the people shared by no other flower. Because of its significance as a symbol of purity and faith, because of the many associations, legends and traditions surrounding it, because of its sheer beauty, it has been loved and revered by countless generations throughout the world.

The romance of the rose has come down to us in song and story and it is interwoven into the very fabric of our history. The Greek poetess, Sappho, sang of its beauty in the sixth century B.C. The Roman matron of the first century A.D. took pride and pleasure in arranging her roses for the flower shows of her day. The symbols of the two factions contending for supremacy in strife-torn England during the fifteenth century were the white rose of York and the red rose of Lancaster. "The War of the Roses" was so called because of these symbols.

One of the first flowers to become domesticated, the rose has been faithfully protected and treasured, and wherever civilization has spread there roses have been planted. Universal in its appeal to the spirit of man, it is equally at home over the cottage doorway and within the proud gates of royal palaces.

Since the dawn of science, and its application to the study of plants, no other flower has received so much attention as has the rose. Plant explorers and botanists have discovered and named more than two hundred species in the northern hemisphere and, after a century of plant breeding, we have hundreds of varied forms. When we compare the wealth of material available to us today with the very limited number of varieties and types which were available only a few generations ago we realize what a

debt of gratitude we owe to our modern plant hybridizers.

Today there is a rose for every place and purpose; for formal beds and borders, for arbors, trellises and fences, for hedges, for ground covers on steep banks, for edgings, for accent plants in perennial borders, for use as specimen shrubs, and as decorative features on terrace and patio, and even for planting in little rose bays along crowded streets in the heart of great cities. Roses are one of the most versatile and exciting plant groups with which the designer and gardener work today in creating landscape compositions.

The Rose Garden—Its Design

Partly because of the special esteem in which the rose is held, partly because the cultural requirements of the rose differ from those of other flowers, and partly because the rose lacks the fullness of growth of many cultivated plants and so needs special compositional arrangement, a separate garden for roses is the most satisfactory method of planting. A garden devoted entirely to roses may seem to be too great an undertaking but it is not impossible of attainment even on a small place, and where resources are limited. It need not be large in scale or lavish in details of construction.

A few well-planted beds or borders can be a source of pleasure throughout the season and the satisfactions of such a planting will far outweigh the work involved.

In planning a rose garden in the traditional style there are a few essential considerations which should be borne in mind: an enclosure which is not too close and airless, yet gives adequate shelter from the wind and provides a

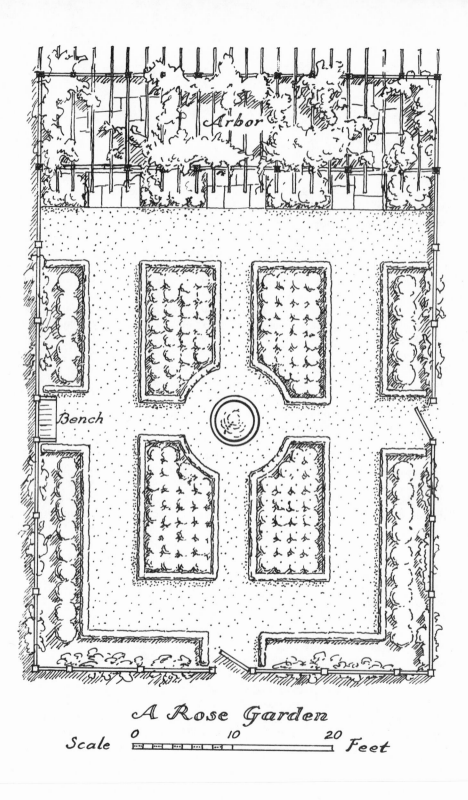

A Rose Garden

Scale 0 10 20 Feet

SUNKEN ROSE GARDEN

background against which the blooms may be seen to the best advantage; a geometric pattern to give the design definite form, so that the garden will have a beauty of its own quite independent of the flowers; and paths of some material such as brick, flagstone or turf which will be in harmony with the surroundings.

In a rose garden of contemporary design the composition will be more casual and more varied, and will permit greater freedom. The rose beds may be designed to create an interesting and dramatic pattern within the surfaced area of the patio, or roses may be planted in raised beds against the free-sweeping curve of the patio wall. Planted in tubs, roses may be used as specimen or accent plants to highlight a planting composition.

If the grounds of a suburban home are too cramped to permit the development of even a very small garden, roses may still be grown and enjoyed—perhaps a single lovely bush beside the door, or a few Floribundas planted in a group near the corner of the house, or some of the graceful, climbing hybrid tea roses on a low fence. There are few flowers which bring the touches of warmth and graciousness, of color and beauty to the surroundings of the modest home such as the rose imparts.

425

Cultural Requirements

The factors which contribute to success in growing roses of fine quality include—a suitable location; a fertile, congenial soil; good drainage; the selection of vigorous, disease-free plants; correct planting; and good cultural practices—pruning, fertilization, mulching, winter protection and the control of insect pests and diseases.

Location: In order to produce good bloom, roses require a minimum of six hours of sun during the day. Shade during the afternoon is preferable to morning shade. In fact, some afternoon shade is desirable, as the blooms tend to retain their color for a longer period. Roses will not thrive in situations where the shade is too dense, and they should not be planted in close proximity to trees, shrubs or hedges which are heavy surface feeders as, under such conditions, the roses will be deprived of both food and moisture.

The matter of air circulation is also important. Roses do not make satisfactory growth in closely confined areas where the air becomes stagnant, due to insufficient circulation of air currents.

Soil Requirements

The actual structure of the soil is not as important as its drainage capacity and its fertility. Roses will thrive in fairly heavy clay and in sandy-loam soils, provided the requirements of drainage and fertility are met. The ideal soil is a good garden loam, well supplied with organic matter.

Drainage: Good drainage is absolutely essential. While roses require large quantities of water for their best growth, they are seriously injured by an excess of standing water in the soil. They will not thrive in soils which do not drain readily or where the water table rises to within a few feet of the surface at any time of the year.

If the natural drainage is not adequate to take care of surplus water the beds may either be under-drained with tile or with crushed stone or cinders.

Four-inch agricultural tile should be used, being laid at the bottom of a 2-foot trench. The tile should be laid end to end and the joints should be covered with strips of tar-paper to keep the soil out of the tile while the trench is being refilled. There should be a fall of at least 3 inches in every 50 linear feet.

If crushed stone or cinders are used, a 6-inch layer placed at the bottom of the trench will usually be sufficient to provide adequate drainage.

Acidity of the Soil: Recent experiments show that roses prefer a slightly acid soil with a pH ranging between 5.5 and 6.5. If the soil is too strongly alkaline, or if it becomes too acid, roses have a tendency to become chlorotic, this condition being indicated by a very characteristic mottling of the leaves, the veins remaining dark green and the leaf areas between the veins becoming yellow, or in extreme cases, almost white. When such a condition becomes evident the soil should be tested to determine whether the trouble is due to too much acidity or to too high a degree of alkalinity, known as lime-induced chlorisis, or to a lack of available iron. (See page 166 for the use of iron chelates). If the chlorosis is caused by too high a degree of acidity the condition may be remedied by an application of lime. (See Chart on page 171 for rate of application.) In the preparation of new beds the soil should be tested and a pH ranging between 5.5 and 6.5 should be definitely established.

Preparation of the Soil

It is important that the soil for roses be well prepared. The roots of a vigorous rose bush will extend to a depth varying from 15 to 20 inches, and it is prior to planting that one has the best opportunity to improve the fertility and texture of the soil in the area where the roots can derive the greatest benefit from it.

If the soil is of a decidedly sandy character its texture may be improved, and its water-holding capacity may be greatly increased, by the admixture of clay-loam, compost, peat moss and other organic materials. In like manner the texture and aërability of extremely heavy clay soils may be improved by the addition of sand, compost, strawy manure, or some similar material.

The method of soil preparation for the rose beds will depend to a considerable extent upon the desires of the owner. If one's means are limited and if labor is not readily available, the old English practice of double-digging will give satisfactory results. If, however, time, labor and expense do not have to be taken into consideration, and if one wishes to provide conditions which will be as nearly ideal as possible, the beds should be trenched.

Double-digging is a simple, comparatively rapid and very efficient method of soil preparation. It consists of removing the top spadeful of soil from one end of the bed and placing it at the other end of the bed, ready for later use. A generous layer of well-rotted cow manure or rich compost, to which a few handfuls of superphosphate have been added, should then be worked well into the lower stratum of soil which has been left exposed after the top spadeful was removed. The next layer of top-soil is then spaded forward upon this lower stratum and the process is continued until the end of the bed has been reached. The pile of top-soil removed from the first trench is used to fill the last trench. The organic matter should, if possible, be applied at the rate of 5 to 6 bushels per 100 square feet of area.

Essentially the same procedure may be followed when individual holes are being prepared for specimen roses.

If the roses are to be planted in the spring the beds should, if possible, be prepared the previous autumn. The preparation of the bed should be completed at least three weeks before planting in order that the soil may have time to settle.

The final level of the bed should be about an inch or two below the surface of the surrounding area.

Maintenance of Soil Fertility

If the rose beds have been well prepared, no further fertilization will be necessary during the first season of growth. During the second year it will be well to adopt a definite program of fertilization which may be followed from year to year, in order that the soil may not become depleted. Roses are vigorous feeders and require a soil well supplied with the essential elements of fertility. An adequate supply of nitrogen is necessary in order to promote rapid, vigorous growth and good foliage. Phosphorus induces good root development and stimulates flower bud formation, and also increases the size and color of the blooms. Potash is essential in that it gives strength to the cell walls, increases the resistance of the plant to disease, and aids in the ripening and hardening of the wood in the autumn.

In planning a program for the maintenance of soil fertility the following points should be taken into consideration: the time of application, the analysis of the fertilizer to be used, and the method and rate of application.

In order to obtain vigorous growth and abundant bloom at least two feedings a year should be made and, if weather permits, a third may be given. The first application should be made in the spring soon after the pruning has been done. The second should be made in June about the time that the roses are coming into bloom, and the third may be given in the summer provided the weather is not too hot nor too dry. No application of fertilizer should be made after the middle of August, as it will tend to encourage succulent fall growth which will be subject to winter injury.

Most rose growers use a complete, commercial fertilizer such as a 5-10-5. Some prefer to use a fertilizer with an organic base containing the trace elements.

The soil should be fairly moist when the application is made. The fertilizer should be sprinkled on the soil about the plant and worked in lightly with a hand weeder. Unless a rain occurs shortly afterward the soil should be watered in order that the fertilizer may go into solution and thus be made readily available for absorption by the roots. The foliage of the plants should be dry at the time that the application is made and no fertilizer should be allowed to come into contact with the leaves or the canes as it may cause severe burning, particularly if the foliage is wet.

The rate of application will vary somewhat according to the fertility of the soil. For soils of high fertility 2 tablespoonfuls of 5-10-5 fertilizer per plant at each application is recommended. For soils of average fertility the amount should be increased to 3 tablespoonfuls and for poor soils 4 tablespoonfuls are recommended.

High-analysis, soluble fertilizers may also be used if desired, but are considerably more expensive than the commercial fertilizers. Instructions given on the container should be carefully followed.

UNIVERSITY OF WISCONSIN
METHOD OF FEEDING

A revolutionary system of feeding trees, shrubs and roses has been developed by the University of Wisconsin (page 166).

When this method is used for roses directions are:

At Planting Time: Place one 2 oz. packet in contact with the lower portion of the root system. This should provide sufficient nutrients for three years.

For Established Roses: Bore a small hole beside each plant and place one 2 oz. packet in close contact with the roots.

Selection of Stock

The importance of purchasing good stock from a reliable source can hardly be overemphasized. It is never a wise practice to purchase cheap rose bushes or "bargain" stock. Such plants are almost invariably of inferior quality and rarely will they make vigorous growth or bloom satisfactorily.

For the protection of the buyer roses are now graded into several standard classes. The top grade is listed as No. 1. In order to be graded No. 1 a bush must have 3 to 4 vigorous canes and, if carefully planted, it is almost certain to develop into a satisfactory plant.

Time of Planting

Roses may be planted in the autumn after the bushes have stopped active growth and are dormant but before the ground freezes; they may be planted in early spring while the plants are still dormant; or they may be planted as potted roses after growth is well started. Some growers are enthusiastic over autumn planting, while others prefer very early spring planting. A method which, in some ways, is a combination of both fall and spring planting has been employed very successfully in some cases and is now being highly recommended by rose authorities. The plants are dug and shipped in the autumn, and upon arrival they are placed in a trench, the bushes being completely covered with soil. In the spring, when the soil is in ideal condition, the plants are lifted and placed in their permanent position in the bed. When this method is followed the wood and buds remain plump and firm throughout the winter, and the bushes are in perfect condition for planting in the spring. Planting does not have to be delayed until a spring shipment arrives, but may be done when both soil and weather conditions are most favorable; and one also has the advantage of being able to obtain superior stock. Most of the large commercial rose growers and seed firms dig their plants in the autumn, and store them during the winter in specially constructed storage houses. Consequently orders shipped out in the autumn are filled before the stock has become depleted, and plants of the finest quality may be obtained.

Spring planting should be done as early in the spring as the ground can be worked. Spring-shipped roses have usually been held in storage over winter. They should be completely dormant upon arrival and should be planted immediately.

If a delay in planting is necessary because of weather conditions they should be unpacked and buried in a trench. If the stems are dry and shrivelled this will help to "plump" up the buds.

Many retail growers now lift their roses in the autumn, or have wholesale orders shipped to them, and pot them up during the winter in deep, heavy, tar-paper pots, ready to sell in the spring after the bushes have leafed out, or later when they are in bud or in bloom. If good, top-grade plants are used and if they are potted with skill and are well cared for, roses may be handled very successfully in this way. When planting potted roses care must be taken to make sure that the ball of earth is not broken.

Method of Planting

Planting distances will depend almost entirely upon the type of rose. Because of their very vigorous habit of growth, the hybrid perpetuals should be planted from 2 feet to 2½ feet apart. For the hybrid teas and the tea roses a distance varying from 18 inches to 2 feet is sufficient except in the case of some of the very vigorous varieties. Floribundas and Grandifloras should be spaced from 18 to 36 inches apart. There is great variance in spread among the varieties of Floribundas.

Never let the roots be exposed to sun or wind prior to planting. They should be kept wrapped in wet sphagnum moss or wet paper until ready to be placed in the hole.

Before planting, all injured or broken roots should be carefully pruned away, a clean, slanting cut being made. Any long, straggly roots should be cut back sufficiently so that they will not have to be twisted or bent when the plant is set. A hole of ample size should be dug for each plant. If the loose soil is mounded slightly in the bottom of the hole one will be able to place the roots in a natural position, extending both outward and downward.

The depth of planting is a very important factor. The plant should be placed so that the bud, or crown, which is the point of union between the stock and scion, is between 1 and 2 inches below the surface of the soil. If the bush is planted too deeply, with the point of union more than 3 inches below the surface, the roots will receive an inadequate supply of oxygen from the air and the growth of the plant will be seriously injured in consequence. This factor is of particular importance in heavy clay soils.

After the plant is in place the soil should be packed firmly about the roots. Many failures are caused by loose, careless planting, and if success is to be assured it is necessary that a few simple rules be observed. Packing the soil about the roots with the blunt end of a trowel handle is very effective, care being taken not to bruise the roots. When the hole has been filled almost to the top, the soil may be tramped firmly about the bush with the feet. The plants should then be watered thoroughly, and the beds should not be allowed to dry out until the plants have become well established. This is quite as necessary for roses planted in the autumn, as it is for roses planted in the spring, as the soil about the roots should always be

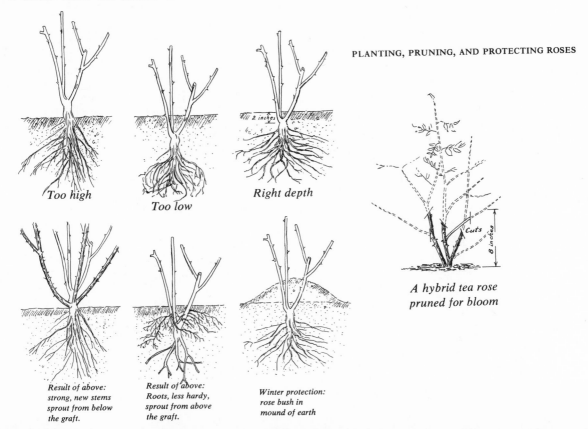

PLANTING, PRUNING, AND PROTECTING ROSES

Too high

Too low

Right depth

Result of above: strong, new stems sprout from below the graft.

Result of above: Roots, less hardy, sprout from above the graft.

Winter protection: rose bush in mound of earth

A hybrid tea rose pruned for bloom

moist when the ground freezes. Immediately after the first watering has been given at the time of planting, the soil should be mounded up about the plants. In the case of roses planted in the autumn this will serve as a winter protection for the plants, and the beds may be mulched in the usual manner. When roses are planted in the spring this hilling up of the soil is equally advisable, as it protects the canes from the drying effects of sun and wind while the new feeding roots are being developed which will, later in the season, supply the moisture which the plant needs. In the spring these temporary mounds of earth should be left about the plants for three or four weeks and the soil may then be gradually worked back into the beds.

Pruning

The method and the time of pruning depend, to a large extent, upon the type of rose and the locality. However, there are a few fundamentals which apply to all types and to all areas.

The objectives in pruning roses are twofold—to remove dead, weak and diseased wood, and to maintain the desired height and form of the bush. All dead canes should be removed at the base. Canes should be examined for wounds, split bark and signs of canker or other disease, and such canes should be cut back below the point of injury or attack. Where tips of canes have died back during the winter they should be cut back to sound wood. Canes which interfere with the desired height or the pleasant shape of the bush should be cut back or removed, and where canes rub against each other one cane should be removed to at least below the point of contact.

Sharp pruning shears are an essential. Dull shears will make a jagged cut and will tend to bruise the stems, thus making conditions more favorable for the entrance of fungi and bacteria. A clean, slanting cut should be made just above a vigorous bud, the slant being in the same direction as the bud. The cut should be made as close as possible to the bud without causing

injury to it. It should never be more than $\frac{1}{4}$ inch above the bud. Long stubs tend to permit the entrance of fungi. As a precaution against fungi the end of the stems may be treated with tree-wound paint. This is, however, a tedious process and is not practical on a large scale.

Climbing Roses: The large-flowered climbers, such as Silver Moon and Dr. Van Fleet, require rather drastic pruning in order to restrain their rampant growth. Pruning should be done in late winter or early spring. Several of the oldest canes should be removed at the base each year to make room for new, vigorous growth, and long, unwieldy canes should be cut back. Most of the large-flowered climbers bear their blooms on the new shoots which are produced by the strong branches which form the framework of the bush, and after bloom these laterals should be cut back to 6 to 12 inches. It is unwise to permit a large-flowered climber to become too rampant. With careful training and judicious pruning the full beauty of the bush may be maintained, but if it is allowed to grow unrestrained it will, in the course of a few years, become a tangled, unsightly mass. Where growth must be very much restricted it is wiser to plant a climber of more delicate habit.

The Climbing Hybrid Teas are much less vigorous in growth than the other type of large-flowered climbers and require little pruning beyond the cutting back of canes which may have winter-killed at the tip.

Floribundas: Pruning should be done in the spring just as the buds begin to swell. As a class the *Floribundas* require very little pruning. They should be allowed to grow to their natural height unchecked. Dead and diseased wood and crowding canes should be removed. Occasionally an old cane will die back and a new cane grow up.

Grandifloras: The same methods apply as to the Floribunda class.

Hybrid Perpetuals: Prune in early spring as the buds begin to swell. Cut out dead and diseased wood. Prune back canes to the desired height and prune canes where necessary to maintain the symmetry of the bush.

Hybrid Teas: Prune in the spring as the buds begin to swell. If *Hybrid Tea Roses* are pruned severely, leaving only two to four buds on a cane, it will result in a few, somewhat late but very large blooms suitable for exhibition purposes. If this practice is continued over a period of years, however, it may result in shortening the life of the bush.

Unless exhibition blooms are specifically desired, moderate pruning is recommended. When canes are pruned back to a height of 12 to 18 inches an abundance of bloom will be assured and the bush will produce sufficient foliage to manufacture the food so necessary for its continued vigor. The beauty and symmetry of the bush should be maintained by the removal of crowding or angular canes. Whenever possible the cut should be made just above an *outside* bud as this tends to keep the center of the bush open.

Polyanthas: Roses in this class require very little pruning. Dead or unhealthy wood should be removed and each spring, before the buds swell, a few of the old canes should be cut out in order to induce the growth of young, vigorous shoots.

Ramblers: The members of this class should be pruned immediately *after* their period of bloom is passed. Much of the old, recently flowered wood may be cut away, as the true ramblers will produce their flowers the following season on the new canes arising from the base of the plant. In this respect they differ markedly from the large-flowered climbing roses. Unless pruned vigorously Ramblers will become an unsightly mass of briers.

Shrub Roses: Remove dead, unhealthy or crowding branches to maintain a bush of pleasing shape.

Cutting Roses

When roses are cut for decorative purposes, many of the same principles may be applied which are used in the pruning of the plants. A clean, sharp, slightly slanting cut should be made, approximately $\frac{1}{4}$ of an inch above a leaf-bud. The symmetry of the bush may be maintained by cutting either at an outside or inside bud, it being advisable to direct the growth outward whenever it is possible to do so. The quality and abundance of future bloom will depend upon the number of leaf-buds left on the stem after the flower has been cut. If the shoot is strong and vigorous, three buds may be left—two if the shoot is weak. The length of the stem of the cut flower will, therefore, be determined by the number of buds to be left on the cane. Roses should preferably be cut early in the morning before they have been touched for many hours by the sun.

Watering

Roses make their best growth during moderately cool weather when the soil is well supplied with moisture. Although roses resent a soil that is too saturated with moisture, or a water table that has risen above the level of the roots, they require an adequate and fairly abundant supply of moisture throughout the growing season. During periods of drought, roses should be watered thoroughly once a week. The bed should be soaked until the water has penetrated into the soil to a depth of at least a foot. Frequent light waterings are of little value and do more harm than good.

Overhead watering is not recommended as it is conducive to the spread of black spot and other diseases. It is preferable to use a soil soaker or underground irrigation.

Diseases and Insect Pests—see page 662.

Summer Mulches

Roses benefit greatly from a summer mulch. This is particularly true of roses of the bush type. There are a number of materials which may be used—buckwheat hulls, ground corncobs, peat moss, shredded sugar cane fiber, sawdust and tobacco stems. Of these buckwheat hulls have proved one of the most satisfactory. They are light in weight and easy to handle, they may be applied dry, they are permeable to water, do not cake, and have a dark, pleasing color. If peat moss or sawdust is used it is essential that it be thoroughly wet before being applied. The long-continued use of peat moss year after year may cause the soil to become too loose in texture and may tend to increase its acidity slightly. If corncobs or sawdust are used extra nitrogen must be supplied to compensate for the loss of nitrogen from the soil during the period of decomposition.*

The soil should always be moist at the time the mulch is applied. The mulch should be at least one inch in depth.

See Chapter XXXIV on Mulches.

Winter Protection

The amount of winter protection which may be necessary depends upon three factors—the severity of the climate; the exposure of the rose

* See page 500.

garden; and the natural hardiness of the varieties which have been selected.

Winter injury is usually attributable either to the actual freezing of the twigs and roots, which breaks down the cell tissues, or to the loss of moisture from the twigs caused by excessive evaporation. Winter injury is quite as likely to be caused by strong, drying winds and by brilliant sunshine as by extreme cold. Throughout the winter the roots continue to absorb water from the soil and a slow evaporation of moisture continues from the canes. If an undue amount of wind and sunshine increases evaporation beyond the point where the roots can supply sufficient moisture to the twigs, the canes will begin to shrivel, and if the process is prolonged, the plant will die, even though no actual freezing of the plant tissues has taken place. Therefore one of the first preparations for winter should be to see that the soil is well supplied with moisture. The normal autumn rains will often provide for an adequate storage of moisture, but if the autumn season is deficient in rainfall, artificial watering should be done before the ground freezes.

In the South roses require practically no winter protection. In sections of the North, however, where the cold is of such severity that the thermometer will range much below 10 degrees F. it is wise to provide adequate protection for the majority of the hybrid teas, for all the tea roses, for some of the floribundas, hybrid perpetuals and polyanthas, and for a few of the more tender climbers.

In a normal season the early frosts of autumn will harden and ripen the wood and the plants will gradually become dormant. It is a wise precaution to rake and burn all fallen leaves and bits of twig in order to prevent them from harboring bacterial and fungous diseases. Soil brought into the beds may be mounded up about the bushes to a height of from 10 to 12 inches. This mound of earth will afford considerable protection about the crown of the plant and will also prevent the wood and buds of the lower portion of the stem from drying out. After the ground has frozen, a mulch of salt hay or some

similar material may be spread over the beds. It is important that the mulch should not be applied until after the ground has frozen. In the case of the less hardy varieties each individual bush may be protected with a covering of salt hay or dry leaves, and in sections where the winters are of extreme severity a generous covering of salt hay or dry leaves may be heaped over the entire bed until only the tips of the bushes are left exposed. The covering may be held in place by evergreen boughs or by a wire framework. If leaves are used for this purpose, only those should be chosen which do not rot readily, such as oak leaves. Leaves from maples and elms soon form a soggy mat when used for winter covering and usually do more harm than good.

There are various climatic conditions which frequently contribute to the winter-killing of roses, conditions over which one has very little control. If there is a long spell of warm, growing weather in the autumn the plants will not become sufficiently hardened to withstand the rigors of a severe winter. Under such conditions the bushes will have a tendency to continue growth until late in the autumn and the shoots will be so soft and succulent that considerable injury may result. In such cases it is wise to provide careful protection for the bushes, even though it may not usually be necessary.

Protection for Climbers

Some of our most beautiful climbers, such as Jacotte and Emily Gray, are not able to survive the extreme severity of a Northern winter unless given sufficient protection.

Some very interesting experiments have been carried out at Cornell University to determine the most satisfactory method of affording protection for climbing roses. It has been found that cornstalks and evergreen boughs, while affording satisfactory protection, often harbor field mice and rabbits to such an extent that considerable damage may be done. Burlap is not satisfactory, as it holds too much moisture. The most approved method, and one that has given absolute satisfaction, consists of removing the canes from the trellis or support early in October while they are still supple, and allowing them to remain procumbent upon the ground, where the grass will grow up among them and where the falling leaves which are blown in upon them will afford natural protection. Soil is then mounded up about the base of the plant, and after the ground has become frozen a mulch of salt hay or straw is placed over the mound of soil. In order to hold the canes in a procumbent position two strong pieces of wood may be driven into the earth at right angles to each other, forming a wedge to hold the canes in place. This method of protection has proved so satisfactory that even during several winters of extreme severity, when the temperature reached 20 degrees below zero, no injury resulted. Early in the spring, after danger from frost is over, the mounds of soil may be removed from the base of the plant gradually, and the canes may easily be re-fastened to their supports.

Protection of Standard Roses

Standard or Tree Roses require careful winter protection. The soil should be removed from the side of the roots, the rose tree should be bent down into an improvised trench and it should then be covered with a heavy layer of soil.

Classification of Roses

Roses may be grouped into several classifications, one of the most logical being their adaptability to certain uses.

For the formal pattern of beds and borders in the rose garden the six types which are of the greatest value are the Floribundas, the Grandifloras, the Hybrid Perpetuals, the Tea Roses, the Hybrid Teas and the Polyanthas.

For use on arbors, lattices, pergolas and walls the large-flowered climbing roses, the climbing Hybrid Teas, the pillar types, and the semi-climbing, everblooming types are the most desirable.

As a ground cover on steep banks some of the species roses are of value, and in this group we

also find a number of recent introductions which are of outstanding merit.

For massed shrubbery plantings, for hedges and for beautiful specimens, the Brier roses, the Rugosas and some of the delightful species roses may be used.

And, quite in a class by themselves, we have the old-fashioned roses—the Moss Rose and the Damask Rose; the Bengal and Bourbon roses; the Noisette roses and many others.

ROSES FOR GARDEN BEDS AND BORDERS

Floribunda Roses

Seldom has a new type of rose gained so rapidly in popularity as has the Floribunda class which is a comparatively recent introduction. The result of a cross between the low-growing polyanthas and the chaste and lovely Hybrid Tea rose, the Floribundas have inherited many of the best characteristics of each parent. Hardy and vigorous, almost prodigal in their bloom, lovely in form and coloring, and adaptable to many uses, the Floribundas have won the hearts of rose lovers throughout the country.

Varieties vary greatly in size, some being semi-dwarf in habit and others, such as Betty Prior, reaching a height of 5 to 6 feet. There is also considerable variance in the flower form, from single to semi-double and fully double. And there is a wide range of color, white, pink, salmon, coral, scarlet, deep red, yellow and two-tone. The Floribundas are generous with their bloom, flower over a long season, and are less demanding of care and attention than are the more fastidious Hybrid Teas.

The versatility of the Floribunda is one of the qualities which has made it so popular with gardeners everywhere. Its charm and piquant beauty make it a welcome addition to the formal rose garden, it is happily at home in the foreground of a shrubbery planting, it can be used as a hedge or as a solid border along the base of a wall, it gives added interest to the planting in a perennial border, and if there is space for only a bush or two on a tiny suburban plot the floribundas are the ideal choice.

VARIETIES OF MERIT

Betty Prior: The single flowers resemble those of the pink dogwood in coloring, outside of petals carmine, inside shell pink. Vigorous, tall growing, 4 to 6 feet. Never out of bloom.

Cocorico: Large clusters of red-scarlet, semi-double flowers, 3 to 3½ feet.

Fanfare: Coral with tints of yellow, orange and pink. 3½ feet, vigorous, in almost continuous bloom. Rome Gold Medal, 1955.

Fashion: An exquisite shade of coral pink, 2 to 2½ feet. All-American Award, 1949. One of the most popular of the Floribundas.

Floradora: Orange-scarlet, vigorous, 3 to 4 feet. Always dependable and in almost continual bloom.

Frensham: Fine, unfading scarlet, good flower clusters, 3 to 3½ feet. Dense foliage, vigorous growth.

Golden Slippers: All American 1962. Dainty and exquisite in form, color a blend of gold and orange, almost continuously in bloom, low, sturdy growth.

Jiminy Cricket: Orange-coral, vigorous, 2½ to 3 feet, abundant bloom, thrives well anywhere.

Ma Perkins: Shell-pink with gold tints, 2½ to 3 feet. All-American Winner for 1953.

Saratoga: All American 1964. Fragrant white blooms resembling camellias, lustrous foliage. Blooms resistant to rain and wind.

Spartan: Orange-red, free-blooming, vigorous, 3 to 3½ feet, fine foliage, disease-resistant. Almost never out of bloom.

Vogue: Flame to cherry-coral, compact, upright growth, 2½ to 3 feet.

Grandiflora Roses

The lovely Grandiflora class, recently developed, attests the skill of the modern rose hybridizer and has been enthusiastically received by rosarians throughout the country.

Roses in this class are extremely vigorous, free blooming, and among the easiest roses to grow. The buds and flowers have the exquisite perfection of the Hybrid Tea but are borne in clusters. The flowers are long and tapering, the blooms large and delicately formed, often measuring more than four inches across. The Grandiflora roses are noted particularly for their almost incredible profusion of bloom, their robust growth and healthy foliage, and for the long-lasting qualities of the flowers. Some varieties are fragrant and others almost thornless.

VARIETIES OF MERIT

Buccaneer: The large flowers, 4½ inches across, are a bright, clear yellow—"veritably, sunshine in the garden". Buds are long and tapering. Extremely vigorous, tall and erect in growth.

Camelot: All American 1965. Luminous coral-pink. Large, fragrant semi-double flowers, vigorous, uniform growth.

Montezuma: A bright scarlet-orange in color with pointed buds and beautiful, long-lasting blooms. Vigorous, free-blooming, fine foliage. Winner of the Geneva Gold Medal in 1955.

Queen Elizabeth: The first of the Grandiflora roses and the All-American Winner in 1955. The superbly-formed, fragrant flowers are a lovely, clear pink in color and unusually long-lasting when cut. A tall, erect plant with handsome foliage.

Hybrid Perpetuals

The hybrid perpetuals were introduced in 1830 by Laffray, who had succeeded in crossing the lovely old Damask rose with the China rose. The name, hybrid perpetual, is, unfortunately, very misleading, as the members of this group bloom freely during the month of June and yield but occasional, scattered bloom throughout the rest of the season. The term perpetual was originally intended to refer to the hardiness of the plant instead of to its blooming period. The hybrid perpetuals are the "June Roses" which were so cherished by gardeners a half century or more ago, and even today, when they are no longer classed among our favorites, we recognize the fact that they possess many virtues and that they will never be entirely replaced by the newer hybrid teas. The hybrid perpetuals are very hardy, able to withstand winters of extreme severity. In habit of growth they are strong and vigorous. The flowers are large and well formed and are produced on long, strong stems.

VARIETIES OF MERIT

Arrillaga: Large, glowing pink buds developing into immense flowers of a vivid pink with a golden glow at the base of the petals; blooms fragrant and long-lasting.

Frau Karl Druschki: Considered the best white rose in cultivation and often called "the white American Beauty". The large, pure white blooms are borne on long, strong stems and are unexcelled for cutting. The flower is of beautiful form, and its one failing seems to be that it has no fragrance.

George Arends: The pink form of Frau Karl Druschki; very fragrant.

Paul Neyron: Very large blooms of a deep pink shade.

Ulrich Brunner: Brilliant scarlet-crimson; a rose of vigorous habit and very hardy.

Tea Roses

Tea roses were introduced from China in the year 1810 and they have long been classed among the favorites.

Wherever tea roses can be grown they are greatly prized. The foliage has a coppery tint and the sweetly scented flowers are exquisite in form. Unfortunately tea roses are not hardy in the North unless very elaborate winter protection is provided. They are, therefore, seldom grown except in the lovely rose gardens of the South. They prefer a rich, well-drained soil and require severe pruning.

VARIETIES OF MERIT

Lady Hillingdon: Beautifully pointed buds, flowers a clear saffron yellow.

Maman Cochet: Large, fragrant flower of carmine-pink.

William R. Smith: Flowers creamy white, tinged with pink.

Hybrid Tea Roses

The first hybrid tea rose was produced by Guillot in 1867 as the result of crossing the hybrid perpetual rose Mme Victor Verdier with the tea rose Mme Bravy. This cross resulted in the lovely hybrid tea rose known as La France, which has maintained its popularity for more than half a century. Many later crosses were made between hybrid perpetuals and tea roses and again between hybrid tea roses and other hybrid teas and as a result of these crosses many strains have been developed.

Our finest and most desirable garden roses are to be found in this group. Most varieties within the group are of a sturdy, vigorous habit of growth and are hardy in the North if given moderate winter protection. Under favorable cultural conditions the hybrid tea roses will give generous bloom from June well into October. During the heat of midsummer the bloom is more scattered and the different varieties vary somewhat in their blooming habits, some giving better autumn bloom than others. There is also considerable variance in habit of growth, some varieties attaining a height of 3 feet or more, while other varieties are somewhat low and spreading in form and produce but scanty foliage. Some varieties are exceptionally vigorous and very long-lived, while other varieties have a

tendency to die out after a few years, even when grown under the most favorable cultural conditions. The hybrid teas possess a wide range of color and form, and they are the most desirable type for the average garden.

VARIETIES OF MERIT

Apricot Queen: Long, pointed buds. Flowers orange-apricot at base of petals, merging to salmon-rose. (All-America Selection, 1940.)

Charles Mallerin: A very dark, velvety red. A rose of great beauty, and exceptional quality.

Charlotte Armstrong: Extremely vigorous; foliage leathery, deep-green, very resistant to mildew. Long tapering buds, flowers a rich cerise. Very floriferous. (All-America Selection, 1941.)

Chrysler Imperial: Dark rich red, very fragrant. (All-American, 1953.)

Confidence: A blend of peach-pink and yellow, very long, tapering buds, large flowers. Bagatelle and "Most Beautiful Rose of France" awards.

Duquesa De Penaranda: Large, fragrant flowers of a cinnamon-peach color. Vigorous, upright habit of growth with splendid foliage. Exceedingly fine autumn bloom.

Golden Scepter: Golden yellow, long-lasting flowers, vigorous growth, abundant bloom.

Granada: All American 1964. Large, fragrant flowers, a striking blend of rose-bengal with reddish yellow. Vigorous growth.

Helen Traubel: Luminous apricot-pink, tapering buds, long-lasting flowers, fragrant, vigorous, easy to grow. (All-American, 1952.)

Katherine T. Marshall: One of the most outstanding pink roses. Long, tapering buds of deep coral-pink suffused with yellow. Stems strong, fine for cutting. Flowers are beautiful in form and coloring.

Mirandy: The long, pointed buds are a deep red with black shadings, the flowers a rich chrysanthemum red, with an alluring damask fragrance. Good growth, excellent foliage. Thrives well in warm climates. (All-America Selection, 1945.)

Mission Bells: In bud a deep, glowing salmon, opening to a brilliant, clear shrimp-pink. Vigorous, free branching and floriferous. (All-America Selection, 1950.)

Mister Lincoln: All American 1965. Deep, velvety red flowers, large and perfectly formed. Vigorous growth, disease resistant.

Mojave: The flower combines the brilliant tones of a desert sunset—orange, red and vermilion. (All-American, Bagatelle and Geneva Awards, 1954.)

Nocturne: Buds very long and slender. Flowers a bright, cardinal-red with darker shadings of crimson. Vigorous in growth. (All-America Selection, 1946.)

Peace: One of the most sensational roses ever introduced. The flowers are unusually large and long-lasting, borne singly on strong, stout stems, and in color combine tints of pale gold, cream, ivory and alabaster with a faint flush of apple-blossom pink or cerise on the edge of the slightly ruffled petals. Hardy and of very vigorous growth. (All-America Selection, 1946.)

Peaceful: Coral pink, suffused with apricot, exceptionally large blooms, vigorous growth.

Polynesian Sunset: A superb rose with iridescent coral-orange tones. Vigorous growth.

Sutter's Gold: The beautiful, tapering yellow buds are shaded with coppery red. The open flower is clear yellow with coppery veins through the petals. Very vigorous and free branching in growth.

Taffeta: Buds are of medium size with fluted edges, a rich carmine in color. The semi-double flowers are a combination of begonia-pink, salmon, and apricot with yellow tones at the base. Vigorous in growth with good foliage. (All-America Selection, 1948.)

Tallyho: Beautiful two-tone, rich pink and crimson blush, fragrant, vigorous, hardy and easy to grow.

Tropicana: Winner of 14 International Awards. Flowers are a brilliant, glowing orange-red. Tall, vigorous growth, disease resistant.

White Swan: Long, graceful buds of alabaster white, large flowers, excellent for cutting, vigorous, disease resistant.

Single Hybrid Tea Roses

In this group we find some of our most beautiful hybrid tea roses, exquisite both in form and in coloring. They are decorative and lovely in the garden and offer most delightful possibilities for cut-flower arrangements.

VARIETIES OF MERIT

Cecil: Large, single flowers of a soft primrose-yellow. Plants vigorous and bushy in habit of growth, with splendid foliage.

Dainty Bess: A rose of most striking form and color. The flower is composed of six broad petals of a soft rose-pink with a large cluster of deep wine-colored stamens which give it a most unique appearance. The flowers are borne in clusters and vary considerably in size.

Irish Elegance: A rose of exquisite beauty, bronze-pink when in bud, the open flowers being a delicate shade of apricot.

Irish Fireflame: The flowers are an orange-crimson shaded with pink and gold, and are lovely for cutting. The bush is of vigorous growth and gives generous bloom.

Isobel: Beautiful, large, single flowers of a bronzy tone with shades of flaming orange-pink.

Old Gold: Flowers sweetly fragrant, of a delicate pinkish-buff shade.

White Wings: Perfectly formed, large white flowers, borne in pyramidal sprays. Striking amethyst stamens tipped with gold.

Polyantha Roses

The Polyantha or cluster roses are used extensively for mass plantings, for the foreground of shrubbery borders and for edging purposes. They are very hardy and require comparatively little care and attention. Gay and colorful, they give generous bloom throughout the season, and they are rapidly gaining in popularity.

VARIETIES OF MERIT

Cameo: The tiny flowers are borne in great profusion and are of a most lovely tone of shell-pink shading to orange-salmon.

Improved Cecile Brunner is known also as the Sweetheart rose. The flowers are small and exquisitely formed, being particularly charming when in bud. The color is a delicate shade of pink, tinted with yellow at the base.

Gloria Mundi: The flowers are borne in clusters and are of a most unusual scarlet-orange hue.

Golden Salmon: The small flowers, produced in great abundance, are of a bright scarlet-salmon hue.

The Fairy: A polyantha with unique and endearing qualities. Hardy and vigorous, it reaches a height of $1\frac{1}{2}$ to 2 feet and often attains a spread of 3 feet. The rosette-type flowers are a charming shade of pink and are borne in great abundance in small clusters. The Fairy is seldom out of bloom.

ROSES FOR WALLS, PERGOLAS AND TRELLISES

Climbing Roses

In this class we find roses which are of particular value for use on arbors, fences, pergolas, pillars, trellises and walls.

Some are very robust, inclined to be rampant in habit of growth, and require ample room for development and adequate support. Others are more restrained in growth and less apt to outgrow their location. Some give a profusion of bloom during the height of the rose season and do not bloom again, while others continue to produce either abundant or intermittent bloom after the peak of bloom is passed. Some varieties are extremely hardy, and others are suited only to a mild climate. Some are particularly well adapted to growing on pillars and low fences, while others are best when allowed to climb on arbors or pergolas, or when trained on a trellis against a wall.

ROSES IN A LATTICE BAY

VARIETIES OF MERIT

Aloha: Deep, coral-pink buds, very large, rose-pink, double flowers with waxy petals. Blooms prolifically in June and continues to bloom frequently throughout the balance of the season. An excellent pillar rose.

Blaze: A very hardy, vigorous, everblooming climber, bearing an abundance of flowers of an intense scarlet-red hue. One of the best of the climbers in this color range.

City of York: Buff-yellow buds opening to creamy-white flowers. Awarded the National Gold Medal of the American Rose Society in 1950, the highest honor accorded a rose in this country.

Climbing Dainty Bess: The dainty, single flowers of sun-tan pink are borne in profusion. Vigorous growth.

Climbing Etoile De Hollande: Very fragrant, deep red blooms.

Climbing Mrs Sam McCredy: Abundant, salmon-copper blooms; a thing of dramatic beauty when in flower.

Climbing Peace: A luxuriant, fast-growing climber bearing flowers which are a replica of the beautiful hybrid tea rose, Peace.

Dream Girl: Coral-pink, full-petaled blooms, very fragrant, fine, healthy foliage, excellent on low fences.

Gladiator: An everblooming climber, flowers red in bud, rose-red in bloom. Vigorous, very hardy.

Golden Showers: Produces cascades of golden yellow blooms. Almost continually in flower. An excellent pillar rose and may also be used as a cascading shrub or as a climber. (All-American, 1957.)

High Noon: Because of the beauty of its golden yellow blooms and its fine habit of growth, High Noon received the regional All-America Award for mild climates.

CLIMBING ROSES

Jacotte: One of the most beautiful of all climbing roses. The foliage is glossy and holly-like in appearance and the large, semi-double flowers, which are borne in profusion, are an exquisite shade of apricot-orange. It is not hardy without protection where the winters are severe.

Mermaid: Large, single flowers of pale, sulphur yellow to ivory. Glossy foliage is evergreen in mild climates. May be used as a climber, a pillar rose or on banks. Adapted to mild climates.

New Dawn: One of the few large-flowered climbers with true everblooming characteristics. It is a sport of Doctor Van Fleet, the large, double flowers of a soft shell-pink color being produced continuously throughout the season.

Silver Moon: There is no other climber which possesses the unusual qualities of Silver Moon. The flowers are beautiful in form, being large and semi-double. In color, the flowers are a glistening white, shading to soft cream, and the brilliant golden stamens add greatly to the beauty of the blooms. It is one of the most vigorous of all the climbers.

Sparrieshoop: Beautiful in form and color. The single, shell-pink flowers are borne in abundance throughout the season. Lovely as a pillar rose or on a low fence.

White Dawn: Very hardy, everblooming, double, fragrant white flowers.

Ramblers

The rambler roses are particularly well suited for the covering of rough banks. Unfortunately some of the more common sorts such as the Crimson Rambler and Dorothy Perkins have been very much over-planted and it is usually possible to find roses which can be grown under similar conditions and which are far superior both in habit of growth and in quality of bloom. As a group the ramblers are very subject to attacks of mildew and the foliage is apt to become unsightly.

VARIETIES OF MERIT

Aviateur Blériot: Saffron buds and flowers in small clusters, light yellow fading white; magnolia fragrance.

Evangeline: One of the strongest-growing climbers with excellent glossy foliage, and bearing its soft pink, single flowers in enormous clusters. Lovely fragrance.

Phyllis Bide: A graceful rambler with exquisitely formed little buds of pale gold and pink, opening to small buff-yellow flowers.

Sanders' White Rambler: Flowers pure white, double and sweetly fragrant, in huge clusters. A strong grower with good, disease-resistant foliage.

White Dorothy: A pure white counterpart of the common pink Dorothy Perkins.

SHRUB ROSES

Roses of numerous types, many of them species roses or hybrids, fit into this class. They have considerable decorative value when used as specimens or accent plants, and some are happily at home in the shrub border. Most are hardy and vigorous and require comparatively little care and attention.

Austrian Brier Rose (R. foetida): A shrub rose reaching a height of 8 to 10 feet. Flowers bright yellow, single.

Austrian Copper (R. foetida bicolor): A lovely brier rose with single flowers of an intense coppery-red hue, the reverse side of the petals being a bright, golden yellow.

Harison's Yellow (R. foetida hybrid): Originated in 1830 by the Rev. Mr. Harison, this lovely brier rose has maintained its popularity for more than a century. It is hardy and vigorous in habit of growth and the semi-double yellow flowers are produced in great profusion. When it is in flower every branch and twig seem to have blossomed forth, so full is it of starry blooms.

Persian Yellow: Is a fine, old-fashioned shrub rose producing myriads of small, golden flowers.

Father Hugo's Rose (R. hugonis): Was first discovered growing wild in northern China by Father Hugo, a missionary, and was named in his honor. It is one of the loveliest plants known to cultivation and no rose garden is complete without it. It is the first rose to come into flower, and in late spring the slender, graceful branches are covered with myriad blooms. The flowers are single and exquisite in form, and they are of the softest shade of primrose yellow. It blooms more profusely if not fertilized.

Frueling's Gold (R. spinosissima hybrid): A recent introduction with lovely, golden, cup-shaped flowers, sweetly scented. Blooms are produced in great abundance. Vigorous growth, 3 to 5 feet high, spreading clumps. Very hardy, thrives on soil of moderate fertility.

Sweetbrier

The *Sweetbrier* or *Eglantine Rose* (Rosa Rubiginosa) is a native of England and is famed in song and story. The Eglantine rose, with its hybrids, is the only rose which possesses sweet-scented foliage. Tiny glands on the under-surface of the leaves give out a most delightful perfume, and when the plants are wet with dew, or after a warm summer shower, the fragrance is most alluring. The small, single flowers are a bright pink in color.

The *Penzance Sweetbriers* are hybrids of the Eglantine rose and were originated by Lord Penzance. The exquisite beauty of the small, single flowers and the scent of the foliage have endeared them to many gardeners and they are worthy of wider recognition.

Brenda: Fragrant, single flowers of a light peach-pink.

Lady Penzance, with bright, copper-colored flowers and its sweetly-scented foliage, is one of the most desirable of this group.

Lord Penzance bears exquisite single flowers of a delicate fawn tint shading to ecru, and the foliage is sweetly scented.

Meg Merrilies: Very vigorous in habit of growth. Single, fragrant flowers of a rosy crimson.

Minna: Flowers white, opening with the palest tinge of pink.

Rose Bradwardine: Flowers a clear, rose-pink. Foliage heavily scented.

Rugosa and Rugosa Hybrids

The name, rugosa, was given to this group because of the very wrinkled appearance of the foliage. The Rugosa roses are natives of Japan, China and Korea and they are noted for their hardiness and their ability to withstand very adverse conditions. They will thrive in almost any type of soil, will endure extreme cold and will withstand neglect better than almost any other rose known. They are of particular value for planting in exposed situations and at the seashore, where they are able to withstand the effects of salt spray. They range in height from 6 to 7 feet and produce numerous erect, very spiny stems. The foliage is a deep green in color, thick and wrinkled in texture, and is practically disease- and insect-proof.

VARIETIES AND HYBRIDS OF MERIT

Agnes: Coppery yellow buds, double flowers, pale amber-gold and very fragrant.

Doctor Eckener: Flowers are large, very fragrant, semi-double and of a beautiful coppery-rose shade, blended with yellow.

Flamingo: The flowers are borne in clusters. Buds are pointed. The single, five-petaled blooms are a flamingo pink, the color deepening as the season advances. Flowers throughout the summer and autumn. Hardy and vigorous. Height 4 to 5 feet.

Frau Dagmar Hartopp: A low-growing Rugosa hybrid. Flowers silvery pink, single with ruffled petals. Abundant bloom from June until frost. Rugged and hardy. Thrives on poor, sandy soil. Good under seashore conditions.

TRAILING ROSES

There are a few roses which are of such low, trailing habit that they are particularly well suited for use as a ground cover on hillsides and embankments. A number of new varieties have recently been introduced which are admirably adapted for this purpose.

VARIETIES OF MERIT

Coral Creeper: Buds deep red, flowers apricot-orange, fading to pink, semi-double in form and of good size.

Little Compton Creeper: Flowers single, deep rose-pink borne in large, open clusters. Foliage dark green and glossy.

Max Graf: Sprays of large, single, clear pink flowers.

Wichuraiana: A species rose of exceedingly rapid growth often producing canes from 12 to 15 feet long in a single season. The foliage is a glossy, pale green and the small white flowers are rather inconspicuous. The Wichuraiana rose is extremely hardy and will grow in almost any type of soil. It is well adapted to washed clay banks and other unfavorable situations.

OLD-FASHIONED ROSES

Beloved by countless generations of gardeners, these old-fashioned roses are seldom seen in gardens of the present day. There are, however, a few rosarians who have made a study of them and have brought together collections which are greatly cherished.

The Provence Rose

The *Provence* or *Cabbage Rose* derives its name from the Provence section of France where it was grown so abundantly. Legends tell us that it was cultivated by the Romans and was later introduced into other sections of Europe. The foliage is deeply wrinkled, broad and heavy, the blooms are large and globular in shape, and sweetly scented. Because of the great number of petals, folded upon each other like the leaves of a cabbage, it has been called the "Cabbage Rose". It blooms but once during the season. Although the Provence rose will grow in almost any soil and will withstand considerable neglect, it responds remarkably to good care and cultivation, and for best growth it should be heavily pruned.

VARIETIES OF MERIT

Anais Segalas: Flowers a deep tone of almost Tyrian-pink.

Konigin von Danemark: Flowers a delicate flesh-pink.

Unique Blanche: Deeply cupped, pure white flowers.

The Moss Rose

These roses are characterized by the distinctly mossy growth on the outer side of the calyx of the opening buds. As a group they are quite hardy but require severe pruning if good bloom is desired. In order to secure a succession of bloom, half of the canes may be pruned in October and half the following May, the shoots being cut back to 4 or 5 buds.

VARIETIES OF MERIT

Blanche Moreau: Buds heavily mossed, the double flowers being borne in clusters. Color, white tinged with pink. Vigorous and fine-flowering.

Crested Moss: The Crested Moss Rose is an offshoot of the Provence rose and was first discovered in 1827 growing in the crevice of a wall in Fribourg, Switzerland. The large, full flowers are a bright, rose-pink in color.

Gloire De Mousseux: One of the finest of the Moss roses. The flowers are of a carmine-salmon-pink shade and are produced in great abundance.

Old Pink Moss: One of the oldest roses of this type. Buds heavily mossed, flowers pale rose-pink.

The Damask Rose

This rose is a native of Damascus and Syria and was brought to Europe by the early Crusaders upon their return from the Holy Land. It is known to have been in cultivation in England in 1573. Damask roses are very hardy and vigorous and thrive well in almost any type of soil. The foliage is large and rough and light green in color. The flowers are usually produced in trusses of three or more.

VARIETIES OF MERIT

Damascena officinalis: The original Rose of Damascus, intensely fragrant, and bearing double, rose-pink flowers.

Marie Louise: Double flowers of a rich, deep pink. An old variety found growing in the gardens of Malmaison in 1813.

Mme Hardy: Flowers pure white, occasionally tinged with pink. One of the most beautiful and most fragrant of the Damask roses.

The Bourbon Rose

These roses were introduced into France in 1820 from the Isle of Bourbon and are closely related to the China or Bengal Roses. They are moderately hardy and vigorous and bloom freely throughout the early summer, some varieties blooming also in the autumn. The foliage is dark and lustrous.

VARIETIES OF MERIT

Adam Messerich: Fragrant flowers of a clear, rose-red. Bushy in habit of growth.

Louise Odier: Flowers, flesh-pink, of good form, and produced freely throughout the season.

Martha: Flowers a lovely shade of salmon-orange, produced freely on thornless canes.

Souvenir De La Malmaison: Very fragrant flesh-colored flowers. Of dwarf habit—hardly more than 2 feet in height.

The Noisette Rose

This rose was originated by Mr. Philip Noisette of Charleston, South Carolina, in 1817, as a result of crossing the China Blush Rose with the Musk Rose. Mr. Noisette sent the rose to his father in France and he, in turn, originated from it the beautiful Maréchal Niel rose, so beloved throughout the South.

VARIETIES OF MERIT AMONG THE NOISETTE HYBRIDS

Bouquet D'Or: Flowers large and full, pale yellow, shaded with coppery salmon.

Crépuscule: A beautiful variety with flowers of an orange-pink shade, fading to apricot yellow.

Maréchal Niel: Double, fragrant flowers of a deep, golden yellow. Not hardy in the North, but one of the most beautiful of all roses for Southern gardens.

Rêve D'Or: Fragrant, double flowers of a soft buff-yellow shade. Very vigorous in habit of growth.

China or Bengal Rose

These are noted for their fine, almost evergreen foliage, which is extremely resistant to disease, and for their profuse, everblooming habit.

VARIETIES OF MERIT

Comtesse Du Cayla: Semi-single flowers, buds coppery orange, flowers reddish-orange and yellow.

Laurette Messimy: Flowers rose-pink, tinted with yellow.

Old Blush: The original China Rose introduced in 1796. Flowers bright pink, darkening with age.

XXX

PLANTS IN THE HOME

HOUSES designed in the contemporary manner have presented to the gardener new opportunities and a new challenge for the dramatic use of plants. Great expanses of glass reaching from ceiling to floor; room dividers with built-in boxes for plants; walls of brick or stone near the raised hearth—such areas, if treated with imagination and skill, may have great distinction and charm, and plants thus used will add immeasurably to the decor of the home.

Architects have designed floor wells into which potted plants of large size may be set to give dignity and scale to the planting in front of large windows, and long, deep boxes are especially designed for use in front of windows slightly above floor level.

And never before has such a wealth of plant material been available. Plant explorers, sent into Central and South America, have discovered, growing in the dim light of tropical jungles, new plants which are admirably adapted to growing in the subdued light of room interiors in the modern suburban home and in the city apartment. Some of these new plants, with their huge, glossy, deeply-lobed leaves are exotic and exciting in appearance, while others are valued for their more gentle qualities of delicate leaf patterns and iridescent hues on the undersurface of the foliage.

In recent years the plant scientists have developed many new hybrids with interesting leaf forms and with variegated foliage, splashed with white and dusted with gold, which bring life and animation to indoor planting compositions. Especially suited to the more traditional type of home are the new varieties of ivy and begonias and saintpaulias which bring color and warmth and bloom to the window garden. There are few foliage plants more decorative than some of the new hybrid begonias, and a pebble-filled tray containing a number of varieties with contrasting leaf forms and subtle colorings possesses great beauty and distinction.

Practical Considerations

In order to attain success with plants in the house it is necessary to have a knowledge of their cultural requirements. Selections should be made with care and the specific requirements of each plant should be met as completely as possible. In order to provide favorable growing conditions the following points should be taken into consideration: light, temperature, ventilation, humidity, watering, feeding, potting, soil, general care and the control of pests and diseases.

Light

Light is essential to the growth of all plants which contain chlorophyll or green coloring matter. The leaves serve as a manufacturing center for plant foods, and this process is carried on under the direct influence of light. If the leaves are entirely deprived of light, they are unable to perform the function of food manufacture, and they gradually turn yellow and die.

Plants vary tremendously in the amount of light which they require for their best development. Many of the ferns, which in their native habitat grow in dense woodland shade, require comparatively little light. Most foliage plants, particularly those which are native to the tropical jungles and rain forests of Central America, thrive best in diffused natural light. In the home a north window will best meet their needs, and some may be grown successfully in the interior of the room. There are comparatively few foliage house plants which can tolerate direct sunlight, particularly midday sun. Foliage plants with variegated foliage require more light than others, due to the fact that the leaf cells in the white portion contain little or no chlorophyll and are therefore unable to carry on the manufacture of food.

Most flowering plants require full sunlight, or sun for at least the major portion of the day. Such plants thrive best in a window with a southern or southeastern exposure. A few flowering plants, however, such as Achimenes and the Italian Bellflower, prefer limited sun and should be grown in a window with an eastern exposure.

When house plants are left in one position for any length of time, the leaves and stems will turn toward the light, and the growth of the plant will become very unsymmetrical. In order to avoid this tendency the pots should be turned at frequent intervals so that all portions of the plant may receive an equal amount of light. The growth will then remain symmetrical and well balanced.

Temperature

Every plant has an optimum temperature range which provides conditions favorable for maximum growth. Some plants suffer seriously when there are fluctuations of temperature much above or below this range, while other plants are able to withstand great fluctuations without serious damage.

The majority of house plants thrive well in a moderate temperature, ranging between 62 and 70 degrees F., with a somewhat cooler temperature at night.

Some plants require a very warm temperature, between 75 and 80 degrees F., and will not make satisfactory growth unless this requirement is met. Other plants require a very cool temperature, 50 to 60 degrees F., and will not thrive well in even moderately warm temperatures. Plants in this group are best suited to growing on a cool porch.

When plants are grown on window sills or ledges it is a wise precaution to place a heavy layer of newspaper between the plants and the window on severely cold nights, as such a measure will afford excellent protection.

Ventilation

House plants require an ample supply of fresh air, but must be protected from direct drafts and from being suddenly chilled. Ventilating should, therefore, be done in such a way that they are protected from direct currents of cold air. Either muslin or metal slat ventilators are very satisfactory for use in rooms where house plants are grown, as they provide for an excellent circulation of fresh air without causing a draft. It is wise to provide a change of air at least twice a day in a room where plants are grown. In mild weather the doors or windows of the room may be opened. In severe weather it may be advisable to open the windows in an adjoining room. Ventilation has a very direct influence in mitigating the effect of coal gas and illuminating gas. Some plants, such as the Jerusalem cherry, are extremely sensitive to escaping gas, and even a very minute quantity of gas in the atmosphere, a quantity so minute that it can hardly be detected, will have a very damaging effect, causing a blackening of the buds and a discoloration of the leaves. In the fruiting stage, the fruits will drop prematurely.

Humidity

Closely associated with the problems of ventilation and watering is the problem of humidity. A moist atmosphere is essential to the health and vigor of most house plants. There are comparatively few plants which will thrive, or even survive, in a dry, almost desert-like atmosphere. It is impossible, therefore, to expect satisfactory growth unless every effort is made to increase the humidity of the atmosphere, and this may be accomplished in several very simple ways. Some of the newer heating systems are equipped with humidifying devices, and special water-holding compartments are attached to some of the more modern types of radiators. If such devices are not already part of the heating system, water pans may be purchased and attached to the radiators. Another excellent method of increasing the humidity is to set the plants on metal trays which have been filled with pebbles and water. The bottom of the pots should rest on dry pebbles which are slightly above the level of the water. This same method may be used with flowerpot saucers, care being taken to make sure that the water does not reach the bottom of the pot, which would cause the soil to be too constantly saturated.

A daily syringing of the foliage with a fine spray of clear water will not only greatly increase the humidity but will also help to keep the foliage clean and in healthy condition, as it keeps the stomata or breathing pores open. It is also of benefit in helping to keep certain insect pests in check. Plants with hairy leaves, such as gloxinias and saintpaulias, should not be syringed, as the effect of moisture upon the leaves is often more harmful than beneficial. A small rubber bulb syringe such as may be procured at any hardware store is excellent for a small number of plants. A glass jar fitted with a small spray attachment is also very satisfactory. It is possible, also, to use a larger type of sprayer, provided that it will throw a fine, mist-like spray. If an adjustable nozzle is used it will be possible to reach the undersurface of the leaves.

Watering

The watering of house plants is a task which requires good judgment. It is quite as important not to overwater as it is to avoid underwatering. Not only do different species of plants vary tremendously in their moisture requirements, but individual plants also vary considerably according to the stage of growth. When plants are making active growth, forming new shoots and flower buds, they require much more water than they do when they are in the resting, non-flowering stage. Although daily watering is not necessary for all house plants it is wise to make a daily survey in order to ascertain their needs. When the surface of the soil in the pot is dry to the point of being crumbly to the touch, or if the pot gives a hollow, ringing sound when it is tapped lightly with the knuckle, the indications

are that the plant needs water. If water is applied to the surface of the soil by means of a watering can, the surplus water will drain out through the opening in the bottom of the pot. If watering is done by placing the pot in a pan of water it should be allowed to remain in the receptacle until the surface of the soil becomes dark and moist in appearance. It should then be removed and the surplus water should be allowed to drain away. This method of watering is excellent for those plants which have dense, fuzzy leaves such as the African violet (saintpaulia) and gloxinia. Pots should never be allowed to stand in saucers which are filled with water, as the soil in the bottom of the pot will soon become soggy and sour and the growth and vigor of the plant will be seriously affected. Water which is approximately the same temperature as the room should be used.

Feeding

Many house plants will be benefited by a regular feeding. Applications of fertilizer should be made when the plants are making active, vigorous growth, preferably after the flower buds have formed but before the flowers have begun to show color. At this period of growth a light application of fertilizer may be made at intervals of every two weeks. No application should be made when the plants are in a resting stage.

When feeding potted plants according to the method developed by the University of Wisconsin place a single package near the bottom of the pot. (see page 166)

There are many excellent, quickly-soluble fertilizers on the market which are suitable for house plants. A preparation should be chosen which contains the trace elements, as well as the major elements. The instructions on the container concerning the rate of application should be followed with care. (See pages 165–166 covering Soluble Fertilizers.)

General Care

Keeping Foliage in Good Condition: Plants transpire through their leaves and when the foliage becomes coated with a film of fine dust particles, or with soot from oil-burning or coal heaters, it seriously interferes

A WINDOW GARDEN IN A MODERN HOME. A BUILT-IN FLOOR WELL OFFERS DELIGHTFUL OPPORTUNITIES FOR GROWING PLANTS OF CONSIDERABLE SIZE.

with this natural process, and the plants suffer in consequence. In order to keep the foliage of house plants with glossy leaves clean and in healthy condition the leaves should be syringed or cleansed at periodic intervals, at least once or twice a month. Plants with thick, hairy leaves such as the African violets and gloxinias should not be treated in this manner.

If one has only a few plants which require attention, and if they are not too large, they may be placed in the sink or in a laundry tub and syringed with a fine, but fairly strong, spray of lukewarm water from the faucet. Both the upper and under surfaces of the leaves should be covered. The foliage should be allowed to dry before the plants are placed again in full sunlight in order to avoid the possibility of burning tender leaves.

In the case of large plants which cannot be moved easily, the leaves may be wiped with a damp cloth or sponge. A mild soap and water solution will leave a gloss on the leaves.

If plants are kept on pebbles in a metal tray a small hand syringe may be used very effectively. The syringing should be done on a dry day and the foliage should be protected from direct sunlight while it is wet.

Dividing House Plants: Many foliage plants benefit greatly from occasional division and replanting. Not all plants can be handled in this way, however, because of their habit of growth. In general, plants which grow in clumps, with several stems rising from below the soil, each with a separate root system, may be divided successfully.

The procedure is simple. The plant should be removed from the pot. The soil should then be shaken away from the roots, and the sections should be pulled gently apart. It is important that each section have good roots. In some cases it may be necessary to cut the sections off the main stock-plant with a sharp knife.

Long, straggly roots should be cut back, and in some cases it may be advisable to remove one or two of the old leaves, retaining the younger, more vigorous growth.

Each section should be planted in a pot of sufficient size, using a good potting mixture. The soil should be worked well about the roots in order to prevent air pockets, and should be well firmed. The plant should be watered and should be placed in subdued light for several days.

Potting

House plants should be repotted only when they will derive very definite benefit, and it has been found that plants vary greatly in their needs for frequent potting. Most flowering plants will, like the geraniums, give better bloom if they are allowed to become somewhat pot-bound. Such plants as amaryllis, the various palms, and pandanus will also thrive well in very small pots and seem to suffer no ill effects from becoming extremely pot-bound. Many house plants may be grown in comparatively small pots if sufficient nutrients are provided in the form of occasional applications of a complete fertilizer (see page 679 on Feeding).

Young plants, grown either from seed or from cuttings, must be shifted on at frequent intervals from small pots to slightly larger pots. The general practice is to repot such plants as soon as the pots which they occupy have become well filled with roots. Unless this is done, the plants may become stunted, and will be unable to make normal and vigorous growth. A pot from $\frac{1}{2}$ inch to 1 inch larger in size is usually sufficient for the next stage of growth.

When plants are grown in pots it is essential that ample drainage be provided. In small pots a piece of broken crock placed over the hole in the bottom of the pot will usually be sufficient. When large pots are used, and particularly if the plant is to remain in the pot for some time, it is wise to place a layer of broken crock in the bottom, and above the crock a thin layer of moist sphagnum moss in order to prevent the soil from sifting down and clogging the drainage area.

In potting young seedlings or rooted cuttings the pot may be partially filled with soil. The plant should then be held in place with the roots spread out in a natural position. The remaining soil should be added and pressed firmly into place with the fingers. In small pots a space of approximately $\frac{1}{2}$-inch should be left between the surface of the soil and the rim of the pot. In potting rooted cuttings a soil mixture consisting of 2 parts sharp sand, 1 part loam, and 1 part leaf mold or peat is recommended. For young seedlings in the early transplanting stages, a mixture of 1 part sand, 1 part loam and 1 part leaf mold or peat moss will give excellent results. The pots should be watered thoroughly and should be shaded from direct sunlight for several days in order that the plants may have an opportunity to become re-established.

In repotting an established plant, the plant may be removed by inverting the pot and tapping the rim on the edge of a firm surface, such as the edge of a potting bench or a work table. The soil in the pot should be fairly moist so that it does not crumble, and while the pot is held in an inverted position the fingers of the left hand should be held firmly over the ball of earth. A small quantity of soil should be placed over the drainage material and the plant should be placed in the center of the pot. If the pot is only slightly larger than that previously occupied by the plant it will be necessary to remove some soil from the bottom and sides of the ball of earth surrounding the roots. This should be done with care in order to keep the root system as nearly intact as possible. The space between the old ball of earth and the side of the pot should be filled with the new potting soil, which should be firmed into place with the fingers or with a small potting stick.

(For details concerning sizes and types of pots, see page 38.)

Soil Mixtures

An excellent general-purpose potting mixture consists of 1 part sand, 2 parts fibrous loam, 1 part humus in the form of compost, leaf mold or peat, $\frac{1}{2}$ part of well-rotted cow manure—to which mixture has been added a 5-inch pot of bone meal per bushel of soil.

Certain groups of plants have very definite soil preferences. The azaleas and all the members of the Heath family prefer an acid soil, and the following potting mixture is recommended: 2 parts sand, 2 parts loam, 2 parts acid peat, 1 part leaf mold, and $\frac{1}{3}$ of a part of cow manure.

The succulents, on the other hand, prefer a highly alkaline soil and the following mixture will give excellent results: 2 parts sand, 2 parts loam, $\frac{1}{2}$ part leaf mold—to which mixture there has been added, per bushel of soil, one 5-inch pot of bone meal, and one 5-inch pot of finely ground limestone. The mixture may be further improved by adding a small quantity of finely chipped brick particles or broken crock.

Ferns and begonias thrive best in a soil well supplied with humus, such as a mixture of 2 parts sand, 2 parts loam, 2 parts leaf mold or some other form of humus, and $\frac{1}{2}$ part rotted cow manure.

Further details concerning potting mixtures for individual plant groups may be found under the specific cultural requirements.

Control of Pests and Diseases

It is important to know how to identify the various insect pests which attack house plants and to recognize the first signs of infestation in order that prompt and effective measures of control may be undertaken. Conditions under which house plants are grown are very favorable to the rapid increase of many insect pests and the importance of being on the alert to detect trouble when it first starts cannot be overemphasized.

There are on the market excellent all-purpose sprays for house plants which come in small plastic spray bottles and in metal containers of the aerosol type. When using the latter type it is very important to follow the directions implicitly. The spray "bomb", as it is sometimes called, should always be held 12 to 18 inches away from the plants. If the spray is applied at too close a range the solvent may not evaporate quickly enough and severe burning of the foliage may result. A circular or sweeping motion should be made with the hand while making the application and the spray should be applied in short bursts rather than as a continuous spray. The foliage of the plants should not appear visibly wet after the application has been made.

Most of these sprays are formulated to provide effective control for all the common house plant pests. However, when purchasing it is wise to make certain that the spray selected is effective against the particular pest which you desire to eradicate. This information is always given on the spray container. Instructions concerning the method of application are also given on the container and should be followed with care.

Insects on House Plants

Aphids are often very troublesome on house plants. There are various species, some living only on one type of plant while others thrive on many kinds. They are small, lice-like insects and may be either green, black, or brown in color. They are found usually on the tips of the young, growing shoots, both on the leaves and clustered closely along the stem. Being equipped with delicate, tuber-like mouth-parts they are able to pierce through the outer tissues and suck the juices from the plant, causing a general lack of vigor and stunted growth. All species may be readily controlled by a good contact poison, a poison which will come into direct contact with each insect, causing death by stopping up the breathing pores.

Cyclamen-mites are usually found on cyclamen plants but they also attack geraniums, fuchsias, chrysanthemums, and a number of other plants. They are minute creatures, hardly visible to the naked eye, but if they are present in sufficient numbers they are capable of doing considerable damage. The injury caused by cyclamen-mites is very characteristic. When a plant is attacked, the leaves begin to curl from the outside, taking on a curiously deformed appearance, and if the infestation is severe the plant loses its foliage entirely. The flower buds wither before they open or become badly distorted and drop prematurely.

Mealy-bugs belong to the group of scale insects and are often found on plants which have been purchased from a greenhouse or a florist. They are not only very unsightly but they sap the vitality of the plants and every effort should be made to keep them under control. Although found on many kinds of plants they seem to have a particular fondness for abutilon and coleus. They may be easily distinguished from other insects by their white waxy covering. At the time the females are ready to deposit their eggs, this covering increases until it resembles a little tuft of cotton.

Red Spiders are very small mites which cause considerable trouble if they become sufficiently numerous. They collect on the undersurface of the leaves and suck the juices from the plant, causing the foliage to become whitish and unhealthy in appearance.

Scales. House plants are attacked by various forms of scale, ferns, palms, rubber plants and orange plants being particularly susceptible. Some scales have soft bodies while others have hard, shell-like coverings, but they may all be controlled by contact sprays.

White-flies have a special fondness for fuchsias, heliotrope, lantana, and geraniums, and in some seasons they become very troublesome. They are found usually on the tender new shoots, and as they suck the juices from the plants they cause stunted growth. They are small, whitish flies. Although they are provided with wings they usually settle on the underside of the leaves and seldom fly unless disturbed.

FLOWERING PLANTS OF MERIT

Achimenes: This charming, tuberous plant which is so generous with its bloom throughout the summer months is happily at home indoors and makes a most unusual and lovely house plant. It prefers an exposure where it is protected from midday sun, and thrives particularly well in an east window. It may be grown as a potted plant on the window sill or may be used in a hanging pot or basket. (For complete description and culture see page 394.)

African violet (Saintpaulia ionantha): Few plants have obtained such wide acclaim within recent years as has the lovely African violet. It is now rated as the most popular and most widely grown of all house plants. Under favorable growing conditions, and with proper care, it will remain almost continually in bloom. It is a delightfully decorative little plant with thick, fuzzy leaves and myriad flowers in soft tones of violet, purple and pink. During recent years many new varieties have been introduced which have greatly extended the color range and given a variety of leaf forms. The African violet is one of the most charming and satisfactory of house plants, provided its rather exacting cultural requirements are met.

Culture:

Exposure: The African violet thrives best in low light intensity and may be grown very satisfactorily in either an east or west window. If grown in a south window it should be protected from direct sunlight by a thin curtain. In a north window it will live and make some growth but will usually give little or no bloom during the winter months. The African violet is particularly well adapted to growing under artificial light (see page 462).

Temperature: A range of temperature between 65° and 75° F. best meets the needs of the African violet. The plants will not thrive if the temperature drops below 60° F. If the plants are grown in too cool a temperature they develop a condition known as epinasty, which causes the growth to curl downward.

Soil: African violets require a mellow, friable soil, rich in humus, with a pH ranging between 6.0 and 6.5. Any of the following mixtures will give excellent results:

(1) 1 part garden loam, 1 part leaf mold, 1 part sand.
(2) 1 part loam, 1 part sand, 1 part *rotted* manure, 1 part peat moss or leaf mold.
(3) 2 parts loam, 2 parts leaf mold, 1 part sand, 1 part dried manure.

Watering: Careful attention must be given to watering. African violets are particularly well adapted to wick-watering and this is the ideal method to use. Wick-fed pots have many advantages: the plant receives the exact amount of water which it needs, the pot never becomes too wet or too dry, the danger of crown rot is lessened and there is no spotting of the leaves. An adaptation of this method is to place the pot in a saucer of water until the soil at the surface begins to appear moist. The pot should then be removed. If surface watering is done, great care must be taken not to let water settle in or around the crown of the plant, as it is apt to cause crown rot. Another precaution which must be strictly observed is always to use water which is about blood warm.

Care: African violets require loose potting. The plants are extremely sensitive to gas fumes. One must be on the alert to detect the first signs of mite infestation, as African violets are particularly susceptible. Trouble is evidenced by a dwarfed appearance of the plants, a blighting of flower buds and malformation of the flowers. The leaves are either cupped upward or rolled downward, and frequently have a whitish pubescence on the upper surface. (See page 646 for measures of control.) Faded blooms should be snipped off in order to induce continued flowering. Dust may be removed from the leaves with a small camel hair brush. Leaf cuttings taken in March usually root readily. (See Chapter XXXIII on Propagation.)

Culture of African Violets under Artificial Light

African violets do extremely well when grown under artificial lights. In fact experimental tests have proved that African violets will thrive better when grown under lights than when grown under natural conditions either in the home or in a greenhouse. The plants will come into flower earlier, will produce more abundant bloom, the foliage will be larger and will possess deeper color, the plants will be more symmetrical in shape and the color of many varieties will be deeper and richer in tone. At Ohio State University salable plants were produced from rooted cuttings in two months when grown under fluorescent lights.

Tests at various experiment stations have determined that for maximum growth and flowering African violets require a rather low light intensity, from 300 to 600 foot-candles of light, depending upon the size and stage of growth of the plant. Small plants in 2-inch pots will make best growth if placed about 3 to 4 inches below the light tubes. Mature plants should be placed from 12 to 18 inches below the lights. If the foliage turns yellow it is an indication that the plants are probably receiving too much light. If the leaves are a very deep green and the stems spindly and weak, and the plants fail to flower satisfactorily it is usually an indication that the plants are not receiving enough light.

(For the general culture of plants under artificial lights see page 642.)

Amaryllis. The species amaryllis from which our modern types have been developed are dainty and graceful. In the hands of the hybridizers they have lost these particular qualities, but have gained in range of coloring, in robustness and in size.

These modern hybrid amaryllis have increased rapidly in popularity within recent years and are now widely grown for winter flowering in window gardens and in greenhouses. In mild climates they may be brought into flower out-of-doors and used with dramatic effect in the garden or as a foreground planting in the shrub border.

The longevity of amaryllis bulbs is a constant source of amazement to gardeners. When properly handled a bulb will continue to produce flowers for 50 to 75 years, and may become almost an heirloom in a family. It is this characteristic which often justifies the purchase of expensive, named varieties of superior quality.

The blooms of the amaryllis are borne on tall, straight flower stalks, high above the foliage which develops at the base of the plant. The flowers of the American-grown strains are trumpet shaped, and vary greatly in size according to the variety and the culture which they receive. Some individual blooms measure as much as 10 to 12 inches across. In the Dutch strains the flowers have what is known as "pansy-faced" blooms, the rounded petals being widely flared. The colors found in the Royal Dutch amaryllis are usually very pleasing, seldom being garish or striped, and many of the blooms have a luminous, iridescent quality. Some of the exceptionally large Dutch bulbs produce as many as three flower stalks.

Selection of Bulbs: Large quantities of amaryllis bulbs are produced from seed by commercial growers. Bulbs grown from naturally pollinated seed are considerably less expensive than those grown from hand-pollinated seed. For blooms of superior quality and of selected color the bulbs from hand-pollinated seed are to be preferred. Named varieties of Amaryllis are propagated vegetatively, either by division of the parent bulb or by the forced production of bulblets. Such bulbs are far more expensive than bulbs produced from seed, but when exhibition blooms of outstanding quality are desired the additional cost is more than justified.

A good amaryllis bulb should be from 4 to 6 inches in diameter and should have numerous roots. Bulbs purchased early in the season (October to December) will usually be of better quality than those purchased later. The roots will be more fleshy and the bulb will become established more quickly than it will if the roots have become very dry.

Potting: For satisfactory winter bloom indoors amaryllis bulbs should preferably be started in November or December.

The pot should be comparatively small in relation to the bulb. A 4-inch pot is usually adequate for an amaryllis bulb of average size. For larger bulbs a pot of more ample size is necessary. Most growers prefer "three-quarter" or "azalea-type" pots. Amaryllis bulbs will produce better flowers when somewhat root bound. A pot may be considered large enough if there is room for an inch of soil between the bulb and the pot. New pots should always be soaked before they are used.

At least one half-inch of broken crocks or gravel should be used in the bottom of the pot to insure good drainage. Above this an inch layer of rich compost or rotted cow manure (if it is available) should be placed. A good general potting mixture for amaryllis bulbs consists of one part leaf mold or compost, one part good garden loam and one part sand. To this mixture a handful of steamed bone meal should be added for each pot. The optimum pH for amaryllis ranges between 6.0 and 6.8.

The bulb should be placed in the pot so that about one-third protrudes above the soil. It is advisable to make sure that the soil is worked in well around the roots at the time of potting and that no air spaces are left. The soil should be pressed around the bulb firmly, and at least one inch should be left between the surface of the soil and the rim of the pot in order to provide adequate space for watering.

Watering: Immediately after potting the bulb should be watered thoroughly. From then on, until growth starts, it should be watered sparingly, being kept barely damp. Too much water at this stage may cause basal rot. As soon as the flower stalk appears the amount of water should be increased. When in bloom amaryllis require large quantities of water and can hardly be kept too moist. It is not advisable, however, to place the pot in a receptacle of water.

Exposure: When amaryllis are grown indoors a window with a southern exposure will provide the most ideal conditions, although they may also be brought into flower reasonably well in windows with either an eastern or western exposure. If the only available space is a north window a fair degree of success may be obtained by placing a 100-watt electric bulb over the plant for a few hours every evening.

Temperature: Amaryllis are among the most adaptable of plants when it comes to temperature requirements. They will thrive well in over-heated city apartments, and will also adapt themselves quite happily to the wide fluctuation in temperature often encountered in country houses. The time from planting to flowering will depend to a considerable extent upon the temperature in which the plants are grown. If the pot is placed on a tray over a hot water radiator an amaryllis bulb can be forced into bloom weeks ahead of one grown on a cool window sill. It is therefore possible to bring them into bloom very rapidly or to hold them back. This is a great advantage when flowers are desired for some special date, such as Valentine's Day, or Easter, or for a flower show. The normal months for flowering are February, March, April and May. If exceptionally early blooms are desired for Christmas or New Year's, specially treated bulbs may be obtained.

The temperature also has a great influence upon the lasting qualities of the blooms. In a warm room where the day temperature ranges around 75° the blooms will last about three weeks. In a cool window where the temperature seldom goes above 65° flowers will often last for 10 weeks.

Fertilization: It is advisable to apply a soluble fertilizer (at half the usually recommended strength), every two or three weeks throughout the growing period.

Care after Flowering: As soon as each flower fades it should be cut off with a sharp knife. After the last bloom is over the flower stalk should be cut down within 2 inches from the top of the bulb.

The foliage will continue to grow and the average bulb will produce from 8 to 10 large leaves by October. This leaf growth is necessary in order to prepare the bulb for the next season of bloom.

The bulb may be kept in the pot indoors throughout this growing period, or it may be planted out-of-doors in a semi-shaded spot. If it is removed from the pot, care must be taken not to break the root ball.

If the bulb is kept in the pot, watering and feeding should be continued until about October 1. Water should then be withheld. After the leaves have wilted they should be cut off and the pot should be turned on its side for a rest period. During this curing period, which lasts from three to four weeks, the temperature should range from 70° to 75°. At the end of this period the pot may be placed in a cooler temperature and held there until December. The bulb can then be repotted if it has become too crowded in the pot, or the pot may be placed in its accustomed window where the growth cycle will start again. Repotting is advisable when the bulb practically fills the pot. A pot an inch larger than the old one should be used. There will be less set-back if care is taken not to disturb the ball of earth around the roots.

When amaryllis bulbs have been planted out-of-doors after flowering they should be lifted just before the first frost. A spading fork can be used to loosen the soil, and care should be taken to see that the roots are not injured. The leaves should be cut back to the neck of the bulb and the bulbs should then be stored for three to four weeks at a temperature of 70° to 75°. They should then be moved to a cool, dry place until they are potted in December.

Amaryllis will flower year after year, and each season will usually produce a greater number of blooms.

Bouvardia: This lovely, evergreen Southern shrub makes an attractive house plant and is particularly beloved because of the delightful fragrance of its tubular white flowers. It reaches a height of 2 to 3 feet and is of particular value for use in front of a large sunny window, or in a floor well.

Culture:

Exposure: Thrives best in a sunny window.

Temperature: Requires a cool temperature between 55° and 60° F.

Soil: Thrives best in a mixture of leaf mold, peat moss and sand.

Care: See page 526.

Bulbs: A great variety of bulbs may be brought into flower indoors during the late winter and early spring months and will add greatly to the charm of the window garden. Many of the smaller bulbs may be forced, as well as the bulbous iris, the narcissus and the tulips.

For full cultural directions for forcing—

Bulbous Iris: See page 532.
Narcissus: See page 534.
Tulips: See page 537.

A BROAD WINDOW SILL FOR POTTED PLANTS

Campanula isophylla (Italian Bellflower): This is one of the most charming of the trailing house plants. It graces many a window in the homes of New England and should be more widely grown. The starry flowers are a soft lavender-blue and the foliage has a gray-blue cast. The flowers of the variety *alba* are a sparkling white and the foliage is a deep green. When the plants are in bloom they are literally covered with flowers and a large, well-grown specimen is a thing of great beauty. They can be used very effectively on a plant stand, or a plant may be placed on an inverted pot on a window sill. But they are at their best when grown in a hanging pot in the window. The period of bloom usually extends from August to December.

Culture:

Exposure: Campanula isophylla thrives well in either an east or west window, although morning sun is preferred. During late spring and summer light protection should be given against strong sunlight. During the long days of summer not more than six hours of sunlight is advisable.

Temperature: Cool growing conditions are essential, and a good circulation of air is necessary.

A DRAMATIC ARRANGEMENT OF HOUSE PLANTS

A WINDOW GARDEN

Soil: A light, rich soil will best meet their needs, such as a mixture composed of 2 parts garden loam, 1 part leaf mold, 1 part sand, and 1 part rotted cow manure or dehydrated manure.

Watering: Throughout much of the year the plants should be kept rather on the dry side, but they should never be allowed to dry out entirely. During the budding and flowering period the plants should be watered more freely but should never be kept too wet. It is wise to let the plants dry out slightly before watering again.

Fertilization: Begin monthly feedings of a high-analysis, soluble fertilizer in May after plants are well established. After the buds begin to form, feed every two weeks. When the plants come into flower reduce feedings to three-week intervals.

Care: The Italian Bellflower should be grown under roof throughout the year. A cool, covered porch will provide excellent growing conditions during the summer months. The plants are unable to tolerate heavy rains and it is not advisable to put the pots out of doors at any time. During the heat of summer the plants should be kept as cool as possible. After bloom is over the plants should be cut back to the base and carried through the winter in a very cool room with full sun, being kept on the dry side. Cuttings may be taken from January to April. Side shoots may also be picked off and rooted. Repot old plants in March or April in fresh soil and begin to water more freely. Pinch back shoots as they start to run up and do not allow them to trail. Repot plants when they become pot bound. Keep plants pinched back until early June. Give plants about six hours of morning sun. After plants come into flower pick off dead blooms to improve appearance.

Fuchsias (Ladies' Ear-drops): The fuchsias, with their colorful, pendent blooms, are among the most decorative of house plants. A well-grown specimen plant is a thing of great beauty when in full flower. The colors range through tones of blush-pink, violet, reddish purple and cerise, many varieties producing flowers with striking contrasting shades. Fuchsias normally flower during the summer and mature plants will not bloom during the winter unless they have had a rest period. For winter bloom it is usually most satisfactory to purchase vigorous young plants in the autumn. Plants may, if desired, be grown at home from cuttings taken in the spring. If old plants are to be used they must be given a rest period during November and December in a very cool, dimly lighted place where the temperature range is from 45° to 50° F. The plants should receive only enough water to keep the wood plump. In January the plants may be brought into the house and watered sparingly until active growth starts, being kept in a temperature of 60° to 65° F. during the day, lower at night. Plants should be pruned to shapely form when the buds begin to swell, dead and weak wood being cut out.

Culture:

Exposure: Fuchsias require good light but protection from full sun. They thrive best in east or west windows.

Temperature: Fuchsias require a cool temperature for good growth, 50° to 65° F. best suiting their needs. They will not thrive in over-heated rooms.

Soil: A mellow, garden loam well supplied with humus will give satisfactory results. Good drainage is essential.

Fertilization: Fuchsias respond well to liberal feeding. During the period of active growth and bloom biweekly applications of a high-analysis, soluble fertilizer may be given at half the usual strength.

Care: As fuchsias are shallow rooted, careful attention must be paid to watering. Ample water is required during the growing and flowering period. Young plants grown from cuttings should be pinched back to induce bushy, stocky growth. Fuchsias may be easily trained to the standard form if desired.

Geraniums: For generations the geraniums have been among the most popular and beloved of house plants. (For description and complete cultural details, see page 530.)

Gloxinias: Although the lovely gloxinias thrive best under greenhouse conditions they may also be grown as house plants and are becoming increasingly popular. (For description and complete cultural details, see page 531.)

Impatiens (Patience Plant): Impatiens is one of the few house plants which will give almost continuous bloom throughout the year if conditions are favorable. The two species most commonly grown are *I. sultani*, the old-fashioned type, and *I. holsti*. Many lovely hybrids of these two species have recently been introduced and plants are now available in a wide variety of colors; white, soft pink, salmon, coral, pale lavender, purple, cerise and brick-red. The dainty, five-petaled flowers are borne in great profusion and the plants are sometimes literally covered with bloom.

Culture:

Exposure: The plants thrive best in full sun during the winter months and in partial sun during the summer.

Temperature: Impatiens prefers cool to moderately warm growing conditions and resents sharp fluctuations in temperature.

Soil: Any good, well-drained, non-acid garden soil will give satisfactory results.

Care: Impatiens requires abundant water and wilts quickly if allowed to become too dry, although it revives promptly upon the application of water, even when badly wilted. Cuttings may be taken at any time of year and root easily. Cuttings taken in the late spring or early summer will develop into plants ready to give good bloom the following winter. Old plants which have become too large may be cut back severely and will send up vigorous young growth from near the base. With Impatiens it is necessary to be on the alert to detect infestations of aphids, mites and white fly.

Marica (Twelve Apostles): This interesting member of the iris family derives its common name from the fact that the fans of foliage usually contain 12 leaves. The sword-like leaves are from 18 to 24 inches in length and have some decorative value when the plant is not in bloom. The flowers, iris-like in appearance, are borne on the tips of long flower scapes in late winter and are very fleeting. The two species most commonly grown are *M. northiana*, with 3- to 4-inch flowers, white with lavender markings, and *M. gracilis*, which bears smaller white flowers, marked with blue, brown and gold.

Culture:

Exposure: Thrives best in either an east or west window.

Temperature: Prefers a moderately warm temperature.

Soil: Any ordinary soil will give good results.

Care: Marica requires little beyond ordinary, routine care. Old plants may be divided after flowering. Little plantlets develop along the flower stalks and these may be removed and potted up.

Annuals for Bloom Indoors

Among the annuals there are several which, if taken up in the autumn and brought indoors, will give generous bloom for several months. Ageratum, browallia, nicotiana, phlox drummondii, petunias, and torenias are among the most satisfactory. In most cases the period of bloom may be considerably prolonged if some of the little self-sown seedlings are also brought in, as these will come into flower just as the older plants are beginning to grow shabby. If self-sown seedlings are not available a special sowing may be made early in August and the young plants may be grown on in pots.

FOLIAGE PLANTS OF MERIT

Aglaonema modestum (Chinese Evergreen): This is an adaptable foliage plant of easy culture which reaches an eventual height of about three feet. The broad, lance-shaped leaves, light green in color, are borne on long, thick stalks. There are also variegated types with attractive, silver-splashed foliage. The Chinese Evergreen is well adapted to growing in room interiors because of its low light requirements and it may be used on tables and in room-dividers. As it may be grown in water it is especially well suited for use in wall pockets and for hollow glass blocks.

Culture: Thrives best in a moderate to warm temperature. May be grown either in water or in soil. If grown for long periods in water a soluble fertilizer should be added occasionally, the water being completely changed. When grown in soil abundant moisture is required. Adapted to low light intensity. Will thrive well in a north window or room interior.

Araucaria excelsa (Norfolk Island Pine) is a very slow-growing tree which may be grown in a pot or small tub when young and will remain attractive for many years. It is symmetrical in form, with tiers of spreading branches of evergreen foliage. It is an excellent plant for a cool sun-porch.

Culture: Requires a cool temperature, 45° F. at night and not much over 55° F. during the day and abundant moisture throughout the year. Soil mixture, equal parts of garden loam, sand and peat.

Begonias: Among the most decorative of foliage plants are some of the begonias. They have very definite cultural requirements and one should not attempt to grow them unless these requirements can be met.

Among the many species and varieties which are highly valued for their attractive foliage only a few can be mentioned. (These also produce flowers but are valued chiefly for their foliage.)

B. argentes-guttata (Trout Begonia): The leaves are somewhat oval, pointed and coarsely toothed. In color they are an olive-green with white spotting. This is a begonia of easy culture and one of the best for a moderately warm temperature.

B. feasti (Beefsteak Begonia): The leaves, which resemble those of a water-lily in shape, are green on the upper surface and a lustrous rose on the lower surface. Well adapted for growing in a north window.

B. rex: There are many beautiful hybrids and named varieties of the Rex Begonia. Among the most decorative are:

Can-Can: Interesting and decorative, oak-leaved foliage.

Glory of St. Albans: An outstanding English hybrid. Leaves medium to small, a metallic rose in color with a silver sheen. Exacting in its cultural requirements.

Lucy Closson: Very decorative, brilliantly colored foliage.

Merry Christmas: Colorful, decorative foliage.

Princess Margaret: Vigorous in growth; foliage green, splashed with silver on the margin, shading to rose in the center.

Sheezar is an attractive, hybrid type of bushy habit with medium to small, silvery, rippled leaves.

B. sunderbruchi: Bronze-green leaves, often 10 inches in length.

Culture: Begonias require a mellow, fibrous soil, rich in humus and well drained, a moderate to cool temperature, a fresh, moist atmosphere and good light. Some varieties are particularly sensitive to drafts. Begonias usually thrive best when grown in trays filled with pebbles. Water should be kept constant just below the surface of the pebbles, so that the pots are resting on the pebbles but are not touching the water. This will provide increased humidity for the plants and create favorable conditions for good growth.

Caladium bicolor (Fancy-leaved Caladium): The Fancy-leaved Caladiums are among the most decorative of foliage plants. Many of the new named varieties are of striking beauty and may be used with dramatic effect in the house, the pots being sunk in floor wells or in deep planting boxes or set on trays filled with pebbles.

Culture: If dormant tubers are obtained and started in the autumn some varieties, such as Candidum, may be brought into full leaf as early as January. If started in February or March they will be in full leaf by April or May and will give a lavish display throughout the summer and early autumn when there is often little color in the window garden.

(For detailed description and culture, see page 400.)

Coleus: Some of the new strains are so decorative and the colors so beautiful that coleus has begun to regain the popularity which it enjoyed in the Victorian era. No other group of plants produces foliage with such richly varied colors. The dull and often garish colors so characteristic of coleus a generation ago have today been replaced by new strains with the most beautiful and subtle color harmonies. Among these many excellent strains are the Avalon Strain, Park's Brilliant and the Rainbow Hybrids.

Culture: Coleus may be grown from seed and from cuttings with the utmost ease. When a particularly desirable plant has been obtained it is wise to propagate it by cuttings. Although coleus will thrive well in shade, better coloration will be obtained if it is grown in a sunny window. A moderate to warm temperature is preferred, and any good garden soil will be satisfactory.

Dieffenbachia (Dumb Cane): The dieffenbachias are valued for their decorative foliage. As the foliage is large and the plants reach considerable size they are best adapted for flanking north or west windows, or for use in low planting boxes or beds at floor level. In time the plants will usually reach a height of 3 to 4 feet. There are many species and varieties. Among the most valuable for use as house plants are:

D. amoena: This species was discovered in Colombia in 1948 by Walter Singer of the New York Botanical Garden. The leaves are a dark green with white featherings.

D. picta: Erect and thick-stemmed. Leaves oval in shape, green, usually spotted or blotched with white.

Variety genmanni has narrow leaves, the parallel bands of white running diagonally from the mid rib.

Variety Rudolph Roehrs, which is a sport of D. picta, has very striking foliage and is most popular. The pale, yellowish leaves with narrow bands of green are blotched with ivory and have an unusual and exotic appearance. This variety is more exacting in its cultural demands than some of the other varieties.

Culture: The dieffenbachias prefer a warm temperature and good light, but no direct sunlight. A moderately acid loam best meets their needs and the plants should be kept on the dry side, as they will not tolerate soggy, water-logged soil. The plants are sensitive to drafts and will not thrive well if the temperature is too low.

Dracæna (Corn Plant): Some of the dwarf types of dracæna are well suited to the modern home. Being native to west equatorial Africa, they are able to withstand the dry, overheated conditions so often encountered in apartments better than most other plants.

D. deremenis warnecki is rugged and the one best adapted to unfavorable growing conditions.

D. godseffiana, which is called the "gold-dust" dracæna, is a compact, bushy plant seldom exceeding a height of 18 inches, although under exceptionally favorable conditions it may attain a height of 2½ feet. The glossy green leaves, oval in shape, are dusted with yellow and cream. This variety is more exacting in its cultural demands than many other types and prefers a moist but well-drained soil, rich in humus.

D. sanderiana is of dwarf habit and the gray-green leaves are banded with white. It is of easy culture and will withstand dry conditions exceptionally well.

D. terminalis, variety *E. Andre:* A colorful plant with broad, coppery-red leaves.

Culture: The dracænas do well in either a moderately warm or very warm temperature. They may be grown in strong light or in partial sun and are well adapted to windows with eastern or western exposures. With an occasional exception, they are undemanding concerning soil and will withstand dry conditions well. An occasional syringing of the foliage will be of great benefit.

Fatshedera lizei (Tree Ivy) is an interesting and attractive foliage plant, of erect habit. The leaves are large and glossy and in form resemble those of the ivy. They are borne on an erect, central stem which may eventually reach a height of 5 feet or more. By pinching out the center of a plant when small and by occasional pruning a low bushy growth may be obtained.

F. l. variegata is an attractive variegated form but of more difficult culture than the type.

Culture: Tree Ivy thrives best in a moderately cool temperature and it does not do well in an overheated room. It is particularly well adapted for use on a cool sun-porch and will even withstand light frost. It is not exacting in its soil requirements, doing well in any ordinary soil. It prefers a location in partial shade but also may be grown satisfactorily in fairly low light intensity, and on the whole survives adverse conditions well. It requires a moderate amount of moisture. It is somewhat subject to mite infestations.

Fatsia japonica (Aralia sieboldi) (Aralia japonica): This evergreen shrub which is used so extensively in California to create boldly dramatic effects may also be grown successfully in the house and has great decorative value when skillfully used. The dark green leaves are very large and deeply lobed, and the small white flowers are borne in clusters. It must be grown in a large pot or small tub, as it eventually becomes a large shrub.

F. j. moseri is a dwarf, compact form and is the one best adapted for use as a house plant in the average home.

Culture: The plants thrive well in full shade or in full sun, in any ordinary soil, are tolerant of varying temperatures, and require a moderate amount of moisture. In intense light the foliage tends to lack luster and sometimes becomes yellow.

Gardenia jasminoides: Gardenias all too frequently fail to do well as house plants. This is particularly true if they have grown in a greenhouse. Due to the high temperature, the low humidity and the low light intensity found in the average home the buds tend to drop before opening. Some plants will continue to make foliage growth under these conditions but will produce little or no bloom. A cool sunporch offers reasonably favorable conditions.

Osmanthus fragrans (Oleo fragrans) (Sweet Olive): This is the lovely Sweet Olive so beloved in southern gardens. It may be grown very successfully in a large pot or in a tub, and is well adapted to cool sun-porches. The leaves are lance-shaped or oval and are a deep, glossy green. The small, white flowers, which are almost hidden by the foliage, are borne in spring and are delightfully fragrant, with the scent of orange blossoms.

Culture: Thrives in full sun or partial shade. Requires a moderate to cool temperature and grows well in ordinary soil with moderate moisture.

The plants should be pinched back when small to induce compact growth, as they have a tendency to become leggy.

Peperomia: Among the low-growing plants of easy culture are the peperomias which seldom exceed a height of more than 10 inches. They are interesting little plants, many varieties having highly decorative foliage. Among the species most commonly grown as house plants are the following:

P. obtusifolia is very popular and widely grown. The waxy leaves are roundish and are borne on erect or sometimes partially procumbent stems.

P. o. variegated: Leaves are attractively marked with cream and white.

P. sandersi argyreia is known as the watermelon begonia and is one of the most decorative of the group. The leaf stalks develop from a central crown and make a very symmetrical small plant. The dark green, heart-shaped leaves are interestingly marked with silver stripes.

There are many other interesting types and varieties.

Culture: The peperomias thrive best in a moderately warm temperature and prefer good light but no direct sunlight. They are excellent for growing in a north window. For good growth they require plenty of water and high humidity. They do particularly well when placed on pebble-filled trays kept partially filled with water. A woodsy soil, rich in humus, best meets their needs.

Philodendron: These non-climbing and self-heading types of philodendron have considerable decorative value, and they can be used with dramatic effect in room interiors. Among the most desirable varieties are:

P. bipinnatifidum which is an attractive species attaining considerable size. The foliage is feathery and finely cut.

P. selloum has attractive, deeply cut leaves.

P. undulatum with erect, waxy, heart-shaped leaves.

P. wendlandi with oblong, glossy leaves which emerge from the crown of the plant. This species is more dwarf in habit than many, and is often called the "bird's-nest" type because its leaves are arranged in a rosette.

Culture: The philodendrons thrive best in a warm temperature in indirect light. They should not be exposed to direct sunlight. They are suited to a north window and will do well in the interior of a room if they receive reasonably good light. A good loam, moderately on the acid side, will best meet their needs. They require a moderate amount of moisture, but will not thrive in a water-logged soil. Frequent syringing of the foliage or sponging of the leaves with soapy water will help to keep them glossy and in good condition.

Pilea cadieri (Watermelon Pilea): An interesting foliage plant recently introduced into this country from Europe by Mr. T. H. Everett of the New York Botanical Garden.

The foliage is very decorative, elliptical in shape, the bright green leaves being blotched with silvery white. Plants reach a height of about two feet.

Culture: Of easy culture. Plants thrive best in a shady location, prefer a moderate temperature and a fairly moist soil, rich in humus.

Pittosporum tobira (Japanese Pittosporum): This lovely shrub, which is so frequently seen in southern gardens and in California, is very slow-growing and when grown in a pot or tub it makes a most attractive house plant. By judicious pruning it may be kept to a reasonably small size for many years.

The leathery, dark green foliage is always fresh and attractive in appearance and the creamy-white flowers which are borne in clusters have the fragrance of orange blossoms.

P. t. variegata is a very decorative form, the grayish-green leaves being outlined in white.

Culture: The pittosporums do well in a sunny location and are also tolerant of shade. They prefer a moderately cool temperature and a moderate amount of moisture and will thrive well in any ordinary soil.

Sansevieria (Snake Plant): This is one of the toughest of all house plants and will survive poor growing conditions and amazing abuse. It is often used in combination with other plants in room dividers. There are numerous species and varieties.

S. hahni is a dwarf form not more than 6 inches in height. The dark green, pointed leaves are banded with gray-green.

S. h. variegata has leaves marked with narrow, yellow stripes.

S. trifasciata is the species most commonly grown. The leaves are erect and pointed, gray-green, with dark green bands. It reaches a height of 2 to 3 feet.

S. t. Craigi has leaves which are dark green in the center with broad, yellow bands.

Culture: Sansevierias are of the easiest possible culture. They will endure dry air, poor soil and a minimum of light, but thrive best in a moderately fertile soil, which is allowed to become dry between waterings.

Schefflera actinophylla is a comparatively recent introduction. It is a tree but may be grown very satisfactorily indoors in a large pot or small tub. The large, hand-shaped leaves, which are borne on long stalks, are a bright, glossy green. Where a plant of some size is desired it has great decorative value.

Culture: It is of easy culture, thriving well in a moderate temperature, and it makes good growth in ordinary soil. It should be kept moderately moist, but not overwet.

FLOWERING VINES

Gloriosa rothschildiana (Glory Lily): The lovely, exotic, red and yellow flowers of the Gloriosa lily, with their gracefully recurved petals, make it a very decorative vine for the house. It clings to its support by means of little tendrils at the tips of the long, pointed leaves. It may be used to frame a window and is dramatically lovely when in flower.

Exposure: Full sun is preferred.

Temperature: Thrives best in a moderately warm temperature.

Soil: Prefers a sandy loam but is tolerant of soils of widely varied types.

Culture: Tubers are usually shipped in the autumn. They should be potted as soon as the little red buds begin to show. One of the secrets of success in growing the Gloriosa lily is to make sure that tubers have begun to sprout before they are potted. The pots should be placed in subdued light and watered sparingly until growth has started. The pots should then be placed in full sunlight. After flowering water should be gradually withheld, and when the plants have become dormant the pots may be stored in a damp cellar where the temperature can be maintained above freezing.

Morning Glory (Ipomoea purpurea): Morning glories grow exceedingly well in the house during the winter months and are gay and charming when used to frame a sunny window.

Exposure: Full sun.

Temperature: Moderately warm.

Soil: Garden loam of moderate fertility.

Culture: For early winter bloom seeds should be sown in pots about the middle of August. They may also be started in the autumn and will come into flower by midwinter or early spring. The seeds should be soaked in warm water for two hours before sowing, or should be notched, in order to hasten germination. Plant three seeds in a 4-inch pot and after they have begun to grow leave the most vigorous plant and discard the other two. Provide string or light wire upon which the plant can climb. Any of the following varieties are excellent: Heavenly Blue, Rose Marie, Scarlett O'Hara, Pearly Gates.

Nasturtium: Nasturtiums are a great favorite among children and offer excellent material for an interesting

A RECESSED SHELF FOR PLANTS

indoor project during the winter months. The climbing varieties make rapid growth when grown in pots indoors and will soon clamber up to the top of a window if provided with string or wire.

Exposure: Full sun.

Temperature: Moderately warm.

Culture: Plant several seeds in a 3- or 4-inch flowerpot and thin out later to one sturdy plant. If seeds are sown in August the plants will be in bloom by late autumn. They may be sown later on, or at any convenient time.

Passion Flower (Passiflora): The Passion Flower is a vine of vigorous growth which blooms intermittently throughout the winter months. The flowers, which are about 4 inches across, are intricate in detail and beautiful in coloring, the white on the outer edge of the petals shading to soft mauve and blue near the crown.

Exposure: Prefers sun, but will do well in partial sun.

Temperature: Best suited to moderately cool temperatures.

Soil: Will thrive well in any good garden loam.

Culture: The plants should be grown in 6- or 8-inch pots. They make rapid growth and require plenty of moisture. A fine, but strongly attached, wire placed up the sides and along the top of the window will provide adequate support for the tendrils.

FOLIAGE VINES

Cissus adenopodus: This charming vine resembles its close relative, the Grape ivy, but the trifoliate leaves are hairy instead of glossy. They are an olive-green on the upper surface and a soft rose color on the lower surface, as are the young stems and tendrils.

Culture: A moderately warm room, high humidity and partial sun best meet the needs of this lovely vine. A definite rest period is required and when active growth ceases water should be reduced and the pot should be placed in a shady place until growth is resumed.

Cissus antarctica (Kangaroo Vine): This is one of the most vigorous and foolproof of the vines suited to indoor culture. It may be allowed to trail or may be trained as a vine to frame a window. The pointed, oval leaves are a very dark green and are slightly toothed.

Culture: Thrives best in partial sun and is well adapted to both eastern and western exposures. It does well in a moderately warm room, yet is unaffected by comparatively low temperatures. Grows well in any soil, but requires a moderate degree of moisture.

Cissus rhombifolia (Grape Ivy): The lovely grape ivy is one of the most popular and most decorative of vines for the house. The three-parted leaves have a glossy

sheen and the young growth is particularly attractive. It may be allowed to trail or may be trained to frame a window with its delicate tracery of leaf forms.

Culture: It is at its best when grown in a fairly warm room. It prefers a moderate amount of sun and is well adapted to growing in windows with eastern or western exposures. Does well in any ordinary soil.

Hedera helix (English Ivy): The exciting new varieties of English ivy which have been introduced within recent years have become tremendously popular, and are highly valued for their decorative effect. They may be allowed to trail over the edge of a plant tray or planting box; they may be trained upward to frame a window; they may be trained along lattice strips against the wall in a sun room or on a ceiling; or, if desired, some varieties may be kept to a compact, bushy form and used as part of the decor in the interior of the room.

Among the many excellent types and varieties are:

GREEN VARIETIES

　Albany: Trailing, medium-leaved, branching
　Conglomerata erecta: Erect, slow-growing, leaves curled
　Lady Kay: Bushy, trailing, small, lance-shaped leaves
　Manda's Crested: Trailing, ruffled, star-shaped leaf

VARIEGATED VARIETIES

　Jubilee: Slow-growing, branches freely, becoming a shapely plant
　Glacier: Small-leaved, attractive
　Hahn's variegated: Free-growing, leaves have thin white edge
　Williamsiana: Leaves have crisp white edge

Culture: The ivies are very adaptable as house plants. They will grow well in windows with any exposure and will also grow well in indirect light in the interior of a room. They thrive best in a cool temperature. They will grow in any type of soil and may also be grown in water over long periods if soluble fertilizers are occasionally added. They require a moderate amount of moisture and the leaves should be syringed at frequent intervals or sponged with soapy water.

Monstera deliciosa (Swiss Cheese Plant): (This is often sold under the name of Philodendron pertusum.) The leaves of this tall-growing, tropical climber are very decorative, being large and rounded, cut at the margins and having conspicuous holes. It is usually given a moss stick or piece of bark for support.

Culture: Moderately warm temperature, ordinary soil, keep fairly moist but not saturated. Will make satisfactory growth in poor light.

Philodendron (Climbing Types): The climbing types of philodendron are widely grown as indoor plants. Their slender stems permit them to be grown as trailing vines or to be trained as a climber on a moss stick or piece of bark. They may also be trained on a wire to frame a window, a mantle or a doorway.

There are a number of species and varieties.

P. erubescens: The heart-shaped leaves are medium in size, deep green on the upper surface, coppery on the undersurface. This is one of the best types for growing on moss sticks or tree bark.

P. hastatum: Leaves dark green, long and narrow, arrow or heart-shaped.

P. imbe: Broad, lance-shaped leaves, red on undersurface.

P. oxycardium: (often listed by nurseries as P. cordatum). The deep green, heart-shaped leaves are smaller than most other types. Stems are slender and it makes an excellent trailer but may also be trained on a moss stick.

P. panduriforme: The deep green leaves are fiddle-shaped.

P. sodiroi: The large, heart-shaped leaves have a silvery hue, stems are reddish. Neat and trim in habit of growth.

Culture: The philodendrons thrive well in ordinary room temperatures and have the ability to grow well in poor light, which makes them particularly valuable for room interiors. A good loam, containing considerable organic matter, is ideal. They require moderate watering, but the soil should never be allowed to become soggy. They thrive best in an atmosphere which is not too dry.

Scindapsus aureus (Pothos aureus) (Ivy-arum): This is an attractive vine with very glossy, pointed, oval leaves, the green being marked with yellow. It may be grown either as a trailing vine or may be trained on a moss stick or tree bark for support.

S. a. variety Marble Queen has leaves marked with white.

Culture: Ordinary soil, moist but not saturated. Moderately warm temperature. Will grow well in rather poor light.

Syngonium: (Often sold as Nephthytis). These vine-like tropical plants are very satisfactory for use in room dividers as they thrive well in indirect light. They may be allowed to trail, or may be trained on a piece of tree bark or a moss stick. The stems cling by means of fleshy, aerial roots.

There are many excellent species and varieties.

S. auritum: The bright green leaves are very glossy, and have one large lobe with two small lobes at the base.

S. erithrophyllum has small, coppery leaves which are covered with tiny, pink dots.

S. hoffmani has a grayish-green leaf with a silver center.

S. podophyllum: The long-stemmed, arrow-shaped leaves are a pleasing, glossy green.

S. p. albolineatum has white midribs and veins.

S. xanthophilum, known as Green Gold, has smooth leaves which have an ivory variegation in the center.

Culture: The Syngoniums are of easy culture. They thrive best in a warm temperature in indirect light. They require moderate watering and do well in ordinary soil. The foliage will benefit from occasional syringing.

HOUSE PLANTS WHICH PREFER FULL SUNLIGHT

Astilbe japonica	Euphorbia (Crown of
Azalea	Thorns)
Beloperone (Shrimp Plant)	Kalanchoë
Cactus	Gardenia
Calceolaria	Geranium
Crassula	Jerusalem Cherry
Genista (Broom)	Impatiens or Balsam
Heliotrope	Lantana
Cineraria	Poinsettia
Clivia	Bulbs of all varieties

HOUSE PLANTS REQUIRING PARTIAL SUNLIGHT

Abutilon (Flowering Maple)	Cyclamen
Anthericum (Spider Plant)	Dracæna
Anthurium (Flamingo Flower)	Fuchsia
Ardisia crenulata (Coral Ardisia)	Peperomia maculosa
Asparagus plumosus	Peperomia arifolia
(Asparagus Fern)	Pothos aureus
Asparagus Sprengeri	Primula malacoides
Begonia (in great variety)	Primula obconica
Coleus Blumei (Coleus)	Primula sinensis

Many bulbs will also thrive well in partial sunlight

HOUSE PLANTS FOR NORTH WINDOWS

Aglaonema modestum (Chinese Evergreen)
Araucaria excelsa (Norfolk Island Pine)
Aspidistra lurida (Iron Plant)
Begonia Rex (Rex Begonia)
Billbergia perringiana (Livingvase Plant)
Cissus rhombifolia (Grape Ivy)
Crassula arborescens (Chinese Rubber Plant)
Cryptanthus acaulis (Pineapple Plant)
Dieffenbachia Seguine (Dumb Cane)
Fittonia Verschaffeltii (Fittonia)
Ivies (in great variety)
Monstera deliciosa (Swiss Cheese Plant)
Pandanus Veitchii (Ribbon Plant)
Philodendron cordatum
Saintpaulia (African Violet)
Sansevieria zeylanica (Snake Plant)
Sempervivum Haworthii (Hen and Chickens)
Sedum Adolphi
Sedum dendroideum
Sedum treleasi
Tradescantia (Wandering Jew)

XXXI

GROWING HOUSE PLANTS
UNDER ARTIFICIAL LIGHT

As a result of extensive research it has been found that some of our most popular and decorative house plants will thrive better when grown under artificial light than when grown under normal home conditions.

This new development offers fascinating possibilities, as it no longer limits the use of house plants to window areas. Foliage plants and certain flowering plants may now be grown in any part of the room, and very decorative and exciting effects may be obtained. In regions where there are long periods of fog and dull weather the growing of plants under artificial light is a particular boon to house-bound gardeners. And to apartment dwellers, and to others with sunless windows, it offers delightful possibilities for dramatizing their plants.

In the average home it is difficult, if not impossible, to maintain uniform light. At certain times of the day the light intensity may be too high, at other times too low, and it is seldom that the optimum intensity for growth and flowering can be maintained.

With artificial light plants may be grown under completely controlled conditions. There need be no seasonal adjustments for, as far as the plants are concerned, every day becomes a sunny day. Since plants grown under these conditions receive equal light from all sides they tend to be much more symmetrical in shape than plants grown under average home conditions, and in the case of flowering plants the period of bloom will be accelerated, flowers will be produced in greater abundance and their color will often be enhanced.

Not all plants are adapted to growing under artificial light. In general plants which prefer conditions of low light intensity may be grown most satisfactorily and will thrive best under artificial illumination. It is not practical to attempt to grow plants under artificial light which require exceptionally high light intensity.

FLOWERING PLANTS

Achimenes
Begonias
    Calla Lily Begonia
    B. Evansiana
    Rex begonia
    Wax begonia: B. semperflorens
Bletilla hyacinthina
Episcia (Flame violet)
Fuchsias
Gloxinia
Kæmpferia (Ginger Lily)
Kohleria
Lily-of-the-Valley (convallaria)
Pansies
Rechsteineria
Saintpaulia (African violet)
Smithiantha

FOLIAGE PLANTS

Alocasia
Anthurium
    A. crystallinum
Bromeliads
Caladiums
Cissus rhombifolia (Grape Ivy)
Crytomium rockfordianum
Dieffenbachia
Dracæna
Peperomia
    P. obtusifolia
    P. sandersi

462

Philodendron   Pothos (scindapus) Aureus
P. cordatum   Sansevieria
P. dubium
P. hastatum

Where Plants May be Grown

Plants may be grown under artificial light in any part of the house, from attic to cellar, provided suitable temperatures can be maintained. The possibilities are almost unlimited. They may be grown in dim hallways, on windowless walls, in dark corners, on room dividers, which can be especially designed for the purpose, in recessed wall planters, in basement areas, on empty book shelves, in unused cabinets—even on closet shelves, if no other space is available.

Regardless of where they are grown, the plants may be removed at any time and used as part of the decor of the home. If, after a time, they begin to look a bit straggly they may be returned to their place under the light and will soon recover.

Type of Light Required

Considerable research has been done in order to determine the kind of light and the amount of light which will best meet the requirements of specific plant groups. It has been found that for the majority of plants fluorescent lights are superior to incandescent lights. However, under certain conditions, and with certain plants, incandescent lights are preferred, and in some cases a combination of the two types is recommended. Practically all flowering plants will grow best under fluorescent light. Most foliage plants may be grown under either fluorescent or incandescent light, but as a result of extensive research it has been found that many foliage plants will thrive best when grown under a combination of both types of illumination.

There are a number of types of fluorescent light, but for use in growing plants under artificial illumination *white* or *daylight tubes* should be used, as these will give the best results.

Light Intensity

Plants vary considerably in their light intensity requirements for maximum growth. Some plants thrive best under low light intensity, others require a medium light intensity, while others will not thrive except under high light intensity. It is therefore necessary to know within which group the plants with which one is working are classed.

The intensity of light is measured in terms of foot-candles, each foot-candle being a unit of light illumination. The number of foot-candles of light in a given area, which designates the light intensity, may be determined with a special meter which may be procured at small cost.

Planning the Set-up

There are numerous very satisfactory commercial set-ups available for growing plants under artificial illumination. However, if one prefers to do so, one may easily, and more economically, construct one's own. A commercial-type fluorescent fixture containing two 40 watt daylight tubes may be purchased, or, at less expense, two single tube strips with built-in starters may be obtained and mounted on a board which has either been covered with aluminum foil or has been painted white in order to increase reflection of light down on to the plants. If a light-reflecting material is used at the back and on the sides of the cabinet or tray, such as a piece of plywood covered with foil or painted white, it will further increase the efficiency of the set-up.

Fluorescent tubes 48 inches in length are very satisfactory for the average set-up. Two such tubes will supply light for an area 2½ ft. by 4 ft. Shorter tubes may be used for small areas. Tubes should last from 12 to 16 months, but after six months the light intensity begins to decrease. When placing plants under the tubes it must be borne in mind that the area under the center of the tube always receives somewhat stronger light than the area at either end.

The lights may be suspended over the plants by a chain, a pulley attachment being added, if desired, in order to make the fixture adjustable. If preferred, the lights may be mounted on either a metal or a wooden frame. Wrought iron legs suitable for this purpose can often be purchased in furniture stores. Lights may also be installed in a cabinet or used on a wall bracket.

The distance between the fluorescent lights and the pots will depend to some extent upon the specific needs of the plants being grown. For most flowering plants the lights should be from 12 to 18 inches above the plants. The measurement should always be taken from the tube to the rim of the pot. If, for some reason, it is necessary to suspend the lights at a higher level, it will be essential to leave the light on for a greater number of hours in order to obtain satisfactory growth.

When foliage plants are grown under artificial light they are often placed on stands or brackets or in room dividers and are lighted by fluorescent lights suspended at some distance above the plant and by incandescent spot lights. In many instances they are grown where they will receive the full benefit of light from a table lamp or floor lamp.

Hours of Artificial Light Required

The number of hours of artificial light required for optimum growth will depend upon the needs of the specific plant and the distance between the lights and the plants. The usual range is between 12 to 18 hours. It does not matter which portion of the 24 hours is covered, but the schedule should be regular. An inexpensive time switch can be purchased which will give automatic control.

If lights are suspended from 12 to 18 inches above the plants a 12 hour day is usually sufficient. For such plants as African violets from 300 to 600 foot-candles of light should be provided at leaf level. If two 40 watt daylight fluorescent lights are suspended 12 inches above the plants it will normally produce an intensity of light within this range and a 12 hour day is sufficient. If the lights are suspended at a level of $2\frac{1}{2}$ to $3\frac{1}{2}$ feet it would be necessary to provide 16 hours of light in order to compensate.

In general the amount of artificial light available to the plant is approximately the foot-candles of light multiplied by the hours of light supplied to the plant. For example—30 foot-candles of light intensity supplied over a period of 10 hours would be approximately equal to 20 foot-candles over a period of 15 hours.

Length of Time Plants Can be Grown Under Lights

Some plants, such as African violets and Episcias, may be grown on for many years under artificial lights, and will continue to bloom well and to show no ill effects from long periods of growth under such conditions.

General Cultural Requirements

The general cultural requirements for most plants grown under artificial illumination are much the same as for those grown under normal conditions.

Temperatures are, as always, an important consideration, a range between 60° and 70° being considered suitable for the majority of plants.

The *humidity* may be checked very easily with a Humidiguide, a small instrument obtainable in almost any hardware store. A humidity range between 60 and 70% is considered optimum for many plants but is not readily obtainable under average home conditions and most plants will thrive reasonably well within a range of 45 to 50%. If extensive operations are carried on in a basement room it may be advisable to invest in an electric humidifier. Setting pots on trays filled with moist sand or pebbles helps to maintain good humidity, but it is important to see that the water on the pebbles is kept below the level of the pot.

Ventilation is a matter which requires important consideration when plants are grown under artificial light. Drafts must be avoided, but provision must be made for the circulation of fresh air, as few plants thrive well in a close, stagnant atmosphere. In the average room a circulation of fresh air may readily be provided, but in a basement area it may prove wise to use a small electric fan. Basement windows should preferably be hinged at the bottom and open inward.

Watering must be done with regularity and with care. If pots of flowering plants are sunk up to the rim in deep trays filled with $\frac{1}{2}$ moist sand and $\frac{1}{2}$ vermiculite the frequency of watering will be greatly reduced, as the soil in the pots will stay moist for several weeks.

Fertilization practices are followed as usual, an application of a liquid fertilizer being made about every two to three weeks when the plants are in active growth.

Special Recommendations for Foliage Plants

When foliage plants are grown under artificial illumination they will usually be most satisfactory if they make rather slow growth and maintain good proportion. Too rapid growth often results in soft, spindly shoots which detract from the appearance of the plant. A method developed by Dr. O. Wesley Davidson at the New Jersey Experiment Station has given excellent results and is being widely used in hotels and offices, as well as in homes. The pot is set either in a jardiniere, or deep tray or trough, the space between the clay pot and the larger container being filled with moist peat moss or sphagnum moss. When the plant needs water it is applied one time directly to the pot, allowing the pot to overflow slightly, and the following time the water is applied to the peat moss or sphagnum. This procedure is followed with regularity, and tends to keep the soil moderately dry, thus producing slow but healthy growth and attractive form. The plants must also be fertilized very sparingly, only about one third the amount being given which would normally be used if the plant were being grown under good natural light. Foliage plants grown under favorable light intensity by this method will remain attractive in appearance over a period of many months.

Automatic Controls

If one's time is limited, or if one is away from home for occasional periods the problem of growing plants under artificial light may be solved by making it an almost automatic procedure. A time switch may be installed to control the turning on and off of the lights and if the plants are grown in wick-type pots watering may be done by means of an automatic pump.

However, whether one has time to work at leisure with one's plants or is able to devote only an occasional spare moment to them, growing plants in the home under artificial light offers many delightful possibilities and brings rich rewards.

XXXII

FLOWER BOXES

IN many towns and villages in Europe the flower boxes contribute almost as much to the charm and beauty of the community as does the picturesque architecture. One sees them everywhere —at windows, on balconies, on lamp posts, between gas pumps at filling stations. Flower boxes are used not only at the windows of private homes but also on public buildings, hotels, hospitals, banks, office buildings and shops. And in the poorer districts material poverty is often so clothed with flowering beauty and living green that one realizes that there is no poverty of the spirit among those who dwell there.

Within recent years there has been a tremendous upsurge of interest in flower boxes in this country. One sees window boxes more and more frequently on city homes, as well as on homes in the suburbs and country. And many a porch and terrace and patio is made gay with flower boxes. Indeed these portable planting boxes may be used to create a veritable garden in miniature. If a wise selection of plant materials is made the boxes can be kept bright with color and bloom from early spring until mid-autumn and will be a source of joy throughout the season.

In order to provide the most favorable conditions for the plants there are a number of points which must be given consideration; the size and type of box, the material of which the box is made, the provision for drainage, the soil mixture, the selection of plants best suited to the exposure and the program of general maintenance.

Size of box: The size of the box is a matter of considerable importance. Small boxes have several disadvantages. They tend to dry out very quickly and in extremely hot weather the soil may become overheated. When this occurs the plants suffer seriously, as it is difficult for them to obtain the nutrients from the soil

which they need. Overheating of the soil is the cause of frequent failures in maintaining flower boxes in good condition. On the other hand, large boxes become extremely heavy when filled with soil, and hanging them properly from a window or balcony may become a problem.

For window and porch boxes the most satisfactory dimensions are: length from 32 to 48 inches, depending upon the length of the window; minimum width 10 inches; minimum depth 8 inches (inside measurements). In flower boxes root development is necessarily very restricted and there is considerable competition between the plants for available nutrients. In boxes which are too narrow or too shallow plants fail to make good growth.

For use on terraces and patios and in penthouse gardens planting boxes may be built according to dimensions which are suited to the location and best meet the specific needs of the plants to be grown.

Materials: The materials of which flower boxes are made has an important bearing upon the growth and vigor of the plants.

Metal boxes have decided limitations. The cheaper types rust out after a year or two and must be replaced. And since metal is a conductor of heat the soil in metal boxes tends to become seriously overheated in hot weather, which greatly retards the normal development of the plants. Metal boxes are also often too shallow to permit good root development and frequently lack adequate provision for drainage.

Fiberglass has come into use for flower boxes within recent years and has much to recommend it. Plant boxes of this type are molded from fiberglass and polyester resins. They are light in weight, do not rust or crack and are extremely durable (some firms even offer a 25-year guarantee). Fiberglass boxes provide good insulation against heat and cold, are resistant to acids and chemicals and the color does not fade. Flower boxes of this type can be used as window boxes and can also be used as easily movable, decorative features on terraces and patios. Indoors they may be used on deep window sills, on plant stands and on room dividers.

Wood is an excellent material for plant boxes of all types. If a suitable wood is selected and the box is well made a wooden box should give service for many years. The two woods which possess remarkable ability to resist decay are cypress and redwood. They are more expensive than other woods but will outlast them by many years. Cedar is also excellent, and a good grade of white pine may be used. Cheap grades of lumber or kinds which are subject to decay should not be used. In the long run it is a matter of economy to use the best wood available, preferably cypress or redwood with cedar and white pine as second and third choice.

Construction: There is a great difference between a really well built flower box and one which is carelessly constructed. As there is considerable pressure against the sides of a flower box it is essential that it be constructed with care. Boards from $\frac{7}{8}$ of an inch to $1\frac{1}{4}$ inches in thickness should be used, depending upon the size of the box. Brass screws should be used throughout instead of nails, as nails are likely to pull out if the boards begin to warp. The corners should be reinforced with angle irons screwed onto the inside near the top. This will strengthen the box and prevent the boards along the front and rear from pulling away from the end pieces. Holes to permit the drainage of surplus water should be bored in the bottom of the box. The holes should be about $\frac{1}{2}$ inch in diameter and should be spaced from 6 to 8 inches apart.

In hot climates or in situations where boxes will be exposed to long hours of hot sun an insulated type of box may be constructed which will prevent the soil from becoming seriously overheated. A $\frac{3}{4}$ inch board may be used along the front, faced with a light $\frac{3}{16}$-inch board, a dead air space of about $\frac{1}{2}$ inch being left between the two boards. This space will provide excellent insulation if it is filled with dry sphagnum moss.

After the construction of the box has been completed the inside should be brushed over with cuprinol or some equally good wood preservative which is non-toxic to plants. Creosote should not be used as it is toxic to plants. The outside of the box should be painted with a good quality paint.

There are various styles in which wooden boxes may be made. A molding around the front of a box or a little scalloped apron at the base adds greatly to the attractiveness of the box.

A self-feeding, self-watering window box may be built if desired. Such a box has a double bottom. The lower portion, which should be approximately 3 inches in depth, provides a place for the removable metal tray which contains the nutrient solution. Wicks made of glass wool carry the nutrients to the plants. Vermiculite or some other equally satisfactory material should be used in the box instead of soil. The plants should be taken from their pots and planted, with the ball of earth surrounding their roots, directly in the vermiculite.

There should be a row of holes in the bottom of the box spaced approximately 9 inches apart and the wicks should be about 9 inches long. Five inches of the wick should be poked down through the hole in the box into the metal tray. The remaining portion of the wick should be slit down into four sections, each section being spread out flatly over the bottom of the box on which an inch of vermiculite has been placed. Both the vermiculite and the wicks should be thoroughly wet with the solution. The remaining vermiculite should then be moistened with the solution and placed in the box. The box is then ready for planting.

The tray should be kept filled with the nutrient solution. Beyond this no further feeding or watering is needed.

Provision for Drainage: It is important that adequate provision be made for drainage in all types of flower boxes. Unless this is done the soil in the boxes becomes completely saturated with water during periods of heavy rain and under such conditions plants become starved for oxygen and fail to thrive. Before the soil is put into the box a 1 inch layer of small pieces of broken flower pots, small stones, sifted hard-coal cinders or old bricks smashed with a hammer into small pieces should be spread over the bottom of the box. Above this a piece of wet burlap or a thin layer of sheet sphagnum moss which has been thoroughly moistened should be spread in order to prevent the soil from sifting down into the drainage area.

Soil Mixture: A good garden loam well supplied with humus is ideal for flower boxes. If the soil is of a heavy texture it tends to become very compact and provides unfavorable conditions for the development of the plants. Before such soil is used several quarts of well decomposed leaf mold or good compost, or a mixture of two parts moist peat moss and one part sand should be worked well into it. A good soil conditioner, in addition to the materials suggested above, may also be used to improve the texture of a heavy clay soil (see page 170). A soil with a pH range between 6.3 and 7.0 will be satisfactory for practically all plants which are commonly grown in window boxes. The box should be filled to within about $\frac{3}{4}$ of an inch of the top.

Keeping the Plants in Pots: If desired, the flower boxes may be filled with moist peat moss and the pots containing the plants may be sunk in the moss. This procedure has several advantages. It makes it easy to change the plants from season to season or to replace a plant which is not doing well, and it obviates the necessity of obtaining soil which, in city areas, is often a great problem. The peat moss should be kept moist at all times and the potted plants should be watered whenever the soil appears dry on the surface. The disadvantage of this method is the expense involved. Plants in pots cost considerably more than plants in plant bands, flats, or other commercial containers, and it is sometimes difficult to procure certain plants such as lobelia, alyssum and marigolds in pots.

Maintenance: In caring for flower boxes the three essentials of good maintenance are watering, feeding and the removal of faded blooms.

The soil in flower boxes dries out much more rapidly than the soil in garden beds and the plants therefore need more frequent watering. A mulch of peat moss on the surface of the soil will help to conserve the moisture and will be of great benefit. The peat moss should be moistened well before it is used. A mulch ½ to 1 inch in depth is sufficient. Watering of the boxes should preferably be done in the late afternoon or early evening. In extremely dry, hot weather it may be necessary to water boxes which have a south or southwestern exposure early in the morning and again during the middle of the day. In watering when the sun is on the plants care must be taken not to get water on the foliage or on the

blooms as it will cause a spotting of the petals due to burning. Syringing the foliage with a fine spray several times a week will help to keep the plants in good condition. This is very necessary in the case of window boxes in the city in order to remove the coating of soot which forms on the leaves and is a serious hindrance to the normal transpiration of the plants.

Overwatering is almost as serious as underwatering as few plants can thrive in saturated, water-logged soil. Therefore watering must be carefully regulated and in cool, cloudy weather should be withheld until the soil appears dry.

In order to encourage vigorous growth and abundant flowering a good program of feeding is recommended. Beginning about a month after planting a weekly application of a high-analysis, quickly soluble fertilizer which also contains the various trace elements should be made, being mixed at the rate of 1 teaspoonful to 1 gallon of water (see pages 165–166). A small portion may be sprayed over the foliage if desired (see page 167 on Foliar Feeding), or it may all be applied directly to the soil.

If such plants as petunias, pansies, lantanas, verbenas, marigolds and a number of others are to be kept in continuous bloom throughout the season it is necessary to remove the faded flowers in order to prevent the formation of seed pods. The removal of dead flowers also greatly improves the appearance of the box. Some plants, such as pansies, will give a second period of bloom if they are cut back severely and allowed to develop a new growth of vigorous young shoots.

Planning for Succession of Bloom

If expense does not have to be considered, it is possible to have bloom in window boxes from very early spring until late autumn.

During the early spring the boxes can be gay and charming with pansies, English daisies, violas, forget-me-nots, wallflowers and a few pots of scillas, poet's narcissus or some of the other spring bulbs.

By late spring geraniums, potted petunias and verbenas, lobelia and lantanas and many other plants will be in flower and, with good care, will continue in bloom until early autumn.

In August some of the colchicums and autumn crocus may be planted near the front of the box and will provide a gay bit of color when the annuals are removed to make way for the chrysanthemums which will carry the season of bloom well into the autumn.

During the winter small evergreens, such as very small box bushes, may be planted in the boxes, being removed and planted elsewhere in the early spring when the pansies and their gay companions are ready to again hold the center of the stage for a brief time.

PLANTS SUITABLE FOR FLOWER BOXES

FULL SUN	LIMITED SUN	PARTIAL SHADE	FULL SHADE
Ageratum	Browallia major	Achimenes	English Ivy
Candytuft (Iberis umbellata)	Coleus	Coleus	Ferns
English daisy	Heliotrope	Fuchsia	Syngonium
Forget-me-nots	Impatiens	Impatiens	
Geraniums	Lobelia	Tuberous begonias	
Lantana	Nemesia	Wax begonia	
Lobelia	Torenia		
Nasturtium	Wax begonia		
Nierembergia cærulea			
Pansies			
Petunias			
Phacelia campanularia			
Phlox drummondii			
Portulaca			
Snapdragons			
Sweet alyssum			
Verbena			
Viscaria			
Wallflowers			

PLANTS OF LOW GROWTH
(*suited to front of box*)

Achimenes
Ageratum
English daisies
Forget-me-nots
Lobelia
Nierembergia cærulea

PLANTS OF MEDIUM HEIGHT

Browallia
Candytuft (Iberis umbellata)
Heliotrope
Nemesia
Nasturtium
Petunias

PLANTS SUITABLE FOR FLOWER BOXES—continued

PLANTS OF LOW GROWTH

Pansies
Phacelia campanularia
Phlox drummondii, nana compacta
Portulaca

Sweet alyssum
Torenia
Violas

PLANTS OF MEDIUM HEIGHT

Verbena
Viscaria
Wax begonia

PLANTS OF TALL GROWTH
(capable of reaching considerable size)

Coleus
Fuchsia

Geraniums
Impatiens

Lantana
Tuberous begonias

FLOWERING PLANTS OF TRAILING HABIT

(SUITABLE FOR FLOWER BOXES)

Achimenes
Fuchsia: trailing form
Lantana: trailing form

Lobelia: trailing form
Nasturtiums: trailing form
Sand verbena

Sweet verbena
Thunbergia alata

VINES SUITABLE FOR FLOWER BOXES

Canary Island Ivy (Hedera canariensis variegata)
English Ivy (Hedera helix)
Lotus bertheloti
Grape Ivy (Cissus rhombifolia)

Ground Ivy (Nepeta hederacea)
Strawberry geranium (Saxifraga sarmentosa)
Vinca major variegata (Large-leaved vinca)
Vinca minor (Periwinkle)

GOOD COMBINATIONS

SUNNY EXPOSURE

Geraniums: pink
Petunias: white
Lobelia: light blue
Variegated vinca

Lantana: yellow
Nasturtium: orange-yellow
Verbena: white

PARTIAL SHADE

Achimenes: purple
Fuchsias: purple to mauve
Impatiens: soft pink

Browallia major: blue
Impatiens: coral
Nemesia: blue
Torenia: white

Petunias: purple
Verbena: pink
Ageratum: lavender
Sweet alyssum: white

Geraniums: red
Petunias: white
Lobelia: deep blue
Grape ivy

Wax begonias: pink
Coleus: pink tones
Torenia: deep blue

Tuberous begonias: pink
Achimenes: trailing–purple

XXXIII

PROPAGATION

THERE are few subjects of more vital interest to the gardener than that of propagation.

Many of the old and established practices may still be followed, but within recent years new discoveries have been made which have revolutionized some of the techniques of the propagator. With the discovery of the hormone-like substances which are now available to the gardener it has been possible to stimulate the rooting of cuttings to a remarkable degree, thus making possible the propagation of hitherto difficult species. The newly discovered uses of colchicine, that substance derived from lily bulbs which, in some mysterious way, has the ability to upset the normal behavior of the chromosomes, holds much of interest for the plant breeder. Although the art of propagation dates back to time immemorial, more progress has been made by scientists within the past few decades than had occurred in many previous centuries.

REPRODUCTION BY SEED

Growing Annuals from Seed

All annual flowers and vegetables may be grown very readily from seed. They may be grouped into three general classifications: those which are extremely hardy and may be sown in the open ground early in the spring as soon as the soil is in condition for planting; those which are half-hardy and may be sown in the open ground after all danger of frost is over; and those which are either extremely tender and delicate, or which make such slow growth that it is advisable to sow them in either the greenhouse or hotbed where they may be kept under carefully controlled conditions until they are well started.

If early bloom is desired many of the hardy and half-hardy annuals may also be started under glass. The rapidly growing kinds such as the zinnias and marigolds should not be sown more than six weeks before time for transplanting to the garden as they will become spindly and leggy if held too long indoors. The slow-growing annuals such as lobelia, petunia, snapdragon, salpiglossis and verbena may be sown from eight to ten weeks before the time for transplanting to the open.

Raising Biennials from Seed

Practically all biennial flowers may be grown very easily from seed. The seeds are usually sown in coldframes during the summer months. When the seedlings have reached sufficient size they are transplanted and are usually carried on in the frames until autumn. Those that are tender are wintered in the frames, while those that are hardy may be transplanted to the open ground. For details regarding time of sowing and method of handling, see Chapter XXV on Biennials.

Raising Perennials from Seed

There are many perennials which may be raised very successfully from seed. However, this method of propagation is not suitable for all perennials, as there are some which have become so highly developed that they do not produce seed, and some perennials, such as iris and phlox, do not come true from seed. There are others which develop so slowly when grown from seed that it is far more practical to resort to the division of old clumps or to some other means of vegetative reproduction.

PERENNIALS PROPAGATED BY SEED

SCIENTIFIC NAME	COMMON NAME
Achillea	Yarrow
Aconitum	Monkshood
Althea rosea	Hollyhock
Alyssum saxatile	Goldentuft
Amsonia	
Anchusa	Bugloss
Aquilegia	Columbine
Arabis	Rockcress
Arenaria	Sandwort
Artemisia	Mugwort
Asclepias tuberosa	Butterflyweed
Aubrietia	Purple Rockcress
Baptisia	False-indigo
Bocconia	Plume poppy
Boltonia	
Campanula	Bellflower
Centaurea	
Centranthus	Valerian
Cerastium tomentosum	Snow-in-summer
Chelone	Turtlehead
Cimicifuga	Bugbane
Coreopsis	
Delphinium	Larkspur
Dianthus (single types)	
Dicentra	Bleeding-heart
Dictamnus	Gas Plant
Digitalis	Foxglove
Eupatorium	Mistflower
Gaillardia	Blanketflower
Geum	
Gypsophila	Baby's-breath
Helenium	Sneezeweed
Helleborus	Christmas Rose
Hesperis	Sweet Rocket
Heuchera	Coral Bells
Iberis	Candytuft
Linum perenne	Perennial flax
Lobelia	
Lupinus	Lupine
Monarda	Horsemint
Myosotis	Forget-me-not
Œnothera	Evening-primrose
Penstemon	Beard-tongue
Physostegia	False dragonhead
Platycodon	Balloon flower
Primula	Primrose
Pyrethrum	Painted Daisy
Salvia	Sage
Scabiosa	Pincushion-flower
Sedum	Stone crop
Thalictrum	Meadowrue
Veronica	Speedwell
Viola	

Seeds

In order to raise plants successfully from seed, it is necessary to provide conditions which are as nearly ideal as possible. The essential con-siderations are: good seed; favorable tempera-ture; correct degree of moisture; and a medium suitable for seed germination.

Good Seed. Some seeds retain their vitality for many years whereas certain seeds must be planted as soon as they are ripe if good germination is to be secured. The seeds of most of our commonly grown annual and perennial flowers retain their vitality for at least a year and some of them for two years or even longer. Weed seeds are notoriously hardy in this respect, and records show that seeds of some of our common weeds will germinate readily after fifty years of dormancy. One of the most outstanding examples of longevity in seeds is to be found in the case of the Lotus. Recent experiments have proved that Lotus seeds still retain their viability after a period of four hundred years.

With the majority of our garden flowers we can ex-pect a percentage of germination ranging from 75 to 85%, and in some cases an even higher percentage may be obtained if conditions are extremely favorable.

If seed has been carried over from one season to another, or if there is any reason to doubt its viability, it is wise to run a test for germination before the seed is sown. There are a number of methods which may be used in testing seed, one of the simplest being the blot-ting paper method. The seeds should be placed between two sheets of blotting paper which are kept con-stantly moist and at a temperature ranging between 65° and 70° F. If several varieties of seed are to be tested, the paper may be marked off into small squares. The per-centage of germination may be determined by dividing the number of seeds which have sprouted by the total number tested.

When seeds are to be held for any length of time they should be stored in a dry place with a range of tempera-ture varying from 45° to 50° F.

Meeting Special Requirements. Many seeds will germi-nate under widely varying conditions of temperature and light. However, there are some seeds which have special requirements and maximum germination can-not be obtained unless these requirements are met.

The seeds of some flowers will not germinate well if the temperatures at the time of sowing are too high; other seeds will not germinate well if the temperatures are too low. Recent research has determined the opti-mum temperature range within which seeds in these two groups will give the best germination, other conditions being favorable. Seeds with definite temperature re-quirements for maximum germination will, with a few exceptions, sprout under less favorable temperature conditions but the percentage of germination will become increasingly lower as the temperature moves further away from the optimum.

In the case of seeds in the low temperature range (see list) every effort should be made to provide conditions which are as nearly ideal as possible in order to secure the best germination. Such seeds should be sown during cool weather whenever possible, or the seed flats should be placed in as cool a location as is available. For seeds in the very low temperature group a special procedure may be followed. The seeds may be mixed with damp, sterile sand and moist peat moss and placed in the refresher compartment of the home refrigerator. As soon as the seed has germinated the sand, peat moss and sprouted seed may be sown in drills in a flat, cold frame or seed bed, and from this point on they may be handled in the usual manner.

Seeds in the high temperature range should not be sown out-of-doors until the soil is thoroughly warm. If started early indoors the seed pans or flats should, if possible, be placed in a location where a temperature above 68° F. can be maintained.

Pansy seed has rather unique requirements, as it fails to germinate well unless there are wide fluctuations in temperature. When sown where a constant temperature is maintained, with no fluctuations whatsoever, pansy seed will not germinate at all. It will sprout with moderate variations in temperature but the wider the fluctuations the better the germination. This explains why pansy seed usually germinates best in the early autumn when hot days follow cool nights.

Some seeds pass through alternating periods of dormancy. They will germinate well when fresh, then, a few months later, will become completely dormant and will appear to have lost their vitality. Six months later they will again show a high percentage of germination. Primrose seed is in this class. Perennial seed which does not sprout, yet which remains firm and shows no signs of rotting, may be passing through such a period of dormancy and should be left in the seed bed.

It has been found that some seeds will germinate best in the dark, other seeds will give the highest percentage of germination in the light, other conditions being favorable, while other seeds are indifferent and germinate well either in the dark or in the light.

Some seeds, such as delphinium seeds and the seeds of the double petunias, lose their vitality very rapidly if kept under average storage conditions but if stored at a cold temperature will retain their viability for many months. Some of the best seed houses now provide special storage facilities for seeds in this group. If such seed, whether home produced or purchased, is to be kept for any length of time before it is sown, it should be stored in the refrigerator in a moisture-proof container.

Some seeds will not germinate readily when freshly gathered but will sprout well after a few months of storage. However, if the fresh seed is chilled to 42° F. and then sown in a temperature of 68° F. it will germinate well.

OPTIMUM TEMPERATURE RANGE FOR BEST GERMINATION

HIGH (68° to 86° F.)	LOW (55° to 68° F.)	INDIFFERENT	VERY LOW (42° to 55° F.)
Ageratum	Alyssum	Asters	Annual Larkspur
Balsam	Antirrhinum	Mignonette	Delphinium
Cleome	Calendula	Phlox drummondii	Lettuce
Columbine	Clarkia		
Dahlias	Pansies	VARIABLE	
Lobelia	Phacelia	Petunias	
Marigolds	Tahoka daisy		
Morning Glory	Torenia		
Nicotiana	Violas		
Salvia farinacea			
Verbena			
Zinnias			

LIGHT REQUIREMENTS FOR BEST GERMINATION

PREFER LIGHT	PREFER DARK	INDIFFERENT
Ageratum	Balsam	Aster
Alyssum	Dahlias (Seedling)	Calendula
Antirrhinum	Larkspur (Annual)	Marigold
Clarkia	Scabiosa	Mignonette
Lobelia	Verbena	Phlox drummondii
Nicotiana	Zinnia	Salvia farinacea
Pansies		Torenia
Petunias		
Violas		
Bluegrass seed		

FRESH SEED REQUIRING CHILLING TO GERMINATE

Antirrhinum	Dianthus	Stock
Candytuft	Lupine	Sweet alyssum
Carnation	Phlox drummondii	Sweet pea

PERIOD OF GERMINATION AND LONGEVITY OF FLOWER SEEDS

NAME	PERIOD OF GERMINATION (DAYS)	APPROXIMATE LONGEVITY (YEARS)	NAME	PERIOD OF GERMINATION (DAYS)	APPROXIMATE LONGEVITY (YEARS)
Achillea, the Pearl	14	4	Dimorphotheca (African orange daisy)	15–21	1
Acroclinium	14–20	3	Erigeron	14	2
Ageratum	14	4	Eschscholtzia	10	2
Agrostemma	10–14	4	Euphorbia heterophylla	7	2–3
Alyssum	10–20	4	Euphorbia marginata	19	3–4
Amaranthus	6–10	4–5	Gaillardia grandiflora	15–20	4
Ammobium	14	1–2	Gaillardia picta	15–20	2
Anagallis	21	4–5	Geranium	30–40	1
Anchusa italica	14–20	3	Gerbera	14	1
Anemone	28–40	2	Geum	21	2
Anthemis	14	2	Godetia	15	3
Antirrhinum	10–14	3–4	Gourds, small mixed	14	3–4
Aquilegia	30–50	2	Gourds, large mixed	14	3–4
Arabis	21	2–3	Gypsophila elegans	10–14	2
Armeria	14	2	Gypsophila paniculata	10–14	4
Aster	8–12	1–2	Helianthus cucumerifolius	10–14	2–3
Aubrietia	25	2	Helianthus, double chrysanthemum flwd.	10–14	2–3
Balsam	10–14	5–6	Helichrysum	14	1–2
Bartonia	5–10	1–2	Heliotrope	21	1–2
Bellis (English Daisy)	10–14	2–3	Hesperis	18	3–4
Boltonia	20	5	Hibiscus	15–30	3–4
Brachycome	10	3–4	Hollyhock	21	2–3
Browallia	28–40	2–3	Hunnemannia	14	2
Calendula	14	5–6	Impatiens Holstii	15	2
Calliopsis	14	2–3	Ipomœa, Cardinal Climber	10	5
Candytuft	14	2–3	Ipomœa, Cypress Vine	10	4–5
Canna	14	3	Ipomœa, Japanese selected	21	2–3
Canterbury bells	14	3	Ipomœa noctiflora	40–60	2–3
Carnation	10	4–5	Larkspur, annual	20–28	1–2
Celosia	6–10	4	Lathyrus latifolius	21	3–4
Centaurea americana	10–13	1–2	Lavatera	14–35	4–5
Centaurea gymnocarpa	14–30	1–2	Lilium regale	21	1
Centaurea imperialis	15	1–2	Linaria	15	2–3
Centaurea moschata	12–14	1–2	Linum perenne	21–30	1–2
Cheiranthus Allionii	14	2–3	Linum (Scarlet Flax)	14	5
Chelone	20–30	1–2	Lobelia	10–15	3–4
Chrysanthemum, annual	11–18	4–5	Lunaria (Honesty)	14–21	1–2
Cineraria	15	3–4	Lupinus Hartwegii	10	2
Clarkia	14	2–3	Lupinus nanus	10	2
Cobæa	21	2	Lupinus polyphyllus	21–30	2
Coleus	14	2	Lychnis	21–30	2–3
Coreopsis	21	2	Marigold, African	8	2–3
Cosmos, Mammoth	10–14	3–4	Marigold, French	8	2–3
Cosmos, Orange Flare	14		Marvel of Peru	14	2–3
Cyclamen	21	4–6	Matricaria	11–14	2–3
Cynoglossum	10	2–3	Mesembryanthemum	14	3–4
Dahlia	10	2–3	Mignonette	11–14	2–4
Datura	15–21	3–4	Myosotis	14	2
Delphinium	15–21	1	Nasturtium, Golden Gleam	12–14	6–7
Dianthus	6–10	4–5	Nasturtium, tall single mixed	12–14	6–7
Didiscus	12–14	2–3			
Digitalis	15	2			

PERIOD OF GERMINATION AND LONGEVITY OF FLOWER SEEDS--continued

NAME	PERIOD OF GERMINATION (DAYS)	APPROXIMATE LONGEVITY (YEARS)	NAME	PERIOD OF GERMINATION (DAYS)	APPROXIMATE LONGEVITY (YEARS)
Nemesia	18–21	2–3	Scabiosa, annual	14–21	2–3
Nepeta	17	2–3	Schizanthus	21–30	4–5
Nicotiana	10	3–4	Shasta Daisy	10–14	1–2
Nigella	14	1–2	Smilax	32	1
Œnothera	31	2	Statice sinuata	14–21	2–3
Pansy	14	1–2	Stocks	6–10	5–6
Penstemon	17	2	Stokesia	28	2
Petunia hybrids, mixed	10	2–3	Sweet Peas	10	2–3
Phlox	10–15	1–2	Sweet William	6	2
Physostegia	25	2–3	Thalictrum	30	1
Platycodon	12–15	2–3	Thunbergia alata	21	2
Polemonium	20	2	Thunbergia Gibsoni	10–14	2
Poppy, carnation flowered	10–14	4–5	Tithonia	25	2
Poppy, glaucum	10–14	4–5	Torenia	14	1–2
Poppy, nudicaule	10–14	3–4	Tritoma	21	2
Poppy, oriental	10–14	5	Verbena	14	1
Poppy, Shirley	10–14	5–6	Vinca rosea	14	1–2
Portulaca	14	3	Viola	14	1
Pueraria (Kudzu Vine)	30–50	4	Virginian Stock	12	1–2
Pyrethrum aureum	21	1	Wallflower	10–14	5
Pyrethrum roseum	21	1	Wisteria	7	2
Ranunculus	30–40	6–7	Zinnia, dahlia-flowered, mixed	5–10	6–7
Salpiglossis	14	6–7	Zinnia, Lilliput, mixed	5–10	6–7
Salvia (Scarlet Sage)	14	1			
Saponaria Vaccaria	10	2			

Preventing Damping-off

One of the greatest handicaps in sowing seeds in soil is the prevalence of the fungi which cause the damping-off of young seedlings. Therefore when seeds are to be sown in coldframes, hotbeds, or in soil indoors, every possible precaution should be taken to prevent the growth and spread of these fungi which attack the young seedlings before they emerge, or at a later stage, causing the stem to rot away at the ground level. The loss of one or two plants may not seem serious, but it is the danger signal, as the fungus spreads rapidly and hundreds of plants may become affected in a very short time. Unfortunately the very conditions which are the most favorable for the germination and growth of young seedlings are also favorable for the growth and spread of the fungi which cause damping-off. These fungi cannot grow in absolutely dry soil, but under conditions of warmth and moisture they develop rapidly. Consequently the disease is apt to be more serious in damp, cloudy weather than it is in bright, sunny weather; and it is more serious where there is inadequate ventilation than it is where there is good circulation of air. Weak plants are invariably more susceptible to attack than strong ones, and the overcrowding of young seedlings tends to aggravate the spread of the disease.

In order to insure complete control of damping-off, the seed, the soil, and the containers (if old pots or flats are used) should be sterilized.

Seed Treatment. The treatment of the seed is very simple and will insure the pre-emergence control of damping-off. This protection of the seeds has become an accepted practice in many commercial greenhouses, and it should be quite as generally adopted by home gardeners, as it is a very important factor in the successful control of the disease. The most effective means of protecting seeds is to dust them at the time of sowing with a good seed protectant. There are a number of excellent commercial products of this type on the market which will give good control against seed decay, damping-off and various seedling blights. Some seed firms now offer seeds which have been treated with a protectant.

To insure control of post-emergent damping-off seeds should be sown in a sterile medium. Milled sphagnum moss and vermiculite provide a medium which is completely sterile. If soil is to be used it should be sterilized, if complete control is desired.

Soil Sterilization

Method No. 1—Formaldehyde Drench

This is one of the simplest and most effective methods of sterilizing soil, in coldframes and in the open ground, also in preparing soil for seed flats or for potting mixtures. Directions: Use 1 cupful of formalin (40% formaldehyde) to 3 gallons of water.

1. Apply with a watering can with sprinkler spout. The soil should be thoroughly moistened but not made soggy.
2. Cover the soil with a piece of plastic material or a clean piece of burlap.
3. Allow the soil to remain undisturbed for 24 hours.
4. Turn it over daily for three days with a spading fork or trowel in order to aërate it well. The implements used for turning should be thoroughly washed and disinfected before use.
5. Do not sow seed or set out plants until the process of aëration has been completed and all odor of formaldehyde has disappeared.
6. Flats, seed pans and other containers should be disinfected before use.

Method No. 2—Baking

This method is suitable for the sterilization of small quantities of soil for use in seed pans.

The seed pan, pot or container should be sterile. Fill the container with soil.

Cover and place in oven heated to 200° F.

Bake for 15 minutes (*not* longer).

The temperature should not be allowed to go over 200° F.

One of the most satisfactory ways for the home gardener to disinfect seed pans and pots is to place them in a large kettle, such as a canning kettle, and boil them for one-half hour.

If seeds are sown in an unsterile medium and damping-off occurs, immediate measures of control should be undertaken. There are a number of excellent commercial preparations on the market which may be used to reduce losses. See Oxyquinoline, page 618.

Seed Sowing in the Open

The seed of many annual flowers may be sown directly in the garden where they are to bloom. Some of the perennials and biennials, as well as many annuals, may be sown in out-of-door seed beds, being transplanted to their permanent position in the garden after they have made some growth in the nursery plots. The disadvantages of sowing seeds in the open ground are that one is unable to control conditions of temperature and moisture, and it is more difficult to provide an ideal seed bed. Heavy rains often cause the soil to become too firmly compacted before the seeds germinate and may also seriously injure the delicate young seedlings. Long hours of hot sunshine may cause the soil to dry out too rapidly and to form a hard crust unless constant attention is given to watering, but in spite of all these handicaps, seed sowing in the open can be done successfully in the majority of cases if careful attention is given to a few essential details. A well-prepared seed bed will do much to offset the vagaries of nature.

The time of sowing will depend, to a large extent, upon the kind of seed. A few of the very hardy annuals such as the California poppies, the Shirley poppies, larkspur, cornflowers and nigella may be sown in the autumn where they are to flower. The secret of success in autumn sowing lies in the fact that the seeds should not be sown until late in the season. They will then lie dormant in the soil throughout the winter and will germinate with the first warm days of spring, many weeks before the soil is in condition for the sowing of seeds. These autumn-sown seedlings are unusually sturdy and vigorous and will give an abundance of early bloom. For the more tender annuals spring sowing is preferable and it is wise to wait until the soil is mellow and warm and workable. It is unwise to attempt the sowing of seed when the soil is wet and heavy and sticky. Unless the soil will crumble readily after it has been pressed firmly in the hand, it is best to wait.

If the garden soil is a mellow loam one need not be greatly concerned about the preparation of a special seed bed, particularly in the case of the more sturdy plants such as the lupines, zinnias, and marigolds. If, however, one is dealing with a heavy soil which will have a tendency to form a hard, baked crust, it is necessary to prepare a special seed bed. This may easily be done by working compost, sand and finely pulverized moist peat moss into the upper 3 inches of soil. This will make the soil more retentive of moisture and, most important of all, will prevent it from forming a hard crust through which the young seedlings cannot penetrate. In the case of very fine seeds, such as petunias, nicotiana, and ageratum, it is advisable to sift the top inch of soil and the final light covering. With larger seeds this precaution is not necessary. The depth of sowing will depend upon the size of the seed. In general, seeds should be sown at a depth corresponding to twice the diameter of the seed. Large seeds such as lupines and sweet peas should be planted about $\frac{1}{4}$ of an inch deep; zinnias and marigolds about $\frac{1}{4}$ to $\frac{1}{2}$ inch; while petunia, nicotiana and ageratum seeds are so fine that they need only be barely covered with a light sprinkling of sand or mellow soil.

After the seeds have been sown, the soil should be watered with a very fine spray and should not be allowed to dry out until the seeds have germinated and the young plants have become well established. It is advisable to provide some light shade. If the seeds have been sown in the garden where they are to flower this is usually not feasible, but in an outdoor seed bed in the nursery it is readily possible. A lath frame forms a very satisfactory shade as it permits free circulation of air and admits a small amount of direct sunshine. Inexpensive shades may be easily made by tacking pieces of burlap on plasterer's lath.

In preparing a seed bed in the nursery it is essential to select a well-drained location, and the natural drainage will be improved if the bed is raised a few inches above the surrounding ground.

Sowing Seeds Indoors

In Soil. When sowing seeds indoors it is well to realize that the texture of the soil is of far greater importance than the fertility of the soil. In order to provide a good medium for seed germination the soil must be loose and mellow. An excellent soil mixture for seed pans and flats consists of one part sterile garden loam or compost, one part coarse sand, and one part moist peat moss.

As it is essential that adequate drainage be provided, broken pieces of crock, small stones, or a layer of moist sphagnum moss should be placed in the bottom of the seed pan or flat. After the container has been filled with the prepared mixture the soil should be levelled off and lightly firmed with a flat block of wood or some such object. This should bring the surface of the soil about $\frac{1}{8}$ of an inch below the rim. When pots or seed pans are used the seeds are usually sown broadcast over the surface of the soil. The seed should be sown as evenly as possible, and too heavy seeding should be avoided, as it will result in spindly, weak plants due to overcrowding. When very fine seeds are sown no covering is necessary, as they may be pressed gently into the soil with a float or small tamper. Larger seeds should be covered with a finely sifted layer of the soil mixture or with sand. When flats are used the seeds may be sown either broadcast or in drills, the rows being spaced from $1\frac{1}{2}$ to 2 inches apart. The soil should be firmed lightly after the seeds have been sown.

As soon as sowing has been completed the flats or seed pans should be watered. The most satisfactory method, particularly in the case of very fine seed, is the sub-irrigation method. The seed pan or flat should be placed in a pan of water and allowed to remain until the surface of the soil has become dark and moist in appearance. It should then be removed and any surplus water should be allowed to drain off. This method is far superior to the overhead method. If, however, the overhead method is employed a very fine spray should be used such as a fog nozzle. A rubber bulb sprinkler is very satisfac-

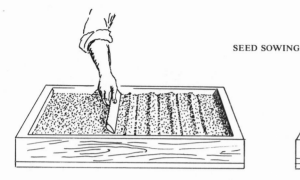

SEED SOWING

tory for the purpose if only a small number of pots are being handled. At no time should the seed boxes be allowed to dry out, and they should be kept carefully shaded until the seeds have germinated. Shading will greatly facilitate the conservation of moisture and will hasten germination. A pane of glass covered with newspaper or a small burlap frame may be used very satisfactorily. It is essential, however, that some provision be made for the circulation of air, and the covering should be raised very slightly, being laid on small sticks placed across the pot or flat. A covering of light, plastic material is excellent, as it retains the moisture and also provides for a movement of air.

Germination will be hastened if the pots or flats are placed in a warm, dark place, the ideal temperature ranging from 60 to 70 degrees. In a greenhouse the seed boxes are sometimes placed along the heat pipes underneath the benches, and in the house a radiator may be made to serve the same purpose. As soon as the seeds have germinated, the covering should be removed and the seedlings should be place in full light. If the seed pans or flats are placed in a sunny window they should be turned every two or three days, as the seedlings have a tendency to lean towards the light. Watering must be done with regularity and with care. The seed boxes must never be allowed to dry out, but an excess of moisture must also be avoided.

In Sphagnum Moss. Shredded or milled sphagnum moss offers one of the most ideal mediums for the germination of seeds, and new techniques for its use have recently been developed by the Department of Agriculture at the Plant Introduction Garden at Glendale, Maryland. It is inexpensive, readily procurable from any horticultural supply house, easy to use, a high percentage of germination is usually secured, there is no danger of over-watering, and, as it is a completely sterile medium, it entirely eliminates all danger of damping-off. Germination takes place in an incredibly short time, the young seedlings make rapid growth, and if mineral nutrient solutions are supplied many plants may be carried on in the sphagnum well beyond the seedling stage.

Sphagnum moss grows in bogs in certain sections of the country, most of it being obtained from bogs in New Jersey and Wisconsin. As it comes from the bog it is long and stringy and it must be shredded before it is suitable for use as a medium for seed germination. Horticulturally milled sphagnum is available commercially. Shredding may also be done at home by rubbing the long, dry sphagnum through a wire screen such as hardware cloth. Sphagnum moss may be used for starting seedlings in flats, in seed pans, in pots, in hotbeds and in coldframes. In flats, pots and seed pans it may be used either as the entire medium, or an inch of fine sphagnum moss may be used on top of a light sandy sterile soil or a mixture of sterile sand and peat moss.

When sowing seeds on sphagnum moss the procedure is very simple. The moss should be moistened slightly to increase the ease of handling and the flat or seed pan should be filled until it is level. The surface should then be firmed until the moss is about $\frac{1}{2}$ inch below the rim and it should be watered thoroughly. As this firm, smooth surface is favorable to the growth of green algæ it has been found advisable to add, after the flat or pot has been allowed to drain for a few minutes, an additional layer of finely shredded moss about $\frac{1}{8}$ of an inch in depth. This should be given a light sprinkling and the seeds should then be sown either broadcast or in drills. When sowing fine seeds no covering is necessary, but with larger seeds, such as zinnias and marigolds, it is advisable either to poke them down into the sphagnum or to add a light covering of the shredded moss. After the seed has been sown a light sprinkling should be given, a fine, mist-like spray from an atomizer being ideal, and the flat or seed pan should then be covered with a pane of glass or with a sheet of translucent glass substitute which has been tacked on a frame. The seed boxes should not be exposed to direct sunlight until after the seeds have germinated. Little watering is necessary, merely enough to keep the sphagnum moist. As soon as germination has taken place the covering should be removed and from this time on considerable care must be taken to see that the sphagnum does not dry out. Fortunately there is no danger of over-watering.

Seedling plants which are to be transplanted while still quite small may be grown very satisfactorily in sphagnum without the use of nutrient solutions. If, however, the seedlings are to be held for any length of time beyond the cotyledon stage it will be found advisable to apply a well-balanced solution, as more vigorous growth will be obtained. The solution should be applied at intervals of every few days in a quantity sufficient to saturate the moss. A commercially prepared mixture may be used, or a very satisfactory mixture may be made at home by using either of the following formulas:

1. Add 2 teasp. of a 12–12–6 fertilizer to 1 gal. of water
2. Add 6 teasp. of a 4–12–4 fertilizer to 1 gal. of water

By withholding the nutrient solution seedlings growing in sphagnum moss may be held for some time in an arrested state of development without suffering any permanent set-back. When transplanted from the flat or seed pan they will continue normal growth. Under certain conditions this offers definite advantages. Where the viability of seeds is affected by even a brief period of storage they can be germinated immediately on sphagnum and held in a retarded state until normal growth is desired. In other cases a succession of plants ready for transplanting may be obtained from one sowing by holding some of the seedlings in a retarded state.

One of the greatest advantages of growing plants in sphagnum is the ease with which they may be transplanted. If removed carefully there is usually much less disturbance to the root system than when seedlings are grown in soil. Seedling plants may also be shipped with ease when grown in pots or bands filled with sphagnum, as it is so light in weight. If they are knocked out of the pots for shipment the sphagnum ball will hold its shape well.

The most important advantage of all, however, in starting seedlings in sphagnum is the fact that absolutely no losses are encountered from damping-off, which frequently takes such a toll when seedlings are started in non-sterile mediums.

In Vermiculite. This new material is rapidly gaining favor as a medium for starting seeds. Vermiculite is made from a mica-like ore which is composed of thousands of separate layers with a very small amount of water between each layer. When subjected to very intense heat, expansion of the moisture takes place and each layer is separated into many tiny cells. Vermiculite, which is put out under a number of trade names, is light in weight, easy to handle, has the ability to hold large quantities of water and yet provide free circulation of air, and, being entirely sterile, eliminates all danger of damping-off. The vermiculite may be used as the sole medium or an inch layer may be spread over sterile soil in the flat or seed bed. After the vermiculite has been spread, it should be leveled off but should not be packed down, and it should then be moistened thoroughly. The seed should be sown broadcast over the surface. Seeds of medium or large size should be covered by sifting over them a thin layer of the very fine particles of the vermiculite. When sowing very fine seed, such as petunia or foxglove seed, it is advisable to sift such a layer over the surface before the seeds are sown, as this will prevent them from working their way down to too great a depth. No covering is needed for very fine seed, and surface watering is not advised, as there is a tendency for the seeds to be washed down into the vermiculite. When watering becomes necessary the pan or flat should be placed in a receptacle containing several inches of water and left until the surface is moist. When larger seeds are being germinated watering may be done with a bulb spray or with a hose with a very fine nozzle. As soon as the first true leaves appear a mineral nutrient solution should be applied. This may be done by sub-irrigation or by surface feeding. (See page 479 for formulas for nutrient solutions.)

A mixture of one part vermiculite and one part milled sphagnum moss also makes an excellent medium for starting seeds.

In Sand. Seeds may also be germinated very successfully in pure sand. If the sand is sterile all danger of damping-off will be eliminated. Sand of a somewhat coarse grade is preferable to very fine sand. If seedlings are to be held for any length of time a nutrient solution should be applied. Many growers using this method feel that it is advisable to apply a nutrient solution before the seeds are sown. This may be done by placing the pot or seed pan in a pan of the solution and leaving it until the surface has become moist. The solution is commonly used at the rate of one cupful of the solution to each quart of sand. The usual procedures in sowing seeds in other mediums are followed when seeds are being germinated in sand.

Hastening Germination

Most seeds germinate readily under average conditions. There are, however, some seeds which, because of an unusually hard outer coating, require special treatment if a good percentage of germination is to be obtained. In this group we find seeds of such plants as canna, moonflower, morning-glory, sweet peas, honey locust, Kentucky coffeetree, beets, parsley, carrot, celery, parsnip, and a few others. In some instances, as in the case of apple and peach seeds, special treatment of the seed may take the place of stratification, if desired.

Method No. 1: Soaking. The length of time will vary considerably, some seeds requiring only twenty-four hours, other seeds requiring several weeks. As a general rule the seeds should be soaked until they begin to swell. After the seeds have been soaked, they should not be allowed to dry out before sowing and the soil should be moist but not excessively wet at the time that they are sown. During the process of soaking, the seeds should be kept uniformly damp but not too wet, and if the process is continued for more than a few days the mass of seed should be stirred and aërated occasionally.

Method No. 2: Scalding. In the case of some very dry, hard-shelled seeds, such as seeds of the Kentucky coffeetree, scalding water may be used with considerable success. Boiling water is poured over the seeds and allowed to cool gradually.

Method No. 3: Mechanical Aids. There are also a number of mechanical aids which may be employed very successfully, such as filing and clipping. In the cases of some extremely large seeds a very minute hole may be bored. The germination of some seeds is greatly increased if they are scarified previous to sowing. Scarification is usually done by a machine, designed especially for this purpose, which scratches the surface of the hard seed coat, making it more permeable to water.

Transplanting

When the first or second pair of true leaves has developed young seedlings should be transplanted, in order to prevent overcrowding and to induce better root development. They may be transplanted into other flats, or they may be transplanted singly into small, 2½-inch pots. If the young seedlings are strong and vigorous and if weather conditions are favorable, they may be transplanted into the coldframes, and in some exceptional cases, they may be transplanted directly into the open ground.

The soil should be a slightly richer mixture than that prepared for the seed bed, the follow-

PROPAGATING POT

ing mixture being recommended: one part sand, one part leaf mold, two parts loam, one part well-rotted, sifted cow manure or good compost. It is essential to see that good drainage is provided. The soil should be neither too wet nor too dry at the time of transplanting. If it is moist enough to form a fairly firm ball when pressed together in one's hand, yet dry enough to crumble when the ball falls to the ground, it is of excellent consistency for transplanting. After the soil has been made level it should be firmed and marked off into rows from 2 to 3 inches apart. The young plants should be spaced from 2 to 3 inches apart in the row, depending upon their size and vigor.

In order that the roots may receive as little injury as possible, the seedlings should be very carefully removed from the seed bed. The pointed end of a small label is excellent for this purpose. If the small seedling plants are massed together in a clump, as so often happens when the seeds have been sown thickly, the soil should be shaken gently from the roots and the individual plants should be carefully separated from the group. Only a small number of seedlings should be removed at a time, as only a few moments should elapse between the time when the young plants are lifted from the seed bed and when the operation of transplanting is completed. If the roots are exposed for any length of time the plants may suffer a serious check. The roots should be kept covered with soil as much as possible and under no condition should the young plants be exposed to direct sunlight.

Long, straggly roots should be pinched back in order to induce a vigorous, well-branched, fibrous root system. A hole large enough to receive the roots without crowding should be made with the pointed end of a label or small stick. The roots of the plant should be placed in the hole and the soil should be pressed firmly about the roots and stem. Most seedling plants should be set a little deeper than they were when growing in the seed flat. In the case of very spindly plants, which have suffered as a result of overcrowding or because of other unfavorable conditions, it is advisable to set them quite deeply. In transplanting delphinium seedlings, care must be taken not to cover the crown with soil as the plants are very apt to rot unless the crown is slightly above the surface of the soil.

Most seedlings may be very easily handled, being picked up by the leaves with the thumb and forefinger. In the case of very tiny seedlings, such as begonias and primroses, it is sometimes a matter of convenience to use a small pair of forceps.

In transplanting seedlings into small pots, place sufficient rubble in the bottom of the pot to provide good drainage, and then fill the pot with the prepared soil mixture without packing it down. Make a hole in the center, place the seedling so that it will be at the desired depth and firm the soil about it with both thumbs. The surface of the soil should be about three-quarters of an inch below the rim of the pot.

As soon as the transplanting has been completed, the flats, pots or frames should be watered with a fine spray or fog nozzle and the plants should then be shaded until they have had an opportunity to re-establish themselves. Transplanting is a severe shock to young seedling plants, as many of the tiny root hairs which supply moisture and nutrients to the plant are injured or destroyed. It is, therefore, necessary to provide conditions which are as nearly ideal as possible during this critical period when the plant is re-establishing itself.

For the use of plastic sprays to prevent wilting see page 683.

VEGETATIVE REPRODUCTION

Propagation by Cuttings

Many greenhouse and garden plants, the majority of shrubs, and a few perennials may be successfully propagated by cuttings. The term "cutting" is applied when a small portion of a plant is removed and is treated in such a way that root growth is induced, a new plant being formed which is similar in every respect to the parent plant. Cuttings may be made from various portions of a plant, some plants being propagated more readily by one type than by another. In general garden practice, cuttings are usually made from a portion of the stem, from leaves, from tubers, and from roots.

Rooting Medium

Cuttings of some plants may be rooted very easily in water, in moist sphagnum moss, or in a light sandy loam soil, but in general practice the following rooting mediums will prove the most satisfactory:

1. Moderately coarse, sterile sand
2. One part coarse sand, one part peat moss
3. One part coarse sand, one part vermiculite

Propagating Cases

If a greenhouse propagating bench is not available, flowerpots, small shallow boxes, greenhouse flats and old fish aquariums may all be converted into very satisfactory propagating cases. The receptacle should have a depth of at least 4 inches and some provision should be made for shading the cuttings. When only a few cuttings are to be rooted the double flowerpot is one of the most satisfactory devices. A small 3- or 4-inch pot is placed within a larger pot, the hole in the bottom of the small pot being tightly closed with a cork. The rim of the small pot should be level with the area of sand in the large pot. The intervening space below and about the sides should be filled with sand or with sand-peat moss mixture. The small pot should be kept filled with water and there will be a gradual seepage through the porous clay of the pot which will keep the rooting medium uniformly moist. If a large glass jar, such as a bell jar, is inverted over the pot, it will prevent an excessive evaporation of moisture and will provide very favorable conditions for the rooting of the cuttings. A shallow box may also be easily converted into a very satisfactory propagating case if a pane of glass is placed at each end and on each side with a large pane on top. It is not necessary for the glass to fit closely at the corners, as a small amount of ventilation is desirable. An old aquarium makes an ideal small propagation case if adequate provision is made for drainage. In greenhouses special benches are usually provided for propagating. The lower portion of the bench is enclosed to conserve the bottom heat and the bench is usually provided with a hinged sash which may be raised or lowered to any desired height. A hotbed or coldframe may also be used very successfully during the more mild seasons of the year if shaded and protected from drafts.

A Home Propagating Unit

Until recently it has been difficult for the home gardener to propagate trees or shrubs from cuttings unless he was fortunate enough to possess a special propagating bench in a greenhouse where temperature, humidity and ventilation could be controlled.

However, with the introduction of plastics it is now possible to construct an inexpensive and very satisfactory home propagating unit which will give excellent results in rooting both softwood and hardwood cuttings.

Plastic materials, such as polyethylene and vinyl plastic, are readily available and possess unique qualities. They are permeable to air and thus permit air to flow freely in and out, and at the same time they possess the remarkable ability to hold moisture within. This makes it possible to obtain the desired degree of humidity and adequate ventilation when a propagating unit is covered with a plastic material.

A very small unit of this type may be made by using a standard greenhouse flat measuring $1' \times 2' \times 3''$. The flat should be filled with a rooting medium such as peat moss, vermiculite, sand, or a mixture of 1 part vermiculite and 1 part sand. The medium should be thoroughly moist when the cuttings are inserted. After the cuttings have been taken the cut ends should be dipped in a hormone powder to hasten rooting and they should then be inserted in the moist medium in the flat. A wooden or wire frame, somewhat higher than the cuttings, should be placed within the flat with an upright at each of the four corners, and the plastic material should be stretched tightly over the frame, being securely tucked in around the bottom so that the unit will be completely sealed. The flat should be placed in a location where the cuttings will receive good light but no direct sunlight. The north wall of a building will afford an excellent location.

If a larger unit is desired a pit from 4 to 6 inches deep and of any convenient width and length can be prepared in some suitable location where it will be protected from direct sun. A number of flats can be placed in the pit or the rooting medium may be put directly in the pit. A rigid wooden or wire frame, high enough to comfortably clear the cuttings (eight inches is usually sufficient), should be placed over the pit. After the rooting medium has been moistened and the cuttings have been inserted the frame should be covered with small-mesh chicken wire, or with turkey wire, and the plastic material should be drawn securely over it. There should be an overlap of about 5 inches on all sides which should rest flush on the ground and should be covered with several inches of soil to insure complete sealing.

As the water vapor inside the propagator cannot escape, high humidity is maintained within the unit, and as air passes freely through the plastic a slight but fairly constant circulation of air is obtained. Therefore frequent watering and ventilation are not necessary. However, occasional attention is desirable. If, after a period of 3 or 4 weeks, there is a marked decrease in the amount of condensation on the inside of the plastic, and if, upon examination, the rooting medium appears to be slightly dry, watering should be done. During exceptionally hot weather a piece of moist burlap should be spread over the plastic to prevent the cuttings from being burned.

As the conditions which favor the rooting of the cuttings also provide excellent conditions for the growth of fungi it is advisable to spray the cuttings every week or 10 days with a good fungicide such as Captan 50 W, used at a concentration of 2 teaspoonfuls per gallon of water.

The cuttings should be examined occasionally to determine whether they are well rooted and ready for potting. Softwood cuttings taken from a propagating unit of this type require special treatment, as they would suffer badly from wilting if they were handled in the ordinary manner. After the rooted cuttings have been potted the pots should be placed in a shady place and covered tightly with sheets of plastic, supported by a frame. The plastic should be removed for a brief time for the first few days and then for a longer period on successive days until the cut-

tings show no signs of wilting. This will require from 5 to 6 days, according to the type of cutting. Hardwood cuttings do not require this special treatment.

Substances Which Promote Root-formation

Within recent decades research scientists have developed various root-forming substances. These chemical compounds, which are known as plant hormones, have a very direct influence upon plant growth, and hasten the root development of both succulent and hardwood cuttings.

There are a number of excellent commercial preparations on the market. Detailed instructions are given for their use on the container and the directions should be followed with care.

These plant hormone substances may be used with a wide variety of cuttings and they mark a distinct advance in the technique of propagation, as root formation can be stimulated on many plants which have formerly been difficult to propagate. They are of particular value in rooting cuttings of such plants as Azalea, Blueberry, Dahlia, Dogwood, Holly, Magnolia and Taxus.

Experiments have shown that in many cases root development is hastened and subsequent growth is improved if the cuttings are dipped for a few minutes in a dilute solution of a high-analysis, quickly soluble fertilizer. This should be done just before they are inserted into the propagating medium. A solution no stronger than one ounce to six quarts of water should be used. The following plants have shown excellent response to this treatment: Arabis, Lady Mac Begonia, Boxwood, Fuchsia, Geranium, Heliotrope, Lantana and various types of Ivy and Euonymus.

Mist Sprays for Cutting

The development of mist spraying has been a great boon to propagators. It is a practice now widely used by commercial growers and can be adapted for use by the home gardener who wishes to propagate plants by softwood cuttings on a fairly large scale. Ohio State University and the Arnold Arboretum have pioneered in the development of this new method.

Mist spraying of softwood cuttings has many

advantages. At no point in their development do the cuttings dry out, as the foliage is kept constantly moist. As shade is not necessary when mist spraying is used the plants receive ample sunlight and the danger of having the cuttings suffer from lack of sufficient air circulation is greatly lessened. As a consequence there is less opportunity for disease to gain headway. A high percentage of rootage is usually obtained, and resultant growth is healthy and vigorous. Under this method it is possible to root cuttings of larger size, which is a decided advantage when propagating trees and shrubs, as it is often possible to save from one to three years of growing time. This method has also made it possible to propagate plants which were hitherto extremely difficult to grow from cuttings and which can now be easily rooted.

The procedure is simple and can be adapted for use in greenhouses, in coldframes and in outdoor propagating beds. However, with this method good drainage of the area is essential. Pipes containing a series of nozzles which give off a very fine mist are installed above the propagating area. The mist spray may be regulated by hand or may be controlled automatically by a time-clock, or by an "electronic leaf." The number of applications required will depend to a considerable extent upon the weather, and good judgment must be exercised on the part of the operator if it is controlled manually. Constant mist will supply far more water than is needed and is definitely detrimental to cuttings of most types. A time-clock may be set so that it will go on and off—so many seconds on, so many seconds off; but here, again, the intervals must be regulated to some extent according to the weather. The most satisfactory control is through the use of a remarkable device known as an "electronic leaf." This consists of two carbon contact points, embedded in a small block of plastic which is on a short stand. This is inserted in the rooting medium with the cuttings. The surface of the plastic dries off a little more rapidly than do the leaves of the cuttings, and when there is no longer a film of moisture covering the plastic the contact is broken and the mist

spray is automatically turned on, going off again as soon as the leaves are thoroughly moist.

When cuttings are first inserted in the medium the "leaf" is placed at its farthest point from the jets. As the cuttings begin to root it is gradually moved closer to the jets, which reduces both the frequency and quantity of mistings. After the cuttings are rooted the application of mist should gradually cease, lath shade should be provided and they should go through a hardening-off process before being removed from the bed.

Stem Cuttings

Stem cuttings may be grouped into three separate classes: softwood cuttings; cuttings made from half-ripened wood; and those made from hard or dormant wood, known as hardwood cuttings. Practically all greenhouse plants and all herbaceous perennials as well as some shrubs may be propagated by softwood cuttings. Many shrubs, vines, and some trees are propagated by cuttings made from half-ripened wood, while others are most successfully propagated by hardwood cuttings.

Softwood Stem Cuttings of Herbaceous Plants

Stem cuttings are sometimes referred to as "slips," the term being frequently applied to small shoots which are pulled or slipped from a plant for the purpose of propagation.

Time of Making Cuttings. Softwood stem cuttings of herbaceous perennials such as delphiniums, phlox and chrysanthemums should preferably be taken in the spring just as the plants are starting into growth, although they may be taken at any time during the growing season when young, non-flowering shoots are obtainable. Cuttings of violas and of the majority of rock plants such as phlox divaricata, phlox subulata, arabis, and iberis are most successful when taken during June and July after the flowering season is over.

Making the Cutting. The parent plants from which the cuttings are taken should be vigorous, healthy and preferably well branched. The cuttings should usually be taken from the terminal growth, preferably from non-flowering shoots. Growth that is too soft and succulent should be avoided as cuttings taken from such shoots are apt to rot before root formation has taken place. Shoots that are somewhat older and are brittle enough to snap when bent double should be selected. Old fibrous stems are also unsatisfactory as they root very slowly and have a tendency to produce inferior plants. In some cases old plants can be headed back in order to induce a growth of new lateral shoots suitable for cuttings.

Softwood cuttings vary in length from 2 to 4 inches; 2 inches being sufficient in the case of small plants such as arabis, alyssum saxatile, and many of the rock plants, 4 inches for geranium cuttings. A sharp, clean, slightly diagonal cut should be made a short distance below a node or joint, a node being the point at which the leaf is attached to the stem. There are occasional exceptions to this generally accepted rule of cutting slightly below a joint, as a few plants have been found to root more readily if the cut is made midway between the nodes or slightly above a node. After the cuttings have been taken, it is advisable to plunge them in cold water or to wrap them in damp newspaper for a brief time, a half hour or more, as it will prevent them from wilting. This practice does not apply to geraniums or to other plants which exude a milky juice. Cuttings from such plants should be sprinkled lightly with water and spread out on a surface where they will be exposed to the air for several hours. This will give the bleeding cells an opportunity to become sealed and there will be less danger of rot after the cutting is placed in the propagating case.

In preparing the cutting, all flower buds should be removed and the leaf surface should be slightly reduced. The leaves should be removed from one or two nodes at the base of the cutting, being cut with a sharp knife, not pulled or stripped off. The leaf area at the top should not be reduced unless there is an excessive amount. In the case of coleus and a few other plants with large, succulent foliage a portion of the leaves may be removed, but as a general practice it is well to leave as much leaf area at the top of the cutting as possible. The leaves of a softwood cutting aid in the manufacture of food for the plant and they consequently have an important part to play in the development of the new root system.

Planting the Cutting. After the cuttings have been prepared, they should be inserted in the propagating case. The depth will vary somewhat with the type of cutting but, in general, the depth should be such that one or two nodes are buried. The rooting medium should be pressed firmly about the cuttings and a thorough watering should be given after the cuttings are in place. Shade should be provided for the first few days at least, and in some cases for a much longer period. One may be guided by the condition of the foliage. The leaves should be firm and should never be allowed to show any appearance of wilting. Plants differ greatly in this respect. As the roots begin to form it is important that full sunlight be provided.

Temperature. The matter of temperature is of considerable importance. For the majority of plants a temperature ranging between 65 and 75° F. is ideal, although some plants require somewhat lower or a much higher degree of heat. Root formation is usually greatly stimulated if bottom heat is provided. If possible, the temperature of

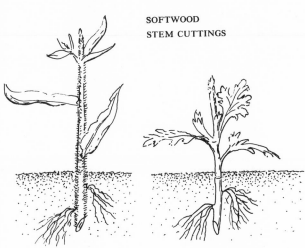

SOFTWOOD
STEM CUTTINGS

the rooting medium should be 5 to 10° warmer than the surrounding air. In greenhouses the bottom heat is supplied by the pipes which comprise the regular heating system or by an automatically controlled electric heating cable. In a hotbed it may be supplied by manure or by an electric cable, while in the house it may be supplied by radiator pipes, if they are accessible.

Moisture. An adequate supply of moisture and sufficient circulation of air are also important factors. For the majority of plants a moderate degree of moisture is desirable. The sand of rooting medium should never be allowed to dry out completely, nor should it be allowed to become wet to the point of being soggy. Cacti and other succulents require a rather dry environment, while a few of our large-foliaged greenhouse plants prefer a very high degree of humidity.

Air Conditions. There should be a sufficient circulation of air so that moisture does not remain on the leaves constantly or for too long a time, and direct drafts should always be avoided, as the effects are usually very harmful.

Potting-up. From three to four weeks will be required for the rooting of most softwood cuttings. Evidence of root formation will usually be indicated by the beginning of new top growth. When the roots are well developed, having reached a length of $\frac{1}{2}$-inch or more, the cuttings should be removed from the sand. They may then be potted up in small pots or planted in flats or frames. A sandy loam with a small proportion of leaf mold is ideal for this first potting, and after the young plants have become well established they may be allowed a richer diet.

PERENNIALS PROPAGATED BY STEM CUTTINGS

SCIENTIFIC NAME	COMMON NAME
Althæa rosea	Hollyhock
Alyssum saxatile	Goldentuft
Amsonia	
Arabis	Rockcress
Arenaria	Sandwort
Artemisia	Mugwort
Asclepias tuberosa	Butterflyweed
Aster (all hardy asters)	
Aubrietia	Purple Rockcress
Boltonia	
Campanula	Bellflower
Caryopteris	
Centaurea dealbata	
Ceratostigma plumbaginoides	Blue Leadwort
Chrysanthemum	
Clematis (herbaceous types)	
Daphne cneorum	Garland flower
Delphinium	Larkspur
Dianthus	Pink
Dicentra	Bleeding-heart
Eupatorium cœlestinum	Mistflower
Epigæa repens	Trailing Arbutus
Gaillardia	Blanketflower
Geum (Avens)	
Gypsophila	Baby's-breath
Helenium	Sneezeweed
Helianthus	Sunflower
Heliopsis	Orange Sunflower
Hesperis	Sweet Rocket
Heuchera	Coral Bells
Iberis	Evergreen Candytuft
Lobelia	
Lychnis	Campion
Lupinus	Lupine
Lythrum	Loosestrife
Monarda	Horsemint
Myosotis	Forget-me-not
Nepeta	
Penstemon	Beard-tongue
Phlox	
Potentilla	Cinquefoil
Pyrethrum	Painted Daisy
Rudbeckia	Coneflower
Salvia	Sage
Saponaria	Soapwort
Sedum	Stonecrop
Silene	Catchfly
Teucrium	Germander
Tradescantia	Spiderwort
Verbascum	Mullein
Veronica	Speedwell
Viola	

Half-ripened Stem Cuttings of Shrubs and Trees

The majority of shrubs may be readily propagated by half-ripened stem cuttings. The cuttings may be taken during the late summer months, the exact time depending upon the growth of the plant. The cuttings should be taken from the tip end of the shoots and the wood should be just brittle enough to snap off when bent double. The cuttings will vary in length from 4 to 6 inches and a clean cut should be made below a node. The leaves should be removed from the lower portion of the stems and the cuttings should be inserted in the home propagating unit described on page 482.

Hardwood or Dormant Stem Cuttings

Many deciduous trees and shrubs may be propagated very readily by means of dormant or hardwood cuttings. These cuttings should be taken in the autumn after the leaves have fallen.

HARDWOOD STEM CUTTINGS

In the case of a few shrubs, such as Hibiscus and Diervilla, only the tips of the branches should be used. With the majority of shrubs and trees, however, the branches may be cut into sections varying from 6 to 10 inches in length. The cuttings should be made from healthy wood of the current season's growth. In most cases there should be at least three or four buds on each section of stem used as a cutting. A clean, slightly diagonal cut should be made just above a bud at the top and just below a bud at the bottom of each cutting. After the cuttings have been made, they should be tied in bundles of convenient size with the lower or butt ends even and the cuttings facing in the same direction. A label should be attached to each group and the bundles should then be buried in slightly moist sand, soil, peat moss or sawdust. A cool cellar with a temperature ranging between 40 and 45 degrees Fahrenheit provides an ideal storage place for hardwood cuttings during the winter months. If such a place is not available, however, the bundles of cuttings may be buried out of doors in sand or in light, sandy soil, a well-drained spot being selected, and the bundles should be buried below the frost line. During this period of storage, a callous will form over the butt ends of the cuttings. In the spring when the ground is workable the cuttings may be removed from storage and may be planted out in nursery rows. The depth of planting will vary somewhat according to the type of cutting. The general practice is to set the cutting so that only the tip shows above the surface of the ground. In the case of cuttings containing a large number of buds, one third of the stem may protrude above the surface of the soil, thus allowing several buds to develop into new shoots. By autumn the cuttings should be well rooted and the young plants may be shifted to more ample quarters in the nursery.

Evergreen Cuttings: Coniferous

Many evergreens may be readily propagated by cuttings. The usual practice is to take cuttings during October and November from growth of the current season. In the case of some of the rather slow-rooting evergreens, the heel or mallet type of cutting is preferred. (See illustrations.) The cuttings should be inserted in a propagating case and kept at a moderately cool temperature of approximately 60° F. with mild bottom heat. The cuttings should be protected from strong sunshine and, for best results, there should be a reasonably high degree of humidity. Some evergreens will root readily in any medium such as sand, peat moss, or a combination of the two, while other types of evergreens such as yews prefer sand as a rooting medium. Some of the very quick-rooting evergreens such as the aborvitæs and the retinosporas may also be propagated by cuttings taken in August. These late summer cuttings may be inserted in an outdoor propagating frame and will root readily.

Leaf Cuttings

Among our more commonly grown house plants there are several which may be very easily propagated by leaf cuttings, various methods being used to meet the requirements of the individual plant. In general, plants with thick, fleshy leaves may be most readily propagated in this manner as the leaves contain a sufficient supply of reserve food.

The Saintpaulia, Gloxinia, Peperomia, and the Begonias of the Gloire de Lorraine group may be propagated by removing an entire leaf from the plant and inserting the petiole, or leaf stem, in the rooting medium. Sansevierias may be increased by cutting the leaves into lengths varying from 3 to 5 inches and inserting them in the propagating case. In the case of Bryophyllum or Kalanchoë, the leaf should be removed from the plant and laid flat upon the surface of the sand, being weighted down with pebbles. The new plants are produced in the indentations along the margins of the leaves. Occasionally

Part-leaf cutting, rooted and sprouting.

Cuts and sprouts

Pebble Anchors

BEGONIA whole-leaf cutting

Sprouted

ST. PAULIA LEAF CUTTINGS

these young plantlets begin to grow while the leaf is still attached to the parent plant. In the propagation of Rex Begonias, the usual practice is to make a slight cut through the main veins of the leaf just below the point where they fork. The leaf is then placed flat on the sand or other rooting medium, being pinned in place with small wire hairpins or weighted down with pebbles. Another method of propagating Begonias is to cut the leaf into the shape of a V, each piece containing a large vein. The point of the V is then inserted in the sand and the new plant will develop at this point. A propagating

case with glass sides and top such as that described on page 482 is ideal for the rooting of leaf cuttings if a greenhouse propagating frame is not available.

Root Cuttings

After the plants have been lifted, the roots may be cut into lengths varying from 2 to 3 inches. These small pieces of root should then be planted in greenhouse flats or in frames, being placed in a horizontal position at a depth of approximately an inch. Pure sand, sand and peatmoss in mixture, or a light sandy soil will all give satisfactory results as a rooting medium.

If the cuttings are taken in the autumn, they may be carried over the winter in the coldframe, and by spring the new plants will be ready to set out in the nursery. If the cuttings are given mild bottom heat in the greenhouse propagating bench, the development of new root and top growth will be very rapid. Root cuttings may be taken at almost any season of the year, but the most favorable time will usually be indicated by the natural habit of growth of the plant. Anemone Japonica, which flowers in the autumn, may be propagated most successfully if lifted late in the season after the blooming period is over. The Oriental Poppies and Bleeding-heart become dormant soon after flowering, and root cuttings should preferably be made during this period. Phlox may be successfully propagated by this method at almost any season and the root cuttings develop new plants so readily that they may even be planted in small shallow drills in the open ground.

PERENNIALS PROPAGATED BY ROOT CUTTINGS

SCIENTIFIC NAME	COMMON NAME	SCIENTIFIC NAME	COMMON NAME
Anchusa	Bugloss	Œnothera	Evening Primrose
Anemone Japonica	Japanese Anemone	Papaver orientale	Oriental Poppy
Asclepias	Butterflyweed	Phlox	
Bocconia	Plume Poppy	Polygonatum	Solomon's Seal
Ceratostigma		Romneya	Canyon Poppy
plumbaginoides	Blue Leadwort	Stokesia	Stokes Aster
Dicentra Spectabilis	Bleeding-heart	Thermopsis	
Dictamnus	Gas Plant	Trollius	Globe-flower
Echinops	Globe Thistle	Verbascum	Mullein
Gypsophila paniculata	Baby's-breath	Yucca	Adam's-needle

Propagation by Division

Clumps

The division of old clumps is one of the most simple of all methods of propagation. A few shrubs and many of the herbaceous perennials may be propagated very successfully in this way.

The plants should be lifted from the soil and pulled apart with care in order that the roots and crown may be injured as little as possible. In cases where the crowns have become tough and hard, two spading forks or hand forks may be used to loosen them. In occasional instances where no alternative seems possible, a clean, sharp cut can be made with a strong butcher's knife or with a spade.

In the case of certain herbaceous perennials, the frequent division of the clumps is desirable from the standpoint of good cultural methods; in other cases it is employed only when there is a desire to increase the stock. Hardy Asters and Chrysanthemums deteriorate rapidly if left undisturbed over a period of many years, and they should, therefore, be systematically lifted and divided every two or three years, whether new plants are desired or not. Peonies should preferably not be divided more frequently than once in seven or eight years and they may often be left undisturbed for many years with no apparent injury to the plant. Bleeding-heart should never be disturbed unless an increase of stock is desired as the plants will increase in beauty as the years pass.

The season of the year most favorable for the division of old clumps will vary with the natural habit of growth of the plant. Hardy asters and chrysanthemums should be divided in very early spring just as growth starts. Phlox should preferably be divided in the early autumn after the period of bloom has passed, although it may be divided at almost any season of the year with reasonable success. Bleeding-heart should always be divided in the autumn, never in the spring if one wishes to have bloom the same season. Peonies should be lifted and divided early in September.

PERENNIALS PROPAGATED BY DIVISION OF CLUMPS

SCIENTIFIC NAME	COMMON NAME	SCIENTIFIC NAME	COMMON NAME
Achillea	Yarrow	Doronicum	Leopard's-bane
Aconitum	Monkshood	Echinops	Globe Thistle
Ajuga	Bugle	Eupatorium	Mistflower
Alyssum saxatile	Goldentuft	Euphorbia	Spurge
Amsonia		Filipendula	Meadowsweet
Anchusa	Bugloss	Gaillardia	Blanket-flower
Aquilegia	Columbine	Helianthus	Sunflower
Arabis	Rockcress	Hemerocallis	Daylily
Artemisia	Mugwort	Heuchera	Coral Bell
Aster (all hardy types)		Iris	
Astilbe	Herbaceous Spirea	Linum perenne	Perennial Flax
Aubrietia	Purple Rockcress	Lupinus	Lupine
Baptisia	False-indigo	Mertensia	Virginia Bluebells
Bocconia	Plume Poppy	Monarda	Horsemint
Boltonia		Œnothera	Evening-primrose
Campanula	Bellflower	Penstemon	Beard-tongue
Centranthus	Valerian	Peony	
Cerastium tomentosum	Snow-in-summer	Phlox (all hardy types)	
Ceratostigma plumbaginoides	Blue Leadwort	Physostegia	False-dragonhead
		Primula	Primrose
Chelone	Turtlehead	Pyrethrum	Painted Daisy
Chrysanthemum		Rudbeckia	Coneflower
Cimicifuga	Bugbane	Scabiosa	
Clematis (herbaceous types)		Sedum	Stonecrop
Coreopsis		Statice	Thrift
Delphinium	Larkspur	Thalictrum	Meadow Rue
Dianthus	Pink	Trollius	Globeflower
Dicentra	Bleeding-heart	Veronica	Speedwell

In cases where the plant grows from a definite crown, the hard, woody center should be discarded and the vigorous outside growth should be selected for purposes of propagation. After the divisions have been reset, they should be kept watered until new root growth has started and they have become well established.

PERENNIALS PROPAGATED BY RHIZOMES

SCIENTIFIC NAME	COMMON NAME
Achimenes	
Canna	
Convallaria majalis	Lily-of-the-Valley
Helleborus niger	Christmas Rose
Hosta	Plantain Lily
Iris (all rhizomatous types)	
Podophyllum	Mayapple
Polygonatum	Solomon's Seal
Primula Sieboldii	Primrose
Sanguinaria	Bloodroot
Smilacina	False Solomon's Seal
Trillium	Wake-robin

Rhizomes

Botanically a rhizome is an underground, or partially underground, stem which, in most cases, produces roots, shoots, and leaves. A rhizome may be distinguished from a root by the presence of nodes. A true root has no nodes. The rhizomes of some plants penetrate quite deeply into the soil, while in the case of certain Irises, the rhizomes rest upon the surface of the ground, being only partially subterranean. Plants of this type may be readily propagated by a division of the rhizomes. In the case of the bearded iris, the plant may be lifted from the soil and the rhizomes gently separated, each rhizome having two or three sprouts for new growth.* The rhizomes of some plants bear no prominent shoots and in such cases the rhizome should be cut into short pieces. These sections should then be planted in sand until they have rooted. The majority of rhizomatous plants should be propagated when dormant. In the case of the bearded iris, however, the most favorable time is the season immediately following the blooming period.

* See page 361 for illustration.

Tubers

Tubers are thickened underground stems bearing conspicuous buds or eyes. Among flowering plants, the Dahlia is the most prominent member of this group while the Irish potato and the Jerusalem artichoke are well known among the vegetables. The tubers may be cut into sections, as in the case of the Potato, or they may be planted whole, as in the case of the Dahlia. It is essential that each tuber have at least one healthy bud. When Dahlias are propagated by tubers, a small portion of stem should be attached to each tuber.

"Bulbous" Propagation

Bulbs and Bulbils

There are numerous bulb-like structures, commonly called "bulbs," but which in reality may be tubers or rhizomes (as described above) or corms. Bulbs are, botanically, modified leaves and stems which occur usually underground. They are composed largely of fleshy, scale-like leaves and they contain large quantities of stored plant food. There are two general types of bulbs, the tunicated type composed of close-fitting layers of leaf tissue covered with a dry husk, such as the hyacinth and tulip; and the scaly type which is composed of thick, loose, overlapping scales, such as the lily.

Many bulbs are readily increased by natural separation. A fully matured bulb, known as a "mother bulb", will, under favorable conditions, produce one or more bulbs of flowering size and a number of small bulbils. These small bulbils should be removed when the mother bulb is dug and should be planted in flats or in nursery plots, as they will usually require several years to reach blooming size.

Lilies may be propagated by the separation of the bulbs, by bulblets produced in the axils of the leaves, and by the fleshy scales. The bulblets produced in the axils of the leaves should be planted in the same way as the bulbils from the base of the bulb. After the flowering period, the bulbs should be lifted and three or four of the outer scales may be removed. These scales should be placed in damp sphagnum moss in a warm greenhouse. Tiny bulbils will develop at the base of the scales and will reach flowering size in from two to four years.

Another method of propagation which has proved successful with some lilies is to remove the scales and plant them in the nursery during the summer. They should be set about 2 inches deep and they will usually produce flowering bulbs in about three years.

Madonna lilies may be propagated by removing the lower portion of the flower stems from the bulb. After the blooming season is over and the flower stalk has been cut off, the base of the stem may be pulled out and planted in sand, being placed in a horizontal position. Small bulbs will be produced along the stem and will flower in from two to three years.

Hyacinths may be increased very rapidly by notching or scooping the bulbs. The usual practice is to dig the bulbs in late spring or early summer. In notching, a transverse cut is made through the base of the bulb. In scooping, the entire basal section of the bulb is removed in such a manner that the various layers of scales are slightly severed. In order to hasten the production of new bulbils, the notched or scooped bulbs are dusted with slaked lime and are then placed, bottom up, in a moist atmosphere where a high temperature, ranging around 80° F., can be maintained. If this procedure is followed, the new bulbils will begin to form within a few weeks and in the autumn the mother bulbs with the small bulbils still attached should be planted in the nursery. When the bulbils have reached maturity they may be separated from the mother bulb. Notched bulbs will produce a small number of large bulbils which will reach blooming size in from three to four years. Scooped bulbs will produce a larger number of small bulbils which require from four to five years to reach blooming size.

Tulip bulbs, when they have reached maximum size, usually split up into a number of smaller bulbs. These should be lifted and planted in nursery rows, and, if conditions of soil and climate are favorable, they will reach blooming size in from two to four years.

Narcissus, Scilla, Muscari and many other bulbs may be easily increased by division or separation as the bulbs multiply very rapidly under natural conditions.

Corms and Cormels

A corm is a fleshy, underground base of a stem, rounded in shape. It is solid, being composed almost entirely of stem tissue, and is unlike a bulb in this respect. A bulb consists largely of leaf tissue, and when a crosswise section is cut from it a number of concentric scaly rings are revealed, whereas a corm thus cut reveals only solid tissue. Among the most familiar examples of plants grown from corms are the Calochortus, Crocus, Cyclamen, Gladiolus, Ixia,

and Tritonia. Each year one, and in some cases several new corms of flowering size are formed on top of the mother corm which deteriorates at the end of the growing season. Many small cormels are also usually formed at the base of the new corm. When the plants are dug in the autumn, the new, flowering-size corms may be separated and stored for spring planting. In general practice these corms are planted the following season to produce bloom. If, however, a very rapid increase of stock is desired, as in the case of a new or very expensive variety, these large corms may be cut into sections in order that more plants may be produced. The tiny cormels should be stored until planting time in the spring. They may then be planted in rows, being treated very much like seed, and they will reach blooming size in from one to three years.

Propagation by Specialized Shoots

Layering

Layering is one of the simplest and most dependable methods of propagation although it is adapted only to those plants which possess a characteristic habit of growth and which root readily when their branches come into contact with the soil. It is a method which is of especial value in the propagation of some of the broadleaved evergreens such as certain varieties of Rhododendrons and Magnolias. Daphne cneorum may also be propagated by layering.

There are several different types of layering: tip-layering, simple layering, serpentine layering, mound layering, and air layering.

Tip-Layering is the method commonly used in the propagation of Black Raspberries and plants of a similar habit of growth. In late summer the supple canes are bent over, the tip being anchored in the soil. A new plant will soon form which may be severed from the parent plant and transplanted to any desired position.

Simple Layering is usually done during the spring and summer months. If the branch is woody in character, a notch should be cut in it about 18 inches from the tip. The notch should be propped open with a match or some very small piece of wood. The branch should then be bent over to the ground, the portion where the notch occurs being covered with soil. The leaves should be removed from that portion of the stem which is to be buried. The tip end of the branch should be left exposed. If necessary the branch may be pegged down with a forked stick, or it may be held in place by the weight of a small stone. After the layer has rooted, it may be severed from the parent plant and when the new plant is well established, it may be transplanted the following spring.

Serpentine Layering is a method frequently used in the propagation of vines with long flexible stems, and enables one to obtain a large number of new plants. (See sketch below.) In continuous layering the entire shoot except the tip is covered with soil. Continuous layering can be used only with a rather limited group of plants as many types will not send up shoots from buds which are buried in the soil. This method is of particular value in the propagation of Ivy, Willow and Highbush cranberry.

Mound Layering. Plants of a characteristically bush habit of growth may frequently be propagated successfully by mound layering. This method is of particular value in the propagation of Hydrangeas, Cotoneasters, Cydonia, Calycanthus and Gooseberries. The plants should be pruned back severely, preferably a year before the layering is to be done, in order to encourage the production of new shoots at the base. The soil should be mounded up about the entire base of the plant in the spring and these new basal shoots will strike root at the nodes. This method of propagation is somewhat slow, as it will frequently require from one to two years for the new plants to become well established.

Air Layering is a method used more than 2,000 years ago by the Chinese. Until recently, however, its use in this country has been largely limited to the propagation of a few greenhouse plants, such as the Rubber plant and certain of the Dracænas. But today, due to the development of new techniques and to the use of plastic materials which have the ability to hold moisture in without hindering the movement of air, air layering has come into much wider use, and both professional and amateur gardeners are finding it an excellent method of propagating such plants as the hollies, rhododendrons, oleanders and gardenias.

The most favorable time for air layering is just as the buds start into growth in the spring. A stem or branch of the previous season's growth should be selected. A cut should be made from $1\frac{1}{2}$ to 2 inches in length extending approximately one third of the way through the stem. The cut should be made with a sharp knife and may be made with either an upward or downward motion. The flap of bark made by the cut should be entirely removed. The cut should then be dusted with a dusting powder such as Hormodin No. 3. A small sash brush is an excellent thing to use for this purpose. Fine sphagnum moss which has either been horticulturally milled or rubbed through a $\frac{1}{2}$ inch screen should be used to bind the wound. The moss should be thoroughly moistened and then squeezed until no water drips from it. Moss that is soggy when it is applied will cause fermentation and discourage rooting. After the moss has been moistened and the excess water squeezed out it should be rolled into a ball and then cut in half. These two pieces should be bound around the wounded area on the stem. A 6 inch by 6 inch piece of plastic, such as polyethylene or vinyl plastic, should then be wrapped tightly around the ball of moss. The plastic should be sealed at both the top and bottom with strips of black Scotch Electrical Tape #33. The strip of tape should completely seal the plastic and be bound several times around the stem of the plant, as it is important that a complete seal be made which will prevent rain water from seeping through.

When roots have formed at the point where the cut

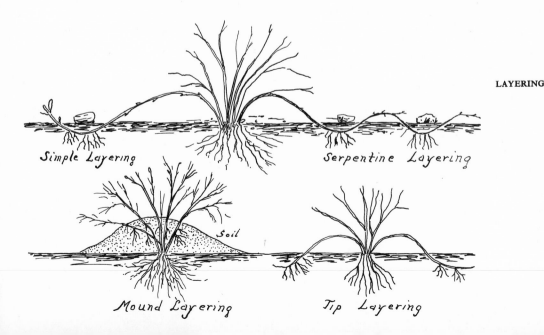

LAYERING

Simple Layering

Serpentine Layering

Soil

Mound Layering

Tip Layering

was made, the branch should be severed from the parent plant, the plastic covering should be removed, and the newly rooted plant should be planted either in a pot of ample size or in a nursery bed.

Suckers

Some plants may be propagated by means of suckers which are leafy shoots produced from adventitious buds on the underground parts of a plant. Certain varieties of Cherries and Plums produce suckers very rapidly, and Lilacs may be propagated by this method. If the tree or shrub which is to be thus propagated has been grafted it is important to make certain that the sucker has been produced from a bud above the graft. If it happens to have come from a bud below the graft it will be similar to the stock upon which the tree or shrub was grafted and will not possess the desirable characteristics of the grafted plant. Willows, Poplars, Black Locust and Sassafras may be very readily propagated by means of suckers.

Runners

Some plants, such as the Strawberry, the Boston Fern and the Strawberry Saxifrage, may be readily propagated by means of runners. In plants of this type the stems creep along the surface of the ground and strike root at the nodes, producing new plants which continue to receive nourishment from the parent plant until they are well established. The connecting stem may be severed at any point between the old plant and the new plant, and the new plant may then be moved to its new location.

Stolons

A stolon is a slender branch which, under favorable conditions, will take root. Stolons may be produced either above ground or below ground, the new plant being produced from the bud at the end of the solon. Some of the bent grasses may be very readily increased by the planting of stolons. The sod is broken into small pieces and the stolons are strewn upon the surface of the well-prepared seed bed, being covered with approximately $\frac{1}{2}$-inch of soil. The soil should be kept moist until growth has started,

and at no time should the stolons be allowed to dry out.

Some shrubby plants also take root very naturally by means of stolons and may be readily propagated in this way. In this group we find Forsythia, the red-twigged Dogwood, Matrimony-vine, many of the Willows and the Red raspberries.

Grafting

Fruit trees do not come true from seed, as most of our orchard varieties are hybrids. In order to perpetuate a variety, vegetative propagation or a vegetative union is necessary.

Grafting and budding are the two common methods of propagating fruit trees. An undesirable variety may be changed to a more desirable one by grafting. Pollination troubles can be solved by grafting the proper variety on part of an unproductive tree, because the presence of another or pollinating variety will result in cross-fertilization, causing fruits to form on the heretofore non-productive variety. When the trunk of a tree has been girdled by mice, grafting will save the tree.

The Tree Peony is also propagated by grafting, as is the herbaceous perennial, Gypsophila paniculata floreplena, the double-flowered baby's-breath.

Bridge Grafting

This is the only method to save trees girdled by mice.

1. Remove soil from around the trunk of the tree until the live bark on the roots is exposed.
2. Trim off rough edges of the bark with a sharp knife at the base of the tree and also on the root.
3. Take a piece of dormant one-year-old wood (previous season's growth) and measure the distance to be bridged over. Allow $1\frac{1}{4}$ inches on the bark and also on the root, and cut with a sharp knife.
4. Cut out a piece of bark above and below the girdled area, into which the ends of the scion should fit snugly. (Def.—A *scion* is a young shoot used for grafting.)
5. Make a slanting cut, $1\frac{1}{4}$ inches long on each end of the scion and place each end in the part where the bark was removed.

6. Place the scions 2 inches apart around the trunk.

7. Two small brads without heads should be used to hold the scion firmly in place at each end. They should be nailed through the middle two-thirds of each scion, each end of which is properly fitted above and below the girdled area.

8. Apply grafting wax over the united areas to keep them airtight.

Whip Grafting

This graft is used to propagate nursery stock and may be done in midwinter when most orchard operations are at a standstill.

One-year-old root stocks should be used. (Def. —*Stock* is that part which is to receive the scion.) They may be grown from seed or purchased from firms in mid- and far-western States which make a speciality of this. The procedure is as follows:

1. Cut the root from the one-year whip and below any green tissue.

2. Cut the root into 3-inch lengths.

3. Make a clean slanting cut about $1\frac{1}{2}$-2 inches in length. The next cut on the root is made parallel to the edge of the root and should be $1\frac{1}{4}$-$1\frac{1}{2}$ inches long.

4. Select a piece of scion wood from the middle of one-year terminal growth with three buds on it. Cut it $1\frac{1}{4}$ inches below the third bud and proceed as in No. 3.

5. Join the two tongues together and be sure that the cambium layer of one side of the root is in contact with one side of the scion. (Def.—*Cambium* is a layer of cells which is between the bark and the wood; these cells grow and multiply rapidly.)

6. Wrap tightly with waxed string and store in moist sand or leaves in a damp, cool place with a temperature of approximately 45 degrees until they have united. As soon as the soil can be prepared in the spring set the plants 6 inches apart in rows 3 feet apart. Set deep enough to cover all but the top bud. Remove the string before planting.

This method may also be practiced on young trees in the nursery row which are not over one year old. If older, the smaller branches may be successfully grafted in this manner.

Cleft Grafting

Cleft grafting is a method used to top-work trees, especially when the limb to be grafted is somewhat larger than the one-year scion to be grafted. A limb may vary from $\frac{1}{2}$ to 2 inches in diameter. This type of grafting is most successful if done early in the spring when the bark is loose, before growth has made much progress. It may be done after that, however, if the scions are dormant. The procedure is as follows:

1. Saw the limb off at the desired point where the limb is to be grafted.

2. With a sharp knife smooth the edges so the cambium layer may be easily seen.

3. A grafting chisel is placed on the center of the stump and driven into the stock to a depth of 3 to 4 inches with a wooden mallet or club.

4. The scion of the desired variety should have been taken from the terminal growth of a bearing tree which should be the previous season's growth.

5. The tip of the scion should be cut off, and the second cut is made $1\frac{1}{2}$ inches below the third bud.

6. That part of the scion below the third bud is cut to make a wedge. The side with the bud should be slightly thicker than the side which will be in toward the center of the stump. This wedge should be $1\frac{1}{4}$ inches in length.

7. The cleft is opened with the end of the chisel which is wedge-shaped and the scion inserted so that its cambium layer is in direct contact with that of the stock. One scion is inserted on each side of the stock if it is more than an inch in diameter, and the chisel is removed. The pressure from the sides of the split stock holds the scions firmly in place. It is well to remember that the scions should be uniform in size to fit well and have equal pressure from both sides of the stock.

8. Cover the exposed area immediately with grafting wax to prevent drying out, the entrance of disease organisms, and the entrance of excess moisture.

An extra large branch may be cleft grafted by making two clefts at right angles to each other. In this case four scions are necessary. A small piece of wood, or a wedge, must be put in the center to prevent the scion from being crushed, as the larger the limb, the greater the pressure.

When the grafting of an individual limb is finished, the entire exposed area should be waxed over to prevent the entrance of moisture, disease organisms or drying out. The grafts should be checked occasionally to make sure that the wax is properly protecting it. When grafting is done after considerable growth has been made, it is best to cover the entire scion with wax, which keeps it in a dormant state a little longer while the scion is uniting with the stock.

Cleft grafting is very satisfactory on Apples and Pears but more difficult on Plums and Cherries and almost impossible with Peaches.

Bark Grafting

Bark grafting must be done in the spring after the sap starts to flow, or the bark will not easily separate from the cambium layer. This graft is most practical on limbs which are too large to be cleft grafted. The limb is removed at the desired place and a smooth area is selected where the graft is to be placed.

Preparing the Scion

1. The scion should contain three buds and be cut from the terminal growth 1½ inches below the third bud for all three types of bark grafting.

2. (a) Directly opposite the lower bud make an abrupt cut to the center and then straight down to the end; *or*

(b) Make a sloping cut on the side opposite the lowest bud to the end of the scion, or 1½ inches.

There are three ways of bark grafting.

1. (a) Make a cut 1¼ inches in length on the stock and at right angles to the stub which is to receive the graft.

(b) Pry the two corners up with a sharp knife and insert the scion prepared as in either (a) or (b). Force it under the bark until the outer bud is directly at the point of the stock and the scion.

(c) Fasten it securely by driving two small brads into it through the bark.

(d) Put the grafts 2 inches apart around the stub, cover exposed tissues (newly cut) with grafting wax. Best results are obtained if, in addition, raffia is wound around the stub two to three times and tied securely. The purpose is to hold the bark tightly against the scion.

2. Bark grafts may also be made in the same way as a bridge graft. Preparation for the scion has been discussed. A piece of bark is removed as described in

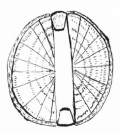

CLEFT GRAFT

SCION SET IN STOCK

SCIONS TRIMMED FOR
CLEFT GRAFT

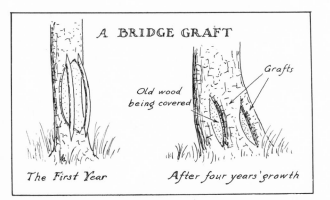

A BRIDGE GRAFT

Grafts

Old wood being covered

The First Year

After four years' growth

CLEFT GRAFT COMPLETE
EXCEPT FOR WAXING

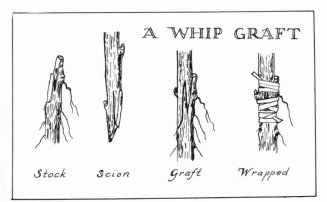

A WHIP GRAFT

Stock   *Scion*   *Graft*   *Wrapped*

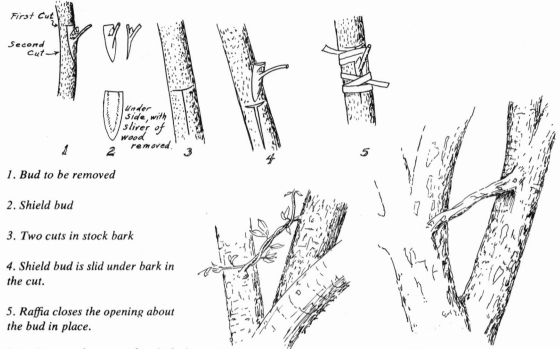

First Cut

Second Cut →

Under Side with sliver of wood removed.

1   *2*   *3*   *4*   *5*

1. *Bud to be removed*

2. *Shield bud*

3. *Two cuts in stock bark*

4. *Shield bud is slid under bark in the cut.*

5. *Raffia closes the opening about the bud in place.*

Sometimes used to strengthen forked branches. The illustration is self-explanatory.

A brace graft after one year

A brace graft after six years

bridge grafting. One side of the scion is cut as described in (*a*) or (*b*), inserted, fastened with brads and waxed over. This is the easiest method for the amateur to follow.

3. Budding. This type of grafting is done during the month of August or in the early part of September when the bark slips easily. Its main use is to propagate young trees of the desired variety.

(*a*) At the point where the budding is to be done, that is, as close to the ground as possible, make a cut in the shape of a T; its vertical distance $\frac{3}{4}$ of an inch long and the horizontal distance, $\frac{1}{2}$ inch.

(*b*) The bud to be used is selected from the terminal growth on the current season's growth. Be sure that the bud is well developed. Remove the leaf next to the bud, but leave on part of its stem.

(*c*) Using a sharp knife remove the bud with some of the wood and bark attached to it. When properly removed it looks like a shield.

(*d*) Loosen carefully the corners of the T-shaped cut in the stock and slip the bud in under the corners.

(*e*) Use raffia, rubber bands or waxed string to wind above and below the bud.

(*f*) Two weeks later the bud should be united. The bud remains dormant until the following spring. The

stock is cut back to the bud which develops into the desired limb.

Pruning and Training of Grafts

Grafts, especially those on large limbs which have been cleft or bark grafted, must be properly understood. If two or more grafts are made on a stub only one should be allowed to fully develop. The best one should be selected before next season's growth starts. It is cut back to promote lateral branches. The other is cut back to two or three buds. The purpose is to keep it alive so that it will help to heal over the stump but not to compete with the one selected. The principle used to train them until maturity or bearing is the same as with young trees planted in the ground.

It is best to graft one side of a tree at a time if it is more than eight years old. The side not grafted can be grafted the following year.

XXXIV

MULCHES

MULCHES not only have a very beneficial effect upon plant growth but also reduce to a minimum the time and labor required for garden maintenance. On the well-managed home property mulching becomes a year-round operation.

A good mulch, consisting of suitable materials properly applied at the correct time, serves many functions. The most important function of a mulch is the conservation of moisture. A good mulch readily permits the penetration of water into the soil. During periods of heavy precipitation it checks the full force of the rain, lessening the danger of surface run-off, and permits the water to sink gently into the soil. It also protects the soil from the drying effects of sun and wind, thus preventing the evaporation of moisture from the soil surface. On soils protected by a mulch one never finds a hard, baked crust such as one finds all too frequently on soils which are exposed to the sun's rays. Even during periods of intense summer heat and drought the soil under a heavy mulch will remain cool and moist. It is usually dark in color, and crumbly in texture, characteristics of a soil which will provide favorable conditions for good root development.

The application of a mulch is also one of the most effective measures of weed control. There are few weeds which can push up through a heavy mulch and if they occasionally succeed they are so straggly that they can easily be pulled out.

A mulch also serves as an insulating material and helps to maintain more even soil temperatures. In summer the soil under a mulch is sometimes as much as 20 degrees F. cooler than surrounding soils and in winter the soil under a blanket of mulch retains some of its heat and is warmer than surrounding soil areas. More uniform soil temperatures usually result in better plant growth and, in the case of vegetables, in superior quality.

The end result of an organic mulch is that it eventually decomposes and adds humus to the soil. During this process of decomposition valuable plant nutrients are released which increase the fertility of the soil. In the course of time soil under a heavy mulch will resemble woodland soil which is always so richly supplied with natural humus resulting from the slow decay of fallen leaves and branches. It will become crumbly to the touch, dark in color and have a clean, woodsy smell. The upper few inches of soil will be full of healthy feeding roots and will be well supplied with earthworms and beneficial soil micro-organisms. If plants are kept mulched with organic materials year after year there will be a constantly replenished supply of humus for their needs.

Selecting Materials for Mulches

The points in favor of mulching are so convincing that the gardener is usually not faced with the problem of whether to mulch or not to mulch, but rather with the question of which kind of mulch to use.

In selecting materials for mulches there are a number of factors which should be taken into consideration: the availability of the material; the cost, compared with that of other materials; the appearance of the mulch; the effect which it will have upon the soil; the acidity of its reaction upon the soil; its durability; whether it presents a fire hazard; whether it decomposes rapidly or slowly; whether it is comparatively weed-free; and whether there is danger of introducing disease through its use. In general, organic mulches are to be preferred to inorganic mulches, because of their benefit to the soil.

Aluminum Foil: In experimental tests aluminum foil has proved to be an effective mulch. It conserves moisture well, the moisture content of the soil under an aluminum mulch usually being at least 8 percent higher than that of the surrounding soil. This is due in part to the fact that water vapor coming to the surface of the soil condenses on the underside of the foil and drips back into the ground. Aluminum foil also serves as an insulating material against both heat and cold. As it reflects the sun's rays it has an extraordinarily cooling effect upon the soil in summer. Tests show that on a hot, sunny day the soil under an aluminum mulch will often be 20° F. cooler than that of the surrounding soil. And on cold nights the soil under the mulch will retain its heat and remain 8° to 10° F. warmer than the surrounding area. This even soil temperature results in more uniform growth and, in the case of vegetables, in improved quality. Aluminum foil is also one of the most fire-resistant of all mulches.

In spite of its many good qualities aluminum foil has certain limitations as a mulch. It is comparatively expensive, it adds no humus or nutrients to the soil, it must be anchored down along the edges to prevent blowing and tearing, and it is suitable only for plants grown in rows. It has proved of special value as a mulch in vegetable gardens, in areas where flowers are grown in rows for commercial production or for cutting, in nurseries where small plants are set out in rows, and for strawberries. It has resulted in increased yields of both vegetables and flowers, in an improvement in quality, and in better disease and insect control.

In applying an aluminum foil mulch the soil should be completely covered with the foil except for a two-inch strip where the plants come through. The most suitable grade for garden use is a .001 or a .0015-inch gauge. The foil is obtainable in widths varying from one to three feet.

Buckwheat Hulls are an excellent mulch for rose beds and flower borders. They are clean, light in weight and easy to apply. They are weed-free, and make a mulch which is inconspicuous in appearance and which can be raked up and re-used a second year if desired. Its greatest disadvantage is that in exposed areas it has a tendency to blow. It should be applied in a layer from one to three inches in depth.

Corncobs ground into small pieces, make a very satisfactory mulch, and in some sections they are readily obtainable at moderate cost. They are weed-free, clean, light in weight and easy to handle. They rot down into excellent humus but in order to avoid a deficiency of nitrogen in the soil during the period of decomposition extra nitrogen should be applied in some form (see page 500). When used on roses or on shrubs a three- to four-inch layer should be applied, while on perennial beds a two-inch layer is sufficient. If canker on roses is prevalent it will be advisable to spray the canes and the mulch with Fermate (see page 663).

In some sections very finely ground corncobs are being used as a mulch on greenhouse crops and have given excellent results on roses, carnations, chrysanthemums, snapdragons and stocks. A three- to four-inch mulch is recommended for greenhouse roses, an inch mulch for other crops.

Glass Wool: This material has been used experimentally and provides an effective mulch, one of its chief advantages being that it is completely fireproof. It is too expensive for extensive home or commercial use and lacks the many good qualities of an organic mulch.

Grass Clippings: Raked-up grass clippings provide a good home-grown mulching material. Because they tend to form a rather dense mat it is advisable to mix them with some coarse material such as partially rotted leaves, sawdust, or corncobs.

Hay: Rain-damaged hay which is unfit for livestock feed may sometimes be procured in rural areas for a very low cost and it makes an excellent mulch for the vegetable garden and for shrubbery borders. It may be used either as long hay or as chopped hay. It rots down into good humus, and is very beneficial to the soil. If the hay is from a legume crop, such as alfalfa, clover, soybeans or cowpeas, it will supply a considerable amount of additional nitrogen to the soil as it decomposes.

Hops: In some areas spent hops from breweries are readily available and have much to recommend them as a mulch for shrub plantings and for use around specimen trees. They decay very slowly and need to be renewed only once in every three or four years. And they are one of the most resistant of all mulches to fire. They do not catch fire as do most dried materials, they do not even smolder, they merely blacken. When first applied there is an objectionable odor but this is soon dissipated. Spent hops are used extensively at the Arnold Arboretum as a deep mulch on some of the prized shrubbery plantings and around valuable specimen trees.

Leaves are nature's favorite mulching material and are ideal for mulching trees and shrubs. A mulch of leaves four to eight inches in depth applied to a shrub border or to trees in the autumn will afford excellent protection and will add large quantities of humus to the soil. Oak leaves are acid in their reaction on the soil and are the standard mulch for broad-leaved evergreens. Some leaves, such as those of silver maple, elm and birch trees have an unfortunate tendency to mat down and soon become a soggy mass. In the flower garden there is danger of having leaves of this kind mat down and destroy the crowns of valuable plants. Shredded leaves do not mat as readily as whole leaves and have the added advantage of decomposing more quickly. If shredding is impracticable the leaves may be composted for a season before they are used, or they may be mixed with straw, ground corncobs or some other light material. Leaves of oak, beech and sycamore do not have a tendency to mat down.

Manure: Most animal manures available for mulches are mixed with straw, sawdust or some other form of absorptive organic material which has been used as bedding. They are, therefore, mulches with "built-in" fertility and are of great value. Such materials could be easily obtained half a century ago, but they are at a premium today and usually available only to people living in rural areas. When used for mulching purposes manures are most satisfactory if they have been composted.

Paper first came into use as a mulch on the pineapple plantations in Hawaii. A heavy grade of tough, black paper has been developed for mulching purposes which is very effective in controlling weeds and in conserving moisture. However, it is higher in cost than many other mulching materials, it must be weighted down to prevent blowing and tearing, it is suited only to row crops and it lacks the values of an organic mulch. It is particularly useful for killing such weeds as quack grass, Canada thistle and bindweed on very small areas where it can be heavily weighted down with boards or stones, as it will exclude all light.

Peat Moss is one of the most widely used of all mulching materials. It is obtainable in medium-sized bags or in large burlap-covered bales. It makes a mulch which is attractive in appearance, it is clean, easy to handle and weed-free, it is slow to decompose and therefore has to be renewed less frequently than many other organic materials, and its reaction is so mildly acid that it may be used on a wide variety of plants. It is suitable for use in the flower garden, on rose beds, on shrubbery borders and around specimen plants. Peat moss should be thoroughly moistened before it is applied as a mulch and the mulch should be kept moist and loose. If it is permitted to dry out it has a tendency to form a crust which is almost impervious to water, creating a condition which is extremely detrimental to plant growth. Peat moss is very absorptive and if it is partially dry it sometimes does not permit light rains to percolate down into the soil. Under conditions of normal rainfall this is not apt to occur.

Pine Needles make an airy, attractive mulch and in many areas are available for the raking. In the South they are widely used as a mulch for camellias. They are slightly acid in reaction, light in weight, clean, weed-free and pleasant to handle.

Plastic Mulches: Black polyethylene plastic is widely used as a mulch in many commercial vegetable areas, and to some extent in home gardens. It is usually spread between the rows, being weighted down with soil or with stones. Plants may also be set out through slits in the mulch. Its advantages are that it eliminates the need for cultivation as it prevents the growth of weeds completely, it conserves the moisture in the soil, and, since it is dark in color, it absorbs the rays of the sun and therefore maintains a high soil temperature.

On cold nights the soil temperature is from 10° to 15° F. warmer under a black plastic mulch. This is of great advantage in starting crops in the vegetable garden early in the spring. A plastic mulch is also valuable for strawberries as it results in early maturity, clean berries free from grit, and reduced decay in ripening berries. The disadvantages for the home garden are that it is not an organic mulch, it is not attractive in appearance, and in midsummer soil temperatures under it may become too high for some plants. It is obtainable in rolls of various widths and may be used for a number of seasons.

Redwood Bark: Shredded redwood bark is a mulching material which is in general use on the Pacific Coast. It is clean, attractive in appearance, weed-free and pest-free. Although it is an organic mulch it is not a good source of humus as it is extremely rot-resistant.

Salt Hay: Salt or Marsh hay is extensively used as a mulch in many sections. It is light, clean, pest-free and weed-free and is long lasting. After a season of use it may be raked up, stored and used again. It never mats down, and it makes an excellent winter mulch for perennial beds and borders, being of particular value for mulching plants with leafy crowns. A bale of salt hay will provide a light covering for an area of approximately 1,200 square feet.

Sawdust makes a very effective mulch and in areas where it is readily available is widely used. As a year-round mulch on blueberries and other small fruits, and in vegetable gardens, a mulch four to six inches in depth is usually applied. Sawdust is less desirable as a mulch in flower gardens, as it is apt to encourage the development of crown rot in plants which are particularly susceptible, probably due to the fact that moisture is held so closely about the crown. The acid reaction of sawdust will depend upon the source. Sawdust from some trees is very acid in its reaction, from other trees it is nearly neutral (see table on page 500). For some plants it is desirable to use an acid type of sawdust, for other plants a neutral type will best meet their requirements. To lessen the effect of an acid type of sawdust 100 pounds of ground limestone may be used per ton of dry sawdust which will help to maintain a more nearly neutral pH. When using sawdust as a mulch it is essential that additional nitrogen be applied to the soil (see page 500).

Stones: Flat stones can be used as a mulch in areas where they are readily available and in a location where a permanent mulch is desired. They will conserve the moisture in the soil, will prevent the growth of weeds, and will provide a cool root-run for the plants but, on the whole, organic materials are to be preferred. Stone chips are excellent for use in rock gardens as they prevent erosion in the soil pockets and help to lower soil temperatures.

Straw: All of the cereal straws, such as wheat, oat, barley and rye straw, provide excellent mulching material. Long straw may be used satisfactorily in the vegetable garden and for the mulching of trees and shrubbery, but straw is not suitable for use in the flower garden unless it is shredded. After one season straw is usually pretty well decomposed and becomes valuable humus. Nitrogen should be applied when straw is used as a mulch (see opposite column).

Tobacco Stems: In sections where they are available tobacco stems make an effective and economical mulch. Because of the danger of introducing mosaic disease they should never be used on bulb plantings, or even near lilies or tomato plants.

Walnut Shells: In some areas ground black walnut shells are available as a mulching material and they have much to recommend them. They provide a mulch which is fairly permanent, as they do not rot readily and therefore do not have to be replaced as frequently as many other mulches. They are pleasing in appearance, being a cinnamon brown in color, they do not wash away during heavy rains, and since the shells do not actually absorb any moisture themselves even light rains percolate down into the soil. A mulch of this type is also very resistant to fire, and since the material is extremely rot-resistant it has little tendency to reduce the supply of nitrogen in the soil.

Wood Chips: With the introduction of the mechanical chipper wood chips have become available in many sections. They are very effective as a mulch and will, in time, become completely decomposed and add humus to the soil. Extra nitrogen should be supplied when wood chips are used (see opposite column).

ACID MULCHES

Apple pomace from cider mills
Oak leaves: very acid
Peat moss: slightly acid
Pine needles: moderately acid
Sawdust

> Black oak: moderately acid
> Cypress: very acid (pH 3.5 to 3.9)
> Maple: mildly acid
> Red oak: mildly acid
> White oak: moderately acid

Acid mulches are recommended for use on azaleas, rhododendrons, pieris, camellias and other broad-leaved evergreens, and on blueberries.

NON-ACID MULCHES

Buckwheat hulls	Straw
Corncobs	Sawdust
Grass clippings	Elm
Leaves (except oak)	Hemlock
Salt hay	Locust

Non-acid mulches are recommended for use on perennial flower beds, on rose beds, in the vegetable garden and on deciduous shrub borders.

Peat moss is so mild in its acid reaction that it may also be used safely on most plants in this group.

Need for Additional Nitrogen

Certain raw organic materials, such as sawdust, wood chips, corncobs and, to some extent, the cereal straws will cause a depletion of nitrogen in the soil during the process of decomposition. This is due to the fact that the bacteria in the soil which cause the breakdown of raw organic materials into humus require large amounts of nitrogen during the process and they make use of the available nitrogen in the soil, sometimes causing the plants to suffer from nitrogen starvation. This may be prevented by increasing the supply of nitrogen in the soil at the time that such mulches are applied so that there will be sufficient to meet the needs of both the soil bacteria and the plants. Ammonium sulfate, nitrate of soda, ammonium nitrate or a complete fertilizer high in nitrogen may be used. The following amounts are recommended for use on soils of average fertility, per 100 square feet.

$\frac{1}{2}$ pound of ammonium sulfate or nitrate of soda
or $\frac{1}{3}$ pound of ammonium nitrate
or 1 pound of a complete fertilizer 10–6–4

On large areas the fertilizer is usually applied directly to the soil. If it is necessary to apply it after a mulch has been put on, it may be applied on the surface of the mulch and watered in, or it may be dissolved in water and applied to the mulch in the form of a solution.

In using small quantities of sawdust for mulching individual plants the fertilizer may be mixed with the sawdust as it is applied.

Summer Mulches

Summer mulches are of great value in conserving moisture and controlling weeds and are widely used in flower gardens, vegetable gardens, on small fruits and trees and shrubs.

In the Flower Garden: The summer mulch in the flower garden should be applied in the late spring or early summer after the ground has become thoroughly warm. Buckwheat hulls and peat moss are recommended as the most satisfactory materials for use on flower beds, as they are weed-free, clean, easy to handle and make a mulch which is inconspicuous in appearance. A mulch two inches in depth will usually be sufficient. When plants have low, leafy crowns the mulch should be worked in carefully about the plant in order to avoid covering the crown. If peat moss is used it should be thoroughly wet before it is applied and should be maintained in a moist, fluffy condition, never being allowed to dry out and form a crust.

If slugs are troublesome precautions must be taken in mulching herbaceous plants and annual flowers. A slug killer should be applied to the soil before the mulch is put on, and careful watch should be kept. If the slug killer was not applied to the soil an application on the surface of the mulch may prove helpful.

In the Vegetable Garden: A summer mulch in the vegetable garden will reduce to a minimum the labor required and will also appreciably increase yields and improve the table quality of the crops. And if an organic mulch is used the benefit to the soil will be great. Sawdust, straw, aluminum foil and paper may be used.

On Small Fruits: When summer mulches are used on small fruits such as raspberries, blackberries and blueberries it will not only result in the control of weeds and a consequent saving in labor but in more vigorous growth and increased production. Sawdust, straw, and hay are excellent mulching materials. A year-round sawdust mulch on blueberries is recommended.

On Trees and Shrubs: Broad-leaved evergreens, being shallow rooted, thrive best under a permanent mulch which should remain undisturbed. As the older layers decompose new material should be added. This may be done whenever materials such as leaves and grass clippings are available. Permanent mulches may also be maintained on deciduous trees and shrubs. Permanent organic mulches of leaves, straw or sawdust should be maintained at a depth of 4 to 6 inches.

Winter Mulches for the Flower Garden

Purposes of the Winter Mulch: In the North a winter mulch serves several important functions in the flower garden. It protects the plants from severe cold; it protects the foliage of certain plants from the effects of drying winds and brilliant winter sunshine which are apt to sear and scorch tender growth; it prevents plants from starting into growth too early in the spring; and, perhaps most important of all, it prevents the alternate freezing and thawing of the soil which is apt to occur during the late winter and spring months which is so harmful to many herbaceous plants, heaving the crowns out of the soil and leaving the roots exposed. Young plants whose roots are very near the surface, and shallow-rooted plants, such as columbines, are the most likely to be injured. In many sections winter-killing is more often due to this cause than to the effect of extremely low temperatures.

Materials for Winter Mulches: A number of materials may be used very satisfactorily as winter mulches in the flower garden, such as salt hay and straw.

If small evergreen boughs are available, they offer excellent material for winter covering, as they are light in weight and permit a good circulation of air. They may also be used to hold leaves, straw or other light materials in place. Fallen leaves are one of nature's own coverings, but if they are to be used as a winter protection on garden beds only those kinds should be selected which will not mat down and will not become a soggy mass before spring. Leaves from oak, beech and sycamore trees are excellent, while leaves from maples, elms and other hardwood trees should not be used.

When to Apply the Mulch: The winter mulch should not be applied until the plants are completely dormant and the ground is frozen. The purpose of the mulch is not only for the protection against cold but also to protect the plants from the temporary warmth of late winter and early spring days which can be so deceptive and so damaging to herbaceous plants when it is followed by a return to severe weather.

Depth of the Mulch: The depth of the winter mulch will depend upon the type of material used and the severity of the winter climate. It is as disastrous to apply too heavy a mulch and smother the plants as it is to apply too light a covering. Care should be taken not to cover the crowns of such plants as foxgloves, Canterbury bells, hollyhocks, heuchera, garden pinks or anchusa, all of which retain their succulent foliage throughout the winter. The mulch should be worked in about the roots with only a few light wisps of salt hay over the foliage.

Removal of the Winter Mulch: The removal of the winter mulch is always a matter of concern to the gardener. If a fairly heavy mulch was used it should be removed gradually and the final covering should, if possible, be lifted off on a cloudy day in order that any young shoots which have started into growth may not be too suddenly exposed to brilliant sunshine.

It is unwise to leave the winter mulch on too late in the spring as it will seriously retard the growth of the plants, and shoots which have tried to push through will be spindly and weak. It is usually safe to begin to remove the mulch as soon as the cold weather seems to be over and the early, small bulbs such as the squills and species crocus are in bloom.

Winter Mulches for Evergreens

The evergreens, particularly the broad-leaved evergreens, are greatly benefited by a winter mulch. Under an adequate winter mulch the soil does not freeze as quickly or as deeply as soil which is exposed. This is a matter of considerable importance with evergreens, as they are never completely dormant. They continue to need water during the winter, and are able to obtain it much more readily from heavily mulched soils than from bare, frozen ground. Under a system of permanent mulching this advantage is gained.

XXXV
TOOLS,
TOOL HOUSES, AND GARDEN EQUIPMENT

GARDENING is a craft. Good craftsmen have good tools. For the greatest efficiency in all gardening operations good tools are essential. Not only should the gardener know how to select tools which are strong and durable and which will give good service over a period of many years, but he should also know how to care for tools properly in order that they may be kept in good condition.

It is a matter of sound economy to buy well-made tools. A good tool differs from a poor one in the materials used in its manufacture and in its type of construction. Good tools are more durable than cheap tools and they are usually more efficient. Particularly is this true in the case of tools used for cutting purposes such as lawn mowers, pruning shears, grass shears, and hedge trimmers, as they may be sharpened more readily and will retain a better edge.

The most satisfactory type of spade is that with a metal shank which extends part way up the handle, as this makes for additional strength. The same type of construction is desirable for spading forks and for long-handled shovels. Trowels made from a single sheet of metal pressed into shape are not so strong or so durable as trowels with wooden handles driven into a metal shank.

The most satisfactory type of small hand cultivator for use in flower borders is the weeder with three claw-like prongs which are not rigid. It is capable of doing very rapid and efficient work and it leaves the soil in excellent tilth. It is also possible to work with it among very small seedling plants. There are a number of other

types on the market which are reasonably satisfactory.

The garden hoe has been designed in a great variety of sizes and shapes. A hoe that is too large and heavy is cumbersome and is better fitted for the mixing of cement than for garden work. The 6-inch draw hoe, the 6-inch scuffle hoe and the lightweight pointed type of hoe are all satisfactory for general garden cultivation. The pointed type is of particular value for opening seed drills in the vegetable garden. If the broad-bladed type of hoe is used, its efficiency will be greatly increased if it is kept well sharpened.

Aluminum wheelbarrows, with rubber tires, are light, durable and easy to handle, and have largely replaced the heavy, cumbersome, wooden wheelbarrows which had been standard equipment for so many years.

The garden hose is one of the most indispensable pieces of equipment on any country or suburban place. If a hose of good quality is purchased and if it receives good care, it should last for many years, whereas a cheap hose of inferior quality will need to be replaced within a comparatively short time. A one-ply rubber hose has the advantage of being light and is therefore easily handled, and if it is of superior quality it will give excellent service. A two-ply rubber hose will give longer wear as it is made for heavy service and it has the added advantage that it will not kink, but it is heavy to move from place to place. The light, plastic hose has been a great boon to the gardener and is beginning to replace the rubber hose. It is supple and easy to handle, and may be moved from one part of the garden to another with little effort. A plastic hose of good quality has a long life of service. Soil soakers are available both in plastic and in canvas and are exceedingly useful where a gentle flow of water which will soak into the ground is desired.

Various new hose attachments have made watering less of a problem for gardeners. The fog nozzle gives a very fine, mist-like spray and is excellent for watering newly sown seed beds and young seedlings. It is also valuable for syringing the foliage of broad-leaved evergreens, and for increasing the humidity for tuberous begonias, achimenes and other plants which thrive best in a moist atmosphere. A hose attachment for applying liquid fertilizers is used by many commercial growers and is also a useful piece of equipment for the home gardener.

Care of Tools

Tools should be cleaned immediately after use and before they are returned to their place. It is far easier to remove soil from a spade or hoe when it is still moist than when it is hard and dry and has become encrusted onto the metal. A blunt stick of the type used to mix paint is a very convenient thing to use in removing the soil from spades and hoes. If the soil has been allowed to become badly encrusted, it may be removed by rubbing the surface vigorously with a wet cloth or with a rag soaked in kerosene.

When tools are to be put away for the winter, they should first be thoroughly cleaned. Rust can easily be removed with steel wool. A protective coating of wax or grease should then be applied. Ordinary floor wax may be used or almost any type of grease which happens to be available— a cheap grade of vaseline is excellent, cup grease is entirely satisfactory, or lard may be used. It is a wise plan to see that such tools as pruning shears, lawn mowers, knives and hoes are sharpened before they are put away in order that they may be ready for use when the rush of spring work begins.

Sprayers should always be rinsed out after use. The plunger rod and leather plunger should be oiled at frequent intervals during the spraying season and when the sprayer is to be stored for the winter in order to keep the leather from drying out. Before storing, worn washers should be replaced and the hose should be cleaned with a mild vinegar solution and then rinsed with clear water. During the winter the sprayer should be stored in a dry place. This is of particular importance in the case of galvanized iron sprayers in order to prevent them from rusting. The lawn fertilizer distributor should be thoroughly cleaned after use and the wheels should be oiled to prevent rusting. It should be kept in a dry place.

Most fertilizers are very corrosive to metal and the period of usefulness of the distributor will be greatly extended if these simple precautions are followed.

When not in use a garden hose should be kept on a reel or a mounted fixture designed for the purpose. Nothing shortens the life of a hose more rapidly than to allow it to lie out in the sun day after day. When a hose is put away for the winter, care should be taken to see that it is carefully drained.

The lawn mower should be given a thorough cleaning at the end of the season. All grass clippings, dirt and grease should be removed. A steel brush is excellent for this purpose. Any parts which show evidence of rust should be cleaned with steel wool. All exposed metal parts should receive a coating of oil. All bearings should be oiled. The oil filter should be cleaned and rinsed in gasoline and clean oil should be added. All gasoline should be removed from the tank, as it is liable to leave a gummy residue as it evaporates. Run the engine until all the gasoline in the tank, fuel line and carburettor is used up. Drain the crankcase oil while the engine is still warm in order to remove all sediment and then add fresh oil. Remove the spark plug and pour one ounce of No. 20 grade oil on the cylinder. Cover the mower with a plastic, waterproof cover to protect it from dampness and dust.

THE ANCIENT
SPRING-HOUSE
NOW SERVES
AS A
TOOL HOUSE.

AN ATTRACTIVE TOOL HOUSE

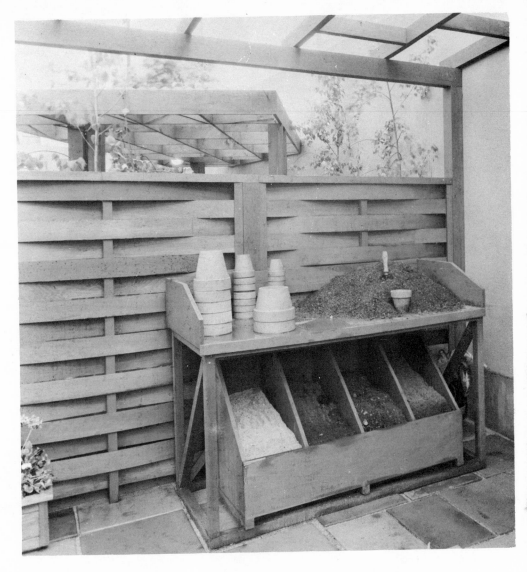

A
WORK YARD
WITH
POTTING BENCH
IN
CALIFORNIA

Equipment for the Small Place

Under the heading "Recommended Tools and Equipment" are included the tools and equipment necessary for the maintenance of the average small home property.

The supplementary list includes tools which would be necessary or desirable where gardening is done on a more extensive scale.

RECOMMENDED TOOLS

Garden line
Grass shears
Hand cultivator or weeder
Hand duster or sprayer
Hoe, small, triangular type
Hose and attachments
Iron rake
Lawn edger
Lawn fertilizer distributor
Lawn mower
Lawn rake
Pruning shears
Shovel, rounded, short D-handle
Spading fork
Trowel
Watering can
Wheelbarrow

EQUIPMENT

Bamboo stakes
Flower pots
Labels
Measuring cup
Measuring spoon set
Twistems for tying plants

505

A TOOL HOUSE IN CALIFORNIA

SUPPLEMENTARY LIST

Grass whip	Lawn hand spiker	Soil soaker
Knapsack or bucket sprayer	Long-handled loppers for pruning	Sprinkler attachment
Ladder	Pruning saw	Wheelhoe or power cultivator

Storage Facilities

A well-organized tool room where the tools may be kept in good order and where supplies, such as spray materials, stakes, labels and other garden accessories, may be kept readily at hand will be a source of constant satisfaction.

The ideal arrangement is to have a small building which has been specially designed for such a purpose, with racks and hanging space for the tools, shelves and cupboards for supplies, a small potting bench, bins for soil and compost, and floor space for the wheelbarrow and lawn mower. Such a building need not be large, a floor area 60 to 100 square feet is ample, but it should be conveniently arranged and, although simple in design, it should have architectural merit and be in harmony with the style of the house.

It is not always possible to plan for a separate tool house and various compromises may be evolved. A portion of the garage may be used, the mower being stored in one corner and the tools hung along one of the side walls. The simplest arrangement for hanging the tools is to nail a 2″ × 4″ strip on the wall about 4 feet above the floor and screw into it a half dozen broom holders which are procurable at any hardware store and are inexpensive. All the tools with long handles, such as rakes, hoes, spading fork, etc. can be easily kept in place in this way, the handle of each being slipped into its holder when it is not in use. A piece of composition peg-board nailed against the wall will provide more adequate facilities, as the small tools may be hung on it as well as the larger tools, and it presents a neat appearance.

When a garage with a gable roof is being constructed it may be possible, at very little additional expense, to extend the roof-line on one side to include a separate area for tools. Such an arrangement can be very functional, and also quite attractive. In some cases a small projection can be built at the rear of the garage which can serve as a storage space for tools.

In providing storage for supplies it must be borne in mind that all spray materials should be stored in locked cupboards where children will have no access to them. The importance of this can hardly be overemphasized.

Seeds should be stored in tight metal containers where they will be protected from dampness and from mice.

Fertilizers which are not to be used within a short time should be stored in large glass jars or earthenware crocks, and should be labeled. If left in paper or cloth bags the containers will soon disintegrate entirely.

XXXVI

COLDFRAMES AND HOTBEDS

COLDFRAMES

A COLDFRAME is an indispensable adjunct, even to the smallest garden. It is, as the name implies, an unheated frame, the plants receiving heat from the penetration of the sun's rays through the sash.

There seems to be a very general idea that coldframes are useful only for the protection of plants during the winter months and that at other seasons of the year they lie idle. Winter protection, however, is but one of the many uses to which coldframes may be put. Indeed, a really enterprising gardener will find that his frames are in use during every month of the year—that there is never a time from one season's end to another when they lie fallow.

Uses of Coldframes

Early Spring

(*Hardening-off Plants*). During the early spring months, coldframes may be used to harden off seedlings which have been started in the greenhouse or in the house. This hardening-off process is a factor of considerable importance, as young seedlings often suffer a serious setback if moved directly from indoors to the garden. The coldframe provides an ideal transition, as the plants may be protected from sudden drops in temperature and will have an opportunity to become gradually hardened-off. When pots or flats are moved to the frames, they should be placed on a bed of cinders, in order that drainage may be facilitated. There is also less danger of trouble from slugs and pill-bugs if cinders are used.

Spring and Summer

(*Seed Sowing*). A coldframe also offers very satisfactory facilities for the starting of young seedling plants throughout the spring and summer months. (See directions for seed sowing, Chapter XXXIII.) The hardy and half-hardy annuals may be sown in the frames early in the spring, many weeks before seed could be sown in the open ground; perennials may be sown in the spring, and the young transplanted seedlings may be carried

508

on in the frames until they are ready to be moved to the nursery rows or to their permanent place in the garden; biennials may be sown during the summer months, and as many of them, such as the foxgloves, Canterbury bells and wallflowers, need winter protection in cold climates they may be carried on in the frames until spring.

(*Propagation by Cuttings*.) During the late spring and summer months, a portion of the coldframes may be converted into a propagating case, the soil being temporarily replaced with sand or peat moss or some other medium which is satisfactory for the rooting of cuttings. (See plant propagation, Chapter XXXIII.)

Autumn

(*Seed Sowing*.) Most perennials and a few of the annuals may be sown very successfully in the autumn, and there are many benefits to be gained if such a practice is followed. The object is not to secure germination during the autumn, but to have the seeds remain dormant during the winter months. They will then germinate very early in the spring and the young seedlings will have a vigor and lustiness which usually surpasses that of spring-sown seedlings. Better germination is also frequently secured. A coldframe offers ideal conditions for autumn sowing. The seeds may be sown either in a well-prepared seed bed or in flats. It is essential that good drainage be provided and if flats are used they should be placed on a layer of cinders. The seeds should not be sown until just before the onset of winter, as the ground begins to freeze. There will then be no danger of having the seed germinate before spring. At the time of sowing the soil should be watered so that it is moderately damp, but not excessively wet. If the soil becomes dry during the winter a light watering should be given, preferably during a spell of warm weather. It is a wise practice to inspect the frame every few weeks to check up on the condition of the soil. After the seeds have been sown, the sash should be placed over the frames, being raised slightly to provide adequate ventilation. In order to exclude the winter sunshine and to maintain a more even soil temperature, it is well to place a lath sash over the glass. This slat shade should be removed very early in the spring in order that the soil may warm up as rapidly as possible. As soon as the soil in the frame has begun to thaw out the seeds should be given the usual care. The soil should not be allowed to dry out, adequate ventilation should be provided and the sash should be removed on warm, sunny days.

Winter

(*Protection of Less Hardy Plants and Tender Bulbs.*) Not only are coldframes useful during the winter months for the protection of the less hardy plants and newly started perennials, but they also make it possible to grow some of the tender bulbs which cannot be grown in the open ground in sections where the winters are of extreme severity. In this group we find the lovely bulbous iris, the dwarf gladioli of the nanus and Colvillei types, which are so decorative as cut flowers, and the St. Brigid anemones. If planted in the autumn in the frames these bulbs will give abundant bloom in the spring.

(*Storage of Bulbs and Plants for Forcing.*) Coldframes may also be used for the storage of bulbs and plants which are later to be forced indoors. Such plants as bleeding-heart, astilbe japonica, and mertensia may be handled very successfully in this way. Chrysanthemum plants which are of the less hardy type may be lifted in the autumn and carried over the winter in the frames, and cuttings may be made from these stock plants in the spring.

Location

Coldframes should preferably be located on ground that is very gently sloping in order that good drainage may be assured, a south or southeastern exposure being considered ideal. The frames should be placed with the high end towards the north, the sash sloping towards the south in order that full benefit may be obtained from the rays of the sun. Whenever possible a sheltered spot should be chosen with a wall or hedge upon the north to afford protection against winter winds. If a sheltered spot is not available, however, a temporary winter windbreak may be constructed of corn stalks, or boughs braced against a snow fence. If a cinder walk is laid immediately in front of the frames it will greatly facilitate easy access in wet weather and will be a matter of great convenience. Sufficient space should be left at the rear of the frames for the comfortable removal of the sash. The frames should be easily accessible and water should be piped to them.

It is occasionally possible to make use of a steep bank for the construction of coldframes, and much of the backbreaking work usually associated with the management of coldframes may be eliminated. A concrete or cinder-block wall should be built up along the upper side of the path to a level of approximately 3 feet. The frames may be placed upon the top of the bank if the height of the bank corresponds with the desired height of the frames, or a section of the bank may be dug back to provide a level area for the frames. Thus, the frame is raised to a position where it can be reached as easily as a greenhouse bench. Sashes of small size should be used, since they can be reached only from the front.

Construction

Of the many materials which are available, wood and cinder-block are the most satisfactory for the construction of coldframes. Stone, brick, and solid concrete may be used, and while they are extremely durable materials, the additional expense is hardly justifiable. Sometimes in old colonial gardens one will come upon ancient frames of brick, built a century or more ago and still providing shelter for young seedlings.

Wood is the least expensive material and if a good grade of cypress is selected, wooden frames will last for many years. Cypress will resist decay better than almost any other wood and it is, therefore, particularly well adapted for locations where it will be exposed to dampness and to the weather. It is folly to construct frames of cheap lumber which does not possess the ability to resist decay, as the boards will have to be replaced after a few years. Wooden frames are very easily constructed and as they do not require highly skilled workmanship, they may readily be made at home. It is also possible to purchase good cypress frames from some of the large seed firms and greenhouse-construction companies. These are shipped "knocked down" and are easily assembled. These commercial frames are very satisfactory, and they may readily be moved from one section of the garden

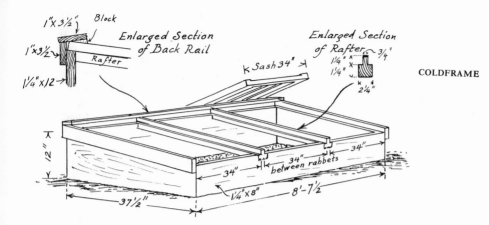

to another if a change in the general arrangement of the working area should be desired, or if one is moving to a new property. These ready-made frames may be obtained both in the standard size and in a small size which is admirably adapted for use in suburban gardens.

Frames constructed of cinder-blocks are of a more permanent nature than are wooden frames as they cannot be moved from one location to another. The initial cost is considerably higher than for wooden frames, but it is the only cost, as no replacement will be necessary. The cinder-blocks should extend into the ground a few inches below the frost line for the locality, and the blocks should be laid with mortar joints. The appearance of the frames will be greatly improved if a cement-sand mortar finish is applied as a surface coat over the cinder-blocks.

Regardless of the material used, coldframes should be so constructed that the back is approximately 6 inches higher than the front. This slope will permit the water to drain easily from the sash and will also offer the maximum amount of surface for the penetration of sunlight.

The front of the frame may vary in height from 6 to 12 inches. If the frames are to be used as a seed bed and to winter small plants such as pansies and English daisies a height of 6 inches will be sufficient. If large plants such as foxgloves and Canterbury bells are to be wintered over in the frames a height of 12 inches will be needed. Cross-ties usually extend from the back of the frame to the front at intervals of every 3 feet in order to provide additional support for the sash. These ties should be dovetailed into the walls of the frame and a projection in the center of each cross-tie will keep the sash from slipping out of position.

The standard size for coldframe sash used by practically all commercial growers and by most private gardeners is 3 feet by 6 feet. For the home garden, where operations are on a limited scale and where convenience is a matter of considerable importance, a smaller size is often more satisfactory. Small sash measuring 2 feet by 4 feet, or 3 feet by 3 feet, may be obtained from several firms, and they have many advantages. They are much lighter and are, therefore, easier to handle than the standard size sash, and the entire area within the frame may be reached from the front with comparative ease, which greatly facilitates such operations as seed sowing and transplanting.

Most coldframe sash are made of glass, and they may be purchased either as glazed or unglazed sash. The process of glazing is a rather simple one and considerable expense may be saved if this is done at home. A small portion of

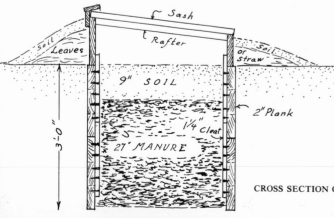

CROSS SECTION OF HOT BED

putty should be worked in the warmth of the hands until it is smoothly pullable without breaking. If the putty is too thick, a little linseed oil may be added to make it of the right consistency. With a putty knife, a thin layer should be spread the entire length of the sash—not too much, but just enough to cover. The first pane is then laid in place at the top, or back, of the sash. The next is then laid underneath, underlapping about ½-inch. The number of panes of glass will depend upon the size of the sash. After all the panes have been evenly spaced the length of the sash, each pane is then snugly fastened in place by several brads, which are tiny pieces of zinc. The triangular shaped brads which measure about ½-inch are most satisfactory. Then a layer of putty is spread along the edge of the pane against the wooden frame which, when dried, keeps out moisture. A layer of green paint, special for coldframe and sash use, may be applied after several days when the putty has become firm but not brittle. This application will both protect the wood from deterioration and the putty from cracking.

Coldframe sash may also be made of celoglass, a glass substitute, which has the advantage of allowing the penetration of ultra-violet rays. Sash made of celoglass is lighter in weight than glass sash and is easier to handle. It is, however, less transparent, and does not provide as much protection against extreme cold as does sash made of glass.

When not in use during the summer months, the sashes should be neatly stacked, preferably under cover where they will not be exposed to the weather. It is a matter of sound economy to keep coldframe sash in good condition. All cracked or broken panes of glass should be replaced and the sashes should be kept well painted. If attention is given to these details, coldframe sash should last for many years.

Management

There are a few general rules which should be followed in the management of coldframes. The most important factors to be considered are ventilation, watering, protection from extreme cold, and protection from extreme heat.

Ventilation. During the late winter and early spring, the sash should be partially raised for a brief period on clear, sunny days, when the temperature ranges above 45° F., the object being to keep an even temperature. As the season advances, the sash may be raised for a longer period each day and on warm days it may be removed entirely during the middle of the day. The sash should be lowered or replaced before the temperature begins to drop in the afternoon, in order to conserve as much heat as possible. On windy days, the sash should be raised on the opposite side from the direction of the wind in order to protect the plants from a direct draft. With the approach of warm weather, the sash may be removed entirely. When sashes are to be raised slightly, small blocks of wood may be placed between the edge of the frame and the sash. A block measuring approximately 1 inch × 4 inches × 6 inches is excellent for this purpose as it enables one to regulate the size of the opening.

Watering. It is an accepted rule among gardeners that plants grown under glass, either in greenhouses or in frames, should be watered when the temperature is rising rather than when it is falling. It is, therefore, advisable, and particularly so early in the season, to water the frames in the morning, in order that the foliage of the plants may be dry at night. In cold, cloudy weather water should be withheld as much as possible in order to avoid trouble from various fungous diseases.

Protection Against Extreme Cold. During periods of extreme cold, additional protection should be given. Straw mats, light frames filled with straw, heavy sisal-craft paper and similar materials may be used for this purpose. In mild climates no protection other than that of the sash is necessary, but in localities where the thermometer reaches zero, it is advisable to provide extra protection.

Summer Shade. In the summer months some provision must be made for protecting the seed beds and the young seedling plants in the frames from intense sunshine. Lath sashes which may be obtained from most seed houses are very satisfactory for this purpose. They are light and easy to handle, permit a free circulation of air, and a filtered sunshine reaches the plants. Burlap tacked on lath frames also makes a very satisfactory shade.

HOTBEDS

Hotbeds differ from coldframes in that they are supplied with some form of artificial heat. They may be heated by the old, time-honored method of fermenting manure, or they may be heated by the more modern method of specially devised electric cables. In occasional instances, where hotbeds may be located in close proximity to a greenhouse, they may be heated as a part of the greenhouse unit, which is a very satisfactory arrangement. The construction and management of the hotbed will usually be determined by the type of heating which is to be used.

Uses of Hotbeds

Since the soil in a hotbed is maintained at a warm and fairly constant temperature, it provides excellent facilities for the germination of seeds and for the growing of a wide variety of young seedling plants. Some plants with a short season of growth, such as lettuce, may be carried through to maturity in the hotbed, although the majority of plants started in the hotbed are later transplanted to the garden or field. Seeds may be sown in the hotbed several weeks before it is advisable to make use of the coldframes, and the young seedlings will make much more rapid growth. Later in the season when there is no longer any need for artificial heat the hotbed may serve as a coldframe and may be used to fulfill the same functions.

Types of Hotbeds

Manure Hotbeds. A pit approximately 2½ feet deep is necessary if manure is to be used, the dimensions for width and length being determined by the size of the frames and the number of frames desired. If the earth walls of the pit are firm, no inside wall need be constructed. If, however, there is any danger that the earth walls may crumble, it will be necessary to construct supporting walls. Walls made of wood will be of only temporary value as they will lack durability in such a location, but materials such as cinder-block, stone and brick are excellent. The upper part of the frame is similar in construction to a coldframe.

Manure-heated hotbeds should be started in early March and it is necessary to use fresh horse manure obtained from stables where straw has been used for bedding. Approximately four cubic yards of manure will be required for a single sash hotbed. The manure should be piled near the hotbed and every three or four days the heap should be turned, throwing the outside toward the center. When the entire pile has begun to heat evenly, which is evidenced by steam arising from the pile, the manure may be placed in the pit. It should be spread evenly in 6-inch layers, each layer being firmly tramped and packed. After the manure has been placed in the pit to a depth of 2 feet, a thin layer of straw should be spread over it and the soil should then be added. The depth of soil may vary from 4 to 6 inches and it should be of a mixture suitable for a seed bed. A soil thermometer should be placed so that the mercury extends well down into the soil and the sash should remain tightly closed. For the first few days the thermometer will register a high degree of heat, ranging well above 90° F. When the soil temperature has cooled down to 75° F. the bed is ready for use and the seeds may be sown.

In extremely cold climates it is well to bank manure about that portion of the bed which extends above the surface of the ground, as this will increase the warmth within the frame to a very appreciable extent.

Electric Hotbeds. There are various types of electric units which have been especially designed for the heating of hotbeds. One of the most satisfactory types is the insulated electric cable which may be buried in the soil and which will provide uniform heat. The procedure for the construction of such a bed is as follows: A pit approximately 1 foot deep should be excavated and it should be of sufficient size to extend a foot or more beyond the sides and ends of the proposed frame. The pit should be filled with 6 inches of slag or good clinker cinders, free from fine ashes. The frame may be placed directly on the bed of cinders. The outside of the frame should be banked with cinders or soil in order to provide insulation against the penetration of cold air. A layer of burlap or of sphagnum moss should be placed over the cinders and 1 inch of sand should be spread over the surface of the bed. The electric cable is then laid upon the sand in uniform loops in order that the heat may be evenly distributed. (See diagram A.) No. 19 or No. 20 Nichrome wire protected with a lead sheath having a resistance of one-half ohm per foot is recommended by several authorities as being the best for this purpose. Sixty feet of this flexible, lead-covered cable will be required for a two-sash hotbed, if the voltage is 110–120. This will provide for 10 coils spaced approximately 7 inches apart, the ends of the cable being connected with a thermostat. The thermostat should be installed on the inside of the frame with the switch box on the north side of the bed. The thermostat should be regulated so that a uniform temperature is maintained. Tender plants will require a temperature ranging from 60° to 75°F.; half-hardy plants will prefer a temperature of 50° to 60°F., and those that are truly hardy will thrive well in a temperature ranging from 45° to 60°F.

Approximately 400 watts will be required to provide heat for a two-sash hotbed (6 feet × 6 feet) in a moderately cold climate. Operating costs will usually average one kilowatt hour per square yard of hotbed per day.

The soil which is to be used for the seed bed may be placed over the cable to a depth of 6 inches. If flats are to be used, 3 inches of sand may be spread over the cable and the flats may be placed upon the sand.

The one great disadvantage of an electric hotbed is that the current may go off during a severe storm or because of some other emergency, In such a case the plants are apt to suffer serious injury, and every effort should be made to protect them, through the use of straw mats or other materials which will provide temporary insulation.

Hot Water or Steam Pipes. One of the most satisfactory and also one of the most economical ways to provide heat for the hotbeds is to install a system of pipes which may be connected with the heating system in the dwelling house or the greenhouse. The pipes may be placed around the top of the frame on the inside or they may be placed beneath the soil. (See two diagrams B.) Such a system provides for a uniform heat which may be maintained at a minimum of expense and labor.

Management

The management of a hotbed is similar in most respects to the management of a coldframe. There is, however, more danger from trouble with damping-off, as the plants are somewhat more susceptible to attack, because of the greater degree of heat and humidity. Every precautionary measure should, therefore, be taken to control an outbreak of this disease. (See Chapter XXXIII for the control of damping-off.)

Since artificial heat is provided, the plants grown in a hotbed are more tender than those grown in a coldframe and are more sensitive to sudden fluctuations in temperature. Ventilation and watering must, therefore, be done with care.

Hotbeds are usually started upon the approach of spring weather. In the latitude of New York and Philadelphia, early March is usually the most favorable time. If severe cold spells occur extra protection for the young plants may be provided by the use of straw mats or other similar materials.

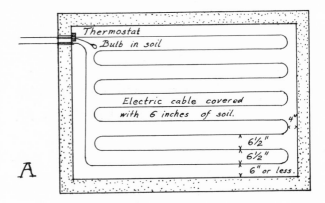

Plan of an Electric System of Heating Soil in Hotbed.

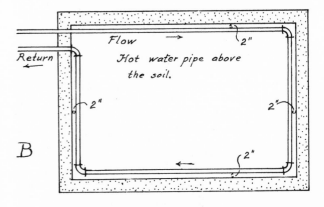

Plan of a Water or Steam System for Hotbed.

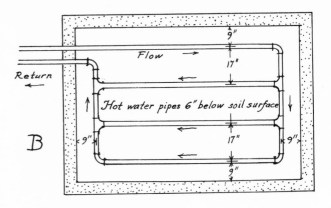

Plan of a Water System of Heating Soil in Hotbed.

XXXVII

THE SMALL GREENHOUSE AND
THE LATH HOUSE

For many, gardening is a joyous adventure from the opening of the first winter aconite in the spring until the frosts of autumn have robbed the garden of its beauty and driven us indoors to await the arrival of the first seed catalogs. Fortunate, indeed, are those favored few among gardeners who possess a small greenhouse and can carry on their gardening activities throughout the year.

Small, private greenhouses have always been considered such a luxury that many gardeners have assumed they were something quite beyond their means and have given the matter little thought. However, new types have been designed along such simple and efficient lines that construction costs have been greatly reduced, and the small greenhouse is now well within the range of many a gardener. It need not be elaborate or expensive; a small lean-to, built against the house, may be constructed for only a few hundred dollars and will offer delightful possibilities for winter gardening. The money thus invested will pay big dividends in beauty and in joyous activity. Even the unheated greenhouse offers many opportunities and is a challenge to the skill and ingenuity of the gardener.

Location

If the greenhouse can be attached directly to the house it may usually be operated on the same heating unit, which not only reduces the cost of operation, but also reduces the labor item to a minimum. Such a location also has the advantage of providing shelter from strong winds. If a greenhouse is attached to the house, it should preferably have a south or southeastern exposure.

If the greenhouse is not attached to the house,

it should be located so that it receives a maximum amount of sunshine and is protected, if possible, from the prevailing winds. If the topography of the ground presents no problem, the greenhouse should preferably be oriented so that the length of the house runs from north to south, as this will provide for a maximum amount of sunlight during the winter months.

The Unheated Greenhouse

Although the unheated greenhouse has decided limitations, it offers many delightful opportunities.

In sections of the country where the climate is severe, it is difficult, if not impossible, to obtain any actual bloom in an unheated greenhouse during the midwinter months, but with the first warm days of spring, such a greenhouse may become a veritable garden, and it will offer a wealth of material for flower arrangements in the house. Bulbs of all kinds may be forced into early bloom, and astilbe japonica, bleeding-heart, mertensia, aquilegia, pansies, and primroses may be brought into flower. Antirrhinums, calendulas, annual larkspur, and wallflowers may be sown in the early autumn and the young plants may be carried over the winter in the benches. Although they will make comparatively little growth during the winter, they will develop into sturdy plants with strong, vigorous root systems and will come into flower months ahead of spring-sown seedlings.

During the spring months, the unheated greenhouse serves the purposes of a somewhat glorified coldframe as it affords ideal conditions for the starting of young seedlings.

It is a decided advantage to have the unheated greenhouse in as protected a location as possible and in some cases it is feasible to have it built so that it is partially below ground. Straw mats, or burlap frames packed with straw, may be used to provide added protection during extremely cold weather.

Construction

In the construction of a greenhouse, even though it be a very simple structure, there are many details which must be taken into consideration and it is well to have the house erected by a man who is thoroughly conversant with the problems which must be met. It is essential that the house be built of sturdy, durable materials; that satisfactory provisions be made for ventilation; that the benches be designed to meet any special needs which may be designated; and that the heating unit be entirely adequate.

Aluminum has recently come into use for the construction of greenhouses and is gaining rapidly in favor. It is very durable and will not be affected by rust or rot. Although the initial cost may be somewhat higher than that of wood, the costs of maintenance will be reduced to a minimum, as the aluminum will require no painting and almost nothing in the way of repairs and replacements. A combination of wood and aluminum is also a very satisfactory type.

The least expensive type of greenhouse is one in which plastic is used instead of glass. This new type was first developed at the University of Kentucky and is being widely used in some sections by commercial growers. The cost is but a small fraction of the cost of a glass greenhouse and much of the construction can be on a "do-it-yourself" basis if a man is handy with tools. In appearance a plastic house is not so attractive as the standard type of greenhouse, but it offers great possibilities for the home gardener whose budget is limited.

The advantages of a plastic greenhouse, in addition to its low cost, are that it has greater moisture retention and less heat loss than a glass greenhouse. The light transmission is about 90 percent that of glass and some plants actually thrive better in this lower light intensity than they do in a glass greenhouse. On the other hand, there are some plants which thrive less well. The chief disadvantage to a house of this type is that the plastic slowly deteriorates under strong sunlight and must be renewed each year. This may be done at a very moderate cost for materials but involves something in the way of labor.

The material to be used for the construction of the benches is usually a question for the owner to decide. Wood is the most economical, if only the initial cost is considered, but it is the least satisfactory, for it is not durable and will have to be replaced after a few years. If wood is used, the best grade of cypress should be selected, as cypress is more resistant to decay than any other wood which is available. Solid concrete is sometimes used but it is very expensive. One of the most satisfactory types is a combination of metal and tile which is pleasing in appearance, durable, and yet not prohibitive in cost.

Benches which are constructed with pipe legs and an angle-iron frame are the most satisfactory. Benches in which crops for cut flowers are to be grown should be from 6 to 8 inches deep. Adequate provision for drainage must be provided in the form of narrow openings between the boards or tiles which form the bottom of the bench. Benches upon which potted plants are to be placed need be but 2 or 3 inches deep. Such benches, which resemble shallow trays, should be filled with pebbles or cinders upon which the pots may rest. This will not only facilitate drainage but will aid in maintaining the desired degree of humidity as well.

The greenhouse should be piped with water and a sufficient number of outlets should be provided at convenient points. The faucets should be threaded so that a hose may be easily attached.

Concrete walks are the most satisfactory type for greenhouses, although cinders and gravel are sometimes used where it is necessary to maintain a very high degree of humidity, as in orchid houses. Concrete walks are easy to keep clean, will withstand wear, are impervious to dampness, and are, in general, entirely satisfactory.

It is a matter of great convenience to have a small work room or potting shed attached to the greenhouse, but if space is not available, or if the various items of expense must be kept to a minimum, the north end of the house may be utilized for this purpose. A bench of convenient height and length should be provided for use in the preparation of soil mixtures, and for such operations as seed sowing, transplanting and potting, which are an almost daily part of the greenhouse routine. Bins may be constructed underneath the bench as a storage place for surplus flats and pots and to hold the loam, sand, leaf mold and compost used in the various soil mixtures. Adequate shelf space should also be provided for insecticides, fumigants, labels and other small items.

In the management of a small greenhouse, the most important considerations are the matters of temperature control, ventilation and watering.

Heating

Hot water is the most satisfactory form of heat for the small greenhouse. The heat is more evenly distributed than in the case of steam heat and there is less danger of a sudden drop in temperature. And it is an accepted fact that practically all plants thrive better under a system of hot water heat than under steam heat. It is a more natural kind of heat and is more nearly like the heat of the sun. Hot water heat has the added advantage of being more economical than steam, as it is possible to maintain a very low fire in mild weather.

Thermostatically controlled oil heat is the most satisfactory type of heating unit for greenhouses today. However, for a very small home greenhouse in a protected location the possibility of using an electric heating unit should be considered. For a greenhouse of considerable size the cost of operation would be prohibitive, but for a small home greenhouse operating costs are not excessive. Such a unit is, of course, automatically controlled.

Bottled gas may also be used for heating and is the type often selected for use in plastic greenhouses. It is also coming into use in greenhouses in northern New England in which large quantities of young plants are grown in the spring but which are not heated during the very cold winter months.

Temperature

If the house is of sufficient size it is well to have it divided into at least two sections, and to have the heating system so planned that it is possible to maintain a moderately high temperature in one section and a much lower temperature in the other section. This will make it possible to grow a wider variety of plants, as some plants have a preference for a cool temperature, while others will prefer a comparatively high temperature. If, however, the greenhouse is small, and it is not feasible to provide for more than one temperature, it need not be considered too great a handicap. The choice of plant materials will, of necessity, be somewhat more limited, but even the smallest greenhouse, maintained at a rather low temperature, will offer delightful opportunities for winter gardening.

In general commercial practice, greenhouse temperatures range from 40–45 degrees F. in extremely cool houses, to 65–70 degrees F. in houses where semi-tropical plants are grown. These figures refer to night temperatures. During the day the temperatures will naturally rise from 10 to 15 degrees higher. The thermometer in a greenhouse should not be placed where the direct heat of the sun will fall upon it. For a small greenhouse where but one temperature is to be maintained, a range between 50 and 55 degrees F. at night with a temperature varying from 10 to 15 degrees higher during the day will usually prove most satisfactory. Some plants are able to endure severe fluctuations in temperature, while other plants are extremely sensitive to changes in temperature, and it is wise for the amateur to choose the less temperamental plants. If one is an experienced gardener and can provide conditions which will very nearly approximate the ideal, it will be possible to grow some of the more exotic greenhouse plants, but if one is a novice it is well to devote one's efforts to the more sturdy types which are less exacting in their demands.

Ventilation

An abundance of fresh air is essential for the normal, healthy growth of all plants, and at the time of construction adequate provision must be made for ventilation. Some greenhouses are equipped with ventilators on the sides as well as on the glass span which forms the roof, and this is the most desirable type of construction. It requires care, skill, and good judgment to control a ventilating system efficiently. As a general practice the ventilators should be opened in the morning when the temperature is rising. On warm days when there is brilliant sunshine and little wind, the ventilators should be opened to the fullest extent. On very cold days a mere crack may be sufficient. The ventilators should be closed early enough in the afternoon to conserve as much heat as possible. When a strong wind is blowing it is wise to open the ventilators

A SMALL GREENHOUSE. ADJOINING THE LIVING ROOM THIS SMALL GREENHOUSE BECOMES AN INDOOR GARDEN.

on the opposite side of the house from the direction of the prevailing wind in order to prevent a direct draft of air on the plants. Sudden changes in temperature and sudden shifting from brilliant sunlight to dark clouds mean more or less constant attention to the regulation of the ventilators in a greenhouse if the heating unit is to function at its maximum degree of efficiency.

So important is fresh air to the welfare of the plants that even on days in early autumn and in the spring when it would be possible to maintain the desired temperature within the house, provided that the ventilators were kept closed, it is preferable to admit fresh air even if it necessitates maintaining a low fire.

There are on the market today, excellent mechanically controlled devices for regulating the ventilators in greenhouses. Such a device is well worth the extra cost, as it relieves the owner of much care and anxiety. When fluctuations in temperature occur the ventilators are automatically opened and closed.

Watering

Greenhouse plants vary tremendously in their moisture requirements, and individual plants also vary considerably at different stages of growth. In a program of successful greenhouse management it is, therefore, essential to fully understand the moisture requirements of the plants which one is handling. The moisture requirements of all the important greenhouse plants and plant groups are discussed in detail under the section on Cultural Requirements of greenhouse plants, which is to be found at the end of this chapter.

There are, however, certain general principles which should be observed. Watering should preferably be done when the temperature is rising, and it is, therefore, part of the usual morning routine in the greenhouse. To secure the best results, the temperature of the soil in the beds and benches should be approximately that of the surrounding air in the greenhouse. Water absorption by the plant takes place very slowly in cold soils. Greenhouse plants in ground beds frequently fail to do well because of this

factor. Such a condition may be remedied, however, by running heating pipes along the sides of the beds, or placing pipes in tiles underneath the beds. Some plants are so sensitive to the matter of temperature that it is advisable, whenever possible, to supply them with water which has been warmed to a room temperature, approximately 70 degrees F. In this group we find such plants as poinsettias, gardenias, gerberas, lilies, and roses. Tanks or barrels may be kept in the greenhouse for the storage of sufficient water to supply the needs of such plants.

Most plants will make their best growth, other conditions being favorable, in soils which are uniformly supplied with a sufficient amount of moisture. In the case of greenhouse plants grown in beds and benches the optimum moisture conditions may best be maintained by heavy watering at rather infrequent intervals. Both the amount of water and the frequency of application will be determined, to a considerable extent, by the age of the plants, the type of root system which the plants possess, and the physical structure of the soil. Large plants which are making active growth will require relatively large amounts of water. Plants with fibrous root systems will require larger amounts than those with tap roots. Heavy soils will require less frequent applications than light, sandy soils. If greenhouse beds and benches are given a fairly heavy watering at rather infrequent intervals, the plants will make a vigorous root growth which will extend deeply into the soil. If frequent, light waterings are given, the plants will have a tendency to become shallow rooted, and will be less vigorous in consequence.

The force with which the water is applied is also a factor which must be taken into consideration. A heavy stream of water should be avoided, as it causes the soil to become more and more compact and thus reduces aëration. An adjustable hose nozzle, or a rose nozzle of a size to permit a moderately fine spray, may be attached to the hose. For the watering of small seedlings and young growing plants a fog nozzle or a watering can is preferred. The regulation greenhouse watering can with a long spout is ideal for this purpose and a series of rose nozzles of various sizes may be obtained.

Careful attention must always be given to the watering of young seedlings, and on bright, sunny days it is often necessary to water more than once. Seed flats and young transplanted seedlings should never be allowed to dry out.

The watering of potted plants also requires skill and good judgment, and the plants vary tremendously in their moisture requirements. Some plants, such as the azaleas, maidenhair ferns, and certain types of begonias, should never be allowed to dry out. Other plants such as the poinsettias, fuchsias, callas, clivia, and many others, require a definite rest period, during which time the amount of water should be appreciably decreased or, in some cases, entirely withheld. The requirements of the individual plants are discussed at the close of the chapter. In general, potted plants should be watered only when necessary. Plants which are making active growth and plants which are in full flower will usually require liberal quantities of water. In some cases it may be necessary to water more than once a day. An excellent way to determine a potted plant's need for water is the method used by many old English gardeners—that of tapping the pot with the knuckle. If the tap resounds in a dull thud, it is an indication that the plant does not need water. If, however, the tap resounds with a hollow, ringing sound, additional moisture should be supplied to the plant. The majority of plants with smooth leaves may be watered by the overhead method without any danger of injury to the foliage. Plants with hairy or very fleshy leaves, such as the Saintpaulias, should preferably be watered in such a way that no moisture comes into contact with the foliage. A watering can may be used very successfully for this purpose if the rose nozzle is removed. In some cases it is advisable to place the plants in a pan of water and to allow them to remain thus until the surface of the soil in the pot has become moist.

There are excellent automatic sub-irrigation systems for greenhouse benches. Such a system, which should preferably be installed at the time the house is built, has many advantages but involves considerable expense.

Syringing

There are several very direct advantages to be gained from syringing. It increases the humidity, and very appreciably reduces the evaporation power of the air. Thus the transpiration of water from the leaves is reduced to a point lower than the actual absorption of water by the roots.

Syringing also has a very direct influence upon the control of red spider.

During the winter, syringing should be done on bright, sunny days when the temperature is rising. It is not advisable to syringe plants late in the afternoon when the temperature is dropping, as the result will be a condensation of moisture on the foliage, which may prove injurious to the plant. During the summer, plants may safely be syringed in the late afternoon.

In general, all plants that have smooth foliage will benefit from syringing. But plants with fleshy or hairy foliage should not be syringed, as the effects are more harmful than beneficial.

Humidity

The maintenance of a proper degree of humidity in the greenhouse is a matter of vital importance. Plants vary greatly in their optimum humidity requirements, just as they vary greatly in their moisture requirements. The fact that roses require a humidity of 75 percent or more, while members of the cactus family thrive best where the humidity is less than 50 percent, means that these two plant groups must be accorded very different treatment. Every gardener should be familiar with the general humidity requirements of the various plant groups. In some cases, the optimum humidity requirements of specific plants have been very definitely determined, and these have been included under the section on culture.

Humidity is closely associated with the respiration of plants and with the manufacture of food within the plant. It is a generally accepted fact that high humidity makes it possible for the leaf stomata to open wider and to remain open longer than is possible under conditions of low humidity. If plants are grown in an atmosphere in which the degree of humidity is far below the optimum, the transpiration from the leaves will be greater than the intake of moisture by the roots and the growth and vigor of the plants will suffer seriously in consequence.

There is a very direct relation between humidity and the factors of light and temperature. During dull, winter days an overabundance of humidity is not to be desired, as it may have a definitely detrimental effect upon the plants, whereas on bright, sunny days when the temperature is comparatively high, the effect will be decidedly beneficial. It is particularly needed on cold, bright days in winter when the heater is being forced to maintain the desired temperature.

There are various ways in which the humidity in a greenhouse may be increased: by syringing the plants, by wetting-down the walks, by spraying beneath the benches, particularly on the heating pipes. It is possible to maintain a higher degree of humidity in a house where the walks are made of gravel or cinders than it is in a house where the walks are of concrete. However, most growers prefer concrete because the degree of humidity may be more definitely controlled and the house may be kept dry except when moisture is artificially applied at times when it may seem desirable to increase the humidity. In orchid houses, where a very high degree of humidity is necessary, a sprinkling system is sometimes installed under the benches.

It is advisable to record definitely the degree of humidity in a greenhouse and this may be done by means of a hydrometer, or some similar device designed especially for this purpose.

For the control of diseases and pests of greenhouse plants, see Chapter XLI.

Summer in the Greenhouse

With the approach of summer, the intensity of the heat in a greenhouse would become unbearable both for the plants and for the gardener if some form of shade were not provided. The ideal device for such a purpose is a roller type of shade made of small strips of wood or thin pieces of bamboo. These may be regulated by means of a pulley and may be rolled up and down at will. It is a decided advantage to be able to lower them on cool, cloudy days and to roll them up on bright, sunny days when the temperature within the house is soaring. If it is not possible to obtain shades of this type the most satisfactory substitute is a coating of some suitable preparation applied to the outside of the glass. The following formula is recommended for this purpose.

A WELL PLACED HOME GREENHOUSE

MISSOURI BOTANICAL GARDEN PREPARATION

3 gallons of water	6 pounds of cement
5 pounds of whiting	½ pound of powdered glue

Mix all ingredients together with the exception of the glue. Dissolve the glue in hot water and add to the mixture. The mixture must be stirred frequently to keep it well agitated and it should be applied immediately with a brush or sprayer. This preparation has the advantage of gradually wearing off and does not have to be scraped off.

During the summer months when most of the plants have been removed, the greenhouse may be given a thorough cleaning. Any necessary repairs or repainting may be done at this season, the soil from the benches may be removed and fresh soil brought in, and the greenhouse may be made ready for the winter season.

Effect of Increasing or Decreasing the Amount of Light

During the past decade a number of interesting experiments have been carried on at several of the State Agricultural Experiment Stations to determine the effect on plant growth of increasing or decreasing the amount of light. It has been found that plants vary tremendously in their response to light. In the case of some plants it is possible to hasten the blooming period and to increase the quantity and quality of the bloom by prolonging the day. This is accomplished by means of electric lights placed above the plants. In the case of other plants, the reverse procedure, the shortening of the day, has resulted in the production of early bloom, and

this, in turn, is accomplished by shading the plants with black cloth in order to exclude all light for a portion of the day. Extensive experiments have proved that some plants are not affected by either of these treatments, and in other cases the effect has been so slight that the additional labor and expense involved have not been justified.

Increasing the Length of the Day. Additional light may be supplied for a period varying from 4 to 8 hours either at the beginning or the end of the day. The method most commonly employed by commercial growers is to provide additional light for a period of 5 hours, beginning at 5 p.m. and continuing until 10 p.m. The method employed in supplying the light is of considerable importance. The lights should be placed approximately 18 to 24 inches above the plants. For the majority of plants a 40-watt bulb may be used with excellent results. For some plants which are unusually responsive to light a 15-or 25-watt bulb will be sufficient. Either clear or frosted incandescent Mazda lamps may be used. Nitrogen-filled Mazda lamps have, in the majority of cases, proved to be more satisfactory than mercury, neon, or sun lamps. It is essential that reflectors be used. The most desirable type of reflector is one which is about 8 inches in diameter and which is deep enough so that only the tip of the bulb extends beyond the rim. The plants should be given an opportunity to become well established in the benches before extra light is supplied.

Reducing the Length of the Day. The usual procedure in shortening the length of the day in order to induce early flowering is to drape black cloth or some other dark, opaque material over the plants. Closely woven, black sateen has proved to be one of the most satisfactory materials for this purpose, and if proper care is taken it will give good service for several seasons. In most cases a reduction of 4 to 5 hours in the length of the day is sufficient, and the practice which is most generally followed is to place the cloth over the plants at 5 in the afternoon, allowing it to remain until 7 o'clock the following morning. The time when the short-day treatment should be initiated will depend entirely upon the normal bud-forming period of the plants.

Selection of Plant Materials

If the potentialities of a small greenhouse are to be realized to the fullest extent, the plant materials which are to be grown must be selected with great care. The usual desideratum is to have as much bloom as possible in the greenhouse from early autumn until late spring and to have a wide variety of flowers which are of particular value for cutting and for decorative purposes in the house.

Annuals, perennials, bulbs and potted plants all have an important part to play, and with careful thought and planning an abundance of bloom may be had throughout the winter months.

Many of the annuals which grow so luxuriantly out-of-doors during the summer months and which are so valuable for cutting will give an equally good account of themselves in the greenhouse. And to this list we are able to add some of the more temperamental annuals which cannot always be grown so successfully under the trying conditions of midsummer temperatures and humidity. This makes it possible for us to introduce into the greenhouse some of the annuals which we greatly admire when we see them growing so luxuriantly in English gardens. Heliophila will not thrive in many sections of the country during the summer months, but it is one of the loveliest flowers we have for greenhouse culture. It will give abundant bloom from October until May and the airy grace of its clear, blue flowers will add charm to many a winter bouquet. Clarkia, schizanthus and many other annuals are also in this group and in some sections will give much better bloom under greenhouse culture than out-of-doors.

In order to obtain a succession of bloom from autumn until spring it is necessary to plan one's program of work well in advance and to follow the schedule with exactitude and care.

Plants for the Home Greenhouse

Agathæa cœlestis (Blue Daisy): Lovely both as a potted plant and for cutting, Agathæa cœlestis is admirably adapted to the small greenhouse. The daisy-like flowers, of a soft powder-blue with golden centers, are borne in profusion throughout the winter and early spring months, and the fact that the plants remain in flower over such a long period of time makes them of particular value as potted plants for house decoration.

Propagation: Agathæa may be raised from seed or from cuttings. In plants grown from seed there is a slight variation in color, and after a stock has been established it is wise to make cuttings from the most

COMMON NAME	BOTANICAL NAME	INTENSITY OF LIGHT	REMARKS
Blue Laceflower	Didiscus	40 Watt	Early and more profuse bloom. Stems somewhat shorter when plants are forced early.
Boston Yellow Daisy	Chrysanthemum sp.	25–40 Watt	Earlier and more abundant bloom. Early planting desirable
Butterfly Flower	Schizanthus	15–40 Watt	Flowers 4–6 weeks earlier. Too rapid growth undesirable
Calceolaria		40–60 Watt	Flowers 6 weeks earlier. Apply lights when plant is nearly mature. Cool temperature necessary
Cornflower	Centaurea cyanus	25–40 Watt	Earlier bloom, longer stems
Corn Marigold	Chrysanthemum segetum	40–60 Watt	Early bloom and an increase in flowers up to 50%
Clarkia		40 Watt	Earlier bloom, longer stems. Do not apply lights until plants are very well established
Coreopsis		40 Watt	Earlier flowering and more abundant bloom.
Feverfew	Matricaria capensis	40 Watt	Flowers 6–8 weeks earlier and with more profuse bloom
Gardenia	G. Veitchii	150 Watt	6 hours of light necessary to produce earlier flowers
Gaillardia		40 Watt	Earlier and more abundant bloom, longer stems
Gypsophila	G. elegans	25–40 Watt	4 hours of light will produce earlier bloom
Iris (bulbous)	I. tingitana	75–100 Watt	Longer stems and almost 50% increase in bloom
Marigold	Tagetes	40 Watt	Earlier and more abundant bloom
Nasturtium	Tropaeolum majus	40–60 Watt	Earlier bloom and almost 50% increase
Pansy	Viola tricolor	40 Watt	Flowers 6–8 weeks earlier and a tremendous increase in bloom
Salpiglossis		40 Watt	Earlier bloom and longer stems
Scabiosa		40 Watt	Earlier bloom, longer stems, more abundant flowering. Not advisable to force too early
Shasta Daisy		40 Watt	Earlier bloom, longer stems and larger flowers. Increase up to 150%
Shirley Poppy		40–60 Watt	Long stems and abundant bloom
Snapdragon	Antirrhinum majus	40 Watt	Earlier and more abundant bloom but stems are short and not heavy. Lights are of doubtful value
Stock	Mathiola incana	40–60 Watt	Earlier flowers, longer stems
Violets		40 Watt	Earlier and more abundant bloom

PLANTS WHICH RESPOND PROFITABLY TO SHORT-DAY TREATMENT

Bouvardia—Treatment should be started from six to eight weeks previous to the date when flowers are desired.

Chrysanthemum—Treatment should be started when standard type plants have reached a height of 18 to 24 inches and pompon types a height of 14 to 18 inches.

Euphorbia fulgens—Plants treated from Sept. 1 to Oct. 20 will flower in December.

Kalanchoë—Short-day treatment: July 20–Sept. 20, flowers Oct. 20; Aug. 1–Oct. 1, flowers Dec. 1–15; Sept. 1–Oct. 20, flowers Dec. 20.

Poinsettia—Late varieties such as Oak Leaf may be brought into flower by Christmas if short-day treatment is given between Oct. 1 and Oct. 20.

Stevia—Plants treated from Sept. 15 to Oct. 10 will flower November 20.

CALENDAR OF BLOOM

October
Chrysanthemums predominating
Antirrhinums

November
Chrysanthemums
Antirrhinums
Heliotrope

December
Agathæa
Antirrhinums
Bouvardia
Clarkia
Freesias
Gerberas
Heliophila
Larkspur, annual
Lupines

January
Agathæa
Antirrhinums
Bouvardia
Calendulas
California Poppies
Clarkia
Freesias
Gerberas
Heliophila
Larkspur, annual
Narcissus
Schizanthus
Stocks

February
Agathæa
Antirrhinums
Bleeding-heart
Calendulas
California Poppies
Clarkia
Freesias
Gerberas
Gladiolus
Heliophila
Iris, bulbous
Larkspur, annual
Lupines
Narcissus
Schizanthus
Stocks

March
Agathæa
Antirrhinums
Aquilegia
Bleeding-heart
Calendulas
California Poppies
Clarkia
Freesias
Gerberas
Gladiolus, also dwarf
Heliophila
Iris, bulbous
Larkspur, annual
Lupines
Narcissus
Schizanthus
Stocks
Tulips

desirable plants. Cuttings made during the early spring root readily, and the young plants may be carried on in pots through the summer.

Culture: In early autumn the plants may be transferred to the greenhouse bench if the flowers are to be used only for cutting, or they may be shifted into 6 or 8 inch pots or bulb pans, to be grown on as potted plants. The plants thrive well in a moderately cool house.

Soil Requirements: Agathæa is not particular in regard to soil. A good potting compost is all that is necessary.

Antirrhinum (Snapdragon): The Antirrhinums are among the most satisfactory of all greenhouse plants and will give a wealth of bloom throughout the winter months.

Propagation: If autumn or early winter bloom is desired, the seeds should be sown early in June. The young seedlings should be pricked out before they become in the least crowded, and they may be carried on in flats or in pots until they are ready to be benched in late August or early September.

Soil Requirements: A rather heavy, coarse soil, well supplied with organic matter and of good fertility, is considered ideal, although snapdragons will do well on widely varying types of soil. A soil with a slightly acid reaction is preferred. A soil which is too alkaline in its reaction will cause a yellowing of the leaf margins and veins. An application of superphosphate, 5 pounds per 100 square feet, made at the time of planting will give excellent results, and additional feeding is usually not necessary.

Culture: When the young seedlings have developed 5 or 6 sets of leaves they should be pinched back. The plants should be spaced 10 inches apart each way in the bench. Antirrhinums prefer a cool temperature and will succeed extremely well if given a night temperature approximating 45 to 48° F. with a rise of 10 to 15 degrees during the day. They are one of the few plants which can be grown successfully in an unheated greenhouse, and will give an abundance of bloom during the late winter and early spring months if grown under such conditions. In the heated greenhouse they are often used to follow chrysanthemums and in this way excellent use is made of all available bench space. For a late planting such as this, the seeds should be sown in late August and the young seedlings carried on in flats or in pots until the chrysanthemums have been removed and bench space is available. These plants will usually not come into flower until late winter but will give luxuriant bloom throughout the early spring months. It is a common practice among commercial growers not to water the foliage of the antirrhinums, watering merely the roots, as a precautionary measure against the spread of rust. Throughout the flowering season the plants should be disbudded, the small shoots appearing at the base of

the leaves and in the axils of the flower stalks being removed. Snapdragons prefer a relatively low humidity of approximately 60 percent.

VARIETIES OF MERIT

Antirrhinums of the forcing type, suitable for growing in the greenhouse, may be obtained in many lovely colors, white, yellow, apple-blossom pink, rose, apricot, scarlet, deep Indian red and wine color. Among the most popular varieties are:

Afterglow	Cheviot Maid
Ball Red Hybrid No. 7	Ethel
Better Times	Mary Ellen

Aquilegia (Columbine): It is, perhaps, difficult to think of Aquilegia as a greenhouse plant, yet it can be forced so easily and the flowers are so exquisite for cutting that a few clumps should be included. Plants which have flowered the previous season in the garden or in the nursery should be selected. It is well to mark the clumps at the time that they are in bloom, as it is then possible to choose plants which are unusually beautiful in form or in coloring and which will therefore be of particular value for cut flowers.

Culture: The clumps should be lifted in the autumn and placed in a coldframe where they can be given some slight protection. Late in January or early in February the dormant plants may be brought into the greenhouse, being planted in a bench, or being potted in 10- to 12-inch pots. Growth will start within a few days and by March or early April the plants will be in full flower. A cool temperature, ranging between 45 and 55°F., is preferred, as Aquilegias will not do well if subjected to too high a degree of heat. After the plants have been forced, they may be replanted in the nursery.

Soil Requirements: Good potting compost.

Azaleas: There are few plants more decorative than the Azaleas when they are in bloom, and there are a number of species and varieties which may be grown very successfully under greenhouse conditions, being forced into bloom either for Christmas or for Easter.

VARIETIES OF MERIT

Mme Petrick: pink	Prof. Walters: pink
Petrick superba: white	Empress of India: salmon-rose
Paul Schoen	Mme Vander Cruyssen: pink
Jean Haerens	Orange Beauty
Sweetheart Supreme	Salmon Beauty
Mrs. Fred Sanders:	Coral Bells
double cerise	

Propagation: Some varieties may be propagated most successfully from cuttings, while other varieties are usually grafted. As the propagation of azaleas is a highly specialized field, it is advisable for the owner of the small greenhouse to purchase a few plants which have been especially prepared for forcing.

Soil Requirements: Azaleas require a highly acid soil with a pH between 4.5 and 5.5. The potting soil should consist of a mixture of 2 parts loam and 1 part imported acid peat. Yellowing of the foliage and poor root development are indicative of a soil which is too highly alkaline and of a lack of available iron. In order to correct an iron deficiency an application of one ounce of a 12 percent chelated iron per 100 square feet of bench area, or four ounces in 100 gallons of water for application to potted plants will give excellent results.

Culture: Azalea plants are shipped with a small ball of earth and as soon as they have been unpacked the ball should be immersed in a bucket of water until it has become thoroughly saturated. It should then be allowed to drain before it is potted. For the first two or three weeks the plants should be placed in a cool greenhouse where the night temperature ranges around 45 degrees. Azaleas require an abundance of water and a moist atmosphere. Frequent syringing of the foliage with warm water is beneficial. If the plants are to be brought into flower by Christmas, they should be kept in a temperature of 45 to 48 degrees until November 5. They should then have a night temperature of 60 degrees with a somewhat higher temperature of 65 degrees during the day. If the plants are desired for Easter bloom they should be kept in a very cool house (45 to 50 degrees) until six weeks before Easter. All new growth which appears at the base of the flower buds should be pinched out. If this is not done the flowers will be small and there will be many blind buds.

After the flowering period is over the plants should be trimmed back lightly, and they should be placed in a warm, moist house in order that vigorous new growth may be encouraged. In June the pots may be sunk in the open ground or the plants may be shifted to the nursery rows. A soil mixture similar to that of the potting mixture should be used. The symmetry of the plant should be maintained by the occasional pinching back of any awkward shoots. No pinching should be done after July 1. In early autumn the plants may be lifted and brought into the greenhouse.

Begonias may be grouped into four general classes: the semi-tuberous-rooted; the tuberous-rooted; the foliage group; and the fibrous-rooted.

(1) *Semi-tuberous Group*

VARIETIES OF MERIT FOR CHRISTMAS FLOWERING

Lady Mac   Melior   Marjorie Gibbs

Propagation: The plants are propagated by petiole leaf cuttings taken from medium sized, well-ripened leaves

in November and December. The petioles should be inserted in the propagating case in such a way that the leaves do not come into contact with the sand. The formation of roots requires from four to five weeks but the cuttings should not be potted up until new shoots have begun to develop from the base. A potting mixture of 1 part loam, 1 part sand and 1 part peat moss should be used and the crown of the cutting should be placed as near the surface as possible.

Soil Requirements: A soil with a pH between 6.8 and 7.2 is preferred. For the final potting soil a mixture of 3 parts loam, 2 parts rotted manure, 1 part peat moss, and 1 part sand is recommended. To each 2½ bushels of soil may be added a 4-inch pot of a 4–12–4 complete fertilizer and a 4-inch pot of horn shavings.

Culture: The young plants may be grown on with a bottom heat of about 70 degrees, and as they develop they may be shifted into larger pots. The final potting in a 6- or 7-inch pot should be done in September. A humid atmosphere and partial shade during the summer are desirable, and pinching should be practiced in order to produce stocky, well-developed plants. Staking is advisable, as the stems are very brittle. During the growing period a night temperature of 58 to 60 degrees F. is desirable, with a slightly higher temperature during the day.

(2) *Tuberous-Rooted Group*

See Summer-flowering Bulbs and Tubers, page 394.

(3) *Foliage Group*

VARIETIES OF MERIT

For list of varieties see page 455.

Propagation: Members of this group are propagated by means of leaf cuttings. Well-matured leaves should be selected. One inch of the margin of the leaf should be cut away and the remaining portion of the leaf should be cut into triangular sections, with a small section of the petiole at the base and a vein running through the middle. The cutting should then be inserted in the propagating case, the section of petiole being well buried.

Soil Requirements: }
Culture: } See Semi-tuberous Group.

(4) *Fibrous-rooted Group* (Begonia semperflorens)

VARIETIES OF MERIT

Bonfire	Prima Donna
Gloire de Chatelaine	Pride of Newcastle
Luminosa	Westport Beauty

Propagation: The fibrous-rooted begonias may be propagated by seed, by stem-cuttings and in the case of a few varieties, such as Gloire de Chatelaine, by division.

Seeds may be sown at any time from November to January. The seeds are exceedingly fine and should be handled with care. (See Chapter XXXIII on Propagation.) The seedlings should be pricked out as soon as they have developed their second leaf. Cuttings may be taken at any time of the year but will root most readily in March and April.

Soil Requirements: ⎱
Culture: ⎰ See Semi-tuberous Group.

Bleeding-heart (Dicentra spectabilis)*:* There are very few perennials which can be forced as successfully as Bleeding-heart, and there are few flowers more beautiful or more appealing. After you have once grown them in the greenhouse, you will not want a season to pass without having at least a few plants for decorative purposes in the house or in the conservatory.

Soil Requirements: Good potting compost.

Culture: Two-year-old clumps should be lifted in the autumn and heeled in in a frame. Late in January the plants should be brought into the greenhouse and potted up in ample 10- to 12-inch bulb pans. They should be placed in the coolest temperature available and forced slowly. During this period of growth, the plants will require abundant moisture. By late March or early April the lovely, pendent, heart-shaped flowers will begin to open and the plants will remain in bloom for many weeks if they are kept in a moderately cool temperature. After the flowering period is over, the plants may be replanted out of doors, and will show no ill effects from this gentle process of forcing.

Bouvardia: The waxy, orange-blossom-scented flowers of the Bouvardia are a source of constant joy during the brief months that they are in bloom. The flowers are so lovely for cutting and the fragrance is so delightful that a few clumps should be grown in every small greenhouse.

Propagation: New plants may be started very readily from cuttings made in late winter or early spring, and the young plants may be grown on in pots. Bouvardia may also be propagated by means of root cuttings. The roots may be cut into pieces 1 to 2 inches long and these may be planted horizontally in flats containing a mixture of $\frac{1}{2}$ sand and $\frac{1}{2}$ peat moss.

Soil Requirements: Bouvardia prefers a very fibrous, mellow soil, abundantly supplied with leaf mold or some other form of organic matter. The soil should have a neutral or slightly alkaline reaction, preferably testing between pH 7.0 and pH 7.5. If the soil is too acid in its reaction it will cause a browning of the foliage, and in some cases a complete defoliation.

Culture: During the summer months the young rooted cuttings may be planted in the open, being benched late in August, or they may be planted directly in the greenhouse bed or bench in May, being carried over the summer in their permanent location. The plants should be kept pinched back until the end of August in order that they may become well branched. When the plants are moved from the open ground into the greenhouse they must be lifted with an ample quantity of earth and the roots should be disturbed as little as possible. It is also wise to shade the plants for a few days after transplanting until they have become well established. Bouvardia prefers a moderately cool temperature, a night temperature of 55 degrees F. being considered ideal, with a rise of 10 degrees or so during the day. The plants will usually begin to flower late in September and will continue to give generous bloom throughout November and December. When the plants have finished blooming, they should be cut back, lifted, and placed under the bench, water being withheld gradually. Late in January the soil may be shaken from the roots of the old plants, and they may be potted up in 5 or 6-inch pots. Cuttings may be made from these plants as growth starts, or the old plants may be carried over for another season of bloom. They will often do their best during this second season.

VARIETIES OF MERIT

Bouvardia ternifolia: red-flowering species
Bouvardia Humboldti: white-flowering species

Calendulas are among the most satisfactory of all plants for the cool greenhouse, and their gay, jaunty blossoms, in shades of orange and gold, are borne in profusion throughout the winter months. The plants are of easy culture, and will repay one generously for the small amount of labor expended upon them.

VARIETIES OF MERIT

Gold: golden yellow, large flowers with long stems
Lemon Queen: bright yellow
Masterpiece: deep orange with dark center
Art Shades

Soil Requirements: Calendulas may be grown with a reasonable degree of success in almost any soil, but they thrive best in a rather heavy loam of high fertility. A cool, deep, rich soil is ideal, and in the preparation of the beds 1 part rotted manure should be used to every 3 parts of soil, and an application of 5 pounds of superphosphate per 100 square feet should be made. The plants are more or less indifferent to soil reaction but, in general, a neutral reaction is considered best. A mulch of peat moss is beneficial in that it helps to maintain a cool soil temperature.

Propagation: The seeds may be sown at any time from mid-July to late October. Seeds sown the last week in July will come into flower about the middle of October.

Seeds sown about October 10 will flower early in February. The young seedlings make rapid growth and after being transplanted into pots or flats the plants will be ready for benching about the middle of September.

Culture: The new, improved varieties should be spaced from 12–15 inches apart each way. The size of the flower, the length and stiffness of the stem, and the quality of the foliage will depend to a large extent upon the temperature under which the plants are grown. In order to produce flowers of maximum size with strong, stiff stems, the night temperature should be about 45 degrees. A slightly higher temperature ranging between 50 and 55 degrees will produce earlier and more abundant bloom but the flowers will be somewhat smaller.

California Poppies: Although California Poppies are seldom thought of as greenhouse flowers, a few plants may well be included if one's aim is to provide a pleasant variety of flowers for cutting. Some of the large-flowering types which have been recently introduced are very decorative and lovely.

VARIETIES OF MERIT

Aurora: a delicate peach-pink in color
Sutton's Fireglow
Sutton's Rosy Queen

Soil Requirements: A good greenhouse compost.

Propagation: The seeds should be sown in the greenhouse bench where they are to flower, as the young seedlings do not take kindly to transplanting.

Culture: The plants should be thinned out to a distance of 8 to 10 inches. A cool house will provide conditions which are very nearly ideal. The plants will come into flower in about eight to ten weeks from sowing.

Calla (Zantedeschia): Callas are grown for the decorative quality of their blooms when used in cut-flower arrangements.

TYPES

White Calla (*Zantedeschia æthiopica*)
Yellow Calla (*Zantedeschia Elliottiana*)

Propagation: The small offsets which form around the parent rhizome may be removed. Several years of growth are required before these young plants will come into bloom.

Soil Requirements: Callas require a very rich soil. A mixture of 2 parts heavy, rich loam and 1 part well-rotted cow manure will give excellent results.

Culture: Callas may be grown either in solid beds, in raised benches, or in pots. A night temperature of 55 degrees and a day temperature ranging between 60 and 65 degrees are preferred. The plants require an abundant supply of moisture throughout their growing period. After the flowering period is over, the plants are gradually dried off and are given a period of rest. Occasional waterings may be given but all active growth is allowed to cease. In August the top soil from the beds may be removed and after the plants have been given a thorough soaking a heavy mulch of stable manure may be applied. Active growth will soon be resumed and the plants will begin to flower late in the autumn.

Carnations (Dianthus): Carnations are among the ever-dependable and ever-popular greenhouse flowers.

Propagation: Carnations are propagated by means of cuttings. The most accepted practice is to take the cuttings from established plants in November or December. Cuttings may be taken later in the winter season but plants grown from cuttings taken earlier in the season will make more vigorous growth and will produce more abundant bloom the following year. The cuttings should be taken from disease-free plants which are in vigorous growing condition. Cuttings are taken from the axillary shoots, preferably from the lower portion of the flowering stem. Cuttings will range from 3 to 5 inches in length and they should be inserted in the propagating case, clean, sharp sand being the best rooting medium. Although it was formerly a common practice to remove a portion of the foliage, recent experiments have proved that a higher percentage of rootage is obtained if the foliage is not reduced. Under favorable conditions the cuttings should root in about 4 weeks, although some varieties will root more readily than others.

Soil Requirements: Carnations prefer a medium sandy loam, high in organic matter, and the plants are indifferent to soil reaction, thriving equally well in neutral, mildly acid or slightly alkaline soil, within a range of pH 5.5 to 8.0. At the time of planting an application of superphosphate, 10 pounds per 100 square feet, may be made. Beginning eight weeks after benching, monthly applications of a 4–12–4 commercial fertilizer may be made at the rate of 4 pounds to every 100 square feet. Planting distances vary from 6 to 12 inches apart according to the variety and, to some extent, to the fertility of the soil in the benches.

Culture: When the cuttings are well rooted, the roots being from $\frac{1}{2}$ to 1 inch long, the cuttings should be removed from the propagating bench and potted up in $2\frac{1}{2}$-inch pots, a mixture of 1 part compost, 1 part sand and 1 part peat moss being used. Before the plants become in the least pot-bound, they should be shifted on to larger pots, as carnations suffer seriously from any check of this sort, the plants becoming hard, yellow, and stunted in appearance. Carnations are one of the few plants which should not be potted very firmly, and care should be taken not to set the plants too deeply. Watering must also be done with care, as overwatering is often fatal to the welfare of the plant.

Soon after the plants have been potted for the first time they should be pinched back to within about 3 inches. The lateral shoots should be pinched back as they develop, in order to produce symmetrical, well-branched plants. Pinching should continue until one desires to let the flower buds mature. If early bloom is desired pinching should cease early in July. If late bloom is desired pinching may be continued until after the plants are benched. It requires from ten to twenty weeks for a newly pinched shoot to produce a flower. The plants may be carried on in pots until they are ready to be benched or, as soon as danger of frost is past, they may be set in the open ground. If field culture is practiced a more vigorous growth and greater disease resistance are obtained, while the pot-grown plants will give earlier bloom. The plants should be benched in late summer, and early summer benching is sometimes practiced.

Disbudding: The flowering stems of carnations should be kept disbudded, all the axillary buds and shoots being removed from the upper portion.

Watering: Watering must be done with care. Carnation plants thrive best in a soil which is uniformly moist but which is not saturated.

Chrysanthemums: There is no other flower which can take the place of the Chrysanthemums during the autumn months. They are so generous with their bloom, so lovely in form and coloring, so entirely satisfactory, both for cutting and as potted plants, that they should be included in every greenhouse, no matter how limited the space may be. Many varieties which are not hardy out-of-doors may be grown successfully in the greenhouse, and with careful planning the period of bloom may be extended over several months.

Propagation: Rooted cuttings of many desirable varieties may be purchased from commercial growers and after the first season cuttings may be made from the stock thus obtained. These rooted cuttings should be potted up in March or early April, and they may be carried on in pots, being shifted to larger pots as the plants develop, or they may be transferred to the benches. During the summer the plants should be syringed at least twice a day.

Soil Requirements: The soil in the benches should be carefully prepared. A one-inch layer of rotted sod or coarse, strawy manure should be placed in the bottom of the bench and a soil mixture consisting of 1 part well-decomposed manure and 3 parts good sandy loam is recommended. An application of 20 percent super-phosphate at the rate of 8 pounds per 100 square feet

may be made at the time of planting. The soil should be very slightly acid in its reaction.

Culture: If the plants are to be trained to single stems they should be spaced from 8 to 10 inches apart. For the more branching types, 12 inches should be allowed. If large flowers borne on tall single stems are desired, all side shoots and all growth from the base of the plants should be removed. The pompon types should be kept pinched back until the middle of August in order to obtain sturdy, well-branched plants, six or eight flowering branches being allowed to develop. Commercial growers consider it a good practice to bench their chrysanthemums during May, June and July as this enables the young plants to become well established during the summer.

A few weeks after the plants have been benched, a one-inch mulch of domestic peat moss should be applied. Such a mulch has a most startling effect upon the growth and vigor of the plants, sometimes causing as much as a 50 to 100 percent increase in growth.

When the buds begin to show, weekly applications of ammonium sulphate may be made, 1 ounce dissolved in 2 gallons of water.

Chrysanthemums prefer a night temperature which does not exceed 50 degrees F.

After the flowering season is over the plants may be lifted from the bench and placed in a coldframe, cuttings being taken from these stock plants in the early spring.

Clarkia: The copper-colored stems of the Clarkias, studded with crisp little whorls of bloom, are very lovely for cutting, and a few plants will add welcome variety for flower arrangements. If the flowers are cut just as the buds begin to open, they will last extremely well.

Propagation: For early bloom the seeds should be sown before mid-September; for later bloom, a sowing should be made in October or early November.

Soil Requirements: Clarkia is rather indifferent to soil conditions and will thrive in any good greenhouse compost.

Culture: The young plants make rapid growth, and they may be grown either in pots or in raised benches, the plants being spaced from 10 to 12 inches apart. Clarkia prefers a decidedly cool temperature of 50 degrees F. at night.

Cyclamen: The blooms of the Cyclamen are like miniature butterflies poised on slender stems. If the plants are well grown they will flower abundantly during the winter and will add their full share of beauty to the indoor garden.

Exposure and Temperature: When used for decorative

purposes in the house, a window with an eastern exposure is ideal. If maximum growth and development are desired, the temperature throughout the growing period should range between 50 and 60 degrees.

Propagation: Cyclamen may be propagated either by seed, or by cutting the corm into sections with one or two leaves attached. The seed should be sown in the early autumn in order to produce flowering plants for the following winter. A mixture of 1 part loam and 1 part German peat may be used for the seed bed and the seeds may be planted about an inch apart. If kept in a temperature ranging between 55 and 60 degrees F. they will germinate in from four to five weeks. After several leaves have developed, the plants should be transplanted into small 2½-inch pots. At the time of this first transplanting, the tiny corm which is forming should be placed so that its top is level with the surface of the soil. At each subsequent repotting the corm should be placed slightly higher until at the time of the last shift it is entirely above the surface of the soil.

Soil Requirements: A slightly acid soil with a pH between 6.0 and 7.0 is considered ideal. A soil decidedly light in texture should be used for cyclamen plants in the early stages of growth. For plants reaching maturity, the following soil mixture is recommended: 3 parts good loam, 1 part manure, ½ part imported peat, ½ part sand. At the time of the final potting, a 4-inch potful of a 4–12–4 complete fertilizer and a 4-inch potful of horn shavings should be added to each 2½ bushels of soil.

Culture: During the summer months, the young plants should be kept in a cool, semi-shaded spot, a well-ventilated, partially shaded greenhouse being satisfactory. Frequent syringing of the foliage and the maintenance of high humidity is desirable. The shade should be removed in the autumn. If, at this time, the pots are set on a staging or are elevated on overturned flower pots, the development of the plant will be hastened. Cyclamen plants should be grown in clay pots, rather than in glazed containers. Watering must be done with care. The plants should usually be watered twice a day, the pots being set in a saucer or pan until the surface of the soil has become moist. Faded blooms and any yellowing leaves should be removed by giving the stem a quick jerk in order that it may snap off at the base. The plants may be carried over for a second year by resting them after the period of bloom is over.

Euphorbia (Euphorbia fulgens): The brilliant orange-red flowers of the Euphorbias are very decorative and lovely and a few plants are a welcome addition to the stock of a small greenhouse.

Propagation: Euphorbias may be propagated by softwood cuttings taken from the stock plants about the first of May, or by hardwood cuttings taken in January after the parent plants have flowered. The cuttings should consist of 2 or 3 nodes and should be rooted in a medium of half peat and half sand.

Soil Requirements: A rather heavy, slightly acid soil is preferred for Euphorbias.

Culture: The rooted cuttings may be benched or potted up early in July. The plants should be pinched back so that 3 or 4 stems develop from the lower portion of the plant. The plants should be spaced from 10 to 12 inches apart in the bench. A growing temperature of 60 degrees F. is preferred. Sudden changes in temperature are to be avoided, as they have a very harmful effect upon the plant.

Freesias: Freesias may be obtained in a wide range of colors—mauve, lavender, blue, yellow, orange, pink, and carmine-rose. The delicately formed, sweetly scented flowers are lovely for cutting and Freesias are exceedingly well adapted for greenhouse culture.

Propagation: If bloom is desired throughout the winter months the bulbs may be planted in succession from August until the middle of December. They may be grown in pots or in flats. For early bloom only large-sized bulbs should be used; for later bloom the smaller sizes will be entirely satisfactory. The bulbs should be spaced approximately 2 inches apart each way.

Soil Requirements: A potting soil consisting of 2 parts loam, 1 part leaf mold and 1 part sand is recommended.

Culture: After planting, the bulbs should be placed in a cool, dark place until the leaves appear. In the summer, the pots or flats may be placed in a coldframe, being shaded with lath sash. The pots should be kept moist but not too wet. As soon as leaf growth has started the shade should be removed. The pots should be brought into the greenhouse before there is danger of frost. A night temperature ranging between 55 and 60 degrees F. is satisfactory. As the flower stems are very delicate, some support is necessary and very small bamboo stakes may be used with a number of strings criss-crossed between them. After the plants have finished flowering, water should be gradually withheld and the bulbs should be allowed to ripen. After the foliage has ripened sufficiently, the bulbs may be removed from the soil and the largest ones may be saved for bloom the following year, being stored during the summer in a cool dry place.

Gardenia jasminoides is well adapted to greenhouse culture and is widely grown for the florist trade. The blooms are in great demand for corsages and there is also a demand for pot-grown plants. The flowering period varies according to the climate. On the West Coast a long flowering period is attained. In other sections it is comparatively short, depending upon the interval of night temperature which remains below 65° F. Plants thrive best in raised benches. Soil should be sterilized as a protection against nematodes and canker. Gardenias thrive best with a night temperature between 62 and 65° F. and a day temperature above 70° F. Humidity should be kept very high and the soil moist. (For soil requirements see page 255.)

Geraniums (Pelargonium): The popularity of the Geranium as a house plant has endured over a period of many years. Beloved and cherished by our grandmothers, geraniums were among the few flowering plants which could be grown in the window garden a generation or more ago; and they are still beloved today, their popularity being quite undiminished in spite of the wealth of new material which is available.

SPECIES AND VARIETIES

P. domesticum. Lady Washington Geranium

VARIETIES   Easter Greeting   Lucy Becker

P. graveolens. Rose Geranium
P. odoratissimum. Nutmeg Geranium
P. peltatum. Ivy-leaf Geranium
P. zonale. Horseshoe or Common Geranium

VARIETIES

Enchantress: light pink	Mme Buchner: white
Improved Poitevine:	Radio Red: red
salmon pink	Red Fiat: brick red
Mme Landry: salmon pink	Suzanne: cerise

Exposure and Temperature: Full sunlight at all times. A temperature ranging between 65 and 70 degrees F. during the day and between 60 and 65 degrees F. at night is considered ideal.

Propagation: Geraniums are propagated by means of softwood stem cuttings. When winter bloom is desired, cuttings should be made in May. (See Chapter XXXIII on Propagation.)

Soil Requirements: Geraniums require a soil low in nitrogen and relatively high in phosphorus and potash. An excess of nitrogen in the soil induces a rank, vegetative growth and prevents flowering. Geraniums will thrive reasonably well in almost any ordinary garden soil. If, however, maximum growth and abundant bloom are desired, the following soil mixture will give the best results when used in the final potting: 8 parts good garden loam to 1 part well-rotted manure. To 2½ bushels of soil, add one 5-inch flower potful of superphosphate and one 4-inch potful of a 2–10–10 commercial fertilizer. This should be thoroughly mixed with the soil before potting. This same mixture may be used in repotting old plants. If a good potting mixture is used, it is not advisable to make any subsequent application of fertilizer. A soil with a pH between 6.5 and 7.6 is preferred.

Culture: After the cuttings have rooted, they should be potted up into small 3-inch pots and as the plants develop they may be shifted on into 4- and 5-inch pots. Geraniums require very firm potting, and as they flower more abundantly when they are allowed to become slightly pot-bound they should be carried through the winter in 4 or 5 inch pots. Old plants should be grown in 6- and 8-inch pots. During the first summer of growth the young plants should be pinched back frequently, in order that they may become symmetrical and well branched, and no flower buds should be allowed to develop until early September. The plants should then give ample bloom from October until April. In May these plants which have bloomed through the winter months should be severely pruned back, leaving about 3 strong shoots, 3 or 4 inches long to each plant. During the summer they should be placed in a partially shaded place, and they should be kept fairly dry. It is important not to encourage new growth during this rest period, as the plant is storing up a reserve of strength for winter bloom. In the early autumn, the plants may be repotted in fresh soil and should give abundant bloom during the winter months.

Watering: Geraniums should not be watered too liberally. The plants will give better bloom if they are kept somewhat on the dry side. Overwatering and poor ventilation are frequently the cause of a physiological leaf spot which is very disfiguring to the foliage.

Gerbera (Transvaal Daisy): Coming to us from the fields of the Transvaal in South Africa the Gerbera has gained rapidly in popularity as a greenhouse plant. The flowers are unusually fine for cutting and are obtainable in many exquisite shades of salmon, apricot, orange-pink, and cerise. Gerberas are true perennials in their native habitat but they are too tender to withstand the rigors of our winters north of Virginia and in many sections they are, therefore, best adapted to greenhouse culture.

Propagation: They may be readily propagated both by seed and by the division of old established clumps. As Gerbera seed loses its vitality rapidly, only fresh seed should be used. The seed should be sown in March and as soon as 4 or 5 small leaves have developed the seedlings should be transplanted directly into the beds where they are to flower. Established plants may be divided in June.

Culture: Gerberas should preferably be grown in solid beds. During the summer the plants should be given a light mulch, they should be kept carefully watered, and the house should be well ventilated. The plants should be spaced 12 to 15 inches apart. A moderately cool night temperature of 55 to 60 degrees F. is preferred, and if given good care the plants will give abundant bloom throughout the winter and early spring months.

Soil Requirements: Gerberas prefer an open, well-drained soil of good fertility, with a pH value of approximately 7.0 to 7.5. In the fall and spring a weekly application of urea, 1 ounce to 7 gallons, is recommended.

Gladiolus: Both the large-flowered types of gladiolus and the primulinus hybrids, as well as many of the very exquisite dwarf types, may be forced in the greenhouse for early spring bloom. The culture of the latter group is, however, quite distinct from the culture of the large-flowered types; consequently the two groups will be treated separately as regards culture and soil requirements.

VARIETIES OF MERIT

LARGE-FLOWERED TYPE

Oregon Gold: yellow   Snow Princess: white
Pacific Skies: pale lavender
Picardy: shrimp-pink   Spring Maid: deep salmon

PRIMULINUS TYPE

Butterboy: yellow   Golden Frills: deep yellow
Early Orange: bright orange   White Butterfly: white
Giralda: magenta rose

MINIATURE TYPE

Arctic Star: white   Gypsy: rose-red
Charming: rose-pink   Salmon Ruffles
Elf: orange-salmon

Large-flowered, Primulinus and Miniature Types

Soil Requirements: Any good loam is satisfactory.

Culture: If the large-flowered and primulinus types are to be grown, corms which have been especially prepared for forcing should be obtained. These may be planted directly in a bench, the rows being spaced 12 inches apart and the corms 4 inches apart in the row, or they may be planted in flats or in pots. The method of planting will usually be determined by the space which happens to be available at the time. When pot culture is followed, three corms may be planted in a 6-inch pot. In flats the corms may be spaced 4 inches apart each way. The corms should be planted at a depth of approximately an inch, and the soil should be at least an inch below the rim of the pot or flat in order to allow for watering. Greenhouse culture is practically identical with outdoor culture. The plants should be given full sun, they should be watered adequately, and a moderate temperature is preferred. If bench space is not available

at the time of planting, the pots or flats may be placed beneath the benches for a brief period, until the corms have started into growth, and the shoots have obtained a height of about 4 inches. They should then be brought into full light. The primulinus hybrids are particularly well adapted to forcing, and as cut flowers they are far lovelier than the large-flowered types.

Dwarf Types

Soil Requirements: A light, sandy-loam soil is preferred.

Culture: There are few flowers more exquisite in form and coloring than some of the dwarf gladioli and no greenhouse should be without them. Although many of these dwarf types are not hardy enough to be grown out-of-doors in the North, they may be grown to perfection in the small greenhouse. Most of these dwarf species, and their hybrids, have come to us from South Africa and it is to be regretted that they are not hardy enough for general culture out-of-doors, for they are so utterly charming. The corms should be planted in November, either in pots or in flats. The pots should be stored in a coldframe until mid-January, when they may be brought into the greenhouse and forced in a moderately cool temperature. The graceful flower spikes will begin to open in late March, and if a succession of bloom is desired during the spring months, the pots should be brought in from storage at intervals of every ten days.

Gloxinias: In a 1956 popularity poll for the most popular house plants the gloxinia was accorded second place, yielding first place to its close relative, the African violet. It is a colorful, lovely plant, bountiful with its bloom, and it well deserves the popularity which it has attained.

The large-flowered hybrids have a wide color range and the handsome, showy blooms sometimes measure as much as 6 to 7 inches across. However, many gardeners prefer the more modest slipper type, with smaller, more delicate flowers.

The colors of the gloxinias range from white, delicate pink and rose to sparkling red and purple, with many lovely intermediate hues.

In many sections of the country gloxinias are not adapted to outdoor culture and should be grown either in the greenhouse or as house plants.

Propagation: Gloxinias may be grown from tubers, from leaf cuttings and from seed. Tubers may be planted at any time from November to February if favorable growing conditions can be provided. If tubers have been shipped it is wise to plant them as soon as possible after they arrive. They may be started in small pots or in trays, vermiculite or milled sphagnum moss being used as the starting medium, or they may be planted directly in the pots in which they are to flower;

small tubers in 5-inch pots, large tubers in 6- to 8-inch pots. The top third of the tuber should be exposed above the level of the soil in the pot.

Leaf cuttings may be taken from mature, flowering plants during the spring and early summer. The leaf should be cut close to the main stem and should be placed in the shade for half an hour in order to give the end a chance to dry. The leaf may then be inserted in moist sand or vermiculite in the propagating case. Cuttings also root very readily in water or in any simple, home-made device. When new growth appears and the original leaf dies the plant may be transplanted into a pot. Plants grown from leaf cuttings will bloom the following spring and summer.

Gloxinias may also be grown easily from seed. The seeds are very fine and require careful handling (see page 477 for details). The seeds germinate in about ten days and the young seedlings should be transplanted into flats when they have two or three pairs of leaves, being later shifted into 5- or 6-inch pots. When grown from seed gloxinias will come into flower in from six to ten months. Seed sown in early January should produce flowers by midsummer.

Soil Requirements: Gloxinias require a rich, porous, well-drained soil with a high content of organic matter. The following mixtures will give excellent results.

(1) 1 part garden loam, 1 part sand, 1 part peat moss.

(2) 1 part garden loam, 1 part leaf mold, 1 part sand. To the above mixture add one 4-inch pot of bonemeal per bushel of soil.

Culture: For their best development gloxinias require a moist atmosphere, a favorable temperature, a sufficient amount of light, protection from brilliant sunshine, and a congenial soil.

The plants are not difficult to grow, yet they are not of easy culture and they present something of a challenge, particularly when they are grown in the house where conditions cannot be as readily controlled as in a greenhouse.

The ideal range of temperature for gloxinias is from 68 to 72 degrees F. during the day and 62 to 65 at night, although they are adapted to some fluctuation. If temperatures range much above 75 degrees F. growth will tend to suffer.

Gloxinias should be given as much light as possible but should be shaded from strong sun. Insufficient light will produce leggy, spindly growth. When grown in the house gloxinias will usually do well in a south or east window during the winter months.

Watering must be done with care. The most satisfactory method is to place the pot in a pan of water and leave it until the surface of the soil appears moist. It should not be watered again until the soil begins to look dry. It should never be allowed to stand in water for a long period of time. If overhead watering is practiced the water should be poured close to the rim of the pot in order to avoid wetting the leaves or the crown of the plant. When water stands in the crown it is conducive to crown rot and to the spread of gray mold. Ample drainage material should be placed in the bottom of the pot at the time of potting, as good drainage is essential.

When the period of bloom is over and the foliage begins to die down, water should be gradually withheld so the plants may become dormant. The pots should be stored in a cool place, at a temperature of about 50 degrees F., and should be watered just enough to keep the tubers from shrivelling. If desired, the tubers may be removed from the pot and stored in peat moss in a cool place until their period of dormancy is over. They may then be potted up again in fresh soil in February or March.

Plants which flower in early spring can be cut back to the first pair of leaves and will usually produce excellent second bloom within eight to ten weeks. After the second period of bloom is over they should be prepared for their rest period.

Heliophila is one of the most charming of the group of South African annuals, and as it becomes more widely known its popularity will undoubtedly increase. The long sprays of lovely clear blue flowers, similar in coloring to the flowers of the perennial flax (Linum perenne), are borne in profusion throughout the late winter months, and they are perfectly delightful for cut-flower arrangements. The fact that a few plants will produce such an abundance of bloom, and that they may be cut almost continually over a period of several months, makes them of unique value as a greenhouse flower.

Propagation: The seeds may be sown at any time during the late summer and early autumn months.

Soil Requirements: Good greenhouse compost.

Culture: Heliophila prefers a moderately cool temperature. The plants may be grown either in pots or in raised benches, the latter being preferred. A distance of from 8 to 10 inches between the plants will give ample space for their best development.

Bulbous Iris: Of all the varieties and types of bulbous Iris which may be grown in the greenhouse, the Iris tingitana hybrid, *Wedgwood,* is the most beautiful. It is extremely well adapted to forcing and the lovely, clear blue flowers are of great value for cutting. The Spanish, English, and Dutch Iris may all be forced into early bloom very successfully and they may be had in a wide range of colors. (For a list of varieties, see page 408.)

Soil Requirements: A soil mixture of 1 part compost, 1 part loam and 1 part sand is recommended.

Culture: The bulbs may be planted in September in shallow bulb pans or in flats, being spaced 1½ inches apart. A thorough watering should be given in order to start root action. They should be stored in a coldframe until the middle of November and may then be brought in and placed in a cool house with a night temperature of 45 to 50 degrees F. If a succession of bloom is desired a few pots or flats should be brought in from the frames at intervals of every ten days. When the buds begin to show the temperature may be raised to 55 degrees F., but the plants should never be subjected to a high temperature, as the quality of bloom will be seriously affected. The bulbous iris requires abundant water during the growing period, but the amount should be reduced when the buds begin to develop. Only the largest size bulbs should be used for forcing. Bulbs which have been especially prepared for forcing may now be obtained and the variety Wedgwood may be brought into flower by Thanksgiving. This method of preparing bulbs for early forcing was developed by Doctor David Griffiths of the U.S. Department of Agriculture and consists of subjecting the bulbs to a temperature of 80 degrees F. for three weeks after they are dug in July. From the middle of August to the 25th of September they are held at a temperature of 50 degrees F. and they are then ready for potting.

Larkspur, annual: Some of the new and greatly improved varieties of annual Larkspur are exceedingly lovely and they are well adapted for greenhouse culture. The plants will come into flower several months after sowing and it is possible to plan either for an early winter crop or for a later crop to follow on after the chrysanthemums have been removed from the benches.

Propagation: The annual larkspur is propagated by seed, and the young seedlings may be carried on in pots or in flats until bench space is available.

Soil Requirements: A light, fertile soil, neutral or slightly alkaline, is preferred.

Culture: A decidedly cool temperature, ranging around 50 degrees at night, is most favorable for the development of the annual larkspurs, and the plants are in no way exacting in regard to their soil requirements. The plants should be given ample room in which to develop, being spaced 8 by 10 inches apart. Coming in shades of lavender-blue, rose, white, and pink, the annual larkspurs offer a wealth of bloom, and the tall, stately flower spikes are exceedingly fine for cutting.

Lilies, Easter: There are several species of lilies which are used for forcing, the most popular being Lilium longiflorum giganteum, and Lilium longiflorum erabu.

Propagation: Bulbs are obtainable in three sizes, 5- to 7-inch bulbs, 7- to 9-inch, and 9- to 11-inch. Most commercial growers purchase the 7- to 9-inch size. The larger size, 9- to 11-inch, will give more flowers per stem, but in price they are considerably higher. Northern-grown bulbs will produce shorter plants with more blooms on a plant than Southern-grown bulbs, and they are usually preferred.

Soil Requirements: Easter lilies prefer a somewhat heavy, yet porous, soil with a pH ranging between 6.0 and 7.0. A soil mixture of 4 parts silt loam, 1 part sand, and 1 part well-rotted, composted manure is recommended.

Culture: Approximately thirteen weeks are required from the time of planting to the time of bloom. The bulbs should be planted in 6-inch pots, being set at a depth of an inch or more, and they should be placed on a bench in a house where the temperature can be maintained between 54 and 56 degrees F. The potting soil should be fairly dry and very little water should be given until root growth has started, at which time the temperature of the house should be increased to 60 degrees F. It is desirable that the plants be watered with warm water of a temperature of approximately 70 degrees F. After active growth has started, and the plants have attained a height of 6 inches, bi-weekly applications of a liquid fertilizer may be given, 1 oz. of ammonium sulphate being dissolved in 2 gals. of water. The time of bloom may be slightly hastened or retarded by raising or lowering the temperature a few degrees.

Lupines, annual: The annual Lupines are well adapted to greenhouse culture.

The most satisfactory varieties for cutting are Hartwegii, Azure Blue, with flowers of a delicate mist-like hue, and Sutton's Tall Pink, with flowers of a lovely soft shade of pink.

Propagation: The seeds may be sown in the bench where the plants are to flower or they may be sown in flats, being transplanted into small pots.

Soil Requirements: A moderately rich soil, well supplied with organic matter, will produce fine bloom. The soil should be neutral or slightly alkaline in its reaction.

Culture: The plants may be shifted into the benches as soon as space is available, being spaced 12 inches apart. A cool house with a night temperature of 50 to 55 degrees F. is preferred.

Mignonette (Reseda odorata)*:* Although Mignonette is prized more for its fragrance than for the beauty of its bloom, some of the new and greatly improved forms are valuable for cutting and they are admirably adapted to greenhouse culture.

Propagation: Mignonette is readily propagated by seed. If bloom is desired throughout the winter months, three successive sowings should be made, one early in July, another early in August and the last early in September.

The seeds should always be sown where they are to flower as the plants suffer such a check from transplanting that they never fully recover. The procedure followed in most commercial greenhouses is to mark the bench area off into rows 6 by 8 inches apart. From 6 to 8 seeds are planted at the intersection of the rows, being covered very lightly. Watering should be done with a very fine spray. After the seeds have germinated and the small seedling plants have developed the third leaf, the three strongest plants should be left and the remaining plants should be thinned out. The young seedling plants should be shaded from intense sunlight during the middle portion of the day until they have become well established.

Soil Requirements: A medium, light, rather turfy loam is preferred. The usual practice is to place an inch of well-rotted stable manure on the bottom of the bench. The remaining portion of the bench is then filled with compost.

Culture: Mignonette prefers a very cool temperature. A night temperature ranging between 45 and 48 degrees F. and a day temperature between 55 and 65 degrees F. is considered ideal. Watering must be done with care. As the plants may be seriously injured by an overabundance of moisture, watering should be done only on bright mornings. If water is allowed to remain on the foliage for any length of time, the leaves become spotted. When the flower spikes begin to form, all side shoots should be removed from around the top of the stem. Three or four vigorous shoots may be left at the base of the plant for later bloom. A top-dressing of one part sheep manure and two parts rich loam may be applied when the plants are ready to come into flower.

Narcissus: All the members of the Narcissus group may be easily forced into early spring bloom in the greenhouse.

VARIETIES OF MERIT

Among the most beautiful varieties for forcing are:

TRUMPET GROUP	SMALL-CUPPED GROUP
King Alfred	Firetail
Beersheba	Silver Star
Lord Wellington	Pomona
Spring Glory	Lady Kesteven
Mrs. E. H. Krelage	Bonfire

LARGE-CUPPED GROUP	POETICUS GROUP
Fortune	Actæa
John Evelyn	Snow King
Sir Watkin	Thelma
Scarlet Leader	Dulcimer
Carlton	
Firebird	JONQUIL GROUP
Red Marley	Odorus regulosi
Mary Blonck	General Pershing

Soil Requirements: The bulbs should be planted in a good general purpose soil mixture of two parts loam, one part leaf mold and one part sand.

Culture: The planting should take place in the autumn, either in pots or in flats, and they should be placed in storage for a minimum period of twelve weeks. A coldframe or outdoor pit will provide satisfactory conditions for storage and the pots or flats should be covered with several inches of sand or coal ashes. The pots may be brought in from storage in succession if desired, but if bulbs of the various Narcissus types are planted this will hardly be necessary as there will be considerable variance in the time of bloom and a succession of bloom will automatically be obtained. When the bulbs are first brought in from storage they should not be placed in full light for several days. If forced at a cool temperature, 50 to 55 degrees F. at night, the blooms will be of a superior quality and will last as well as cut flowers.

Poinsettias are the most decorative of all plants for the Christmas season, and if conditions are favorable it is possible to have well-grown, specimen plants even in the small greenhouse.

Propagation: Poinsettias are propagated by cuttings taken from mature stock plants. After the flowering season is over, the stock plants are usually lifted and placed under a bench for a period of ten or twelve weeks. The temperature of the house should range between 50 and 60 degrees F. and the plants should be kept very dry—not dry enough, however, to allow the wood to shrivel. About the first of April the plants should be potted up or replanted in the bench, being pruned back heavily. They should be watered thoroughly and the stems should be syringed occasionally. A rich soil should be used for the stock plants consisting of 3 parts loam and 1 part rotted manure with a light application of superphosphate. The first cuttings may be taken early in July. They may be cut at a node or with a slight heel of old wood from the parent stem. As the plants bleed readily, the cuttings should be dropped into cold water for a few moments (not over five minutes). The cuttings should be trimmed so that only the two top leaves remain, and they should be rooted in a medium of moderately fine, sterilized sand, being shaded during the day. The cuttings should be well rooted and ready for potting in about three weeks. A mixture of 2 parts loam, 1 part sand and 1 part well-rotted manure is recommended.

Soil Requirements: Poinsettias thrive best in a soil of medium fertility with a slightly acid reaction, the pH ranging between 6.0 and 7.0. For the final potting or benching soil, the following mixture is recommended: 2 parts silt loam, 1 part manure, 1 part sand. To each $2\frac{1}{2}$ bushels of soil add a 4-inch flowerpotful of superphosphate and a 4-inch pot of horn shavings. Peat should not be used in any form, as it is detrimental to the best development of the plants.

Culture: The plants may be shifted into larger pots as they develop or they may be benched. If well branched, symmetrical plants are desired poinsettias may be pinched back until early September. The ideal temperature for poinsettias ranges between 60 and 65 degrees F. The temperature should never be allowed to drop below 60 degrees F. at night. The plants are extremely sensitive to drafts and are very easily injured by chilling or by overwatering. Under such conditions the leaves will turn yellow and drop.

Primroses (Primula): There are several species of Primula which are excellent when grown as potted plants in the greenhouse. They are very decorative when in flower and bloom over a long season. Among the most popular species for greenhouse culture are P. Forbesii, P. kewensis, P. malacoides, P. obconica and P. sinensis.

Propagation: Primroses are propagated by seed which should be sown in February or early March. Germination will be hastened if the seeds are soaked for a few hours previous to sowing. When the young seedlings have attained sufficient size they may be transplanted into flats or into small pots, a soil mixture of 3 parts good loam and 1 part well-rotted manure being used. As the plants develop they may be shifted into larger pots. As the plants have a tendency to wilt badly they should be shaded after each transplanting.

Soil Requirements: Primulas prefer a slightly acid soil with a pH ranging between 6.0 and 7.0. The final potting mixture should consist of 3 parts good loam, 2 parts well-rotted manure and 1 part sand. To each 2½ bushels of soil a 4-inch pot of a 4–12–4 complete fertilizer should be added. No peat should be used in the potting mixture.

Culture: Primroses require an abundance of moisture, and the pots should never be allowed to dry out. During the summer the pots may be kept in a lightly shaded greenhouse or they may be placed on a bed of ashes in a coldframe under a lath shade. The plants prefer a moderately cool temperature during the winter—a temperature ranging between 50 and 60 degrees F. being considered ideal.

Roses: There are many varieties of roses which are admirably adapted to greenhouse culture and which will give abundant bloom throughout the winter months. Among the most popular varieties are:

Better Times	Golden Sceptre	R. M. S. Queen Mary
Copper Lustre	Happy Days	Talisman
Golden Rapture	Joanna Hill	

Propagation: Greenhouse roses may be propagated by budding, by cuttings or by grafting. Grafting is the most approved method and the one most commonly employed by commercial growers. As the propagation of roses is a highly specialized business it is advisable for the owner of a small greenhouse to purchase strong, healthy pot-grown plants which are suitable for forcing.

Soil Requirements: Roses prefer a slightly acid soil with a pH ranging between 6.0 and 7.0. A rich compost, consisting of 3 parts good loam and 1 part rotted manure will give excellent results.

Culture: A temperature ranging between 58 and 62 degrees F. at night and between 70 and 75 degrees in the daytime is considered ideal for roses. Roses may be grown either in raised benches or in solid beds. Good drainage is essential and beds or benches should be narrow, preferably not over 4 feet wide, as the best blooms are invariably produced on the outside plants. The plants may be set in their permanent position in the greenhouse between the middle of May and the first of July, being spaced from 12 to 14 inches apart. The plants should be set a little deeper than they were when growing in the pots. During this period when the plants are becoming established, they should be watered thoroughly, but at no time should the soil be allowed to become too saturated with moisture; the walks of the house should be kept damp and the foliage should be sprayed several times a day during sunny weather. The temperature should be kept as low as possible and the house should be well ventilated. No flower buds should be allowed to form until early in September. As the plants develop, wire may be stretched along the side of the benches and wire stakes may be placed beside the plants to provide support. During the growing season very shallow cultivation should be given, and at the time of flowering applications of a complete fertilizer, 4–12–4, may be given every three or four weeks, being applied at the rate of 1 pound to every 100 square feet of bench area. Greenhouse roses will usually continue to give good results over a period of three or four years, sometimes longer. Plants which are to be carried over in the benches should be given a period of rest during the summer. Beginning about the middle of June water should be withheld gradually. The plants should not be allowed to become too dry, however. During this period the plants should be pruned vigorously. Weak stems should be pruned more severely than strong ones. The plants should be cut back to within approximately 18 or 20 inches. A few inches of top-soil may be removed and the bed or bench may be refilled with rich compost.

Saintpaulia (African Violet)
For cultural details see page 449.

Stevia: The chief value of Stevia is a filler-in for mixed bouquets. The small, white flowers are produced in abundance on long stems which are heavily clothed with deep green foliage.

Propagation: Stevia is propagated by stem cuttings taken from the stock plants in January. As soon as the cuttings have rooted they may be potted up in 2½-inch pots.

Soil Requirements: A good rich greenhouse compost will give excellent results. If a light application of superphosphate is made at the time that the plants are brought into the greenhouse the danger of oversucculent soft-stemmed growth will be reduced.

Culture: As the plants develop, they may be shifted on into 4-inch pots and later into 7-inch pots, being grown in a cool temperature of 40 to 45 degrees F. As soon as all danger of frost is over, the pots may be set on a bed of cinders in a coldframe, or the plants may be transferred to nursery rows. During the summer the plants should be kept pinched back in order that they may become bushy and symmetrical. In the autumn, before the first frost, the plants should be brought into the greenhouse. They may be grown on in pots or they may be planted in beds or benches, being spaced 12 inches apart. Stevia prefers a cool house with a night temperature of approximately 50 degrees F. The plants will normally come into flower shortly before the Christmas season. The flowering period may be hastened by shading the plants with black cloth for four hours a day for a period of thirty days, beginning September 1.

Stocks: The delicate fragrance of the Stocks adds greatly to their appeal as a cut flower, and they do extremely well under greenhouse conditions.

VARIETIES OF MERIT

Antique Copper	Deep Apricot Improved
Apple Blossom	Lilac-Lavender
Chamois Pink	Santa Maria

Propagation: The seeds should be sown in flats in early August, the young seedlings being transplanted either directly into the benches where they are to flower, or carried on in pots or flats until bench space is available.

Soil Requirements: A light, porous and well-drained soil of good fertility is considered ideal.

Culture: When the young plants are shifted to the benches they should be spaced from 8 to 10 inches apart each way. The plants should be pinched back once in order to induce branching, and they will begin to flower late in the winter. The coolest possible temperature is to be desired, a night temperature of 48 to 50 degrees F. being considered ideal. Stocks are often used to follow on after the chrysanthemums have been removed from the benches.

Schizanthus (Butterflyflower): Seldom at its best in the garden under the heat of our summer sun, the lovely Schizanthus is one of those annuals admirably adapted to greenhouse culture. Only indoors does it reach full perfection, and a well-grown pot of Schizanthus is a thing of beauty. The small, orchid-shaped flowers in tones of luminous pink, lavender, and white, are borne in great profusion and are lovely both for cutting and as potted plants.

Propagation: Seed may be sown in early September and the plants grown on in pots for early spring bloom.

Soil Requirements: A soil composed of 2 parts good, fibrous loam and 1 part well-rotted cow manure will give excellent results.

Culture: The plants may either be grown on in pots, or they may be benched when they have reached sufficient size, being spaced not less than 12 inches apart. They thrive best in a moderately cool temperature of 45 to 50 degrees F. at night. If the plants are allowed to become somewhat potbound, the blooming period will be hastened.

Sweet Peas (Lathyrus odoratus): So delightfully decorative are sweet peas for cut flower arrangements that they are an important crop in the small home greenhouse, even though little space can be allotted to them. Some of the winter flowering types are exquisite both in form and in coloring, the flowers being borne on long, slender stems.

VARIETIES OF MERIT

Ball Rose Supreme	Majestic Rose
Bridesmaid	Michigan
Daphne	Rhapsody
Fiesta	Treasure Island
Gardenia	Triumph
Hiawatha	Twilight

Propagation: Sweet peas are propagated by seed. As the seeds have a hard outer covering, germination may be hastened by soaking them for 24 hours previous to sowing. The seeds may be sown directly in the beds or benches where they are to flower, or they may be sown in small pots or in flats, being later transplanted to their permanent position in the greenhouse. A light soil mixture should be used, consisting of equal parts of sand and loam. The time of flowering will depend to a considerable extent upon the date when the seed is sown. Seeds of the early or winter-flowering type, which is the type best suited for greenhouse culture, sown about the middle of July will flower from October through January. If sown September 1 the flowering period will extend from February to the middle of March, and if sown late in September the plants will flower in March, April and May. For early bloom it is therefore necessary to start the seeds in midsummer.

Soil Requirements: Sweet peas thrive best in a soil which is very nearly neutral in its reaction and which is of an open and porous texture. Good drainage is essential, as the plants are seriously injured by excessive amounts of water in the soil. A good, rich, fibrous compost is considered ideal. To this may be added a 0–10–10 commercial fertilizer, applied at the rate of 4 to 5 pounds per 100 square feet of soil area. An excess of nitrogen in the soil is detrimental to the best development of the plants.

Culture: Sweet peas prefer a cool growing temperature and from the time the young seedlings have begun growth they should be kept as cool as possible in order that they may develop good root systems. During the summer the greenhouse should be well ventilated, and adequate shade should be provided for the seedlings. Throughout the entire growing period low temperatures should be maintained. During the winter the night temperature of the greenhouse should not go above 50 degrees F. and day temperatures should not range over 55 to 60 degrees F., with 65 degrees F. as a maximum high. Solid beds are preferred, rather than raised benches. The rows may be spaced from 3 to 4 feet apart, double drills being approximately 6 inches apart. The plants are allowed to remain thickly in the rows, being spaced hardly more than a few inches apart. As soon as the plants have become well established they should be provided with adequate support. Wire or stout twine on wire supports may be used. When the plants come into bloom all flowers should be kept picked. If seed pods are allowed to form, subsequent flowering will be seriously checked and the flowers will have a tendency to become short stemmed.

Tulips: Both as potted plants and as cut flowers, Tulips add their share to the galaxy of bloom in the greenhouse during the spring months, and a succession of bloom may be had over a period of many weeks.

VARIETIES OF MERIT

The early varieties force more readily than the Darwin and Breeder types, but under favorable cultural conditions most varieties may be forced with a fair degree of success. Some of the varieties best suited to forcing are:

SINGLE EARLY

Cottage Maid	La Reine
General de Wet	Rose Luisante
Golden Queen	Le Rêve

DOUBLE EARLY

Murillo	Peach Blossom

COTTAGE TYPE

Inglescombe Pink	Dido
Moonlight	Griselde

DARWIN TYPE

Anton Mauve	The Bishop
Faust	Venus
Kathryn Watson	Clara Butt
Margaret	William Copeland

BREEDER TYPE

Cherbourg	Bronze Queen
Indian Chief	

SPECIES TULIP

Clusiana

Soil Requirements: A soil mixture consisting of 2 parts good loam, 1 part leaf mold and 1 part sand is recommended.

Culture: The bulbs should be planted in November, either in pots or in flats. Ample drainage should be provided and the tip of the bulb should be from 1 to 2 inches below the surface of the soil. Unless bulbs which have been especially prepared for forcing are used, tulips require a long period of storage in order to make good root growth. They should be kept in storage for a period varying from twelve to fourteen weeks. They may be placed in a coldframe or in an outdoor pit. It is a wise plan to place a light layer of straw or excelsior over the pots or flats to afford protection for any shoots which may push through, and a 6-inch layer of ashes or sand may then be added. Early varieties may be brought in after twelve weeks of storage, late varieties at the end of fourteen weeks. If a succession of bloom is desired, the pots may be brought in at intervals of every 10 days. When first brought in from storage the pots should preferably be placed in a cool, semi-dark place, as it is wise not to expose them to direct sunlight for several days. Tulips should be forced at a comparatively low temperature, 55 to 60 degrees F. approximating the ideal. A high temperature is conducive to more rapid development, but the quality of the flowers is seriously affected. After the pots have been placed in full sunlight they should be turned every few days in order that the flowers and leaves may develop evenly.

Violets: Violets are admirably suited to the cool greenhouse and if the plants are grown under favorable conditions they will give an abundance of bloom during the winter months.

Propagation: The method of propagation usually preferred by commercial growers is that of cuttings taken from healthy terminal shoots between the middle of January and the middle of March. Violets may also be propagated by the division of the parent plant after the flowering season is over and by root cuttings taken during February and March. After the young plants are well established they may be planted in flats. During the summer the plants may be kept in coldframes or they may be planted in the open ground. Some growers prefer to transplant the young plants into their permanent position in May. If this practice is followed adequate ventilation must be given and the house must be heavily shaded during the summer.

Soil Requirements: Violets prefer a rather heavy, sandy loam soil, well drained, yet retentive of moisture. A good, moderately rich compost is considered ideal.

Culture: Violets may be grown either in solid beds or in raised benches. Most growers prefer solid beds as it is easier to maintain a cool, moist soil. Cool growing conditions are one of the essentials for success. Single-flowering varieties prefer a night temperature of 45 to 50 degrees F. and a day temperature ranging between 60 and 65 degrees F. Double-flowering varieties prefer a temperature of about 5 degrees lower. High temperatures are conducive to an excessive amount of vegetative growth which is produced at the expense of flowers. The plants require an abundance of moisture and an adequate supply of fresh air.

Wallflowers (Cheiranthus Cheiri)*:* The English Wallflowers are prized for their delightful fragrance and for their quaintly decorative quality. They are of easy culture and are admirably adapted to the cool greenhouse.

Propagation: Wallflowers are propagated by seed. For bloom during the winter months the seeds should be sown the previous March. The young seedlings may be pricked out into small pots or into flats as soon as they have made sufficient growth.

Soil Requirements: A good, rich compost will give excellent results.

Culture: During the summer months the young plants may be carried on in pots or they may be planted in nursery beds in the open ground. Wallflowers require a very cool growing temperature. The night temperature should range between 45 and 50 degrees F. and the day temperature but a few degrees higher. Throughout their growing period, the plants require a liberal amount of water. Wallflowers may be grown in pots, in raised benches, or in solid beds, the plants being spaced approximately 12 inches apart.

PLANTS WHICH MAY BE GROWN IN POTS FOR DECORATION IN THE HOUSE

Abutilon hybridum	Chrysanthemum	Kalanchoë
Acacia armata	Cineraria cruenta	Lantana Camara
Drummondii	Cyclamen	Poinsettia
Agathæa cœlestis	Cytisus canariensis (Genista)	Primula—in variety
Astilbe japonica	racemosus	Saintpaulia ionantha
Azalea—in great variety	Dicentra spectabilis	Solanum (Jerusalem Cherry)
Begonia—in great variety	Euphorbia fulgens (jacquiniæflora)	Strelitzia reginæ
Bougainvillea glabra	Fuchsia hybrida	(Bird of Paradise Flower)
Browallia var. speciosa major	Gardenia Veitchii	Streptosolen Jamesonii
Camellia japonica	Geranium	Zygocactus truncatus
Chorizema ilicifolium	Gloxinia	(Christmas Cactus)

PLANTS TO BE GROWN FOR CUT FLOWERS

Antirrhinum	Chrysanthemum	Lupine	Scabiosa
Bouvardia	Cynoglossum amabile	Mignonette	Schizanthus
Boston Yellow Daisy	Didiscus cœruleus	Myosotis	Stevia
Buddleia	(Bluelace Flower)	Nemesia	Stock
Calendula	Gerbera Jamesonii	Orchid	Ursinia
Carnation	Heliophila	Rose	Violet
Clarkia	Larkspur	Salpiglossis	Wallflower

BULBS, CORMS, AND TUBERS SUITABLE FOR FORCING

Amaryllis—Hippeastrum vittatum hybrids	Lilium candidum	Narcissus—all species
Anemone coronaria	elegans	and varieties
Calla	Krameri	Ornithogalum lacteum
Convallaria majalis (Lily-of-the-Valley)	longiflorum—in variety	Ranunculus acris
Freesia	Formosanum	Tulip: in great variety
Gladiolus	regale	
Hyacinth	speciosum album	
Iris (Bulbous)	speciosum rubrum	
Lilium auratum	tenuifolium	
Batemanniæ	tigrinum	

CUT BRANCHES OF SHRUBS WHICH MAY BE FORCED

Flowering Cherries—all species and varieties
Flowering Crabs—all species and varieties
Flowering Dogwood (Cornus florida)
Forsythia—in great variety

Japanese Quince (Chænomeles japonica)
Star Magnolia (Magnolia stellata)
Thunberg Spirea (Spiræa Thunbergii)
Viburnums—in great variety

SHRUBS WHICH MAY BE FORCED IN POTS OR TUBS

Astilbe japonica
Azaleas—in great variety
Chænomeles japonica (Japanese Quince)
Clethra alnifolia (Sweet Pepperbush)
Daphne cneorum (Garland Flower)
Deutzia—in variety

Philadelphus Lemoinei (Lemoine's Mock-orange)
Pieris floribunda (Lily-of-the-Valley Shrub)
Prunus tomentosa (Nankin Cherry)
Rhododendron—in variety
Spiræa prunifolia (Bridalwreath Spirea)
Spiræa Thunbergii (Thunberg Spirea)

PLANTS FOR THE COOL GREENHOUSE

FOR CUT FLOWERS

Antirrhinum	Didiscus	Larkspur	Statice
Bouvardia	Dimorphotheca	Lupine	Stevia
Calendula	Erlangea	Mignonette	Stock
Carnation	Eupatorium	Myosotis	Streptosolen
Centaurea	Euphorbia	Nemesia	Sweet Pea
Chrysanthemum	Feverfew	Salpiglossis	Violet
Clarkia	Gerbera	Scabiosa	Wallflower
Cynoglossum	Gypsophila	Schizanthus	

POTTED PLANTS

Acacia	Begonia	Cineraria cruenta	Primula
Agathæa	Browallia	Cyclamen	Solanum
Ardisia	Calceolaria	Cytisus	Strelitzia
Astilbe japonica	Camellia japonica	Hydrangea	Zygocactus
Azalea	Chorizema ilicifolium	Kalanchoë	

FOLIAGE PLANTS AND VINES

Araucaria	Cissus rhombifolia (Grape Ivy)	Grevillea robusta	Peperomia
Asparagus plumosus	Dracæna	Hedera helix	Philodendron
Sprengeri	Ficus—in variety	Palms—in variety	Senecio mikanioides
Aspidistra	Ficus repens (vine)	Pandanus	Vinca major

BULBS

Anemone coronaria	Gladiolus	Lilium longiflorum	Ranunculus acris
Calochortus	Hyacinth	speciosum	Tulip
Calla	Iris (bulbous)	candidum	
Freesia	Ixia	Narcissus	

VINES FOR THE GREENHOUSE

Allamanda Hendersonii
Antigonon leptopus (Coral-vine)
Asparagus plumosus
Asparagus Sprengeri
Clerodendrum Thompsonæ
Ficus repens (Climbing Fig)
Ficus repens, variety minimus
Hedera helix (English Ivy)—in great variety
Jasminum grandiflorum

Passiflora (Passion Flower)
Philodendron cordata
micens
pertusum
Senecio mikanioides (German Ivy)
Stigmaphyllon ciliatum
Tradescantia fluminensis (Wandering Jew)
Vinca major

PALMS FOR DECORATIVE PURPOSES

Areca lutescens	Kentia Belmoreana	Latania borbonica	Phœnix rupicola
Cocos Weddelliana	Kentia Forsteriana	Livistona rotundifolia	

FERNS FOR DECORATIVE PURPOSES

Adiantum cuneatum (Maidenhair fern)
  farleyense

Asplenium Nidus (Bird's-Nest fern)
Cyrtomium falcatum

Nephrolepsis exaltata (Sword fern)
Pteris cretica

FOLIAGE PLANTS

Araucaria excelsa (Norfolk Island Pine)
Ardisia
Aspidistra lurida
Caladium bicolor (Fancy-leaved Caladium)
Codlæum variegatum (Croton)
Dieffenbachia Seguine (Dumb Cane)
Dracæna
Ficus elastica (Rubber Plant)

Fittonia argyroneura
  Verschaffeltii
Grevillea robusta (Silk Oak)
Pandanus utilis
  Veitchii
Peperomia cordata
  Verschaffeltii
Sansevieria (Bowstring-Hemp, Snake Plant)

PLANTS FOR THE INTERMEDIATE OR WARM GREENHOUSE

FOR CUT FLOWERS

Begonia—some varieties
Cattleya
Cypripedium

Gardenia
Gloxinia

Easter Lily
Lily-of-the-Valley

Poinsettia
Rose

POTTED PLANTS

Azalea—in variety
Bougainvillea

Clerodendrum
Fuchsia

Hydrangea
Kalanchoë

Lantana
Poinsettia

FOLIAGE PLANTS AND VINES

Asparagus plumosus
  Sprengeri
Aspidistra

Ferns—in variety
Ficus, in variety

Ficus repens (vine)
Palms—in variety

Pandanus
Philodendron

BULBS

Hyacinth   Tulip

LATH HOUSES

A small lath house is a valuable adjunct to the garden and serves many uses. It makes it possible to grow to perfection certain plants which require protection from full sunlight and hot, drying winds, such as tuberous begonias, achimenes, streptocarpus, clivias, fuchsias, gesnerias, African violets and ferns. It provides an excellent holding area for potted plants and hanging baskets which are to be used on patios and terraces when they have reached full development. It offers ideal conditions for hardening off young seedlings, and started tubers, and for giving a few days of much needed protection to young transplants. It is useful also in many phases of propagation, particularly if no greenhouse is available, as it provides an excellent place to start seed flats and to develop a small propagating area for cuttings.

Within recent years lath houses have come into very general use in commercial nurseries and on home properties in areas where the climate is hot and dry, and they are also considered a valuable asset in humid areas. Not only does a lath house reduce the intensity of the sunlight but it also provides a cooler temperature, and makes it possible to maintain a higher degree of humidity.

A lath house is easy to construct and is relatively inexpensive. The orientation of the house is important. It should always be constructed so that the laths run north and south, in order to provide for alternating sun and shadow within the house. If the laths run east and west the

A LATH HOUSE IN CALIFORNIA

shadows are thrown on the same area for long periods through the day and the remaining area receives direct sunlight, which tends to defeat the purpose of the house. The shape and size of the house will be determined by the site available and the needs and preferences of the owner. A lean-to against the side of a garage or some other building is one of the most economical types as far as construction is concerned. The size of the house should be in multiples of lath lengths in order to avoid extra cutting. Laths are usually obtainable in standard four, six and eight foot lengths. The spacing of the laths on the frame will be determined to some extent by the climate. In most areas the width of a single lath will prove the most satisfactory spacing. However, in areas of long periods of intense sunshine somewhat closer spacing is recommended, and in areas where there is considerable cloudy weather slightly wider spacing may be desirable.

Although lath houses are very often constructed with flat roofs there are certain advantages to the sloping roof. If the laths are laid from the ridge to the eaves on a sloping roof the rain will tend to run down the laths and the plants will be protected from too much drip. This is a matter of much greater importance in areas of heavy rains than it is in hot, dry climates.

The permanence of a lath house will depend, to a considerable extent, upon the type of material used in its construction. Plaster lath can be used in small houses but it is thin and sometimes warps badly. Lattice strips two to three inches in width and $\frac{1}{4}$ of an inch in thickness will prove more durable and will more than justify the additional cost involved. Cedar, cypress and redwood are the most desirable woods to use, as they have remarkable ability to resist decay and will give lasting satisfaction. However, they are expensive in many areas and when costs of construction are a major consideration it is possible to use cheaper types of lumber which have been chemically treated to retard decay.

The most permanent type of lath house is one built of aluminum. The construction is easy, as the aluminum strips and supports come cut to specified measurements, and upkeep and repair are reduced to a minimum.

A lath house may take the form of merely a lath roof over the area, or it may be enclosed at the rear, or on two, three or all four sides. Climatic conditions will help to determine the type of house best suited to one's needs. In areas where there are hot, drying winds and intense summer sunshine more protection will be needed than in cooler, more humid sections.

Within the lath house ground-beds, benches and various forms of shelving may be used for the growing and staging of plants. Plants in a lath house should not be crowded, as it is important to provide for a good circulation of air. Watering must be done with care and with the needs of the individual plant in mind. It is possible to have a house equipped with a humidistat and an automatic watering system which will maintain the desired degree of humidity.

XXXVIII

THE HOME FRUIT GARDEN

*By John A. Andrew, Jr.**

THE small home fruit garden, if it is carefully planned and well maintained, will yield a bountiful and varied supply of fruit throughout the season and will be a constant source of pleasure and of profit. Many choice varieties of fruit, far superior in quality to those grown commercially, may be produced in the home garden. When fruit is to be shipped a great distance it is often necessary to pick it long before it is fully ripe and much of its sweetness and flavor is lost in consequence. Fruit grown in the home garden may be harvested at its finest stage of ripeness and will possess a quality which is unobtainable in the commercial market.

Fruit Trees for Ornamental Purposes

In addition to their purely utilitarian uses, most fruit trees have a decidedly decorative value. There are few things more beautiful than an apple tree when in full bloom, and both pears and apples are often very picturesque in outline. On a place of modest size, fruit trees may play a very important part in the landscape development of the property. They may be used as shade trees upon the terrace or upon the lawn, they may be planted along the driveway, or they may be trained against some supporting structure such as a fence or wall. Espaliered fruit trees are often seen in English gardens and in France, and they are becoming increasingly popular in this country. An "Espalier" is a trellis or open support upon which a vine or a woody plant may be trained. Apple trees, pears, peaches, plums, nectarines and quinces may be very readily used in this way. Such trees are usually trained to a given number of branches (see illustration), and

* Revised by Stephen Patronsky, Assistant Professor of Pomology, Rutgers University.

they should preferably be grown on a wall facing southeast.

Purchasing and Planting Nursery Stock

Where to Buy

When one considers the initial cost of nursery stock he may be inclined to shop around for lower prices. One should know that the initial cost is the lowest cost of all. The years of pruning, spraying and general upkeep necessary to bring trees into a successful fruiting period cost much more. Therefore, the reputation of the nurseryman should be your guide, as there are many factors under his control which insure you against getting poor stock. Many people prefer to buy their stock directly from the nurseryman, but this is not necessary provided the firm with whom you are doing business is honest and reputable. Remember that you get what you pay for, and that if the initial cost of a good tree is slightly more than a second-grade type, the first tree won't have to produce much more in later years to make up for this difference.

When to Buy

It is necessary first to decide and plan what fruits are needed for the home garden. When this decision has been made, the order for stock should be placed well in advance of planting time. If ordering is delayed nurseries will be in their rush season and certain varieties may be exhausted. Therefore, by ordering early and stating shipping date, the stock will arrive in ample time for best planting. One should plan to set the stock as soon as the frost is out of the ground.

543

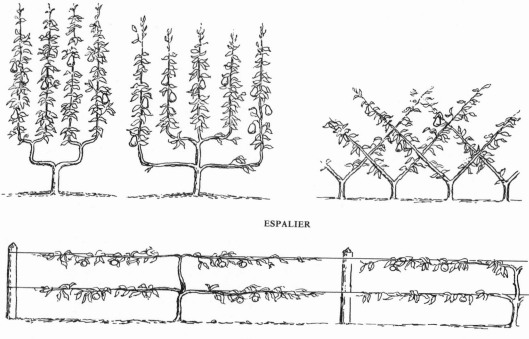

ESPALIER

CORDON

Choosing Varieties and Dwarfed Trees

The home gardener should specify the varieties which he desires, but should avoid new highly advertised varieties and species which may not be adapted to the local conditions. It is best to check with the local county agent or agricultural experiment station for recommended varieties.

A dwarf tree is a standard variety grafted to a dwarfing root stock. This root stock causes the tree to make less annual growth and remain a smaller tree throughout its life. These dwarf trees are better suited to the home garden because they come into bearing at an earlier age, require less space, and are easier to spray and prune.

The root stock for the dwarf trees should be specified in order that the gardener may know that the trees are actually dwarfs rather than weak, standard trees. Dwarfing root stock has a shallow root system. Therefore it is advisable to stake these trees.

The point of the graft should be left above ground in planting because, if it is covered, roots will form above the union and the tree will become standard in size.

Grade to Buy

Trees. Trees are graded according to their height and thickness of trunk, and are priced accordingly. Fruit trees are offered in two or three sizes of one- and two-year-old stock. The A, or best, grade costs only a few cents more than a smaller tree. It seems to be a matter of preference as to whether one- or two-year-old stock shall be planted. However, there is no doubt that the best should be purchased, regardless of age.

The main advantages in purchasing one-year trees are as follows:

1. Not as many roots are broken off in transplanting
2. Easily pruned to desired height
3. No branches broken in shipping
4. Better selection of main branches the following year
5. More quickly handled and planted

Bush Fruits. Bushes are more easily handled and set out than trees. A well-grown two-year-old bush will give excellent results and possibly produce fruit sooner and in larger quantities than a one-year-old bush. The only reason for buying a one-year-old bush is to be sure that it is of the best grade, as sometimes a two-year-old bush is inferior in size and appearance at the end of its first year's growth.

Care of Stock Before Planting

Often the stock is received before planting conditions are satisfactory. The land may not be prepared, or it may be too wet. Other things coming at the same time of year may also necessitate a delay in planting for a short time.

As soon as the stock is received, it should be removed from the package to prevent sweating and possible deterioration. It may be planted temporarily in a trench or kept in a cool damp cellar for several days. The roots should not be permitted to dry out. Plant the stock before the buds begin to open; otherwise, if dry soil conditions exist, watering may be necessary. Also the roots should have a chance to establish themselves before the warm weather begins. For this reason the earlier the stock is planted in the spring, the greater the chance it will have to establish its root system before the buds begin to swell. This should result in a greater shoot growth the first season when planted.

When to Plant

Nursery stock may be planted either in the spring or in the fall. In some cases, fall planting is advisable especially if the stock is to be planted on heavy land which is apt to be too wet at the proper planting time in the spring. Fall planting also enables a tree to get its root system established so that the period of adjustment after transplanting is long past when conditions are favorable for growth in the spring. Weather conditions are more stable in the fall and the soil may be in better condition for planting.

The advantages of spring planting are as follows:

1. The stock makes considerable top and root growth before winter.

2. There is one winter less to control rodents.

3. In a severe winter the stock may winter-kill if set in the fall.

Laying Out The Orchard

Definite planting distances are recommended for each fruit. These should be closely observed. The distances in most cases seem enormous especially after the trees are planted. These distances are the recommendations obtained from many experiments. In many cases, one is puzzled when trees are set next to each other which have different planting distances. This is easily solved as follows. Apples and sour cherries are to be planted in adjacent rows. How far should the sour cherries be planted from the apples? Take the sum of the two planting distances as 35 feet for apples and 20 feet for sour cherries, which equals 55 feet and divide by two. Twenty-seven feet will be about the correct distance to plant the sour cherries from the apples.

Be sure to plant the trees in a straight line, as once they are set they are a picture of your accuracy. Establish a base line along which the first row of trees is to be planted and take all your measurements from it. Wire or coarse string is very practicable to use for this purpose. Then measure off the required distance for each tree on this line and insert a small stake at that point. To lay out the second row, measure the required distance from the base line at each end and set up another line. The formula which is used to insure unquestionable accuracy is: "The square of the hypotenuse of a right-angled triangle is equal to the sum of the squares of the other two sides."

Therefore, letting y equal the unknown distance,

$$y^2 = A^2 \text{ (or } 40^2) + B^2 \text{ (or } 40^2)$$
$$y^2 = 1600 + 1600$$
$$y^2 = 3200$$
$$y = 56.56 \text{ feet.}$$

If the trees are set out correctly, the line C (see diagram on page 546) will be just 56.56 feet long.

Planting the Orchard

The equipment for planting consists of a round pointed shovel and a planting board.

To make a planting board, take a board approximately 3 feet long and 6 inches wide. Make a V-shaped notch in each end and one in the middle.

Place the notch in the middle of the board up to the peg which marks the spot where a tree is to be set. Place a peg in the notches at each end of the board and remove the board. Then remove the peg in the middle. Dig a hole between the two pegs which are left. First remove the top-soil and lay it aside. When the sub-soil, which is yellowish in color, appears, place it in a separate pile. Make the hole just wide enough to receive the roots without crowding. Dig deep enough to allow the tree to be set 2 or 3 inches deeper than in the nursery. Make the two sides of the hole parallel and thus have the bottom as wide as the top. This will allow the soil to be packed uniformly around the roots and avoid any danger of leaving air spaces which would dry them out.

Next, put the planting board back in place so that the two outside pegs will fit into the V-shaped notch in each end. Then place the tree in the hole with its trunk fitting snugly into the notch in the middle. Have one person hold the tree in place while the other puts in the top-soil first. Move the tree up and down several times with a vertical motion. This will permit the soil to sift in around the roots. When the roots are covered, the soil should be firmed if it is not too wet. Then the sub-soil should be put on top and firmed again. The planting board is removed, the tree is in the correct spot, and the next tree is waiting to be planted. Manure or fertilizer should not be put in the hole at planting time.

Pollination

Some years ago, between 1820–1830, in a thriving Ohio village called Cincinnati, several farmers noticed that one of their neighbors obtained better and larger yields of strawberries than they did. Their problem was solved when the son of this successful grower told one of his neighbors that practically all of his plants were imperfect or pistillate varieties and that flowers which contain pollen are necessary for pollination. Therefore, a staminate or pollen-bearing variety must be planted with one which has insufficient pollen.

Pollination may be defined as the transfer of pollen from the stamen to the stigma or female part of the blossom. Pollen of many varieties of fruits is not borne in large quantities and is not carried far by the wind. The pollen merely falls on the stigmas or is carried on the bodies of insects that visit the flowers.

In some varieties of fruits the pollen produced is capable of fertilizing the ovules of the same variety, while others must receive pollen from another variety to be successfully cross-fertilized. The causes of self-unfruitfulness are as follows:

1. Lack of visible pollen.

2. Discharge of pollen at a time when pistil is not receptive.

3. Production of insufficient visible pollen by some varieties.

4. In some fruits and varieties the male flowers and female flowers are borne on separate plants.

These causes of self-unfruitfulness show that plants are somewhat modified in order to avoid self-fertilization and to secure cross-fertilization.

Many years ago, fruit trees were grown from seed. This resulted in the introduction of many worthless varieties. Little was known or done about pollination. However, this was not very important as so many different varieties were interplanted that cross-pollination took place naturally.

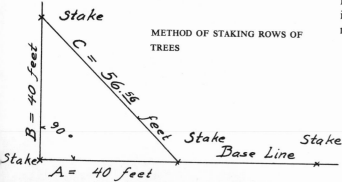

METHOD OF STAKING ROWS OF TREES

PLANTING BOARD

As new varieties were developed, fruit growers began to select fewer but better varieties. These varieties were arranged in rows, planted apart at a definite distance, and given proper cultural methods.

However, many trees of a single variety planted on a large acreage were too far away from trees of another variety for cross-pollination to be successful.

Many crosses have been made using the same plant to supply, as well as to receive pollen, from another variety. For example, at an Eastern Experiment Station, the Wealthy variety of apple formed seven fruits from each hundred blossoms pollinated with its own pollen. When the pollen of the Delicious variety was applied to the stigmas of the Wealthy a 31 percent set was the result.

If a fruit tree fails to set fruit because of lack of proper pollination, this condition may be corrected in several ways:

1. The quickest method is to place bouquets of blossoms of another variety in the tree at blooming time. These bouquets should be placed in a pail of water so that the flower will last as long as possible, and should be hung in the uppermost part of the tree. This method to be successful depends entirely on the presence of bees or other insects.

2. Another method is to top-graft the tree to a different variety. It usually requires three or four years to get results by this method. Meanwhile bouquets of blossoms may be used in order to keep up production as heretofore described.

Before planting varieties of tree fruits it is well worth the time to write to your State Experiment Station for further advice.

Growing and Fruiting Habits

The greatest disappointment an amateur receives in growing fruits is due primarily to a lack of understanding of the essential principles of growing and bearing. One is disappointed if a tree, several years after planting, fails to bear fruit, though he may have pruned, sprayed, and fertilized it conscientiously. There is considerable variation in the time it takes a tree to come into bearing, but with other con-

ditions being favorable, it may be only a varietal difference. Some varieties of apples take as long as eight years to begin bearing while most varieties of peaches and sour cherries fruit within three years.

Until a tree begins to produce blossom buds, it usually makes a rapid vigorous growth if it is in a healthy condition. Young trees may make as much as 4 or 5 feet of growth in a single season. The buds formed are vegetative and contain only leaves. As the tree gets ready to bear fruit, a marked change is noticeable. Fruit buds are larger and more plump, as they have flower parts in them. Short spur-like growths occur on the pear and apple, while modifications of this appear on cherries and plums. Peach buds become larger, with two large ones surrounding a center one. A change has taken place in the vigor of the tree. Terminal growth has slowed down to 18 or 20 inches. The tree is leaving its vegetative period to enter its productive period (fruit bud formation).

Apple. Apples are borne terminally on spurs and laterally and terminally on shoots. The fruit bud is a mixed bud and contains three to eight blossoms, normally five blossoms, and a whorl of leaves.

The spurs are rough looking and irregular in their method of growth. When a spur fruits, a small bud forms at one side of it. This bud cannot fruit the next year because it has no flowers in it. This is due to the fruit on that spur which has prevented it from further development. It must have one season's time in which to develop into a fruit bud other than the year when fruit is borne. Therefore, it is conclusive that a spur will not produce fruit every year but may every other year. When a tree bears a heavy crop one year and none the next, its fruit spurs have all borne at the same time and it is called a biennial bearer. An annual bearing tree has some spurs which bear each year, but no spur bears in successive years.

Fruit spurs are productive until ten or twelve years old, and may not be more than 6 to 10 inches long at that time.

Pear. This fruit is very similar to the apple.

Peach. Peaches are borne from lateral buds formed on the previous season's growth. The buds are borne one, two, or three at a node. If three, the two outside buds are fruit buds and contain only one blossom each and no leaves, while the center bud is a leaf bud.

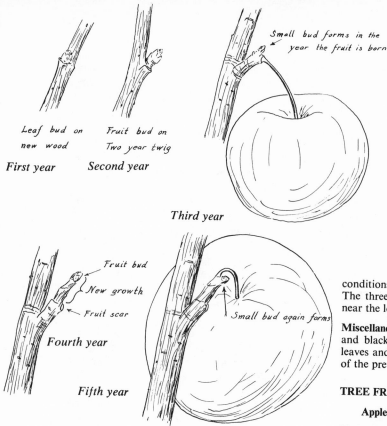

Leaf bud on new wood
First year

Fruit bud on Two year twig
Second year

Small bud forms in the year the fruit is born
Third year

Fruit bud
New growth
Fruit scar
Fourth year

Small bud again forms
Fifth year

Plum. Fruit buds are borne axially on spurs. Each fruit bud contains from one to three blossoms. Leaf buds are also on the same spur but are smaller in size. The terminal bud, as in the peach, is always a wood bud.

Cherry. The fruiting habits are very similar to those of the plum. The sour cherry often produces fruit buds on the previous season's growth, the fruits being formed near the lower part of it. Each bud usually contains from two to four flowers.

Quince. Fruit buds are lateral on the previous season's growth. The bud expands as a shoot in the spring, and after making several inches of growth, a single flower blossoms on the end of it. This habit of growth makes the quince a very twiggy bush.

Grape. Grape buds are produced on the current season's growth. The bud, which is within a single covering, is divided into three parts. The primary or main fruit-producing bud is the largest. The secondary bud is somewhat smaller and not as productive, while the smallest or tertiary bud expands as a shoot but produces no fruits. Usually, when the primary bud is not damaged by a late spring frost, the other buds fail to develop. This bud grows as a shoot and with favorable

548

conditions may make between 10 and 20 feet of growth. The three to five clusters of blossoms are borne very near the lower end.

Miscellaneous. The flowers of red and black raspberries and blackberries are borne in clusters which contain leaves and which come from axillary buds on the cane of the previous season's growth.

TREE FRUITS

Apple

Name: Pyrus malus.

Soil: A deep, well-drained, loamy soil, well supplied with organic matter, gives excellent results. Heavy, clay soils, with a hard and impervious sub-soil, should be avoided.

Planting

Age of Trees: One- and two-year-old trees are the best as they recover very quickly from the effects of transplanting and are lowest in price and easily handled. Older trees may be planted if sufficient soil is moved with the roots, but this operation is expensive and the tree's recovery is not very rapid.

Time of Planting: Apple trees may be planted during the late fall or early spring months when they are in a dormant condition, or leafless. In sections north of Philadelphia, early spring planting is preferable to fall planting as a precaution against winter injury. It is well to bear in mind that the root system of a tree is active when no noticeable top growth is taking place. Therefore, late fall or early spring planting is most desirable in order that the root system will become established before the growing season begins. A tree which is well established on its root system before top growth actually begins will make a more vigorous growth the first season.

Planting Distance: Apple trees should be planted 40 feet apart in the row and between the rows. They may, however, be set as close as 30 feet apart each way if space is extremely limited and the varieties are not of the most vigorous types.

Method of Planting: Dig a hole just large enough to receive the roots without crowding and deep enough to set the tree 2 inches deeper, except dwarf trees, than it was formerly growing in the nursery. When removing the soil keep the top- and sub-soil separate. Be sure to make the sides of the hole parallel and the bottom as wide as the top.

Trim off any broken, injured or too lengthy roots to within bounds and place the tree in the hole. Put the top-soil in first and firm it around the roots. Then put the sub-soil in and firm it again. Place the sod, grass down, around the base of the tree.

Pruning

The purpose of pruning and training young trees is to establish a strong framework of branches which will satisfactorily carry the future load of fruit.

One-year Tree: The top of a one-year-old apple tree should be cut back to a height of 36 inches from the ground after it has been set out.

Two-year Tree: Two-year-old trees may contain many branches. In this case it is essential to choose the branches for the framework and remove the others when the tree is planted. Choose three or four branches making at least a 45-degree angle with the trunk, and about 6 inches apart. They, of course, are not on the same plane but are spaced uniformly around the tree for balance. The lowest branch should be at least 18 inches from the ground. Trees which are less vigorous should be pruned back more severely, but the principle is the same in every case. Crossing, closely parallel, weak, broken, and low branches should be removed. However, it is best to leave branches which are not too thick or which do not directly compete with each other, as they materially aid in increasing the total growth.

Time of Pruning Young Apple Trees: Pruning may be done at any time that the trees are in dormant condition, or leafless. However, as winter-killing begins at the tip of a branch, pruning should not be practiced until the coldest part of the winter is past, and not later than the time at which the buds begin to swell.

Pruning Non-Bearing Young Apple Trees: Pruning should be as light as possible until the tree reaches its bearing age. This age varies greatly according to the variety. Remove one of two closely parallel branches; one of two crossing branches, as well as branches which are weak, crowding or diseased. Do not remove any branch which may not be interfering at present just to get rid of it. Such branches are a great help to the tree

for several years. Do not allow any of the so-called scaffold branches to grow beyond the leader. This will necessitate some cutting back each year as the leader should be several inches longer than the others. Always cut back to buds on one-year-old wood or to lateral branches on older wood. Permit some branches to fill in the center of the tree without overcrowding.

Pruning Young Bearing Trees: For several years after a tree begins to bear, its crops are not very heavy. Pruning should be light, so as not to cause an over-vegetative condition which will throw it out of bearing.

Pruning Bearing Trees: Pruning is beneficial to a certain point, but it may be overdone if not thoroughly understood. A man who is paid three dollars a day may cause more than fifty dollars' worth of damage if he knows little about it. Therefore, before one prunes or permits others to prune his trees, he should be thoroughly informed on the subject and should understand its principles. Less damage is caused by non-pruning than by pruning the wrong way. When a fruit tree reaches the bearing stage it can be kept in a high state of production for many years.

When a tree begins to bear and form fruit-producing points, it becomes less vegetative and vigorous than it was previously. The amount of terminal growth is less, and is made within a period of three to four weeks. Fruit spurs have formed which are to bear the fruit. Severe pruning may throw it out of bearing. The procedure for the amateur, or one not fully experienced, is as follows:

1. Look the tree over at a distance of 15 to 20 feet. Try to visualize how it should look when properly pruned.

2. First remove dead and diseased wood, water sprouts, and suckers.

3. If any large branches must be removed, make your decision on the ground and not up in the tree. They look entirely different from the two points of view. One is justified in removing a large branch if it is:

    (*a*) Rubbing against another.
    (*b*) Running parallel to another only a few inches away.
    (*c*) Heavily shaded by a branch above it.
    (*d*) Growing up through the center of the tree through many other branches.
    (*e*) Too close to the ground.
    (*f*) Growing back toward the center, and interfering with other branches.
    (*g*) Broken or diseased.
    (*h*) Long and spindly (weak).

4. Thin out the remaining branches by removing:

    (*a*) Crossing, crowding, parallel, broken or diseased branches.
    (*b*) Weak and spindly branches.
    (*c*) Branches growing in the wrong direction.

5. If the branches are extra long and growing out of bounds, cut them back to within the same area as the others. Always cut back to a lateral branch on wood more than one

year old. One-year growth may be cut back to an outside bud. Cut back to promote bushy, lateral growth.

6. Scrape the loose bark off with the back of the saw, a hoe or tree scraper. This will remove hibernating places for the coddling moth, scale and other insects.

Duration of Bearing: Many varieties of apple trees bear in from four to five years after planting and reach full bearing around the twelfth to fifteenth year, while some varieties do not begin to bear until they are at least eight years old. Some varieties are much longer lived than others, while other factors, such as soil, fertilization, insects and diseases, etc., should not be overlooked. However, with good cultural methods, a tree should bear over a period of forty years.

Overcoming Failure to Bear: The principal causes of failure to bear fruit are:

1. Insufficient nitrogen.
2. Severe pruning.
3. Lack of pollinating insects.
4. Wrong varieties.

(See Pollination, page 546 and Fertilization, below).

Cultivation: Weeds compete with trees for food and water. This competition is most harmful when the trees are newly set or are just about to bear. By keeping weed growth suppressed, the tree is able to make a better and faster start. Cultivation should consist of removing weeds from around the trees while young and mowing the weeds between the rows, or by frequent disking. Cultivation should cease from four to six weeks before fall begins so the trees will be hardened off and be in good condition to withstand the cold winter months. By allowing the weeds to grow at the above late date they actually compete with the tree for favorable results.

If cultivation is not possible, as is the case in some backyards, on lawns or on stony ground, the next best treatment is to keep the weed or grass growth cut. Two cuttings per season is usually sufficient. If possible, these cuttings should be used as a mulch under the tree.

Fertilization:

Non-bearing trees

Non-bearing trees are referred to as trees which have not reached the bearing age. The importance of feeding them to produce a large bearing framework for future years is apparent. If a tree is making from 12 to 18 inches or more of terminal growth each year an application of fertilizer will not be beneficial. If, however, such a tree is making only 1 to 4 inches of growth, fertilization would prove to be extremely valuable and would be justifiable.

A non-bearing tree should be fertilized with particular reference to its age. A two-year-old tree should receive from 4 to 8 ounces, and this amount may be gradually increased as the tree gets older. However, the maximum

amount which seems to give best results on a bearing tree is between 5 and 7 pounds.

A high-grade complete fertilizer or some form of nitrogen may be used. For best results the nitrogen should be available as soon as spring growth begins. Nitrate of soda can be applied as soon as growth starts as its nitrogen is in a quickly available form. Sulphate of ammonia should be applied a week earlier and cyanamide six weeks earlier.

All fertilizers should be spread under the outer branches around the tree. It is not necessary to spade or rake them into the soil.

When trees are growing on a lawn the best method is to make holes with a stick or bar under the outer branches from 12 to 18 inches apart, 1½ inches in diameter, and about 6 inches deep. Fill them almost to the top with fertilizer. It is not necessary to cover them with soil or other material. This method puts the fertilizer down where the roots will get it, and also prevents an unsightly and uneven lawn which would otherwise be the result.

Bearing trees

Bearing trees should be fertilized regularly in most cases. Besides producing a crop of fruit, a bearing tree should make from 8 to 14 inches of terminal growth each year. Many bearing trees are biennial bearers, which means that they bear a heavy crop one year and few if any fruits the following year. However, fertilization should be just as regular as with an annual bearer, since a fruit spur will not bear two years in succession and each type of tree requires about the same amount of food. Fertilizers help to form fruit buds for the succeeding year's crop and to materially aid in the setting of blossoms which form fruits. Five to seven pounds of a complete fertilizer is sufficient for a full-grown tree.

Thinning: When a tree contains an overabundance of fruits, some should be removed to prevent branches from breaking as well as to increase the size of those left. Thinning should be practiced from four to five weeks after the fruits have begun to form. Only one apple should be left in a cluster and individual apples should be from 6 to 8 inches apart on a limb or branch. If one side of a tree has practically no fruits and the other side is heavily laden, good-sized fruits will develop with little thinning. When removing fruits, leave the stem on the spur and use a pair of shears.

With early ripening varieties such as the Early Harvest, Yellow Transparent, and Red Astrachan, thinning may be delayed until six weeks after the blossoms have set. Then the fruits removed are large enough and soft enough to use for pies, apple sauce and the like, and come at a time of year when apples are particularly high in price.

Harvesting: Apples are mature and ready to be picked when their stems part easily from the spurs on which they are growing. They should be handled very carefully and not be bruised or left in the sun. They will keep longer if put into storage immediately and wrapped or packed with oiled paper. A temperature of 35 to 40 degrees F. is not too low, but a good circulation of moist air is essential for long keeping.

Spraying and Disease and Pest Control: See schedule and table at the end of this chapter.

VARIETIES OF MERIT

APPLES

Yellow Transparent: An early yellow variety ripening in July. Bears early, heavy annual crops. When the fruits are half mature they may be thinned and used for cooking.

Milton: A cross between Yellow Transparent and McIntosh. Very high quality, tree very vigorous and hardy.

Wealthy: One of the best varieties, ripening the last two weeks in August. Fine for culinary and dessert purposes. Comes into bearing young and bears heavy crops. Usually bears every other year.

McIntosh: Ripens in September. One of the finest varieties for general purposes. Tree is very hardy and vigorous. Plant Wealthy with it for pollination purposes. (See section on pollination.)

Delicious: A popular, well-known variety. Bears young and biennially.

Cortland: A cross between Ben Davis and McIntosh to extend the McIntosh season. A good keeper and very high in quality.

McCoun: A variety similar to Cortland but ripening later.

Stayman Winesap: Ripens October 5–10. A very profitable apple for the middle Atlantic and Central states. Good keeper. Bears biennially, usually. Should be planted with Delicious, McIntosh or Grimes Golden for pollination purposes.

Paragon: One of the longest keeping varieties—similar to Winesap.

Rome Beauty: All purpose fall and winter cooking apple.

CRAB APPLES

Transcendent: Ripens in September, a very good variety. Large size.

Hyslop: Pale yellow covered with dark crimson.

Dolgo: Ripens in mid-August. Brilliant crimson.

Cherry

Name: Prunus avium—Sweet Cherry.
Prunus Cerasus—Sour Cherry.
Prunus avium x P. Cerasus—hybrids of the sweet and sour varieties, also known as the Dukes.

Soil: A well-drained, loamy soil is suitable for all species.

Planting

Age of Trees: Grade A one- or two-year-old trees are preferable as they are, figuratively speaking, the "cream of the crop."

Time of Planting: Same as for Apple.

Planting Distance: Sweet Cherry Trees, 30 feet by 30 feet; Sour or Pie, 20 feet by 20 feet; Dukes or Hybrids, 25 feet by 25 feet.

Method of Planting and Overcoming Failure to Bear: See Apple.

Duration of Bearing: Twenty-five years for the Sour, and up to forty years for the Dukes and Sweet cherries.

Pruning

One-year Tree: A one-year-old cherry tree usually contains a few lateral branches. Cut the top back to within 24 to 36 inches from the ground and prune all strong laterals back to 6 to 8 inches. Weak growth should be removed.

Two-year Tree: Select from three to five branches within 15 inches from the ground which are uniformly spaced 3 to 5 inches apart, and which are not on the same plane, but which nevertheless balance the tree. This procedure is very simple to follow if the tree was planted when one year old. If a two-year tree is being pruned at planting time it is best to leave the three to five best branches for the framework and cut back the center branch to the uppermost one which is left. Those branches selected are then cut back to at least 15 to 20 inches if the tree has made a vigorous growth during the first year it was planted. The laterals on a newly set two-year tree should be cut back to 6 or 8 inches in length.

Time of Pruning: Same as Pear or Peach.

Pruning Young Non-Bearing Trees: Most varieties of cherry trees bear in two or five years after setting out. Pruning should be very light and consists of removing only weak, competing, and diseased branches. Slight heading back of the one-year wood is usually necessary in order to promote a bushy habit of growth.

Pruning Bearing Trees: The bearing cherry tree requires but light pruning until it reaches an age of 15 to 20 years, at which time it responds to a heavier pruning which is necessary in order to invigorate it and prolong its life.

Cultivation: See Apple.

Fertilization: Pie or Sour cherries and the hybrids, or Dukes, may be fertilized with the same materials and in the same manner as apple trees, except that the amount should be from one-half to two-thirds as much. Sweet cherry trees, or excessively large Pie cherry trees, should receive the same amount as a full-sized bearing apple tree.

Thinning: This is unnecessary with all cherry trees in the home garden.

Harvesting: Sour or Pie cherries may be harvested as soon as they begin to turn red. They may be used for cooking at this stage, but may be left on the tree over a period of approximately three weeks.

Sweet and Duke varieties should not be harvested until they are sweet but firm and ready to eat. Do not allow these varieties to remain on the tree after they once become ripe, as a rain will cause great loss from cracking and possibly brown rot.

All varieties of cherries will keep much longer if picked with the stems attached to the fruit.

Spraying and Disease and Pest Control: See schedule and table at the end of this chapter.

VARIETIES OF MERIT

SWEET CHERRIES

All varieties described bear in four years:

Bing: One of the largest, black oxheart varieties. Tree is quite small and a slow grower.

Lambert: Very large, purplish red color. Very vigorous.

Napoleon: A yellow-fleshed variety with a red cheek. Known also as Royal Ann.

Black Tartarian: A very large, vigorous growing oxheart. Fine in quality and black in color.

Note: The Bing, Lambert, and Napoleon will not bear cherries if planted separately or together. If any one or all of these varieties are planted, a Black Tartarian should also be planted for cross-pollination purposes.

SOUR CHERRIES

All varieties are self-fertile and may be planted alone.

Early Richmond, Montmorency: Both are hardy, vigorous varieties, ripening a week apart. The Montmorency is more highly colored.

Peach and Nectarine

Name: Prunus Persica.

Soil: A sandy loam soil is best. Silt will, however, give fair results.

Planting

Age of Trees: One year old.

Planting Distance: 18 to 20 feet apart each way is the standard distance, although 16 feet apart each way is not too close for the home orchard.

Method of Planting: See Apple.

Pruning

One-year Tree: The purpose of pruning and training young peach trees is to develop a framework of bowl-shaped branches which will produce the greatest load of fruit close to the ground.

Low-headed peach trees are preferred which branch between 18 and 22 inches from the ground. Oftentimes one-year peach trees contain several small branches. After cutting the main stem back to the height described, the remaining lateral branches should be cut back to 4 to 6 inches in length. This should be done as soon as the tree is planted.

After First Season: When the tree is in its second season, remove all side branches that form at an angle of less than 45 degrees with the trunk. Remove any branches that are but a few inches above ground level. Prune out suckers or strong branches that fill in and shade the center of the tree. Delete one of two limbs of equal size that tend to divide the tree and form a Y. Cut back slightly the stronger framework branches.

Time of Pruning: Pruning should not be done until all danger of near or below freezing temperatures is past as many varieties are susceptible to these low temperatures.

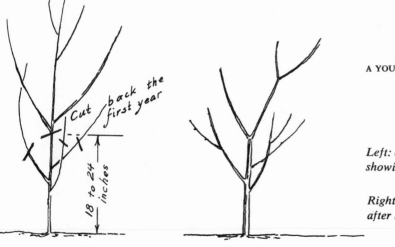

Cut back the first year

18 to 24 inches

A YOUNG PEACH

Left: one year old showing pruning cuts

Right: two years old after second pruning

PEACH. *Right: leaf bud has become a spur.*

Pruning Young Non-Bearing Peach Trees: Peach trees come into bearing during their third or fourth year so that their non-bearing period is very short. During this period a vigorous, spreading, bushy framework should be developed. Eighteen to 24 inches of terminal growth is most satisfactory. Pruning should consist of thinning out weak and inferior wood; cutting back several inches on the one-year wood to produce a bushy and stocky framework and to remove competing or crossing and too closely parallel branches. The center should be allowed to become filled in but not clogged.

Pruning Bearing Peach Trees: Peaches are borne on growth formed the previous season. The principle involved is to have a good supply of fruiting wood each year which makes cutting back a necessary practice instead of an injury, as would be the result with apple trees. If peach trees were not pruned the fruit would be borne on the terminal ends of the branches at such a height as to cause the limbs to break. Fourteen feet is a good height for a peach tree.

The necessary procedure to prune a peach tree is as follows:

1. Cut out dead, diseased, and broken branches.
2. Thin out weak, crossing, and parallel branches.
3. Keep the center open and allow water sprouts to grow, but thin them out if too many are present.

(A *water sprout* is a type of vigorous, succulent growth which develops on the trunk or limbs of a tree. Severe pruning encourages water sprouts to develop.)

4. Cut back to strong lateral branches to promote vegetative growth.
5. Do not allow the center to become clogged with non-fruiting wood.
6. Cut back one-year growth to 15 inches in length. Lateral growth will be encouraged.
7. Keep the tree within bounds.

If a healthy tree fails to grow vigorously after several years of bearing, the branches should be cut back severely, but always to a lateral branch. This will invigorate new growth better than fertilizers.

Duration of Bearing: A peach tree is an annual bearer of heavy crops over a period of twenty to twenty-five years, although some trees may be productive for as long as forty years.

Overcoming Failure to Bear: Early spring frosts, killing winter temperatures, and lack of food are the main causes of failure to bear. The first two mentioned may be avoided by planting resistant varieties, and the food supply may be given them in the form of commercial fertilizer and organic matter. Very few varieties are self-unfruitful when grown alone, but it is well to look into this matter before planting some of the newer varieties. The J. H. Hale should be planted with another variety.

Cultivation: Peach trees give their best response to cultivation, although results may not be poor if otherwise grown. The soil should be disked or cultivated at frequent intervals during the growing season and cultivation should cease when the varieties begin to ripen. Cultivate at intervals sufficient to prevent weed growth from competing with the trees and to keep a 2-inch soil mulch at all times.

Fertilization: A general rule is to apply from half to two-thirds as much fertilizer to a peach tree as to an apple tree, and the application should be made at approximately the same time. See Apple.

Thinning: When about the size of a 25-cent piece, peaches should be thinned to about 4 inches apart. This practice will result in larger and higher quality fruits. When a tree is overcrowded with fruits the stone will be as large in a small fruit as in a larger fruit. Therefore, thinning tends to increase the proportion of flesh to the size of the stone or peach seed.

Harvesting: Peaches should be harvested when they are mature, but firm. If they are left on the tree until fully ripe too many will drop and become inferior in appearance and salability. At the time of maturity the undercolor which changes from green to yellow or white is very apparent. Two or three days after picking, the peaches are in prime condition for eating or preserving. Some varieties first become soft on one side, usually the most highly colored side. If packed in this stage the other side will soften up within a short time.

VARIETIES OF MERIT

PEACHES

1. Early Yellow: Jerseyland, Golden Jubilee, Triogem.
2. Early White: Raritan Rose, Carman.
3. Midseason Yellow: Sunhigh, Halehaven, Elberta.
4. Midseason White: Red Rose, Champion.
5. Late Yellow: Afterglow.
6. Late White: Belle of Georgia, Late Rose.

Bonanza: a very dwarf peach suited to small backyards. May be grown in tubs.

NECTARINE

Surecrop: Recommended for the home fruit garden.
Garden State: Yellow.

Pear

Name: Pyrus.

Soil: A deep, loamy soil with good drainage.

Planting

Age of Trees for Planting: See Apple.

Time of Planting: See Apple.

Distance Between Trees: 30 feet by 30 feet.

Method of Planting: See Apple.

Duration of Bearing: Thirty to forty years or more.

Pruning

One-year Tree: A one-year-old pear tree should be pruned back to a height of 30 to 36 inches. Usually it is a straight whip without any lateral branches. If lateral branches are present, prune them back to 4 to 6 inches in length if they are vigorous. If lateral growth is weak it is best to cut it out entirely.

Two-year Tree: Four or five branches are selected as scaffold branches for the future framework of the tree. The same principles are practiced as with apples, which see. The reason for leaving more scaffold branches than with apples is that the pear is quite susceptible to fire blight. If it developed on a limb from which all the main laterals developed, the entire tree would be killed within a short time. By training several branches as described, the removal of one will not seriously injure the tree.

Time of Pruning: The pear is hardier than the peach but not as hardy as the apple. Therefore, do not prune until freezing weather has passed in order to avoid winter-killing.

Pruning Non-Bearing Trees: Light pruning is the answer to this question for reasons discussed in the case of the apple. There are many varietal habits of growth, so allow the tree to grow naturally with a little thinning and heading back when necessary.

Pruning Bearing Trees: See Apple.

Overcoming Failure to Bear: See Apple.

Cultivation: Not entirely necessary, as with the peach, although it is helpful to give young trees a good start when possible. Keep weed growth suppressed as with the apple.

Fertilization: This may vary somewhat according to the variety and its ultimate size. Medium-sized trees may be fertilized like the peach. Large-sized trees should receive the equivalent amounts which are supplied to bearing apple trees.

Harvesting: Pears contain their best flavor if not allowed to fully mature on the tree. Pick them when they begin to turn yellow, or, with green or russet varieties, when they part easily from the spur. They should be juicy and sweet several days later.

Spraying and Disease and Pest Control: See schedule and table at the end of this chapter.

VARIETIES OF MERIT

PEARS

Varieties listed all bear within four years, except Beurre Bosc.

Bartlett: This variety needs no introduction. It is as well known as the Elberta Peach. It should be planted with another variety as in most cases it is self-sterile.

Clapps Favorite: Resembles the Bartlett, ripening about a week earlier. Has a tendency to become soft when fully ripe more quickly than the Bartlett.

Seckel: One of the highest quality small russet pears. A vigorous grower. Not as subject to fire blight as the Bartlett.

Beurre Bosc: A very large russet yellow color and one of the longest keepers. Does not bear until eight or nine years old.

Tyson: Small to medium, pale yellow, very good quality for an early dessert pear.

Gorham: A similar variety to Bartlett, about ten days later.

Anjou: Very good quality, green late variety, best for eating and salads.

Plum

Name: Prunus domestica—European Plum.
Prunus salicina—Japanese Plum.
Prunus insititia—French or Damson Plum.

Soil: A heavy silt or clay loam is most desirable, although some varieties give good results in the lighter soils.

Planting

Age of Tree: See Apple.

Time of Planting: See Apple.

Planting Distance: 30 feet by 30 feet for domestica and salicina species. Twenty to 25 feet apart each way for the insititia species.

Method of Planting: See Apple.

Overcoming Failure to Bear: See Apple.

Duration of Bearing: Usually twenty to thirty years.

Pruning, Cultivation, Fertilization, and Thinning: See Cherry.

Harvesting: The European types may be harvested when mature but firm. They include the prune plums which will keep for as long as two weeks under ordinary conditions. However, they have the best flavor when allowed to fully mature on the tree. This is indicated by the stem easily parting from the twig.

The Japanese types are much softer and, once they begin to ripen, deteriorate rather soon. They may, however, be picked when firm to prolong their keeping period.

The insititia types keep as well, if not better, than many of the domestica types. They usually ripen several weeks later.

Spraying and Disease and Pest Control: See schedule and table at the end of this chapter.

VARIETIES OF MERIT

PLUMS

Burbank: A yellow-fleshed variety with a dark red skin. Good for culinary and dessert purposes. Hardy.

Italian Prune: A dark purplish skin with greenish yellow flesh. Very solid and fine for canning or eating.

Green Gage: A yellowish green variety which is very high in quality.

Damson: Not used for eating but an excellent variety for canning in various ways. Very vigorous and prolific.

Quince

Name: Cydonia oblonga.

Soil: A well-drained, rich, loamy soil.

Planting

Age of Trees for Planting: Two-year-old trees are most desirable as the quince is a comparatively slow grower.

Time of Planting: Early spring planting gives excellent results but fall planting is permissible in regions where the temperature does not go below zero.

Distance Between Trees: Quince bushes are set from 15 to 20 feet apart each way.

Method of Planting: See Apple.

Pruning

First Year: The quince is pruned back slightly to stimulate new shoot growth. No definite system is followed.

Second Year: Thin out the weaker, inferior branches and cut back the remaining shoots from one-third to one-half their length, especially if the tree has been set out that season. Two-year-old trees which have been growing in their permanent position for a year do not require as severe pruning as those just planted.

Pruning the Bearing Quince Bush: Remove a small amount of the twiggy growth each year and cut back any branches which have the tendency to grow out of bounds.

Duration of Bearing: A quince bush will bear for twenty-five years or more.

Overcoming Failure to Bear: There should be no trouble in this respect. See Apple.

Cultivation: See Apple.

Fertilization: See Peach.

Thinning: Fruits will be larger if thinned out from 6 to 8 inches apart. In most cases, however, there is little need of it.

Harvesting: The quince may be harvested when it has attained its fullest development which is around 3 inches in diameter. It is such a hard fruit that it will keep from 4 to 6 months without any special care except careful handling.

Disease and Pest Control: See Spraying Schedule at the end of this chapter.

SMALL BUSH FRUITS

Blackberries

Name: Rubus (various).

Soil: The Blackberry will grow on any fertile soil where the moisture conditions are satisfactory. As it bears its crop in midsummer, lack of moisture is often the cause of low yields. Once it is established, it will spread rapidly if not kept within bounds.

Planting: The plants are usually set out in the early spring months. Early planting is most favorable for the best results. The tops are cut back to 12 to 18 inches and the plants are set 3 feet apart in the row; 6 to 8 feet between the rows is not too far apart. Suckers may be set out any time after August 1, but the results are apt to be questionable because of weather conditions at that time of year. Set the plants slightly deeper than they grew in the nursery.

Culture: Vigorous, vegetative suckers grow up one year, fruit the following summer and die. It is therefore necessary to permit suckers to grow but they must be kept within bounds. Plants may be trained to wires, or several canes may be tied to a stake. The plants must be kept in rows or hills, which makes it necessary to remove all suckers appearing in the middle of the row. This should be done by pulling up the roots and not by cutting, as new ones will readily sprout from the old stumps. Enough space should be left to allow for cultivation and care in picking.

Cultivation or Mulching: If cultivation is the method chosen to follow, it should be done frequently enough to keep weed growth suppressed. Blackberry roots are close to the surface, so cultivation should be shallow.

A mulch will suppress weed growth and conserve moisture, and if this method is chosen, enough mulch should be applied between the plants and in the row to keep weeds from growing up through it. Grass clippings, hay, leaves, etc., will give satisfactory results.

Fertilizers: Fertilizers should be applied early in the spring when growth begins, to encourage good strong sucker development which is to fruit the following year. A complete fertilizer containing nitrogen, phosphorus, and potash is strongly recommended. The rate of application will depend on the fertility of the soil. Some cases have been known in which blackberries did better without any fertilizer than others did with a heavy application, due to soil and moisture differences. An application of 1 pound to 50 feet of row early in the spring when the plants begin to fruit heavily is a medium application. Manure may also be applied with good results.

Pruning: Fruiting canes may be removed at any time after the crop is harvested until growth begins the following spring. Weak and broken canes should be removed. Thin the others out so that they are at least 6 inches apart. This is not necessary if plants are grown in hills, but never allow more than five or six canes per hill. Cut the tops back to a height between 4 and 5 feet. This varies with the variety and the vigor of growth. Three or four strong laterals may be left per cane if cut back to three or four buds. Cut out the weak ones entirely.

Cutting back should be practiced only in the spring as winter killing always starts at the tip. If the canes are cut back in the fall, winter killing will begin at the point of detachment.

If some of the weak suckers are removed during the growing season, those left will have more room in which to develop.

Disease and Pest Control: See table at the end of this chapter.

VARIETIES OF MERIT

Eldorado: The largest and sweetest variety. Very hardy, vigorous and productive.

Blowers: Midseason, good quality, productive.

Brewer: Midseason, productive, glossy attractive berry.

Iceberg: A novelty, white-fruited.

Blueberries

Name: Vaccinium corymbosum.

Blueberry culture is of most recent origin, which is due in part to the increased market demand for a greater supply of large, high-quality berries. The problem is to adapt them to many soils which have been growing other crops with different soil requirements.

Soil: Blueberries produce best results on a soil which is acid in reaction and which is well drained, but retentive of moisture. Soil which has previously grown garden crops is usually not suitable because it is not acid enough. However, the addition of decomposed leaves, peat, woodland turf or sawdust will materially help to make the soil acid. Aluminum sulfate may be applied at the rate of 1 pound to 75 or 100 square feet, but its effect is only temporary. Aluminum sulfate should not supplant the addition of the above materials suggested, but it may be used satisfactorily in conjunction with them if applied each year and worked into the soil.

Land which has not previously been planted to garden or other crops is suitable for growing blueberries, especially if acid-loving plants such as sweet ferns, wild blueberries, white cedar, oak or pines are growing on it.

The land should be plowed after all superfluous growth is removed and allowed to lie fallow for one season. Frequent cultivation or disking during the year will prevent growth and also improves its physical condition. If water has the tendency to stand on the surface for a period of several days during the growing season, the plant roots will suffer from lack of oxygen. Such places should be drained.

Setting the Plants: Blueberry plants are set during early spring or late fall months. Early spring planting usually gives best results. Do not allow the roots of the plants to dry out before setting in the ground. The plants are set 4 feet apart in the row and from 6 to 8 feet apart between the rows. Dig the holes wide enough to avoid crowding the roots and deep enough to set the plants two inches deeper than they were growing before. Firm the soil around the plants and water if the soil is dry. Several varieties should be planted, as cross-pollination is necessary to produce good yields.

Soil Management: Blueberry plantations may be managed by two methods: clean cultivation and mulching.

If clean cultivation is practiced it should be shallow, at intervals of two or three weeks apart from early spring to midsummer to control weeds and thus conserve moisture. Deep cultivation or hoeing to a depth of more than 2 inches will destroy part of the plant's fibrous root system. Do not cultivate within several inches of the base of the plant for this reason.

Plants may be mulched with satisfactory results but cultivation should precede this treatment for at least a year after the plants are set. Shavings, peat moss, pine needles or oak leaves are suitable materials for using as a mulch. Lawn clippings may also be used. The important point is to apply enough of the mulching between the rows and around the plants to prevent weed growth and to conserve moisture. Three or 4 inches are usually necessary.

Fertilization: Fertilizers are applied just as growth begins in the spring and again four to six weeks after the first application. A 4–12–4 fertilizer applied at the rate of 1 pound to 100 square feet will give good results. Cultivate the fertilizer into the soil soon after applying it if the mulch system is not used.

Pruning: Pruning should be done early in the spring before growth begins. During the first three years pruning consists of removing a few of the smaller lateral shoots and thinning out the bushy growth. The plants should not be permitted to bear fruit for the first two years after setting. To prevent bearing, remove the flower clusters when they appear. Pruning after the third year consists in removing from one-fourth to one-third of the old wood, besides removing weak twigs and branches lying on the ground.

Varieties: As many new varieties are being developed, it is strongly recommended that you write to your State Agricultural Experiment Station for their advice on this subject. The Cabot, Pioneer, Rancocas, Jersey, Dixie and Rubel are excellent varieties.

Currants and Gooseberries

Names: Currant—Ribes, various.
Gooseberry—(American) R. hirtellum.
(European) R. Grossularia.

The growing, fruiting and cultural methods are so similar that currants and gooseberries may be discussed together.

Both are very hardy and winter injury is an uncommon occurrence.

Soil and Location: A moist, fertile, well-drained loam soil, supplied with organic matter, is ideal. They should not be planted in low places where late frosts occur, as they bloom early.

Planting: Both fruits may be planted in the fall or spring with equally good results, although in some cases fall planting is preferable.

Good strong one- or two-year-old plants may be set. The planting distance is from 4 to 6 feet apart in the row with 6 feet between the rows.

Broken and extra long roots should be cut back. The tops are cut back to a height of 6 to 8 inches. Cutting back depends to a great extent on the size of the root system and the size of top.

Set the plants slightly deeper than originally growing in the nursery and firm the soil around them.

General Care: Practice shallow cultivation to suppress weed growth. Plants may be mulched with leaves, straw or other material during the growing season but the mulch should be removed in the early fall to discourage rodents.

Fertilizers: Stable manure may be broadcast around the plants early in the spring. Complete fertilizers give most satisfactory results as they contain more readily available plant food. Four ounces per plant as growth begins in the spring is usually sufficient. This is applied in a narrow band 6 to 8 inches away from the main stalk and raked or hoed in.

Pruning: Both bear fruit at the base of the one-year-old wood and on spurs of older wood. The principle of pruning is to maintain a steady supply of new wood and to prevent old, partially fruiting canes from accumulating in any great number so as to interfere with the younger growth. All wood four years or older should be removed at the base of the plant. Remove at the same time spindly and short shoots. Eight or ten strong shoots are sufficient, ranging in age from one to four years. By keeping the old canes going we keep the new canes coming.

A little heading back of the new canes is necessary. In some sections where borers are a pest it is not recommended to any great extent.

Gooseberries are more difficult to propagate than currants. By heaping soil around the plant and covering 3 or 4 inches of the base of the one-year canes, roots will form. This should be done in late June or July. By the middle of September, the soil may be removed and those which have rooted may be severed from the plant and set in another location. Another method is to cut back the one-year growth 6 inches, remove the tips, and plant in the open ground. They will root quite readily. This is best done in the early spring before the growth process is perceptible.

Disease and Pest Control: See table at the end of this chapter.

VARIETIES OF MERIT

GOOSEBERRIES

American varieties produce twice as many berries as other varieties but they are very small.

European varieties are more susceptible to mildew than American ones.

Downing: Adapted to all conditions in this country. Very productive, high in quality. American.

Poorman: One of the largest American kinds. Pinkish, sweet, excellent. Produces about 2 quarts when five years old. Berries hang on a long time.

Chautauqua: European. Large. Comparatively free from mildew. Seeds large. Plant hard to propagate.

Houghton: Small. Old, well-known variety. Adapted to a good many soils.

RED CURRANTS

Perfection: Berries large, bright crimson, sprightly sub-acid, midseason, clusters compact, very long, easy to pick. A heavy yielder. Berries sometimes scald in hot weather if not picked as soon as ripe. Bush more or less spreading, throwing up canes from below the ground; canes break easily.

Wilder: Berries large, dark red, mild sub-acid, hang on bushes well. Midseason; clusters large, compact, easy to pick. Bush upright and large.

London Market: (London Red)—Berries medium to large, deep red, rather acid, midseason to late; clusters compact, with short stems. Bush upright, somewhat resistant to borers and diseases; most resistant of any variety to the white pine blister rust. (See Chapter XLI.)

Red Cross: Berries large, firm, light red, sub-acid, hang on to bushes well; midseason, but later than the Cherry; clusters of medium length, well filled, easy to pick. Cracks easily. Plant is not long-lived. Fruit ripens unevenly.

Cherry: Berries large, becoming smaller as the bush grows older. Deep red, very acid, midseason. Bush somewhat spreading. Unproductive. Canes have a tendency to go blind.

WHITE CURRANTS

White Dutch: Earliest and sweetest of white ones. Small berries and not uniform. Good in quality. Sweeter than the red ones.

White Grape: The best. Medium in size, berries fairly large, but not uniform. Rich flavor. Bush very productive.

White Imperial: Berries large, pale yellow, almost sweet; clusters medium length, and loose. Bush spreading, very productive. A desirable variety; considered to have the best dessert quality of all currants.

BLACK CURRANTS

Champion: Wild flavor. Ripens after the red currants. Mildest of the black varieties. Larger than Perfection (Red). Most susceptible to white pine blister rust.

Red Raspberries

Name: (European) Rubus idaeus.
          (American) Rubus idaeus strigosus.

Soil: A deep loamy soil is most desirable for red raspberries because it is best for the plants and easier to cultivate. Heavy silts and clay soils should be avoided because of poor growth and lower yields. Thorough drainage and an adequate supply of moisture are essential.

The soil should be thoroughly pulverized previous to planting. Sod land should be prepared by growing some vegetable on it at least two years in advance.

Planting: New stock or suckers which developed the previous year should be planted in the following spring, before growth begins. Suckers may also be dug up and planted during the month of August but the first suggestion gives best results under average conditions.

Plants are set 3 to 4 feet apart in the rows, allowing 6 to 8 feet between the rows. Before planting, the tops of the plants, if set in the spring, should be cut back to 12 inches. Set the plants 3 inches deeper than they were formerly growing to protect them from drought.

Cultivation: Tillage should be thorough and more regular than for most other crops. The root system is quite shallow and cultivation should not be deeper than 3 inches.

Fertilizer: The application of commercial fertilizers should be planned with caution since too much nitrogen will cause excessive growth and weak canes which may bend over and touch the ground. A fertile soil is

necessary to begin with. Given sufficient cultivation to suppress weed growth, it should be sufficient.

Training and Pruning: Red raspberries fruit on the same principle as do blackberries. Suckers grow one year, fruit the next, and die. The principle of pruning is also the same. Varieties vary greatly in their habit of growth and should be treated accordingly when thinned out. The tops are cut back before growth begins in the spring. Cut the canes back from 6 to 18 inches. Severe cutting will reduce the crop. With some very vigorous varieties more cutting back is practical than with others. The canes should be cut back to a height of $3\frac{1}{2}$ to $4\frac{1}{2}$ feet.

Disease and Pest Control: See table at the end of this chapter.

VARIETIES OF MERIT

Sunrise: Earliest, long picking, good quality.

Latham: Fruit very large, plants hardy and resistant to mosaic. Flavor is only fair.

New Milton: A late variety. Excellent for market and home use. Vigorous, productive and hardy.

Taylor: An outstanding variety. Vigorous, hardy, very productive. Berries of superior quality.

EVERBEARING VARIETIES

Indian Summer: The first crop ripens early in July, the second from early September to severe frost.

September: An outstanding everbearing variety. Hardy, vigorous and productive. Berries of fine quality.

Purple and Black Raspberries

Name: (Black Raspberries) Rubus occidentalis.
          (Purple Raspberries) R. occidentalis x R. idaeus.

Soil: Soil requirements are practically the same as for the red raspberry. Although its water requirements are greater, it may do well on the heavier soils. Its root system is much more vigorous.

Planting: Early spring planting is most satisfactory. The plants should be spaced 4 feet in the rows and 6 feet between the rows. They should be cut back to 6 inches when setting out and the spot should be marked with a stick.

Propagation: Purple and black raspberries do not produce suckers as do red raspberries. All new growth comes from a definite place in the crown of the plant and propagation is done by covering the ends of the new growth with soil during the months of July and August. This is called tip-layering.

Pruning: Three fruiting canes are sufficient for each plant. These are summer pinched to a height of $3\frac{1}{2}$ to 4 feet. The following spring laterals are pruned so they are 8 to 10 inches long.

A BLACK RASPBERRY
BEFORE AND AFTER
PRUNING

Other requirements are the same as for the red raspberry. *Disease and Pest Control:* See table at the end of this chapter.

VARIETIES OF MERIT

Black Beauty: Excellent, everbearing, fine flavor.

Morrison: Bushes vigorous, productive, resistant to disease. Berries of superior quality and flavor.

New Dawn: Ripens early, excellent flavor.

Purple Autumn: First crop late spring; autumn crop continues until frost.

Sodus: Hardy, vigorous, productive.

Strawberries

Name: Fragaria.

Remarks: A large patch of strawberries may be planted at a small cost and will bring quicker returns and high yields sooner than any other fruit crop. It is the first fresh fruit to appear on the markets in early spring.

Soil: Soil is more important than location. A soil for strawberries should contain plenty of organic material, be well drained and fertile. The time of ripening may be extended or delayed several days. A sandy soil warms up most quickly in the spring months. Plant growth will therefore be stimulated sooner than on silt or heavy loam soils which do not warm up as quickly. Too much nitrogen will cause excessive plant development which will result in crowding and lower yields. The soil should be well firmed before planting.

Getting the Plants: Strawberry plants are said to be perfect or imperfect. A perfect blossom has both stamens and pistils while an imperfect blossom has only one or the other. Imperfect varieties should be interplanted with perfect ones so that cross-pollination will insure a good yield of berries. The perfect and imperfect varieties should bloom at the same time. However, over 99 percent of the varieties sold today are perfect ones.

Time to Plant: Early spring is the best time to plant and the earlier the better. Plants may be set in the fall but this practice is not recommended as the yield is reduced

the following year and heaving is very apt to occur during the winter.

The planting distance depends on the variety, method of training, and fertility of the soil. The usual distance is 15 to 20 inches in the row and $3\frac{1}{2}$ to 4 feet between the rows.

Plants are prepared for planting by removing old and decayed leaves and trimming the roots to about three inches. Soak the roots in a pail of water and keep them in the shade.

Setting the Plants: The ideal time to set plants in the garden is on a cloudy day or late in the afternoon. Be sure to keep the roots moist at all times by keeping them in a container which is covered with paper or wet burlap. Do not allow the roots to be exposed to the sun for over two minutes before planting.

Mark out the rows with a tight line. If planting is difficult because of the line a furrow $1\frac{1}{2}$ inches deep may be made with a hoe or other garden implement, using the line as a guide before removing it. The crown center of the plant where the tiny leaves are developing should be just flush or level with the surface of the soil. If set too deeply, it will be covered with soil and will rot; if set too high, the roots will dry out, as they will not be in contact with a sufficient supply of moisture. The plants should be well firmed in the soil to prevent drying out, and to keep the moisture in contact with the roots.

The following method of setting has proven most satisfactory.

1. Have the rows properly marked.
2. Have the plants properly trimmed.
3. Have someone drop the plants on the row 15–18 inches apart.
4. The setter takes a trowel in the right hand, plunges it into the soil and pulls it toward him about 3 inches.
5. The plant which has been dropped is put in the hole in back of the trowel at the proper depth. The roots are spread out. The trowel is removed and the soil firmed around the plant by pressing with both hands. Twenty plants per minute can be set out with excellent results.

Care of Newly Set Plants: Blossoms which will appear after the plants are set out should be removed to allow

559

all the strength to go into the formation of plants instead of fruit the first year.

Keep weed growth suppressed by practicing shallow cultivation.

About a month to six weeks after planting, runners will appear. The first two plants on each one will develop first and will, therefore, produce more fruit the following year than those rooting late in the season. Four runners per plant is sufficient. Others may be cut off. If these runners are spaced around the plant and a small stone is placed next to where the leaves are appearing, they will take root very easily. On a commercial basis, very little training and pruning is practiced and so by the end of the growing season the row has a matted appearance and is called the matted row system. As the new plants form, the row gradually closes in and more hand weeding is necessary as it is impossible to hoe or cultivate between the plants.

However, if plants are not going to be dug up from the middle of the row for planting the following spring, they might just as well be kept hoed out during the first year. Leave a path 12 inches wide which will facilitate harvesting the next summer.

When new runners appear the soil should be slightly mounded 12 inches each side of the parent plant and 2 to 3 inches higher than the level of the field. This will supply soft soil in which the runners will root, besides facilitating better drainage.

The bed should be weeded late in the fall and all weeds, especially clover and chickweed which overwinter, removed.

Manures and Fertilizers: An application of well-rotted manure is a decided advantage. One horse load to a plot 50 feet × 50 feet will bring good results. It should be plowed in at any time previous to planting. A cover crop should be plowed under a year in advance of setting the plants to allow time for decomposition to take place if it is used as a substitute for manure.

Lime is not essential and should not be applied in any great quantity if at all, as the strawberry prefers an acid soil.

A complete fertilizer should be used for best results. It may be applied at the time of setting the plants at the rate of 1 pound to 50 square feet and raked in or applied after the plants are established. In the latter case, it is applied on a dry day by broadcasting it over the plants at the mentioned rate. An old broom or fine brush should be used to remove any of it from the leaves, which will be burned if moisture is present. This application should be raked or cultivated into the soil.

Winter Protection: In sections where winter weather is variable and accompanied by alternate freezing and thawing, the plants should be protected to prevent them from heaving. Coarse material such as straw or hay is best applied after the ground freezes. Cover to a depth of $\frac{1}{2}$ to 1 inch. This material prevents the soil from thawing out very rapidly and thus prevents heaving. Fine material in any quantity, such as pine needles, should be avoided as it may pack too tightly and kill the plants.

Spring Treatment: Winter covering should be removed after all danger is past of a heavy frost which would kill the blossoms. About two-thirds of the straw is removed and placed in the space left between the rows. It serves as a mulch and makes kneeling a pleasure instead of a pain. The plants will grow up through the remaining covering which will settle down around the base of them and keep the berries clean and off the ground.

There has been much discussion as to the feasibility of spring fertilization. It is well to remember at this point that the fruit buds were formed the season before. Nitrogenous fertilizers promote vigorous succulent growth which may result in overcrowding and in soft berries. The main requirement until the fruit is harvested is water. It is the care the plants receive the first season that is so important for the production of the next year's crop.

Harvesting: The picking season for a particular variety ranges from seven to fourteen days. Beds fruiting the second or third time are earlier than those bearing their first crop.

Pick the berries in the coolest part of the day and do not pick when the vines are moist, unless absolutely necessary. Gather the fruit at least every other day, as it becomes soft very quickly after reaching maturity. Put the fruit in the shade and in a cool place immediately after picking. Do not hold more than two berries in the hand at a time.

Renewing or Renovation: After the crop has been harvested, a vigorous treatment is necessary to instigate new life in the patch.

1. Remove all material used for a mulch and burn or compost it.

2. Rake the patch very vigorously. Many plants will be removed but this is unimportant as concerning future yields.

3. Cultivate the rows to a width of 2 feet. This will narrow them considerably but it must be done.

4. Apply a complete fertilizer—1 pound to 50 feet of row.

5. Keep weed growth suppressed.

It is not advisable to keep a patch for more than three years, and two is more generally recommended.

Potted Plants: Some nurserymen sell potted plants which can be set out in August and which will bear fruit the following spring. One hundred such plants cost as much as a thousand dug from the patch in the spring. Also the yield is a comparatively small one.

Pots filled with soil are plunged into the earth next to spring-set plants when the runners are somewhat developed. The first joint on each runner is placed on the soil in the pot. The roots which develop grow into the soil in the pot. Plants from later joints which develop are firmly rooted in the ground by August and need no help from the parent plant. The runner on both sides of the plant growing in the pot is cut and the pot removed with its plant.

Home-grown plants will give excellent results if the bed has received reasonable care and if they are free from disease. Nurserymen sell excellent plants which are satisfactory, provided they are properly packed and shipped.

Plants may be dug from the patch with a trowel and moved to their new location with soil on the roots. Old and decayed leaves should be removed before planting. Two or three leaves per plant are sufficient to begin with.

If plants are received by mail or express, the package should be opened as soon as received to avoid sweating and deterioration. Set the plants in a trench temporarily, to prevent the roots from drying out.

Disease and Pest Control: See table at the end of this chapter.

VARIETIES OF MERIT

Pathfinder: early midseason
Fairfax: early midseason
Temple: midseason
Sparkle: late midseason
Redwing: midseason to late

EVERBEARING VARIETIES
Gem, Superfection, and Mastodon

VINE FRUITS

Grapes

Name: Vitis Labruscana.

Soil: The grape does well on any fertile soil but shows a preference for the medium to silt-loam types.

Planting

Age of Vines for Planting: One- or two-year-old vines.

Time of Planting: Early spring as soon as the frost is out of the ground.

Distance Between Vines: 6 feet by 6 feet, or 6 by 8 feet.

Method of Planting: Set 2 inches deeper than they were originally growing in the nursery.

Pruning and Training: The best time for pruning is in late winter or very early spring before the sap starts to run. There are several systems of training and pruning the grape. They will not be discussed in detail, but the important facts about pruning and training will be stated.

1. The best fruits are borne on pencil-sized canes and between the second and twelfth bud from the base.
2. A vine can supply 40 to 60 buds.
3. Therefore, the best system is one which contains four pencil-sized canes, each cane having from 10 to 15 buds.

Grade A, one- or two-year vines should be planted early in the spring before the buds begin to swell. Cut the vine back to two or three buds at planting time. As the new shoots develop, train them off the ground to a stake or two wires which have been fastened to posts.

Set posts 3 feet in the ground and 4½ feet out of the ground, 15 to 18 feet apart. Attach the first lengthwise wire 18 inches from the ground, the second 18 inches from the first, and the third 18 inches from the second.

The vine should be trained up to the top wire and tied and cut. This is to form the trunk. The following year, growth will appear from all the lateral buds and the system of training will be established when the vine is pruned early the following spring. Select two pencil-sized canes near the middle wire. Train one on each side of the main stem and cut back to 10 to 12 buds. Repeat this process on the top wire, and tie the canes in place with soft string or binder twine. Tight tying is not necessary as the string serves only as a support for the canes. The other canes should be removed, but be sure to leave two buds on four of them, so that they will be fully developed to produce the crop near each cane the following year.

Oftentimes only two wires are used, as the bottom wire serves mainly for support.

Lateral growths on one-year-old canes are cut back to four buds if pencil-sized.

The new wood should be kept as close to the head as possible. This is to keep the fruiting wood from growing out of bounds. As a vine gets old, 8 to 10 years, its vigor diminishes, which is well attested to by the shortening of the annual growth. As the vigor decreases it is time to renew the vine. One will notice in most

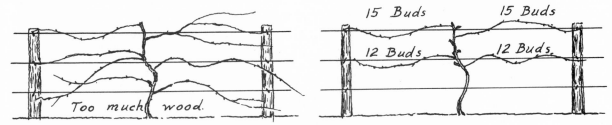

PRUNING GRAPE VINE: VINE NOT PRUNED (LEFT) AND VINE PRUNED TO FOUR BRANCHES

GROWTH AND
PRUNING OF A GRAPE
VINE

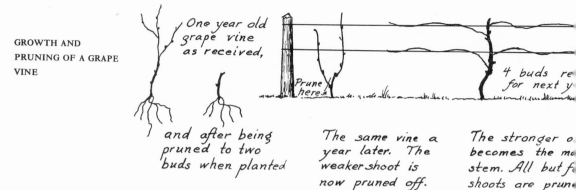

One year old grape vine as received,

Prune here

4 buds re for next y

and after being pruned to two buds when planted

The same vine a year later. The weaker shoot is now pruned off.

The stronger o becomes the mo stem. All but f shoots are prun

instances that canes are persistent in growing at the base of the trunk. Cut the trunk off so as not to injure these canes and train one up to take the place of the old one removed. The results obtained will be remarkable, with an increase of vigor to a productive result for several years to come.

Training and Pruning a Grape Arbor

A grape arbor, besides furnishing shade, should also be productive. As much more space is allowed each vine than when trained to wires the system of training is somewhat different. Vines may be planted 4 feet apart on the sides. The general tendency is to permit the vines to grow year after year without pruning. Then, when someone begins to prune it properly, the owner thinks that it is being ruined.

The vigor of a vine is considerably increased by pruning. Cutting back the previous season's growth will give better results than additional fertilizer. Cut back the previous season's growth approximately one fourth of its length each year until the arbor is covered. Thin out canes less than pencil-sized and leave several of those larger cut back to two or three buds. Practice thinning out and cutting back each year thereafter and do not allow a vine to go without any pruning.

When a vine becomes unproductive and there is an excess of non-fruiting wood present, severe pruning is essential. It may be necessary to cut it back almost to the ground in order to stimulate vigorous growth, which, in turn, is trained up as previously described.

Duration of Bearing: 50 years or more.

Cultivation: Weed growth should be suppressed by using a mulch or by cultivation and hoeing.

Fertilization: Apply approximately one-half pound of a complete fertilizer to a bearing vine in a ring about 2 feet away from the trunk, or broadcast over the surface just as growth begins in the spring. Young non-bearing vines should receive from one-half to one-third of the above amount and at the same time.

Thinning: Thinning is not necessary if a bearing vine is pruned and trained as suggested, as it can comfortably care for the entire crop.

Harvesting: Grapes should not be harvested until they are fully ripe, at which time they have reached their highest sugar content and flavor. Each bunch should be handled carefully and preferably removed with a pair of scissors to prevent shattering or other injury.

Pest and Disease Control: See the Spray Schedule at the end of this chapter.

VARIETIES OF MERIT

Moore's Early: Black in color, ripens two weeks earlier than the Concord. Not so high in quality. Not such good color. Berries crack easily. Bunch not compact. Shoulders (upper part of grapes) not very good.

Worden: Ripens ten days before the Concord. Berries larger than the Concord. In wet, rainy weather, the berries will crack. When ripening on the bunch, those that ripen first will not wait until the others ripen (tend to shell). Highly recommended, more so than the Concord.

Concord: An old variety. Widely grown except in the warmer sections. Can be depended upon. Still sort of wildish. Will grow without any cultivation. Likes moisture.

Agawam: Large, red. About 2½ times as large as the Concord. Not highly colored. Good flavor. Drawback, hard to swallow. Very vigorous grower.

Caco: Red in color. Yield and quality good. One of the best all-round grapes.

Brighton: Never plant alone. About the only variety that must be cross-pollinated. Recommended for cooler parts. On heavy soil, plant 8 by 8 feet. It is usually planted 6 by 6 feet.

Delaware: About three-sixteenths inch in diameter. Leaves are tiny and many. Must spray thoroughly on account of mildew. Small, red, compact. Late and excellent flavor. Red, small bunches.

Portland: Early white, vigorous and excellent flavor.

Green Mountain: Medium late, white, dark green, sprightly flavoured.

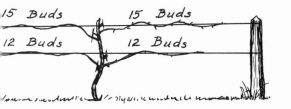

15 Buds   15 Buds

12 Buds   12 Buds

Next year the four fruiting branches are pruned off and the four buds become branches, but are cut to 12 and 15 buds.

SPRAYING OF FRUIT TREES AND BUSH AND VINE FRUITS

Equipment: Any type of hand- or machine-driven sprayer will give satisfactory results from the disease and insect control standpoint, if all parts of the leaves and fruit are covered. One cannot figure on over forty hours of good spraying weather per week. Therefore, the size of the sprayer should be such that complete coverage can be given to all trees to be sprayed within a week.

For a small home orchard consisting of 15 to 20 trees and other small fruit, a five-gallon knapsack sprayer will be sufficient if the trees are not over 15 feet in height. A stepladder will increase efficiency and thoroughness in covering taller trees.

For a small orchard of 25 to 150 trees a hand barrel-pump, 30–60 gallons in capacity, has a pressure capacity of 75–125 pounds and will spray from 1 to 3 gallons per minute.

A small, power sprayer with a capacity of 100 gallons may be purchased in place of the barrel-pump for orchards consisting of 5 to 15 acres. Such a sprayer has a capacity of delivering 3 to 5 gallons of spray per minute at a pressure of 250 pounds.

No machines, even when new, can be depended upon to deliver advertised capacities when placed in service. The average sprayer will not generally deliver over 70 percent capacity after the newness is worn off. No machine will stand up if operated at full capacity. Therefore, get a machine that need not be operated at full speed in order to get the job done satisfactorily.

Spray Schedules: The spray schedules which follow are not intended to be discussions from the commercial viewpoint, but rather to give the home grower an insight into insect and disease control.

Trees and fruits are attacked by insects and disease at various stages in their development. Prevention is better than cure, for once an insect or disease attacks a fruit, it decreases in value. Therefore, sprays should be applied to prevent them from gaining a foothold. Certain insects and diseases must be controlled at a definite time or over a definite period. Some materials, especially those which keep fungous diseases under control, may be used in place of others. These substitutions should be closely observed.

BEARING YIELDS

TREE FRUITS	ANNUAL YIELD PER PLANT
Apple-Dwarf	1¼ to 1½ bushel
Standard	5 to 10 bushel
Pear-Dwarf	1¼ to 1½ bushel
Standard	1 to 4 bushel
Plums	1 to 2 bushel
Peaches	2 to 4 bushel
Sour Cherry	1 to 2 bushel
Sweet Cherry	1 to 2 bushel
Quince	½ to 1 bushel

SMALL FRUITS	ANNUAL YIELD PER PLANT
Blackberries	1 to 1½ quarts
Blueberries	4 quarts
Currants	3 quarts
Grapes	1¼ to ½ bushel
Gooseberries	3 to 4 quarts
Raspberries	1½ quarts
Strawberries	¾ to 1 quart

Yields vary according to size, age, vigor of plant and growing conditions.

APPLE AND PEAR SPRAY SCHEDULE

NO.	TIME OF APPLICATION	MATERIALS	GALLONS OF WATER			INSECTS AND DISEASES TO CONTROL	SUGGESTIONS
			5	10	100		
1	Dormant—before green tips appear.	One of the Dinitro compounds at manufacturer's recommendation.				Aphids.	
2	Delayed Dormant until buds show ½" green.	Regular Dormant Oil (3%) or Miscible Oil at manufacturer's recommendation. Copper Sulfate Hydrated Lime	2½ cups. ⅙ cup. ¾ cup.	5 cups. ⅓ cup. 1½ cups.	3 gals. 2 lbs. 3 lbs.	Scale, Red Mite.	
3	Ten days later.	Captan.	⅓ cup.	1⅓ cups.	2 lbs.	Scab.	Repeat weekly to Calyx cup if scab.
4	Calyx cup, or when petals have fallen.	Lead Arsenate. Captan or Single Package Spray or All Purpose Mixture.	⅔ cup. ⅔ cup.	1⅓ cups. 1⅓ cups.	3 lbs. 2 lbs.	Codling Moth, Curculio, Leaf Roller, Scab.	Very important against Codling Moth: add ½ cup 50% Wettable DDT per 5 gal. water; use in balance of sprays as needed but no closer than 1 mo. before harvest.
5	Seven days after Spray #4.	Same as Spray #4.				Codling Moth, Curculio, Leaf Roller, Caterpillars, Scab.	
6	Ten days after Spray #5.	Same as Spray #4.				Codling Moth, Curculio, Leaf Roller, Caterpillars, Scab.	
7	Fourteen days after Spray #6.	Same as Spray #4.				Codling Moth, Scab, Fruit Spot.	
8	Ten days after Spray #7.	Same as Spray #4.				Codling Moth, Leaf Roller, Apple Maggot, Fruit Spot.	

NOTES: 1. Spray #7 and #8 may be dropped for early varieties.
2. Aphids are controlled by 40% nicotine sulfate or Malathion according to manufacturer's recommendations.
3. See Peach Schedule for Single Package or All Purpose Mixture.

PEACH AND NECTARINE SPRAY SCHEDULE

Explanation: On all stone fruits (peaches, nectarines, cherries, and plums) there is a husk which covers the young developing fruit in its early stages of development. As the fruit grows, this outer covering or shuck finally drops off, exposing the young fruit.

No.	Timing	Recommendation				Pest/Disease	Notes
	swell.	recommendation: Copper Sulfate *plus* Hydrated Lime *or* Liquid Lime-Sulfur.	½ cup. ¾ cup. 2 qrts.	1 cup. 1½ cups. 1 gal.	6 lbs. 3 lbs. 10 gals.		
2	When all blossom buds are pink.	Wettable Sulfur.	1½ cups.	3 cups.	8 lbs.	Brown Rot.	
3	When most of the blossoms are open.	Same as Spray #2.				Brown Rot.	Do not use more lead arsenate or less lime than recommended.
4	When shucks begin to split	Lead Arsenate. Zinc Sulfate. Hydrated Lime *plus* Wettable Sulfur *or* Single Package Spray (see footnote) *or* All Purpose Mixture (see footnote)	½ cup. 1¼ cups. 2 cups 1¼ cups.	1 cup. 2½ cups. 4 cups. 2½ cups.	2 lbs. 5 lbs. 8 lbs. 6 lbs.	Curculio and Brown Rot.	
5	Ten days later.	Same as Spray #4.				Curculio, Scab, Brown Rot.	
6	Fourteen days later.	Wettable Sulfur *or* Single Package Spray *or* All Purpose Mixture.	1¼ cups.	2½ cups.	6 lbs.	Scab and Brown Rot.	
7	Fourteen to 21 days later.	Same as Spray #6.					
8	Depends on section of country; check with County Agent on Oriental Fruit Moth Control.	DDT (50% Wettable Powder). Wettable Sulfur *or* Single Package Spray *or* All Purpose Mixture.	½ cup. 1¼ cups.	1 cup. 2½ cups.	2 lbs. 6 lbs.	Oriental Fruit Moth, Japanese Beetle, Brown Rot.	
9	Fourteen to 21 days later.	DDT (50% Wettable Powder). Wettable Sulfur *or* Single Package Spray *or* All Purpose Mixture.	¼ cup. 1¼ cups.	½ cup. 2½ cups.	1 lb. 6 lbs.	Oriental Fruit Moth, Brown Rot.	

NOTES: Single Package Spray Mixtures:
1. Should be used at manufacturer's recommendation regarding the amount to be used.
2. Where not shown in spray schedule apply specified materials.
3. Where many plants are to be sprayed, the cost is higher with single package sprays.
4. No mixing of materials is necessary.
5. Mixing incorrect amounts is eliminated.

All Purpose Mixture:
1. May be purchased as a single package or may be mixed at home.

Metoxychlor	50% Wettable Powder	5 oz.
Malathion	25% Wettable Powder	5 oz.
	plus	
Captan	50% Wettable Powder	5 oz.
	or	
Ferbam	70% Wettable Powder	5 oz.
Water		10 gals.

Do not use any form of Sulfur other than that recommended in Schedule.

CHERRY AND PLUM SPRAY SCHEDULE

(See explanation at top of Spray Schedule for Peaches)

NO.	TIME OF APPLICATION	MATERIALS	GALLONS OF WATER			INSECTS AND DISEASES TO CONTROL	SUGGESTIONS
			5	10	100		
1	In early spring before buds swell.	Liquid Lime Sulfur *or* Dry Lime Sulfur.	½ gal. 2½ cups.	1 gal. 5 cups.	10 gals. 24 lbs.	Scale and Black Knot.	
2	When outer covers or shucks are splitting from mature fruits.	Lead Arsenate. Captan *or* Ferbam *or* Single Package Spray *or* All Purpose Mixture.	½ cup. ⅔ cup. ½ cup.	1 cup. 1⅓ cups. 1 cup.	3 lbs. 2 lbs. 2 lbs.	Curculio, Brown Rot, and Leaf Spot.	Watch for presence of aphids.
3	Fourteen days after Spray #2.	Same as Spray #2.				Curculio, Brown Rot and Leaf Spot.	
4	When fruit begins to color.	Captan *or* Ferbam *or* Single Package Spray *or* All Purpose Mixture.	⅔ cup. ½ cup.	1½ cups. 1 cup.	2 lbs. 2 lbs.	Brown Rot and Leaf Spot.	
5	Immediately after fruit is harvested.	Same as Spray #4.				Leaf Spot.	Not needed for plums.

NOTES: If aphids present use 40% nicotine sulfate or Malathion at manufacturer's recommendation.
Single Package Sprays may not contain material for aphid control. All Purpose Mixture contains Malathion.
See Peach Schedule for All Purpose Mixture.

QUINCE SPRAY SCHEDULE

NO.	TIME OF APPLICATION	MATERIALS	GALLONS OF WATER		INSECTS AND DISEASES TO CONTROL	SUGGESTIONS
			5	10		
1	Dormant.	Oil Emulsion (3%) *or* Miscible Oil at manufacturer's recommendation.	2½ cups.	5 cups.	Scale.	If Scale not present omit this spray.

			5	10		
	Lead Arsenate					
	Hydrated Lime	1 cup.	2 cups.			
	Wettable Sulfur	1½ cups.	3 cups.			
	or					
	Single Package Spray					
	or					
	All Purpose Mixture.					
4	Same as Spray #3.			Codling Moth, Curculio, Scab.	
5	Same as Spray #3.			Codling Moth, Curculio, Fruit Moth, Scab.	Important for Fruit Moth.

NOTES: 1. By leaving out Lime in Spray #3, Fermate may be substituted for Wettable Sulfur all through the Schedule at the rate of 1 cup to 10 gals. of water.
2. Add Nicotine if aphids are present.
3. See notes under Peach Schedule for Single Package Spray or All Purpose Spray.

GRAPE SPRAY SCHEDULE

NO.	TIME OF APPLICATION	MATERIALS	GALLONS OF WATER		INSECTS AND DISEASES TO CONTROL	SUGGESTIONS
			5	10		
1	When new growth ½" to ¾" long.	Copper Sulfate. Hydrated Lime. Soap Chips.	½ cup. 1½ cups. ½ cup.	1 cup. 3 cups. 1 cup.	Black Rot.	Important for Black Rot.
2	When shoots are 10" to 12" long.	Copper Sulfate. Hydrated Lime. Soap Chips.	½ cup. 1½ cups. ½ cup.	1 cup. 3 cups. 1 cup.	Black Rot.	Very important for Black Rot.
3	One week after bloom when small grapes evident.	Copper Sulfate. Hydrated Lime. DDT (50% Wettable). Soap Chips.	⅓ cup. 1 cup. ½ cup. ¼ cup.	⅔ cup. 2 cups. 1 cup. 1 cup.	Black Rot, Mildew, Berry Moth, Root Worm, Leaf Hoppers, Rose Chafer.	Important for Black Rot and Berry Moth.
4	Three weeks later.	Same as Spray #3.	Same as Spray #3.	Same as Spray #3.	Black Rot, Mildew, Berry Moth, Root Worm.	May be omitted if Black Rot and Berry Moth not present.
5	Four weeks before harvest.	Same as Spray #3.	Same as Spray #3.	Same as Spray #3.	Same as Spray #4.	Same as Spray #4.

NOTES: If mildew no problem, Fermate may be substituted for (Bordeaux) Copper and Lime at rate of 1 cup to 10 gals. water. DDT will control Japanese Beetle. Do not apply DDT within 3 weeks of harvest. Wash fruit if residue noticeable. Bordeaux Mixture: Dissolve Copper Sulfate first, then add Lime. Commercial Bordeaux may be used at manufacturer's recommendation. Commercial spreader or sticker may be used in place of soap at manufacturer's recommendation. Single Package Spray may be used if no Sulfur present.

CONTROL OF FRUIT DISEASES AND INSECTS NOT INCLUDED IN SPRAY SCHEDULES

FRUIT	DISEASE	INSECT	DAMAGE	CONTROL
Apple, Pear		Codling Moth		Chemically treated bands. Gathering of worm infested apples.
		Borers	Large white grubs bore into limbs, thereby weakening them. Presence is indicated by sawdust exuding from their holes.	Dig out borers with knife or wire. Wrap trunks of trees with paper.
	Fireblight		Spreads very rapidly, causing the affected parts to turn dark brown in color and also to shrink. Leaves turn dark brown to black and hang on very tenaciously.	Do not fertilize trees too heavily. Prune out several inches below injury. Use Fireblight Canker solutions and preventive sprays of Bordeaux. Use antibiotic sprays.
Peach		Peach Tree Borer	Larvæ bore through bark and outer sapwood leaving brown sawdust combined with gum-like substance.	Paradichlorobenzene, applied September 1–20 when soil is dry. Remove trash and grass from base of trees. Use $\frac{3}{4}$ oz. of PDB in complete circle around trunk 2″ from trunk and 1″ wide. Cover PDB with 3″ of soil; remove soil covering in 3–4 weeks; if wet, 5–6 weeks. On young trees, dig borers out with knife or wire. Paint trunks with DDT (check time of application with County Agent).
	Brown Rot		Peaches turn brown and shrivel.	Remove brown dried peaches, rake up fallen brown dried peaches, burn.
Plum	Brown Rot		See Peach	Practice clean cultivation (see Peach).
Bramble Fruits, Raspberry, Blackberry, etc.	Anthracnose		Grayish spots on leaves and canes, dieback of fruiting shoots.	Spray, just as green tips appear with 1 gallon liquid lime sulfur to 20 gallons of water; or $2\frac{1}{2}$ tablespoons of Dinitro Paste per gallon of water.
	Galls		Knobby growths on crowns, canes, and roots.	Healthy plants, uncontaminated soil, and crop rotations.
	Orange Rust		Plants dwarfed, stunted appearance, at first with slight orange tinge, later leaves covered with orange looking powder.	Ferbam sprays, early removal of infected plants and removal of wild brambles. Before infected plants are removed scorch with blow torch to kill spores.
	Virus		Plants stunted, dwarfed, leaves curled, mottled, stunted, and crumbly berries.	Disease free plants, isolation, and rogue plantings regularly. Resistant varieties.
		Raspberry, Byturus or Fruit Worm	Light brown beetle, somewhat hairy. Skeletonizes newly formed leaves. Larvæ tiny white worm, completely hidden from view in berry.	Against beetle 4 lbs. lead arsenate to 100 gals. water. Dust plants with Rotenone. $\frac{1}{2}$ cup DDT (50% Wettable) to 5 gals. water.

NOTE: Spray raspberries only when insects and diseases require it. 1% Rotenone Dust may be used near harvest if raspberry beetles or Japanese Beetles appear serious.

FRUIT	DISEASE	INSECT	DAMAGE	CONTROL
Bramble Fruits, Raspberry, Blackberry, etc.		Raspberry Sawfly	Spiny, many legged, pale green worm, ¾″ long. Feeds on foliage.	Lead arsenate to 3 lbs. to 100 gals. water. ½ cup DDT (50% Wettable) to 5 gals. water.
		Raspberry Caneborer	Young shoots girdled with two rings approximately 1″ apart. Larvæ leaving hole in cane below girdle.	3 lbs. lead arsenate to 100 gals. water. Cut off infected part and burn.
		Rose Chafer	Yellow brown beetles ½″ long. Eat foliage and fruit buds.	DDT (50% Wettable) 2 lbs. to 100 gals. of water.
Currants and Gooseberries		Scale		Spray Oil.
		Aphids	Small yellowish insects on under sides of leaves causing leaves to curl.	Nicotine sulfate.
		Currant Worms	Green worm with black spots. Eats foliage.	1% Rotenone Dust Lead arsenate, 3 lbs. to 100 gals. water.
		Currant Borers	Small grayish white larvæ which bores into stems causing wilting.	Remove infected part.
	Powdery Mildew		Whitish powdery mold later turning reddish brown.	Fermate ¾ cup to 5 gals. water or 4–6–100 Bordeaux (copper sulfate, hydrated lime, water).
	Leaf Spot		Small brownish spots causing foliage to turn yellow and drop.	Same as above.
	Anthracnose		Same as above.	Same as above.
Strawberry		Strawberry Leaf Roller	Leaflets folded and webbed together by small greenish worm.	2 cups lead arsenate to 10 gals. water or TDE before blossoms appear.
		Spittle Bug	Wet gummy masses in berry clusters or leaf crotches covering small green insects.	Lindane 25% Wettable Powder ⅓ cup to 5 gals. water; or ¾% Rotenone dust.
		Root Worms	Small beetles which eat leaves, larvæ feed on roots.	At planting time: work lightly into soil 40% Chlordane Wettable Powder at the rate of 30 lbs. per acre.
		White Grubs	Large white grubs attacking roots.	Same as above.
	Leaf Spots		Purplish spots with gray centers.	Spray with 4–4–50 Bordeaux at 10-day intervals; or Fermate ¾ cup to 5 gals. water.
	Red Stele		Dying of feeding roots. Roots show red cores.	Resistant varieties.

NOTE: For more detailed information concerning the above diseases, insects, damage and controls, consult your County Agent or State Experiment Station.

XXXIX

THE HOME VEGETABLE GARDEN*

By John A. Andrew, Jr. *

THE home garden, when properly planned and planted, will supply a variety of vegetables for home use throughout the entire growing season, and will furnish enough for canning, freezing and storing. It is also one of the greatest sources of pleasure and recreation for the home owner. Much satisfaction comes from careful planning and planting. As fresh vegetables are an important item on one's diet, the necessity of having them fresh and in sufficient amount is apparent.

One will do well to consider the following points:

1. Plan and plant the garden so that it will be a pleasure. Figure out how much of each vegetable you will need for canning, for eating fresh, or for storing, and grow only those vegetables which will give high yields.

2. Figure out just how much ground you can properly care for. It is better to have a small garden properly cared for than to plant so much that you will be discouraged with it by midsummer. A plot 40 feet wide and 60 feet long will furnish an adequate supply of fresh vegetables for a family of six grown people and enough extra to can and store.

3. If the ground has not been previously planted, dig it up in the fall. Freezing and thawing weather will improve its physical condition. Fork in a good application of manure or compost if it is available. One ton will not be too much for a plot 40 feet by 60 feet.

If lime has not been applied for several years, have the soil tested. Lime is best applied after the manure has been dug in. It should be raked in to a depth of 2 inches if possible. If it is not possible to prepare the land in the fall, the same suggestions also hold true for spring preparation.

4. During the early or late winter months before it is possible to plant outside, plan your garden on a piece of paper so that no time will be lost or mistakes made at planting time.

* Spray Schedules were revised by Stephen Patronsky, Assistant Professor of Pomology, Rutgers University.

570

Order your seed from a reputable seedsman at an early date so as to be sure of getting the best varieties. Remember that several varieties of the same vegetable may be planted at the same time which will mature several weeks apart.

5. When planning a garden, the following points should be observed:

(a) The earliest and latest planting date. Beets, for example, may be planted as soon as the ground is workable in the spring and planted until midsummer. Most varieties mature in sixty days.

(b) The time of year at which each vegetable grows best. The small, quick-maturing varieties of radishes do best when planted in the spring and fall and should not be planted during the hot summer months. They mature in 25 to 30 days.

(c) Period over which the vegetable may be harvested. Sweet corn may be harvested over a period of 10 to 14 days while radishes may last for only several days if the weather is hot and the soil quite dry. Tomatoes are harvested over a period of two months.

(d) Those vegetables which mature at the same time should be planted together. Asparagus and rhubarb are two examples and are perennials. They should be planted at one end of the plot, where they will not interfere with soil preparation each year.

(e) The planting distances of vegetables in the home garden may be somewhat modified where hand cultivation is to be practiced entirely. Cabbage, broccoli, cauliflower are usually set 2½ to 3 feet apart when cultivated with horse-drawn implements; 2 feet is sufficient for hand cultivation.

(f) Plant tall-growing crops at one end of the garden and not next to the smaller ones which would be shaded too much. For example, beets should not be planted next to sweet corn but tomatoes or potatoes would give equally good results.

(g) Plant those vegetables next to each other which are susceptible to the same insects and diseases so that they may be controlled more easily. Cabbage, broccoli, brussels sprouts, and cauliflower belong to the same group, while eggplant, peppers, potatoes and tomatoes belong to another. Vine crops which include squashes, pumpkins, melons and cucumbers are also in one group.

(*h*) Plan to have the soil producing all the time. As soon as one crop is removed, plant another in its place. Early peas will mature in 70 to 80 days or about July 15. They may be followed by late beets, turnips, lettuce, snap beans, or spinach. This is known as successive cropping.

(*i*) Practice intercropping by planting a quick-maturing crop between those which take a longer time to mature. Radishes or lettuce may be intercropped with peas.

(*j*) Rotation. Some vegetables give better results if not planted in the same place the same year. It is poor practice to plant cabbage or any of its close relations after the early crop has been removed, as the following crop may be very inferior in quality and size.

Other points which might be helpful are as follows:

(1) If parsley is planted, have it on the outside edge next to the house so you won't have to walk through the entire garden to get to it.

(2) A path 4 feet wide and 60 feet long through the garden may be bordered with ageratum, zinnias, marigolds, calendulas or other such flowers. This will allow for rows 18 feet long each side of the path which can be easily cared for.

(3) With only a limited amount of time such as evening hours, a garden 50 feet by 50 feet is most practical.

Garden Equipment

A good many garden operations can be done with little effort if the equipment is at hand.

A spade and fork are necessary for preparing the soil as well as for harvesting some of the crops.

A rake is used for smoothing or fining the soil just after it is spaded and also to rake in fertilizers which have been applied.

A hoe is necessary to make rows, cover the seed, move the soil toward some plants, cut off weeds, and make holes for setting plants.

A stout line and stakes are necessary for making rows straight.

Other implements which may be used with a great deal of efficiency are hand weeders, trowels and hand cultivators, which have several attachments for marking rows, cutting weeds, and making furrows.

Commercial Fertilizers

Commercial fertilizers cannot take the place of organic matter in the soil, but do much to supplement it and are especially desirable where land is intensively cropped.

The three elements most essential for garden crops are nitrogen, phosphorus and potash. Generally speaking, nitrogen is used to promote leaf and vegetative growth; phosphorus promotes root growth and hastens maturity, and potash increases general sturdiness and resistance to disease.

A complete fertilizer is one which contains nitrogen, phosphorus and potash. It is usually described by figures giving the percentages of each element, *i.e.*, a fertilizer which contains 4 percent of nitrogen, 8 percent of phosphorus, and 4 percent of potash, is called a 4–8–4.

As plants need a well-regulated diet, an understanding of the use of fertilizers and of the reasons for their application will greatly help the gardener.

Every plant has three stages, the germinating and sprouting, the vegetative, and the fruiting. In the germinating stage, the seed absorbs moisture which, when added to heat, changes the concentrated food contained in each seed to a simple form and is sufficient to make a sprout appear through a surface of soil.

From the time the first true leaves begin to turn green until the fruit begins to form, the plant is in the vegetative state. From the time the fruit first begins to form, the plant is in the fruiting stage.

As plants such as lettuce and spinach are eaten in the vegetative stage, tomatoes, peppers and eggplant in the fruiting stage, it is easy to understand that fertilizer requirements vary greatly. Both phosphorus and potash when placed in the soil are available to plants over a long period, but nitrogen has various forms differing widely in the quickness with which they become available. Nitrogen may be classified into three types: (1) Inorganic, available as soon as dissolved in water; example, nitrate of soda, which is available under all soil conditions. (2)

Organic, which must undergo complete decomposition before nitrogen is available; examples, tankage and dried blood, available in about a month if the soil is warm, as the bacteria which promote decay are not otherwise active. (3) Those which are halfway between (1) and (2) must be changed to the nitrate form; example, ammonium sulphate which becomes available in a week or two after being applied. No. (1) is used early in the spring when the soil is cold and at all times for quick results. The effect of an application lasts only two or three weeks and for continuous quick growth over a long period, (1), (2), and (3) should be mixed together.

Many complete fertilizers are on the market, some having fancy trade names, others using the firm name and having the contents described by figures.

As already noted, a one-hundred-pound bag of a good complete fertilizer each season is a great aid in the production of a 50-foot by 50-foot garden.

Where fertilizers have been applied to the first crop, the succeeding crop's requirements are practically satisfied without applying additional fertilizer.

Methods of Applying Fertilizer

1. Broadcasting it over the surface and raking it in just previous to planting.

2. Scattering it in the drill or furrow and raking it into the soil just previous to planting.

3. Broadcasting between the rows during the growing season.

4. Drilling it in with an attachment on the seed planter.

5. Applying it in narrow bands, 3 to 4 inches away from the plants and covering it with soil.*

Note: Fertilizer will prevent germination if it comes in contact with the seed and will burn the foliage if it is spread on it.

Control of Vegetable Diseases

Precaution in Use of Frames and Hotbeds. In many cases when vegetables have been started early in coldframes or hotbeds, instead of in the garden, diseases will appear after their trans-

* The most approved method.

planting into the open. The cause can often be traced to insufficient care in preparing the seed bed. Many diseases are able to winter-over in old seed beds and gardens, while many of the more damaging ones are also carried over by the seed, such as early and late blights of celery; leaf blights and fruit rots of cucumbers, eggplant, melons, and squashes; black rot and black leg of cabbage, turnips and cauliflower; early blight, leaf spot and bacterial canker of tomatoes and others. Therefore, it is highly important to use clean seed and also clean seed bed soil in starting the crop. This may be assured to a large extent by observing the following points:

1. Save seed only from disease-free plants and as early in the season as possible.

2. Purchase seed from reputable seedsmen.

3. Disinfect seed when necessary in order to kill disease germs. (See "Seed Treatment", page 475.)

4. Change the soil every year in hotbeds, coldframes, benches, etc., or, if practicable, move the site of the hotbeds or coldframes to soil previously used for other crops. Disinfect containers, sides and covers of beds with formaldehyde (1 part F. to 45 parts water).

5. Do not use old seed beds unless soaked with formaldehyde solution. This process kills parasites before sowing the seed. Add formaldehyde dust to the soil, using 8 ounces of a 6 percent dust to each bushel of soil; sow seed, and water. Gas will diffuse through the soil, kill the damping-off fungi and disinfect the seeds as well. For full instructions see page 476.

6. Do not use manure or compost under seedlings or transplants if you know it contains old vegetable refuse.

Investment in good seed justifies safeguarding the crop in the seed bed. While the use of disease-free seed and clean seed bed soil are important steps in producing strong healthy plants, so is good seed bed management also. Healthy plants in seed beds usually mean a disease-free crop in the garden.

Precaution Against Infection from Outside Sources. Since many important garden diseases of vegetables secure their start in the seed bed or coldframe, even in spite of precautions already mentioned, we must guard against infection from outside sources. Such sanitary and protective steps consist of the following:

1. Avoid too frequent watering and excess watering of beds; instead, water more heavily at longer intervals; water only in the forenoon and ventilate well to hasten drying as soon as possible. Proper watering, heating and ventilating of beds not only insure sturdy, vigorous-growing plants, but also provide conditions that are not favorable for damping-off and other diseases.

2. Avoid handling or disturbing the plants while they are wet; otherwise where there are only traces of the disease it might spread in the bed.

3. Discard spotted, wilted and otherwise diseased plants for they are starters of infection.

4. Avoid introducing old plant debris and contaminated soil into seed beds and coldframes.

5. Treat the celery bed at ten- to fourteen-day intervals with copper-lime dust or Bordeaux Mixture when plants are 1 inch high.

Remember that thorough protection of the vegetable crop against diseases may be accomplished easily while it occupies so limited a space.

APPROXIMATE SEED QUANTITIES

Asparagus	1 oz.—800–1,000 plants
Beans	1 lb.—100 feet
Beet	1 oz.—50–75 feet
Broccoli	
Brussels Sprouts	
Cabbage	¼ oz. will give 700 plants
Cauliflower	
Kale	
Chard	1 oz.—100 feet
Carrots	1 oz.—100 feet
Celery	¼ oz.—500–800 plants
Corn (Sweet)	1 lb. for 125 hills
Cucumbers	½ oz.—25 hills
Endive	¼ oz.—50 feet
Eggplant	¼ oz.—750 plants
Kohlrabi	¼ oz.—75–100 feet
Leek	1 oz.—100 feet
Lettuce	¼ oz.—750 plants
Muskmelon	1 oz.—35–50 hills
Watermelon	1 oz.—35–50 hills
Parsley	½ oz.—100 feet
Onion seed	1 oz.—100 feet
Onion sets	1 quart—50 feet
Parsnip	¼ oz.—100 feet
Peas	1 lb.—40–50 feet
Peppers	¼ oz.—600 plants
Pumpkin	1 oz.—20 hills
Rhubarb	1 oz.—75–100 feet
Radishes	1 oz.—75–100 feet
Spinach	1 oz.—75 feet

CAN BE TRANSPLANTED

Asparagus	Broccoli	Celery
Beets	Brussels Sprouts	Swiss Chard

Cabbage	Lettuce
Cauliflower	Onion
Endive	Parsley
Eggplant	Peppers
Kale	Rhubarb
Kohlrabi	Tomatoes
Leek	

CAN BE GROWN IN POTS AND PLANTED OUTSIDE

Beans, Lima	Cucumbers	Melons
Corn, Sweet	Gourds	Watermelons

Storing Home-grown Vegetables

Many people who have vegetable gardens like to grow surplus crops for winter consumption, especially beets, carrots, turnips, onions, cabbage, potatoes, winter squash, parsnips, and salsify. All crops must be matured late in the season for successful storage. Crops maturing earlier will not store successfully. Root crops, including carrots, beets, potatoes, salsify, and parsnips, require cool and fairly moist conditions. Onions and winter squash must be kept warm and dry.

In the House. A cool room in a house cellar should be about 8 by 8 feet to provide sufficient space for a family of five or six from a garden of 5,000 square feet. This room should be built so that it will keep the vegetables from freezing and prevent them from becoming too warm. The floor should be of soil and the walls and ceilings made of 2-inch by 2-inch studs about 3 feet apart and covered on both sides with paper and insulating lumber.

In a Mound of Soil. Root crops including potatoes and cabbage may be piled on level ground, the pile being 3 feet long at the base and tapering to about 2 feet at the top. A 4- to 6-inch layer of straw is put over the vegetables except at the top which is left open about 4 inches to make provision for ventilation. A piece of pipe may be placed on top to allow for ventilation. Then the hay or straw is covered with 12 to 18 inches of soil. In cold weather, a board or stone is placed over the top of the pipe.

The disadvantage of such a pit is that it cannot be opened in cold weather, but serves the purpose of keeping vegetables until the spring months.

A Storage Pit

This type of storage pit should be situated in a location which has adequate drainage. It may be built where the ground is level if the soil is well drained and water does not remain on the surface for any length of time.

The pit to be described has been used successfully for several years with the most satisfactory results. Apples, potatoes and other vegetables which will not keep well in a warm, dry cellar have been kept in this pit until May with very little loss.

1. Dig a pit 9 feet long, 6 feet wide and 5 to 6 feet deep.

2. Place three 6-foot posts on each side as close to the soil as possible and set 1 foot into the soil which is firmed around them.

3. Brace these posts with 2 × 4's, one for each side and one across the back and front ends.

4. Place 2 × 4's across the tops of the posts on the sides and also on the ends.

5. Cover the top and sides with rough but strong boards.

6. Remove soil so a door may be used as an entrance in the front end.

7. A door 4 feet high and 2½ feet wide will be very satisfactory and is supported against two 2 × 4 uprights which are used for the framework.

8. Use waterproof paper to cover the top.

9. Fill in with soil the space between the sides of the frame and the earth walls of the pit.

10. Cover the top with 12 to 18 inches of hay when the weather gets cold. Hay is also packed around the door to prevent freezing.

This pit contains approximately 250 cubic feet. It can be built for a moderate sum and will last for many years with slight repairs. It will more than make up for its cost the first year.

CULTURAL DIRECTIONS

Artichoke—Globe

The Globe Artichoke is a tender perennial which must be protected to withstand freezing temperatures.

Botanical Name: Cynara Scolymus.

Soil Preparation: The Globe Artichoke requires large amounts of plant food. The soil should be manured at the rate of ¼ ton to 500 square feet and should also receive an application of a 4-8-4 or 5-10-5 fertilizer at the rate of 1 pound to 35 square feet. Heavy clay soils should be avoided for best results.

Propagation: Seed is sown in flats during February or the early part of March in a greenhouse or hotbed. When the seedlings are 3 inches high, transplant to 3-inch pots and plant outside after all danger of freezing temperatures has passed. The plants are set 3 feet apart in rows which are 4 feet apart.

During the following year, many suckers will develop at the base of the plant. Remove all but six to eight of them when about 8 inches high. If removed with a knife so as to obtain a root system with them, they may be transplanted to a new location.

As the parent plants are unproductive after the fourth year, constant renewing is necessary to keep up production.

Fertilization and Cultivation: A complete fertilizer may be applied during the growing season if needed. The plants should receive clean cultivation to suppress weed growth and thereby conserve moisture.

Harvesting: Plants grown from seed do not produce buds the same year. Suckers will in many cases produce a few buds the same year.

Artichoke—Jerusalem

Botanical Name: Helianthus tuberosus.

Origin: A perennial plant which was known to be cultivated by the Indians. The edible portion is the tuber which develops in the ground. The part above ground closely resembles the sunflower when in bloom.

Soil: Practically any type of soil will give good results if it is in a fair state of productivity. An application of manure plus the use of a 4-8-4 or 5-10-5 commercial fertilizer broadcast at the rate of 1 pound to 50 square feet just previous to planting will be beneficial.

Planting: The tubers may be planted whole or cut like potatoes just previous to planting, which takes place in early spring or fall. The planting distance is 18 to 24 inches in the row and 3½ to 4 feet between the rows; they should be covered with 2 inches of soil.

Harvesting: The tubers may be dug in the fall after top growth ceases, or left in the ground until spring. It is important that all of the tubers be removed; otherwise those left will become a nuisance if other crops are grown in that place.

Storage: The tubers may be stored by putting them in any type of container with sufficient soil to prevent drying out. They may be left outdoors in this container all winter and even if the temperature falls to 20° below zero they will not be affected; in fact a little frost improves the flavor.

Asparagus

Botanical Name: Asparagus officinalis, derived from the Greek word meaning to swell or be ripe.

Origin: Known as food in Europe more than two thousand years ago; grown in this country since colonial days.

Soil: Asparagus will grow on almost any soil, but its growth and development are retarded by too much moisture. A sandy, well-drained soil is best. Also, as a sandy soil warms up quickly in the spring, maturity is hastened. Soil should be plowed or spaded deeply, 10 inches is not too much. Before plowing, well-rotted manure should be spread over the whole area about 2 inches deep; fork or disk the soil until it is very fine.

Planting: Asparagus roots will produce a crop one or two years earlier than if they are grown from seed. One-year-old roots are preferable, because they can stand transplanting much better than the larger ones at two years of age. Plant in trenches 6 to 8 inches deep, 18 inches apart in the rows, with rows 4 feet apart. Cover with 3 inches of soil and as the plants grow, pull more soil around them.

Sowing: Sow the seed as soon as frost is out of the ground in rows 18 inches apart, two seeds to the inch. Germination is slow, but may be hastened by soaking seed in water for two to three days before planting. Germination takes about thirty days, and it is advisable to mix radish seed, $\frac{1}{4}$ radish to $\frac{3}{4}$ asparagus, to keep rows marked and the soil from packing. Sow one ounce of asparagus seed to each 40 feet, and cover seed $\frac{1}{2}$ inch.

Transplanting: When the plants are 3 inches high, thin out 4 inches apart. In the latter part of August or in the following spring move to permanent position, setting plants 18 inches apart in trenches 8-10 inches deep and 4–5 feet apart. Cover plants with 2 inches of soil and as they begin to grow, add more soil. Plants must be set in trenches as they have a tendency to rise as they grow old. No crop can be expected for the first two years, as it takes that length of time for the roots to become well established. With good care an asparagus bed should last ten to fifteen years.

Inter-cropping: When first set out, asparagus plants are so small that there is sufficient space between the rows to plant lettuce, radishes, spinach, beets, turnips, carrots, etc.

Cultivation: Keep ground well loosened at all times to a depth of 1 inch to suppress weed growth and to conserve moisture.

Fertilizers: An application of well-rotted manure applied in the late fall or early spring will promote quick, succulent growth. Nitrate of soda, $\frac{1}{2}$ ounce to each plant, applied just before growth starts in the spring, will promote good growth and high quality. Stop harvesting as soon as hot weather begins and broadcast a complete fertilizer, formula 4-8-4, at the rate of 1 pound to 75 feet between the rows. This application promotes vigorous growth, resulting in a large

amount of food being stored in the roots, which will really furnish the next season's crop. The fertilizers which are applied one season as well as the care given that season are materially responsible for next season's crop.

Harvesting: Cut the shoots 1 to 2 inches below the ground, either early in the morning, or late in the afternoon; the best length is 6 to 8 inches. In hot weather, cut twice a day to prevent the shoots from becoming spindly. If not cut immediately before cooking, keep in a cool, moist place. An asparagus bed can be cut over a period of six to eight weeks.

Remarks: If white tips are desired, set the plants in rows 7 to 8 feet apart and ridge plants up in early spring before growth starts. Forty plants are sufficient for a family of six.

Varieties: Mary Washington—rust resistant, produces good shoots, and is not sensitive to hot weather. Martha Washington is very similar. Both are recommended for freezing.

Bean

Botanical Name: Phaseolus.

Origin: The American cultivated beans were first known to cultivation only three to four hundred years ago in North and South America. The string bean is the oldest, having been introduced about the end of the fifteenth century. This also applies to the lima bean which came into cultivation soon afterwards. There are two types of beans: those grown for their edible pod as the string or snap bean, and those grown for the seed as the shell, kidney, and lima bean.

Soil Type and Preparation

Bush Snap Beans: For the first and second crop, the soil should be fairly light, but for the summer and fall crops, the soil may be much heavier. The soil does not have to be as fertile as for most of the other crops as too much vine growth, encouraged by a rich soil, lessens the productivity. Add a little well-rotted manure or a commercial fertilizer such as a formula 4-8-4 and fork it in to a depth of 6 to 8 inches, but if the soil is not poor, such an application of manure or fertilizer is not advisable.

Bush Limas: These require a much more fertile soil and one which is retentive of moisture during the hot summer months.

Pole Snap Beans and Pole Lima Beans: Require much more fertile soil than either of the bush beans.

When and How to Plant

Bush Snap Beans (String Beans): May be planted after all danger of frost is over until the middle of August, 2 inches apart in the row and 2 feet apart between the rows. Cover with an inch of soil. Seed should germinate in a week, and the plants should be mature in 45 to 60 days. One pound of seed per 100 feet of row.

Bush Limas: Seed may be sown after all danger of frost is over until the first week in June—4 inches apart in the row and 2 feet apart between the rows. Recent experiments have proven that a much higher percentage of germination results when care is taken to plant lima beans eye-downward. Cover with 1½ inches of soil and they should germinate in ten days. Beans should mature in 85 to 100 days. One pound of seed per 100 feet of row.

Pole Snap Beans: Plant after all danger of frost is over until the first of July in hills 3 feet apart each way. To make hills, remove one or two shovelfuls of soil, put in a shovelful of manure, cover with 4 inches of soil. Use poles about 7 feet long, inserting 1 foot of it into the ground and set before planting the seed. Plant 6 to 8 seeds, cover with 1 inch of soil and when 4 inches high thin out, leaving the four best plants. One-half ounce per pole.

Pole Lima Beans: Seed may be planted eye-downward after all danger of frost is over until the third week in May. Prepare hills and plant in the same way as for pole snap beans. One-half ounce of seed per pole.

Succession and Inter-cropping

Bush Snap Beans: For a succession, plant every ten days to two weeks.

Pole Snap Beans: An early and late planting.

Bush Lima Beans: Two plantings are best.

Pole Lima Beans: Only one planting is necessary, as they bear all season.

Moisture Requirements: When too much moisture is present, excessive vegetative growth reduces the yield. The soil should be kept only slightly moist for the best results. Limas require more moisture than the string beans.

Cultivation: Shallow and frequent to remove weeds.

Manures and Fertilizers

Pole Snap Beans and Pole Lima Beans: A small handful of formula 4-8-4 applied in a ring around each hill when the blossoms first appear will give good results. When the first crop has been picked, a second application will invigorate the plants to produce a second crop.

Bush Lima Beans: These may also have a complete fertilizer broadcast between the rows, when they are beginning to bloom, at the rate of 1 pound to 75 feet.

Harvesting

Bush Snap Beans and Pole Snap Beans: These beans should be harvested any time before the pods begin to

toughen and before the bean itself begins to mature. Both the quality and flavor are superior when the beans are harvested while still young. Do not allow the beans to become overripe as this condition has a tendency to stop plant growth and affects future development. Pick every two or three days, and only when the vines are dry, to prevent Bean Rust. This disease does not harm the vines but impairs the appearance of the pods. Keep the beans in a cool place after harvesting to prevent deterioration by loss of moisture.

Bush Lima Beans and Pole Lima Beans: These should not be harvested until the pods are well filled. This may be determined by holding them up to the light. Harvest while the pods still have their attractive green color; do not leave them until they begin to turn yellow. Keep them in a cool, moist place after harvesting. The quality is best if they are eaten as soon after picking as possible.

Remarks: 100-foot row yields 50 pounds Snap, or 20 pecks Pole Snap, or 75 pounds Bush Lima, or 20 pecks Pole Lima.

VARIETIES

Bush Snap Beans: Green Bountiful, Black Valentine, Burpee's Stringless Green-Pod*, Fulcrop*, Giant Stringless Green-Pod*, Rival*, Tendercrop*, Tenderpod*. Varieties starred are recommended for freezing.

Bush Wax Beans: Brittle Wax, Surecrop Wax, Round-pod Kidney Wax, Puregold Wax. All are recommended for freezing.

Pole Snap: Kentucky Wonder (Green) and Kentucky Wonder Wax, both 65 to 70 days to maturity. Recommended for freezing.

Bush Lima: Baby Fordhook, Fordhook 242, Peerless, Triumph; all are recommended for freezing.

Pole Lima: King of the Garden (recommended for freezing) and Challenger mature in 80 to 90 days.

Beet

Botanical Name: Beta vulgaris. Derived from fancied resemblance of the seed to the second letter of the Greek alphabet, beta.

Origin: Originating in the Canary Islands and countries around the Mediterranean Sea, beets have been under cultivation for over two thousand years.

Soil Preparation and Fertilizer: Beets may be grown in practically all types of soil, but one which is friable and well drained gives best results. Plow or fork over soil to a depth of 6 to 8 inches, and then fork or disk in a liberal application of well-rotted manure to a depth of 4 to 6 inches. Pulverize soil thoroughly, rake it over very evenly, broadcast and rake in a complete fertilizer, at the rate of 1 pound to every 50 or 75 square feet.

Sowing: As soon as the frost is out of the ground, sow seed in rows 15 inches apart, 3 seeds to an inch; cover with ½ inch of soil, firmly pressed. These seeds germinate in ten to fourteen days.

Thinning: When the plants are 2 inches high, they should be thinned to 1½ inches apart. These thinnings may be eaten as greens. When the beets are 1¼ inches in diameter, pull up every other one; these will be large enough to eat and those which are left will have room to develop properly.

Succession: For a continuous supply, plant seed every two weeks. One ounce of seed plants 75 feet.

Starting Under Glass: Seed may be started indoors, three weeks before outdoor planting date, in finely pulverized ordinary garden soil. Avoid excess watering. Plants may, if desired, be transplanted while still indoors, 1½ inches apart each way. These plants set out-of-doors the same time as seed is planted will mature two to three weeks earlier. Growth may be further hastened by broadcasting a complete fertilizer formula 4-8-4, at the time of transplanting, at the rate of 1 pound to 50 to 75 square feet.

Cultivation: Beets need shallow cultivation until plants are half grown; after this, it is not necessary as their leaves will shade the ground, control weed growth, and hold moisture in the soil.

Harvesting: Beets are ready for pulling when they are 1½ to 3 inches in diameter; size depending on variety. Keep in a cool moist place until they are used. After they are mature, they can be left in the ground a week or two before they begin to deteriorate.

Storing: Seed should be sown between the first and twentieth of July for the winter-storing crop. Harvest and remove tops early in October; store in moist sand at a temperature between 40 and 50 degrees. In a good root cellar they will keep in boxes or barrels without sand.

VARIETIES

Early: maturing in 45 to 50 days: Early Wonder, Eclipse.

Main crop: maturing in 55 to 60 days: Crosby's Egyptian and Detroit Dark Red. Longest keeping variety is the Blood Turnip which is grown only for winter use, but the main crop varieties may also be stored with good success.

For freezing: Detroit Dark Red, Edmond's Blood, Ohio Canner.

Broccoli

Botanical Name: Brassica oleracea var. italica.

Origin: Known in western Asia for over two thousand years, it has only recently become popular because of its newly discovered food value.

Soil: Any soil is satisfactory, if it is well provided with organic matter and a moderate supply of moisture. As the root system is very shallow and fibrous, proper preparation cannot be over emphasized. Soil should be well worked to a depth of 6 to 8 inches.

Fertilizer: A good application of well-rotted manure or 4-8-4 fertilizer forked in and then well pulverized.

Sowing: As Broccoli prefers a cool season, it is best to make two plantings, one in the spring (as soon as frost is out of the ground) and the other two months later, both sown at the rate of ⅛-ounce seed to 50 feet of row. Sow seed indoors in flats ¼-inch deep, in rows 2 inches apart. Several hundred seeds should germinate in seven days. When 4 inches high, transplant 18 inches apart in rows 2½–3 feet apart; transplant only the best plants. Seed may be started in coldframe or hotbed eight weeks before it can be sown in the open.

Moisture: A continuous supply of moisture is necessary for good growth and production; otherwise the plants will bear prematurely and the quality will be inferior.

Cultivation: Shallow, clean cultivation should be practiced frequently to conserve moisture whenever the soil has a tendency to pack.

Harvesting: The first crop looks like heads of green cauliflower and should be about 3 inches in diameter. It should be cut just before the heads begins to separate with 4–6 inches of stem. The second and succeeding crops come as small individual heads from shoots which appear after the first head has been cut. It has the best flavor when cut early in the morning. To prevent wilting and to conserve the flavor, keep in a shallow pan of water in a cool place until used.

Fertilizer: Just before the first crop is mature, a good commercial fertilizer (4-8-4) may be applied at the rate of 1 tablespoonful to each plant. Make a ring of fertilizer 6 inches from the stem of the plant and cover with 1 inch of soil.

VARIETIES

Calabrese: Ninety days to maturity. Italian Green Sprouting and De Cicco are recommended for freezing.

Brussels Sprouts

Botanical Name: Brassica oleracea var. gemmifera.

Remarks: This vegetable is grown for its small buds which mature in the axis of leaves along the main stem.

Soil and Fertilizer: The same as for Broccoli.

Planting: Two crops, the spring and fall ones, are the most satisfactory as the buds are not firm when grown in hot weather. Seed may be sown inside the same as Cabbage and the plants set out when the ground thaws out; or it may be sown inside at the same time the plants are set. Seed for the late crop is sown outside between May 20 and June 15. Cultural requirements are the same as for Cabbage.

Harvesting: The buds are mature when they are hard and from 1–1½ inches in diameter. They may be broken off, trimmed, and stored in a cool, moist place. A well-developed plant will produce from two-thirds to a quart of the best grade of buds. The plants may be left outside during freezing weather as they are very hardy.

VARIETIES

The Long Island Improved is the standard variety, and is recommended for freezing. Dobbie's Exhibition Variety from Dobbie Brothers in Edinburgh, Scotland, when planted in the spring, has produced buds all season but those produced in hot weather are not as firm. This variety grows to a height of $4\frac{1}{2}$ feet and should be planted $2\frac{1}{2}$ feet apart in the rows.

Cabbage

Botanical Name: Brassica oleracea var. capitata.

Origin: Cabbage was known as food more than four thousand years ago in western Asia.

Soil Type and Preparation: May be grown on any fairly fertile soil, but a sandy loam is best for the early crop as well as for the late crop, if the ground is well supplied with manure.

Fertilizer: The same as for Broccoli.

When and How to Plant: For a continuous supply, three crops should be planted. Seed for the first crop should be sown indoors or in a hotbed between the first and the middle of February, six to eight weeks before the date for setting out. Sow the seed in fairly light soil in rows 3 inches apart and cover with $\frac{1}{4}$-inch of soil. Seed should germinate in a week. When plants are 2 inches high, prick out 2 inches by 2 inches. They should be grown in a temperature of 70 degrees. Plants may be transplanted 3 inches by 3 inches, or in individual 3-inch pots, three weeks later, but this is not necessary. Plants may be transplanted to the garden as soon as the ground is workable, but the plants must be hardened off beforehand in order to withstand the unfavorable weather conditions. Set out in the garden 18 inches apart in the rows and $2–2\frac{1}{2}$ feet apart between the rows. Set the plants out a little deeper than they were inside.

Succession and Inter-Cropping: Early crop should mature the first week in July. The second crop planted the middle of March to the first of April should be ready to harvest from the last of July till the middle of August. Seed for the late crop may be sown outdoors in the open ground from the middle of June until the first of July. This should mature by October, and it may be stored. Inter-cropping is not practical.

Moisture Requirements: Cabbage requires a liberal supply of moisture for maximum development. Lack of moisture causes the heads to form prematurely. Too much moisture causes improper soil conditions.

Cultivation: The root system of the Cabbage is very fibrous and extremely close to the surface of the ground. For this reason cultivation should be light, but frequent enough to control weeds.

Manures and Fertilizers: Cabbage requires large amounts of nitrogen, phosphorus, and potash. Manures when applied in liberal amounts keep the soil in good physical condition and furnish a part of the nutrients, but unless the soil is very rich commercial fertilizers high in nitrogen, phosphorus, and potash, such as formulas 4-8-4 or 5-8-7, should be used. This should be broadcast at the rate of 1 pound to 25 square feet and raked in just before planting. It may be applied broadcast between the rows when, or just after, the plants are set out.

Harvesting: Do not harvest until the heads are solid, for soft heads are inferior and undeveloped. Cut several of the outer leaves with the head, for these will protect the head and keep it from deteriorating until used. If it is not harvested as soon as the heads are hard, the heads will burst. If the heads become hard, but the cabbage is not to be used for a week or so, simply give the plant a good jerk to break some of the roots, and leave it in the field until the head is wanted.

Storing: The late crop is the one most satisfactorily stored, especially for winter use. Pull plants up by the roots; place in a cellar with a temperature of 40 degrees and a fairly moist atmosphere. Store between the first and the middle of November. Although early varieties may be planted so as to mature late, they cannot be stored as satisfactorily.

VARIETIES

Early: Golden Acre, round; Early Jersey Wakefield, pointed head.

Midseason: Copenhagen Market, round head; Glory of Enkhuizen, round head.

Late: Penn State Ball, round head; Drumhead Savoy, drum-shaped and crinkly leaves.

Red: Mammoth Redrock, and a smaller variety, the Red Dutch.

Cabbage—Chinese

Botanical Name: Brassica pekinensis.

Origin: Probably a native of China, where it has been under cultivation for fifteen hundred years. Known to the authorities here for some time, but only recently used here in home gardens.

When and How to Plant: Does best on a rich soil, which will retain moisture. Sandy loam or loam soil well enriched with decayed manure before plants are set out is excellent. Seed may be sown outside as soon as the soil is slightly warm, or about May 1, and any time up until July 1. Distances should be $2–2\frac{1}{2}$ feet between the rows and 8–12 inches between plants. For fall crop, seed is sown about July 1; thin out when plants are 3 inches high. For general care and cultivation see Cauliflower. This vegetable cannot be transplanted.

Moisture: Plenty of moisture is required. Should the supply fail, a seed stalk will form before the head has fully developed. For this reason a muck soil, which is also rich in organic matter, will give good results.

Fertilizer: A good commercial fertilizer, such as a 4-8-4 formula, is very beneficial if applied ten days to two weeks after thinning. Apply at the rate of 1 pound to 100 feet between the rows.

Harvesting: Heads should be harvested when fully matured and developed. They should be firm, but the size depends on the variety. Cut from the roots as with Celery. Remove the loose outer leaves, until the bleached interior shows. Keep in a cool moist place; consume as soon as possible. It may, however, be kept several weeks under proper conditions.

VARIETIES

Chihili—18–20 inches, very solid with tapering head.
Pe-tsai—12–14 inches, fairly compact with broad head.
Wong bok—8–12 inches, rather loose, with broad head.

Carrot

Botanical Name: Daucus Carota var. sativa.

Origin: Carrots were known as food in temperate sections of Asia over two thousand years ago.

Soil: The best soil for this vegetable is a deep, mellow loam, which will not become too compact. Since carrots have a deep-root system and cannot penetrate a hard soil, the soil should by all means be fairly light. A hard, compact soil tends to force the carrots to put forth fibrous roots which are very disfiguring. Never plant this crop on a sod land, but on a land which has been prepared well beforehand by thorough plowing or forking. Apply a liberal amount of well-rotted manure, disk or fork this in, and then rake over the soil, making sure all the lumps are out and the soil is finely pulverized. If sod land is to be used, plant two or three deep-rooted crops over the area first, such as corn or potatoes.

When and How to Plant: The seed should be planted in early spring, as soon as the ground is workable. There are usually two crops: the spring one, for summer consumption, and the fall one, sown in June or July, depending on the locality, and harvested in November. Those harvested late are usually stored for winter use. Since both crops are treated alike, they can be discussed together, except for dates. Sow the seed at the rate of 1 ounce per 100 feet. Allow 1 foot between the rows, and since the seed is usually a long time in germinating, lettuce seed may be mixed with it. The lettuce seed will quickly germinate and mark the rows, so that cultivation will be easier until the carrots appear. Plant the seed as soon before or after a rain as possible, for they require a good deal of moisture in order to germinate. In a month's time, the carrots should be from 3 to 4 inches in height. At that time they should

be thinned, and the lettuce should be removed. Thin the carrots $\frac{3}{4}$ inch to $1\frac{1}{2}$ inches apart. The lettuce may be transplanted if desired. These thinnings are very young and tender and are delicious when served whole.

Succession: The early crop is followed by a fall crop which should be planted about the first of June. This receives the same treatment as the first one.

Moisture Requirements: Carrots need plenty of moisture particularly when the seeds are germinating. However, they should receive only a moderate supply when they really begin to grow, for too much moisture will make the roots crack, especially when they are reaching full size.

Cultivation: Cultivate to keep all the weeds out. However, the cultivation should be fairly shallow to prevent the formation of adventitious side roots which disfigure the main root so much. After the plants are 8 inches high, the tops will begin to fall over a bit, thereby making a natural mulch or ground cover which will prevent the weeds from coming up, and will conserve all the moisture necessary for the proper maturity of the crop.

Fertilizers: Three to four days after thinning, it is advisable to apply a good commercial fertilizer such as a formula 5-10-5, scattered over the area on a dry day. See Beet for rate of application.

Harvesting: The early crop is harvested about the first of July, depending on the date planted, and the nature of the weather of the locality. They should be pulled only as they are needed, for the fresher they are when cooked, the better they will be. The late crop is harvested about November and is usually stored.

Storing: Carrots should be stored in slightly moist sand if they are to be put in an ordinary cellar. This sand keeps them from drying out too much while in storage. However, if they can be stored in a good root cellar, they need only be put in bags. The natural dampness of a root cellar makes the damp sand unnecessary. Pull the carrots and let them dry out in the field for at least half a day before storing them either in sand or in a root cellar.

VARIETIES

The best varieties are the Red-cored Chantenay and Guerande, which are early and of the 3-inch stump-rooted size; the Danver's Half-long is the finest midseason carrot, being long, slender, and pointed. It usually is from 6–8 inches long, and it always pulls easily. For the late planting the best variety is the Long Orange, which is about 12 inches long, pointed, and large-cored. This is a good variety for storing. It should always be thinned to the width of three fingers and no more in order to encourage the root to be long and slender, as it should be.

Recommended for freezing: Chantenay, Nantes, Tendersweet.

Cauliflower

Botanical Name: Brassica oleracea botrytis.

Origin: Known as food in western Asia two thousand years ago.

Soil: Same as for Cabbage, Brussels Sprouts, and Broccoli.

When and How to Plant: Being a cool season crop, seed should be sown indoors about February 15. Sow in a sandy loam soil, 3 inches between rows; cover with ¼ inch of soil. When the plants are 1½ inches high, transplant to 2 inches apart each way. Keep at 55–60 degrees to develop a good root system and stocky tops. One more transplanting is advisable, but not usually practiced. Harden off plants a week before setting out, about April 15, 18 inches apart in rows 2½–3 feet apart.

Seed for the second or fall crop may be sown in the open ground between the middle of June and the first of July. One-eighth ounce of seed should produce at least 100 plants. Germination takes one week.

Moisture: Soil should be well supplied with moisture, especially when heads are beginning to form.

Cultivation: Keep weed growth suppressed at all times, but cultivation should be shallow to avoid root injury. For best results, cauliflower should be grown as quickly as possible.

Manures and Fertilizers: Manure is most effective if applied when the ground is being prepared. A complete fertilizer, 4-8-4, will hasten growth and may be applied at the rate of a good tablespoonful to each plant, two weeks after the plants have been set out. A second application at the same rate may be applied just as the tiny heads appear.

Shading: As the heads begin to form, the outside leaves should be brought together and tied at the top to keep heads completely shaded.

Harvesting: In two weeks to a month after the head has been tied up, depending on the variety and weather, it should be ready to harvest. Properly matured heads should be firm and show no signs of discoloration or breaking. Cut the head off at the junction of head and leaves; trim off any discolored leaves, leaving a few trimmed to within 1 inch of the top of the head. These will give protection until the head is ready for use. Store in a cool, moist place.

Storing: If the plants mature too quickly for consumption, as they may in hot weather, the entire plant may be pulled up by the roots and stored in a cool, moist place for about two weeks.

VARIETIES

Dwarf Erfurt and Snowball. These mature in from 100 to 120 days, depending on growing conditions. Both are recommended for freezing.

Celeriac

Botanical Name: Apium graveolens var. rapaceum.

Origin: Probably first grown in Europe although the date is not known. Same family as the celery and like it in many ways. The thick tuberous underground stem is the edible portion; the leaves resemble those of celery, but they are a darker green and smaller. Celeriac has a hollow stem.

Soil: The soil requirements are the same as for celery. Celeriac is a much slower growing plant.

Planting: The seeds may be started in the open ground, but there may be two crops, the first one started indoors and the second one in the open ground. The first crop should be sown indoors not later than the first of March, since it is slow to germinate and to grow, and it should be transplanted once about the first of April. Plants should be ready to set out in the open ground the middle of April, but this depends mainly on the locality and the seasons. This crop is set out in the open ground as celery is, but the distance between the rows may be lessened, for this vegetable is not hilled up more than 2 inches to be bleached. The leaves and stems are never used, only the enlarged root stem.

Harvesting: This first crop should be harvested on or before the first of September; the second or late crop will provide the succession. Pull up, clean off side roots and top, and use as soon as convenient.

Succession: The second crop should be started in the open ground from the middle to the last of May, with the same distance between the rows. When the plants are 2 inches high, they should be thinned to 6 inches apart.

After thinning or transplanting, from a week to ten days later, an application of a good commercial fertilizer should be put on at the rate of 1 pound to 35 square feet. Put it down the rows as close to the plants as possible and then cultivate it in. If the soil was not very rich with manure to begin with, another application equal to the first may be made a month later.

Cultivation: Shallow cultivation is necessary. The leaves should eventually grow so that no weed growth will be possible. Then cultivation need be done only occasionally.

Storing: Pull up, clean off the side roots, twist off the tops, and then store in moist sand at a temperature of 40–50 degrees.

Celery

Botanical Name: Apium graveolens. Derivation is speculative. Possibly from the Greek word for parsley —selinon.

Origin: In its wild state, celery has a wide range. It was not used for food until the sixteenth century.

Soil: Celery does best on soils which are well supplied with organic matter and which do not contain an over-abundance of clay. Land which has not previously been planted for several years should be manured and dug or plowed the fall previous to planting and these operations should be repeated in the spring. If manure is not available, any organic matter such as leaf mold may be used with good results. A complete fertilizer, such as a 4-8-4, 5-10-5, or 4-12-4, should be broadcast at the rate of 1 pound to 50 square feet and raked in just before setting out the plants.

When and How to Plant: Celery does best in the cooler parts of the year, and the spring and fall crops are most practical. All varieties do not mature at the same time; so it is possible to plant several at the same time and have a continuous supply for home use.

(1) *Early Crop:* For the first crop, sow seed in a hot-bed or coldframe about ten weeks before planting in the open ground, which may be done as soon as danger from heavy frost is past. Broadcast the seed after watering the soil and cover very lightly with fine sand. The temperature should be between 60° and 75° F. Four to five weeks after planting the seed, the plants will be large enough to transplant, though this is not necessary, as a little thinning in the seed bed will prove to be more satisfactory and faster growth will be made if transplanting is not practiced. Ten days before the plants are set in the field, withhold all water to harden them off. The plants are set 6 inches in the row and 2–3 feet between the rows.

Cultivation: Shallow cultivation will control weeds and thereby conserve moisture. The root system is very fibrous and shallow, so cultivation should not be more than 1 inch deep.

Bleaching: Celery must be bleached in order to get rid of the green coloring which gives it a bitter taste, and to cause the rapid growth of the undeveloped stalks in the crown. Boards 8 inches wide may be placed on both sides of the plants as close as is possible without injury, and kept in place by stakes 18 inches long, driven 6–10 inches into the ground at sufficient intervals to hold the boards upright. The distance between the boards at the top should be 3–4 inches. Be sure to have all leaves in a vertical position to protect the center leaves during bleaching. These small undeveloped leaves receive a stimulus when light is withheld, and in two weeks they should be the same height as the outside leaves. Then it is ready to be harvested. By bleaching only a few plants at a time, the early crop will last at least six weeks. There are numerous other methods of bleaching, but the principle is to exclude light from the leaves, make the plant compact, and force the heart to respond to the stimulus of light.

Waterproof bleaching paper and cardboard collars are some of the other materials used for this purpose. Soil should not be used for the early crop as there are too many injurious organisms in soil when it is warm.

Harvesting: The early crop is harvested by cutting off the stalk 2 inches below the ground. Trim off outside leaves, which are usually tough in warm weather. Store in a cool place.

(2) *Late Crop:* Seed is planted in a prepared seed bed, in a coldframe or in the garden from April 10 to May 10. Plants should be set in the garden between June 20 and July 20. Transplant 6 inches apart in the row and leave 4 feet between the rows. Inter-cropping with radishes, beets, lettuce or any other quick-maturing crop is practical.

Bleaching: The late crop is of the highest quality when bleached with soil. It can remain in the ground and survive a heavy freeze if the tops are adequately protected. About two months after the plants have been set in the field, begin to hill them up by pulling the soil toward them. Keep it even with the center of the plant but do not allow the soil to reach the center, or growth will be inhibited. Hill up ten days later and repeat if necessary until the plants are 12–18 inches in height.

Fertilizers: 1 pound of a high grade complete fertilizer containing nitrogen, phosphorus, and potash is applied to every 25–50 square feet at planting time. A quick-acting nitrogenous fertilizer such as nitrate of soda or Cal-Nitro, applied just before the bleaching process, will hasten the development of tender succulent stalks. One pound to 100 feet of row is sufficient.

Storing the Late Crop: If the crop has not been bleached with soil it may be trenched to prevent it from freezing. Dig a trench 2 feet wide and deep enough to allow the leaves to be on the same level as the ground and pack the celery, roots and all, in a close, upright position. Decayed or broken stalks should be removed before trenching. Mulch with hay in cold weather. It will keep outside until Thanksgiving. When bleached with soil, it may be dug with roots intact, put in boxes in a cool damp place, and kept for a much longer period.

VARIETIES

The Easy Blanching and Golden Self-Blanching types are the earliest to mature, requiring about 120 days. The Golden Plume type matures 2 weeks later and is excellent for an early or late crop. Many prefer the large Giant Pascal which is entirely a late, green variety, blanching creamy-white.

Swiss Chard

Botanical Name: Beta vulgaris, var. Cicla.

Origin: Of garden origin, but the date is unknown.

Soil: Fairly rich soil is good, and an application of well-decayed manure turned under before planting is beneficial.

Sowing: Sow seed as early in spring as the ground can be worked, in rows 18–30 inches apart, and when plants are 3 inches high, thin 3 inches apart. Thinnings may be used as greens. When plants are 7–9 inches high, thin to 9 inches apart. A crop matures in sixty days, but careful cutting before that time does no harm. One sowing will last until the crop is killed by autumn frost.

Cultivation: Cultivate shallowly and sufficiently often to keep down weeds.

Fertilizers: Two weeks after the last thinning, an application of 4-8-4 at the rate of $\frac{3}{4}$ of a pound to 75 feet will be beneficial, but it is not absolutely necessary. Spread in rows between plants and cultivate in shallowly. A second application, same method and amount, about the middle of August, will help insure the crop for the rest of the season, but it is not necessary unless poor growth is being made.

Harvesting: Harvest by removing the outer leaves with a sharp twist, taking care not to injure the small, undeveloped leaves in the center. Keep in a cool moist place, and use as soon as possible.

VARIETIES

Lucullus and Rhubarb, both suitable for freezing.

Remarks: May be overwintered if protected with salt hay. Will produce a good early crop, but will not last very long. Also may be started indoors in pots and transplanted out.

Chicory

Botanical Name: Cichorium Intybus.

Origin: Also known as French Endive and Witloof Chicory; the origin and date of introduction are doubtful, but it is definitely known not to have been cultivated by the ancients.

Soil: Will give good results on any soil which will grow root crops, such as carrots, etc.

Planting: Start outside the first of June, for the crop will mature and go to seed if started earlier. Top of plant is of no value. The roots are used as a substitute for coffee and they may be forced at any time during the winter. Seed is sown in rows, 18 inches to 2 feet apart, covered with $\frac{1}{2}$ inch of soil. When plants are 2–3 inches high, thin 6–8 inches apart.

Moisture: A constant and well-regulated supply of moisture is necessary to make good plants and to prevent the plants from sending up a seed stalk.

Inter-Cropping: One crop is sufficient, and inter-cropping is not practicable.

Cultivation: Cultivation is the same as for any root crop.

Fertilizers: Thorough preparation in the beginning, before putting in the crop, is best for good results. No additional feeding should be really necessary. The addition of manure or a complete fertilizer after this crop has been planted will do very little toward producing good results. Nothing can make up for a lack of complete soil preparation in the beginning.

Harvesting: Roots should be harvested late in the fall before the ground freezes; they should be removed with a fork or a spade so completely and carefully as not to injure them in any way. Tops should be removed and the roots stored in a cool, moist place. They may be stored in sand kept slightly moist. Injured or diseased roots should never be stored. The roots store best at a temperature of 40 degrees.

Forcing: The main use of Chicory is for forcing during the winter months, using the tender bleached shoots for salad. To force the roots properly, they may be taken out of storage at any time, using only a few for each forcing, so that the supply will last all winter. They should be started at intervals of every two weeks, for one crop will last about a month, and the next crop may be coming on to take its place when it is exhausted. The roots should be placed upright in sand; if there is no sand, ashes may be used; all light should be excluded, and they should be kept moist at a temperature of 50–55 degrees. As they sprout, they should be covered with the sand until the shoots are 3 inches long. Then they should be cut and used as soon as possible. Each crop may be cut on the average of three times during the month they are forced, and much better shoots are obtained from the good strong roots.

The Witloof is the only variety.

Sweet Corn

Botanical Name: Zea Mays, var. saccharata.

Origin: Grown by the Indians in Mexico and eastern North America before this continent was discovered.

Soil: Corn requires a well-drained soil, high in organic matter. A good application of a well-decayed manure is the best source of organic material. Early crops do best on a sandy loam soil which warms quickly in the spring, but later crops prefer a heavier soil which retains moisture.

When and How to Plant: Seed may be sown as soon as the soil has warmed up, or about May 1 to 10. Plant 3–4 seeds in hills from 2–3 feet apart each way. Mix a small handful of commercial fertilizer with the soil in the bottom of each hill and cover the seeds with $1-1\frac{1}{2}$ inches of soil. Seed germinates in one week to ten days. Thin to three plants to each hill, when plants are from 3–6 inches high.

Inter-Cropping: May be practiced with squash, melons, or pumpkins, string beans, lettuce, and other quick-maturing crops. Plant every ten to fourteen days for a continuous supply.

Cultivation: Should be frequent, beginning when plants first appear. Practice shallow cultivation, pulling the soil toward the hills each time. Three to four cultivations are all that are necessary. Cultivation should cease as soon as the tassel shows.

Manures and Fertilizers: When plants are 4–8 inches high, broadcast 4-8-4 between the rows at the rate of 1 pound to 50–75 feet and cultivate in carefully and shallowly. Another application is sometimes made just before the tassels appear, but is not necessary in every case, being advisable if growth is not satisfactory.

Harvesting: Harvest when the silk has begun to turn brown. Corn should be used just as soon as picked, as the sugar content is higher at that time. If it cannot be used at that time, husk and keep in a cool place, but the quality deteriorates very quickly.

VARIETIES

Golden Bantam*: Yellow, sweet, 70 days to maturity.

Golden Sunshine*: Larger than the Golden Bantam; matures in 70 to 75 days.

Golden Cross Bantam*: Matures in 90 days.

Spanish Gold: Matures in 70 to 80 days.

Country Gentleman Shoe-Peg: Matures in 90 days; white.

Stowell's Evergreen: Matures in 95 to 100 days.

Varieties starred are recommended for freezing.

Remarks: Too much emphasis cannot be placed on the fact that corn should be eaten as soon as picked. Husking immediately after picking is an aid in preventing deterioration. Corn may be picked early in the morning, or late in the afternoon, husked and kept cool and shaded. In this way, it will keep in good condition for twelve hours, but is at its best if picked immediately before using.

Cress

Botanical Name: Lepidium sativum—Garden Cress.
Nasturtium officinale—Water Cress.

Origin: Probably of Persian origin; its cultivation dates from a very early period.

When and How to Sow: Garden cress is a cool season crop, the leaves being used for salad or for garnishing. Goes quickly to seed in hot weather. Sow seed in any garden soil as weather conditions permit. Sow in rows 12 inches apart and thin as needed for use.

If leaves are cut without injuring the crown, the plant will keep bearing for several weeks. It should be ready for use four to six weeks after planting.

Water cress may be grown in any stream where the water is pure and fresh. Once established in a good stream, it will last indefinitely. It is a perennial which will throw out roots from the joints and which may also be propagated from seed or pieces of stem. It may also be grown in the garden in well-prepared, very moist soil, by starting the seed indoors and transplanting to the garden. If given plenty of moisture, plants should last some time. If grown like ordinary vegetables it will be a failure.

Cucumber

Botanical name: Cucumis sativus.

Origin: Native of southern Asia, in cultivation for over four thousand years.

Soil: Heavy soil is best because it tends to be more fertile and retentive of moisture. If well-decayed manure is available, it should be used in liberal quantities and should be well forked in before planting.

Sowing: When ground has become thoroughly warm (May 1 to 15), plant in hills 4 feet apart each way. If available, a forkful of well-rotted manure placed at the bottom of each hill and covered with 4 inches of soil gives excellent results. In each hill plant 12 seeds, $\frac{1}{2}$ inch deep. Seeds germinate in ten days and plants should be thinned out gradually, so that when they are 4 inches high there should be four plants to each hill. A less satisfactory method is to sow seeds in rows 4–6 feet apart, 6 or 8 seeds to 1 foot, and thin plants to 1 foot apart after they are 2–4 inches high. Cucumber plants cannot be satisfactorily transplanted. Four to six hills is enough for a family planting.

Succession: For a continuous supply, there must be at least two plantings between May 1 and July 10. If a few radish seeds are sown in each hill, they will germinate quickly and attract all the insects. As soon as the cucumbers appear, pull up the radishes and destroy them, insects and all.

Moisture: Vines will not develop properly and fruit will be small without a continuous supply of moisture. Heavy land, well prepared, is an excellent method of insuring moisture.

Cultivation: Should be shallow and constant until vines cover the ground. Do not step on the vines—it will kill them, as they cannot put out new shoots below the injury.

Fertilizer: Cucumbers must have a maximum amount of nitrogen; if the soil is rich, a complete fertilizer, applied when plants are 4 inches high, will promote satisfactory growth. If it was impossible to put manure in the hills before planting, complete fertilizer should be applied, a small handful to each hill, when the plants are about 3 inches high. Applied to plants grown in rows, 1 pound is sufficient for 50 feet.

Harvesting: Do not pick cucumbers until leaves are dry in the morning, as disease is easily spread by disturbance of damp foliage. Harvest fruit before it begins to turn yellow; in a cool moist place, it will keep a week.

VARIETIES

Longfellow, Davis' Perfect, White Spine, Early Fortune, Straight Eight, and Stokes Windermoor Wonder.

Remarks: The Gherkin used for pickling is planted July 1 and given the same treatment as the Cucumber. As the plants are somewhat smaller, they need only be thinned to 6–7 plants per hill. There are two varieties: West India Gherkin is round, and the Boston Pickling is long, from 2 to 4 inches.

Eggplant

Botanical Name: Solanum Melongena.

Origin: Known as food in India several thousand years ago. The varieties cultivated in America are long and ovate in shape, while those cultivated in India are even longer, slender and slightly curved.

Soil: A sandy loam soil yields the best crop. It should have plenty of well-decayed manure forked in to a depth of 6 inches and it should be finely pulverized, at any time before the plants are set.

Sowing: Eggplant requires warm soil conditions and a long period in which to mature, and north of Virginia it must be started indoors. Seed may be sown in flats from February 15 to March 15, in soil with a high percentage of sand. Seed germinates in ten days to two weeks. When plants are $1\frac{1}{2}$ inches high, transplant 2 inches each way. The temperature should be 75 degrees F. at all times; when plants begin to crowd, transplant to individual 3-inch pots, transplanting to larger pots as the plants grow. They should be in 6-inch pots one month after they are in 3-inch pots. If plants show any tendency to turn yellow, water with nitrate of soda (1 ounce dissolved in 1 gallon of water). Plants should not be set out before June 1, and later if the ground is not thoroughly warm; if set out earlier they are checked by cool nights and cool soil conditions. When set out, plants should be 4–6 inches high. Planting distance should be 3 feet between rows, 2 feet between plants.

Moisture: Eggplant is distinctly fussy about moisture; if it has too little, leaves turn yellow, become spotted and drop; if too much, flowers will not set fruit.

Cultivation: Should be exceedingly shallow as roots are very near the surface. Cultivate just enough to keep down weeds.

Fertilizer: A small handful of a complete fertilizer, 4-8-4, should be placed in a ring around each plant when it is set out. This should be cultivated in lightly. At any time satisfactory growth is not being made, a second application is advisable.

Harvesting: Always cut the fruit from the plant. It is best when about 4 inches in diameter. Keep in a cool place until ready to use; do not keep more than 4 days.

VARIETIES

Black Beauty and New York Purple are the two main varieties, both high in quality. Black Beauty is usually preferred because of its attractive appearance.

Endive

Botanical Name: Cichorium Endivia.

Origin: In very early times endive was cultivated in Egypt.

Soil: Should be rich and heavy. Prepare with plenty of organic matter (compost or well-decayed manure) to a depth of 6 inches before planting. Ground at the base of a slope is advisable because of the greater supply of moisture available.

Sowing: Sow seed from June 1 to August 1 in rows 18 inches apart. When plants are 2 inches high, thin to 1 foot apart. Thinned plants may be transplanted. One-fourth ounce of seed will plant 50 feet of row. An early sowing may be made as soon as the ground can be worked in spring, but is not as satisfactory as the later one, for the ground warms up too quickly.

Moisture: A continuous supply is essential for good endive.

Cultivation: Three weeks before crop is harvested, plants must be bleached to make them more tender and less bitter. Draw outside leaves over the heart and center leaves until they come together at the top. Put a piece of waterproof paper around them to hold them in place and tie with string or an elastic band. This must be done on a dry day as the inside leaves rot quickly if tied when wet. When the endive is bleached, the plants should be cut as close to the ground as possible and stored in a cool, moist place.

VARIETIES

Broad-leaved Batavian or Escarole is mainly used for culinary purposes and is hardier, but of poorer quality than French Green Curled, which is the best salad variety; when properly raised and bleached the latter is of excellent quality.

Kale

Botanical Name: Brassica oleracea var. acephala.

Origin: First known in Europe, and cultivated for several thousand years.

Soil: A well-drained, sandy loam, well prepared with plenty of decayed manure or other organic matter is ideal for Kale. Prepare to a depth of 6–8 inches and dig in manure any time before planting. Kale will, however, grow on any soil which is fairly rich.

Sowing: Sow in place, $\frac{1}{8}$ ounce seed to 50 feet in rows 18 inches to 2 feet apart, as soon as the soil can be worked in the spring. Seed germinates in seven to ten days, and when plants are 3 inches high, they should be thinned to one plant to 8–10 inches. Sow again in midsummer for fall and winter crop. Plan on sixty to eighty days to maturity.

Cultivation: Should be frequent and shallow. All weed growth must be suppressed.

Fertilizer: A complete fertilizer, 4-8-4, applied to plants a month after thinning, will prove beneficial. Apply at the rate of $\frac{1}{2}$ pound to 25 feet of row.

Harvesting: When leaves are sufficiently mature, they should be bright green and of an attractive appearance. When old, they become dark green and tough. Cut and keep in a cool, damp place and use as soon as possible. If allowed to remain on the plant too long, they become tough. The fall or winter crop may be left in the field, covered lightly with salt hay or straw, and the leaves cut when desired. They will keep until late into the winter.

VARIETIES

First crop: Dwarf Green Curled or Dwarf Curled Scotch.

Fall and Winter crop: Dwarf Siberian or Bloomsdale Double Extra Curled.

Scotch types are usually used for the early crop, while Siberian is more hardy and is used for the late crop.

Kohlrabi

Botanical Name: Brassica caulorapa.

Origin: Date of introduction uncertain, for there are no wild types. Known as an extreme varietal form of Wild Cabbage.

Soil: Any well-prepared soil is satisfactory. After first working, an application of manure should be well turned under and the soil should be pulverized. Soil should be prepared to a depth of 6 inches.

Sowing: No advantage is gained by early or by indoor sowing. First crop should be sown as soon as the frost is out of the ground; then sow every two weeks until August 1. Sow in rows 18 inches apart at the rate of $\frac{1}{4}$ ounce seed to 75 feet. Cover lightly with soil, and when plants are 3–4 inches high, thin to 6–8 inches apart. The thinnings may be transplanted to another row and will take about an extra week to develop. Leave and transplant only the best seedlings. Days to maturity, 50–60.

Cultivation: Keep soil loose at all times, but do not cultivate deeply near plants.

Fertilizer: About five days after thinning, plants will be in condition to benefit by additional fertilizer, and a small amount ($\frac{3}{4}$ pound to row of 50 feet) of nitrate of soda or ammonium sulfate may be broadcast between rows and lightly raked in. If fertilizer remains on the leaves, it will burn the plants.

Harvesting: Kohlrabi is a member of the Cabbage family and is peculiar because the edible portion is a swollen stem which develops just at the level of the ground; it should be used when this is the size of a silver dollar. It becomes tough and flavorless as it grows larger. Pull up the entire plant to avoid disease from rotting roots and leaves.

VARIETIES

Early Purple Vienna, Early White Vienna, and Smooth White Vienna, which is short-lived.

Leek

Botanical Name: Allium Porrum.

Origin: First known in Mediterranean countries, leeks have been grown since prehistoric times.

Soil: Leeks prefer a soil which is very rich, supplied with plenty of decayed vegetable and animal matter. Prepare as early as weather will permit by plowing or digging and then pulverizing.

Sowing: About February 15, seed should be sown indoors in any good garden soil in a temperature of 60–70 degrees. Will germinate in about ten days. When plants are 2–4 inches high, transplant 2 inches apart each way. First week in May, set plants out 6 inches apart in rows 2–3 feet apart.

Seed sown in open ground does not give leeks of large size and highest quality, but does give satisfactory results. Seed should be sown $\frac{1}{4}$ inch deep at the rate of 1 ounce to 100 feet, in rows 2–3 feet apart, as soon as ground is in workable condition. As the root system is meager, leek plants take at least two weeks to become established before noticeable growth takes place. Since the plants do not all mature at the same time, only one planting is necessary. Leeks may be left in the ground until the soil freezes.

Cultivation: Keep the soil friable at all times; as the plants begin to grow, hoe the soil toward them.

Fertilization: When the plants are from 4–6 inches high, apply a complete fertilizer, about one teaspoonful to each plant; put over each plant a paper collar made of waterproof paper. Collar should be 3 inches high and 2 inches in diameter. This hastens upward growth; they should grow 3–4 inches in three weeks. Move collar up 3 inches, hilling the soil about the plants; continue to do so until plant grows, always keeping soil hilled up to the collar. Some of the plants will be mature about August 15, but will not deteriorate if left in the ground until late fall.

Another method of planting: set the plants in trenches 6 inches deep, 4 feet apart, and, as they grow, fill in soil to bleach them.

Moisture: Plants must have a continuous and liberal supply of moisture in order to make maximum growth.

Harvesting: Plants may be dug before freezing weather and stored in a trench as celery is, where they will keep from four to six weeks.

VARIETIES

American Flag attains a diameter of 1–1$\frac{1}{2}$ inches and a white stalk 8–12 inches high when properly bleached.

Prizetaker and Musselberg attain a diameter of 1$\frac{1}{2}$–2 inches and do not grow quite as tall.

Lettuce

Botanical Name: Lactuca sativa.

Remarks: Lettuce is best if grown in the cooler parts of the year. Only the Cos, or Romaine, type is adapted to warmer conditions.

Soil Preparation: Lettuce likes an abundance of decayed organic matter and just as good results may be obtained with it as with commercial fertilizers, on soils of a fine structure. The soil should be spaded to a depth of 6 inches or more and plenty of well-rotted manure worked in. A complete fertilizer may be added at this time if deemed necessary.

Planting: April to May 15, then again in August. Seed may be sown in flats in a greenhouse or hotbed for transplanting outside. Seed should be sown six to seven weeks before transplanting outside. The young plants grow most satisfactorily at a temperature between 50 and 60 degrees. Too high a temperature makes the plants spindly and non-heading. At high temperatures the sugar changes rapidly to starch which results in a disagreeable and bitter flavor. When the plants are about 2 inches high they are pricked into other flats, 2 inches apart each way. They are kept in these flats until set in the garden, which should be preceded by a hardening-off period. The plants are set 8 inches apart in rows 15 inches apart.

Lettuce seed may be planted in the open ground as soon as the frost has disappeared, the plants being thinned out to 8 inches apart when crowding begins to occur. These plants may be set out and will mature a week or so later than those which have not been moved One ounce of seed is sufficient for 3,000 plants.

Cultivation: Shallow, and frequent enough to control weeds.

Succession: For a continuous supply sow seed every two weeks or plant varieties that mature at different dates.

Fertilizers: Lettuce responds to nitrogen very quickly which, with plenty of moisture available, will promote a rapid, succulent, crisp growth. Nitrate of soda, Cal-Nitro, or sulphate of ammonia, applied at the rate of 1 pound to 100 feet of row two weeks before harvesting, may be used to hasten maturity.

Harvesting: Loose-leaf varieties may be harvested in any stage of development before they become tough. Heading varieties should be allowed to mature. As only a few heads mature at a time, it will not be a case of a feast or a famine if seed is sown every two weeks. The root may be cut close to the ground, removing all leaves with it. If the heads are pulled up some of the leaves may be injured.

Storing: Lettuce may be stored in a cold place such as an ice chest for a period of ten to fourteen days if the humidity is relatively high.

VARIETIES

Grand Rapids is a loose-leaved, non-heading, early variety. May King is a very early variety with a very small head. Big Boston is a standard heading, commercial variety, as are the New York or Iceberg types. The Cos (Romaine) varieties are able to mature in hot weather. Bibb and Oakleaf are excellent varieties for the home garden.

Muskmelon

Botanical Name: Cucumis Melo.

Origin: Origin doubtful; presumably they were first known either in Africa or Asia. Not cultivated before the Christian era.

Soil Type and Preparation: Melons grow well in many soils which are either sandy or slightly sandy in character. Heavy clay soils should be avoided. The more sand the soil contains, the earlier a crop may be planted. An application of well-rotted manure is advisable before planting, or it may be somewhat supplemented by a complete fertilizer broadcast at the rate of 1 pound to 35 square feet and raked in before planting.

When and How to Plant: Melons are very tender, and must not be planted until the soil is thoroughly warm, from the tenth of May until the middle of June. For best results, sow seeds in hills 4 feet apart each way, and for large varieties, 4–6 feet apart. This is for hand cultivation. For horse cultivation, they should be planted 6–8 feet apart. To make a hill, remove 2 shovelfuls of soil, insert 1 shovelful of well-rotted manure, and cover with 6 inches of well-firmed soil. Plant 6–8 seeds per hill and cover with $\frac{1}{2}$ inch of soil. Hills should be at least 12 inches in diameter, and the seeds placed 2 inches apart in the hill. One ounce of seed is enough for 20 hills. Seed should germinate and appear above the ground in about two weeks; when plants are 3–4 inches high, thin out to the three best plants. Seed may also be sown indoors in pots a month previous to setting out of doors. Two plants may be grown in each pot and two pots set out in each hill.

Succession: By one planting of two or more varieties, early and late, a continuous supply may be obtained, without successive plantings.

Moisture: A continuous supply of moisture is very necessary to insure proper vine development and maximum fruit production. Plants require much more moisture when fruit begins to mature than they do in the growing stage.

Cultivation: Keep soil lightly cultivated between rows at all times, but do not cultivate too close to the plants; weeds near the plants should be carefully pulled out to avoid disturbing roots of vines. As the vines give shade, they conserve the moisture near the plants, and cultivation is most needed where ground is exposed to sun.

Fertilizers: A commercial fertilizer is needed for good growth and production. Apply 4-8-4, at the rate of

¼ ounce per hill in a ring around each hill, 4–6 inches away from the plants, and cover with 1 inch of soil taken from between the rows. Apply after thinning.

Harvesting: Yield: 10–15 melons per hill. Melons are ready for harvesting when the stems part easily from the fruit with a very slight pull. They are not mature until the stems begin to separate and should never be cut if highest quality is desired. If not picked at this stage, they will become overripe and too soft for use. In four or five days after reaching this state, they will completely detach themselves. If picked when stems part easily, flesh is firm, but will mellow if kept in a cool place, 60–70 degrees. Vines will continue producing fruits from three weeks to a month.

VARIETIES

Hearts of Gold: 80 to 90 days, high in quality, deep orange flesh.

Rocky Ford: 100 days, flesh light green, weight 2–3 pounds.

Hale's Best, 4–6 pounds yellow flesh, and *Bender's Surprise,* same weight, golden fleshed, are two of the best larger varieties.

Okra

Botanical Name: Hibiscus esculentus.

Origin: Asiatic in origin, but not cultivated during ancient times. Grown in the warmer parts of the United States since the eighteenth century.

Soil Type and Preparation: Any good garden soil will give good results if enriched before planting with manure or commercial fertilizer.

When and How to Plant: Okra is a tender plant, giving good results only in hot weather. Sow seeds from the middle of May to the middle of June, in rows 2½–3 feet apart. When plants are 3–4 inches high, thin the dwarf varieties 12–18 inches apart, and the larger varieties 18–30 inches apart. Not easily transplanted unless enough soil is moved to prevent root disturbance.

Cultivation: Keep soil well stirred and weeds suppressed.

Fertilizers: A liberal application of manure or complete fertilizer should be well worked in when the soil is prepared. If plants do not grow steadily, apply one teaspoonful of fertilizer to each plant as a side dressing.

Harvesting: Pods should be gathered while young—1–2 inches long. For continuous growth, do not allow pods to mature. Two plantings are often made in the South, but only one is possible in the North.

VARIETIES

White Velvet: 3½–5 feet high, white and smooth.

Dwarf Green: 15–18 inches high, green and furrowed.

Onion

Botanical Name: Allium Cepa.

Origin: Probably first known in parts of Asia. Grown by the ancient Egyptians, it is one of the oldest of cultivated vegetables.

The onion is one of the hardiest vegetables and may be sown as soon as the frost is out of the ground in the spring. Onion sets may also be planted at the same time.

Onion Sets are immature onions which have been produced by close seeding the season before. Those best suited for planting range from ½ to ¾ inches in diameter. The seed may also be sown in flats in a hotbed or greenhouse and the plants transplanted to the garden at any time soil and weather conditions permit.

Soil Preparation: Thorough preparation cannot be over-emphasized. The organic and nutrient and water content should be high. The onion plants feed within a limited range, due to their sparse root system. Heavy applications of commercial fertilizers are often necessary, at the rate of 1 pound to 20 or 25 square feet, being worked into the soil before planting.

Planting: Seed may be sown in flats in a greenhouse two months before the earliest planting date in the field. Four to five seeds are sown per inch. Before setting in the field the tops are cut back to a height of 3 or 4 inches. They are set 4–6 inches in rows 15–18 inches apart. Seed may be sown in rows, planting three or four seeds per inch. The plants are thinned to 4–6 inches apart when well established but before the onion begins to swell.

Onion sets are planted the same distance apart, in and between the rows, as transplanted plants. One pound of small onion sets will plant 100 feet.

Succession: If sets are planted early and followed by plants from seed, either indoors or out, there should be a steady supply, as sets mature in ninety to one hundred days, and seed onions in one hundred and fifty to one hundred and eighty days. Plants started from seed should be put in the open ground when sets are put out.

Moisture: A continuous, well-regulated supply of moisture is absolutely necessary. In experiments conducted at the School of Horticulture, onions at the lower end of a 100-foot row on a slight slope were twice as large as those at the top, due to the greater amount of moisture.

Cultivation: Should be shallow and constant and should begin as soon as the plants appear. Wait until tops straighten out, about one week, before weeding between the seedlings, to avoid disturbing plants. Keep rows free from weeds.

Harvesting: Tops are practically dead before plants are mature. Pull or dig and leave in sun for a few days to dry out and to toughen skins. This will improve the keeping quality.

Storing: Onions should be thoroughly cured by being exposed to sun for several days. Do not try to remove the soil until onions are thoroughly cured; then it will come off easily without washing. Only the onions grown from seed will keep for any length of time. Store in a cool, dry place spread out on a flat, dry surface. They do not need moisture and should keep five to six months.

VARIETIES

Yellow Glove Danvers, Yellow Strassburg, Southport Red Globe, and Southport White Globe are the best varieties for the main crop. Prizetaker and Ailsa Craig are two very large varieties, often weighing a pound or more. One variety of sets is as good as another.

Parsley

Botanical Name: Petroselinum hortense.

Origin: Indigenous to southern Europe. Known to the Greeks only as a wild plant. Mentioned in a list of plants for Charlemagne's garden, and introduced into England in 1548.

Soil: Variety used for leaves may be grown in any soil, but requires ample food material; that which is grown for its root system needs a deep, 6–8-inch, well-drained soil.

Sowing: Seed requires about 3 weeks to germinate and may be sown in the open ground at any time after soil can be easily worked until August 1. Sow in rows 18 inches apart; barely cover with soil. One packet of seed is sufficient for a family. Seed may also be started in hotbeds two months before it can be sown outside. Transplant when 1 inch high, 2 inches each way, and later move into the garden when the ground is workable. Transplant 8 inches apart in rows 18 inches apart.

Parsley may also be sown in coldframes about August 1. Keep plants covered with hay in the frames all winter and transplant to garden in early spring.

Cultivation: Keep soil lightly cultivated and free from weeds.

Moisture: In dry weather parsley is greatly benefited by thorough watering two or three times a week.

Fertilizer: Plants will thrive without fertilization, but will be much larger if commerical fertilizer, 4-8-4, or well-rotted manure, is applied just before planting. A little nitrate of soda applied after planting out in the field is often beneficial.

Harvesting: First leaves may be picked about 75 days after seed is sown. Kept in water, they will remain fresh for several days. Never pick plant clean; some leaves should be left around the center of the crown to insure continuous growth.

VARIETIES

Champion Moss Curled is a good leaf variety. Hamburg (Turnip-Rooted) is grown mainly for its roots, which are used for flavoring.

Remarks: Plants may be taken up before ground freezes and kept in a coldframe where they will produce in early spring, or they may be potted and kept in the house in a sunny window.

Parsnip

Botanical Name: Pastinaca sativa.

Origin: Grown since the beginning of the Christian era. Native of Europe and Asia.

Soil: Parsnips need a very fertile, but fairly heavy soil, deep and well drained. If too heavy, roots become distorted; if too sandy, superfluous fibrous roots form.

Fertilizers: To get long, straight roots, apply all manures and fertilizers, such as a 4-8-4, before the land is plowed, and turn under to a depth of at least 8 inches. The long tap root forms before the parsnip begins to develop, and if fertilizer is too close to the surface, roots will not be encouraged to grow down.

Sowing: Sow seed as early as possible in spring, 1 inch deep, at the rate of $\frac{1}{8}$ ounce to 50 feet. They should be in rows 18 inches to $2\frac{1}{2}$ feet apart. They germinate in 12–18 days and rows may be marked by radish seed mixed with parsnip seed. When plants are 2–4 inches high, thin 4–6 inches apart.

Inter-Cropping: Parsnips, being a long-season crop, may be inter-cropped with any quick-maturing crop such as beets, lettuce, radishes, or spinach.

Cultivation: Should be constant, but not deep.

Moisture: A constant supply of moisture is essential for smooth, long, well-developed roots.

Harvesting: Parsnips may be harvested before the ground freezes, or may remain in the ground, protected by coarse hay or straw, until spring. Freezing tends to reduce the bitter flavor present in the fall. Dig parsnips out, never try to pull them.

Storing: Store in moist sand or in root cellar like carrots at a temperature of 40–50 degrees.

VARIETIES

Guernsey and Improved Hollow Crown.

Pea

Botanical Name: Pisum sativum.

Origin: This vegetable is a native of Europe, and has been cultivated since antiquity.

Soil: Peas should be grown in a sandy loam which is rich in organic matter. The soil should be well prepared the fall previous to planting, for the crop is planted early in the spring, often before the frost is all out of the ground. If the soil is well worked over in the fall, very little work is necessary in the spring. Plenty of well-rotted manure well mixed in with the soil will give the best results.

Planting: Peas are divided into two groups, smooth-seeded and wrinkled. The smooth varieties may be planted two weeks before the wrinkled sort, because they can stand moister and cooler soil conditions—as soon as enough of the frost is out of the ground to make it easily workable. The wrinkled sorts should be put in two weeks later, for by that time the soil is drier and warmer, which is essential for this type. The seed for both types should be sown in rows 2½ feet apart and 1½–2 inches in the row. Thin them if it seems necessary. Make a trench 4 inches deep, and cover the seed to the depth of an inch, filling in the trench as the plants grow. One pound of seed is sufficient for 50 feet of garden row. The plants cannot be transplanted successfully.

Succession: For a continuous supply, seed should be sown every ten days. They should not be planted after hot weather sets in, for they will not mature nor thrive properly. A fall crop may be sown about August 1, but it is not nearly as productive as the spring crop. They should be mature in from 60–80 days, depending on the variety.

Moisture: Peas do not require an abundance of moisture, but they do need a continuous supply. Practice clean, shallow cultivation for the best results.

Training: Peas do not need a definite system of training unless they grow to a height of more than 2 feet. Training is then necessary to keep them off the ground and to facilitate harvesting.

Birch brush or any twiggy brush is the best for training the taller growing varieties. The brush should be put from 6–10 inches apart in the row any time before the peas begin to spread.

Fertilizer: An additional application of a complete fertilizer may be given during the blooming period, if the land is not very fertile. Use the fertilizer at the rate of 1 pound for every 75 feet, broadcast between the rows, and lightly cultivated in.

Harvesting: The wrinkled varieties should be harvested when the pods are well filled out, while the smooth-seeded sorts are best when the pods are only about half full, for the peas lose their flavor as they grow larger and more mature. Both varieties are best when harvested either early in the morning or late in the evening, never during the hot part of the day. The quality becomes inferior in a very short time, if, after picking, they are not kept in a very cool place.

VARIETIES

Smooth-seeded sort: Alaska, 2–2½ feet high. Plant for the first crop only.

Wrinkled-seeded: Blue Bantam, 65 days to maturity, 18 inches high and very productive, with large pods. Little Marvel, 2 feet high, small podded, high in quality, mature in 65 days. Laxtonian, 18 inches high, large podded, high in quality, and mature in 65 days. Potlatch, 2 feet in height, pods from 4–5 inches in length, 75 days to maturity. Telephone, from 4–5 feet high, 80–85 days to maturity. Prince Edward, 4–5 feet in height, and 80–85 days to maturity. For freezing: Alderman, Dark Podded Telephone, Improved Gradus, Laxton's Superb, Oneida, Onward, Shasta, Thomas Laxton.

Pepper

Botanical Name: Capsicum fruticosum.

Origin: Native of South America, and cultivated for centuries.

Soil Type and Preparation: Sandy loam is best, though any type will give fair results. For preparation, see Eggplant.

When and How to Plant: Should be started indoors from the first of February to the first of March. Sow in soil composed of two parts garden loam to one part sand. Put in rows 3 inches apart, and cover seed with ¼ inch of soil. Seed will sprout in 10 days to 2 weeks, and when plants are 1½ inches high transplant 2 inches by 2 inches. The temperature should not be lower than 70 degrees. A month to six weeks later, transplant again to 3 inches by 3 inches or 4 inches by 4 inches. Set out of doors as soon as the ground has warmed up and all danger of frost is over. Set 18 inches in the row and 2½ feet between the rows.

Moisture Requirements: Continuous moisture supply is necessary but too much will promote excessive leaf growth with less fruit.

Cultivation: Practice shallow cultivation. The plants may be slightly hilled up, as they grow. When the first peppers are ready to harvest, cultivation should cease. Keep all weeds out even when the time for cultivation has ended.

Fertilizers: A complete fertilizer such as 4-8-4 or 5-8-7 should be used, as the average soil is usually deficient in nitrogen, phosphorus, and potash. If the soil is not very fertile, fertilizer should be applied just before or when the plants are set out. If applied when setting out, mix about two tablespoonfuls with the soil at the bottom of the hole into which the plants are to be set. Another application may be made when the fruits are just beginning to form, to hasten growth and maturity. This is applied in the form of a circle around each plant 3 inches to 4 inches away from the stem of the plant, and covered with soil. Two tablespoonfuls per plant is enough.

Harvesting: All sweet peppers are green until they reach a stage where they no longer increase in size, and at that time they turn red. They are usually harvested in the green stage. Red sweet peppers are usually used only for their color. They may be picked at any time after they have reached the desired size, being kept in a cool place to prevent them from wilting. They may be kept this way for as long as two weeks.

Storing: If the entire plant is pulled up and hung upside down in a cellar, the peppers will remain in good condition for as long as three weeks.

VARIETIES

Ruby King, Ruby Giant, and California Wonder are good. These will mature in 150 days. The California Wonder is thick-fleshed, very solid, and a rather late-bearing variety unless started early and given proper care. Hungarian Wax, Long Red Cayenne, the Red Cayenne, and Red Chili are the best pungent varieties.

Potato

Botanical Name: Solanum tuberosum.

Origin: Native of South America; found here in the latter part of the sixteenth century.

Soil Type and Preparation: A light, well-drained, loamy soil is best. Potatoes are very heavy feeders, so the soil should be plowed or forked as deeply as possible and a liberal amount of well-decayed manure incorporated. Fresh manure should never be used unless it is applied the fall previous to planting. If fresh manure is applied in the spring it will make a good deal of nitrogen available to the plants right away, which will cause them to make an excessive amount of top growth, and little root growth. Lime should never be applied to the soil as it activates organisms which cause potato diseases. All manure which is applied should be turned under as deeply as possible.

When and How to Plant: Early crop may be planted as soon as the frost is out of the ground, and succeeding crops may be planted until the first week in July. Make the trenches from 4–6 inches deep and 2½–3 feet apart. Plant the potatoes 15–18 inches apart in the trench and cover with 2 inches of soil. Use only disease-free or certified seed. Potatoes should be prepared for planting 10 days beforehand, being cut so there are at least two eyes for each section, with a small piece of the potato attached. Spread the pieces in a box not more than two layers deep, and sprinkle them with sulfur. The sulfur should come in contact with all the cut surfaces, causing them to dry out and to toughen up. This is known as suberization, for it prevents the potato from becoming diseased before the plant gets a good start. Potatoes are sometimes planted without this treatment. Potato skins are also planted, but the results in both cases are variable. They should be planted at the rate of 3–4 pounds every 50 feet. Sprouts should appear above the ground in two weeks. The later crops are all treated in the same way.

Cultivation: Keep the soil loose and friable at all times. When the plants are from 4–6 inches high, begin to hoe the soil toward them. Kill all weeds before they have a chance to develop enough to compete with the potatoes. Hoe the soil around the plants gradually at intervals of ten days to two weeks, taking the soil from between the rows. Continue until the plants have grown so that working between the rows is impossible.

Manures and Fertilizers: An application of a complete commercial fertilizer, 4-8-4, at the rate of 1 pound to 50 feet may be broadcast between the rows one month after the plants have sprouted, if the soil was not very fertile to begin with.

Harvesting: The early crop may be dug from the time vines begin to die until they are actually dead. Leaving the potatoes outside on the ground in the sun for a day to toughen up the skin makes them easier to handle, and prevents them from bruising so easily. The late crop should not be dug until the vines are dead. Leave outside for a day in the sun, as with the early crop.

Storing: Requirements for storing potatoes are: temperature of 50 degrees, medium amount of humidity, uniform conditions. They may be stored in bags, boxes, or in piles, provided there is an allowance for proper air circulation. Will keep for five months or more.

Yield: 1–2 bushels per 100 feet for early crop. Larger yield for late crop.

VARIETIES

Best early variety is the Irish Cobbler. Midseason varieties: Katahdin, Green Mountain, Rural New Yorker, Gold Coin, Rose. These varieties are also good used for the late crops. Jersey Redskins may be planted around the first of July, and because of their resistance to disease and freedom from insects, the crop is seldom a failure. Early crops mature in 90–115 days. Late crops mature in 150 days.

Pumpkin

Botanical Name: Cucurbita Pepo.

Origin: Grown for thousands of years, for rinds have been found in the Swiss lake dwellings.

Soil, Sowing, Cultivation, etc.: See Squash.

VARIETIES

Connecticut Field Pumpkin, chiefly used for decoration, indifferent for cooking. Small Sugar Pumpkin, 3–5 pounds, is the best cooking variety, being sweet and of fine texture.

Remarks: The chief difference between Squash and Pumpkin is in the stems. Squash stems are round and tender, Pumpkin stems are hard, square and woody. Pumpkins cannot stand freezing, so they should be picked before a heavy frost.

Radish

Botanical Name: Raphanus sativus. The name is derived from the Latin, *radix*, meaning root.

Origin: The radish is probably native to Western Asia, but it has been under cultivation for so long that it is impossible to know its origin. The turnip, the onion, and the radish are the oldest vegetables known.

Sowing: Sow as early as possible. The seeds need a cool moist period in which to germinate. Sow 4 seeds to the inch at the rate of 1 ounce to 100 feet, rows 12 inches apart. Thin when plants are 2 inches high to ¾ inch apart, or 12 plants to a foot. Sow seed every two weeks to provide a continuous supply. Seed of the early spring varieties may be sown April 15 to June 1. Seed of summer types may be sown from June 1 until July 15. Seed for the early spring varieties may be sown from the first of August until the first of September, as they will not mature in hot weather. A sowing may also be made in the hotbed, where they will come to maturity for an early delicacy.

Cultivation: Cultivate at least once a week; or four times before harvesting.

Moisture: Plenty of moisture is needed for germination and for growing. If too moist when they mature, they will crack; if too dry, they will become pithy and pungent much sooner than otherwise.

Harvesting: If roots remain in the ground too long, they become woody and crack. Pull as soon as mature. The large summer or fall varieties may be stored in moist sand at a temperature of 40–50 degrees.

VARIETIES

The best quick-growing varieties are Scarlet Globe, Crimson Giant, French Breakfast, White Icicle, which mature in 25–35 days. The best summer or storing varieties are Long Black Spanish and China Rose.

Rhubarb

Botanical Name: Rheum rhaponticum.

Origin: Discovered after the Christian era in the desert and sub-alpine regions of southern Siberia and the Volga River.

Soil: Any soil is satisfactory; if it is well prepared before plants are set out, they should last for eight or nine years. Work in a liberal application of well-decayed manure as deeply as possible and cultivate until it is finely pulverized.

Planting: As seed does not always come true to type, it is best to buy good one- or two-year-old plants. Set them out as early as possible in the spring, 18 inches apart in rows 30–36 inches for hand cultivation. The advantage of spring planting is that the soil is in the best condition, but Rhubarb can easily be transplanted whenever the tops are dead.

Cultivation: Cultivate regularly, but not deeply. Keep all weed growth out, as the weeds compete with the plants, lessen the productivity of the bed, and reduce the quality of the stalks.

Harvesting: Always pull the stalks, never cut them. Do not harvest the first year the plants are set out and only lightly the second year, but from the third year on, heavy harvesting does not hurt the roots. Do not allow the plants to go to seed.

Remarks: Plants may be forced very early in the spring by putting boxes or barrels, with the top and bottom knocked out, over them, and heaping fresh horse manure 18 inches high around the barrel. If the top can be covered with glass, heat is kept in and sunlight is allowed to enter. Even without manure, a glass-covered box or barrel over the plant gives protection from cold and causes shoots to grow up for light. If glass and manure are both used, forcing may be started in really cold weather, at least two weeks earlier than if only boxes are used.

VARIETIES

Victoria and Linnæus.

Rutabaga (*See Turnip*)

Salsify

Botanical Name: Tragopogon porrifolius.

Origin: Salsify is also known as the Oyster-plant, for its flavor is said to slightly resemble that of the oyster.

Soil and Fertilizers: See Parsnip.
   Punch holes in the ground a foot in depth. Put manure in the bottom, then add garden soil with a teaspoonful of commercial fertilizer. Leave the level about 2 inches below that of the ground. Put in four to five seeds per hole, and when they are up, thin to one seed per hole. The rows should be 15–18 inches apart, and the holes should be 6 inches apart.

Planting: As early in the spring as possible, or as soon as the ground can be worked. One-eighth ounce of seed to 50 feet of row is sufficient.

Inter-Cropping and Harvesting: See Parsnip.

Mammoth Sandwich Island is the best variety.
Giant Prague is the best.

Spinach

Botanical Name: Spinacia oleracea.

Origin: Probably Persian in origin, introduced into Europe in the fifteenth century. The New Zealand type has very recently been introduced from that country.

Soil Preparation and Type: For both the cool season or

broadleaved type and the warm-season or trailing type (New Zealand), the soil should be rich and well prepared by spading to a depth of 6 inches, with well-rotted manure disked or forked in. Soil should be finely pulverized. Both types give a high response to lime, which should not be applied in direct contact with the manure, but after the manure has been spaded in, at the rate of 1 pound to 35 square feet. Lime should be used if the soil has not been limed for several years.

When and How to Plant:

(1) *Cool-season type:* Plant in the open ground as early in the spring as possible. Can be planted during a February or March thaw; sow seed at the rate of 1 ounce to 50 feet in rows 12 inches apart. The plants are not usually thinned. Mature in 40–50 days. May also be sown in late September or October, and protected by a covering of salt hay before the ground freezes. This crop is ready to use very early the following spring.

(2) *Warm-season type:* New Zealand Spinach seed germinates slowly, and should be soaked in water 24–48 hours before planting. May be sown in the open ground from May 1 to June 1. Plant in rows 3 feet apart, 6–8 seeds to each foot, and thin 12 inches apart when plants are 3–4 inches high. Seed may also be started indoors about April 1 in flats or in pots. If started in flats, plants when 2 inches high should be transplanted to pots, one plant to a pot containing good garden soil. About May 15, they may be transplanted into the open ground, same distance as above.

Cultivation:

(1) *Cool-season type:* Keep soil well loosened, keep weeds down.

(2) *Warm-season type:* Cultivate carefully and shallowly until plants begin to run; after that pull weeds, do not cultivate.

System of Training: For New Zealand Spinach, or warm-season type, plants grow quickly when well established. Rapid growth usually takes place 3–4 weeks after the seeds have germinated. As crop is dependent on well-established plants, nothing should be picked until growth is well established, about June 15. All yellow leaves should be removed.

Manures and Fertilizers:

(1) *Cool-season crop:* When plants are half-grown, top-dress with nitrate of soda or ammonium sulfate at the rate of 1 pound to 100 square feet applied as for beets, and cultivated in.

(2) *Warm-season crop:* Will be benefited by an application of either a complete fertilizer or nitrate of soda, if applied just as cultivation is stopped.

Harvesting:

(1) *Cool-season type:* Can be picked only once. Best method is to cut individual plants by the roots, and wash.

(2) *Warm-season type:* Harvested by breaking off the tips, 3–4 inches long. Plant continues to send out new shoots until killed by frost.

VARIETIES

Cool-season type: King of Denmark, smooth-leaved, slow to bloom, long standing. Bloomsdale Savoy, mosaic resistant, an excellent variety, savoy-leaved, which should be cut when 3–4 inches high.

Recommended for freezing: Giant Noble, King of Denmark, Long Standing Bloomsdale, Old Dominion.

Warm-season type: New Zealand is the only variety. This is not spinach, but Tetragonia expansa, like spinach in flavor.

Squash

Botanical Name: Cucurbita, various species.

Origin: Tropical America, about 1490.

Types: Squash is of three types, summer, fall and winter. The summer or bush type will mature in 60–70 days and should be used before it reaches maturity and while the skin is still soft. The fall type matures more quickly and does not store as well as the winter type, which it otherwise resembles. The winter type will take 90–130 days and should be well matured before harvesting.

Soil: Squash likes a fairly light soil, containing plenty of organic matter. Work the soil to a depth of 6–8 inches and spade in a liberal quantity of well-rotted manure, as the squash plant is a heavy feeder. Summer squash should be planted in hills 4 feet apart each way; fall and winter squash in hills 6–8 feet apart each way.

Sowing: For summer types, it is advisable to make at least two plantings for a continuous supply. For the fall and winter types one planting is sufficient. Except in regard to distance of hills, planting, cultivating, and fertilizing are the same for all types. Sow seed as soon as the frost is out of the ground in hills prepared by removing one or two shovelfuls of earth and putting in a shovelful of manure; this should be packed firmly and covered with 4 inches of soil. A good squash hill should be about 1½ feet in diameter and about 3 inches above ground level. If commercial fertilizer such as 4-8-4 is substituted for manure, mix one handful with at least one shovelful of soil before planting the seed. Plant 6 seeds to the hill, 2 inches apart; cover with 1 inch of soil and pack down firmly. Seed should germinate in about 10 days. When the plants are about 3 inches high, thin out to the three best plants. If more are left, the size and the quality of the fruit will be inferior.

Plants may also be started indoors in small containers about three weeks before seed is sown in the open ground. Use any good garden soil, and sow several seeds in each container. Thin out to two and set out when all danger of frost is past, being careful not to disturb the soil about the roots.

Moisture: Squash requires a continuous but not a heavy supply of moisture to insure steady growth and maximum production.

Cultivation: Practice shallow cultivation from the time the plants begin to grow until they have extended into the rows so far that cultivation would injure them. Do not cultivate within 6 inches of the plant, to avoid injury to the fibrous roots which are very close to the surface. After cultivation is impracticable, plants should be weeded to prevent the weeds from taking nourishment needed by the plants. To avoid disturbing the roots of the squash plants, cut large weeds growing close to them rather than pull them out.

Fertilizer: If soil has not been thoroughly enriched before seeds were planted, a good commercial fertilizer may be added, just after thinning the plants. Another application is made just before the vines begin to run, at the rate of $\frac{1}{2}$ ounce to 1 ounce per hill, applied in a ring 6 inches away from the plants and covered with 1 inch of soil, taken from between the rows.

Harvesting: Summer squash may be harvested any time before the skin hardens; they should be used immediately, or kept in a cool place to prevent evaporation. Pick all fruits before the skin hardens. If fruit is allowed to ripen, the vines will stop growing.

Fall or winter types are mature when the stems turn to a light greenish yellow. They may then be cut and exposed to the sun for two weeks until the stem turns grayish and shrivels, or they may be left on the vines until the same condition is reached. Do not pull the fruit; cut it. Winter squash should remain in the sun two weeks after reaching maturity, as evaporation reduces the high water content, making the fruit more edible and in better condition for storing.

Storing: Many vegetables prefer a damp atmosphere, but Squash must have a dry one. Handle each fruit so carefully that the skin is not broken or bruised in any way. Do not pile in more than two layers, to prevent bruising. Storing temperatures should be 45–55 degrees.

VARIETIES

Summer types: Golden Straight Neck, an improved strain of the old-fashioned Crooked-Neck.

Early White Bush, Patty pan types. Early Yellow Bush. Cocozelle and Zucchini are Italian Vegetable Marrows which are greenish in color at the edible stage.

Fall types: Boston Marrow, 5–20 pounds when mature.

Des Moines, Table Queen, or Acorn Squash, 1–1½ pounds when mature. Suitable for fall use, but will also keep during the winter.

Winter types: Golden Hubbard, 4–8 pounds when mature, very hard skin, bright orange in color.

Blue Hubbard, 10–30 pounds when mature, good keeper.

Golden Delicious, medium-sized fruits of high quality. This and Hubbard squash are recommended for freezing.

Remarks: Squash and pumpkins may be inter-planted in corn when the corn is about 3 inches high. Plant 2–3 seeds in every fourth row to every four to five hills.

Tomato

Botanical Name: Lycopersicon esculentum.

Origin: First known as food in Peru. Until comparatively recently tomatoes were cultivated for ornamental purposes only. Even in colonial days, the fruit was considered deadly poisonous to eat, and was known as the ornamental Love Apple.

Soil: The soil should not be very acid in reaction, nor should it react as alkaline. It should be well drained; a sandy loam is the best. Early tomatoes particularly require a light soil and do best with a south-eastern exposure. Land which has grown corn or potatoes the previous year is good for tomatoes, especially if it is plowed or forked over in the autumn. Just before setting out the plants, fork in a very liberal supply of well-decayed manure and work the soil well to a 6-in. depth, being certain that the texture is very fine.

When and How to Plant: North of the latitude of Philadelphia the season is too short to insure fruit from seed planted in the open ground for the first crop; therefore, people buy their tomato plants, which should be set out when all danger from frost is past. Plants 6–10 inches in height, set 2 inches deeper than they were growing in the seed bed, are the best size to set out.

Seed may, however, be sown indoors in March in a light loam soil. Sow in rows 3 inches apart, four seeds to the inch, and cover with ½ inch of soil. In a temperature of 75 degrees, they should germinate in about 10 days. The best plants for transplanting come from the seeds which germinate first. When plants are a week old, about 2 inches high, with true leaves showing, transplant 2 inches apart each way into flats of the same soil as that in which they were sown; 2–3 weeks later, transplant 4 inches apart each way into the same soil and at the same temperature. Should the seedlings turn yellow, let them dry out slightly and then water with 1 ounce of nitrate of soda to a gallon of water. As with the purchased plants, the best plants should be 6–10 inches high. Set out deeper than they were in the flats indoors. Set out when all danger of frost is past. If the plants are not to be staked, set out 4 feet apart each way. When the fruit begins to ripen, dry hay beneath the plants will prevent rotting due to moisture.

Staking is, however, a much more satisfactory method for the early crop, although it does not give as large a crop. Set out 3 feet between rows and 1½ feet between plants. Put stakes 3 inches away from the plants a week after they have been set out, or put them in before planting. Stakes should be 6 feet high, and driven 18 inches into the ground. Plants should be tied to stakes in three or four places; use raffia or soft rope and a figure-8 knot to prevent the plants coming too close to the stake or being cut. A second method is to fasten three wire hoops, 2 feet in diameter, to three stakes and to slip these over the plants, so that the plant can spread inside the hoops but cannot touch the ground.

Pruning: All suckers should be pruned off until the fruiting period is well advanced, as they sap the strength of the good fruit and will set fruit of poor quality and size. The suckers grow in the joints of the stems, between the leaf and the main stalk. True fruiting spurs come directly from the stem. Unstaked plants are practically impossible to prune.

Cultivation: Cultivate carefully and shallowly until plants are established and really begin to grow. In any case, cultivate sufficiently often to keep soil stirred and to suppress weed growth. When they are well started begin to hill them very slightly. Cultivate until plants have so grown together that it is impossible to get through the rows without disturbing the plants. By this time they should be covering the ground enough to prevent weed growth and to conserve moisture.

Fertilizing: When plants are set out, put a small handful of good fertilizer, preferably 4-8-4, in each hole and thoroughly mix with the soil. Or scatter a handful in a ring, 6 inches in diameter, around each plant one week after they are set out. This should be covered with soil. At the last cultivation, apply a 4-8-4 or a 5-8-7, 2 pounds to 100 feet, broadcast lightly down the row and hoed in.

Harvesting: Allow tomatoes to ripen on the vines and do not pick them when the foliage is wet. They may also be picked when the first tinge of red shows and stored in a warm, dark place, where they will take about a week to ripen. Well-grown plants should each yield 12 pounds of tomatoes.

Storing: Tomatoes may be picked while green, before frost has touched them, and buried in hay in coldframes under glass where they will keep warm and ripen slowly. It is essential that they be picked while firm, and kept dry. The whole vine may also be pulled and hung up in a frost-proof, dry place, and the fruit will ripen for some time. Tomatoes which show white on the blossom end will ripen.

VARIETIES

Earliana: good for home garden, but fruit is not very uniform.

Valiant: a large, round, early maturing variety.

Break o' Day: also good, coming one week later.

Bonny Best: standard midseason variety. Can always be depended on.

Pritchard's Marglobe: standard midseason to late variety, and also dependable.

Rutgers: the most widely planted variety for eating and canning.

Queen Anne and *Tangerine:* yellow varieties.

Turnip

Botanical Name: Brassica Rapa.

Origin: Native of southern Europe, and under cultivation for more than 4,000 years.

Soil: Any good garden soil is satisfactory. Should be prepared to a depth of 6–8 inches.

Sowing: Sow in open ground as soon as soil can be worked, at the rate of ¼ ounce to 50 feet, in rows 18 inches apart. Cover seed with ¼ inch of soil, and when plants begin to crowd, thin to 3 inches apart. For fall crop, maturing in 60 days, sow July 15–August 10.

Cultivation: Should be shallow and sufficiently frequent to prevent soil packing.

Fertilizer: Complete fertilizer, applied before the spring crop is planted. Late crop does not need any, as fertilizers are not all used up by preceding crop.

Harvesting: Spring crop should be harvested when 1½–2½ inches in diameter. Fall crop any time before ground freezes.

Storing: Fall crop may be stored like Carrots.

VARIETIES

White Egg, Purple Top Globe, White Globe and Golden Ball, for either early or late crop. Purple Top Globe is recommended for freezing.

Remarks: The spring crop is a quick-maturing crop which is good only in cool weather. Fall crop much superior to spring crop.

Rutabaga, Golden Neckless, is given the same treatment as Turnip, but should be planted only from July 10 to 20, for winter use.

Watermelon

Midget type is excellent for the home garden. (For culture see Muskmelon, page 586.)

VARIETIES

New Hampshire Midget   Takii Gem

VEGETABLE DISEASES AND INSECTS AND THEIR CONTROL

VEGETABLE	DISEASE	INSECT	DESCRIPTION	DAMAGE	CONTROL
Asparagus.	Rust.		Yellowish brown.	Needle-like leaves.	Plant-resistant varieties.
		12-spotted Asparagus Beetle.	Dark orange, ¼" long with black spots.	Chews the newly developing shoots from spring to summer.	During cutting season Rotenone dust. After cutting season Methoxychlor.
		Asparagus Beetle.			Same as above.
Bean.	Anthracnose.		Circular black sunken areas with a pinkish center.	Leaves, stems and fruits.	Resistant varieties; do not work when plants are wet.
	Bacterial Blight.		Irregular large brownish areas on leaves, smaller irregular spots on the pods, with reddish brown margin.	All parts of the plant and seed.	Disease free seed; do not pick beans when wet.
		Mexican Bean Beetle.	Adult: Roundish oval in shape with copper-colored wings each containing 8 black spots. Larvæ: Lemon yellow with many spines of the same color.	Larvæ feed on undersides of the leaves, skeletonizing them.	Rotenone dust; handpicking of beetles.
		Bean Weevil.	Small and grayish.	Eats round holes in dried beans especially after they have been harvested or stored.	Fumigate the seed with carbon bisulphide or paradichlorobenzene.
Beet.	Leaf Spot.		Brownish circular spots which dry up and fall out, leaving holes.	Leaves.	Bordeaux Mixture, Ziram or Zineb.
		Aphids.	Small greenish soft-bodied lice.	Dwarf leaves by sucking juice from them.	Nicotine dust or spray.
Broccoli, Brussels Sprouts, Cabbage, Cauliflower.	Blackleg.		A depressed brownish canker which girdles the stem and in late stages is covered with black dots. Leaves have same characteristics of this disease on the stem.	Stem, leaves and seed pods.	Clean seed, rotation, hot water treatment of seed. Disease free soil.
	Clubroot or Finger-and-Toe Disease.		Club-like swellings on the roots which cause a derangement of their function and prevent normal growth and development of the above ground parts. Plants may wilt during hot part of the day but appear normal in early forenoon.	Root.	Crop rotations 1 : 1, 5,000 solution of corrosive sublimate for watering plants at planting time. Keep soil pH between 6.0 and 7.0
		Cabbage Worms.	A greenish caterpillar from one-half to over an inch in length with yellow spots along its sides.	Foliage is devoured.	Before heads form DDT or later Rotenone.
		Cutworms.	Caterpillar 1-2" in length, pale brown with variegations.	Chew stems of newly set plants close to the ground. May also eat roots and leaves.	A prepared poison bait.

VEGETABLE DISEASES AND INSECTS AND THEIR CONTROL—continued

VEGETABLE	DISEASE	INSECT	DESCRIPTION	DAMAGE	CONTROL
Broccoli, etc.—contd.	Clubroot, etc.—continued.	Maggots.	Small white larvæ, ¼–⅓" long.	Burrow in roots, preventing the plant from functioning properly.	Add 1 oz. of bichloride of mercury to 7½ gals. of water. Apply ¼ cupful around the base of each plant soon after setting in field. Twice at 10-day intervals.
	Cabbage Yellows.		In seedling stage, the whole plant dies. Partly matured plants have a dwarfed yellow appearance. The lower leaves drop in succession.	Stems and leaves.	Resistant varieties.
		Aphids.	See Beet.	See Beet.	See Beet.
Carrot.	Bacterial Soft Rot.		A water-soaked appearance followed by decay.	Carrot root.	Place only healthy roots in storage at temperature 40° F. in sand.
	Phoma Root Rot.		A brown canker on or near the top of the root with black dots on it.	Carrot root.	Plant seed in good loam. Select best roots for storage.
Celery.	Early Blight.		At first, minute yellowish spots which enlarge and darken, changing from a yellow to a gray color with a thin papery texture.	Leaves.	Dust or spray with Bordeaux or fixed coppers or organic fungicides containing Zineb, Nabam, Ziram.
	Late Blight.		Circular yellowish spots which turn black and have minute black dots on them.	Leaves and stems.	Same as Early Blight but start spraying in seed bed.
Cucumber.	Bacterial Wilt.		Entire plant wilts and finally dies.	Leaves and stems.	Pull and burn diseased plants. Control cucumber beetle.
	Leaf Spot.		Leaves develop water-soaked areas which later become gray.	Leaves.	Bordeaux mixture.
		Striped Cucumber Beetle.	Dark yellow in color, ¼" long with 3 black stripes.	Eats foliage of young tender plants. Spreads Bacterial Wilt.	Rotenone dust; tobacco dust repellent; clean up refuse in fall; burn.
Eggplant.	Phomopsis Blight.		Stems of seedlings next to ground turn brown and shrivel, causing plant to fall over. Circular, defined gray to brown area on the leaves with black dots, causing leaf to yellow and finally die. On fruit, spots are pale sunken areas with numerous black dots on them.	Stems, leaves and fruit.	Bordeaux mixture (see Blackleg of Cabbage). Treat seed with 1 : 1,000 corrosive sublimate for 10 minutes.
		Flea Beetle.	Tiny shiny black beetles.	Make tiny holes in the leaves, giving them the appearance of a sieve.	Rotenone or DDT as dust or spray.
		Colorado	Medium-sized reddish larvæ. Beetles are	Eats the foliage.	Same as for Flea Beetle.

	Cucumber.	Cucumber.		
Onion.	Neck Rot.	Dark sunken spots on the neck of the onion which rots the entire bulb.	Bulb.	Well dried before storing and stored at a temperature of 50–60° F.
Parsley.	Crown Rot.	A soft rot which gradually spreads, rotting off the roots from the leaves.	At junction of leaves and roots.	Rotation.
Pea.	Root Rot.	Stems decay, causing above ground parts to die.	Roots.	Rotation, resistant varieties and well drained soil.
	Aphids.	See Beet.	See Beet.	See Beet.
	Ascochyta Blight.	Pods: Grayish areas covered with brown dots. Stems: Sunken cankers which may surround the stem and cause death. Leaves: Poorly defined circular grayish areas with black dots.	Pods, stems and leaves.	Rotation and resistant varieties.
Pepper.	Bacterial Spot.	Leaf: Upper side of leaf is slightly sunken in small spots with a corresponding bulge on the lower side. Fruit: Spots very visible, brownish black in color with a roughened surface.	Leaves and fruit.	Treat seed with 1 : 2,000 corrosive sublimate or red copper oxide; or spray plants with Bordeaux.
	Phoma Rot.	Small, water-soaked areas which enlarge and turn black.	Fruit.	Rotation of crops. Careful handling of the fruit.
Potato.	Early Blight.	Dark brown circular spots on the foliage which enlarge as the disease spreads.	Leaves.	Bordeaux mixture; Zineb; plant decay free tubers.
	Late Blight.	Water-soaked areas with no definite margins.	Leaves.	Same.
	Rhizoctonia.	Tiny dark fungous bodies on the tuber. Sprouts are attacked when growth begins. Sprouts are only partially affected, which causes many small tubers to form in a hill.	Tubers.	Use disease-free seed for planting.
	Scab.	Small swollen or depressed areas on the surface with a corky ridge.	Tubers.	Clean tubers for seed. Plant seed on soil that is slightly acid in reaction.
	Potato Beetle.	See Eggplant.	See Eggplant.	See Eggplant.
	Flea Beetle.	See Eggplant.	See Eggplant.	See Eggplant.
	Aphids.	See Beet.	See Beet.	See Beet.
Pumpkin.	See Cucumber.	See Squash.		

VEGETABLE INSECTS AND DISEASES AND THEIR CONTROL—continued

VEGETABLE	DISEASE	INSECT	DESCRIPTION	DAMAGE	CONTROL
Spinach.	Yellows.		A dwarfing and yellowing of the leaves.	Leaves.	Resistant varieties.
Squash.	*See Cucumber.*				
		Squash Bug.	Grayish to dark brown hardshell insects.	Sucks juices from the plant, stunting it.	Hand pick adults and eggs; dust with sabadilla powder.
Sweet Corn.	Bacterial Wilt.		Wilting of plant before mature.	Leaves and stalk.	Resistant varieties.
	Smut.		Large black powdery substance.	Ear and tassel.	Cut and burn as soon as noticed.
		Corn Borer.	Grayish caterpillar.	Bores into ears.	Spray plant with 2 lbs. Wettable (50%) DDT to 100 gals. water; or spray with derris cube root.
		Corn Ear Worm.	Very similar.	Bores into ears and develops.	Spray green silks with 5% Wettable DDT. Repeat in 4 days; or place 20 drops of white oil plus pyrethrum on 6-day old silks.
Tomato.	Anthracnose.		Small water-soaked areas which enlarge, shrink and turn dark. Larger areas show a distinct zonation or circling.	Ripening fruits.	Bordeaux mixture.
	Early Blight.		*See Potato.*	*See Potato*	*See Potato*
	Late Blight.		*See Potato.*	*See Potato.*	*See Potato.*
	Phoma Rot.		*See Pepper.*	*See Pepper.*	*See Pepper.*
	Blossom End Rot.		A physiological disease which causes a breakdown of the rapidly growing tissues. Appears as a water-soaked area at first, gradually turning black and sunken in appearance.	Fruit.	Good cultural methods including proper amount of water and fertilizers will help. Weather conditions may play an important part.
		Potato Beetle.	*See Eggplant.*	*See Eggplant.*	*See Eggplant.*
		Flea Beetle.	*See Eggplant.*	*See Eggplant.*	*See Eggplant.*
		Aphids.	*See Beet.*	*See Beet.*	*See Beet.*
		Tobacco Worm.	A long greenish caterpillar with white stripes, yellowish spots and a spine protruding from the posterior end.	Eats the leaves and green fruits.	Hand pick. Dust with Rotenone.

NOTES: Use good garden practices to help control insects and diseases. Where possible resistant varieties should be used.

Precaution should be taken with insecticides and fungicides.

XL

THE CONTROL OF WEEDS
AND UNDESIRABLE PLANTS

In the larger sense every tree, vine, shrub and herb is a weed if it grows in the wrong place or if its habit of growth is such as to crowd out more desirable plants. One of the fundamental characteristics of most plants is to extend their dominion, often at the expense of their neighbors.

In forest country the encroachment of seedling trees very quickly pushes the margins of the woodlands out into the fields, and one of the annual chores of the farmer in such regions is to cut back the young seedlings in order to maintain the meadows. In a well-balanced agriculture, however, many native weeds are held in check by the very completeness of the use of the land. The annual cutting of a hayfield will usually destroy seedling trees and weeds in their first season of growth, while the cultivation of crop fields eliminates many weeds in an early stage of growth and prevents them from maturing. Thus it is only along the fence rows and the stone walls that separate the fields that the seedling trees and shrubs and weeds survive, and here they serve a very definite purpose in providing shelter for birds and wild life.

But on land that has been left idle in that zone which seems to surround so many of our cities, where it is no longer profitable to farm and where the time for real-estate development is not yet ripe, the weeds and weed-trees often have a twenty-year start on the ultimate home-owner. By the time there is a demand for suburban home sites in such areas, they have all too frequently become jungles of honeysuckle, sumac, poison ivy and ailanthus, and the new owner of the property is faced with serious problems. And even on well-established and carefully maintained home properties it is necessary to exert constant vigilance in order to prevent the introduction and encroachment of undesirable plants. Many a gardener and many a property owner has lived to regret the day when he failed to realize the danger of permitting a few trailing runners of Japanese honeysuckle to form a pleasant mat of green beneath some trees, or when he failed to take immediate action against the small patch of poison ivy which had established itself along the fence-row at the far end of his property, or when he failed to dig out quite ruthlessly the lovely tawny daylilies which had suddenly appeared as volunteers in his flower border.

There are some trees and shrubs, such as the ailanthus and the sumacs, which, if left to their own devices, tend to form such rank jungles of growth that their eradication involves a costly program. There are certain vines which, although of great ornamental value when kept within bounds, can become devastatingly rampant if neglected. In this group we find akebia and wisteria. There are also the ubiquitous, rank-growing perennials, such as the tawny daylily, the plume poppy and bouncing bet which form vigorous colonies on the perimeter of our cultivated areas and threaten to invade our gardens whenever they are afforded an opportunity to do so. And there are other plants which are frankly weeds—some of them comparatively harmless, others with dangerous potentialities. It is therefore important for every home owner and gardener to know which trees and shrubs and which vines and herbaceous plants have a tendency to become over-dominant and to crowd out more desirable plants, and which weeds are likely to become a serious menace. It is important, also, that he become familiar with the latest and most approved means of eradication, if a controlled economy of plants is to be maintained.

Trees Which May Become Weeds

Ailanthus (Ailanthus glandulosa). The Ailanthus, known also as the Tree of Heaven, was imported into this country from China, where it is greatly revered. No other tree is able to thrive under such adverse conditions and it is found growing in city yards and in alley-ways where scarcely any other green thing could gain a root-hold. Under favorable conditions it grows very rapidly, often, when young, making as much as six feet of growth in a single season, and it attains an ultimate height of about 75 feet. Although it has definite value as a tree for city planting, it deserves no place in more open areas. It reseeds prolifically and the young seedlings soon grow into dense, jungle-like thickets, often crowding out desirable native trees and other plant materials of superior quality. In parts of New England, in New York and Pennsylvania, in California and in certain other States the ailanthus has thus "gone wild".

Measures of Control: Young seedling trees should either be cut down as soon as they appear, or they should be destroyed by spraying. Fortunately the wood of the Ailanthus is soft and light and the task of cutting is therefore comparatively easy, but it is a task which should not be postponed. Ailanthus may also be controlled effectively by spraying with a brush-killer containing 2,4,5–T plus 2,4–D. The spray may be applied as a dormant spray during the winter months or it may be applied during the summer. (See page 608.) If sprouts from unkilled sections develop they should be sprayed as soon as they are a foot or two high.

Sumac: Both the Staghorn Sumac (Rhus typhina) and the Smooth Sumac (Rhus glabra) are weed-trees common in the eastern part of the United States. They are soft-wooded, quick growing, shrub-like trees which form continuous thickets and rapidly convert open fields into jungles. They spread both by underground stems and by seeds, and often take over abandoned land by the acre. The sumacs are decorative in form, the foliage has brilliant autumn coloring, and the red-berried seed heads are strikingly handsome, but their weediness far outweighs their beauty, and they should never be allowed to spread out of bounds.

Measures of Control: Merely cutting the plants down is not a satisfactory measure of control, as they spring up again the following year with a growth more dense than before, although they can be eradicated by grubbing out the roots, which is a long, slow task. The most effective means of control is a brush-killer containing 2,4,5–T plus 2,4–D. This may be applied either as a dormant spray during the winter or as a summer spray (see page 608). One thorough application will usually result in the complete eradication of sumac. If subsequent growth occurs a second application should be made.

Miscellaneous Weed Trees: In this group we have such trees as the wild cherry, the poplars, some of the maples, birches and pines, the hackberry and the mulberry.

The wild cherries harbor tent-caterpillars which spread to orchard trees and to the flowering crabs, and they should be eliminated from the home grounds, from roadsides and from hedgerows. A watchful eye, the axe, and the bonfire constitute one method of eradication. They may also be controlled by either summer or dormant spraying with 2,4,5–T plus 2,4–D (see page 608).

Under certain conditions some of the birches, poplars and pines, in spite of their many fine qualities, may become weed-trees, as they reseed prolifically and have a tendency to spread into open land, thus re-establishing the forest. Therefore if open fields are to be maintained, or if a cherished view or vista is to be kept clear of encroachment, it is imperative that these young seedling trees be systematically destroyed through the annual use of the axe, brush-hook, chopping-knife, mower or sprayer. All of these trees may be successfully controlled by either summer or dormant spraying with one of the brush-killers containing 2,4,5–T plus 2,4–D (see page 608).

The *Hackberry* (Celtis occidentalis) and the *Mulberry*, both Morus alba and Morus rubra, may be considered weed-trees in almost any situation, and, under most circumstances, should be completely eliminated. Small seedling trees may be readily cut down, or eradicated by spraying with a brush-killer as directed (page 608).

Vines with Dangerous Potentialities

Akebia (Akebia quinata). Akebia is a small-stemmed vine with attractive foliage, and it is often planted as an ornamental vine on fences, porches, and pergolas. Unless care is taken to keep its growth within bounds, however, it is capable of spreading as a dense mat over the ground and of obtaining a strangle hold on all shrubs and trees in its path, and eventually killing everything within its reach.

Measures of Control: Keep the vine strictly within bounds by judicious pruning. If it has been permitted to grow unchecked it may be eradicated by spraying with one of the brush-killers containing 2,4,5–T plus 2,4–D (see page 608).

Bittersweet (Celastris scandens and Celastris chinensis). Although Bittersweet is loved for the brilliant coloring and decorative qualities of its fruits, it must be kept within bounds, as it has a propensity to clamber over surrounding trees and shrubs and in time will cause considerable damage.

Measures of Control: Careful pruning will keep bittersweet under control, and in cases where eradication is desired it may either be cut down or it may be sprayed with one of the brush-killers containing 2,4,5–T plus 2,4–D (see page 608).

Dodder (Cuscuta): Known also as love-vine, strangleweed, and hellbind, dodder is one of the few parasitic plants which invade the garden, and it can become a very insidious and destructive pest. It is a leafless, annual vine. After the seed has germinated the slender, orange tendrils reach out until they come into contact with some neighboring plant, and they then entwine themselves about the stem. Being a true parasite, the tiny, sucker-like stems pierce the stalk, and thenceforth the dodder draws its nourishment entirely from the host plant, completely losing its contact with the ground. The dodder plant has the appearance of a tangled mass of tiny, orange, threadlike suckers and tendrils. It produces no green foliage, but bears clusters of small, white flowers. The seeds mature in August and drop to the ground where they lie dormant during the winter, germinating the following spring. When allowed to go unchecked, dodder can become a very serious problem in the garden. It attacks annuals, perennials and vines, and once it has become well established it is difficult to eradicate it completely.

Measures of Control: It is useless to attempt to disentangle the dodder plant from the plant which it has attacked, as new growth will start again if the tiniest piece is left attached to the host plant. The only sure measure of control is to root up or cut down the entire host plant, or such portion of the plant as has been attacked, and to burn it immediately. Dodder can also be eradicated by spraying with 2,4-D, but this will also usually kill the host plant as well.

Japanese Honeysuckle (Lonicera japonica). About seventy-five years ago there was imported into this country a new decorative climber which unfortunately was destined to become one of our most troublesome and devastatingly destructive weed-vines—the Japanese honeysuckle. Because of its attractive appearance and its fragrant blossoms it is frequently planted by property owners who are completely unaware of the liability which they are incurring. When it once gets out of bounds it spreads rapidly under trees and in open, sunny areas as well, and it obtains a stranglehold on anything which comes within its reach. In some sections it has destroyed acres of young forest growth. It has smothered out large areas of crop land, and entire farms have been abandoned because of its devastations.

Measures of Control: In the past Japanese honeysuckle has been one of the most difficult of all plants to control, once it gained headway, but the new brush-killers have proved very effective, and it can now be eradicated completely by spraying with 2,4,5–T plus 2,4–D (see page 608). The spray should be applied when the plants are in full leaf and are making active growth, from June to September being the most favorable period. If the growth is dense, more than one application will be necessary. A vigorous and thorough program of spraying, followed by a careful check-up the next season will be necessary if effective control is to be secured. Better than eradication, however, is prevention. Don't plant it! Don't tolerate it on your property under any circumstances!

Poison Ivy (Rhus toxicodendron). The tremendous increase in the spread of poison ivy during the past fifty years gives emphatic proof that we have been playing a losing contest with some of our weed enemies. Poison ivy is a vine native to the United States which is now found growing rampantly from New Hampshire southward to Virginia, and it is extending its habitat annually. In some woodlands which, twenty years ago, were a joy to explore for the wealth of wild flowers they contained, poison ivy has gradually established itself as a permanent ground cover and has completely overwhelmed the lovely native azaleas and viburnums, the ferns and the wild flowers. It has become a serious economic pest in many an orchard and its rampant growth along roadsides and hedgerows spoils the enjoyment of the countryside for those who are susceptible to it, and there are very few who are immune.

In areas where poison ivy is only starting its invasion prompt action on the part of the property-owners may avert disaster. Here the rule should be: Don't let it become established! In sections where it has already become rampant a united effort should be made on the part of the entire community to eradicate it.

Measures of Control: If poison ivy spread only by extending its runners over the surface of the ground its control would be a reasonably simple matter, as these ground trailers seldom bear fruit, but once it has attained height by attaching itself to a fencepost, a tree, or the wall of a building it blooms and sets seed. Birds carry the seeds to new locations and its spread thus becomes much more rapid. Therefore wherever poison ivy has started to ascend trees or posts or walls its stems should be cut with an axe or pruning saw if it is inadvisable to spray it, due to the possibility of injury to the host plant or to nearby plants. Needless to say, this should be done by someone who is not susceptible. Otherwise a curved pruning saw blade may be attached to a long pole which will enable the worker to stand at a considerable distance.

In the past, the eradication of large areas of poison ivy was an almost impossible task, but some of the chemical and hormone sprays which are now available have proved remarkably effective and it is now a relatively easy matter to eliminate it completely.

The following sprays have proved effective controls.

1. *Amino Triazole:* (See page 607.) (Available under the trade name ACP Poison Ivy Killer.) This is one of the most effective controls for poison ivy. One application will usually result in complete eradication. Application may be made at any time after the leaves have become fully expanded until they begin to change color in the autumn. Early spring and dormant applications are not advisable. A fairly coarse spray is preferable to a fine, mist-like spray, and the application should be made on a day when there is little wind in order to avoid the danger of having the spray drift onto other plants which might prove sensitive.

It is essential to obtain a thorough coverage. The leaves and stems should be sprayed down to the base to the point of run-off. Within a short time after the application has been made the leaves will become dry and brittle and a complete kill is usually obtained.

A number of trees (see list on page 607) are not sensitive to amino triazole and one of its great advantages over most other measures of control is that poison ivy may be sprayed when it is growing under or on such trees without causing injury. When application is being made the spray should be confined as far as possible to the foliage of the poison ivy. Amino triazole does not penetrate the bark of trees.

2. *Ammonium sulfamate* (see page 605).

3. *2,4,5–T plus 2,4–D* (see page 608).

Now that poison ivy may be so effectively eradicated with these new sprays, entire communities are undertaking to rid themselves of this scourge. Roadside spraying is being done on an extensive scale in many sections, and in some areas spraying is being done for individual property owners on a custom basis.

Wisteria: Although one of the most beautiful of all vines, wisteria can become a rampant weed-vine if allowed to get out of bounds. Its capacity to reach ever higher and to wrestle with anything with which it comes in contact and to pull it from its fastenings makes it a bad neighbor for shutters, rain-conductors, gutters, and shingles. Another unfortunate characteristic of wisteria is its habit of spreading by long, trailing runners on the surface of the ground, or just below the surface, from which it sends down roots at intervals and forms new plants. Thus, if left unchecked, it can take possession of a large area very rapidly and can completely crowd out all existing growth. There is a tragic example near an old, deserted house in the South where a single wisteria vine has spread out in every direction until its rampant, unrestrained growth now covers an area of more than an acre, forming an almost impenetrable jungle.

Measures of Control: The pruning saw and pruning shears are the most important tools for the control of wisteria, and a vine should never be allowed to get out of control.

When young plants spring up from runners they may be controlled by spraying with a brush-killer containing 2,4,5–T plus 2,4–D. Wisteria is fairly resistant to sprays of this type, however, and several applications may be necessary (see page 608).

Shrubs with Undesirable Characteristics

There are some shrubs which seem to possess an unquenchable spirit for conquest and which will quickly encroach upon more desirable plantings if given the least opportunity. And there are other shrubs which are so weedy in character that they do not deserve a place in any well-studied planting scheme. In these two groups we find matrimony vine and the ubiquitous knotweed, coralberry and St. Johnswort, and a number of other shrubs.

Matrimony Vine (Lycium halimifolium) is a shrub with slender, drooping branches. It is useful as a ground cover on eroded banks, but it should never be used in a shrubbery border or in plantings about the house. It spreads rapidly from underground suckers and in a comparatively short time will completely take over quite an extensive area. It is difficult to eradicate it by cutting it down or grubbing it out, as young suckers will almost invariably appear and it will soon re-establish itself. It is, however, extremely sensitive to sprays containing 2,4,5–T plus 2,4–D and may be completely killed by one application (see page 608).

Knotweed (Polygonum Sieboldii) spreads rapidly from deep, underground roots, is very persistent and is difficult to eradicate. Because of the very rank character of its growth it will quickly crowd out everything in its path, and it is the part of wisdom never to permit it to become established on one's property. It may be brought under control by spraying with a brush-killer containing 2,4,5–T plus 2,4–D although more than one application may be necessary as it is fairly resistant (see page 608).

St. Johnswort (Hypericum aureum) is not only of a weedy nature, but also possesses the unfortunate characteristics of reseeding so prolifically that young plants spring up all over the place, making it a doubly undesirable resident upon one's property. The *Coralberry* (Symphoricarpus vulgaris) spreads rapidly, also, and both of these shrubs should be watched and kept within bounds.

Perennials with Aggressive Tendencies

There are a number of perennial plants which, when they escape from the confines of the garden, tend to spread rapidly and have potentialities of becoming serious pests in lawns and woodlands and less well cultivated areas. And there are other undesirable perennial plants which are sometimes unwittingly brought into the garden, the owner being entirely unaware of their aggressive characteristics. In some instances such plants appear suddenly as voluntary invaders in the garden, and unless immediate steps are taken to eliminate them they will soon gain such headway that they will crowd out the more desirable plantings. Some of these perennials, such as the Plumepoppy (Bocconia cordata) reseed so prolifically that they very soon become a source of annoyance on one's property unless all the flower stalks are cut off before the seed has matured. The piquant and dainty little English Daisy can also become a source of annoyance in lawns unless the flower heads are cut off before the seeds have formed and ripened, and they hold a very strategic position, since they are always used as edging plants along the front of beds or borders and are thus in close proximity to areas of turf in the garden.

Other plants, such as False Dragonhead (Physostegia virginiana), send their long, underground shoots out in every direction and in an incredibly short time will completely take over large areas in the garden at the expense of less aggressive plants. When a plant such as the Tawny Daylily (Hemerocallis fulva) has once gained a root-hold in the flower garden it seems ruthless in its determination to take command. To eradicate it every particle of the root must be dug out, as the plant will grow again if even a small portion is left.

Since the eradication of these undesirable perennials is such a laborious undertaking, it is well to know which plants possess dangerous potentialities and to prevent their introduction into the garden, and, if they appear as volunteers, to undertake immediate measures of control. An informed mind, eternal vigilance and prompt action will bring their rewards.

Some of the worst offenders among herbaceous plants are included in the following list:

BOTANICAL NAME	COMMON NAME
Ajuga genevensis	Bugle
Apios americana	Tuberosa
Bellis perennis	English Daisy
Bocconia cordata	Plumepoppy
Campanula rapunculoides	Grandmother's Bluebells
Coronilla varia	
Hemerocallis fulva	Tawny Daylily
Physalis Alkekengi	Chinese Lantern
Physostegia virginiana	False Dragonhead
Plumbago larpentæ	Leadwort
Saponaria officinalis	Bouncing Bet
Sedum sarmentosum	Stringy Stonecrop

Weeds that are Frankly Weeds

There are many plants that are frankly weeds and do not masquerade as decorative vines or handsome shrubs, or ingratiate themselves by producing such attractive flowers that they thus gain admittance to one's garden. Among these weeds some are comparatively innocuous, causing little trouble and being easy to control. In this group we find such weeds as lambsquarters, Pennsylvania smartweed, Indian mallow, chickweed, rough pigweed, purslane, ragweed and many other annual weeds which may be readily controlled by ordinary cultivation. There are other weeds, however, which present a very different problem—weeds which are capable of becoming a definite menace in the flower bed, vegetable garden or orchard. It is important to know which weeds are in this class and to be able to recognize them when they first appear. And it is important also to undertake immediate measures of control, as it is often a comparatively simple matter to eradicate such weeds in the very beginning, but it becomes increasingly difficult to do so after they are once established and have begun to spread. The worst offenders in this group are bindweed, Canada thistle, Johnson grass, the palmetto, prickly pear cactus, and quackgrass.

Bindweed is an exceedingly pestiferous weed and has been one of the most difficult of all weeds to control. In certain sections of the country it has become so rampant that it has made necessary the abandonment of great areas of agricultural land. Its habit of obtaining a stranglehold on all plants with which it comes into contact makes it a most serious menace in garden and crop fields, and immediate measures of control should be undertaken as soon as it appears, as it spreads very rapidly from underground runners.

Measures of Control:

1. Benzac is one of the most effective controls for bindweed and kills of 95 percent to 100 percent have been obtained. It is applied as a spray and should be used in accordance with the manufacturer's instructions as given on the container.

2. 2,4–D (see page 607). As bindweed is somewhat tolerant of sprays of this type more than one application may be necessary. The most favorable time to make the first application is when the plants are just coming into bloom, although reasonably good results may be obtained at other times if the plants are making vigorous growth. Poor results are usually obtained from spraying during the hot, dry summer months when plants are making but little growth.

3. Sodium chlorate has been widely used on large-scale operations for the control of bindweed but is less desirable for use by the home gardener than some of the other recommended controls (see page 606).

4. Complete eradication may be obtained on very small areas by treating the soil with Methyl Bromide (Dowfume MC–2), applied at the rate of 1 lb. per 100 sq. ft. Application should be made during mild weather, as moderate temperatures are necessary for the material to be completely effective. After the application has been made the area should be covered for 48 hours with a heavy, plastic sheeting, weighted at the edges with soil.

    Directions of the manufacturer as given on the container should be followed with care.

Canada Thistle. The Canada thistle is one of the most pernicious of all weeds, and legal measures have been taken in many states to prevent its spread. The roots are tough and deep lying and spread out in every direction from the parent plant, new shoots being formed at frequent intervals. Within the space of a single season a few plants will develop into an extensive patch, and when once firmly entrenched Canada thistles are capable of crowding out most other plants. Many a gardener and many a farmer has lived to rue the day when he failed to take prompt action against this invader which can become such a very serious menace in the garden, in the orchard, and on farm fields.

Measures of Control:

1. Small patches may be smothered out (see page 605).

2. Spray with amino triazole (see page 607). This amino triazole herbicide has proved an excellent control for Canada thistle. For best results it should be applied to young growth in the spring when the plants are between 6 and 15 inches high. Results are not good if spraying is done after the plants have reached the bud or bloom stage. Good coverage with the spray is essential. Plants should not be mown or otherwise cut down after treatment. About three weeks after application of the spray the plants should be plowed or deeply spaded under.

3. Spray with sodium chlorate (see page 606).

4. Spray with 2,4–D (see page 607). As Canada thistles are somewhat resistant to sprays of this type more than one application is usually necessary. The first application should be made when the plants are in the bud stage. Following this initial application a careful watch should be kept and as new shoots appear they should be sprayed while still in the rosette stage, being at this time between 4 and 6 inches in height.

Johnson Grass: In some sections of the country Johnson grass is a serious pest, being the most troublesome of any of the perennial grasses. It is a deeply rooted grass, spreads very rapidly, and prior to the introduction of some of the new chemicals it has been difficult to control.

Measures of Control:

1. Small patches may be smothered out (see page 605).

2. Spray with dalapon (see page 607). Application should be made in the spring when the grass is well developed and is making active, fast growth. Good coverage is essential. A second application may be necessary.

3. Spray with TCA (see page 606). The first application should be made when the grass is about a foot high. Subsequent applications will usually be necessary in order to eradicate it completely. Best results will be obtained if the spraying is done when the grass is growing vigorously and when optimum moisture conditions prevail.

Palmetto: Where palmettos constitute a weed menace they may be controlled by spraying with TCA (see page 606), or with 2,4,5–T (see page 608).

Prickly Pear Cactus: This has formerly been a very difficult weed to eradicate, but may now be brought under control very readily by spraying thoroughly with TCA (see page 606).

Quackgrass: This is one of the perennial grasses which has become a source of very real annoyance to gardeners in many sections of the country. It spreads very rapidly, as the long, underground stems trail along for great distances just below the surface of the ground and root at every joint.

Measures of Control:

1. Small patches may be smothered out (see page 605).
2. Spray with amino triazole (see page 607). Application should be made in the spring when the grass is 4 to 6 inches high. When the grass shows a whitish color, usually about two weeks after treatment, it should be plowed or spaded deeply under so that all the treated grass is completely covered.
3. Spray with dalapon (see page 607). Application should be made in the spring when the grass is in full leaf and is making fast, active growth. Good coverage is essential. A second treatment may be necessary if a complete kill is not secured with the first application.
4. Spray with TCA (see page 606). Either of the methods outlined below may be followed:
   (*a*) Apply TCA and spade or plow from two to four weeks following the application.
   (*b*) In the autumn spade or plow to a shallow depth all infested areas. Apply TCA at the rate of 50 to 100 pounds per acre. The lower amount should be used on very light, sandy soils. The ground should be left undisturbed during the winter, and may be planted to whatever crop is desired in the spring.

Effective Measures of Weed Control

In general the most effective measures of control for weeds and other undesirable plants include cultivation, smothering by means of an effective mulch, and eradication through the use of chemical and organic sprays.

Cultivation: Many annual weeds in the flower garden, the vegetable garden and the orchard, as well as some perennial weeds, may be controlled very satisfactorily by good cultivation. It is the age-old method of weed control and will probably continue to be used by gardeners throughout the world for centuries to come. It is the method most frequently employed for the control of weeds in the flower garden, where other methods, such as the use of chemical and hormone sprays, are not feasible, although to some extent in the flower garden and very definitely in the vegetable garden it is being replaced by the use of mulches.

Cultivation should be timely and thorough. In normal seasons a good cultivation every ten days or two weeks will keep most of the weeds under control, although in very rainy seasons more frequent cultivations may be necessary. The soil should never be stirred with a cultivator when it is too wet, as it will tend to injure the structure of the soil, making it lumpy and cloddy. This is particularly true when one is working with heavy loam or clay soils. A good way in which to determine whether the soil is dry enough for cultivation is to pick up a handful of earth and squeeze it tightly in the palm of the hand. If, when it is dropped, it breaks up into a crumbly mass it is a sign that it is sufficiently dry.

If it remains in a solid lump it is evident that it is too moist to receive a cultivation.

Mulches: There are various materials which may be used very satisfactorily for mulches (see page 498).

The application of a mulch has become an increasingly popular practice among gardeners within recent years, and mulches have proved their value in the flower garden, the vegetable garden, and the orchard. In addition to being a very effective method of controlling weeds a mulch also helps to conserve the moisture in the soil and to maintain lower soil temperatures, thus creating more favorable growing conditions for the plants.

On small areas where one wishes to kill out weedy grasses which spring up again so readily from bits of trailing roots and stems if one tries to remove them by spading up the ground, one of the most effective methods of eradication is to smother all growth with a very heavy, impervious mulch. Boards, building paper, or heavy layers of newspapers may be used. At the end of several weeks both the roots and tops will be dead, provided that all light and air have been excluded. Small patches of Canada thistle, bindweed and other weeds of this type may also be eradicated in this way.

Sprays: The United States Department of Agriculture, the State Experiment Stations and many large commercial concerns have carried on extensive experiments in an effort to discover and develop effective measures of weed control through the use of chemical and hormone sprays, and remarkable advances have been made. In fact, so great has been the progress in these fields that large-scale operations have practically been revolutionized in many areas, and it is now possible to eradicate weeds along roadsides and in crop fields and in gardens and orchards where heretofore it had seemed useless even to make an attempt to do so, so limited were the measures of control available.

Chemical Sprays

Ammonium sulfamate (sold under the trade name "Ammate"). This chemical weed-killer is non-poisonous to men and to animals and has no lasting ill effects upon the soil. It is effective against certain types of weeds and against many woody plants such as blackberry and other brambles, green briar, hickory, poison ivy, poison oak, the sumacs and the willows. As there is less danger of drifting than with sprays of certain other types it is particularly well suited to use as a control for underbrush and weeds in orchards. One disadvantage of ammonium sulfamate is that it will injure grasses, and care must therefore be taken when it is used under certain conditions. Directions concerning rate and method of application, as given on the container, should be followed with the utmost care.

Borax is one of the most effective of all weed-killers on areas where complete soil sterilization is not a detriment. It renders the soil toxic to all plant growth for a number of years, and is therefore of particular value for use on tennis courts, driveways and areas of this nature. It should be applied in the powder form at the rate of three to four pounds per square rod.

Sodium chlorate has given excellent results in the eradication of certain weeds, and it is widely used in many farming areas for the control of such troublesome plants as Canada thistle, bindweed, Johnson grass and quackgrass. It may be used in the form of a powder or as a spray. When used in the dry form it should be applied at the rate of four pounds per square rod. For the control of bindweed and Johnson grass, applications made in October or November have proved most effective. When used in the liquid form it should be applied as a fine, mist-like spray. It kills the top of the plant to which it is applied by absorbing the food supply in the new leaves. This in turn exhausts the stored food in the roots and the plant eventually turns yellow and dies. For the majority of plants the most favorable time of application is when the plant is coming into bloom. The spray should be applied thoroughly, especially to the young, growing tips, and the application should preferably be made when the air is moist. Spraying on damp days or early in the morning when the plants are wet with dew will give the best results. If the growth is rank, more than one application may be necessary. Sodium chlorate is known as a non-selective weed-killer, as it is destructive to all vegetation and it must therefore be applied with care. If heavy applications are made it will sterilize the soil for a period of six months to a year or more, making it impossible to grow crops during this period. There are areas where it may be advisable to prevent the growth of all vegetation, but the hazards of soil sterilization must definitely be borne in mind when sodium chlorate is being used. A form of sodium chlorate which is put out under the trade name of "Altacide" is a safer type to use than the pure form, which must be used with great care as, under certain conditions, it is inflammable.

TCA (trichloroacetate) is an effective control for such pestiferous grasses as Johnson grass and quackgrass, as well as for a number of other grasses. It is used in the form of a spray, and it renders the soil sterile for a time, the effect of the chemical lasting anywhere from one to three months. The type of soil and the amount of rainfall both have an influence upon the length of the sterile period. During a season of heavy rainfall the effects of the chemical will disappear within a month or six weeks. TCA is most effective if application is made when the soil is fairly moist and when there is a minimum amount of rain following the application. Some grasses, such as Bermuda grass, are very sensitive and may be eradicated with but one application, while other grasses, notably Johnson grass, require at least two applications. TCA is also of value in killing both annual and perennial grasses in the seedling stage and, when it is used in low dosages, it will suppress the growth of grasses without actually killing them. Such treatment might be of value along highways and rights-of-way where a sod is desired but where long grass constitutes a fire hazard.

Hormone Type Sprays

One of the most revolutionary advances in recent years in the weed control field has been the development of the completely new type of hormone weed-killers. Sprays of this type possess the quality of translocation. They move through the plant and produce formative effects within the plant. Some act as growth-regulating substances which kill a plant either by upsetting its balance of growth so completely that it is no longer adapted to its environment, or by exciting it into such activity that it literally grows itself to death. In some cases the leaves become distorted in shape; in other cases development is arrested and flowers do not open. The parts below ground become enlarged and at length split open, causing the plant to die within a short space of time. Other hormone type sprays affect the formation of chlorophyll within the plant.

These hormone sprays, which are organic compounds, are known as selective weed-killers, as some plants are extremely sensitive to them, while others are markedly resistant. In general, most broad-leaved plants are sensitive, while many narrow-leaved plants, such as the grasses, are not seriously affected. Sprays of this type do not sterilize the soil. Hormone sprays are obtainable under various trade names. They should be applied in the form of a fine, mist-like spray, preferably on a calm, sunny day when the absorption by the leaves will be accelerated. Directions on the container should be carefully followed. When plants are growing in deep shade more than one application will usually be necessary in order to obtain effective results. For small areas a one-quart hand sprayer will be entirely satisfactory, provided that it gives a fine, mist-like spray. On somewhat larger areas a knapsack sprayer with a short hose attachment will prove more practical, and for large-scale operations a power sprayer should be used.

Precautions: When using any of the hormone type sprays certain precautions should be observed. It must be borne in mind that most broad-leaved plants are susceptible and the spray should not be allowed to drift onto nearby vegetation lest severe damage be done. A sprayer used for the application of a hormone spray should never be used for any other purpose. It is extremely difficult to eliminate all traces of the spray, no matter how carefully the sprayer is cleaned, and there have been instances where serious damage has resulted.

Amino Triazole. This hormone type spray (put out under such trade names as ACP Poison Ivy Killer and Weedazole) has proved particularly effective against many hard-to-kill plants. It affects the formation of chlorophyll, interfering with the normal growth of the plant, as chlorophyll is basic to the manufacture of food within the plant. Amino triazole possesses outstanding qualities of translocation and has proved superior to some of the other hormone type sprays in controlling certain plants. It is most effective if applied when the plants are in active growth and after they are well leafed out, and it may be used effectively up to within a few weeks of frost. Early spring and dormant applications are not advisable. One application is usually sufficient for complete eradication, but under some conditions a follow-up treatment may be necessary.

Amino triazole has many advantages as a herbicide. It does not volatilize and form vapors which might prove harmful to sensitive plants. It dissolves readily in water and is easy to apply; it is non-toxic to humans and animals; it is not a fire hazard; and it is not corrosive to spray equipment. It is readily inactivated in heavy soils and does not build up a toxic residue if it is used at the prescribed rates.

As amino triazole is a comparatively non-selective weed-killer, precautions must be taken in its use. However, unless plants which are sensitive to it come into direct contact with the spray there is no danger of permanent damage. If a small amount of spray drifts onto evergreens or deciduous trees or shrubs the leaves may turn white, but unless the entire plant has been soaked with the solution it will not die. The new growth of grass may turn white but will resume its normal color within a few weeks.

WEEDY PLANTS WHICH ARE SENSITIVE TO AMINO TRIAZOLE

(One application usually required for eradication)

Bermuda Grass	Quackgrass
Buck Brush	Russian Knapweed
Canada and Sow Thistles	Poison Ivy
Cattails and Tules	Poison Oak

Horsetail Rush	Prickly Ash
Leafy Spurge	White Ash
Nut Grass	White, Scrub and Red Oak

PLANTS WHICH ARE COMPARATIVELY RESISTANT TO AMINO TRIAZOLE
(at rates required for ordinary control)

Apple	Sassafras
Dogwood	Smooth Sumac
English Ivy	Spice Bush
Japanese Honeysuckle	Viburnum
Lilacs	Virginia Creeper
Pachysandra	Vinca Minor
Red Maple	Walnut
Rhododendron	Wild Grape

Dalapon is a systemic herbicide of the hormone type which has proved very effective in the control of weedy grasses such as Bermuda grass, Johnson grass and quackgrass. It possesses qualities of translocation within the plant and causes a gradual yellowing of the leaves. It induces a dormancy of the crown and rhizome buds and if used at prescribed rates the dormant buds fail to develop and a high percentage of kill results.

It should be applied when the grasses are in full leaf and are making active, fast growth. Good coverage is essential in order to provide for sufficient absorption by the plant.

In using dalapon certain precautions should be taken. Direct contact with the skin should be avoided as it may cause irritation. All spraying equipment should be flushed out after use and before storage.

2,4–D. The scientific name of this hormone spray is 2,4 dichlorophenoxyacetic acid, which, for common usage, has been shortened to 2,4–D. It was one of the first of these new organic sprays to be developed and it is now widely used as a weed-killer. It is an effective control for most of the broad-leaved lawn weeds, such as buckhorn, dandelion, English plantain, lawn pennywort and ground-ivy, and it is also used extensively to control such weeds as mustard and yellow rocket when they become troublesome in grain fields. It is a selective weed-killer, as it has the ability to kill many of the weeds which are troublesome on lawns and in grain fields without injuring the lawn grasses or the grain crop itself. Among the other advantages of 2,4–D are the facts that it is non-toxic to man and to animals, it is non-inflammable, and it has only a very temporary effect upon the soil, which is soon dissipated after a few good rains. However, seeds should not be planted immediately in soil which has been sprayed with 2,4–D. It has been found that 2,4–D is less effective when used during periods of excessive rainfall or during periods of prolonged drought than it is when used under more normal conditions. Under these less favorable conditions additional applications may be necessary. 2,4–D is available both as a dust and as a spray, For use as a spray 2,4–D is available in three formulations, ready for mixing with water.

1. 30 to 50 percent esters in liquid form
2. 30 to 50 percent amine salts dissolved in a liquid
3. 70 to 80 percent sodium salt as a powder

Extensive experiments have shown that the ester form is the most effective. This has been found to be particularly true when conditions are unfavorable or when hard-to-kill plants are to be eradicated.

2,4,5–T. Known scientifically as Trichlorophenoxyacetic Acid, 2,4,5–T is similar in many respects to the ester form of 2,4–D but has been found to be a more effective measure of control for certain types of plants such as the brambles, blackjack oak and Osage orange. It has also been found effective for the basal treatment of brush during the dormant season. For this dormant spraying a 2,4,5–T butoxy ethanol ester should be used, being mixed with either oil or water. The base of the plant should be thoroughly wet with the spray from the ground level to a height of from two to three feet. For a foliage spray it should be mixed with water.

2,4,5–T plus 2,4–D. A combination of 2,4,5–T and 2,4–D (put out under various trade names such as Brush Killer 32) has been found to be more effective against hard-to-kill woody plants than either 2,4–D or 2,4,5–T used alone. It represents a distinct advance in weed-killers and is being widely used on home properties, in park areas and for roadside spraying. It is effective against an exceedingly wide range of woody plants and is one of the best means of eradicating poison ivy and Japanese honeysuckle. It is also effective in killing stumps and preventing resprouting. It will kill weeds and woody plants without harming grasses, it is non-poisonous to man and to animals, it does not cause a fire hazard and it is non-corrosive to spray equipment. It may be mixed with water for high volume spraying or with oil for low pressure spraying.

Best results will be obtained if the plants are in full leaf at the time that the application is made. In the majority of cases the most effective results have been obtained when the spraying was done between midsummer and early autumn. Complete coverage of the foliage is necessary. When areas of brush are being sprayed the size of the bushes or saplings is very important. Spraying should not be attempted on brush that is over six feet in height. If the brush exceeds this height it is advisable to cut it back and then to spray the stubble with 2,4,5–T plus 2,4–D mixed with oil. This may be done at any time of the year, either during the growing season or during the winter when the plants are dormant. The tops and sides of the stumps should be sprayed thoroughly. This same treatment may be accorded the stumps of trees which have been cut down. A single application will usually reduce resprouting as much as 75 percent, although a few stumps may require a second application. Stumps can be treated at any time.

Many weed-trees and shrubs may be effectively controlled by dormant spraying with 2,4,5–T plus 2,4–D. Thorough coverage of all trunks, stems and basal parts to a height of two to three feet above the ground is essential. Some species may begin to leaf out in the spring, but growth will soon be arrested and the plants will eventually die.

As many broad-leaved ornamental plants as well as many vegetable and farm crops are sensitive to sprays of this type, care must be taken to prevent the drifting of the spray onto nearby vegetation.

Some woody plants are very sensitive to 2,4,5–T plus 2,4–D and are readily killed by one application, while other plants are more tolerant and more than one application may be necessary. There are a few plants which have proved somewhat erratic in their reaction, and there are others that are extremely resistant.

Pre-emergence Weed-killers: A number of hormone type sprays will prevent weed seeds from germinating and will kill very young seedling weeds such as chickweed, crabgrass, pigweed, lambs-quarters and purslane.

Sprays of this type are widely used in the preparation of land for the production of farm crops and for certain commercial vegetable and flower crops and they are being used to an increasing extent by the home gardener. Such sprays may be applied to bare soil or to areas where non-sensitive, established plants are growing and will prevent all growth of weeds for a period varying from three to six weeks.

Pre-emergence sprays are also being used to a considerable extent on lawn areas to prevent the germination of crabgrass seeds and to kill very young seedlings. They are not effective in controlling older plants.

The following pre-emergence sprays will give good control under favorable conditions:

1. *Crag Herbicide 1.* In the vegetable garden Crag Herbicide 1 may be used in plantings of asparagus before and after cutting, and on potatoes at any time after planting. In the fruit garden it is effective in controlling weeds in strawberry beds and may be used at any time after the plants are well established.

On ornamentals it may be used around well established shrubs and evergreens and on roses, gladioli, narcissi and lilies. Among the perennials on which it may be used are iris, phlox and violets.

Crag Herbicide is also effective in controlling young crabgrass seedlings on lawns and preventing the germination of crabgrass seed.

2. *2,4–D* is widely used on commercial areas as a pre-emergence spray. However, in the home garden it must be used with caution as many vegetable crops are sensitive to it. Its chief value is for use on asparagus beds and on corn, and it may be used on strawberries and raspberries.

As a pre-emergence spray for crabgrass on lawns 2,4–D is very effective under normal conditions.

The manufacturer's directions on the container should be followed with care when making applications.

For further details concerning 2,4–D see page 607.

WEEDS WHICH ARE VERY SENSITIVE TO 2,4–D SPRAYS

(one normal application usually required)

Beggar ticks
Buckhorn
Bull thistle
Burdock
Carpetweed
Chickweed
Chicory
Cocklebur
Dandelion
False flax
Four-o'clock

Galinsoga
Ground ivy
Hedge bindweed
Jerusalem artichoke
Jewel weed
Jimson weed
Kochia
Loco weed
Marsh elder
Morning-glory
Mustard

Nettle (stinging)
Pennywort
Peppergrass
Pigweed
Plantain
Puncture vine
Ragweed
Shepherd's purse
Sow thistle
Spurge nettle

Sunflower
Vervain
Virginia Creeper
Water hemlock
Wild parsnip
Wild sweet potato
Winter cress
Wormwood
Yellow rocket
Yellow sorrel

WEEDS SOMEWHAT LESS SENSITIVE TO 2,4–D SPRAYS

(a stronger spray or repeated applications usually required)

Bindweed
Bouncing Bet
Buckwheat (wild)
Bur Ragweed
Buttercup
Canada thistle
Orange hawkweed
Chickweed (mouse
  ear)

Climbing milkweed
Coreopsis
Dock
Dodder
Dogbane
Fleabane
Goldenrod
Gourd (wild)
Henbane

Ironweed
Knotweed
Lambs-quarters
Lettuce (prickly)
Mallow
Marestail
Mayweed
Pokeweed
Purslane

Russian thistle
Silverleaf horsenettle
Smartweed
Speedwell
Wild carrot
Wild garlic
Wild lettuce
Yarrow

WEEDS RESISTANT TO 2,4–D SPRAYS

Barnyard grass
Bermuda grass
Black nightshade
Bracken
Buffalo bur
Cactus (prickly pear)
Cheat

Corn cockle
Crabgrass
Ferns
Foxtail grasses
Goosegrass
Ground cherry
Horsenettle

Johnson grass
Milkweed
Mullein
Oxalis
Oxeye Daisy
Quackgrass

Sandburs
Skelton weed
Sorrel (red ox)
Sorrel (wood)
Toad flax
Wild onions

TREES, SHRUBS AND VINES SENSITIVE TO 2,4,5–T PLUS 2,4–D

Ailanthus
Akebia
Alder
Apple
Aspen
Birch
Blackberry
Black Locust
Boxelder
Buckbrush
Buckeye
Catalpa
Cherry (choke)
Cherry (wild)
Chestnut
Chinaberry
Cottonwood
Currant

Elderberry
Elm
Fir
Grape
Gum (black)
Gum (sweet)
Hackberry
Hawthorn
Hazel
Hazelnut
Hercules Club
Honey Locust
Honeysuckle
Hornbeam
Horsechestnut
Juneberry
Larch
Maples (except Red)

Mulberry
New Jersey Tea
Pear
Pecan
Pine (in oil spray)
Poison Ivy
Poison Oak
Poplar
Prickly Ash
Raspberry
Rose
Sage brush
Salt Cedar
Sand Plum
Sassafras
Scotch broom
Shadbush
Silverberry

Skunkbrush
Spicebush
Sumac
Sweet fern
Sycamore
Trumpet Vine
Tulip-tree
Tung
Virginia Creeper
Walnut
Wild Plum
Willow
Winterberry
Wisteria
Witchhazel
Wolfberry
Wormwood

SOMEWHAT TOLERANT UNDER CERTAIN CONDITIONS

(more than one application, or basal or stump treatment)

Barberry
Dewberry

Dogwood
Greenbriar

Hemlock
Hickory

Juniper
Oak

Osage Orange
Snowberry

RESISTANT

Ash
Basswood

Beech
Cedar (Red)

Holly
Laurel
Maple (Red)

Mesquite
Persimmon

Rhododendron
Spruce

XLI

PLANT DISEASES AND INSECT PESTS

PLANT DISEASES

PLANT diseases may be grouped into three general classes—those brought about by unfavorable environment or by some physiological disturbance, those caused by fungi and by bacteria, and those caused by a virus.

In the first group we find plants suffering from malnutrition, from an improper balance of food elements in the soil, from an excess of one or more food nutrients, from extreme soil acidity, or from extreme alkalinity as is the case in lime-induced chlorosis. The symptoms are very much the same in most cases. Growth is retarded, the foliage becomes a sickly, yellowish green, and the root systems are poorly developed. For the control of such physiological diseases, refer to Chapter XVI on Soils and Soil Management.

In the second group we find the majority of our common plant diseases, those caused by fungi and bacteria. Fungi are minute forms of plant life, too small, for the most part, to be seen with the naked eye. They differ primarily from other plants in that they possess no green coloring matter, which is known as chlorophyll. All fungi are classed as parasites as they cannot live except on some other plant or animal. Some forms, such as the rust fungi, can exist only on living plants; other forms can live only on dead plants, and a few forms can live on either living or dead plant tissue. Some fungi attack many different plants, while other forms can live on but one kind. Some forms are very short lived, while others live on in the soil for many years. Most fungi produce small seed-like bodies which are called spores. These tiny spores are very easily carried from one plant to another by the wind and other agencies, and the spread of

fungous diseases is therefore often very rapid. When supplied with sufficient moisture these spores germinate and produce new fungus plants. Since they require a certain amount of moisture in order to germinate, it may be readily understood why fungous diseases are apt to be much more prevalent in wet seasons than in dry seasons.

Bacteria are also a form of plant life, being even more minute in size than the fungi. There are many different kinds of bacteria but those that attack plants do not usually produce spores. They differ from fungi in this respect, and since they cannot be blown about by the wind they do not spread as rapidly from plant to plant. They must depend upon some mechanical means such as human hands, insects, garden tools and things of this nature, or upon the splashing of raindrops from leaf to leaf, or the spattering caused by heavy rains upon the surface of the soil. It is in just this way that the dreaded Leaf Spot of delphiniums is spread. The bacteria winter over in the soil, and with the spring rains they are spattered up onto the lower leaves.

The infections due to viruses seem to be an increasing group of plant diseases. As yet it is not known just what viruses are. The virus which causes tobacco mosaic has been found to be a complex protein molecule. But we do not know if this is generally the case. Viruses are spread by contaminated pruning instruments, by insects, and, in some cases, they seem to be transmitted in the seed.

Some of the commonest symptoms of a virus infection are curling of leaf tissue, yellowing of leaves, a mottled effect due to the alternating of green and yellow patches, and a bushy type of growth.

610

INSECT PESTS

Many scientists have devoted their lives to the study of insects and, as a result of their patient investigations, information is now available regarding the habits and life histories of practically all our common insect pests. Nearly seven hundred thousand species of insects have already been classified, nor is this figure astonishing when we realize that insects constitute the largest group in the animal kingdom. It has been estimated that 75 percent of all known kinds of living animals belong to the insect world, and there are probably many species in remote sections of the earth that have not, as yet, been discovered.

Continual warfare has been waged between man and insects since the dawn of history, and it is disheartening to learn that in spite of all that modern science has done no insect species has ever been known to be completely exterminated. So probably the best that we can hope for in our gardens is to keep them under control, and this can be done only by prompt and concerted effort. In order to give our gardens intelligent care, there are certain things which we should know regarding the common insect pests. We should know something about their life histories, their feeding habits, and the various measures of control.

Insects, in common with all other animals, begin life from a single cell known as the egg. In most cases the eggs are fertilized by the male and are then deposited in some suitable place by the adult female. In some cases, however, fertilization does not seem to be necessary and the females produce living young without mating. This remarkable phenomenon is known as parthenogenesis and the most common example is the aphid. Throughout the summer months generation after generation is produced, consisting entirely of females which have developed from unfertilized eggs. As many as 98 generations have been produced in this manner. In the autumn males suddenly appear and the eggs which are to carry the species over the winter are fertilized.

Insect eggs vary greatly in size, shape, and coloring, most of them being very small. The number laid by one female varies from a single egg, which is exceptional, to as many as one million. The average number is probably about one hundred. The eggs of some species are laid all at one time; in the case of other species they are laid in successive batches. Instinct almost invariably guides the female to lay her eggs where the newly-hatched young will be able to find suitable food. After the eggs are laid the mother's responsibility usually comes to an end and she gives them no further heed. From the moment of hatching the young insects are thrown entirely upon their own resources. There are a few cases where the adult insects prepare elaborate nests and provision them with food for the young, but this is the exception rather than the rule. The time spent within the egg varies considerably. In the majority of cases it is about two weeks. In the case of the house fly it is only 8 hours, and in other cases the period is decidedly prolonged, the winter frequently being passed in the egg stage. The life cycle of most insects is completed within the year. A few species such as the ants, the honey bees and wire worms live longer than a year. The shortest life cycle as yet known among insects is ten days.

In studying the life histories of insects we find that they are grouped into three classes, those without a metamorphosis, those with a simple, or gradual metamorphosis, and those with a complete or complex metamorphosis. A metamorphosis may be defined as a noticeable change in the form of an animal between the time of hatching, or birth, and the time of maturity.

Those insects which do not undergo a metamorphosis constitute a relatively small group and include such species as spring tails and fish moths which are of little or no importance to the gardener. When the young are hatched they are perfectly formed and resemble the adults in every respect except in size.

In the second group, those having a simple or gradual metamorphosis, we find many of our old acquaintances such as the grasshoppers, squash bugs, the scale insects and the aphids. In the case of many species in this group the newly-hatched young are very similar to the adults except for the absence of wings. In some species, however, the difference is more widely marked. The young insects in this group are spoken of as nymphs. In general they have the same feeding habits as their parents and are often found together. As they grow, their wings develop and they become more and more like the adults.

We find the largest number of insect species in the last group, those which pass through a complete metamorphosis, having four distinct life stages: the egg stage, the larva stage, the pupa stage and the adult stage. In most cases the newly-hatched young in no way resemble the adults and have totally different habits. The young are known as larvæ (singular larva). When the larvæ become full grown they pass into the pupa stage and later the adult form emerges. All growth is made in the larva stage. No growth ever occurs in the adult stage. Little beetles never grow into big beetles or little butterflies into big butterflies.

The way in which insects make their growth is very interesting. They do not grow gradually, almost imperceptibly, as do the young of most other animals. The body wall is incapable of expanding, and increase in size can take place only through a series of molts. An entirely new skin is created within the old skin and when this is ready a fluid known as the molting fluid is poured forth by certain specialized cells in the body. This loosens the outer skin and the insect crawls forth. Ordinarily four or five molts occur before the nymphs or larvæ become full grown. In some species an insect passes through as many as 20 molts. In the case of a nymph the final molt results in a fully developed adult, whereas in the case of a larva the final molt carries the insect into the pupa stage.

The pupa stage is one of the most important in the life of an insect for it is during this period that it undergoes the wonderful transformation from a sluggish larva into an alert, highly developed adult—a bee, a moth, a beetle, a fly— according to the species. Most larvæ make very careful provision for the safeguarding of the pupa, protecting it under bark or rubbish of some kind, hiding it in the long grass, enfolding it within a leaf or burying it in the soil. In a few species, such as the lady beetles, the pupa is found exposed, with the tip of the body merely fastened to a leaf. The protection about the pupa varies considerably with the different species. In the case of many of the flies the larva retains its own mottled skin and pupates within it. The skin undergoes something of a change, however, becoming hard and forming a water-proof and in most cases a completely airtight case. In some species the larva spins a cocoon for the protection of the pupa and in other species it constructs intricate little cells within the soil. The period of pupation varies greatly. Many species pass the winter in the pupa stage while others spend only a few days within the pupa case.

The Control of Insect Pests

There are various natural factors which enter into the control of insect pests. Weather conditions have a considerable influence upon the prevalence of some species. For example, most of the eggs of the gypsy moth are killed during a cold, open winter, whereas they will survive a snowy winter. If heavy rains occur during the time that the eggs are hatching certain species suffer severe losses. This may help to explain the reason why certain insects are much more numerous in some seasons than in others.

On farms we use drop rotations to control certain insects and resort to deep plowing in order to expose the larvæ of other species at a critical time in their development. But here the farmer has a decided advantage over the gardener, for it would be neither practicable nor possible to use these methods in the flower garden.

Probably few realize what staunch allies we have in the birds, when it comes to the control of insects. But when we stop to consider the fact that the number of insects eaten in a day by certain birds is equal to the weight of the bird itself, we begin to appreciate the extent of their usefulness. Some birds are, of course, much more valuable as insect destroyers than others. Many of the smaller mammals are also useful. Moles, skunks, toads, and some species of snakes depend almost entirely upon insects for their food. Predatory parasites also play an important part in insect control. These are insects which are harmless in themselves from the viewpoint of the gardener but which prey upon other insects. In most sections of the country natural parasites exist and are a constant source of help. When new insects are brought into the country—and more than one half of our pests are of foreign origin—one of the most effective means of control is the introduction of these predatory parasites. When the gypsy moths were working such havoc in New England a decade or so ago insect parasites were imported from Europe and Asia, and were of inestimable value. The Australian lady beetle was imported into California to help control the Cottony cushion scale on the citrus fruits, and one of the most interesting examples is found in the case of the Japanese beetles. The beetle has existed for many years in Japan but has never become a serious pest because it has been kept practically under control by its natural enemies. Some years ago a few beetles were brought into this country on a shipment of plants from Japan. For a year or so they escaped notice and then, too late, we woke up to the fact that they were increasing in alarming numbers and that they threatened to become a very serious pest.

It is doubtful whether, in the history of this country, any pest has increased so rapidly or proved so destructive. The Government appropriated millions of dollars to aid the fight against the Japanese beetles and to prevent their spread into uninfested territory. And one of the most important measures of control has been the importation of some of the natural parasites which have so successfully kept the beetle in check in its native home. The two that have proved most valuable are a parasitic fly which lays its eggs upon the adult beetle, the larvæ boring their way into the body of the beetle, and

a parasitic wasp which attacks the beetle in the larva stage.

In spite of the fact, however, that these natural factors are constantly at work to prevent the increase and spread of insect pests, the gardener will find that he cannot depend upon them for entire control, save in rare instances. It is necessary, therefore, to resort to other means, such as chemical control through the use of poison sprays, dusts and fumigants; or to mechanical control through the use of traps, tree bands, and hand picking. In controlling insect pests by these means it is necessary to determine the type of pest which one is fighting, to decide upon the remedy to be used, and to apply it promptly and thoroughly.

Insects are grouped into two distinct classes: those with chewing mouth parts and those with sucking mouth parts. In the first group we have caterpillars and beetles, of every kind and description, and other less important insects such as grubs, grasshoppers and some "slugs." These feed largely upon the foliage of growing plants and in the case of grubs and borers upon the roots; and among them we find some of our worst enemies, such as the aster beetles, the iris borer, the rose beetle, the Japanese beetle, the yellow woolly-bear caterpillar, the cabbage looper and many others. The insects in this group chew and swallow solid plant tissues and they may, with very few exceptions, be controlled by stomach poisons.

In the second group, those insects having sucking mouth parts, we find such familiar enemies as the aphids, the various scale insects and the leaf-hoppers. Instead of being equipped with jaws with which they can tear off and chew their food, these insects have delicate tube-like mouth parts with which they are able to pierce through the outer layer of plant tissue and suck the juices from within. These long, needle-like beaks are usually jointed and they may point forward, upward or downward. When not in use they are generally laid back on the breast between the front legs. It is not possible to control the insects in this group by coating the outer surface of the plant with poison dusts or sprays, as they are able to pierce through the poisoned layer and can then draw their nourishment from the plant, quite unharmed. It has been found, however, that these sucking insects can be controlled by contact poisons—poisons which come into direct contact with the body.

The Garden Medicine Shelf

It is wise for every gardener to become familiar with some of the standard and reliable remedies which are used in controlling insect pests and diseases and to keep a sufficient quantity on hand for ordinary use. An orderly, well-stocked medicine shelf for the garden is not only a great source of satisfaction in itself but also means that in an emergency you will find yourself prepared.

For the average flower garden comparatively little is needed in the way of equipment. A quart measure, a measuring spoon (the kind that comes in little sets is very useful), a sprayer, and a dust gun are really all that are necessary. The size of the sprayer and dusting outfit will depend largely upon the extent of one's gardening operations. In a small garden a hand sprayer such as may be purchased from any hardware store will probably be entirely adequate. For a large garden a sprayer of the knapsack or bucket type would be more satisfactory.

Insecticides

In order to be satisfactory as a means of control for insect pests in the garden, an insecticide must measure up to certain definite requirements. It must not repel the insects against which it is to be used; it must give reasonably quick results; it must not burn the foliage of tender plants; it must spread uniformly when applied and adhere well to the foliage of the plant; it must keep its strength during storage; it must be reasonable in price; and it should have as low toxicity as possible for humans and animals.

Within recent years, as the result of extensive scientific research, many new insecticides have been discovered and developed which make it possible for the gardener to obtain complete control of many insect pests which heretofore were difficult to combat.

Stomach poisons are used as a control for insects with chewing mouth parts, such as beetles of various types, cabbage worms, etc., which actually eat the foliage, fruit or flowers. Contact insecticides are used to control insects with sucking mouth parts which suck the juices from the plant tissues, such as the aphid, red spider, etc. In order to be effective most contact insecticides must come into direct contact with the body of the insect, as they kill the insect either by clogging up the breathing tubes or by entering the body and causing a chemical reaction upon the body tissues. Some contact sprays are effective against certain sucking insects and are not effective against others, and it is important that the right spray or dust be selected for use. Some of the newer chemicals are effective both as contact and stomach poisons.

Aramite: An excellent miticide which controls red spiders, the two-spotted spider mite and the spruce spider mite. Does not harm beneficial insects and is one of the best for use in the home garden as it is comparatively non-toxic to plants and to humans.

Arsenate of Lead: Within recent years arsenate of lead has been replaced to a considerable extent in the home garden by DDT and Rotenone, although it is still extensively used for large scale operations, such as the commercial spraying of shade trees and in orcharding. Arsenate of lead is highly effective as a control for most chewing insects, but it must be used with care and discretion. It is a deadly poison, toxic to both humans and animals. As it is not readily washed away it should never be used on fruits or vegetables shortly before they are to be eaten, and it should not be used on vegetables which form heads, such as cabbage, as it may remain within the folded leaves and cause injury to consumers.

Chlordane: One of the most valuable of the recently developed insecticides is Chlordane, a chlorinated hydrocarbon. It is effective against beetles of many types, Japanese beetle grubs, chinch bugs, squash aphids, house flies and numerous other pests. It acts both as a contact poison and as a stomach poison, is quick in action, and is extremely long-lasting in its effects. When sprayed on a surface where it is not washed off it will remain effective over a period of several months. It is available as a 50% wettable powder, as a 5% dust and as an emulsion.

DDT was developed during World War II. It proved a very successful control for malarial mosquitoes and was also helpful in controlling typhus epidemics, thus saving the lives of many men in the armed services. It also proved effective in the control of many insect pests which it had been impossible to eradicate and it became widely used.

However, after scientific tests it became evident that DDT had cumulative effects which were very damaging. It proved highly toxic to fish, bees and many insect eating birds. It also destroys beneficial insects as well as harmful ones. It destroys the natural parasites of the red-spider mites.

To-day DDT has become widespread in soils, in streams and lakes as evidenced by the kill of enormous numbers of salmon in Lake Michigan due to the high concentration of DDT residues. In many areas the use of DDT has been banned.

Among the many pesticides on the market that are harmless to man are the Pyrethrums and Rotenone. For general use in the home garden Malathion is excellent. To be avoided are Aldrin, DDT, Dieldrin, Endrin and Heptachlor.

Precautions in Handling Pesticides: Follow instructions on container. Store cans, bottles and other material where children will never have access to them. Destroy all empty containers. Avoid inhaling sprays and dusts. Some pesticides, such as the nicotines, are absorbed through the skin. It is important to wash if only a small spot occurs. When applying insecticides as dusts or sprays use special precautions. Wear long sleeves and gloves. Surgeons' gloves are excellent. Use goggles to protect eyes and mask to cover nose and mouth.

Among reliable sources of information concerning pesticides which are rated as safe for the home garden are: The U. S. Department of Health, Education and Welfare, Washington, D.C., The U. S. Department of Agriculture, Washington, D.C., and The Audubon Society, with offices in New York City and Lincoln, Massachusetts.

Dimite (DMC): A miticide which is particularly effective against cyclamen mites, common on delphiniums and African violets, European red mites and the privet mite. It is, however, injurious to some trees.

Lindane: A purified form of benzene hexachloride which is an excellent control for woolly aphids, lace bugs, leaf rollers, some leaf miners, flea beetles, thrips and cutworms. Available as a 25% wettable powder, as a dust, and in emulsions.

Malathion: A phosphate spray which is much less toxic than parathion and therefore recommended for use in the home garden. It is one of the most effective controls for aphids, mealy bugs, mites, leaf hoppers, lace bugs, certain scales in the crawling stage, thrips, white flies and many other pests on ornamentals, fruit trees and vegetables. Malathion is available as a 25% wettable powder and as a 50% emulsifiable liquid. It is one of the few chemicals which will control both mites and aphids, which is a great boon to the amateur gardener. It is available in a small, convenient container for use in the home garden. Malathion is an ingredient of many general-purpose dusts and sprays.

Methoxychlor (*DMDT*) (sold under the trade name Marlate): An insecticide closely related to DDT but far less toxic to warm-blooded animals. An effective control for Mexican bean beetles, and many other fruit and vegetable pests. It may be used safely on cucurbits. Available as a 50% wettable powder, as a 25% emulsifiable liquid and as a dust, and it is frequently used as an ingredient in general-purpose dusts.

Miscible Oils: An effective control for many forms of scale when used as a dormant spray in early spring.

In applying miscible oil sprays certain precautions should be observed. Spraying should not be done when the temperature is below 45° F. or when it is apt to go below freezing during the night. The spray should be applied early in the day so that the foliage will be dry before nightfall. Spraying should be done early in the spring just before the buds are ready to burst. A dormant spray should not be used after the buds have burst. The trees should not be drenched when the spray is applied. Never more than one dormant spray should be applied in a season.

Miscible oil sprays should *not* be used on the following trees; sugar maples, Japanese maples, black walnut, butternut, beech, magnolia, chamæcyparis, cryptomeria, Douglas-fir, true firs, hemlocks or yews.

Nicotine: For most species of aphids and for a number of other sucking insects, a good nicotine dust or spray is a satisfactory control. Nicotine is a yellowish, oily liquid extracted from tobacco and put on the market under a number of trade names, most brands containing 40 percent nicotine. Black Leaf 40 is an old stand-by and is very reliable. When mixing any of these nicotine sprays, soap should be added, not only to serve as a spreader, but also to aid in liberating the nicotine. One cubic inch of soap per gallon is sufficient, dissolved in hot water and added to the spray. Nicotine is also available in dust form, often being mixed with sulphur, hydrated lime, or some other substance. These nicotine dusts should be applied when the plants are perfectly dry as they are not as effective in their action if the plants are wet. Nicotine in all forms should be stored in air-tight containers, as it readily loses its strength when exposed to the air. The liquid forms lose their effectiveness if they are allowed to freeze. As nicotine in concentrated form is very toxic, care must be taken not to inhale the fumes or to spill any upon the body, as absorption through the skin is extremely dangerous.

Parathion: Because of its extreme toxidity parathion is not recommended for use by the home gardener.

Pyrethrum is made from the heads of certain flowers belonging to the same family as the chrysanthemum. It may be used either as a spray or as a dust and is an effective control against many sucking insects, such as aphids and thrips, as well as against some of the chewing insects.

Rotenone is an insecticide which is toxic to both chewing and sucking insects and which has the advantage of being non-toxic to man and animals. It is derived from the roots of certain tropical plants, such as derris and cube. It is on the market in various commercial forms and may be used either as a dust or as a spray. Its chief disadvantage is that when it is used as a stomach poison it loses its toxic properties within a few days, as it decomposes rapidly.

Systemic Insecticides

Systemic insecticides are chemical compounds which can be absorbed through the roots or the leaves of actively growing plants and which are toxic to insects which feed upon the plants or, as in some cases, breed within the tissues of the plant.

Insecticides of this type are most frequently used in the form of a solution applied to the soil about the plant or are sprayed upon the foliage.

Some of the systemic insecticides have proved extremely valuable in the control of aphids, mealy bugs and mites, and will remain effective for as long as a month following application. They have also proved one of the most effective controls for root aphids and leaf nematodes. The systemic insecticides are used extensively by many commercial growers for the control of insect pests on roses, chrysanthemums and carnations, both in the greenhouse and in outdoor plantings.

Scope: Among the systemic insecticides Scope is one of the most suitable for use on the home grounds. It comes in a granular form and should be worked into the surface of the soil and then watered in thoroughly.

It may be used on trees and shrubs, on roses, on garden flowers, and on potted plants. It may also be applied to flower beds before planting. For rate of application follow directions as given on the container.

Scope will give excellent control over a period of 6 to 8 weeks for many common insect pests, among them, aphids, birch leaf miner, lace bugs, leaf hoppers, mimosa web worms, pine tip moth, spider mites, thrips and white flies.

In handling the systemic insecticides certain precautions should be observed. Direct contact with skin, eyes and clothing should be avoided, and precaution should be taken not to breathe the dust.

Sodium selenate is a selenium compound which is an effective control not only for aphids and mites but also an excellent control for leaf-inhabiting nematodes on such plants as chrysanthemums. It is available as a powder to be dissolved in water and applied to the soil about the plants, and in a 2% mixture absorbed on superphosphate (trade name P–40) for direct application to the soil. It also comes in capsule form (trade names Kapsulate and Sel-Kaps) for use on African violets and other potted plants.

Precaution. Sodium selenate is a deadly poison and must be used with extreme care. It should never be used on soils where vegetables, fruits or crops fed to livestock might be grown at any time, as it is not known how long its effect will remain in the soil.

Fungicides

Captan (Orthocide 406): An organic fungicide for use on fruits, vegetables and ornamentals. Controls various turf diseases such as brown patch and copper spot, early and late blight on potatoes, and has proved an effective control for black spot and leaf rust on roses. It is also used for treating rose cuttings as a preventive against crown gall. It should not be used in combination with oil sprays or with lime, but it is compatible with most insecticides. It is available as a wettable powder and a dust. It is not effective against mildew.

Dithane Z 78 has proved an excellent control for azalea petal blight, and is also used as a control for black spot on roses and for downy mildew on cucurbits. It may be used either as a dust or as a spray.

Fermate is one of the most valuable of the new organic fungicides. It is an excellent control for certain plant diseases such as septoria leaf diseases of chrysanthemums, rusts on antirrhinums and carnations, some Botrytis blights and anthracnoses, downy mildew, black spot on roses, black rot on grapes, apple scab, apple rust and brown rot of stone fruits. Fermate is not so effective against powdery mildew in midsummer as sulphur or Mildex. It is generally used at the rate of 2 tablespoons to one gallon of water with a spreader when used as a spray. It is also obtainable as a 7 to 10% dust. It is often used in combination with sulphur as a fruit spray and may also be used in combination with arsenate of lead. Although Fermate is dark in color it does not noticeably disfigure foliage and causes no burning.

Karathane (Available under trade name Mildex): A fungicide which has proved one of the most effective controls for powdery mildew on roses, phlox, tuberous begonias and other plants. It should not be applied when the temperature is above 85° F. or during periods of very humid weather, as it is apt to cause damage under such conditions. It is important to follow with care instructions concerning rate of application. Karathane also has some value as a miticide.

Lime-Sulphur is used as a standard dormant spray for fruit trees and is also sometimes used for roses. As a summer spray it is used for Volutella blight of boxwood. As a dormant spray it is used at a dilution of 1 to 9; as a summer spray at a dilution of 1 to 50. It should not be used when the temperature is over 85°F.

Manzate: A good control for black spot on roses and for cercospora leaf spot and downy mildew. It is a protectant and should be applied before infections appear. Manzate controls all common tomato and potato diseases including early and late blight.

Sulphur is an effective control against black spot, rust and mildew. It may be used either as a spray or as an 80 to 90% dust. It is not wise to apply sulphur when the temperature is above 85° F., as it may cause severe burning.

Systemic Fungicides

The systemic fungicides have opened up a new approach to the control of plant diseases. These systemic compounds can be absorbed by plants through their roots and leaves and are proving helpful in the control of some of the most baffling plant diseases.

Carolate was one of the first systemic fungicides to be developed and has proved effective in the cure of bleeding canker of maple trees. Benox is used to prevent elms from being attacked by bleeding canker and to prevent its spread in the case of young trees which have already become infected. Another systemic fungicide is being used in the control of Dutch elm disease. This is not effective when used as a soil drench, being applied to the foliage in the form of a quick-breaking oil emulsion.

Many of the Agricultural Experiment Stations are doing extensive research in this new field of disease control, and the possibilities for future development are great.

Antibiotics

The antibiotics which have proved to be so spectacularly effective in the treatment of many diseases which affect humans and animals are also proving to be "wonder drugs" in the treatment of certain plant diseases.

The antibiotics are substances produced by fungi which have the power to destroy other fungi or the toxins produced by them. The chemical structure of many of the antibiotics has been determined, which has made it possible for them to be produced synthetically in laboratories.

Some of the results from the use of antibiotics on plants have been almost as dramatic as have the cures effected through their use in human diseases. As the result of a single application of the antibiotic, Actidione, to the galls on red cedars which spread cedar-apple rust, spore production was completely arrested. And through the use of a Streptomycin spray fire-blight, one of the most dreaded diseases among orchardists, and one heretofore extremely difficult to combat, has been brought under almost complete control. Such bacterial diseases as tobacco wildfire, bacterial spot of peppers and tomatoes, bacterial soft rot of potato seed pieces, angular leaf spot of cucumber and bacterial blight of celery have all been controlled experimentally with the new antibiotics.

Aureomycin has proved an effective form of treatment for seed infected with bacterial black rot. Another antibiotic, Cyclohexamide, sold under the name Acti-dione Ferrated, has proved an excellent control for a number of turf diseases such as brownpatch, dollarspot, melting out and snow mold.

The production of antibiotics is costly and they are therefore so expensive that their use is frequently not justified on large-scale operations, but for certain hard-to-control diseases which have not yielded to other measures, they offer great possibilities.

General Purpose Dusts and Sprays

There are many excellent all-purpose dusts and sprays on the market. In order to be of greatest value to the home gardener an all-purpose dust or spray should offer good control for the following: *Insect pests*—aphids, red spider mites, caterpillars and beetles of most types. *Diseases*—the various leaf spots, mildews and rusts. This is by no means an all-inclusive list but covers the pests and diseases most likely to be a problem in the average home garden.

In purchasing an all-purpose dust or spray it is wise to know what ingredients it contains and what pests and diseases it may be expected to control.

It is possible to prepare an all-purpose spray mixture which will be equally as effective as a commercial product and which will be considerably less expensive. Such a mixture should contain a good general fungicide, a miticide, and a control for both sucking and chewing insects. It is very important that the ingredients used be compatible, as otherwise serious complications may result.

The following mixtures are recommended. The tablespoons and teaspoons should be slightly rounded.

1. 2 tbsp. Malathion, 25% wettable powder
   3 tbsp. Methoxychlor, 50% wettable powder
   2 tbsp. Manzate or Orthocide 406
   1 gal. of water
   plus—a sticker-spreader used according to manufacturer's directions.

2. 4 tbsp. Malathion, 25% wettable powder
   2 tbsp. DDT, 50% wettable powder
   1 tbsp. Zineb, 65% wettable powder
   2 tbsp. Sulfur, 95 to 100% wettable powder
   $\frac{1}{2}$ tsp. Karathane (or Mildex) 25% wettable powder
   1 gal. of water
   plus—a sticker-spreader used according to manufacturer's directions.

3. 4 tbsp. Malathion, 25% wettable powder
   2 tbsp. Methoxychlor, 50% wettable powder
   2 tbsp. Captan, 50% wettable powder
   $\frac{1}{2}$ tsp. Karathane or Mildex, 25% wettable powder
   1 gal. water
   plus—a sticker-spreader used according to manufacturer's directions.

TABLE OF MEASUREMENTS

3 teaspoonfuls	equal	1 tablespoonful
4 tablespoonfuls	equal	$\frac{1}{4}$ cupful
16 tablespoonfuls	equal	1 cupful
2 cupfuls	equal	1 pint
4 cupfuls	equal	1 quart
2 pints	equal	1 quart
4 quarts	equal	1 gallon
8 fluid ounces	equal	1 cup

TABLE OF DILUTIONS
Number of tablespoonfuls to 1 *gallon of water*

TABLESPOONFULS		DILUTION
$\frac{1}{4}$	..	1 to 1,000
$\frac{1}{2}$	..	1 to 500
1	..	1 to 250
$1\frac{1}{4}$	..	1 to 200
$2\frac{1}{2}$	..	1 to 100
5	..	1 to 50
10	..	1 to 25

PRECAUTIONS

As many insecticides and some fungicides are deadly poisons they must be handled with care.

Every possible precaution should be taken to protect children, birds, dogs and other animals.

Such materials should always be kept in a locked cupboard, never on open shelves.

Soil Fumigants

Chloropicrin (Sold under the trade name of Larvacide): An excellent soil fumigant. Destroys nematodes, weed seeds and some fungi. It causes injury to living plants and should only be used on fallow ground or on bare soil in benches or in containers being prepared for planting. Directions should be followed with great care as it is somewhat dangerous to use.

D–D Mixture: A soil fumigant which is an effective control against root-knot nematodes, wireworms and other insects and some weeds. It is most effective on sandy soils. It is available in liquid form. On large scale operations it should be applied with a special applicator. On small areas application can be made by hand.

Ethylene Dibromide: An effective soil fumigant which is available in liquid form for large scale operations and also in capsule form, which is a very convenient form for home gardeners to use, as the capsules can be easily pressed into the soil. Toxic to both plants and animals. It is most effective when the soil is moist and the temperature 60° F. or above. No planting should be done for at least two weeks after application.

Oxyquinoline: A soil fumigant which is of special value as a post-emergent control of the damping-off of seedlings. It should never be used on cabbage, cauliflower or broccoli. It is sold under various trade names such as Anti-damp, Damp Not, Oxyquin and Sunox.

Vapam: Effective in the control of nematodes, weed seeds, and certain fungi and undesirable soil organisms. It can be mixed with water and applied with a sprinkling can.

PLANTS SELDOM ATTACKED BY PESTS AND DISEASES

ANNUALS

Acrolinium (Everlasting)
Ageratum
Alyssum
Arctotis grandis
Balsam
Brachycome (Swan River daisy)
Browallia
Calliopsis (Coreopsis)
Candytuft
Celosia (Cockscomb)
Clarkia
Cynoglossum (Houndstongue)
Didiscus (Blue lace flower)
Dimorphotheca (African orange daisy)
Eschscholtzia (California poppy)
Euphorbia marginata (Snow-on-the-mountain)
Gilia (Thimble flower)
Godetia
Gypsophila (Baby's-breath)
Helichrysum (Straw flower)
Hunnemannia (Goldencup)
Incarvillea
Larkspur
Lupin
Mirabilis
Nemesia
Nemophila
Nierembergia
Nigella (Love-in-the-mist)
Nicotiana (Flowering tobacco)
Portulaca
Salpiglossis
Salvia splendens (Scarlet sage)
Scabiosa
Schizanthus
Shirley poppy
Stocks

PERENNIALS

Achillea (Yarrow)
Aconitum (Monkshood)
Adonis
Ajuga (Bugle)
Alyssum
Anchusa
Anemone
Arabis (Rockcress)
Artemisia
Asclepias tuberosa (Butterflyweed)
Aubrietia
Baptisia australis
Boltonia
Cerastium tomentosum (Snow-in-summer)
Cimicifuga (Black snake root)
Coreopsis
Crucianella (Crosswort)
Dicentra eximea (Fringed bleeding-heart)
Dicentra spectabilis (Bleeding-heart)

PERENNIALS—continued

Echinops (Globe thistle)
Erigeron (Fleabane)
Eupatorium
Geum
Gypsophila (Baby's-breath)
Helenium (Sneezewort)
Helianthemum (Sunrose)
Helianthus (Hardy sunflower)
Hemerocallis (Daylily)
Hesperis (Sweet rocket)
Heuchera (Coral Bells)
Hibiscus
Iberis sempervirens (Hardy candytuft)
Liatris
Linum perenne (Perennial flax)
Lupin
Lychnis (Campion)
Mertensia (Virginia bluebells)
Myosotis (Forget-me-nots)
Nepeta Mussini
Papaver nudicaule (Iceland poppy)
Papaver orientale (Oriental poppy)
Papaver pilosum (Olympic poppy)
Penstemon
Physostegia (False-dragonhead)
Platycodon (Balloonflower)
Plumbago larpentæ (Leadwort)
Potentilla (Cinquefoil)
Rudbeckia (Coneflower)
Salvia azurea (Azure sage)
Saponaria ocymoides (Rock soapwort)
Scabiosa
Sedum (Stonecrop)
Sempervivum (Houseleek)
Silene (Catchfly)
Spiræa Filipendula
Statice (Thrift)
Stokesia cyanea (Stoke's aster)
Thalictrum (Meadowrue)
Thermopsis
Tritoma (Red hot poker)
Trollius (Globe flower)
Verbascum (Mullein)
Veronica (Speedwell)

BIENNIALS

Bellis perennis (English daisy)
Canterbury Bells
Pansies
Sweet Williams
Violas
Wall Flowers

DISEASES AND INSECT PESTS OF TREES AND SHRUBS

Arborvitae

Insect Pests

Arborvitae Leaf Miner

Identification: Larvae very small, $\frac{1}{5}$ of an inch long, color green with reddish tinge, head black.

Injury: Larvae make tunnels in the terminal leaves as they feed. Tip growth appears whitish and finally turns brown. In severe infestations the entire tree may be affected.

Life History: The small, gray moths emerge from the infested leaves in late spring or early summer. Eggs are laid, hatch within a few weeks, and the larvae begin to feed.

Control: If infestation is very slight cut off and burn affected tips. Spray early in July with nicotine sulfate, 2½ teaspoonfuls per gallon of water, or with DDT. If the latter is used be on the alert for possible mite infestations.

Bagworm

Attacks: Arborvitae, hemlock, red cedar, larch, junipers, pine and spruce. Sometimes found on locust, soft maples, linden and sycamore.

Identification: The characteristic, grayish, spindle-shaped bags, an inch or two long, make identification of the bagworm easy. The bags are usually seen hanging near the tips of the branches, and they vary somewhat in appearance, as the outer covering is made from the needles, leaves and twigs of the host tree. The larvae are dark, brownish-black in color with white to yellowish, black-spotted head and thorax. When full grown they are about an inch long.

Injury: The larvae feed upon the needles or leaves of the host tree and if present in great numbers they can do considerable damage, sometimes completely defoliating a tree and after several years, if left unchecked, causing its death.

Life History: The eggs winter over in the bag and the larvae hatch out in late spring. As it feeds, each larva constructs its own case, weaving a band of silk about itself and attaching it to a leaf or petiole whenever it stops to eat. Four molts take place and pupation occurs in late summer. The male moth mates with the female through an opening in the base of her bag. The maggot-like female lays from 500 to 1,000 eggs in the pupal case in her bag and then dies.

Control: If the infestation is light the bags may be picked off during the winter and burned. When the infestation is heavy spraying with Diazinon (25% wettable powder) Malathion, or Sevin (50% wettable powder) will give excellent control.

Spruce Spider Mite

Attacks: Arborvitae, hemlock, juniper and spruce.

Identification: Minute, dark green to nearly black mites with pinkish legs. Webbing between the needles may often be detected.

Injury: The mites cause the foliage of the arborvitae to turn brown, the hemlock needles appear nearly white, the junipers appear yellowish and the spruce needles grey. If the infestation is severe, young trees die quickly. The lower branches of older trees are usually the first to show injury and die. Injury is most pronounced in hot, dry seasons.

Life History: The winter eggs are laid in October at the base of the needles. These eggs hatch in April or May. As a new generation occurs every 4 to 5 weeks the mite population builds up very rapidly.

Control: As soon as infestation is noted spray with a good miticide such as Aramite, used at the rate of 1 tablespoon of 50 percent wettable powder to 1 gallon of water or with Kelthane 18% 2 tbsp. to 1 gal. water, or with Ovotran which is more effective against the egg stage. One application in May and one in August is recommended.

A dormant spray of miscible oil will destroy many of the winter eggs, but should *not* be used on hemlocks.

Azalea

Diseases

Azalea Flower Blight (also called Flower Spot and Petal Blight)

A most devastating disease which is prevalent from Maryland southward to Florida and along the Gulf to Texas, and also in California.

Symptoms: Infection is first evidenced by a white, slimy spot on the petals. Flowers on the lower branches are the first to become affected. The disease spreads with incredible speed, particularly in warm, humid weather, and all the flowers become limp and slimy, the beauty of the blooms being completely ruined.

Nature of Disease: A fungous disease. The summer spores are formed inside the petals during periods of moist weather and are spread from flower to flower and bush to bush by wind, rain and insects. The spots on the petals, white spots on colored petals, brownish spots on white petals, indicate where each spore has landed. Within 24 hours in rainy or humid weather tiny black Sclerotia form within the limp, slimy petals. Many of these drop to the ground or remain in the shrivelled flowers. In very early spring the Sclerotia on the ground send up little stalks and from the tiny sacs which develop on the top of the stalks the spores are catapulted into the air and find lodgement on the lower petals and the cycle begins again.

Control: Sanitary precautions are of little help because of the rapid spread of the spores. However, excellent control may be obtained with a systematic spraying program. When mid-season varieties show color begin spraying 3 times a week for a month or 6 weeks. Either of the following sprays is recommended.

Dithane Z-78, one ounce to 5 gallons of water

Parzate, $\frac{4}{5}$ of an ounce to 5 gallons of water

Insect Pests

Lace Bugs

Identification: Small insects about $\frac{1}{8}$ of an inch long, whitish and lace-like in appearance are found on the undersurface of the leaves. Brown droplets of liquid are sometimes evident.

Injury: Lace bugs, both in the adult and nymph stage, suck the juices from the plant causing a whitish speckling of the foliage and a gradual blanching and dying.

Life History: During the winter the eggs are inbedded in the undersides of the leaves. The young nymphs hatch out in the spring and begin feeding. Several generations are produced during the year, damage being continued quite late into the autumn.

Control: As soon as any evidence of infestation is noted spray with lindane or malathion. It is important that the spray reach the undersurface of the leaves. The application should be repeated later in the season if necessary. Scope is an excellent control (see page 616).

Mites (*Southern Red Mite*)

Identification: The mites, almost infinitesimal in size, are found on the lower surface of the leaves, and tiny webs are sometimes observed. Foliage appears greyish, unhealthy and dusty.

Injury: Mites feed on both upper and lower surfaces of leaves, and if numerous will cause complete defoliation.

Life History: Eggs are laid on leaf surfaces, hatch in a few days and populations build up rapidly.

Control: Spray with a good miticide such as aramite, dimite or ovotran.

White Fly

Identification: Tiny white flies on under surface of leaves.

Injury: Grayish speckling on the leaves. Bush appears unhealthy if infestation is heavy.

Life History: See page 632.

Control: At first sign of infestation spray with malathion. Make 3 applications at 10 day intervals.

Birch

Insect Pests

Leaf Miner: Attacks Gray, Paper and European White Birch.

Identification: Mature larvae are about $\frac{1}{2}$ inch long, whitish with black spots on thorax. The adult sawfly is black and about $\frac{1}{16}$ of an inch long.

Injury: The larvae feed upon the tissues between the upper and lower leaf surfaces, causing a browning of the foliage. If the infestation is severe the tree appears blighted.

Life History: The adult sawfly emerges in spring when the leaves are about half open and the eggs are laid in the new leaves. Upon hatching the young larvae begin feeding within the leaf. There are several generations. The eggs are always laid in the new leaves. Infestation is therefore heaviest when the first brood hatches, later broods being confined more to the tips of the branches. The mature larva passes the winter in an earthen cell in the soil at the base of the tree.

Control: Excellent control may be obtained by spraying in May as soon as infestation is observed with malathion or lindane emulsion used at the rate of 1 to 2 teaspoonfuls to 1 gallon of water. Later applications should be made about July 1 and again in mid-July to control the second and third broods. Scope is an excellent control (see page 616)

Tent Caterpillar

Attacks: Chiefly blackcherry, chokecherry and apple, Also sometimes found on birch, elm, hawthorn, maple, oak, pear, plum and roses.

Identification: Hairy caterpillars which are black with a white stripe down the back and brown and yellow stripes along the sides. At maturity the caterpillars measure 2 to $2\frac{1}{2}$ inches in length. The moths are a light, reddish-brown with two diagonal stripes across each forewing.

Injury: The tent caterpillars are a serious and a very unsightly pest of orchard and roadside trees in many sections. They are voracious feeders and can completely defoliate a tree in a remarkably short time.

Life History: The female moth lays from 150 to 350 eggs, depositing them in a circle about a twig or branch on the host tree. The egg mass is covered with a sticky substance which is dark brown in color and becomes very hard and shiny. The young larvae hatch out in early spring and gather in the fork of the tree where they spin their web-like nest. They remain in the nest during the night and on dark, rainy days. but leave it on clear days to feed nearby. The caterpillars become full grown in about a month. The pupa stage is passed in a yellowish-white cocoon usually found on tree trunks or on buildings. The adult moths emerge in about three weeks. The winter is passed in the egg stage.

Control: There are various measures of control.

1. Locating and destroying egg masses during the winter.
2. Destroying the young caterpillars as soon as the web is noticed. This may be done by removing the nest in the evening or on a rainy day when all the young caterpillars are at home and burning it, or by dipping a swab (a cloth tied to the end of a stick) into

a can of discarded crank case oil and then poking it into the nest. Use of a torch is *not* recommended as it too often damages the tree.

3. Spraying with arsenate of lead, 1½ lbs. to 50 gallons of water.
4. Spraying with DDT.

Box

Disease

Nectria Canker *or* **Volutella Blight** (Leaf Cast or Twig Blight)

Symptoms: In midsummer, particularly during a long spell of damp weather, some branches turn straw-color. Salmon-pink spore pustules will be found on the backs of the leaves and along the stems. In the canker form the disease often follows severe winter injury.

Nature of the Disease: A fungous disease.

Control: Remove and burn all affected twigs. Cut out all branches where winter injury is evident, and if signs of canker are found spray with liquid lime sulphur, 1 to 50 dilution, before midsummer. As a precautionary measure clean out all dead leaves from interior of bushes and cut out all dead twigs once a year. Spread papers under the bush or hedge and burn the accumulated debris. Avoid too drastic trimming.

Insect Pests

Box Leaf Miner

Identification: The adult form of the box leaf miner is a yellowish fly, slightly smaller than a mosquito. These flies may readily be distinguished by their very definite yellow coloring. The larvae are small, being only about $\frac{1}{10}$ of an inch long when full grown, and they are a muddy white in color.

Injury: The lower, more protected branches are usually the first to become infested. Leaves in which the miners are at work gradually turn yellow and drop prematurely. Bushes that are badly infested present a scraggly, unthrifty appearance.

Life History: The adult flies emerge from the pupa stage in late April or early May. The emerging period for the entire brood extends over several weeks. The average life of the adult fly is about 2 days and soon after emerging the females deposit their eggs within the leaf tissues, piercing through the epidermis on the undersurface. The eggs hatch during the next 2 or 3 weeks and the tiny larvae feed within the tissues of the leaves throughout the summer and autumn and the early spring of the following year. In late March or early April the larvae pass into the pupa stage and 3 or 4 weeks later the adult flies emerge and the life cycle begins again.

Control: Spray with DDT, 1 to 2 tbsp. of 50 percent wettable powder to 1 gallon of water, or 1 tsp. of DDT emulsion to 1 gallon of water. It is imperative that the spray be applied just prior to the emergence of the adult flies, as they alight immediately and deposit their eggs.

One application is usually sufficient. However, if emergence is delayed because of weather and the spray is applied sometime before it occurs, a second application may be desirable.

If a pre-emergent spray has not been applied, many of the young miners may be killed by spraying twice in early summer with lindane emulsion, 1 tsp. to 1 gallon of water, or with malathion, 1 tsp. to 1 gallon of water.

Box Psylla

Identification: Small, greenish insects about ⅛ of an inch in length, the body being covered with a white, waxy secretion. They are usually found at the tips of the young terminal shoots.

Injury: The young nymphs feed upon the young, growing shoots, sucking the juices from the plant and causing a very characteristic curling of the leaves at the tips of the branches. The damage done by the Box Psylla is usually not very serious unless the bushes are heavily infested.

Life History: The adults emerge in late April or early May and the females lay their eggs upon the tips of the young shoots. Several weeks later the nymphs hatch out and begin feeding.

Control: Spray with lindane 25 percent emulsion 1 tsp. to 1 gallon of water. Two applications should be made, the first between early and mid-May, the second in early June. Or—spray with nicotine sulfate 1 tsp. per gallon of water. Three applications are advisable, early May, June and July.

Nematodes

Indication: Foliage becomes yellow, growth appears stunted and unhealthy for no apparent reason. Shallow root mat observed upon examination.

Control: The systemic insecticide, sodium selanate, will give the best control. Apply ¼ gram per square foot of ground area about the bush and soak the soil thoroughly. See page 675.

Precaution: A deadly poison which must be handled with extreme care. It must never be used on any soil where fruits, vegetables or crops fed to livestock would be grown.

Oyster Shell Scale

Identification: Small, grayish-white scales, resembling an oyster shell in shape. They are usually found clustered in masses along the lower branches and the innermost twigs.

Injury: The scales suck the juices from the bush, greatly lowering its vigor and vitality. If the infestation is not checked they will in time cause its death.

Life History: During the winter the eggs are protected by the hard, shell-like covering of the old scales. The young hatch out about the end of May or early in June. At this stage they are soft-bodied and look like small, yellowish-white specks crawling about on the branches. Soon after hatching they select a place to feed and pierce through the outer bark. As the season advances the hard, shell-like covering is formed.

Control: It is possible to destroy the young scales while they are in the soft-bodied stage, and the spraying should be done at this time. It is wise to spray about June 1 and again on June 15.

Spray formula: Spray with malathion or with nicotine sulfate. Prune out branches which are heavily encrusted and burn.

Mites (Boxwood)

Identification: Minute animals hardly visible to the naked eye. Their presence may usually be detected by their characteristic injury.

Injury: The mites suck the juices from the young, tender leaves of the new growth, causing the foliage to lose its fresh, bright green color. The infested leaves at first become mottled, later taking on a dull, grayish-brown appearance and dropping prematurely.

Life History: The winter is passed in the egg stage, the eggs being infinitesimal, round, pinkish dots. The first brood hatches in April and as they breed rapidly four or five generations are produced during a single season.

Control: Spray with a good miticide such as aramite, 50 percent wettable, 1 tbsp. to 1 gallon of water, or dust thoroughly with sulphur dust. The number of applications will depend upon the severity of the infestation.

Camellia

Diseases

Camellia Flower Blight: A blight which first appeared in California in 1938 and which has now spread to Oregon and to some sections of the South. Areas where it has been found have been placed under rigid quarantine and every precaution has been taken to prevent its further spread.

Symptoms: Small, brown specks appear on the petals, a darkening of the veins is evident, and the flower becomes brown in the center, the entire bloom gradually turning brown, but not becoming slimy, a symptom which is a characteristic of azalea flower blight.

Nature of the Disease: A fungous disease. When infected flowers drop the moist soil and mulch become infected. From January to March the large, black Sclerotia,

which have formed about the plant, develop mushroom-like apothecia from which the spores are catapulted, alighting on the opening petals.

Control: Sanitary precautions are all-important in the control of Camellia flower blight, and every effort should be made to prevent infection from being brought in on new plants or in infected soil. It is wise to remove and burn all faded blooms and to be ever on the alert to detect the first signs of trouble.

In infected areas quarantine regulations require that, for two years after the detection of the disease, all flower buds be removed and that all old mulch be removed with the top 3 inches of soil, being replaced with a new 4-inch layer of soil or mulch. It is further required that from January to May the area be drenched once a month with a solution of 1 pound of Fermate to 25 gallons of water.

Insect Pests

Nematodes

Indication: Foliage becomes yellow, growth appears stunted and unhealthy for no apparent reason.

Control: See pages 622 and 675.

Mites (Southern Red Mite)

Identification: Leaves become unhealthy in appearance with a yellow or grayish cast.

See page 621 for *Injury* and *Life History.*

Control: Spray with a good miticide such as aramite, or ovotran.

Tea Scale

Identification: The scales are found on the undersurface of the leaves. The female when young is light yellow and thin, later becoming brown, elongated and hard. The male is soft, white and narrow. White cottony threads seem to entangle the scales.

Injury: The upper surface of the leaves has a yellowish, blotched appearance. Bush appears unhealthy, foliage drops prematurely.

Life History: The eggs hatch in from one to three weeks, depending upon the weather. The newly-hatched crawlers which are flat and yellow in color reach the new growth in a few days and attach themselves. The first molt occurs in 18 to 36 days, the second 7 days later. Eggs are laid 41 to 65 days after birth and there are many overlapping generations, during the spring, summer and early fall months.

Control: The most effective control is to spray in the spring when cold weather is passed and the blooming period is over with a white oil emulsion such as Florida Volck at the rate of 6 tablespoonfuls per gallon of water. The spray should be applied with considerable force and it is very important to cover the underside of the leaves. Another application may be necessary.

Malathion may also be used as a spray.

Clematis

Insect Pests

Root-Knot Nematode

Indication: Plant appears stunted for no apparent reason. Wilting sometimes occurs, resulting in death.

Control: See pages 622 and 675.

Crabapple
(ornamental)

Disease

Cedar-Apple Rust

Symptoms: In midsummer orange-yellow spots appear on the leaves.

Nature of Disease: See page 629.

Control: See page 629.

Dogwood

Insect Pest

Borers (Dogwood Borer) (Thamnosphecia Scitula)

Identification: Adult moths small with blue-black margins on their clear wings. Caterpillar, whitish with brown head, approximately ¼ inch long.

Injury: The young borers penetrate the bark and feed in the cambium layer. A badly infested tree may have as many as 50 borers. The trunk may become completely girdled, causing the death of the tree, or branches may be girdled at the base and die. Tree greatly weakened.

Life History: Moths emerge from the pupa stage from late spring to midsummer. The eggs are laid by the female moths in roughened places on the bark. Young larvae hatch and begin their feeding.

Control: About June 1, and again in late July, apply a drenching spray of DDT or dieldrin to the bark. Use 4 to 6 teaspoonfuls to 1 gallon of water.

Precautions: As young, newly transplanted dogwood trees are particularly susceptible to attacks from borers because of their reduced vitality, it is a wise precaution to wrap the trunk with burlap. It is also wise at all times to prevent dogwood trees from being damaged by rabbits, or by the lawn mower or in any other mechanical way, as it is in such roughened areas that the eggs of the adult moths are laid.

Elm

Diseases

Dutch Elm Disease

Symptoms: In the case of acute attacks the foliage of the entire tree may wilt rather quickly. The leaves may or may not turn yellow before wilting. Soon afterwards the tree may drop its leaves. However, the disease usually presents a more chronic condition, and only a few branches at a time are attacked. For this reason it is often difficult to distinguish from other diseases. The presence of branches bearing wilted or yellow leaves should be investigated at once. A diagonal section through the twig will show, if the disease is present, a whole or partial brown ring. Sometimes the ring consists of a series of brown spots. The symptoms of the disease are so similar to other diseases that it is often difficult in the case of minor infections to recognize it.

Nature of the Disease: The disease is caused by the fungus, Ceratostomella ulmi (Schwarz) Buisman. The European elm-bark beetle has proved to be the principal carrier of the disease. The beetles winter over in dead or diseased wood, emerging in the spring. They migrate to healthy trees where, during the process of feeding in newly formed twig crotches they inject fungus spores of the disease into the wounded tissues of the tree, whence it soon spreads through the entire vascular system.

Control: Much research has been undertaken in order to develop effective controls for Dutch Elm Disease. A very promising control is the systemic insecticide, Bidrin, developed by Shell Chemical Company, for which the U. S. Department of Agriculture has granted clearance for its distribution.

However, because of the nature of this material its sale is restricted to qualified, licensed firms, whose men are trained in its use. Bidrin is dangerous if safety precautions are not taken, or if it is carelessly applied. Inoculations must be accurate.

Bidrin is injected into the vascular system of the tree. Timing of the injections is essential to success. The elm bark beetles winter over under the bark and upon emergence in the spring they carry the spores on their bodies and thus infect new trees. Inoculations with Bidrin should be done when the beetles emerge and begin feeding on the bark of the young twigs.

Insect Pests

Cankerworm

Both the Fall and the Spring Cankerworm usually appear in cycles. For several successive years they will be present in vast numbers, and they will then almost disappear for a few years, only to return for another upswing of the cycle.

Fall Cankerworm

Attacks: Elms, oaks and apples. Sometimes attacks birch, linden and maple trees, cherry, plum and other fruits. During the end of their feeding period they occasionally attack roses, rhododendron and other shrubs growing nearby.

Identification: Male moths brownish-gray with a 1¼ inch wing spread. Female moths are gray, and completely wingless, $\frac{1}{2}$ inch in length. Larvae are about an inch long, brownish on the upper surface, green below, with three narrow, white stripes along the body above the spiracles, and a yellow stripe below. They have a characteristic of dropping from a branch or leaf on a silken thread and then climbing back again.

Injury: Larvae feed on the foliage, causing great damage if the infestation is heavy.

Life History: The moths emerge in the late autumn, usually after there have been freezing temperatures. The wingless females crawl up the trunk of the host tree to deposit their grayish eggs in a compact, single-layered mass. The eggs hatch in early spring about the time the leaves begin to unfold and the larvae feed on the foliage until early summer. When fully mature they drop to the ground and spin a silken cocoon in which they pass the pupa stage, at a depth of one to four inches. Only one generation is produced in a year.

Control: Spraying is the most satisfactory measure of control. Application should be made as soon as the leaves have expanded in the spring, and before damage has become serious. Arsenate of lead, three pounds to 100 gallons of water, is very effective. DDT may be used in a 6% emulsion for a mist sprayer or at the rate of two pounds of 50% wettable powder to 100 gallons of water.

As a precautionary measure a 4 to 6 inch band of heavy paper, cotton batting or Balsam wool may be bound about the trunk of a tree and smeared with Tanglefoot in late September. This will entangle many of the female moths as they ascend the trunk to lay their eggs. Great care must be taken not to let the Tanglefoot come into direct contact with the bark of the tree as it may cause serious injury. This measure of control is, at best, only partially effective, but many moths will be destroyed. It is best suited to use on individual trees on a lawn rather than trees grouped closely in a grove or woodland.

Spring Cankerworm

Attacks: Elms and apples. Less often injures oaks, hickory, cherry and maple.

Identification: Female moths are gray, wingless, and may be distinguished from the Fall Cankerworm moth by the dark stripe down the back and the rows of stiff, reddish spines on the first seven joints of the abdomen. The larvae are about an inch long and vary in color from green to brownish black, usually having a yellow stripe under the spiracles.

Injury: The caterpillars are voracious feeders, often completely skeletonizing the leaves, and causing defoliation of a tree. They are one of the most annoying of tree pests as, when they are present in great numbers, one can actually hear the crunching of the leaves as they feed, and their droppings fall in the form of tiny black pellets on terraces, furniture and unwary guests. Where infestations are very severe for a number of years the ravages of cankerworms may cause the death of trees through defoliation. At best, the trees are so weakened that they become ready prey to other pests and diseases.

Life History: Moths hatch in early spring, and the wingless females crawl up the trunk to lay their eggs. The eggs are oval in shape, a brownish-purple, and are laid in loose clusters under the bark scales on the main trunk of the tree and on some of the larger branches. The eggs hatch in about 30 days, and the caterpillars begin their feeding period. When mature they drop to the ground and pass the period of pupation in the soil at the foot of the host tree.

Control: See control for Fall Cankerworm. If the practice of tree banding is followed the material should be freshly applied before the female moths begin to ascend the tree trunks in the spring.

Elm Leaf Beetles

Attacks: American, English and Scotch elms. The slippery, rock and winged elms are usually not attacked by the elm leaf beetle.

Identification: Adult beetle slender, about $\frac{1}{4}$ inch in length, yellow to olive green in color, with a dark line near the outer edge of each wing, which becomes less distinguishable prior to hibernation. Larvae are yellow but so spotted and striped that they appear almost black, about $\frac{1}{2}$ inch in length.

Injury: The adult beetles feed on the young foliage of the tree in the spring as it unfolds, making many small holes, but most of the damage is done in the larvae stage. The larvae are voracious feeders and when infestation is heavy they practically skeletonize the leaves. Foliage takes on the appearance of brown lace, and the tree may become completely defoliated. The vigor of the tree is greatly weakened and it becomes an easy victim of other pests and diseases. Three years of defoliation will usually cause the death of the tree.

Life History: The adult beetles emerge from their winter hiding places in early spring and begin feeding. They lay their yellow, lemon-shaped eggs in clusters of 5 to 25 on the underside of the leaves in late spring and early summer. The egg laying period continues for several weeks, a single female laying about 500 eggs. The eggs hatch in five to six days and the larvae begin their feeding period which lasts from 15 to 20 days. The larvae then drop or crawl to the ground and pass into the pupa stage at the base of the tree. The period of pupation is very brief and in 6 to 10 days the adult beetles emerge and the life cycle of the second generation begins. The number of generations in a season varies from one to four, depending upon the climate.

During the latter part of the summer the beetles usually crawl into houses to hibernate until spring, often being found in cellars or attics.

Control: Spraying with arsenate of lead has long been the standard control for elm leaf beetles. Used at the rate of four pounds per 100 gallons of water, with 1 pint of fish oil added as a spreader, it will give excellent control. Two applications are recommended, the first when the leaves are nearly expanded to kill the adult beetles while feeding (this will also control canker-worm) and the second about three weeks later to control the larvae in their feeding stage. The second is the more important of the two applications.

DDT is also a very effective control but its application may destroy the natural enemies of mites, aphids and certain scales and result in an increase of these pests. A 6% emulsion of DDT in a mist blower is not as serious in its effect as is the much used 50% wettable powder, two pounds to 100 gallons of water, applied with a hydraulic spray.

English Ivy

Insect Pests

Aphids

Identification: Small black plant lice clustered along the tips of the shoots.

Control: See pages 631 and 632.

Spider Mites

Indication: Foliage appears unhealthy, dusty, grayish brown in appearance.

Control: See page 623.

Euonymus

Insect Pests

Euonymus Scale

Attacks: Euonymus and bittersweet, and is sometimes found on pachysandra and ivy growing near Euonymus.

Identification: Female scale resembles a tiny, dark brown oyster shell, males are white and very slender. In a severe infestation the leaves and stems may appear almost completely covered with the white males, with a smaller proportion of brown females.

Injury: Foliage turns yellow, leaves drop prematurely, branches begin to die back. Euonymus trained to a vine form is most apt to become seriously affected.

Life History: The eggs are laid under the shell of the female and hatch in late spring. The pale yellowish crawlers are usually seen in late May or June. A second brood appears in late August or early September.

Control: Spray in spring before new growth starts with a dormant oil spray. Some defoliation may occur but new growth will soon take its place.

In the crawler stage DDT emulsion and malathion are both effective. A 57% emulsion of malathion should be used at the rate of 2 tsp. to 1 gallon of water.

If old stems have become encrusted with scales before measures of control are undertaken it may be advisable to cut them off and burn them.

Hawthorn

Disease

Cedar-Apple Rust

Symptoms: In midsummer orange-yellow spots appear on the leaves. One type of spore is borne on the upper surface of the leaf and another type on the lower surface.

Nature of Disease: See page 629.

Control: See page 629.

Hemlock

Insect Pest

Spruce Spider Mite

Indication: Needles appear whitish, giving the tree an unhealthy appearance.

Control: See page 620.

Lilac

Disease

Powdery Mildew

Symptoms: Late in the summer a white coating appears on the foliage, giving it a dusty appearance.

Control: Spray with Karathane (Mildex) or dust with fine dusting sulphur when disease first becomes evident.

Insect Pests

Lilac Borer

Attacks: Lilac, ash, mountain ash and privet.

Identification: Larvae from ¾ to 1½ inches in length, white with brown head. Adult a clear-winged moth.

Injury: The larvae tunnel under the bark and into the wood. Sawdust from new borings is sometimes noted. Old branches may become riddled with holes and die slowly. If the infestation is heavy and no measures of control are undertaken the health and vigor of the entire bush may be seriously affected.

Life History: The borer passes the winter in its tunnel within the branch, usually near the ground. Feeds for a short time in the spring and then pupates in its tunnel near the outer bark. Adults emerge during the spring and summer, according to the locality, and the females lay their eggs at the base of the branches or in roughened places on the bark. After hatching the young larvae start tunneling into the stems. There is only one generation a year.

Control: Spray or paint the trunks with DDT or with Dieldrin (4 to 6 tsp. to 1 gallon of water) as this will prevent egg laying. Several treatments should be made, the first about June 1, the second about July 20 and the third a month later.

Scale (Oystershell Scale)

Identification: Grayish scales, resembling miniature oysters are found on twigs and branches.

Injury: The health and vigor of the bush is affected and heavily infested twigs and branches die.

Life History: The winter is passed in the egg stage under the female shells. The young crawlers hatch in late May or June. After moving about for a few hours they penetrate the bark with their beaks.

Control: A dormant oil spray should be applied in spring just before the buds break. A 1 to 5 dilution of miscible oil is recommended. In the crawling stage a spray of malathion will give excellent results. Heavily encrusted branches should be cut off and burned.

Magnolia

Insect Pest

Magnolia Scale

Identification: The Magnolia Scale is the largest of any of the scale insects. The female is $\frac{1}{2}$ inch across and is covered with a whitish wax. If the infestation is severe the branches appear to be covered with a white, cottony substance.

Injury: Trees become unhealthy and leaves are small.

Life History: The young nymphs hibernate in young wood. They molt early in the spring and again in June, starting the secretion of wax. By August they produce living young.

Control: A dormant oil spray will give effective control. In late summer an application of malathion, timed to reach the young crawlers, will be advantageous. If the infestation is light and only a few branches are affected the scales can be readily scrubbed off during the summer with a stiff brush.

Mountain Laurel

Disease

Leaf Spot

Symptoms: Brown or grayish spots appear on the leaves and the foliage may become badly disfigured.

Cause: A fungous disease which is most apt to be troublesome on Mountain Laurel when it is growing in a very shady or damp location.

Control: Spray with Bordeaux, Captan or Ferbam, beginning when the new growth is young, and repeating the application several times during the season.

Oaks

Disease

Anthracnose (Leaf and Twig Blight)

Most common on Sycamores but sometimes attacks oaks.

Symptoms: The usual type of lesion appears as elongated brown spots along the main veins of the leaf. The infected tissue causes the death of the surrounding leaf tissue, and two or more lesions may involve an entire leaf. A tree so infected may appear from a distance to be scorched. The leaves soon drop after they are dead, and the tree may become completely defoliated by early summer. Sometimes the young twigs become infected and turn brown as they start to grow. This symptom is often confused with frost injury. Cankers may also appear on the twigs. The center of the canker is usually sunken with a slightly raised margin. The repeated killing of the young branches often produces a gnarled type of growth.

Nature of the Disease: The disease is caused by the fungus, Gnomonia Veneta (Sacc. and Speg.) Klebahn. Of the oaks, those belonging to the red and white groups are most commonly affected. Frequent rains and a humid atmosphere promote the spread of the disease.

Control: All infected leaves should be raked up after they have fallen, and burned. Twigs bearing cankers should be carefully pruned out. Spray by means of a power sprayer with Bordeaux mixture (4–4–50 or 5–5–50). Be careful that all leaves are covered. The first application should be made after the buds have burst and before the leaves are half grown. A second application should be made about a week later. Three or four applications should be made if the season is a rainy, humid one.

Pines

Disease

Blister-rust

Symptoms: The injury is very characteristic. The young shoots are the first portion of the tree to become affected. When infection first takes place the bark becomes somewhat swollen, but it is not until the spring of the second or third year that the orange-colored fruiting bodies appear. At the point where these fruiting pustules appear on the tree a cankerous scar is left, and in many cases the branch becomes completely girdled and dies. If the infection extends into the trunk of the tree the growth becomes characteristically stunted and compact, and there is a decidedly yellowish cast to the foliage.

Nature of the Disease: There are many forms of blister-rust which attack various species of pine, the most common being the fungus Cronartium Ribicola, which causes the stem blister-rust of the white pine and of other five-needle pines. Young trees are most susceptible, and on older trees it is the young branches which are first attacked.

Part of the life cycle of the fungus must be passed on an alternate host plant, the currant and the gooseberry being the hosts. When the covering of the blister-like fruiting bodies on the pines has broken, the fine, powdery spores are liberated and are blown in every direction. However, these spores cannot infect other pine trees, as in order to complete their cycle they must find lodgment on the leaves of the currant or gooseberry.

Control: The disease may be brought under complete control through the eradication of all currant and gooseberry bushes within a radius of 500 feet of the pine trees.

Cankerous growths should be cut out as soon as infection is detected, and all affected branches pruned off and burned.

Insect Pests

Red-headed Pine Sawfly

Identification: The larvae are whitish with brown heads when young, later becoming yellow with 6 rows of black spots.

Injury: The larvae live in groups and feed voraciously upon the needles of the pine, often completely defoliating young trees. They begin feeding about May and continue until late autumn.

Life History: The larvae winter over in the pupa stage, encased in tough, papery cocoons in the ground beneath the trees. The adult fly lays her eggs in slits in the needles. Young larvae begin feeding as soon as hatched. There are often two overlapping broods.

Control: Spray with DDT or with arsenate of lead when the larvae are young.

White-pine Sawfly

Identification: Larvae yellowish with four rows of black dots.

Control: Same as for the Red-headed Pine Sawfly.

Pine Spittlebug

Most injurious on Scotch pine but also attacks white, pitch, red and Virginia pines and Norway Spruce.

Identification: The young nymphs live in a frothy substance resembling the lightly beaten white of an egg.

Injury: The young feed on the twigs, ejecting undigested sap which causes the branches to become covered with a black, sooty mold. If infestation is not checked it may cause the death of the tree within a few years.

Life History: The eggs are laid during the summer months at the base of the terminal buds, hatch the following May and the young begin feeding.

Control: Spray in June with pyrethrum extract or with lindane.

Pine False Webworm

Identification: Larvae about an inch long, greenish-gray striped with purplish red.

Injury: Larvae feed within a loose webbing, chewing off the needles and pulling them into the web. Trees can become completely defoliated if infestation is severe.

Life History: The adults emerge from their earthen cells between mid-April and early May, and the eggs, which are laid on the needles, hatch within a few weeks and the larvae begin feeding. In late June the mature larvae make silken tubes along the twigs and drop to the ground.

Control: Spray in May, before the needles become webbed, with DDT or arsenate of lead.

Pine Webworm

Identification: Larvae are a yellowish brown with two dark stripes along each side.

Injury: The larvae feed in silken webs near the ends of the terminal shoots.

Life History: The winter is passed in the pupa stage in the ground near the tree. Adults emerge from June to August.

Control: Spray with DDT or arsenate of lead before the webbing starts. If infestation is light cut off and burn infested tips.

White-pine Weevil

One of the most serious pests on white pines in the East. Sometimes attacks Scotch and pitch pines and Norway Spruce.

Identification: Adults are about $\frac{1}{4}$ inch long, reddish brown, with a long, curved snout. Grubs are yellow, footless, $\frac{1}{3}$ of an inch in length.

Injury: The grubs kill the terminal leader, girdling it as they mine into the bark, and causing it to turn brown and then die. Wilting and drooping of terminal shoots in the spring is the first sign of infestation.

Life History: Adults hibernate under trashy cover on the ground. Begin feeding in May and the female lays two to three eggs in cavities which she cuts in the bark of the leader shoot. Grubs hatch in six to ten days and begin feeding on the inner bark. They pupate in the wood and emerge as beetles during the summer.

Control: Cut off and burn all infested shoots as soon as they are noticed. Cut below the point of infestation. To protect shoots from infestation spray in early spring, just as the buds begin to swell, with a 3% DDT emulsion or with lead arsenate.

Pyracantha

Disease

Fire Blight

Attacks: Apples, pears, quinces, crabapples, hawthorns and pyracantha.

Symptoms: The branches begin to die back, and look as if they had been burned by fire.

Nature of the Disease: A bacterial disease which is spread from one plant to another by insects and by contaminated pruning shears.

Control: Good sanitation is one of the best measures of control. All diseased branches should be cut off at least 6 inches below the point of infection. It is essential that the cut be made well below the visibly blighted portion, as the bacteria progress downward inside the tissues. All pruning shears should be disinfected after use.

The antibiotic Streptomycin sprays have proved most effective in the control of fire blight. The spray should be applied during the blossoming period at 4 to 5 day intervals. The first application should be made when the first blossom opens and the last when the period of full bloom has been reached.

Insect Pests

Lace Bug

Identification: Small insects about ⅛ of an inch long, whitish and lace-like in appearance are found on the undersurface of the leaves.

Life History: See page 621.

Control: See page 621.

Webworm

Identification: Small caterpillars feeding near the tips of the branches within a web.

Life History: See page 628.

Control: See page 628.

Red Cedar

Diseases

Cedar-Apple Rust

Attacks: Apples, hawthorns and ornamental crabapples. Bechtel's and many native crabs are very susceptible. Asiatic varieties show more resistance.

Symptoms: This fungus, like many rusts, has to have two different plants as hosts in order to complete its life cycle. In this case the two hosts are the ordinary cedar, Juniperus Virginiana, and the crab or ordinary domestic apple. On the leaves of apples, the infection first appears as small yellow spots which enlarge, deepen in color, and frequently have reddish borders. On the under-surface of the leaf the tissue develops a cushion or blister on which small tubular projections appear. Likewise on the twigs small swollen areas develop, bearing many tubular projections. In the case of the cedar, galls, commonly called apples, are produced with small round indentations. In the spring, gelatinous raylike processes arise from these indentations. In this stage, the infection is sometimes called a cedar flower.

Nature of the Disease: The fungus, Gymnosporangium Juniperivirginianae Schw., causes the disease. The fungus winters over in the galls on cedars. In the spring, the gelatinous rays are produced which bear many spores. These spores infect the apple. Several stages of the life cycle are completed on the apple. In June, re-infection of the cedar may occur.

Control: If possible remove all red cedars or all of the alternate host trees, apples, crabs and hawthorns, as the fungus must have both plants to complete its life cycle.

The antibiotic, Actidione, applied as a spray in April to trees producing the galls will completely prevent spore production, and thereby arrest the spread of the disease to the alternating host plants.

If the spread of the spores has not been arrested apples, ornamental crabs, and hawthorns growing in proximity to the cedars should be dusted with 1–40 lime-sulphur when the blossoms show good color, again within one or two days after the first blossom opens, when one-half to two-thirds of the petals have dropped, then four successive times at four to five-day intervals.

Rhododendron

Insect Pests

Rhododendron Borer

Sometimes attacks azaleas and mountain laurel.

Identification: Larvae are yellowish-white and about ½ inch long. Adult moths black with 3 yellow bands.

Injury: The larvae bore into the sapwood under the bark and usually cause the branches to wilt or break off. The general vigor of the bush is affected and leaves turn brown.

Life History: The eggs are laid by the female moth on the twigs in May and June. The young larvae begin tunnelling into the branches soon after hatching.

Control: Spray or paint the trunks and branches with DDT in spring before the eggs are deposited. As a precautionary measure cut out and burn all infested branches.

Lace Bug

Indication: Leaves begin to show yellowish stippling on upper surface, with rusty flecks on the underside; small, whitish, lace-like insect found on the undersurface of leaves.

Life History: See page 621.

Control: See page 621.

Spruce

Insect Pest

Spruce Spider Mite

Indication: Foliage becomes grayish and unhealthy in appearance. Tiny webs are sometimes evident.

Life History: See page 620.

Control: See page 620.

Sycamore

Disease

Anthracnose (Leaf and Twig Blight)

Most common on sycamores. Sometimes attacks oaks.

Symptoms: Foliage appears to be scorched. Leaves drop after they are dead and the tree may become defoliated.

Nature of Disease: See page 627.

Control: See page 627.

Taxus

Insect Pests

Taxus Mealybug

Identification: The female is small, about ⅜ inch long and is covered with a white, waxy substance.

Injury: The mealybugs suck the juices from the plant and cause a decline in vigor and appearance.

Life History: The nymphs winter over in crevices in the bark. They become mature about June and give birth to living young. There are 2 or 3 broods during the season. The adults disappear in the autumn.

Control: Spray with nicotine sulfate, 2 tsp. per gallon, or with malathion emulsion or wettable powder used at the rate of 2 to 4 tsp. per gallon of water. Late May is the most favorable time for the application to be made. It is important to have sufficient pressure to reach the inside of the bushes.

Tulip-tree

Insect Pests

Tulip-tree Scale

Usually found on tulip-trees. Occasionally attacks magnolia and linden.

Identification: Large, dark brown, soft scales are found along the twigs and branches.

Injury: Reduces the vigor of the tree and in the case of very heavy infestations may cause its death.

Life History: The winter is spent in the nymph stage, the small, partly grown nymphs clinging tightly to the twigs of the host tree. The nymphs grow rapidly during the spring and begin producing young by midsummer.

Control: Dormant spray of miscible oil.

DISEASES AND INSECT PESTS OF FLOWERING PLANTS

Antirrhinum (Snapdragon)

Diseases

Anthracnose

Symptoms: Small, brownish spots with a dark, narrow margin appear on the leaves. Cankerous formations develop on the stems, frequently girdling them. Growth is seriously affected and badly diseased plants may succumb entirely.

Nature of the Disease: A fungous disease caused by Colletotrichum antirrhini Stew. It is rather common on greenhouse plants and is frequently found on outdoor plants which have been started under glass.

Control: Thorough spraying every 10 days with either Bordeaux or Fermate. Pick off infected leaves. Destroy badly infected plants.

Blight

Symptoms: Yellowish, somewhat circular spots appear on the foliage. Stems brownish. Occasionally dark shrunken areas resembling cankers are found on the stems. In the center of each leaf spot there is a minute black pimple which readily distinguishes Blight from other diseases attacking antirrhinums. Young seedlings die off rapidly when affected with Blight, apparently rotting off at the ground line. Older plants are more resistant but will succumb in time unless the disease is checked.

Nature of the Disease: A fungous disease caused by Phyllostictia antirrhini Sydow, which is very prevalent in some sections.

Control: Same as for anthracnose (see above).

Flower Spike Disease

Symptoms: Flowers die prematurely. The lower blossoms at the base of the spike die first and the disease extends upward to the tip.

Nature of the Disease: A fungous disease caused by Sclerotinia sclerotiorum (Lib.) Mass. The fungus is carried to the stigma of the flower by bees and it is spread rapidly from plant to plant in this manner.

Control: All diseased flowers should be cut off and burned in order to remove sources of infection. Aside from this no effective measure of control is known.

Rust

Symptoms: Stems and leaves become covered with rusty, brown pustules. If rust is allowed to gain headway the plants will be killed in a comparatively short time.

Nature of the Disease: A fungous disease caused by Puccinia antirrhini Diet. and Holw. The spores of the fungus are readily blown about by the wind and the disease spreads rapidly from plant to plant. As the spores require a certain amount of moisture for germination the disease is more prevalent during a rainy season than during a dry season.

Control: Once rust has gained headway no sprays or dusts are entirely effective. Infected plants should be pulled up and burned. Surrounding plants should be dusted thoroughly or sprayed with any one of the following materials: superfine dusting sulphur, Parzate, Fermate, or a rosin lime-sulphur spray, made by dissolving 1 oz. of rosin soap in 1 gallon of water and adding 1 oz. of lime sulphur. In greenhouse culture, copper-naphthenate has been effective in controlling rust when applied as an aerosol.

Rust-resistant varieties should be selected and are now obtainable in a variety of colorings.

Wilt

Symptoms: Plants suddenly wilt and die as if from lack of water. When the stem is split open the sap tubes will be found to be dark and discolored.

Nature of the Disease: A fungous disease which attacks the plant through the roots. It is usually first introduced on infected seed and the fungus lives over in the soil for many years. Extremely moist conditions favor its spread.

Control: Pull up and burn all diseased plants. Disinfect the soil thoroughly before planting other antirrhinums.

METHOD NO. 1—Soak the soil thoroughly with a solution of Semesan used at the strength of 1 tablespoon to 1 gallon of water.

METHOD NO. 2—Use 1 pint of 40 percent formaldehyde to 12½ gallons of water. Apply at the rate of one gallon of the solution to every square foot of soil.

Let stand for twenty-four hours, then fork the soil over and aërate it well. Do not plant any seed or set out plants for several days.

Aquilegia (Columbine)

Diseases

Root Rot or Crown Rot

Symptoms: Plants show general lack of vigor and rot off at the crown. They may be attacked at any time during the growing season or they may fail to winter over.

Nature of the Disease: A fungous disease caused by certain fungi known as Sclerotinia sclerotiorum (Lib.) Mass. It is becoming more and more prevalent and causes serious losses in some sections. The long-spurred types seem to be more susceptible than the old fashioned short-spurred varieties.

Control: Water the soil about the plants with either of the following solutions as soon as trouble is detected. As a safeguard against the disease it is well to make an occasional application through the growing season.

Semesan, 1 tablespoonful to 1 gallon of water, *or*

Corrosive sublimate solution, 1 oz. to 20 gallons of water. (When using the corrosive sublimate be sure that the soil about the plants is moist before it is applied.)

Insect Pests

Aphids

Identification: Soft-bodied, lice-like insects which are usually found clustered near the tips of the young, growing shoots. They are light green in color and vary in size, the newly-hatched young being considerably smaller than the adults.

Injury: Aphids suck the juices from the plant and cause a general lack of vigor and stunted growth.

Life History: In the North aphids pass the winter in the egg stage, while in the South where the winters are mild they continue to breed throughout the year. The eggs, which are small, black and glossy in appearance, hatch early in the spring and the young aphids begin feeding immediately. This first brood becomes mature in about two weeks and from then on, until autumn, living young are produced from unfertilized eggs. These are all females and reproduction takes place with startling rapidity as each mature female gives birth daily to several young and nearly one hundred generations are sometimes produced in a single season. In the autumn males appear and the eggs which carry the aphids over the winter are fertilized. The life history of the aphids is one of the most remarkable in the entire animal kingdom.

Control: The following controls are recommended for aphids. Application should be made as soon as any infestation is noticed, and should be repeated as necessary. The dusting or spraying should be done with the utmost thoroughness.

1. Malathion—50% emulsion, 1 tsp. to 1 gal. of water
2. Nicotine sulfate—1 tsp. to 1 gal. water. Add 2 tsp. of a detergent, such as Dreft, as a spreader
3. Pyrethrum
4. Rotenone
5. An all-purpose spray or dust
6. Scope (see page 616)

Leaf Miner (Phytomyza aquilegiæ Hardy)

Identification: Small worms which feed within the tissues of the leaf making a white serpentine trail. The trail usually crosses itself several times and ends in a small spot about ⅛ of an inch in diameter. Eight to ten larvae sometimes develop within a single leaf.

Injury: The foliage becomes badly disfigured and the vitality of the plant is lowered.

Life History: The adult flies which are small and dark brown in color appear early in May. They feed for a short time, doing no noticeable damage, and then deposit their eggs on the underside of the leaves. The eggs hatch within a few weeks and the larvae immediately tunnel their way into the leaves where they feed for about 10 days. They then pass into the pupa state, the tiny pupa being attached to the leaf. A short time later the adult flies emerge and the life cycle begins again. There are several generations during the summer, the last appearing about the middle of September. The winter is passed in the pupa state, the pupa case being buried in the soil close to the plants.

Control: Apply 5% chlordane dust early in the spring to the surface of the soil around each plant. Cultivate it in *very* lightly.

If infestation is light, remove and burn affected leaves. Spray foliage with either nicotine sulfate or lindane.

Rose Beetles

Identification: Long-legged beetles, grayish-fawn in color and about ½ inch in length.

Injury: The adult beetles feed upon the flowers, completely destroying them in a very short time.

Life History: Refer to page 665.

Control: Picking the beetles off by hand and dropping them in a receptacle of water with a thin film of kerosene over it is one satisfactory measure of control.

Spray with DDT 50% wettable powder, 3 level tbsp. to 1 gallon of water. Application should be made as soon as infestation is noted.

Clean cultivation in and about the garden is also advisable.

White Fly

While white flies are generally regarded as greenhouse pests, they occasionally attack plants in the open. This is particularly apt to happen if the garden is located near a greenhouse or conservatory.

Identification: Very small, whitish flies about $\frac{1}{16}$ of an inch long with four wings. They are found usually on the under surface of the leaves.

Injury: White flies suck the juices from the plant, causing a general lack of vigor. The leaves turn yellow and if the infestation is severe the plant eventually dies.

Life History: The females deposit their minute, yellow eggs on the under side of the leaves upon which they are feeding. The young nymphs which hatch from the eggs are very small and almost flat, being a pale green, somewhat transparent color. The nymphs feed for about four weeks and pass through four molts before they become full-grown. The average life of an adult fly is between 30 and 40 days and many generations are produced during the year.

Control:

1. Dust with DDT.
2. Spray thoroughly with a Nicotine solution, making sure to reach the under surface of the leaves. Several applications should be made 3 or 4 days apart. Use standard formula (see top of previous column).
3. Spray with malathion. Use standard formula (see top of previous column).
4. Spray with Rotenone.
5. Scope (see page 616)

Aster, annual (Callistephus)

Diseases

Leaf Spot

Symptoms: Small dark spots appear on the leaves, gradually becoming larger.

Nature of the Disease: A fungous disease which is prevalent in some sections. It is caused by Septoria callistephi Gloyer, ascochyta asteris Gloyer, Botrytis sp.

Control: Spray thoroughly, at intervals of one month, or oftener if necessary, with Captan (Orthocide 406) or Maneb.

As the disease is carried on the seed it is a wise precaution to disinfect all aster seed before planting. This may be done by soaking it for 1½ hours in a 3% solution of hydrogen peroxide.

Rust

Symptoms: Orange-colored patches of rust appear on the leaves and unless the disease is checked the leaves turn yellow and die.

Nature of the Disease: A fungous disease caused by Caleosporium Solidaginis (Schw.) Thum., one stage of which is passed on asters or closely related plants, the other stage being passed on pine trees.

Control: Occasional dusting with fine sulphur will, to a large extent, prevent attacks of rust. It is not, however, an effective remedy after the disease has gained headway. All infected plants should be pulled up and burned in order to prevent the spread of the spores. Some varieties seem to be much more susceptible to rust than others.

Wilt

Symptoms: Young plants in the seed bed are frequently attacked and rot off at the ground line. The time of transplanting and of blossoming seem to be susceptible periods for older plants. The lower leaves are usually affected first, turning a yellowish green in the early stages, later becoming withered and black. Occasionally only one side of the plant is affected. Dark streaks develop in the cortex of the stem and in severe cases the stems and roots rot away entirely. Plants sometimes die quickly when attacked and sometimes linger on for months, producing a few small blooms.

Nature of the Disease: Wilt is a fungous disease caused by Fusarium conglutinans vr. callistephi Beach. which attacks the plant through the roots. It is usually first introduced on infected seed and the fungus lives over in the soil for many years. Extremely moist conditions favor its spread.

Control: Wilt-resistant varieties are now available. Use clean seed and be sure that the soil, both in the seed bed and in the garden, is free from infection. If there is danger of infection treat the seed and soil as follows:

Soak the seed for $1\frac{1}{2}$ hours in a 3% solution of hydrogen peroxide, or for $\frac{1}{2}$ hour in a 1–1,000 solution of mercuric chloride, or in Semesan.

Disinfect the soil with Semesan solution, 1 tablespoon to 1 gallon of water.

Yellows

Symptoms: Plants become dwarfed if attacked when young. Older plants have a curiously bushy and erect habit of growth, the young branches which arise from the axils of the leaves being thin and yellowish in color. Leaves that are not mature at the time infection takes place turn bright yellow. This is first evidenced by a slight yellowing along the veins. Occasionally only one side of a plant is affected. The injury to the flowers is very characteristic of the disease, the blossoms becoming dwarfed and distorted and frequently developing only on one side. Plants are practically never killed outright, usually living on until cut down by frost.

Nature of the Disease: The Yellows is caused by a virus in the sap of the plant. A leaf-hopper (Cicadula sexnotata Fall.) is the principal and probably only carrier. The disease apparently cannot be spread in any other way. One can handle badly diseased plants without any fear of spreading the infection. Many other closely related plants are attacked by the Yellows and the disease is carried over the winter by perennial hosts.

Control: In order to control the Yellows it is first necessary to control the leaf-hoppers, which spread the infection by injecting the virus into the plant when they feed. The following measures of control are recommended:

1. Nicotine: spray or dust every week or ten days
2. DDT
3. Pyrethrum
4. Rotenone

Destroy all diseased plants in order to remove sources of infection. When grown commercially, asters are frequently grown under cheesecloth.

Insect Pests

Black Blister Beetle, also known as *Aster Beetle*

Identification: A slender, jet-black beetle about $\frac{1}{2}$ inch in length with prominent head and neck.

Injury: The beetles feed voraciously upon the flowers, completely destroying them in a short time.

Life History: The winter is passed in the larva stage, the grubs pupating early in the spring. The adult beetles appear about the middle of June.

Control: The following controls are recommended:

Pick beetles off by hand and drop into kerosene. (Wear gloves when hand picking.)

Spray with Cryolite, 2 tbsp. to 1 gallon of water *or* dust with 5% DDT.

Buffalo Tree Hopper

Identification: A small, green insect about $\frac{3}{8}$ of an inch long, triangular in shape with a two-horned enlargement at the front.

Injury: The nymphs and adult insects feed upon the plants and do considerable damage if they become numerous.

Life History: The eggs are deposited in slits in the bark of trees and occasionally in the bark of rose bushes. The winter is passed in the egg stage and late in the spring the small, green nymphs hatch out and begin feeding on the sap of various plants. They become full grown by August and the adult females die as soon as they have deposited their eggs.

Control: The only satisfactory measure of control for the Buffalo Tree Hopper seems to be clean cultivation in and about the garden. Hand picking may also be resorted to on small areas.

Leaf Miner

Identification: Small worms which feed within the tissues of the leaf, making a white serpentine trail. The trail usually crosses itself several times and ends in a small spot about ⅛ of an inch in diameter. Eight to ten larvae sometimes develop within a single leaf.

Injury: The foliage becomes badly disfigured and the vitality of the plant is lowered.

Life History: See page 632.

Control: Cultivate the ground about the plants as early as possible in the spring in order to destroy the pupa cases before the flies emerge.

See page 632.

Leaf Roller

Identification: Small caterpillars about ¾ of an inch in length when full grown. They vary in color from yellow to light green.

Injury: The caterpillars feed upon the flower buds and the foliage, rolling and tying the leaves in a very characteristic manner with fine silken threads.

Life History: The moths deposit their eggs in tiny masses upon the foliage of the host plants. The young caterpillars hatch out a few weeks later and begin feeding. They become full grown in about a month and pupate within the rolled leaves. The pupa stage extends over a period of about two weeks. The adult moths then emerge and the life cycle begins again. Two broods are generally produced during the season.

Control: If infestation is light, open the leaves which have been rolled and destroy the caterpillars or pupae.

Dust with 5% DDT or with Pyrethrum or spray with arsenate of lead.

Root Aphids

Identification: Soft-bodied, whitish-gray insects found clustered along the roots or near the crown of the plant.

Injury: Root aphids suck the juices from the plant causing it to become dwarfed and stunted. The foliage frequently turns yellow, indicating general lack of vigor.

Control: Pour ½ cupful of nicotine solution (¼ teaspoonful of Black Leaf 40 to 1 quart of water) about the base of each plant, making sure that the soil is cupped out about the crown in order that the solution may reach the roots and not run off the surface.

Keep the ground about the plants well cultivated.

Treat the soil with 5% chlordane dust to control the ants which act as nurses to the aphids. The ants collect the eggs in the autumn and store them in their own nest during the winter. In the spring ant nurses carry the young to the plants.

Stalk Borer (Common)

Identification: Slender caterpillars about an inch or two in length. The young caterpillars are brown with white stripes. When full grown they lose their stripes and become a solid, dirty gray in color.

Injury: The stalk borer makes a small, round hole in the stem and tunnels up through the stalk, causing the injured shoot to wilt suddenly and break over.

Life History: The Common Stalk Borer passes the winter in the egg stage, the eggs being laid on grasses and weeds in the autumn. The larvae hatch very early in the spring and when small they attack the stems of grasses but as they grow they become more ambitious and attack larger plants. They change frequently from the stem of one plant to that of another, seldom remaining for any length of time in one place. The caterpillars become full grown about the first of August and pass into the pupa stage within the stem of the plant upon which they happen to be feeding at the time. Late in September the adult moths emerge and the females deposit their eggs.

Control: Clean cultivation about the garden in order to destroy breeding places is one of the most important measures of control.

Cut off and burn infested shoots or insert a small wire with a hook on the end of it into the tunnel and drag the borer out. If this is done as soon as trouble is detected the shoot may sometimes be saved.

If plants are dusted with DDT it may act as a repellent.

Tarnished Plant Bug

Identification: A small, very active bug about ¼ inch in length. The body is oval in shape, being somewhat triangular in front. Coppery-brown in color with dark brown and yellow flecks on the back.

Injury: The bugs puncture the shoots just below the flower heads, causing the buds to droop and die. The injury completely destroys any chance of bloom. It is thought that while feeding the Tarnished Plant Bug injects some substance into the sap that is highly injurious to the plant and has the effect of a poison.

Life History: The adults live over the winter in the shelter of long grasses and with the first warm days of spring they become very active and begin feeding. The eggs are usually laid in the stems of herbaceous plants, occasionally in growing fruit such as peaches. Two generations are produced during the season.

Control: The Tarnished Plant Bug has been one of the most difficult pests to control but may now be kept in check.

Dust plants with 5% DDT powder, *or*

Spray with 50% wettable DDT, 2 tbsp. to 1 gallon of water.

The dust or spray should be applied to the flower buds as they start to form, and should be repeated again just as they open.

Clean cultivation both in and about the garden will destroy breeding places and help to keep the Tarnished Plant Bug under control.

White Fly

Identification: Very small whitish flies, about $\frac{1}{16}$ of an inch in length. Four wings. Usually on the undersurface of the leaves.

Injury: White flies suck the juices from the plant causing a general lack of vigor. Leaves turn yellow and if the infestation is severe the plant will eventually die.

Life History: See page 632.

Control: See page 632.

Grubs

The grubs of the Asiatic garden beetle, the Japanese beetle, the June beetle and various other species cause damage to garden plants.

Identification: Large, fleshy grub worms, grayish-white in color with a brown head and six prominent legs. They are usually found in a curled position, buried in the soil.

Injury: The grubs feed upon the roots causing the plant to become stunted and weakened. If the infestation is severe the plants may die.

Life History: Both the larvae and the adult beetles winter over in the soil. In the spring the adults emerge from the soil at night, feeding while it is dark and returning to the soil at daybreak. The females deposit their eggs several inches below the surface of the soil, generally selecting grassy fields or weedy areas. The eggs hatch in two or three weeks and the young grubs begin feeding on the roots of nearby plants. Some species complete their growth in 1 year while others require from 2 to 4 years. The most common species requires 3 years and the grubs cause the greatest damage during the second feeding season. During the winter they burrow down below the frost line. Grub worms are particularly troublesome on grassy or weedy ground.

Control: Grub-proof the soil (see page 195). In the garden late summer or autumn spading is helpful as it kills some larvae.

Calendula

Diseases

Mosaic

Symptoms: The foliage has a curiously mottled appearance, being blotched and streaked with yellow. In some cases the leaves become distorted in shape.

Nature of the Disease: Aphids and leaf-hoppers are probable carriers of the disease in very much the same way as mosquitoes carry malaria to human beings. In sucking the juices of a diseased plant these insects pick up the infectious virus, later transmitting it to healthy plants.

Control: When once injected the virus penetrates to every portion of the plant and there is no known cure for the disease.

All diseased plants should be pulled up and burned in order to lessen sources of infection.

Nicotine dusts and sprays may be used to keep both the aphids and leaf-hoppers in check.

Soft Rot

Symptoms: Plants rot away. The rotted tissues are frequently covered with a white mold.

Nature of the Disease: A fungous disease which is apt to be prevalent during damp seasons. The resting bodies of the fungus, known as sclerotia, resemble little hard, black balls.

Control: Remove and destroy all infected plants.

Do not let young seedlings become too crowded.

Water plants and soak the ground about them with some organic mercury solution such as

Semesan, 1 tablespoonful to 1 gallon of water

Insect Pests

Aphids

Identification: Soft-bodied, louse-like insects which are usually found clustered near the tips of the young shoots. They are light green in color and vary in size, the newly-hatched young being considerably smaller than the adults.

Injury: Aphids suck the juices of the plant and cause stunted growth and a general lack of vigor.

Life History: See page 631.

Control: See page 632.

Black Blister Beetle, also known as *Aster Beetle*

Identification: A slender, jet black beetle about $\frac{1}{2}$ inch in length with prominent head and neck.

Injury: The beetles feed upon the flowers, completely destroying them in a short time.

Life History: See page 633.

Control: See page 633.

Cabbage Worm

Identification: Small, velvety, green caterpillars, somewhat more than an inch in length when full grown.

Injury: Large, irregular holes eaten in the foliage.

Life History: The winter is passed in the pupa stage and the adult butterflies which are white with three or four black spots on the wings emerge early in the spring. The females lay their small, yellow eggs one at a time upon the undersurface of the leaves of the various host plants. Several hundred eggs are laid by each female. The very small, green caterpillars hatch out in about a week and begin feeding immediately. They develop rapidly, becoming full grown within a few weeks, and they then pass into the pupa stage. Several weeks later the adult butterflies emerge and one generation swiftly succeeds another throughout the summer until sometimes as many as five or six broods are produced.

Control: The following controls are recommended: DDT, toxophene, cryolite, Rotenone.

Stalk Borer

Identification: Slender caterpillars about 2 inches in length when full-grown. The young caterpillars are brown with white stripes. When full-grown they lose their stripes and become a solid, dirty gray in color.

Injury: The stalk borer makes a small round hole in the stem and tunnels up through the stalk, causing the injured shoot suddenly to wilt and break over.

Life History: See page 634.

Control: See page 634. Clean cultivation about the garden in order to destroy breeding places is important.

Cut off and burn infested shoots or insert a small wire with a hook on the end of it into the tunnel and drag the borer out.

White Fly

Identification: Very small, whitish flies about $\frac{1}{16}$ of an inch in length. Four wings. Found usually on the undersurface of the leaves on plants near greenhouses.

Injury: White flies suck the juices from the plant causing a general lack of vigor.

Life History: See page 632.

Control: See page 632.

Calla Lily

Diseases

Root Rot

Symptoms: The plants appear normal for a time, then the outer leaves begin to yellow along the margins, and gradually the whole leaf yellows and droops. Other leaves are affected progressively inward. However, new leaves continue to develop. If flowers are developed the spathe usually does not open properly. The tip of the spathe may turn brown.

Nature of the Disease: The disease is caused by the fungus, Phytophthora richardia. If the roots are examined, they are found to be infected. The feeder roots start rotting at the tips, and the infection sometimes spreads through the root to the corm. The rot in the corm is more or less dry and spongy.

Control: As the infection lives over in the soil, it is best to change or sterilize the soil before replanting. As a preventive measure corms may be treated as follows:

1. Soak for 1 hour in bichloride of mercury (2 oz. to 7½ gal. of water)
2. Soak for 1 hour in a 2% formaldehyde solution

Soft Rot

Symptoms: The leaf stalks are often attacked near the base. Water-soaked areas develop which later become dark and slimy. The leaf blade yellows at the tip and along the margins, and as the infection spreads, becomes entirely yellow, shrivels and dies. If the flower is attacked, the flower turns yellow and the stalk eventually falls over.

Nature of the Disease: The disease is caused by the bacterium, Bacillus carotovorus. The top of the corm at or just below the top of the soil is usually attacked first. The plant may rot off at this point. Sometimes it spreads downward through the corm producing a soft, mushy rot with a foul odor.

Control: See Calla Root Rot.

Carnation

Diseases

Rust

Symptoms: The rust is first characterized by yellow swollen areas on the leaves and stem. These soon break open and expose the brown spores. The whitish ruptured edges of the epidermis give the pustules a ragged appearance.

Nature of the Disease: The disease is caused by the fungus Uromyces caryophyllinus. The infection usually extends throughout the entire plant.

Control: Cuttings should be taken only from healthy plants. Cultural practices are important in controlling rust. Good ventilation is essential, the foliage should be kept as dry as possible, therefore syringing should be avoided and surface watering should be done. Dusting with sulphur or spraying with lime-sulphur will help. Fermate and Zerlate will also aid in the control of rust.

Stem Rot

Symptoms: This is a very common disease of carnations. It may attack cuttings or older plants. In the case of cuttings and plants which have recently been potted, the plants may appear to damp-off. On older plants, the rot usually starts at an injury in the cortex of the stem. As the infection spreads it girdles the stem and the plant then wilts and dies. In this type of infection, the rot is more or less dry and corky.

Nature of the Disease: The disease is caused by the fungus, Rhizoctonia solani.

Control: Take cuttings from healthy stock; sterilize benches; use sterilized soil; avoid over-watering.

Leaf Spot

Symptoms: Circular or oblong spots which are blanched or pinkish with purple borders develop on the leaves. In the center of the spot are small black dots. The stem may also become infected.

Nature of the Disease: The disease is caused by the fungus, Septoria dianthi. The disease is most abundant on the lower part of the leaves. The diseased part often becomes contracted, causing the leaves to be bent and curled.

Control: Remove and burn all infected leaves. Spray with Fermate.

Alternaria Leaf Spot

Symptoms: The disease appears as spots on the leaves, which become infected near the tip and die back, and sometimes on the stems, especially at the nodes. The spots are white with the center occupied by a black fungous growth.

Nature of the Disease: The disease is caused by the fungus, Alternaria dianthi. The lower leaves are usually more seriously infected than those at the top of the plant. When the stem becomes infected, the part of the plant above the infection dies.

Control: Spray before and after benching at 2 to 3 week intervals with Bordeaux, lime-sulphur, Fermate, or Zerlate. Use a spreader.

Bud Rot

Symptoms: This disease affects only the flowers of the plant. In some cases the buds do not open, others fail to expand perfectly while others are only slightly abnormal. The petals are first infected, then the sepals. The entire flower may rot and turn brown.

Nature of the Disease: The disease is caused by the fungus, Sporotrichum anthophilum. Mites are usually found associated with the disease and are believed to carry the spores. The fungus can sometimes be seen with the naked eye.

Control: Destroy infested buds; avoid high humidity; control the mites.

Campanula

Disease
Root Rot

Symptoms: Plants show signs of wilting; tips of the branches dry up, foliage turns a pale, yellowish green, roots become rotted. Occasionally only a single branch is affected.

Nature of the Disease: The Root Rot of the Campanula is caused by the fungus, Sclerotium Rolfsii Sacc., and it is particularly troublesome during hot, wet weather. The fungus produces small, brown, resting bodies resembling mustard seed.

Control: Remove and burn badly infected plants.
Water plants thoroughly with an organic mercury solution such as

Semesan, 1 tablespoonful to 1 gallon of water

Insect Pest
Rose Beetle

Identification: Long-legged beetles, grayish-fawn in color and about ½ inch in length.

Injury: The beetles feed upon the flowers.

Life History: See page 665.

Control: See page 665.

Canna

Disease
Bud Rot

Symptoms: The young buds become a mass of rotted tissue and the foliage becomes spotted. The disease is seldom fatal and vigorous plants will often entirely outgrow it. When plants are severely attacked, however, it causes considerable loss of bloom.

Nature of the Disease: A bacterial disease caused by Bacterium cannae Bryan. Some varieties seem to be much more susceptible to it.

Control: Root stocks should be selected from clean, healthy plants.

Insect Pests
Corn Ear Worm

Identification: Large striped worms about two inches in length when full-grown. They vary in color from light green to brown and the stripes, which run lengthwise with the body, are alternating light and dark. The head is yellow, the legs almost black.

Injury: The caterpillars feed upon both the foliage and the flower buds, causing considerable damage.

Life History: The adult female moths deposit their eggs upon the host plants, flying only in the evening or on dark, cloudy days. The eggs are laid singly and an individual moth will deposit anywhere from 500 to 2,000 during her lifetime. The eggs hatch in from 3 to 5 days and the larvae feed ravenously for about 3 weeks. At this time they have reached their full growth and drop to the ground where they burrow into the soil and form a small cell-like structure in which the pupa stage is passed. Two to three weeks later the adult moths emerge and the life cycle begins again. From two to three generations are produced each year and the winter is passed in the pupa stage 4 to 5 inches below the surface of the soil. Before entering the pupa stage the larvae carefully prepares a small exit tunnel through which the moths may crawl when they are ready to emerge. The moths vary in color from light gray to brown.

Control: Dust or spray with arsenate of lead.

Greenhouse Leaf Tier

Although primarily a greenhouse insect the leaf tier is often troublesome on garden flowers.

Identification: Slender, yellowish green caterpillars having a broad white stripe running lengthwise down the back with a dark green band in the center of the stripe. When full-grown they are about ¾ of an inch in length.

Injury: The caterpillars feed upon the leaves, often completely skeletonizing them. They also form a light web which draws the edges of the leaves together in a very characteristic way.

Life History: The adult moths, which are of a brownish color, fly usually at night and the females lay their eggs upon the underside of the leaves of the host plants. The eggs hatch in about 2 weeks and the larvae begin feeding. When the caterpillars are full-grown and ready to pupate they roll the edge of the leaf over and fasten it with a delicate web. Within this shelter they spin their silken cocoons and 10 days later the adult moths emerge. The life cycle takes 40 days and several generations are produced each season.

Control: Dust plants with 5% DDT dust or with pyrethrum.

Leaf Rollers

Cannas are attacked by two distinct species of leaf rollers. These are both very prevalent in some sections of the South but are seldom seen in the North.
Lesser Canna Leaf roller. Larger Canna Leaf roller.

Injury: The caterpillars feed upon both the foliage and the blossoms, rolling and tying the leaves together with fine silken threads.

Control: See page 634.

Rose Weevil

Identification: Dull, brownish gray beetles slightly over ¼ inch in length with a white line running diagonally across each wing.

Injury: The beetles feed upon the foliage, unopened buds and flowers. Most of their feeding is done at night.

Control: The beetles may be trapped under boards placed on the surface of the soil beneath the plants in the daytime. The plants may also be protected by banding them with little strips of fly paper or other sticky material. If the infestation is very severe, carbon bisulphide may be used. Make a round diagonal hole about an inch in diameter and about four inches deep. Insert a funnel into the hole and pour in one teaspoonful of carbon bisulphide. Plug up the opening and leave undisturbed for several days.

Saddle-back Caterpillar

Identification: A caterpillar about an inch in length and of very striking appearance. It is brown at each end, the main part of the body being light green with a little purple saddle over the back. It also possesses stinging, poisonous hairs.

Injury: The caterpillars feed upon the foliage and the flowers.

Control: Spray or dust with arsenate of lead; Rotenone dust.

Be careful not to touch the caterpillars with the bare hands as certain hairs on the body inject a poison into the skin which causes a very unpleasant, stinging sensation.

Spotted Cucumber Beetle

Identification. A yellowish green beetle about ¼ inch in length with twelve very conspicuous black spots on its back. The head and antennae, which are almost two-thirds as long as the body, are black.

Injury: The beetles feed upon the leaves, buds and flowers.

Life History: The adult beetles hibernate during the winter in long grass and about the base of woody plants. They become active very early in the spring and begin feeding. The females deposit their eggs in the ground and upon hatching the young larvae bore into the roots of nearby plants where they feed until they become full grown. Early in July they pass into the pupa stage which lasts for about a week and the adult beetles then emerge. Two generations are produced each season in the South and one or two in the North.

Control: Spray with DDT, cryolite or lindane.
Dust with Rotenone or pyrethrum.

Centaurea

Disease

Root Rot

Symptoms: Plants become sickly and rot off near the crown and white mold is often found on the lower portion of the stem.

Control: Space plants well apart to permit a good circulation of air. Water thoroughly with some organic mercury solution such as

Semesan, 1 tablespoonful to 1 gallon of water

Rust

Symptoms: Rusty spots appear on the leaves and stems.

Control: Destroy all diseased plants. Dust thoroughly with sulphur as a preventive.

Insect Pest

Root Aphids

Identification: Soft-bodied white or grayish-green insects found clustered along the roots or near the crown of the plant.

Injury: Root aphids suck the juices from the plant causing it to become dwarfed and stunted. Foliage turns yellow.

Control: See page 634.

Chrysanthemum

Diseases

Blight

Symptoms: Dark blotches about ½ inch in diameter appear on the foliage. The disease spreads rapidly. The leaves turn yellow, become somewhat shrivelled and drop. Severely infected plants die in a comparatively short time.

Nature of the Disease: A disease caused by the fungus, Cylindrosporium chrysanthemi.

Control: Destroy all badly infected plants. Spray thoroughly with Bordeaux mixture.

Leaf Spot

Symptoms: Dark brownish black spots of circular or somewhat irregular outline appear on the leaves. The spots enlarge until they merge together and the entire leaf becomes involved. The lower leaves are usually the first to be affected. The vitality of diseased plants is seriously affected and growth is stunted. The diseased leaves become black and shrivelled and drop prematurely. In severe cases the plant may become entirely defoliated.

Nature of the Disease: A fungous disease caused by Spetoria chrysanthemi Cav. It is very prevalent in some sections and causes severe losses.

Control: Pick off and burn all affected leaves; keep foliage dry; use sterilized soil; provide good ventilation. Spray with Fermate at weekly intervals for 3 weeks. Use only healthy plants for propagation.

Mildew

Symptoms: Leaves become covered with a white, powdery growth. In the most advanced stages the affected areas turn black.

Nature of the Disease: A fungous disease caused by Erysiphe cichoracearum D. C. It is particularly prevalent in damp, rainy weather.

Control: Mildew can be kept under complete control with frequent dusting or spraying. If dusting is done early, before the disease has gained any headway, and is continued throughout the season, fine dusting sulphur will prove very satisfactory. However, if mildew has gotten a start a spray of wettable sulphur or Karathane (Mildex) will prove more effective.

Some of the general-purpose sprays containing ammoniacal copper carbonate or a general-purpose dust with 60 to 75% sulphur will also give excellent control.

Precaution: Sulphur may burn the foliage if applied when temperatures are high, 80 degrees F. or over.

Root Rot

Symptoms: Plants show signs of wilting—the tips of the branches dry up and the foliage turns a pale, yellowish green, roots become rotted. Occasionally only a single branch is affected.

Nature of the Disease: A fungous disease caused by Sclerotium Rolfsii Sacc. The resting bodies of the fungus resemble small, brown mustard seeds. The disease is particularly troublesome during hot, wet weather.

Control: Remove and destroy badly infected plants. Water plants thoroughly with an organic mercury compound such as:

Semesan, 1 tablespoonful to 1 gallon of water

Rust

Symptoms: In the early stages small, rusty blisters about the size of a pinhead are found on the lower surface of the leaves. Very occasionally they occur on the upper surface. At this stage the blister is covered by the epidermis of the leaf. As the disease progresses the epidermis breaks away, exposing a mass of dark, brownish spores. When plants are badly affected the undersurface of the leaves may be almost entirely covered with these rust spores. The leaves gradually shrivel and die, and the plants become stunted and fail to produce good bloom.

Nature of the Disease: Rust is a fungous disease caused by Pucinia chrysanthemi Roze. It is thought to be a native of Japan and was introduced into this country in 1896 by way of Europe. It has spread very rapidly until it is now prevalent in almost every section where chrysanthemums are grown. It attacks only the chrysanthemum, as yet having been found on no other host plant. The fungus is comparatively short lived and soon dies out unless it is continually transmitted from one living plant to another. Some varieties seem to be more susceptible than others.

Control: Pick off and burn all diseased leaves as soon as trouble is detected. Use only healthy, disease-free plants for propagating purposes. Inspect all newly purchased stock with great care in order to avoid bringing infection into the garden. Reject or destroy any plants which show the least sign of infection.

The use of fine dusting sulphur is advocated not as a control after the plants are attacked but as a preventive measure. It is of great value in keeping healthy plants free from infection.

Stunt

Symptoms: Plants are stunted in growth, leaves pale green.

Nature of the Disease: A disease first found in 1945 on greenhouse chrysanthemums. Transmitted by vegetative propagation.

Control: Use only healthy, disease-free plants for propagation. When purchasing plants, obtain only those which are guaranteed to be free of the disease.

Wilt

Symptoms: Plants wilt suddenly and die, the lower portion of the stem becoming black.

Nature of the Disease: A fungous disease caused by Verticillium alboatrum McA. The fungus lives for some time in the soil. The disease is more prevalent on greenhouse plants than on plants grown in the open, although it sometimes causes considerable trouble in the garden.

Control: Destroy diseased plants. Use fresh soil which is known to be free from infection. Use only healthy plants for propagation.

Yellows

Symptoms: Leaves turn yellow. Plants become stunted and fail to produce normal bloom, the blossoms being distorted and frequently developing only on one side. The plants are only infrequently killed.

Nature of the Disease: See page 633.

Control: See Yellows of Asters, page 633.

Insects

Aphids

Identification: Soft-bodied, louse-like insects which are usually found clustered near the tips of the young shoots or on the underside of the leaves. Chrysanthemums are attacked by several different species, some being pale green in color while others are brown and black.

Injury: Aphids suck the juices from the plant, causing a general lack of vigor and stunted growth.

Life History: See page 631.

Control: See page 632.

Greenhouse Leaf Tier

Although primarily a greenhouse insect the leaf tier is often troublesome on outdoor chrysanthemums.

Identification: Slender, yellowish green caterpillars having a broad white stripe running lengthwise with the body with a dark green band in the center of the stripe. When full grown they are about $\frac{3}{4}$ of an inch in length.

Injury: The caterpillars feed upon the leaves, often completely skeletonizing them. They also form a light web which draws the edges of the leaves together in a very characteristic way.

Life History: See page 638.

Control: See page 638.

Gall Midge

Identification: Small, cone-shaped galls about $\frac{1}{2}$ inch in length are found on the leaves, stems and flower buds. When on the leaves they are almost always on the upper surface. Within the galls small maggot-like larvae are found.

Injury: The foliage becomes disfigured and the flowers are badly distorted. If the infestation is very severe the tips of the stems become dwarfed and curiously gnarled, and no flower buds develop.

Life History: The adult midge is a tiny, two-winged fly and the females deposit their bright, orange-colored eggs on the tips of the young tender shoots. The larvae hatch within from 1 to 2 weeks, depending upon temperature conditions, and for several days after hatching they move about upon the surface of the plant. They then bore into the tissues and as a result of the irritation the little galls are formed. The larvae feed until they reach full development and then pupate within the gall. When the pupa is fully developed and while it is still enclosed in the pupal skin, it pushes itself out of the gall and the adult flies emerge. It is a peculiar fact that the flies always emerge shortly after midnight and the females lay their eggs very early in the morning about dawn. Frequently the discarded pupal skin may be seen protruding from the opening of the empty gall. The period from the time the larvae penetrate the tissues of the plant until the adults emerge from the pupa stage varies from 21 to 46 days.

Control: If the infestation is light pick off and destroy all infested leaves, Pull up and burn all heavily infested plants. Examine all newly purchased plants with care in order to make sure that they are free from galls. Cut plants close to the ground in the autumn and burn all refuse.

Spray with 25% lindane emulsion, 1 tsp. to 1 gallon of water *or* with wettable lindane powder, 1 tbsp. to 1 gallon of water. Make 2 or 3 applications at 5 day intervals. Spraying should be done toward evening.

Tarnished Plant Bug

Identification: A small, very active bug about $\frac{1}{4}$ inch in length. The body is oval in shape, being somewhat triangular in front. Coppery-brown in color with dark brown and yellow flecks on the back.

Injury: The bugs puncture the shoots just below the flower heads, causing the buds to droop and die. The injury completely destroys any chance of bloom. It is thought that, while feeding, the Tarnished Plant Bug injects some substance into the sap that is highly injurious to the plant and has the effect of a poison.

Life History: See page 634.

Control: See page 634.

Nematodes

Identification: The Chrysanthemum Leaf Nematode is a dreaded pest in both garden and greenhouse. Too small to be seen except under a microscope, it is best identified by the characteristic injury to the plant.

Injury: The first indication of trouble is the appearance of dark spots on the undersurface of the foliage. The leaves begin to turn brown or black between the veins and gradually wither and hang down along the stem, giving the plant an unsightly appearance.

Life History: The nematodes enter the plant through the stomata on the undersurface of the leaves, and they move about on the plant by swimming up the stems in a film of water when moisture is present.

Control: The systemic insecticide, sodium selenate, will give excellent control. This is available in capsule form and directions should be followed with care.

See page 675.

Precaution: Sodium selenate should be used only on areas where the soil would never, under any circumstances, be used for the growing of vegetables or fruits, or for crops to be fed to livestock, as it would be absorbed by the plants and is extremely poisonous to humans and to animals.

Parathion is used as a measure of control in commercial greenhouses and gardens but is too highly toxic to humans to be recommended for use in the home garden.

Cleome (*Spider-Flower*)

Insect Pest

Harlequin Bug (Harlequin Cabbage Beetle)

Identification: The body is flat, shield-shaped and about $\frac{1}{2}$ inch in length, the back being gaily decorated with red and black markings.

Injury: Both the young nymphs and the adults suck the sap from the plant tissues and if the infestation is severe it will cause the death of the plants.

Life History: The Harlequin bug is a distinctly Southern insect as it is incapable of surviving the cold of Northern winters. In the extreme South it feeds and breeds during the entire year. In the more northerly part of its range the adults find shelter in long grass or under piles of rubbish in the winter, emerging with the first warm days of spring. The eggs are usually laid on the underside of the leaves of host plants, and they are very amusing in appearance, as they resemble tiny white kegs. They are set on end, about a dozen being glued together, and each one is bound with two black bands which look like miniature barrel hoops. There is even a black dot set in the very place for a bung hole. The time of hatching varies from 4 to 25 days, according to weather conditions. The young nymphs begin feeding as soon as they have hatched and at the end of 8 weeks, after passing through five molts, they become full-grown. Three and sometimes four generations are produced during the season.

Control: Handpick bugs on small areas. Dust with 10% DDT, toxaphene, or Rotenone.

Coleus

Insect Pests

Orthezia

Identification: The young nymphs are very tiny, dark green in color and wingless, with a row of waxy plates extending back over the body. The adult females have a very conspicuous white, fluted egg sack which extends back from the body for a distance of two or more times the diameter of the body.

Injury: Although primarily a greenhouse insect the orthezias frequently infest bedding plants when grown in the open and cause considerable trouble. They are closely related to the scales and mealybugs and suck the juices from the plant tissues.

Control: Spray with malathion or with nicotine sulfate.

White Fly

Identification: Small, whitish flies about $\frac{1}{16}$ of an inch long with four wings. They are usually found on the undersurface of the leaves.

Injury: White flies suck the juices from the plant causing a general lack of vigor and if the infestation is severe the plant eventually dies.

Life History: See page 632.

Control: See page 632.

Yellow Woolly-bear Caterpillar

Identification: A caterpillar about 2 inches in length when full grown. The body is completely covered with long hairs which vary in color from pale yellow to reddish brown.

Injury: The caterpillars feed upon the foliage.

Life History: The winter is passed in a cocoon made from the woolly coat of the caterpillar and silk which it spins. These pupa cases are usually found under piles of dead leaves or loose brush. The adult moths which emerge early in the spring are pure white with a few black spots on each wing. The females deposit the eggs in small patches on the leaves of the host plants. The larvae hatch out within a few days and begin feeding, attaining full size in about two months. There are usually two generations during the season.

Control: Spray or dust with arsenate of lead.

Cosmos

Diseases

Botrytis Rot

Symptoms: Attacks foliage, stems and flower buds. The affected parts appear to be covered with a greenish mold.

Nature of the Disease: A fungous disease which is seldom prevalent except in very wet seasons.

Control: Pull up and burn badly infected plants.
   Spray with Bordeaux mixture or dust with copper-lime dust.

Wilt

Symptoms: Leaves turn a sickly yellow. Plants wilt and die.

Nature of the Disease: A bacterial disease caused by Bacillus solanacearum E. F. S. which also causes the wilt of potatoes and tomatoes.

Control: No remedy has as yet been discovered. All diseased plants should be destroyed.

Insect Pests

Aphids

Identification: Soft-bodied, louse-like insects which are usually found clustered near the tips of the young shoots. They are light green in color and vary in size, the newly hatched young being considerably smaller than the adults.

Injury: Aphids suck the juices from the plant and cause a general lack of vigor and stunted growth.

Life History: See page 631.

Control: See page 632.

Spotted Cucumber Beetle

Identification: A yellowish green beetle about $\frac{1}{4}$ inch in length with twelve very conspicuous black spots on its back. The head and antennae, which are about two-thirds as long as the body, are black.

Injury: The beetles feed upon the leaves, buds and flowers.

Life History: See page 638.

Control: See page 638.

Stalk Borer

Identification: Slender caterpillars about an inch or two in length. The young caterpillars are brown with white stripes. When full grown they lose their stripes and become a solid, dirty gray in color.

Injury: The stalk borer makes a small round hole in the stem and tunnels up through the stalk, causing the injured shoot to wilt suddenly and break over.

Life History: See page 634.

Control: See page 634.

Dahlia

Diseases

Mildew

Symptoms: Leaves become covered with a powdery, white growth. In the most advanced stages the affected areas turn black.

Nature of the Disease: A fungous disease caused by Erysiphe polyoni D. C. which is apt to be prevalent in damp, rainy weather.

Control: See page 639.

Root Rot

Symptoms: Affected tubers rot during storage, becoming soft in the center and having a spongy, water-soaked appearance.

Nature of the Disease: A fungous disease caused by Botrytis sp. which always gains entrance through bruised areas on the surface of the tubers.

Control: Handle tubers with care in order to avoid bruising. Store in a cool and dry place. Dust any scarred places with fine dusting sulphur.

Stunt

Symptoms: Plants become a yellowish green in color, leaves are small, flowers poor and malformed. The growth of the plant is curiously bushy and stunted and the flower buds do not show until very late in the season.

Nature of the Disease: A disease closely resembling mosaic. It is transmitted through the roots.

Control: Pull up and burn all diseased plants. Use tubers from healthy plants for propagating.

Dahlias are subject to various physiological disorders caused by lack of water at time of blossoming, hot weather and intense sunshine, too much shade, too rich soil, etc. Such conditions are apt to cause stunted growth, distorted blossoms, and burning along the tips of the leaves. Such troubles can usually be overcome by good cultural methods.

Insect Pests

Corn Ear Worm

Identification: Large, striped worms about two inches in length when full-grown. They vary in color from light green to brown and the stripes which run lengthwise with the body are alternating light and dark. The head is yellow, the legs almost black.

Injury: The caterpillars feed upon the foliage and the flower buds, causing considerable damage.

Life History: See page 637.

Control: Spray or dust with arsenate of lead.

European Hornet

Identification: A small hornet with a dark body and two gauzy wings.

Injury: European hornets cause serious trouble in some sections by gnawing or peeling off the tender bark on the stems of dahlia plants. In some cases the stem becomes completely girdled and the plant dies.

Control: Locate the nest and destroy it. This should be done at night when all the hornets are in and it may be speedily accomplished with a kerosene torch.

Cutworms

Identification: Smooth, plump little caterpillars, about an inch in length when full-grown and varying in color from greenish gray to muddy brown.

Injury: Cutworms are exceedingly destructive as they sever the stem at or near the ground line, causing the immediate death of the plant attacked. Young plants are most susceptible to attack but older plants are frequently injured.

Life History: There are numerous species of cutworms which are injurious to flowering plants. In the case of most species the adult moths deposit their eggs on the stems of weeds and grasses. The larvae conceal themselves in the ground during the day, emerging to feed only at night. They start feeding early in the spring and continue until midsummer when they pass into the pupa stage. Most species produce only one generation a year, the winter being passed in the larval stage in little cell-like structures in the soil.

Control: Apply 5% DDT dust to the soil about the plants at the rate of $\frac{1}{2}$ lb. per 1,000 sq. ft. Work the dust lightly into the soil, or spray the soil with 50% DDT wettable powder, 6 tbsp. to $2\frac{1}{2}$ gallon of water per 1,000 sq. ft.

Greenhouse Leaf Tier

Although primarily a greenhouse insect the leaf tier is often troublesome on dahlias.

Identification: Slender, yellowish green caterpillars having a broad white stripe running lengthwise down the back with a dark green band in the center of the stripe. When full-grown they are about $\frac{3}{4}$ of an inch in length.

Injury: The caterpillars feed upon the leaves, often completely skeletonizing them. They also form a light web which draws the edges of the leaves together in a very characteristic way.

Life History: See page 638.

Control: See page 638.

Leaf-cutter Bee

Injury: The bees first make a tunnel in the stem and then construct their nest within it. In most cases they cause the death of the shoot.

Life History: The bees cut a neat circular piece of some growing leaf, usually preferring roses, and with this they build a nest composed of thimble-shaped cells within the tunnel which has already been prepared in the stem of some half-woody plant. The cells are arranged one above another and when they are completed each contains a single egg, some nectar and some pollen. The young bees develop within the nest until ready for flight.

Control: Remove and burn infested shoots.

Spotted Cucumber Beetle

Identification: A yellowish green beetle about $\frac{1}{4}$ inch in length with twelve very conspicuous black spots on its back. The head and antennae, which are almost two-thirds as long as the body, are black.

Injury: The beetles feed upon the leaves, buds and flowers and do considerable damage if they become numerous.

Life History: See page 638.

Control: See page 638.

Stalk Borer

Identification: Slender caterpillars about an inch or two in length. The young caterpillars are brown with white stripes. When full-grown they loose their stripes and become a solid, dirty gray in color.

Injury: The stalk borer makes a small round hole in the stem and tunnels up through the stalk, causing the injured shoot to suddenly wilt and break over.

Life History: See page 634.

Control: See page 634.

Tarnished Plant Bug

Identification: A small, very active bug about ¼ inch in length. The body is oval in shape, being somewhat triangular in front. Coppery-brown in color with dark brown and yellow flecks on the back.

Injury: The bugs puncture the shoots just below the flower heads, causing the buds to droop and die. The injury completely destroys any chance of bloom. It is thought that while feeding the Tarnished Plant Bug injects some substance into the sap which is highly injurious to the plant and has the effect of a poison.

Life History: See page 634.

Control: See page 634.

Delphinium

Diseases

Bacterial Leaf Spot

Symptoms: Dark spots of irregular outline appear upon the leaves. The lower leaves are usually the first to be affected. The spots occasionally appear on the stems and flower buds and in some cases the leaves become distorted.

Nature of the Disease: A bacterial disease of an insidious nature caused by Bacterium delphinii (E. F. S.) Bryan. The bacteria remain alive in the soil during the winter and are spattered up onto the leaves with the early spring rains. The disease spreads rapidly and the entire plant is soon affected. The original source of infection may usually be traced to the purchase of diseased plants. In rare instances it has been found that infection was carried on the seed.

Control: Pick off and burn all affected leaves in order to prevent the spread of the disease.

In early spring before growth starts drench the soil about the plants with Bordeaux. Repeat this operation several times during the season and spray the foliage thoroughly at the same time.

In severe cases cut the plants back to the ground in late July and drench the soil with corrosive sublimate solution:

1 tablet to 1 quart of water, *or* 1 ounce to 14 gallons of water.

Be sure that the ground about the plant is moist before this application is made.

Black Rot, also known as Root Rot and Crown Rot

Symptoms: Plants wilt and die suddenly, rotting off at the crown, or plants fail to come through the winter. The crown and roots sometimes become covered with a yellowish, moldy growth which has a characteristically strong odor of decay.

Nature of the Disease: A fungous disease caused by Sclerotium delphinii (Welch). The fungus spreads rapidly through the soil and is particularly prevalent on low, poorly drained land. It is also favored by damp, rainy weather.

There is also a form of crown rot which is caused by a bacterium. This organism enters the plant through wounded surfaces and causes the crown to decay. In appearance it is very characteristic, being wet and shiny, and it possesses a very strong and unpleasant odor.

Control: There is no known remedy; infected plants should be dug up and burned, and the adjacent soil should be removed and subjected to fire. In order to lessen the danger of infection to other plants it is well to scrape away the soil from around the crown of each plant, replacing the soil with sand or coal ashes. Do not allow animal manures of any kind to come into direct contact with the crown of the plant.

If the disease is prevalent, water the crown of the plants with a corrosive sublimate solution:

1 tablet to 1 quart of water, *or* 1 ounce to 14 gallons of water.

Be sure that the ground about the plants is moist before this application is made, and care should be taken not to water the foliage with the solution as it is liable to cause injury.

Mildew

Symptoms: Foliage becomes covered with a white, powdery growth. In the most advanced stages the affected areas turn black.

Nature of the Disease: A fungous disease caused by Erysiphe polygoni D. C. It is particularly prevalent in damp, rainy weather. It is very disfiguring to the appearance of a plant but seldom causes its death.

Control: See page 639.

Burning of the Leaves

Symptoms: Leaves have a curious metallic sheen on the undersurface and in some cases the edges begin to dry and curl up.

Nature of the Disease: Although this condition may appear alarming it is not in the true sense a disease. It is a physiological condition caused by intense summer sunshine and it seldom results in any permanent injury to the plant.

Insect Pests

Aphids

Identification: Soft-bodied, louse-like insects which are usually found clustered near the tips of the young shoots. The species that infest delphiniums are usually black in color and they vary considerably in size, the newly hatched young being smaller than the adults.

Injury: Aphids suck the juices from the plant, causing a general lack of vigor and stunted growth.

Life History: See page 631.

Control: See page 632.

Cyclamen Mite (Pallid Mite)

Identification: A very minute creature hardly visible to the naked eye. The adult mites are pale brown in color, somewhat glossy and have four pairs of legs. The presence of cyclamen mites is usually detected by their very characteristic injury.

Injury: Both the leaves and flower spikes become blackened and very much distorted. Stems become twisted and flower buds fail to open. Injury usually is evident on young, succulent growth.

Life History: The eggs, which are infinitesimal in size, are laid either about the base of the plant or on the leaves. The young begin feeding as soon as they have hatched.

Control: The only completely successful control for the pallid mite on delphiniums is the immersion of the plants in hot water. Although this treatment entails a considerable expenditure of time and effort on the part of the gardener, it is so entirely successful that the extra work is more than justified. It is fortunate that the plants are able to withstand a temperature which proves fatal to the mites in all stages of their development. Any convenient receptacle may be used for the treatment, provided it is of sufficient size to permit a complete immersion of the plants. A laundry tub, an old-fashioned wash-boiler, an ash can or a bucket may be used. The water should be heated to a temperature of 110 degrees F. and it should be maintained within a degree of this temperature throughout the treatment. A small quantity of hot water may be added occasionally during the treatment to prevent the temperature from dropping. Young seedling plants, or plants which have been lifted from the open ground, should have all soil washed off the roots. They may then be placed on trays or within a loose roll of small-meshed wire. They should never be tied in tight bundles. The plants should be entirely immersed in the hot water (110° F.) and should be held for a period of 10 to 15 minutes. If the plants are potted it is not necessary to remove them from the pots, as the pot and plant may be immersed together. It is necessary to immerse potted plants for a period of 25 minutes in order to kill all the mites below the surface of the soil. When the plants are removed, the pots should be tilted, in order to allow the water to drain off. Plants with bare roots should be spread out and allowed to cool off and dry slightly before they are replanted. It is advisable to shade the plants for several days after they have been replanted in order to reduce the danger of shock, and to give them an opportunity to become re-established as promptly as possible. As little time as possible should elapse between the digging of the plants, the treatment, and the replanting.

There are several other measures of control which are reasonably effective against mites, but none is so efficacious as the hot water treatment.

Dusting the plants at intervals of every week or ten days with very finely ground sulphur dust (300 mesh) will help to keep the mites under control as it is fairly effective against those which are actually exposed.

Regular applications of a Rotenone spray at the rate of 1 tablespoonful to 1 gallon of water is also effective to some extent against mites which are exposed. The plants should be sprayed at weekly or ten-day intervals from April until the time of bloom. Spraying should be resumed after the flower stalks have been cut down and new growth has started.

Dimite is a fairly effective control when used as a spray at the rate of 1 teaspoonful to 1 gallon of water. Spraying should begin soon after the plants start growth and continue through the season.

As a matter of general precaution, all infected shoots and flower stalks should be removed and burned.

The importance of keeping a garden free from infestation in the beginning can hardly be overemphasized.

In bringing new plants into the garden, it is a wise precaution to give them the hot water treatment in order to avoid any possibility of introducing mites. It is far easier to thus prevent the introduction of mites than it is to control them after they have once gained headway and have caused a serious infestation.

Stalk Borer (Common)

Identification: Slender caterpillars about two inches in length when full grown. The young caterpillars are brown with white stripes. When full-grown they lose their stripes and become a solid dirty gray in color.

Injury: The stalk borer makes a small round hole in the stem and tunnels up through the stalk, causing the injured shoot to suddenly wilt and break over.

Life History: See page 634.

Control: See page 634.

Dianthus (Pink)

Diseases

Anthracnose

Symptoms: Leaves turn yellow and the plant gradually dies.

Nature of the Disease: A fungous disease caused by Volutella dianthi (Hal.) Atk.

Control: Spray with Bordeaux, or dust with copper-lime dust.

Root Rot

Symptoms: Leaves wither and die. Plants rot off at the crown.

Nature of the Disease: Caused by the same fungus which attacks many other plants, Sclerotium Rolfsii Sacc.

Control: The most satisfactory measure of control seems to be the use of gypsum. Several handfuls should be cultivated in about the plants early in the season.

Digitalis (Foxglove)

Disease

Leaf Spot

Symptoms: Leaves have an unhealthy, rusty-brown appearance. Young seedlings are very subject to attack and older plants are also susceptible.

Nature of the Disease: A fungous disease caused by Phyllostictia digitalidis. Very prevalent in some sections.

Control: Leaf spot may be readily controlled by spraying with Bordeaux as soon as trouble is detected.

Insect Pests

Mite (*Red Spider*)

Identification: Minute mites, some red in color, others greenish-yellow and black.

Injury: Red spiders feed usually on the undersurface of the leaves, puncturing the outer tissues and sucking the juices of the plant. The foliage has an unhealthy, white, curiously glazed appearance and frequently drops prematurely. Fine silken threads will be found, spun across the undersurface of the leaves.

Life History: The very minute eggs are laid on the undersurface of the leaves, usually being attached to the web. Each female lays from two to six eggs per day, depositing about seventy in all. The eggs hatch in four

to five days and the young mites begin feeding. The females pass through three molts, the males through only two. The life cycle covers a period of 35–40 days.

Control: Thorough dusting with fine sulphur will kill both mites and eggs. Spraying with a good miticide, such as Aramite, Dimite or Ovotran will also give effective control.

Thrips

Identification: Young thrips are lemon-yellow, adults amber, about $\frac{1}{20}$ of an inch in length. Usually found on inside of infested flower buds.

Injury: Flowers are affected, not the foliage. Flower buds turn brown and fail to open or are distorted.

Life History: See page 668.

Scope is an excellent control (see page 616), *or* spray with Lindane, malathion or Dieldrin. Cut down and burn all affected flower stalks.

Fritillaria Imperialis (Crown Imperial)

Disease

Gray Bulb Rot

Symptoms: Dry rot begins at the nose of the bulb. The flesh of the bulb becomes a reddish-gray in color. In the advanced stages of the disease the bulbs rot away entirely.

Nature of the Disease: Caused by the same fungus that attacks tulips and various other bulbs, Rhizoctonia tuliparum (Kleb.) Whetzel and Arthur.

Control: Dig up and burn all diseased bulbs. Disinfect the soil with formaldehyde before planting any of the following bulbs: narcissus, hyacinths, tulips, scilla sibirica. See page 670.

Gaillardia

Disease

Yellows

Symptoms: Plants become dwarfed if attacked when young. Older plants have a curiously bushy habit of growth. Leaves that are not mature at the time that infection takes place turn a bright yellow. Occasionally only one side of the plant is affected. The blossoms become dwarfed and distorted. Plants are practically never killed outright, living on until frost.

Nature of the Disease: See page 633.

Control: See page 633.

Galtonia (Hyacinthus Candicans)

Insect Pest

Bulb Fly (Merodon equestris Fab.)

Identification: Small, brown scars are sometimes found upon the outer scales. Bulbs are suspiciously soft and light in weight. Upon cutting the bulb open, large, fat, grayish to yellowish-white maggots are found, $\frac{1}{4}$ to $\frac{3}{4}$ of an inch in length.

Injury: The maggots feed upon the tissues and render the bulbs practically worthless.

Life History: See page 652.

Control: Discard and burn badly infested bulbs that have become light and soft.

If there is danger of infestation it is wise to treat the bulbs as follows:

Submerge bulbs for $2\frac{1}{2}$ hours in hot water which is held at a temperature of 110 to $111\frac{1}{2}$ degrees F. Then plunge immediately in cold water. This will destroy the larvae in all stages of their development and will not harm the bulbs if they are sound.

Geranium

Diseases

Bacterial Leaf Spot

Symptoms: The affected area first shows as a water-soaked dot which can be seen only in transmitted light. As the spots become older they are brown in color and usually irregular though sometimes circular in shape. Several spots may appear on a single leaf. The tissue between the spots may turn brown and die, but the original spots show up clearly in the dead area.

Nature of the Disease: The disease is caused by Bacterium pelargoni Brown. It may be present on young as well as old leaves.

Control: Out-of-doors the plants should be planted so that they will get plenty of sunlight and air. In the greenhouse, plants should be kept in a well-ventilated house and care should be taken that the tops are not splashed in watering. Plants may be sprayed with Bordeaux mixture or colloidal sulphur, or with fermate.

Bacterial Spot

Symptoms: The soft leaf tissue is invaded between the veins which give rise to a rather large elongated area which converges toward the base of the leaf. Occasionally the infected areas are more or less round. The affected area may retain the original color or become brownish or pinkish in color.

Nature of the Disease: The disease is caused by the Bacterium erodii Lewis. The disease may start at the margin of the leaf and give rise to the angular areas or it may start by a small translucent spot.

Control: See Bacterial Leaf Spot.

Cercospora Leaf Spot

Symptoms: The spots are small, light brown or pale brick-red in color, more or less circular in shape, and have a narrow, slightly raised and darker border. It can be differentiated from bacterial spot in that the borders of the spots are raised and darker in color than in the center of the spot, while in bacterial spot the borders are colorless.

Nature of the Disease: The disease is caused by the fungus, Cercospora brunkii Ell. and Hall.

Control: See Bacterial Leaf Spot.

Dropsy

Symptoms: The leaves develop water-soaked areas which later become brown and corky. The leaf yellows first around the spot, and later becomes entirely yellow and drops off. The stems and petioles develop corky ridges.

Nature of the Disease: Dropsy is believed to be caused by a warm, damp soil which stimulates root growth and a moist, cool air which inhibits transpiration. The disease is more common in late winter.

Control: Give the plant plenty of light and good ventilation. Avoid over-watering.

Gladiolus

Diseases

Bacterial Blight

Symptoms: In the early stages, dark, water-soaked spots appear on the leaves. The diseased areas spread gradually until the entire leaf is affected. There is usually a very characteristic, somewhat sticky, exudation of the infected areas which gradually dries until it becomes a thin film. The corms are seldom affected.

Nature of the Disease: A bacterial disease caused by Bacterium gummisudans McCulloch. Some varieties seem very susceptible while others are quite resistant.

Control: Cut off and burn all infected leaves. Soak the corms before planting in any of the following:

Corrosive sublimate. Soak for $1\frac{1}{2}$ hours. Use 1 tablet to 1 pint of water or 1 ounce to 7 gallons of water.
Formaldehyde. Soak for $1\frac{1}{2}$ hours. Use 1 cup in 15 gallons of water.
Semesan. 1 tablespoonful to 1 gallon of water.
Spray at 10-day intervals with Bordeaux, Fermate, or Zerlate.

Dry Rot

Symptoms: Dark, reddish-brown spots are found on the corms. These spots are sunken with raised margins and are usually most numerous on the lower part of the corm near the old bulb scar. When corms which are badly diseased are planted the growing plants may become affected later in the season, the leaves turning yellow and rotting off at the ground level. In advanced stages the roots and the corm itself rot away. When diseased corms are lifted and stored in the autumn the dry rot continues and frequently the corms become entirely mummified before spring.

Nature of the Disease: Dry Rot is a fungous disease caused by Sclerotium gladioli Mass. which is becoming more and more prevalent and causes severe losses. The Primulinus varieties seem to be particularly susceptible. The fungus lives over the winter in the soil in the form of minute resting bodies known as sclerotia which are found on the base of decayed leaves.

Control: After the corms have been harvested in the autumn any of the following treatments are recommended:

Always remove the husks before treatment.

1. Soak corms for 7 hours in Semesan solution
   1 tablespoonful to 1 gallon of water
2. Soak corms in water for 15 minutes. Place corms between pieces of moist blotting paper for several hours. Then soak for 20 minutes in a corrosive sublimate solution, 1 tablet to 1 pint of water or 1 ounce to 7 gallons. Rinse immediately in clear water after treatment. Allow corms to dry thoroughly before storing away.
3. Soak corms in water for 15 minutes. Keep moist as above for several hours. Soak in formaldehyde, 1 cupful to 15 gallons of water for 30 minutes. Allow corms to dry thoroughly.

Hard Rot

Symptoms: Reddish-brown spots appear on the leaves, producing a rusty caste. As the disease advances minute black specks appear in the center of the leaf spots. These are the fruiting bodies of the fungus and later on this center frequently drops out, giving the leaves a shot-hole appearance. The corms are also affected, dark brown spots with a water-soaked margin being found on both the upper surface and the base. In severe cases the corm becomes a hard, shrivelled mummy. When badly diseased corms are planted spindly, unthrifty growth results and the plants eventually die.

Nature of the Disease: Hard Rot is a fungous disease caused by Septoria gladioli Pass. It is particularly prevalent on young plants grown from seed or from small cormels. It may spread directly from the old corm to the new corm and cormels, or it may first attack the leaves. In an apparent endeavor to resist the disease and to check its spread on the corm a layer of cork-like tissue is frequently built up around the infected area.

Control: Destroy all infected plants as soon as the disease is detected.

Give the corms the same treatment as recommended for Dry Rot.

Neck Rot or Scab

Symptoms: This disease usually first manifests itself by the appearance of light-brown streaks on the lower leaves near the ground line. Upon close observation minute brown spots are apparent which, as they enlarge become black and merge into one another. The blackened leaves rot off at the base and frequently the entire plant is killed.

The corms are also affected. Dark, burnt-looking streaks are found on the bulb scales and the corms are covered with brownish or blackened sunken spots having a slightly raised margin. In the advanced stages of the disease the entire corm presents a rough, scabby appearance and is covered with a varnish-like secretion. The outer husk is frequently stuck to the corm with this sticky exudation. In some cases the husk is entirely destroyed.

Nature of the Disease: A bacterial disease caused by Bacterium marginatum. The bacteria are carried on infected corms.

Control: The same as for Dry Rot. See page 647.

Penicillium Rot

Symptoms: The entire corm becomes a mass of dark, porous, rotted tissue.

Nature of the Disease: A fungous disease caused by Penicillium gladioli Machk. It always gains entrance through wounded tissues. Small, light brown sclerotia or resting bodies are found in the infected corms.

Control: Since rot fungi live in the soil, rotation is essential in controlling disease. Spray small plants from seed or cormels with Bordeaux mixture at 10-day intervals. Potash fish-oil soap should be added to spray for a spreader at the rate of 1 ounce to 1 gallon of spray. Handle the corms carefully.

Insect Pests

Black Blister Beetle

Identification: A slender, jet-black beetle about ½ inch in length with prominent head and neck. Its best means of identification is a yellow exudate.

Injury: The beetles feed upon the flowers.

Life History: See page 633.

Control: See page 633.

Corn Ear Worm

Identification: Large striped worms about two inches in length. They vary in color from light green to brown and the stripes which run lengthwise with the body are alternating light and dark. The head is yellow, the legs almost black.

Injury: The caterpillars feed upon the foliage and the flowers.

Life History: See page 637.

Control: Spray or dust with arsenate of lead.

Stalk Borer

Identification: Slender caterpillars about two inches in length. The young caterpillars are brown with white stripes. When full grown they lose their stripes and become a solid, dirty gray in color.

Injury: The stalk borer makes a small, round hole in the stem and tunnels up through the stalk causing the injured shoot to suddenly wilt and break over.

Life History: See page 634.

Control: See page 634.

Gladiolus Thrips

Identification: The adult thrips are black-winged insects about $\frac{1}{16}$ of an inch in length. In the immature stage they are wingless, pale yellow in color and very active.

Injury: The thrips feed upon the leaves, buds and flowers of the gladioli, causing a very characteristic injury. Affected flowers open imperfectly, the flower spike is apt to nod, and small, silvery-white streaks may be found on both the flowers and the leaves.

Life History: The adults appear early in the spring and feed within the tissues of the leaf, where the eggs are laid. The eggs hatch into small, wingless insects that continue feeding until they are full grown when they pass into a quiescent stage and emerge as adults.

Control: After the corms have been harvested all the tops should be removed and burned as soon as they are dry. The corms should then be treated in order to destroy any thrips which may be present. One of the most simple and yet one of the most effective treatments is the use of DDT. Put corms in a paper bag, add a small quantity of DDT dust and shake until all the corms are lightly coated.

Corms which have not been treated at time of harvest may be soaked for 3 hours just before planting in a Lysol solution, $1\frac{1}{2}$ tablespoon to 1 gallon of water.

There are a number of treatments which are recommended for the control of thrips on growing plants.

1. Dust at 10-day intervals with a 5% DDT dust after the plants are 6 inches high. This will usually give excellent control.
2. Dust with 5% Chlordane or with Lindane, *or*
3. Spray with malathion.

Woolly Aphids

Gladiolus corms are occasionally attacked by woolly aphids during storage. This is particularly true if they are stored in or near a conservatory or greenhouse.

Identification: Small, soft-bodied insects with a whitish woolly covering are found clustered on the corms.

Injury: The insects suck the juices from the tissues of the corms and weaken their vitality.

Control: Soak corms in a solution of Nicotine sulfate, 1 teaspoonful to 1 gallon of water. Allow the corms to dry thoroughly before replacing them in storage.

Golden Glow
Diseases
Mildew

Symptoms: Foliage becomes covered with a white, powdery growth. In the most advanced stages the affected areas turn black.

Nature of the Disease: Caused by the fungus Erysiphe cichoracearum D. C.

Control: Dust thoroughly with fine dusting sulphur.

Root Rot

Symptoms: Plants show signs of wilting, the tips of the branches dry up and the foliage turns a pale yellowish green, roots become rotted.

Nature of the Disease: See page 637.

Control: See page 637.

Insect Pests
Aphids

Identification: Soft-bodied, louse-like insects, usually found clustered along the tips of the growing shoots. The species that attacks golden glow is a dark reddish-brown in color.

Injury: Aphids suck the juices of the plant, causing general lack of vigor and stunted growth.

Life History: See page 631.

Control: See page 632.

Stalk Borer

Identification: Slender caterpillars about two inches in length. The young caterpillars are brown with white stripes. When full grown they lose their stripes and become a solid, dirty gray in color.

Injury: The stalk borer makes a small, round hole in the stem and tunnels up through the stalk, causing the injured shoot to wilt suddenly and die.

Life History: See page 634.

Control: See page 634.

Grape Hyacinth (*Muscari*)
Diseases
Rot

Symptoms: A white, moldy growth appears on the surface of the ground about the plants. Bulbs become rotten.

Control: Water the ground about infected plants with an organic mercury solution:

> Semesan, 1 tablespoonful to 1 gallon of water

Also soak bulbs in the same solution for two hours before planting.

Smut

Symptoms: The flowers are imperfect and become covered with a greenish-brown smut. The smut spores replace the ovaries and anthers of the flowers and utterly ruin their beauty.

Control: Pick off and burn all infected flowers as soon as the disease is detected in order to prevent the spread of the smut spores.

Before planting soak the bulbs for three hours in water kept at a temperature of 110 degrees F. Plunge in cold water immediately after the hot bath.

Heliotrope

Insect Pests

Greenhouse Leaf Tier

Identification: Slender, yellowish-green caterpillars having a broad white stripe running lengthwise down the back with a dark green band in the center of the stripe. When full-grown they are about $\frac{3}{4}$ of an inch in length.

Injury: The caterpillars feed upon the leaves, often completely skeletonizing them. They also form a light web which draws the edges of the leaves together in a very characteristic way.

Life History: See page 638.

Control: See page 638.

Orthezia

Identification: The young nymphs are very tiny, dark green in color and wingless, with a row of waxy plates extending back over the body. The adult females have a very conspicuous white, fluted egg sack which extends back for a distance of two or more times the diameter of the body.

Injury: The orthezias are closely related to the scales and suck the juices from the plant tissues.

Control: See page 641.

Hemerocallis

Insect Pests

Tarnished Plant Bug

Identification: Small, coppery-brown very active bug about $\frac{1}{4}$ of an inch long.

Injury: The bugs puncture the stems just below the flower bud, causing the buds to droop and die.

Control: See page 634.

Thrips

Identification: Young thrips are lemon-yellow, adults amber, about $\frac{1}{20}$ of an inch long.

Injury: Petals are streaked, foliage often has a silvery sheen.

Control: See page 646.

Hollyhock

Diseases

Anthracnose

Symptoms: The foliage becomes covered with irregular, dark brown spots and the leaves wither and fall. Sunken spots varying in color from pale yellow to black appear on the stems and petioles of the leaves. When young plants in the seed bed are attacked the stems usually collapse.

Nature of the Disease: A fungous disease, Colletotrichum malvarum (Br. & Casp.) South, which causes severe losses in some sections.

Control: Spray thoroughly with Bordeaux mixture. If one is troubled with this disease in the seed bed, spraying should begin as soon as the first true leaves appear and subsequent applications should be given every few days until the seedlings are well started.

Dusting with superfine sulphur is also recommended as a measure of control.

Rust

Symptoms: Leaves and stems become covered with raised pustules, a light, rusty-brown in color. If the infection is severe the whole plant may wither and die. In mild cases, however, the lower leaves are killed but the plant continues to grow and flower.

Nature of the Disease: A fungous disease caused by Puccinia malvacearum Bert. It was first discovered in Chili and from thence it was introduced into France. It was brought into this country in 1886 upon some infected seed and has spread with alarming rapidity to almost every section of the United States where hollyhocks are grown. It renders the plants most unsightly and is a very insidious disease.

Control: As soon as the leaves appear in the spring dust the plants thoroughly with superfine sulphur. Make subsequent applications every week or 10 days throughout the season. This is more in the nature of a preventive than a cure. When rust has once gained headway it is very difficult to control.

Cut all hollyhock plants down to the ground in the autumn and burn the stalks, leaves, and all other refuse.

Cercosporose

Symptoms: Large, dark, angular spots appear on the leaves. The spots are surrounded by darker margins and as the disease progresses the center becomes a light, ashen gray in color. Upon this light center small black dots may be distinguished. When the infection is severe the plants lose nearly all of their foliage.

Nature of the Disease: A rather uncommon fungous disease caused by Cercospora althaeina Sacc.

Control: Spray every 10 days with Bordeaux or with ammoniacal copper carbonate.

Insect Pests

Japanese Beetles

Identification: Large, handsome beetles, a metallic, greenish-bronze in color, with two conspicuous and several small white spots near the tip of the abdomen. During the middle of the day they are very active, making rapid flight when disturbed.

Injury: The beetles feed upon both the foliage and the flowers and will completely demolish a plant in a very short time.

Life History: See page 664.

Control: See page 664.

Leaf Roller

Identification: Small, active caterpillars about ¾ of an inch long, olive-green in color.

Injury: The caterpillars feed upon the foliage, their work being very characteristic as they roll and tie the leaves together with fine silken threads.

Life History: See page 634.

Control: See page 634.

Stalk Borer

Identification: Slender caterpillars about two inches in length. The young caterpillars are brown with white stripes. When full grown they lose their stripes and become a solid, dirty gray in color.

Injury: The stalk borer makes a small, round hole in the stem and tunnels up through the stalk, causing the injured shoot to wilt suddenly and die.

Life History: See page 634.

Control: See page 634.

Yellow Woolly-bear Caterpillar

Identification: A caterpillar about two inches in length when full-grown. The body is completely covered with long hairs which vary in color from pale yellow to reddish-brown.

Injury: The caterpillars feed upon the leaves.

Life History: See page 642.

Control: See page 642.

Hyacinth

Diseases

Black Rot

Symptoms: Bulbs become a mass of black, rotted tissue. Small black resting bodies of the fungus known as Sclerotia are frequently found within the bulb.

Control: Bulbs which are badly affected should be destroyed. If only very slightly affected the rotted portion may be cut away and the bulbs soaked in an organic mercury solution:

Semesan, 1 tablespoonful to 1 gallon of water. Soak for two hours.

Gray Bulb Rot

Symptoms: Dry rot begins at the nose of the bulb, and the flesh of the bulb becomes a reddish-gray in color. In the advanced stages of the disease the bulbs rot away entirely.

Nature of the Disease: See page 670.

Control: See page 670.

Soft Rot

Symptoms: Flower stalks rot off at the base. Bulbs come "blind", failing to form flower buds, or the flower head becomes distorted.

Nature of the Disease: A bacterial disease caused by Bacillus caratovorous Jones.

Control: The treatment is preventive rather than curative. Avoid excessive watering and also avoid too high a temperature when the bulbs are being forced.

Yellow Rot

Symptoms: The tip of the leaf is usually affected first and a characteristically yellow or brownish stripe appears down the mid-rib, causing the leaf to die. The sap tubes of the bulb become filled with a yellowish, slimy substance and in time the entire bulb is destroyed.

Nature of the Disease: Caused by the Pseudomonus hyacinthi (Walker) E. F. S. Some varieties seem much more susceptible to Yellow Rot than others.

Control: No measure of control has as yet been discovered. All diseased bulbs should be dug up and destroyed.

Insect Pests

Bulb Mite

Identification: Minute, whitish mites, bead-like in form. These are found in large numbers within the bulb scales. Reddish-brown spots appear at the point of injury.

Injury: The mites suck the juices from the plant tissues and the bulbs become soft and mushy. The vitality of the bulb is weakened and as a result growth is generally stunted—the leaves turn a sickly yellow and the flower buds either fail to develop or produce distorted flowers.

Life History: The eggs are laid inside the bulb scales and hatch out into six-legged nymphs. After passing through a molt these change to an eight-legged form and it is in this stage that they are the most destructive. They molt again before becoming adults and several generations are produced each year. The mites frequently migrate through the soil from decaying bulbs to healthy ones.

Control: Discard and burn all badly infested bulbs. If the infestation is not severe treat the bulbs as follows:

Submerge bulbs for 3 hours in water which is kept at a temperature of 110° F. This will kill all the mites but will not injure sound healthy bulbs in which root growth has not started.

Or: Soak bulbs for ten minutes in a solution of nicotine sulfate held at a temperature of 122° F. Nicotine sulfate—$2\frac{1}{2}$ teaspoonfuls to 1 gallon of water.

Or: Store in airtight containers with a 2% nicotine dust.

Bulb Fly (Merodon equestris Fab.)

Identification: Bulbs are suspiciously soft and light in weight and small, brown scars are sometimes found upon the outer scales. Upon cutting the bulb open large fat maggots, grayish to yellowish-white in color, are found.

Injury: The maggots feed upon the tissues and render the bulbs practically worthless.

Life History: The adult fly is yellow and black in color and very hairy, resembling a bumble bee in appearance although it is considerably smaller. The female lays her eggs either in the neck of the bulb or at the base of the leaves. Upon hatching the young maggots bore their way into the bulb and begin feeding. They are equipped with strong, slightly hooked mouth parts which are admirably adapted for this purpose. The pupa stage is passed sometimes within the bulb, sometimes in the soil.

Control: Discard and burn badly infested bulbs that have become light in weight and soft.

If there is serious danger of infestation the following treatment is recommended:

Submerge bulbs for $2\frac{1}{2}$ hours in hot water which is held at a temperature of 110° F. Immerse in cold water as soon as they are removed. This will kill the larvæ in all stages of development and will not harm the bulbs if they are sound and have not started root growth.

The following pre-planting treatment will give excellent protection from attacks of the bulb fly in the field.

Dip bulbs for 10 minutes in a solution of 25%

Heptachlor emulsifiable concentrate, $\frac{1}{2}$ ounce to 4 gallons of water.

Lesser Bulb Fly (Eumerus strigatus Fall)

Identification: Bulbs become soft and light in weight and upon examination maggots will be found feeding within the tissues. The maggots are grayish to yellowish-white in color, about $\frac{1}{2}$ inch in length when full-grown, and the body is decidedly wrinkled in appearance. They may be distinguished from the larvae of the Bulb Fly (Merodon equestris) by this characteristic.

Injury: The maggots feed upon the tissues and ruin the bulbs.

Life History: The adult fly is blackish-green in color with white markings on the sides of the abdomen. It is about $\frac{1}{3}$ of an inch long with an almost hairless body, and in general appearance it resembles a small wasp. The eggs are laid at the base of the leaves or in the neck of the bulb, and the larvae tunnel down into the bulb as soon as they have hatched. Two generations are usually produced during the season.

Control: Same as for Bulb Fly (Merodon equestris).

White Grubs

Identification: Large, fleshy grub worms, grayish-white in color, with a brown head and six prominent legs. They are usually found buried in the soil in a curled position.

Injury: The grubs feed upon the roots, causing the plant to become stunted and weakened.

Life History: See page 635.

Control: See page 195.

Iris

Diseases

Leaf Spot

Symptoms: In the early stages small brown spots appear on the leaves. The spots enlarge as the disease progresses, the center becoming lighter and the margin decidedly darker. The foliage gradually turns brown and is killed entirely.

Nature of the Disease: A fungous disease caused by Didymellinia Iridis (Desm.) Hoehn. It is becoming more and more prevalent in many sections and causes severe losses. The fungus lives over the winter on the dead leaves and infection on the new growth usually becomes apparent about the middle of June. Some varieties seem to be very much more susceptible than others.

Control: Leaf Spot on Iris may be controlled to a very large extent by destroying all foliage during the winter months.

During the growing season spray with Fermate as soon as there is evidence of infection. If the disease has gained headway it may be advisable to cut back the entire clump to within five or six inches of the ground and allow it to make new growth.

Lime and superphosphate worked into the soil about the plants are both considered helpful in keeping the disease in check.

Sclerotial Rot

Symptoms: Leaves turn a yellowish-brown. Leaf stalks and flower stalks rot off at the base.

Nature of the Disease: Sclerotial rot of iris is caused by the fungus Sclerotium delphinii Welch., the same fungus which attacks many other plants. It is particularly prevalent during damp weather and where irises are planted on low, poorly drained land.

Control: 1. Sprinkle copper salt powder over the rhizomes. 2. Work several handfuls of gypsum into the soil about the plant.

Soft Rot

Symptoms: The affected leaves and stems have a yellowish, unhealthy appearance, and at the base they become a mass of ill-smelling, rotting pulp. This disagreeable odor is very characteristic of the disease and distinguishes it from the less serious Sclerotial Rot.

Nature of the Disease: A bacterial disease caused by Bacillus caratovorous. It is very prevalent and destructive in some sections.

Control: Dig up and burn all seriously affected plants. If the infection is slight apply one of the following treatments:

1. Sprinkle copper salt powder over the rhizomes, liberally.
2. Lift the rhizomes, scrape away all rotted portions, soak for 30 minutes in a 1:1,000 mercuric chloride solution (2 tablets to 1 gal. of water). Dry in the sun for several days.
3. Dip in a solution of Semesan (1 tablespoonful to 1 gal. of water).
4. Dip in a pink solution of potassium permanganate.
5. Dust the rhizomes thoroughly with fine sulphur.

   If the disease is prevalent it is well to take precautionary measures and occasionally to water all iris clumps with either the Semesan or permanganate solution.

   Lime and superphosphate worked in about the plants are also effective in keeping Soft Rot under control.

Insect Pest

Iris Borer

Identification: The borers are a pinkish-white in color with a row of dark spots on each side of the body. When full grown they measure about two inches in length. In spring the presence of the borers may be detected by the characteristic "bleeding" of the leaves at the point where they enter.

Injury: The borers tunnel down through the leaf into the rhizome, feeding upon the plant tissues as they continue their peregrinations. They weaken the vitality of the plant to a very serious extent and cause sickly, stunted growth.

Life History: The winter is passed in the egg stage and the young larvae hatch out late in March or early in April. The tiny caterpillars crawl up the leaves, make a small hole in the outer surface, and as soon as they are safely within the tissues of the leaf they begin tunnelling their way down into the rhizome, feeding as they go. They become full-grown about the first of August and pass into the pupa stage. At the end of three weeks the adult moths emerge, and early in the autumn they lay their eggs near the base of the leaves or on the roots which appear above the surface of the ground. The moths fly only at night.

Control: In the spring, when the leaves are about 6 inches high, dust thoroughly with 5% DDT powder or spray with 50% wettable DDT, 3 tablespoonfuls to 1 gallon of water. Repeat every 7 to 10 days until the flower spikes show.

As a precautionary measure pull off and burn all old leaves in the autumn, leaving only the short fans of young leaf growth.

Lantana

Insect Pests

Orange Tortrix

Identification: Whitish, brown-headed caterpillar. Adult moths are grayish fawn with dark mottlings.

Injury: The caterpillars roll and tie the leaves upon which they feed. They are a distinctly Southern pest and sometimes cause considerable injury.

Control: Spray or dust with arsenate of lead, cryolite, or pyrethrum.

Orthezia

Identification: The young nymphs are very tiny, dark green in color, and wingless, with a row of waxy plates extending back over the body. The adult females have a very conspicuous white, fluted egg sack which extends back for a distance of two or more times the diameter of the body.

Injury: The orthezias are closely related to the scales and suck the juices from the plant.

Control: See page 641.

White Fly

Identification: Very small, whitish flies about $\frac{1}{16}$ of an inch in length. They are usually found on the under-surface of the leaves.

Injury: White flies suck the juices from the plant causing a general lack of vigor. Leaves turn yellow and if the infestation is severe the plant will eventually die.

Life History: See page 632.

Control: See page 632.

Lilies

Diseases

Botrytis Rot

Symptoms: Spots which range in color from orange to brown appear on the leaves, stems and flower buds. A small dark area will be found in the center of each lesion. The spots gradually increase in size and in the latter stages of the disease, when the spores of the fungus begin to develop, the affected areas appear to be covered with a grayish mold. In severe cases the stem of the plant rots off, the flower buds fail to develop and the disease spreads down into the bulb.

Nature of the Disease: A fungous disease, Botrytis illiptica (Berk.) Cooke., which is very prevalent in some sections. Its spread is particularly favored by cool, wet weather. The spores are carried from one plant to another by wind and other agencies. The fungus lives over the winter on dead and decaying leaves and other garden refuse.

Control: Botrytis Rot can be almost entirely controlled by thorough and systematic spraying.

Spray with Bordeaux every week or ten days during the growing season, or spray with livers of sulphur,* 2 ounces to 3 gallons of water. When the disease is first detected pick off and burn all affected leaves. If the disease has gained considerable headway cut off and burn all portions of the plant above the ground, lift the bulbs, and either dust them thoroughly with superfine sulphur before replanting them, or soak them in Semesan, 1 tablespoonful to 1 gallon of water, for several hours. They should be replanted in fresh soil.

It is also a wise precaution to practice clean cultivation and to rake up and burn all dead leaves and other refuse in the autumn.

Bulb Rot

Symptoms: In the early stages a slightly darkened appearance is noted in the flesh of the bulb about the roots. As the disease progresses the bulb softens at the base and the entire heart may become rotten. The rotted portion is brown and cheesy. When bulbs are seriously affected the flower stalks are usually dwarfed

* Potassium sulphide.

and frequently break over and if any blooms are borne they are distorted and malformed.

Nature of the Disease: A fungous disease caused by Rhizopus necans Mass.

Control: If the bulbs are badly rotted discard them entirely. If, however, they are of considerable value and are only slightly affected it may prove worthwhile to treat them. The rotted portions should be carefully scraped out and the bulbs may then be given the following treatment:

Soak bulbs for $1\frac{1}{2}$ hours in a solution of 1 part carbolic acid to 40 parts of water. After this treatment dust the bulbs thoroughly with powdered charcoal.

Leaf Spot

Symptoms: Brown spots appear on the foliage and as the disease progresses the spores of the fungus form a powdery, mildew-like substance on the surface of the leaves.

Nature of the Disease: A fungous disease caused by Cercospora richardiæcola Ptk.

Control: Dust thoroughly with sulphur every week or ten days or spray with livers of sulphur, 2 ounces to 3 gallons of water.

Mosaic

Symptoms: In the early stages the leaves have a curiously mottled appearance, being blotched and streaked with yellow. The disease usually progresses slowly. The second year the leaves and stems become twisted and distorted and no flowers are formed. Eventually the plant succumbs entirely but it will usually linger on for a number of years.

Nature of the Disease: Mosaic disease is becoming more and more serious and in some sections it is entirely wiping out large colonies of Lilies. The disease is carried from one plant to another by aphids in very much the same way that mosquitos carry malaria to human beings. In sucking the juices of a diseased plant the aphids pick up the infectious virus, later transmitting it to healthy plants. The virus penetrates to every portion of the plant. If infection occurs late in the summer the disease may not become active until the following season. Therefore apparently healthy bulbs may be carriers of the disease.

Control: At present no effective cure for mosaic disease is known. Pull up and burn all diseased plants in order to reduce sources of infection.

The importance of protecting lilies from aphids cannot be over-emphasized. Frequent checks should be made to detect infestation and spraying or dusting should begin immediately. Nearby plants should also be checked as possible sources of infestation. For control of aphids see page 632.

Rust

Symptoms: Small, brown, rusty patches appear both on the upper and undersurface of the leaves.

Nature of the Disease: A fungous disease. Some varieties are much more susceptible than others. Regal and Bermuda lilies are seldom attacked. Candidum lilies are very susceptible, particularly so when planted in shady places.

Control: Dust thoroughly with superfine sulphur or spray with livers of sulphur, 2 ounces to 3 gallons of water. After rust has once gained headway it is very difficult to control and this treatment is more in the nature of a preventive rather than a cure.

Insect Pests

Aphids

Identification: Soft-bodied, louse-like insects which are usually found clustered near the tips of the young, growing shoots. They vary in size, the newly hatched young being considerably smaller than the adults.

Injury: Aphids suck the juices from the plant, causing a general lack of vigor and stunted growth. They are also carriers of the Mosaic disease on lilies and every effort should therefore be made to keep them under control.

Life History: See page 631.

Control: See page 632.

Stalk Borer

Identification: Slender caterpillars from 1 to 2 inches in length. The young caterpillars are brown with white stripes. When full grown they lose their stripes and become a solid, dirty gray in color.

Injury: The stalk borer makes a small, round hole in the stem and tunnels up through the stalk causing the injured shoot to wilt suddenly and break over.

Life History: See page 634.

Control: See page 634.

Lobelia

Insect Pest

Red-banded Leaf Roller

Identification: Small, active caterpillars, about $\frac{3}{4}$ of an inch in length. Greenish in color with a distinctive red band from which they derive their name.

Injury: The caterpillars feed upon the leaves, rolling them together in a very characteristic fashion.

Life History: See page 634.

Control: Dust or spray with arsenate of lead.

Lunaria (Honesty)

Insect Pest

Harlequin Bug (Harlequin Cabbage Beetle)

Identification: The body is flat, shield-shaped and about $\frac{3}{8}$ of an inch long, the back being gaily decorated with red-and-black markings.

Injury: Both the young nymphs and the adults suck the sap from the plant tissues and if the infestation is severe it may cause the death of the plant.

Life History: See page 641.

Control: See page 641.

Marigold

Diseases

Wilt

Symptoms: The lower leaves turn yellow in the early stages and this condition gradually spreads over the entire plant. The sap tubes become brown and the plants eventually wilt and die.

Nature of the Disease: The wilt of marigolds is caused by the same bacteria that affect tomatoes and various other vegetables.

Control: At present no remedy is known. Diseased plants should be pulled up and burned.

Yellows

Symptoms: Leaves turn yellow. Plants become stunted and fail to produce normal bloom. The plants are seldom killed outright, usually lingering on until frost.

Nature of the Disease: See page 633.

Control: See page 633.

Insect Pest

Tarnished Plant Bug

Identification: A small, very active bug about $\frac{1}{4}$ inch in length. The body is oval in shape, being somewhat triangular in front. Coppery-brown in color with dark brown and yellow flecks on the back.

Injury: The bugs puncture the shoots just below the flower buds, causing the buds to droop and die. The injury completely destroys any chance of bloom. It is thought that while feeding the Tarnished Plant Bug injects some substance into the plant which is highly injurious and has the effect of a poison.

Life History: See page 634.

Control: See page 634.

Mignonette

Diseases

Leaf Spot or Blight

Symptoms: Small, slightly sunken spots with pale yellowish-brown margins appear on the leaves. As the disease progresses dark specks which are the fruiting bodies of the fungus develop in the center of the spots and the leaves gradually wither and die.

Nature of the Disease: A fungous disease caused by Cercospora resedæ. Fckl.

Control: Spray with Bordeaux every week or ten days during the growing season.

Insect Pests

Cabbage Looper

Identification: Greenish caterpillars with a white line along each side of the body and two lines near the middle of the back. The middle half of the body is without legs, and when resting or moving the caterpillar is usually in a very characteristic humped position.

Injury: The caterpillars feed upon the leaves.

Life History: The winter is passed in the pupa stage, the delicate, white pupa cases being attached to a leaf of some host plant. The small, grayish-brown moths emerge in spring and the females lay their eggs singly upon the upper surface of the leaves of the host plants. The moths fly only at night. After hatching the larvae feed for three to four weeks and then pass into the pupa stage. During the summer the pupa stage covers a period of only two weeks and there are usually three or four generations during the season.

Control: See page 636.

Cabbage Worm

Identification: Small, velvety-green caterpillars somewhat more than an inch in length when full grown.

Injury: Large irregular holes eaten in the foliage.

Life History: See page 636.

Control: See page 636.

Morning Glory

Insect Pest

Golden Tortoise Beetle or Gold Bug

Identification: A small, golden-colored beetle about $\frac{1}{4}$ of an inch long. Occasionally black stripes or dots are found on the body. The beetle is turtle-shaped, being flat on the underside with the head and legs partially hidden.

Injury: The beetles feed upon the foliage.

Life History: The adult beetles hibernate during the winter in dry, sheltered places, and they usually do not come out of hiding until late in the spring. The eggs, which are laid on the leaves of the host plants, hatch in about a week or ten days and the larvae begin feeding. Their feeding is confined largely to the underside of the leaves. After feeding for a short time they pass into the pupa stage and a few weeks later the adults emerge.

Control: Spray or dust thoroughly with arsenate of lead, DDT or Cryolite.

Narcissus

Diseases

Botrytis Bulb Rot

Symptoms: Leaves and stems become covered with unsightly spots. Small, black, resting bodies known as sclerotia are frequently found in the rotting tissues of the bulbs.

Nature of the Disease: A fungous disease similar to that which affects tulips.

Control: Dig up and burn badly infected bulbs. Soak bulbs for two hours before planting in

Semesan, 1 tablespoonful to 1 gallon of water

Gray Bulb Rot

Symptoms: Dry rot begins at the tip of the bulb. The flesh of the bulb becomes a reddish gray in color and the diseased portions are often covered with dark brown sclerotia or resting bodies. The bulbs finally rot away entirely.

Control: Dig up and burn all diseased bulbs. Disinfect the soil with formaldehyde before planting any other bulbs in the same area.

Insect Pests

Bulb Fly (Merodon equestris Fab.)

Identification: Small brown scars are sometimes found upon the outer scales. Bulbs are suspiciously soft and light in weight. Upon cutting the bulb open large, fat maggots are found. The color varies from grayish to yellowish white and when full-grown they are about $\frac{3}{4}$ of an inch in length.

Injury: The maggots feed upon the tissues and render the bulbs practically worthless.

Life History: See page 652.

Control: See page 652.

Lesser Bulb Fly (Eumerus strigatus Fall.)

Identification: Bulbs become soft and light in weight and upon examination maggots will be found feeding upon the tissues. The maggots are grayish to yellowish-white, about $\frac{1}{2}$ inch in length when full grown and the body is very much wrinkled. They may be readily distinguished from the larvæ of Merodon equestris by this characteristic wrinkled appearance.

Injury: Same as that of the Bulb Fly.

Life History: See page 652.

Control: See page 652.

Bulb Mite

Identification: Minute, whitish mites, bead-like in form, found in large numbers within the bulb scales. Reddish-brown spots appear at the point of injury.

Injury: The mites suck the juices from the plant tissues and the bulbs become soft and mushy. The vitality of the bulb is weakened and as a result growth is stunted. The leaves turn a sickly yellow and the flower buds either fail to develop or produce distorted blooms.

Life History: See page 651.

Control: See page 651.

Nematodes

Identification: Upon cutting open an infested bulb a brown ring will be found, and with the use of a hand lens one may detect the nematodes, which are minute worms of à transparent color and hardly more than 1/25 of an inch in length.

Injury: Plants make stunted growth. The leaves become curiously twisted and distorted and lie prostrate on the ground, turning yellow and dying prematurely. Thickened specks or speckles are produced upon the leaves and are very characteristic of infestation.

Life History: The eggs, four to five hundred being laid by a single female, are deposited within the tissues of the plant. Upon hatching, the larvae usually remain within the plant but occasionally they migrate through the soil to other hosts. It is during this stage that they so often find their way into the greenhouse or into the garden when fresh soil is brought in. Located in the mouth of each worm is a sharply pointed, spear-like apparatus which is used to bore through the root tissues when a new host plant is attacked, and it is also used while feeding. During the first two to three weeks after hatching the male and female larvae are identical in size and shape. During the molting period, however, when the old skin is shed, the female undergoes a distinct change and becomes pear-shaped, being pearly white in color. The male remains spindle-shaped.

In the South the worms winter over in the open. In the North they are usually killed by the cold unless harbored in frames or in greenhouses.

Controls: Destroy all badly infested bulbs. Bulbs which are only lightly infested or of which one may be suspicious may be given the following treatment:

Submerge bulbs for three hours in water kept at a temperature of 110° F. Plunge immediately in cold water after treatment.

Nasturtium

Disease
Wilt

Symptoms: The lower leaves turn yellow in the early stages and this condition gradually spreads over the entire plant. The sap tubes become brown and the plants eventually wilt and die.

Nature of the Disease: The wilt of nasturtiums is caused by Bacterium solanacearum E. F. S., the same bacteria that causes the wilt of potatoes.

Control: At present no remedy is known. Diseased plants should be pulled up and burned.

Insect Pests
Aphids

Identification: Soft-bodied, louse-like insects usually found clustered on the tips of the young, growing shoots. The species that infests nasturtiums is black in color.

Injury: Aphids suck the juices from the plant, causing the leaves and stems to become curled and distorted.

Life History: See page 631.

Control: See page 632.

Cabbage Looper

Identification: Greenish caterpillars with a white line along each side of the body and two lines near the middle of the back. The middle half of the body is without legs, and both when resting and when moving the caterpillar is in a very characteristic humped position.

Injury: The caterpillars feed upon the leaves.

Life History: See page 656.

Control: See page 636.

Cabbage Worm

Identification: Small, velvety-green caterpillars somewhat more than an inch in length when full grown.

Injury: The caterpillars feed upon the foliage.

Life History: See page 636.

Control: See page 636.

Œnothera (Evening Primrose)

Insect Pest
Primrose Flea Beetle

Identification: A small, very active beetle, a metallic blue in color.

Injury: Both the larvæ and the adult beetles feed upon the foliage. If the infestation is severe the leaves may become completely skeletonized.

Life History: The adult beetles usually appear early in June and the females deposit their eggs upon the leaves of the host plant. Upon hatching, the larvae feed for a short time and then pass into the pupa stage, the second generation emerging late in July. The winter is passed either in the pupa or adult stage.

Control: Dust with 5% DDT.

Pansy

Diseases

Anthracnose

Symptoms: Small brown spots with a narrow, dark border appear on the foliage and the petals. The flowers are usually malformed and fail to produce seed. If the disease is not checked the plants eventually die.

Nature of the Disease: A fungous disease caused by Colletotrichum violæ-tricoloris Smith. The spores of the fungus are carried on the seed and infection may usually be traced to this source.

Control: Spray thoroughly with Bordeaux as soon as trouble is detected. It is also wise to pull up and burn all badly infected plants in order to check the spread of the ripened spores.

Leaf Spot

Symptoms: Dead-looking spots appear on the leaves. In the very early stages the spots are small with dark margins but they rapidly become larger until the whole leaf is involved. The petals of the flowers also become blotched and spotted; flower buds fail to open or produce distorted bloom.

Nature of the Disease: A fungous disease caused by Cercospora violæ Sacc.

Control: Spray every few weeks with Bordeaux or with ammoniacal-copper carbonate. Destroy badly diseased plants.

Rust

Symptoms: Small, reddish-brown pustules found upon the leaves and stems.

Nature of the Disease: A fungous disease caused by Puccinia violæ.

Control: Pull up and burn all infected plants. Dust remaining plants with superfine sulphur as a precautionary measure.

Yellows

Symptoms: Plants become dwarfed and stunted. Foliage turns a greenish yellow.

Nature of the Disease. See page 633.

Control: At present no effective control is known. Pull up and burn all diseased plants.

Insect Pests

Aphids

Identification: Soft-bodied, louse-like insects usually found clustered along the tips of the young growing shoots. The species that most commonly infests pansy plants is pale green.

Injury: Aphids suck the juices from the plant, causing it to have a sickly, unhealthy appearance.

Life History: See page 631.

Control: See page 632.

Violet Sawfly

Identification: Small, slug-like larvæ, bluish black in color with conspicuous white spots on the back and sides. When full grown they are about $\frac{1}{2}$ inch in length.

Injury: The larvæ are usually found close to the ground, feeding upon the lower leaves, but if the infestation is severe the entire plant may be eaten.

Life History: Eggs are laid on lower surface of the leaves; pupation takes place in stalks of pithy plants and adults emerge in about 2 weeks.

Control: Spray or dust thoroughly with arsenate of lead, or Rotenone, making sure to reach the lower leaves.

Peony

Diseases

Anthracnose

Symptoms: Spots appear on the stems and leaves. In the early stages the center is almost white with a dark, reddish border. Later in the season, the spots become sunken with a small black pimple in the center.

Nature of the Disease: A fungous disease which occasionally attacks peonies.

Control: Spray frequently with Bordeaux mixture. Remove and burn diseased portions of the plant.

Botrytis

Symptoms: Young shoots rot off at the ground line when 5 to 8 inches tall, the stems having a water-soaked, cankerous appearance. The rotted portion later becomes covered with a soft brown mass of spores. The flower buds turn brown and fail to open and the flower stalk is usually affected for several inches below the bud. During a severe outbreak of the disease 90 percent of the flower buds may fail to develop. Open flowers also occasionally become affected, turning dark brown and becoming a mass of rotting petals. The leaves are usually the last part of the plant to show any trace of infection, being attacked first at the tips. Large, irregular spots appear, being dark in the early stages, later fading to light brown. There are dark concentric rings within the lesions on both the leaves and the stems which are very characteristic of the disease.

Nature of the Disease: A fungous disease caused by Botrytis pæoniæ Oud. which is very destructive in many sections of the country. It is particularly prevalent in damp, rainy seasons. Small, black resting bodies, known as sclerotia, are formed in the diseased stems and the fungus is carried over the winter in this manner.

Control: As soon as the shoots poke through the ground in the spring spray with Bordeaux or with ferbam. Repeat at 10-day intervals until 4 applications have been made.

One of the most effective measures of control consists in the removal of all dead stubble. The soil should be scraped away from the base of the plant and the old stalks should be cut as close to the crown as possible.

During the growing season any shoots, leaves or flower-buds that show the least sign of infection should be immediately removed and burned. It is important that the disease be detected in the early stages as the spores are produced very rapidly and in great abundance.

Leaf Blotch

Symptoms: Large spots, 2 to 3 inches in diameter, appear on the leaves late in the season. The spots are very characteristic, being purple on the upper surface and dull brown on the lower surface. In damp weather the spots on the lower surface appear to be covered with a felt-like substance, olive-green in color.

Nature of the Disease: A fungous disease caused by Cladosporium pæoniæ Pass.

Control: As the fungus lives over the winter on the old leaves the disease may be kept almost entirely under control by cutting off and burning all top growth after the plants have become dormant in the autumn.

Mosaic Disease

Symptoms: Leaves become blotched with alternating rings of light and dark green. The spots vary considerably in size, some being small with narrow margins and others being large with much wider margins. Frequently only one or two stalks in the clump are affected.

Nature of the Disease: See page 635.

Control: See page 635.

Phytophthora Blight

Symptoms: Large, dark brown spots appear on the leaves resembling those of Botrytis but lacking the concentric markings. The buds are usually blighted and fail to open and the crown of the plant may become rotted.

Nature of the Disease: The disease is caused by the fungus Phytophthora pæoniæ Coop. and Port.

Control: Spray with Bordeaux as soon as growth begins in the spring and every few weeks during the growing season. Destroy all top growth in the autumn.

Stem Rot

Symptoms: Stalks suddenly wilt, due to rotting at the base. Large black resting bodies or sclerotia are found in the pith at the base of the plant and readily distinguish this disease from any other.

Nature of the Disease: A fungous disease caused by Sclerotiorum (Lib.) Mass. Damp, rainy weather is particularly favorable to its spread.

Control: As soon as the disease is detected, the infected stalks should be cut away close to the crown. As the fungus spreads from stalk to stalk through the soil it is well to remove the soil from about the crown, replacing it with clean sand. Manure should never be allowed to come into direct contact with the crowns. All growth above ground should be burned in the autumn.

Wilt

Symptoms: Plants show signs of wilt and gradually die. The sap tubes become clogged and when the stem is split open they appear as greenish streaks.

Nature of the Disease: The disease is caused by the fungus Verticillium albo-atrum Reinke and Berth.

Control: See page 631.

Insect Pests

Ants

Ants are frequently found on peonies, being attracted by the sweetish, sticky substance which is exuded from the buds. While they do no direct harm themselves, it is very probable that they carry the spores of fungous diseases from one plant to another provided such spores are present. It is recommended that the soil about the plants be treated with a 5% chlordane dust to control the ants.

Rose Beetle

Identification: Long-legged beetles, grayish-fawn in color and about ½ inch in length.

Injury: The beetles feed upon the flowers, completely destroying them in a very short time.

Life History: See page 635.

Control: See page 635.

Rose Cucurlio

Identification: Bright red beetles with black legs and snout, about ¼ inch in length.

Injury: The beetles eat holes in the unopened buds and also feed to some extent upon the leaves. Buds either fail to open or produce flowers riddled with holes.

Life History: See page 666.

Control: See page 666.

Nematodes causing *Root Gall*

Identification: Swollen places are found on the roots which are caused by microscopic worms. The roots are often short and stubby, the fine rootlets being covered with galls. The crown of the plant is also occasionally swollen.

Injury: The growth of the plant is very seriously affected if the infestation is severe.

Life History: See page 675.

Control: See page 675.

Oyster Shell Scale

Identification: Small, grayish white scales, resembling an oyster shell in shape, are found clustered in masses along the stems.

Injury: The scales suck the juices from the plant, causing general lack of vigor and the eventual death of the infested shoots.

Life History: During the winter the eggs are protected by the hard, shell-like covering of the old scales. The young hatch out about the end of May or early in June. At this stage they are soft-bodied and look like small, yellowish-white specks on the stems. Later in the season the hard, shell-like covering is formed.

Control: About June 1st and again about June 15th spray with one of the following: DDT, malathion, or nicotine sulfate.

It is possible to destroy the scales at this time while they are in the soft-bodied stage. Later in the season after the hard scale-like covering has formed it is practically impossible to reach them as any spray strong enough to be effective would be injurious to a growing plant.

As a means of destroying wintering places, all growth above ground should be cut down and burned in the autumn after the plants have become dormant.

Stalk Borer

Identification: Slender caterpillars about 2 inches in length. The young caterpillars are brown with white stripes. When full-grown they lose their stripes and become a solid, dirty gray in color.

Injury: The stalk borer makes a small round hole in the stem and tunnels up through the stalk, causing the injured shoot to wilt suddenly and break over.

Life History: See page 634.

Control: See page 634.

Petunia

Disease

Mosaic

Symptoms: The foliage becomes a mottled yellow and green in color. The leaves are frequently distorted and the growth of the plant is stunted.

Nature of the Disease: See page 635.

Control: See page 635.

Insect Pests

Orthezia

Identification: The young nymphs are very tiny, dark green in color and wingless with a row of waxy plates extending back over the body. The adult females have a very conspicuous white, fluted egg sack which extends back from the body for a distance of two or more times the diameter of the body.

Injury: The orthezias are closely related to the scales and suck the juices from the plant tissues.

Control: See page 641.

Potato Flea Beetle

Identification: Small, very active beetle about $\frac{1}{16}$ of an inch long, black in color. The hind legs are longer than the front legs and enable the beetle to jump like a flea when disturbed.

Injury: The beetles feed upon the foliage, making many small holes either round or irregular in shape. The leaves have the appearance of being peppered with fine shot. The foliage becomes badly disfigured and if the infestation is very serious it may cause the death of the plant.

Life History: The adults hibernate during the winter under leaves or trash and emerge early in the spring. The eggs, which are minute in size, are laid in the soil about the plants. The larvae are small, slender, whitish worms. They feed to some extent upon the roots and underground stems of weeds and cultivated plants but do comparatively little damage. After feeding for a few weeks they pass into the pupa stage in the soil and a short time later the adult flea beetles emerge. There are usually two generations a year.

Control: Spray or dust with DDT or Rotenone.

Yellow Woolly-bear Caterpillar

Identification: A caterpillar about 2 inches in length when full-grown. The body is completely covered with long hairs which vary in color from pale yellow to reddish brown.

Injury: The caterpillars feed upon the foliage.

Life History: See page 642.

Control: See page 642.

Phlox

Diseases

Leaf Spot

Symptoms: Dark spots, ranging in color from brown to black, appear on the leaves and in time the plant may become almost completely defoliated.

Nature of the Disease: A fungous disease caused by Septoria divaricata Ell. and Ev. The fungus lives over the winter on the fallen leaves and is ready to reinfect the new growth in the spring.

Control: Spray with Captan or Fermate; or dust with copper-lime dust when the plants are wet with dew. Rake up and burn all dead leaves in the autumn.

Mildew

Symptoms: The foliage becomes covered with a white, powdery substance. In the most advanced stages the affected areas turn black. Mildew is very disfiguring to the plant and is injurious to its growth. Especially prevalent in damp seasons.

Nature of the Disease: The disease is caused by the fungus Erysiphe cichoracearum D. C.

Control: See page 639. In the autumn remove the tops and rake up and burn fallen leaves. It is well to divide the clumps and give the plants plenty of space.

Phlox Blight

Symptoms: The lower leaves of the plant become spotted and gradually turn brown and die. In the majority of cases only the lower portion of the plant is affected. The upper portion of the plant continues to make good growth, appears healthy and vigorous, and produces normal bloom. In occasional instances the disease progresses slowly upward, eventually killing the entire stem.

Nature of the Disease: In the past it has been thought that Phlox Blight was caused either by a fungus or by injury from some insect or mite, but investigations carried on at Cornell and at the New Jersey Agricultural Experiment Station tend to prove that the trouble is attributable to the peculiar growth habits of certain types of phlox. In the paniculata types the new shoots in the spring are borne on the stem of the previous season's growth, and these new shoots obtain their water and nutrients through the old stems. As growth advances the old stems begin to decay and there is an apparent disturbance in the flow of nutrients into the young and vigorously growing shoots, causing the characteristic symptoms of phlox blight, the theory being that the growing tips draw the moisture from the lower leaves. Some varieties appear to be much more susceptible than others, and when phlox plants are grown in a very moist climate the trouble is less severe.

The suffruticosa types of phlox seldom suffer from blight, due to the fact that the new shoots start from a much lower point on the old stems or directly from the crown, and they soon become established on their own roots.

Measures of Control: Various measures of control are recommended. The removal of the first shoots in early spring will induce the formation of new bud growth, either directly from the crown of the plant or at a point lower down on the old stem, and it has been found that such growth is comparatively free from blight. Another measure of control which is proving very satisfactory is to prune back the old stalks to sound wood and to paint them with Bordeaux paste.

Insect Pests

Black Blister Beetle

Identification: Slender jet black beetles about $\frac{1}{2}$ inch in length with very prominent head and neck. It exudes a yellow oily fluid from joints of legs when disturbed.

Injury: The beetles feed upon the flowers, completely destroying them in a very short time.

Life History: See page 633.

Control: See page 633.

Corn Ear Worm

Identification: Large striped worms about 2 inches in length when full-grown. They vary in color from light green to brown and the stripes which run lengthwise with the body are alternating light and dark. The head is yellow, the legs almost black.

Injury: The caterpillars feed upon the plants.

Life History: See page 637.

Control: See page 637.

Nematodes

Identification: Minute, microscopic worms. Their presence is usually detected by their characteristic injury to the plant.

Injury: Plants are dwarfed and stunted. Few flowers develop. Foliage frequently becomes spotted and distorted. Small, swollen, knotty growths are found upon the roots.

Life History: See page 675.

Control: See page 675.

Physalis Francheti (Japanese Lantern Plant)

Insect Pest

Tortoise Beetle or Gold Bug

Identification: A small golden beetle about $\frac{1}{4}$ inch in length. Occasionally black spots or stripes are found on the body. The beetle is turtle-shaped, being flat on the underside with the head and legs partially hidden.

Injury: The beetles feed upon the foliage.

Life History: See page 656.

Control: See page 656.

Primrose
Diseases
Chlorosis

Symptoms: Leaves become somewhat mottled in appearance, yellow and white. Plants fail to make vigorous growth.

Nature of the Disease: A physiological disease which is thought to be due to intense acidity in the soil.

Control: An application of the following is recommended. Three applications should be made, one week apart.

1 oz. sulfate of iron   1 oz. nitrate of soda   15 gal. water

Rot

Symptoms: Plants rot off at the crown, becoming covered with a gray mold.

Nature of the Disease: The disease is caused by Botrytis vulgaris Fr. which is very prevalent under conditions of extreme dampness.

Control: Spray with Bordeaux or dust with copper-lime dust.

Insect Pest
Potato Flea Beetle

Identification: A small, very active beetle, metallic blue in color. The hind legs are longer than the front legs and enable the beetle to jump like a flea.

Injury: The beetles feed upon the foliage, making many small holes, either round or irregular in shape. The leaves have the appearance of being peppered with fine shot.

Life History: See page 660.

Control: See page 660.

Pyrethrum
Disease
Yellows

Symptoms: Plants become dwarfed if attacked when young. Leaves that are not mature at the time infection takes place turn bright yellow. Blossoms become dwarfed and distorted, frequently developing only on one side. Plants are seldom killed outright, usually living on until cut down by frost.

Nature of the Disease: See page 633.

Control: See page 633.

Rose
Diseases
Black Spot

Symptoms: Black spots appear on the foliage. Leaves turn yellow and drop prematurely. The spots are somewhat circular in shape, having irregular margins, and they occasionally reach a diameter of half an inch or more. They are confined entirely to the upper surface of the leaf. The disease first makes its appearance early in the summer and becomes particularly virulent later in the season. It saps the vitality of the plant to a great extent and in severe cases causes complete defoliation.

Nature of the Disease: Black Spot is caused by a fungus known as Diplocarpon rose. The winter spores, which are protected during the cold months by minute sacs, mature at about the time that roses begin their growth in the spring. These spores are carried to the leaves by wind, splashing rain, and other agencies and when conditions of temperature and moisture are favorable they germinate, sending out tiny germ-tubes which penetrate the outer covering or cuticle of the leaf. When safely within the leaf these germ-tubes develop a vegetative, thread-like structure which is known as mycelium. About two weeks after infection has taken place these mycelium produce millions of spores which are spoken of as secondary or summer spores. These are readily blown about by the wind, finding lodgment on nearby plants. If conditions happen to be extremely favorable they germinate within a few hours. Thus successive crops of these summer spores are produced throughout the season at intervals of from two to three weeks and the disease gains tremendous headway as the season advances unless proper measures of control are taken. The fungus lives over the winter on dead and decaying leaves, special winter spores being produced.

Control: Black Spot cannot be cured but it *can* be kept under control. After a leaf is once attacked, after the minute germ-tubes have once penetrated through the outer tissues, there is no chemical known which will kill the fungus and not be injurious to the growing plant. The problem, therefore, is to prevent infection, and fortunately, with a reasonable amount of care, this is possible. The importance of prompt and systematic attention cannot be overemphasized. If the foliage is coated with an effective fungicide the spores will fail to germinate, and will be unable to start new centers of infection. As a matter of further precaution all leaves which drop to the ground should be immediately raked up and burned. As the spores require a certain amount of moisture in order to germinate it is essential that the foliage be protected particularly well during rainy weather.

The following controls are recommended:

Captan, Dithane, Fermate, Parzate, Sulphur, and Zerlate.

There are a number of excellent commercial products on the market which are combination sprays or dusts for the control of Black Spot and other rose diseases, as well as many insect pests. The convenience of using a preparation of this nature is very great and it is the practical solution to the problem of disease and insect control for the average gardener. Such sprays or dusts usually contain a good fungicide such as Fermate, a stomach poison, and a contact poison.

Regardless of the type of spray or dust used, frequent applications must be made if good control is to be obtained. During periods of rainy weather applications should be made at 5- or 6-day intervals, during dry weather at 8- to 9-day intervals. A two-week interval between applications is too long and will not give satisfactory control. Both the upper and the under surfaces of the leaves must be reached. There are few accomplishments which bring greater satisfaction to the gardener than rose beds filled with vigorous, healthy bushes with luxuriant, disease-free foliage. If spraying is done thoroughly and frequently, it is an achievement which is well within the realm of possibility, and one in which a rose grower may take justifiable pride.

Brown Canker

Symptoms: In the early stages small, purplish-red areas appear on the stems and the petioles of the leaves. As the disease progresses the spots develop a lighter center with a definite purple margin. When the leaves and flowers are affected the same characteristic spots appear, being more or less cinnamon-buff in color. Usually only the outer, more exposed petals of the flowers are affected. When the flower buds are attacked they either fail to open or produce distorted, malformed blooms. In some cases a branch becomes completely girdled by Brown Canker and occasionally an entire plant will succumb to the disease if it is not checked.

Nature of the Disease: Brown Canker is caused by cryptosporella umbrina, a disease which has gained much headway during the past decade and it causes severe losses in many sections.

Control: Recent experiments have proved that thorough and systematic spraying with Bordeaux mixture will keep Brown Canker pretty well under control. Spraying should begin early in the spring and continue throughout the growing season.

All diseased canes should be removed at time of pruning. Do not use any type of winter mulch which will keep the canes moist for long periods, such as peat moss or leaves.

Stem Canker

Symptoms: In the early stages Stem Canker appears as a slender, purple stripe on the branches. As the disease progresses the affected area becomes dry and brown and somewhat sunken and the stem may become partially or entirely girdled. It reduces the vigor of the plant, causing sickly, weakened growth above the point of attack.

Nature of the Disease: Stem Canker is caused by Coniothyrium frickelii Sacc., the same fungus which causes the cane blight of raspberries.

Control: The fungus of stem canker usually enters through wounds or scars on the stems. The best measure of control is to prune stems back to a point below infection, and when cutting blooms always to cut close to a bud or leaf axil. It is a wise precaution to dip the shears in a corrosive sublimate solution.

Leaf Rust

Symptoms: In the early stages bright orange-colored pustules are found on the undersurface of the leaves. As the disease progresses the pustules become brick-red in color.

Nature of the Disease: Leaf Rust is a fungous disease caused by Phragmidium sp. It causes the foliage to become unhealthy in appearance and if the infection is severe the vitality of the plant is seriously affected.

Control: Frequent dusting with superfine sulphur will keep the disease under control to a considerable extent. Captan, Fermate and Parzate are also recommended.

Affected leaves should be picked off and burned. All fallen leaves should be raked up and burned in the autumn.

Mildew

Symptoms: In the early stages grayish or whitish spots are found on the young leaves and shoots. These spots gradually enlarge and the stems, foliage and unopened buds become almost completely covered with a white, powdery substance. In the most advanced stages the affected areas turn black. Not only is mildew very disfiguring but it also seriously affects the vigor and growth of the plants. If it is not checked the foliage and flower buds become dwarfed and malformed and many of the leaves drop prematurely.

Nature of the Disease: Mildew is a fungous disease caused by Sphærotheca pannosa. It is a mold-like growth, the greater portion being confined to the outer surface of the leaves. The minute white threads form a network with their numerous strands and at frequent intervals chains of egg-shaped spores are borne on upright branches. When mature these pores are blown about by the wind and find lodgment on nearby plants. As soon as temperature and moisture conditions are favorable they germinate and establish new centers of infection. The individual spores are comparatively short-lived but new ones are constantly being produced. Special spores are produced to carry the fungus over the winter months and these are ready to start growth as soon as spring comes.

The original source of infection may usually be traced to spores brought into the garden when new plants were purchased. Mildew is often very troublesome on roses grown under glass, and as the spores are blown about by the slightest wind it is probable that roses growing in a garden some distance away might become infected in this manner.

Mildew is especially prevalent during damp, rainy seasons as the spores are then provided with ideal conditions for germination. Some varieties are much more susceptible to mildew than others. The Crimson Ramblers and closely related forms are highly susceptible.

Control: Mildew can be kept under complete control with frequent dusting or spraying. If dusting is done early, before the disease has gained headway, and is continued throughout the season, fine dusting sulphur will prove very satisfactory. However, if mildew has gotten a start a spray of wettable sulphur or Karathane (sold as Mildex) will prove more effective. Some of the general-purpose sprays containing ammoniacal copper carbonate or general-purpose dusts containing 60 to 75% sulphur will also give excellent control.

Precaution: Sulphur will burn the foliage if applied when temperatures are high, 80° F. or above.

Stem Rust

Symptoms: Canker-like spots, bright orange in color, appear on the petioles of the leaves and the stems of the young shoots. The affected shoots frequently become distorted.

Nature of the Disease: A fungous disease caused by Earlea speciosa.

Control: All infected shoots should be cut off and burned.

Bronzing of Leaves

Symptoms: A single leaf or several leaves on the same shoot become a mottled bronze in color, turn yellow and drop prematurely.

Nature of the Disease: A physiological disease due to some functional disturbance in the growth of the plant. It may sometimes be due to very rapid growth caused by the drastic pruning of some particular shoot.

Insect Pests

Aphids

There are two species of aphids that attack roses, the Rose Aphid (Macrosiphum rosæ L.) and the Small Green Rose Aphid (Francoa Myzaphis rosarum) (Kalt). The latter is usually the most troublesome in greenhouses but it is also frequently found on outdoor roses in the South and in California. The identification, injury and control of the two species are practically the same.

Identification: Soft-bodied, louse-like insects. Body globular or pear-shaped, green in color. Usually found clustered along the tips of the young growing shoots.

Injury: Aphids suck the juices from the plant, reducing its vigor and vitality and in many cases causing the leaves and flowers to become unsightly and distorted.

Life History: In the North the Rose Aphids pass the winter in the egg stage. The eggs are small, glossy black in color and are attached to the bark near the buds. The eggs hatch early in the spring, as soon as plant growth begins, and the young aphids begin feeding. The first brood which hatches out from the eggs becomes mature in about two weeks and from then on, through the balance of the season, living young are produced. As each female gives birth daily to several young they multiply with startling rapidity. These living young are produced from unfertilized eggs and are all females. In the autumn males appear and fertilize the eggs which are to carry the species over the winter. In the South they do not pass through an egg stage as the winters are mild and they breed throughout the year.

Control: See pages 631 and 632.

Japanese Beetles

Identification: Large, handsome beetles, a metallic, greenish-bronze in color with two conspicuous and several small white spots near the tip of the abdomen. During the middle of the day they are very active, making rapid flight when disturbed. During the evening they are more sluggish.

Injury: The Japanese beetles are among the most destructive of any of our garden pests. They feed voraciously upon the foliage, buds, and open flowers, and will completely skeletonize a bush in a very short time. They are gregarious in habit and sometimes as many as twenty or thirty beetles will be found clustered on a single flower bud.

Life History: The adult beetles appear early in July and for a period of about six weeks they ravage the entire countryside, feeding upon fruit and shade trees, field crops and vegetables, and many ornamentals. The female beetles deposit their eggs in the soil, usually selecting an open, sunny area where the grass is short. The larvae hatch in several weeks and begin feeding on decaying vegetable matter in the soil and also to a considerable extent upon the roots of grasses and other plants. At this stage they do considerable damage to lawns and golf courses. At the approach of cold weather the grubs burrow down into the soil to a depth of six to twelve inches and construct a little earthen cell in which they pass the winter. In the spring the grubs work their way toward the surface again and feed for several weeks before passing into the pupa stage. The pupa stage extends over a period of about six weeks and the adult beetles then emerge.

Control: In order to effectively control Japanese beetles the foliage must be kept coated with a dust or spray as soon as the beetles appear. Weekly spraying is often necessary in order to keep the foliage sufficiently coated. One of the most effective controls is Sevin, used as a spray. All-purpose sprays containing lindane or malathion are also effective.

Beetle traps are satisfactory in isolated gardens but in areas where beetles are prevalent they tend to attract the beetles unless neighbors use them also.

Reduce the population of Japanese beetle grubs by treating lawn areas (see page 195).

These measures of control are effective against most other beetles which are occasionally found on roses.

Leaf Rollers

There are a number of caterpillars of this type which attack roses. The life history, injury and control are practically the same in all cases.

Identification: Rose Leaf Roller (Archips rosaceana Harr.). Small, active caterpillar, about ¾ of an inch long. Olive-green in color with a black head.

Rose Leaf Tier (Archips [Cacœcia] rosaceana Harr.). Small caterpillar varying in color from yellow to light green and distinguished by an oblique band running across the body.

Red-banded Leaf Roller (Eulia velutiana Wlk.). Small caterpillar, similar to the above but readily distinguished by the red band on the body.

Injury: The caterpillars feed upon the foliage and the blossoms, their work being very characteristic, as they roll the leaves together and web them with fine, silken threads.

Life History: The moths vary somewhat in appearance according to the species. They deposit their eggs in tiny masses on the foliage and within a few weeks the caterpillars hatch and begin feeding. They become full-grown in about a month and pupate within the rolled leaves. Several weeks later the moths emerge and the life cycle begins again. Two broods are usually produced during the summer.

Control: See page 634.

Mites (Red Spider)

The species of mite most commonly found on roses and on many other garden plants, such as phlox and hollyhocks, is the two-spotted spider mite, commonly called red spider.

Identification: Almost infinitesimal in size, being less than 1-50 of an inch. Body is oval with two dark spots on the back.

Injury: The mites feed on the undersurface of the foliage. Leaves take on an unhealthy appearance, becoming gray, reddish- or yellowish-brown. If the infestation is severe and remains unchecked the plant may become completely defoliated. Tiny webs are made on the undersurface of the leaves, and sometimes on the tips of new shoots and on flower-buds.

Life History: The female lays her eggs on the under-surface of the foliage. Upon hatching the young mites feed for a few days, then pass into a resting stage, molt, begin active feeding again, then pass into the resting stage again before developing into adults. The time required from egg to adult depends upon the temperature. When temperatures are low, ranging around 55° F. it requires 40 days. When temperatures reach 75° F. it requires only 5 days. In midsummer, particularly when the humidity is high, mite populations build up very rapidly.

Control: Measures of control should be undertaken as soon as infestation is noted. Any of the following will give excellent control if used frequently: Aramite, Dimite and Malathion. There are a number of all-purpose insecticides on the market which will also give good control.

Precaution: When DDT is used frequently or in large amounts it tends to kill the natural enemies of the mites and when this occurs mites are apt to become a serious problem.

Rose Beetle, also known as **Rose Chafer** or **Rose Bug**

Identification: Long-legged beetles, grayish fawn in color and about ¼ inch in length.

Injury: The beetles feed chiefly upon the flowers. Sometimes a dozen or more will be found clustered upon a single bloom which will be completely demolished. Rose beetles are, beyond any doubt, the most destructive of our rose pests. They appear in hordes just as the first roses are coming into bloom and their depredations continue throughout the height of the rose season.

In closely built suburban areas rose bugs are seldom seen and cause little damage, due probably to the fact that conditions are not so favorable for them, as the land is too intensively cultivated. In open country districts, however, where open fields abound, and particularly where the soil is of a sandy texture, conditions are ideal for them and they make the most of their opportunities by increasing in alarming numbers. They are not apt to be so numerous in sections where the soil is of a heavy clay texture, as it is almost impossible for the females to deposit their eggs, and consequently they never gain much headway.

Life History: The adult rose beetles appear early in June and feed for about six weeks. Toward the end of this period the females deposit their eggs. Under normal conditions each female deposits three sets of eggs, about twelve being laid at one time. The beetle selects a rough, grassy place where the soil is somewhat sandy, burrows into the ground for a depth of three to six inches and lays her eggs singly in tiny soil pockets. The eggs, which are oval, white and smooth in appearance, hatch in about two weeks. The larvae feed both on decaying vegetable matter and upon the roots of weeds and grasses, reaching maturity about the latter part of October. They then burrow down into the soil to a depth of about twelve inches and curl themselves up in little earthen cells for the winter. In the spring the grubs work their way up toward the surface again and usually feed for a short time before they pupate. The pupa stage varies from three to four weeks and the adult beetles then emerge just as the first roses are coming into bloom.

Control: Apply 5% DDT dust about every 4 days as the flowers open, or spray with 50% wettable DDT, 2 tablespoonfuls to 1 gallon of water.

Protection: As a means of protection against rose beetles, where infestations are severe, beds may be temporarily covered by mosquito netting or a cheap grade of tobacco cloth tacked onto a light frame.

Rose Cucurlio

Identification: Bright red beetles with black legs and snout. Small in size, measuring only about $\frac{1}{4}$ inch in length.

Injury: The beetles eat holes in the unopened buds and in the fruits and they also feed upon the leaves and flower stems to some extent. Many of the injured buds fail to open and the petals of those that do expand are usually riddled with holes.

Life History: The beetles appear early in June. The eggs, which are oval in shape, are deposited in the holes which the beetles bore in the buds and young fruits. Within a week or ten days the eggs hatch and the small, white, legless larvae feed upon the seeds and flower petals until they are full-grown. In late summer the grubs migrate down to the ground near the base of the plant where they enter the pupa stage and pass the winter.

Control: If the infestation is light the beetles may be picked off by hand. All dried-up buds and fruits should be cut off and burned as they are likely to contain eggs or larvae. Wild roses growing in the vicinity may become a serious source of infestation and if so they should be destroyed.

Spraying with arsenate of lead, 1 ounce to $1\frac{1}{2}$ gallons of water, or with DDT, will help to keep the beetles under control.

Rose Leaf hopper

Identification: Small, narrow, yellowish-white insects. Very active, hopping quickly from one leaf to another when disturbed.

Injury: The nymphs and adults feed usually from the undersurface of the leaves, sucking the juices from the plant. The leaves at first appear yellow and somewhat faded and if the infestation is severe they later turn brown and die.

Life History: The adult females deposit their eggs in late summer under the bark of the rose bushes. The winter is passed in the egg stage and the young nymphs hatch out early in May. They begin feeding immediately and pass through several molts before reaching the adult stage.

Control: Nicotine sulfate will kill hoppers which are hit by the spray. General-purpose sprays containing pyrethrum or Rotenone are fairly effective. DDT is very effective but sometimes results in an increase in the mite population.

Rose Midge

Identification: Adult a very minute, yellowish-brown fly; larvae small, whitish to orange.

Injury: The maggots feed on the flower buds, causing a blackening and distortion of the buds.

Life History: The adult female lays her eggs within the flower and leaf buds. Larvae feed on the buds, and when grown drop to the ground and pupate. The life cycle covers only two to three weeks in midsummer and successive generations are produced.

Control: At the first indication of trouble spray the foliage and the ground about the plants with 50% wettable DDT, 2 tablespoonfuls to 1 gallon of water. Two or three applications ten days apart will usually give good control.

Rose Scale

Identification: Small scale insects, snow-white in color, usually found clustered thickly along the branches and twigs. The female scales are circular in shape, being about $\frac{1}{10}$ of an inch in diameter. The male scales are considerably smaller, being long and narrow in shape.

Injury: The scales feed upon the plant juices, causing weakened growth and general lack of vigor. If they become sufficiently numerous they cause the death of the plant.

Life History: The young scales emerge from beneath the scale of the female parent and for the first few days they crawl about actively upon the plant. They find a favorable location and then insert their thread-like mouth parts into the bark and begin feeding. After a short time they pass through the first molt and at this stage they lose their legs, and the scale-like covering forms over the body. The scale is composed of fine threads of wax which have exuded from the wall of the body and have become practically welded together. The female scales molt twice, remaining under the scale for the period of their entire life. The males pass through four molts, and at the end of this period they become minute, two-winged, yellowish insects with three pairs of legs, and with eyes and antennæ. They do not feed in this stage but move about actively, mating with the female scales. The female scales continue to feed for a short time after mating.

Control: Prune out badly infested canes. Spray in early spring while plants are still dormant with commercial lime-sulphur, 1 part to 9 parts of water. The temperature should be above 45° F. when the application is made.

A miscible oil, applied as a dormant spray, will give fairly satisfactory control.

Malathion, applied as a spray during the summer, will eliminate some of the scales in the crawler stage.

Rose Slugs

There are three distinct species which are apt to be troublesome on roses:

American Rose Slug

Identification: Greenish when young, becoming more yellow as they grow older. $\frac{1}{2}$ to $\frac{3}{4}$ of an inch in length.

Injury: The slugs do most of their feeding at night, skeletonizing the upper surface of the leaves. The foliage becomes unsightly and eventually dries up and drops off.

Life History: The adult flies are black in color, about $\frac{1}{5}$ of an inch long, and they possess four wings. They appear at about the time that the rose bushes start growth in the spring, and the females deposit their eggs between the tissues of the leaves. The eggs hatch about 10 days later and the slugs begin feeding, attaining full growth in from two to three weeks. When mature they burrow into the soil to a depth of an inch or two and construct a cocoon in which to pupate during the winter. The following spring the flies emerge and the life cycle begins again.

Control: Various measures of control are recommended. A strong spray of water from a hose will usually dislodge and kill many of the slugs.

Arsenate of lead, used as a spray, is very effective.

Nicotine sulfate may be used with good success provided each individual slug is reached.

Bristly Rose Slug

Identification: Yellowish-green in color, about $\frac{3}{8}$ of an inch in length, the body being covered with little bristly hairs.

Injury: When young the slugs merely skeletonize the leaves, feeding upon the undersurface, but as they grow older they eat large irregular holes along the edge of the leaves.

Life History: The adult is a black, four-winged fly, slightly larger than that of the American Rose Slug. The female deposits her eggs just under the surface of the leaf petiole. The eggs, which are small, white and

round, hatch in from 7 to 10 days and the young slugs make rapid growth. Six or more generations are produced during the season and the winter is passed in the pupa stage, the cocoons, which are very thin and transparent, being protected by rubbish and old leaves.

Control: Same as for American Rose Slug.

Coiled Rose Slug

Identification: The upper surface of the body is green with a metallic sheen. There are numerous white spots on the body and a wide band runs across the middle of the abdomen. The slug is about $\frac{3}{4}$ of an inch in length.

Injury: The slugs feed along the edge of the leaves with the tip of the body usually coiled beneath the leaf. The entire leaf surface will, in time, be destroyed by them.

Life History: The adult flies appear in early spring and the females deposit their eggs, singly, upon the undersurface of the leaves. The larvae hatch out within a few days and begin feeding. When full-grown they bore into the pith of a dead or decaying branch and pass into the pupa stage. Two broods are produced each season, the winter being passed in the pupa stage.

Control: Same as for American Rose Slug.

Rose Stem Borer

Identification: The larvae, which are seldom seen unless an infested shoot is slit open, are small, whitish caterpillars.

Injury: The larvae feed within the shoots, making small tunnels which weaken the branches and eventually cause their death.

Life History: The adult of the Rose Stem Borer is a wasp-like insect which appears early in the summer. The females puncture the shoots and deposit their eggs within the tissues. A short time later the larvae hatch out and begin feeding within the stem.

Control: Infested shoots should be cut off and burned.

Rose Stem Girdler

Identification: Small, whitish caterpillars. Their presence may be detected by the characteristic swelling of the shoot.

Injury: The larvae tunnel their way into the stem, making short, spiral mines. The shoots swell over the affected area.

Life History: The adult beetles appear in June and July and the females deposit their eggs on the bark of the branches. Upon hatching the larvae tunnel their way into the shoots and begin feeding. When full grown they construct little cells in the pith of the plant and pass into the pupa stage.

Control: Cut off and burn all infested shoots.

Rose Weevil, also known as **Fuller's Rose Beetle**

Identification: Dull, brownish-gray beetle, slightly over ¼ inch in length with a white line running diagonally across each wing.

Injury: The larvae feed upon the roots to some extent and the adult beetles feed upon the foliage, buds, and open blooms. They are most commonly found on greenhouse roses but occasionally they become a serious menace to roses grown in the open. Most of their feeding is done at night.

Life History: The female beetle lays her eggs in late summer in crevices of bark or at the base of the host plant. The larvae feed on the roots and the pupae stage is passed in the soil.

Control: Dust with DDT, Chlordane or Lindane.

Thrips

The Flower Thrip is the species most commonly found on roses.

Identification: Adults are very small, about $\frac{1}{20}$ of an inch, brownish-yellow to amber in color with an orange thorax. The young are lemon yellow.

Injury: The thrips feed only upon the flowers, causing the buds to turn brown. Blooms are distorted and buds frequently fail to open. The thrips may often be observed inside the petals, usually near the base. They have a preference for light colors.

Life History: The thrips breed in grasses and weeds and migrate to the garden. The entire life cycle covers only two weeks, and generations build up very rapidly.

Control: Spray with Lindane. A bomb may be used for spot treatment. As a precautionary measure infected flower buds should be cut off and burned.

Salvia Farinacea (Mealycup Sage)

Insect Pest

Aphids

Identification: Soft-bodied, louse-like insects, usually found clustered near the tips of the young, growing shoots and along the flower stems. The species that attacks Salvia farinacea is black.

Injury: Aphids suck the juices from the plant, causing a general lack of vigor and stunted growth. The leaves at the tips of the growing shoots become curled and distorted and the flower heads are stunted and malformed.

Life History: See page 631.

Control: See page 632.

Sweet Pea

Diseases

Anthracnose

Symptoms: The growing tips of the plant wilt and die, becoming white and brittle. As the disease progresses the entire plant becomes affected and the flower buds dry up and fail to open. When an infected leaf is examined under a hand lens it is found to be covered with very small pustules of a peculiar salmon-pink color. These pustules are also prominent on the seed pods. Small cankers are sometimes produced on the stems and leaf petioles.

Nature of the Disease: The anthracnose of the sweet pea is caused by Glomerella rufomaculans (B.) V. Sch. and Sp., the same fungus which produces the bitter rot of the apple and the ripe rot of the grape. It is confined almost entirely to sweet peas grown in the open. Only in rare instances has it been found on greenhouse plants. The spores of the fungus are carried on the seed and the disease is usually transmitted in this way.

Control: Remove and destroy all diseased plants and nearby refuse. Soak the seed for five minutes, just before planting, in a 5 percent solution of formaldehyde. Spray occasionally with Bordeaux as a preventive.

Collar Rot, also known as Stem Rot

Symptoms: Young seedlings are particularly susceptible to this disease although older plants are occasionally attacked. The plants wilt at the tip, the leaves show a peculiar flagging, and the stem rots off at the ground line. The roots are practically never affected. The disease spreads quickly from plant to plant and is always fatal.

Nature of the Disease: Collar Rot is caused by Sclerotinia libertiana Fckl., the same fungus which attacks a number of different plants. The fungus penetrates the stem at the ground level, clogging up the vessels and preventing the flow of sap from the roots to the upper portion of the plant. After a plant has succumbed it soon becomes covered with a white, moldy growth which is the mycelium of the fungus. The small black sclerotia or resting bodies of the fungus are later found both on and within the affected parts of the plant. The fungus lives over in the soil from year to year.

Control: If Collar Rot has proved troublesome it will be advisable to use fresh soil which is known to be free from the disease, or the soil may be sterilized with formaldehyde. Use 1 pint of 40 percent formaldehyde to 12½ gallons of water at the rate of 1 gallon to every square foot. Let the soil stand for 24 hours. Fork over and aërate well and do not plant seed for several days.

Mildew

Symptoms: Leaves turn yellow and drop prematurely. The white, powdery growth so typical of mildew is more apt to be found on the dead and fallen leaves than on the growing plant.

Nature of the Disease: This disease is caused by the fungus, microsphæra alni (Walk.) Wint.

Control: See page 639.

Mosaic

Symptoms: Leaves become a mottled yellow and green in color and have a tendency to curl. Flower stalks become twisted and fail to make normal growth. If the plants are affected when young they frequently remain dwarfed and stunted.

Nature of the Disease: See page 635.

Control: See page 635.

Root Rot

Sweet Peas are attacked by several forms of Root Rot. The control is practically the same in all cases:

Black Root Rot (Thielavia basicola (B. and Br.) Zopf.)

Symptoms: Plants affected with Thielavia Root Rot have practically no root system except a dark, charred-looking stub. The new roots are destroyed as soon as they are formed. The disease occasionally spreads up the stem for some two or three inches above the ground. The affected plants seldom die but remain dwarfed and stunted, being a sickly color and producing no bloom.

Rhizoctonia Root Rot (Rhizoctonia solani Khun)

Symptoms: Roots become rotted, plants wilt and finally collapse entirely. Stems frequently become affected, being covered with reddish, sunken spots. Young seedlings seem to be more susceptible to attack than older plants.

Shredded Root Rot (Aphonomyces entiches)

Symptoms: The underground portion of the stem becomes rotted and the tissues have the appearance of being shredded. The roots usually rot away entirely.

Control: Destroy all diseased plants. Disinfect the soil thoroughly with formaldehyde. Use 1 pint 40 percent formaldehyde to 12½ gallons of water at the rate of 1 gallon to every square foot. Let the soil stand for 24 hours, then fork it over and aërate it well. Do not plant the seed for several days.

Streak

Symptoms: The disease usually makes its appearance just as the plants are coming into bloom. Peculiar spots or streaks, varying in color from light reddish-brown to dark brown, appear on the stems. This condition is usually first apparent near the ground line but spreads gradually to other portions of the plant. In some cases the streaks merge and the stem becomes entirely girdled, the plant being killed. In the advanced stages of the disease, water-soaked spots are found on the leaves, petioles and flowers.

Nature of the Disease: Streak is a bacterial disease caused by Bacillus lathyri Manns and Taub. The bacteria are carried on the seed and are spattered up onto the plant by heavy rains. The bacteria gradually destroy the tissues of the plant.

Control: Root up and burn all diseased plants. Little can be done after the disease has once gained headway, the only satisfactory measure of control being the treatment of seed before planting.

Soak seed for five minutes in a 5 percent solution of formaldehyde.

Insects

Aphids

Identification: Soft-bodied, louse-like insects usually found clustered along the tips of the young growing shoots. The species that most commonly infests sweet peas is pale green in color.

Life History: See page 631.

Control: See page 632.

Nematodes causing *Root Knot*

Identification: Swellings are found on the roots, singly, in pairs or in strings, often giving the root a beaded appearance. The swellings are sometimes very small, and sometimes almost as large as the root nodules, with which they must not be confused. The root nodules which are peculiar to sweet peas and all other members of the legume family are lobed outgrowths which are attached to the root at one end, whereas the galls or swellings caused by nematodes produce a swelling of the entire affected portion of the root. Upon cutting open a swelling the minute worms may frequently be seen with a hand lens.

Injury: Infested plants become sickly and fail to make normal growth. Leaves turn yellow and flower production is seriously affected. The plants usually linger on for a long time before dying.

Life History: See page 675.

Control: See page 675.

Root Aphids

Identification: Soft-bodied, grayish-white insects found clustered along the roots or near the crown of the plant.

Injury: Root aphids suck the juices from the plants, causing them to become dwarfed and stunted. The foliage frequently turns yellow, indicating a general lack of vigor.

Control: See page 634.

Tulip

Diseases

Blossom Blight

Symptoms: The flower stalks turn white and gradually shrivel just below the flower buds. Buds drop over and fail to develop.

Nature of the Disease: A fungous disease caused by Phytophthora cactorum (Leb. & Cohn) Schröt. It seems to be particularly prevalent when tulips are planted in wet locations.

Control: Pick off and burn all diseased flower stems. Very little is as yet known about Blossom Blight and no satisfactory measure of control has been found.

Botrytis Blight, also known as Fire Disease

Symptoms: The leaves, stems and flowers become covered with unsightly spots. In the early stages the spots appear as small, yellowish areas with a dark, water-soaked margin. As the lesions enlarge they become covered with a moldy growth and appear a light gray in color. The bulbs are also frequently affected, deep, yellowish brown lesions being found in the fleshy scales. Black sclerotia or resting bodies develop on the dead stalks and are also found within the outer scales of the bulbs. When plants are severely affected the stalks rot and break over; the leaves become twisted and distorted and the flower buds are blighted.

Nature of the Disease: A fungous disease caused by Botrytis tulipæ (Lib.) Hopk. It is causing severe losses in many sections of the country and every effort should be made to keep it under control.

Control: Every precaution should be taken to see that newly purchased bulbs are free from disease. It is far easier to keep the disease out of one's garden than to try to control it after it has gained entrance. The outer scales of the bulbs should be removed in order to make sure that they are healthy and absolutely free from infection. As an additional measure of precaution the bulbs may be soaked in some organic mercury solution before planting. Soak for two hours in a solution of Semesan, 1 tablespoonful to 1 gallon of water. Remove and destroy infected plants in order to prevent the spread of the disease. Thorough spraying will keep the disease under control to some extent, but is very disfiguring to the foliage. Bordeaux is reasonably effective but may be injurious to the plants in cool spring weather.

Fermate has proved to be one of the most satisfactory controls, used at the rate of 4 ounces to $12\frac{1}{2}$ gallons of water. Begin spraying when the plants are about 4 inches high and repeat at intervals of 10 to 14 days.

Gray Bulb Rot

Symptoms: Dry rot begins at the tip of the bulb. The flesh of the bulb becomes a reddish gray in color and the diseased portions are often covered with dark brown sclerotia or resting bodies. The bulbs finally rot away entirely.

Nature of the Disease: A fungous disease caused by Rhizoctonia tuliparum (Kleb.) Whetzel and Arthur, which affects tulips and various other bulbs.

Control: Dig up and burn all diseased bulbs. Disinfect the soil with formaldehyde before new bulbs are planted. Use 1 pint of 40 percent formaldehyde to $12\frac{1}{2}$ gallons of water at the rate of 1 gallon to every square foot. Let the soil stand for 24 hours. Then fork it over and aërate it well before planting.

Insects

Bulb Mite

Identification: Minute, whitish mites, bead-like in form, are found in large numbers within the bulb scales. Small, reddish-brown spots appear at the point of injury.

Injury: The mites suck the juices from the plant tissues and the bulbs become soft and mushy. The vitality of the bulb is weakened and as a result growth is stunted. The leaves turn a sickly yellow and the flower buds either fail to develop or produce distorted blooms.

Life History: See page 651.

Control: See page 651.

Sweet Alyssum

Insect Pests

Cabbage Worm

Identification: Small, velvety-green caterpillars, somewhat more than an inch in length when full grown.

Injury: The caterpillars feed upon the foliage.

Life History: See page 636.

Control: See page 636.

Potato Flea Beetle

Identification: Small, black beetle $\frac{1}{16}$ inch long, which jumps like a flea when disturbed.

Injury: Feeds on foliage, making many small holes.

Life History: See page 660.

Control: See page 660.

Tuberous Begonias

Diseases

Tuberous begonias grown out-of-doors are comparatively free from pests and diseases. Plants grown in greenhouses or indoors are more subject to trouble, and difficulties are sometimes encountered.

Bacterial Leaf Spot. Seldom causes trouble if tubers are obtained from a reliable source.

Symptoms: Spots appear on the leaves, disfiguring the foliage of the plant.

Control: Remove and burn all affected leaves. Spray with a 2-2-50 solution of Bordeaux mixture. Repeat every week or ten days. Three to four applications recommended.

Precautions: Isolate affected plants. Water only at base to avoid moisture on leaves.

Poor ventilation, high temperatures and inadequate drainage encourage the spread of the disease.

Mildew. A disease which has become very troublesome in many sections.

Symptoms: Leaves become affected with a powdery, grayish-white mildew which spreads rapidly over the entire surface of the leaf unless checked. Plants become sickly and fail to flower well.

Control: Spray thoroughly, at the first sign of trouble, with Karathane (Mildex) and repeat as necessary.

Stem Rot

Symptoms: Stem rots away at the base.

Control: Same as for leaf spot (see above).

Prevention: Same as for leaf spot.

Insect Pests

Mealy Bug

Identification: Scales covered with a white, waxy secretion appear on the stems and sometimes on the undersurface of the leaves.

Life History: Entire life cycle completed on the plant. Female deposits eggs in a wax covered sac at rear of body, then dies. Sacs usually found in axils of stems or leaf petioles. Hatch in 10 days and young nymphs begin feeding.

Control: Spray with malathion.

Mites

Identification: The young shoots are attacked and the underside of the leaves turn a rusty brown, having a glazed appearance. The leaves have a tendency to curl. Infinitesimal mites may be seen under a hand lens. The plants gradually become sickly and unhealthy in appearance and fail to bloom well. Infestation is most likely to occur when tuberous begonias are grown near gloxinias, cyclamen and other susceptible plants.

Life History: See page 646.

Control: See page 646.

Thrips

Identification: Dark streaks appear on the stems, leaves and flowers. Plants appear stunted and malformed.

Life History: See page 668.

Control: See page 668.

Slugs and Snails

Identification: Slugs and snails can cause severe damage if present in great numbers. They feed at night, chiefly upon the petals of the flowers and the tender foliage of young shoots.

Control: Use a good commercial bait. Such mixtures usually contain metaldehyde, which is the most effective control.

Verbena

Insect Pests

Leaf Roller (oblique-banded)

Identification: Small caterpillar varying in color from yellow to light green and distinguished by an oblique band running across the body.

Injury: The caterpillars feed upon the foliage and the flowers, their work being very characteristic as they roll the leaves together and web them with fine silken threads.

Life History: The female moths deposit their eggs in tiny masses on the foliage and within a few weeks the caterpillars hatch out and begin feeding. They become full-grown in about a month and pupate within the rolled leaves. Several weeks later the moths emerge and the life cycle begins again. Two broods are usually produced during the season.

Control: See page 634.

Mites (*Red Spider*)

Identification: Minute mites, some red in color, others greenish, yellow or black.

Injury: Red spiders feed usually on the undersurface of the leaves, puncturing the outer tissues and sucking the juices of the plant. The foliage has an unhealthy, whitish, and curiously glazed appearance. Fine silken threads are sometimes found, spun across the undersurface of the leaves.

Life History: See page 646.

Control: See page 646.

Yellow Woolly-bear Caterpillar

Identification: A caterpillar about two inches in length when full-grown. The body is completely covered with long hairs which vary in color from pale yellow to reddish-brown.

Injury: The caterpillars feed upon the foliage.

Life History: See page 642.

Control: See page 642.

Wallflower

Insect Pests

Diamond-Back Moth Caterpillar

Identification: Small, slender caterpillars about $\frac{2}{5}$ of an inch in length, light green in color. The caterpillars are very active and when disturbed they usually drop from the plant, suspending themselves by a fine silken thread.

Injury: The caterpillars feed upon the foliage, often completely skeletonizing it.

Control: Dust or spray with DDT or Rotenone.

Potato Flea Beetle

Identification: Small, very active beetles about $\frac{1}{16}$ of an inch long, of a dark, somewhat metallic color. The hind legs are longer than the front legs and enable the beetle to jump like a flea when disturbed.

Injury: The beetles feed upon the foliage, making many small holes either round or irregular in shape. The leaves have the appearance of being peppered with fine shot. The foliage becomes badly disfigured and the vitality of the plant is greatly weakened.

Life History: See page 660.

Control: See page 660.

Zinnia

Diseases

Leaf Spot

Symptoms: Large, dark spots appear on the leaves. Usually not troublesome except in very wet weather.

Nature of the Disease: A fungous disease caused by Cercospora atricinata.

Control: Spray with Bordeaux, or dust with copper-lime dust as soon as trouble is detected.

Mildew

Symptoms: Foliage becomes covered with a white, powdery growth. In the most advanced stages the affected areas turn black.

Nature of the Disease: This disease is caused by Erysiphe cichoracearum D.C.

Control: Dust thoroughly with fine dusting sulphur.

Sclerotium Disease of Zinnia

Symptoms: The disease attacks the plant at ground level and works upward. The stems become blackened and the leaves turn yellow and wilt. The stem finally collapses. The reproductive bodies may be seen as small bumps on the surface of the stem. Sometimes they become quite large.

Nature of the Disease: The disease is caused by the fungus, Scleroinia sclerotiorum Mass. It attacks the plant at ground level. The vegetative growth of the fungus completely fills the vessels of the plant and thus deprives the leaves of water.

Control: Diseased stems should be burned. In flower beds where the disease has occurred, the top-soil to a depth of 2 inches should be removed. New soil which has been mixed with a little quicklime should be added. Green manure favors the development of the disease.

Insect Pests

Black Blister Beetle

Identification: A slender jet-black beetle about $\frac{1}{2}$ inch in length with prominent head and neck. The best identification is the yellow oily, blistering fluid exuded when handled.

Injury: The beetles feed upon the flowers.

Life History: See page 633.

Control: See page 633.

Japanese Beetles

Identification: Large, handsome beetles of a metallic, greenish-bronze color. There are two conspicuous and several small white spots near the tip of the abdomen. During the middle of the day they are very active, making rapid flight when disturbed. During the evening they are more sluggish.

Injury: The beetles feed upon both the foliage and the flowers, completely demolishing a plant in a very short time.

Life History: See page 664.

Control: See page 664.

Leaf Roller (Red-banded)

Identification: Small caterpillar varying in color from yellow to light green, readily distinguished by the red band on the body.

Injury: The caterpillars feed upon the foliage, their work being very characteristic, as they roll and tie the leaves together with fine silken threads.

Life History: See page 634.

Control: See page 634.

Stalk Borer

Identification: Slender caterpillars about two inches in length when full-grown. The young caterpillars are brown with white stripes. When full-grown they lose their stripes and become a solid, dirty gray in color.

Injury: The stalk borer makes a small, round hole in the stem and tunnels up through the stalk, causing the injured shoot to suddenly wilt and break over.

Life History: See page 634.

Control: See page 634.

Tarnished Plant Bug

Identification: A small, very active bug about ¼ inch in length. The body is oval in shape, being somewhat triangular in front; coppery brown in color with dark, brown and yellow flecks on the back.

Injury: The bugs puncture the shoots just below the flower heads, causing the buds to droop and die. The injury completely destroys any chance of bloom. It is thought that while feeding, the Tarnished Plant Bug injects some substance into the sap which is highly injurious to the plant and has the effects of a poison.

Life History: See page 634.

Control: See page 634.

MISCELLANEOUS INSECT PESTS, RODENTS AND ANIMALS

Mice

Meadow Mouse

Identification: Small, dark brown mouse with coarse fur. The ears are almost entirely concealed and the tail is much shorter than that of our common house mouse. The meadow mice make little runs readily visible just under the surface of the soil.

Injury: The meadow mouse does most of its feeding at the surface of the ground, nibbling at the roots and crowns of many herbaceous plants and gnawing the bark of trees, shrubs and vines at or just above the ground level, in many cases completely girdling them and causing their death.

Pine Mouse

Identification: The pine mouse is smaller than the meadow mouse, it is a reddish-brown in color and has an exceedingly short tail, the tail being about the same length as the hind foot. The burrows of the pine mouse are well below the ground level with occasional small openings upon the surface.

Injury: The pine mouse does all of its feeding below the surface of the ground. It has a particular fondness for tulip and lily bulbs, and it feeds also upon the roots of herbaceous plants, trees and vines. In sections that are severely infested with pine mice the destruction is often alarming. Literally thousands of bulbs may be destroyed in a single season and fruit trees forty or fifty years of age have been known to be killed outright by the work of pine mice. One of the greatest tragedies is that one is seldom aware of their presence until considerable damage has been done.

Control: The use of poison bait is probably the most satisfactory measure of control for these field mice, and the following baits are recommended:

1. Use any rat or mouse bait containing Warfarin. Place in protected receptacles in or near mouse runs. Keep the supply replenished as long as the bait is being eaten.

2. Sweet potato bait. Cut the sweet potatoes into small cubes. Mix together equal parts of powdered strychnine and baking soda. Sift this over the potatoes, making sure that each cube is thoroughly coated. The bait should be used immediately, while it is fresh, and it should be dropped directly into the runs or placed in crevices in dry stone walls known to be infested with mice.

   Precaution: Strychnine is a deadly poison and must be handled with extreme care.

Protection of Trees, Plants and Bulbs: Field mice seldom trouble narcissus and hyacinth bulbs, but they seem to have a particular fondness for tulips and lilies and in sections that are badly infested with mice it is quite useless to attempt to grow them unless some protection is given them. One of the surest and most satisfactory means of protection is to plant them in wire baskets with open tops. They may be made of ¼-inch mesh wire and will do duty for a number of years. Camphor flakes may also be placed about the bulbs at the time of planting and will afford some protection, although in time the effects will wear off.

As a protection for trees, shrubbery, and vines, sulphonated oil has proved remarkably satisfactory. It may be applied to the lower part of the trunk or to the stems with an ordinary paint brush, or a sprayer may be used if preferred. The mixture consists of one part flowers of sulphur to nine parts of linseed oil by weight. In preparing the mixture the linseed oil should be heated to a temperature of about 470° F. It should then be placed out of doors and the flowers of sulphur should be sifted slowly into the hot oil, the mixture being stirred constantly. The heat will increase until all the sulphur has been dissolved. When cool it is ready for use. Where application of this sulphonated oil has been made, trees will practically never be touched by field mice.

See page 674: Protection against rabbits.

Moles

In sections where moles are prevalent they are classed among the most troublesome of our garden pests. The natural food of moles consists of beetle grubs, cutworms, and other insects of various kinds found in the soil. Moles do not normally feed upon the roots of plants or upon bulbs. Their annoyance to the gardener is caused by the upheaval of the soil when they are tunneling close to the surface. Not only are these tunnels unsightly, but they are often most damaging to lawn areas and to garden plants as they break the contact between the upper inch or so of soil with the soil beneath, thus depriving the grasses or plants of water and food. Unless the damage is quickly repaired the plants suffer seriously and eventually die. Where mole infestations are heavy the damage may be very great, as a lawn or a garden bed may become a network of underground tunnels.

Moles live in colonies and they maintain certain tunnels as regular routes used by all members of the colony. From these main runways side tunnels diverge which are made by individual moles in their search for food. These minor tunnels are used only once and are usually fairly short and end abruptly. When attempting to eradicate moles it is necessary to determine which tunnels are the main runways. This may be done by pressing down all tunnels which are evident in a given area. The main tunnel will soon be heaved up again, whereas the side tunnels will not be. Traps should always be set in the main runs and poisons placed in the main runs.

Mole runs are often used by mice, rats, shrews and pocket gophers. These are usually old runs abandoned by the moles in search of new feeding grounds. They may be distinguished by the presence of openings through which the other creatures using them enter and emerge.

Control: One of the most effective measures of control is to reduce to a minimum the grub population in lawns and garden beds. (See page 195.)

Rat bait containing Warfarin placed in the runs has proved effective in some instances. Place a heaping teaspoonful in the run. Replace the sod but do not press down.

Poison gas is also effective. A commercial preparation known as Cyanogas is probably the most satisfactory thing for this purpose. A small opening should be made in the run and a teaspoonful of the material should be placed upon the bottom. The opening should then be covered over with an inverted saucer or something of this nature. Care must be taken not to use too much Cyanogas in the garden as large quantities of it are liable to prove injurious to the growth of plants in surrounding areas.

Traps: There are several types of strong, steel mole traps on the market and some of them are very satisfactory if properly handled. It is well to handle the traps with rubber gloves, and the results will be better if several traps are set at the same time. One trap should be set at the point where the main tunnel divides and one or two others along the branch tunnels. The soil should be pressed down very firmly at the spot where the trap is set.

Rabbits

During the winter rabbits often seriously damage trees and shrubs by gnawing the bark just above the ground level. If the plant is completely girdled it will die and many valuable specimens have been lost as a result of damage done by rabbits. Young trees are more susceptible to damage than older trees.

Protecting Trees and Shrubs: Fine-meshed chicken wire, "hardware cloth" with a ¼-inch mesh, or ordinary screen wire may be used to protect the trunks of trees and to encircle shrubs, but this method involves considerable labor and expense if done on a large scale. Very satisfactory protection may be obtained with the use of a homemade mixture which can be painted on the trunks and stems. Mix powdered rosin (which can be purchased at any drugstore) with denatured alcohol until it is the consistency of thick paint. Let it stand overnight. Brush the mixture on the trunks and branches from the ground level to the height which a rabbit could reach. Allow for the depth of a drifted snow in the North in addition to the normal reach of a rabbit. The application should be made after the trees or shrubs are leafless and dormant. If the weather is near or below freezing the mixture should be warmed before it is applied. Do *not* place the mixture near an open flame. One application will give protection throughout the winter. This mixture also provides effective protection against field mice.

Protecting Young Plants: Powdered aloes have proved to be one of the most satisfactory repellents for use on young plants. The material may be dusted lightly over the plants with a flour shaker. It will be necessary to repeat the application after a rain. Rabbits will seldom bother plants which have been treated in this way.

Dried blood scattered around an area where rabbits are troublesome will prove an excellent repellent, although the odor is objectionable if the area is close to the house.

Thiram has proved an effective control against rabbits, mice and deer. When sprayed on roses, trees, shrubs and ornamentals it penetrates the bark, stems and leaves making them so bitter that they are distasteful. Thiram is harmless to plants, animals and people. It is on the market under the trade name Chaperone.

Ants

Injury: Although ants seldom cause any direct injury to plants, they can be a source of great annoyance in the flower garden. They are often found on peony buds, where they feed on the sweet secretions which are exuded by the opening flowers, and they are very frequently found on plants which are infested with plant lice as they are fond of the honey dew which is given off by the aphids. In some sections of the South, ants are very troublesome, as they carry off newly sown seed before it has had time to germinate.

Control: The most effective means of control is to destroy ants in their nest and any of the following methods will give satisfactory results. Treatment should be made in the evening after the ants have returned to their nest.

Nematodes

Description: Nematodes are microscopic, thread-like creatures, and they have become one of our most devastating plant pests in many areas. Some nematodes are harmless and live only on dead organic matter, but there are many species which feed on living plants, causing varying degrees of damage. Nematodes are equipped with a minute, spear-like feeding mechanism which enables them to pierce the plant cells and suck out the juices.

Injury: The root-knot nematodes puncture the roots of the host plant just behind the root tip where they drain the food supply of the plant. Small, characteristic root knots are found in the area surrounding the female nematode.

Some species damage the stems, leaves and flowers, and it is often difficult to trace such injury to nematodes. The plants become yellow and stunted and wilt badly on hot days. Among the plants thus attacked by nematodes of this type are camellias, lilies, sweet peas and boxwood.

The stem nematodes attack narcissus, iris, crocus and freesias. They live in the scales, flower stalks and leaves of bulbous plants, causing short, stubby flower stalks, deformed flowers, and twisted, thick, crescent-shaped leaves, yellowish in color. Small, scaly, raised lumps on the leaves and flower stalks indicate the presence of nematodes.

The chrysanthemum nematode is one of the more common types. It lives within the leaves and buds of the chrysanthemum and other closely related plants, causing triangular shaped, dark brown spots. Eventually the entire leaf becomes brown and limp, and if the infestation is severe the plant may become completely defoliated.

How Nematodes are Spread: Nematodes can move only very short distances under their own power and are usually introduced into a garden when infected plants are unknowingly brought in. Once they have gained entrance to a garden they are spread by cultivators, on the hands and shoes of those working in the garden, by animals, by the splashing of raindrops, or water from a hose, and in countless other mechanical ways.

Every possible precaution should be taken to prevent the introduction of nematode-infested plants. New plants obtained either through gift or purchase should be carefully inspected for any evidence of infestation.

Control: Where nematodes are known to exist, measures of control consist of strict sanitation and soil sterilization. In greenhouses, and where small plants are grown, all pots, flats, benches and tools should either be scrubbed with or dipped in a formalin solution (one part commercial formalin to 50 parts of water). Such equipment should not be used until all of the formaldehyde odor has disappeared. All soil used for potting or in benches, and all sand used in propagating beds should be sterilized.

When areas of garden soil have become infested with nematodes all plants must be removed preparatory to thorough soil fumigation. The materials that are recommended are D–D, ethylene dibromide, vapam and chloropicrin. When any of these fumigants are injected into warm, moist soil they vaporize and kill all nematodes with which they come in contact. When soil is to be fumigated all debris must be raked off and the soil should then be turned with a spade or spading fork. It should be raked again and watered lightly.

There are several methods of application. Holes 8 to 10 inches deep may be made 10 inches apart in a square pattern over the area to be treated. The amount of fumigant applied should comply with the directions on the container, the usual quantity being approximately 2 quarts per 1,000 square feet or 15 gallons per acre. Injectors are available which are hand-operated and greatly facilitate the work. These are regulated to release the desired amount in each hole. Capsules containing the fumigant are also available which can be inserted into the soil by hand. Whatever the method, the hole should be closed and tramped down and then watered to seal in the gas.

The treated area can be planted in about three weeks, provided all odor of the fumigant has gone. It is wise, however, to turn the soil before planting.

The most favorable time to apply the fumigant is in the spring after the soil is warm. The soil temperature should preferably be between 55° and 60° F. Treatment can, however, be done at any time during the summer or early autumn.

Nematodes which are confined to the stems, leaves and flowers of plants and which do not inhabit the soil may usually be satisfactorily controlled by spraying with one of the phosphate insecticides such as parathion or demeton, but such materials are not recommended for use by the home gardener because of their extreme toxicity.

Certain flowering plants require specific treatment.

For bulbs such as Narcissus, see page 657.

For chrysanthemums, see page 641.

For boxwood, see page 622.

Deer

One of the most effective controls for deer is bone tar oil which is an odor-producing chemical. It is available under the trade name of Magic Circle Deer Repellent.* The chemical should be mixed with water according to the directions on the container and should either be sprayed on the ground in a circle about the plants or sprayed directly on the plants which are to be protected. It should not be used on young seedlings.

The first application should, if possible, be made before the deer develop the habit of feeding on an area, and subsequent applications should be made at monthly intervals. If deer have already formed a feeding habit, a solution stronger than normal should be used. Evergreens, fruit trees, shrubs, flowers and vegetables may all be effectively protected.

* Manufactured by State College Laboratories, University Park, Pennsylvania.

The odor is repellent not only to deer but also to beavers, woodchucks, sheep, skunks and raccoons. It is not, unfortunately, repellent to rabbits.

See control with Thiram on page 674.

Woodchucks

Woodchucks may be controlled by the use of poisonous gas, by trapping, and by repellents such as a Magic Circle Deer Repellent (see description under Deer).

In some states "bombs" are available through the Fish and Wild Life Service or through the local Game Warden. These may be placed in the mouth of the den, and instructions should be followed with great care. There are usually two openings to a woodchuck den and it is necessary to locate both in order to plug up the exit with soil before the bomb or poisonous gas is used. Carbon monoxide gas may be piped through a hose from the exhaust pipe of a car into the mouth of a den, closed except for the small opening made for the hose. This must be done with care and there must be no leakage. Control measures of this type should preferably be taken in early spring before the adult woodchucks become active and before the young leave the den.

There are a number of very effective traps on the market and special woodchuck lures may be obtained as bait. These may be used at any time during the growing season.

XLII

GARDEN PRACTICES

A GOOD garden program includes several general practices such as soil preparation, cultivation, watering, feeding, pruning, winter protection, protection against frost, preventing transplanting losses, and control of pests and diseases.

The application of these garden practices to various types of gardens and to special plant groups has been discussed in the various chapters, but it is well to understand some of the underlying principles involved.

Digging

Double Digging. Dig an initial trench two feet in width, one foot deep, across the end of the bed. This soil is moved to the farther end of the bed to be used in filling the final trench. Spread manure in the trench and fork it into the ground as deeply as possible. Dig the next trench two feet wide and one foot deep, turning the soil into the first trench and enriching it with a layer of manure when half the soil has been moved in. Break up and enrich the bottom of the second trench and continue across the bed in this matter.

Trenching. This operation is the same as double digging except that two feet of soil are removed in each trench. The top-soil of the second trench is placed in the bottom of the first and the lower foot of soil becomes the top-soil of the first trench. This is only practical when the garden soil is a very deep loam. Where the top-soil is only one foot in depth, fresh soil can be hauled in for the fill and the lower foot of sub-soil discarded.

Cultivation

The cultivation of the soil serves several important functions. It destroys weeds; breaks the crust which forms on heavy soils after a rain; aërates the soil, thus permitting air to reach the roots of the plants; and establishes a dust mulch on the surface which helps to conserve the moisture in the soil.

Under normal conditions the ground should be cultivated as soon as possible after a rain. If the soil is extremely sandy it may be cultivated almost immediately. In the case of heavy clay soils it is necessary to wait until they have dried out sufficiently, as it is imperative that such soils should not be worked when they are too wet, as it will cause the formation of many hard little lumps and will seriously injure the physical condition of the soil. There are occasional instances when it is unwise to cultivate the soil after a rain. Such a situation occurs during a period of drought when but a light rain has fallen. Under such circumstances it is wiser to allow the plants to derive what refreshment they can from the meager supply of surface moisture, which would be almost entirely dissipated and lost if the surface were stirred.

Certainly one of the most important functions of cultivation in the garden is the destruction of weeds, and it is essential that cultivations be given so frequently that the weeds never have an opportunity to gain headway. If the weeds are very small, less than an inch in height, at the time that the cultivation is given, it will not be necessary to remove them, as they will wilt as soon as they have been uprooted and will disappear entirely within a very short time.

For the cultivation of flower beds and borders and nursery plots various types of small hand weeders are available. A small inexpensive type with three flexible wire prongs is one of the most efficient. For more extensive areas, such as shrubbery borders and the vegetable garden, there are the long-handled prong cultivators, hoes of many and varied types, the small half-moon type being one of the most satisfactory, and the wheel hoes, which are exceedingly useful in the cultivation of long rows.

Watering

As all plants derive their nutrients from the soil in the form of a solution, it may readily be understood what an important part water plays in the maintenance and welfare of the garden.

In order to be fully effective very thorough watering is necessary. Frequent light waterings tend to do infinitely more harm than good. If only the few surface inches of soil are moist, and if there is not enough water to allow for a sufficient depth of penetration, the plant roots, in their search for moisture, will be drawn upward toward the surface, and if this process continues the plants will become more and more shallow rooted. And it is a well-established fact that shallow-rooted plants are less vigorous than those which are deeply rooted, as they can derive their nutrients from only a very limited soil area, and suffer seriously during periods of drought. It is therefore the wise practice to water thoroughly, even if less frequently.

The most favorable times for watering are late afternoon and evening, or very early in the morning, evening being preferable. The evaporation of moisture is considerably less at such times, and the plants are consequently able to derive more lasting benefit from the application. It is not wise to water during the heat of the day, except in the case of young seedling plants which must never be allowed to suffer from lack of moisture.

The method of watering, or of supplying constant moisture, will vary considerably, being dependent upon the type of plants which is being handled and, to some degree, upon the extent of one's gardening operations. One of the most satisfactory ways of maintaining a constant and uniform supply of moisture in the soil is to sink pieces of 4-inch drain tile in the ground, one open end being level with the surface of the soil. If these pieces of tile are kept filled with water there will be a gentle and very gradual seepage of moisture through the soil. Such a method is of particular value in providing moisture for trees and shrubs. It may also be used in flower beds and borders of ample size, as the tile openings are inconspicuous and are seldom noticed. English primroses, which are extremely dependent upon moisture, will usually thrive well when water is supplied by this method.

The usual method of supplying water to plants is through the use of a sprinkling can or a garden hose. There are various attachments which are available for the hose. An adjustable nozzle which is capable of throwing both a fine, mist-like spray and a comparatively heavy stream of water is one of the most useful. Rose attachments similar to those used on a watering can may also be obtained and are very useful for certain types of watering where a gentle, steady spray is desired. There are also various types of automatic sprinklers which are very satisfactory and which will relieve the tedium of hand watering. Sprinklers should be left in place until an area is thoroughly soaked, and should then be moved on to another section of the garden or lawn. There is also a device, known as a water sword, which may be attached to a hose and plunged deeply into the ground, being of special benefit in the watering of trees and shrubs.

There is comparatively little danger of too liberal applications of water when watering is done artificially, but during prolonged periods of excessively heavy rains the soil may become so saturated with moisture that plant growth suffers seriously in consequence. Under such conditions much of the available nitrogen in the soil is leached away and plants are unable to make normal growth. The ground also becomes so densely saturated with water that the aëration of the soil is seriously checked and plants fail to thrive, due to the fact that their roots are unable to obtain sufficient air. Large trees sometimes die as a result of such a condition. Under such circumstances it is well to apply additional nitrogen to the soil in order to stimulate plant growth, and to make up for the deficiency in nitrogen due to leaching. In areas where trees are beginning to show ill effects from such a condition, evidenced by a browning of the leaves and a generally unthrifty appearance, it is wise to bore holes in the soil beneath the spread of the branches, in order to increase the supply of oxygen and to permit air to reach the roots.

Feeding

As all plants are dependent upon mineral nutrients for their growth and development, it is essential that an adequate supply of those elements which are necessary be maintained in the soil. A detailed discussion of the value of soil tests, the mineral nutrients needed for plant growth, and the form in which these nutrients may be applied, will be found in Chapter XVI on Soils and in various other chapters dealing with special plant groups.

There are, however, a few fundamental principles which should be observed in the application of all fertilizers.

Under no condition should commercial fertilizers be allowed to come into contact with seeds at the time that they are sown, or into direct contact with the roots of trees, shrubs, or herbaceous plants at the time of planting. The germination of most seeds will be seriously affected if commercial fertilizers are used in the drill at the time of sowing. The most approved method of supplying nutrients to young plants is to place the fertilizer in drills 3 or 4 inches away on each side of the row. The drills should be from 2 to 3 inches in depth and the fertilizer should be covered with a small quantity of soil. This method is especially recommended for vegetables and for flowers in the cutting garden which are grown in rows.

The most satisfactory way to apply fertilizer to garden beds and borders is to broadcast it over the surface of the soil at the prescribed rate and to cultivate it in very lightly. The soil should then be thoroughly watered in order that the fertilizer may become more readily available to the plants. If individual plants within the border are to be fertilized a shallow furrow in the form of a ring may be made several inches from the crown of the plant and the fertilizer may be placed in the furrow. Care must be taken not to allow the fertilizer to come into contact with the foliage, as it may cause severe burning.

When fertilizers are to be applied in the form of a solution they may be dissolved in the desired quantity of water and applied with a watering can from which the rose or sprinkler has been removed.

Pruning

It is important that every gardener should have a knowledge of the fundamental principles of pruning. One should know why pruning is necessary, and at what season of the year it should be done. And one should also be familiar with the most approved pruning practices.

These are the primary purposes of pruning: to restore a proper balance between root and top growth at the time of transplanting; to remove injured, diseased or dead wood; to increase both the quantity and quality of flowers and fruit; to control the structure of a tree or shrub and to guide its growth; to improve the appearance and symmetry of a plant; and to aid in the rejuvenation of old trees, shrubs or vines.

To be able to prune a tree or shrub intelligently it is necessary to understand that there is always a very definite relation in all plants between root growth and top growth. If there is a reduction in normal root growth there must be a compensating reduction in top growth. It is for this reason that the judicious pruning of trees and shrubs at the time of transplanting is a matter of such paramount importance. In bare-root transplanting it is almost inevitable that some of the roots will be severed entirely or severely injured. Therefore, in order to compensate for this reduction in root growth, the top must be pruned; moreover, because the plant has suffered more or less shock and will require some time to re-establish itself, it is not able to sustain its usual amount of top growth; consequently severe pruning is recommended.

Although each tree and shrub has a natural form, its symmetry and appearance may be controlled to a considerable degree by judicious pruning. No attempt should be made, however, to radically change the shape or form of a plant.

Pruning should serve merely as an aid in building a strong framework, and in guiding the natural growth. After ornamental trees have attained their full development, and have been trained to the desired form, comparatively little pruning is necessary. Systematic yearly care includes the removal of broken branches and of any dead or diseased wood, and the cutting away of any branch which may be interfering with the development of other branches. In the case of shrubs the same general principles hold true, with the exception of the fact that in many cases some of the old wood should be cut away entirely in order to stimulate the production of vigorous new growth. The pruning requirements of the various groups of shrubs are discussed fully in Chapter XX.

Just as the removal of roots necessitates the reduction in top growth, so does the severe pruning of top growth disturb the equilibrium of the normal function of the roots, and nature tends to restore the balance by the production of new shoots and branches. In many cases this is what is desired, as with fruit trees and with flowering shrubs, where the production of vigorous, young, flowering and fruiting wood is the desideratum. Some plants bear flowers and fruit on new growth, and such growth may be encouraged by the annual pruning-out of old wood. Many of our flowering shrubs, most roses, the small bush fruits, and the grapevines may be found in this group.

Such pruning is also associated with the rejuvenation of old trees and shrubs which have become weak and unthrifty through age or neglect. Invariably, vigorous pruning is followed by an increase in top growth, but moderation must be practiced. Particularly is this true in the rejuvenation of old trees. If very severe pruning of large trees seems necessary or advisable, the process should be extended over a period of several years. If excessively heavy pruning of top growth is attempted at one time it will usually cause the formation of much undesirable growth in the nature of water sprouts and suckers. These rampant, upright shoots are entirely unproductive, injure the form and appearance of the tree, and rob the more desirable growth of nourishment. Not only should they be removed if they occur, but their production should be controlled by judicious pruning.

Pruning Equipment. Elaborate pruning equipment is not necessary. Practically all of the pruning on a place of average size may be accomplished efficiently with three or four tools—a pair of good pruning shears, a pair of lopping shears with extended handles, one or two pruning saws, and a pair of pole pruners are the only tools necessary. It is essential that the shears be sharp, as much damage may be done with dull tools. Pruning shears should always be kept well sharpened and properly tightened, and they should be oiled at frequent intervals.

Pruning Practices. To make a close, clean cut, and to avoid injury to the bark, the shears should be held with the blade next to the portion of the twig or branch which is to remain upon the plant. A ragged cut, with torn and mutilated bark, reflects only discredit upon the one who is responsible for the pruning. In cutting back small branches the cut should be made at a slight angle, just above a bud (see sketches). If the cut is made above an outside bud the growth will be directed outward, and the form will be open and spreading. If a more compact, upright growth is desired the cut should be made above an inside bud. When branches have opposite rather than alternate buds, one of the buds may be removed, and the growth may thus be guided in any desired direction.

If large branches are to be removed the final cut should be made as close to the main trunk as possible, in order that the wound may heal rapidly and that there may be no disfiguring stump. If the limb is of any size, more than one cut may be advisable. The first cut should be made from below, about a foot from the main trunk, and it should extend but halfway through the branch. The second cut should be made from above, at a distance 3 or 4 inches further out on the branch, and it should sever the limb entirely. The final cut should consist of the removal of the stub as close to the trunk as possible. (See sketches.)

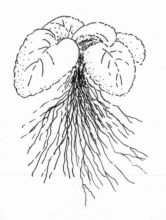
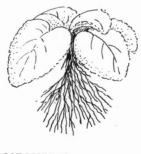

ROOT PRUNING

Control of Insect Pests and Diseases

It requires constant vigilance on the part of the gardener to keep insect pests and diseases under control, and it is necessary to be able to recognize the first symptoms of disease, or the first manifestation of the presence of injurious insects. The effectiveness of any treatment depends upon the promptness and the frequency with which it is applied and the thoroughness of the application.

The identification and full description of all the more common insect pests and diseases are given in Chapter XLI. The most approved measures of control and the methods of application are also given in detail.

Winter Protection

The problem of providing adequate winter protection for trees, shrubs and flowers is one which all gardeners in Northern climes must face. The amount of protection necessary depends upon the natural hardiness of the plants, upon the severity of the climate, and upon the exposure.

Winter injury to plants is usually attributable to two factors: either to severe cold or to the loss of moisture from shoots and branches. Extreme cold will cause the twigs, stems and roots to freeze, with a consequent breaking down of the cell tissues. Excessive loss of moisture, which is quite as frequently a cause of winter-killing as is severe cold, is due largely to the effect of strong, drying winds during periods of brilliant winter sunshine. It is a well-known fact that the evaporation of moisture from the twigs, branches, canes, and, in the case of evergreens, from the leaves, continues at a slow rate throughout the winter, and that in order to supply this moisture the roots of the plant must continue to absorb water. When the evaporation is unduly accelerated by prolonged periods of winter wind and sunshine, the roots are unable to supply moisture rapidly enough, and the branches and canes become shrivelled in consequence. If this condition becomes sufficiently aggravated it fre-

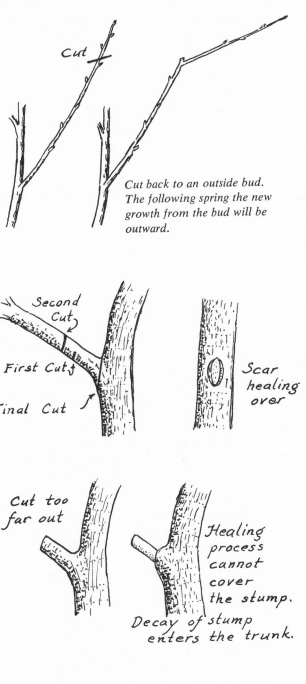

Cut back to an outside bud. The following spring the new growth from the bud will be outward.

PROPER METHOD AND IMPROPER METHOD OF CUTTING BRANCHES

quently results in the dying back of a large portion of the plant, or in its death.

Therefore, one of the most important preparations for winter in the case of all woody plants, and most particularly in the case of broad-leaved evergreens, is to see that the soil is adequately supplied with moisture. If rainfall has been light during the autumn months, it will be necessary to see that the ground is thoroughly soaked before it freezes. Many trees and shrubs may be saved from winter injury if this precaution is taken, and for many plants a winter protection against wind and sun is quite as important as a protection against extreme cold.

The most approved practices for providing winter protection for herbaceous perennials, rock plants, roses, trees, and shrubs have been discussed in detail in the various chapters.

Protecting Plants from Frost

When sudden cold spells occur plants may be protected from frost in numerous ways.

If only a small number of plants need protection they may be covered with baskets, boxes, or lath frames over which burlap, muslin or sheets of plastic have been spread.

Smudge pots may also be used on cold nights.

One of the most effective ways of lessening frost damage is through the use of water. If plants can be subjected to a fine, gentle, continuous spray of water during a sudden drop in temperature, satisfactory protection can be obtained in many cases, even where the thermometer drops as low as 20° F. When the air temperature drops below freezing the water sprayed onto the plants begins to form into ice. During the process of freezing the water gives off heat and enough of this heat is absorbed by the plants to prevent them from freezing, with a resultant breakdown of cell structure. As long as water is applied continuously the plant remains above its freezing point. The application of water should begin when the temperature at plant level drops to 34° F. It must be constant throughout the period when the air temperature is below freezing, and must be continued until all the ice has melted off the plants.

This method is used by many commercial growers, particularly where sprinkler irrigation systems are available, and often means the saving of an entire crop. Much less water is required than the amount normally used for irrigation purposes, however, as a fine, light spray is essential. In the home garden a stationary or rotary sprinkler on the end of a hose will give very satisfactory results, although it is possible to cover only a comparatively small area in this way unless a number of hoses and water connections are available. When a light frost is forecast sufficient protection may often be obtained by watering the plants with a fine, mist-like spray several times during the evening and again early in the morning, keeping them wet until the temperature has risen above freezing.

Tall, slender plants, such as dahlias and gladiolas, are not as well adapted to this method of frost protection as are lower, more bushy types, due to the weight of the ice load which builds up on the plant and is apt to cause breakage of the stalks. This does not usually happen, however, unless the temperature drops below 27° F.

If a sudden, light frost has caught one unaware and no precautions have been taken, plants can sometimes be salvaged by protecting them immediately from direct sunshine so that they will have a chance to thaw out gradually. In the case of potted plants the pots can be moved to a completely shaded area.

Preventing Transplanting Losses

At the time of transplanting many of the feeder roots are often injured or destroyed and the water-absorbing capacity of the root system is consequently greatly reduced. Unless the top growth is also appreciably reduced, or measures are taken to reduce the transpiration of water from the leaves, wilting usually occurs, as the plant is unable to maintain a balance between water intake and outgo. Some plants tend to wilt more rapidly than others and are slower in making a recovery. In very severe wilting there is a complete destruction of the cells and the plant dies.

The usual precaution taken by the gardener is to do the transplanting on a cloudy day when there is an abundance of moisture in the air, but this is not always possible. Artificial shade may be provided temporarily for newly transplanted stock but this involves considerable labor and expense.

The most approved practice is to spray the plants with a plastic spray before they are transplanted. In order to be effective such a spray must have the ability to control the amount of water transpired by the leaves without stopping it completely, and it must not interfere with the proper gas exchange. A number of plastic sprays have been developed which meet these requirements, put out under various trade names. Such sprays are a great boon to the gardener, as they cut transplanting losses and setbacks to a minimum.

Plastic sprays may be used on trees and shrubs, both deciduous and evergreen, on vegetable plants, and on all types of flowering and foliage plants. In fact they make it possible to transplant deciduous trees and shrubs when they are in full leaf, providing a thorough application of the spray is given prior to moving. The entire tree or shrub should be coated with the spray, the trunk as well as the foliage. Losses in transplanting evergreens may also be reduced to a minimum if they are sprayed before they are dug.

A foliage spray is not effective on plants which have already wilted. It is essential, therefore, that the spray be applied *before* the transplanting is done, or before any signs of wilting are evident. Good results may also be obtained by dipping the top of a plant into the spray solution while it is still in its container, or as soon as it has been lifted from the soil. This would apply only to vegetable plants and small-sized annuals, biennials and perennials.

In order to secure a good film on the surface of the leaves, rapid drying of the spray is necessary, and its use is not recommended when the temperature is below 50° F. The optimum temperature for application is around 70° F.

The advantages of using plastic sprays at the time of transplanting are great and it is a practice which is strongly recommended.

GARDENER'S MISCELLANY

GARDEN CALENDAR

GLOSSARY

MAPS

INDEX

ACKNOWLEDGEMENTS

GARDENER'S MISCELLANY
NOTABLE GARDENS OPEN TO THE PUBLIC

(* *Indicates a garden of exceptional interest and merit*)

ALABAMA

Birmingham

Avondale Park Rose Garden

Vestavia Temple and Gardens
Rose garden; azaleas, camellias, narcissus

Arlington, 331 Cotton Avenue
Ante-bellum plantation house and garden

Mobile
*Bellingrath Gardens (notable planting of azaleas and camellias)

ARIZONA

Mesa: Garden at the Arizona Temple

Phoenix

Papago Park (Desert Botanical Garden)

Valley Garden Center (Rose Garden)

Somerton: Arizona Mission Gardens

Tombstone

Lady Banksia Rose (famous rose tree)

Tucson: Memorial Rose Garden

ARKANSAS

Little Rock

Arkansas Territorial Restoration
An interesting restoration preserving the early history of Arkansas as a territory (1820–1836). Gardens of the period faithfully reproduced

CALIFORNIA

Arcadia: Los Angeles County Rose Garden

Berkeley: Municipal Rose Garden

Carmel: Mission Dolores: old mission garden

Fresno:
Underground Gardens (fantastic and interesting)

La Canada (near Pasadena)
*Descanso Gardens (notable plantings of camellias and roses)

San Francisco
Civic Center Gardens (seasonal plantings)

*Japanese Garden, Golden Gate Park

Union Square
Garden constructed above an underground garage (seasonal plantings)

Santa Rosa:
Home of Luther Burbank (experimental gardens)

COLORADO

Denver
City Park (rose garden)

Washington Park (rose garden)

Greeley: Glenmere Park (rock gardens and pools)

CONNECTICUT

Hamden: East Rock Park (Pardee Rose Garden)

Hartford: Elizabeth Park Rose Garden

Norwich: Memorial Rose Garden

Waterford: Harkness Memorial Gardens

DELAWARE

Wilmington
*Longwood Gardens (P.O. Kennett Square, Penna)
Formal gardens; beautiful conservatories; displays of great horticultural interest

DISTRICT OF COLUMBIA

*Bishop's Garden of St. Alban's Cathedral
A garden of great distinction and charm including a Mediæval Herb Garden

687

Dumbarton Oaks
(roses and boxwood)
Kenilworth Aquatic Gardens

FLORIDA

Clearwater: Eagle's Nest Gardens (exotic plants)

Dania: Flamingo Tropical Gardens

Gainesville: Wilmot Memorial Camellia Gardens

Jacksonville: Oriental Gardens

Lake Wales: Bok Tower and Gardens; Bird Sanctuary

Leesburg: The Venetian Gardens

Palm Beach

Cluett Memorial Gardens

Society of the Four Arts Gardens

St. Petersburg: Turner's Sunken Gardens (exotic trees, shrubs and flowers)

Tallahassee: *Killearn Gardens (notable planting of azaleas, gardenias, camellias)

Vero Beach: McKee Jungle Gardens

Winter Haven:

*Florida Cypress Gardens (notable planting of azaleas)

Idylwyld Gardens (azaleas and gardenias)

Winter Park: Kraft Memorial Azalea Garden

GEORGIA

Athens: Founder's Memorial Garden (honoring the oldest Garden Club in America)

Atlanta

Druid Hills Municipal Rose Garden

Municipal Park (rose, iris and lily gardens)

Savannah: U.S. Foreign Plant Introduction Garden

Thomasville: Municipal Park Rose Garden

IDAHO

Caldwell: Municipal Rose Garden

ILLINOIS

Chicago

Garfield Park
Conservatory of great horticultural interest; extensive gardens

Grant Park (beautiful waterfront; extensive plantings)

Humboldt Park (Rose Garden)

Jackson Park
An Island Park; extensive plantings; Perennial Garden; Oriental Garden

Lincoln Park (conservatory and gardens)

Evanston

Merrick Park Rose Garden

Shakespeare Garden
(Northwestern University Campus)
Beautiful in design; historically correct

Highland Park: Municipal Rose Garden

Lombard: Lilacia Park (fine collection of lilacs)

Peoria: Dr. Ernest H. Wilson Memorial Garden

St. Charles: "Grangemead Lodge" (Wildflower Preserve and Bird Sanctuary)

Springfield: The Abraham Lincoln Memorial Garden

INDIANA

Fort Wayne: Municipal Rose Garden (sunken garden; bird sanctuary)

Michigan City: International Friendship Gardens

IOWA

Des Moines

Ewing Park (lilacs)

Greenwood Park Rose Garden

Union Park (formal gardens; trial gardens)

Dubuque: Grandview Park (Peony Trail)

Oskaloosa: Edmondson Park (peonies)

KANSAS

Manhattan: Municipal Park Rose Garden and Rock Garden

Topeka: Reinisch Rose and Rock Gardens

KENTUCKY

Bardstown: My Old Kentucky Home State Park (interesting old garden)

Frankfort: Liberty Hall: Restored Gardens (maintained by the Garden Club of Kentucky)

Lexington: "Ashland": A lovely garden (maintained by the Garden Club of Kentucky)

Louisville: Reservoir Park Rose Garden

LOUISIANA

Hammond: Zemurray Gardens (azaleas, camellias, dogwood, wild flowers)

Many: Hodges Gardens, notable plantings, holds great interest for all visitors

New Iberia: Avery Island Jungle Gardens (camellias, azaleas, iris, sub-tropical plants; bird refuge)

New Orleans: City Park Rose Garden

St. Francisville: "Afton Villa"
(ante-bellum home and azalea garden)

MAINE

Portland: Henry Wadsworth Longfellow House (restored garden)

MARYLAND

Annapolis: Baltimore Museum of Art (rose garden and perennial garden)

Baltimore: Druid Hill Park Rose Garden

Beltsville: U.S. Dept. of Agriculture (chrysanthemums and lilies)

Towson: Hampton Mansion (restored terraced gardens)

MASSACHUSETTS

Barnstable: St. Mary's Church Garden (a small garden of great charm and significance)

Boston

    Boston Public Gardens (established in 1839)
    Tulips in springtime: seasonal displays

    Fenway Park Rose Garden

    Isabella Stuart Gardner Museum
    Inner Court of great beauty and horticultural interest; Garden featuring tulips, roses and unusual ground covers

Quincy: John Quincy Adams House (interesting old gardens)

Salem

    First Church of Salem
    A period garden of great beauty
    Horticulturally and architecturally perfect

    House of the Seven Gables
    Interesting garden of the colonial period

Stockbridge: Berkshire Garden Center
Interesting plant collections; herb garden

Waltham: Waltham Field Station (University of Massachusetts) Perennials in great variety

Westfield: Chauncy Allen Park
Colonial herb garden: "Grandmother's Garden"

MICHIGAN

Adrian: Hidden Lake Gardens (iris, bulbs, rock garden)

Dearborn: *Greenfield Village
(English Cotswold Garden)

Detroit: Oak Park
Iris, dahlias, native plants, rock plants

Lansing: Cooley Gardens, Potter Park (roses)

MINNESOTA

Minneapolis: Lyndale Park (rose garden, rock garden, bog garden)

MISSISSIPPI

Jackson: Municipal Rose Garden

Natchez: *Home and Garden tours in March

MISSOURI

Cape Girardeau: Ten Mile Rose Garden (along Highway 61 between Jackson and Cape Girardeau)

Centralia: Chance Gardens (more than 450 varieties of flowers)

Independence: Glendale Rose Garden (formal planting of over 5,000 roses)

Jefferson City: State Capitol Grounds (flowers and shrubs in great variety)

Kansas City: Jacob L. Loose Memorial Park (Municipal Rose Garden)

Kirksville: Sunken Garden (State Teachers' College)
Iris, dahlias, magnolias, flowering crabs

St. Louis

    Forest Park
    The Jewel Box Gardens: roses, iris, peonies, chrysanthemums

    Shaw's Garden
    Lilies, roses, orchids, chrysanthemums

    Tower Grove Park
    Lily ponds

Springfield: Phelps Grove Park (roses, dahlias, annuals)

MONTANA

Glacier National Park: Display of annuals and perennials

Great Falls: Gibson Park (rock garden)

Missoula: Sunset Park
(American Rose Society Test Garden)

NEBRASKA

Lincoln: Lincoln City Park
(rose garden; sunken garden)

Omaha: Mt. Vernon Municipal Garden
Reproduction of George Washington's Garden

NEW HAMPSHIRE

Cornish: St. Gaudens Memorial Garden

Exeter: Exeter Wild Flower Gardens

NEW JERSEY

Elizabeth: The Henry S. Chatfield Memorial Garden
Spring bulbs, annuals, Japanese cherries, rock garden

Plainfield: Cedar Brook Park
Shakespeare Garden, Peony and Iris Garden, Wild Flower Preserve

Upper Montclair: The Presby Memorial Iris Garden

NEW MEXICO

Albuquerque
Native Plant Trial Garden
(project of Council of Albuquerque Garden Clubs)

Rose Garden and Cactus Garden on the University Grounds

Raton: Library Park
Memorial Rose Garden
(project of the Raton Garden Club)

Roswell: Museum Grounds (Municipal Rose Garden)

Santa Fe
Art Museum
Beautiful patio
(project of the Santa Fe Garden Club)

Old Governor's Palace (interesting patio)

State Capitol
A patio of great distinction
(project of the Las Jardinieras Garden Club)

NEW YORK

Monticello: "Shofu-den": a replica of a Japanese palace
Extensive and beautiful gardens

New York City
*The Cloisters, Fort Tryon Park
Mediæval gardens in a perfect setting. Outstanding

Museum of Modern Art
Modern garden

Van Cortlandt House, Broadway and 242nd Street
House built in 1748; formal Dutch garden of the period

Stillwell–Perine House, 1476 Richmond Road, Dongan Hills, S.I.
House built 1679; colonial garden of the period

Niagara Falls: Hyde Park (rose garden)

Oyster Bay: "Planting Fields"
(azaleas, camellias, rhododendrons)

Rochester
Cobbs Hill Park
(lilacs and Chinese shrubs)

Durand-Eastman Park
(azaleas, peonies, roses, rhododendrons)

Highland Park (lilacs, roses, rhododendrons)

Maplewood Park
(rose garden; crab-apples, hawthorns)

Saratoga Springs
Congress Park
Italian Garden; displays of annuals and perennials

Petrified Sea Gardens
Area of petrified plants of earliest types; large rock garden

"Yaddo" Estate
Formal rose garden; rock garden

Schenectady: Jackson's Gardens, Union College
Historical restoration: rose garden, perennials, wild garden

Syracuse
Thornen Park
Rose Garden (10,000 bushes), herb garden, perennial garden

Burlingham Memorial Garden
Alpine plants

NORTH CAROLINA

Ashville
Biltmore House (large formal gardens, greenhouse)

Craggy Gardens (rhododendrons)

Blowing Rock: Rhododendron Garden

Charlotte: Municipal Rose Garden

Durham: Sarah P. Duke Memorial Garden (iris)

Manteo: Elizabethan Garden
On the site of the "Lost Colony" an Elizabethan Garden is being constructed under the auspices of the Garden Club of North Carolina

Wilmington: Orton Plantation
Azaleas, camellias, holly, cypress swamps

NORTH DAKOTA

Fargo: Island Park (rose garden)

OHIO

Cincinnati: Auit Park (formal gardens)

Cleveland
Cleveland Garden Center (interesting roof garden)

Wade Park (fine arts garden)

Mansfield: *Kingwood Center
Interesting gardens and plant collections

Toledo: Ottawa Park Municipal Rose Garden

OKLAHOMA

Muskogee: Honor Heights Park (rose garden)

Oklahoma City: Will Rogers Park (rose garden)

Tulsa: Municipal Rose Garden

Brookings: Azalea State Park

Portland

Peninsula Park, Sunken Rose Garden
Chrysanthemum Society Test Garden

Salem: Schreiner Iris Gardens
Ware Lily Gardens

PENNSYLVANIA

Harrisburg

Municipal Rose Garden

Breeze Hill Gardens (interesting plant collections)

Hershey: Hershey Garden (tulip display; outstanding rose garden)

Philadelphia

Azalea Garden near the Art Museum in Fairmount Park

Bartram's Garden (home of America's first great botanist)
Of historical interest

Valley Forge: Valley Forge State Park
Magnificent dogwood display in May

Washington's Crossing

*Bowman's Hill State Wild Flower Preserve
Notable development of a natural area

RHODE ISLAND

Providence: Roger Williams Park
Azalea and tulip displays; rose garden

SOUTH CAROLINA

Charleston

*Magnolia Gardens
Notable for its superb display of azaleas and camellias

Middleton Place
Fine old plantation home and gardens; azaleas, camellias

*Cypress Gardens
Magnificent cypress trees; notable azalea display

Columbia: Memorial Gardens
Azaleas, camellias, superb boxwood; wall garden

Georgetown: Brookgreen Gardens
Southern plantation home, sculpture featured in the garden

Orangeburg: Edisto Gardens (azaleas, roses, wisteria)

Sumtu: Dunndell Gardens (Japanese Iris)

SOUTH DAKOTA

Rapid City: Municipal Rose Garden

Sioux Falls: State Rose Garden (hardy roses)

Vermillion: Iris Garden

TENNESSEE

Chattanooga

Warner Park
Iris garden; rose garden

Great Smoky Mountains National Park
Azaleas, laurel, rhododendron, dogwood, redbud, wild flowers

Memphis: Overton Park (Memorial Rose Garden)

Nashville: "The Hermitage"
Home and garden of Andrew Jackson

TEXAS

Austin

Laguna Gloria Art Gallery Garden; historical site
Italian building and beautiful gardens

Dallas

Cloister Garden, 3300 Mockingbird Lane

Iris Bowl

Lambert Gardens, 3800 Northwest Highway
Interesting plant materials

Oak Cliff Park Rose Garden

Houston

Herman Park (rose garden)

Museum of Fine Arts Garden

San Antonio: Brackenridge Park (Formal Garden; Chinese Garden)

Tyler: Municipal Rose Garden

Weatherford: Chandor Gardens
Extensive, beautiful gardens

UTAH

Salt Lake City: Liberty Park (Rose Garden)

VERMONT

Bennington: Memorial Garden
Interesting plant material (project of the Plain Dirt Gardeners of Bennington)

Brattleboro

Living Memorial Park
Interesting garden (project of the Garden Club of Brattleboro)

"Naulahka", home of Rudyard Kipling
Perennial garden, wall garden (house and garden in the English tradition)

Shelburne: Shelburne Museum Garden
Old-fashioned roses and herbs

VIRGINIA

Alexandria

Gunston Hall (15 miles south of Alexandria)
Home of George Mason. Beautiful garden (restored by The Garden Club of Virginia)

Bowling Green: "Hampton Manor"
Unusual garden by Salvador Dali

Charlottesville

"Ash Lawn", home of James Monroe
Boxwood garden, well preserved and with much charm

"Monticello", home of Thomas Jefferson
Garden faithfully restored (by The Garden Club of Virginia)

Fredericksburg

"Kenmore", home of Betty (Washington) Lewis
Gardens restored (by The Garden Club of Virginia)

"Stratford Hall" (42 miles east of Fredericksburg)
Home of the Lees. Garden restored (by The Garden Club of Virginia)

Jamestown: Old English Rose Garden

Mt. Vernon: *Home and garden of George Washington
A notable garden restoration; great historic interest

Norfolk: *Azalea Gardens
Azaleas, laurel, rhododendron, Japanese Iris

Staunton: Birthplace of Woodrow Wilson
Garden of Victorian design

Williamsburg: *A notable colonial restoration of homes and gardens; of great interest to all Americans

Yorktown: York Hall Gardens (restored colonial gardens)

WASHINGTON

Seattle

Rain Forest
Giant trees; ferns, lichens and mosses

Woodland Park (rose garden)

Tacoma: McKinley Park
Rose Garden; perennial garden; water garden

Grandview: Municipal Rose Garden

Spokane: Manito Sunken Gardens (lilacs and roses)

WEST VIRGINIA

Huntington: Ritter Park (Municipal Rose Garden)

WISCONSIN

Lake Geneva: Chrysanthemum Test Garden

Milwaukee

Mitchell Park (conservatory and sunken garden)

Skittnall Park
Extensive flower gardens; roses, tuberous begonias, chrysanthemums

WYOMING

Cheyenne: Cheyenne Horticultural Station
Gardens and plant collection

ARBORETUMS AND BOTANICAL GARDENS

ARIZONA

Boyce Thompson Southwestern Arboretum—(*Superior*)
(Succulents, woody trees and shrubs)

Desert Botanical Garden of Arizona—(*Tempe*)
(Succulents, woody trees and shrubs)

CALIFORNIA

Rancho Santa Ana—(*Claremont*)
(Succulents, perennials, woody trees and shrubs)

University of California Botanical Garden—(*Berkeley*)
(Succulents, evergreens, woody trees and shrubs)

Botanical Garden, University of California—
(*Los Angeles*)
(Succulents, perennials, evergreens, woody trees and shrubs)

Institute of Forest Genetics—(*Placerville*)
(Evergreens, woody trees and shrubs, pines)

Strybing Arboretum at Golden Gate Park—
(*San Francisco*)
(Native annuals, evergreens, woody trees and shrubs)

Huntington Botanical Garden—(*San Marino*)
(Succulents, evergreens, woody trees and shrubs)

Santa Barbara Botanic Garden—(*Santa Barbara*)
(Perennials, woody trees and shrubs)

COLORADO

Glenmore Arboretum—(*Buffalo Creek*)
(Evergreens, native woody trees and shrubs)

CONNECTICUT

Marsh Botanical Gardens, Yale University—
(*New Haven*)
(Evergreens, woody trees and shrubs)

CONNECTICUT—continued

Connecticut Arboretum at Connecticut College—
(*New London*)
(Native evergreens, native woody trees and shrubs)

DISTRICT OF COLUMBIA

National Aboretum—(*Washington*)

National Botanic Garden—(*Washington*)

FLORIDA

Fairchild Tropical Garden—(*Coconut Grove*)
(Palms and other tropical trees, vines and shrubs)

McKee Jungle Gardens—(*Vero Beach*)
(Evergreens, palms, woody trees and shrubs, vines, orchids)

The Mead Botanical Garden—(*Winter Park*)
(Orchids and other tropical plants)

ILLINOIS

Garfield Park Conservatory—(*Chicago*)
(Exotics chiefly)

Morton Arboretum—(*Lisle*)
(Evergreens, woody trees and shrubs, 150 hedges, 100 ground covers, and a garden of old-fashioned roses containing 285 varieties; as complete a collection of every genus as possible)

Lilacia Park—(*Lombard*)
(Perennials—tulips; shrubs—lilacs)

INDIANA

Butler Botanical Garden, Butler University—
(*Indianapolis*)
(Perennials, annuals, woody trees and shrubs)

Christy Woods (formerly Ball Arboretum)—(*Muncie*)
(Annuals, woody trees and shrubs)

IOWA

Iowa State College Arboretum—(*Ames*)
(Evergreens, woody trees and shrubs)

KANSAS

Indian Hill Arboretum—(*Topeka*)
(Woody trees and shrubs, pines, lilacs, oaks, junipers and thorns)

LOUISIANA

McIlhenny Arboretum—(*Avery Island*)
(Evergreens, woody trees and shrubs)

MASSACHUSETTS

Arnold Arboretum, Harvard University—
(*Jamaica Plain*)
(Evergreens, woody trees and shrubs)

Lexington (Mass.) Botanic Gardens, Inc.—(*Lexington*)
(Perennials—Iris, Primula, Sedum, Phlox, Saxifraga, Hemerocallis)

Smith College Arboretum—(*Northampton*)
(Succulents, perennials, annuals, evergreens, woody trees and shrubs)

Garden in the Woods—(*South Sudbury*)
(Native plants—wild flowers)

Alexandra Botanic Garden and Hunnewell Arboretum, Wellesley College—(*Wellesley*)
(Evergreens, woody trees and shrubs)

Walter Hunnewell Arboretum—(*Wellesley*)
(Conifers and Rhododendrons)

MICHIGAN

Nichols Arboretum, University of Michigan—
(*Ann Arbor*)
(Peonies, evergreens, woody trees and shrubs)

Slayton Arboretum and Botanical Garden—(*Hillsdale*)
(Perennials, evergreens, woody trees and shrubs)

MINNESOTA

Eloise Butler Wild Flower Garden in Theodore Wirth Park—(*Minneapolis*)
(Wild flowers and plants of Minnesota, in more than 1,000 varieties)

MISSOURI

Missouri Botanical Garden—(*St. Louis*)
(Succulents, evergreens, woody trees and shrubs)

NEW JERSEY

Arboretum of Horticultural Farm, New Jersey Agricultural Experiment Station—(*New Brunswick*)
(Perennials, woody trees and shrubs—Rhododendron)

NEW YORK

Brooklyn Botanic Garden—(*Brooklyn*)
(Trees and shrubs; extensive gardens)

Long Island Agricultural and Technical Institute—
(*Farmingdale*)
(Perennials, annuals, evergreens, woody trees and shrubs)

Cornell Plantations, Cornell University—(*Ithaca*)
(Evergreens, woody trees and shrubs)

New York Botanical Garden—(*New York City*)
(Representatives of all plant groups maintained)

Thomas C. Desmond Arboretum—(*Newburgh*)
(Woody trees and shrubs)

Highland and Durand-Eastman Park Arboretum, Rochester Parks Department—(*Rochester*)
(Evergreens, woody trees and shrubs—Syringa, Malus, coniferous evergreens)

Arboretum of the Boyce Thompson Institute for Plant Research—(*Yonkers*)
(Evergreens, woody trees and shrubs)

OHIO

Mt. Airy Forest Arboretum—(*Cincinnati*)
(Evergreens, woody trees and shrubs)

PENNSYLVANIA

Masonic Home Arboretum—(*Elizabethtown*)
(Hardy cacti, perennials, annuals, evergreens, woody trees and shrubs—Ilex, Syringa)

John F. Tyler Arboretum—(*Lima*)
(Woody trees and shrubs—unusually large specimens of Sequoia, Cedrus libani, Picea orientalis)

Bowman's Hill State Wild Flower Preserve in Washington Crossing Park—(*New Hope*)
(Woody trees and shrubs but especially ferns, fern allies and wild flowers native to Pennsylvania)

Morris Arboretum, affiliated with University of Pennsylvania—(Philadelphia—*Chestnut Hill*)
(Wall plants and ferns; evergreens; woody trees and shrubs—Rhododendrons and Azaleas; Clematis species, varieties and hybrids)

Botanical Garden of the Reading Public Museum and Art Gallery—(*Reading*)
(Perennials, annuals, evergreens, woody trees and shrubs)

PENNSYLVANIA—continued

Arthur Hoyt Scott Horticultural Foundation, Swarthmore College—(*Swarthmore*)
(Woody trees and shrubs—Magnolia, Malus, Prunes, Rhododendrons, Syringa, Pæonia, Iris)

TEXAS

Fort Worth Botanic Garden—(*Fort Worth*)

VIRGINIA

The Blandy Experimental Farm Arboretum—(*Boyce*)
(Evergreens, woody trees and shrubs)
Norfolk Botanical Garden—(*Norfolk*)
(Azaleas, Camellias, Crape Myrtles, rhododendrons, roses)
Maymont Park—(*Richmond*)
(Perennials, evergreens, woody trees and shrubs)

WASHINGTON

University of Washington Arboretum—(*Seattle*)
(Evergreens, woody trees and shrubs—Rhododendron)

WISCONSIN

University of Wisconsin Arboretum—(*Madison*)
(Evergreens, woody trees and shrubs, prairie studies, woods, wild flowers)
The Botanical Gardens, Charles B. Whitnall Park—(*Milwaukee*)
(Perennials, annuals, evergreens, woody trees and shrubs)

SERVICES AVAILABLE TO THE HOME GARDENER THROUGH THE STATE AGRICULTURAL COLLEGES AND UNIVERSITIES

Publication of bulletins and circulars on flowers, fruits, lawns, shrubs, trees, vegetables, etc. (List of publications usually available upon request.)

Demonstration gardens and experimental and test gardens are maintained at most of the State Colleges. These gardens are open to the public and usually contain much of interest for the gardener.

A Soil Testing Service is offered to residents of the State by some State Colleges.

Through the Extension Service, with headquarters at the State College, and through the local County Agricultural Agent advice on individual problems may be obtained.

The 4-H Clubs for boys and girls which are organized through the Extension Service offer interesting flower, fruit and vegetable projects.

STATE COLLEGES AND UNIVERSITIES

ALABAMA
Alabama Polytechnic Institute, *Auburn*

ARIZONA
University of Arizona, *Tucson*

ARKANSAS
University of Arkansas, *Fayetteville*

CALIFORNIA
University of California,
Department of Landscape Arch., *Berkeley*
Department of Floriculture, *Davis*

COLORADO
Colorado Agricultural and Mechanical College,
Fort Collins

CONNECTICUT
University of Connecticut, *Storrs*

DELAWARE
University of Delaware, *Newark*

FLORIDA
University of Florida, *Gainesville*

GEORGIA
University of Georgia, *Athens*

IDAHO
University of Idaho, *Moscow*

ILLINOIS
University of Illinois, *Urbana*

INDIANA
Purdue University, *LaFayette*

IOWA
Iowa State College of Agriculture, *Ames*

KANSAS
Kansas State College of Agriculture, *Manhattan*

KENTUCKY
University of Kentucky, *Lexington*

LOUISIANA
Louisiana State University,
University Station, Baton Rouge

MAINE
University of Maine, *Orono*

MARYLAND
University of Maryland, *College Park*

MASSACHUSETTS
University of Massachusetts, *Amherst*

MICHIGAN
Michigan State College of Agriculture, *East Lansing*

MISSISSIPPI
Mississippi State College, *State College*

MISSOURI
University of Missouri, *Columbia*

MONTANA
Montana State College, *Bozeman*

NEBRASKA
University of Nebraska, *Lincoln*

NEVADA
University of Nevada, *Reno*

NEW HAMPSHIRE
University of New Hampshire, Durham

NEW JERSEY
Rutgers University, *New Brunswick*

NEW MEXICO
New Mexico College of Agriculture, *Mesilla Park*

NEW YORK
New York State College of Agriculture,
Cornell University, *Ithaca*

NORTH CAROLINA
North Carolina State College of Agriculture, *Raleigh*

NORTH DAKOTA
North Dakota Agricultural College,
State College Station, Fargo

OHIO
College of Agriculture, University of Ohio, *Columbus*

OKLAHOMA
Oklahoma Agricultural College, *Stillwater*

OREGON
Oregon State College, *Corvallis*

PENNSYLVANIA
Pennsylvania State University, *University Park*

RHODE ISLAND
University of Rhode Island, *Kingston*

SOUTH CAROLINA
Clemson Agricultural College, *Clemson*

SOUTH DAKOTA
South Dakota State College of Agriculture,
State College Station

TENNESSEE
University of Tennessee, *Knoxville*

TEXAS
Texas Agricultural College, *College Station*

UTAH
Utah State Agricultural College, *Logan*

VERMONT
University of Vermont, *Burlington*

VIRGINIA
Virginia Polytechnic Institute, *Blacksburg*

WASHINGTON
State College of Washington, *Pullman*

WEST VIRGINIA
West Virginia University, *Morgantown*

WISCONSIN
University of Wisconsin, *Madison*

WYOMING
University of Wyoming, *Laramie*

PLANT SOCIETIES

African Violet Society of America, Inc.   Dues $3.00
Secretary: Mrs. George Mayer,
  1014 Forrest Hills Ave.,
    Calumet City, Ill.

American Begonia Society   Dues $2.50
Secretary: Mr. Jack MacLanahan,
  3734 Overland Ave.,
    Los Angeles 34, Calif.

American Camellia Society   Dues $5.00
Secretary: Mr. Arthur C. Brown,
  Box 2398, University Station,
    Gainesville, Florida.

American Daffodil Society
Secretary: Mr. Willis H. Wheeler,
  3171 N. Quincy St.,
    Arlington 7, Va.

American Dahlia Society, Inc.   Dues $4.00
Secretary: Mr. Edward B. Lloyd,
  10 Crestmont Rd.,
    Montclair, N.J.

American Delphinium Society   Dues $3.00
President: Mr. Arthur Brooks,
  Van Wert, Ohio.

American Fern Society
Secretary: Mildred E. Faust,
  501 University Place,
    Syracuse 10, N.Y.

American Fuchsia Society   Dues $1.50
Secretary: Mr. Clelle T. LeHew,
  1633 Moreland Drive,
    Alameda, Calif.

American Gloxinia Society   Dues $1.50
Secretary: H. E. Dillard,
  3810 Bales Ave.,
    Kansas City 28, Mo.

American Hemerocallis Society   Dues $2.50
Secretary: Olive M. Hindman
  404 Weigle Ave.,
    Sebring, Florida

American Hibiscus Society   Dues $3.00
Secretary: Mrs. Ruth Stuart Allen,
  355 N.E. 59 St., Miami, Fla.

The American Horticultural Society, Inc.   Dues $5.00
Secretary: Dr. Francis de Vos,
  1600 Bladensburg Rd., N.E.,
    Washington 2, D.C.

American Iris Society   Dues $4.00
Secretary: Dr. L. F. Randolph,
  Sheldon Rd., Ithaca, N.Y.

American Orchid Society, Inc.   Dues $7.00
Secretary: Dr. O. Wesley Davidson,
  Rutgers University,
    New Brunswick, N.J.

American Penstemon Society   Dues $1.00
Secretary: Mrs. E. M. Babb,
  213 Lambert St., Portland, Maine

American Peony Society   Dues $5.00
Secretary: Mr. George W. Peyton,
  Box 1, Rapidan, Va.

American Plant Life Society   Dues $3.00
Secretary: Mrs. Lydia Barnett,
  3162 Haven Park,
    Del Monte, Calif.

American Primrose Society   Dues $2.50
Secretary: Mrs. Louise H. Gee,
  923 Avenue "A", Oswego, Ore.

American Rhododendron Society   Dues $5.00
Secretary: Mrs. Ruth M. Hansen,
  3514 N. Russet St.,
    Portland 17, Ore.

American Rock Garden Society   Dues $3.50
Secretary: Mr. E. L. Totten,
  238 Sheridan Ave., Hohokus, N.J.

American Rose Society   Dues $4.50
Secretary: James P. Gurney,
  4048 Roselea Place,
    Columbus 14, Ohio.

The Bromeliad Society   Dues $3.50
Secretary: Victoria Padilla,
  647 S. Saltair Ave.,
    Los Angeles 49, Calif.

The Cactus and Succulent Society of America, Inc.   Dues $3.00
Secretary: Mrs. Ethel G. Rush,
  820 W. 115 St.,
    Los Angeles 44, Calif.

The Canadian Rose Society   Dues $2.00
Secretary: Mrs. G. P. Amos,
  38 Golf Club Rd., Toronto 13,
    Ontario, Canada.

Epiphyllum Society of America
Secretary: Mrs. Martha F. Maxwell,
  500 Grove Place,
    Glendale 6, Calif.

The Gourd Society of America, Inc.   Dues $2.00
Secretary: Mrs. Raymond Wheeler,
  Horticultural Hall, Boston, Mass.

The Hemerocallis Society   Dues $3.50
Secretary: Mrs. Daisy L. Ferrick,
  416 Arter Ave., Topeka, Kan.

The Herb Society of America   Dues $5.00
Secretary: Mrs. Francis R. Williams,
  234 Highland Ave.,
    Winchester, Mass.

Holly Society of America, Inc.	Dues $6.00
Secretary: Mr. Charles A. Young, Jr., Bergner Mansion, Baltimore 16, Md.	

International Geranium Society　　　　Dues $3.00
　Secretary: Mrs. Vernon Ireland,
　　　1413 Bluff Drive,
　　　　Santa Barbara, Calif.

National Chrysanthemum Society, Inc.　Dues $3.00
　Secretary: Miss Dorothy P. Tuthill,
　　　345 Milton Rd., Rye, N.Y.

The National Tulip Society, Inc.　　　Dues $3.00
　Secretary: Mr. Felix R. Tyroler,
　　　55 West 42 St.,
　　　　New York 36, N.Y.

New England Gladiolus Society　　　　Dues $3.00
　Secretary: Miss Marion P. Ayer,
　　　12 Newbury Park,
　　　　Needham, Mass.

North American Gladiolus Council　　　Dues $2.00
　Secretary: Mr. Henry S. Sentman,
　　　820 Ontario St.,
　　　　Havre de Grace, Md.

North American Lily Society　　　　　Dues $3.00
　Treasurer: P. M. Byam,
　　　47 Denvale Rd., Toronto 16,
　　　　Ontario, Canada.

Society for Louisiana Irises
　Secretary: Miss Aline Arceneaux,
　　　Box 55, Southwestern Louisiana
　　　　Institute, Lafayette, La.

Southern California Camellia Society, Inc.　Dues $5.00
　Secretary: Col. C. M. Gale,
　　　40 N. San Rafael Ave.,
　　　　Pasadena 2, Calif.

Spuria Iris Society (Spuria Section of The
　American Iris Society)
　Secretary: Mrs. Charles A. Johnson,
　　　2233 Pelham, Houston, Tex.

The Wild Flower Preservation Society, Inc.　Dues $2.50
　Secretary: Edna L. Stone,
　　　3740 Oliver St., N.W.,
　　　　Washington 15, D.C.

GARDEN CALENDAR

(Pages for full instructions are listed after some of the topics.)

SPRING GARDEN CALENDAR

The Flower Garden

Mulch: The mulch on flower borders may be gradually removed or, if composed of manure, it should be lightly forked in. (Page 501.)

Lime: Lime may be broadcast *after* manure is forked in (if considered necessary). (Page 170.)

Edging: Edge the garden beds, and as soon as the soil is warm and mellow give the first cultivation. (Page 677.)

Fertilizer: Apply a top-dressing of a good complete fertilizer to the perennial beds. (Page 343.)

Hotbeds: Start manure-heated hotbeds in very early spring. (Page 512.)

Roses: New roses should be planted as soon as the ground is workable. Prune the bush roses before growth starts. Remove hills and the winter mulch. Top-dress the rosebeds with a good commercial fertilizer. Later, after leaf growth begins, keep up a regular spray or dust schedule. (Page 426.)

Lily Pool: Drain and clean pool before growth begins. Plant new hardy water lilies early.

Wood Ashes: Wood ashes from winter fire places may be spread at the rate of 1 pound to 200 square feet and cultivated in.

Division of Perennials: Lift and divide such perennials as the hardy asters, chrysanthemums, phlox, and physostegia, which have a tendency to become overcrowded.

Hardening-off: Seedlings started in the greenhouse or indoors should be hardened off by use of coldframes.

Coldframes: Lift sash on coldframes when temperature rises above 45° F. (Page 511.)

Seed Sowing:

1. In very early spring, start seeds indoors or in the greenhouse in flats, pots, or nutrient solution. (Page 477.)
2. Start spring-sown perennials and hardy and half-hardy annuals early in frames. (Page 508.)
3. Sow lily seed (or in fall). (Page 416.)
4. Sow very hardy annual seeds in open ground as soon as the ground is workable. (Page 476.)
5. Sow half-hardy annual seeds in open as soon as frost is over. (Page 476.)

Cuttings: Take softwood stem cuttings of such perennials as delphinium, phlox, chrysanthemum—when new growth is tender.

Dahlias: Divide dahlias, and plant after all danger of frost is over.

Gladioli: Treat gladiolus corms with bichloride of mercury, and make several plantings for succession of bloom.

Tender Bulbs: Plant tender summer-flowering "bulbs" —galtonia, tritonia, tigridias, gladioli, anemones, kniphofia, ismene. (Page 394.)

Tuberous-rooted Begonias: May be planted out of doors after all danger of frost is over. (Page 396.)

House Plants: Remove house plants to shady place in garden in late spring when night temperatures do not drop too low.

Peonies: In late spring an application of complete fertilizer or liquid manure may be made. Pinch off any side buds to encourage larger bloom.

Pinching Back: Pinch back annuals which need to be trained for bushiness when 4 to 6 inches high—zinnias, petunias, salvia, etc. (Page 307.)

Weeding: Keep ahead of the weeds with cultivator or hoe.

Staking: Place garden stakes as plants reach medium height.

The Vegetable Garden

Preparation of Soil: If fall cultivation with strawy manure was done, spread lime in very early spring, several weeks before seeding. If fall cultivation was not done, then fork in strawy manure as early as possible.

Rhubarb: An early crop may be had by covering the plants with tall baskets and mounding manure about them in very early spring. (Page 591.)

Hotbed: Make a sowing of melon and cucumber seeds for an early crop as soon as there is room after transplanting other seedlings into the open ground.

Weeds: Keep ahead of the weeds with cultivator or hoe.

Lawn

Fertilizer: Make an early application of commercial fertilizer. (Page 183.)

Mowing: Do not mow the lawn until the grass has reached a height of about 2 inches. It is at this season that the roots are renewed and it is essential that the plants have an opportunity to make vigorous top growth.

Rolling: Rake and roll in order to level any mounds caused by freezing action.

Seeding: Bare spots on lawn may be seeded when the soil is not soggy. New lawns may be started at this time, but a better time is the fall. (Page 193.)

Trees and Shrubs

Transplanting: When transplanting trees and shrubs, place several shovelfuls of damp peat moss in the hole. The great benefits to be gained in following this practice are explained on page 212.

Wax Spray: If trees and shrubs are sprayed with a specially prepared wax at the time of transplanting, they will suffer comparatively little shock. (Page 210.)

Pruning: Spring-flowering shrubs should be pruned after bloom. (Page 241.)

Evergreens: Prune evergreens just before growth starts.

Fertilizers: Fertilize trees and shrubs before growth begins. (Page 219.)

Spraying: If there is any evidence of scale, spray with dormant spray early, before buds open, and again in the fall.

Fruit

Strawberries: Set strawberry plants in early spring. Gradually remove straw mulch from strawberry plants wintered over and place in between rows when danger of frost is over.

New Stock: Plant blueberries, blackberries, currants, and gooseberries very early in spring.

SUMMER GARDEN CALENDAR

The Flower Garden

Mulch: Mulch lily borders or bulb clumps. Mulch perennials where soil is clayey and inclined to bake hard into a crust. (Page 500.)

Propagating Case: Use part of frames for propagating case, replacing soil with sand and peat moss, for cuttings. (Page 682.)

Cuttings: Take cuttings of violas, phlox divaricata, phlox subulata, arabis, iberis and other rock plants. Take softwood and half-ripened cuttings of woody plants and shrubs before wood ripens. In late summer, take cuttings of garden-flowering plants for house-plant use.

Lilies: Propagation of lilies by scales after flowering period. Any transplanting may be done after the foliage dies back, toward the end of the summer.

Division: Divide Bearded iris. Divide old clumps of narcissus, hyacinths and other spring-flowering bulbs in early summer after blooming.

Insect Control: Watch for insects now and keep to spray schedule on those plants which need it throughout the summer.

Tropical Water-Lilies: Plant tropical water-lilies early in summer.

Roses: Ramblers and climbers should be pruned immediately after blooming. (Page 430.)

Hollyhocks: Gather and sow hollyhock seed where plants are to bloom.

Annuals: Keep faded blooms of annuals cut off so that seed will not set, if longer blooming period is desired.

Weed Control: Weed killers may be applied to poison ivy and any other rank growers.

Delphiniums: Cut delphiniums back after blooming to prevent seeding. A second bloom will thus be encouraged late in summer.

Everlastings: Cut, dry and store everlastings in paper bags toward the end of the summer.

Seed Sowing: Many perennial seeds may be sown now. (Page 476.)

The Vegetable Garden

Succession: Make replantings as soon as early crops are harvested.

Cultivation: Keep ahead of the weeds with hoe or cultivator, which at the same time forms a dust mulch beneficial to the plants. (Page 677.)

Insect Control: Watch for insects on each crop and apply proper controls.

Late Crops: A late crop of beans, beets, lettuce, peas, and spinach may be planted toward the end of summer (as late as the middle of August in the vicinity of Philadelphia).

Lawn

Crabgrass: If crabgrass is troublesome, make an application of a good control in late July or early August in order to prevent seed formation. (Page 198.)

Cutting: Lawns should not be cut as closely during the summer as during the faster growing periods. Therefore, raise the cutting blades of mower.

New Lawn: Make plans and preparations for any new lawn areas toward the end of the summer, in order to do the seeding in early fall. (Page 173.)

Trees and Shrubs

Box: Trim box in late summer after new growth is made.

Lilacs: When cutting branches of bloom for indoor bouquets, it is best to keep in mind the shape of the shrub at the same time. Often this is all the pruning lilacs need. However, if the shrub is inclined to be leggy, this may be remedied by cutting off dead heads after blooming, with somewhat long branches.

Mulch: A mulch of humus on box increases the vigor and protects the roots from summer heat.

Dead Heads: Remove dead flower-heads from rhododendrons and azaleas for neatness and strength of the plant.

Wisteria: A light pruning should be made during the summer to shorten lengthy vegetative strands and to promote better bloom the following year.

Hedges: Early in the summer, trim sheared deciduous hedges before the new growth hardens, which makes it difficult to prune. Late in the summer, evergreen formal hedges can be clipped. Deciduous hedges may have a second light trimming.

Evergreen Plantings: Evergreens should be planted toward the end of the summer.

Fruit

Layering: Many plants may be propagated during the summer by layering. Black Raspberries, and plants similar in habit of growth, may be tip-layered in late summer.

Raspberries: Plant suckers of raspberries in late summer.

Thinning: The fruit of apples, pears, peaches, plums, etc., need thinning if they are too thick on the branches.

Pruning: Cut out blackberry and raspberry canes which have fruited.

AUTUMN GARDEN CALENDAR

The Flower Garden

Seed Sowing: Most perennial and some annual seeds may be planted in the fall in frames, late enough to leave them dormant during the winter without germinating until very early spring. Sow certain annuals very late in the autumn in the open ground. For list, see page 316. Sow lily seed as soon as ripe (or in the spring). See page 414.

Lilies: Plant lily bulbs as soon as received and mulch over winter in Northern regions. (Page 413.)

Tender Bulbs: Lift certain tender summer-flowering "bulbs"—tritonia, galtonia, tigridias, gladioli. Lift tuberous-rooted begonia, tender anemones, kniphofia, ismene.

Peonies: Plant new peonies and fertilize established plants in early fall. (Page 368.)

House Plants: Pot up any garden plants which are to be used indoors, and bring house plants in early in the fall. (Page 446.)

Roses: Order bushes early in fall for late planting. Hill up earth around roses in late fall while the soil is still workable. (Page 430.) Make certain climbers and ramblers are fastened securely against winter blasts.

Dahlias: Dahlia tubers may be lifted after the first killing frost and may be placed in storage for the winter. (Page 404.)

Planting of Bulbs: Plant certain hardy summer-flowering "bulbs" such as Eremurus.

Plant tulips and small spring-flowering bulbs in middle to late autumn. Plant hyacinths in early to mid-autumn.

Division of Perennials: If necessary, divide lilies, oriental poppies, bleeding-heart, Japanese iris, phlox, peonies. (Page 489.)

Temporary Protection: Have on hand some heavy paper, boxes, etc., to cover tender garden plants on first nights of frost. Often if the tender plants can be protected from the first early frost, they will bloom for several more weeks.

Transplanting: Any changes in perennial borders should be made in mid-autumn. New perennials may be planted at this time.

Plants and Bulbs for Forcing: Pot up in late fall, for forcing, narcissus, hyacinths, lily-of-the-valley, mertensia, bleeding-heart, astilbe japonica, and store in coldframes for the required period.

Cuttings: Make root cuttings of phlox, Japanese anemones, and other plants.

Soil: Bring a supply of soil into the house for potting purposes during the winter and for seeding indoors in early spring.

Sweet Peas: Prepare trench and sow sweet peas in late fall for seeds to lie dormant for spring germination. (Page 314.)

Pools: Protect any pools by covering, or by floating logs in the water in late autumn. (Page 135.)

Clean Cultivation: Clean up and burn all refuse which may harbor insects.

Insects: Gather and burn insect cocoons, nests, and webs.

The Vegetable Garden

Harvesting: Harvest and store the late vegetable crops such as carrots, winter squash and cabbage.

Celery: Bank celery plants with earth.

Spinach: Prepare a plot of ground for a late winter sowing of spinach seed. Spade or fork it over lightly and leave a roughly raked surface.

Fall Preparation of Soil: Prepare the ground in the fall preferably, by digging and leaving the soil in large clods for the winter action of freezing and thawing to work it into good physical condition. If manure is available, it may be dug in also at the same time. An alternate plan is to work in the lime in the fall, spreading the manure in the spring. The first plan is preferred in order to give the strawy manure a longer time to decay.

Cover Crops: Any free area may be planted with a cover crop to be turned under for green manure the following spring.

Storage: Gather winter squashes and pumpkins after the first frost and store in a pit or mound. Gather any late summer squashes and green tomatoes before frost. The tomatoes can be ripened indoors and will last for several weeks. Harvest the root crops (except parsnips and salsify which are improved by freezing).

Clean Cultivation: Gather any garden refuse—vegetable roots, stalks or leaves—and burn, to avoid harboring insects over the winter.

Lawn

Seeding: Early autumn is the best season of the year for the sowing of grass seed. (Page 186.)

Trees and Shrubs

Planting: Many trees and shrubs may be planted very successfully in the autumn. The few which are the exception to this rule are listed in the chapters on trees and shrubs.

Fertilizer: Trees may be given an application of commercial fertilizer late in the fall to be used for the growth made the following spring.

Evergreens: Be sure that the area surrounding broad-leaved evergreens is well supplied with moisture. Such plants suffer seriously during the winter if the ground is dry, as the transpiration of moisture from the leaves continues, and the roots must be able to absorb sufficient moisture to meet this demand.

Cuttings: Take hardwood and dormant cuttings of deciduous trees and shrubs after the leaves fall. Take evergreen cuttings.

Manure Mulch: A mulch of manure on small trees and shrubs will add fertility to the soil as well as protect them during the winter.

Spraying: If there is any evidence of scale, spray in late fall with dormant spray and again in early spring.

Fruit

Planting: Plant blueberries, currants, gooseberries in late fall.

Borers: Apply paradichlorobenzene to peaches and other trees attacked by borers in early fall. (Page 568.)

WINTER GARDEN CALENDAR

The Flower Garden

Mulch: The winter mulch should not be applied until after the ground is well frozen. (Page 501.)

Coldframes: On days when the temperature rises above 45° F., raise the coldframe sash a few inches in order that the plants may have the benefit of good ventilation. Protect frames with straw mats or similar coverings during extreme cold.

Seeds: Water the seeds which have been sown in the frames if the soil becomes too dry.

Tender Plants: Half-hardy plants, newly started perennials, and tender bulbs may be stored in the frames.

Plants for Forcing: The potted plants and bulbs placed in the coldframes in late autumn may be brought indoors after the necessary period for root development has elapsed.

Cuttings: Take cuttings of saintpaulia, begonia and other house plants.

Tools: Clean tools and rub rusty places with grease or oil before putting away. (Page 503.)

Wood Ashes: Save all wood ashes from the fireplace to be incorporated into the soil in the spring.

Storage:

1. Inspect tubers of dahlias to make certain of right moisture conditions. Sprinkle with water if too dry.
2. Inspect all bulbs, corms, etc. Cut off portions which show decay, and dust with sulphur.

Seed Catalogs: Study seed catalogs and place orders for spring plantings.

Hardy Plants for Forcing: Bring into greenhouse plants which have been stored dormant in frames.

The Vegetable Garden

Seed Sowing Outdoors: In January or early February sow spinach seed on the ground which was prepared for it in the autumn. Cover lightly with strawy manure. The seed will germinate in very early spring and an excellent crop may be obtained.

Seed Sowing Indoors: Celery, cabbage, and onion seed may be sown in late winter for an early crop.

Rhubarb Forcing: Rhubarb dug up in the fall may be forced in the cellar.

Seed Catalogs: Study seed catalogs and place orders for spring planting.

Trees and Shrubs

Protection: Protect young evergreens and newly planted trees and shrubs from wind and severe cold. Corn stalks, burlap tacked on to wooden frames, and straw mats may be used to advantage. Shake snow off evergreen branches to avoid bending and breaking.

Pruning: During the late winter months, prune the shrubs which bear their flowers on the current year's growth. (Page 679.)

Ornamental trees and fruit trees may be pruned during the late winter months. (Page 679.) Burn any parts with disease or insects.

Spraying: Late winter is the most advisable time to apply the dormant spray for various scale insects and other pests and diseases. The chart on page 564 will give full details. Do not use a miscible oil spray when the temperature is below 40° F., as it is liable to cause considerable damage.

Insects: Watch for nests, webs, and tents of various insects. Burn, and use proper spray.

Wisteria: Prune wisteria during its dormant period. (Page 291.)

Mice and Rabbits: Protect trees and shrubs from mice and rabbits by baiting. (Pages 673 and 674.)

Shrub Branches for Forcing: Cut sprays of early-flowering shrubs—forsythia, quince, etc.—in late winter for indoor bloom.

Fruit

Strawberries: Cover strawberry plants with straw ½ to 1 inch deep. (Page 560.)

GLOSSARY

Anther: The terminal part of the reproductive organ or pollen-disseminating part of the "male" flowering plant.

Broadcast: To scatter seed, rather than to sow it in rows or drills.

Cambium: The layer of growing cells just under the bark and outside the wood.

Casein: A substance contained in milk which, when added to sprays and dusts, adds to their adhesive and spreading qualities.

Coniferous: Pertaining to a tree which bears woody cones containing naked seeds.

Crop Rotation: The practice of alternating crops in a garden or field to avoid (1) the plant's taking the same food elements out of the soil year after year which are necessary to the plant's growth, and (2) the increase of the insects and diseases characteristic of one plant.

Cultivation: The practice of stirring the surface of the soil (1) to aërate the soil, (2) to break the crust which sometimes forms after the wet soil has dried in the sun, (3) to discourage weed growth, (4) to form a dust mulch.

Deciduous: A term applied to trees which drop their leaves annually, in contrast to "evergreen".

Decomposition: Decay, usually of strawy manure, compost, or some similar substances.

Diœcious: A term applied to plants which bear staminate and pistillate flowers.

Dormant: The period during which a plant makes no active growth. Most plants are completely dormant during the winter season. The rest period of a plant is not identical but is controlled by internal factors, characteristic of the plant itself.

Drying-off: A method of preparing bulbs for ripening or plants for resting between periods of forcing. It may be done by gradually reducing the amount of water or by laying the pots on their sides in a spot protected from the sun.

Emulsion: A liquid mixture in which a fatty substance is suspended in minute globules, usually appearing like milk.

Erosion: The washing away of soil or rock. Often it is advantageous. More often it is destructive, as when rainfall starts gullies in a field which grow to the proportions of a deep ditch, washing away the valuable top-soil and sometimes even sub-soil.

Everlastings: Flowers which are grown for their winter effects, as they hold their shape and color.

Fertilization: (1) the application of fertilizer, (2) the union of the "male" reproductive body (pollen) with the "female" reproductive body (egg) to produce offspring (seeds).

Flats: Shallow boxes, usually $16 \times 22\frac{1}{2}$ inches and varying in depth from 2 to 4 inches. The young stages of plant growth may be carried on in flats, thus eliminating the back-breaking work of planting and transplanting tiny seedlings in nursery rows indoors or out of doors.

Forcing: A process (1) of making plants or bulbs bloom at a time that is not natural for them to do so, or (2) of making them bloom in a shorter length of time than is normal. In the first case, only duplication of their normal growing conditions may be necessary, while in the second excess heat and moisture are necessary.

Fumigation (Plant): The control of injurious infestation by the use of toxic fumes given off by chemical substances.

Grafting: A process whereby a part of one plant, usually tree or shrub (scion), is made to unite with a part of another plant (stock). There are many ways of performing this process.

Habitat: The region in which a plant is found growing wild.

Hardening-off: The process of gradually reducing the amount of water and lowering the temperature for plants grown indoors or under glass, in order to toughen their tissues, making it possible for them to withstand colder conditions.

Heaving: The lifting of plants out of the ground, produced by alternate freezing and thawing during the winter. In some cases, roots may be left exposed, which may prove injurious if they are not pressed back into the soil. A light, porous texture of the soil, or a mulch will help to prevent this injury.

Heel: A small piece of two-year-old wood left on a cutting of one-year-old wood, for a certain method of propagation.

Heeling-in: A method of storing plants in the ground until conditions are favorable for planting. They are usually laid on their sides in trenches and covered with soil until only a small part of their top growth is left exposed.

Hilling-up: A practice of mounding the earth about a plant, performed for various purposes (1) protecting half-hardy plants during the winter, (2) bleaching celery, (3) strengthening the stand of aerial-rooted plants, as corn, (4) to protect shallow roots or tubers from sun-scorch.

Hybrid: A variety or individual resulting from the crossing of two species. The result of cross-fertilization; a cross.

Insecticide: A substance which kills insects by poisoning, suffocation, or paralysis. There are stomach poisons, contact poisons, and fumigants. A repellent is not really an insecticide as it does not kill, but repels insects by its disagreeable properties.

Leaching: The diminishing or complete loss of soluble fertilizers from the soil caused by the percolation of water downward.

Mat (Hotbed): A straw or fabric covering used to protect plants in coldframes and hotbeds against excessive cold.

Monœcious: A term applied to plants which bear flowers of different "sexes", that is, staminate and pistillate, on the same individual plant.

Naturalizing: The planting of trees, shrubs, flowering plants, bulbs, mosses, etc., in such a way as to bring about the effect of natural wild growth.

Nitrification: The change of crude forms of nitrogen first into ammonia, then into nitrites and finally into nitrates, in which form the nitrogen is available to the plant.

pH: A term which represents the hydrogen ion concentration by which scientists measure soil acidity. The pH acidity scale measures from 1 (acid) to 14 (alkaline) with 7 as neutral.

Pinching Back: The shortening of young shoots either to achieve bushy plant form, to encourage the development of a greater quantity of buds, or to enhance flower or fruit development.

Pistil: The central organ or reproductive part of a pistillate flower.

Pistillate: Often referred to as "female" flowers because they contain cells which, when fertilized, become seeds.

Pollen: The dusty substance found on the anther or terminal part of the reproductive organ of the opening "male sex" flowers.

Pollination: The transfer of pollen from the anther of the "male" flower to the stigma of the "female" flower, accomplished by wind, insects, or man.

Pot-bound: A stage of potted plant growth when the roots become a mass of fibers and no longer can reach out freely to make growth. Normally potted plants should be transplanted before they become pot-bound, but some prefer to be slightly so.

Potting-on: A term applied to the repeated transplantings of a plant from seedling stage to maturity in graduating sizes of flowerpots, each transplanting taking place as soon as the roots have filled the pot.

Potting-up: The transplanting of seedling plants from flats or seed pans into flower pots; the transplanting of mature plants from outdoor positions into pots, usually for the purpose of winter or ornamental effects.

Pricking-out (Pricking-off): The process of transplanting tiny seedlings from the seed pans, pots, or other containers, into flats. The purpose is to give the seedlings more room to develop leaf and branch growth, and to help them develop more compact masses of roots by the breaking off of the tiny tips of rootlets.

Propagation: The increase or multiplication of plants. For different methods, *see* chapter on Propagation.

Repellents: Substances which, when used alone or in combination with other substances, protect plants by warding off, without killing, insects or animals.

Respiration: The process by which a plant takes in oxygen, oxidizes matter, and gives off the product.

Scabrous: Rough or gritty to the touch, as leaves.

Scarification: (1) A process of loosening the soil without turning it over, (2) a method of scratching hard-coated seeds to hasten germination.

Scion (Cion): A term given to a bud or cutting of an improved variety which is to be inserted into the rooted "stock" in the process of grafting.

Seedlings: A term usually applied to very young plants. It is also sometimes applied to mature plants which have been produced from seed, in order to distinguish them from similar plants grown from cuttings, grafts, budding, etc.

Species: A group of individuals forming a subdivision of a genus with similar characteristics, but differing from the genus too slightly to form another genus. In "Anchusa italica" "Anchusa" is the genus, and "italica" is the species.

Stamen: The reproductive organ of the "male", pollen-bearing flower, the top part of which is the anther.

Staminate: A term used to describe a flower containing only stamens, or male reproductive organs.

Sterilization (Soil): A term commonly given to the process of making a soil, or similar material, free from all harmful organisms before it is used for sowing seed, or for transplanting purposes.

Stigma: The terminal part of the reproductive organ, or pollen-receiving part, of the "female" flowering plant.

Stock: In grafting, the plant into which the scion is to be inserted, and which will assume the rooting function of the new plant. Any leaf or stem growth from the stock should be cut back close to the root or branch, as only new growth from the scion is desired.

Stomata: Minute openings on the undersurface of a leaf through which transpiration of moisture takes place.

Stratification: An artificial method of reproducing Nature's way of preparing seeds for germination. Some seeds require a longer period of storage than others before germination will take place, and this is usually done by placing them between layers of peat moss, soil, or similar materials which are kept moist to prevent them from drying out. Stratification is usually done in the winter so that frost action will help split hard-shelled seeds.

Sub-soil: A stratum of soil lying beneath that commonly referred to as top-soil. It is less fertile. Since it contains practically no humus and no micro-organisms essential to plant growth, roots do not penetrate it, except those of very large vigorous plants.

Sucker: Vegetative growth which comes from the roots of a tree near the base or at a short distance.

Tamping: The process of lightly firming down freshly loosened soil, either in the open or in containers, with a flat surface such as a block of wood or a board.

Top-dressing: Any material such as manure, compost, fertilizer, etc., which is placed on the surface of the ground, and which may in some cases be cultivated in. It differs from a mulch in that its primary function is to feed the plant, while the primary purpose of a mulch is to hinder weed growth and to protect from heat or cold, although a mulch may have some food value.

Transpiration: The process by which excess water is given off by the leaves of a plant, through *stomata*, or minute openings, primarily on the undersurface of the leaf. The greatest amount of moisture is given off when the heat rays of the sun reach the plant.

Transplanting: The process of moving seedlings or mature plants from one location to another. The first transplanting process out of the seed pan or pot is referred to as "pricking-out".

Variety: A group of individuals forming a subdivision of a species with similar characteristics, but differing from the species too slightly to form another species. In "Anchusa italica Dropmore", "Dropmore" is the variety.

Water Sprout: A quick, succulent shoot growth which may appear on the trunk, or limbs.

MAPS OF THE UNITED STATES

SHOWING REGIONS OF APPROXIMATELY SIMILAR GROWING CONDITIONS AND FROST DATES FOR SPRING AND AUTUMN

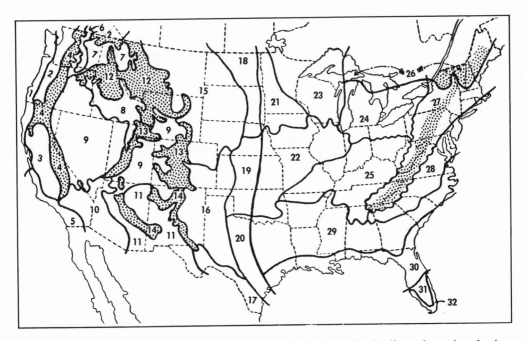

A map of the United States showing, by numbers within the heavy border lines, the regions having approximately similar growing conditions for the same elevation. The stippled areas are mountain regions. *Reproduced through the courtesy of the United States Department of Agriculture.*

MAP OF ZONES OF HARDINESS

The zones of hardiness are indicated in the lists and descriptions of trees, shrubs, and vines. The data in those lists are derived largely from "Manual of Cultivated Trees and Shrubs," by Alfred Rehder, and the map was published in the "Atlas of American Agriculture," U. S. Department of Agriculture, 1936.

Each zone represents an area in which similar climatic conditions prevail. The zones are based on average annual minimum winter temperatures for the years 1895 to 1935, but rainfall and soil are factors not taken into consideration.

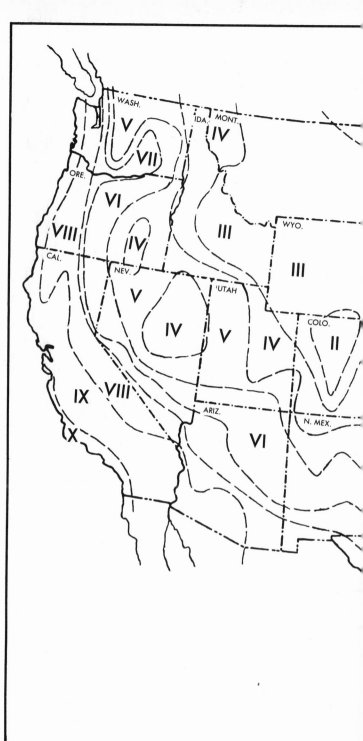

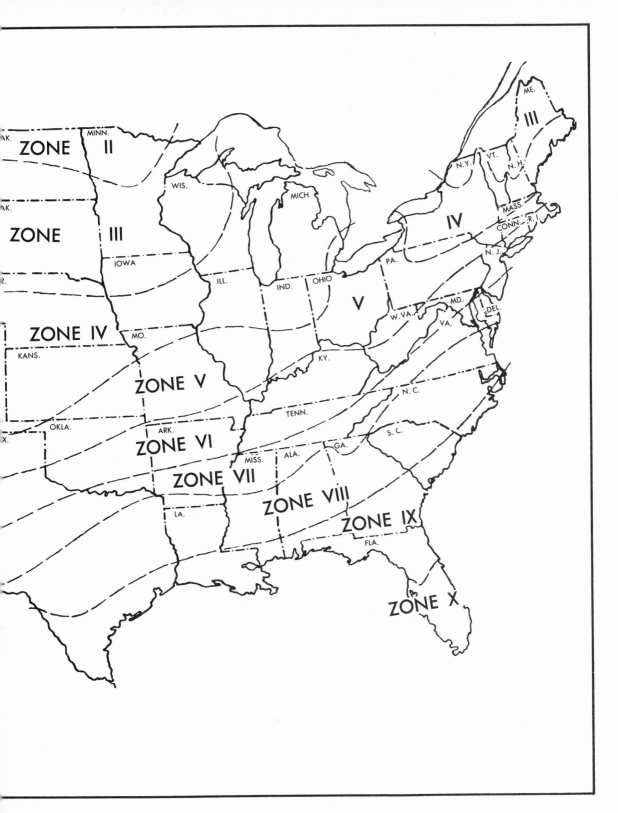

ZONE

ZONE

ZONE IV

ZONE V

ZONE VI

ZONE VII

ZONE VIII

ZONE IX

ZONE X

II

III

II

IV

V

III

MINN.

WIS.

MICH.

IOWA

ILL.

IND.

OHIO

PA.

N.Y.

VT.

N. H.

ME.

MASS.

CONN.

R. I.

N. J.

MD.

DEL.

W.VA.

VA.

KANS.

MO.

KY.

N. C.

OKLA.

ARK.

TENN.

S. C.

MISS.

ALA.

GA.

LA.

FLA.

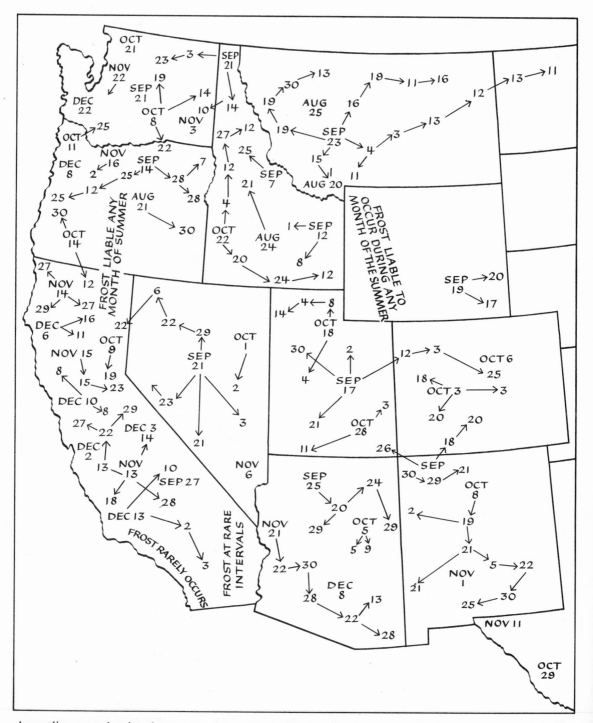

An outline map showing the average date of the killing frost in the autumn in the western portion of the United States. *Reproduced through the courtesy of the United States Department of Agriculture.*

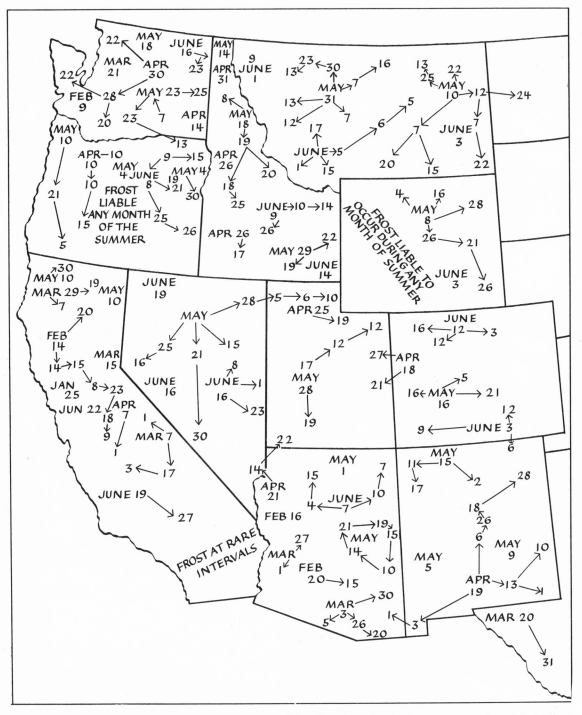

An outline map showing the average date of the last killing frost in spring in the western portion of the United States. *Reproduced through the courtesy of the United States Department of Agriculture.*

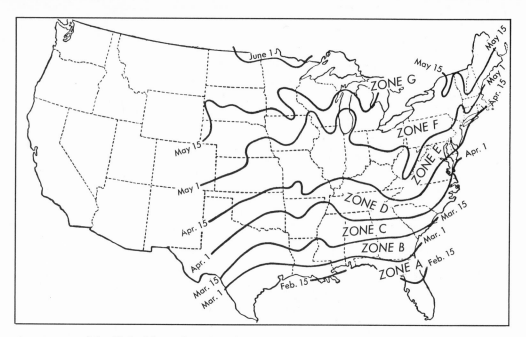

A zone map of the United States based on the average dates of the latest killing frost in spring east of the Rocky Mountains. *Reproduced through the courtesy of the United States Department of Agriculture.*

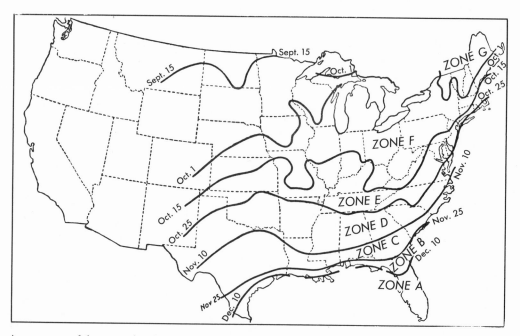

A zone map of the central and eastern part of the United States based on the average dates of the first killing frost in autumn. See page 707 for the latest safe date for planting any crop in any one of the various regions. *Reproduced through the courtesy of the United States Department of Agriculture.*

INDEX

Important descriptive references are indicated in bold face numerals
See also Supplementary Index, p. 753

Abelia grandiflora, **244**, 267, 297
Abies balsamea, 235
  concolor, **225**, 235
  homolepis, 235
  Nordmanniana, 235
  Veitchii, 235
Abronia umbellata, 322
Acacia, Rose, 275
Acanthopanax pentaphyllum, 267
Acanthus mollis, 377
Acer campestre, **220**, 229
  dasycarpum (A. saccharinum), 229
  ginnala, 229
  japonicum, 229
  negundo, 229
  palmatum, 229
  pennsylvanicum, 229
  platanoides, 229
  pseudoplatanus, 229
  rubrum, 229
  saccharum, **220**, 229
  spicatum, 229
  tataricum, 229
Achillea clavennae, 81
  filipendulina, 377
  millefolium, 377
  ptarmica, 377
  tomentosa, 81
Achimenes, **394**, 448
Acid Soil, 168
Aconite, 377
Aconitum, **344**, 377
  autumnale, **345**, 377
  fischeri, **345**, 377
  lycoctonum, 377
  napellus, **345**, 377
  N. var. sparksii, **345**, 377
  wilsonii, **345**, 377
Acorus calamus, 105
Actaea rubra, 92
Acti-dione Ferrated (cyclohexamide), 617
Actinidia polygama, **282**
Activators, 157
Adam's-needle, 383
Adiantum pedatum, 94
Adonis aestivalis, 322
  Amur, 377
  amurensis, 377

Spring, 377
  vernalis, 377
Aesculus carnea, 229
  glabra, 229
  hippocastanum, 229
Aethionema cordifolium, 377
  grandiflorum, 377
African Daisy, **308**
African Violet, **448**
Agapanthus africanus, 46
Agathaea coelestis, 522
Ageratum houstonianum, **308**, 322
Aglaoenema modestum, **455**
Ailanthus altissima (A. glandulosa), 229
Ailanthus, Control of, 600
Ajuga genevensis, Control of, 603
  reptans, 32, 81, **202**
Akebia quinata, **282**
  Control of, 600
Alder, Black, 229
  Common, 229
Alfalfa, 158
Algae, 99
Allamanda cathartica, **282**
Alnus glutinosa, 229
  incana, 229
Alpines, 69
Althaea rosea, 331
Aluminum foil, 498
Aluminum Sulphate, 169
Alumroot (Coral Bells), 82, 93
Alyssum argenteum, 81, 377
  maritimum, **308**, 322
  montanum, 377
  saxatile, 81, 377
  saxatile citrinum, 377
  saxatile compactum, 81, 377
  Silver, 81, 377
  Sweet, **308**, 322
Amaranthus caudatus, 322
Amaryllis, **449**
  Halli, 410
Ambrosia, 103
Amelanchier canadensis, 229, 267
American Ash, 231
American Columbine, 81, **86**, 92
American Cowslip, **89**, 92
American Elm, **225**, 234

711

American Holly, 225
Amino Triazole, 607
Ammobium alatum, 322
Ammonium Phosphate, 162
Ammonium Sulphate, 162
Ammonium sulfamate, 605
Ampelopsis brevipedunculata, **282**
Anagallis indica, 322
Anaphalis margaritacea, 377
Anchusa barrelieri, 377
  italica, **345**, 377
  myosotidiflora, 377
Andromeda, Japanese, **258**, 274
  Mountain, 274
Anemone blanda, 391
  Canada, 92
  canadensis, 92
  coronaria, **396**
  hupehensis, 377
  japonica, **345**, 377
  pulsatilla, 81
  quinquefolia, **86**, 92
  Rue, 92
  Wood, 86, 92
Anemonella thalictroides, 92
Anethum graveolens, 104
Angelica archangelica, 103
Anise, 103
Annual Larkspur, 311
  in the greenhouse, 533
Annuals, 305
  blue, 319
  border plan, 305
  culture of, 307
  difficult to transplant, 317
  diseases, 630
  fall sown, 316
  fertilizer for, 306
  Lists for
    acid soil, 316
    alkaline soil, 316
    city gardens, 60
    conservatory, 321
    cool places, 321
    cut flowers, 321
    drought, 316
    edging, 320
    everlastings, 321
    Flower-Pot Gardens, 39
    greenhouses, 321
    heat, 316
    hedges (temporary), 320
    indoor bloom, 455
    moist soil, 321
    mountains, 320
    neutral soil, 316
    penthouse gardens, 66

    poor soil, 316
    porch boxes, 320
    pot culture, 39
    roof gardens, 64
    seashore, 320
    shade, 315, 316
    window boxes, 320
  insect pests, 630
  lavender, 319
  mauve, 319
  orange, 319
  pinching back of, 307, 317
  pink, 318
  propagation of, 306, 471, 472
  purple, 319
  red, 318
  rose, 318
  scented, 321
  seldom attacked by pest or disease, 619
  selection of varieties, 308
  self-sown, 317
  short blooming season, 317
  slow-growing, 317
  soil requirements for, 306
  tabular list, 322
  thinning, 307
  transplanting, 307
  white, 318
  yellow, 320
Antennaria dioica, 81
Anthemis nobilis, 103
  tinctoria, 377
Anther, defined, 703
Anthriscus cerefolium, 103
Antibiotics, 617
Antigonon leptopus, **283**
Antirrhinum, **314**, 322
  diseases, 630
  in the greenhouse, 524
Ants, 674
  poison for, 674
Aphids, 448, 631
Apios americana, Control of, 603
Apple, 548
  duration of bearing, 548
  fertilization, 550
  fruiting habits, 547
  planting, 548
  pollination, 546
  pruning, 549
  spray schedule, 564
  varieties of merit, 551
Apple, Flowering Crab, 232
Aquilegia, **346**, 377
  diseases, 631
  in the greenhouse, 524
  insect pests, 631

Species and Hybrids
  alpina, **346**
  caerulea, 81, 92, **346**, 377
  canadensis, 81, **86**, 92, **346**, 377
  chrysantha, **347**, 377
  glandulosa, **347**, 377
  Hybrid strains, **347**, 377
  siberica, 377
  skinneri, 377
  vulgaris, **347**, 377
  vulgaris nivea, 377
Arabis albida, 81, 377
  alpina, 32, 81, 377
  aubrietioides, 377
Aralia japonica, 457
  sieboldi, 457
  spinosa, 229, 267
Aramite, 614
Araucaria excelsa, 455
Arboretums, 692
Arborvitae, American, **226**, 236, 298
  Giant, 236
  insect pests, 619
  Leaf Miner, 619
  Oriental, 236
  Siberian, 236
Arbutus, Trailing, 89
  unedo, **244**, 267
Architectural features, 18
Arctostaphylos uva-ursi, 202
Arctotis grandis, 322
Arenaria grandiflora, 81
  montana, 32
  verna, 32, **181**
Argemone grandiflora, 322
  mexicanum, 322
Arisaema triphyllum, **88**, 92, 99
Aristolochia durior, **283**
Armoracia rusticana, 104
Aronia arbutifolia, **244**, 267
  a. var. brilliantissima, 267
  melanocarpa, 94
Arrow-wood, 277
Arsenate of Lead, 614
Artemisia, **348**, 377
  abrotanum, 105, 377
  absinthium, 105, 377
  albula, 377
  dracunculus, 105
  lactiflora, **348**, 377
  montana, 377
  pontica, 105
  purshiana, 377
  stelleriana, 105, 377
Artichoke, Globe, 574
  Jerúsalem, 574
Artificial Light for Plants, 462

Aruncus sylvester, 378
Asclepias incarnata, 378
  tuberosa, **348**, 378
Ash, Flowering, 231
  Green, 231
  Water, 231
  White, 231
Ashes, Wood, 164
Asparagus, 574
  disease and insect control, 595
Aspen, Largetooth, 233
Asperula azurea setosa, 322
  odorata, 105, 378
Asplenium platyneuron, 94
  trichomanes, 94
Aster, 349, 378
  diseases (Annual), 632
  insect pests, 633
  Species
    alpinus, 81
    amellus, 378
    China, **309**
    cordifolius, 378
    Mauve Cushion, 81
    novae-angliae var., **349**, 378
    novi-belgii var., **349**, 378
    Rock, 81
    subcaeruleus, 378
Aster Beetle, 633
Astilbe, 378
  davidii, 378
  David's, 378
  grandis, 378
  Great, 378
  japonica, 378
Athyrium filix-femina, 94
  pycnocarpon, 94
Aubrietia deltoidea, 81
  in variety, 378
Aucuba, Greenleaf, 267
  japonica, 267
Aureomycin, 617
Austrian Pine, **226**, 235
Autumn Sun, 382
Azalea, **244**, 268
  Culture, 244
  diseases, 620
  insect pests, 621
  in the greenhouse, 524
  Species and Hybrids
    arborescens, 268
    calendulacea, **245**, 268
    canadense, 268
    Chinese, 268
    Downy Pinxter, 268
    Flame, 268
    Ghent Hybrids, **245**, 268

Azalea—*continued*
  Species and Hybrids—*continued*
    Glendale Hybrids, 245
    indica, 268
    Indian Group, **245**, 268
    kaempferi, **246**, 268
    Kurume, 246
    Mollis Hybrids, **246**, 268
    nudiflora, **247**, 268
    Pink Shell, **247**, 268
    Pinxter, **247**, 268
    pontica hybrids, 268
    rosea, 268
    Schlippenbachii, **247**, 268
    Species and Hybrids of Merit, 245
    Swamp, 268
    Sweet, 268
    Torch, 268
    Vaseyi, **247**, 268
    viscosa, 268

Baby Blue-eyes, 326
Babysbreath, 324
Babysbreath, Creeping, 82
Bachelors-Button, 310
Bacteria, 610
Bagworm, 620
Bald Cypress, **224**, 234
Balloonflower, 382
Balm, 103
  Lemon, 103
Balm of Gilead, 233
Balsam, Garden, 324
  Patience, 324
  Sultan, 324
Banks, 117
  planted, 117
  plants for, 117
  turf, 117
Baptisia australis, 378
  tinctoria, 378
Barbarea verna, 104
Barberry, Dwarf Japanese, 268
  Dwarf Magellan, 268
  Japanese, 268
  Korean, 268
  Warty, 268
  Wilson's, 268
Bartonia, 322
Basic Slag, 163
Basil, 103
Basketflower, 323
Bay, Bull, 225
  Sweet, 232, 273
Bayberry, 274
  Northern, 274
Beans, 575
  disease and insect control, 595

Bean, Soy, 159
Bearberry, 202
Beardtongue, 326
Bearsbreech, 377
Beaumontia grandiflora, **283**
Beautyberry, Chinese, 269
  Japanese, 269
Beautybush, **257**, 273
Bechtel's Crab, 232
Bedstraw, 380
Beebalm, 103, 381
Beech, American, 231
  European, **221**, 231
Beet, 576
  disease and insect control, 595
Beetle (see Insects)
Begonia, 455
  in the greenhouse, 525
  Species
    argenteo-guttata, 455
    Beefsteak, 455
    feasti, 455
    Fibrous-rooted Group, 525
    Foliage Group, **455**, 525
    rex, 455
    Semi-tuberous, 525
    Sunderbruchi, 456
    Trout, 455
    Tuberous-rooted, **396**
Bellflower, 350
  Bluestar, 323
  Carpathian, **350**, 378
  Milky, 378
  Peachleaf, **350**, 378
  Spotted, 378
Bellflowertree, 271
Bellis perennis, **330**
Belvidere, 325
Bent grass, 174
  Colonial, 174
  Creeping, 174
  Velvet, 174
Benzoin aestivale, 268
Berberis, 247, 268
  buxifolia, var. pygmaea, 268
  julianae, **247**, 268
  koreana, 268
  mentorensis, 268, **297**
  Sargentiana, 268
  Thunbergii, 268, **297**
  T. var. erecta, 268
  T. var. minor, 268, **297**
  verruculosa, 268
  wilsonae, 268
Bergamot, 103
Bermuda grass, 179
Bethlehem Sage, 382

Betony, 383
  Woolly, 383
Betula alba (B. pendula), **220**, 229
  lenta, 229
  lutea, 229
  maximowicziana, 230
  nigra, 230
  papyrifera, **221**, 230
  pendula, **220**, 229
  populifolia, 230
Biennials, 328
  for City Gardens, 60
  for Pot Culture, 41
  seldom attacked by pests or diseases, 619
  selected list, 328
Bignonia jasminoides, 289
  radicans, 283
Bindweed, Control of, 603
Birch, **220**, 229
  insect pests, 621
  Species (Common name)
    Canoe (White), **221**, 230
    European White, **220**, 229
    Gray, 230
    Monarch, 230
    River, 230
    Sweet (Black), 229
    Yellow, 229
Bird of Paradise Flower, 46
Birds, 302
  attracting, 302
  flowers attractive to, 303
  nesting sites, 303
  shrubs attractive to, 304
  trees attractive to, 303
  winter feeding, 302
Bishop's Cap, 93
Bittersweet, Control of, 601
  Species (Common name)
    American, **284**
    Oriental, 284
Blackberries, 555
  Spray schedules, 568
Blackhaw, 278
Black Snakeroot, **88**, 92
Bladdernut, 276
Bladder Senna, 269
Blanketflower, 380
Blazing-star, 381
Bleeding-heart, **355**, 379
  in the greenhouse, 526
  Species
    Fringed, 82, 379
    Wild, 92
Blister-rust, 627
Bloodroot, **90**, 93
Bluebeard, 252, 269, 378

Bluebells, 92
  Virginia, 381
Blueberries, 556
  Dwarf Late, 95
  Highbush, 277
  Lowbush, 277
Blue Phlox, 90
Blue Pimpernel, 322
Bluets, 82, 92
Blue-wings (Torenia), **315**, 327
Blue Woodruff, 322
Bocconia cordata, **350**, 378
Bog Gardens, 99
  Plants for, 99
  Soil for, 99
Boltonia, Dwarf Pinkray, 378
  latisquama, 378
  nana, 378
  Violet, 378
Bone Meal, 163
Bone Tar Oil, 676
Borage, 103
  officinalis, 103
Borax, 606
Borer, Dogwood, 624
  Iris, 653
Boron, 164
Boston Ivy, 290
Botanical Gardens, 692
Botrychium virginianum, 94
Bougainvillea glabra, **283**
Bouvardia, **451**
  in the greenhouse, 526
Box, 247
  disease, 622
  insect pests, 622
  Leaf Miner, 622
  Species (Common name)
    Common, 247
    Dwarf, **248**, 269
    Japanese, **248**, 268
    Korean, **248**, 269
    Tree, **248**, 269
Brachycome iberidifolia, **314**, 322
Bridal Wreath, **261**, 276
Broadcast, defined, 703
Broccoli, 577
  disease and insect control, 595
Broom, 270
  Scotch, 270
Broussonetia papyrifera, 230
Browallia demissa (B. elata), 322
  speciosa major, **309**, 322
Brownpatch, 196
Brunnera macrophylla, 378
Brussels Sprouts, 577
  disease and insect control, 595

Buckeye, Ohio, 229
Buckhorn, Control of, 200
Buckthorn, 95
Buckwheat hulls, 498
Buddleia Davidi, **247**, 268
    D. var. veitchiana, 268
Buffalograss, 179
Bug, Chinch, 195
    Lace, 621
    Mealy, 671
    Rose, 665
    Tarnished Plant, 634
Bugbane, 379
    Cohosh, 379
    Kamchatka, 379
Bugle, Carpet, 81, **202**
    Geneva, 603
Bugloss, **345**, 377
    Early, 377
    Siberian, 377, 378
Bulbils, propagation by, 490
Bulbous Iris, 408
    in the greenhouse, 532
Bulbs, 384
    Autumn-Flowering, 409
    for city gardens, 60
    for pot culture, 42
    for the greenhouse, 534, 537
    for the house, 451
    planting chart, 410
    planting in sod, 385
    Propagation by, 490
    Protection from mice, 390
    Small Spring-Flowering, 391
    Spring-Flowering, 384
    Summer-Flowering, 394
Burnet, 103
Burning-bush, 271
    Evergreen, **255**, 271
Butterflybush, 268
    Veitch's, 268
Butterflyflower, **309**, 327
Butterflyweed, **348**, 378
Butternut Tree, 231
Buttonwood, 233
Buxus, **247**, 268, 269
    microphylla var. japonica, **248**, 268
    microphylla var. koreana, **248**, 269
    sempervirens
    s. var. arborescens, **248**, 269
    s. var. suffruticosa, **248**, 269, 297

Caladium bicolor, 456, **671**
    Fancy-leaved, 456, **671**
Calandrinia grandiflora, 322
    speciosa, 322
Calcium, 161

Calcium Nitrate, 162
Calendar, Garden, 698
    Spring, 698
    Summer, 699
    Autumn, 700
    Winter, 701
Calendula, diseases, 635
    in the greenhouse, 526
    insect pests, 634
    officinalis, 104, **309**, 322
California Poppy, **309**, 324
    in the greenhouse, 527
Calla, 527
    diseases, 636
Callicarpa japonica, 269
    purpurea, 269
Calliopsis, 323
Callistephus chinensis, 322
Calluna vulgaris, 269
Calonyction aculeatum, **283**
Caltha palustris, 99
Calycanthus floridus, 249, 269
Cambium, 703
Camellia, Culture, 249
    diseases, 623
    insect pests, 623
    Species
        japonica, 249
        reticulata, 251
        sasanqua, 251
Camomile, 102
    Yellow, 377
Campanula, **350**, 378
    diseases, 637
    insect pests, 637
    Species
        caespitosa, **350**, 378
        calycanthema, 328
        carpatica, 81, **350**, 378
        drabifolia, 323
        garganica, 202, 350
        glomerata, **350**, 378
        glomerata acaulis, 32
        isophylla, **452**
        lactiflora, 378
        medium, **328**
        persicifolia, **350**, 378
        punctata, 378
        pyramidalis, **350**, 378
        ramosissima, 323
        rapunculoides, 603
        rotundifolia, 81, 92, **350**
Campion, Clammy, 381
    Sea, 82
    Sweet-william, 327
Campsis chinensis, **283**
    grandiflora, **283**

radicans (Tecoma r., Bignonia r.), **283**
Camptosourus rhizophyllus, 94
Canada thistle, Control of, 604
Canary Island Ivy, 287
Candidum lily, 417
Candytuft, Annual, 324
    Evergreen, 82, 204, 381
    Purple, 324
    Tenore, 82
Cankerworm, 624, 625
Canna, 401
    diseases and insect pests, 637
Canterbury Bells, **328**
    Annual, 323
Cape Honeysuckle, 291
Cape-marigold, **310**, 323
Cape Plumbago, 290
Captan, 616
Caragana arborescens, 269
Caraway, 103
Cardinal flower, 99, 381
Carmel Creeper, 203
Carnation, 527
    diseases, 636
Carolate, 624
Carpathian Harebell, **350**, 378
Carpenteria californica, 252, 269
Carpinus betulus, 230
    caroliniana, 230
Carrot, 579
    disease and insect control, 596
Carum carvi, 103
Carya alba, 230
    glabra, 230
    laciniosa, 230
    ovata, 230
Caryopteris incana (C. mastacanthus), 252, 269, 378
Casein, defined, 703
Cassia marilandica, 378
Castor Pomace, 163
Catalpa speciosa, 230
    Western, 230
Catananche caerulea, 378
Caterpillars, Tent, 621
    Yellow woolly-bear, 642
Catmint, mussin, 381
Cauliflower, 580
    disease and insect control, 595
Ceanothus grisens horizontalis, 203
Cedar, Atlas, **225**, 235
    Deodar, **225**, 235
    Incense, 235
    Indian, **225**, 235
    of Lebanon, **225**, 235
    Red, **225**, 235
    Temple, 235
    White, 235

Cedar-Apple Rust, 629
Cedrus atlantica, **225**, 235
    Deodara, **225**, 235
    libani, **225**, 235
Celandine-poppy, 378
Celastrus orbiculatus, 284
    scandens, 284
Celeriac, 580
Celery, 580
    disease and insect control, 596
Celosia argentea (C. plumosa), 323
    dwarf, 323
    cristata, 323
Celtis occidentalis, 230
Centaurea americana, 323
    diseases, 639
    insect pests, 639
    Species
        babylonica, 378
        cineraria (C. candidissima), 323
        cyanus, **310**, 323
        Globe, 378
        gymnocarpa, 378
        imperialis, 323
        macrocephala, 378
        montana, 82, 378
        moschata (C. suaveolens), 323
        Syrian, 378
        Velvet, 378
Centranthus macrosiphon, 323
    ruber, 378
Cephalaria alpina, 378
    Yellow, 378
Cerastium biebersteinii, 82, 378
    taurus, 82, 378
    tomentosum, 82, **203**, 378
Ceratostigma plumbaginoides, 203
Cercidiphyllum japonicum, **221**, 230
Cercis canadensis, **221**, 230
Chaenomeles japonica (Cydonia Maulei), **253**, 269
    lagenaria, **253**, 269
Chafer, Rose, 665
Chamæcyparis Lawsoniana, 235
    obtusa, 235
    o. compacta, 235
    o. crippsii, 235
    o. gracilis, 235
    o. nana, 235
    pisifera, **225**, 235
    p. plumosa, 235
    p. squarrosa, 235
    thyoides, 235
Chamaedaphne calyculata, 269
Chamomile, 103
    Allium schoenoprasum, 103
    False, 103
    Sweet, 103

Chard, Swiss, 581
Chaste-tree (Vitex Agnus-castus), 278
Checkerberry, 92
Checkerbloom, 383
    Satin, 383
Cheiranthus allioni, 333
    cheiri, 333
Chelidonium majus, 378
Chemical sprays, 605
Chenopodium botrys, 103
Cherry, 551
    Black, 233
    Higan, 224
    Japanese, 233
    Japanese, Early, 233
    Nankin, 233, 274
    Yoshino, 233
Chervil, 103
Chewing Insects, 613
Chicory, 582
Chickweed, 200
China-aster, **309**, 322
China Pink, 323
Chinch Bug, 195
Chinese Cabbage, 578
Chinese Evergreen, 455
Chinese Fleece Vine, 290
Chinese-houses, 323
Chinese lantern, 603
Chinese Matrimony Vine, 602
Chinese Scholar tree, **224**, 234
Chionanthus virginica, **253**, 269
Chives, 103
Chlordane, 614
Chloropicrin, 618
Chlorosis, lime induced, 170
Chokeberry, Black, 94
    Red, 94, **244**, 267
Christmas Berry, **258**, 274
Christmas Rose, 82, 380
Chrysanthemum, **350**, 379
    diseases, 639
    insect pests, 640
    for pot culture, 41
    for greenhouse culture, 528
    Species and Varieties
        Annual, 323
        arcticum, 379
        balsamita, 104
        carinatum, 323
        coccineum, 379
        coronarium, 323
        Garden, **350**, 379
        leucanthemum, 379
        maximum, 379
        morifolium (C. hortorum), **350**, 379
        nipponicum, 379

        parthenium, 323
        segetum, 323
        uliginosum, 379
Cimicifuga cordifolia, 379
    foetida simplex, 379
    racemosa, **88**, 92, 379
Cinquefoil, Nepal, 382
    Pyrenees, 82
    Shrubby, 274
Cissus adenopodus, 460
    antarctica, 460
    rhombifolia, 460
Citrus trifoliata, 269
City Gardens, 51
    design of, 51
    fences for, 53
    flowers for, 60
    paths for, 53
    plants for, 59
    shrubs for, 60
    soil for, 57
    trees for, 59
    utility features for, 55
    vines for, 60
Cladrastis lutea, 221, 230
Clarkia elegans, **310**, 323
    in the greenhouse, 528
    pulchella, 323
Clary, 104
Clay Soils, 155
Claytonia virginica, **88**, 92
Clematis, **284**
    cultural requirements, 285
    insect pests, 624
    Species and Hybrids
        armandii, 284
        crispa, 284
        Ground, 379
        Henryi, 286
        heracleaefolia, 379
        Hybrids (large-flowered), 286
        integrifolia, 379
        Jackmani, 286
        lanuginosa, 284
        montana, 284
        m. rubens, 285
        paniculata, 285
        recta, 379
        Tube, 379
Cleome, spinosa, 323
    insect pests, 641
Clethra alnifolia, **253**, 269
Clintonia borealis, 92
    pulchella, 323
Clock Vine, 327
Closed Gentian, 92, 99

Clover, Mammoth Red, 159
  Sweet, 159
  White, 159
Clytostoma callistegioides, **286**
Cobaea scandens, 286
Cockscomb, 323
Cockspur Thorn, 230
Colchicum, 409
Coldframes, 508
  construction of, 509
  location of, 509
  management of, 511
  protection of, 511
  summer shade, 511
  uses of, 508
  ventilation of, 511
  watering of, 511
Coleus, 456
  insect pests, 641
Collinsia bicolor, 323
Collomia coccinea, 323
Colorado Columbine, 377
Colorado Spruce, 235
Columbine, **346**, 377
  diseases, 631
  insect pests, 631
  in the greenhouse, 524
  Species (Common name)
    Alpine, **346**
    American, **92**, **346**, 377
    European, **347**, 377
    Golden, **347**, 377
    Mexican, 377
    Munstead, 377
    Rocky Mountain, 92, **346**
    Siberian, 377
Columnberry, 268
Colutea arborescens, 269
  orientalis, 269
Common Pussytoes, 81
Complete fertilizers, 164
Compost Pile, 156
    making weed-free, 157
Comptonia asplenifolia, 269
Concrete pools, 131
Coneflower, Autumn, 382
  Great, 382
  Pinewoods, 326
  Purple, 379, 382
  Showy, 382
  Sweet, 382
Coniferous, defined, 703
Convallaria majalis, 82, 92, 204, **393**
Copper, 164
Copper Spot, 197
Coral Bells, **357**, 380
Coralberry, 277
Coral-vine, **283**

Coreopsis drummondii, 323
  grandiflora, 379
  Rose, 379
  rosea, 379
  Stillman, 325
  Threadleaf, 379
  tinctoris, 323
  verticillata, 379
Coriander, 104
Coriandrum sativum, 104
Cork Tree, 232
Corms, 384
Corn (Sweet), 582
  disease and insect control, 598
Corn Cobs, 498
Cornflower, 310, 323
Corn-marigold, 323
Corn Plant, 456
Cornus, 221, 230
  insect pests, 624
  Species
    alba, 269
    a. siberica, 269
    Amomum, 269
    florida, **221**, 230
    kousa, 230
    mas, 269
    paniculata, 270
    racemosa, 95
    sanguinea, 269
    stolonifera, 269
Corylopsis spicata, 270
Corylus americana, 270
  avellana fusco-rubra, 270
  rostrata, 270
Cosmos, 323
  diseases and insect pests, 642
  Species
    bipinatus, 323
    diversifolius, **310**, 323
    sulphureus, **310**, 323
    Yellow, **310**, 323
Costmary, 104
Cotinus coggygria, **260**, 270
Cotoneaster adpressa, 270
  apiculata, 270
  Creeping, 270
  dielsiana (Diel's), 270
  divaricata, 270, **297**
  francheti (Franchet's), 270
  horizontalis, 204, **253**, 270
  microphylla, 270
  Rock, **253**, 270
  rotundifolia, 270
  Round-leaf, 270
  salicifolia, 270
  Spreading, 270

Cottonseed Meal, 163
Cover Crops, 157
  leguminous, 158
  non-leguminous, 159
Crab, 232
  disease, 624, 629
  Species (Common name)
    Arnold, 232
    Bechtel's, 232
    Carmine, 232
    Chinese Flowering, 232
    Fragrant, 232
    Japanese Flowering, 232
    Parkman, 232
    Redvein, 232
    Scheidecker, 232
    Siberian, 232
Crabgrass, 198
Cranberry Bush, Dwarf, 278
  Highbush (European), 278
Cranesbill, Armenian, 380
  Bigstem, 82
  Lilac, 380
  Meadow, 380
  Rocky Mountain, 380
Crape-Myrtle, 273
Cratægus cordata, **221**, 230
  crus-galli, 230
  mollis (c. coccinea), 230
  oxyacantha, **221**, 230
  phaenopyrum, **221**, 230
  punctata, 230
Creeping Bent, 174
Crepis barbata rubra, 323
Cress, 104, 583
  Garden, 583
  Water, 583
Crested Iris, 82, 93, **365**
Crocus, 391
  autumn-flowering, 410
  sativus, 105
  Species, 391
Crop Rotation, 703
Crowndaisy, 323
Crown Imperial, diseases, 646
Cryptomeria japonica Lobbii, 235
Cucumber, 583
  disease and insect control, 596
Cucumber Tree, 232
Cultivation, 677, 703
Culver's-physic, 383
Cumin, 104
Cuminum Cyminum, 104
Cup-and-saucer vine, **286**
Cuphea ignea, 323
  Fiery, 323
Cupid's-dart, 378

Currant, Flowering, 275
Currants, 557
Cuttings, 481
  evergreen, 487
  leaf, 487
  mist spraying, 483
  propagating cases for, 482
  root, 488
  root-forming substances, 483
  rooting medium, 482
  stem, 484
  stem dormant, 486
  stem half-ripened, 486
  stem hard wood, 486
  stem soft wood, 484
Cut-worms, 643
Cyanamid, 157, 162
Cyanogas, 674
Cyclamen, 529
Cyclamen Mite, 645
Cynoglossum amabile, 323
Cypress, Bald, **224**, 234
  Dwarf Hinoki, 235
  Hinoki, 235
  Lawson's, 235
  Moss, 235
  Plume, 235
  Sawara, **225**, 235
  Slender Hinoki, 235
Cypress Vine, 290
Cypripedium, 88
  acaule, **88**, 92
  hirsutum, 92
  pubescens (C. parviflorum), **88**, 92
Cyrilla racemiflora, 270
Cystopteris bulbifera, 94
Cytisus hirsutus, 270
  scoparius, 270

Daffodil (see Narcissus), 384
Dahlia, **402**
  Classification, 402
  Culture, 403
  diseases, 642
  insect pests, 643
  Propagation, 403
  Varieties of Merit, 402
Daisy, Arctic, 379
  Blue, 522
  English, 330
  Giant, 379
  Kingfisher, 324
  Nippon Oxeye, 379
  Oxeye, 379
  Shasta, 379
  Transvaal, 530
Dalapon, 607

Damping-off, 475
Dandelion, 200
Danesblood, 378
Daphne cneorum, 270
    February, 270
    Genkwa, 270
    Lilac, 270
    Mezereum, 270
    Rose, 270
Datura chlorantha, 323
    fastuosa (D. cornucopia), 323
Daylily, **355**, 380
    Hybrid, 356
    Japanese, **356**, 380
    Lemon, **356**, 380
    Orange, **356**, 380
    Species, **356**, 380
    Tawny, **356**, 380
Davidia involucrata var.
    Vilmoriniana, 230
D-D Mixture, 618
DDT, 615
Deciduous, defined, 703
Decomposition, defined, 703
Deer, 676
Defoliation, 210
Delphinium, **352**, 379
    diseases, 644
    insect pests, 644
    Species and Hybrids
        ajacis, 323
        belladonna, **350**, 379
        bellamosum, 379
        cardinale, 379
        consolida, 323
        grandiflorum, 379
        hybrids, **352**, 379
        nudicaule, 379
        Siberian, 379
        Yellow, 379
        Zalil, 379
Demeton, 616
Dennstaedtia punctilobula, 94
Deodar, 235
Desert Candle, 405
Design, 6
    built-in planting beds, 14
    Contemporary, 7
    creating a, 10
    fundamental qualities, 6
    of the home property, 10
    style in, 6
    use of plant material in, 19
Deutzia gracilis, **254**, 271
    Lemoinei, **254**, 271
    Slender, **254**, 271

Dianthus, 379
    diseases, 646
    Species
        allwoodii, 379
        barbatus, **333**, 379
        caesius, 379
        chinensis, **313**, 323
        cruentus, 379
        deltoides, 82, 379
        latifolius, 379
        plumarius, 82, 379
Diascia barberae, 323
Dicentra canadensis, 92
    cucullaria, 92
    eximia, 81, 92, 379
    spectabilis, **355**, 379
    s. in the greenhouse, 526
    s. for pot culture, 41
Dichondra carolinensis (D. repens), 181
Dictamnus albus, 379
Didiscus (Trachymene), 323
Dieffenbachia, 456
    amoena, 456
    picta, 456
Dieldrin, 615
Diervilla florida, 271
    hybrida, 271
Digging, Double, 677
Digitalis, 88, **330**
    diseases and insect pests, 646
    Species
        ambigua, 88, 379
        a. Isabellina, 379
        lutea, 88
Dill, 104
Dilutions, Table of, 618
Dimite (DMC), 615
Dimorphotheca aurantiaca, **310**, 323
Dioecious, defined, 703
Diospyros virginiana, 231
Diseases (General), 610
    of flowers, 630
    of fruits, 564
    of shrubs, 619
    of trees, 619
    of vegetables, 595
    Plants seldom attacked by, 619
Diseases (Specific)
    Alternaria Leaf Spot, 637
    Anthracnose of
        Antirrhinum, 630
        Dianthus, 646
        Hollyhock, 650
        Oaks, 627
        Pansy, 658
        Peony, 658
        Sweet Pea, 668

Diseases—*continued*
  Anthracnose of—*continued*
    Sycamore, 630
  Azalea Flower Blight, 620
  Bacterial Blight of Gladiolus, 647
  Bacterial Leaf Spot of
    Delphinium, 644
    Geranium, 647
    Tuberous Begonia, 671
  Bacterial Wilt, 631
  Black Rot of Bulbs, 651
  Black Rot of Delphiniums, 644
  Black Spot of Roses, 662
  Blight
    Azalea, 620
    Beans, 395
    Chrysanthemum, 639
    Phlox, 660
  Blister Rust of Pines, 627
  Blossom Blight of Tulips, 670
  Botrytis Blight of Tulips, 670
  Botrytis Bulb Rot of Narcissus, 656
  Botrytis of Peony, 658
  Botrytis Rot of
    Cosmos, 642
    Lilies, 654
  Bronzing of Leaves, Roses, 664
  Brown Canker of Roses, 663
  Bud Rot of
    Canna, 637
    Carnation, 637
  Bulb Rot of Lilies, 654
  Camellia Flower Blight, 623
  Cedar-Apple Rust, 629
  Cercospora Leaf Spot of
    Geranium, 647
    Hollyhock, 650
  Chlorosis of Primrose, 662
  Collar Rot of Sweet Peas, 668
  Crown Rot, 631
  Dropsy, 647
  Dry Rot of Gladiolus, 647
  Dutch Elm Disease, 624
  Fire Blight, 629
  Flower Spike Disease, 631
  Gray Bulb Rot of
    Fritillaria Imperialis, 646
    Hyacinth, 651
    Narcissus, 656
    Tulips, 670
  Hard Rot of Gladiolus, 648
  Leaf Blotch of Peony, 659
  Leaf Rust of Roses, 662
  Leaf Spot of
    Aster, 632
    Carnation, 637
    Chrysanthemum, 639

    Digitalis, 646
    Iris, 652
    Lilies, 654
    Mignonette, 656
    Mountain Laurel, 627
    Pansy, 658
    Phlox, 660
    Zinnia, 672
  Leaf and Twig Blight, 627, 630
  Mildew of
    Chrysanthemum, 639
    Dahlia, 642
    Delphinium, 644
    Golden Glow, 649
    Phlox, 660
    Roses, 663
    Sweet Peas, 669
    Tuberous Begonia, 671
    Zinnia, 672
  Mosaic of
    Calendulas, 635
    Lilies, 654
    Peony, 659
    Petunia, 660
    Sweet Pea, 669
  Neck Rot of Gladiolus, 648
  Neck Rot of Onions, 597
  Nectria Canker, 622
  Penicillium Rot of Gladiolus, 648
  Phoma Root Rot, 596, 597
  Phomopsis Blight, 596
  Phytophthora Blight of Peony, 659
  Rhizoctonia, 597
  Root Rot of
    Aquilegia, 631
    Calla, 636
    Campanula, 637
    Centaurea, 639
    Chrysanthemum, 639
    Dahlia, 642
    Dianthus, 646
    Golden Glow, 649
    Sweet Peas, 669
  Rot of Muscari, 649
  Rot of Primrose, 662
  Rust of
    Antirrhinum, 631
    Aster, 632
    Carnation, 636
    Centaurea, 639
    Chrysanthemum, 639
    Hollyhock, 650
    Lilies, 655
    Pansy, 658
  Scab, 597
  Sclerotial Rot of Iris, 653
  Sclerotium Disease of Zinnias, 672

Smut of
  Corn, 598
  Muscari, 650
Soft Rot of
  Bulbs, 651
  Calendula, 635
  Calla, 636
  Hyacinth, 651
  Iris, 653
  Peony, 659
Stem Canker of Roses, 663
Stem Rot of
  Carnation, 636
  Tuberous Begonia, 671
Stem Rust of Roses, 664
Streak of Sweet Peas, 669
Stunt of
  Chrysanthemum, 640
  Dahlia, 643
Twig Blight, 627, 630
Wilt, 631
Wilt of
  Aster, 633
  Chrysanthemum, 640
  Cosmos, 642
  Marigold, 655
  Nasturtium, 657
  Peony, 659
Yellow Rot of Bulbs, Hyacinth, 651
Yellows of
  Aster, 633
  Chrysanthemum, 640
  Gaillardia, 646
  Marigold, 655
  Pansy, 658
  Pyrethrum, 662
Disodium Methyl arsonate, 198
Distictis cinerea, 286
  lactiflora, 286
  riversi, 286
Dithane Z, 78, 616
Dittany (see Gasplant), 379
Division, 489
Dockmackie, 277
Dodder, Control of, 601
Dodecatheon meadia, **89**, 92
Dog-tooth Violet, **89**, 92
Dogwood, **221**, 230
  insect pest, 624
  Species (Common name)
    Blood-twig, 270
    Coral, 269
    Cornelian, 269
    Flowering, **221**, 230
    Gray, 95, 270
    Japanese Flowering, 230
    Red Osier, 270

    Silky, 269
    Tatarian, 269
Dolichos lablab, 287
Dollarspot, 197
Dormant, defined, 703
Doronicum austriacum, 379
  caucasicum, 82, 379
  plantagineum, 379
Double Digging, 677
Douglas Fir, **226**, 236
Dovetree, 230
Dracaena, 456
  deremenis warnecki, 456
  godseffiana, 456
  sanderiana, 456
  terminalis, 456
Dracocephalum ruyschiana, 379
Dragonhead, 379
Drainage, of surface water, 109
  in the Rock Garden, 72
  of terrace, 32
  size of pipe required, 109
  under-draining wet land, 110
Drains, Tile, 109, 110
  grade of, 110
  table to determine size, 110
Dried Blood, 163
Dropwort, 380
Drying-off, defined, 703
Dryopteris clintonia, 94
  cristata, 94
  dilatata, 94
  hexagonoptera, 94
  linnaeana, 94
  marginalis, 94
  phegopteris, 94
  spinulosa, 94
Dumb-Cane, 456
Dusts and Sprays, General Purpose, 617
Dusty-miller, 323
Dutch Elm Disease, 624
Dutch Iris, 409
Dutchman's Breeches, 92
Dutchman's Pipe, **283**
Dwarf Asiatic Elm, 234

Ear Worm, Corn, 637
Easter Lilies, 533
Easter Lily Vine, **283**
Echinacea purpurea, 379
Echinops humilis, 379
  ritro, 379
  sphaerocephalus, 379
Echium creticum, 324
  plantagineum, 324
  plantagineum hybrids, 324

Edgings, Perennial, 375
Eelworms (see Nematodes), 675
Eggplant, 584
　disease and insect control, 596
Elæagnus angustifolia, 231, **254**, 271
　argentea, 271
　Cherry, **254**, 271
　longipes (E. multiflora), **254**, 271
　pungens, 271
Elder, 95
　American, 276
　European Redberried, 276
Electronic leaf, 484
Elm, American, **225**, 234
　diseases, 624
　insect pests, 624
　Species
　　Augustine ascending, 225
　　Dwarf, 234
　　Wych, 234
Elsholtzia stauntoni, 271
Emilia flammea, 324
　sagittata, 324
Empress Tree, 232
Emulsion, defined, 700
Endive, 584
English Bluebell, 393
English Daisy, **330**
English Hawthorn, 230
English Iris, 408
English Ivy, 287, **460**
　insect pests, 626
English Wallflower, **333**
Enkianthus campanulatus, 271
　Nikko, **254**, 271
　subsessilis, **254**, 271
Epaulette Tree, 233
Epigæa repens, **89**, 92
Equipment, Garden, 502
　for the small place, 505
Eranthis hyemalis, 392
Eremurus, **405**
Erica carnea, 271
Erigeron multiradiatus, 379
　speciosus, 379
Erosion, defined, 703
Eryngium alpinum, 379
　amethystinum (Amethyst), 379
　maritimum, 379
　oliverianum, 379
　planum, 379
Eryngo, Bluetop, 379
Erythronium americanum, **89**, 92, 99
Eschscholtzia californica, **309**, 324
　in the greenhouse, 527
Espaliered Trees, 543

Ethylene Dibromide, 618
Euonymus
　insect pests, 626
　Scale, 626
　Species
　　alatus, **254**, 271
　　a. compactus, 271, **297**
　　americanus, 271
　　atropurpureus, 271
　　Dwarf Winged, 271
　　europaeus, 231
　　fortunei radicans, 287
　　japonicus, **255**, 271
　　patens, 271
　　radicans, **204**, 271, 287
　　r. acutus, 271
　　r. carrieri, 271
　　r. coloratus, **204**, 271
　　r. kewensis, **204**, 271
　　r. vegetus, 271
　　Winged, **254**, 271
Eupatorium coelestinum, 380
　purpureum, 380
　urticaefolium, 380
Euphorbia fulgens, **529**
　in the greenhouse, **529**
　Species
　　corollata, 380
　　cyparissias, 380
　　epithymoides, 380
　　heterophylla, 324
　　marginata (E. variegata), 324
European Hornbeam, 230
European Linden, 234
Evening-primrose, 326
　drummond, 326
　insect pests, 657
Evergreen Candytuft, 381
Evergreens, Dwarf, for Rock Gardens, 81
　for City Garden, 59, 60
　shrubs, for shade, 267
Evergreen Trees, **225**, 235
　Disease and Pest Free, 227
　for rapid growth, 227
　for sandy soil, 226
　for the seashore, 227
　for wet soil, 228
　for windbreaks, 228
　for the woodland garden, 85
　tabular list of, 235
Everlasting, Mangles, 324
　Pearl, 377
　Rose, 324
　Winged, 322
Everlastings, defined, 703
Exochorda grandiflora, 271

Fading-out, 197
Fagus americana (F. grandiflora), 231
  sylvatica, **221**, 231
False-dragonhead, 382
False-spiraea, Kashmir, 276
Farewell-to-Spring, 324
Fatshedera lizei, 457
  l. variegata, 457
Fatsia japonica, 457
  j. moseri, 457
Feeding, 679
Felicia bergeriana, 324
Fences, 144
  Basket-weave, 150
  Board, 146, 147
  Canvas, 151
  Cast Iron, 153
  Grape Stake, 150
  Hurdle, 146
  Lattice, 147
  Louver, 148
  Picket, 149
  Plastic, 151
  Post and Board, 146
  Post and Rail, 145
  Snake, 145
  Snow, 150
  Spindle, 149
  Split Rail, 145
  Split Sapling, 148
  Wire, 151
  Wrought iron, 152
Fennel, Florence, 104
Fennel Flower, 104
Fermate, 616
Fern, American Maidenhair, 94
  Berry Bladder, 94
  Christmas, 94
  Cinnamon, 94
  Climbing, 94
  Clinton, 94
  Crested, 94
  Crested Wood, 94
  Ebony Spleenwort, 94
  Hartford, 94
  Hayscented, 94
  Interrupted, 94
  Lady, 94
  Leatherwood, 94
  Maidenhair Spleenwort, 94
  Mountain Wood, 94
  Narrow Beech, 94
  Narrowleaf Spleenwort, 94
  Oak, 94
  Ostrich, 94
  Polypody, 94
  Rattlesnake, 94

  Royal, 94, 99
  Sensitive, 94
  Toothed Wood, 94
  Walking, 94
  Winged Wood, 94
Ferns for Woodland Gardens, 94
Fertilization, defined, 703
Fertilizers, Complete, 164
  Mineral, 161
  Soluble, 165
  Urea-form, 162
Fescue, 178
  Red, 178
Feverfew, 323
Ficus lyrata (F. pandurata), 457
  pumila, 287
  repens, 287
  r. var. minimus, 287
Fiddle-leafed Fig, 457
Fig, Creeping, 287
Filipendula hexapetala, 380
  palmata, 380
Fir, Balsam, 235
  Colorado, 225
  Douglas, **226**, 236
  Nikko, 235
  Nordmann's, 235
  Veitch's, 235
  White, 235
Fire Blight, 629
Firethorn, **259**, 274, 298
Five-leaf Aralia (see Acanthopanax pentaphyllum), 267
Flagstone Paths, 124
Flats, 703
Flax, Alpine, 82
  Blue, **366**, 381
  Flowering, 325
  Golden, 381
  Narbonne, 381
  Perennial, 82, **366**, 381
  Prairie, 82
Fleabane, 379
Flea Beetle, Potato, 660
  Primrose, 657
Fleece Vine, Chinese, 290
  Primrose, 657
Florence Fennel, 104
Floripondio, Cornucopia, 323
  Yellow, 323
Flower Boxes, 466
  construction of, 467
  drainage for, 467
  maintenance of, 467
  materials for, 466
  plants for, 469
  sizes, 466
  soil mixtures, 467

Flower Garden Calendar, 698
Flower-of-Jove, 381
Flower-Pot Gardens, 37
  Cultural requirements of, 38
  Plants for, 39
  Selection of Pots for, 38
  Watering, 39
Flower-Tub gardens, 44
  Maintenance of, 45
  Plants for, 46
  Types and sizes, 45
Flowers, attractive to birds, 303
Flowers for Penthouse Gardens, 66
Flowering Cherry, **224**, 233
  Crab-apple, **224**, 232
  Dogwood, **221**, 230
  Quince, Japanese, 269
  Tobacco, **311**
Fly, Bulb, 652
  White, 632
Foamflower, 93
Foeniculum officinalis, 105
  vulgare, var. dulce, 104
Foliar Feeding, 167
Forcing, 700
  bulbous iris, 526
  lilies, 533
  narcissus, 534
  shrubs, 539
  tulips, 537
Forget-me-not, 93, **330**, 381
  alpestris, 381
  Alpine, 381
  Swiss, 381
  True, 381
Formaldehyde, 476
  Drench, 476
Forsythia, **255**, 271
  intermedia, 271
  i. spectabilis, **255**, 271
  ovata, **255**, 271
  suspensa, **255**, 272
  s. fortunei, 272
  viridissima, 271
Fothergilla, Alabama, 272
  Gardeni, 272
  monticola, 272
Foundation planting, 13
Fountains, 135
Four-o'clock, 325
Foxglove, **330**
  diseases and insect pests, 646
  Yellow, 379
Foxtail Lily, 405
Franklin Tree, **221**, 231
Franklinia, **221**, 231

Fraxinus americana, 231
  caroliniana, 231
  lanceolata, 231
  ornus, 231
Freesia, 529
Fringe Tree, **253**, 269
Fringed Gentian, 92
Fritillaria Imperialis, diseases, 646
Frost Protection for Plants, 682
Fruit Garden, 543
  care of stock, 545
  choosing varieties, 544
  disease and pest control, 564
  growing and fruiting habits, 547
  laying out, 545
  planting, 546
  pollination, 546
  spraying, 563
Fruit Trees, Apple, 547, **548**
  Cherry, 548, **551**
  Nectarine, 552
  Peach, 547, **552**
  Pear, 547, **554**
  Plum, 548, **554**
  Quince, 548, **555**
Fruit Trees, Cordon, 543
  Espaliered, 543
  Ornamental, 543
Fruits, Bush, 555
  disease and pest control, 568, 569
  spraying schedules, 568, 569
  Blackberries, 555
  Blueberries, 556
  Currants, 557
  Gooseberries, 557
  Raspberries, 558
  Strawberries, 559
Fruits, Vine, Grapes, 561
  spraying of, 563
  spraying schedules, 564
Fuchsia, 42, 454
Fumigation of Soil, 703
Fungi, 610
Fungicides, 616
Fungicides, Systemic, 617
Funkia, **358**, 381

Gaillardia, 324
  diseases, 646
  Species
    amblyodon, 324
    aristata, 380
    Maroon, 324
    pulchella, 324
    Rose-ring, 324
Galanthus, 392
Galax aphylla, 92

Gale, Sweet, 274
Galega officinalis, 380
Galium boreale, 380
    verum, 380
Galtonia candicans, 405
    insect pest, 646
Gamolepis tagetes, 324
Garden Balsam, 324
Garden Calendar, 698
Garden Lighting, 28
Gardens open to the Public, 687
Garden Practices, 677
Garlic, Control of, 200
Gasplant, 379
Gaultheria procumbens, 92
Gayfeather, Cattail, 381
    Grassleaf, 381
    Spike, 381
Gaylussacia baccata, 272
Gazania splendens, 204
Gelsemium sempervirens, 287
Gentian, Bottle, 92
    Closed, 92, 99
    Fringed, 92, 99
Gentiana andrewsii, 92, 99
    crinita, 92, 99
Geranium, 454
    diseases, 647
    for Pot Culture, 42
    in the greenhouse, 530
    Species
        armenum, 380
        fremontii, 380
        grandiflorum, 380
        ibericum, 380
        Ivy-leaved, 530
        Lady Washington, 530
        Lilac, 380
        macrorrhizum, 82
        maculatum, 82
        pratense, 380
        Rose, 530
        Scented, 104
        Wild, 82
Gerbera jamesonii, 530
Germander, 383
Geum, chiloense florepleno, 380
    montanum heldreichii, 380
Gilia, Birdseye, 324
    capitata, 324
    coccinia, 324
    coronopifolia, 324
    Globe, 324
    Scarlet, 324
    tricolor, 324
Ginkgo biloba, **221**, 231
Gladiolus, **405**

diseases, 647
    insect pests, 648
    in the greenhouse, 531
Gleditsia aquatica, 231
    triacanthos, 231
    t. inermis moraine, **221**, 231
Globe-Amaranth, 324
Globeflower, 383
    Chinese, 383
Globethistle, Common, 379
    Low, 379
    Steel, 379
Gloriosa rothschildiana, 458
Glory Lily, 458
Glossary, 703
Gloxinia, 531
Goatsbeard, 378
Goatsrue, 380
Godetia amoena, 324
    grandiflora, 324
    Whitney, 324
Goldenbells, Border, 271
    Drooping, **255**, 272
    Green-stem, 272
    Showy Border, **255**, 271
Goldencup, 324
Goldenglow, 382
    diseases and insect pests, 649
Golden Rain Tree, **222**, 231
Goldenrod, Alpine, 383
    Canada, 383
    Stiff, 383
    Tall, 383
    Wreath, 383
Goldentuft, 81, 377
    Dwarf, 81, 377
Goldenwave, 323
Goldflower, 272
Goldwings, 383
Gomphrena globosa, 324
Gooseberries, 557
    disease and pest control, 569
Gordonia alatamaha, **221**, 231
Grading, 106
    finished, 109
    plan, 106
    without a plan, 108
Grafting, 493, 703
    bark, 495
    bridge, 493
    cleft, 493
    Pruning and Training of
        Grafts, 496
    whip, 494
Grape Hyacinth, 393
    diseases, 649
Grape Ivy, 460

Grapes, 561
  planting, 651
  soil requirements, 651
  spray schedules, 567
  training and pruning, 561
  varieties of merit, 562
Grasses for lawns
  Bent, 174
  Bermuda, 179
  Buffalograss, 179
  Fescues, 178
  Kentucky Bluegrass, 175
  Merion Kentucky Bluegrass, 175
  Mixtures, 178
  Poa Trivialis, 177
  Redtop, 178
  Roughstalk Bluegrass, 177
  St. Augustine, 179
  Zoysia, 178, 179
Gravel Walks, 127
Greek-valerian, 382
Greenhouse, 514
  additional light, 523
  benches, 515
  calendar of bloom, 523
  construction, 515
  heating, 516
  humidity, 519
  light, 521
  location, 514
  selection of plants, 522
  Short-Day Treatment, 523
  summer in the, 520
  syringing, 519
  temperature, 516
  unheated, 514
  ventilation, 517
  watering, 518
Greenhouse Plants, 522, 538
  Detailed culture of, 522
  Lists of
    bulbs, corms and tubers, 538
    cut branches, 539
    cut flowers, 538
    ferns, 540
    foliage plants, 540
    for cool greenhouse, 539
    for intermediate greenhouse, 540
    for warm greenhouse, 540
    palms, 539
    pot plants, 538
    shrubs in pots, 539
    vines, 539
Grill, 143
  Construction, 143
Ground Cover Plants, 201
  of merit, 202

  selection of, 201
  troublesome, 202
Groundsel-Bush, purple, 327
Grubs, in lawns, 195
Guinea Gold Vine, 288
Gum, Sweet, 222
Gymnocladus dioica, 231
Gypsophila, **355**, 380
  Bristol Fairy, 355
  Creeping, 355
  Cushion, 324
  elegans, 324
  muralis, 324
  paniculata, 355
  repens, 32, 82, 355

Habitat, defined, 703
Habenaria ciliaris, 92
  fimbriata, 92
  psycodes, 92
Hackberry, 230
Hairy Vetch, 158
Halesia carolina, **221**, 231
  diptera, 231
  tetraptera, 231
Hamamelis japonica, 272
  mollis, 272
  vernalis, 272
  virginiana, 272
Hanging Pots and Baskets, 46
  Planting of, 47
  Plants for, 48
  Types of, 47
Hardening-off, defined, 703
Hardy Orange, 269
Harebell, Carpathian, 81
  Peach-leaved, **350**, 378
  Tufted, **350**
Hawkweed, 323
Hawthorn, **221**, 230
  Downy, 230
  English, **221**, 230
Hay, 498
Hay (Salt), 499
Hazel, Purple, 270
  Winter, 270
Hazelnut, American, 270
  Beaked, 270
Heath, Spring, 271
Heather, 269
Heaving, defined, 703
Hedera canariensis, 287
  c. variegata, 287
  helix, 204, **287**, 460
  h. baltica, 287
  h. conglomerata, 288

h. hahnii, 288
h. minima, 288
Hedge Maple, **220**, 229
Hedges, 293
 care of, 295
 forms of, 296
 growth inhibitors, 296
 planting, 294
 Plants of merit, 297
 material for, 298
  deciduous shrubs, 300
  deciduous trees, 300
  dwarf evergreens, 299
  evergreen shrubs, 299
  evergreen trees, 298
Heel, defined, 703
Heeling-in, defined, 703
Helenium autumnale, 380
 a. pumilum, 380
 Hoopesii, 380
Helianthus angustifolius, 380
 annuus, **314**, 324
 atrorubens, 380
 debilis, 324
 decapetalus, 380
 Maximiliani, 380
 orgyalis, 380
 scaberrimus, 380
Helichrysum bracteatum, 324
Heliophila, 324
 in the greenhouse, 532
Heliopsis pitcheriana, 380
 Pitcher, 380
 scabra var. excelsa, 380
Heliotrope, 324
 insect pests, 650
Heliotropium peruvianum, 324
Helipterum manglesii, 324
 roseum, 324
Helleborus niger, 82, 380
Hemerocallis, 355
 aurantiaca, **356**, 380
 citrina, **356**
 dumortierii, **356**, 380
 hybrids, **356**
 flava, **356**, 380
 fulva, **356**, 380
 middendorffi, **356**, 380
 thunbergii, **356**, 380
Hemlock, **226**, 236, 298
 Carolina, 236
 insect pest, 626
 Japanese, 236
 Weeping, 236
Hepatica acutiloba, 93
 triloba, **89**, 93
Herald Trumpet, **283**

Herbaceous Perennials, 334
 acid tolerant, 341
 diseases, 630
 fertilizing, 343
 Lists for
  alkaline soil, 341
  background, 376
  bold effects, 376
  borders of ponds, 375
  borders of streams, 375
  city gardens, 60
  dry, sandy soil, 374
  edging, 375
  light shade, 374
  old-fashioned gardens, 376
  poor soil, 374
  pot culture, 41
  semi-shade, 374
  sub-tropical effects, 376
  well-drained situations, 375
  wet situations, 375
 fragrant, 376
 insect pests, 630
 long blooming, 376
 maintenance, 341
 planning the border, 335
 planting plans, 337, 339
 preparation of soil for, 340
 propagation,
  by division, 489
  by division of tubers, 490
  by grafting, 493
  by layering, 491
  by leaf cuttings, 487
  by rhizomes, 490
  by root cuttings, 488
  by seed, 471
  by softwood stem cuttings, 481
 renewal of plants, 344
 seldom attacked by pests and diseases, 619
 selected list of, 344
 soil reaction for, 340
 staking, 342
 summer mulches for, 344, 500
 tabular list of, 378
 watering, 342
 winter mulches for, 344, 501
 winter protection, 501
Herbs, 100
 classification, 101
 for flavoring, 102
 for fragrance, 103
 harvesting, 102
 indoor culture, 102
 tabular list, 103
 uses, 101
Hercules Club, 229, 267

Herniaria glabra, 32
Hesperis matronalis, 380
Heuchera, **357**, 380
  americana, 92
  lithophila (brizoides), **358**
  sanguinea, 82, **358**, 380
  s. Rosamondie, 358
  s. Perry's White, 358
Hibbertia volubilis, 288
Hibiscus syriacus, 272
Hickory, 230
  Shagbark, 230
  Shellbark, 230
Highbush Blueberry, 277
Hilling-up, defined, 703
Holly, American, **225**, 235
  Chinese, 272
  English, **225**, 235
  Finetooth, 255
  Japanese, 272
Hollygrape, Leather-leaf, 274
  Oregon, 274
Hollyhock, **331**
  diseases, 650
  insect pests, 651
Holly-olive, 274
Honesty, 325
Honeysuckle, Amur, 273
  blue-leaf, 273
  fragrant, 273
  Giant Burmese, 289
  Hall's climbing, 289
  Japanese, Control of, 601
  Morrow, **257**, 273
  privet, 273
  scarlet trumpet, 289
  shiny, 273
  Tatarian, **257**, 274
Hops, 498
Horehound, 104
Hormone sprays, 606
  Plants resistant, 609
  Plants sensitive, 609
Hornbeam, American, 230
  European, 230
  Hop, 232
Horsechestnut, 229
  red, 229
Horseradish, 104
Hosta, 358
  caerulea, 381
  japonica, 381
  plantaginea grandiflora, 381
  sieboldiana, 381
Hotbeds, 511
  electric, 512

hot water, 513
management, 513
manure, 512
steam pipes, 513
types of, 511
uses of, 511
Houndstongue, 323
House Plants, 442
  annuals for, 455
  artificial light for, 462
  bulbs, 451
  diseases, 447
  dividing, 446
  feeding, 444
  flowering plants, 448
  foliage plants, 455
  for partial sunlight, 461
  for north windows, 461
  general care, 444
  humidity, 443
  insects, 448
  light, 442
  potting, 446
  potting mixtures for, 447
  preferring sunlight, 461
  temperature, 443
  ventilation, 443
  vines, flowering, 458
  vines, foliage, 460
  watering, 444
Houstonia caerulea, 93
  purpurea, 93
Hovenia dulcis, 231
Huckleberry, Black, 272
Humulus japonicus, 288
Humus, 155
Hunnemannia fumariaefolia, 324
Hyacinth, 391
  diseases, 651
  insect pests, 651
Hyacinth-bean, 287
Hyacinthus candicans, insect pest, 646
Hybrid, defined, 703
Hydrangea arborescens, 272
  Climbing, 288
  Oak-leaf, 272
  Panicle, 272
  paniculata, 272
  petiolaris, 288
  quercifolia, 272
Hydrocotyle rotundifolia, 200
Hymenocallis calathina, 407
Hypericum moserianum, 82, **204**, 272
  prolificum, 272
Hyssop, 104
Hyssopus officinalis, 104

Iberis affinis, 324
  amara (I. coronaria)
  sempervirens, 82, **204**, 380
  tenoreana, 82
  umbellata, 324
Ibota Privet, 273, 300
Iceland Poppy, **332**
Ice Plant, 205
Ilex aquifolium, **225**, 235
  cornuta, 272
  c. Burfordii, 272
  crenata, **255**, 272
  c. convexa, **255**, 272, 297
  c. latifolia, 255
  c. microphylla, **255**, 272, 297
  glabra, 272
  opaca, **225**, 235
  serrata, 255
  verticillata, **255**, 272
Immortelle, 327
Impatiens balsamina, 324
  Holstii, 454
  Sultani, 324, **454**
Incarvillea variabilis, **311**, 324
Inch Worm (see Canker Worm), 624
Inkberry, 272
Insect Pests (general), 611
  in the lawn, 194
  of flowering plants, 630
  of fruit, 564–569
  of house plants, 447
  of shrubs and trees, 619
  of vegetables, 595
  Plants seldom attacked by, 619
Insecticides, 614, 703
  General Purpose, 617
  List of, 614
  Systemic, 616
Insects, 611
  Control of, 612
Insects (specific)
  Ants, 659
  Aphid, 631
  Asparagus Beetle, 595
  Aster Beetle, 633
  Bagworm, 619
  Bean Weevil, 595
  Birch Leaf-miner, 621
  Black Blister Beetle, 633
  Borer, Dogwood, 624
    Lilac, 626
    Rhododendron, 629
  Box Leaf Miner, 622
  Box Psylla, 622
  Buffalo Tree Hopper, 633
  Bulb Fly, Galtonia, 646
    Hyacinth, 652

Bulb Mite, 651
Cabbage Looper, 656
Cabbage Worm, 635
Canker Worm, 624
Chinch Bug, 195
Codling Moth, 564, 568
Corn Borer, 598
Corn Ear Worm, 637
Cucumber Beetle, 596
Curculio, 564
Currant Worm, 569
Cutworm, 643
Cyclamen Mite, 645
Elm Leaf Beetle, 625
Euonymus Scale, 626
European Hornet, 643
Flea Beetle, 596
Gall Midge, 640
Gladiolus Thrip, 649
Golden Tortoise Beetle, 656
Grape Berry Moth, 567
Greenhouse Leaf Tier, 638
Grubs, 195, 635
Grubs in the lawn, 195
Harlequin Bug, 641
Inch Worm (see Canker Worm), 624
Iris Borer, 653
Japanese Beetle, 664
June Bug, 195
Lace Bug, 621
Leaf-cutter Bee, 643
Leaf-miner (Aquilegia), 632
  (Arborvitae), 619
  (Birch), 621
Leaf Roller, 634
  of Rose, 665
Lesser Bulb Fly, Hyacinth, 652
Lilac Borer, 626
Maggots
  Apple, 564
  Broccoli, 596
  Cabbage, 596
  Cauliflower, 596
Magnolia Scale, 627
Mealy Bug, 671
Mexican Bean Beetle, 595
Midge, 666
Mites (Cyclamen), 645
  (Red Spider), 646
  (Southern Red), 621
Nematodes, **675**
  of Chrysanthemum, 641
  of Narcissus, 657
  of Peony, 660
  of Sweet Peas, 669
Orange Tortrix, 653
Oriental Fruit Moth, 655

Insects—*continued*
  Orthezia, 641
  Oyster Shell Scale, 660
  Pallid Mite, 645
  Pine False Webworm, 628
  Pine Leaf-miner, 628
  Pine Sawflies, 628
  Pine Spittlebug, 628
  Pine Webworm, 628
  Pine Weevil, 628
  Potato Beetle, 596
  Potato Flea Beetle, 660
  Primrose Flea Beetle, 657
  Raspberry Byturus, 568
  Raspberry Cane Borer, 569
  Red-banded Leaf Roller, 655
  Red Spider, 564
  Rhododendron Borer, 629
  Root Aphids, 634
  Rose Beetle, 665
  Rose Curculio, 666
  Rose Leafhopper, 666
  Rose Leaf Roller, 665
  Rose Leaf Tier, 665
  Rose Midge, 666
  Rose Scale, 666
  Rose Slugs, 667
  Rose Stem Borer, 667
  Rose Stem Girdler, 667
  Rose Weevil, 638, 668
  Saddle-back Caterpillar, 638
  Scale (Apple), 564
  Slugs, 671
  Southern Red Mite, 621
  Spotted Cucumber Beetle, 638
  Spruce Spider Mite, 620
  Squash Bug, 598
  Stalk Borer, 634
  Tarnished Plant Bug, 634
  Taxus Mealybug, 630
  Tea Scale, 623
  Tent Caterpillar, 621
  Thrips,
    Digitalis, 646
    Gladiolus, 649
    Hemerocallis, 650
    Rose, 668
  Tulip Tree Scale, 630
  Violet Sawfly, 658
  White Fly, **632**
  White Grubs, 195
  Woolly Aphids, 649
  Yellow Woolly-bear Caterpillar, 642
Ipomoea purpurea, **288**, **458**
Iris, **358**
  diseases, 652
  insect pests, 653

Species and types
  American beardless, 365
  apogoniris, 361
  autumn-flowering, 360
  bearded, **359**, **360**
  bearded varieties of merit, 360
  bulbous, 408
  bulbous, in the greenhouse, 532
  crested, 82, 93, **365**
  cristata, 82, 93, **365**
  Dutch, 409
  Dwarf Bearded, 359
  Dwarf Crimean, 82
  English, 408
  fulva, 99
  gracilipes, **366**
  Japanese, 361
  kaempferi, 361
  Louisiana, 364
  pogoniris, 359
  pseudacorus, 99, **365**
  pumila, 82
  reticulata, 409
  siberica, 362
  Spanish, 408
  spuria, 364
  tectorum, 366
  tingitana, 409
  verna, 82, 93
  vernal, 82, 93
  versicolor, 99, **365**
  vesper (dichotoma), 364
  xiphioides, 408
  xiphium, 408
Iron, 166, 170
Iron Chelates, 166, 170
Iron, Deficiency in association with lime, 166, 170
Ironwood, 230
Ismene, 407
Italian Bellflower, **452**
Ivy, Algerian, 287
  Boston, 290
  Canary Island, 287
  English, 204, **287**, 460
  Grape, 460
Ivy-arum, 461

Jack-in-the-Pulpit, **88**, 92, 99
Jacobaea, 324
Japanese Anemone, 345
Japanese Barberry, 268
Japanese Beetle, 664
Japanese Holly (see Ilex crenata), **255**, 272
Japanese Honeysuckle, Control of, 601
Japanese Hop Vine, 288
Japanese Maple, 229
Japanese Spurge, 205

Japanese Tree Lilac, **224**, 234
Japanese Yew, 236
Jasmine, Carolina, 287
  Chilean, 289
  Poet's, 288
  Primrose, 288
  Winter, **256**, 272, 288
Jasminum mesnyi, 288
  nudiflorum, **256**, 272, 288
  officinale, var. grandiflorum, 288
  Stephanense, 288
Joe-pye-weed, 380
Johnson grass, Control of, 604
Jonquil (see Narcissus), 384
Judas-Tree, **221**, 230
Juglans, 231
  cinerea, 231
  nigra, 218, 231
  regia, 231
  sieboldiana, 231
June Bug, 195
Juniper, Andorra, **256**, 273
  Chinese, 235
  columnar Chinese, 235
  common, 235, 273
  creeping, 235, 273
  Douglas, 273
  Greek, 235
  Pfitzer, 235, **256**, 272
  prostrate, 204, 235
  Savin, 235, **256**
  Swedish, 235
  Waukegan, 204, 235, 273
Juniperus chinensis, 235
  c. Pfitzeriana, 235, **256**, 272
  c. pyramidalis, 235
  communis, 235, 272
  c. depressa, 235
  c. depressa plumosa, 273
  c. succica, 235
  excelsa stricta, 235
  horizontalis, 204, 235, 273
  h. Douglasii, 204, 235, 273
  h. depressa plumosa, **256**, 273
  procumbens, 235
  sabina, 235, **256**
  s. tamariscifolia, 235, 273
  squamata, var. Meyeri, 235, 273
  virginiana, **225**, 235
  v. Canaertii, 235
  v. elegantissima, 235
  v. glauca, 235
  v. Schottii, 235
Jupitersbeard, 378

Kale, 584
Kalmia (Mt. Laurel), diseases, 627

latifolia, **256**, 273
Kangaroo Vine, 460
Karathane, 616
Katsura-tree, 230
Kentucky Bluegrass, 175
Kentucky Coffeetree, 231
Kerria japonica, **256**, 273
Kniphofia, **407**
  foliosa, 381
  rufa, 381
  uvaria, 381
  u. pfitzeriana, 381
Knotgrass, 200
Knotweed, Control of, 602
Kochia scoparia, 325
  trichophylla, 325
Koelreuteria paniculata, **222**, 231
Kohlrabi, 585
Kolkwitzia amabilis, **257**, 273

Laburnum vulgare, 273
Lace Bugs, 621
Laceflower, Blue, 327
Lady's Slipper, Pink, **88**, 92
  Showy, 92
  Yellow, **88**, 92
Lagerstroemia indica, 273
Lantana, for pot culture, 42
  insect pests, 653
  Species and types
    callowiana, 204
    trailing, 204
Larch, American, 231
Larix americana (L. laricina), 231
Larkspur (Annual), **311**
  in the greenhouse, 533
  Species and types
    cardinal, 379
    field, 323
    orange, 379
    Rocket, 323
    Siberian, 379
    Yellow, 379
Larvacide, 618
Lath Houses, 540
Lathyrus (see Sweet Pea)
  dwarf, 325
  odoratus, **314**, 325
Lathyrus, in the greenhouse, 536
Laurel, Cherry, 274
  Grecian, 297
  Mountain, 256
Laurus nobilis, **225**, 273, 297
Lavandula dentata, 104
  officinalis, 104
  spica, 104, 381
  vera, 104, 381

Lavatera alba splendens, 325
  rosea splendens, 325
  trimestris, 325
Lavender, Spike, 381
  True, 104, 381
Lavender-Cotton, 104
Lawns, 173
  aeration of, 192
  diseases, 196
  establishment of, 173
  fertilization, 183, 188
  for poor soil, 185
  grasses, 174
  grass substitutes for, 180
  growth inhibitors, 192
  lime for, 191
  maintenance, 187
  mowing, 191
  organic matter for, 181
  pests, 194
  preparation of soil, 181, 184
  renovation, 193
  rolling, 188
  seeding, 186
  shady areas, 185
  sodding, 186
  soil acidity for, 183
  sub-irrigation, 193
  temporary, 185
  top dressing, 190
  watering, 193
  weed control, 197
  weeds, 198
  weed-free seed bed, 184
Lawn Leaf, 181
Layering, 491
  air, 492
  mound, 492
  serpentine, 492
  simple, 491
  tip, 491
Layia elegans, 325
Leaching, 703
Lead, Arsenate of, 614
Leadwort, Blue, 82, 203
Leaf Miner, 621
Leaf Spot, 627
Leaves, for Mulches, 498
Leafmold, 156
Leatherleaf, 269
Leatherwood, 270
Leek, 585
Legumes, 158
Leiophyllum buxifolium, 95
Lemon Verbena, 104
Leopard-bane, 379
  Caucasian, 82

Leptosiphon hybrida, 325
Leptosyne maritima, 325
  stillmanii, 325
Lettuce, 586
Levisticum officinale, 104
Leucojum, 392
Leucothoë catesbaei, 257, 273
  Drooping, 257, 273
Liatris graminifolia, 381
  pycnostachya, 381
  scariosa, 381
  spicata, 381
Libocedrus decurrens, 235
Lighting in the garden, 28
Lights for Growing Plants, 462
Ligustrum amurense, 273
  ibolium, 273
  ibota, 273
  japonicum, 273
  lucidum, 257, 273
  obtusifolium var. regelianum, 273
  ovalifolium, 273
  sinense, 297
Lilac, Common, 262, 277
  Culture, 262
  diseases, 626
  insect pests, 626
  Species (Common name)
    Japanese Tree, 224, 234, 262
    Himalayan, 277
    Persian, 262, 277
    Rouen, 262, 277
Lilies, 412
  Culture, 412
  diseases, 654
  exposure, 413
  for the Bog Garden, 99
  for city gardens, 60
  for the greenhouse, 533
  for pot culture, 44
  for special purposes, 416
  healthy bulbs, 413
  insect pests, 655
  of special merit, 416
  planting, 413
  propagation, 414
  soil requirements, 413
  summer mulches, 414
  winter mulches, 413
  Species
    amabile, 416
    auratum (Gold-banded), 417
    a. platyphyllum, 417
    batemanniae, 417
    canadense (Meadow Lily), 99, 417
    candidum (Madonna Lily), 417
    concolor, 418

elegans, 418
 formosanum, 418
 hansoni, 418
 henryi, 418
 longiflorum erabu (Easter Lily), 533
 Martagon, 418
 pardalinum (Leopard Lily), 418
 p. Giganteum, 418
 regale (Regal Lily), 419
 r. Royal Gold, 419
 speciosum, 419
 superbum, 99
 testaceum (Nankeen Lily), 419
 Strains and varieties, 421, 422
Lily-of-the-Nile, 46
Lily-of-the-valley, 82, 92, 204, **393**
Lime, 170
 danger of excessive application, 170
 ground limestone, 170
 hydrated, 170
 rate of application, 171
Limestone, 170
Lime-Sulphur, 617
Limonium bonduellii, 325
 gmelini, 381
 latifolium, 381
 perezii, 42
 sinuatum, 325
 suworowi, 325
 tataricum, 381
Linaria bipartita, 325
 macedonica, 381
 maroccana, 325
Lindane, 615
Linden, American, 234
 European, **225**, 234
 Littleleaf, 234
Linum alpinum, 82
 flavum, 381
 grandiflorum, 325
 lewisii, 82
 narbonense, 381
 perenne, 82, **366**, 381
 p. album, **366**, 381
Lippia canescens (L. repens), 181
 citriodora, 104
Liquid Manure, 160
Liquidambar styraciflua, 218, **222**, 231
Liriodendron tulipifera, **222**, 231
 insect pests, 630
Liverwort, **89**, 92
Loam Soil, 155
Lobelia, Annual, **311**, 325
 insect pests, 655
 Species
  cardinalis, 99, 381

 erinus, 325
 tenuior, 325
Locust, Black, 234
 Clammy, 275
 Honey, 231
 Moraine, **221**, 231
 Water, 231
Lonicera fragrantissima, 273
 heckrottii, 289
 hildebrandtiana, 289
 japonica chinensis, 289
 japonica halliana, 289
 korolkowii, 273
 Maackii, 273
 Morrowi, **257**, 273
 nitida, 273
 pileata, 273
 sempervirens, 289
 tatarica, **257**, 274
Loosestrife, Clethra, 381
 Purple, **367**, 381
Lotus berthelotii, 48
Lovage, 104
Love-in-a-mist, 326
Love-lies-bleeding, 322
Lunaria annua, 325
 insect pests, 655
Lupine, Annual, **312**, 325
 greenhouse culture, 533
 Species (Common name)
  Blue, 93, 325
  dwarf, 325
  Hartweg, 325
  Washington, 381
  Yellow, 325
Lupinus, **367**, 381
 greenhouse culture, 533
 Species
  dwarf, 325
  hartwegii, 325
  hirsutus, 325
  luteus, 325
  mutabilis, 325
  perennis, 93
  polyphyllus, 381
Lychnis chalcedonica, 381
 coeli-rosa, 325
 flos-jovis, 381
 viscaria, 381
Lycoris squamigera, 409
Lygodium palmatum, 94
Lysimachia clethroides, 381
Lythrum superbum, **367**, 381
Lycium halimifolium, 602

Maclura pomifera, 231
Madagascar Jasmine, 291

Madonna Lily, 417
Magnesium, 161
Magnolia, **223**, 232, 235
  insect pest, 627
  transplanting, 217
  Species
    acuminata, 232
    Bigleaf, 232
    Cucumber, 232
    denudata (M. conspicua), 232
    glauca, 232
    grandiflora, **225**, 232, 235
    kobus, 232
    macrophylla, 232
    Saucer, **223**, 232
    soulangeana, **223**, 232
    Star, **223**, 232
    stellata, **223**, 232
    Swamp, 232
    tripetala, 232
    Umbrella, 232
    virginiana (M. glauca), 232
    yulan, 232
Mahonia aquifolium, **257**, 274
  beali, 274
Majorana Onites (see Origanum), 104
Malathion, 615
Malcomia maritima, 325
Maleic Hydrazide (MH)
  for hedges, 296
  for lawns, 192
Mallow-wort, 325
Malope trifida grandiflora, 325
Maltese Cross, 381
Malus arnoldiana, 232
  atrosanguinea, 232
  baccata, 232
  coronaria, 232
  floribunda, **224**, 232
  halliana parkmanii, 232
  ioensis, 232
  i. plena, 232
  neidzwetzkyana, 232
  scheideckeri, 232
  spectabilis, 232
Mandevilla suaveolens, 289
Manganese, 164
Manure, 159
  animal, 159
  artificial, 160
  cow, 160
  dehydrated, 160
  fresh, 160
  green, 157
  horse, 160
  in hotbeds, 512
  liquid, 160

pig, 160
poultry, 160
sheep, 160
Manzate, 617
Maple
  Species
    Amur, 229
    Hedge, **220**, 229
    Japanese, 229
    Mountain, 229
    Norway, 229
    Red, 229
    Silver, 229
    Sugar, **220**, 229
    Sycamore, 229
    Tatarian, 229
Marica, 455
Marigold, **312**, 327
  diseases, 655
  insect pests, 655
  Species
    African, **312**, 327
    French, **312**, 327
    Mexican, 327
Marjoram, 101, 102, 104
  Perennial, 104
  Pot, 105
  Sweet, 105
Marrubium vulgare, 104
Marsh Marigold, 99
Martynia fragrans, 325
Maskflower, 322
Mat, defined, 703
Mathiola bicornis, 325
  incana, **314**, 325
  in the greenhouse, 536
Matricaria chamomilla, 103
Matrimony Vine, Control of, 602
Mayapple, 93
Mayflower, **89**, 92
May Tree, **221**, 230
Mazus reptans, 204
  rugosus, 32
Meadow Lily, 417
Meadow Saffron, 409
Meadowrue, Columbine, **373**, 383
  Dusty, **373**, 383
  Early, 82
  Low, 383
  Tall, 383
  Yunnan, **373**, 383
Meadowsweet, 380
Mealy bug, 671
Measures, Table of, 618
Meconopsis cambrica, 381
Medicine Shelf, 614
Melissa officinalis, 103

Melon, 586
Mentha crispa, 104
   piperita, 104
   rotundifolia, 104
   spicata, 105
Merion Kentucky Bluegrass, 175
Mertensia virginica, **90**, 93, 381
Mesembryanthemum crystallinum, 205
Metaldehyde, 671
Methoxychlor (DMDT), 615
Mexican Ageratum, 322
Mexican Bean Beetle, 595
Mexican Poppy, 322
Mexican Shellflower, 407
Mice, Control of, 673
   Meadow mouse, 673
   Pine mouse, 673
Midge, 666
Mignonette, 326
   diseases, 656
   greenhouse culture, 533
   insect pests, 656
Milkweed, Swamp, 378
Mimulus luteus, 325
   tigrinus, 325
Miner, Leaf,
   Birch, 621
   Box, 622
   Perennials, 632
Mineral Nutrients, 161
Mint, Apple, 104
   Curled, 104
Mintshrub, 271
Mirabilis jalapa, 325
Miscible Oils, 615
Mistflower, 380
Mist spraying, 483
Mitchella repens, 93
Mitella diphylla, 93
Mites, 621
   Boxwood, 623
   Cyclamen, 645
Moccasin Flower, **88**, 92
Mock-orange, 274
   Big Scentless, **258**, 274
   California, **252**, 269
   Lemoine's, 274
   Virginal, **258**, 274
Mockernut, 230
Moles, 196, 674
Monarda didyma, 103, 381
   fistulosa, 103
   f. alba, 103
Monkeyflower, 325
Monkshood, Autumn, 377
   Azure, 377
   Violet, 377

Monoecious, defined, 703
Monstera deliciosa, 460
Montbretia, 408
Moon Flower, **283**
Moosewood, 229
Morning Glory, **288**, **458**
   insect pests, 656
Morus alba, 232
Moss Pink, 205
Moss Vervain, **315**, 327
Moth, codling, 564, 567
Mother-of-Thyme, 205
Mountain Ash, American, 224
   European, 224
Mountain Bluet, 378
Mountain Laurel, **256**, 273
   disease, 627
Mountain Pine, 235
Mourning Bride, **313**
Mulberry, Paper, 230
   Control of, 600
   White, 232
Mulches, 497
   acid, 500
   for the rock garden, 74
   for trees, 218
   for weed control, 605
   Materials for, 497
   Need for Additional Nitrogen, 500
   non-acid, 500
   summer, 500
   winter, 501
Muriate of Potash, 164
Muscari, 393
   diseases, 649
Muskmelon, 586
   disease and insect control, 597
Myosotis, 330
   alpestris, 381
   dissitiflora, 325, 381
   laxa, 93
   palustris, 381
   p. semperflorens, 82, 205
   scorpioides, 93, 381
Myrica pennsylvanica, 274
   Gale, **258**, 274
Myrrhis odorata, 105
Myrtle, 205
   Crape, 273
   Sand, 95

Nandina domestica, 274
Nankeen Lily, 419
Nannyberry, 95
Narcissus, 384
   classification, 384
   culture, 385

Narcissus—*continued*
  diseases, 656
  greenhouse culture, 534
  insect pests, 656
  varieties of merit, 386
Nasturtium, 327, 458
  diseases, 657
  insect pests, 657
  Species
    aquaticum, 105
    Dwarf, 327
Naturalizing, defined, 703
Nectarine, 552
Nectria canker, 622
Nematodes, 675
Nemesia strumosa, 326
Nemophila insignis, 326
  maculata, 326
  Spotted, 326
Nepeta mussini, 82, 205, 381
Nephthytis, 460
Nicotiana, **311**, 326
  alata (N. affinis), **311**, 326
  sanderae, **311**, 326
  sylvestris, **311**, 326
Nicotine, 615
Nigella damascena, 326
  sativa, 104
Nitrate of Soda, 162
Nitrification, defined, 704
Nitrogen, 161
  inorganic, sources of, 161
  organic, sources of, 163
  in complete fertilizers, 165
  increase through bacteria, 158
Nitrogen-fixing bacteria, 158
Nitrophoska, 162
Norfolk-Island Pine, 455
Nymphaea alba, 96
  a. candidissima, 96
  marliacea, 96
  m. albida, 96
  m. chromatella, 96
  m. rosea, 96
  odorata, 96
  o. caroliniana, 96
  o. minor, 96
  o. rosea, 96
Nyssa sylvatica, 218, 232

Oak, Basket, 234
  Black, 234
  Burr, 233
  diseases, 627
  English, 234
  Laurel, 233
  Live, **226**, 234

  Pin, 233
  Red, 233
  Scarlet, 233
  Spanish, 233
  Swamp White, 233
  Water, 233
  White, **224**, 233
  Willow, 233
Ocimum basilicum, 105
  minimum, 103
Oenothera americana, 326
  caespitosa, 381
  drummondii, 326
  fruticosa, 381
  insect pests, 657
  missouriensis, 381
Okra, 587
Oleander, 46
Olive, Russian, 231, **254**, 271
Onion, 587
  disease and insect control, 597
Onoclea sensibilis, 94
Orange, Hardy, 269
Orchard, Fruit, 545
Orchid, Purple Fringed, 92
  Showy, 93
  Small Purple Fringed, 92
  Yellow Fringed, 92
Orchis spectabilis, 93
Organic Matter, 181
Organic Nutrition, 163
Oriental Poppy, 382
Origanum, 104
  Majorana, 105
  M. hortensis, 105
  vulgare, 105
Osage Orange, 231
Osmanthus aquifolium, 274
  fragrans, 457
Osmunda cinnamomea, 94
  claytoniana, 94
  regalis, 94, 99
Ostrya virginiana, 232
Outdoor Grill, 143
Oxydendrum arboreum, **224**, 232
Oxyquinoline, 618
Oyster Shell Scale, 622

Pachistima canbyi, 95
Pachysandra terminalis, 205
Paeonia, **367**, 381
Painted Lady, 379
Painted Spurge, 324
Painted Tongue, **312**
Palmetto, Control of, 604
Pandorea jasminoides, 289

Pansy, 327, **332**
  diseases, 658
  insect pests, 658
  Tufted, 82, 383
Papaver alpinum, 382
  nudicaule, **332**, 382
  orientale, **370**, 382
  pilosum, 382
  rhoeas, 326
  somniferum, 326
Paper Mulch, 499
Paradichlorobenzene, 568
Parathion, 615
Parsley, 104, 588
  disease and insect control, 597
Parsnip, 588
Parthenocissus quinquefolia, 289
  tricuspidata, 290
Partridge-berry, 93
Pasqueflower, European, 81
Passiflora, 290, **460**
  alato-caerulea, 290
  incarnata, 290
  manicata, 290
  mollissima, 290
Passion Flower (Passion Vine), 290, **460**
Paths, 121
  brick, 122
  brick and cement, 123
  city garden, 53
  edgings, 129
  flagstone, 124
  gravel, 127
  lines and grades, 111
  stepping stones, 127
  tanbark, 128
  turf, 129
Patience, 324
Patios, 33
  pavements for, 35
  plants for, 37
Paulownia imperialis, 232
  tomentosa, 232
Pavements, for patios and terraces, 35
Paving Stones, Plants between, 32
Pea, 588
  disease and insect control, 597
Pea Tree, Siberian, 269
Peach, 552
  disease and insect control, 564, 568
  spray schedule, 564
  varieties of merit, 553
Pear, 554
  disease and insect control, 564, 568
  spray schedule, 564
  varieties of merit, 555
Pearlbush, 271

Peat, Domestic, 156
  Imported, 156
Peat Moss, 156
Pelargonium, 104, **530**
  greenhouse culture, 530
  for pot culture, 42
  Species
    domesticum, 530
    graveolens, 530
    peltatum, 530
Pennywort, 200
Penstemon alpinus, 82
  barbatus, 382
  Blue, 82
  digitalis, 382
  Foxglove, 382
  glaber, 82
  gloxinioides, 326
  grandiflorus, 382
  laevigatus, 382
  Pink Beauty, 382
  Shell-leaf, 382
  Smooth, 382
  torreyi, 382
Penthouse Gardens, 61
  maintenance of, 68
  plant materials for, 64
  practical considerations, 57
Peony, **367**, 381
  diseases, 658
  insect pests, 659
  Tree, **369**
  Varieties, 369
Peperomia, 457
  obtusifolia, 457
  o. variegated, 457
  sandersi argyreia, 457
Pepper, 589
  disease and insect control, 597
Peppermint, 104
Perennials (see Herbaceous Perennials), 334
Perennial Garden, 334
  feeding, 343
  general maintenance, 341
  planning, 335
  renewal of plants, 344
  soil preparation, 340
  staking, 342
  summer mulching, 344, 500
  watering, 342
  winter protection, 344, 501
Periwinkle, 205
  Madagascar, 327
Persimmon, 231
Pests of
  flowering plants, 630
  fruit, 568

Pests of—*continued*
  house plants, 448
  lawn, 194
  shrubs, 619
  trees, 619
  vegetable, 595
Petroselinum hortensis, 104
Petunia, **312**, 326
  disease and insect pest control, 660
pH, 168, 704
Phacelia, 326
  campanularia, 326
  ciliata, 326
  Harebell, 326
  tanacetifolia, 326
  viscida, 326
Phaseolus coccineus, **290**, 326
Phellodendron amurense, 232
Phenyl mercuric acetate, 199
Philadelphus coronarius, 274
  grandiflorus, **258**, 274
  lemoinei, 274
  virginalis, **258**, 274
Philodendron, 457, 460
  bipinnatifidum, 457
  selloum, 457
  undulatum, 457
  wendlandi, 457
Philodendron (Climbing Types), 460
  erubescens, 461
  hastatum, 461
  imbe, 461
  oxycardium (cordatum), 461
  panduriforme, 461
  sodiroi, 461
Phlox, **371**
  diseases, 660
  insect pests, 660
  Species
    amoena, 82
    Annual, **313**
    arendsii, 382
    Arends, 382
    Blue, 82, **90**, 205, 382
    creeping, 82
    decussata, **371**, 382
    divaricata, 82, **90**, 93, 205, 382
    drummondii, **313**, 326
    Downy, 82
    Dwarf Magenta, 82
    Garden, **371**, 382
    Mauve, 82
    Moss, 82
    paniculata, **371**, 382
    pilosa, 82
    Smooth, **371**, 382
    stellaria, 82

    stolonifera, 82
    subulata, 82, 205
    s. alba, 82 ·
    suffruticosa (P. glaberima), 382
Phosphorus, 163
  in complete fertilizers, 165
  sources of, 163
Photinia serrulata, 274
  villosa, **258**, 274
Physalis alkekengi, 603
  francheti, insect pest, 661
Physostegia virginiana, 382
Picea alba (p. glauca), 235
  engelmanni, 235
  excelsa (p. abies), 235
  glauca, 235
  mariana (P. nigra), 235
  orientalis, 235
  pungens, 235
  rubra, 235
Pickerel Weed, 99
Pieris floribunda, 95, 274
  japonica, **258**, 274
Pignut, 230
Pilea cadieri, 458
Pimpinella anisum, 103
Pinching Back, 704
Pincushion flower, **313**
Pine
  disease, 627
  insect pests, 628
  Species
    Austrian, **226**, 235
    Cluster, 236
    Dwarf Mountain, 235
    Himalayan, 235
    Japanese Black, 226, 236
    Japanese Red, 235
    Japanese Table, 235
    Japanese White, 235
    Korean, 235
    Lace-bark, 235
    Limber, 235
    Mountain, 235
    Mugho, 235
    Pitch, 236
    Red, 236
    Scots, 226, 236
    Stone, 235
    Western Yellow, 236
    White, **225**, 236
Pine Needles (Path), 84
Pink, Allwoods, 379
  Annual, 313
  Blood, 379
  Cheddar, 379
  Double Cluster, 379

Grass, 82, 379
  Maiden, 82, 379
Pinus Bungeana, 235
  Cembra, 235
  densiflora, 235
  d. umbraculifera, 235
  excelsa, 235
  flexilis, 235
  koraiensis, 235
  montana, 235
  m. mugo, 235
  nigra, **226**, 235
  parviflora, 235
  Pinaster, 236
  ponderosa, 236
  resinosa, 236
  rigida, 236
  Strobus, **226**, 236
  sylvestris, 226, 236
  Thunbergii, 226, 236
Pinxter Azalea, 268
  Downy, 268
Pistil, defined, 704
Pistillate, defined, 704
Pitcher plant, 99
Pittosporum, Japanese, 274, **298**, 458
  phillyraeoides, **259**, 274
  tobira, **259**, 274, 298, 458
  t. variegata, 458
  Willow, 274
Plane, London, **224**, 233
Plant Diseases, 610
Plantain, 200
Plantainlily, 381
Plants, between paving stones, 32
  for Pots, 37
  for tub culture, 44
  seldom attacked by pests and diseases, 619
Planting Design, 19
Plastic Mulches, 499
Plastic Spray, 210
  for transplanting, 210, 682
  for winter protection, 243
Platanus acerifolia, **224**, 233
  occidentalis, 233
Platycodon grandiflorum, 382
  g. mariesii, 382
Plum, 554
  diseases and pest control, 566
  Beach, 233, 274
  spray schedule, 566
Plumbago capensis, 290
  larpentae, 82, 203
Plume poppy, **350**, 378
Poa trivialis, 177
Podophyllum peltatum, 93
Poinsettia, 534

Poison Bait of Mice, 673
Poison Ivy, Control of, 601
Polemonium caeruleum, 382
  reptans, 93, 382
Pollen, defined, 704
Pollination, defined, 704
  of Fruit, 546
Polyethylene, 482
Polygonatum biflorum, 93
  commutatum, 93
Polygonum auberti, 290
  Sieboldi, Control of, 602
Polypodium vulgare, 94
Polypody, Common, 94
Polystichum acrostichoides, 94
Pontederia cordata, 99
Pools (Garden), 130
  clay-lined, 133
  concrete, 131
  copper, 135
  fiberglass, 134
  lead, 132
  maintenance, 135
  reducing cost of, 135
  stone, 133
Pools (Swimming), 138
  accessories, 141
  concrete, 139
  construction, 139
  enclosure, 142
  fiberglass, 140
  filters, 138
  materials for, 140
  obligations, 143
  plastic, 141
  size and location, 139
  steel, 141
Poplar, 233
  Balsam, 233
  Lombardy, 233
  Tulip, 231
  White, 233
Poppy, Alpine, 382
  Annual, 313
  California, 309
  California, in greenhouse, 527
  Canyon, 582
  Iceland, **332**, 382
  Olympic, 382
  Opium, 326
  Oriental, **370**, 382
  Shirley, 326
Populus alba, 233
  a. pyramidalis, 233
  balsamifera (P. deltoides), 233
  candicans, 233
  grandidentata, 233

Populus—*continued*
  nigra italica, 233
  tremuloides, 233
Portable Planting Boxes, 49
  Bulbs for, 50
  Maintenance of, 50
  Plants for, 50
  Types of, 50
Portulaca grandiflora, 326
Potash, in complete fertilizers, 165
Potassium, 163
  in complete fertilizers, 165
  sources of, 164
Potassium chloride, 164
Potassium cyanate, 199
Potassium sulphate, 164
Potato, 590
  disease and insect control, 597
Pot-bound, defined, 704
Potentilla alba, 82
  fruticosa, 274
  nepalensis, 382
  nitida, 82
  pyrenaica, 82
  warrensii, 382
Pothos aureus, 461
Pot-marigold, 105, **309**, 322
Pot Marjoram, 105
Potted Plants, **37**
  Annuals for, 39
  Biennals for, 41
  Cultural Requirements of, 38
  for city gardens, 60
  Perennials for, 41
  Plant material for, 37
  Selection of pots for, 38
  Watering, 39
Potting, 39
Potting Mixtures, 38
Potting-on, defined, 704
Potting-up, defined, 704
Powdery Mildew, 626
Prairie Mallow, 383
Pre-emergence Weed-killers, 608
Pricking-out, defined, 704
Prickly pear cactus, Control of, 604
Pricklepoppy, 322
Primrose, 90
  diseases, 662
  insect pests, 662
  in the greenhouse, 535
  Species
    Cowslip, 382
    English, 382
    Himalayan, 382
    Japanese, 382
    Polyanthas, 382
    Silverdust, 382

Primula, **90**
  diseases, 662
  insect pests, 662
  Species
    acaulis, 382
    auricula, 382
    bulleyana, 99
    cockburniana, 99
    denticulata, 382
    helodoxa, 99
    japonica, 99, 382
    kewensis, 535
    malacoides, 535
    obconica, 535
    polyantha, 382
    pulverulenta, 382
    sieboldii, 382
    sinensis, 535
    veris, 382
    vulgaris, 382
Primulas in the greenhouse, 535
Privet, Amur, 273
  California, 273
  glossy, **257**, 273
  ibolium, 273
  ibota, 273
  Japanese, 273
  Regel, 273
Propagating Cases, 482
Propagation, 471
  Bulbs and Bulbils, 490
  Corms, 491
  Cuttings, 481
  Division, 489
  Grafting, 493
  Layering, 491
  Rhizomes, 490
  Runners, 493
  Seeds, 471
  Stolons, 493
  Suckers, 493
  Tubers, 490
  Vegetative, 481
Protecting Plants from Frost, 682
Pruning, 679
  hedges, 295
  practices, 679
  roses, 430
  shrubs, 241
  trees, 220
Prunus laurocerasus, 274
  maritima, 233, 274
  serotina, 233
  serrulata, 233
  sieboldii, 233
  subhirtella, **224**, 233
  tomentosa, 233, 274
  yedonensis, 233

Pseudotsuga taxifolia (P. douglasii), **226**, 236
Pteretis nodulosa, 94
Pterostyrax hispida, 233
Pulmonaria officinalis, 382
    saccharata, 382
Pumpkin, 590
    disease and insect control, 597
Pussy Willow, 276
Pyracantha coccinea, 298
    c. Lalandi, **259**, 274
    disease, 269
    insect pests, 629
Pyrethrum, 616
Pyrethrum roseum, 382
    diseases, 662

Quackgrass, Control of, 604
Quaker Ladies, 92
Quamoclit pennata, 290
Queen's Wreath, **283**
Quercus, disease, 627
    Species
        alba, **224**, 233
        bicolor, 233
        borealis, 233
        coccinea, 233
        falcata, 233
        laurifolia, 233
        macrocarpa, 233
        nigra, 233
        palustris, 233
        Phellos, 233
        Prinus, 234
        robur, 234
        rubra, 233
        velutina, 234
        virginiana, **226**, 234
Quince, 555
    diseases and insect pests, 566
    spray schedule, 566
    Species
        Japanese Flowering, **253**, 269
        Lesser Japanese Flowering, **253**, 269

Rabbits, 674
Radish, 591
Raisin Tree, 231
Raspberry, Black, 558
    disease and pest control, 568
    Purple, 558
    Red, 558
Red Baneberry, 92
Redbud, **221**, 230
Red Cedar, 235
    diseases, 629
Red Clover (Mammoth), 159
Red copper-oxide, 597

Red-headed Pine Sawfly, 628
Red-hot Poker Plant, 407
Redtop, 178
Redwood Bark, 499
Regal Lily, 419
Rehmannia angulata, 326
Repellents, defined, 704
Repotting
    house plants, 447
    soil mixtures for, 447
Reseda odorata, 326
Respiration, defined, 704
Retaining Walls, 111
Rhamnus cathartica, 95
Rhizomes, Propagation by, 490
Rhododendron, **244**, 259
    diseases and insect pests, 629
    winter protection, 243
    Species
        carolinianum (Carolina), 95, **260**, 275
        catawbiense (Catawba), 95, **260**, 275
        maximum, 95, **260**, 275
        minus, 95, 275
        mucronulatum (Korean), 260
        obtusum kaempferi, 246
        Rosebay, 95, **260**, 275
Rhodotypos kerrioides, 275
Rhubarb, 591
Rhus cotinus, **270**, 275
    glabra, 275
    typhina, 275
Ribes odoratum, 275
Robinia hispida, 275
    pseudoacacia, 234
    viscosa, 275
Rockcress, Alpine, 377
    Wall, 377
Rock Gardens, 69
    construction of, 72
    design of, 70
    dwarf evergreen for, 81
    grading for, 72
    maintenance, 74
    planting of, 73
    shrubs for, 78
    soil for, 73
    winter mulches, 74
Rock Phosphate, 163
Rock Plants, Dwarf Evergreens, 81
    easy to grow, 81
    for acid soil, 79
    for lime soil, 79
    hardy, 80
    tender, 80
Rock Spray, 204
Rocket, 380
Romneya coulteri, 382

Roof Gardens, 61
  maintenance, 68
  plant material for, 64
Root-forming substances, 483
Rooting Medium, 482
Rosebay, 275
Rose Mallow, 381
Rosemary, 105
Rose-of-Heaven, 325
Rose-of-Sharon, 272
Roses, 423
  acidity of soil for, 426
  Climbing, 436
  cultural requirements, 426
  cutting of, 431
  diseases, 662
  drainage for, 426
  insect pests, 664
  in the greenhouse, 535
  maintenance of soil fertility, 427
  method of planting, 428
  Old-fashioned, 440
  preparation of soil for, 426
  pruning, 430
  soil requirements, 426
  selection of stock, 428
  Shrub, 439
  summer mulches, 431
  time of planting, 428
  Trailing, 440
  watering, 431
  winter protection, 431
  varieties of merit, 433
  Species and Hybrids
    alba, 275
    Bengal, 441
    blanda, 275
    Bourbon, 441
    Brier, 439
    Bristly, 275
    Cabbage, 275
    carolina, 275
    centifolia, 275
    China, 441
    cinnamomea, 275
    damascena (Damask), 275, **441**
    Eglanteria (rubiginosa), 275, **439**
    Eglantine, 275, **439**
    Father Hugo's Rose, 275, **439**
    Floribunda, 433
    French, 275
    gallica, 275·
    Grandiflora, 434
    Harisonii, 275
    Harison's Yellow, 275, **439**
    Hugonis, 275
    Hybrid Perpetual, 434

    Hybrid Tea, 435
    Japanese, 275
    Max Graf, 205
    Memorial, 276
    micrantha, 275
    moschata, 275
    Moss, 441
    multiflora, 275
    Musk, 275
    nitida, 275
    Noisette, 441
    palustris, 275
    Pasture, 275
    persica, 275
    Persian, 275
    Prairie, 276
    Polyantha, 436
    Provence, 440
    Rambler, 439
    Rugosa, 276, **440**
    Scotch, 276
    setigera, 276
    spinosissima, 276
    Swamp, 275
    Sweetbrier, 439
    Tea, 434
    virginiana (Virginia), 276
    Wichuraiana, **205**, 276
Rosmarinus officinalis, 105
Rotenone, 616
Rowan Tree, 234
Rudbeckia bicolor, 326
  laciniata, 382
  maxima, 382
  nitida, 382
  purpurea, 382
  speciosa, 382
  subtomentosa, 382
Rue, 105
Rue Anemone, 92
Rumex acetosa, 105
Russian Olive, 231
Rust, Blister, of pines, 627
  Cedar-Apple, 629
  of bramble fruits, 568
  of hollyhock, 650
  of lilies, 655
Ruta graveolens, 105
Rutabaga, 591
Rye, 159

Saffron, 105
Sage, 105
  Azure, **372**, 383
  Bog, 383
  Gentian, 326

Meadow, 383
Mealycup, 326, **373**, 383
Pitcher, 383
Scarlet, 326
Silver, 383
Welwyn, 326
St. Augustine grass, 179
St. Johnswort, 82, 204
Control of, 602
Saintpaulia ionantha, **448**
Salix alba, 234
babylonica, **224**, 234
caprea, 276
discolor, 276
fragilis, 234
nigra, 234
pentandra, 234
vitellina, 234
Salpiglossis sinuata, **312**, 326
Salsify, 591
Salt Hay, 499
Salvia
insect pests, 668
Species
argentea, 383
azurea grandiflora, **372**, 383
farinacea, 326, **373**, 383
officinalis, 105
patens, 326, 383
pitcheri, 383
pratensis, 383
sclarea, 104
splendens, 326
s. var. Welwyn, 326
uliginosa, 383
Sambucus canadensis, 276
pubens, 95
racemosa, 276
Sand-verbena, 322
Sandy Soil, 155
Sandwort, Showy, 81
Sanguinaria canadensis, **90**, 93
Sanguisorba minor, 103
officinalis, 103
Sansevieria hahni, 458
h. variegata, 458
trifaseiata, 458
t. Craigi, 458
Santolina chamaecyparissus, 104
Sanvitalia procumbens, 326
p. flore pleno, 326
Saponaria calabrica, 327
ocymoides, 82
vaccaria, 327
Sarcococca hookeriana humilis, **261**, 276, 298
Sarracenia flava, 99
purpurea, 99

Sassafras, 234
variifolium, 234
Satureia hortensis, 105
montana, 105
Saucer Magnolia, **223**, 232
Savory, 105
Summer, 105
Winter, 105
Sawdust, 499, 500
Sawfly, 628
Saxifraga caespitosa, 82
cordifolia, 82
Scabiosa atropurpurea, **313**, 327
caucasica 383
graminifolia, 383
japonica (Japanese), 383
Sweet, 327
Scabrous, defined, 704
Scale, Apple, 564
Euonymus, 626
Oyster Shell, 660
Rose, 666
Tulip Tree, 630
Scarification, defined, 704
Scarlet Runner Bean, **290**, 326
Schefflera actinophylla, 458
Schizanthus pinnatus, 327
in the greenhouse, 536
Scholar Tree, **224**, 234
Chinese, **224**, 234
Schradan, 616
Sciadopitys verticillata, 236
Scilla hispanica (S. campanulata), 393
nonscripta (nutans), 393
sibirica, 394
Scindapsus aureus, 461
Scion, 704
Scots Pine, **226**, 236
Scutellaria alpina lupulina, 383
baicalensis, 383
Seaholly, 379
Sea-lavender, 325
Notchleaf, 325
Suworow, 325
Sedum acre, 33, 82, 205
album, 82
altissimum, 82
reflexum, 82
rupestris, 82
sarmentosum, 82
Seed sowing, 472
Seedlings, 704
Damping-off of, 475
Transplanting, 480
Seeds, 472
annuals from, 471
biennials from, 471

Seeds—*continued*
  hastening germination of, 480
  longevity of, 474
  meeting special requirements of, 472
  perennials from, 471
  pre-treatment of, 472
  sowing indoors, 477
    in sphagnum moss, 478
    in sand, 480
    in vermiculite, 479
  sowing in the open, 476
  treatment of, 475
Sempervivum, 82
  arachnoideum, 33
  atlanticum, 33
Senecio elegans, 327
Senna, Wild, 378
Serviceberry, 229
Sesame, 105
Sesamum officinalis, 105
Shadbush, 229, 267
Shooting Star, **89**, 92
Showy Orchis, 93
Shrubs, 237
  as part of landscape, 15
  attractive to birds, 304
  diseases, 619
  evergreen, for shade, 267
  evergreen for the rock garden, 81
  Lists for
    autumn foliage, 264
    covering banks, 267
    cut flowers, 266
    dry places, 265
    fruit effects, 265
    Penthouse Gardens, 66
    rapid growth, 266
    shady places, 267
    the city garden, 60
    the rock garden, 81
    the woodland garden, 94
    wet places, 266
    windbreaks, 266
  heeling-in, 241
  insect pests, 619
  low, of neat habit, 266
  old-fashioned, 264
  planting, 238
  preparation of soil for, 241
  propagation from cuttings, 486
  pruning, 241
  reliable, 265
  selected list of, 245
  selection of, 238
  tabular list of, 267
  transplanting, 238
  winter protection, 243
Siberian Wallflower, 333

Sidalcea candida, 383
  malvaeflora, 383
  m. listeri, 383
Silene acaulis, 33
  Armeria, 327
  maritima, 82
Silverbell Tree, **221**, 231
Silverberry, 271
Silver Lace Vine, 290
Silver Vine, 282
Skullcap, 383
  baikal, 383
Sky Flower, 291
Slime Molds, 197
Slugs, 671
Smoke Tree, Smoke Bush, 270, 275
Snake Plant, 458
Snakeroot, Black, **88**, 92
Snapdragon, **314**, 322
  diseases, 630
  Dwarf, 322
  in the greenhouse, 524
Sneezeweed, 380
Sneezewort, 377
Snowball, Japanese, 278
Snowbell, Fragrant, **224**, 234
  Japanese, **224**, 234
Snowberry, 277
Snowdrop, 392
Snowflakes, 392
Snow Mold, 197
Snow-in-Summer, 82, 203, 378
Snow-on-the-Mountain, 324
Soapwort, Calabrian, 327
  Rock, 82
Sod Webworms, 196
Sodding New Lawns, 186
Sodium Chlorate, 606
Sodium Selenate, 616
Soil, acidity, 168
  conditioners, 170
  formation of, 154
  fumigants, 618
  obtaining samples of, 168
  sterilization of, 476
  tests, 168
  types of, 154
Solanum integrifolium, 327
Solidago alpestris, 383
  altissima, 383
  caesia, 383
  canadensis, 383
  rigida, 383
  virgaurea, 383
Solomon's-Seal, 93
Soluble Fertilizers, 165
Sophora japonica, **224**, 234

Sorbaria aitchisonii, 276
Sorbus americana, 224
  aucuparia, **224**, 234
Sorrel, 105, 232
Sorrel Tree, 232
Sourgum, 232
Sourwood, **224**, 232
Southernwood, 105
Soybeans, 159
Spanish Iris, 408
Spearmint, 105
Species, defined, 704
Speedwell, Bastard, 383
  Cliff, 82
  Clump, 383
  Spike, 383
  Woolly, 383
Sphagnum moss, 478
Sphenogyne speciosa, 327
Spicebush, 268
Spiderflower, 323
Spinach, 591
  disease and insect control, 598
Spindletree, European, 231
Spiraea arguta, 276
  billiardii, 276
  bumalda, 276
  b. var. Froebeli, 276
  Garland, 276
  prunifolia, **261**, 276
  Thunbergii, 276
  Vanhouttei, **261**, 276, 298
Spittlebug, 628
Spleenwort, Ebony, 94
  Maidenhair, 94
  Narrowleaf, 94
Spray formulas, all-purpose, 618
Spring Beauty, **88**, 92
Spruce, insect pest, 620
  Species
    Colorado, 235
    Engelmann's, 235
    Norway, 235
    Oriental, 235
    Red, 235
    White, 235
Spur-valerian, 323
Spurge, Cushion, 380
  Cypress, 380
  Flowering, 380
  Japanese, 205
Squash, 592
  disease and insect control, 598
Squills, 394
Squirrel Corn, 92
Stachys Betonica, 383
  grandiflora, 383
  lanata, 383

Staking, 342
Stamen, defined, 704
Staminate, defined, 704
Staphylea colchica, 276
Star Jasmine, 291
Star Magnolia, 223
State Colleges and Universities, 695
Statice, 325, 381, 383
  armeria, 33, 383
  Bigleaf, 381
  Laucheana, 383
  montana (S. alpina), 383
  perezii, 42
  plantaginea (S. dianthoides), 383
  Tatarian, 381
Stephanandra incisa, 276
  flexuosa, 276
Stephanotis floribunda, 291
Stepping stones, 127
Steps, 118
  arrangements, 120
  foundations, 120
  ramped, 120
Sterilization, defined, 704
Sterilization of soil, 476
Sternbergia lutea, 411
Stevia, 535
Stewartia, Japanese, 234
  pentagyna, 276
  pseudo-camellia, 234
Stigma, defined, 704
Stock, defined, 704
Stock, 314, 325
  in the greenhouse, 536
Stokes-aster, 383
Stokesia laevis, 383
Stolons, 180, 493
Stomata, defined, 704
Stonecress, Lebanon, 377
  Persian, 377
Stonecrop, 82, 205
Storage Pit, 573
Stranvaesia davidiana, 276
Stratification, defined, 704
Straw, 500
Strawberries, 559
  disease and pest control, 569
Strawberry Shrub, 249
Strawberry Tree, **244**, 267
Strawflower, 324
Strelitzia reginae, 46
Streptosolen jamesonii, 46
Styrax japonica, **224**, 234
  obassia, 234
Sub-soil, defined, 704
Suckers, 704
Sulphate of Ammonia, 162

Sulphur, 617
Sumac, Control of, 600
  Smooth, 275
  Staghorn, 275
Summer Adonis, 322
Summer Cypress, 325
Summer Hyacinth, 405
Summer Savory, 105
Sundrops, 381
  Ozark, 381
  Tufted, 381
Sunflower, **314**, 324, 380
  Cucumber, 324
  Maximilian, 380
  Mexican, 327
  Prairie, 380
  Swamp, 380
  Thinleaf, 380
Superphosphate, 163
Supports for vines, 279
Swan River Daisy, **314**, 322
Sweet Alyssum, **308**, 322
  insect pests, 670
Sweet Basil, 105
Sweet Bay, **225**, 232
Sweet Cicely, 105
Sweet Corn, 582
Sweet Clover, 159
Sweet Fennel, 105
Sweetfern, 269
Sweet Flag, 105
Sweetgum, **222**, 231
Sweetleaf, Asiatic, 277
Sweet Marjoram, 105
Sweet Olive, 457
Sweet Pea, **314**
  diseases, 668
  insect pests, 669
  in the greenhouse, 536
Sweet Pepperbush, **253**, 269
Sweet Rocket, 380
Sweet Shrub, **249**, 269
Sweet-sultan, 323
  Royal, 323
Sweet William, **333**, 379
Sweet Woodruff, 105
Swiss Chard, 581
Swiss Cheese Plant, 460
Sycamore, 233
  disease, 630
Symbiosis, 158
Symphoricarpos albus (S. racemosus), 277
  vulgaris, 277
Symplocos paniculata, **261**, 277
Syngonium auritum, 461
  erithrophyllum, 461
  hoffmani, 461

  podophyllum, 461
  p. albolineatum, 461
  xanthophilum, 461
Syringa, culture, 262
  diseases, 626
  insect pests, 626
  Species and hybrids
    chinensis, **262**, 277
    japonica, **224**, 234, 262, 277
    microphylla superba, 261
    pekinensis, 263
    persica, **262**, 277
    villosa, **262**, 277
    vulgaris, **262**, 277
Systemic Fungicides, 617
Systemic Insecticides, 616

Tagetes (Marigold), 327
  erecta, 327
  patula, 327
  signata pumila, 327
Tamarisk, 277
  Five stamen, 277
Tamarix africana, 263
  parviflora, 277
  pentandra, 277
Tamping, defined, 704
Tanacetum vulgare, 105
Tanbark, 128
Tansy, 105
Tarragon, 105
Tasselflower, 324
Taxodium distichum, 218, **224**, 234
Taxus, insect pests, 630
  Species
    baccata, 236
    b. adpressa, 236
    b. fastigiata, 236
    b. repandens, 236, 277
    canadensis, 236, 277
    canadensis stricta, 298
    cuspidata, 236
    c. capitata, 236
    c. fastigiata, 299
    c. hicksii, 236
    c. media, 236
    c. nana (brevifolia), 236
    media Hatfieldi, 298
TCA, 606
Tea Scale, 623
Tecoma radicans, 283
Tecomaria capensis, 291
Tent caterpillars, 621
Terraces, 31
  Architectural Functions of, 31
  drainage, 32
  pavements for, 35

plants for, 37
raised, 31
scale and proportion, 31
sunken, 31
Teucrium chamaedrys, 383
Texasplume, 324
Thalictrum, **373**, 383
    adiantifolium, **373**
    aquilegifolium, **373**, 383
    dioicum, 82
    dipterocarpum, **373**, 383
    glaucum, **373**, 383
    polygamum, 383
Thorn, Cockspur, 230
    Dotted, 230
    Washington, **221**, 230
Thoroughwort, 380
Thrift, 383
    Rosalie, 383
Thrips, Digitalis, 646
    Gladiolus, 649
    Roses, 668
Thunbergia alata, 327
    grandiflora, 291
Thuya occidentalis, **226**, 236, 298
    o. compacta, 236
    o. douglasii pyramidalis, 236
    o. globosa, 236
    o. Hoveyi, 236
    o. pyramidalis, 236, 298
    o. vervaeneana, 236
    o. Wareana, 236
    orientalis, 236
    o. compacta (sieboldii), 236
    o. elegantissima, 236
    plicata, 236
Thyme, 105
    Lemon, 205
Thymus, 105
    citriodorus, 33, **205**
    serpyllum, 33, **205**
    s. lanuginosus, 33
    s. vulgaris, 33
Tiarella cordifolia, 93
Tidytips, 325
Tiger Flower, 407
Tigridia, 407
Tile drains, 110
    table to determine size, 110
Tilia americana, 234
    cordata, **225**, 234
    glabra, 234
    vulgaris, 234
Tithonia rotundifolia (T. speciosa), 327
Toadflax, 325
Tobacco, Flowering, **311**, 326
Tobacco Stems, 500

Tomato, 593
    disease and insect control, 598
Tool Houses, 504
Tools, 502
    care of, 503
    essential, 502
    recommended, 505
    storage facilities, 507
    supplementary, 507
Top-dressing, defined, 704
Torchlily, 381
    Bonfire, 381
    Early, 381
Torenia fournieri, **315**, 327
Toxylon pomifera, 231
Trace Elements, 164
    in complete fertilizers, 165
Trachelospermum jasminoides, 291
Trachymene caerulea, 327
Trailing Arbutus, **89**, 92
Trailing Lantana, 48
Transpiration, defined, 704
Transplanting, defined, 704
    preventing losses, 682
    seedlings, 480
    shrubs, 238
    trees, 210
Tree Ivy, 457
Tree-of-Heaven, 229
Trees, 206
    as part of landscape composition, 15, 207
    attractive to birds, 303
    care after transplanting, 218
    defoliation, 210
    diseases, 619
    distance apart, 207
    espaliered, 543
    feeding, 219
    Lists for
        dry, sandy soil, 226
        city gardens, 59
        hedges, 298
        penthouse gardens, 65
        rapid growth, 227
        the seashore, 227
        the small place, 208, 209
        the street, 227
        wet soil, 228
        windbreaks, 228
    foreign, 207
    free from pests and diseases, 227
    grading around, 218
    insect pests, 619
    malnutrition of, 219
    native, 207
    of merit, 220
    planting of, 208

Trees—*continued*
  preparation of soil for, 209
  protection from mice, 673
  pruning, 679
  selection, 208
  tabular list of, 229
  transplanting, 210
  watering, 219
  weed, 600
Treemallow, 325
Trenching, 677
Trillium erectum, 93, 99
  grandiflorum, **91**, 93, 99
  Large flowering, **91**, 93
  Southern Pink, 93
  stylosum, 93
  White, **91**, 93
Tritoma, 407
Tritonia, 408
Trollius asiaticus, 383
  europaeus, 383
  ledebouri, 383
  sinensis, 383
Tropaeolum majus, 327
  minor, 327
Trout Lily, **89**, 92, 99
Trumpet Creeper, 283
Trumpet Vine, Royal, 286
  Vanilla-scented, 286
Tsuga canadensis, **226**, 236, 298
  c. microphylla, 236
  c. pendula, 236
  carolineana, 236
  diversifolia, 236
Tuberous-rooted Begonia, **396**
  diseases, 671
  insect pests, 671
Tubers, 384
  propagation by, 490
Tubs, 44
Tulip, 387
  care after blooming, 390
  culture, 387
  diseases, 670
  for Southern gardens, 390
  greenhouse culture, 537
  insect pests, 670
  Planting, 388
  Soil, 388
  Species, 390
  Varieties of Merit, 390
Tulip Poplar, **222**, 231
Tulip poppy, 324
Tulip Tree, **222**, 231
  insect pests, 630
Tunica saxifraga, 82, 383
Tunicflower, 82, 383

Tupelo, 232
Turnip, 594
Twelve Apostles, 455
Twinspur, 323
2, 4-D, 607
2, 4, 5-T, 608
2, 4, 5-T plus 2, 4-D, 608

Ulmus
  diseases, 624
  insect pests, 624
  Species
    americana, **225**, 234
    americana ascendens, 225
    glabra, 234
    pumila, 234
Umbrella Tree, 232
Undesirable Plants, Control of, 599
Urea, 162
Urea-form fertilizers, 162
Ursinia anethoides, 327
  hybrids, 327

Vaccinium canadense, 277
  corymbosum, 95, 277
  pennsylvanicum, 95, 277
  vacillans, 95
Valerian, 383
  Greek, 93
Valeriana officinalis, 383
Variety, defined, 704
Vanhoutte's Spiraea, **261**, 276
Vegetable Garden, 570
  cultural directions, 574
  disease control, 522
  equipment, 571
  fertilizers, 571
  insect pest control, 595
  seed quantities, 573
  storage pit, 573
  storing, 573
Venidium fastuosum, 327
Verbascum phoeniceum, **333**
Verbena, **315**, 327
  canadensis, 383
  erinoides, 327
  hybrida, **315**, 327
  insect pests, 671
Veronica incana, 383
  maritima, 383
  repens, 33
  rupestris, 33, 82
  serpyllifolia, 33
  spicata, 383
  spuria, 383
  virginica, 383
Vermiculite, 479

Viburnum acerifolium, 277
  americanum (V. trilobum), 277
  Burkwoodii, 277
  carlcephalum, **263**, 277
  Carlesii, **263**, 277
  cassinoides, 277
  dentatum, 277
  dilatatum, **263**, 277
  Doublefile, **263**, 278
  Fragrant, 277
  Kentucky, 277
  Lantana, 277
  Leatherleaf, **263**, 278
  Lentago, 95
  Linden, 277
  molle, 277
  opulus, 278
  o. nanum, 278
  Oriental, 278
  prunifolium, 278
  rhytidophyllum, **263**, 278
  setigerum, **263**, 278
  sieboldii, 278
  theriferum, **263**, 278
  tomentosum, **263**, 278
  t. plicatum, 268
  trilobum, 278
  wrightii, 278
Vinca major, 470
  minor, 205, 470
  rosea, 327
Vines, 279
  Lists for
    flower boxes, 470
    the city garden, 60, 292
    the house, 458, 460
    the penthouse garden, 66
    the rock garden, 81
    window boxes, 470
  maintenance, 281
  recommended, 282
  Southern, 292
  supports for, 279
Viola blanda, 93
  canadensis, 93
  conspersa, 93
  cornuta, 83, **373**, 383
  palmata, 93
  pedata, 93
  tricolor, 327
Violet
  in the greenhouse, 537
  Species, 93
    Bird's-foot, 93
    Canada, 93
    Common Blue, 93

Dog, 93
    Sweet White, 93
Violet Trumpet Vine, 286
Viper's Bugloss, 324
Virginia Bluebell, **90**, 93, 381
Virginia Cowslip, **90**, 93
Virginia Creeper, 289
Virginian-stock, 325
Viruses, 610
Viscaria, 325
Vitex agnus-castus, 278
Vitis rhombifolia (see Cissus), 468
Volutella blight, 622

Wake-robin, 99
Walks (see Paths), 121
Wallcress, 81
Wallflower
  insect pests, 672
  greenhouse culture, 538
  Species
      English, **333**
      Siberian, **333**
Wall Gardens, 76
  plants for, 80
Wall Plants, Easy to grow, 81
Walls, 111
  dry retaining, 113
  free-standing, 111
  mixture for masonry, 113
  retaining, 111
  reinforced concrete, 116
Walnut, Black, 231
    English, 231
    Japanese, 231
Walnut Shells, 500
Washington Thorn, 230
Watercress, 105
Water Gardens, 96
  control of algae, 99
  insect pests, 97
  plants for, 96
  winter care, 97
Water-hyacinth, 97
Watering, 678
Water Lilies, 96
Water-lily
    Cape Cod, 96
    Carolina, 96
    cultural requirements, 97
    propagation, 96
    species and varieties, 96
    winter care, 97
Watermelon, 594
Watermelon Pilea, 458

Water plants, 97
  pests on, 97
  oxygenating, 97
  shore, 97
Water Sprout, 704
Weed, Perennials, 603
  Shrubs, 602
  Trees, 600
  Vines, 600
Weeds, 603
  Control of, 599, 605
  Control of, in the Lawn, 197
Weeping willow, 234
Weevil, 628
Weigela amabilis, 264
  florida, 271
Welsh-poppy, 381
White Fly, 632
White Kerria, 275
White-Pine Sawfly, 628
White-Pine Weevil, 628
Wild Cherry, Control of, 600
Wild-indigo, 378
  Yellow, 378
Willow, Bay (Shiny), 234
  Black, 234
  Brittle, 234
  Goat, 276
  Pussy, 276
  Weeping, **224**, 234
  White, 234
  Yellow, 234
Windbreaks, 228
Windflower, 86
  Japanese, **345**, 377
Window Boxes, 466
Winter Aconite, 392
Winterberry, 272
Wintercreeper, 271
Wintergreen, 92
Winter Jasmine, 272
Winter Mulches, lilies, 413
  perennials, 344
  rock garden, 74
Winter Protection, 681
  roses, 431
  shrubs, 243
Wisteria, 291
  Control of, 602
  Species
    Chinese, 291
    floribunda, 291
    f. multijuga, 291
    Japanese, 291
    sinensis, 291

Witchhazel, 272
  Chinese, 272
  Common, 272
  Japanese, 272
  Spring, 272
Wolfbane, 377
Wood Ashes, 164
Woodbine (see Virginia Creeper), 289
Wood Chips, 500
Woodchucks, 676
Woodland Flowers, 86
Woodland Garden, 83
  design of, 83
  ferns for, 94
  flowers, 86, 92
  paths, 84
  shrubs for, 85, 94
  site, 83
  soil, 85, 91
Woodland Plants, 92
  soil requirements, 91
  tabular list of, 92
Woodruff, 378
Wormwood, 105, 377
  Beech, 105, 377
  Common, 377
  Cudweed, 377
  Piedmont, 377
  Roman, 105

Xeranthemum annuum, 327

Yarrow, 377
  Fernleaf, 377
  Silver Alpine, 81
  Woolly, 81
Yellow root, 205, 278
Yellow-wood, **221**, 230
Yew, Canadian, 236
  Dwarf Japanese, 236
  English, 236, 277
  Irish, 236
  Japanese, 236
Yucca filamentosa, 383

Zanthorhiza apiifolia, 205, 278
Zinc, 161, 164
Zinnia, **315**, 327
  diseases, 672
  insect pests, 672
  Species and types
    Dwarf, 327
    elegans, 327
    Giant, 327
    Haageana, 327
Zoysia, 178, 179

SUPPLEMENTARY INDEX 1965

DELETIONS

Crataegus oxyacantha
Ilex serrata
Lilies
  Species
    Batemanniae
    canadense
    elegans
    Hansoni
    pardalinum
    p. Giganteum
    testaceum

ADDITIONS

Actaea spicata, 91
Albizzia julibrisin, 220
Baneberry, White, 91
Barronwort, 91
Cornus canadensis, 91
    kousa, 221
Epimedium sulphureum, 91
Euonymus Corlissi, 225
False Solomon's Seal, 91
Gardenia jasminoides, 255, 457, 530
Lilies
  Species
    amabile luteum, 417
    auratum Virginale, 417
    speciosum album novum, 419
    s. Lucy Wilson, 419
    s. Magnificum, 419
    s. Superstar strain, 419
    s. White Champion, 419
    s. White Pearl, 419
  Strains and varieties, 417
Merrybells, 91
Scope, 616
Smilacena racemosa, 91
University of Wisconsin method of feeding, 128, 166, 219, 248, 444
Uvularia grandiflora, 91

ACKNOWLEDGMENTS

PHOTOGRAPHERS

Baer, Morley, 36
Baker, Eric J., 517
Beals, Jessie Tarbox, 41, 43, 54, 85, 222, 417, 438
Braun, Ernest, 27, 28, 57, 67 top, 223, 541
Bush-Brown, James, 3, 114 top, 136, 281 bottom, 282
Costain, Harold H., 21, 77
Frick Charles, 504 top
Genereaux, Paul E., 17, 20, 23 top, 26, 29, 40, 53, 55, 65, 115, top, 127, 140, 148, 149, 150, 249, 342, 356, 363, 395, 401, 415, 420 top right and bottom, 453, 459
Gottscho, Samuel H., 203
Gottscho-Schliesner, 8-9, 11, 24, 25 top, 34, 35, 47, 56, 58, 62, 71, 87 top, 115 bottom, 116, 124, 142, 386, 445, 452, 468
Hewitt, Mattie Edwards, 23 bottom
Lincoln, F. S., 177
McFarland, J. Horace, Company, 75, 87 bottom, 98, 240, 246, 248, 281 top, 329, 331, 332, 346, 347, 353, 397, 419, 504 bottom
Morse, A. B., Company, 392, 420 top left, 421
Palmer, Phil, 49 bottom, 141, 152
Partridge, Rondal, 137
Robinson, John, 280
Saunders, Silvia, 126
Smith, Richard Averill, 52, 62-63, 126 top, 217, 239, 335, 387, 388-389, 414
Van Anda, George H., 114 bottom, 437
Wall, Herman V., 419, 420 bottom
Wallace, Philip B., 16, 134, 425
Weymouth, Mason, 128
Wilder, Walter Beebe, 86, 216

DESIGNERS AND LANDSCAPE ARCHITECTS

Baylis, Douglas, 128
Chamberlin, Noel, 52, 114 bottom
Church, Thomas, and Associates, 280
Clark, Agnes Selkirk, 124
Dean, Ruth, 62-63, 239
Ehrenpfort, Burnett S., 49 top
Finletter, Frances V., 134
Fowler, Clarence, 8-9
Halprin, Lawrence, 25, 27, 28, 30, 36, 37, 47, 57, 67, 137, 223, 541
Innocenti & Webel, 11
Landscape Associates, 142
Lawrence, Milford, 23 top, 26, 40, 140, 150
Lindeberg, H. T., 127
Lylton, R. Burton, 151
May, Ruth S., 54
Platt, William and Geoffrey, 452
Rucker, Ned, 49 bottom
Scott, Geraldine, 152
Sears, Thomas W., 136, 177
Sears, Thomas W., and Okie, R. Brognard, 16
Steinmetz, Katy and Paul, 141
Tibbits, Armand R., 203
Ward, Robertson, 24, 56
Weed, Robert Law, 34
Wheelwright, Robert, 18, 22
Wilson, Mrs. Helen, 29

The photographs on pages 517, 520 and 521 are from the Lord and Burnham Company; the material on pages 49, 64, 128, 141, 151, 152, 280, 505 and 506 is reproduced through the courtesy of the California Redwood Association. The maps between pages 705 and 708 are based on material from the United States Department of Agriculture.